Warman's
ANTIQUES
AND COLLECTIBLES
PRICE GUIDE

28th Edition

The Essential Field Guide to the
Antiques and Collectibles Marketplace

Edited by
Harry L. Rinker

Completely illustrated
and authenticated

Wallace-Homestead Book Company
Radnor, Pennsylvania

ISBN 0-87069-709-9
ISSN 0196-2272
Library of Congress Catalog Card No. 82-643542
Manufactured in the United States of America

1 2 3 4 5 6 7 8 9 0   3 2 1 0 9 8 7 6 5 4

EDITORIAL STAFF, 28TH EDITION

Mark R. Brown and
   Tim M. Sublette
Seekers Antiques
P.O. Box 10083
Columbus, OH 43201
(614) 291-2203
Staffordshire, Romantic

Lissa L. Bryan-Smith and
   Richard M. Smith
Box 208, R.D. 1
Danville, PA 17821
(717) 275-7796
Christmas Items

Craig Dinner
P.O. Box 4399
Sunnyside, NY 11104
(718) 729-3850
Doorstops

Roselyn Gerson
12 Alnwick Rd.
Malverne, NY 11565
Compacts

Ted Hake
Hake's Americana &
   Collectibles
P.O. Box 1444
York, PA 17405
(717) 848-1333
*Disneyana, Political
   Items*

John High
415 E. 52nd St.
New York, NY 10022
(212) 758-1692
Stevengraphs

Joan Hull
1376 Nevada
Huron, SD 57350
(605) 352-1685
Hull Pottery

David and Sue Irons
Irons Antiques
R.D. #4, Box 101
Northampton, PA 18067
(610) 262-9335
Irons

Lon Knickerbocker
20 William St.
Dansville, NY 14437
(716) 335-6506
Whimsies, Glass

Judy Knauer
1224 Spring Valley Lane
West Chester, PA 19380
(610) 431-3477
Toothpicks

Robert Levy
The Unique One
2802 Centre St.
Pennsauken, NJ 08109
(609) 663-2554
Coin Operated Items

Ron Lieberman
The Family Album
R.D. #1, Box 42
Glen Rock, PA 17327
(717) 235-2134
Books

Robert A. Limons
R.D. #1, Box 162
Hellertown, PA 18055
(610) 838-8931
Pewter

Joyce Magee
7219 Auld Rd.
Bradford, OH 45308
(513) 447-7134
Children's Books

Clarence and Betty Maier
The Burmese Cruet
P.O. Box 432
Montgomeryville, PA
   18936
(215) 855-5388
*Burmese Glass, Crown
   Milano, Royal Flemish*

Norman Martinus
Nostalgia Gallery
148 Marlin Drive
Kitty Hawk, NC 27949
(919) 261-2002
Paper Ephemera

James S. Maxwell, Jr.
P.O. Box 367
Lampeter, PA 17537
(717) 464-5573
Banks, Mechanical

Wayne McPeek
1211 Pembroke Rd.
Newark, OH 43055
(614) 344-7846
Verlys Glass

Joan Collett Oates
685 S. Washington
Constantine, MI 49042
(616) 435-8353
Phoenix Bird Pattern

Evalene Pulati
National Valentine
   Collectors Association
P.O. Box 1404
Santa Ana, CA 92702
Valentines

John D. Querry
R.D. 2, Box 137B
Martinsburg, PA 16662
(814) 793-3185
Gaudy Dutch

Ferill J. Rice
302 Pheasant Run
Kaukauna, WI 54130
Fenton

Harry L. Rinker
5093 Vera Cruz Rd.
Emmaus, PA 18049
(610) 965-1122
Puzzles

Christie Romero
521 N. Zeyn St.
Anaheim, CA 92805
(714) 778-1828
Jewelry

George Theofiles
Miscellaneous Man
Box 1776
New Freedom, PA 17349
(717) 235-4766
Posters

Lewis S. Walters
2640 Washington St.
Allentown, PA 18104
(610) 820-5088
Phonographs, Radios

Kathy Wojciechowski
P.O. Box 230
Peotone, IL 60468
(708) 258-6105
Nippon

INTRODUCTION

A NEW NAME, SAME QUALITY PRODUCT

Warman's Antiques and Their Prices is now **Warman's Antiques and Collectibles Price Guide**. The new name more clearly reflects the broad range of coverage found in **Warman's**. However, no matter what its title, this book will continue to be known simply as **Warman's** to those in the trade, a fitting tribute to a man of vision and his product.

Warman's, the antiques and collectibles "bible," covers objects made between 1700 and the present. It always has. Because it reflects market trends, **Warman's** has added more and more twentieth century material to each edition. Remember, 1900 was ninety–four years ago—the distant past to the new generation of twentysomething and thirtysomething collectors.

The general *antiques* market consists of antiques (objects made before 1945), collectibles (objects of the post–World War II era that enjoy an established secondary market), and desirables (contemporary objects that are collected, but are speculative in price). Although **Warman's** contains information on all three market segments, its greatest emphasis is on antiques and collectibles. The new title reflects this.

Also note the book's new subtitle: *Essential Field Guide to the Antiques and Collectibles Marketplace*, first introduced in the 26th Edition. It indicates that **Warman's** is much more than a list of object descriptions and prices. It is a basic guide to the field as a whole, providing you with the key information you need every time you encounter a new object or collecting category.

"WARMAN'S IS THE KEY"

Warman's provides the keys needed by auctioneers, collectors, dealers, and others to understand and deal with the complexities of the antiques and collectibles market. A price list is only one of many keys needed today. **Warman's 28th Edition** contains many additional keys including: histories, reference books, periodicals, collectors' clubs, and museums. Useful buying and collecting hints also are provided. Used properly, there are few doors these keys will not open.

Warman's is designed to be your first key to the exciting world of antiques and collectibles. As you use the keys this book provides to advance further in your specialized collecting areas, **Warman's** hopes you will remember with fondness where you received your start. When you encounter items outside your area of speciality, remember **Warman's** remains your key to unlocking the information you need, just as it has for over forty–six years.

ORGANIZATION

Listings: Objects are listed alphabetically by category, beginning with ABC Plates and ending with Zsolnay Pottery. If you have trouble identifying the category in which your object belongs, use the extensive index in the back of the book. It will guide you to the proper category.

We have made the listings descriptive enough so that specific objects can be identified. We also emphasized items that are actively being sold in the marketplace. Some harder–to–find objects are included to demonstrate market spread, useful information worth considering when you have not traded actively in a category recently.

Each year as the market changes, we carefully review our categories—adding, dropping, and combining to provide the most comprehensive coverage possible. **Warman's** quick response to developing trends in the marketplace is one of the prime reasons for its continued leadership in the field.

Wallace–Homestead Book Company also publishes the Warman's Encyclopedia of Antiques and Collectibles, volumes in the Warman format that concentrate on a specific collecting group, e.g., Americana, Country, English & Continental Pottery & Porcelain, Furniture, Glass, Oriental Antiques, and Paper. Several are in their second edition. Their expanded coverage compliments the information found in **Warman's**.

History: Collectors and dealers enhance their appreciation of their objects by knowing something about their history. We present a capsule history for each category. In many cases this history contains collecting hints or tips to spot reproductions.

References: References are listed in each category to help you learn more about their objects. Included are author, title, publisher [if published by a small firm or individual, we have indicated "published by author"], and date of publication or most recent edition.

Finding these books may present a problem. The antiques and collectibles field is blessed with a dedicated core of book dealers who stock these specialized publications. You will find them at flea markets and antiques shows and through their advertisements in trade publications. Many dealers publish annual or semi–annual catalogs. Ask to be put on their mailing lists. Books go out–of–print quickly, yet many books printed over twenty-five years ago remain the standard work in a category. Used book dealers often can locate many of these valuable reference sources.

Periodicals: The newsletter or bulletin of a collectors' club usually provides the concentrated focus sought by speciality collectors and dealers. However, there are publications, not associated with collectors' clubs, about which collectors and dealers should be aware. These are listed in their appropriate category introductions.

In addition, there are several general interest newspapers and magazines which deserve to be brought to our user's attention. These are:

Antique Review, P.O. Box 538, Worthington, OH 43085
Antique Trader Weekly, P.O. Box 1050, Dubuque, IA 52001
Antique Week, P.O. Box 90, Knightstown, IN 46148
Antiques (The Magazine Antiques), 551 Fifth Avenue, New York, NY 10017

Antique & The Arts Weekly, Bee Publishing Company, 5 Church Hill Road, Newton, CT 06470

Antiques & Collecting Hobbies, 1006 South Michigan Avenue, Chicago, IL 60605

Collector News & Antique Reporter, Box 156, Grundy Center, IA 50638

Collectors Journal, P.O. Box 601, Vinton, IA 52349

Collectors' Showcase, P.O. Box 837, Tulsa, OK 74101

Inside Collector, 225 Main Street, Suite 300, Northport, NY 11768

Maine Antique Digest, P.O. Box 358, Waldoboro, ME 04572

MidAtlantic Monthly Antiques Magazine, P.O. Box 908, Henderson, NC 27536

New England Antiques Journal, 4 Church Street, Ware, MA 01082

New York-Pennsylvania Collector, Drawer C, Fishers, NY 14453

Southern Antiques, P.O. Box 1107, Decatur, GA 30031

West Coast Peddler, P.O. Box 5134, Whittier, CA 90607

Yesteryear, P.O. Box 2, Princeton, WI 54968

Space does not permit listing all the national and regional publications in the antiques and collectibles field. The above is a sampling. See David J. Maloney, Jr.'s *Maloney's Antiques & Collectibles Resource Directory 1994–1995* [Wallace–Homestead, 1993] for a more detailed list.

Collectors' Clubs: Collectors' clubs adds vitality to the antiques and collectibles field. Their publications and conventions produce knowledge which often cannot be found elsewhere. Many of these clubs are short–lived; others are so strong that they have regional and local chapters.

Museums: The best way to study a specific field is to see as many documented examples as possible. For this reason, we have listed museums where significant collections in that category are on display. Special attention must be directed to the complex of museums which make up the Smithsonian Institution in Washington, D.C.

Reproductions: Reproductions are a major concern to all collectors and dealers. Most reproductions are unmarked; the newness of their appearance is often the best clue to uncovering them. Specific objects known to be reproduced are marked within the listings with an asterisk (*).

A subscription to *Antique & Collectors Reproduction News,* a monthly report on fakes, frauds, and facts, is highly recommended. Send $32 for twelve issues to: ACRN, Box 71174, Des Monies, IA 50325. This publication completed its second year of publication at the end of 1993. Consider buying all available back issues. The information they contain will be of service long into the future.

Index: A great deal of effort has been expended to make our index useful. Always being by looking for the most specific reference. For example, if you have a piece of china, look first for the maker's name and second for the type. Remember, many objects can be classified in three or more categories. If at first you do not succeed, try, try again.

Photographs: You may encounter a piece you cannot identify well enough to use the index. Consult the photographs and marks. If you own several editions of **Warman's**, you have available a valuable photographic reference to the antiques and collectibles field. Learn to use it.

PRICE NOTES

In assigning prices we assume the object is in very good condition. If otherwise, we note this in our description. It would be ideal to suggest that mint, or unused, examples of all objects exist. The reality is that objects from the past were used, whether they be glass, china, dolls, or toys. Because of this, some normal wear must be expected. In fact, if an object such as furniture does not show wear, its origins may be more suspect than if it does show wear.

Whenever possible, we have tried to provide a broad listing of prices within a category so you have a "feel" for the market. We emphasize the middle range of prices within a category, while also listing some objects of high and low value to show market spread.

We do not use ranges because they tend to confuse rather than help the collector and dealer. How do you determine if your object is at the high or low end of the range? There is a high degree of flexibility in pricing in the antiques field. If you want to set ranges, add or subtract 10% from our prices.

One of the hardest variants with which to deal is the regional fluctuations of prices. Victorian furniture brings widely differing prices in New York, Chicago, New Orleans, or San Francisco. We have tried to strike a balance. Know your region and subject before investing heavily. If the best prices for cameo glass are in Montreal or Toronto, then be prepared to go there if you want to save money or add choice pieces to your collection. Research and patience are key factors to building a collection of merit.

Another factor that affects prices is a sale by a leading dealer or private collector. We temper both dealer and auction house figures.

PRICE RESEARCH

Everyone asks—where do we get our prices? They come from many sources.

First, we rely on auctions. Auction houses and auctioneers do not always command the highest prices. If they did, why would so many dealers buy from them? The key to understanding auction prices is to know when a price is high or low in the range. We think we do this and do it well.

Second, we work closely with dealers. We screen our contacts to make certain they have full knowledge of the market. Dealers make their living from selling antiques; they cannot afford to have a price guide which is not in touch with the market.

Over fifty antiques and collectibles magazines, newspapers, and journals come into our office regularly. They are excellent barometers of what is moving and what is not. We don't hesitate to call an advertiser and ask if their listed merchandise sold.

When the editorial staff is doing field work, we identify ourselves. Our conversations with dealers and collectors around the country have enhanced this book. Teams from **Warman's** are in the field at antiques shows, malls, flea markets, and auctions recording prices and taking photographs.

Collectors work closely with us. They are specialists whose devotion to research and accurate information is inspiring. Generally, they are not dealers. Whenever we have asked them for help, they have responded willingly and admirably.

BOARD OF ADVISORS

Our Board of Advisors are specialists, both dealers and collectors, who feel a commitment to accurate information. You'll find their names listed in the front of the book. Several have authored a major reference work on their subject.

Members of the Board of Advisors file lists of prices in the categories for which they are responsible. They help select and often supply the photographs used. If you wish to buy or sell an object in their field of expertise, drop them a note along with an SASE. If time or interest permits, they will respond.

BUYER'S GUIDE, NOT SELLER'S GUIDE

Warman's is designed to be a buyer's guide to what you would have to pay to purchase an object on the open market from a dealer or collector. **It is not a seller's guide to prices.** People frequently make this mistake. In doing so, they deceive themselves. If you have an object listed in this book and wish to sell it to a dealer, you should expect to receive approximately fifty percent (50%) of the listed value. If the object will not resell quickly, expect to receive even less.

A private collector may pay more, perhaps seventy to eighty percent of our list price. Your object will have to be something needed for his or her collection. If you have an extremely rare object or an object of exceptionally high value, these guidelines do not apply.

Examine your piece as objectively as possible. As an antiques and collectibles appraiser, I spend a great deal of time telling people their treasures are not ''gold'' at all, but items readily available in the marketplace.

In respect to buying and selling, a simple philosophy is that a good purchase occurs when the buyer and seller are happy with the price. Don't look back. Hindsight has little value in the antiques and collectibles field. Given time, things tend to balance out.

COMMENTS INVITED

Warman's Antiques and Collectibles Price Guide: The Essential Field Guide to the Antiques and Collectibles Marketplace continues to be the leader in the antiques and collectibles price guide field because we listen to our readers. Readers are encouraged to send their comments and suggestions to Harry L. Rinker, c/o Rinker Enterprises, Inc., 5093 Vera Cruz Road, Emmaus, PA 18049.

ACKNOWLEDGMENTS

Although my name appears on the cover and title page as editor, **Warman's Antiques and Collectibles Price Guide** is a team effort. The Rinkettes, the Rinker Enterprises, Inc., staff, are largely responsible for the descriptions, listings, and photographs that appear in this book. Their names rightfully head up the staff and advisor listing in the front of this book.

My role is that of composer and conductor. I compose the Warman music and make the final decision about how it is to be played. I also direct the composition. However, like any conductor, my reputation rests on the strength of the orchestra. Fortunately, I work with the best professionals in the business. While Harry and the Rinkettes remain rock 'n' rollers at heart, we respect the classics and annually look forward to another rendition of **Warman's**. Hopefully, you do as well.

It has been a year of accomplishments at Rinker Enterprises, Inc. New titles by the staff include Ellen Schroy's *Warman's Pattern Glass* and Harry, Jr.'s *Price Guide To Flea Market Treasures, Second Edition*. My pride and joy, *Warman's Americana & Collectibles*, appeared in its sixth edition.

On the personal side, you will note that Terese Oswald is now Terese Yeakel. We wish Peter and her the very best in their new life together. Harry, Jr. and Paulanne, my daughter, both received their college degrees. Hallelujah!!!

With the increasing number of antiques and collectibles price guides available in the market and the tendency during a recession to cut back, I want to thank those users of **Warman's** who continually purchase, support, praise, and value this book. We value the trust we have earned and promise to do our best to preserve it.

One of my greatest joys in the antiques and collectibles field is the willingness to share information that I encounter on a daily basis. From auction houses to dealers in the field, ''what can I do to help'' is the answer to almost every request we make for assistance. The Rinkettes and I express our sincerest appreciation to everyone who responded positively in 1993.

We have worked on **Warman's** with the editorial, production, and sales staff at Chilton Books, parent company of Wallace–Homestead, enough times that a comfortable annual routine has evolved. This level of comfort is due to the skills of Edna Jones, Troy Vozzella, Elsie Comninos, and the other professionals on the Chilton staff.

As 1994 dawns, Rinker Enterprises, Inc., is about to depart significantly from the way it has operated in the past. New computer equipment will allow us to enter the world of typesetting, page layout, and newsletter production. I plan to greatly increase my media presence. My teaching commitment will be significantly increased.

The Rinkettes and I assure you that all these new activities are designed to enhance the quality of information, descriptions, and prices found in subsequent editions of **Warman's** and titles in the Warman's Encyclopedia of Antiques and Collectibles. Most of all we are looking forward to your support in our new efforts and to better serving the field we love so much.

Rinker Enterprises, Inc.   Harry L. Rinker
5093 Vera Cruz Road   Editor
Emmaus, PA 18049
January 1994

STATE OF THE MARKET

IT'S TOUGH OUT THERE. 1993 was not a great year for most individuals involved with the antiques and collectibles field. While not disastrous, it was a year filled with uncertainties. Every day, week, month, and quarter was a struggle. Everyone stressed persistence. The key goal was to survive. The good news is that most have, albeit often in somewhat reduced circumstances.

This is quite a contrast from the optimism that I expressed in the *State of the Market Report* that appeared in the twenty–seventh edition of **Warman's Antiques and Their Prices**. Allow me to refresh your memory:

"As 1993 dawns, the national economic forecast is optimistic. Many economic barometers suggest that America is slowly coming out of the recession. A sense of recovery is in the air . . . I favor a strong recovery by the middle or end of 1994. Momentum builds slowly in our field . . . The light at the end of the tunnel is in sight. Those who are still in the game by 1994 will enjoy the sunlight."

Add one year to each of the dates above. Deep in my heart, I believe the real number is plus two; but, I do not want to be labeled a nay-sayer. In my mind, the train is stalled on the tracks within sight of the light at the end of the tunnel. While not moving backward, it is not moving forward either. The train needs a push, something to overcome its current state of inertia. The shove must come from outside the antiques and collectibles field. We are economic followers, not leaders. President Clinton—are you listening?

Prices remained stable throughout 1993. The declining prices of the early 1990s are apparently in the past. Prices are as low as they are going to go. In 2003 today's prices are going to seem like unbelievable bargains.

It is a buyer's market. The individual with cash to spend is in command, especially if buying middle and low end merchandise. Cash rich buyers are besieged. It is amazing how quickly word spreads about them. Sellers are literally "giving away" some items in an attempt to get a piece of the cash cow. The problem is that this overwhelming abundance of buying opportunities all too quickly taps out these buyers. It is feast or famine. There is little middle ground.

The previous price discount plateau of ten percent for one's best customers has given way to fifteen, twenty, and even as high as thirty-three and one third percent. This practice is fraught with danger, threatening to undermine confidence in the sticker price of objects. One wishes sellers would mark objects with what they must receive to recover their cost and make a fair profit and hold firm to these prices.

It is a proven adage in the trade that quality items sell no matter what the economic state of the market. This is certainly true in the antiques and collectibles trade. High priced items continue to sell well. Because of this, many sellers are concentrating on making the *big* kill rather than a number of smaller ones.

Few are catering to the low end buyer, i.e., the individual who can afford to spend $5 to $50 per purchase. The longer this persists, the longer it is going to take for the antiques and collectibles market to recover. The strength of the market rests with these buyers. These are the new collectors, individuals who are just entering the market. Properly cultivated, these buyers become the $100, $500, and $1,000 buyers. They do not deserve to be ignored.

The field also seems to have lost sight of the relationship between the sales price of antiques and collectibles and what it cost to buy a similar item new. Put aside aesthetics, age, quality, and nostalgia, some of the traditional reasons cited as to why antiques and collectibles are worth buying. Go back to basics.

One of the principal reasons individuals bought antiques and collectibles in the past is that they were cheaper than buying new. Not any more, at least not in a large number of collecting categories. When it is cheaper to buy new, the antiques and collectibles field has lost one of its major sales advantages.

This argument carries even greater weight in a recession. This is a period when *reuse* rather than *shelf display* makes good buying sense. It is time to rediscover the reuse value of antiques and collectibles and reduce the investment emphasis that dominated the 1980s and early 1990s.

The number of reproductions, copycats, and fantasy items increased significantly during the past year. Many individuals only want the look. They do not care if the item is old or new. Rather than risk damaging a multi-hundred dollar item, they are willing buy a reproduction, copycat, or fantasy item at one tenth to one quarter of the value of a period piece. In 1993 the ''reproduction'' problem shifted from how to tell whether or not an object was a reproduction, copycat, or period to what is the price relationship between the reproduction, copycat, or fantasy object and the period piece. As the price difference continues to widen, the number of reproductions, copycats, and fantasy items will increase. The market is flooded now; it may soon be deluged.

For decades the antiques and collectibles market's biggest competitor for collector dollars was the limited edition market. The drain was enormous. Within five years, these numbers are going to seem miniscule when compared to the dollars being sucked out of the market by the shop-at-home cable television channels. Everything about the objects that they sell indicates trouble—from the superficial hype to large production numbers. Quality is often unsatisfactory. Most are overpriced. Early examples that have entered the secondary collectibles market sell at pennies on the dollar. It is so tragic that instead of crying, I find myself laughing. Cable shopping is the best proof I know of the greater fool theory.

The success of national, regional, and mail auction houses during the recession has turned everyone into an auctioneer. Hardly a week passes without my receiving a letter that ends with ''make a bid'' or ''I'm taking quotes.'' Greedy sellers prey on greedy buyers. Those who participate deserve each other. I refuse. I hope you will as well. It is the seller's responsibility to set the selling price and the buyer's responsibility to say yes, no, or counteroffer. This is how most purchases are made in the traditional retail environment. Why is it that the antiques and collectibles marketplace always wants to be different? Sometimes tried and true methods are the best.

1993 witnessed the increased use of the telephone, fax machine, and mail for sale purposes. Sellers have found that they must sell to a national or international base to survive. Further, it is far better to conclude a deal by telephone and receive cash quickly than to hold goods for several months in hopes that a specific buyer will attend a show or mall where the seller is set up.

Collectors became more aggressive in 1993. The number of seeker classified advertising increased. Collectors finally realized that they could not be everywhere at once. They need two, three, and four pairs of eyes searching for material. Further, they could buy more if they stayed home and generated income rather than hunting. Actually, many continue to hunt, but on a much more restricted basis.

Few question any longer that the American antiques and collectibles market is part of a larger, worldwide market. While this is most noticeable in the fine arts area, it is also true for decorative accessories and many trendy, post–World War II collectibles. The worldwide recession, especially the economic decline in Japan, finally impacted negatively on the American antiques and collectibles market in 1993. The market lost a major jump start possibility.

The vast majority of American sellers continue to remain passive, relying on foreign buyers to come to them rather than reaching out. They have trouble dealing with individuals who do not speak English. Look for major changes in the years ahead. First, antiques and collectibles trade periodicals are springing up everywhere, becoming important advertising vehicles for American sellers. Second, American sellers are expanding their horizons. Australia, the Far East, and South America offer important new markets. The toy community continues to set the pace. The rest of the market is playing catch-up.

One of the biggest news stories of 1993 is the growth of the information highway, from CD-ROM technology to communication links between television, telephone, and other media companies. The newest generation of collectors, the twentysomething children of hippies and yuppies are computer literate. The traditional information and business practices of the antiques and collectibles field are alien to them.

As 1993 comes to a close, the auction catalog listings of major American and European houses with prices realized are available on CD-ROM disc, antiques and collectibles image discs are in production, a few image catalog discs are available, several antiques and collectibles bulletin boards have been established, and a number of software programs have been written specifically for the antiques and collectibles community. The surface has just been scratched. Look for existing price guides to be available on CD-ROM and one or more national bulletin boards within the next five years, perhaps within the next two.

Until now, the changes in the antiques and collectibles field have occurred within its traditional framework. The antiques mall was an extension of the antiques shop. Independent mail auctions are copycats of national and regional catalog houses. Specialized periodicals adopted the approach of the national parents. Expansion was gradual and comfortable—a logical, systematic growth.

This is about to change. Growth in the late 1990s promises to be explosive.

When the dust settles in the twenty-first century, the antiques and collectibles market will have experienced the greatest changes in its history. If a poll was taken today, most would say I am crazy. History is full of crazy visionaries. Perhaps I am one. Time will tell.

AUCTION HOUSES

The following auction houses cooperate with Rinker Enterprises, Inc., by providing catalogues of their auctions and price lists. This information is used to prepare *Warman's Antiques and Collectibles Price Guide*, volumes in the Warman's Encyclopedia of Antiques and Collectibles, and Wallace–Homestead Book Company publications. This support is most appreciated.

Sanford Alderfer Auction
  Company
501 Fairgrounds Rd.
Hatfield, PA 19440
(215) 368-5477

Andre Ammelounx
P. O. Box 136
Palatine, IL 60078
(708) 991-5927

Al Anderson
P. O. Box 644
Troy, OH 45373
(513) 339-0850

Ark Antiques
Box 3133
New Haven, CT 06515
(203) 387-3754

Arthur Auctioneering
R. D. 2
Hughesville, PA 17737
(717) 584-3697

Noel Barrett Antiques
  and Auctions Ltd.
P. O. Box 1001
Carversville, PA 18913
(215) 297-5109

Robert F. Batchelder
1 West Butler Ave.
Ambler, PA 19002
(215) 643-1430

Biders Antiques, Inc.
241 South Union St.
Lawrence, MA 01843
(508) 688-4347

Butterfield & Butterfield
7601 Sunset Blvd.
Los Angeles, CA 90046
(213) 850-7500

Butterfield & Butterfield
220 San Bruno Ave.
San Francisco, CA 94103
(415) 861-7500

Cerebro
P. O. Box 1221
Lancaster, PA 17603
(800) 695-2235

W. E. Channing & Co.
53 Old Santa Fe Trail
Santa Fe, New Mexico
  87501
(505) 988-1078

Christie's
502 Park Ave.
New York, NY 10022
(212) 546-1000

Christie's East
219 E. 67th St.
New York, NY 10021
(212) 606-0400

Christmas Morning
1850 Crown Rd.,
  Suite 1111
Dallas, TX 75234
(817) 236-1155

Cincinnati Art Galleries
635 Main St.
Cincinnati, OH 45202
(513) 381-2128

Clinton-Ivankovich
  Auction Co. Inc.
P. O. Box 29
Ottisville, PA 18942
(610) 847-5432

Cohasco, Inc.
Postal 821
Yonkers, NY 10702
(914) 476-8500

Marvin Cohen Auctions
Box 425, Routes 20 & 22
New Lebanon, NY 12125
(518) 794-9333

Collector's Auction
  Services
P. O. Box 13732
Seneca, PA 16346
(814) 677-6070

Marlin G. Denlinger
RR 3, Box 3775
Morrisville, VT 05661
(802) 888-2774

William Doyle Galleries,
  Inc.
175 E. 87th St.
New York, NY 10128
(212) 427-2730

Early Auction Co.
123 Main St.
Milford, OH 45150
(513) 831-4833

Steve Finer Rare Books
P. O. Box 758
Greenfield, MA 01302
(413) 773-5811

William A. Fox
  Auctions, Inc.
676 Morris Ave.
Springfield, NJ 07081
(201) 467-2366

Freeman/Fine Arts Co. of
  Philadelphia, Inc.
1808 Chestnut St.
Philadelphia, PA 19103
(215) 563-9275

Garth's Auction, Inc.
2690 Stratford Rd.
P. O. Box 369
Delaware, OH 43015
(614) 362-4771 or
  369-5085

Glass-Works Auctions
P. O. Box 187-102
  Jefferson St.
East Greenville, PA
  18041
(215) 679-5849

Grandma's Trunk
The Millards
P. O. Box 404
Northport, MI 49670
(616) 386-5351

Guerney's
136 East 73rd St.
New York, NY 10021
(212) 794-2280

Ken Farmer Realty &
  Auction Co.
1122 Norwood St.
Radford, VA 24141
(703) 639-0939

Hake's Americana and
  Collectibles
P. O. Box 1444
York, PA 17405
(717) 848-1333

Harmer Rooke
  Numismatists, Inc.
3 East 57th St.
New York, NY 10022
(212) 751-4122

Morton M. Goldberg
  Auction Galleries
547 Baronne St.
New Orleans, LA 70113
(504) 592-2300

Norman C. Heckler &
  Company
Bradford Corner RD.
Woodstock Valley, CT
  06282
(203) 974-1634

Leslie Hindman, Inc.
215 West Ohio St.
Chicago, IL 60610
(312) 670-0010

James D. Julia, Inc.
P. O. Box 830
Fairfield, ME 04937
(207) 453-7904

Charles E. Kirtley
P. O. Box 2273
Elizabeth City, NC
  27906
(919) 335-1262

Howard Lowery
3818 W. Magnolia Blvd.
Burbank, CA 91505
(818) 972-9080

Alex G. Malloy, Inc.
P. O. Box 38
South Salem, NY 10590
(203) 438-0396

Martin Auctioneers, Inc.
Larry L. Martin
P. O. Box 477
Intercourse, PA 17534
(717) 768-8108

Robert Merry Auction
  Company
5501 Milburn Rd.
St. Louis, MO 63129
(314) 487-3992

Mid-Hudson Auction
  Galleries
One Idlewild Ave.
Cornwall-On-Hudson,
  NY 12520
(214) 534-7828

Milwaukee Auction
  Galleries
318 N. Water
Milwaukee, WI 53202
(414) 271-1105

Neal Auction Company
4038 Magazine St.
New Orleans, LA 70115
(504) 899-5329

New England Auction
  Gallery
Box 2273
W. Peabody, MA 01960
(508) 535-3140

New Hampshire Book
  Auctions
Woodbury Rd.
Weare, NH 03281
(603) 529-1700

Nostalgia Publications,
Inc.
21 South Lake Dr.
Hackensack, NJ 07601
(201) 488-4536

Richard Opfer
Auctioneers Inc.
1919 Greenspring Dr.
Timonium, MD 21093
(410) 252-5035

Pettigrew Auction
Company
1645 South Tejon St.
Colorado Springs, CO
80906
(719) 633-7963

Phillips Ltd.
406 East 79th St.
New York, NY 10021
(212) 570-4830

Postcards International
P. O. Box 2930
New Haven, CT
06515-0030
(203) 865-0814

David Rago Arts &
Crafts
P. O. Box 3592 Station E
Trenton, NJ 08629
(609) 585-2546

Lloyd Ralston Toys
173 Post Rd.
Fairfield, CT 06432
(203) 255-1233 or
366-3399

Renzel's Auction Service
P. O. Box 222
Emigsville, PA 17318
(717) 764-6412

R. Niel & Elaine
Reynolds
Box 133
Waterford, VA 22190
(703) 882-3574

Roan Bros. Auction
Gallery
R.D. 3, Box 118
Cogan Station, PA 17728
(717) 494-0170

Selkirk Gallery
4166 Olive St.
Saint Louis, MO 63108
(314) 533-1700

L. H. Selman Ltd.
761 Chestnut St.
Santa Cruz, CA 95060
(408) 427-1177

Robert W. Skinner Inc.
Bolton Gallery
357 Main St.
Bolton, MA 01740
(508) 779-6241

C. G. Sloan & Company,
Inc.
4920 Wyaconda Rd.
North Bethesda, MD
20852
(301) 468-4911

Smith House Toy Sales
26 Adlington Rd.
Eliot, ME 03903
(207) 439-4614

Sotheby's
1334 York Ave.
New York, NY 10021
(212) 606-7000

Rex Stark
49 Wethersfield Rd.
Bellingham, MA 02019
(508) 966-0994

Swann Galleries, Inc.
104 E. 25th St.
New York, NY 10010
(212) 254-4710

Theriault's
P. O. Box 151
Annapolis, MD 21401
(301) 224-3655

Victorian Images
P. O. Box 284
Marlton, NJ 08053
(609) 985-7711

Vintage Cover Story
P. O. Box 975
Burlington, NC 27215
(919) 584-6990

Western Glass Auctions
1288 W. 11th St.,
Suite #230
Tracy, CA 95376
(209) 832-4527

Winter Associates
21 Cooke St., Box 823
Plainville, CT 06062
(203) 793-0288

Wolf's Auction Gallery
13015 Larchmere Blvd.
Shaker Heights, OH
44120
(216) 231-3888

Woody Auction
Douglass, KS 67039
(316) 746-2694

ABBREVIATIONS

The following are standard abbreviations which we have used throughout this edition of **Warman's**.

4to	= 8 x 10″		k	= karat
8vo	= 5 x 7″		l	= length
12mo	= 3 x 5″		lb	= pound
ADS	= Autograph Document Signed		litho	= lithograph
adv	= advertising		ls	= low standard
ah	= applied handle		LS	= Letter Signed
ALS	= Autograph Letter Signed		mfg	= manufactured
AQS	= Autograph Quotation Signed		MIB	= mint in box
C	= century		MOP	= mother of pearl
c	= circa		NE	= New England
circ	= circular		No.	= number
cov	= cover		opal	= opalescent
CS	= Card Signed		orig	= original
d	= diameter or depth		os	= orig stopper
dec	= decorated		oz	= ounce
dj	= dust jacket		pat	= patent
DQ	= Diamond Quilted		pcs	= pieces
DS	= Document Signed		pgs	= pages
ed	= edition		pr	= pair
emb	= embossed		PS	= Photograph Signed
ext.	= exterior		pt	= pint
Folio	= 12 x 16″		qt	= quart
ftd	= footed		rect	= rectangular
gal	= gallon		sgd	= signed
ground	= background		sngl	= single
h	= height		SP	= silver plated
hp	= hand painted		SS	= Sterling silver
hs	= high standard		sq	= square
illus	= illustrated, illustration		TLS	= Typed Letter Signed
imp	= impressed		unp	= unpaged
int.	= interior		vol	= volume
irid	= iridescent		w	= width
IVT	= inverted thumbprint		#	= numbered
j	= jewels			

ABC PLATES

History: The majority of early ABC plates were manufactured in England, imported into the United States, and achieved their greatest popularity from 1780 to 1860. Since a formal education was limited in the early 19th century, the ABC plate was a method of educating the poor for a few pennies.

ABC plates are found in glass, pewter, porcelain, pottery, and tin. Porcelain plates range in diameter from 4⅜ to slightly over 9½ inches. The rim usually contains the alphabet and/or numbers; the center features animals, great men, maxims, or nursery rhymes.

References: Susan and Al Bagdade, *Warman's English & Continental Pottery & Porcelain, Second Edition*, Wallace–Homestead, 1991; Mildred L. and Joseph P. Chalala, *A Collector's Guide to ABC Plates, Mugs and Things*, Pridemark Press, 1980.

GLASS

6" d
Christmas Eve, Santa on chimney, clear. 65.00
Dog, standing on grass, center tree, clear. 65.00
Ducks, amber 45.00
Elephant with howdah, three waving Brownies, Ripley & Co, clear. 125.00
Little Bo Peep, center scene, raised alphabet border 45.00
Star Medallion, clear 40.00
7" d
Centennial 1776–1876 Exhibition, American eagle center, clear. 100.00

Clock face center, Arabic and Roman numerals, alphabet center, frosted and clear. 65.00

PORCELAIN OR POTTERY

5" d, black transfer, Staffordshire
Alpine shepherd, polychrome enamel, red rim stripe, small edge flake . . . 65.00
Child reading, polychrome enamel, short hairline, small back edge flakes 25.00
5¼" d, Stilt Walking, black transfer, polychrome enameling, imp "Meakin," stains and hairline 95.00
6" d
Ironstone, black transfer of monkey and cat, polychrome enamel, titled "Take your time Miss Lucy," molded hops rim, red rim, imp "Meakin". 115.00
Staffordshire, Zoares, black transfer, polychrome enamel, light stains. . . 135.00
6⅜" d, red transfer print of children playing, tea party center, sign language around inner edge, emb alphabet border, blue rim band 190.00
7¼" d, brown transfer of boy, stringed instrument, bird on fence, emb alphabet border, marked "Adams" 75.00
7½" d, brown transfer of Old Mother Hubbard, polychrome enamel trim, alphabet border above scene, marked "Tunstall". 200.00

TIN

3½" d, girl on swing, lithographed center, printed alphabet border 55.00
4¼" d, two kittens playing with basket of wool. 75.00
7¾" d, Who Killed Cock Robin? 120.00
8" d
Frogs playing leapfrog, emb alphabet border. 125.00
Mary Had A Little Lamb, light rust . 110.00
Who Killed Cock Robin? 85.00

ADAMS ROSE

History: Adams Rose, made 1820–40 by Adams and Son in the Staffordshire district of England, is decorated with brilliant red roses and green leaves on a white ground.

G. Jones and Son, England, made a variant known as "Late Adams Rose." The colors are not

Porcelain, Staffordshire, 8½" d, $80.00.

as brilliant and the ground is a "dirty" white. It commands less than the price of the early pattern.

Reference: Susan and Al Bagdade, *Warman's English & Continental Pottery & Porcelain, Second Edition,* Wallace–Homestead, 1991.

Plate, late, marked "England," 7½" d, $24.00.

Bowl, 8¾" d, early	600.00
Creamer, early	345.00
Cup and Saucer, handleless, late	65.00
Cup Plate, 4½" d	50.00
Milk Pitcher	
4⅞" h, c1840	75.00
6¾" h, bulbous, emb	135.00
Plate	
7¼" d, early	145.00
7½" d, late	40.00
8½" d, late	50.00
8¾" d, late	50.00
9¼" d, early	175.00
9½" d, late	75.00
10½" d, early	225.00
Platter, 15" l, oval, early, c1820	300.00
Soup, flange rim, late	75.00
Sugar, cov, late	165.00
Teapot, late	220.00
Vegetable Dish, cov, 12⅝" l, c1850	500.00
Wash Bowl and Pitcher, early	1,000.00

ADVERTISING

History: Before the days of mass media, advertisers relied on colorful product labels and advertising giveaways to promote their products. Containers were made to appeal to the buyer by the use of stylish lithographs and bright colors. Many of the illustrations used the product in the advertisement so that even an illiterate buyer could identify a product.

Advertisements were put on almost every household object imaginable and were constant reminders to use the product or visit a certain establishment.

References: Al Bergevin, *Drugstore Tins and Their Prices,* Wallace–Homestead, 1990; Al Bergevin, *Food and Drink Containers and Their Prices,* Wallace–Homestead, 1988; Douglas Congdon–Martin, *America For Sale: A Collector's Guide To Antique Advertising,* Schiffer Publishing, 1991; Douglas Congdon–Martin and Robert Biondi, *Country Store Antiques,* Schiffer Publishing, 1991; Douglas Congdon–Martin and Robert Biondi, *Country Store Collectibles,* Schiffer Publishing, 1990; Douglas Congdon–Martin, *Tobacco Tins: A Collector's Guide,* Schiffer Publishing, 1992; Warren Dotz, *Advertising Character Collectibles: An Identification and Value Guide,* Collector Books, 1993; Ted Hake, *Hake's Guide To Advertising Collectibles,* Wallace–Homestead, 1992; Bob and Sharon Huxford, *Huxford's Collectible Advertising,* Collector Books, 1993; Jerry Jankowski, *Shelf Life: Modern Package Design 1920–1945,* Chronicle Books, 1992; Vivian and Jim Karsnitz, *Oyster Cans,* Schiffer Publishing, 1993; Ray Klug, *Antique Advertising Encyclopedia,* Vol. 1 (1978, 1993 value update) and Vol. 2 (1985), L–W Promotions; Ralph and Terry Kovel, *Kovels' Advertising Collectibles Price List,* Crown Publishers, 1986; Norman E. Martinus and Harry L. Rinker, *Warman's Paper,* Wallace–Homestead, 1994; Tom Morrison, *Root Beer: Advertising and Collectibles,* Schiffer Publishing, 1992; Alice L. Muncaster, Ellen Sawyer, and Ken Kapson, *The Baby Made Me Buy It!,* Crown Publishers, 1991; James H. Stahl, *Collectors Guide To Key–Wind Coffee Tins With Price Guide,* L–W Book Sales, 1991; Dawn E. Reno, *Advertising: Identification and Price Guide,* Avon Books, 1993; Bob and Beverly Strauss, *American Sporting Advertising,* Vol. 1 (1987, 1992 value update), Vol. 2 (1990, 1992 value update), published by authors, distributed by L–W Book Sales; Robert W. and Harriett Swedberg, *Tins 'N' Bins,* Wallace–Homestead, 1985.

Collectors' Clubs: The Antique Advertising Association, PO Box 1121, Morton Grove, IL 60053; The Ephemera Society of America, PO Box 37, Schoharie, NY 12157; Tin Container Collectors Association, PO Box 440101, Aurora, CO 80014.

Periodicals: *National Association of Paper and Advertising Collectibles,* PO Box 500, Mount Joy, PA 17552; *Paper Collectors' Marketplace,* PO Box 128, Scandinavia, WI 54917.

Additional Listings: See *Warman's Americana & Collectibles* for more examples.

Ashtray	
Dunhill, iron, cobra top	75.00
Kool Cigarettes, milk glass, penguins	10.00
Michelin Tires, 4¾ x 6", molded plastic, man sitting on edge, 1940s	75.00
Bank, figural	
Atlantic Premium, 5" h, tin, gas pump shape, red, white, blue, and black	45.00

Esso, 6½" h, plastic, red man saluting, red, white, and blue logo. **110.00**
Blotter, Medusa Cement, 3½ x 6", pastoral scene and June 1925 calendar, unused. **4.00**
Booklet, Hood's Sarsaparilla **12.00**
Bottle, glass
  Soconu, 15½" h, emb lettering, metal cap. **75.00**
  Tiolene, 18" h, emb logo, lettering, and vertical lines **60.00**
Bottle Carrier, "Buy Pepsi Cola," wood, 1930 . . . . **115.00**

Box, Grandpa's Wonder Soap, Beaver Soap Co., Dayton, OH, 2½ x 4¼ x 1½", $12.50.

Box
  Balkan Sobranie Turkish Cigarettes, yellow, mountains, wagons, and two women, black lettering **25.00**
  Hood Tire Tube, 13" h, 5" w, 5" d, man wearing uniform, cream lettering, cardboard. **185.00**
  Magnolia Brand Condensed Milk, 7" h, 19" w, 13" d, wood **25.00**
  Royal Baking Powder, 8½" h, 14¾" w, 7¾" d, wood, red paper label **25.00**
  Tootsie Roll, cardboard **15.00**
Bracelet, Lucky Strike, Bakelite **250.00**
Cabinet
  Rainbow Dye, 14" h, 13¼" w, countertop type, metal, wood base, orig dye packets. **145.00**
  Rit Dye, 16" h, 14" w, 10" d, wood and tin, slant top, litho slogan, 64 compartment drawers, three orig handles. **225.00**

Calendar
  Collins Baking Co, 1909, girl wearing blue bonnet, 8" h, 8" w **25.00**
  Finotti Beverage Co, 1961, girl with globe and maps, 33⅓" h, 16" w. . . **25.00**
Canister, cov, La Paloma 5¢ Cigar, glass **30.00**
Change Tray
  Quick Meal Ranges **75.00**
  Stollwerck, 5⅛" d, metal, hot pink, gold and black globe, gold border . **15.00**
  The Fair's Millinery Opening/Fall Season 1905/Champion Cininnatus Pride, hunting dog, forest and lake scene **10.00**
Cigarette Lighter
  Ford Falcon, 2¼" l, chrome **20.00**
  Richfield, 2¼" l, chrome metal, brushed silver side panels, yellow and black Richfield delivery truck, 1950s. **40.00**
Clock
  Nu–Grape, plastic **75.00**
  Oilzum Motor Oil, 14½" d, blue border, blue and white lettering. **950.00**
  Simmon's Liver, regulator **225.00**
  Vanderbilt Premium Tires, 14½" d, leopard jumping through V center, red, black, and white lettering, Pam Clock Co, Inc, NY, c1958 . . . . **125.00**
Display
  Alka Seltzer, 9½" h, 12" w, metal, painted, red, white, and blue **30.00**
  Olin Winchester Flashlights and Batteries, 34" h, blue, red, and white lettering, silver rack **50.00**
Door Push
  Duke's Mixture, porcelain **90.00**
  Salada Tea, porcelain **85.00**
Figure
  Beefeater Gin, 17" h, 8½" w, wood and composition, man holding spear, red, black and yellow, yellow lettering. **75.00**
  Lamb Knit, 15" h, papier mache, old white and black repaint, some wear **360.00**
Glass, Wm Bierbaw Brewing Co, Mankato, MN, acid etched **195.00**
Good Luck Token, Green River Whiskey, brass, emb **25.00**
Jar, Schepp's Coconut **125.00**
Matchbook, 3½ x 4½", Carstairs White Seal Blended Whiskey, blue, gold, and red printing, unused, c1940 . . . . **10.00**
Mirror
  Angelus Marshmallow, pocket **58.00**
  Ceresota Flour, 2⅛", celluloid, trademark illus, dark brown rim, white lettering, early 1900s **50.00**
  Consolidated Ice Cream, hand held type, polar bear, hunter, ship and icebergs, gold handle **80.00**

Defiance Tick Mitten Co, World's Most Modern Glove & Mitten Factory, Toledo, OH, 2¾ x 1¾″, celluloid, yellow, red, white, and black, red printing, 1920s **16.50**

Garland Stoves and Ranges, 1¾″, tin covered, emb logo, inscribed "Sold Everywhere/The World's Best," early 1900s **25.00**

H H Debolt, Morgantown, WV, 2½″ d, celluloid, black and white **20.00**

Monitor Stoves and Ranges, 1¾″, celluloid, black and white, logo design, c1914 . . . . **25.00**

Morton's Salt, 2⅛″, celluloid, blue and white, pocket, c1920. . . . . **35.00**

Old Dutch Cleanser, pocket **25.00**

Pepsi–Cola, 2⅛″, celluloid, red and white, 1930s style name **40.00**

Robin Hood Flour, 1½″, None So Good As Robin Hood, aluminum covered, emb Robin Hood image, c1930 . . . . **28.00**

The Derby Oil, 2¼″, celluloid, red, white, and blue, star logo **55.00**

Mug

Bishop's Chocolate **20.00**

Liebig Hot Drink **27.00**

Sign, E & J Burke Ale, paper, Chicago New York World Series baseball team captains toasting each other, c1881, 20 x 26″, framed, $36,300.00. Photograph courtesy of James D. Julia, Inc.

Oil Can, 1 qt

Air Race Motor Oil, 5½″ h, yellow plane, cream background, yellow bands, red and blue outline dec, 1935–45 . . . . **110.00**

Champlin Motor Oil, 5¼″ h, cream lettering, blue background **55.00**

Gebhart's Motor Oil, 5½″ h, blue and gold comet **75.00**

Penn–Aero, 5½″ h, blue, red, and cream lettering, red propellers in center **135.00**

Rocket Motor Oil, 5½″ h, green and silver lettering **55.00**

Viking Chief Motor Oil, 6½″ h, red, white, and blue design **110.00**

Paperweight, The Badger Mutual Fire Insurance Co, cast iron **45.00**

Pinback Button

Flying Merkel Motorcycle, ⅞″ d, yellow, red, black, and white slogan, early 1900s **50.00**

Pin Holder, Ely's Cream Balm, 1½ x 1¾″, tin, diecut, litho, black and white, profile face image on front and back, 1890–1900 . . . . **75.00**

Poster

Anheuser–Busch, color, Clydesdale horses, 10 x 26″. **150.00**

Buster Brown, 40⅞ x 27″, George Ali photo and Tige red, black, yellow, and blue lettering, "Melville B Raymond presents The Newest in Musical Comedy Creations," cloth back **325.00**

Satin Skin Powder, 42½″ h, 28″ w, paper, yellow, woman holding blue fan, black lettering **30.00**

Puzzle, Kellogg's, 6 x 8″, framed, dated 1933 . . . . **20.00**

Rubbers, pr, child's, Goodyear, 1910, MIB **40.00**

Ruler, folding

H Chapins Sons, No. 39 . . . . **25.00**

John A Roeblings Sons Co, wire rope measure **225.00**

Sign

Acme Quality Paints, 20″ h, 14½″ w, porcelain, double sided, white paint can, black highlights, red background **55.00**

Atlantic Pure White Lead and Atlantic Linseed Oil, 35″ h, 20¾″ w, boy sitting on shelf with paintbrush and pail, titled "The Dutch Boy Painter," black frame **150.00**

Bates Market, 30″ l, 13½″ h, wood, fish dec **1,300.00**

Beacon Shoes, 20½″ h, 14⅜″ w, reverse painted glass, blue and gold, green center trademark **75.00**

Bickmore Easy Shave Cream, 31″ h,

21″ w, cardboard, litho, diecut, man wearing undershirt applying shave cream on shaving brush, blue, white, yellow, and orange 15.00

Borden's Ice Cream, 15″ h, 24″ w, metal, flanged, double sided, Elsie with yellow daisies 300.00

Bulova, 28″ h, pocket watch, cast outer ring, rest wood, gold, white, and black paint, face on each side 915.00

Campbell & Co's Ales, 22⅝″ h, 28½″ w, paper, gold crest, green and black lettering, wood frame 25.00

Canada Dry, 34″ h, 28″ w, cardboard, winter stream scene with ginger ale, club soda bottle, and glass, blue background 15.00

Corona Extra, 20″ h, 5¼″ w, tin, bottle shape, yellow, white, and navy blue 40.00

Cunningham Farm & Garden Machines, tin 25.00

Dr Pepper, 10½″ h, 26½″ w, porcelain, red, white and black lettering, white and green border 180.00

Electric Auto–Lite Service, 25½ x 35¾″, porcelain, white, yellow, and blue background, red, white, and blue lettering 150.00

Empire Fire Insurance, aluminum, framed, 15 x 21″ 75.00

Fatima Turkish Cigarettes, 36½″ h, 27″ w, yellow, Turkish girl, black and orange lettering, orig frame 175.00

Feen–A–Mint, 7″ h, 29¼″ w, porcelain, orange, blue lettering 55.00

Fidelity–Phoenix Fire Insurance Co, 11¾″ h, 23¼″ w, yellow, red outline, black and yellow lettering 80.00

Fisk Tires, 47 x 31″, wood, cream and blue lettering, young boy holding tire, wrought iron bottom 425.00

Galliker's Ice Cream, 24″ h, 9½″ w, tin on cardboard, white, maroon, and pink ice cream carton, maroon and white border 35.00

General Arthur Cigar, 34½″ h, 27″ w, reverse painted glass, red, gold lettering and border, framed 125.00

Goodyear Tires, 8 x 25″, reverse painted glass, yellow and silver lettering, blue background, wood and metal frame. 55.00

Grape Nuts, 30¼″ h, 20¼″ w, tin, girl carrying basket and St Bernard, house and mother in background, blue and black lettering. 1,100.00

Hamilton Brown Shoe Co, 14″ h, 19½″ w, metal, flanged, painted, red, black and white lettering 25.00

Hartford Insurance, tin 35.00

Helmar Cigarette, 3⅝″ h, 21⅝″ l, card-

board, dark green, cigarette pack illus, white emb lettering, wood frame 10.00

Hoffman's Ice Cream, 22″ h, 25¾″ w, porcelain, wrought iron bracket, double sided, center logo, red and green lettering 140.00

Huyler's Candies, 7″ h, 20¼″ w, porcelain, flanged, red background, white letters. 50.00

Independent Gasoline, 30″ d, porcelain, white, blue lettering, yellow and black logo, red border. 210.00

Keen Kutter, 10¾″ h, 20¾″ w, cardboard, black and red lettering 30.00

Keystone Ice Cream, 20″ h, 28″ w, porcelain, wrought iron bracket, white and red. 140.00

Marathon Products, 29½″ d, porcelain, green, black center, cream marathon runner 355.00

Sign, Klondike Head Rub, emb cardboard, blue letters, 11 x 8⅜″, $20.00.

McCormick–Deering, 10″ h, 27½″ w, tin, painted, black and yellow, emb 75.00

Melox Dog Foods, 26″ h, 18″ w, porcelain, blue, white lettering, dog on red ball 750.00

M H & M Shoes, 6½″ h, 28″ w, tin, diecut, emb, yellow, hand with pointing finger, black lettering and highlights. 220.00

Mississippi Pacific Lines, 19″ h, 13″ w, metal, red and cream lettering, green background 85.00

Opex Paints, 16″ h, 22″ w, porcelain, flanged, double sided, orange and white lettering 200.00

Pabst Blue Ribbon Beer, 60″ h, 26″ w, tin, white and silver can, red and white lettering, blue ribbon 40.00

Peoples Department Store, Bangor, ME, 8" w, 77" l, brass, late 19th C 660.00

Peter Schuyler Cigar, 12" h, 36" w, porcelain, dark blue, white line border, blue, yellow, and white lettering 45.00

Pittsburgh Brewing Company, 22" h, 40½" w, cardboard, top center logo, white, red, and dark blue. 55.00

Poll Parrot Shoes, 38" h, 22" w, porcelain, neon, red, orange, yellow, green, and blue parrot, dark red lettering. 1,150.00

Remer's Tea Store, 6¼" h, 10" w, cardboard, diecut, standup, cat in cup and saucer 25.00

Royal Crown Cola, 59¾" h, 15¾" w, metal, yellow, white, and red lettering. 130.00

Royal Insurance Co, 31¼" h, 22¼" w, wood, red, black, gold, and white crest emblem with crown, gold lettering, framed 80.00

Sweet–Orr Pants, Shirts, Overalls, 10" h, 24" w, pale yellow, people playing tug of war with overalls, blue lettering. 200.00

Van Houten's Cocoa, 30¼" h, 24¼" w, cardboard, woman wearing straw hat, peach ribbon and dress, green and black lettering, orig oak frame with etched product name 40.00

Watchmaker's, 21" d, 29" h, carved and painted wood, old weathered surface, New England, late 19th C 1,540.00

Western Union, 19½" h, 18" w, porcelain, flanged, yellow and white, blue and black lettering. 450.00

White Star Gasoline, 30" d, porcelain, white star, blue lettering and background. 450.00

Whitman's Chocolates, 13½" h, 39½" w, porcelain, green, white lettering and border. 125.00

Will's Cigarettes, 24" h, 13" w, green, gold and green lettering 150.00

Wrought Iron Range Company, 16½" h, 22½" w, paper, pink, yellow, blue, green, wood frame. 300.00

Zerolene, 27" sq, porcelain, white, blue lettering, blue and white logo . 110.00

Spoon, Coon Chicken Inn 35.00

Stereoscope, Kis–Me–Gum, tin 95.00

Stickpin

    J I Case Threshing Machine Co, brass, trademark symbol, early 1900s 15.00

    John Deere, 1 x 1¼", brass, diecut, detailed image of plow trademark, early 1900s 20.00

    Yale/The Everlasting Motorcycle, 2½" l, brass, diecut celluloid pennant dec, multicolored logo, white background, blue lettering, early 1900s 75.00

String Holder, O.L.O. Soap, tin 325.00

Thermometer

    Abbott's Bitters, 21" h, 5⅛" w, wood, yellow, man on top, blue outline, black letters. 185.00

    Amalic Motor Oil, 9" d, metal and glass, red logo, white and black lettering. 65.00

    DuPont Denatured Alcohol, 38¾" h, yellow, gold, red, and black design 75.00

    Freeman/Headbolt Engine Heater, 15" h, metal, white, black and brown lettering. 80.00

    Goodyear Tires, 11½" h, wood, yellow, blue lettering and highlights 55.00

    Mail Pouch Tobacco, 38¾" h, porcelain. 155.00

    Merrill Transport Company, 15" d, tire form, green, red, yellow, brown, and black 160.00

    Mobiloil, 23" h, blue and red lettering, red horse, blue shield, white background. 250.00

    Satin Luminall, 38½" h, 8⅛" w, metal, painted, yellow, blue and red lettering. 35.00

    Tums, 9" h, 4" w, blue, cream and yellow lettering, marked "Made in USA" 50.00

Tie Clasp, Charlie Tuna 18.00

Tin

    Airee Renewal Flints 18.00

    Bagshaw's Brilliantone Phonograph Needles 20.00

Sign, Full Weight Cigars, tin, $14,850.00.

China Tea Peacock Brand, 6½" h, 4"
d, green and gold, peacock illus .. 10.00
Columbia Ideal 200 Phonograph
Needles 15.00
Globe Tobacco 375.00
Hope Denture Powder 35.00
Jewel Tea Orange Spice 15.00
Luzianne Coffee, red, handle, 3 lb,
1928.................... 90.00
Peterson's Nut, 4½ x 6¾", 1928
copyright.................. 15.00
Silvertone 200 Phonograph Needles 20.00
Sunshine Biscuit, 12" h, litho, girl .. 20.00
The Planters Peanut, 9¾" h, 8½" d,
dark blue, red lettering 35.00
Victrola Tungstone Phonograph
Needles 18.00
Winner Cut Plug Tobacco, 4" h, racing
scene, brown and blue lettering... 60.00
Tire Rack
Astrostar, 9" h, 13" w, tin, painted,
black and green............. 45.00
Mohawk, 8" h, 15" w, tin, green and
yellow lettering, white background 60.00
Tray
Hub Bottling Works 65.00
Valentine, Beech–Nut Gum, animated,
orig box 85.00
Washboard, Cupples Co, glass
scrubber.................. 25.00
Watch Fob
Caterpillar 45.00
Columbian Stove, 1½", silvered
brass, emb, "C" around patriotic
shield design, red and blue enamel
accents, early 1900s 40.00
De Laval 25.00
G Heileman Brewing Co 25.00
Goodyear, 1½", brass, emb, automo-
bile tire, diagonal bar inscribed
"Goodyear," and flying foot symbol,
1920s.................... 35.00
Heinz 57, 1½", silvered brass, raised
"57" symbol, home office building
on back, inscribed "Heinz Pure
Food Products/Pittsburgh, USA,"
early 1900s................ 55.00
Lauson Frostking, 1¼ x 2", brass,
dark bronze color, emb, long
bearded king wearing crown, inscribed on reverse, early 1900s... 50.00
Mutual of Omaha 15.00
NCR, 1½", silvered brass, emb, company initials in wreath border design, cash register detail on reverse, inscribed "National Cash
Registers Benefit Everybody/Over
800,000 In Use".............. 45.00
Poll Parrot Solid Leather Shoes,
metal, enamel center with parrot,
back with raised lettering, "Star
Brand Shoes Are Better," c1915 .. 20.00

Sheep Union Stock Yards, Ogden 65.00
Union Pacific, The Overland Route 125.00

ADVERTISING TRADE CARDS

History: Advertising trade cards are small, thin cardboard cards made to advertise the merits of a product and usually bore the name and address of a merchant.

With the invention of lithography, colorful trade cards became a popular advertising medium in the late 19th and early 20th centuries. They were made especially to appeal to children. Young and old alike collected and treasured them in albums and scrapbooks. Very few are dated; 1880 to 1893 were the prime years for trade cards; 1810 to 1850 cards can be found but rarely. By 1900 trade cards were rapidly losing their popularity. By 1910 they had all but vanished.

References: Kit Barry, *The Advertising Trade Card,* Book 1, published by author, 1981; Robert Jay, *The Trade Card In Nineteenth–Century America,* University of Missouri Press, 1987; Norman E. Martinus and Harry L. Rinker, *Warman's Paper,* Wallace–Homestead, 1994; Jim and Cathy Mc-Quary, *Collectors Guide To Advertising Cards,* L–W Promotions, 1975, out of print; Murray Card (International) Ltd. (comp.), *Cigarette Card Values: 1992 Catalogue of Cigarette & Other Trade Cards,* Murray Cards (International) Ltd., 1992.

Periodical: *The Trade Card Journal,* 143 Main St., Brattleboro, VT 05301.

Additional Listings: See *Warman's Americana & Collectibles* for more examples.

Eureka Health Corset, text on back, 3¹⁄₁₆ x 5³⁄₁₆", $3.00.

BEAUTY

Djer–Kiss Rouge and Face Powders, set of 6, women with different hair color on each 30.00
Dr Hebra's Viola Cream, folder type, continuous scene when opened 8.00
Miss L A Cummins Ladies Hair Dresser, black and white. 15.00
Parker's Hair balsam, nude nymph with long hair, black design, green background. 11.00
Read's Grand Dutches Cologne 9.00
Richard Hudnut Perfumer's Shop, whimsical nude on water lily, purple and green dec storefront on reverse 80.00

BEVERAGES

Acher Co Coffee, pretty girl, 1904 . . . 18.00
California Brand Condensed Milk . . . 12.00
Charles Wilson Ginger Ale, Soda Water, Toronto, black and buff 34.00
Hills Bros Fine Coffees, San Francisco, black and white. 38.00
Knapp's Root Beer, double sided, multicolored, continuous scene, diecut window. 12.00
Levering's Roasted Coffee, diecut . . . 18.00
Luzianne Coffee, diecut 14.00
R & R MacLeod Tea, London, black and white 18.00
Tyson's Montgomery County Milk . . . 55.00

Koch Brothers, Maude Humphrey illus, 3 x 5″, $10.00.

CLOTHING & ACCESSORIES

Andrew Lester Co Woolens, pink, black, and gold lettering. 38.00
Atwood Suspender, Uncle Sam distributing suspenders to world 42.00
B A Hadsell Ready Made Plain Clothing 28.00
Bicknell & Neal Fine Clothing, photo . 10.00
Black Cat Hosiery, diecut, cat 20.00
Broadhead Dress Goods, folder type, continuous scene when opened 24.00
Brownie Shirt Mfg Co, San Antonio, TX, black and white. 24.00
C A Carruth Fine Clothing, photo . . . 18.00
Ehrich & Co, 8th Ave, New York City, clothing, 1876. . . . . 25.00
F Mayer Boot & Shoe Co, multicolored, boys playing leapfrog. 8.00
Foster's Hook Gloves, folder type, color 20.00
Georgetown Hosiery Co, black and white 32.00
Henderson's Red School House Shoes 20.00
Isaac Remington Shirt Manufacturer, blue and white, writing on back. 10.00
John Kelly's Fine Shoes, black shoe image. 12.00
Jos Meyers & Son Ladies Suits, black and white. 20.00
Oakfords Hats, black and orange . . . 11.00
Paine & Co Hats, black and white . . . 36.00
Queen Bess Corsets 22.00
Reliance Corset Co, Imperial Corset, blue reverse with corset vignettes. . . 12.00
Stevenson Co Clothiers, Christmas Offering, multicolored 8.00
Sweet's Boots & Shoes, diecut, black and violet 17.00
Webb & Wakefield Clothing, comical image. 28.00
Williams Shirts Made to Order, black and white, red diagonal line 12.00

FARM MACHINERY & SUPPLIES

American Standard Corn Planter, Victorian girl illus 26.00
Bay State Lawn Mower, Old Homestead 40.00
D M Osborne Mowers, Reapers, folder type. 22.00
Farmer's Feed & Boarding Stable, S G Ray Proprietor, black and white 8.00
Geo L Myers Grain Thresher, two illus 20.00
J I Case, Racine, WI, black and white illus 34.00
L A May & Co, Union St, Lynn, MA, agricultural tools 15.00
Moline Plow, American Royalty, King Corn & Queen Wheat 55.00
Schuttler Wagon, farm scene 40.00
Syracuse Chilled Plow Co, hunting scene. 12.00

The Deering Binder, black and white illus	15.00
Williams Poultry Food, Makes Hens Lay	8.00

FOOD

Bleim & Leyh Pretzels & Bread, Atlanta, GA.	34.00
Bush Hill Creamery Butter, red and green illus, cream background	10.00
Crosse & Blackwell's Pickles, London, multicolored image	20.00
Geo Hubbard Co Wholesale Groceries, black and white.	12.00
Heinz Tomato Soup, emb	14.00
Holland Butter, diecut, offset printing .	20.00
John B Cancelmo Fancy Fruits, black and cream	12.00
Kennedy's Biscuit, Compliments of the Season on reverse	24.00
Libby McNeill Corned Beef, Uncle Sam illus	24.00
Monarch Teenie Weenie Sweets, diecut, pickle barrel	10.00
Pearl Backing Powder, C E Andrews & Co, c1890.	30.00
Porcelain Ice Cream Co, black and cream	34.00
Swift's Premium Ham & Bacon, multicolored	15.00
Wheatlet Breakfast Food, diecut, standup	40.00
Whitney's Boston Baked Beans, gold and brown	20.00
Wilson Pkg Co Cooked Corned Beef, Russians Partaking	20.00
Wright's Minced Meat, red oval, black and buff	8.00

FURNITURE

Albee's National Upright Parlor Bed, black and yellow	24.00
Burger & Co Fine Furniture, gold borders	46.00
C H Hubbards' Furniture Warerooms, black and white tufted chair illus	17.00
Gately & Hurley Co, Camden, NJ, black and buff	8.00
J C Hand & Co Fine Furniture, multicolored, design on back	10.00
Providence Furniture Co, black and white, vignette illus	20.00
Steven Chair Co, Pittsburgh, black and cream	18.00
Union Wire Mattress Co, black and white	18.00
Wakefield Rattan Co, black and white, ornate rocker on reverse	1.00

LAUNDRY AND SOAPS

Anthony Wayne Washers, Ye Old and Ye New, folder type.	32.00

Calkins Champion Washer, red background.	28.00
Doty's Washer, folder type, red, black, and buff, 1873 price list int.	15.00
French Laundry Soap, diecut, frog . .	8.00
Gold Dust Washing Powder, diecut . .	16.00
Higgin's German Laundry, Uncle Sam bringing soap to Indians.	32.00
J L Larkin Creme Toilet Soap, multicolored	15.00
Lenox Soap, diecut, standup	10.00
New Process Soap, multicolored	15.00
Soapine, rising balloon	20.00
Sapolio, diecut, black boy in watermelon	8.00
Wool Soap, My Mamma used Wool Soap, diecut.	14.00

MEDICAL

A A Marks Artificial Limbs, black and white	12.00
Burdock Blood Bitters, Invalid Ladies! This is for You, descriptions and reasons	10.00
Dr C McLane's Liver Pills & Vermifuge, multicolored, detailed.	20.00
Dr P K Hill Albany Dentist, Rochester, NY, black and buff.	18.00
Hibbard's Rheumatic Syrup, Greatest Blood Purifier Known & Testimonials int., litho, folder type	25.00
Ivory Polish for the Teeth, adv on back with other products	15.00
J C Ayer Co, Weather and Medicine Signal for Daily Reference	14.00
Johnson's Anddoyne Liniment	10.00
Mrs. Wislow's Soothing Syrup, classic image, 1887 calendar on back	12.00
Royal Elixir, Sallie Williams as Peep–Bo, multicolored	8.00
Well's Rough On Corns, reverse with Rough on Rats Too	22.00

MISCELLANEOUS

Akehurst's Paper Products and Cards	24.00
American Roofing Slates, black design, blue background	16.00
Automatic Rug Machine Co	22.00
Bixby's Royal Polish, NY, full color, 1880	30.00
Buffalo Scale Co	34.00
Coach Varnishes, Clarence Brooks & Co, New York City, c1885	15.00
Dayton Autographic Register Co, gold and red	65.00
Edw K Tryron, Jr & Co, Firearms, Philadelphia, c1880.	40.00
Ellis, Knapp & Co Umbrellas & Parasol, blue and light blue, gold circle.	16.00

Henry McShane Plumbers' Steam and Gas Fitters Supplies, black and white — 26.00
Howard Insurance Co, NY, Manhattan view, copyright 1878 — 50.00
J F Lawrence Label & Job Printers, colorful — 12.00
John Ashton Marble & Granite Works, black and white — 40.00
Jones Photographer, Providence, RI — 12.00
Magnesco–Calcite Fire Proof Co, black and white vignette illus — 20.00
Merchant's Gargling Oil, Lockport, NY, full color — 15.00
Mermod, Jaccard & Co Gold Pens — 12.00
Simplex Typewriters, diecut, Santa, 1909 — 15.00
Spencerian Pens, soldier writing letter illus — 12.00
T Wilce Kiln Dried Hardwood Floors, yellow illus — 16.00
Universal Photographic Co, black and red — 12.00

PIANOS AND ORGANS

Cable Co Pianos, Oriental woman, red emb floral border — 12.00
Chas M Stieff Grand & Upright Pianos, black and white, reverse with vignette of plant and Expo medals — 13.00
Emerson Piano Co, multicolored, pink background — 8.00
Mrs A M Barons Teacher of Piano, penciled writing on back with 1806 date — 16.00
Pivolis Organs, Pianos & Music, black and white, Paris Expo medals illus — 14.00
Sohmer Pianos, Are at present the most popular and preferred by the Leading Artists, eight artists photos — 12.00

STOVES AND RANGES

Argand Stoves & Ranges, folder type, pretty girl — 12.00
C Riessner Co, Queen Oil Range, turkey cooking scene — 20.00
Dixon's Stove Polish, Palmer Cox Brownies illus — 20.00
Garland's Stoves 7 Ranges, arctic scene — 14.00
Glenwood Ranges & Heaters, diecut, circus dog act illus — 30.00
Gold Coin Stoves & Ranges, stove vignette — 10.00
Household Ranges, US flag illus — 12.00
John Diamond Electric Paste Stove Polish, Philadelphia, black and white — 12.00
Litchfield Stove Co, Queen Anne, folder type, brown, yellow, and gray — 12.00
Model Grand Portable Range, Uncle Sam being fed by black man — 26.00

Shaker and New Tariff Ranges, Lt Greeley arriving at North Pole — 55.00
Sunshine Stoves and Ranges, folder type, 1898 calendar — 8.00
Union Star Paste Stove Polish, NY, c1885 — 30.00
William Miller Manufacturer of Ranges, double cased range vignette — 15.00

THREAD AND SEWING

Albin Warth Machines for Cutting Clothing, black and violet, medals illus — 32.00
American Button–Hole Machine, black and white — 16.00
Barbours Irish Flax Thread — 10.00
Belding Bros Spool Silk — 34.00
Brainerd & Armstrong Silk Works, A Moonlight Frolic, reverse with crazy stitches — 25.00
Brooks Spool Cotton, Whaling with Brooks Threads, classic image — 15.00
Clark's Mile End Spool Cotton, colorful clowns illus — 8.00
Davis Sewing Machine Co, black over vermilion vignette — 10.00
J & P Coates Spool Cotton, Gulliver and the Lilliputians — 15.00
Monach Tailoring Co, black and red — 15.00
Standard Sewing Machine, stitched cloth border — 18.00
Wheeler & Wilson Sewing Machines, purple illus — 15.00
White Sewing Machine, Cleveland, OH, full color, c1890 — 10.00
Willimantic Spool Cotton, Brooklyn Bridge version — 15.00

TOBACCO

Allen Tobacco Co, black and white Delaware River scene — 26.00
Capadura, lady in sheer slip — 70.00

Wilson & McCallay Tobacco Co., Middletown, OH, color litho illus, text on back, 5¾ x 3½", $5.00.

Choice Smoking	18.00
Domingo Viana Fine Cigars	12.00
Frishmuth Bro & Co Fine Cut & Smoking Tobacco, Philadelphia, reverse with buildings illus	15.00
Geo Edwards Leaf Tobacco & Cigars, black and white, brown logo	44.00
Joe Michl's Fifty Little Orphans Cigar, hanging string	15.00
Ours Smoking Tobacco, pasted color margins	14.00
Scout Smoking Tobacco	26.00

AGATA GLASS

History: Agata glass was invented in 1887 by Joseph Locke of the New England Glass Company, Cambridge, Massachusetts.

Agata glass was produced by using a piece of peachblow glass, coating it with metallic stain, spattering the surface with alcohol, and firing. The result was a high-gloss, mottled appearance of oil droplets floating on a watery surface. Shading usually ranged from opaque pink to dark rose. Pieces are known in a pastel opaque green. A few pieces have been found in a satin finish.

Tumbler, rose, 3¾″ h, $675.00.

Bowl	
5″ d, tricornered	1,450.00
6½″ d, ruffled top	1,800.00
8″ d, 2″ h, green opaque ground, agata staining, gold etching, minor wear to staining	300.00
Celery Vase, 7″ h, sq, fluted top	600.00
Creamer	1,200.00
Finger Bowl, 5¼″ d, 2⅝″ h, crushed raspberry shading to creamy pink, all over gold mottling, blue accents	975.00
Juice Tumbler, 3¾″ h	825.00
Pitcher, 6⅜″ h, crimped rim	1,675.00
Scent Bottle, 3″ h, silver hinged rim, screw cap, marked "Black, Starr & Frost"	250.00

Spooner, 4½″ h, 2½″ w, sq top, wild rose peachblow ground, agata staining, small areas of wear	350.00
Toothpick Holder, 2¼″ h, flared, green opaque, orig blue–spot color, gold trim, New England	770.00
Tumbler, 4″ h, deep rose top	850.00
Vase	
4½″ h, sq, pinched sides, ruffled scalloped rim	600.00
9″ h, lily shape	1,100.00

AMBERINA GLASS

History: Joseph Locke developed Amberina glass in 1883 for the New England Glass Works. "Amberina," a trade name, describes a transparent glass which shades from deep ruby to an amber color. It was made by adding powdered gold to the ingredients for an amber glass batch. A portion of the glass was reheated later to produce the shading effect. Usually it was the bottom which was reheated to form the deep red; however, reverse examples have been found.

Most early Amberina is of flint quality glass, blown or pattern molded. Patterns include Diamond Quilted, Daisy and Button, Venetian Diamond, Diamond and Star, and Thumbprint.

In addition to the New England Glass Works, the Mt. Washington Glass Company of New Bedford, Massachusetts, copied the glass in the 1880s and sold it at first under the Amberina trade name and later as "Rose Amber." It is difficult to distinguish pieces from these two New England factories. Boston and Sandwich Glass Works never produced the glass.

Amberina glass also was made in the 1890s by several Midwest factories, among which was Hobbs, Brockunier & Co. Trade names included "Ruby Amber Ware" and "Watermelon." The Midwest glass shaded from cranberry to amber and resulted from a thin flashing of cranberry applied to the reheated portion. This created a sharp demarcation between the two colors. This less expensive version caused the death knell for the New England variety.

In 1884 Edward D. Libbey was assigned the trade name "Amberina" by the New England Glass Works. Production occurred in 1900 but ceased shortly thereafter. In the 1920s Libbey renewed production at his Toledo, Ohio, plant for a short period. The glass was of high quality. Amberina from this era is marked "Libbey" in script on the pontil.

Reproduction Alert: Reproductions abound.

Beverage Set, Diamond Quilted pattern, 7″ h pitcher, three punch cups, two tumblers, New England, price for six pieces	770.00
Bonbon, 7″ d, 1½″ h, wavy six pointed	

Wash Bowl and Pitcher, Baccarat, 13" h pitcher with applied handle and swirl design, matching 15" d bowl, $1,210.00. Photograph courtesy of James D. Julia, Inc.

1½" w rim, fuchsia shading to pale amber bowl, sgd "Libbey" 600.00

Bowl
4½" d, 4" h, molded Optic Diamond Quilted pattern, Mt Washington . . . 285.00
9" d, 2¾" h, Inverted Thumbprint pattern, melon ribbed 195.00

Butter Pat, 2¾" d, Daisy and Button pattern, sq, notched corners, price for pair 220.00

Butter Tub, cov, 5" d, Daisy and Button pattern, amber faceted cut knob, minor roughness. 550.00

Celery, sq, scalloped top, Diamond Quilted pattern, New England. 450.00

Compote, 6½" d, 4" h, slightly scalloped rim, fuchsia ribbed bowl, baluster stem, marked "Libbey Amberina" . . . 720.00

Cordial, 4½" h, trumpet shape 225.00

Creamer and Sugar, 4½" h, Diamond Quilted pattern, crimped top, amber reeded handles. 625.00

Cruet
6" h, inverted goblet body, swirled ribs, amber faceted stopper. 535.00
6¾" h, deep color, Inverted Thumbprint pattern, chocolate tricorn rim, petticoat form, amber stopper, applied amber handle, price for pair. . 990.00

Curtain Tiebacks, orig pewter shanks, price for pair. 165.00

Decanter, 11" h, Reverse Diamond Quilted pattern, Amberina stopper, handle 650.00

Finger Bowl, 4¾" d, 2⅝" h, faintly ribbed, flared bulbous shape, deep red to

dark amber, one oval label "N.E.G. W Amberina, Pat's...", price for set of five 615.00

Hair Receiver, 4" d, 2" h, ribbed, fuchsia, marked "Libbey". 660.00

Ice Cream Set, Daisy and Button, large serving bowl, six ice cream plates, Hobbs & Brockunier, price for seven pc set. 925.00

Milk Pitcher, 6" h, sq top, bulbous body, Inverted Thumbprint pattern, applied amber reeded handle, New England 450.00

Pickle Castor, 6¾" h, Inverted Thumbprint pattern, enameled floral dec, pewter cov, Mt Washington 250.00

Pitcher
6¾" h, tankard, Diamond Quilted pattern, deep color, New England . . . 770.00
7" h, sq rim, Inverted Baby Thumbprint pattern, applied amber reeded handle, New England. 400.00
7¼" h, Optic Diamond Quilted pattern, bulbous, applied amber reeded handle. 300.00
8½" h, Inverted Thumbprint pattern, applied clear reeded heart shaped handle 175.00

Punch Bowl Set, 15½" d x 7½" h bowl, eight handled 3" d x 2" h cups, Expanded Diamond Quilted pattern, price for nine piece set. 1,800.00

Punch Cup, 2½" h, Inverted Baby Thumbprint pattern, applied amber plain handle, New England. 90.00

Rose Bowl, 6½" h, Inverted Thumbprint pattern, feet chipped 125.00

Spooner, 4½" h, Inverted Coin Spot pattern, fold–in crimped rim. 335.00

Toothpick, Diamond Quilted pattern, sq mouth, Libbey. 235.00

Tumble Up, Inverted Thumbprint pattern, water carafe and matching tumbler. 325.00

Vase
4¼" h, gently waisted form, vertical paneling, attributed to Libbey. 175.00
8½" h, 3½" d, paneled, applied amber edge, deep color 325.00
10½" h, 7½" d, ftd, applied amber edge, aesthetic style dec, fan with bird on branch, gold floral dec. . . . 300.00

AMBERINA GLASS—PLATED

History: The New England Glass Company, Cambridge, Massachusetts, first made Plated Amberina in 1886; Edward Libbey patented the process for the company in 1889.

Plated Amberina was made by taking a gather of chartreuse or cream opalescent glass and dipping it in Amberina and working the two, often utilizing a mold. The finished product had a deep amber to deep ruby red shading, a fiery opalescent lining, and often vertical ribbing for enhancement. Designs ranged from simple forms to complex pieces with collars, feet, gilding, and etching.

A cased Wheeling glass of similar appearance had an opaque white lining but is not opalescent and the body is not ribbed.

Bowl, bulbous, scalloped top, New England Glass Co., 7¾″ w, 3 to 3¾″ h, $2,750.00.

Bowl, 8″ d, 3¼″ h, ruffled 1,600.00
Celery Vase 2,600.00
Cruet, 6¾″ h, faceted amber stopper . 3,200.00
Lamp Shade, 14″ d, hanging, swirled, ribbed 4,750.00
Milk Pitcher, applied amber handle, orig "Aurora" label. 7,000.00
Parfait, applied amber handle, c1886 1,250.00
Punch Cup, vertical ribs, applied handle 1,500.00
Salt Shaker, vertical ribs, orig top . . . 1,000.00
Tumbler, 4″ h, deep fuchsia shading to ruby to amber, opalescent white lining, horizontal ribs. 800.00
Vase
  3½″ h, flared twelve ribbed bowl, raspberry red shading to amber, opal white casing 3,960.00
  7¼″ h, lily shape, raspberry red shading to bright amber, opal white casing. 2,650.00

AMPHORA

History: The Amphora Porcelain Works was one of several pottery companies located in the Teplitz–Turn region of Bohemia in the late 19th and early 20th centuries. It is best known for art pottery, especially Art Nouveau and Art Deco pieces.

Several markings were used, including the name and location of the pottery and the Imperial mark, which included a crown. Prior to World War I, Bohemia was part of the Austro–Hungarian Empire, so the word "Austria" may appear as part of the mark. After World War I the word "Czechoslovakia" may be part of the mark.

Reference: Susan and Al Bagdade, *Warman's English & Continental Pottery & Porcelain, Second Edition,* Wallace–Homestead, 1991.

Additional Listings: Teplitz.

Cat Pitcher, tail handle, white, brick red bow, black paws, dark green base, imp "Austria, Crown, Amphora, 1906/39," 10¼″ h, $275.00.

Bowl, 12 x 15″, reticulated, applied leaves and chestnuts, ftd, two double twisted gold handles, sgd. 635.00
Centerpiece, 18½ x 18½″, matte glaze, baby Dionysius wearing wreath of grapes on head, holding two thyrsus, sitting on ram, two empty basket molded containers, rect base, painted amber and green, gilt highlights, cream ground, imp "Amphora" and crown mark. 425.00
Ewer, 9½″ h, handles, spout, oval reserve of gladiator. 125.00
Figure
  15″ h, bird of prey, gray, brown and white, imp "Amphora 38/17," initialed "MZ" 825.00
  28″ h, female, shades of blue and gold, cream ground, signature stamp, imp mark and number, designed by E Stellmacher, c1904, minor losses 2,310.00

Vase

5½" h, olive Art Nouveau portrait and landscape dec, gold highlights, cream ground, stamp, imp numbers, sgd "Amphora/Turn," c1915 .... **550.00**

8¾" h, blue–green irid ground, applied pink leaves and blueberries, double handles, imp Amphora mark at base. **275.00**

11" h, pink roses, green shaded ground, imp crown and Amphora marks, minor chips. **300.00**

15¾" h, raised stylized octopus and crab dec, matte mottled green glaze, gold and maroon highlights, imp marks, c1918. . . . . **4,125.00**

ANIMAL COLLECTIBLES

History: The representation of animals as a theme in fine arts, decorative arts, and utilitarian products dates back to antiquity. Some religions endowed certain animals with mystical powers. Authors throughout written history embodied them with human characteristics.

Collecting by animal theme has been practiced for centuries. Until the early 1970s most collectors were of the closet variety. However, the formation of collectors' clubs and marketing crazes, e.g., flamingo, pig, and penguin, brought most collectors out into the open.

The animal collector differs from other collectors in that they cares little about when an object was made or even its aesthetic quality. The key is that the object is in the image of their favorite animal.

References: Pauline Flick, *Cat Collectibles,* Wallace–Homestead, 1992; Marbena Jean Fyke, *Collectible Cats: An Identification and Value Guide,* Collector Books, 1993; Lee Garmon and Dick Spencer, *Glass Animals of the Depression Era,* Collector Books, 1993; Everett Grist, *Covered Animal Dishes,* Collector Books, 1988, 1993 value update; Peter Johnson, *Cats & Dogs: Phillips Collectors Guides,* Dunestyle Publishing, 1988; Alice Muncaster and Ellen Yanow, *The Cat Made Me Buy It,* Crown, 1984; Alice Muncaster and Ellen Yanow Sawyer, *The Cat Sold It!,* Crown, 1986; Herbert N. Schiffer, *Collectible Rabbits,* Schiffer Publishing, 1990; Mike Schneider, *Animal Figures,* Schiffer Publishing, 1990.

Periodicals: *MOOsletter,* 240 Wahl Ave., Evans City, PA 16033; *The Canine Collector's Companion,* PO Box 2948, Portland, OR 97208.

Collectors' Clubs: Canine Collectibles Club of America, Suite 314, 736 N Western Avenue, Lake Forest, IL 60045; Cat Collectors, 33161 Wendy Dr., Sterling Heights, MI 48310; Folk Art Society of America, PO Box 17041, Richmond, VA 23226; The Frog Pond, PO Box 193, Beech Grove, IN

46107; The National Elephant Collector's Society, 380 Medford Street, Somerville, MA 02145.

Museums: American Kennel Club, New York, NY; American Saddle Horse Museum Assoc., Lexington, KY; Frog Fantasies Museum, Eureka Springs, AR; International Museum of the Horse, Lexington, KY; Stradling Museum of the Horse, Patagonia, AZ; The Dog Museum, St Louis, MO.

Additional Listings: See specific animal collectible categories in *Warman's Americana & Collectibles.*

BIRDS

Bonbon Dish, 4" h, 9" l, peacocks, sterling silver, stamped, chased, dish formed by spreading tail feathers, Durgin for Gorham, Concord, NY, price for pair. **1,320.00**

Bottle Opener, figural, cast iron

3¼" h, cockatoo, orange and yellow chest, red and orange comb, green base, black ground, John Wright Co **100.00**

3⅜" h, pelican, red and black, yellow beak, orange feet, green base, Wilton Products **50.00**

Candy Dish, cov, swan, luster blue and gold, Japan, raised star mark **55.00**

Carving, 8¼" h, 11¼" l, bluejay, wood, relief carved, orig yellow and alligatored paint, burl base, early to mid 20th C **450.00**

Decanter, pelican, marked "Germany" **125.00**

Dish, 6" h, 8½" l, swan, sterling silver, glass molded body, silver chased wings, neck, and head, price for pair **2,475.00**

Figure, 6" h, chalk, old worn polychrome paint, old chips, minor head damage **215.00**

Iron, 2¾" h, swan, miniature, cast iron, orig trivet, worn red paint **65.00**

Paperweight, 3" h, swan, cast lead, price for pair. **70.00**

Poster

41 x 15", The Swans, pair of swans swimming, iris and foliage in foreground, trees in background, arched Art Nouveau stylized window border, sgd "Mary Gobley" in matrix lower left, publisher identified as Depose in matrix lower left, lithograph, printed in colors, framed . . **660.00**

63 x 47", peacock, Cognac Jacquet, Bouchet, Vercasson, Paris, multicolored peacock, green and yellow ground, red letters **550.00**

Shaker, 5½" h, 11" l, pheasants, sterling silver, chased, male and female, long folded pointed tails, removable necks, perforated breasts, monogram on male, retailed by Marshall Field & Co, Chicago, set of four. **3,020.00**

BOVINE

Carousel Animal, 19" h, 39" l, bull, carved and painted wood, full body, horns, sweeping tail, running position, black and white, minor repairs **1,760.00**

Folk Art, 21" h, 15" w, carved wood, stylized head of steer, brown paint, light brown stripe, white markings, leather ears, real steer horns, 19th C **880.00**

Painting, 26 x 37", G Brasseur, Pasture with Cows, oil on canvas, modern frame **850.00**

Weathervane, 29" l, cow, molded copper, cast tail and horns, applied ears, verdigris surface **3,000.00**

CATS

Bank, 9½" h, chalk, full body, seated, worn polychrome paint. **200.00**

Children's Book, Kittens and Cats, Eulalie Osgood Grover, Houghton Mifflin Co, 1911 . . . . **25.00**

Doorstop, litho, wooden wedge back . **55.00**

Figure
Beswick **55.00**
Hagenauer, Austria, c1925, bronze, stylized, slightly cubist version, imp marks, minor abrasion **220.00**

Folk Art, 4½" h, 5" l, carved wood, cross hatched coat, orig white, black, and brown paint, red trim, Schimmel type **350.00**

Match Holder, hanging kitchen type . . **35.00**

Painting, 15 x 22", Daniel Merlin, The Captivating Toy, sgd, four kittens and ball of yarn, c1900. . . . . **10,500.00**

Pip–Squeak
4⅜" h, papier mache, orig black paint, polychrome trim, wear, damage to ears, replaced leather. **45.00**
7¾" h, composition, seated cat, white, orange and black markings, bellows base. **1,200.00**

Tambourine, black Halloween cat face **40.00**

Toy, 5" l, pull, wood, orig polychrome paint, platform with wheels. **75.00**

DOGS

Advertising, American Brakeblok Dog, name "Stopper" on collar, 1930s . . . **45.00**

Bookends, pr, puppies playing, Frankart **145.00**

Boot Scraper, 9¼" h, cast steel, Scottie, low relief, edge tooling, old black paint **95.00**

Figure
Boxer, sitting, Morten **75.00**
Bulldog, bronze, standing **225.00**
Cocker Spaniel, Morten **35.00**
Dachsund, Royal Dux **60.00**
Dalmatian, sitting, Morten **55.00**

English Sheep Dog, raised flowered bow, c1950, 10" h **65.00**

Hunting Dog, head, terra cotta, brown glazed imp "U & C/'879," J Uffrecht & Co, Germany, late 19th C **715.00**

Irish Setter, Arnart, 1950s **22.00**

Poodle, black, Goebel, 1988, 7" h . **85.00**

Pug, chalk, full body, worn red and black paint, 10" h **300.00**

Whippet, seated, Majolica, amber and white glaze, 31" h, repairs. **1,870.00**

Whippets holding rabbits, standing, Staffordshire, 19th C, price for pair **625.00**

Folk Art, 3⅞" h, primitive carved wood, good patina, late **105.00**

Humidor, bulldog **145.00**

Inkwell, 10" l, bronze, hound lapping at dish, French, 19th C **1,670.00**

Jewelry, pin, two Scottie heads, red . **42.00**

Painting, oil on canvas
Dogs in the Field, School of George Smith Armfeld, 1840–75, indistinctly sgd lower left, 16 x 24", framed, conserved. **935.00**
Young girl in White with a Dog, Anglo/ American School, 18th C, unsigned, 38 x 27", framed, good condition, retouched **1,950.00**

Pitcher, Scottie, mottled black and brown, Japan **22.00**

Sculpture
12" h, white marble, King Charles spaniel, sgd "Rebaldi," Italian, 19th C **6,735.00**
16" h, bronze, retriever with pheasant in mouth, Jules Moigniez, c1870 . . **5,280.00**

Textile, 19¾ x 18¾", needlepoint panel, dog on cushion, shaded brown, blue, white, and olive, sgd and dated "H 1885," old worn gilt frame **475.00**

Weathervane, 16" h, 31" l, molded copper, setter, good verdigris surface, bullet hole, E G Washburne & Co, Danvers, MA, late 19th or early 20th C **5,250.00**

EAGLES

Figure
15" h, bisque, soft coloring, marked "Bald Eagle by Andrea, Japan". . . **85.00**
17½" h, 23½" wingspan, cast iron, good details, old gold paint, modern wood base **135.00**

Folk Art
13½" h, carved pine, old natural finish, traces of gilt, minor damage to spread wings. **275.00**
13¾" h, carved and painted pine, glass eyes, naturalistic colors, green painted base **1,300.00**

ELEPHANTS

Bookends, pr
4½" h, 4½" w, brass and Bakelite, stylized tubular elephants, rect base, Chase Chrome and Brass Co **275.00**
4½" h, weighted iron, imp "Made in Italy". **200.00**
Bottle Opener, 3¹⁄₁₆" h, figural, sitting, trunk in circle, gray, pink, nostrils, white details **35.00**
Figure
2⅝" l, pink quartz, wood base **45.00**
8½" h, bronze, running Senegal elephant, after A L Barye, sgd and imp "ZZ," late 19th C **1,650.00**
20" l, bronze, walking, Oriental, wood base, one ivory tusk glued **375.00**
Screen, 96" w, 84" h, three panel, elephant family moving through jungle, brightly colored parrot in tree, sgd "Ernest Brierly" **2,750.00**

FOWL

Bottle Opener, 3⅞" h, figural, metal, black body, red comb, orange–yellow beak and feet, green base, John Wright Co. **50.00**
Box, cov, 10½" l, porcelain, two ducks, bright enamels, Oriental. **550.00**
Carousel Animal, 32" h, 35" l, rooster, laminated wood, relief carving, layers of old worn polychrome paint, glass eyes, age cracks, old repairs, replaced base **1,500.00**
Figure
Ducks, colorless glass, gold dust and controlled bubbles, partial label on base for Archemede Seguso Bullicante, 8¼" h **440.00**
Geese, Duncan Miller, glass, fat . . **220.00**
Folk Art
5⅞" h, rooster, carved pine, old patina, red comb, Mountz type, damaged comb **65.00**
6⅛" h, chicken, pine, old patina, glass eyes, Mountz type, damaged beak **25.00**
6¼" h, chicken, wood and papier mache, orig polychrome paint, minor edge flaking, damage to beak and legs **145.00**
12¼" h, rooster, carved wood, antiqued polychrome paint, minor wear. **275.00**
15" h, rooster, sheet metal, hammered three dimensional body, edge tooling, wrought iron legs . . . **2,300.00**
Game Plates, turkey, 21" l platter, eight 10" d plates, brown transfer, polychrome, marked "Ralph Wood, Bur-

slem, England," price for nine piece set. **150.00**
Painting, 5 x 6¾", Adrien Joseph Verhoeven–Ball, Farmyard Fowl and Roosters, Chickens and a Peacock in a Landscape, oil on panel, sgd and dated 1870, price for pair. **2,000.00**

Animal Covered Dish, hen on nest, white milk glass, red glass eyes, 6⅞" l, 6½" h, $50.00.

Weathervane, rooster
20½" h, 21¾" l, copper and cast zinc, strutting, perched on arrow, gilt loss **1,300.00**
25" h, cast iron and tin, hollow zinc body, traces of old paint, name "James" as balance. **350.00**
33" h, 32" w, molded copper, swell body, cut copper comb, crop, and tail, painted green, yellow, brown, and white, repairs. **5,225.00**

FOXES

Painting, 40¼ x 32½", Carl Fredrik Kioeboe, The Escape/Winter Scene with Fox and Rabbit, oil on canvas, sgd lower right, framed. **2,500.00**
Poster, 40½ x 30", La Fleche, Backer, Dresden, brown fox, green and brown ground. **330.00**
Weathervane, 13¾" h, 31" l, copper, verdigris surface, traces of bolle, 19th C **1,700.00**

HORSES

Carousel Animal, 28½" h, 38" l, laminated wood, good relief carving, old worn polychrome repaint, glass eyes, worn velvet seat, old repairs, modern stand **1,800.00**

Diorama
9″ h, 60″ l, Amish farm scene, full bodied carved wood animals and figures, five horse–drawn wagons, painted background, early 20th C .   **700.00**

14¾″ h, 60″ l, livery stall, nine full bodied cast iron horses, individual illuminated stalls, painted details, early 20th C. **1,500.00**

Figure, 9¾″ h, 12″ l, bronze, rearing, raised forelegs, pricked ears, flared nostrils, long curly mane falling over right side of neck, partly bound tail flying, rear legs resting on later brass plaque, attributed to workshop of Francesco Fanelli, mid 17th C **19,800.00**

Flower Arranger, gray colt, Hull **35.00**
Necktie, hand painted **40.00**

Painting
10 x 12½″, watercolor, primitive brown and black horse, pink cloth belt, blue grass, sgd on back "Henry Lapp 1873," rosewood veneer frame **1,150.00**

16 x 19″, Suzanne Wamsley, Paris Prince, pastel on paper, sgd and dated lower right, 1983. . . . .   **1,045.00**

23 x 28″, Catherine Bloomfield, Premier Ministre, gouache on paper, sgd and dated lower left, 1982 . . .   **1,210.00**

Poster
33 x 23″, James Montgomery Flagg, "Help Him To Help U.S.!," The American Red Star Animal Relief, National Headquarters, Albany, NY, Uncle Sam with horse. **440.00**

49½ x 35″, Horse Super Cigarettes, red horse, deep blue ground **250.00**

Vase, mare and foal, Royal Copley, price for pair. **60.00**

Weathervane
18″ h, painted, J Howard & Co, Bridgewater, MA, third quarter 19th C **4,000.00**

19″ h, 43½″ l, molded copper, full body, Dexter, fine verdigris surface, Cushing and White, Waltham, MA, second half 19th C, hole at underside **4,250.00**

19½″ h, 35½″ l, molded zinc, full body, flowing mane and tail, painted black, repairs to tail **1,210.00**

22″ w, copper, stallion, patina, sgd "Westervelt" on bar, AB and WT Westervelt, Church, NY, 1883. . . .   **5,500.00**

28″ l, copper, running, Black Hawk, hollow body, molded detail, green patina, soldered repairs, modern wood base. **1,750.00**

OWLS

Andirons, 14″ h, cast iron, copper wash, perched on branch, yellow glass eyes, c1920, price for pair. **150.00**

Barometer, 11″ h, carved walnut, English. **65.00**

Calendar, 8½″ w, 18¾″ h, twelve color lithographs, different bird on each month, muted tones surround, Theo van Hoytema, Holland, 1908. . . . . . .   **1,100.00**

Calendar Plate, owl on open book, 1912, Berlin, NE. **30.00**

Candelabrum, 13½″ h, hammered wrought iron, central stylized owl center, brass dec, brown–black patina, imp marks, Gobert, Austria, c1925 . .   **300.00**

Candy Container, 4⅜″ h, stylized feathers, gold tin screw cap. **85.00**

Fairy Lamp, 4″ h, bisque, glass eyes .   **250.00**

Folk Art
3¾″ h, primitive carving, hardwood, old brown finish, round base **45.00**

12½″ h, carved wood, relief carving, orig paint, glass eyes **125.00**

Humidor **145.00**

Inkwell, 8 x 4″, brass, glass inset, hinged lid, pen tray, 2″ owl figure. **85.00**

Mask, papier mache, c1915 . . . .   **90.00**

Medallion, 3 x 4″, oval, Wedgwood, solid light blue jasper ground, white relief owl, imp modern mark **150.00**

Stein, half liter, Bibite on shield held between claws, Mettlach #2036. . . . . .   **950.00**

Vase, 12½″ h, ruffled rim, two handles, marked "Royal Nishiki Nippon Hand Painted". **365.00**

PARROTS

Figure
13″ h, porcelain, bright polychrome, marked "Germany," minor edge damage, painted repair. **125.00**

24″ h, porcelain, pink, blue, green, yellow, and rust, trunk form base, applied and molded trailing fruiting vines, scattered flowers, dome scrolled base, underglaze blue crossed arrows mark, French, early 20th C, price for pair. **3,575.00**

Folk Art, 17¼″ h, carved wood, orig polychrome paint, glass eyes, seated on perch, 20th C **350.00**

Tape Dispenser, parrot, figural **58.00**

Urn, cov, 17¾″ h, baluster, domed cov, waisted circular stepped base, applied overall flowering vines and scattered insects, three perched parrots, lid with parrot finial, Potschappel, overglaze blue factory mark, minor repairs, price for pair. **2,100.00**

SHEEP

Magazine Cover, orig art, Harper's, May,
1895, Edward Penfield illus, woman
with ship, green, red, and blue **250.00**
Painting
  22 x 28″, British School, Sheep and
  Poultry in a Landscape, oil on cra-
  dled panel, 19th C **2,100.00**
  22¼ x 31″, AF Tait, Sheep in a Pas-
  ture, oil on canvas, sgd "AF Tait, NA
  NY '95," modern gilt frame **4,750.00**
Stamp, 4¼″ h, carved stone ram, dark
patina, Oriental characters **145.00**

WILD ANIMALS

Architectural Element, 29½″ h, 38″ w,
lions, cast stone, painted white, curly
manes, open jaws, one forepaw resting on sphere, molded rect base, price
for pair **990.00**
Box, cov, green, seal on cov, Rook-
wood, 1932. . . . . **215.00**
Carving, 6½″ l, leopard, wood, painted
spots, one tooth chipped **45.00**
Doorstop, 13″ h, lion, cast brass, ram-
pant lion, dark patina, wood base . . . **85.00**
Figure
  3¾″ h, monkey, stylized and slightly
  cubist version, bronze, Hagenauer,
  Austria, c1925 . . . . **470.00**
  8½″ h, 29½″ l, panther, bronze, left
  forepaw outstretched, curling tail
  resting on ground, laid–back ears,
  snarling jaws, base inscribed
  "Andre Basseire, Cire Perdu Lebl-
  anc Barbedienna A Paris 18/25,"
  later granite oblong base, French . **1,650.00**

ARCHITECTURAL ELEMENTS

History: Architectural elements are those items
which have been removed or salvaged from buildings, ships, or gardens. Many are hand crafted.
Frequently they are carved in stone or exotic
woods. Part of their desirability is due to the fact
that it would be extremely costly to duplicate the
items today.

The current trend of preservation and recycling
architectural elements has led to the establishment
and growth of organized salvage operations that
specialize in removal and resale of these elements.
Special auctions are now held to sell architectural
elements from churches, mansions, office buildings, etc. Today's decorators often design an entire
room around one architectural element, such as a
Victorian marble bar or mural, or use several as
key accent pieces.

References: Ronald S. Barlow (comp.), *Victorian Houseware: Hardware and Kitchenware,*
Windmill Publishing Co., 1991; Margaret Lindquist
and Judith Wells, *The Official Price Guide To Garden Furniture and Accessories,* House of Collectibles, 1992; J. L. Mott Iron Works, *Mott's Illustrated
Catalog of Victorian Plumbing Fixtures for Bath-
rooms and Kitchens,* Dover Publications, 1987;
Alan Robertson, *Architectural Antiques,* Chronicle
Books, 1987; *Stable and Barn Fixtures Manufactured by J. W. Fiske Iron Works,* Apollo Books,
1987; J. P. White's Pyghtle Works, Bedford, England, *Garden Furniture and Ornament,* Apollo
Books, 1987.

Additional Listings: Stained Glass.

Aviary, 60 x 144″, iron and wirework, faceted onion dome top, rect vertical
cage, arched sides, radiating span-
drels, painted white, French **4,500.00**
Baluster, 18½″ h, walnut and inlaid ivory,
late Georgian, early 19th C. **120.00**
Bird Bath, 32″ h, 24″ d, carved stone,
circular, steeply tapering sides, separate sq section pyramidal stand, 19th
C **375.00**
Boot Scraper
  12¾″ l, wrought iron, arc welded, good
  detail, old pitted surface **215.00**
  13″ l, 9⅛″ h, cast iron, double griffin **275.00**
Bracket Shelf, 10¾″ w, 9″ h, eagle, detailed carved pine, gesso and old worn
gilt, old edge damage **600.00**
Ceiling, 31 x 5′, pressed copper, elabo-
rate floral dec **1,200.00**
Cistern, 12½″ h, 31½″ l, granite, sq . . **275.00**
Door
  Arts and Crafts, oak, hammered iron
  hardware, woven iron grating,
  unsgd, weathered ext., 41⅛″ w,
  80½″ h **220.00**
  Federal, New England, 19th C, six
  raised panels, grained to simulate
  bird's eye and tiger maple, 35½″ w,
  90″ h, price for pair. **500.00**
Door Knocker, 7¾″ h, brass, engraved
"J Frey, 1805". **85.00**
Drying Rack, hanging, triangular cut out
ends, geometric designs with three
bars extending between ends, old
gray–white wash, found in Zoar, OH,
area, 53″ l. **220.00**
Elevator Door, Aesthetic Movement,
brass, bordered, ascending design,
drilled, 19″ w, 71″ h **275.00**
Fencing, 47″ l, 41″ h, cast iron, America,
19th C **440.00**
Fire Mark, 11½″ h, 7¼″ w, cast iron,
oval, hose and "F.A.," worn old dark
green repaint **75.00**
Fireplace Facade, 54 x 44 x 14″, Art
Deco, blue mirror, acid etched iris dec,

Ornamental Arch, wrought iron, early 20th C, 122″ w, 37¾″ h, $8,250.00. Photograph courtesy of Freeman/Fine Arts of Philadelphia.

matching 52 x 35″ wall mirror, price for set.............................. **2,200.00**

Fountain, 54″ h, terra-cotta, shallow circular basin, deeply everted lip, molded relief laurel and flowers, putto on one side, naked winged mermaid with crossed arms as baluster, coved circular base, acanthus cast scrolled feet, weathered patina, minor losses, repaired basin................... **4,125.00**

Garden Bench, 46″ l, cast iron, good scrolling details, old white repaint ... **545.00**

Garden Chair, arm, cast iron
28″ h, vintage design, painted white, price for pair **175.00**
36″ h, center seat medallion, label "Mfg by the Kramer Bros Fdy Co, Dayton, O," old worn white repaint **440.00**

Garden Gate
Cast Iron, 45½″ h, 19th C **385.00**
Picket, 35¼″ w, 49″ h, New England, 19th C, wood, gray painted weathered surface **220.00**

Garden Ornament
29″ l, cast concrete, lion, rect base, broken front corner............ **360.00**
40″ l, 28½″ h, painted cast iron, dog, long thin tail, American, 19th C ... **3,100.00**
52″ l, 35½″ h, Newfoundland Dog, painted cast iron, detailed coat, America, mid 19th C.......... **24,200.00**
80″ h, zinc, classical figure, marked "AB and WT Westervelt, New York," late 19th C............. **6,600.00**

Garden Seat
13″ h, Staffordshire, 19th C, Chinese style, barrel form, coral red ground, price for matched pair.......... **990.00**
19″ h, Minton Majolica, England, 1871, hexagonal, cobalt blue ground, polychrome enamels, pierced floral and geometric side panels, imp mark and date code, surface wear, price for pair **3,300.00**

Garden Suite, cast iron, three tables, plant stand, five chairs, labeled "Woodard," white repaint, old cushions, price for nine piece set **525.00**

Garden Table, cast iron, round
18½″ d, 17¾″ h, plate glass top, yellow paint................... **75.00**
39″ d top, 28″ h, floral design, white repaint **110.00**

Gate Pediment, 32″ h, 89″ l, arched form, scrolls and foliate dec, two dragon heads, wrought iron, painted black, parcel gilt, Continental **715.00**

Hinges, wrought iron
10″ h, H–L, price for pair **45.00**
20″ l, strap hinge, rect plate pintels, price for set of six **90.00**
24″ l, strap hinge, extended "Y" ends, pitted, price for pair **140.00**
30″ l, strap hinge, "Y" ends, pitted, price for pair **140.00**

Hitching Post, 40″ h, cast iron, whip shape, round base with fastening holes **275.00**

Latch Handle, 12″ l, wrought iron, leaf ends, pitted, rust, thumb piece missing................... **150.00**

Lawn Sprinkler, 11″ w, 7″ h, bronze and copper, revolving sphere, arched tripod base with vertical striations, imp "37," design attributed to Rockwell Kent, c1925 .... **800.00**

Lock
4 x 7¼″, cast iron, rect vertical mounted box, keeper, worn green paint, one Rockingham doorknob, brass key **60.00**
4½ x 5¾″, cast iron, rect vertical mounted box, brass key, one Rockingham doorknob, traces of old white paint.................. **68.00**
6½ x 11″, wrought iron, box, spring lever latch, large key, round cast

brass escutcheon, old worn white
paint.   80.00
Mailbox, 44″ h, painted metal, pagoda
form, front and sides molded in relief
of equestrian postmen, foliage cast
baluster pedestal, rect base, painted
dark green, Victorian 675.00
Mantel
   Classical Revival, pine, old tan repaint, 62½″ w, 44½″ h 200.00
   Federal
      Attributed to Salem, MA, c1800,
      wood, carved florals and swags,
      51½″ w opening, 73½″ w overall,
      50″ h 1,320.00
      New England, c1810, combed col-
      umns and central plaque, painted
      white, 52½″ w x 44″ h opening,
      78¾″ w, 66″ h. 770.00
Pedestal, 52″ h, 12″ d, columnar, circular
top, fluted shaft molded plinth base,
painted white, price for pair 525.00
Plaque
   15″ w, 8½″ h, brass, hinged, painted
   and gilded, Massachusetts state
   seal 660.00
   44½″ l, carved eagle, gold paint, red,
   white, and blue shield, 20th C 600.00
Road Sign, 14½″ w, 28½″ h, cast iron,
tombstone shape, rounded top, pointing hands, "Wooster" and "Cleave-
land" [sic] uneven bottom edge. 880.00
Snowbirds, cast iron
   6½″ wingspan, 7¼″ l, eagles, price for
   set of four 85.00
   8½″ w, 14″ l, double bird heads, pitted,
   price for set of six. 165.00
Sundial, 41″ h, carrara marble, acanthus
carved baluster, fluted and volute
carved capital, chamfered gray marble sq top, cast bronze dial, Greek
Key border, quadruple paw footed
base, concave sloped plinth, Neoclass-
ical, Continental, 19th C 2,200.00
Trophy, 27″ w, 99″ h, wall, carved and
gilded, military dec, from the Guard's
Club, London, England, price for pair   3,575.00
Urn
   27″ h, lead covered, woven wicker
   vase form, pierced sides. 715.00
   34″ h, cast iron, floral detail, labeled
   "Walbridge & Co, Buffalo, NY,"
   cleaned, repainted, light rust,
   cracks in reservoir, price for pair . .   650.00
Window Pane, lacy glass, 5″ h, 4″ w,
minor chips
   Amber, floral corners 40.00
   Blue–Green, ivy dec 45.00
   Cobalt Blue
      Floral corners 50.00
      Ivy dec 35.00
   Sapphire Blue, ivy dec 50.00

ART DECO

History: The Art Deco period was named for an
exhibition, "l'Exposition Internationale des Arts
Décorative et Industriels Modernes," held in Paris
in 1927. It is a later period than Art Nouveau, but
sometimes the two styles overlap since they were
closely related in time.

Art Deco designs are angular with simple lines.
This was the period of skyscrapers, movie idols,
and the cubist works of Picasso and Legras. Art
Deco motifs were used for every conceivable object being produced in the 1920s and 1930s, such
as ceramics, furniture, glass, and metals, not only
in Europe but in America as well.

References: Victor Arwas, *Glass: Art Nouveau
To Art Deco*, Rizzoli, 1977; Lillian Baker, *Art Nou-
veau & Art Deco Jewelry: An Identification & Value
Guide*, Collector Books, 1981; Bryan Catley, *Art
Deco And Other Figures*, Antique Collectors' Club;
Tony Fusco, *Art Deco Identification and Price
Guide*, Avon Books, 1993; Mary Gaston, *Collec-
tor's Guide To Art Deco*, Collector Books, 1989,
1994 value update; Robert Heide and John Gilman,
*Popular Art Deco: Depression Era Style and De-
sign*, Abbeville Press, 1991; Richard J. Kilbride, *Art
Deco Chrome Book Z: A Collectors' Guide, Indus-
trial Design in the Chase Era*, Jo–D Books, 1992;
Katherine Morrison McClinton, *Art Deco: A Guide
For Collectors*, reprint, Clarkson N. Potter, 1986;
Wolf Uecker, *Art Nouveau and Art Deco Lamps
and Candlesticks*, Abbeville Press, 1986; Howard
and Pat Watson, *Collecting Art Deco Ceramics*,
Kevin Francis, 1993.

Collectors' Clubs: Chase Collectors Society,
2149 W. Jibsail Loop, Mesa, AZ 85202; National
Coalition of Art Deco Societies, One Murdock Terrace, Brighton, MA 02135.

Museums: Art Institute of Chicago, Chicago, IL;
Corning Museum of Glass, Corning, NY; Jones Museum of Glass and Ceramics, Sebago, ME.

Additional Listings: Furniture and Jewelry.
Also check glass, pottery, and metal categories.

Ashtray, 10″ h, figural, nude holding tray
over head, copper colored metal,
marked "Rembrandt". 185.00
Bookends, pr
   4½″ h, elephants, weighted iron, imp
   "Made in Italy". 200.00
   5⅞″ h, McClelland Barclay, patinated
   metal, stylized leaf form, green and
   gold applied patina, sgd 220.00
Bowl, 12″ d, black glass, silver deposit
border 30.00
Box, cov, 3½ x 2″, green malachite
glass, two nude women, long hair entwined on cov, additional nude frolicking woman around base. 125.00
Cigarette Box, cov, 8½″ l, 5¼″ d, 2¾″ h,
burlwood, rect hinged lid, rounded

Desk Clock, rect, green enameled dial, black stone case, two pierced jadite balls, stepped base, eight day movement, Gubelin, 8" l, estimated price $3,000.00 to $3,500.00.

ends, light and dark veneers, fitted int., c1920 . . . .   145.00

Cigarette Case, 3 x 3½", silver, hinged rect case, horizontal reeded bands, 14k red and green gold bands, medallion with engraved monogram, Elgin, c1915–30. . . . .   300.00

Clock
  Mantel
    13" l, 13" h, bronze, gilt metal case, floral dec, verdigris finished base, sgd "G Beal," France, c1925, replaced works 360.00
    19" l, 12½" h, marble, black and gold, stylized female nude, white metal clock face, sgd "Geo–Luc," France, 1925 . . . .   330.00
  Table, 11⅝" l, 9" h, ceramic, stylized deer and nude figures, blue and white on gold, white field with purple highlights, steel face, attributed to Jean Mayodon, France, c1925, hairline, crazing 220.00

Cocktail Shaker, nickled silver, tapering body, applied handles, imp mark, spout cap missing, wear to finish . . .   200.00

Cologne Bottle, acid treated glass, enameled cobalt blue and yellow stylized flowers, large mushroom stopper   175.00

Cup, 3⅜" h, pottery, Emile DeCoeur, France, c1920, gray marble glaze, black rim, imp mark. 415.00

Desk Set, Bakelite, butterscotch, ink tray, two notepad holders, marked, c1940, price for three piece set. 220.00

Doorstop, 7 x 9", bronze, woman, clinging gown, standing and holding out skirt 175.00

Dresser Set, Catalin, three containers, 10⅜" l tray, butterscotch ground, beige plastic trim and lids. 165.00

Figure
  11" h, cold painted bronze, exotic dancer, after Pierre LeFaguays, black marble base 550.00
  25¼" h, female dancer, metal and simulated ivory, stepped circular marble base, inscribed "Duchamps" 825.00

Flatware Service, sterling silver, Cactus pattern, Georg Jensen, designed by Gundorph Albertus, Denmark, 1930, imp post 1945 mark, monogrammed, price for 27 pcs. 660.00

Furniture
  Chest of Drawers, 44½ x 35", parchment covered, rect top, three tapering drawers, pyramidal mirrored stiles, bracket feet, back branded "Quigley," French, c1925 . . . .   2,750.00
  Vanity, 43 x 23¾", rect top, two drawers, cupboard doors flanking recessed door, mirrored glass panels   425.00

Lamp Base, 10¼" h, Belgian pottery, irid and crystalline light blue, gray, white, and brown streak glaze, floral and foliate stylized hammered iron, incised and painted marks, imp metal, drilled   175.00

Lamp, desk, Saturn, 11½" h, satin glass sphere, reverse painted white stars and planets, blue ground 470.00

Mirror, 22½" w, 42" h, wrought iron, imp marks, attributed to Paul Kiss, c1925   1,210.00

Floor Lamp, chrome and painted wood, round leaded slag glass shade, chrome standard, 52½" h, $357.50. Photograph courtesy of Leslie Hindman Auctioneers.

Paperweight, Egyptian, bronze 38.00

Perfume Bottle, 6″ h, Golliwogg, frosted novelty bottle, orig deVigny Paris label, black face stopper, orig wig, c1920 . . . . 330.00

Perfume Lamp, 8″ h, DeVilbiss, flared opal cylinder, black and orange stylized moonlit enameled scene, gilt metal trifid electrical socket base, conforming perfume holder, reticulated cov 275.00

Plaque, 23¾″ w, 42″ h, carved and polychrome dec wood panel depicting bicycle racing, Federal Art Project, c1930s, splitting 495.00

Powder Box, 5½″ w, black glass base, silverplated cov, wolf hound finial . . . 75.00

Punch Bowl Set, bowl and ten cups, glass, wide rim around center holds ten cobalt blue cups, price for eleven pc set 95.00

Rug, 117″ l, 75½″ w, wool, olive, salmon, light brown, ivory, light blue, and teal irregular areas, brown, rust, light blue, and mauve stylized floral designs, interlocking linear segments border, French, c1925 . . . . 2,750.00

Urn, 10½″ h, patinated metal, repeating red marble and streaked silver segments, yellow linear highlights, sgd "Andrey, Jovenia, France," c1925 . . . 1,045.00

Vase
6″ h, bud, ruby and amber glass, orig price label 45.00
8″ h
Glass, black–amethyst, silver deposit dec of heron and cattails . . 50.00
Metal, applied gold–green patina, raised McClelland Barclay signature 220.00
9″ h, cased yellow to colorless glass, internal red and deep green mottling, circular mark "Scailmont/ Mange/Made in Belgium" 275.00
9½″ h, Boch Frere, designed by Charles Catteau, Belgium, c1925, ceramic, mat yellow, blue, and white stylized leaves, black ground, artist sgd, stamp mark 470.00
12⅞″ h, Boch Frere, c1925, ceramic, shades of blue, yellow and rust blossoms, cream crackle ground, black outlines, imp and stamped marks 360.00
13¾″ h, Jean Verschneider, France, c1925, patinated metal, green shades, repeating linear and geometric pattern, sgd "Jean Verschneider," abrasions, minor denting 1,210.00
16″ h, 12″ w, brilliant orange cutting, mottled white and clear cluthra style

glass ground, large berries and leaves design, sgd "Daum Nancy" with Cross of Lorraine and France 3,000.00

ART NOUVEAU

History: Art Nouveau is the French term for the "new art" which had its beginning in the early 1890s and continued for the next 40 years. The flowing and sensuous female forms used in this period were popular in Europe and America. Among the most recognized artists of this period were Galle, Lalique, and Tiffany.

Art Nouveau can be identified by its flowing, sensuous lines, floral forms, insects, and the feminine form. These designs were incorporated on almost everything produced at that time, from art glass to furniture, silver, and personal objects.

References: Victor Arwas, *Glass: Art Nouveau To Art Deco*, Rizzoli, 1977; Lillian Baker, *Art Nouveau & Art Deco Jewelry: An Identification & Value Guide*, Collector Books, 1981; Giovanni Fanelli and Ezio Godoli, *Art Nouveau Postcards*, Rizzoli, 1987; Albert Christian Revi, *American Art Nouveau Glass*, reprint, Schiffer Publishing, 1981; Wolf Uecker, *Art Nouveau and Art Deco Lamps and Candlesticks*, Abbeville Press, 1986.

Additional Listings: Furniture and Jewelry. Also check glass, pottery, and metal categories.

Ashtray, 2¾″ h, gilt brass, foliate design, wood ground, Fisher–Strand, Germany, c1900 . . . . 140.00

Basket, 9½″ l, sterling silver, monogram, marked "Frank W Smith Silver Co Inc for Bailey, Banks, and Biddle Co" . . . 350.00

Belt, 24″ l, sterling silver, six model female busts plaques, long flowing hair, chain connecting pieces and satin ribbon, marked "Kerr" 715.00

Bowl
10¼″ d, 5¼″ h, glass, maroon, clear, and green bands, controlled veining, WMF Ikora, Germany, c1925 . 250.00
13¾″ d, 2⅞″ h, glass, banded rim, int. shaping, green base highlights, controlled veining, WMF Ikora, Germany, c1925 . . . . 165.00

Bust, 28¼″ h, porcelain, Daphne, finely featured, garland in hair, self base, molded name 1,700.00

Calling Card Tray, 4½ x 7″, pewter, relief molded woman with flowing hair 80.00

Candelabrum, pr
12¼″ h, silvered metal, stylized arms, flaring sq post and base, imp mark, bobeche missing, dents 615.00
19″ h, Britannia metal, four light, elegantly draped woman standard, flowing skirt forms circular base, holding vase beside head with three

Candlestick, sterling silver, Reed and Barton, organic forms flowing into weighted bases, 11¼" h, price for pair, $1,210.00. Photograph courtesy of Freeman/Fine Arts of Philadelphia.

sinuous arms, central taller arm, leafy bud candle socket, removable bobeches, Wurtembergische Metallwaren-Fabric, Germany, "WMF" mark 8,250.00

Charger, 20" d, pewter, large emb profile center bust portrait of woman, long flowing hair, thin gown, wide rim emb with daisies, long stems, scrolling leaves, hallmarked, c1900 . . . . 660.00

Clock, 25" h, green bisque, gold and pink highlights, gilt metal, imp Charenton marks, France, c1900, hand missing, nicks 825.00

Desk Set, London, c1921, onyx, inlaid lapis lazuli band, two inkwells, blotter, note pad, card, and pen holders, imp hallmarks, chips, price for six piece set 275.00

Dish, 6" d, Basse Taille, enamel dec copper, yellow and pink Limoges style floral dec, green and gold leaves, tortoise enamel ground, purple ext., French, sgd "C Faure," c1900 . . . . . 330.00

Dresser Set, silver, rococo floral repousse, engraved "Nellie," and "Dec 1902," brush and matching mirror, cut crystal jars with silver lids, marked "Sterling," price for four piece set . . . 160.00

Figure, 14½" h, gilt bronze, girl, long skirt, low girdle and breastplates over mesh bodice, draped beaded necklace, ivory head, arms, and feet, coved circular gray-green and black marble base, incised "A Gori". 3,200.00

Fire Fender Set, brass, European, c1900
Mushroom finials, scrolling center de-

sign on linear 54" l x 12" h fire fender, matching tools 470.00

Scrolling decor, 19½" h andirons, 53¼" l fire fender, and matching tools 1,100.00

Fire Screen
Copper, 18¼ x 28½" h, wrought iron frame, center blue glazed ceramic insert, England, c1900 . . . . 330.00

Leaded Glass, 48½" w, 32" h, three panels, clear glass top, hammered white glass lower half, central applied floral design, green bull's eye highlights. 2,750.00

Furniture
Bed, 54" w, 57½" h, marquetry, inlaid floral designs, carved tendrils and brass overlay on headboard and footboard, stamped "BL 106 6B," French 1,450.00

Chair, desk, attributed to Louis Majorelle, France, mahogany, curved crest rail continues to outward flaring arms, three upholstered panels over D-shaped overupholstered seat, outward curving molded legs, back uprights supporting setback arms continuing downward as rear leg braces, dark green leatherette upholstery. 9,350.00

Music Cabinet, walnut and marquetry, two doors above two drawers, iris dec, incised "Emile Galle Nancy". . 2,100.00

Parlor Suite, Majorelle style, Escargot pattern, carved mahogany, 55" l settee, two armchairs, two side chairs, molded and dipped crest rails, carved and pierced stiles, rect upholstered seats, cabriole legs, 5 pcs. 4,200.00

Table, side, 22½" l, 27½" h, nest of four, rect top, marquetry, pierced organic trestle supports, shaped stretcher, marquetry includes landscape, seascape, three cats, and flowers 2,250.00

Inkwell
5" d, 1½" h, conical pewter body, raised stylized foliage design, blue-green enamel buttons, glass insert, imp "English Pewter 0521" 275.00

12" w, 6⅞" h, gilt bronze, two nude women in surf, inkwell lid in form of crab, brown composition base, Vve Leonie Ledru, France, c1900. . . . . 525.00

Jardiniere, 12" d, bronze, circular, cast lily pads and buds, dark green patina, c1900. . . . . 550.00

Magnifying Glass, 2⅛" d glass, 6¼" l hollow sterling silver handle, scrolled leaves dec, marked "Blackinton, 1904". 115.00

Mirror

Hand, 8″ l, repousse floral designs, engraved "Lena," marked "Sterling". 50.00

Wall, 43″ w, 72″ h, arch top, rect beveled mirror plate, conforming wooden surround, applied hammered silvered metal stylized blossoms and leaves, textured brass ground 3,575.00

Pitcher

9¼″ h, Bursley–Ware, England, Charlotte Rhead, blue floral dec, white ground, imp stamp, crazing. 110.00

14½″ h, glass, silverplated mountings, cylindrical body, bulbous base, hinged lid, scrolled handle, green leaves, fuchsia blossoms, and band of iris, four scroll feet 335.00

Plaque

14″ d, Ch Spiers, c1880, sunflowers and iris polychrome dec, sgd and imp marks, price for pair. 1,100.00

17″ d, Longwy Faience, E Killiert, pink–white and green Limoges style dec, blue ground, gold highlights, incised sgd, back imp "Longwy D/1182" 880.00

Seal, rock crystal quartz, 18K yg chased collar 385.00

Tazza

10½″ d, 6¼″ h, silver, segmented border inside flaring rim, raised on four posts with vertical striated linear design, stepped disc base, imp Apollo mark. 385.00

Torchere, wrought iron, mottled orange glass shade sgd "Daum Nancy," tapering hexagonal standard, c1930, 19″ d shade, 66″ h, $8,800.00. Photograph courtesy of William Doyle Galleries.

12½″ d, 9¾″ h, gilt bronze, high relief teasel and stalks, fluted bronze stem, brown/green patina, black marble base, French, incised "A Marionnet" 660.00

Tile, 32½″ l, 22″ w, shoreline scene, French, Barbitone School, attributed to Armand Desire Gautier, incised "A Gautier L.L." on reverse, painted cipher "DG," framed, c1800 . . . . 1,100.00

Tray

11½ x 14½″, bronze, lily pad shape, stem handle, male and female figures embracing in relief on one side, imp mark, French, c1900 . . . 660.00

12¼ x 15½″, bronze, cast swirls and pairs of blossoms, pierced stems, slightly upturned sides, case female head, long flowing hair, verdigris patina, imp "Geschutzt 5305" 990.00

Vase

9½″ h, art glass, brilliant butterfly blue, bulbous, sgd "Lustre Art" 550.00

11″ h, Carter, Stabler, and Adams, Poole, England, 1925, pottery, floral polychrome dec, cream ground, imp mark, hairline. 165.00

Wine Glass, gold and copper floral dec, cut swirl stem, gold leaves on base, price for set of eight. 750.00

ART PEWTER

History: Pewter objects produced during the Art Nouveau, Arts and Crafts, and Art Deco periods are gaining in popularity. These mostly utilitarian objects, for example, tea sets, trays, and bowls, were elaborately decorated and produced in the Jugendstil manner by German firms, such as Kayserzinn, and Austrian companies, such as Orivit. In England, Liberty and Company marketed Tudric Pewter, which often had a hammered surface and was embellished with enameling or semiprecious stones. Most pieces of art pewter contain the maker's mark.

FIEN ZINN

Bowl, 9½″ d, large open rim handles, marked "S Rothhan, Fien Zinn" 50.00

Pitcher, 12″ h, marked "Wien, Fien Zinn" 85.00

JUGENDSTIL

Tray, 9″ l, 8½″ w, shaped triangular harp form, relief dec, standing figure of woman with one bare arm resting on top of harp, diaphanous flowing gown swirling at feet, two slender branches form handles, leaves spreading

across dished surface, imp "B" and
"OX" **335.00**

KAYSERZINN

Beaker, 4½" h, poppy motif, c1900,
#436 . . . . **125.00**
Bowl
   13" l, oval, flowers and leaves, open
   handles, #4322 . . . . **150.00**
   16½" d, Art Nouveau styling, car-
   touche dec, scroll legs, handle . . . **375.00**
Chamberstick, Art Nouveau floral dec **75.00**
Flagon, 13" h, squirrel figure on top,
   acorn and leaf motif. **445.00**
Vase, 8" h, iris motif, #4105, peeling
   finish **50.00**

**Bowl, cov, sunflowers dec, handled,
ftd, marked "Kayzerzinn," numbered,
7½" d, $160.00.**

ORIVIT

Pitcher, claret type, green glass insert,
   Art Nouveau vines and floral dec . . . **90.00**
Wine Cooler, 8 x 10½", floral dec . . . **275.00**

TUDRIC

Centerpiece, 9¾" d, two handles, circular dish, raised base, sinuous blossoms and stems, inscribed, stamped
   "Tudric," c1900. . . . . **500.00**
Clock, 5½" h, desk, rect, repousse wind-
   ing vines and berries dec, Arabic numerals enameled in red, green, and
   blue, stamped "Tudric" **350.00**
Pitcher, 5¾" h, cov, blue enamel dec,
   cane wrapped handle, imp Liberty and
   Co, England marks, 1905. . . . . **200.00**

URANIA

Candelabra, 13¼" h, flattened oval
   pierced standard, low relief casting,
   linear motifs, flanking branches at

right angles, conical cup, tapering cylindrical nozzle, imp "Urania/Hutton,
Sheffield/1376," price for pair **550.00**

ART POTTERY (GENERAL)

History: The period of art pottery reached its
zenith in the late 19th and early 20th centuries.
Over a hundred companies produced individually
designed and often decorated wares which served
a utilitarian as well as an aesthetic purpose. Artists
moved about from company to company, some
forming their own firms.

Quality of design, beauty in glazes, and condition
are the keys to buying art pottery. This category
covers companies not found elsewhere in this
guide.

References: Paul Evans, *Art Pottery of the
United States, Second Edition,* Feingold & Lewis
Publishing, 1987; Lucile Henzke, *Art Pottery of
America,* Schiffer Publishing, 1982; Ralph and
Terry Kovel, *The Kovels' Collector's Guide to
American Art Pottery,* Crown Publishers, 1974.

Periodical: *Arts & Crafts Quarterly,* 9 Main St.,
Lambertville, NJ 08530.

Collectors' Club: American Art Pottery Association, 125 E. Rose Avenue, St. Louis, MO 63119.

Additional Listings: See Cambridge, Clewell,
Clifton, Cowan, Dedham, Fulper, Grueby, Jugtown,
Marblehead, Moorcroft, Newcomb, North Dakota
School of Mines, Ohr, Owens, Paul Revere, Peters
and Reed, Rookwood, Roseville, Van Briggle,
Weller, and Zanesville.

Arc En Ciel (1903 to 1907), Zanesville,
   OH, vase, 6½" h, oak leaf rim band,
   trailing stems, pale green–blue gloss
   glaze, imp mark "1/500," 1904, hair-
   line, crazing **250.00**
Arequipa Pottery (1911 to 1918), Marin
   County, CA
   Bowl, 9" d, 4¾" h, flower and leaf
     mold, black and white. **150.00**
   Vase
     3½" h, matte tan glaze ground, teal
      shoulder, imp mark, base pull . . **200.00**
     11⅜" h, Frederick H Rhead, c1913,
      relief stylized wisteria on shoul-
      der and rim band, trailing vertical
      flowers, reticulated highlights,
      matte green and black glaze,
      glaze pulls at base **495.00**
Batchelder Tile Co, Los Angeles
   Ashtray, 4½" d, hexagonal bowl, relief
     lettering, matte light blue glaze,
     c1926, wear, nicks **165.00**
   Center Bowl, 18½" d, wide everted
     rim, int. glazed in pale green, purple
     ext., inscribed "5 EA Batchelder/
     Kinneloa/Kiln" **625.00**
E Bennett Pottery Co (1845–1936), Bal-

Dedham Pottery, vase, sand, high glaze, sgd, Hugh Roberts, 3½″ h, $425.00.

timore, MD, vase, 8½ x 8″, pillow, Arabian man on horseback, brown, green, and cream scene, green ground, base incised "Albion," "E Bennett Pottery Co, 1896," and "KB" **1,100.00**

California Faience (1916–1930), Berkeley, CA

Bookends, pr, eagle, blue matte **675.00**

Box, 1½ x 4½ x 3½″, raspberry tile top, cloisonne dec **100.00**

Potpourri Jar, 4½″ h, Oriental shape, yellow matte, incised mark **225.00**

Vase, 6½″ h, turquoise glaze, relief band of stylized doves, arrowheads, and spruce, incised mark, c1924 **360.00**

Cincinnati Faience, c1890, umbrella stand, 20″ h, applied sea life, blue glaze, gold accents, sgd **990.00**

Kenton Hills (1939–42), Erlanger, KY

Ashtray, 7 x 6½″, stylized horse head shape, turquoise glossy glaze, marked **45.00**

Bowl, 3½″ d, olive glossy glaze **100.00**

Vase, 7 x 6″, brown irid glaze **120.00**

McLaughlin, M Louise (1876–1906), Cincinnati, OH, vase, 4½″ h, 4″ d, bulbous, Impressionist style brown flowers and green leaves, marbled beige ground, sgd in script "L McL Cincinnati 1878″ and "81″ **800.00**

Merrimac Pottery, (1897–1908), Newburyport, MA, vase, 12″ h, 9½″ d, bulbous, smooth feathered matte blue–green glaze, imp mark, small glaze base chips **550.00**

Pewabic Pottery (1903–61), Detroit, MI

Bowl, 6¼″ d, 2¾″ h, matte green glaze, high relief repeating leaves, imp "Pewabic" under maple leaves **1,540.00**

Box, cov, 5″ w, 3¾″ d, 1¾″ h, rect, cut corner top, imp stylized peacock dec, irid blue green glaze, imp "Pewabic, Detroit," early 20th C **275.00**

Plate, 9″ d, hp, cottage scene border **150.00**

Vase, 6½″ h, 4½″ d, gourd shape, cut back design, stylized jonquils, long stems, smooth matte green glaze, die stamped mark **1,760.00**

Teco Pottery (1902 to 1930), Terra Cotta, IL

Coaster, 4¼″ d, Cubs, oatmeal ground, team insignia, imp mark **140.00**

Vase, 4½″ h, green glaze, raised and shaped neck, dimpled body, imp mark twice **250.00**

University City (1910 to 1915), University City, MO, vase

3½ x 3½″, U–shaped, sheets of white snowflake crystals, white porcelain ground, imp "U–C" and "1912" **945.00**

4¼ x 4″, bulbous, heavy, brown to tan flambe glaze, incised "UC" **295.00**

Vance/Avon Faience (1880 to 1905), Tiltonville, OH, vase, 6⅛″ h, elongated, flaring neck, squatty body, stylized orange, green, and light green–blue landscape, black underglaze, incised marks, c1903, hairlines **220.00**

Walley, Sterling, MA, early 20th C

Bowl, 5⅝″ d, 4¾″ h, rolled rim, shouldered, circular ftd base, blue matte glaze, imp "WJW" **360.00**

Vase, 3⅜″ h, gloss brown over blue/green drip glaze, imp "WJW" **220.00**

Walrath Pottery (1900 to 1920), Rochester, NY

Bowl, 4¾″, green florals, brown ground **225.00**

Figure, 6″ l, matte tan and green reposing female nude, int. rust glazed bowl at side, inscribed, dated 1912 **200.00**

Flower Bowl, 9½ x 9½″, brown and green lily pads on ext., center seated nude figure, tall weed flower frogs, incised "Walrath 1412 Pottery". **880.00**

Mug, 6″, brown florals, green matte ground, sgd "RB," incised mark. **250.00**

Pitcher, 3″ h, beige ext., rust int. matte glaze, inscribed mark, c1908. **125.00**

Pot, 2½″ h, purple matte glaze, base chip **95.00**

Wannopee Pottery, New Milford, CT, c1903, table lamp, 18″ h, irid green, blue, black mirror glaze base, canister inset, imp mark, woven wicker shade with silk lining, two light sockets, crazing, liner tears. **715.00**

Wheatley Pottery Co (1880 to 1936), Cincinnati, OH

Bowl, 7½″ d, 3¼″ h, relief dec, open petal flowers and leaves, matte

green glaze, raised mark and number, retail label. **880.00**
Oil Lamp, 7¼" h, 9½" d, four sq buttressed feet, organic curdled matte green glaze. **880.00**
Tile, 7¾" sq, emb lion, organic matte brown glaze. **250.00**
Vase, 12 x 7¾ x 3", oval, Limoges style painting by Martin Rettig on one side, schooners on ocean, deep blue high glaze, artist sgd, incised "No 50, TJW & Co, 1880," some restoration to glaze chips. . . **1,760.00**
Zark Pottery, vase, 7½" h, blue **325.00**

ARTS AND CRAFTS MOVEMENT

History: The Arts and Crafts Movement in American decorative arts took place between 1895 and 1920. Leading proponents of the movement were Elbert Hubbard and his Roycrofters, the brothers Stickley, Frank Lloyd Wright, Charles and Henry Greene, George Niedecken, and Lucia and Arthur Mathews.

The movement was marked by individualistic design (although the movement was national in scope) and reemphasis on handcraftsmanship and appearance. A reform of industrial society was part of the long-range goal. Most pieces of furniture favored a rectilinear approach and were made of oak.

References: Steven Adams, *The Arts & Crafts Movement,* Chartwell Books, 1987; David M. Cathers, *Furniture of the American Arts and Crafts Movement,* New American Library, 1981; Paul Evans, *Art Pottery Of The United States, 2nd Edition,* Feingold & Lewis Publishing, 1987; Malcolm Haslam, *Collector's Style Guides: Arts and Crafts,* Ballantine Books, 1988; Bruce Johnson, *The Official Identification And Price Guide To Arts And Crafts, Second Edition,* House of Collectibles, 1992; Wendy Kaplan, *The Art That Is Life: The Arts And Crafts Movement In America 1875–1920,* Boston Museum of Fine Arts, 1987; Elyse Zorn Karlin, *Jewelry and Metalwork in the Arts and Crafts Tradition,* Schiffer Publishing, 1993; Coy L. Ludwig, *The Arts and Crafts Movement In New York State, 1890s–1920s,* Gallery Association of New York State, 1983; L–W Book Sales, *Furniture of the Arts & Crafts Period With Prices,* L–W Book Sales, 1992; Kevin McConnell, *Heintz Art Metal: Silver–On–Bronze Wares,* Schiffer Publishing, 1990; Mary Ann Smith, *Gustav Stickley: The Craftsman,* Dover Publications, 1983, 1992 reprint.

Periodical: *Arts and Crafts Quarterly,* 9 Main St., Lambertville, NJ 08530.

Museum: Museum of Modern Art, New York, NY.

Additional Listings: Roycroft, Stickleys, and art pottery categories.

Desk Chair, Quaint Furniture, three inlaid stylized tulips on slat, branded mark, c1910, 16" w, 15" d, 38¼" h, $900.00. Photograph courtesy of Skinner, Inc.

Andirons, pr, 16½" h, cast iron, sun personified in relief centers, c1900. . . . . **935.00**
Box, 9" w, 5¾" d, 3½" h, copper, hinged lid, rect ftd box, alternating random hammered pattern, applied arrowheads and silver faux needlework, Shreve, Crump and Low, imp marks, cleaned **700.00**
Candelabrum, 23¼" h, Jessie M Preston, Chicago, bronze, three stylized bud candle nozzles with underleaf, three intertwining stems, disc base, foliate relief, dark brown patina, imp mark **1,320.00**
Candlesticks, pr, 12" h, Jarvie style, brass, candle nozzle over disc, rod stem, disc base, unsigned **165.00**
Chafing Dish, cov, 11" h, 16½" d undulating tray, hammered copper and wood, Shreve, Crump and Low Co, Boston, 1888 . . . . **440.00**
Desk Set, Shreve, Crump and Low, c1910, double inkwell, letter holder, blotter, and thermometer, hammered copper mounted on oak, silvered copper rivets, metal tag, imp marks, price for four piece set. **330.00**
Dish, cov, 4¼" d, ceramic, Mabel A French, Lynn, MA, c1916, dome cov with stylized twisting brown branches, pink buds, green leaves, blue highlights, gold speckled ground and band at rim, shallow round ftd bowl, inscribed artist's name and town **360.00**

Dresser Set, Wallace Sterling, Carthage pattern, three brushes, comb, hand mirror, jar, and tray, hammered and linear design, monogrammed, imp marks, dents, price for seven piece set. 275.00

Floor Screen

48½" w, 65¾" h, three panel, poplar panels, pyrographic and polychrome poppies dec, mahogany frame, unsgd, shrinkage cracks. . .   770.00

79" h, 67½" h, four panel, canvas, beige ground, imp and polychrome aesthetic floral design, brass tacks, metal tag reads "Ferguson Co, Hoboken," wear. 165.00

Furniture

China Closet, No. 2008, c1910, oak, orig medium finish, three int. shelves, 41¾" w, 16" d, 58" h 935.00

Pool Rack, Brunswick–Balke–Collender, c1912, inlaid mahogany, central mirror over ball rack, flanked by cue racks, linear and geometric inlay of wood and mother of pearl, gold stencil and paper label, 48¼" w, 61¾" h 1,760.00

Table

Dining, oak

Hexagonal top, six rect legs, three arched, stacked, and crossed stretchers, central pin, keyed tenons, light refinish, 41¼" d, 29¼" h. 990.00

Round top, pedestal base, five sq posts, four cased leaves, unsgd, branded "No. 804," c1915, finish wear, separation, 48" h, 30½" h 990.00

Library, Lifetime, No. 1015, c1910, oak, medium brown finish, six sided top over two drawers, medial shelf between arched side stretchers, iron hardware, remnants of paper label, retailer's metal tag, water stains, 52" l, 26" d, 29¾" h. 1,430.00

Umbrella Stand, mahogany, pyramidal top sq posts, brass foot cuffs, copper tray base, 13½" w, 28" h . .   135.00

Lamp

Candle, 25½" h, four sided green slag glass shade, oak frame suspended by curved wrought iron strap, triangular oak base with green slag glass inserts, unmarked, price for pair. 1,210.00

Table

23" h, 23" d hexagonal shade, green, red, and brown slag glass panels in oak frame, hexagonal oak base with open lattice work, oil lamp burner 385.00

25" h, hammered copper, orig dark patina, patterned hammered finish, three light sockets, 19" d shade 1,100.00

Painting, A Madrigal, oil on canvas board, Alexis B Many artist, unsgd, identified on exhibition label on reverse, 11 x 10¼", period frame. 360.00

Plaque

Frederick, J William, burned and incised portrait on panel, oak frame, titled "Over The Terrace Wall," inscribed on reverse "This original design was burned on wood with red–hot irons. To my good friend Dellengaugh. The Sherwood, New York, May 2, 1894" 165.00

Hale, Frank Gardner, Boston, enamel, white and transparent, red fish, blue/green and yellow seaweed, black velvet border, framed, sgd, 31" w, 4⁵⁄₁₆" h. 495.00

Print

Baumann, Gustave, Mending The Seine, c1917, sgd "Gustave Baumann" in pencil and with swan chop lower right, titled in pencil lower left, color woodcut on paper, 9¾ x 11¼", unmatted, unframed, toning, subtle water staining, minor tears and creases to margins. 880.00

Hohlwein, Ludwig, Direct China Cotton Importers Wonalancet Company, Nashua, NH, sgd and inscribed "Ludwig Hohlwein Munchen" in lower right matrix, titled in center right matrix, G Schuh & Cie, Munchen, publisher identified in lower center matrix, lithograph in colors on paper, 32 x 23" sheet size, unmatted, unframed . .   770.00

Preissig, Vojtech, Arts and Crafts of the Homelands, monogram of printer and Wentworth Institute, Boston in lower left matrix, lithograph printed in colors on paper, 38 x 25" sheet size, unframed, subtle toning.   1,320.00

Souvenir Scarf, Imperial Hotel, Japan, woodblock style image of Frank Lloyd Wright designed hotel, other Japanese sights, silk, orig box, 29 x 27½"   220.00

Smoking Set, sterling silver, sectioned 11⅞" l x 10" w tray, lamp, and cutter, hammered pattern, monogrammed, imp marks, 30 troy oz, price for three piece set 330.00

Textile, 84" l, 46" w, jacquard woven, design attributed to Samuel Rowe, ascending olive, gold, tan, and green foliate and floral designs, outlined in black, central maroon damask ground, maroon border ground, England, c1900. . . . . 1,320.00

Trophy, auto racing, sterling silver, presentation cup, three stag horn handles, cut–cardwork "Rhode Island Automobile Club Races/Narragansett Park, Providence, October 17th 1901/ First Prize/Steam Class/won by John Shepard Jr," imp Gorham marks, minor dents 470.00

Umbrella Stand, 24½" h, hammered iron, riveted band dec, applied medallion, unsgd 440.00

AUSTRIAN WARE

History: Over a hundred potteries were located in the Austro–Hungarian Empire in the late 19th and early 20th centuries. Although Carlsbad was the center of the industry, the factories spread as far as modern-day Czechoslovakia.

Many of the factories were either owned or supported by Americans; hence, their wares were produced mainly for export to the United States. Responding to the 1891 law that imported products must be marked as to the country of origin, many wares do not have a factory mark but only the word "Austrian."

Reference: Susan and Al Bagdade, *Warman's English & Continental Pottery & Porcelain, Second Edition*, Wallace–Homestead, 1991.

Additional Listings: Amphora, Carlsbad, Royal Dux, and Royal Vienna.

Bouillon, underplate, pink floral dec, white ground, price for six piece set . 90.00

Bowl, 10½" d, glazed pottery, gnarled branch section, grape bunch at one end, incised mark, c1900. . . . . 315.00

Celery Tray, 12" l, scalloped border, pink roses, green leaves, gold trim. 65.00

Ewer, 5" h, 7" w, squatty, gold handle and spout, tan, blue, and cream ground, multicolored mum dec, green leaves, crown Vienna, Austria mark . 100.00

Figure, 7" l, boy fishing, hat, feather plume, shirt, vest, breeches, and clogs, crouching on bank of river, rect plinth, copper–brown patina, inscribed "Berndorf," c1900 . . . . 385.00

Goblet, 12½" h, carved fruitwood, four seasons, attributed to Schwanthaler, 19th C, minor chips 385.00

Jack In The Pulpit Vase, 16" h, naturalistic plant form, amber glass, overall irid, attributed to Pallme Konig, price for pair 800.00

Lamp Shade, 13⅝" d, 11⅜" d rim, 7" h, broad mushroom shape, amber mot-

Figurine, Amphora Teplitz, Arab warrior and horse, oval base imp "8251/38," 10" h, $385.00.

tled glass, int. random red–maroon threading, overall irid 530.00

Plaque, 9" w, hp, acorns, oak leaves, marked "Royal Austria" 50.00

Salt and Pepper Shakers, pr, five hp vignettes 55.00

Stamp Box, cov, 4¼ x 3⅛", ftd, two compartments, hp, roses, gold trim 45.00

Tray, 7" h, two bronze dancers, round green and white marble base, imp mark, abrasions, c1925 . . . . 165.00

Vase
7" h, incised stylized sunflowers, polychrome dec, inscribed "Anton Lang" 165.00
12½" h, green and feathered blue irid cylinder, reticulated pressed metal framework, grapevine and three owl ringed medallions. 385.00
18" h, hanging type, 8" d irid green and maroon glass jardiniere after Pallme Konig, bronzed Art Nouveau hanger frame. 440.00

AUTOGRAPHS

History: Autographs occur in a wide variety of formats—letters, documents, photographs, books, cards, and so on. Most collectors focus on a particular person, country, or category, for example, signers of the Declaration of Independence.

The condition and content of letters and documents bear significantly on value. Collectors should know their source since forgeries abound and copy machines compound the problem. Further, some signatures of recent presidents and movie stars are done by machine rather than by the persons themselves. A good dealer or advanced collector can help one spot the differences.

The leading auction sources for autographs are Swann Galleries, Sotheby's, and Christie's, all located in New York City.

References: Mary A. Benjamin, *Autographs: A Key To Collecting,* reprint, Dover, 1986; Charles Hamilton, *American Autographs,* University of Oklahoma Press, 1983; Norman E. Martinus and Harry L. Rinker, *Warman's Paper,* Wallace–Homestead, 1994; Robert W. Pelton, *Collecting Autographs For Fun And Profit,* Betterway Publications, 1987; George Sanders, Helen Sanders, and Ralph Roberts, *Collector's Guide To Autographs,* Wallace–Homestead, 1990; George Sanders, Helen Sanders, and Ralph Roberts, *The Price Guide To Autographs, 2nd Edition,* Wallace–Homestead, 1991.

Periodicals: *Autograph Collector's Magazine,* 510–A S. Corona Mall, Corona, CA 91720; *The Autograph Review,* 305 Carlton Rd., Syracuse, NY 13207.

Collectors' Clubs: Manuscript Society, 350 N. Niagara Street, Burbank, CA 95105; Universal Autograph Collectors Club, PO Box 6181, Washington, DC 20044.

Additional Listings: See *Warman's Americana & Collectibles* for more examples.

The following abbreviations denote types of autograph material and their sizes.

ADS	Autograph Document Signed
ALS	Autograph Letter Signed
AQS	Autograph Quotation Signed
CS	Card Signed
DS	Document Signed
LS	Letter Signed
PS	Photograph Signed
TLS	Typed Letter Signed

Sizes (approximate):

Folio	12 x 16 inches
4to	8 x 10 inches
8vo	5 x 7 inches
12mo	3 x 5 inches

COLONIAL AMERICA

Dewey, George, PS, 11 x 14″, naval officer, 1898, bust pose, wearing uniform. **350.00**

Greene, General Nathaneal, ALS, 4to, 2 pgs, June 1779, to Col James Abale, supply orders to be sent. **1,600.00**

Gridley, Richard, Revolutionary War General, DS, payment order, Boston, June 25, 1771. . . . . **450.00**

Hamilton, Alexander, ALS, 4to, 1 pg, August 1794, request for tents and camp equipment for New Jersey Militia . . . **850.00**

Harrison, Benjamin, signer of Declaration of Independence, DS, 1783, 6 x 8″, promotion of First Lieutenant paper seal. **650.00**

Hart, John, Revolutionary leader and signer Declaration of Independence, DS, 2 x 4″, currency, March 25, 1776 **450.00**

Mifflin, Thomas, Continental Congress member, DS, 11 x 21″, vellum, land deed, 1798. . . . . **250.00**

Morris, Robert, Signer of Declaration of Independence, ALS, Philadelphia, October 23, 1794, payment of drafts for delivering flour **975.00**

Otis, James, orator and patriot, DS, James Warren appointed sheriff of Plymouth County. **325.00**

Penn, William, DS, 12¼ x 15″, vellum, August 12, 1705, land grant in Philadelphia to Francis and Elizabeth Fox, wax seal. **810.00**

Varick, Richard, Revolutionary soldier, DS, 8vo, 1830, receipt for rent payment. **95.00**

EUROPEAN

Campbell, John, British General, ADS, 3 x 8″, July 13, 1776, pay order for Thomas Sundale. **195.00**

Duke of Wellington, ALS, 4 x 7″, plain stationery, July 22, 1845 . . . . **250.00**

Dumas, Jean Baptiste Andre, French chemist, ALS, 5 x 8″, plain paper . . . **135.00**

Francisco, Franco, PS, 10 x 14″, bust pose, wearing military uniform, inscribed on mat **325.00**

George III, King of Great Britain, DS, 11 x 15″, 1803, military appointment . . . **550.00**

Gladstone, W E, British Prime Minister, ALS, 4 x 7″, 1878, stationery **125.00**

Hitler, Adolf, PS, 8vo, bust pose, wearing suit and tie, black ink signature . . **2,950.00**

Irving, Henry, English actor, post card, 4 x 6″ **150.00**

Lafayette, Gilbert Marquis De, ALS, 4to, 1 pg, January, 1820, discusses news from Spain, framed with portrait **550.00**

Lehmann, Ernest A, German aeronautical engineer, PS, 4 x 6″, bust pose, wearing uniform, smoking pipe **695.00**

Montgomery, B L, PS, 4 x 6″, British General, seated with group of officers, sgd lower left **1,250.00**

Mussolini, Benito, PS, 8 x 12″, bust pose, wearing military uniform, sgd on mat **1,700.00**

Pasteur, Louis, French bacteriologist, ALS, 1882, 5 x 8″, plain paper, French script, reply. **1,600.00**

Pope Pius X, PS, 1906, seated pose, silver, sgd by Pope, Archbishop of Balisa, and Bishop of Sao Paulo. . . . **1,275.00**

Rommel, Erwin, DS, 6 x 8″, February 1942, promotion for Karl Ditmer, blue pencil signature. **2,250.00**

Thackeray, William M, English novelist, ALS, 12mo, requesting arrangements while on lecture tour **675.00**

GENERAL

Bell, Alexander Graham, magazine photo, 3½″ sq, sgd lower margin. . . . **275.00**
Duncan, Isadora, dancer, ALS, 6 x 7″, personal stationery **1,750.00**
Edison, Thomas, cut document signature, 2 x 4″ **450.00**
Hewitt, American Industrialist, ALS, 5 x 8″, 1870, stationery, asking for list of Presbyterian clergyman **95.00**
Hotchkiss, Benjamin B, inventor, ALS, 4to, 3 pgs, business stationery **1,250.00**
Irwin, Jim, astronaut, brochure, 4 x 6″, "Footprints On The Moon," color image on cov **50.00**
O'Keeffe, Georgia, artist, TLS, 4to, regards several drawings given to priest, orig envelope **995.00**
Pershing, TLS, 7 x 9″, stationery, declining invitation to serve on committee, 1924 . . . . **165.00**
Rockwell, Norman, TLS, 6 x 8″, personal stationery **125.00**

LITERATURE

Bloch, Robert, sketch, 6 x 6″, elephant walking on grass, blue ink, mounted on 7 x 10″ white board, sgd and dated **250.00**
Caldwell, Erskine, AQS, 12mo, "Eye do not spel or quot wal" **65.00**
Dickey, James, AQS, 12mo, "It was like riding on a river of air" **35.00**
Doyle, Arthur Conan, ALS, May 5, 1904, to Mackenzie Bell, orig envelope, framed **175.00**
Fitzgerald, F Scott, CS, to Paul Clute **250.00**
Grey, Zane, Oregon hunting license, September 2, 1925, three signatures **900.00**
Kilmer, Joyce, poet, post card, 3½ x 5⅛″, May 15, 1918, bust pose, wearing WWI uniform, penned letter to father on back **2,750.00**
Lewis, Sinclair, TLS, 7 x 8″, December 18, 1945, personal stationery, thank you note to Mrs Barber **395.00**
Longfellow, Henry W, poet, CS, 3 x 4″, ink signature, dated 1881 . . . . **125.00**
Markam, Edwin, PS, 8vo, sepia bust pose, 1927 . . . . **95.00**
Nash, Ogden, TLS, 4to, personal stationery, 1963 . . . . **45.00**
O'Neill, Eugene, book, *Dynamo*, 1929, bound in blue–green vellum, gilt lettering, purple board box **175.00**
Scott, Sir Walter, DS, 3 x 8″, March 12, 1819, bank check **650.00**

Spillane, AQS, 12mo, "It was easy" **25.00**
Torrence, Ridgley, ALS, 8vo, 1922 . . **35.00**

MUSIC

Berlin, Irving, songwriter, sheet music cover, blue ink signature **950.00**
Coniff, Ray, CS, 12mo, dated **30.00**
Dylan, Bob, PS, 4to, black and white, blue felt tip pen signature **350.00**
Gershwin, George, sheet music, 4to, 1925, Rhapsody in Blue for Jazz Band and Piano, inscribed on title page . . . **4,600.00**
Goodman, Benny, PS, 8vo, black and white **75.00**
Holiday, Billie, blues and jazz singer, LS, written by secretary, sgd by Holiday, orig envelope **1,450.00**
Holly, Buddy, 2 pcs, program and black ink signature, matted **1,500.00**
Jones, Spike, PS, 8vo, black and white **75.00**
Lehar, Franz, bandmaster and composer, PS, 12mo, sepia, penned signature and three bars of music **795.00**
Liberace, PS, 8vo, black and white, with sketch **75.00**
Miller, Glenn, book, *Glenn Miller's Method For Orchestra Arranging*, Mutual Music Society, Inc, 1943, blue ink signature **250.00**
Miller, Mitch, PS, 4 x 5″, black and white **12.00**
Pavarotti, Luciano, movie poster, 11 x 14″, Yes, Giorgio. **35.00**
Perlman, Itzhak, PS, 4to, 1966, black and white glossy **45.00**
Strauss, Richard, AQS, 5 x 6″ blank side of Excelsior Hotel, two bars of music and signature **1,000.00**
Welk, Lawrence, PS, 4 x 6″, black and white **35.00**

PRESIDENTS

Adams, John Quincy, ALS, 4to, 1818, to Mr Le Roy de Chaumont, reply of letter by him **3,000.00**
Buchanan, James, ship's paper, August 2, 1858, for Francis E Strawburg, ship *Congress* bound for Pacific Ocean, sgd **1,275.00**
Coolidge, Calvin, DS, 18 x 14″, postmaster appointment, emb seal, 1926 **275.00**
Grant, Ulysses S, DS, 4to, 1 pg, September 1871, order to affix seal on pardon of John Wiggins, framed with engraved portrait. **400.00**
Hayes, Rutherford B, ADS, bank check, August 13, 1866 . . . . **500.00**
Hoover, Herbert, TLS, 4to, February 15, 1931, mentions location of new Veterans Administration hospital **650.00**

Jefferson, Thomas, ALS, April 22, 1826, to Mrs Eleanor Worthington 2,950.00

Madison, James, check, March 27, 1816, Office of Pay and Deposit of the Bank of Columbia, Washington. 1,585.00

McKinley, William, DS, 21 x 16", military appointment, 1923. .... 450.00

Monroe, DS, 8 x 14", land grant, 1817 650.00

Pierce, Franklin, ALS, 4to, 1856, to Josiah Quincy, reply of letter sent by him 2,400.00

Roosevelt, Franklin D, TLS, 4to, 1 pg, December 1944, framed with photo. . 325.00

Roosevelt, Theodore, DS, 22 x 17", postmaster appointment, gold seal, blue ribbon 495.00

Taft, William H, DS, 16 x 19", military appointment, vignette top and bottom 275.00

Truman, Harry, TLS, White House stationery, orig envelope, 1945 ...... 500.00

Tyler, John, DS, 13 x 16", vellum, vignette top and bottom, white paper seal, 1845 .... 1,150.00

Cartoon Drawing, Walter Lantz, orig crayon and ink, matted and framed, 10⅝ x 12½", $85.00.

SHOW BUSINESS

Blocker, Dan, DS, 4to, 1964, affidavit of registration, matted with photo 495.00

Crawford, Joan, TLS, 8vo, 1½ pgs, September 8, 1959, to Walter Smally ... 75.00

Farmer, Frances, 2 pcs, card and magazine photo, matted, pencil signature 225.00

Fields, W C, PS, 11 x 14", October 1928, wearing costume worn in *Poppy*.... 1,700.00

Fine, Larry, ALS, 6 x 8" 375.00

Flynn, Errol, PS, bust pose 950.00

Garbo, Greta, check, Chase Manhattan Bank, envelope.............. 2,500.00

Hart, William S, PS, 7 x 8", sepia, full pose sentiment and signature. 200.00

Heflin, Van, DS, 4to, August 25, 1952, contract for play 65.00

Hopper, DeWolf, TLS, 4to, February 23, 1935, blue ink signature. 95.00

Kern, Jerome, PS, 11 x 14", sitting at piano, sgd and inscribed 1,700.00

Langtry, Lillie, personalized note paper, 4 x 5".................... 175.00

McDaniel, Hattie, PS, 4to, penned inscription, sentiment, and signature, 1941 .... 995.00

Novarro, Ramon, silent film star, PS, 10 x 13", bust pose 250.00

Ross, Lanny, PS, 4to, bust pose, dated 1931 .... 65.00

Wayne, John, PS, 4to, black and white, bold signature. 795.00

SPORTS

Campbell, Malcolm, CS, 2 x 5", blue ink signature 75.00

Clemente, Roberto, magazine cov, 5 x 8", wearing Pirates uniform, blue ink signature 295.00

Cobb, Ty, check, 1945, First National Bank of Nevada, cancellation marks 100.00

Dempsey, Jack, PS, 4to, sepia, boxing pose, sgd and dated Nov 22, '27 ... 75.00

Henie, Sonja, PS, 4to, bust pose, green ink sentiment and signature 150.00

Holm, Eleanor, 1932 gold medal winner, PS, 4to. 45.00

Louis, Joe, PS, 4to, sepia, boxing pose, wearing gloves and trunks, dated 5/31/46 .... 395.00

Ruth, Babe, PS, 7 x 9", sepia, bust pose wearing business suit 3,450.00

Williams, Ted, baseball, sgd, mounted in holder 75.00

STATESMEN

Clinton, De Witt, DS, March 27, 1819, rank appointment 95.00

Darrow, Clarence, clipped letter signature, 1 x 4".................. 250.00

Davis, Jefferson, ALS, April 28, 1853, concerns Allegheny Valley RR Co. .. 485.00

Hall, A Oakley, New York City mayor, ALS, 8vo, 4 pgs, response to inquiry, orig envelope 300.00

Jay, John, DS, April 18, 1800, appointing Henry Saltsman Pay Master to county of Montgomery.......... 790.00

King, Preston, ALS, 4to, 8 pgs, February 6, 1851, to Gideon Welles, concerning the presidential election the following year. 275.00

Marshall, Thurgood, CS, 4½ x 6″, Supreme Court **195.00**
Meriweather, Lewis, promissory note, 8vo, Governor of Louisiana Territory, February 15, 1808. . . . . **1,100.00**
Souter, David, Associate Justice, first day cover, eagle image **55.00**
Sumner, Charles, ALS, 12mo, 1 pg, to Senate Chamber. **25.00**
Warren, Earl, TLS, 4to, Chief Justice, thank you note to Mr Frederick Specht, 1950 . . . . **95.00**

AUTOMOBILES

History: Automobiles can be classified into several categories. In 1947 the Antique Automobile Club of America devised a system whereby any motor vehicle (car, bus, motorcycle, and so on) made prior to 1930 is an "antique" car. The Classic Car Club of America expanded the list, focusing on luxury models from 1925 to 1948. The Milestone Car Society developed a list, for cars in the 1948 to 1964 period.

Some states, such as Pennsylvania, have devised a dual registration system for older cars—antique and classic. Models from the 1960s and 1970s, especially convertibles and limited-production models, fall into the "classic" designation depending on how they are used.

References: Quentin Craft, *Classic Old Car Value Guide, 23rd Edition,* published by author, 1989; James M. Flammang, *Standard Catalog of American Cars, 1976–1986, 2nd Edition,* Krause Publications, 1989; James M. Flammang, *Standard Catalog of Imported Cars, 1946–1990,* Krause Publications, 1992; John A. Gunnel (ed.), *100 Years of American Cars,* Krause Publications, 1993; John A. Gunnel, *Standard Catalog of American Cars, 1946–1975, Third Edition,* Krause Publications, 1992; Beverly Kimes and Henry Austin Clark, Jr., *Standard Catalog of American Cars, 1805–1942, Second Edition,* Krause Publications, 1989; Jim Lenzke and Ken Buttolph, *1994 Standard Guide to Cars & Prices, Sixth Edition,* Krause Publications, 1993; Peter Sessler, *Car Collector's Handbook: A Comprehensive Guide to Collecting Rare and Historic Automobiles,* HP Books, 1992.

Periodicals: *Automobile Quarterly,* 15040 Kutztown Rd., PO Box 348, Kutztown, PA 19530; *Hemmings Motor News,* PO Box 100, Bennington, VT 05201; *Old Cars Price Guide,* 700 E. State Street, Iola, WI 54990; *Old Cars,* 700 E. State Street, Iola, WI 54990.

Collectors' Clubs: Antique Automobile Club of America, 501 West Govenor Rd., PO Box 417, Hershey, PA 17033; Classic Car Club of America, O'Hare Lake Office Plaza, 2300 E. Devon Avenue, Suite 126, Des Plaines, IL 60018; Milestone Car Society, PO Box 24612, Indianapolis, IN 46224.

Note: The prices below are based upon a car in

running condition, with a high percentage of original parts, and somewhere between 60% and 80% restored. *Prices can vary by as much as 30% in either direction.*

Many older cars, especially if restored, now exceed $15,000. Their limited availability makes them difficult to price. Auctions, more than any other source, are the true determinant of value at this level. Especially helpful are the catalogs and sale bills of Kruse Auctioneers, Inc., Auburn, IN 46706.

AMX, 1968, hard top, $2,000.00.

AUTOMOBILES

Auburn, 1935, Model 653, Sedan, 6 cyl. **8,500.00**
Bentley, 1953, Park Ward, Convertible, 4.6 Litre engine. **28,000.00**
Bricklin, 1975, Model SV–1, Gullwing Coupe **8,000.00**
Buick
   1908, Model 10, Touring, 4 cyl. . . . **12,000.00**
   1941, Roadmaster, Sedan, 8 cyl. . . **15,000.00**
Cadillac
   1931, Model 370, Cabriolet, V–12 **42,000.00**
   1956, Sedan, blue body, cream top **11,500.00**
   1963, Convertible, red, white top . . **7,500.00**
Chandler, 1927, Big Six, Sedan, 6 cyl. **4,800.00**
Chevrolet
   1933, Eagle, Coupe, rumble seat, 6 cyl. **6,000.00**
   1953, Sedan, four door **10,000.00**
   1965, Corvair, Convertible, 6 cyl. . . **4,000.00**
   1968, Impala Coupe, V–8 engine . . **1,200.00**
Chrysler
   1932, Imperial, Sedan, 6 cyl. **9,000.00**
   1956, New Yorker, Hemming engine **9,000.00**
   1959, Saratoga, Sedan, V–8 . . . . . **3,000.00**
Columbia, 1925, Six, Sedan, 6 cyl. . . **8,000.00**
Cunningham, 1929, Model V9, Roadster, V–8 . . . . **20,000.00**
Daniels, 1920, Submarine, Speedster, V–8 . . . . **24,500.00**
Dayton, 1913, Tandem, Cycle, 2 cyl. **3,000.00**
Delahaye, 1935, Superflux, Roadster, 6 cyl. **12,000.00**
DeSoto
   1931, Model 31, Coupe, rumble seat, 6 cyl. **4,200.00**

1952, Firedome, Convertible Coupe,
V–8 . . . . **6,000.00**

Dodge
1921, Model 21, Touring, 4 cyl. . . . **3,500.00**
1949, Wayfarer, Roadster, 6 cyl. . . **4,000.00**
1966, Charger, Coupe, V–8 . . . . . **2,200.00**

Dort, 1924, Model 27, Touring, 6 cyl. **4,000.00**
Dragon, 1906, Model 25, Touring, 4 cyl. **5,500.00**
Drexel, 1916, Model 7–60, seven pas-
senger touring, 4 cyl. **5,000.00**
Duesenberg, 1931, LeBaron–J, Con-
vertible Berline, 8 cyl. **125,000.00**
Durant, 1928, Model M, Sedan, 4 cyl. **4,800.00**
Edsel, 1959, Ranger, V–8 engine . . . **2,850.00**
Excalibur SS, 1973, Model SSK, Road-
ster, V–8 . . . . **11,500.00**
Falcon, 1922, Touring, 4 cyl. **5,000.00**
Ferrari, 1956, Tipo 375, Touring, V–12 **27,000.00**

Ford
1903, Model A, Runabout, 2 cyl. . . **11,500.00**
1927, Model T, Coupe, green **6,500.00**
1929, Model A, Coupe, rumble seat,
orig title. **9,000.00**
1930, Model A, Sedan **9,000.00**
1940, Deluxe, Sedan Delivery, V–8 **6,800.00**
1960, Galaxie, Vitoria, V–8 . . . . . . **3,000.00**
1963, Falcon, Convertible **3,500.00**

Franklin
1930, Model 14, Convertible Sedan, 6
cyl. **20,000.00**
1933, Olympic, Cabriolet, 6 cyl. . . . **7,000.00**

Fritchle, 1916, Touring, 4 cyl. **5,000.00**

Gardner, 1929, Model 130, Roadster, 8
cyl. **12,000.00**
Graham–Paige, 1941, Hollywood, Con-
vertible Coupe, 6 cyl. **10,000.00**
Grant, 1921, Model HZ, Sedan, 6 cyl. **4,500.00**
Hillman, 1967, Huskey, Station Wagon,
1.7 litre. **1,250.00**
Hudson, 1935, Terraplane Fordor, Se-
dan, black, brown int. **6,900.00**

Jaguar
1951, Mark VII, Sedan, 6 cyl. **3,600.00**
1966, XKE, Sport Racing, 4.2 litre **6,500.00**

Julian, 1922, Model 60, Coupe, 8 cyl. **10,000.00**
Lambert, 1909, Roadster, 6 cyl. . . . **8,000.00**

LaSalle
1939, hearse **14,500.00**
1940, Model 52, Club Coupe, V–8 **5,000.00**

Lincoln, 1935, Dietrich, Convertible
Coupe, V–12 . . . . **28,000.00**
Lotus, 1966, Mark 46 Europa, Coupe,
1.5 litre. **2,100.00**

Mercedes–Benz
1935, Model 170–V, Limousine . . . **15,000.00**
1956, Model 190SL, Convertible, 4
cyl. **9,000.00**

Mercury
1940, Series 09A, Convertible, 8 cyl. **10,000.00**
1955, Monterey, Sedan **1,500.00**
1963, Comet S–22, Convertible, 8 cyl. **2,400.00**

Nash
1954, Ambassador, two door hardtop,
8 cyl. **1,250.00**
1962, Metropolitan, Convertible, 4 cyl. **4,000.00**

Oldsmobile
1942, Model 66, Station Wagon, 6 cyl. **4,000.00**
1966, Toronado, Coupe, V–8 . . . . **3,100.00**

Opel, 1938, Admiral, Drophead Coupe,
3.6 litre. **1,700.00**

Packard
1928, Model 426, roadster, 6 cyl. . . **14,000.00**
1940, Darrin, Convertible Victoria, 8
cyl. **25,000.00**

Peugeot, 1939, Darl mat, Coupe, 2.1
litre **1,200.00**
Pittsburgh, 1911, Touring, seven pas-
senger, 6 cyl. **6,500.00**

Plymouth
1928, Model Q, Sport Roadster, 4 cyl. **8,500.00**
1942, Model P145, Sedan, 6 cyl. . . **2,500.00**
1957, Fury, Convertible, V–8 cyl. . . **4,000.00**

Pontiac
1955, Star Chief, four door **7,500.00**
1958, Bonneville, two door hardtop,
V–8 . . . . **2,800.00**
1966, GTO, Convertible, V–8 . . . . **5,200.00**

Porsche, 1969, Model 911 T, Coupe, 4
cyl. **6,800.00**
Renault, 1955, Fregate, Convertible, 2
litre **2,000.00**

Rolls Royce
1929, Pall Mall, Touring, 6 cyl. . . . **60,000.00**
1952, Silver Dawn, Touring Limou-
sine, 6 cyl. **18,000.00**
1971, Corniche Coupe **25,850.00**

Studebaker
1933, President, Convertible, 8 cyl. **10,000.00**
1949, Champion, Convertible, 6 cyl. **4,800.00**
1963, Avanti, Coupe, V–8 . . . . . . **5,000.00**

Stutz
1914, Bearcat, Roadster, 6 cyl. . . . **45,000.00**
1927, Black Hawk, Speedster, 8 cyl. **8,000.00**

Sunbeam, 1958, Alpine, Sport, 4 cyl. . **2,800.00**

MISCELLANEOUS

Fire Engine
Diamond T, 1947, pumper **2,500.00**
Dodge, 1945, pumper, American
LaFrance, 6 cyl. **2,500.00**
Ford
1929, Model AA **4,800.00**
1940, pumper, flat V–8 . . . . **6,500.00**
Mack, 1936, pumper, Hale pump . . **4,000.00**

Motorcycle
BSA, 1943, Military **3,800.00**
Harley–Davidson, 1952, Model K . . **1,800.00**
Indian
1930, Scout, Model 101 . . . . **5,500.00**
1948, Chief **7,500.00**
Triumph, 1921, Baby **1,500.00**

Truck
Chevrolet
1932, Huckster **6,000.00**
1937, Sedan delivery, 6 cyl. **5,500.00**
1957, Pickup, ½ ton, Short Bed, V–
6. . . . . **2,300.00**
Dodge
1937, Pickup, ¾ ton, Slant 6 . . . . . **2,000.00**
1957, Sweptside, ½ ton, V–8 . . . .   **850.00**
Ford
1941, F–1 Stake, V–8 . . . . **2,500.00**
1956, F–100, Custom Cab, V–8 . . . **2,500.00**
1962, Falcon, Ranchero, 6 cyl. . . . **2,500.00**
Plymouth, 1938, Pickup, High Side,
Slant 6. **2,400.00**
Stewart, Pickup, 1 ton, 4 cyl. **3,200.00**
VW, Pickup, short bed, 1600 cc **1,400.00**
Willys, 1928, Model 70, Sedan, 6 cyl. **1,800.00**

AUTOMOBILIA

History: The amount of items related to the automobile is endless. Collectors seem to fit into three groups—those collecting parts to restore a car, those collecting information about a company or certain model for research purposes, and those trying to use automobile items for decorative purposes. Most material changes hands at the hundreds of swap meets and auto shows around the country.

References: Gordon Gardiner and Alistair Morris, *The Price Guide and Identification of Automobilia,* Antique Collectors' Club; Brian Jewell, *Motor Badges & Figureheads,* Midas Books, 1978; Jim and Nancy Schaut, *American Automobilia: An Illustrated History and Price Guide,* Wallace–Homestead, 1992; Dan Smith, *Accessory Mascots, The Automotive Accents of Yesteryear, 1910–1940,* published by author, 1989.

Periodical: *Hemmings Motor News,* PO Box 100, Bennington, VT 05201.

Banner, Revere Tires, 11¾" h, 47¾" w,
cloth, yellow, blue lettering **140.00**
Box, tin, Mobil Oil, designed to hold lubrication charts **20.00**
Calendar, Chevrolet, 1920, 30½" h, 16"
w, green, white lettering **145.00**
Carburetor, Buick, 1924–25 . . . . **25.00**
Clock
Atlas Tires & Batteries, wall, 1950s **175.00**
Firestone, 15¼" h, 15¼" w, sq, glass
front, wood frame. **100.00**
Studebaker, 15¼" h, gold metal rim,
red and blue emblem, electric **115.00**
Compression Tester, Hasting's adv on
dial **20.00**
Decanter, spark plug, Motorcraft **25.00**
Display
Champion Spark Plugs, 12" h, 18" w,
5½" d, tin, yellow, black lettering . . **200.00**

Exide Battery, 40" h, tin and metal,
black and orange lettering. **185.00**
Gilmer Fan Belts, 22¼" h, 16½" w, 24"
d, tin, painted, orange, blue trim . . **250.00**
Display Cabinet
Auto Lite Spark Plug, 18½" h, 13⅛"
w, metal, painted, green, glass front **45.00**
Firestone Spark Plugs, 15¼" h, 20⅛"
w, tin, painted, 1940–50 . . . . **325.00**
Emblem, porcelain
Auto Owners Insurance **30.00**
Toledo Motor Club AAA **30.00**
First Aid Kit, Mobil Flying Red Horse . **35.00**
Gas Cap, Ford, metal **8.00**
Hubcap
Chevrolet, 1957 . . . . **15.00**
Edsel, spinner type **35.00**
Packard, 1956, set of four, orig Studebaker Packard envelope **35.00**
Inkwell
Masters Trucks, 5½" h, 7" w, 2¾" d,
cast iron, emb letters **210.00**
Ray Cotton Company Truck, 3¾" h, 8"
w, 3" d, cast iron, truck shape, emb
letters. **80.00**
License Plate Attachment
Automobile Club of Pittsburgh, 3½" h,
3½" d, porcelain, white, black lettering, maroon and green emblem. . . **75.00**
Tydol, 6¾" h, 3½" w, tin, painted, man
carrying lube **50.00**

Broadside, Studebaker Brothers Manufacturing Company, Izzer Buggy adv, steel engraved illus, printed, black and white, 1890s, 4½ x 8", $15.00.

Veedol, 6¾" h, 3½" w, tin, painted, man carrying lube **80.00**
Map
Frontier Gas & Oil **10.00**
Hi–Speed, Michigan, 1938 . . . . . . **9.00**
Map Rack, wall, Cities Service, green **55.00**
Plate, 6" d, Mobil Flying Red Horse emblem **22.00**
Radiator Cap, brass, figural, woman's head, wings **50.00**
Radio, Champion Spark Plug, 14" h, spark plug shape, gray and white . . . **55.00**
Sign
Aetna Automobile Insurance Co, 12" h, 24" w, tin, painted, black lettering **65.00**
B F Goodrich Tires, 23" h, 35" w, tin, painted, blue, yellow and cream lettering. **25.00**
Cooper Tires, 12" h, 32½" w, tin, painted, emb, orange and blue ground, cream and blue lettering. . **200.00**
Delco Battery, 22" h, 30" w, tin, painted, yellow and orange, blue lettering. **160.00**
Fred K Gamash Automobiles, 13⅝" h, 19¾" w, man and woman driving in red car **145.00**
Hudson Rambler, 30" h, 42" w, porcelain, dark blue, white logo **475.00**
National Batteries, 12" h, 20" w, tin, orange, dark blue raised letters . . . **150.00**
Seiberling Tires, 16" h, 30" w, porcelain, double sided, dark blue, orange letters **200.00**
Texas Independent Automobile Dealers Assoc, 9" d, celluloid, gold foil letters **25.00**
Spark Plug, Rentz Visable **55.00**
Thermometer
Buick Motor Cars, 27" h, porcelain, blue, emblem, c1915 . . . . **275.00**
Champion Spark Plugs, 13½" h, yellow, black and white spark plug center. **600.00**
Gold Medal Motor Oils, 9⅛" d, metal, painted **180.00**
Tin, Wadham Motor Oil, one gallon, c1920. . . . . **65.00**
Tire Pump, brass, Ford script on base **55.00**

BACCARAT GLASS

History: The Sainte–Anne glassworks at Baccarat in the Voges, France, was founded in 1764 and produced utilitarian soda glass. In 1816 Aime–Gabriel d'Artiques purchased the glassworks, and a Royal Warrant was issued in 1817 for the opening of Verrerie de Vonôche á Baccarat. The firm concentrated on lead crystal glass products. In 1824 a limited company was created.

From 1823 to 1857 Baccarat and Saint–Louis glassworks had a commercial agreement and used the same outlets. No merger occurred. Baccarat began the production of paperweights in 1846. In the late 19th century the firm achieved an international reputation for cut glass table services, chandeliers, display vases and centerpieces, and sculptures. Products eventually included all forms of glassware. The firm still is active today.

Reference: Jean–Louis Curtis, *Baccarat*, Harry N. Abrams, 1992.

Additional Listing: Paperweights.

Water Bottle, Rose Tiente, rose shading to amber, 7" h, $80.00.

Biscuit Jar, vaseline, shaded frosted to clear, swirling flowers, sgd **200.00**
Bowl
8" d, Rose Tiente, scalloped, ftd, sgd **100.00**
14" d, 3½" h, wide flattened rim, narrow knopped annual foot, etched "Baccarat, France". **500.00**
Candlesticks, pr
10¾" h, Eiffel Tower pattern, Rose Tiente. **225.00**
10⅞" h, leaf design, Museum collection, reissue of 1860s design, limited to 250 prs, orig box **500.00**
Champagne Bucket, 9¼" h, tapering cylindrical, rect stop fluted molded sides, stamped "Baccarat, France". **400.00**
Cigar Lighter, Rose Tiente, SP top . . **125.00**
Cologne Bottle
5½" h, Rose Tiente, Diamond Point Swirl, orig stopper **95.00**
7" h, crystal, frosted rosette ground, gold floral swags and bows, cut faceted stopper, price for pair **330.00**

Crystal Ball, 6" d, clear, acid stamped "Baccarat," 3¼" h clear glass cylindrical dished stand, low circular foot, retailed by Tiffany and Co, price for pair 1,430.00

Decanter, 9¾" h, Rose Tiente, orig stopper. 115.00

Dresser Jar, 5⅜" d, round, double cut overlay, pink cut to clear over opaque white, cut vertical panels, gold dec . .   125.00

Epergne
  10¾" h, four cranberry overlay cut to clear, gilt metal holder 550.00
  15" h, three trumpet shaped vases, scalloped edges, Rose Tiente 450.00

Fairy Lamp, 3⅞" h, shaded white to clear 275.00

Finger Bowl, 4¾" d bowl, 6¼" d underplate, ruby, medallions and flowers gold dec.   325.00

Goblet
  Perfection pattern 36.00
  Vintage pattern, cone shaped amber bowl, etched grape design, cut stem and base, price for six piece set 100.00

Jar, cov, 7" d, cameo cut, gilt metal mounts, imp "Baccarat". 350.00

Jewelry Box, 4" d, 2¾" h, hinged lid, Button and Bow pattern, sapphire blue, brass fittings. 125.00

Lamp, table, crystal and gilt metal, price for pair
  Column form 3,200.00
  Urn form 3,000.00

Paperweight, Joan of Arc, sulfide . . .   70.00

Pitcher, 9¼" h, Rose Tiente, Helical Twist pattern. 275.00

Rose Bowl, 3" h, cranberry, lacy enamel dec 150.00

Sweetmeat Jar, cranberry colored strawberries, blossoms, and leaves, cut back to clear ground of ferns, SP cov and handle, sgd 350.00

Toothpick Holder, 2½" h, scalloped, Rose Tiente 100.00

Tumbler, Rose Tiente, Swirl pattern   60.00

Tumble–Up, Rose Tiente, Swirl pattern, carafe and tumbler 200.00

Vase, 8¼" h, bamboo stalk form, relief molded leaf sprig at side, coiled snake around base, enameled and gilt insects, early 20th C, sgd 500.00

BANKS, MECHANICAL

History: Banks which display some form of action while utilizing a coin are considered mechanical banks. Although mechanical banks are known that date back to ancient Greece and Rome, the majority of collectors center their interests in those

made between 1867 and 1928 in Germany, England, and the United States. Recently there has been an upsurge of interest in later types, some of which date into the 1970s.

Initial research suggested that approximately 250 to 300 different or variant designs of banks were made in the early period. Today that number has been revised to 2,000–3,000 types and varieties. The field remains ripe for discovery and research.

More than 80% of all cast-iron mechanical banks produced between 1869 and 1928 were made by J. E. Stevens Co., Cromwell, Connecticut. Tin banks tend to be German in origin.

While rarity is a factor in value, appeal of design, action, quality of manufacture, country of origin, and history of collector interest also are important. Radical price fluctuations may occur with an imbalance of these factors. Rare banks may sell for a few hundred dollars while one of more common design with greater appeal will sell in the thousands.

The prices on our list represent fairly what a bank sells for in the specialized collectors' market. Some banks are hard to find, and establishing a price outside auction is difficult.

The prices listed are for original old mechanical banks with minor repairs, in sound operating condition, and with a majority of the original paint intact.

References: *Collector's Encyclopedia of Toys and Banks,* L–W Book Sales, 1986, 1993 value update; Al Davidson, *Penny Lane, A History Of Antique Mechanical Toy Banks,* Long's Americana, 1987; Don Duer, *A Penny Saved: Still and Mechanical Banks,* Schiffer Publishing, 1993; Bill Norman, *The Bank Book: The Encyclopedia of Mechanical Bank Collecting,* Collectors' Showcase, 1984.

Periodical: *Heuser's Quarterly Price Guide to Official Collectible Banks,* Heuser Enterprises, 508 Clapson Road, PO Box 300, West Winfield, NY 13491.

Collectors' Club: Mechanical Bank Collectors of America, PO Box 128, Allegan, MI 49010.

Reproduction Alert: Reproductions, fakes, and forgeries exist for many banks. Forgeries of some mechanical banks were made as early as 1937, so age alone is not a guarantee of authenticity. In our listing two asterisks indicate banks for which serious forgeries exist and one asterisk indicates banks for which casual reproductions have been made.

Advisor: James S. Maxwell, Jr.

Acrobats, iron, blue base, polychrome wear **4,625.00**

Australian William Tell, brass, wood, and tin **1,200.00**

Automatic Coin Savings, tin, strong man in leopard skin holding man by hair . .   **2,000.00**

Bad Accident, iron, polychrome paint .   **880.00**

Barking Dog, wood and steel **1,400.00**

Acrobat, J. & E. Stevens Co., Cromwell, CT, designed by Edward L Morris, $1,750.00.

**Bear, standing, iron	350.00
**Bismark, iron	2,350.00
Bowing Man in Cupola, iron	3,000.00
**Boy on Trapeze, iron	875.00
**Boys Stealing Watermelons, iron	850.00
British Lion, tin	850.00
**Bull & Bear, iron	12,000.00
*Bulldog, iron, coin on nose	650.00
Bull Tosses Boy in Well, brass	2,200.00
Bureau	
Tin, Ideal	475.00
Wood, Serrill Pat. Appld. For	400.00
Butting Ram, man thumbs nose	1,700.00
**Calamity, iron	4,500.00
**Called Out, orig unpainted iron	10,000.00
Called Out, lead master pattern	12,000.00
Calumet with Calumet Kid, tin can	150.00
Calumet with Sailor, tin can	1,2000.00
Calumet with Soldier, tin can	1,000.00
**Cannon, U.S. and Spain	1,850.00
Cat & Mouse, iron and brass, cat standing upright	12,000.00
Cat Chasing Mouse in Building, tin	2,400.00
Chandlers, iron	250.00
Child's Bank, Clark Thread	350.00
**Chimpanzee, iron and tin	1,150.00
Chinaman, iron, reclining	1,650.00
**Circus Ticket Collector, man at barrel	800.00
Clown and Dog, tin	850.00
Clown, tin, black face	250.00
**Clown, Harlequin, Columbine, iron	14,500.00
**Clown on Globe, iron	775.00
Coin Registering, iron, domed building	300.00
Confectionery, iron	2,800.00
Crescent Cash Register, iron	125.00
Crowing Rooster, tin	275.00
Dapper Dan, tin	450.00
Darky Bust, tin	450.00
**Dentist, iron	2,200.00
Dog Goes Into House, lead and brass	3,800.00
**Dog With Tray, iron, oval base	1,000.00
Ducks, lead, two	650.00

Electric Safe, steel	150.00
Elephant Baby, lead, with clown at table	3,700.00
**Elephant With Howdah, iron, man pops out	375.00
**Elephant With Locked Howdah, iron, oval base	600.00
**Elephant, iron, "Light of Asia" on wheels	675.00
Elephant, tin, Royal Trick	850.00
**Elephant On Wheels, iron, trunk moves	700.00
Face, wood	875.00
**Feed the Kitty, iron	400.00
**Ferris Wheel, iron and tin, marked "Bowen's Pat."	1,400.00
Fire Alarm, tin	1,250.00
Flip The Frog, tin	950.00
Football, iron, black man and watermelon	14,000.00
Fortune Teller Safe, iron	450.00
Freedman, man at desk	38,500.00
**Forty–Niner, iron	400.00
Frog On Arched Track, tin	2,000.00
Frog On Rock, iron	350.00
Fun Producing Savings, tin	275.00
**Giant Standing, iron	6,800.00
**Girl in Victorian Chair, iron	2,350.00
Give Me A Penny, wood	700.00
**Glutton, brass, lifts turkey	425.00
Golden Gate Key, aluminum	125.00
Grasshopper, tin, wind–up	5,000.00
Guessing, lead and iron, man's figure	2,000.00
Hall's Excelsior, iron and wood, policeman figure	1,400.00
Hall's Lilliput, Type II	250.00
Hall's Yankee Notion, brass	850.00
Harold Lloyd, tin	950.00
Hillman Coin Bank, wood, iron, and glass	3,200.00
**Hold The Fort, iron, five holes	1,400.00
Home, iron	375.00
Home With Dormer Windows, iron	475.00
**Horse Race, iron, tin horses, flanged base	2,000.00
**Humpty Dumpty, iron	425.00
I Always Did 'Spize a Mule, black, sitting on bench	575.00
Huntley And Palmers Readings	250.00
*Indian And Bear, iron, white bear	750.00
**Initiating First Degree, iron	2,800.00
Jack on Roof, iron	300.00
Joe Socko, tin	275.00
John R. Jennings Money Box, wood	2,800.00
Jolly Joe Clown, tin	400.00
**Jolly Nigger	
Aluminum, string tie	100.00
Iron	150.00
Jonah And Whale, iron, ftd base	12,500.00
Key, iron, World's Fair	300.00
Kick Inn, paper on wood	275.00
**Leapfrog, iron	1,250.00
**Lighthouse, iron	600.00
Lion Hunter, iron	1,650.00
Little High Hat, iron	500.00

Little Jocko Musical, tin	900.00
Little Moe, iron, tip hat	450.00
Long May It Wave, iron and wood	400.00
Lucky Wheel Money Box, tin	150.00
**Magic Safe, iron	175.00
**Magician, iron	1,650.00
Mama Katzenjammer, iron, 1905–08, low cut dress with white fringe	3,700.00
Mammy and Child, iron, red dress, minor wear	10,725.00
Man on Chimney	550.00
**Mason, iron	1,450.00
Merry–Go–Round	4,500.00
Metropolitan, iron	150.00
Milking Cow, iron, replaced fence and tail	2,310.00
Minstrel, tin	450.00
Model Railroad Stamp Dispenser, tin	650.00
Model Railroad Sweet Dispenser	650.00
Model Savings, tin	500.00
*Monkey & Coconut, iron	750.00
Monkey & Parrot, tin	200.00
Monkey With Tray, tin	350.00
Moonface, iron	20,000.00
Mosque, iron	450.00
*Mule Entering Barn, iron	650.00
Musical Church, wood, rotating tower	2,500.00
Musical Savings, wood house	1,200.00
New, iron, lever in center	450.00
New Creedmoor Bank, iron	450.00
**Novelty, iron	400.00
Old Woman In The Shoe	180,000.00
*Organ, iron, boy and girl	1,870.00
**Organ Grinder With Performing Bear, iron	4,950.00
Owl, iron, head turns	225.00
*Paddy & Pig, iron	1,600.00
Pascal Savings, tin	250.00
**Peg Leg Begger, iron	600.00
**Pelican With Rabbit, iron	700.00
**Piano, iron, old conversion to musical	2,200.00
Pig In High Chair, iron	450.00
Pistol, stamped metal	325.00
Postman, English	250.00
Presto, iron, penny changes to quarter	3,700.00
Pump & Bucket, iron	425.00
*Punch & Judy, iron	750.00
Punch & Judy, tin	1,500.00
Queen Victoria Bust, iron	5,000.00
**Rabbit, iron, large	275.00
Rabbit In Cabbage	250.00
**Red Riding Hood, iron	5,500.00
Rival, iron	5,000.00
Roller–skating, iron	4,000.00
Safety Locomotive, iron	250.00
Saluting Sailor, tin	500.00
Sam Segal's Aim to Save Target, iron	4,500.00
Savo, tin, round, children	125.00
Scotchman, tin	375.00
Sentry, tin, raises rifle	550.00
Shoot The Hat, brass	2,500.00
Signal Cabin, tin	150.00

Snake & Frog In Pond, tin	1,200.00
*Speaking Dog, iron	750.00
Sportsman, iron, fowler	4,500.00
**Squirrel & Tree Stump, iron	800.00
Stollwerk, tin, Victoria	250.00
Sweet Thrift, tin	150.00
*Tammany, iron	275.00
*Tank and Cannon, aluminum	200.00
Target, iron, fort and cannon	2,750.00
Ten Cent Adding Bank, iron	400.00
Thrifty Tom's Jigger, tin	400.00
Tiger, tin	950.00
Time Lock Savings, iron	1,100.00
Toboggan, SP Britannia metal	850.00
Treasure Chest Music, pot metal	375.00
**Trick Dog, iron, solid base	450.00
*Trick Pony, iron	675.00
Trick Savings, wood, front drawer	125.00
Try Your Weight Scale, tin	250.00
**Uncle Remus, iron	1,650.00
**Uncle Sam Bust, iron	475.00
Uncle Tom, iron, star base	250.00
United States Bank, iron, picture pops up	875.00
Viennese soldier, lead	1,800.00
Volunteer, iron	450.00
Watchdog Safe, iron	250.00
Weeden's Plantation, tin, wind–up	650.00
Wishbone, brass	6,000.00

BANKS, STILL

History: Banks with no mechanical action are known as still banks. The first still banks were made of wood, pottery, or from gourds. Redware and stoneware banks, made by America's early potters, are prized possessions of today's collectors.

Still banks reached a "golden age" with the arrival of the cast-iron bank. Leading manufacturing companies include Arcade Manufacturing Co., J. Chein & Co., Hubley, J. & E. Stevens, and A. C. Williams. The banks often were ornately painted to enhance their appeal. During the cast-iron era, banks and other businesses used the still bank as a form of advertising for attracting customers.

The tin lithograph bank, again frequently with advertising, did not reach its zenith until the 1930 to 1955 period. The tin bank was an important premium, whether it be a Pabst Blue Ribbon beer can bank or a Gerber's Orange Juice bank. Most tin advertising banks resembled the packaging shape of the product.

Almost every substance has been used to make a still bank—diecast white metal, aluminum, brass, plastic, glass, and so on. Many of the early glass candy containers also converted to a bank when the candy was eaten. Thousands of varieties of still banks were made, and hundreds of new varieties appear on the market each year.

References: *Collector's Encyclopedia of Toys*

and Banks, L–W Book Sales, 1986, 1993 value update; Don Duer, *A Penny Saved: Still and Mechanical Banks,* Schiffer Publishing, 1993; Earnest Ida and Jane Pitman, *Dictionary of Still Banks,* Long's Americana, 1980; Andy and Susan Moore, *Penny Bank Book, Collecting Still Banks,* Schiffer Publishing, 1984; Hubert B. Whiting, *Old Iron Still Banks,* Forward's Color Productions, 1968, out of print.

Periodical: *Heuser's Quarterly Price Guide to Official Collectible Banks,* Heuser Enterprises, 508 Clapson Rd., PO Box 300, West Winfield, NY 13491.

Collectors' Club: Still Bank Collectors Club of America, 1456 Carson Court, Homewood, IL 60430.

Museum: Margaret Woodbury Strong Museum, Rochester, NY.

Horseshoe, cast iron, "Good Luck," 4″ h, $125.00.

GLASS

Dog, 3¼″ barrel	75.00
Fruit Jar, Atlas Mason Jar	15.00
House, 4″, brick, orig brown paint, milk glass, orig mustard label on bottom.	40.00
Kewpie, 3⅛″ h, pressed glass with polychrome.	75.00
Liberty Bell, dated 1919	20.00
*Log Cabin, 4″, milk glass	20.00
Milk Bottle, 4½″, Elsie The Cow	25.00
Owl, 7″, carnival glass, marigold	25.00

METAL, Cast Iron unless otherwise stated.

Animal	
Boston Bull, 4⅜″ h, seated, polychrome	85.00
Camel, 7¼″ l, gold, red, and orange	215.00
Cat with ball, 5⅝″ l, gray, gold ball	150.00
*Deer, 9½″, antlers	55.00
*Donkey, 6¾″	100.00
*Elephant, 4″, gold trim	115.00
Goose, 3¾″, "Red Goose School Shoes" adv	100.00
Hippopotamus, 5″ l, black	200.00
Newfoundland, 3⅝″ h, black	40.00
Pig	
2½″, "Decker's Iowana," gold	65.00
4½″ l, seated, gold paint	45.00
7″ l, standing, green over gold paint	40.00
Possum, 2½″, gold or silver	165.00
Rabbit, 5¼″, gold	95.00
Rooster, 4⅞″, red and gold	55.00
*Scottie, 3⁵⁄₁₆″, black	70.00
Seal, 3⅜″, gold	240.00
*Sheep, 5¼″, gold	65.00
Stag, 6¼″, gold	60.00
Turkey, 3½″, brown japanning and red	125.00
Other	
Bank Building, 5½″, cupola, polychrome paint	135.00
Baseball Player, 5¾″, gold or blue	75.00
Battleship, "Maine," 4½″, japan finish	125.00
Beehive, 2½″, gold paint	140.00
Bicentennial, 1776–1976, 6 x 6″	40.00
Boy Scout, 5¾″, gold	65.00
Building, 7″, "Columbia," nickel finish	80.00
Bungalow, 3¾″, polychrome, porch	175.00
Buster Brown and Tige, 5⅛″, gold traces	130.00
Captain Kidd, 5⅝″, c1901	225.00
Castle, 3″, brown japanning, gold trim	250.00
Clock, "Time Is Money," 3³⁄₁₆″, black	55.00
Colonial House, 3″, gold and green	95.00
Coronation, 6¾″, gold	75.00
Devil, 4¼″, two faced, red	285.00
Dutch Girl, 5¼″, flowers	35.00
Fireman	100.00
Frowning Face, 5¾″ h, unpainted	485.00
Garage, 2½″ h, aluminum, two car, red	135.00
Gingerbread House, 2½″, tin, German	35.00
Gothic Bank, 4⅜″, early tin, American	40.00
Globe, 5¾″, on stand, eagle finial, red	90.00
Goodyear Zeppelin Hanger, 2⁵⁄₁₆″, aluminum	130.00
Helmet, German, 4⅞″ l, lead, olive drab, key trap	175.00
High Rise, 5½″ h, silver, gold trim	65.00
Hot Water Heater, Rex, 7¾″ h, green litho finish	20.00
Independence Hall, Tower Bank, bell	220.00
*Junior Cash Register, 5¼″, nickel finish.	75.00
Mammie, 6″ h, polychrome paint	140.00
Mary, 4⅜″, lamb	190.00
Mutt and Jeff, 5¼″ h, gold	165.00
Pass Around The Hat, 2⅜″, black	60.00
Plymouth Rock, 3⅞″, dated "1620," white metal	20.00
Porky Pig, 4⁷⁄₁₆″, tree trunk, white metal	60.00
Radio, 4½″, "Majestic," steel back	45.00

Rose Window, 2¼″ h, brown japanning	145.00
Safe, 4″, "Mascot," tin	25.00
Security Safe Deposit, 5½″, black and gold, brass dial	40.00
Soldier, 6″, tan and red	50.00
Statue of Liberty, 6⅜″, silver	75.00
Stop Sign, 4½″, painted	140.00
Stove, 5⅜″, "Gas Stove Bank," black	80.00
Tank, 4⅜″ l, gold paint	95.00
Taxi, 4″, "Yellow Cab," Arcade	240.00
Teddy Roosevelt, 5″ h, gold, red and silver trim	145.00
US Mail, 5¼″ h, red and gold	50.00
Windmill, 3⅜″, brass, silvered	65.00

POTTERY

Animal

Bear, 12″, ceramic, black and white, Hamm's	30.00
Cat	
4″, head, amber glaze, brown and tan sponging, emb features	110.00
5½″, sitting in basket, blue and green	35.00
Donkey, white, Staffordshire	40.00
Duck, 2¾″, blue and white spongeware	65.00
Elephant	25.00
Frog, 4″	40.00
Owl, 6¾″, brown glaze, yellow eyes	70.00
Peacock, 5″, multicolored glaze	75.00
Pig	
6″ l, blue and brown sponge spatter	100.00
10″, sewer pipe, tooled eyelashes	400.00
Other	
Incense Burner	25.00
Kewpie, chalkware, black	50.00
Mail Box, 3¾″, U.S. Mail, red, white, and blue	40.00
Peach, 2⅝″, pale yellow and peach	50.00
Shoe, 5″, high button, tan	80.00

BARBER BOTTLES

History: Barber bottles, colorful glass bottles found on shelves and counters in barber shops, held the liquids barbers used daily. A specific liquid was kept in a specific bottle, which the barber knew by color, design, or lettering.

The bulk liquids were kept in utilitarian containers under the counter or in a storage room.

Barber bottles are found in many types of glass: art glass with varied decoration, pattern glass, and commercially prepared and labeled bottles.

References: Ronald S. Barlow, *The Vanishing American Barber Shop*, Windmill Publishing, 1992; Richard Holiner, *Collecting Barber Bottles*, Collector Books, 1986; Ralph and Terry Kovel, *The Kovels' Bottle Price List, Ninth Edition*, Crown Publishers, 1992; Philip L. Krumholz, *Value Guide For Barberiana & Shaving Collectibles*, Ad Libs Publishing Co., 1988.

Note: Prices are for bottles without original stoppers unless otherwise noted.

Advertising

Bouquet aux Fleurs by Guitry, 9¾″ h, clear, raised multicolored flowers.	145.00
Koken's Quinine Tonic for the Hair, 7½″ h, clear, label under glass	195.00
LeVarn's Golden Wash Shampoo, label under glass	60.00
LeVarn's Rose Hair Tonic, label under glass.	50.00
Lucky Tiger, red, green, yellow, black, and gilt label under glass, emb on reverse	75.00
Osage Rub, label under glass	100.00
Amethyst, 8″ h, Mary Gregory type dec, child and flowers	250.00
Clear, 10¾″ h, swirled and raised white stripes	220.00
Cobalt Blue	
8″ h, Mary Gregory type dec, girl playing tennis, pontil.	220.00
11″ h, raised white and orange flowers, gold trim, metal over wood and cork stopper	275.00
Cranberry, IVT	125.00
Hand Painted, 7″ h, green and gilt, molded climbing lizard on neck, marked "Lubin/Paris".	495.00
Milk Glass	
Hair Tonic, floral tulip dec, blue background	250.00
Witch Hazel, painted letters and flowers, 9″ h	110.00

Teal, Inverted Thumbprint, made in South NJ, 8¾″ h, $125.00.

Opalescent
8″ h, orange, raised flower and vine
  pattern, marked "Lace Art Cameo"   **110.00**
8¼″ h, Spanish Lace, clear, sq base   **50.00**
Pale Green, 8″ h, white Mary Gregory
  type dec, Vegederma pontil **275.00**
Ruby, 11¼″ h, frosted with gold letters,
  marked "Hair Oil" **55.00**
Sapphire Blue, 8″ h, Mary Gregory type
  dec, seated child and flowers, pontil .   **165.00**
Teal Blue, IVT **125.00**
Wedgwood, 10¼″ h, Victoria Ware,
  salmon glazed ground, raised leaf festoons terminating at ribbons, gilt accents, imp mark, late 19th C, rim
  nicks, hairline, finial repair **330.00**

BAROMETERS

History: A barometer is an instrument that measures atmospheric pressure, which, in turn, aids
weather forecasting. Low pressure indicates the
coming of rain, snow, or a storm; high pressure
signifies fair weather.

Most barometers use an evacuated and graduated glass tube which contains a column of mercury and are classified by the shape of the case.
An aneroid barometer has no liquid and works by
a needle connected to the top of a metal box in
which a partial vacuum is maintained. The movement of the top moves the needle.

**Short and Mason, London, #2404, 26½″
h, $250.00.**

Aneroid, Tynes, carved and painted
  wood, ornate floral frame, 42″ h **475.00**
Banjo
  American, Hepplewhite, mahogany
    veneer, inlaid sunbursts and shells,
    engraved silvered dials and brass
    trim, "D. Gugeri, Boston," small
    piece of mold missing from cornice,
    38¾″ h **900.00**
  English, A Yannini, Sheffield, 19th C,
    chestnut case, 39″ h. **375.00**
  French, Louis XVI, carved giltwood,
    pierced foliate scrolls and swagged
    drapery, two lovebirds under laurel
    arbor cresting, dial inscribed "Rob-
    ert Op, Passage St Pierre 4A Ver-
    sailles," late 18th C, 40″ h. **1,210.00**
Desk, figural, tin, Weather House, chalk
  figures of man and woman, painted
  dec, sgd "Alvan Lovejoy, Boston". . .   **175.00**
Stick
  Abraham, H, Optician, Liverpool, mid
    19th C, walnut and walnut veneer,
    37″ h. **935.00**
  Brenner, Conrad, walnut, worn finish,
    printed paper label under glass
    "Made and sold by Conrad Michael
    Brenner, Columbiana, Ohio," 37″ h,
    no mercury **950.00**
  Central Scientific Co, Chicago, IL, en-
    graved silver brass scale, ebonized
    backboard, 37″ h. **145.00**
  Cray, W, Optician, London Bridge,
    rosewood veneer, applied mold-
    ings, engraved ivory dials, glass
    over mercury tube thermometer
    and several pieces of molding miss-
    ing, minor edge damage, 37½″ h. .   **500.00**
  Lent, DE, Rochester, NY, c1855, wal-
    nut, Dutch ripple moldings, 36″ h. .   **225.00**
  Merrick, John M & Co, Worcester, MA,
    c1857, 37⁹⁄₁₆″ h **200.00**
  Spooner, EC, Boston, mid 19th C,
    walnut, 42″ h **220.00**
Wheel
  Pedrone, L, Liverpool, England, Vic-
    torian, 19th C, broken arch pedi-
    ment, 15½″ dial and thermometer,
    54″ h. **2,100.00**
  Schalfino, J, Taunton, MA, 19th C,
    George III style, mahogany, broken
    arch pediment, minor damage, 38″
    h **420.00**
  Solomons, L, Bath Warantes, Re-
    gency period, early 19th C, mahog-
    any, shaped case, 42″ h **825.00**

BASKETS

History: Baskets were invented when man first
required containers to gather, store, and transport

goods. Today's collector, influenced by the country look, focuses on baskets made of splint, rye straw, or willow. Emphasis is placed on handmade examples. Nails or staples, wide splints which are thin and evenly cut, or a wire bail handle denote factory construction which can date back to the mid 19th century. Painted or woven decorated baskets rarely are handmade unless they are American Indian in origin.

Baskets are collected by (a) type—berry, egg, or field, (b) region—Nantucket or Shaker, and (c) composition—splint, rye, or willow. Stick to examples in very good condition; damaged baskets are a poor investment even at a low price.

References: Frances Johnson, *Wallace–Homestead Price Guide To Baskets, Second Edition,* Wallace–Homestead Book Company, 1989; Don and Carol Raycraft, *Collector's Guide to Country Baskets,* Collector Books, 1985, 1994 value update; Martha Wetherbee and Nathan Taylor, *Legend of the Bushwhacker Basket,* published by author, 1986; Christoph Will, *International Basketry For Weavers and Collectors,* Schiffer Publishing, 1985.

Reproduction Alert: Modern reproductions abound, made by diverse groups ranging from craft revivalists to foreign manufacturers.

Indian, storage, hemp, 11″ d at top, 7¾″ h, $150.00.

Berry, 5″ d, round, splint	15.00
Buttocks, woven splint, weathered gray finish, some damage	
12 x 14″, 7½″ h plus bentwood handle	50.00
14 x 15″, 7″ h plus bentwood handle, square, some age and wear	85.00
14 x 18″, 8″ h plus bentwood handle	95.00
17½ x 20″, 11″ h plus bentwood handle, stripped surface, traces of white paint and some damage. . . .	60.00
21 x 21″, 11″ h plus bentwood handle, some age and damage.	72.00

Cheese, woven splint, round	
15″ d	125.00
21″ d, 7″ h, good age and color, minor damage.	275.00
Field	
Splint, wooden bottom, old natural patina, "H.S.B." painted in red, 15″ d, 11½″ h	60.00
Woven splint, round, good color, bentwood rim handles, minor damage, 18″ d, 12¾″ h.	85.00
Gathering	
Rye straw, rim handles, wear and one handle partially restored, 18″ d, 9″ h	105.00
Woven splint	
Oval	
Flared sides, traces of old red paint, some damage, 10½ x 13½″, 5″ h plus bentwood handle	85.00
Radiating ribs, old varnish, 15 x 16″, 6½″ h plus bentwood handle	210.00
Weathered gray finish, 11 x 16″, 8½″ h plus bentwood handle. .	60.00
Round	
Scrubbed finish, 17″ d, 7¼″ h plus bentwood handle.	115.00
Weathered gray finish, minor damage, 15″ d, 8½″ h plus well shaped bentwood handle	105.00
Goosefeather, woven splint, dome lid, good color, bentwood handles covered by lid, rim of lid broken, minor damage, 25″ h	80.00
Herb Drying, woven splint, open weave base, minor damage, 16″ d, 6¾″ h plus bentwood rim handles.	240.00
Laundry, woven splint	
19 x 27″, oval	75.00
25½″ l, 20½″ w, 10¾″ h, rect, natural, bentwood rim handles	75.00
24″ l, 20″ w, 11″ h, oblong, ribs and open rim handles, damage	95.00
26″ d, 16″ h, rim handles, dark finish, some damage	50.00
31″ l, 21″ w, 10″ h, rect	75.00
40″ l, 22″ w, 12″ h, minor damage .	60.00
Loom, 15″ w, 17″ h, woven splint, hanging, curlique designs, Eastern Woodlands	40.00
Market, 16 x 14″, splint, early 19th C .	70.00
Melon Rib, 15″ d, 7½″ h, round, woven splint, cane wrapped wood handle . .	65.00
Nantucket	
6″ d, 8″ h, lightship type, swing handle, Nantucket Island, MA, early 20th C	1,100.00
8″ d, oval, Stanley Roop	375.00
8″ l, 4½″ h, oval, swing handle, Nantucket Island, MA, early 20th C . . .	245.00
9″ d, oval, oval plaque with whale dec on cov, Formoso Reyes	550.00

11″ l, 5¼″ h, oval, swing handle, Nantucket Island, MA, early 20th C . . . **265.00**
8¾″ d, 10¼″ h, swing handle, Nantucket Island, MA, early 20th C . . . **330.00**
Pea Picking, 10″ l, rect, splint, red . . . **220.00**
Wall Pocket, 9″ l, splint, yellow over white and red, 19th C **110.00**

BATTERSEA ENAMELS

History: Battersea enamel is a generic term for English enamel–on–copper objects of the 18th century.

In 1753 Stephen Theodore Janssen established a factory to produce "Trinkets and Curiosities Enamelled on Copper" at York House, Battersea, London. Here the new invention of transfer printing developed a high degree of excellence, and the resulting trifles delighted fashionable Georgian society.

Recent research has shown that enamels actually were being produced in London and the Midlands several years before York House was established. However, most enamel trinkets still are referred to as "Battersea Enamels," even though they were probably made in other workshops in London, Birmingham, Bilston, Wednesbury, or Liverpool.

All manner of charming items were made, including snuff and patch boxes bearing mottos and memory gems. (By adding a mirror inside the lid, a snuffbox became patch box.) Many figural whimsies, called "toys," were created to amuse a gay and fashionable world. Many other elaborate articles, for example, candlesticks, salts, tea caddies, and bonbonnieres, were made for the tables of the newly rich middle classes.

Reference: Susan Benjamin, *English Enamel Boxes*, Merrimack Publishers Circle, 1978.
Advisors: Barbara and Melvin Alpren.

Snuff, yellow, floral top, 1¼″ d, $250.00.

Bonbonniere, reclining cow, natural colors, grassy mound, floral lid, Bilston, c1770. . . . . **3,500.00**
Candlesticks, 6″ h, pink ground, all over nosegays, pastels, Bilston, 1770. . . . **3,300.00**
Etui, white tapered column, pastoral scenes within reserves, gilt scrolling and diaper work, int. fitted with perfume bottle, writing slide, pencil, and bodkin, Bilston, c1770 . . . . **2,950.00**
Patch Box
1¼″ round, "A Small Token of Friendship," pink, South Staffordshire, c1780 . . . . **450.00**
1½″ oval
Pastoral riverside scene, full color, pale green top and bottom, Bilston, c1780 . . . . **495.00**
Peace and Plenty, cobalt and white doves, Wednesbury, c1780 . . . . **695.00**
1½″ rect, Let Us in Love Unite, yellow, white top, Bilston, c1780. . . . . . . **495.00**
1¾″ oval, Virtue is the greatest ornament of the fair, pink base, white and pastel top, South Staffordshire, c1780. . . . . **595.00**
Potpourri Box, 3½ x 2″, reticulated top, floral cutouts, South Staffordshire, c1770. **1,400.00**
Topsy–Turvy Box, 2¼″ oval, white, Before and After Marriage, humorous drawing of couple whose smiles turn into frowns when box is turned upside down, Bilston, c1780 . . . . **1,200.00**
Traveling Writing Casket, 3 x 1¼ x 1¼″, white, blue, and gold enamel all over geometric pattern, writing implements, polished brass rope mounts, Bilston, c1770. . . . . **3,900.00**

BAVARIAN CHINA

History: Bavaria, Germany, was an important porcelain production center, similar to the Staffordshire district in England. The name Bavarian China refers to companies operating in Bavaria, among which were Hutschenreuther, Thomas, and Zeh, Scherzer & Co. (Z. S. & Co.). Very little of the production from this area was imported into the United States prior to 1870.

Reference: Susan and Al Bagdade, *Warman's English & Continental Pottery & Porcelain, Second Edition,* Wallace–Homestead, 1991.

Bowl, 9½″ d, large orange poppies, green leaves dec. **65.00**
Celery Tray, 11″ l, basket of fruit in center, luster edge, c1900. . . . . **35.00**
Charger, scalloped rim, game bird in

woodland scene, bunches of pink and
yellow roses, connecting garlands. . . 75.00
Chocolate Set, chocolate pot, cov, six
cups and saucers, shaded blue to
white, large white leaves, pink, red,
and white roses, crown mark, price for
set. 245.00
Cup and Saucer, roses and foliage, gold
handle 20.00
Dinner Service, service for twelve, serving pcs, Baronet–Belclaire, black and
platinum rose, platinum rim, c1950,
price for 108 piece set 500.00
Figure, 10½" h, dark blue and pale orange marabou standing beside tan
and navy cactus, marked "Hutschenreuther Selb–Bavaria, K. Tutter". . . . 250.00
Fish Set, thirteen plates, matching
sauceboat, artist sgd, price for four-
teen piece set. 400.00
Hair Receiver, 3½" d, apple blossom
dec, marked "T. S. & Co". 50.00
Pitcher, 9" h, bulbous, blackberry dec,
shaded ground, burnished gold lizard
handle, sgd "D. Churchill" 110.00
Plate
  8½" d, hp, poinsettia dec 45.00
  9½" d, red berries, green leaves,
  white ground, scalloped border . . . 25.00
Platter, 16" l, Dresden flowers 90.00
Portrait Plate, 9" d, lady, sgd "L. B. Chaf-
fee, R. C. Bavaria" 70.00
Punch Bowl, hp roses int. and ext., gold
pedestal base, marked "H & C" 250.00
Ramekin, underplate, ruffled, small red
roses with green foliage, gold rim . . . 40.00

**Salt, white opal int., beige ext., gold rim,
dec, and feet, 2" d, ¾" h, $20.00.**

Salt and Pepper Shakers, pr, pink apple
blossom sprays, white ground, reti-
culated gold tops. 25.00
Sugar, cov, white, green grapes dec . 30.00
Sugar Shaker, hp, pastel pansies . . . 50.00
Toothpick Holder, barrel shape, pink
roses 30.00
Vase, 4¾" h, hp, florals, sgd 20.00

BELLEEK

History: Belleek, a thin, ivory-colored, almost iridescent–type porcelain, was first made in 1857 in
County Fermanagh, Ireland. Production continued
until World War I, was discontinued for a period of
time, and then resumed. The Shamrock pattern is
most familiar, but many patterns were made, including Limpet, Tridacna, and Grasses.

Irish Belleek has several identifying marks, for
example, the Harp and Hound (1865–80) and
Harp, Hound, and Castle (1863–91). After 1891 the
word "Ireland" or "Erie" was added. Some pieces
are marked "Belleek Co., Fermanagh."

There is an Irish saying: If a newly married couple receives a gift of Belleek, their marriage will be
blessed with lasting happiness.

Several American firms made a Belleek–type
porcelain. The first was Ott and Brewer Co. of Trenton, New Jersey, in 1884, followed by Willets. Other
firms included the Ceramic Art Co. (1889), American Art China Works (1892), Columbian Art Co.
(1893), and Lenox, Inc. (1904).

References: Susan and Al Bagdade, *Warman's
English & Continental Pottery & Porcelain, Second
Edition*, Wallace–Homestead, 1991; Richard K.
Degenhardt, *Belleek: The Complete Collector's
Guide and Illustrated Reference, Second Edition*,
Wallace–Homestead, 1993; Mary Frank Gaston,
American Belleek, Collector Books, 1984.

Collectors' Club: The Belleek Collectors' Society, 144 W. Britannia Street, Taunton, MA 02780.

Museum: Museum of Ceramics at East Liverpool, East Liverpool, OH.

Additional Listings: Lenox.

Abbreviations: 1BM = 1st Black Mark; 2BM =
2nd Black Mark; 3BM = 3rd Black Mark; 4GM =
4th Green Mark; 5GM = 5th Green Mark.

AMERICAN

Bowl, 9" d, green, heavy gold trim, white
curled handle, Lenox green wreath
mark 90.00
Cup and Saucer, 6" h, square pedestal
base, undecorated, Willets brown
mark 35.00
Demitasse Cup, liner, gold band border,
SS holder with saucer, Lenox green
wreath mark 55.00
Dresser Set, cov powder box, pin tray,
buffer and container, nailbrush, pincushion, hp violets, artist sgd "M.R.,"

Willets brown mark, price for six
pieces 550.00
Dresser Tray, roses 115.00
Figure
  4" h
    Elephant, white, Lenox green
      wreath mark............. 315.00
    Swan, green, Lenox green wreath
      mark................... 65.00
Loving Cup, three handles, wine keeper
  in wine cellar, artist sgd, SS repousse
  collar, CAC mark............. 185.00
Mask, 7½" h, lady's face, black, Lenox
  green wreath mark 175.00
Mug, 5¾" h, dragon form handle, enameled dog portrait, sgd "GY Houghton,
  1904," printed Willets, Trenton, NJ,
  marks, foot rim nick, price for pair... 825.00
Perfume, figural, rabbit, white, Lenox
  green wreath mark, price for pair ... 525.00
Pitcher, 5½" h, body indentation, tree
  branch shaped handle, gold paste
  floral dec, Willets brown mark..... 375.00
Powder Box, 4 x 6", pink, gold wheat on
  lid, Lenox green wreath mark 40.00
Salt, hearts, crimped gold edges, rose
  dec, Willets................. 55.00
Salt and Pepper Shakers, pr, 1" d salt,
  2" h egg shape pepper, pink roses,
  Lenox green palette mark........ 35.00
Vase
  8½" h, bulbous shape, pinecone and
    branches dec, Lenox green wreath
    mark.................... 55.00
  12" h, 8½" d, applied handles, floral
    ground, artist sgd, CAC mark 475.00

IRISH

Ashtray, 4½" d, shamrock horseshoe,
  4GM 45.00
Basket
  8" d, Melvin, sq, decorative border,
    twig handles, turquoise–blue, four
    applied violet floral sprays, green
    leaves.................. 550.00
  8½" d, Sydenham, three strands, cir-
    cular, twig handles, four applied
    floral sprays, pearl luster glaze, imp
    mark................... 990.00
Box, cov, 3" h, Forget–Me–Not, ftd, glob-
  ular, applied flowerheads, conical
  knop, pearl luster glaze, 3BM...... 385.00
Creamer and Sugar, Lotus, 3BM 130.00
Cup, Neptune, green trim, 2BM 85.00
Cup and Saucer, 6" d, 2" h, Shamrock
  pattern, 2BM................ 200.00
Cake Plate
  Limpet pattern, 2BM 175.00
  Shamrock pattern, 3BM 125.00
Creamer, Lotus pattern, green handle,
  2BM..................... 75.00

**American, vase, calla lily, gold enamel
highlights, Ott and Brewer, c1884–94,
7" h, $750.00.**

Creamer and Sugar
  Lily pattern, 5GM 45.00
  Lotus pattern, 5GM 45.00
  Tridacna, green rim, 3BM 115.00
Dish, 6½" w, heart shape, 3BM 95.00
Figure
  3½" h, Terrier, 4GM 35.00
  4½" h, Swan, 3BM 65.00
  14⅝" h
    Affection, multicolored, 1BM 2,500.00
    Meditation, multicolored, 1BM .. 2,500.00
Flower Holder, 3½" h, Seahorse, one
  with white head, other with brown,
  1BM, price for pair............. 1,200.00
Plate, Shamrock and Basketweave
  7" d 38.00
  8" d 45.00
Sandwich Tray, Mask pattern, 2BM .. 275.00
Sugar
  Cleary pattern, 3BM 60.00
  Shamrock pattern, cov, 3BM 65.00
Tea and Dessert Service, Eugene
  Sheran, partially decorated, c1887,
  price for thirty two pieces........ 7,900.00
Tea Set, Grass Ware, 3⅜" h teapot,
  creamer, cov sugar, waste bowl, two
  teacups and saucers, pink highlights,
  purple luster, brown and gilt trim,
  1BM, price for nine pieces........ 880.00
Tub, 3¼" d, Shamrock pattern, 3BM . 55.00
Vase
  Bird and tree stump, 1BM, few
    chipped leaves.............. 425.00
  Shamrock pattern
    6¼" h, tree trunk, 2BM 145.00
    6½" h, harp, 5GM 40.00
    7⅞" h, panel, yellow gilt, 6GM .. 65.00

BELLS

History: Bells have been used for centuries for many different purposes. They have been traced as far back as 2697 B.C., though at that time they did not have any true tone. One of the oldest bells is the "crotal," a tiny sphere with small holes and a ball or stone or metal inside. This type now appears as sleigh bells.

True bell making began when bronze, the mixing of tin and copper, was discovered. There are now many types of materials of which bells are made—almost as many materials as there are uses for them.

Bells of the late 19th century show a high degree of workmanship and artistic style. Glass bells from this period are examples of the glassblower's talent and the glass manufacturer's product.

Collectors' Clubs: American Bell Association, Alter Rd., Box 386, Natrona Heights, PA 15065; American Bell Association International, Inc., PO Box 19443, Indianapolis, IN 46219.

Museum: Bell Haven, Tarentum, PA.

Brass, Disciples, Matthew, Luke, and John, $45.00.

Bicycle, eagle, cast brass, nickel plated	85.00
Desk	
Bronze, white marble base, side tap, c1875	45.00
Silverplate, wind–up, open filigree skirt, top knob	85.00
Dinner	
Chased foliage design, applied cast copper and brass ornament, tapered cylindrical handle, silver clapper, marked "Dominick & Haff," 1880, 4¼" h.	1,100.00
Sterling Silver, spot hammered, applied leaves and pods, baluster form handle with inlaid polychrome enamel design, Tiffany & Co, New York, 1879–85, 3¾" h.	5,500.00
Victorian, manufacturer sgd, c1875	45.00
Glass	
Amethyst, flint, metal lace trim,	

painted crowing rooster on top of handle.	350.00
Burmese, shaded deep pink to ivory, satin finish, 6¼" h.	70.00
Custard, "Alamo–Built 1718, San Antonio, TX," gilt band	90.00
Heisey, Victorian Belle, frosted	125.00
Vaseline, flint, ornate metal lace trim, elephant with green eyes and red mouth on top of handle.	325.00
Hand, brass, figural	
Bust, woman, quilted pattern bell, 3⅝" h	35.00
Monk, carrying umbrella and basket, 5" h.	75.00
Turtle, bell bracket and striker on shell	30.00
Locomotive, brass, cradle and yoke, 17 x 17"	800.00
Marriage, brown, clear fancy handle, 12" h	125.00
School, hand, brass, turned maple handle, marked "No 6," 6½" h	65.00
Sleigh	
Four bells, nickel plated shaft, arched strap, 12" l.	45.00
Thirty bells, leather strap	125.00
Steeple, cast iron, Hollsboro, OH, 1886	220.00
Table, sterling silver, cupid blowing horn, figural handle, frosted finish, foliate strap work border, Gorham Mfg Co, c1870, 4⅝" h	725.00

J. NORTON
BENNINGTON
VT.

BENNINGTON AND BENNINGTON-TYPE POTTERY

History: In 1845 Christopher Webber Fenton joined Julius Norton, his brother–in–law, in the manufacturing of stoneware pottery in Bennington, Vermont. Fenton sought to expand the company's products and glazes; Norton wanted to concentrate solely on stoneware. In 1847 Fenton broke away and established his own factory.

Fenton introduced the famous Rockingham glaze, developed in England and named after the Marquis of Rockingham, to America. In 1849 he patented a flint enamel glaze, "Fenton's Enamel," which added flecks, spots, or streaks of color (usually blues, greens, yellows, and oranges) to the brown Rockingham glaze. Forms included candlesticks, coachman bottles, cow creamers, poodles, sugar bowls, and toby pitchers.

Fenton produced the little-known scroddled ware, commonly called lava or agate ware. Scroddled ware is composed of different colored clays mixed with cream-colored clay, molded, turned on a potter's wheel, coated with feldspar and flint, and fired. It was not produced in quantity as there was little demand for it.

Fenton also introduced Parian ware to America. Parian was developed in England in 1842 and was known as "Statuary ware." Parian is a translucent porcelain which has no glaze and resembles marble. Bennington made the blue-and-white variety in the form of vases, cologne bottles, and trinkets.

Five different marks were used, with many variations. Only about 20% of the pieces carried any mark; some forms were almost always marked, others never. Marks: (a) 1849 mark (four variations) for flint enamel and Rockingham; (b) E. Fenton's Works, 1845–47, on Parian and occasionally on scroddled ware; (c) U.S. Pottery Co., ribbon mark, 1852–58, on Parian and blue-and-white porcelain; (d) U.S. Pottery Co., lozenge mark, 1852–58, on Parian; and (e) U.S. Pottery, oval mark, 1853–58, mainly on scroddled ware.

The hound-handled pitcher is probably the best-known Bennington piece. Hound-handled pitchers also were made by some 30 potteries in more than 55 different variations. Rockingham glaze was used by more than 150 potteries in eleven states, mainly the Midwest, between 1830 and 1900.

References: Richard Carter Barret, *How To Identify Bennington Pottery,* Stephen Greene Press, 1964; Laura Woodside Watkins, *Early New England Potters And Their Wares,* Harvard University Press, 1950.

Museums: Bennington Museum, Bennington, VT; East Liverpool Museum of Ceramics, East Liverpool, OH.

Additional Listings: Stoneware.

BENNINGTON

Book Flask, 5¼" h, flint enamel, spine imp "Ladies Suffering G," attributed to

Candlestick, 8¼" h, $125.00.

Lyman Fenton & Co, mid 19th C, imperfections **412.00**
Candlesticks, 7½" h, Rockingham glaze, attributed to Lyman, Fenton & Co, mid 19th C, price for pair **420.00**
Curtin Tiebacks, 4¼ and 4½" d, Rockingham glaze, attributed to Lyman, Fenton & Co, mid 19th C, price for set of four **175.00**
Cuspidor
  8" d, flint enamel glaze, Lyman Fenton & Co, mid 19th C **200.00**
  10" d, Rockingham glaze, base marked "Lyman Fenton & Co., Bennington" **225.00**
Figure
  7½" h, lion, Rockingham glaze, attributed to Lyman Fenton & Co, mid 19th C, damage **1,760.00**
  8" h, poodle, Rockingham glaze, attributed to Lyman, Fenton & Co, mid 19th C, minute losses to coleslaw, price for pair **11,000.00**
  9" h, 11" l, lion, mottled flint enamel glaze, marked "Lyman, Fenton & Co, patented 1849, Bennington, VT," imperfections, price for pair . . **11,000.00**
Flowerpot
  3" h, redware, molded, imp "Bennington Centennial Aug 16, 1877," small flake **140.00**
  4½" h, flint enamel, attributed to Lyman, Fenton & Co, mid 19th C, George S McKearin Collection label, star crack **715.00**
Frame, 8" to 11¾" h, attributed to Lyman, Fenton & Co, mid 19th C, each with hollow–cut silhouette, imperfections, price for four piece set **385.00**
Inkwell, Rockingham glaze, attributed to Lyman, Fenton & Co, mid 19th C . . . **165.00**
Paperweight
  Rectangular, mottled flint enamel glaze, sgd on base "Bennington 1849," repaired handle **165.00**
  Spaniel, reclining, c1850, base marked, imperfections, 4½" l **300.00**
Pitcher
  7" h, Rockingham glaze, molded grape dec, marked "Lyman R Fenton East Bennington Vt," 1844–47, repaired **165.00**
  7½" h, Rockingham glaze, attributed to Lyman, Fenton & Co, George S McKearin Collection label **330.00**
  9" h, Rockingham glaze, hound handle, 19th C, imperfections **200.00**
  10½" h, Rockingham glaze, hound handle, 19th C, imperfections **225.00**
  12½" h, flint enamel, attributed to Lyman Fenton & Co, mid 19th C, base marked "E" **825.00**

Pitkin, cov
  5½" d, Rockingham glaze, attributed
    to Lyman, Fenton & Co, mid 19th C   **165.00**
  6¼" h, Rockingham glaze, molded
    ribbed body, indistinct Lyman Fen-
    ton & Co mark, chips **990.00**
Toby Bottle, 10¾" h, Rockingham glaze,
  Lyman Fenton & Co, mid 19th C,
  marked at base, imperfections **715.00**
Vase
  6½" h, flint enamel, hand shape, at-
    tributed to Lyman Fenton & Co, mid
    19th C.   **275.00**
  9" h, flint enamel, tulip, shape, attrib-
    uted to Lyman Fenton & Co, mid
    19th C.   **385.00**

BENNINGTON TYPE

Bank, 6½" h, figural, Rockingham glaze,
  imp "Anna L Curtis Pittsfield Mass,"
  minor imperfections **275.00**
Food Mold, 6⅝" d, turk's head, Rock-
  ingham glaze **95.00**
Pitcher, 10½" h, paneled, Rockingham
  glaze, c1850. . . . .   **225.00**
Soap Dish, 4 x 2½" d, Rockingham
  glaze **95.00**

BISCUIT JARS

History: The biscuit or cracker jar was the forerunner of the cookie jar. They were made of various
materials by leading glassworks and potteries of
the late 19th and early 20th centuries.

Note: All items listed have silver-plated mountings unless otherwise noted.

Crown Milano, 6½" h, opal glass, large
  pink, yellow, and green pansies and
  wild roses, gold tracery, painted Burmese ground, orig SP cov stamped
  "Mt Washington," crown mark, num-
  bered 520. . . . .   **1,000.00**
Doulton, 6½" h, 7" d, tapestry ground,
  highly raised blue dec and peach
  morning glories, orig metal hardware,
  ivory finial and handle, sgd, imp and
  marked "US Patent SIL002 Doulton
  Burselem England" **250.00**
Loetz Type, 7½" h, 5" d, art glass, deep
  irid green, applied amethyst pulled
  feathers, orig metal mountings **225.00**
Mt Washington
  6" h, 6" d, opal glass, scene of whale
    ship caught in iceberg flow, sixteen
    flat panels form continuous scene,
    green, brown, and white dec, pale
    pink accents, sgd "Pairpoint No.
    3932" **600.00**
  7" h, opal glass, molded to simulate

**Wavecrest, pink and blue floral trans-
fer, plated metal top, 7¾" h, $300.00.**

  floral cameo carving, cov stamped
    "M. W. 4413". **250.00**
  8½" h, 5" d, egg crate, pale pink clover
    and green leaves, pale shaded blue
    ground, orig metal hardware **250.00**
Royal Worcester, 7½" h, 6½" d, melon
  ribbed jar, all over pink, blue, purple,
  yellow, coral flowers, green and brown
  leaves, orig matching cov and underplate, sgd "Royal Worcester England
  No. 1412". **375.00**
Webb, 7¼" h, glossy cased peachblow,
  engraved geometric devices, sterling
  silver rim, bale, and cov marked "Tif-
  fany & Co Makers" **935.00**
Wedgwood, 7" h, 6" d, jasper, yellow,
  black, and white, band of classical figures, orig brass hardware **575.00**

BISQUE

History: Bisque or biscuit china is the name
given to wares that have been fired once and are
not glazed.

Bisque figurines and busts were popular during
the Victorian era, being used on fireplace mantels,
dining room buffets, and end tables. Manufacturing
was centered in the United States and Europe. By
the mid 20th century the Japanese were the principal source of bisque items, especially character-
related items.

References: Susan and Al Bagdade, *Warman's
English & Continental Pottery & Porcelain, Second
Edition,* Wallace–Homestead, 1991; Elyse Karlin,
*Children Figurines of Bisque and Chinawares,
1850–1950,* Schiffer Publishing, 1990.

Box, egg shape, relief windmill scene,
  ftd **45.00**
Dish, cov, 9 x 6½ x 5½", dog, brown and
  white, green blanket, white and gilt
  basketweave base. **500.00**

Figure, peasant girl, green dress, pink purse, marked "959," 9" h, $50.00.

Figure, 12½" h, man with axe in one hand, wiping brow with other, lady with baby in one arm, jug in other hand, pastel colors, imp Heubach mark, price for pair **750.00**

Flower Pot, figural, carriage, four wheels, pale blue and pink, white ground, gold dots, royal markings dec **140.00**

Match Holder, figural
   Dog, dressed in man's clothing and top hat, Germany. **70.00**
   Dutch Girl, copper and gold trim . . **35.00**

Nodder
   2½ x 3½", jester, seated holding pipe, pastel peach and white, gold trim. . **75.00**
   4¼" h, lady seated, white and turquoise Oriental style robe, gold trim, holding fan **150.00**

Piano Baby, 6¾" l, lying on stomach, wearing bib, dog and cat, Germany. . **100.00**

Planter, girl with water jug, sitting by well, coral and green. **50.00**

Salt, 3" d, figural, walnut, cream, branch base, matching spoon **70.00**

Tobacco Jar, cov, figural, boy, Heubach **160.00**

Wall Plaque, 10¼" d, figural, cream, scrolled and pierced scallop, white relief figures in center, man playing mandolin, lady wearing hat, c1900, price for pair **250.00**

BITTERS BOTTLES

History: Bitters, a "remedy" made from natural herbs and other mixtures with an alcohol base, often were viewed as the universal cure–all. The names given to various bitter mixtures were imaginative, though the bitters seldom cured what their makers claimed.

The manufacturers of bitters needed a way to sell and advertise their products. They designed bottles in many shapes, sizes, and colors to attract the buyer. Many forms of advertising, including trade cards, billboards, signs, almanacs, and novelties, proclaimed the virtues of a specific bitter.

During the Civil War a tax was levied on alcoholic beverages. Since bitters were identified as medicines, they were exempt from this tax. The alcohol content was never mentioned. In 1907, when the Pure Foods Regulations went into effect, "an honest statement of content on every label" put most of the manufacturers out of business.

References: Carlyn Ring, *For Bitters Only,* 1980; J. H. Thompson, *Bitters Bottles,* Century House, 1947; Richard Watson, *Bitters Bottles,* Thomas Nelson and Sons, 1965.

Periodicals: *Antique Bottle and Glass Collector,* PO Box 187, East Greenville, PA 18041; *The Bitters Report,* PO Box 1253, Bunnell, FL 32110.

American Life Bitters, 9" h, modified log cabin form, amber, sloping collared mouth, smooth base **475.00**

Baker's Orange Grove Bitters, 9½" h, sq with roped corners, light golden amber, sloping collared mouth, smooth base **180.00**

Big Bill Best Bitters, 12⅛" h, tall pyramid form, golden amber, tooled mouth, smooth base. **100.00**

Brown's Celebrated Indian Herb Bitters, 12¼" h, Indian maiden form, golden amber, rolled mouth, smooth base . . **550.00**

Caldwell's Herb Bitters, The Great Tonic, triangular, beveled and latticework panels, yellow–amber, applied tapered lip, iron pontil **385.00**

DeMuth's Stomach Bitters, 9¼" h, sq, beveled corners, light golden amber, sloping collared mouth, smooth base **150.00**

Doyles, amber, raised fruit dec, 1872, 9¾" h, $100.00.

Doctor Fisch's Bitters, 11⅝" h, fish form, golden amber, round collared mouth, smooth base.................. 280.00

Dr C W Robacks/Stomach Bitters, 9¾" h, barrel form, golden amber, sloping collared mouth, iron pontil........ 175.00

Dr J Hostetter's Stomach Bitters, 9¼" h, sq, beveled corners, yellow, sloping collared mouth, smooth base...... 150.00

Greeley's Bourbon and Bitters
9" h, barrel form, pinkish copper, sq collared mouth, smooth base 280.00
9¼" h, barrel form, smoky grayish green, applied collared mouth, smooth base................. 950.00

Hall's Bitters, 9⅛" h, barrel form, yellow, sq collared mouth, smooth base.... 210.00

Holtzermann's Patent Stomach Bitters, 9¾" h, cabin form, golden amber, tooled sloping collared mouth, smooth base 280.00

H P Herb/Wild/Cherry Bitters, 10" h, cabin form, golden amber, tooled mouth, smooth base........... 160.00

Jno Moffat Price $1 Phoenix Bitters, 5¾" h, rect, beveled corners, olive green, tooled mouth, pontil scar......... 350.00

John W Steele's Niagara Star Bitters, 9⅞" h, sq modified cabin form, deep golden amber, sloping collared mouth with ring, smooth base.......... 350.00

Keystone Bitters, 9¾" h, barrel shape, golden amber, applied tapered collar, sq lip, smooth base............ 140.00

Kimball's Jaundice Bitters, 6⅞" h, rect, beveled corners, yellow amber, sloping collared mouth, iron pontil mark.. 400.00

Morning Star Bitters, 12⅝" h, triangular shape, golden amber, applied sloping collared mouth, iron pontil........ 130.00

National Bitters, 12½" h, ear of corn form, deep golden amber, applied collared mouth, smooth base........ 220.00

Old Sachem Bitters And Wigwam Tonic, 9¼" h, barrel form, golden amber, sq collared mouth, smooth base...... 175.00

Rex Kidney and Liver Bitters, The Best Laxative and Blood Purifier, 9⅝" h, amber, smooth base........... 70.00

S O Richardson's Bitters, South Reading, MA, 7" h, deep aqua to teal, open pontil, applied mouth........... 220.00

The Globe Tonic, 9⅝" h, sq, columnar corners, golden amber, applied mouth, smooth base............ 120.00

The Great Tonic/Dr Caldwell's/Herb Bitters, 12⅝" h, triangular, golden amber, applied mouth with ring, smooth base 210.00

Warner's Safe Bitters, 7⅜" h, amber, applied mouth, smooth base........ 250.00

BLACK MEMORABILIA

History: The term "black memorabilia" refers to a broad range of collectibles that often overlap other collecting fields, for example, toys, postcards, and so on. It also encompasses African artifacts, items created by slaves or related to the slavery era, modern black cultural contributions to literature, art, and so on, and material associated with the civil rights movement and the black experience throughout history.

The earliest known examples of black memorabilia include primitive African designs and tribal artifacts. Black Americana dates back to the arrival of African natives upon American shores.

The advent of the 1900s saw an incredible amount and variety of material depicting blacks, most often in a derogatory and dehumanizing manner that clearly reflected the stereotypical attitude held toward the black race during this period. The popularity of black portrayals in this unflattering fashion flourished as the century wore on.

As the growth of the civil rights movement escalated and aroused public awareness to the black plight, attitudes changed. Public outrage and pressure eventually put a halt to these offensive stereotypes during the early 1950s.

Black representations are still being produced in many forms but no longer in the demoralizing designs of the past. These modern objects, while not as historically significant as earlier examples, will become the black memorabilia of tomorrow.

References: Douglas Congdon–Martin, *Images in Black: 150 Years of Black Collectibles,* Schiffer Publishing, 1990; Patiki Gibbs, *Black Collectibles Sold In America,* Collector Books, 1987; Jan Lindenberger, *Black Memorabilia Around The House: A Handbook and Price Guide,* Schiffer Publishing, 1993; Jan Lindenberger, *Black Memorabilia For The Kitchen,* Schiffer Publishing, 1992; Myla Perkins, *Black Dolls 1820–1991: An Identification and Value Guide,* Collector Books, 1993; Dawn Reno, *Collecting Black Americana,* Crown Publishing Co., 1986; Darrell A. Smith, *Black Americana: A Personal Collection,* Black Relics, Inc., 1988; Jackie Young, *Black Collectibles: Mammy and Her Friends,* Schiffer Publishing, 1988.

Periodical: *Black Ethnic Collectibles,* 1401 Asbury Court, Hyattsville, MD 20782.

Collectors' Clubs: Blackin, 559 22nd Ave., Rock Island, IL 61201; Black Memorabilia Collector's Association, 2482 Devoe Terrace, Bronx, NY 10468.

Museum: Museum of African American History, Detroit, MI.

Reproduction Alert: Reproductions are becoming an increasing problem, from advertising signs (Bull Durham tobacco) to mechanical banks (Jolly Nigger). If the object looks new to you, chances are that it is new.

Advertising Trade Card, The Alden Fruit Vinegar, black man caught stealing chickens, $8.00.

Advertising
Display, St Bruno Tobacco, diorama, black men and women picking tobacco, five diecut litho figures, mounted in wood frame 600.00
Sign
Bull Durham Smoking Tobacco, 21½ x 27½", paper, two black hunters, child hunter, and hunting dog, bull in background, matted and framed. 1,500.00
Fern Glen Rye, 23 x 33", tin, black man holding watermelon and chicken 1,800.00
Paul Jones Whiskey, 19½ x 14", tin, black mammy with watermelon, black man holding bottle of whiskey 500.00
Trade Card
Lumbard Bros Druggist, black man and birds 6.00
Sapolio, figural watermelon, black face center. 15.00
Schencks Seaweed Tonic, black boy by fence 15.00
Soapine, black children under umbrella 15.00
Andiron, pr, 17½" h, 15" d, 11½" w, cast iron, figural, black man, c1850 . . . . . 500.00
Ashtray Stand, 35" h, figural, cast iron, black butler holding cigarettes, matches, and ashtray, painted 525.00
Autograph
Ali, Mohammed, 8 x 10" photo, color,

double matted, engraved name plate 45.00
Armstrong, Louis, 8 x 10" photo, glossy, sepia, sgd in green ink . . . 425.00
Dempsey, Jack, post card, color, pictured in ring knocking out Jess Willard, penned inscription, sentiment, and signature. 50.00
Ellington, Duke, 3 x 5" card, sentiment, sgd in gold 95.00
Bank
3" h, pottery, figural, head, black man, yellow glaze. 350.00
6" h, Mammy, polychrome paint . . . 140.00
Book
Black Leaders of the Centuries, S Okechukwu Mezu and Ram Desai, Black Academy Press, 1970, 301 pgs, dj 10.00
Little Black Sambo, 1959 . . . . 45.00
Ole Mammy's Lullaby Songs, 1901, Pepper Publishing Co, 39 pgs, hardback, 12⅜" h, 9½" w 50.00
Ole Mammy's Torment, dated 1897 110.00
Bottle Opener, 4¼" h, cast iron, black man's head, polychrome paint 110.00
Creamer, butler 85.00
Doll
8" h, cornhusk, black farmhand, with basket of cotton, basket sgd "Shuckaninnies by B L Hayden," c1940 . . . . 110.00
17" h, Sukey, composition head, cloth body, American, 19th C 250.00
18" h, rag, black girl, white dress . . 140.00
Figure
5" h, bisque, boy eating watermelon 65.00
25" h, black boy holding machete and bananas, papier mache 425.00
Glass, Coon Chicken Inn 45.00
Greeting Card, birthday, "Say What's Cooking," Mammy holding pie and little boy 6.00
Gum Vendor, 8 x 16 x 6", 1¢, black man holding scoop reaches for gum balls, top marked "Original Manikin Vendor Co" 5,250.00
Marriage Certificate, 16 x 20", black couple, minister, and cherubs, 1910. . . . 50.00
Photograph
Black and White, little girl, framed . 20.00
Carte–de–Viste, black Siamese twins, one holding newspaper, other playing guitar. 175.00
Poster
Black family admiring soldier father, WWI, 16 x 20". 30.00
"Colored Man is no Slacker," 16 x 20", WWI. 35.00
Little black boy and lamb, 16 x 20", 1911. 50.00
Lloyd G Gibbs, Black Patti's Trouba-

Sheet Music, *The Banjo Picker,* printed green on white, 1929, $20.00.

dours, color litho, wood frame, 29 x 20″, 1954	**170.00**
Salt and Pepper Shaker, pr, Valentine girl and boy.	**165.00**
Sheet Music	
Mammy Jimmy's Jubilee, 1913 . . .	**15.00**
The Banjo Picker, Frederic Groton, Carl Fisher Inc, green illus on white background, 1929	**20.00**
The Perfect Song, Pepsodent theme song and *Three Little Words,* Amos and Andy, 1924	**50.00**
When The Robert E Lee Comes To Town, 1927	**8.00**
White Folks Call It Chanticleer but its Just Plain Chicken To Me, Bert Williams, 1910	**15.00**
Sprinkler, 39″ h, metal with wood figural black boy, label on back "The Firestone Tire and Rubber Co".	**225.00**
Tablecloth, Mammy	**125.00**
Toothbrush Holder, black baker, orig tray	**400.00**
Toy, windup, 6¼″ l, Tip–Top, black man pushing cart, tin, Straus	**125.00**

BLOWN THREE MOLD

History: The Jamestown colony in Virginia introduced glassmaking into America. The artisans used a "free blown" method.

Blowing molten glass into molds was not introduced into America until the early 1800s. Blown three-mold glass used a predesigned mold that consisted of two, three, or more hinged parts. The glassmaker placed a quantity of molten glass on the tip of a rod or tube, inserted it into the mold, blew air into the tube, waited until the glass cooled, and removed the finished product. The three-part mold is the most common and lends its name to this entire category.

The impressed decorations on blown-mold glass usually are reversed, that is, what is raised or convex on the outside will be concave on the inside. This is useful in identifying the blown form.

By 1850 American-made glassware was in relatively common usage. The increased demand led to large factories and the creation of a technology which eliminated the smaller companies.

Reference: George S. and Helen McKearin, *American Glass,* reprint, Crown Publishers, 1941, 1948.

Collectors' Club: National Early American Glass Club, PO Box 8489, Silver Spring, MD 20907.

Museum: Sandwich Glass Museum, Sandwich, MA.

Toilet Water Bottle, medium blue, ribbed, 6″ h, McKearin GI–1, type 5, $200.00.

Bottle	
Clear, lavender tint	**40.00**
Cobalt Blue, tam–o'–shanter stopper, pint.	**330.00**
Olive Amber, pint, McKearin GIII–16	**245.00**
Bowl, 5⅝″ d, clear, folded rim, pontil, twelve diamond base, McKearin GII–6	**90.00**
Candlesticks, pr, 7″ h, clear, shaped standard.	**55.00**
Creamer, 3⅞″ h, cobalt blue, sheared rim, pontil	**400.00**
Cordial, clear	**135.00**
Creamer, 3½″ h, applied handle	**90.00**
Decanter	
McKearin GI–6, clear, Vintage Pattern, orig stopper	**75.00**
McKearin GI–29, cobalt blue, flared	

mouth, tam-o'-shanter stopper, pontil, ½ pint 425.00
McKearin GII–26, clear, barrel form, flared mouth, pontil, pint, stopper. . 410.00
McKearin GII–28, sq, sea green, beveled corners, flared mouth, pontil, pint 2,600.00
McKearin GIII–2, clear, flared mouth, pontil, quart, matching stopper. . . . 500.00
McKearin GIII–5, clear, quart 75.00
McKearin GIII–6, clear, flared mouth, pontil, pint, stopper. 175.00
McKearin GIII–16, deep forest green, flared mouth, pontil, quart 2,100.00
McKearin GIII–19, olive amber, sheared mouth, pontil, quart 850.00
McKearin GIII–21, clear 145.00
Dish, 5½" d, clear, McKearin GII–18 . 40.00
Flask, 5¼" h, clear, arch and diamond pattern, sheared mouth, pontil, Continental. 300.00
Flip, clear
3¾" h, etched rim 80.00
4⅞" h, engraved band 165.00
Hat, clear
McKearin GIII–3 . . . . 80.00
McKearin GIII–24 . . . . 90.00
Inkwell
1½" h, 2⅜" d, cylindrical, yellow olive, depressed disc mouth, pontil. 130.00
1¾" h, 2¼" d, cylindrical, light olive yellow, disc mouth, pontil 2,600.00
1⅞" h, 2½" d, cylindrical, deep olive amber, disc mouth, pontil 150.00
Lamp, sparking, 2⅜" h, 1¾" d, cylindrical, clear, sheared mouth, smooth base 325.00
Mustard, 4¼" h, clear, pontil, cork stopper, orig paper label, McKearin GI–15 45.00
Pitcher, 2" h, miniature, clear, inward rolled rim, pontil. 850.00
Salt, 2" h, 3⅛" d, cobalt blue, tooled flared rim, pontil 130.00
Shot Glass, clear, McKearin GII–16 . . 100.00
Toilet Water Bottle, 6" h, cobalt blue, flared mouth, pontil 150.00
Tumbler
2¾" h, clear, barrel shape, McKearin GII–18 . . . . 770.00
4⅜" h, clear, sheared rim, pontil . . 160.00
4⅝" h, clear, pale amethyst tint, sheared rim, pontil 170.00
Vinegar Bottle, cobalt blue, ribbed, stopper, McKearin GI–7. . . . . 275.00
Whiskey, clear, McKearin GI–20 . . . . 45.00

BOEHM PORCELAINS

History: Edward Marshall Boehm was born on August 21, 1913. Boehm's childhood was spent at the McConogh School, a rural Baltimore County, Maryland, school dedicated to caring for homeless boys. He studied animal husbandry at the University of Maryland, serving as manager of Longacre Farms on the Eastern Shore of Maryland upon graduation. During World War II, Boehm joined the air force and was assigned as a therapist to a convalescent center in Pawling, New York. After the war, he moved to Great Neck, Long Island, and worked as an assistant veterinarian.

In 1949 Boehm quit his job to open a potter studio in Trenton, New Jersey. His initial sculptures consisted of Herefords, Percherons, and dogs done in hard–paste porcelain. The first five to six years were a struggle, with several partnerships beginning and ending during the period. In the early 1950s Boehm's art porcelain sculptures began appearing in major department stores. When President Dwight D. Eisenhower presented a Boehm sculpture to Queen Elizabeth and Prince Philip during their visit to the United States in 1957, Boehm's career accelerated.

Boehm had a reputation for being opinionated, prejudiced, and unforgiving. His contributions were the image concepts and techniques used to produce the sculptures. Thousands of prototype sculptures were made, with more than 400 put into actual production. The actual work was done by skilled artisans. Boehm died on January 29, 1969.

In the early 1970s a second production studio was opened in Malvern, England, as Boehm Studios. The tradition begun by Boehm continues today.

Reference: Reese Palley, *The Porcelain Art of Edward Marshall Boehm,* Harrison House, division of Crown Publishers, 1988.

Collectors' Club: Boehm Porcelain Society, PO Box 5051, Trenton, NJ 08638.

BIRDS

American Avocet, #40134 . . . . 1,250.00
American Eagle, #498 . . . . 950.00
Blue Heron, #200–19 . . . . 275.00
Blue Jays, #466 . . . . 4,900.00
Bobwhite Quail, #407 . . . . 1,200.00
California Quail, #433, pr 1,750.00
Canadian Geese, #408, pr 575.00
Capped Chickadee, #438, 9" 450.00
Cardinal, female, #415, 15" h 600.00
Crested Flycatcher, baby, #458C . . . 170.00
Downy Woodpeckers, #427 . . . . 1,000.00
English Nuthatch, #1001 . . . . 650.00
Fledgling Eastern Bluebird, #442 . . . 135.00
Goldfinch, thistle, #457 . . . . 1,000.00
Hummingbird, cactus base, #440, 8½" h 900.00
Kingfisher, #449, 6" h 135.00
Lark Sparrow, #400–35 . . . . 2,750.00
Lesser, Prairie Chicken, #464 . . . . . 2,750.00
Oven Bird, 10" h 725.00
Pelican, #40161, 21" 1,000.00
Prothonotary Warbler, #445 . . . . 575.00

Ring Neck Pheasants, #409 . . . . . . 800.00
Robin, baby, #4375, 3½" h 135.00
Ruby Crowned Kinglets, #434 . . . . . 875.00
Song Sparrow, #400–59 . . . . 475.00
Tumbler Pigeons, #416 . . . . 750.00
Warbler, yellow breasted, #431L . . . 400.00

FLOWERS

Blue Nile Rose, #300–80 . . . . 1,450.00
Daisies, #3002 . . . . 750.00
Grace de Monaco Rose, #300–71 . . 1,900.00
Magnolia Grandiflora, #300–12 . . . . 1,500.00
Pascali Rose, #30093 . . . . 1,500.00
Pussy Willows, #200–28, pr 175.00
Queen Elizabeth Rose, #30091 . . . . 1,200.00
Roy Hartley Begonia, #300–41 . . . . . 1,500.00

BOHEMIAN GLASS

History: The once independent country of Bohemia, now a part of Czechoslovakia, produced a variety of fine glassware: etched, cut, overlay, and colored. Their glassware was first imported into America in the early 1820s and continues today.

Bohemia is known for its "flashed" glass that was produced in the familiar ruby color, as well as amber, green, blue, and black. Common patterns include "Deer and Castle," "Deer and Pine Tree," and "Vintage."

Most of the Bohemian glass encountered in today's market is of the 1875–1900 period. Bohemian–type glass also was made in England, Switzerland, and Germany.

Reproduction Alert.

Beaker, 5½" h, amber flashed, engraved, animals and building, C scroll panels, flared foot, c1860. . . . . 95.00

Decanter, Deer and Castle pattern, ruby, clear stopper, 11¼" h, price for pair, $150.00.

Bowl, 12½" d, double cut overlay, cobalt blue cut to clear 250.00
Box, domed lid, ruby flashed, Vintage, engraved clear and frosted grape clusters and vines, gilt brass fittings . 125.00
Celery Dish, ruby flashed, Deer and Castle, clear and frosted 80.00
Cologne Bottle, 5" h, cobalt blue, tiered body dec, white and gold flowers and scrolls 150.00
Compote, 7" d, amber flashed, cut leaf and floral dec, green band at top, pedestal base. 100.00
Cordial, 3½" h, crystal, deep cutting and engraving, running deer in forest, entire surface cut and polished, slight flakes, price for eight piece set 150.00
Decanter, 14¾" h, crystal, octagonal, greenish tint, engraved forest and deer scene, orig stopper 80.00
Flip Glass, 6 x 6", clear, cut, engraved forest scene with fox and birds 100.00
Goblet, 8" h, 4" d, deep amber, cut to clear, deer, trees, and castle, sq cut base, notched stem, price for set of twelve 250.00
Jar, cov, 7" h, barrel shape, bands of clear engraving, red satin discs, barrel finial. 125.00
Mantel Lusters, 6½" d, 12¼" h, cranberry cut overlay, cut scalloped tops, white overlay panels, multicolored flowers, allover gold flowers and scrolls, clear cut prisms, price for pair 1,000.00
Mug, 6" h, ruby flashed, engraved castle and trees, applied clear handle, sgd "Volmer, 1893". 80.00
Perfume Bottle, 7" h, ruby flashed, Deer and Castle, clear and frosted, gold dec 90.00
Pickle Jar, cov, 6" h, ruby flashed, Deer and Castle, clear and frosted 50.00
Powder Box, 4¼" d, round, straight sides, flat top, ruby flashed, etched cov with leaping stag, forest setting, landscape and birds on sides, clear base 100.00
Rose Bowl, 8½" d, ruby flashed, Deer and Castle, clear and frosted 225.00
Stein, 6½" h, ruby flashed, engraved cathedral panel, leaves, and scrolls, pewter mounts, ruby flashed inset lid 300.00
Sugar Shaker, ruby flashed, Bird and Castle, clear and frosted 70.00
Teapot, 11" w, cranberry cut to clear, panels of flowers, gilt spout and handle 185.00
Tumbler, 4¼" h, engraved scene, early 19th C 150.00
Vase, 10" h, 6" d, cranberry cut to clear, buzz star, shooting star panels, German 350.00

Whiskey Glass, 3¼" h, engraved, clear, early 19th C **95.00**

BOOKS, FORE-EDGE PAINTING

History: Fore–edge painting is a technique whereby the fore–edge of a book is slightly fanned out and painted with an appropriate scene which complements the book's content. The edges are then squared up and gilded. Thus, the painting remains hidden and protected while the book is closed. The painting is revealed when one fans out the edge.

Fore–edge painting was practiced as early as the 15th and 16th centuries, especially in Italy. The technique was popular in London and Edinburgh in the period 1650–1700 and reached new heights in the early 18th century through artists such as John Brindley and Edwards of Halifax. A few binders continued to utilize fore–edge painting throughout the late 18th and 19th centuries.

The 20th century saw a revival of the craft, based in part on a strong demand among collectors. Most artists applied the craft to modern books. However, a number obtained earlier books, decorated the fore–edges, and sold them to unsuspecting dealers and collectors.

References: Allen Ahearn, *Book Collecting: A Comprehensive Guide,* G. P. Putnam's Sons, 1989; Allen and Patricia Ahearn, *Collected Books, The Guide To Values,* G. P. Putnam's Sons, 1991; *American Book Prices Current, Volume 99, 1993,* Bancroft–Parkman, 1993; Marjorie M. and Donald L. Hinds, *How To Make Money Buying & Selling Old Books,* published by authors, 1974; *Huxford's Old Book Value Guide,* Third Edition (1991), Fourth Edition (1992), Fifth Edition (1993), Collector Books; Joseph Raymond LeFonntaine, *The Collector's Bookshelf,* Prometheus Books, 1990; Carl J. Weber, *Fore–Edge Painting: A Historical Survey Of A Curious Art in Book Decoration,* 1966; Carl J. Weber, *A Thousand And One Fore–Edge Paintings,* 1949; Nancy Wright, *Books: Identification and Price Guide,* Avon Books, 1993.

Periodical: *Book Source Monthly,* 2007 Syosett Dr., PO Box 567, Cazenovia, NY 13035.

Collectors' Club: National Book Collectors Society, 65 High Ridge Road, Suite 349, Stamford, CT 06095.

Advisor: Ron Lieberman.

Antiqua Harbor, 1827, panoramic view, James Montgomery, *The Poetical Works,* Edin.: c1860, 8vo, mor gilt. . . **275.00**

Athens, Horace, *Quintus Horatius Flaccus,* Birmingham: Baskerville, 1762, engraved frontispiece and titled vignette, 12mo, vellum gilt, cov with painted landscape, gauffered edges, bookplate, marbled board slipcase . . **715.00**

Berlin, Frederic H Hedge, *Prose Writers of Germany,* Phila.: 1848, 4to, mor gilt, defects. **300.00**

Boston and Philadelphia, double fore–edge street scenes, Richard C Chester and William B Chester, *Poems,* Dublin: 1849, 8vo, 19th C red mor gilt **330.00**

Cain Slaying Abel, Francois Rene de Chateaubriand, *Death of Abel, Idyls,* from the German of Gessner, London: 1825, 12 mo, calf, engraved title and frontispiece. **315.00**

Cashiobury Park, Hertfordshire, England, Richard C Trench, *Notes On The Miracles Of Our Lord,* London: 1886, 8vo, vellum gilt. **265.00**

Cathedral, Taylor and Hessey, stamp signed on cov edges, *The Holy Bible,* London: 1811, thick 12mo, contemp red straight grain mor, wear at edges **360.00**

Cathedral Town, river's edge scene, Taylor and Hessey, stamp signed on board edges, Edward Young, *The Complaint; or Night Thoughts,* London: 1813, plates, small 8vo, contemp black straight grain mor gilt, extremities rubbed **220.00**

City of Oxford

All Souls College and Merton College, Richard Hooker, *Works,* Oxford: 1845, 3 vols, 8vo, contemp mor gilt **650.00**

City view, double fore–edge, William Roberts, *Memoirs of the Life of Mrs Hannah More,* London: 1839, small 8vo, blindstamped leather, wear at joints. **275.00**

Country Scene, *The Book Of Common Prayer,* Oxford: 1793, 12 mo, mor gilt **275.00**

Edinburgh, view, running from inner corner to upper edge of front to inner corner of lower edge, William E Aytoun, *Days Of The Scottish Cavaliers,* Edinburgh: 1872, 8vo, blind–tooled mor. . **500.00**

English Channel, seaside and castle in hills, William C Bryant, *Poems,* London: 1890, 8vo, mor gilt. **250.00**

Faneuil Hall, Boston, *The Holy Bible,* London: John Reeves, 1802, bookplate, tall 8vo, contemp dark blue straight grain mor gilt, edges rubbed **160.00**

Farm House Scene, James Thomson, *The Seasons And The Castle Of Indulgence,* London: 1841, 8vo, mor gilt, defects. **425.00**

Golf, group of men playing golf, Sir Walter Scott, *Poetical Works,* Paris: 1827, 8vo, contemp calf gilt, defects. **375.00**

Hereford View, Sarah Trimmer, *Sacred History,* London: 1810, small 8vo, contemp dark brown straight grain mor, gilt and blindstamped, extremities rubbed **165.00**

House of Seven Gables, Salem, MA, *The Book Of Common Prayer,* Oxford: 1838, 16mo, contemp mor gilt. . **250.00**

Hunting Scene, Thomas Gray, *Poems,* London: 1887, 8vo, calf gilt, gilt by Riviere **190.00**

Lancaster Castle, Luis De Camoens, *Poems,* translated and with notes by Lord Viscount Strangford, second edition, London: 1804, small 8vo, contemp red straight grain mor, spine ends and joints worn **110.00**

London Bridge, IC Robinson, *The Treasury Of Ornamental Art,* London: Day, c1870, 8vo, vellum gilt **295.00**

Military Figures, inscribed to Lord Melbourne, John Rolt, *On Moral Command,* London: 1836, 8vo, contemp mor gilt. **225.00**

Musicians and Muses, double fore–edge, five comic musicians and three dancing muses, Bon, Gaulter, *The Book Of Ballads,* London: n.d., 4to, mor, defects **800.00**

Nude and Putti, sleeping, Samuel Taylor Coleridge, *Poetical And Dramatic Works,* London: c1855, 12mo, contemp mor gilt. **200.00**

Parthenon, George G N Bryon, *Childe Harold's Pilgrimage,* London: 1859, 8vo, contemp mor gilt **350.00**

Philadelphia, 18th C scene of 2nd Street north from Market Street, Thomas Moore, *Poetical Works,* Philadelphia: 1846, 12mo, mor gilt **300.00**

Poe, scene from *The Pit and The Pendulum,* victim standing at edge of pit, top edge under gilt of bats, lower edge with rats, monogram "MF," copy of a plate by Arthur Rackham which appears in 1935 edition of Edgar Allan Poe, *Works,* London: A & C Black, 1899 [1900], standard ed, Vol I only, 8vo, calf gilt extra **1,400.00**

Rhine, John Gregory, *A Comparative View Of The State and Faculties of Man with Those of the Animal World, A New Edition,* London: 1785, 8vo, bookplate, contemp red straight grain mor gilt. **440.00**

Ruins of Roman Temple, William Forsyth, *The Life Of Marcus Tullius Cicero,* London: 1867, 8vo, contemp mor, school prize binding **150.00**

Snipe Hunting Scene at Dawn, *Select Portions of Psalms,* Halifax: 1798, small 8vo, contemp red straight grain mor, spine ends and joints worn **165.00**

St. Albans, Sir Francis Bacon, *Essays,* London: 1840, 8vo, calf gilt **365.00**

Stirling Castle, England, seen from a distance, man and two dogs in foreground, Sir Walter Scott, *Poetical Works,* London: 1862, 8vo, mor gilt. . **250.00**

Tay Bridge Disaster, *The British Almanac,* London: 1880, 8vo, contemp mor gilt, defects **245.00**

Tennis and Golf, Victorian ladies playing tennis, six male golfers on links, Charlotte M Yonge, *Hopes and Fears, or Scenes from the Life of a Spinster,* London: 1860, 2 vols., 8vo, mor **425.00**

Tower of London, Nicholas Harris Nicolas, *Privy Purse Expenses of Elizabeth of York,* London: William Pickering, 1830, 8vo, 19th C mor gilt, some joint wear **330.00**

Venice, canal view, and Windsor Castle, double fore–edge, Titus Lucretius Carus, *De Rerum Natura,* London: 1832, 4to, contemp mor gilt. **450.00**

Westminster Abbey, *The Book Of Common Prayer,* Cambridge: 1782, 8vo, mor gilt. **310.00**

Whaling Scene, harpooning party and ships in ice, *The Book Of Common Prayer,* London: c1873, 8vo, calf prize binding. **375.00**

Windsor Castle and the Thames, John Keble, *The Christian Year,* Oxford: 1827, 8vo, mor **250.00**

BOOTJACKS

History: Bootjacks are metal or wooden devices that facilitate the removal of boots. Bootjacks are used by placing the heel of the boot in the "U"-shaped opening, putting a foot on the back of the bootjack, and pulling the front boot off the foot.

Brass, 10" l, beetle **90.00**

Cast Iron

9¾" l, Naughty Nelly, old worn polychrome repaint **45.00**

Cast Iron, lyre shape, "Try Me," 12" l, $50.00.

10¾" l, lyre shaped	50.00
11½" l, intertwined scrolls form letter M	25.00
11¾" l, cricket, emb lacy design	25.00
12" l	
Tree center, footed	30.00
Vine design	35.00
Wood	
10" l, tiger stripe maple	20.00
13" l, maple, hand hewn	15.00
15" l, Folk Art, monkey, painted suit, c1900	30.00
22" l, walnut, heart and diamond openwork	40.00
24" l, pine, rose head nails, pierced for hanging	40.00
25" l, pine, oval ends, sq nails	28.00

Superior Mineral Water, Twitchel, Phila., graphite bottle, 7⅛" h, $45.00.

BOTTLES, GENERAL

History: Cosmetic bottles held special creams, oils, and cosmetics designed to enhance the beauty of the user. Some of the contents also claimed, especially on their colorful labels, to cure or provide relief from common ailments.

A number of household items, for example, cleaning fluids and polishes, required glass storage containers. Many are collected for their fine lithograph labels.

Mineral water bottles contained water from a natural spring. Spring water was favored by health-conscious people between the 1850s and 1900s.

Nursing bottles, used to feed the young and sickly, were a great help to the housewife because of graduated measures, replaceable nipples, ease of cleaning and sterilizing, and reuse.

References: Ralph and Terry Kovel, *The Kovels' Bottle Price List, Ninth Edition,* Crown Publishers, 1992; Jim Megura, *The Official Identification and Price Guide To Bottles, Eleventh Edition,* House of Collectibles, 1991; Michael Polak, *Bottles: Identification and Price Guide,* Avon Books, 1994; Carlo and Dorothy Sellari, *The Standard Old Bottle Price Guide,* Collector Books, 1989.

Periodicals: *Antique Bottle And Glass Collector,* PO Box 187, East Greenville, PA 18041; *Bottles and Extras,* PO Box 154, Happy Camp, CA 96039.

Collectors' Clubs: American Collectors of Infant Feeders, 5161 West 59th St., Indianapolis, IN 46254; Federation of Historical Bottle Collectors, 14521 Atlantic, Riverdale, IL 60627.

Museum: National Bottle Museum, Ballston Spa, NY.

Additional Listings: Barber Bottles, Bitter Bottles, Figural Bottles, Food Bottles, Ink Bottles, Medicine Bottles, Poison Bottles, Sarsaparilla Bottles and Snuff Bottles. Also see the bottle categories in *Warman's Americana & Collectibles* for more examples.

COSMETIC

Arnold's Vegetable Hair Balsam, 6⅛" h, clear	20.00
Big 4 Dressing Pomade, 2½" h, label, 1930s	8.00
Boswell & Warners Colorific, 5⅝" h, cobalt blue	150.00
Buckingham Whisker Dye, 4⅞" h	8.00
Glover's Royal Scalp & Mange Remedy, amber	15.00
Humphreys Marvel Witchhazel, 5½" h, clear	4.00
John H Woodbury Dermatological Institute, 7" h, man's face	35.00
LaRoque's Oxygenated Cream of Lilies, aqua, label	28.00
Lufkin Eczema Remedy, 7" h, clear, label	8.00
Pond's Extract, 5½" h, amethyst	18.00
Rowland's Macassar Oil, clear	60.00
Sanitol For the Teeth, 4½" h, clear	6.00
St Clair's Hair Lotion, 7¼" h, cobalt blue	125.00
Teel Liquid Dentifrice, 1945	15.00
Zemo Antiseptic Lotion for Skin & Scalp, 6" h, clear	8.00

HOUSEHOLD

American Bluing Co, 5¼" h, clear	4.00
Black Cat Stove Enamel, 6" h, clear	3.00
Dutchers Dead Shot For Bed Bugs, 4⅞" h, aqua, label	75.00
Furniture Cream, amber, label with Indian scene	10.00
Hercules Disinfectant, 6" h, amber	4.00
Inman's Household Ammonia, 10⅞" h, stoneware, tan	58.00
Lazell's Sachet Powder, label, ground stopper	20.00
Osborn Liquid Polish, 3¾" h, olive yellow	350.00

Prices Soap Company, 7¼″ h, cobalt
blue, label. 150.00
Race & Sheldon Boot Polish, eight
sided, green 250.00
Silicious Cement, triangular, aqua . . : 20.00
Triump Superior Clock Oil, 3½″ h, clear 3.00

MINERAL OR SPRING WATER

B W & Co, New York, Soda Water, squat
cylindrical form, cobalt blue, collared
mouth, iron pontil mark, ½ pint 280.00
Highrock Congress Spring, cylindrical,
yellow olive, pint 120.00
John Clar, cylindrical, yellow olive, sloping collared mouth with ring, smooth
base, quart. 110.00
J P Plummer Boston Soda Water, squat
cylindrical, cobalt blue, collared
mouth, iron pontil mark, ½ pint 275.00
Magentic Spring, Henniker NH Mineral
Water, cylindrical, golden amber,
sloping collared mouth with ring,
smooth base, quart 260.00
Missisquoi A Springs Mineral Water, cylindrical, emerald green, sloping collared mouth with ring, smooth base,
quart 80.00
Syracuse Springs Excelsior, cylindrical,
deep reddish amber, sloping collared
mouth with ring, smooth base, pint . . 160.00
Tarr Smith & Clark, Boston, Mineral
Water, squat cylindrical, green, collared mouth, iron pontil mark, ½ pint 145.00
Washington, Lithia Well, Mineral Water,
cylindrical, aquamarine, sloping collared mouth with ring, smooth base,
pint 80.00

NURSING

Acme, W T & Co, 8 oz, star, turtle, 1880 25.00
Baby Bunting, 4 oz, clear 6.00
BB Safety Nursing, flask type, push
base, aluminum collar, 1897. . . . . . . 25.00
Clifton Feeder, 9″ h, pear shape 10.00
Curity, 8 oz, turtle, circle with crown,
1885 . . . . 30.00
Evenflo, 8 oz, hexagon, double lined,
painted red. 8.00
Hygeia, 8 oz, round, emb 5.00
National Baby's Formula Service, sq, or-
ange pyro. 40.00
Rexall Drugs 15.00
Steadifeed, hexagonal, emb, black cap 6.00
Universal Feeder, clear, monogram . . 25.00

BRASS

History: Brass is a durable, malleable, and ductile metal alloy consisting mainly of copper and
zinc. It achieved its greatest popularity for utilitarian
and decorative art items in the 18th and 19th centuries.

References: Mary Frank Gaston, *Antique Brass
& Copper: Identification & Value Guide,* Collector
Books, 1992; Dana G. Morykan and Harry L.
Rinker, *Warman's Country Antiques & Collectibles,
Second Edition,* Wallace–Homestead, 1994; Peter,
Nancy, and Herbert Schiffer, *The Brass Book,*
Schiffer Publishing, 1978.

Additional Listings: Bells, Candlesticks, Fireplace Equipment, and Scientific Instruments.

Reproduction Alert: Many modern reproductions are being made of earlier brass forms, especially in the areas of buckets, fireplace equipment,
and kettles.

**Vase, Art Nouveau, grape leaves and
vine motif, 12″ h, $285.00.**

Andirons, pr
14½″ h, turned shafts with ball finial,
scrolled legs, ball feet. 425.00
16½″ h, spiral stems, rampant lion finials, marked "McKinney". 110.00
18″ h, turned shafts, ball finial, spurred
legs, spayed feet 375.00
20″ h, lemon top, sgd "John Molineux
founder Boston," c1800 . . . . 1,980.00
21″ h, turned shafts, ball finial, spurred
legs, spayed feet, CT, c1800. . . . . 350.00
22″ h
Colonial Revival, fluted standard,
urn finial, spurred legs, ball and
claw feet 3,575.00
Spire and lemon tops, hexagonal
shafts, cabriole legs, ball feet,
c1800 . . . . 1,400.00
24″ h, Federal, paneled standard,
lemon finial, spurred legs, ball feet,
early 19th C. 825.00

28″ h, Colonial Revival, slender column, urn finial, spurred legs, ball feet. 145.00
Ashtray, 4½ x 5″, figural, bull's head, relief, protruding curled horns 50.00
Bedwarmer
43″ l, tooled lid with flowers and peacock, turned wood handle. 360.00
44½″ l, engraved rooster, turned cherry handle 440.00
Book Stand, 9″ h, folding pierced and scrolled, rect base, English. 160.00
Bucket, 22½″ d, tapered cylinder, rolled rim, iron bail handle, 19th C 350.00
Candelabra, 24″ h, Victorian, center cupid figure, three stylized goat legs, three arms 550.00
Candle Box, 12″ l, hanging, scalloped back, minor dents 150.00
Candlestick
5⅝″ h, octagonal base 250.00
6″ h, bell top, oval vasiform shafts, oval base, price for pair 100.00
6¾″ h, sq base, paw feet 250.00
8″ h, sq base, paw feet 300.00
9½″ h, mismatched top, sq base, four short feet. 110.00
9¾″ h, beehive, 19th C, price for pair 130.00
9⅞″ h, Victorian, beehive and diamond quilted detail. 65.00
Candy Scoop, 8″ l 30.00
Chamberstick
4″ h, 9½″ l, threaded stem, loose drip pan, long handle 55.00
4½″ h, oval pan, pushup 100.00
Chenets, pr
16½″ h, dolphins, rect plinth base . 300.00
17″ h, floral and scroll design 350.00
Coal Hod, 9½″ h, hammered, 20th C . 75.00
Desk Lamp, three scroll arms, dish base, red bouillotte shade 375.00
Dipper, 22⅜″ l, flat shape, wrought iron handle with hanger dec, 19th C 75.00
Fire Fender, 49″ l, paw feet 350.00
Fire Tools, 4 pcs, two tongs, shovel, and stand. 1,200.00
Flue Cover, hp scenes, price for pair . 40.00
Garniture Set, two single and one twin light candelabra, Elizabethan lady ornamentation, burnished, mid 19th C, price for three piece set 125.00
Girandoles, 16″ h, single light, young girl feeding her goat and dog form standard, gilt, mid 19th C, price for pair . . 175.00
Inkwell, 11″ l, pierced scrolled back plate, two ink pots, pen tray, Victorian style. 110.00
Kettle, spun brass
11″ d, iron bale handle, "Hayden's Patent" label, some damage, old repair 50.00
17½″ d, iron bale handle, marked

"American Spun Brass Kettle," some damage. 110.00
Ladle, 19½″ l, wrought iron handle . . 140.00
Milk Pail 300.00
Pie Crimper, 4½″ l, wheel on each end 35.00
Pitcher, 7″ h, Continental, late 19th C 50.00
Salt, cov, 3″ d, 4¾″ h, paw feet 75.00
Scissor Wick Trimmer, 9¾″ l, tray . . . 140.00
Scuttle, 7″ h, Victorian, repousse floral dec, scoop 100.00
Skimmer, 26¼″ l, copper rivets, well formed wrought iron handle, heart shape hanger, late 18th–early 19th C 125.00
Tea Kettle, 11″ d, 15¼″ h, unusual spout, copper rivets, 19th C 175.00
Trivet pierced, Renyard The Fox dec, England, c1830. . . . . 30.00
Wafer Iron, 4″ d, 17″ l, geometric floral design, wrought iron handles 65.00
Wash Bowl, 15″ d, Georgian, circular handle, 19th C 90.00
Wedding Mirror, 23″ h, arched repousse panel, Dutch 325.00

BREAD PLATES

History: Beginning in the mid 1880s, special trays or platters were made for serving bread and rolls. Designated by collectors as "bread plates," these small trays or platters can be found in porcelain, glass (especially pattern glass), and metals.

Bread plates often were part of a china or glass set. However, many glass companies made special plates which honored national heroes, commemorated historical or special events, offered a moral maxim, or supported a religious attitude. The theme on the plate could be either in a horizontal or vertical format. The favorite shape for these plates is oval, with a common length being ten inches.

Reference: Anna Maude Stuart, *Bread Plates And Platters,* published by author, 1965.

Additional Listings: Pattern Glass.

China
Nippon, gaudy, green and gold, pink asters 225.00
Noritake, gold handled, hp scene in center, wide border, hp stylized flowers, maroon wreath, 10″ l 65.00
Majolica, green pond lilies and flowers, brown ground, 12″ l, 11″ w 175.00
Milk Glass
Liberty Bell, John Hancock signature, handles. 260.00
William J Bryan 40.00
Wheat & Barley 60.00
Pattern Glass
Actress, HMS Pinafore 125.00
Aurora, large star in center, ruby stained, 10″ d 35.00

**Venus and Psyche pattern, clear glass,
11″ l, 7½″ w, $45.00.**

Be Industrious, clear, handled, 12 x 8¼″, oval.	50.00
Beaded Grape, sq	30.00
Butterfly & Fan, clear	40.00
Canadian, clear, 10″ d	45.00
Continental Hall, 12¾″ l	75.00
Cupid and Venus, amber	75.00
Daisy and Button, apple green, 13″ l	60.00
Deer and Pine Tree, blue	110.00
Egyptian, Cleopatra in center, 13″ l	50.00
Fern	30.00
Give Us This Day, round, rosette center and border	65.00
Good Luck	45.00
Horseshoe, double horseshoe handles, 14″ l	65.00
Iowa, motto	80.00
Lattice, Waste Not Want Not, 11½″ l	32.00
Lion, frosted, including lion handles, GUTDODB, 12″ l	125.00
Maple Leaf, oval, vaseline, 13″ l . .	45.00
Moon and Star, rect, clear	45.00
Nellie Bly, clear, 11″ l	170.00
Old State House, sapphire blue . . .	175.00
Palmette, 9″ l	30.00
Queen Anne	50.00
Rock of Ages, frosted, c1870, 12⅞″ l	175.00
Scroll and Flowers, 12″ d	35.00
Shell and Tassel, round	55.00
Tennessee, colored jewels	75.00
Three Presidents, frosted center . .	85.00
US Coin, frosted coins	315.00
Tin, painted fruit and leaf motif border, brown ground, 19th C, 12¾″ l	3,000.00

BRIDE'S BASKETS

History: A ruffled-edge glass bowl in a metal holder was a popular wedding gift in the 1880–1910 era, hence, the name of "bride's basket." The glass bowls can be found in most glass types of the period. The metal holder was generally silver-plated with a bail handle, thus enhancing the basket image.

Over the years, bowls and bases became separated and married pieces resulted. When the base has been lost, the bowl is sold separately.

Reference: John Mebane, *Collecting Bride's Baskets And Other Glass Fancies*, Wallace–Homestead, 1976.

Reproduction Alert: The glass bowls have been reproduced.

Note: Items listed have silver-plated holder unless otherwise noted.

**Cased glass, white ext., shaded pink
int. with gold floral dec, clear ruffled
rim, stand marked "Superior Silver Co,
Quad Plate 1000," 9⅜″ d, $100.00.**

Cased	
8¼″ w, sq, deep rose and white ext., white int., dragon, floral, and leaf dec, ruffled edge, Mt Washington .	650.00
9⅜″ d, shaded pink int. with gold floral dec, clear ruffled rim, white ext. . . .	100.00
10 x 14¼″, white int., cobalt blue ext., enameled gold flowers and leaves, ruffled rim, SP frame, emb leaves .	400.00
Cranberry, Victorian, ornate ruffled insert	85.00
Custard	
10″ w, sq, melon ribbed, enameled daisies, applied rubena crystal rim, twisted and beaded handle, ftd, emb SP frame, marked "Wilcox" . .	425.00
12″ d, three lobed form, cased pink, amber rim, enameled flower dec, SP stand.	450.00
Hobnail, 10½″ d, pink, enameled flowers, ruffled rim, reticulated SP frame	225.00
Loetz, irid blue, silver threading, coin spots, brass holder	375.00
Opaque, 10⅛″ d, white, apricot satin finished int., white butterflies and flowers, SP holder.	250.00
Pairpoint, pink and white, ornate ruffled edge	325.00

Peachblow
9¼" d, yellow flowers dec, orig SP
  holder 45.00
11½" d, floral dec, sterling silver stand 200.00
Satin Glass
10½" d, pink, ruffled, enameled dec,
  New England, bowl only 100.00
14" d, rose pink, scalloped, rippled,
  ribbed, and swirled, lacy allover
  enamel and gold flower pattern, figural SP base with hummingbird,
  sgd "Eagle & Co". 1,100.00
12" l, 7½" w, 5" h, pale blue shading
  to pink, melon ribbed, Mt Washing-
  ton, bowl only 175.00
Schlegelmilch, floral center, ornate, ftd 50.00
Spangled Glass, 10⅜" d, multicolored,
  ruby, cranberry, and green, ivory–yellow ground, silver flecks, bowl only . . 100.00
Spatter Glass, yellow, brown, and purple, ruffled and crimped, SP holder . . 240.00

BRISTOL GLASS

History: Bristol glass is a designation given to a
semiopaque glass, usually decorated with enamel
and cased with another color.

Initially, the term referred only to glass made in
Bristol, England, in the 17th and 18th centuries. By
the Victorian era firms on the Continent and in
America were copying the glass and its forms.

Biscuit Jar, 6½" h, white, brown leaves
  and white flowers 150.00
Bowl, light blue, cupid playing mandolin,
  gold trim. 35.00
Cake Stand, celadon green, enameled
  herons in flight, gold trim 125.00
Candlestick, 7" h, soft green, gold band,
  pr. 60.00
Cruet, 4¾" h, blue, white flowers, gold
  leaves, applied blue handle, matching
  ball stopper. 90.00
Decanter, 8" h, blue, matching stopper 75.00
Dresser Set, two cologne bottles, cov
  powder jar, white, gilt butterflies dec,
  clear stoppers, price for three piece
  set. 50.00
Ewer, 17" h, white, enameled cupid
  scene. 80.00
Hatpin Holder, 6⅛" h, ftd, blue, enam-
  eled jewels, gold dec 100.00
Marmalade Jar, white, floral dec, plated
  handled frame. 85.00
Mug, 5" h, white, eagle and "Liberty" . 375.00
Perfume Bottle, 3¼" h, squatty, blue,
  gold band, white enameled flowers
  and leaves, matching stopper. 100.00
Pickle Castor, pink, flower dec 300.00
Puff Box, cov, round, blue, gold dec . 30.00

Rose Bowl, 3½" d, shaded blue, crimped
  edge 60.00
Scent Bottle, 6½" h, blue, multicolored
  florals, stopper 100.00
Sugar Shaker, 4¾" h, white, hp flowers 60.00
Sweetmeat Jar
3 x 5½", deep pink, enameled flying
  duck, leaves, blue flower dec, white
  lining, SP rim, lid, and bail handle . 100.00
5¾ x 4½", green, enameled garlands
  of pink, white, yellow, blue, and
  green flowers, four butterflies, SP
  rim, lid, and bail handle. 120.00
Urn, 18" h, pink, boy and girl with lamb
  on gold. 550.00

**Vase, cream colored, raised enameled
floral dec, turquoise flowers, brownish–green leaves and stems, c1880,
8½" h, $85.00.**

Vase
8½" h, cobalt blue dec, price for
  matched pair. 110.00
11" h, tan, coralene flowers and butterflies, gold trim, price for matched
  pair. 300.00

BRITISH ROYALTY
COMMEMORATIVES

History: British commemorative china, souvenirs to commemorate coronations and other royal
events, dates from the 1600s, with the early pieces
being rather crude in design and form. The development of transfer printing, c1780, led to a much
closer likeness of the reigning monarch on the
ware.

Few commemorative pieces predating Queen
Victoria's reign are found today at popular prices.
Items associated with Queen Elizabeth II and her
children, for example, the wedding of His Royal

Highness Prince Andrew and Miss Sarah Ferguson and the subsequent birth of their daughter, Her Royal Highness Princess Beatrice, are very common.

Some British Royalty commemoratives are easily recognized by their portraits of past or present monarchs. Some may be in silhouette profile. Other royal symbols include crowns, dragons, royal coats of arms, national flowers, swords, scepters, dates, messages, and initials.

References: Susan and Al Bagdade, *Warman's English & Continental Pottery & Porcelain, Second Edition,* Wallace–Homestead, 1991; Malcolm Davey and Doug Mannion, *50 Years of Royal Commemorative China 1887–1937,* Dayman Publications, 1988; Lincoln Hallinan, *British Commemoratives: Royalty, Politics, War and Sport,* Antique Collectors' Club, 1993; Peter Johnson, *Royal Memorabilia: A Phillips Collectors Guide,* Dunestyle Publishing, 1988; John May, *Victoria Remembered, A Royal History 1817–1861,* London, 1983; John and Jennifer May, *Commemorative Pottery 1780–1900, A Guide for Collectors,* Charles Scribner's Sons, 1972; Josephine Jackson, *Fired For Royalty,* Heaton Moor, 1977; David Rogers, *Coronation Souvenirs and Commemoratives,* Latimer New Dimensions, 1975; Sussex Commemorative Ware Centre, *200 Commemoratives,* Metra Print Enterprises, 1979; Geoffrey Warren, *Royal Souvenirs,* Orbis, 1977.

Advisors: Doug Flynn and Al Bolton.

Additional Listings: See *Warman's Americana & Collectibles* for more examples.

Beaker
Charles and Diana, 1981 Wedding, 4″ h, Caverswall. **80.00**
Elizabeth II, 1953 Coronation
  3½″ h, Poole **35.00**
  4″ h, official design **14.00**
George V and Mary, 1911 Coronation, 3¾″ h, Foley **70.00**
George VI and Elizabeth, 1937 Coronation, 4″ h, Grindley **42.00**
Bowl
Charles, 1969 Investiture, 5½″ d, Aynsley. **60.00**
Edward VIII, 1937 Coronation, profile in well, pressed glass, 10″ d **65.00**
Elizabeth II, 1953 Coronation, pressed glass, 4¾″ h **60.00**
George V and Mary, 1911 Coronation, color portraits, 5″ d, unmarked. . . .   **50.00**
George VI and Elizabeth, 1937 Coronation, coat of arms, 5½″ d, Paragon **55.00**
Box
Elizabeth II
  1953 Coronation, color and gold dec, 4½″ h, Wedgwood & Co, Ltd   **95.00**
  1977 Silver Jubilee, 1⅞″ d, raised flowers, Crown Staffordshire . . .   **22.00**

1978 25th Anniversary of Coronation, 4½″ d, Coalport **44.00**
Elizabeth, The Queen Mother, 1980, 80th Birthday, color portrait, 4″ d, Crown Staffordshire **70.00**
Chalice
Charles, 1969 Investiture, 4½″ h, black feathers, Grosvenor. **60.00**
Charles and Diana, 1981 Wedding, 4½″ h, color portraits, Coalport . . .   **140.00**
Cup and Saucer
Andrew and Sarah, 1986 Wedding, Colclough **27.00**
Charles and Diana, 1981 Wedding
  Duchess **30.00**
  Royal Albert **28.00**
Edward VII and Alexandra
  1888 Silver Wedding Anniversary, coat of arms. **180.00**
  1902 Coronation, coat of arms, Foley. **50.00**
Edward VIII, 1937 Coronation, color dec, Hammersley. **120.00**
Elizabeth II, 1954 1st Anniversary of Coronation, color dec, Paragon. . .   **95.00**
George V and Mary, 1911 Coronation, color portraits, unmarked **58.00**
Jug
Elizabeth II, 1953 Coronation
  6¼″ h, brown portrait, Royal Doulton **185.00**
  8¼″ h, emb crowning scene, Burleigh Ware. **250.00**
George VI and Elizabeth, 1937 Coronation, musical, Princesses Elizabeth and Margaret on reverse, 8″ h, Shelley. **275.00**
Victoria, 1887, Gold Jubilee, black and white portraits, 5″ h **130.00**
Lithophane
Alexandra, 1902, cup, crown, and cypher, 2¾″ h **185.00**
Edward VII, 1902, mug, crown, and cypher, 2¾″ h **90.00**
George V, 1911, mug, crown, and cypher, 2¾″ h. **160.00**
Mary, 1911, cup, crown, and cypher, 2¾″ h **280.00**
Loving Cup
Charles and Diana, 1981 Wedding, brown on white portraits, limited edition of 5,000, 3½″ h, Royal Doulton   **90.00**
Elizabeth II and Philip, 1972 Silver Wedding Anniversary, 3″ h, Paragon **160.00**
Elizabeth, The Queen Mother, 1980, 80th Birthday, gold profile portrait, limited edition of 500, 3″ h, Royal Crown Derby. **245.00**
George VI and Elizabeth, 1937 Coronation, brown Marcus Adams portrait, 3¼″ h, Sampson Smith **135.00**

Victoria, 1897 Diamond Jubilee, brown portrait, 4″ h, Victoria **175.00**
Medallion, Anne and Mark, 1973 Wedding, molded pale pink portraits, pink frame, 3¼″ d, Hutchenreuther. **55.00**
Mug
 Anne and Mark, 1973 Wedding, brown portraits, 3¾″ h, Crown Staffordshire **60.00**
 Charles, c1953, Marcus Adams sepia portrait, "A Souvenir of Prince Charles," 2¾″ h, Paragon. **150.00**
 Duke and Duchess of Windsor, In Memoriam, black and white portraits, dates, 3⅜″ h, Dorincourt. **60.00**
 Elizabeth II
  1953 Coronation, gold cypher and crown, 3½″ h, Crown Staffordshire. **45.00**
  1986 60th Birthday, color portrait, 3½″ h, Coronet. **22.00**
  1992 40th Anniversary of Succession to Throne, white profile on maroon background, 3″ h, Wedgwood. **50.00**
 Elizabeth II and Philip, 1987 40th Wedding Anniversary, color portraits, 3″ h, Coalport **50.00**
 Henry, 1984 Birth, blue design by R Guyatt, limited edition of 1,000, 4¼″ h, Wedgwood **70.00**
 Victoria, 1887 Gold Jubilee, color beaded crown and ribbon, 3¼″ h, William Whiteley. **100.00**
Paperweight
 Charles and Diana, 1981 Wedding, white sulphide portraits, cobalt blue ground, 2¾″ d, CR Albret, France . **265.00**

Edward VIII, 1937 Coronation, black and white portrait, 4¼″ d. **30.00**
George VI and Elizabeth, 1937 Coronation, black and white Marcus Adams portrait, 2¼″ d. **50.00**
Pin Tray
 Edward VII and Alexandra, 1902 Coronation, sepia portraits, 4″ d. **35.00**
 Edward VIII, 1937 Coronation, 4⅞″ d, Hammersley **50.00**
 Elizabeth II, 1977 Silver Jubilee, black silhouette, 3¾″ d, Coalport **35.00**
 Elizabeth II and Philip, 1959 Canada Visit, sepia portrait, 4¼″ d. **30.00**
Plaque
 Charles, 1969 Investiture, large profile portrait, limited edition of 200, 8″ d, Coalport. **230.00**
 Edward VIII, 1937 Coronation, profile portrait, sgd "F Barbutt," 8 x 6″, Solian Ware. **125.00**

Plate, Victoria, 1887 Jubilee, 7½″ d, $85.00.

Plate
 Andrew and Sarah, 1986 Wedding, silhouette portraits, limited edition of 1,500, 8½″ d, Caverswall **55.00**
 Charles, 1969 Investiture, sepia portrait, 8″ d, Coronet **70.00**
 Edward VII and Alexandra, 1902 Coronation, blue and white, 7″ d, Royal Copenhagen **190.00**
 Elizabeth II
  1986 60th Birthday, large color portrait, limited edition of 20,000, 10½″ d, Coalport **95.00**
  1992 40th Anniversary of Succession, profile portrait and Queen's beasts, white, pale blue jasper-

Plate, Edward VII, 1902 Coronation, sepia portrait, Wedgwood, 9½″ d, $150.00.

ware, limited edition of 5,000, 8″
d, Wedgwood 95.00
Elizabeth, The Queen Mother, 1980,
80th Birthday, large color bust por-
trait, limited edition of 2,500 10¾″ d,
Crown Staffordshire 135.00
George V and Mary, 1911 Coronation,
8½″ d, CT Maling 75.00
George VI and Elizabeth, 1939 Can-
ada Visit, color portraits, 10½″ d,
Royal Winton 100.00
Margaret, 1930 Birth, parakeets and
flowers, blue border, 6″ d, Paragon 80.00
Victoria, 1897 Diamond Jubilee, color
picture of Windsor Castle, crown
and banner above, 9¼″ d 155.00
Playing Cards
Edward VIII, 1919 Canada Visit, color
portrait, single deck, C Goodall &
Co 80.00
Elizabeth II, 1977 Silver Jubilee, sepia
portrait, single deck, Waddington . . 28.00
George V and Mary, 1911 Coronation,
color portraits, double deck 85.00
Shaving Mug
Edward VII and Alexandra, 1902 Co-
ronation, color portraits, 3¾″ h. . . . 115.00
Elizabeth II, 1953 Coronation, color
portrait, 4″ h. 70.00
Sugar Bowl, George V and Mary, 1935
Silver Jubilee, sepia portrait, Art Deco
design, 3″ h, Royal Doulton 120.00
Teapot
Charlotte, 1817 In Memoriam, black
and white dec, 6″ h. 265.00
Edward VII and Alexandra, 1902 Co-
ronation, color portraits, 4¾″ h. . . . 75.00
Elizabeth II, 1953 Coronation, 5″ d
Raised beige profile portrait, brown
ground, Dartmouth Potteries . . . 100.00
Relief white portrait, royal blue jas-
perware, Wedgwood 240.00
George V and Mary, 1911 Coronation,
color portraits with Prince of Wales,
6″ h, unmarked 250.00
Victoria, 1897 Diamond Jubilee, color
coat of arms, Aynsley 225.00
Tea Set, Elizabeth II, 1953 Coronation,
teapot, creamer, and sugar, relief por-
trait, light blue, white Queensware,
Wedgwood 280.00
Tin
Edward VII and Alexandra, 1902 Coronation, color portraits, 4¼ x 5½″ 70.00
Edward VIII, 1937 Coronation, color
portrait, 5¾ x 3¾″, Riley 50.00
Elizabeth II, 1953 Coronation, color
portrait, 10 x 7″, E Sharp 30.00
George VI and Elizabeth, 1937 Coronation, gold portraits, 3″ h, Oxo . . . 20.00
Mary (Princess Royal), 1922 Wed-
ding, color portraits, 4½ x 4″ 45.00

Victoria, color portrait on hinged lid,
6¾ x 4½″ 80.00

BRONZE

History: Bronze is an alloy of copper, tin, and
traces of other metals. It has been used since biblical times not only for art objects but also for utilitarian purposes. After a slump in the Middle Ages,
bronze was revived in the 17th century and continued in popularity until the early 20th century.

Reference: Lynne and Fritz Weber, *Jacobsen's
Thirteenth Painting and Bronze Price Guide*, January 1992 to January 1994, Weber Publications,
1994.

Notes: Do not confuse a "bronzed" object with
a true bronze. A bronzed object usually is made of
white metal and then coated with a reddish–brown
material to give it a bronze appearance. A magnet
will stick to it.

A signed bronze commands a higher market
price than an unsigned one. There also are
"signed" reproductions on the market. It is very
important to know the history of the mold and the
background of the foundry.

**Lacrosse player, Charles Keck, 30″ h,
$9,900.00. Photograph courtesy of
James D. Julia, Inc.**

Bookends, pr, 6¾″ h, cupid, swathed in
swirl of fabric, tiptoeing with bow in
hand, other young girl with flowing hair
and bouquet in hand, inscribed "Cast
By Griffoul, Newark, NJ," early 20th C 400.00
Bowl, 5″ d, four lion head medallions,
linear border, sgd "Tiffany & Co". . . . 190.00
Candelabra, 21″ h, three acanthus and
scrolled arms, reeded urn form candle
sockets, turned and floral banding,
French Empire, price for pair 1,700.00

Dish, 4¼ x 6¼", oval, girl picking apples, naughty view on reverse **40.00**

Dresser Box, cov, 3½" l, woman portrait on cov, sgd "Perin" **135.00**

Figure
10" h, 11½" w, German Shepherd, sitting, rect base, patina, late 19th C **440.00**

12" l, tiger, teak stand, Chinese, price for pair **900.00**

13" h, young boy, Penedo, Paris . . **250.00**

14" h, muscular nude man, throwing discus, dark brown rubbed patina, circular green marble plinth, inscribed "Rudolf Marcuse," 1907 . . **1,980.00**

14½" h, Diana, holding bow in one hand, reaching for arrow with other, sq plinth base **770.00**

16¾" h, Nubian, wearing tunic, holding torches, gilt dec, price for pair . **2,200.00**

19¼" h, Pied Piper, playing pipe, sack over one shoulder, brown patina, inscribed "Bergeron". **1,100.00**

21" h, Admiral Togo, military uniform, flared rect base, copper patina . . . **1,210.00**

23¾" h, woman, partially nude, playing lute and singing, stepped circular base, inscribed "Schener" **1,045.00**

Fire Fender, 22" h, 36" l, hunting dog, boar's head, and hunting dog, foliate tree branches **4,800.00**

Inkwell, 8¼" l, robin perched on branch, cylindrical bark molded holder, cold painted. **660.00**

Jar, 12" h, Oriental design, colored metal inlay. **725.00**

Jewelry Box, 8¾" l, Renaissance style, rect, scrolling foliage, leaf borders and masks, two seated putti on cov, four melon form feet, brown patina, third quarter 19th C. **770.00**

Lamp, argand, 22" h, Classical style, acanthus dec standard surmounted with urn finial, twin arms, molded pedestal, paw feet, second quarter 19th C. **385.00**

Paperweight, figural, dog with ball, Tiffany and Company **150.00**

Pitcher 6" h, Continental, baluster shape, tapering spout, applied scrolled handle, low relief dec, 16th C **550.00**

Planter, 10½" d, high relief marsh marigolds, green patina, stamped "Tiffany Studios New York 3617" **9,900.00**

Plaque, 9⅜ x 10", seated braves, one with outstretched arms offering corn, relief sgd "Raymond Averill Porter 1911–50". **375.00**

Sculpture
7" h, horse, standing, sgd "P E Dolobiena" **250.00**

10" l, horse by fence, oval plinth base, sgd "P J Mene". **350.00**

15" h, La Verglais, marble plinth base **400.00**

16¾" h, Indian on horseback, green marble plinth base, sgd "Ch H Humphries," 1907. . . . . **275.00**

18¼" h, maiden, standing by column holding mirror, sgd "Morceau Mothu". **675.00**

19¼" h, nude female, upraised arms, rect plinth base, sgd "D Dhuperrio" **1,050.00**

Statue
27" h, Joan of Arc, sitting on horse, full armor, holding reins in one hand, furled banner in other, elongated oval rouge marble base, patinated, 19th C. **1,210.00**

36" h, 29" w, eagle, outstretched wings, perched on limb above foliage and flowerheads, circular molded wood base, patina, inscribed, 20th C **935.00**

46" h, crane, standing, neck bent back over folded wings, Japanese. **935.00**

69¼" h, Roman soldier, labeled "Honor Patria," sgd "E Picault" . . . **1,400.00**

Tieback, 14½" l, scrolled plate, reeded scroll arm with leaf and fruit detail, early 20th C, price for set of six **250.00**

Tray, 8" d, Greek Key pattern, dore finish, pedestal base, sgd "Tiffany Studios, New York," numbered **175.00**

Vase
11" h, gilt flowers in relief, Japanese, c1920. . . . . **125.00**

12¼" h, baluster shape, three band relief dec, dark brown patina, imp character signature, Japan, late 19th C. **1,980.00**

33" h, dish top, vasiform, applied bird motif, Chinese, late 19th C **850.00**

BUFFALO POTTERY

History: Buffalo Pottery Company, Buffalo, New York, was chartered in 1901. The first kiln was fired in October 1903. Larkin Soap Company established Buffalo Pottery to produce premiums for its extensive mail-order business. Wares also were sold to the public by better department and jewelry stores. Elbert Hubbard and Frank L. Wright, who designed the Larkin Administration Building in Buffalo in 1904, were two prominent names associated with the Larkin Company.

Early production consisted mainly of dinner sets of semivitreous china. Buffalo was the first pottery in the United States to produce successfully the Blue Willow pattern, marked "First Old Willow Ware Mfg. in America." Buffalo also made a line of hand decorated, multicolored willow ware called Gaudy Willow. Other early items include a series of game, fowl, and fish sets, pitchers, jugs, and a line of commemorative, historical, and advertising plates and mugs.

In 1908–09 and 1921–23, Buffalo Pottery produced the line for which it is most famous, Deldare Ware. The earliest of this olive green, semivitreous china depicts hand-decorated scenes from English artist Cecil Aldin's *Fallowfield Hunt*. Hunt scenes were only done in 1908–09. English village scenes also were characteristic and found throughout the series. Most are artist signed.

In 1911 Buffalo Pottery produced Emerald Deldare, which used scenes from Goldsmith's *The Three Tours of Dr. Syntax* and an Art Nouveau–type border. Completely decorated Art Nouveau pieces also were made.

In 1912 Abino was born. Abino was done on Deldare bodies and showed sailing, windmill, and seascape scenes. The main color was rust. All pieces are artist signed and numbered.

In 1915 the pottery was modernized, giving it the ability to produce vitrified china. Consequently, hotel and institutional ware became their main production, with hand-decorated ware de–emphasized. Buffalo china became a leader in producing and designing the most famous railroad, hotel, and restaurant patterns. These wares, especially railroad items, are eagerly sought by collectors.

In the early 1920s, fine china was made for home use, for example, the Bluebird pattern. In 1950 Buffalo made its first Christmas plate. They were given away to customers and employees from 1950–60. Hample Equipment Company ordered some in 1962. The Christmas plates are very scarce.

The Buffalo China Company made "Buffalo Pottery" and "Buffalo China," the difference being that one is semivitreous ware and the other vitrified. In 1956 the company was reorganized, and Buffalo China became the corporate name. Today Buffalo China is owned by Oneida Silver Company. The Larkin family no longer is involved.

Reference: Seymour and Violet Altman, *The Book Of Buffalo Pottery*, reprinted by Schiffer Publishing, 1987.

Note: Numbers in parentheses refer to plates in the Altmans' book.

Advisor: Seymour and Violet Altman.

ABINO WARE

Candlestick, 9″ h, sailing ships, 1913 (251)	**475.00**
Pitcher 7″ h, Portland Head Light (256)	**700.00**
Plaque	
12¼″ d, sailing ships (241)	**1,000.00**
13½″ d, pasture scene (244)	**2,500.00**
Tankard, 10½″ h, sailing scene (255)	**900.00**

BLUE-AND-WHITE WILLOW

Blue Willow	
Creamer, double lip (30)	**15.00**
Plate, 9¼″ d (75)	**25.00**
Relish (27)	**45.00**
Gaudy Willow	
Pitcher, 8″ h (C*)	**350.00**
Plate, 10½″ d (28)	**125.00**

CHRISTMAS PLATES

1950 (260)	**50.00**
1956 (266)	**50.00**
1962 (271)	**225.00**

Dish, adv, Metropolitan Life Building, New York City, 7½″ d, $85.00.

COMMERCIAL SERVICES

Cake Plate, Roycroft Inn, 10″ d (288)	**150.00**
Plate	
B & O Railroad, Harpers Ferry, 9½″ d (282)	**300.00**
Mont Clair Hotel, 10½″ d (293)	**100.00**
Platter, George Washington Service, (275)	**600.00**

DELDARE

Bowl, 9″ d, 3⅝″ h, Ye Village Tavern, stamped mark, initialed, 1908, crazing	385.00
Cake Plate, 10″ d, Ye Village Gossips, 1908 (142)	325.00
Calendar Plate, 1910	1,800.00
Calling Card Tray, Ye Lion Inn (173)	300.00
Chocolate Pot, 9″ h (163)	1,500.00
Dresser Tray, 9 x 12″, Dancing Ye Minuet, 1909 (144)	550.00
Humidor, 7″ h, octagonal, Ye Lion Inn (174)	675.00
Mug, 3½″ h, Fallowfield Hunt, 1909 (122)	235.00
Nut Bowl, 8″ d, Ye Lion Inn (175)	475.00
Pitcher, 9″ h, With A Cane Superior Air (167)	525.00
Plate	
6½″ d, Fallowfield Hunt, 1909 (132)	120.00
9½″ d, Ye Olden Times, 1908 (145)	160.00
Powder Jar, cov, Ye Village Street (143)	300.00
Relish Dish, Fallowfield Hunt, The Dash (135)	350.00
Sugar, cov, village scenes, 1925 (138)	200.00
Tankard, 12 x 7″, The Fallowfield Hunt, The Hunt Supper scene, six men, two dogs celebrating, painted by L Streissel, ink mark, 1909	725.00
Tea Tile, 6″ d, Traveling In Ye Olden Days (140)	300.00
Teapot, 3¼″ h, Scenes of Village Life, 1909 (138)	250.00
Vase, 8″ h, fashionable men and women (162)	675.00

DELDARE SPECIALS

Humidor, 8″ h, There Was An Old Sailor (227)	750.00
Mug, 4½″ h, Indian scene (231)	500.00
Salt and Pepper Shakers, pr, Art Nouveau	500.00

EMERALD DELDARE

Cup and Saucer, Dr Syntax At Liverpool (181)	275.00
Fruit Bowl, octagonal, Art Nouveau dec, matching underplate (183)	3,550.00
Humidor, 7″ h, Dr Syntax Returned Home	850.00
Inkwell, Art Nouveau dec (196)	5,000.00
Plaque, 13½″ d, Penn's Treaty With The Indians, 1911 (217)	1,500.00
Tea Tray, 10¼ x 13¾″, Dr Syntax Mistakes A Gentleman's House For An Inn (180)	875.00

GAME SETS

Plate	
9″ d, fish, striped bass (60)	70.00
9½″ d, Champion–Bromley Crib Dog (73)	500.00
Platter, oval, Buffalo Hunt, 1907 (62)	175.00

HISTORICAL, COMMEMORATIVE, AND ADVERTISING WARE

Mug, 4½″ h	
Calumet Club (111)	75.00
Fraternity Hall (109)	75.00
Pitcher, Holland	250.00
Plate	
7½″ d, Gate Circle, Buffalo, NY (97)	90.00
9″ d, Women's Christian Temperance Union, 1908 (86B)	150.00

MISCELLANEOUS

Canister Set, cov, 1906, each (353)	40.00
Dinner Set, 100 pcs, Kenmore (315)	500.00
Jug, Landing of Roger Williams (36)	550.00
Plate, 10¼″ d, eleven Roosevelt Bear scenes, 1906	700.00
Punch Set, Tom and Jerry (352)	150.00
Rose Bowl, 3¾″ d, Geranium, 1907 (358)	95.00
Teapot, Argyle, matching tea ball (336)	200.00

BURMESE GLASS

History: Burmese glass is a translucent art glass originated by Frederick Shirley and manufactured by the Mt. Washington Glass Co., New Bedford, Massachusetts, from 1885 to c1891.

Burmese glass shades from a soft lemon to a salmon pink. Uranium was used to attain the yellow color and gold was added to the batch so that on reheating one end turned pink. Upon reheating again, the edges would revert to the yellow coloring. The blending of the colors was so gradual that it was difficult to determine where one color ended and the other began.

Although some of the glass has a surface that is glossy, most of it is acid finished. The majority of the items were free blown but some were blown molded in a ribbed, hobnail, or diamond-quilted design.

American–made Burmese is quite thin, fragile, and brittle. The only factory licensed to make Burmese was Thos. Webb & Sons in England. Out of deference to Queen Victoria, they called their wares "Queen's Burmese."

Reproduction Alert: Reproductions abound in almost every form. Since uranium can no longer be used, some of the reproductions are easy to spot. In the 1950s, Gunderson produced many pieces in imitation of Burmese.

Abbreviations:
MW = Mount Washington
Wb = Webb
a.f. = acid finish
s.f. = shiny finish
Advisors: Clarence and Betty Maier.

Bonbon, 2¾" w, 5" l, 2¾" h, MW, s.f., rect, gently rounded corners. 590.00

Bowl
6½" d, 2½" h, MW, a.f., applied riga-ree edge in unfired yellow, pink blush on bowl, sides turned in. . . . 750.00
9" d, 2¼" h, MW, a.f., ruffled, deep color. 500.00

Cream Pitcher, 2⅝" h, 3½" d, MW, s.f., optic thumbprint design, butter yellow applied handle 535.00

Chalice, Bryden Pairpoint, s.f., 10" h, 3" d, English style stem 140.00

Champagne Glass, 5½" h, shaded rasp-berry to yellow, circular base, two handles 275.00

Cruet, 6½" h, MW, a.f., melon ribbed body, orig mushroom stopper. 1,285.00

Ewer, MW, a.f., cream colored applied handle, cream foot 850.00

Fairy Lamp
5½" h, Wb, dome shaped shade, droopy crimped edge base, turned up at applied Burmese leaf, un-signed clear glass candle cup, orig unused wax candle sgd "The Bur-glar's Horror". 1,450.00
7½" d, Wb, floral dec on shade and open saucer ring, crystal Clarke base and candle cup, minimal chips to saucer base. 1,430.00
7¾" d, MW, crystal Clarke base, very minor chips at shade edge 220.00

Hat, 1¼" h, Pairpoint, s.f., c1930 . . . . 500.00

Ice Cream Dish, 4" d, ¾" h, MW, a.f., deep salmon shading to bright yellow, assembled set of six 400.00

Jack In The Pulpit, 7¼" h, MW, rich color, crimped rim 345.00

Lamp Shade, 5" d, MW, s.f., gas fixture 300.00

Pitcher, 9" h, MW, a.f., tankard, rural scene and florals, Longfellow verse. . 3,250.00

Rose Bowl, 3⅜" h, 3⅜" d, Wb, bronze and gold tinted chrysanthemum blos-soms and leaves, gold outlines, rose colored enameled tinted turned in rim with gold accents 650.00

Salt, master, 5" d, 6¾" h, Wb, s.f., ruf-fled, SP holder 465.00

Sweetmeat, 7" h, Wb, a.f., cylindrical, crimped top, Optic Diamond Quilted pattern, orig paper label. 550.00

Toothpick Holder
2¾" h, MW, two bold blossoms on front, smaller blossom on back, urn shape. 535.00
2⅞" h, MW, powder blue and white blossoms, subdued Burmese shad-ing, coral stripe on sq rim 485.00

Tumbler, MW, s.f., eggshell thin body, shading to 1" w band of pastel yellow at base. 375.00

Vase
4⅝" h, Wb, hp grapes, vines, and leaves, rolled star rim, relief mark, registration mark 725.00
7" h, 4" w, MW, a.f., double gourd shape, green, beige, and pale brown maiden hair fern dec, deep salmon shaded to brilliant yellow base. 950.00
12½" h, MW, a.f., slender neck, bul-bous base, two small handles, wafer base, dainty daisy blossoms, shadow foliage, gold branches . . . 1,950.00

Whiskey Taster, 3" h, MW, a.f., DQ, deep color 175.00

BUSTS

History: The portrait bust has its origins in pagan and Christian tradition. Greek and Roman heroes, and later images of Christian saints, dominate the early examples. Busts of the "ordinary man" first appeared in the Renaissance.

Busts of the nobility, poets, and other notable persons dominated the 18th and 19th centuries, especially those designed for use in a home library. Because of the large number of these library busts, excellent examples can be found at reasonable prices, depending on artist, subject, and material.

Reference: Lynne and Fritz Weber, *Jacobsen's Thirteenth Painting and Bronze Price Guide, Jan-uary 1992 to January 1994,* Weber Publications, 1994.

Additional Listings: Ivory, Parian Ware, Soap-stone, and Wedgwood.

Rose Bowl, satin finish, 2" d, $125.00.

George Washington, plaster, painted black, sgd, dated 1861, 9″ h, $75.00.

Alabaster, 14″ h, Renaissance woman, floral patterned cap, chamfered black marble plinth, c1900 . . . . 935.00

Bisque, 8″ h, Sir Walter Scott 300.00

Bronze

11″ h, Louis Antoine Leon de Saint–Just, brown patina, ebonized wood circular pedestal, early 19th C 825.00

12″ h, Satyr, dark brown patina, sgd 1,045.00

15″ h, Mozart, signed "J Alegro," J Kalmar foundry mark 615.00

20½″ h, maiden, flowing hair, wearing ribbon trimmed gown, waisted plinth, copper–brown patina, inscribed "Fix Masseau," early 20th C 725.00

Lead, 28″ h, Goddess Hera, diadem in parted hair, loose tunic tied at shoulders, 18th C 1,250.00

Majolica, 29½″ h, Charles V, full beard, Order of the Golden Fleece around neck, intaglio dec, scrolling foliage, mustard, rust, and green edged epaulets, 16th C 2,750.00

Marble

17½″ h, Laura, long hair, wearing fitted cap, brocade border gown, sgd "Prof G Besfi, early 20th C" 770.00

18½″ h, Royal Regiment Officer, short waved hair, relief carved uniform collar with badges, buttons, and epaulet, low socle base, incised "E P Papworth/1868" 450.00

23″ h, Napoleon, wearing bicorn hat and high buttoned military topcoat, plinth with applied gilt bronze eagle, inscribed "Napoleon ier, 1812 Par Colombo," bust inscribed "R Colombo" 3,025.00

33″ h, lady, head turned left, hair tied up with ribbons, one exposed breast, polished violet and white marble socle, sgd "Boudet, 43 Bd des Capucins," late 19th C 6,600.00

37″ h, Emperor Augustus, short curly hair, white marble socle, 18th C. . . 9,000.00

53½″ h, man, curled short hair, stern expression, draped shoulders, stone coved circular socle, weathered patination, 18th/19th C 20,900.00

Plaster, 35½″ h, Marquis de Mejanes, white, poetic pose, high brow, receding hairline, long hair resting on back, drilled eyes, open necked chemise, socle base, after Jean–Antoine Houdon, 19th C. 3,950.00

Terra Cotta, 30″ h, Louis XVI style court lady, sgd "Coustou". 575.00

Wedgwood, 16″ h, George Washington, black basalt, modeled after 1785 orig by Jean–Antoine Houdon, 1976 Bicentennial Limited Edition, No. 9 of 10, printed and imp marks, orig box . 990.00

Wood, 15″ h, oak, Benjamin Franklin, old brown alligatored finish, sgd "Harris" 825.00

BUTTER PRINTS

History: Butter prints divide into two categories: butter molds and butter stamps. Butter molds are generally of three-piece construction—the design, the screw–in handle, and the case. Molds both shape and stamp the butter at the same time. Butter stamps are of one–piece construction, sometimes two pieces if the handle is from a separate piece of wood. Stamps decorate the top of butter after it is molded.

The earliest prints were one piece and hand carved, often thick and deeply carved. Later prints were factory made with the design forced into the wood by a metal die.

Some of the most common designs are sheaves of wheat, leaves, flowers, and pineapples. Animal designs and Germanic tulips are difficult to find. Rare prints include unusual shapes, such as half–rounded and lollipop, and those with designs on both sides.

Reference: Paul E. Kindig, *Butter Prints And Molds*, Schiffer Publishing, 1986.

Reproduction Alert: Reproductions of butter prints date as early as the 1940s.

MOLD

Compote with fruit, foliage, and vegetables, rect, old varnish, one foot replaced, 4 x 5″ 250.00

Fish, round, scrubbed finish, cracked case, 3¾″ d 350.00

Pomegranate, round, cased, 4¾″ d . . 45.00

Rose, rect, old varnish finish, 5 x 8″ . 75.00

Roses and cherries, rect, old patina, age cracks, 4 x 7" 95.00
Swan, round, cased, old finish, 5" d . . 110.00

PRINT

Acorn and oak leaf, round, one piece turned handle, old worn patina, 3¾" d 220.00
Bird and flowers, bird looking over shoulder, rect, chip carved edge, old patina, dark stains, 1¾" w, 4¾" l, 2½" h. . . . 225.00
Boat Shape, stylized floral design, old patina, 8¾" d 160.00
Cow, round, turned threaded handle, scrubbed finish, 3⅞ d 125.00
Cow with fence and grain, round, carved edge, turned handle, old patina, 4¾" d 325.00

Eagle, 3¾" d, $135.00.

Eagle and shield, 3⅞" d, round, one piece turned handle, dark finish 140.00
Eagle, foliage, and banner "J Richardson," round, turned handle, old patina, age cracks, 3¾" d 325.00
Eagle, foliage, and starflowers, round, turned handle, old patina, 4¼" d. . . . 175.00
Four hearts and compass star, rect, poplar, good dark patina, 3½ x 5" . . . 165.00
Leaf, long handle, old patina, 4¼" l . . . 60.00
Peacock and branch, round, turned threaded handle, old dark finish, 4¾" d 725.00
Pineapple, semicircular, turned handle, old patina, 3⅜ x 7" 200.00
Pinwheel, deeply cut, round, turned inserted handle, scrubbed white, 4⅜" d 300.00
Rose and thistle, round, one pc turned handle, scrubbed white, 3⅞" d 85.00
Sheaf of wheat, rect, hand grip, 3½ x 4½" 100.00
Stylized floral design
  Lollipop style, chip carved edge, initials, natural patina, 6⅝" l 375.00
  Round
    Double, deeply carved, old dark patina, wear, some edge damage, 4¼ x 4½". 250.00
    Finely detailed carved lines, simple turned handle, old patina, age cracks, 4" d 65.00
Stylized tulip and star design, rect, dark patina, wear, edge damage, and age cracks, 3¼ x 4⅞" 185.00
Thistle, round, inserted turned handle, 4⅞" d. 50.00
Tulip
  Boldly carved, wedge shaped, old patina, 6¾" l 400.00
  Primitive carved, round, pine, old worn patina, 4¾" d. 100.00
  Stylized design, round, turned handle, old patina, wear, edge damage, 4¼" d 225.00

CALENDAR PLATES

History: Calendar plates were first made in England in the late 1880s. They became popular in the United States after 1900, the peak years being 1909 to 1915. The majority of the advertising plates were made of porcelain or pottery with a calendar, the name of a store or business, and either a scene, portrait, animal, or flowers. Some also were made of glass or tin.

Additional Listings: See *Warman's Americana & Collectibles* for more examples.

1907, Christmas scene and holly center 75.00
1908, Pittston, PA, hunting dog 35.00

1910, purple and green grapes, gold trim, marked "Carnation McNicol," 9¼" d, $35.00.

1908, two monks drinking wine, 9½" d	**65.00**
1909, flowers, 8¼" d	**18.00**
1910, Betsy Ross, Dresden	**30.00**
1910, ships and windmills	**20.00**
1910, swimming hole scene	**30.00**
1911, Cash Grocery Store, W C Vanderberg, Hoopston, IL adv, cherub center	**45.00**
1911, Compliments of Hilding Nelson, New Britain, CT, 7½" d	**30.00**
1911, deer in meadow, scenic panels between months	**35.00**
1911, Markell Drug Co, hunt scene, 8" d	**25.00**
1912, Martha Washington, 9¼" d	**35.00**
1913, Quebec country scene	**30.00**
1913, roses and holly	**25.00**
1914, Point Arena, CA, 6¾" d	**25.00**
1915, black boy eating watermelon, 9" d	**35.00**
1916, man in canoe, IA, 7½" d	**25.00**
1916, eagle with shield and American flag, 8¼" d	**32.00**
1917, cat center	**25.00**
1919, ship scene	**25.00**
1920, The Great War, MO	**25.00**
1921, bluebirds and fruit, 9" d	**25.00**
1922, dog watching rabbit	**30.00**
1923, Hudsonville, MI	**35.00**
1929, Valentine, NE, flowers, 6¼" d	**25.00**

CALLING CARD CASES AND RECEIVERS

History: Calling cards, usually carried in specially designed cases, played an important social role in the United States from the period of the Civil War until the end of World War I. When making a formal visit, a caller left his or her card in a receiver (card dish) in the front hall. Strict rules of etiquette developed. For example, the lady in a family was expected to make calls of congratulations, of condolence, and visits to the ill.

The cards themselves were small, embossed or engraved with the caller's name, and often carried a floral design. Many hand-done examples, especially in Spencerian script, can be found. The cards themselves are considered collectible and range in price from a few cents to several dollars.

Note: Don't confuse a calling card case with a match safe.

CALLING CARD CASES

Abalone, 3 x 4", diamond design	**40.00**
Enameled Metal, pink and green florals, c1930.	**250.00**
Gold, 14K yg, alternating polished stripes and reeded sections, Continental, c1936	**500.00**
Ivory, carved	**125.00**
Pearl, carved, classical woman profile, floral engraving	**40.00**

Case, sterling silver, emb Philadelphia scenes, Fairmount Waterworks one side, Christ Church other side, 2⅜ x 3⅜", $245.00.

Silver
2½ x 3¼", rect, large dragon holding pearl, rough sea, China	**70.00**
2½ x 3½", sterling, rect, rounded corners, hinged lid, chased repoussé, cathedral, punch ground, fortress in landscape on reverse, marked "Leonard & Wilson, Phila", c1845	**220.00**
3⅜" l, sterling, chased scrolled borders, chain holder, Nathanial Mills, Birmingham, England, 1849–50.	**200.00**
Tortoise Shell, Oriental carving	**75.00**

CALLING CARD RECEIVERS

Cast Metal, Art Deco, figural lady, painted.	**90.00**
China, 10" l, hp, roses, gold handles	**35.00**
Glass	
Argonaut Shell pattern, Northwood, blue opalescent	**60.00**
Heart with Thumbprint pattern, Tarentum, emerald green	**55.00**
Silver, sterling, marked "S Kirk & Sons," American, 1880.	**145.00**

CAMBRIDGE GLASS

History: Cambridge Glass Company, Cambridge, Ohio, was incorporated in 1901. Initially, the company made clear tableware, later expanding into colored, etched, and engraved glass. More than 40 different hues were produced in blown and pressed glass.

Five different marks were employed during the production years, but not every piece was marked.

The plant closed in 1954. Some of the molds were later sold to the Imperial Glass Company, Bellaire, Ohio.

References: Gene Florence, *Elegant Glassware Of The Depression Era, Revised Fifth Edition,* Collector Books, 1993; National Cambridge Collectors, Inc., *The Cambridge Glass Co., Cambridge, Ohio* (reprint of 1930 catalog and supplements through 1934), Collector Books, 1976, 1991 value update; National Cambridge Collectors, Inc., *The Cambridge Glass Co., Cambridge, Ohio, 1949 Thru 1953* (catalog reprint), Collector Books, 1976, 1991 value update; National Cambridge Collectors, Inc., *Colors In Cambridge Glass,* Collector Books, 1984, 1993 value update; Mark Nye, *Cambridge Stemware,* published by author, 1985.

Periodical: *The Daze,* 10271 State Rd., Box 57, Otisville, MI 48463.

Collectors' Club: National Cambridge Collectors, Inc., PO Box 416, Cambridge, OH 43725.

Museums: Cambridge Glass Museum, Cambridge, OH; Museum of the National Cambridge Collectors, Inc., Cambridge, OH.

Console Bowl, Heliotrope, 10″ w, $65.00.

Animal, swan	
Dark green, 3½″ h	55.00
Pink, 6″ h	85.00
Ashtray	
Caprice, Moonlight Blue, triangular, 3″	12.00
Golf ball, green opaque	25.00
Rosepoint, 2½″	50.00
Basket, Decagon, green, 7″ h	35.00
Bookends, pr, eagle	75.00
Bouillon, underplate, Cleo, green	45.00
Bowl	
Windsor, blue, low, flared, gold encrusted rim, 11½″ d	70.00
#66, forest green, 13″ d	95.00
Brandy Snifter, nude stem	
Amber	100.00
Carmen	125.00
Bridge Set, imp cards, four etched hunt scene tumblers, price for set	175.00
Butter Dish, cov, Wildflower, 5½″	135.00
Cabaraet, Caprice, blue, 14″ d, ftd	65.00
Candlesticks, pr	
Calla Lily, emerald green	35.00
Caprice, blue, orig prisms, 7″ h	75.00
Dolphin, amber, 9¾″ h	180.00
Everglades, crystal	95.00
Rings, blue	60.00
#437, azurite	125.00
#647, two light, wildflower edge, gold encrusted dec	125.00
Candy Dish, cov, Crown Tuscan, three parts	50.00
Celery Tray	
Rosepoint	60.00
Wildflower, gold trim, five parts, 12″ l	50.00
Cereal Bowl, Lorna, yellow	30.00
Champagne	
Caprice, blue, 5¾″ h	25.00
Nude Stem, carmen	135.00
Cheese Compote, Wildflower, pink	95.00
Cigarette Box, cov, Crown Tuscan	75.00
Cocktail	
Martha Washington, blue, 3 oz	12.00
Mount Vernon, clear, 3½ oz	7.50
Nude Stem, amethyst	95.00
Compote, Decagon, light blue, 5″ d	60.00
Cordial, Tally Ho, red	65.00
Creamer and Sugar	
Decagon, green, matching tray	65.00
Farberware, amber, metal tray	38.00
Portia	48.00
Rosepoint	45.00
Cup and Saucer	
Caprice, crystal	15.00
Cleo, blue	40.00
Decagon, light blue	16.50
Decanter	
Farberware, #3400, amethyst, 24 oz	65.00
Hunt Scene, sterling silver overlay, 32 oz.	500.00
Portia, gold encrusted dec, 28 oz	350.00
Decanter Set	
Nautilus, Crown Tuscan, 40 oz decanter, five 2 oz shot glasses, price for set	500.00
Samovar style, Farberware holder, three flat amber tumblers, price for set	100.00
Flower Frog	
Bashful Charlotte	
Clear, green, 6½″ h	145.00
Frosted, blue, 11″ h	500.00
Draped Lady	
Frosted, green, 8½″ h	125.00
Satin, medium pink, 13″ h	175.00
Heron	85.00
Mandolin Lady, clear	195.00
Melon Boy, pink	250.00
Seagull	50.00
Ice Bucket	
Caprice, Moonlight Blue	225.00
Tally Ho, crystal	35.00
Ivy Ball, hanging, nude, amber	125.00

Jug

Rosalie, green, 56 oz	175.00
#3400/141, 80 oz, forest green ...	95.00
Juice Pitcher, Caprice, clear	85.00
Marmalade, cov, Diane	60.00

Mayonnaise, orig liner

Decagon, green	22.00
Rosepoint	55.00
Oyster Cocktail	42.50
Parfait, Caprice, clear	75.00

Plate

Caprice, clear, luncheon, 8½" d ...	15.00
Cleo, blue, luncheon	25.00
Wildflower, 6" d	17.50
Platter, Decagon, green, 10½" l	35.00

Relish

Elaine, two parts	24.00
Portia, five parts	55.00
Tally Ho, red, two parts, 6¼" l	35.00
Wildflower, two parts, 7" l	25.00

Salt and Pepper Shakers, pr, Caprice,

Moonlight Blue	125.00

Sandwich Plate, Daffodil, two handles,

8" d	37.50

Sherbet

Caprice, crystal, ftd, 4¼" d	13.00
Wildflower	20.00
Sherry, Portia, gold encrusted dec, 2 oz	60.00
Syrup, Rosalie	95.00
Torte Plate, Diana, 14" d	50.00
Tumbler, Gyro Optic, blue, 13 oz ...	9.75

Vase

#783, amber, 10" h	55.00
#1237, amethyst, 10" h	95.00
#1299, clear, wildflower etching ..	115.00

Water Set, Twisted Optic, amethyst, 76
oz pitcher, six 13 oz tumblers, price

for seven piece set	175.00

Wine

Rondo, crystal	15.00
Wildflower	55.00

CAMBRIDGE POTTERY

History: The Cambridge Art Pottery was incorporated in Ohio in 1900. Between 1901 and 1909 the firm produced the usual line of jardinieres, tankards, and vases with underglazed slip decorations and glazes similar to other Ohio potteries. Line names included Terrhea, Oakwood, Otoe, and others.

In 1904 the company introduced Guernsey kitchenware. It was so well received that it became the plant's primary product. In 1909 the company's name was changed to Guernsey Earthenware Company.

All wares were marked.

Bank, 3¼" h, 6" l, pig shape, dark glaze	125.00
Bowl, 8½" d, 5¾" h, matte green glaze, ftd, four imp acorn marks	115.00
Custard Cup, Guernsey mark	40.00
Ewer, 5" h, Oakwood, marbleized green, brown, and yellow	85.00
Pitcher, 16½" h, tankard, mold #263, two ears of corn, incised signature ..	650.00
Tile, 6" sq, majolica type glaze, high relief florals	85.00

Vase, Oakwood, yellow, green, and brown, applied shaped handles, high glaze, #235, 8" h, $155.00.

Vase

5½" h, ovoid, grapes and leaves, artist

sgd.	125.00

6½" h, tapering sides, inward flaring collar, raised sq motif with raised circles, green matte finish, acorn

mark.....................	120.00

8" h, Oakwood, mold #235, saucer base, extended body, applied shaped handles, high glaze, tones

of yellow, green, and brown	150.00

CAMEO GLASS

History: Cameo glass is a form of cased glass. A shell of glass was prepared; then one or more layers of glass of a different color(s) was faced to the first. A design was then cut through the outer layer(s) leaving the inner layer(s) exposed.

This type of art glass originated in Alexandria, Egypt, 100–200 A.D. The oldest and most famous example of cameo glass is the Barberini or Portland vase which was found near Rome in 1582. It contained the ashes of Emperor Alexander Serverus, who was assassinated in 235 A.D.

Emile Gallé is probably one of the best-known artists of cameo glass. He established a factory at Nancy, France, in 1884. Although much of the glass bears his signature, he was primarily the designer. On many pieces, assistants did the actual work, even signing his name. Glass made after his death in 1904 has a star before the name Gallé. Other makers of French cameo glass include D'Argental, Daum Nancy, LeGras, and Delatte.

English cameo does not have as many layers of glass (colors) and cuttings as do French pieces. The outer layer is usually white, and cuttings are very fine and delicate. Most pieces are not signed. The best-known makers are Thomas Webb and Sons and Stevens and Williams.

References: Victor Arwas, *Glass Art Nouveau to Art Deco,* Rizzoli International Publications, 1977; Alastair Duncan and George DeBartha, *Glass by Galle,* Harry N. Abrams, 1984; Ray and Lee Grover, *English Cameo Glass,* Crown Publishers, 1980; Charles R. Hajdamach, *British Glass, 1800–1914,* Antique Collectors' Club, 1991; Tim Newark, *Emile Galle,* Apple Press, 1989; Albert C. Revi, *Nineteenth Century Glass,* reprint, Schiffer Publishing, 1981; John A. Shuman III, *The Collector's Encyclopedia of American Art Glass,* Collector Books, 1988, 1991 value update.

AMERICAN

Honesdale, vase
  8¾" h, green, opaque, iris blossom
    and leaves, sgd on base. **450.00**
  9" h, 5¼" d flaring rim, crystal ground,
    medium green overlay, pond lily
    and iris design, gold trim, sgd
    "Honesdale" **950.00**
Mount Washington, oil lamp base, 8" h,
  pink acid etched to white portrait, floral
  band, white metal ball foot platform
  imp "Pairpoint Mfg Co" **220.00**
Tiffany, vase, 11" h, colorless favrile
  glass padded in green, acid etched
  and wheel carved leaves and
  branches, martele background, base
  inscribed "L. C. Tiffany Favrile
  5216C," orig paper label **3,575.00**

ENGLISH

Stevens and Williams
  Lamp, 8" h, yellow ground, red fuch-
    sias and leaves, sgd. **2,750.00**

Le Verre Francais, vase, flaring rim, cylindrical neck, bulbous body, round foot, purple cut to pink floral dec, sgd, 25½" h, $2,200.00. Photograph courtesy of Leslie Hindman Auctioneers.

Vase, 5⅝" h, baluster, translucent
  lime green ground, etched pendant
  dogwood blossoms, flowering rose
  bushes, lower section reserved
  arched frieze of alternating blossoms and squares, waisted neck
  with conforming frieze. **2,500.00**
Unknown Maker
  Marmalade Jar, cov, 5¼" h, carved
    white flowers and leaves, medium
    blue ground, notch in lid for spoon   **1,630.00**
  Perfume, 2¼" h, 2¼" d, green–yellow
    sphere, white overlay, etched and
    carved blossoming branches, fitted
    silver rim, hallmarked screw cap . .   **525.00**
Webb, Thomas
  Berry Bowl, 5" d, 2¾" h, brilliant ruby
    red, white overlay, two etched and
    carved scenes of currants and
    gooseberries, double and leaf and
    blossom border around base rim,
    circular "Thomas Webb & Sons
    Cameo" mark **1,430.00**
  Lamp Shade, 6" d, 4¼" h, 2¼" d fitter
    rim, five carved pink floral swags,
    cream colored Burmese type back-
    ground, sgd "Thos Webb & Son
    Cameo," price for pair **1,500.00**
  Perfume Bottle, 6½" l, elongated tear-
    drop, bright blue, white overlay,
    etched and carved leafy blossom

stem on front, grasses at back, Gorham sterling silver cap **615.00**

Vase

6¼″ h, raisin brown body, white overlay, etched and carved spotty lily blossom, bud, and leafy stems, linear borders. **1,430.00**

6¾″ h, double bulbed ivory colored body, engraved fish and bird bands, repeating medallions, sepia enhancements, marked "Thomas Webb & Sons" **2,310.00**

7½″ h, brilliant blue layered in amethyst, overlaid with white, cameo cut and carved passion flowers, broad leaves, and tendrils, trumpet vine cluster on reverse, strong circular "Thomas Webb & Sons Gem Cameo" mark at base **9,100.00**

8″ h, oval frosted colorless body, deep sapphire blue overlaid with white, etched and carved broad leafy vines and buds, open nasturtium blossoms, double linear borders, semicircular banner mark "Thomas Webb & Sons Cameo". **3,850.00**

9¼″ h, heavy red body, intricate wild geranimum leaves and blossoms, foliage and butterfly on reverse, linear borders **3,300.00**

10″ h, bulbous citron body, white blossoms and leaf design, butterfly on reverse, base marked in banner "Thomas Webb & Sons" **935.00**

13¼″ h, bottle form, luminous citron yellow, white overlay, etched and hand carved digitalis blossoms and twisting naturalistic leaves on front, reverse with thorny branches, two butterflies in flight, offset Webb medallion mark on base **4,950.00**

Woodall School, attributed to Thomas Webb & Sons, vase, 16½″ h, slender elongated pastel yellow oval body, red and white layers, acid etched, wheel cut, and hand carved formal scrolling floral tapestry, lappet border, six vertical panels, six vertical panels of intricately repeating foliate devices . . . **12,100.00**

FRENCH

Arsall, vase

5″ h, flared, pink mottled yellow overlaid ground, green layer etched as decumbent blossoms, buds, and leafy stems, sgd "Arsall" in design **300.00**

10″ h, oval cased pale pink ground, blue and purple etched pond scene, iris, lilies, pads, and tall grasses, side sgd "Arsall" **800.00**

12″ h, tricolor brown, orange, and cased frosted oval, acid etched blossoms, buds, and leafy stems, side sgd "Arsall" **550.00**

Croismare GV, vase, 13″ h, bottle form, yellow ground, beige and green layer, etched orchid blossom, wild grasses **550.00**

D'Argyl, vase, 11¾″ h, transparent amethyst oval, acid etched and dec lilies, silver deposit surface dec, cameo sgd "D'Argyl" **440.00**

Daum Nancy

Compote, 7¼″ d, 6¼″ h, ruffled rim, mottled green and pink bowl, red and green–black acid etched and wheel cut carnation blossoms, spiked leaves, stylized border motif, side marked "Daum Nancy" **2,420.00**

Decanter, 10½″ h, angular quatraform bottle, mottled yellow, white, green, orange swirls, acid etched and enameled flowering leafy stems, "Daum Nancy" etched in design, frosted stopper, small chip at point **2,530.00**

Flagon, ovoid, yellow, red, green, and amber floral dec, gold highlights, sgd on base **1,350.00**

Lamp Base, 26″ h, two part, mottled brown, yellow, red amber, black glass ground, cameo etched falling leaves, enameled bright autumn colors, sgd "Daum Nancy (cross)," gilt metal platform base and harp. . **550.00**

Perfume, 8″ h, transparent green oval, etched and enameled mistletoe, applied handle, conforming dec on stopper, gilt metal cage mount, base inscribed "Daum Nancy," gold worn **1,210.00**

Vase

4⅝″ h, cylinder, amber and maroon cased ground, etched rose hips and thorny branches, naturalistic enameled highlights, base inscribed "Daum Nancy" **770.00**

6¾″ h, 9½″ d, trefoil body, mottled yellow, brown, and red amber, naturalistic gray–brown overlay, cameo etched and wheel engraved, seven broad winged bats in flight, landscaped lower border, sgd in cameo "Daum Nancy (cross)" **5,390.00**

7¼″ h, angular colorless body, deeply etched flowering prunus branch, gilt and pink enameled accents, base inscribed "Daum Nancy" **550.00**

8¼″ h, fire polished, lipped vessel, mottled yellow, red, and maroon ground, pink and dark maroon layers, acid etched and wheel cut blossoms on leafy stems, side sgd in cameo "Daum Nancy France". **3,190.00**

9¾" h, green, lavender, and blue landscape scene, sgd **2,100.00**

15¼" h, mottled pink and green ground, green overlay on pink of persimmons and leafy branches, side sgd in cameo "Daum Nancy" **2,750.00**

21¼" h, elongated quatraform stick, mottled green ground, emerald green and black overlay, acid cut back and etched leafy fern fronds and foliate elements, sgd "Daum Nancy" with Cross of Lorraine . . **1,760.00**

30" h, frosted and mottled white, green, pink, and amethyst baluster form, green layers, etched leaves, padded orange, three wheel engraved poppy blossoms, inscribed "Daum (cross) Nancy" **7,150.00**

Duguersil, vase, 12" h, elongated bottle form, mottled green, orange, and yellow, acid etched thorny thistle, brown enameled accents, side marked "Duguersil/Paris," slightly ground lip **275.00**

Galle

Cruet, 7¾" h, amber fern and flower dec, price for pair. **1,100.00**

Dish, 7" l, 2¾" h, canoe shape, yellow and frosted ground, rose red overlay, acid etched leaves and berries, one pointed, other smoothed. **525.00**

Jar, cov, 2½" h, frosted ground, amethyst dragonfly on cov, leaf and berry motif on jar, cameo sgd "Galle" on both jar and cov. **1,100.00**

Lamp Base, 11" h, baluster, yellow ground, orange, yellow, and brown overlay, etched and wheel cut maple leaves, sgd "Galle" on side, notched at base for cord, gilt metal shade frame **825.00**

Vase

4¾" h, 5¾" d, flattened oval, shaded fiery amber, green, and colorless body, green and brown overlay, acid etched and cut riverscape, man in rowboat, "Galle" with star at side **1,650.00**

6" h, mottled pink and yellow ftd oval body, maroon acid etched and wheel cut layer, polished grapes and leafy vines, side marked "Galle". **990.00**

6½" h, mottled bulbous body, green and red–brown layers, acid etched riverside scene, sgd on

cameo "Galle," paper label on base "Emile Galle, Nancy, Paris" **1,210.00**

7½" h, frosted and polished colorless fiery amber and brown oval, mold blown, naturalistic high relief leaves and seed pods, etched "Galle" on reverse **6,600.00**

7¾" h, bud, flattened oval, mottled yellow and green, brown overlay, etched and engraved tree–lined river scene, sgd on back **1,210.00**

8" h, mottled green frosted oval, amethyst layer etched as pond lily blossoms, pads, and water grasses, side sgd "Galle" **935.00**

8½" h, trefoil rim, frosted clear and amethyst cylinder, green and brown acid etched and wheel cut overlay, blossom and leaf design, reverse sgd "Galle". **990.00**

11½" h, dimpled bulbous body, pink and yellow frosted ground, yellow and amber layers etched as folding nasturtium blossoms and buds, trailing vines, elongated "Galle" on reverse **990.00**

12¼" h, mottled orange and white frosted trumpet form, orange etched layers, floral motif, "Galle" on foot. **825.00**

13¼" h, frosted white, pink, and blue ground, pink, and green etched layers, wheel cut and polished wild geranium blossoms, leafy stems, "Galle" in design . . **1,320.00**

16" h, manipulated raised and flared rim, mottled white, pink, and green body, chartreuse, olive, and dark green etched and wheel cut layers of tree branches, leaves, and seed pods, marked "Galle" on reverse **3,300.00**

23½" h, stick, frosted and mottled ground, orange layers, etched and wheel cut long stemmed chrysanthemum blossoms, buds, and leafy stems, side sgd "Galle" **2,640.00**

Legras

Bowl, 7" d, 4¾" h, opaque oval, amber overlay, cameo cut broad leaf clusters, naturalistic green and red–amber enameled and polished accents, cameo sgd "Legras SD" . . . **715.00**

Vase

4¼" h, transparent amber cased to opaque oval, acid etched grapevines, leaves, and fruit clusters, red–brown enameled accents, cameo mark "Legras" **525.00**

7" h, fiery amber cased to opaque opal, acid etched mistletoe berries and leafy vines, polished

enameled naturalistic accents, side sgd "Legras S + D". 500.00
8" h, flared frosted oval, etched, enameled maroon prunus blossoms, sgd "Legras" in cameo . . 550.00
8¼" h, bulbous colorless oval, etched and cameo carved cherry blossom branches, enameled maroon accents, sgd "Legras" at side. 615.00

Le Verre Francais
Compote, 5⅜" d, 4¼" h, mottled yellow and pink ftd bowl, overlaid polished brown acid etched Art Deco foliate motif, ftd sgd 360.00
Lamp, boudoir, 14" h, 6½" d angular closed top glass shade, mottled white layered in polished amethyst blue, etched stylized repeating Art Deco designs, conforming lighted base, side sgd "Charder," foot sgd "Le Verre Francais" 1,650.00
Vase, 15½" h, angular oval, ftd, mottled yellow ground, polished blue overlay top, orange base, carved exotic seed pods, stylized leafy stems, foot sgd 825.00

Muller Fres
Lamp Shade, half round flared bowl type
12" d, mottled yellow, orange, and blue, three chains affixed for hanging. 415.00
15½" d, mottled orange, blue, and red, hanging ring mount, sgd . . . 825.00
Vase, 9" h, yellow flattened quatraform, orange and brown layers, etched lowland Dutch scene, windmill, cottages, and sailboats, cameo sgd "Muller Fres Luneville" in design. 1,760.00

St Denis, 19½" h, vase, trumpet, colorless crystal frosted ground, etched polished blossoms and leafy vines, gilt highlights, base sgd "St Denis" in gold 175.00
Unknown Maker, lamp base, 13" h, opal white swelled body, gold amber layer, acid etched chrysanthemums, fire polished, gilt metal lamp fittings 275.00
Vessiere, vase, 6" h, frosted oval, amethyst overlay, acid etched freesia blossoms, side cameo sgd "C Vessiere Nancy". 360.00

CAMERAS

History: The collecting of cameras, except in isolated instances, started about 1970. Although photography generally is considered to have had its beginning in 1839, it is very unusual to find a camera made before 1880. These cameras and others made before 1925 are considered to be antique cameras. Most cameras made after 1925 that are no longer in production are considered to be classic cameras. American, German, and Japanese cameras are found most often.

Value of cameras is affected by both exterior and mechanical conditions. Particular attention must be given to the condition of the bellows if cameras have them.

References: John S. Craig, *General Catalog of Photographica, 1993–1*, published by author, 1993; James and Joan McKeown (eds.), *Price Guide To Antique & Classic Cameras, 1992–1993*, 8th Edition, Centennial Photo Service, 1992; Jason Schneider *Jason Schneider On Camera Collecting, Book Three*, Wallace–Homestead, 1985; Douglas St. Denny (ed.), *The Hove International Blue Book Guide Prices for Classic and Collectable Cameras: 1992–1993*, Hove Foto Books, 1992, distributed by Wallace–Homestead; John Wade, *The Camera, From the 11th Century to the Present Day*, Jessop Specialist Publishing, 1990.

Periodicals: *Camera Shopper,* One Magnolia Hill, West Hartford, CT 06117; *Shutterbug,* PO Box F, Titusville, FL 32781.

Collectors' Clubs: American Photographical Historical Society, Inc., 1150 Avenue of the Americas, New York, NY 10036; International Kodak Historical Society, PO Box 21, Flourtown, PA 19301; Leica Historical Society of America, 7611 Dornoch Lane, Dallas, TX 75248; Movie Machine Society, 50 Old Country Rd., Hudson, MA 01749; National Stereoscopic Association, PO Box 14801, Columbus, OH 43214; Nikon Historical Society, PO Box 3213, Munster, IN 46321; The Photographic Historical Society, PO Box 39563, Rochester, NY 14604; Zeiss Historical Society, PO Box 631, Clifton, NJ 07012.

Museums: Cameras and Images International, Boston, MA; George Eastman Museum, Rochester, NY; Smithsonian Institution, Washington, DC.

Additional Listings: See *Warman's Americana & Collectibles* for more examples.

Argus, Model A, 35 mm, f4.5/50mm fixed focus anastigmat lens, 1936–41, (Ann Arbor, MI). 20.00
Baldinette, folding 35mm, f2.9/50, Schneider Radionar, Balda–Werke, 1950, (Dresden, Germany). 48.00
Bell & Howell, Filmo Turret Movie Camera, 8 mm, triple lens holder, variable speeds, 16 64 frames, c1938, (Chicago, IL). 15.00
Busch, Verascope F–40, f3.5/40 Berthiot lens, guillotine shutter to 250, RF, 1950s, (Chicago, IL) 375.00
Ciro, Ciroflex B, c1948, (Delaware, OH) 15.00
Coronet, midget, Bakelite, black, 15 mm roll film, c1935, (Birmingham, England). 35.00

Perfex, One–O–One Camera Corporation of America, Wollensak lens, Alphax Shutter, F4–5/50 mm, 1947–1950, $30.00.

Devry, 16 mm movie camera, c1932, (Chicago, IL). 25.00
Dossert Detective Camera, box, 4 x 5″ plate, reflex viewing, leather cover designed to look like satchel, c1885, Dossert Detective Camera Co (New York, NY) 675.00
Dubroni, Le Photographe de Poche, wooden box, porcelain int. for in camera processing, c1860, (Maison Dubroni, Paris) 3,000.00
Eastman Kodak (Rochester, NY)
 Automatic Kodak Junior, No. 2C, 1916–27 . . . . 15.00
 Boy Scout Camera, 1⅝ x 2½″, 127 roll film, green vest pocket, emblem on bed, 1930–34 . . . . 40.00
 Medalist II, 2¼ x 3¼″, 620 film, f3.5/ 100mm Ektar, flash supermatic shutter, 1946–52 . . . . 150.00
 No. 2, Folding Pocket, 101 roll film, 3½ x 3½″, 1899–1903 . . . . 15.00
 No. 4 Bullet, box, c1896 . . . . 50.00
 Weno Hawk–Eye Box, #7 . . . . . . 25.00
Foth, Derby 11, folding, (Berlin, Germany). 40.00
Genie, brass magazine box, string set shutter, push pull action changes plates and actuates exposure counter, c1892, (Philadelphia, PA) 450.00
Ingento, 3A Folding, Burke & James, (Chicago, IL). 35.00
Kalimar A, 35 mm, non–RF, f3.5/45 mm Terionar lens, c1950, (Japan). 25.00
Leitz (Wetzier, Germany)
 Leica E (Standard), black, 1932–46 275.00
 Leica M2, black, c1950 . . . . 400.00
Nikon, Nikon F Photomatic, 35 mm, c1965, (Tokyo, Japan). 150.00
Revere, Ranger Model 81, 8 mm movie camera, c1947, (Chicago, IL) 10.00

Seneca, Busy Bee, box, c1903, (Rochester, NY). 70.00
Tom Thumb Camera Radio, Automatic Radio Mfg Co, 1948, (Boston, MA) . . 110.00
Tynar, 10 x 14 mm exposures on specially loaded 16 mm cassettes, single speed guillotine shutter, c1950, (Los Angeles, CA) 40.00
Universal Camera Corp (New York, NY)
 Roamer 63, 100 mm f6.3 lens, 120 roll film. 10.00
 Univex AF, compact, collapsing for Number 00 roll film, cast metal body, 1930s. 15.00
Vitar 35 mm, Flash Chronomatic shutter 15.00
Vidmar, Vidax, folding, 120 roll film, c1951, (USA) 250.00

CAMPHOR GLASS

History: Camphor glass derives its name from its color. Most pieces have a cloudy white appearance, similar to gum camphor; the remainder have a pale colored tint. Camphor glass is made by treating the glass with hydrofluoric acid vapors.

Powder Jar, cov, pink salmon, emb flowers, lovebirds finial, 5″ d, 4½″ h, $50.00.

Bowl, 10″ d, fluted rim, polished pontil 125.00
Box, cov, 5″ d, hinged, enameled holly spray dec. 75.00
Candlesticks, pr, 7″ h, hp roses 75.00
Creamer, 3¾″ h 20.00
Cruet, hp enameled roses, orig stopper 35.00
Miniature Lamp, 4½″ h, hp violets, orig burner 80.00

Perfume Bottle, 8½" h, pinch type, mushroom cap	45.00
Place Card Holder, 3¾" h, ftd	35.00
Plate	
6½" d, Easter Greetings	30.00
7¼" d, hp owl dec	35.00
Powder Jar, cov, 4½" d, pink–salmon, emb flowers on lid, figural lovebirds finial.	50.00
Rose Bowl, hp violets, green leaves	48.00
Salt and Pepper Shakers, pr, Swirl pattern, blue, orig tops	45.00
Toothpick Holder, bucket shape	30.00
Vase, 8" h, fan shape, clear leaf design and trim	85.00

Soapstone, red tones, flowers and vases, 5⅛" h, price for pair, $95.00.

CANDLESTICKS

History: The domestic use of candlesticks is traced to the 14th century. The earliest was a picket type, named for the sharp point used to hold the candle. The socket type was established by the mid 1660s.

From 1700 to the present, candlestick design mirrored furniture design. By the late 17th century, a baluster stem was introduced, replacing the earlier Doric or clustered column stem. After 1730 candlesticks reflected rococo ornateness. Neoclassic styles followed in the 1760s. Each new era produced a new grouping of candlesticks.

However, some styles became universal and remained in production for centuries. For this reason, it is important to examine the manufacturing techniques of the piece when attempting to date a candlestick.

References: Margaret and Douglas Archer, *The Collector's Encyclopedia Of Glass Candlesticks,* Collector Books, 1983; Tom Felt and Bob O'Grady, *Heisey Candlesticks, Candelabra, and Lamps,* Heisey Collectors of America, 1984; Ronald F. Michaelis, *Old Domestic Base–Metal Candlesticks,* Antique Collectors' Club; Wolf Uecker, *Art Nouveau and Art Deco Lamps and Candlesticks,* Abbeville Press, 1986.

Brass

6" h, wide scalloped plate shape base, 16th C.	550.00
6½" h, coiled adjustable iron spiral stem, brass base, 18th C	100.00
6⅞" h, Victorian, pushups, pr	55.00
7" h, Victorian, pushups, beehive and diamond quilted detail, pr	75.00
8" h	
Stamped initials, sq base, stamped label	220.00
Turned stem, sq base with four feet	210.00
10" h, Victorian, beehive and diamond quilted detail and pushups, price for set of 4	245.00
11¼" h, faceted knob, turned shafts, octagonal base, 19th C, pr	150.00
11⅝" h, Jarvie style, bulbous candle socket, flaring post, disc base, pr.	360.00
Bronze, 20½" h, rod shafts, wide circular base, gold favrile swirled glass shades, Tiffany & Co, NY, pr	1,200.00
Celluloid, 5" h, creamy ivory	12.00
Copper, 11" h, pear shape, partly hammered, applied silver beads and reeded bands, monogrammed, detachable nozzles, Tiffany & Co, NY, 1891–1902, pr.	4,125.00
Glass	
Cut, 9½" h, hobstars, teardrop stem	230.00
Early American	
5½" h, flint, pressed flower form socket, fluted stems, patterned base, pr.	55.00
6½" h, translucent blue, dolphin stem	770.00
6⅝" h, flint, petal tops, waffle pattern base, pr.	110.00
6¾" h, clear, dolphin stem, hexagonal base, pr	110.00
7" h	
Clear, free blown socket, pressed hexagonal base.	55.00
Medium Sapphire Blue, hexagonal.	660.00
7¼" h, clear, free blown font, hexagonal pressed base.	100.00
8" h, clear, free blown socket, blown molded paneled stem, pressed base	75.00
9½" h, flint, clear, tulip shape socket, unusual stem, stepped base, pr.	225.00
9⅝" h, flint, cobalt blue, Pittsburgh, mid 19th C.	660.00
9¾" h, clear, free blown socket and knop, pressed base.	250.00

Imperial, 7½" h, clear, pressed, orig
sticker. 30.00
Sandwich
   7⅛" h, canary yellow, hexagonal,
    Sandwich, pr 225.00
   7⅝" h, hexagonal, cobalt blue,
    Sandwich. 385.00
   10⅞" h, Acanthus Leaf pattern,
    Sandwich, pr 1,875.00
Iron
   6½" h, pushup with scrolled handle,
    wrought iron spike hanger. 135.00
   7" h, hog scraper, brass ring, lip han-
    ger, stamped initials on underside
    pushup. 200.00
   8" h, hog scraper, pushup, lip hanger,
    brass ring 200.00
   13" h, wrought, spiral shaft, adjusta-
    ble, Japanese tsuba on base. 50.00
Pewter
   7½" h, Jack–O–Diamonds, English,
    19th C, pr 90.00
   8¾" h, pushup, English, 1800–25 . 375.00
Sterling Silver, 10" h, tapered panel
   form, engraved garland dec, oval
   scalloped base, Reed and Barton, pr 550.00

CANDY CONTAINERS

History: In 1876 Croft, Wilbur and Co. filled a
small glass Liberty Bell with candy and sold it at
the Centennial Exposition in Philadelphia. From
that date until the 1960s, glass candy containers
remained popular and served to outline American
history, particularly transportation.

Jeannette, Pennsylvania, a center for the pack-
aging of candy in containers, was home for J. C.
Crosetti, J. H. Millstein, T. H. Stough, and Victory
Glass. Other early manufacturers included: George
Borgfeldt, New York, New York; Cambridge Glass,
Cambridge, Ohio; Eagle Glass, Wheeling, West
Virginia; L. E. Smith, Mt. Pleasant, Pennsylvania;
and West Brothers, Grapeville, Pennsylvania.

Candy containers with original paint, candy, and
closures command a high premium, but be aware
of reproduced parts and repainting. The closure is
a critical part of each container; its loss detracts
significantly from the value.

Small figural perfumes and other miniatures often are sold as candy containers.

References: George Eikelberner and Serge
Agadjanian, *The Complete American Glass Candy
Containers Handbook,* revised and published by
Adele L. Bowden, 1986; Jennie Long, *An Album Of
Candy Containers,* published by author, Volume I:
1978, Volume II: 1983.

Collectors' Club: Candy Container Collectors of
America, PO Box 8708, Canton, OH 44711.

Museums: Cambridge Glass Museum, Cambridge, OH; L. E. Smith Glass, Mt. Pleasant, PA.

Additional Listings: See *Warman's Americana
& Collectibles* for more examples.

Automobile, tin, wheels 825.00
Battleship, 5½" l, clear 25.00
Belsnickle, 8" h, papier mâché, orig
  polychrome paint, white coat with
  mica flecks, red fiber trim, worn
  green feather tree, wear cracks along
  seam, damaged base 275.00
Black Cat For Luck, 4¼" h, glass,
  painted, black 1,540.00
Boot, 3" h, clear, etched "Rick I Love
  You Penny" 20.00
Bulldog, 4¼" h, screw closure 60.00
Bus, Victory Lines Special, gray paint,
  cardboard closure 50.00
Cash Register, 3 x 1½ x 2⅝", clear,
  pressed, gold paint, tin slide closure,
  Dugan Glass Co, Indiana, PA. 325.00
Chest of Drawers, clear, pressed, in-
  serted mirror, painted gold and black
  trim, tin slide closure 125.00
Chick
   3" h, composition, painted, orange,
    yellow, and white, lead legs. 60.00
   3⅛" h, sitting on oblong nest 20.00
   5" h, compos'ion, cardboard base,
    Germany. 12.00
Clarinet, musical, tin whistle, cardboard
  tube. 30.00
Clock, 3¼ x 2½ x 1¾", opaque, white,
  pressed, painted gilt scrolls, pink rose
  and green leaf spray, tin slide closure 150.00
Dog, 3½" h, begging, clear, pressed,
  round open base. 150.00
Elf on rocking horse, 3½" h, pressed
  glass, painted, no closure. 155.00
Fire Truck, with ladders 25.00
Football, tin, Germany 18.00
Ghost Head, 3½" h, papier mâché, flan-
  nel shroud 135.00
Girl, celluloid, crepe paper dress 20.00
Gun, 5¾" l, West Speciality Co 15.00
Hat, clear, opaque white and stained
  colors, screw tin brim. 60.00

**Clear Glass, streamlined auto, Victory
Glass Co., Jeanette, PA, $40.00.**

Horse and Wagon, glass 35.00
House, 3″ h, tin, litho, multicolored, glass
insert with wire trap 110.00
Indian, 5″ l, riding motorcycle with side-
car, pressed glass, no closure 330.00
Kettle, 2″ h, 2¼″ d, clear, pressed, three
feet, cardboard closure, T H Stough
Co. 45.00
Kewpie, 3″ h, glass, painted, no closure 110.00
Lantern, 3¾″ h, marked "Pat Dec 20,
'04" 30.00
Limousine, 4⅛ x 1¹⁵⁄₁₆ x 2½″, clear,
pressed, black painted tin wheels,
open top, 1912–14 . . . . 70.00
Mailbox, 3¼″ h 50.00
Motorcycle, man on top with side car,
clear, pressed, painted, red tin snap
closure, Victory Glass Co, Jeannette,
PA. 350.00
Nursing Bottle, clear, pressed, natural
wood nipple closure, T H Stough Co,
1940–50. 15.00
Owl, 4⅜″ h, orig paint and closure . . . 100.00
Peter Rabbit illus, 2¼″ h, 4½″ w, tin litho,
c1920. . . . . 30.00
Political Elephant, 2¾″ h, GOP 110.00
Pumper, 5″ l, pressed glass, tin wheels
and bottom 100.00
Pumpkin Head, 8¾″ h, composition,
painted, multicolored, paper hat 165.00
Puppy, 2½″ h, papier mâché, painted
white, black muzzle, glass eyes 30.00
Purse, 4⅛ x 2½ x 3⅝″, clear, pressed,
light emerald, alligator leather design,
gilded metal parts, gold souvenir
panel, aluminum closure 275.00
Rabbit
4⅛″ h, pushing wheelbarrow, orig
closure 135.00
4½″ h, laid back ears, rect base . . . 60.00
Record Player, with horn 200.00
Refrigerator, clear, pressed, painted
white, gilded hinges, handles, and
latches, four legs, USA–VG Co–Jean-
nette, PA 1,000.00
Rooster, composition, painted
5⅛″ h, crowing, screw closure 175.00
7½″ h, lead legs 200.00
9¼″ h, policeman, wood jointed neck,
blue, yellow, orange, and green. . . 25.00
Santa Claus
4½″ h, double cuff 65.00
5¼″ h, pressed glass, painted, red,
gold, and white 310.00
6½″ h, cardboard, painted face, upper
body lifts off, Germany 145.00
Soldier, 5⅛″ h, holding sword, molded,
painted, stepped plinth type base, tin
slide closure 800.00
Ship, 6½″ h, SS Colorado 325.00
Squirrel, 5″ h, sitting on stump holding
nut, clear, pressed, emb leaves, twig,

and acorn design, tree bark ground,
metal screw top. 1,200.00
Statue of Liberty, 5¾″ h, clear, lead top 1,100.00
Suitcase, 3⅝″ h, emb straps, tin closure,
wire handle. 35.00
Telephone, 5⅛″ h, cardboard shield, H
B Waters 385.00
Topsy–Turvy, 3¼″ h, composition, card-
board base 110.00
Traffic Sign, 4½″ h, marked "Don't Park
Here". 60.00
Turkey, papier mâché 20.00
Windmill, 5¾″ h, marked "Candy
Guaranteed". 320.00

CANES

History: Canes and walking sticks were important accessories in a gentleman's wardrobe in the
18th and 19th centuries. They often served both a
decorative and utilitarian function. Collectors frequently view carved canes in wood and ivory as
folk art and pay higher prices for them. Glass canes
and walking sticks were glassmakers' whimsies,
ornamental rather than practical.

References: Linda L. Beeman, *The Cane Collector's Directory*, published by author, 1993; Joyce
E. Blake, *Glasshouse Whimsies*, published by author, 1984; Catherine Dike, *Cane Curiosa*, published by author, 1983; Catherine Dike, *La Canne:
Objet d'Art*, published by author, 1987; George H.
Meyer, *American Folk Art Canes: Personal Sculpture*, Sandringham Press, Museum of American
Folk Art, and University of Washington Press,
1992; Jeffrey B. Snyder, *Canes: From The Seventeenth to the Twentieth Century*, Schiffer Publishing, 1993.

Periodicals: *Cane Collector's Chronicle*, 15
Second Street NE, Washington, DC 20002; *Walking Stick News*, Suite 231, 4051 E. Olive Rd., Pensacola, FL 32514.

Museums: Essex Institute, Salem, MA; Remington Gun Museum, Ilion, NY; Valley Forge Historical
Society, Valley Forge, PA.

CANES

31″ l
Bamboo, roothead, convoluted natural growth handle, light natural
patina 40.00
Knobby vine, sterling silver overlay on
handle with foliage scroll tooling
and engraved gothic "K". 90.00
32½″ l, wood, carved snake, refinished 70.00
33″ l, ebony with macrame string dec
painted black, ivory handle with
carved shield, brass collar 250.00
33¼″ l, wood, carved, three ball in cage
segments, old worn patina 160.00

34" l
Knobby sapling, carved alligator on shaft, curved handle, two tone finish ... 50.00
Roothead, carved shaft, old varnish, marked "1950, W J Wenn, N Bloomfield, O". 75.00
34½" l, mahogany, horn handle with carved hoof, silver colored horn shoe and collar. 100.00
34¾" l, carved chain link design, knob head and curved tip, old red finish. . . 85.00
35" l
Hardwood, carved, animals, birds, flowers, silver colored oval medallion with engraved monogram, bird handle, old varnish. 385.00
Roothead, gnarled shaft, carved two face head, black and brown with red 55.00
Willow, stylized diamond type shapes, old dark finish 55.00
35½" h
Ebonized, gold knob with floral tooling, engraved presentation inscription and dated 1881 . . . . 165.00
Knobby shaft, carved alligator handle with metallic eyes, worn finish 110.00
Relief carved, stylized vine with leaves, acorns, and cross hatched stems, Masonic emblems, inscribed and dated 1920, old varnish 330.00
36" l, ebonized, gold knob with floral tooling, engraved monogram, marked "T D & V". 110.00
37" l, carved, snake with rhinestone eyes, ball in cage, and relief insignia, red varnish, old polychrome 220.00

37¼" l, relief carved, tomahawk type handle, decal marked "Souvenir of Wisconsin Dells," old varnish 40.00

WALKING STICKS

29" l, wood, snake, white repaint over black, knob handle 65.00
32½" l, rope turned carved shaft, diamond shaped inlay, carved ivory knop 325.00
34½" l
Ivory, incised shaft, ebony spacers, carved ivory monkey's fist knop, age cracks 1,210.00
Whalebone, tapered shaft, carved walrus ivory serpent handle, inlaid eyes, large cracks, 19th C. 990.00
35" l, wood, painted and varnished, dog head handle 85.00
36" l, maple, carved, polychrome, inscribed "In God We Trust, Liberty, We Will Stand By The Flag" and "To Mary Anna Collins from Edwin H Smith, NYS S & S Home Bath, New York, Sept 2, 1900". 600.00
37", wood, brown and red, lizard, bird, and snake, Indian head knob handle, dated 1926. . . . . 480.00
38½" l, whalebone, turned and incised knob, 19th C. 360.00
47" l, whalebone, horn handle, New England, c1875. . . . . 35.00

CANTON CHINA

History: Canton china is a type of Oriental porcelain made in the Canton region of China from the late 18th and early 19th centuries to the present and produced largely for export. Canton china is hand decorated in light to dark blue underglaze on white. Design motifs include houses, mountains, trees, boats, and a bridge. A design similar to "willow china" is the most common.

Borders on early Canton feature a rain and cloud motif (a thick band of diagonal lines with a scalloped bottom). Later pieces usually have a straight line border. The markings "Made in China" and "China" indicate wares which date after 1891.

Early, c1790–1840, plates are very heavy and often have an unfinished bottom while serving pieces have an overall "orange peel" bottom. Early covered pieces, such as tureens, vegetable dishes, sugars, and so on, have strawberry finials and twisted handles. Later ones have round finials and straight, single handles.

Reference: Gloria and Robert Mascarelli, *Warman's Oriental Antiques,* Wallace-Homestead, 1992.

Reproduction Alert: Several museum gift shops and private manufacturers are issuing reproductions of Canton china.

Walking Stick, blue enameled handle, chased silver overlay, rose quartz set in bezel on top, hallmarked, French, $575.00.

Plate, water edge scene, c1820, 10⅛″ d, $100.00.

Berry Bowl, 5¾″ d, 19th C, price for pair	110.00
Bidet, cov on stand, 25″ l, 15″ h, 19th C	880.00
Bowl	
7¼″ d, scalloped, 19th C	550.00
9¾″ d, shaped, 19th C	880.00
10¼″ d, scalloped, 19th C	770.00
Box, cov, 5½″ h, cylindrical, 19th C	525.00
Butter Chip, 2¾″ d, 19th C, price for set of ten	275.00
Creamer, 4″ h, 19th C	110.00
Cream Pitcher, 3½″ h, 19th C	110.00
Fruit Basket and Undertray, 19th C	
8½″ l	880.00
10¾″ l	615.00
Hot Water Dish, 8½″ d, 19th C	135.00
Pie Plate, 19th C	
8½″ d	220.00
9¼″ d	220.00
Pitcher, 7½″ h, 19th C	935.00
Plate, 8½″ d, 19th C, price for set of six	250.00
Platter, 19th C	
12¾″ l, well and tree	615.00
17¼″ l	500.00
20″ l	330.00
Sauce Tureen and Undertray, 6½″ l	550.00
Serving Dish, 19th C	
Covered	
8¼″ l	275.00
9⅜″ l	412.00
11¼″ l	470.00
Open	
8½″ l, rect	300.00
9⅞″ l, oval	275.00
11¼″ l, oval	300.00
Shrimp Dish, 10″ l, 19th C	500.00
Sugar Bowl, cov, 6″ h, 19th C	500.00
Syllabub, 19th C, price for set of three	385.00
Teapot, cov, 19th C	
5½″ h	550.00
6″ h	275.00

6¼″ h	420.00
8″ h	525.00
Tea Set, 14 pcs, cov ovoid teapot, cov sugar with two twig handles, six tea-bowls, five small bowls, and serving bowl, underglaze blue pattern, tea houses and willow trees, Continental gilt bands of leafy vines	500.00
Tile	
4¾″ square, 19th C	330.00
5⅝″ w, octagonal, 19th C, chips	250.00
Tobacco Jar, 11¼″ h, 19th C	1,430.00
Tureen, cov, 8¾″ h, canted rect form, recessed foot, hog's head handles, underglaze blue, matching 18½″ l platter	1,045.00
Tureen and Undertray, 10¼″ l	770.00
Umbrella Stand, 24½″ h, 19th C	1,430.00
Vase, 9¾″ h, cylindrical, 19th C	440.00

N

CAPO-DI-MONTE

History: In 1743 King Charles of Naples established a soft paste porcelain factory near Naples which made figures and dinnerware. In 1760 many of the workmen and most of the molds were taken to Buen Retiro, near Madrid, Spain. A new factory opened in Naples in 1771 and added hard paste porcelains. In 1834 the Doccia factory in Florence purchased the molds and continued their production in Italy.

Capo-di-Monte was copied heavily by factories in Hungary, Germany, France, and Italy.

Reference: Susan and Al Bagdade, *Warman's English & Continental Pottery & Porcelain, 2nd Edition*, Wallace-Homestead, 1991.

Reproduction Alert: Many of the pieces in today's market are of recent vintage. Do not be fooled by the crown over the "N" mark; it also was copied.

Box, cov, 9″ l, scene on lid of armor making, polychrome enamel and gilt, gilded brass fittings	55.00
Candelabra, pr, 12¾″ h, figural, parrots, floral candle arms	850.00
Compote, cov, 9″ h, oval, relief molded cherubs on sides, cherub finial and handles	225.00
Cup and Saucer, molded cup ext. with sea nymphs swimming in the ocean, gilt int. with painted floral sprigs, molded putti on saucers, underglaze blue crowned "N" mark, price for set of twelve	2,475.00

Urn, raised allegorical scene, sq base, double handles, pastel tones and gilt highlights, $150.00.

Ferner, 11″ l, oval, relief molded and
   enameled allegorial figures, full relief
   female mask at each end. **100.00**
Figure
   3⅜″ h, man with hurdy-gurdy,
     crowned "N" mark **30.00**
   6½″ h, man and woman, pastel enam-
     eling, crowned "N" mark. **250.00**
   9¼″ h, dancing maiden, golden gown **45.00**
Lamp, table, polychrome enamel and
   gilt, orig silk shades, c1930, price for
   pair **795.00**
Plate, nudes bathing beside brook relief,
   floral festoon border. **100.00**
Urn, 7¼″ h, frolicking cherubs and sea
   gods, crowned "N" mark, price for pair **115.00**
Vase, 5⅝″ h, oval columnar shape,
   raised mythical scenes, price for pair **225.00**

Reference: Susan and Al Bagdade, *Warman's English & Continental Pottery & Porcelain, 2nd Edition,* Wallace-Homestead, 1991.

Ashtray, 5¼″ d, multicolored Dutch men
   and women strolling waterfront. **15.00**
Bowl, 8¾″ d, shallow, gold center with
   death of King Lear, green border, art-
   ist sgd **70.00**
Butter Dish, cov, 7½″ d, pink flowers,
   green leaves, wavy gold lines, white
   ground. **55.00**
Chocolate Pot, 10″ h, blue, scenic por-
   trait, marked "Carlsbad Victoria". . . . **110.00**
Creamer and Sugar, Bluebird pattern,
   marked "Victoria Carlsbad" **55.00**
Cup and Saucer, rosebuds, vines, and
   leaves, c1875, price for set of six . . . **125.00**
Ewer
   6″ h, cream, pastel pink, gold, floral
     dec. **75.00**
   14″ h, handles, light green, floral dec,
     gold trim, marked "Carlsbad,
     Victoria" **80.00**
Hair Receiver, 4″ d, cobalt blue flowers,
   emb basketweave at top, gold trim,
   white ground. **30.00**
Oyster Plate, 8¾″ d, lavender flowers,
   gold outlining, white ground **30.00**
Pin Tray, 8½″ l, irregular scalloped
   shape, roses, green leaves, white
   ground, marked "Victoria, Carlsbad,
   Austria" **30.00**
Pitcher
   7″ h, two cherubs at fountain, pink and
     white ground, gold handle. **25.00**
   8″ h, cream, gold floral dec, ornate
     handle. **60.00**
Plate, 9″ d, cherries, hp, sgd **25.00**
Portrait Ware
   Bowl, 10″ d, green border, gold trac-

CARLSBAD CHINA

History: Because of changing European boundaries during the last 100 years, German–speaking Carlsbad has found itself located first in the Austro-Hungarian Empire, then in Germany, and currently in Czechoslovakia. Carlsbad was one of the leading pottery manufacturing centers in Bohemia.

Wares from the numerous Carlsbad potteries are lumped together under the term "Carlsbad China." Most pieces on the market are post-1891, although several potteries date to the early 19th century.

Vegetable Dish, cov, blue bachelor button and light brown floral motif, white ground, 6½ x 8½″, $30.00.

ings, sgd "Boucher, Victoria Carls-
bad, Austria" 60.00
Plate, 7½" d, multicolored portrait of
young girl, pierced for hanging . . . 40.00
Powder Box, cov, 5" d, Bluebird pattern,
Victoria, Carlsbad 45.00
Soup Tureen, cov, white, deep pink and
yellow roses, green leaves, gold trim
buckle handles and finial, imp mark. . 65.00
Sugar Shaker, 5½" h, egg shape, floral
dec 60.00
Urn, 14½" h, rose bouquet, shaded ivory
ground, marked "Carlsbad, Austria" . 145.00
Vase, 9½" h, center medallion of four
Grecian figures, dark blue–green
ground, ornate cream handles 50.00

CARNIVAL GLASS

History: Carnival glass, an American invention,
is colored pressed glass with a fired-on iridescent
finish. It was first manufactured about 1905 and
was immensely popular both in America and
abroad. More than 1,000 different patterns have
been identified. Production of old carnival glass
patterns ended in 1930.

Most of the popular patterns of carnival glass
were produced by five companies—Dugan, Fenton, Imperial, Millersburg, and Northwood. Northwood patterns frequently are found with the "N"
trademark. Dugan used a diamond trademark on
several patterns.

In carnival glass, color is the most important factor in pricing. The color of a piece is determined by
holding the piece to the light and looking through
it.

References: Bill Edwards, *The Standard Encyclopedia of Carnival Glass, Fourth Edition,* Collector Books, 1994; Marion T. Hartung, *First Book of
Carnival Glass to Tenth Book of Carnival Glass*
[series of 10 books], published by author, 1968 to
1982; William Heacock, James Measell, and Berry
Wiggins, *Dugan/Diamond: The Story of Indiana,
Pennsylvania, Glass,* Antique Publications, 1993;
William Heacock, James Measell, and Berry Wiggins, *Harry Northwood, The Wheeling Years, 1901-
1925,* Antique Publications, 1991; Thomas E.
Sprain, *Carnival Glass Tumblers, New and Reproduced,* published by author, 1984.

Collectors' Clubs: American Carnival Glass Association, PO Box 235, Littlestown, PA 17340; Collectible Carnival Glass Association, 2360 N. Old
S.R.9, Columbus, IN 47203; Heart of America Carnival Glass Association, 3048 Tamarak Drive,
Manhattan, KS 66502; International Carnival Glass
Association, Inc., RR #1, Box 14, Mentone, IN
46539; New England Carnival Glass Club, 12 Sherwood Road, West Hartford, CT 06117.

Periodicals: *The Auction Reporter,* PO Box 246,
Scottsburg, IN 47170; *Encore,* PO Box 11734,
Kansas City, MO 64138.

Museum: Fenton Art Glass Co, Williamstown,
WV.

Apple Blossom Twigs, Dugan
Banana Boat, peach opalescent,
ruffled 175.00
Bowl
8" d, marigold 50.00
10" d, purple 250.00
Plate, 9" d, blue 110.00
Vase, amethyst 50.00
Beaded Shell, Dugan
Berry Set, master and three ftd
sauces, purple, price for four piece
set 185.00
Creamer, marigold 60.00
Mug, purple 65.00
Rose Bowl, green 40.00
Spooner, marigold 40.00
Table Set, marigold, price for four
piece set. 250.00
Tumbler
Blue 45.00
Lavender 95.00
Marigold 70.00
Blueberry, Fenton
Pitcher, blue 500.00
Tumbler
Blue 75.00
Marigold 35.00
White 185.00
Brooklyn Bridge, Dugan, 8¾" d, 2⅞" h,
marigold, shiny finish, fluted scalloped
edge 275.00
Carolina Dogwood, Westmoreland
Bowl, 8½" d
Aqua opalescent 375.00
Peach opalescent 150.00

**Water Pitcher, Heavy Iris, marigold, five
matching glasses, price for six pc set,
$500.00.**

Bride's Bowl, peach opalescent ... 325.00
Plate, 8½" d, peach opalescent ... 475.00
Cherry, Fenton
  Bonbon, aqua, two handles 275.00
  Bowl, green 150.00
  Calling Card Tray, aqua 125.00
  Plate, 6" d, marigold 40.00
Cherry Chain, attributed to Fenton,
  bowl, 10½" d, white........... 125.00
Chrysanthemum, Fenton, bowl, large,
  ftd, white 200.00
Coin Dot, Northwood
  Bowl
    6" d, green 20.00
    8" d, aqua, stippled 45.00
    9" d, vaseline, ruffled 55.00
  Pitcher, marigold 150.00
  Plate, purple 60.00
  Rose Bowl, marigold 45.00
  Tumbler, marigold 50.00
Daisy and Plume, Northwood
  Candy Dish, green 65.00
  Compote, aqua 60.00
  Rose Bowl, marigold 80.00
Diamond Lace, attributed to Imperial,
  water set, purple, price for five piece
  set........................ 450.00
Diamonds, attributed to Millersburg,
  water pitcher, marigold.......... 150.00
Dragon and Lotus, Fenton
  Bowl, ruffled
    Amethyst 85.00
    Marigold 65.00
  Ice Cream Bowl
    8" d, green 225.00
    8½" d, white 135.00
  Plate, 9½" d, marigold 650.00
Embossed Mums, Northwood
  Bonbon, pastel 100.00
  Bowl, 9" d, marigold 45.00
  Plate, irid 1,750.00
Fine Cut and Roses, Northwood, candy
  dish, fancy int., ice blue 325.00
Fisherman, attributed to Dugan, mug,
  purple 125.00
Flute, Imperial and Millersburg
  Breakfast Set, individual size, green,
    price for set.............. 115.00
  Goblet, marigold 15.00
  Sauce, green 60.00
  Sherbet 25.00
  Toothpick, amethyst 55.00
Good Luck, Northwood
  Bowl, 9" d
    Green, piecrust edge 425.00
    Marigold, ruffled, ribbed ext. 160.00
  Plate, 9" d
    Green 500.00
    Marigold 225.00
Grape and Cable, Fenton and North-
  wood
  Banana Boat, marigold 140.00

Berry Bowl, master, 9" d, thumbprint
  dec, green.................. 200.00
Berry Bowl, individual, 5" d, thumb-
  print dec, green.............. 30.00
Butter Dish, marigold 145.00
Candlesticks, marigold 235.00
Cracker Jar, marigold 225.00
Creamer, marigold, "N" mark 85.00
Cup and Saucer, marigold 250.00
Ice Cream Bowl, white 130.00
Plate, purple 165.00
Powder Jar, purple 145.00
Punch Cup, marigold 100.00
Spooner, marigold, "N" mark 70.00
Sugar, cov, marigold, "N" mark ... 100.00
Sweetmeat, cov, Northwood, ame-
  thyst, sgd 250.00
Water Set, pastel, price for seven
  piece set................... 625.00
Hanging Cherries, Millersburg, ice
  cream bowl, green, 10" l.......... 175.00
Hobstar and Feather, Millersburg
  Punch Bowl, two pcs, marigold, vase-
    line base, chip on inside rim 525.00
  Punch Cup, green 30.00
  Rose Bowl, green 1,500.00
Holly, Fenton, plate
  Blue 275.00
  White 180.00
Interior Swirl And Wide Panel, maker
  unknown, water pitcher, marigold ... 175.00
Inverted Strawberry, Imperial, tumbler,
  amethyst, marked "Nearcut". 300.00
Jeweled Heart, Dugan
  Bowl, white 165.00
  Calling Card Tray, peach opalescent,
    turned up sides 45.00
  Pitcher, marigold 650.00
  Sauce, purple 40.00
  Tumbler, amber 115.00
Leaf and Flower, Millersburg, compote,
  green...................... 190.00
Little Flowers, Fenton
  Berry Set, master bowl and six
    sauces, green, price for seven
    piece set.................. 240.00
  Bowl
    5" d, marigold 30.00
    8" d, blue 100.00
    10" d, lavender, ruffled 115.00
  Nut Bowl, marigold 65.00
  Plate, 6" d, marigold 185.00
Lotus and Grape, Fenton
  Bonbon, green, two handles 50.00
  Bowl
    5" d, blue, ftd 40.00
    7" d, marigold, ftd 45.00
    8½" d, white, ruffled, low 95.00
  Ice Cream Bowl, 8½" d, Persian blue 400.00
  Plate, 9" d, green 1,500.00
Louisa, Westmoreland
  Bowl, 8" d, green, ftd 45.00

Nut Bowl, marigold, ftd	30.00
Plate, 9½" d, teal blue, ftd	100.00
Rose Bowl, lavender, ftd	70.00
Salt and Pepper Shakers, pr, marigold	20.00
Nautilus, Dugan	
Bowl, ftd, amethyst	130.00
Creamer, purple	170.00
Sugar Bowl, peach opalescent . . .	250.00
Orange Tree, Fenton	
Fruit Bowl, 10" d, white, ftd	200.00
Orange Bowl, white	235.00
Punch Bowl Set, white, price for six	
piece set.	1,000.00
Paneled Dandelion, Fenton, tumbler,	
cobalt blue	65.00
Peacock and Grapes, Fenton, bowl,	
ruffled, amethyst.	85.00
Peacock and Urn, Fenton and Millers-	
burg	
Bowl	
Blue	300.00
Marigold, with bee	350.00
Compote, 5" d, aqua	325.00
Ice Cream Bowl, 10" d, purple	250.00
Plate, 9" d, Bearded Berry ext.,	
marigold.	450.00
Sauce, green	75.00
Peacock at the Fountain, Northwood	
Berry Set, master and six sauces,	
marigold, price for seven piece set	200.00
Butter Dish, cov, purple	225.00
Compote, marigold	400.00
Creamer, purple	90.00
Punch Bowl and Base, marigold . .	350.00
Punch Cup, blue	50.00
Sauce, ice blue	75.00
Sugar Bowl, white	180.00
Water Set, pitcher, six tumblers, co-	
balt blue, price for seven piece set	600.00
Peacocks, (Peacock on Fence)	
Bowl	
8" d, blue, piecrust rim	375.00
9" d, marigold, ruffled rim	200.00
Plate, 9" d	
Ice green	500.00
Purple	600.00
White	400.00
Poinsettia, Northwood, milk pitcher,	
marigold.	85.00
Prisms, Westmoreland, bonbon	
Marigold	60.00
Purple	90.00
Raindrops, attributed to Dugan, bowl,	
7" w, 4½" h, turned up, fluted, peach	
opalescent	85.00
Sailboats, Fenton, bowl, 6" d, ruffled,	
marigold.	25.00
Singing Birds, Northwood	
Mug	
Electric Blue	270.00
Ice Blue	850.00
Marigold, marked "N"	125.00

Sugar, marigold	45.00
Single Flower Framed, Dugan, bowl,	
peach opalescent	85.00
Smooth Rays, Westmoreland, fruit	
bowl, 7¾" w, 2½" h, fluted, raised "N"	
mark, red	100.00

Bowl, Stag and Holly, purple irid, ruffled rim, 11" d, $175.00.

Stag and Holly, Fenton	
Bowl, 10" d, 3 ftd, fluted, ice green .	350.00
Rose Bowl, marigold	375.00
Stork and Rushes, Dugan, tumbler,	
blue.	50.00
Strawberry, Fenton, Millersburg, and	
Northwood	
Bowl	
8½" d, piecrust edge, purple,	
marked "N"	165.00
9" d, ruffled, basketweave ext.,	
green.	110.00
Plate, 9" d, basketweave ext., green,	
irid, marked "N".	425.00
Three Fruits, Northwood	
Bonbon, green	80.00
Bowl, 8½" d, green, ftd	150.00
Compote, marigold	50.00
Plate, marigold	160.00
Tree Bark, Imperial, water pitcher,	
smoky marigold.	45.00
Two Flowers, Fenton, ice cream bowl,	
9" d, marigold	110.00
Windflower, Dugan, bowl, ruffled, blue	65.00
Wreathed Cherry, Dugan, berry bowl,	
master, oval, purple.	150.00

CAROUSEL FIGURES

History: By the late 17th century, carousels were found in most capital cities of Europe. In 1867 Gustav Dentzel carved America's first carousel. Other leading American manufacturers include Charles I. D. Looff, Allan Herschell, Charles Parker, and William F. Mangels.

Original paint is not critical since figures were repainted annually. Park paint indicates layers of accumulated paint; stripped means paint removed to show carving; restored involves stripping and repainting in the original colors.

References: Charlotte Dinger, *Art Of The Carousel,* Carousel Art, 1983; Tobin Fraley, *The Carousel Animal,* Tobin Fraley Studios, 1983; Frederick Fried, *The Pictorial History Of The Carrousel,* Vestal Press, 1964; William Manns, Peggy Shank, and Marianne Stevens, *Painted Ponies: American Carousel Art,* Zon International Publishing, 1986; Dana G. Morykan and Harry L. Rinker, *Warman's Country Antiques & Collectibles, Second Edition,* Wallace–Homestead, 1994.

Periodicals: *Carousel Art Magazine,* PO Box 992, Garden Grove, CA 92642; *Carousel Shopper,* Zon International Publishing, PO Box 47, Millwood, NY; *The Carousel News & Trader,* Suite 206, 87 Park Avenue West, Mansfield, OH 44902.

Collectors' Clubs: American Carousel Society, 3845 Telegraph Rd., Elkton, MD 21921; National Amusement Park Historical Association, PO Box 83, Mount Prospect, IL 60056; National Carousel Association, PO Box 4333, Evansville, IN 47724.

Museums: Carousel Museum of America, San Francisco, CA; Heritage Plantation of Sandwich, Sandwich, MA; Herschell Carrousel Factory Museum, North Tonawanda, NY; International Museum of Carousel Art, Portland, OR; Merry–Go–Round Museum, Sandusky, OH; New England Carousel Museum, Inc., Bristol, CT.

Donkey, rearing, 60″ l, carved bells, expressive face, bell on neck strap, orig handle, Bayol, France, c1895. . . . . . **16,500.00**

Dragon, leaping, 69″ l, scaly body, carved double saddle, fierce expression, etched mirrored and jeweled eye, hinged neck, Anderson, England, c1900. . . . .**11,000.00**

Elephant, walking, 52″ l, painted scalloped blanket, carved saddle, American, c1880 . . . .**11,550.00**

Giraffe, standing, 48″ l, crisscross blanket, Charles Looff, c1895. . . . .**13,200.00**

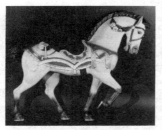

Horse, stander, outside row, Philadelphia Toboggan Co., Muller Period, c1906, $49,500.00.

Horse
Jumper
50″ l, armored, latticework blanket, jeweled trappings, breastplate medallion, C W Parker Amusement Co, c1905 . . . . **6,600.00**
52″ l, tapered head, reverse swept mane, spirited expression, M C Illions, c1910 . . . . **5,500.00**
Prancer, inner row, 54″ l, flowing mane, parted forelock, scalloped straps, draped blanket, Gustav Dentzel, c1900. . . . .**16,500.00**
Standing, outside row
62″ l, protruding peek–a–boo mane, ornately carved, jeweled trappings and blanket, MC Illions & Sons, c1921. . . . .**45,100.00**
64″ l, flowing mane, draped forelock, jeweled trappings, sword and scabbard, fish scale armor, Charles Carmel, c1915 . . . .**29,700.00**
65″ l, carved and polychrome dec, natural painted dappled mare, cordovan with tack and embellished mirrored brasses, saddle with eagle head, attributed to Charles Looff, Coney Island, NY, c1885 . . . .**30,000.00**
Mule, jumping, 52″ l, animated pose, folded blanket, scrolled saddle, Herschell–Spillman, c1914 . . . . **6,600.00**
Pig, running, 42″ l, protruding tongue, painted collar and blanket, Chanvin, France, c1895. . . . . **3,520.00**
Rabbit, running, 46″ l, white body, tassel dec on layered trappings, fur detail, Hubner, Germany, c1890. . . . . **4,950.00**
Rooster, running, 38″ h, 32″ l, Pennsylvania, 19th C **1,750.00**
Sea Dragon, 66″ l, horse front legs, scaly fish tail, fierce expression, jeweled straps and blanket, repainted, Charles Looff, c1900 . . . .**20,900.00**
Stag, leaping, 61″ l, carved and painted, scrolled saddle pommel, real antlers, glass eyes, 61″ l, attributed to Looff, NY, c1895 . . . .**13,200.00**
Zebra, standing, 56″ l, outside row, painted, layered blanket, fringed straps, E Joy Morris, Philadelphia Toboggan Co, c1903. . . . .**22,000.00**

CASTLEFORD

History: Castleford is a soft paste porcelain made in Yorkshire, England, in the 1800s for the American trade. The ware has a warm, white ground, scalloped rims (resembling castle tops), and is trimmed in deep blue. Occasionally pieces are decorated further with a coat of arms, eagles, or Lady Liberty.

Creamer, 4¼″ h, white, parian, deep blue striping, emb classical scenes of cherubs **100.00**
Milk Jug, 4¾″ h, oval, relief of American Eagle on one side, Liberty and cap on reverse, acanthus leaf border **150.00**
Sugar, cov, relief of classical figure leaning on urn, acanthus leaf panel, blue enamel border, scalloped edge, three enamel bands on cov **245.00**

Teapot, salt glazed, cobalt blue trim, 10½″ w, 7″ h, $225.00.

Teapot and Stand, 9¼″ h, blue enamel trim, relief molded classical scenes within panels, leafy borders, floral finial, slide cov, imp mark, minor chips, finial reglued **440.00**
Tea Set, cov teapot, milk jug, cov sugar bowl, relief panels of mythological figures, animals, and shell, bead border, fluted base, dolphin knob, blue enamel line border, glazed int., price for six piece set **400.00**

CASTOR SETS

History: A castor set consists of matched condiment bottles within a frame or holder. The bottles are for condiments, such as salt, pepper, oil, vinegar, and mustard. The most commonly found castor set consists of three to five glass bottles in a silver-plated frame.

Although castor sets were known as early as the 1700s, most of the sets encountered today date from the 1870 to 1915 period, when they enjoyed great popularity.

2 Bottle, China, Quimper, blue sponge trim, male peasant on one, female on other, 5⅜″ h, 8″ w **150.00**

Milk Glass, pink, hp floral dec, fan shaped base, pewter tops, $75.00.

3 Bottle, Cranberry Glass, SP crescent moon shaped stand, orig spoon **185.00**
3 Bottle, Pattern Glass, Daisy and Button pattern bottles, toothpick holder center, matching glass holder **125.00**
3 Bottle, Pattern Glass, Ribbed Palm pattern, pewter tops and stand **175.00**
4 Bottle, Blown Three Mold, pewter holder, McKearin GI–9 . . . . **150.00**
4 Bottle, Blown Three Mold, pewter lids and domed base, loop handle, marked "I Trask," early 19th C, 8″ h . **300.00**
4 Bottle, Cranberry Glass, Inverted Thumbprint pattern, enameled floral dec, SP stand, marked "Meriden" . . . **115.00**
4 Bottle, Pattern Glass, King's Crown pattern, matching glass holder, center metal handle **115.00**
5 Bottle, Amberina Glass, etched dec, cut glass stoppers, gilt frame **2,000.00**
5 Bottle, Baccarat Glass, Rose Tiente, SP frame **180.00**
5 Bottle, Bristol Glass, opaque white, orig dec, orig wood holder **770.00**
5 Bottle, China, Blue Willow pattern, matching china stand **115.00**
5 Bottle, Cut Glass, American, Honeycomb pattern, etched floral bottles, SP stand, marked "Tufts" **190.00**
5 Bottle, Cut Glass, English, allover lunar and geometric cutting, SS mounts and stand, Warwick form, shell shaped foot, English hallmarks, c1750, 8½″ h **620.00**
5 Bottle, Pattern Glass, Bellflower pattern, pewter frame, 11¼″ h **310.00**
5 Bottle, Ruby Overlay, ruby cut to clear, SP frame **200.00**
6 Bottle, Cut Glass, American, clear cut diamond point panels, rotating SS frame, allover floral engraving, paw feet, loop handle, Gorham Mfg Co, c1880, 11½″ h **2,200.00**

6 Bottle, Cut Glass, American, SP pewter frame, mechanical door housing, marked "Gleason" **1,500.00**

6 Bottle, Tiffany Glass, fluted clear bottles, SS stand, circular, vertical fluted border, central ring of cast antheminon and ivy leaf dec, sgd "Tiffany & Co, NY," c1865, 11" h **1,250.00**

CATALOGS

History: The first American mail order catalog was issued by Benjamin Franklin in 1744. This popular advertising tool helped to spread inventions, innovations, fashions, and other necessities of life to rural America. Catalogs were profusely illustrated and are studied today to date an object, identify its manufacturer, study its distribution, and determine its historical importance.

References: Don Fredgant, *American Trade Catalogs: Identification and Value Guide*, Collector Books, 1984; Norman E. Martinus and Harry L. Rinker, *Warman's Paper*, Wallace–Homestead, 1994; Lawrence B. Romaine, *A Guide To American Trade Catalogs 1744–1900*, R. R. Bowker, 1960, 1990 reprint.

Additional Listings: See *Warman's Americana & Collectibles* for more examples.

Akron Cultivator Co, Akron, OH, 1913, 64 pgs, Kraus Cultivators, 5¼ x 7¾"   45.00

American Metal Ware Co, Chicago, IL, 1932, 24 pgs, 8½ x 11" 28.00

American Type Founders Co, Jersey City, NJ, 1923, 1,148 pgs, 7 x 10". . . 90.00

Atwater Kent Mfg Co, Philadelphia, PA, 1926, 24 pgs, 6 x 9". 25.00

Avery Power Machinery Co, Peoria, IL, c1929, 8 pgs, 7¾ x 10" 15.00

Beacon Falls Shoe Co, Beacon Falls, CT, 1899, 63 pgs, 3¼ x 6" 18.00

Bennett Bros, 1942, 438 pgs, compacts, lighters, pens, and housewares and appliances 48.00

Butler Brothers, New York, NY, 1891, 96 pgs, 9¾ x 13¼". 50.00

Carl Zeiss, Berlin, Germany, 1923, 48 pgs, Zeiss field glasses, 4¾ x 7". . . . 40.00

Cavendish Brothers, West Huntington, WV, 1925, 64 pgs, wallpaper, 6 x 9" . 32.00

Columbia Records, January, 1922   . . 15.00

Commonwealth Granite, Atlanta, GA, 1922, 208 pgs, cemetery memorials, 8 x 11" 36.00

Cresent Co, Toms River, NJ, 1940, 20 pgs, birdhouses, 5 x 7" 30.00

David C Cook Publishing Co, Elgin, IL, 1915, 78 pgs, Sunday School and Holiday supplies, 8¼ x 11". 15.00

D R Sperry & Co, Batavia, IL, 1932, 54 pgs, 63rd Annual List, 4 x 6½" 24.00

Empire Gear & Top Co, Newark, NJ, 1903, 47 pgs, 6 x 9". **110.00**

Enterprise Mfg Co of PA, The Enterprise Housekeeper with 200 Tested Recipes & Their Products, 1900, 80 pgs, 4⅝ x 6½" 35.00

Farwell Ozmun Kirk & Co, 1923, 231 pgs, kitchen supplies, 8¼ x 10¼" . . . 36.00

F H Weeks, Akron, OH, 1895, 20 pgs, stoneware, 4 x 6¼". 145.00

Forest City Paint & Varnish, Cleveland, OH, 1924, 13 pgs, 3¼ x 8¼" 25.00

Gately & Fitzgerald, Philadelphia, PA, 1922, 72 pgs, household goods, 5 x 7½" 30.00

Geo H Fuller & Son Co, Pawtucket, RI, 1938, 144 pgs, jeweler's supplies, 7 x 10½" 28.00

Heywood Bros & Co, Gardner, MA, 1890, 10 pgs, furniture, 3½ x 6⅛". . . 60.00

H O'Neill & Co, New York, NY, Spring and Summer, 1901, 112 pgs, 8 x 10½" 50.00

Indestructo Trunk Co, Mishawaka, IN, 1926, 32 pgs, 7¾ x 10½". 30.00

International Sprinkler, Philadelphia, PA, 1901, 137 pgs, roofing supplies, 5¾ x 8¼" 30.00

James Rees & Sons Co, Pittsburgh, PA, 1912, 60 pgs, iron and steel hull freight and passenger steamers, 7½ x 10¼" 285.00

Jersey Keystone Wood Co, Trenton, NJ, 1927, 40 pgs, garden and porch furniture, 5⅝ x 8½" 62.00

John J Frye Manufacturer, Portland, ME, 1870, 16 pgs, farm machinery, 6 x 9" 30.00

Barber's Supplies, **Andrew Domedion, Buffalo, NY, 140 pgs, 7 x 10¼", $10.00.**

Julius King Optical Co, New York, NY, 1898, 203 pgs, 7½ x 10¼" **165.00**

J W Pepper & Son, Philadelphia, PA, 24 pgs, violins and accessories, 9¼ x 12¾" **30.00**

Kendrick & Davis Manufacturers, Lebanon, OH, 1904, 70 pgs, Watchmakers and Jewelers Tools, 6¼ x 7" **68.00**

Knowles Loom Works, Worcester, MA, 1893, 18 pgs, 6 x 9" **75.00**

L & I J White Co, Buffalo, NY, 1912, 60 pgs, tools, 6 x 9" **85.00**

Larkin Soap Co, Buffalo, NY, 1904, 26 pgs, 5½ x 8¼" **30.00**

Lyon Brothers, Chicago, IL, 1898, 32 pgs, clothing, 8½ x 11" **36.00**

Mandel Brothers, Chicago, IL, c1925, 26 pgs, various wigs, 5¼ x 7½" **20.00**

May Hardware, 1915, 128 pgs, enamel ware, tin ware, and kitchen items . . . **30.00**

McCormick Machinery, 1900 . . . . . **75.00**

Model Railroad Shop, Dunellen, NJ, 1939, 28 pgs, model railroad equipment, 8½ x 11" **28.00**

N A Mathews, Corrigansville, MD, 1893, 20 pgs, 9¼ x 11¾" **50.00**

N Shure Co, 1907, 588 pgs, carnival equipment and supplies **45.00**

Olson Rug Co, Chicago, IL, 1927, 32 pgs, 7 x 8" **18.00**

Paramount Electric Supply, Philadelphia, PA, c1927, 52 pgs, lighting fixtures, 9 x 11¾" **48.00**

Peck–Williamson Co, Cincinnati, OH, 12 pgs, Peck Williamson Dryer, 6 x 6¾" **25.00**

Pomeroy–Williams, Springfield, MA, 1903, 16 pgs, surgical appliances, 4 x 6" **35.00**

Powhatan Brass and Iron, 1937, 240 pgs, fire protection items **35.00**

P P Mast & Co, Springfield, OH, c1888, 8 pgs, Buckeye Low Down Shoe & Press Grain Drill, 6 x 9¼" **40.00**

Republic Gear Co, Detroit, MI, 1931, 60 pgs, 8¼ x 10½" **15.00**

R H Macy & Co, New York, NY, 1943, 50 pgs, youth center catalog **12.00**

Rossman Electric Supply, Boston, MA, c1925, electric lighting equipment, 8½ x 11" **37.00**

Roycrofters, East Aurora, NY, 1920, 128 pgs, Roycroft For December, Christmas Gift Suggestions, 5 x 7¼" **30.00**

Sandow Motor Truck Co, Chicago, IL, 1917, 8 pgs, 8½ x 11½" **24.00**

Sears, Roebuck & Co, Chicago, IL, Christmas, 1944, 72 pgs **16.00**

S L Allen & Co, Philadelphia, PA, 1900, 56 pgs, Planet Jr Hill & Drill Seeder, 5¾ x 8¾" **42.00**

Spear & Co, Pittsburgh, PA, Spring and Summer, 1931, 139 pgs. **10.00**

Spiegel, Inc, Chicago, IL, 1939, 76 pgs, 8½ x 11" **8.00**

Switlik Parachute Co, Trenton, NJ, 1942, 48 pgs, 6 x 9" **28.00**

Victor and Bluebird Records, 1943 . . **20.00**

Victor Records, November, 1912 . . . **25.00**

Wallace Nutting, Framingham, MA, 32 pgs, furniture, 6¾ x 10" **85.00**

Whitin Machine Works, Whitinsville, MA, 1911, 198 pgs, cotton yarn machinery, 5¼ x 7" **26.00**

Worthington Mfg Co, Elyria, OH, 1906, 32 pgs, invalid chairs, 5 x 9" **68.00**

CELADON

History: The term celadon, meaning a pale grayish-green color, is derived from the theatrical character Celadon, who wore costumes of varying shades of grayish green, in Honore d'Urfe's 17th-century pastoral romance, *L'Astree*. French Jesuits living in China applied it to a specific type of Chinese porcelain.

Celadon divides into two types. Northern celadon, made during the Sung dynasty up to the 1120s, has a gray to brownish body, relief decoration, and monochrome olive green glaze.

Southern (Lung-ch'uan) celadon, made during the Sung dynasty and much later, is paint decorated with floral and other scenic designs and found in forms which would appeal to the European and American export market. Many of the Southern pieces date from 1825 to 1885. A blue square with Chinese or pseudo-Chinese characters appears on pieces after 1850. Later pieces also have a larger and sparser decorative patterning.

Reproduction Alert.

Bowl

5½" d, barrel shape, two monster masks, stylized floral motifs, band of applied floral bosses, crackled glaze shading from gray–green to brown–green, imperfections, Chinese, Ming Dynasty. **1,200.00**

14¾" d, deep rounded sides, waisted rim, everted lip, ext. with interwoven bands of flowering magnolias, three cylindrical applied monster head feet, pale gray–green glaze, unglazed base, Chinese. **935.00**

Censor, tripod, Chinese

10¾" d, compressed globular form, three monster head supports, ext. carved with Eight Trigrams, thick gray–green crackle glaze, int. central portion and base unglazed, kiln flaws, Longquan, Ming Dynasty. . **660.00**

11⅝" d, shallow rounded form, three paw feet, stylized monster mask heads, ext. with bagua motifs, overhanging lip, pale olive green crackle glaze, unglazed int. well and raised circular base, rim chips and cracks, 19th C 660.00

Dish, 6¾" d, steep sides, everted rim, small ring foot, muted green glaze, wide crackle pattern, Korean, Koryo Dynasty 275.00

Fish Bowl, 8⁷⁄₁₆" d, flattened rim, carved petals, int. with two small swimming fish, luminous glaze. 350.00

Condiment, fish shaped, 5½" l, $60.00.

Ginger Jar, 6" h, bulbous, multicolored relief floral dec, dark green leaves, gold trim. 175.00

Jardiniere, 12" h, circular, pale green glaze, molded alternating shaped medallions with stags and owls, bird and floral border, price for pair 500.00

Libation Cup, 3¾" h, steep taper sides, foliate rim, dragon and clouds, blue–green glaze, 19th C. 200.00

Olive Jar, ovoid, tapering to waisted neck, dished mouth, iron–oxide scrolls beneath translucent olive–green glaze, Korean, Yi Dynasty. . . . 375.00

Planter, 7½" d, cylindrical, molded, bundle of bamboo stalks tied together with blue and white ribbon, stylized calligraphy, glazed deep celadon 225.00

Plate, 8" d, Chinese, 19th C, price for set of seventeen. 1,045.00

Vase, 7¾" h, Hu form, low relief, handles 1,750.00

CELLULOID ITEMS

History: In 1869 brothers J. W. Hyatt and I. S. Hyatt developed celluloid, the world's first synthetic plastic, as an ivory substitute because elephant herds were being slaughtered for their ivory tusks.

Known as "Ivorine" or "French Ivory," celluloid was made of nitrocellulose and camphor. Early pieces have a creamy color with stripes and

grooves to imitate the texture of ivory or bone. The 1897 Sears catalog featured celluloid items. Celluloid was used widely until synthetics replaced it in the early 1950s. Celluloid often is used as a generic term for all early plastics.

Ox, black and white, Japan, 5½" l, 3" h, $30.00.

Bookmark, owl, adv 12.00

Box, cov
  Candy, velvet box with figural celluloid lady 35.00
  Collar, white chrysanthemums and green leaves on cov, velvet lined. . 45.00
  Glove, hp floral dec on cov, pink lining, dated 1869 . . . . 35.00
  Necktie, 2½ x 3 x 4", creamy ivory, gold and floral dec on cov. 42.00
  Powder, round, scalloped ivory top, amber base, marked "Pearltone, Pyralin, DuBarry". 8.00

Candlestick, 5" h, creamy ivory 10.00

Comb, lady's creamy ivory 18.00

Doll, sailor 20.00

Doorknob, creamy ivory 35.00

Figure, Hummel style figures, boy and girl with open umbrella, marked "Atlantic City" 20.00

Frame, 4 x 3", creamy ivory, reticulated border, easel back. 25.00

Hair Receiver, rect, yellow, dark green floral design 8.00

Napkin Ring, creamy ivory 10.00

Perfume Bottle Holder, orig bottle and stopper. 18.50

Rattle
  Cat shape, pink 15.00
  Puffin Bird, 3½" h 10.00

Roly Poly, chicken 10.00

Stickpin, color portrait of woman, yellow and green ribbons, "Welcome to Eugene, Oregon" 25.00

Tatting Shuttle 8.00

Teething Ring, silver bell dec 18.00

Toy, windup
  3" h, penguin, marked "Made In Japan" 30.00

7½″ h, clown, marked "Occupied
Japan" **60.00**

CHALKWARE

History: William Hutchinson, an Englishman, invented chalkware in 1848. It was a substance used by sculptors to imitate marble. It also was used to harden plaster of paris, creating confusion between the two products.

Chalkware often copied many of the popular Staffordshire items of the 1820 to 1870 period. It was cheap, gayly decorated, and sold by vendors. The Pennsylvania German "folk art" pieces are from this period.

Carnivals, circuses, fairs, and amusement parks used chalkware pieces as prizes during the late 19th and 20th centuries. They often were poorly made and gaudy. Don't confuse them with the earlier pieces. Prices for these chalkware items range from $10 to $50.

References: Thomas G. Morris, *Carnival Chalk Prize*, Prize Publishers, 1985; Dana G. Morykan and Harry L. Rinker, *Warman's Country Antiques & Collectibles, Second Edition*, Wallace–Homestead, 1994; Ted Soufe, *Midway Mania: A Collectors Guide To Carnival Plaster Figurines, Prizes, and Equipment 1900–1950*, L–W, Inc., 1985.

Additional Listings: See Carnival Chalkware in *Warman's Americana & Collectibles*.

Bank, 11″ h, dove, orig polychrome
paint, damaged and repairs **100.00**
Bust, 12″ h, monk, brown finish **65.00**
Figure
Bugs Bunny, 9½″ h **50.00**
Cat
7½″ h, seated, orig gray and beige
paint, black eyes. **45.00**

String Holder, kitten, cream colored, red yarn, $45.00.

12″ l, laying, orig black and white
stripe paint, colored bow **165.00**
Donald Duck, 14″ h **60.00**
Robin, 6¾″ h, red, black, brown, and
gold, orig paint, old touch–up
repairs **535.00**
Snow White, 14½″ h **50.00**
Squirrel, 8″ h, solid cast body, old yellow tinted varnish finish, wear and
old chips **65.00**
Stag, 16″ l, 16″ h, reclining, polychrome, American, 19th C, minor
paint loss **935.00**
Pot Holder Hanger, wall type, pickaninnies eating watermelon **20.00**
Santa, Belsnickle, 10½″ h, orig polychrome paint and tree, late. **155.00**
Watch Hutch and Diorama, 13½″ h, bust
of woman, cloth and paper flowers,
mottled brownish yellow paint, bright
red, gold, black, and flesh painted
bust, reset glass, corner chip on case,
paint touch–up **900.00**

CHARACTER AND PERSONALITY ITEMS

History: In many cases, toys and other products using the image of fictional comic, movie, and radio characters occur simultaneously with the origin of the character. The first Dick Tracy toy was manufactured within less than a year after the strip first appeared.

The "golden age" of character material is the TV era of the mid 1950s through the late 1960s. Some radio premium collectors might argue this point. Today, television and movie producers often have their product licensing arranged well in advance of the initial release.

Do not overlook the characters created by advertising agencies, for example, Tony the Tiger. They represent a major collecting subcategory.

This category includes only objects related to fictional characters. Sometimes the line can become very blurred. Bill Boyd's portrayal of Hopalong Cassidy turned Clarence Mulford's fictional hero into a real-life entity in the minds of many.

References: Bill Bruegman, *Cartoon Friends Of The Baby Boom Era*, Cap'n Penny Productions, 1993; William Crouch, Jr., and Lawrence Doucet, *The Authorized Guide to Dick Tracy Collectibles*, Wallace–Homestead, 1990; Warren Dotz, *Advertising Character Collectibles: An Identification And Value Guide*, Collector Books, 1993; Fred Grandinetti, *Popeye: The Collectible*, Krause Publications, 1990; Ted Hake, *Hake's Guide To Comic Character Collectibles: An Illustrated Price Guide to 100 Years of Comic Strip Characters*, Wallace-Homestead, 1993; David Longest, *Character Toys and Collectibles*, Collector Books, 1984, 1992 value update; David Longest, *Character Toys And Collec-*

tibles, Second Series, Collector Books, 1987, 1990 value update; Richard O'Brien, *Collecting Toys, A Collector's Identification & Value Guide, Sixth Edition,* Books Americana, 1993; Brian Paquette and Paul Howley, *The Toys From U.N.C.L.E.: Memorabilia and Collectors Guide,* Entertainment Publishing, 1990.

Additional Listings: See *Warman's Americana & Collectibles* for expanded listings in Cartoon Characters, Cowboy Collectibles, Movie Personalities and Memorabilia, Shirley Temple, and Space Adventurers.

CHARACTERS

Amos 'N Andy
Autograph, 8 x 10″ black and white photo, inscribed in blue ink	**150.00**
Diecut, 3 x 5″, cardboard, Amos, Andy, and Kingfish, 1931	**20.00**
Sheet Music, *Three Little Words,* 6 pgs, 1930 copyright	**25.00**
Toy, Fresh Air Taxi, litho tin windup, Marx, 1929	**395.00**

Andy Gump, booklet, *The Gumps In Radio Land,* Pebeco Toothpaste premium, 96 pgs, 1937 copyright. **25.00**

Annie Oakley
Costume, child's, c1950	**70.00**
Game, Milton Bradley, c1950	**35.00**
Hartland Figure, orig horse, hat, and gun.	**140.00**
Paper Doll, 10½ x 13″, Whitman, 1954, neatly cut	**60.00**
Suspenders, 4½ x 12″, card, multicolored, elastic, Annie Oakley on one, Tagg on other, c1960.	**15.00**

Barney Google
Doll, 7″ h, 10″ l, straw stuffed, fringe mane, applied glass eyes, white leather bridle, 1930s.	**150.00**
Figure, 3 x 3″, lead, painted, Barney riding Spark Plug, 1920s.	**75.00**

Betty Boop
Ashtray, china, 4¼ x 3½″ tray, 3″ h figures of Betty and Bimbo edge, Fleischer Studios copyright, marked "Made in Japan," 1930s . .	**150.00**
Doll, 12½″ h, composition head and body, jointed wood arms and legs, red outfit and shoes, 1930s.	**450.00**
Match Safe, 1¼″ w, sq, celluloid, c1930	**150.00**
Perfume Bottle, 3½″ h, figural, glass, yellow plastic cap, heart shape sticker on front marked "Da Da," c1930	**50.00**
Pin, gold colored metal with attached link chain to Scotty dog, orig sample retail card, Fleisher Studios copyright, 1930s.	**150.00**

Post Card, 3½ x 5½″, dark brown and white glossy portrait image, Netherlands postal mark and stamp, 1935.   **75.00**

Wall Pocket, Betty and Bimbo, luster glaze, Fleisher Studios copyright. .   **100.00**

Blondie and Dagwood
Game, Blondie Goes To Leisureland, orig 8 x 11″ envelope, Westinghouse premium, 1940 copyright. . .	**25.00**
Marionette, 14″ h, Dagwood, wood and plastic, Hazell, 1950s, MIB . . .	**45.00**
Napkin Holder, ceramic	**40.00**
Pinback Button, ¹³⁄₁₆″ d, litho, Dagwood, Kellogg's Pep.	**10.00**

Bonzo
Inkwell, 3¼″ h, camphor glass, figural, silvered metal hinged neck, 1930s	**200.00**
Perfume Bottle, 3″ h, camphor glass, figural, brown plastic cap, marked "Potter & Moore/England," 1930s .	**75.00**

Brownies, Palmer Cox
Book, *The Brownie Primer,* A Flanagan Co, Chicago, 1905, hard cover, 6 x 8″, 96 pgs	**30.00**
Plate, 7″ d, octagonal, china, full color illus of three Brownies, dressed as Uncle Sam, Scotsman, and golfer, soft blue ground, gold trim, sgd "La Francaise Porcelain"	**75.00**
Stickpin, black, white, and green enamel, c1896.	**20.00**

Buster Brown
Bank, iron, horseshoe shape, Buster Brown, Tige, and horse.	**125.00**
Clicker, 1¾″ l, litho metal, "Brown Shoe Co." inscription, c1930.	**15.00**
Mask, diecut, stiff paper, Froggy the Gremlin, 1946	**40.00**
Paddle Board, 5 x 10″, cardboard, rubber ball attached by string, 1946 . .	**60.00**
Pinback Button, ⅞″ d, Buster Brown Hose Supporter, multicolored	**18.00**
Pitcher, 4″ h, china, white, full color illus, early 1900s	**75.00**
Toy, 5″ h, squeaker, rubber, Froggy, Rempel, 1948	**100.00**

Campbell Kids
Child's Utensil Set, knife, fork, and spoon, SP	**50.00**
Salt and Pepper Shakers, pr, 4½″ h, plastic, 1950	**20.00**
Thermometer, tin, figural, adv	**35.00**
Toy, squeeze, figural	**75.00**

Captain Marvel
Game, Shazam, paper, 1944	**30.00**
Pennant, felt, dark blue, maroon picture.	**20.00**
Wristwatch, red strap, orig box, copyright 1948, Fawcett Publications . .	**125.00**

Captain Video
Figure, spaceman, Kellogg's premium	**10.00**
Gun, Rite–O–Lite	**40.00**

Pen, rocketship, 1950s 20.00
Toy, Secret Ray Gun 95.00

Charlie McCarthy
Bubble Gum Wrapper 12.00
Handkerchief, 9 x 9½", linenlike fabric, corner inscribed "Charlie McCarthy In At The Races," white ground, bright red, blue, yellow, and black race horse center, late 1930s 30.00
Pinback Button, ¾" d, celluloid, black and white portrait of Charlie, c1930 65.00
Notepad, 5½ x 9", black, white, and green, lined paper, 1938. . . . . 20.00
Ring, plastic, green, black and white photo, c1940 . . . . 30.00
Valentine, cardboard, diecut 17.50

Charlie The Tuna
Bathroom Scale, 13" w, "Sorry Charlie". 40.00
Lamp, 9" h, plaster, figural 50.00
Wristwatch, "Sorry Charlie," orig case, 1971 . . . . 75.00

Dennis The Menace
Coloring Book, 1960, unused 12.50
Doll, orig box 125.00
Mug, 4" h, plastic, picturing Dennis, 1950s 15.00
Paper Doll, Backyard Picnic Set, punch–out dolls and picnic items, Whitman, 1960 . . . . 25.00
Spoon, 6" l, SP, emb figure at top of handle, name vertically on handle, 1950s 25.00

Dick Tracy
Book, *Secret Service Patrol Secret Code Book,* 12 pgs, Quaker premium, 1938. . . . . 60.00
Camera, 3 x 5", plastic, black, Seymore Products, Chicago. 45.00
Candy Wrapper, Johnson Caramels 20.00
Newspaper, Sunday comic page, 1940, Chester Gould 40.00
Salt and Pepper Shakers, pr, plaster, Dick and Junior 35.00
Toy, 18" l, friction, tin, squad car, Marx 300.00
Water Pistol, plastic, 1955 . . . . 35.00

Elsie The Cow
Bank, 6½" h, marked "Master Caster," 1950 . . . . 75.00
Charm, ½" h, full dimensional Elsie, white hard plastic, c1940 . . . . 18.50
Creamer and Sugar, Elsie and Elmer, orig labels. 75.00
Doll, 15" h, vinyl head, plush, c1950 50.00
Pencil, mechanical 75.00
Pinback Button, 1¾" d, cello, red and white, "Drink Rosenberger's Milk, Smile," white illus of Elsie in center 15.00
Ring, plastic, green, color inset picture, Borden Company copyright, c1950. . . . . 50.00

Felix The Cat
Doll, 8½" l, wood, jointed, decals, leather ears, Schoenhut, c1920. . . 200.00
Figure, 13" h, composition, jointed arms. 350.00
Pin, 1" l, black letter, bright yellow litho, "30 Comics/Herald and Examiner," c1930 . . . . 50.00
Puzzle, 13 x 10½", Built–Rite, 1949 15.00
Sheet Music, *Felix Kept On Walking,* 9¾ x 12¼", 1923 copyright, Lawrence Wright Music Co. 75.00
Yarn Holder, 6½ x 6½", wood, diecut, black images, inscription "Felix Keeps On Knitting" and "Pathe Presents" symbol in center, 1920–30 35.00

Green Hornet
Color Magic Rub–Off, 1966, MIB . . 55.00
Ring, flicker, plastic, silver 7.50
Viewmaster, three reels, 16 pg booklet, 1966 . . . . 48.00

Happy Hooligan
Figure, 8¼" h, bisque, worried expression, tin can hat, orange, black, blue, and yellow. 75.00
Post Card, 3½ x 5½", full color illus, inked inscription, Nov 1905 postmark. 17.50
Stickpin, 2¼" h, brass 35.00

Hopalong Cassidy
Barrette, 2" l, diecut brass, bright luster, initials outlined in bright red, black and red portrait, c1950. . . . . 27.50
Bedspread, chenille, beige and brown 225.00
Bottle Cap, 1¼" stiff cardboard disk, green image, words "Play Money" and "1¢," slight browning, c1950 . . 25.00
Notebook Filler Paper, Hoppy pictured on wrapper, unopened, mint 18.00

Bank, Howdy Doody on pig, 7" h, $45.00.

Pinback Button, 1⅛" d, litho, black picture, bright yellow ground, c1950. . **35.00**
Radio, red, tin saddle back, orig tin tag on bottom, Hoppy on Topper, mint, working condition. **475.00**
Record Album, Hoppy & Square Dance Hold Up, two record set . . . **65.00**

Howdy Doody
Bank, 6½ x 7", ceramic, riding pig . **45.00**
Belt, suede, emb face **30.00**
Game, Flub–A–Dub–Flip–A–Ring . **24.00**
Handkerchief, 8 x 8¼", cotton **15.00**
Lamp, figural **165.00**
Lamp Shade, wall type **275.00**
Marionette, orig box
  Flub–A–Dub **275.00**
  Howdy **225.00**
Puppet Set, Howdy, Clarabelle, Dilly, Princess & Mr. Bluster Put On Your Own Puppet Show, plastic figures, orig pkg. **125.00**
Sand Toy, plastic figural forms, Howdy, Clarabelle, Bluster, and Flub, shovel, orig pkg. **125.00**
Pencil Case, vinyl, red **20.00**
Ukelele, orig box **275.00**

Jiggs and Maggie
Figure, 4" h, set of 3, Jiggs, Maggie, and Nora, King Features copyright, "Made In Japan" 1930s **100.00**
Paperweight, glass **35.00**
Pin, 1" l, Jiggs, black letter, bright yellow litho, "30 Comics/Herald and Examiner," c1930. . . . . **50.00**
Pinback Button, 1³⁄₁₆" d, litho, Maggie, Kellogg's Pep **18.00**
Salt and Pepper Shakers, pr, ceramic **45.00**
Toy, 5½ x 7", windup, litho tin, Maggie holding rolling pin with dog between her feet charges toward Jiggs, spring metal strap, Nifty Toy Co, 1924 copyright. **450.00**

Li'l Abner
Bottle, 7½" h, Shmoo, blue glass, marked "Baldwin Lab, 1950". **30.00**
Coloring Book, Saalfield, #2370, 144 pgs, 1941, some neatly colored pgs. **25.00**
Pinback Button, 2⅛" d, white Shmoo, dark green ground **45.00**
Salt and Pepper Shakers, pr, 4" h, Shmoo, black face details, "Made In Japan" foil sticker, late 1940s . . **85.00**

Little Orphan Annie
Clicker, red, white, and black, Mysto members, 1941 . . . . **35.00**
Doll, ABC Toys, 1940 . . . . **25.00**
Gravy Boat, lusterware, white, orange, yellow, and black **175.00**
Mug, Ovaltine **60.00**
Nodder, 3½" h, painted bisque,

stamped on back "Orphan Annie," 1930s **150.00**
Pastry Set, miniature baking utensils, two aluminum mixing spoons, wood pestle shape rolling pin, flour cup, and 6 x 8" rolling board, boxed, Transogram "Gold Medal" Toy, 1930s **75.00**
Whistle, tin, signal, three tones . . . **30.00**

Lone Ranger
Badge, 1" d, Safety Scout **15.00**
Guitar, 30" l, Jefferson, orig box . . . **80.00**
Hartland Figure, orig box **225.00**
Holster, 9" l stiff cardboard, colored to resemble tan leather, steer design, brand initials "GA," inscription in rope script, khaki web army style belt, includes a 7" l aluminum single shot cap pistol with white plastic grips, boxed, 1942 copyright **75.00**
Pencil Case, 1 x 4 x 8¼", textured stiff cardboard, gold cov design is lightly emb, dark blue background, American Lead Pencil Co, Lone Ranger copyright, 1930s **40.00**
Rifle, 24" l, plastic, simulated metal and wood parts, gold script inscription, emb Indian head and bear in woods on sides of stock, clicking sound, sighting scope, c1960 . . . . **25.00**
Toy, windup, litho tin, Range Rider, Marx, MIB **500.00**

Mr. Peanut
Bank, 8½" h, molded plastic, tan, coin slot in top of hat, inscription on hat brim, c1950 . . . . **40.00**
Pencil, mechanical, 5¼" l, red and white plastic, cylinder at top contains miniature tan figure, inscription on side, c1940–50 . . . . **15.00**

Moon Mullins
Baking Set, Pillsbury Comicookie, 1937, MIB. **35.00**
Nodder, bisque, marked "Germany" **75.00**
Pinback Button, 1½" d, black and white, Moon Mullins Knothole Gang, c1930 . . . . **45.00**
Toy, police truck, blue, yellow wheels, Mullins figure at rear, Tootsietoy . . **100.00**

Nebbs Family, pocket watch, 2" d, Rudy, silver metal, black and white dial, overwound, c1933 . . . . **400.00**
Our Gang, pencil box, 1930s **60.00**

Popeye
Activity Book, Dot–To–Dot, Golden, 1978. . . . . **8.00**
Charm, celluloid **5.00**
Children's Book, *Popeye Borrows A Baby Nurse*, Whitman #712 . . . . . **40.00**
Figure, 14" h, chalkware **125.00**
Lamp, 16 h, figural, dark maroon with gold accent striped shade, gray

metal base with 8" h figure, arms around brown lamp pole **150.00**
Mug, 4" h, Olive Oyl, figural **15.00**
Phonograph, Emerson **40.00**
Salt and Pepper Shakers, pr, 3" h, Vandor **30.00**
Sticker Book, Lowe #2631 . . . . **35.00**
Wristwatch, 1¼" d, silver colored metal case, dial pictures Popeye holding spinach can, gray leather bands, c1960. . . . . **50.00**

Red Ryder
Book, *Red Ryder and Circus Luck,* Whitman Better Little Book #1466, 1949. **25.00**
Glove Case, black enameled metal and cardboard, illus on lid, leather carrying handle, elastic straps for holding supplies, silvered metal spring clip fasteners, 1951 salesman program, Wells–Lamont Glove Company **150.00**
Paint Book, 1941, unused **35.00**
Target Game, litho cardboard, Whitman, 1939. . . . . **55.00**

Reddy Kilowatt
Cookie Cutter **40.00**
Cuff Links **80.00**
Earrings, 1" h, figural, brass, 2¾ x 3" yellow, blue, and red presentation folder with verse, 1955 copyright . . **20.00**
Magic Gripper, 5" d textured rubber disk, yellow, red illus, orig 5¼" sq envelope. **30.00**
Pen and Pencil Set **40.00**

Rocky Jones, Space Ranger
Coloring Book, Whitman, cockpit cov, 1951. **30.00**
Pinback Button, membership **42.00**
Wristwatch **120.00**

Rootie Kazootie
Game, card, Rootie Kazootie Word Game, Ed–U–Cards, 1953 . . . . . . **20.00**
Handkerchief, 9" sq, Gala Poochie Pup **15.00**
Puppet, 11" h, vinyl head, cloth baseball uniform body **30.00**

Skippy
Pinback Button, 1⅛" d, red, white, and blue, litho, "Skippy Ice Cream," c1930 . . . . **15.00**
Sign, 24 x 36", diecut cardboard, "Fro–joy" ice cream container, color, 1930s. **200.00**

Smitty, coloring book, McLoughlin Bros, 1932, 24 pgs. **45.00**

Straight Shooter
Coloring Book, 8½ x 11", health and hygiene, Ralston premium, unused **75.00**
Ring, brass, checkerboard logo on top with steer head and gun design on sides, 1935 . . . . **50.00**

Woody Woodpecker
Clock, 4¾" h, alarm, metal, figural, painted **400.00**
Coloring Book, Learn To Draw, 1958, neatly colored **12.00**
Figure, 5½" h, plastic, red, orig tag **20.00**
Ring, plastic, white, metallic blue and white disk, c1960 . . . . **20.00**

Yellow Kid
Cigar Box, 3½ x 4¼ x 9", wood, illus and name inscription in bright gold, brass hinges, label inside "Smoke Yellow Kid Cigars/Manuf'd By B. R. Fleming, Curwesville, Pa.," tax label strips on back, c1896 . . . . **200.00**
Figure, 7¼" h, paper, full dimensional, hollowed thin papier mache, solid dark red painted back, Pulver Chewing Gum, Old King Cole Papier Machine Co, Canton, OH **225.00**
Pinback Button, No 14, Kid dressed to go to a ball **20.00**
Post Card, 3¾ x 6", full color illus for month of October, issued as reminder from Ohio hardware company, 1911 postmark **40.00**

PERSONALITIES

Ball, Lucille
Magazine, Life, April 6, 1953, five page article, full color cover of Lucy, Desi Arnaz, Desi IV, and Lucy Desiree. **25.00**
Movie Lobby Card, 11 x 14", full color, 1949 Columbia Picture "Miss Grant Takes Richmond". **20.00**
Photo, 8 x 10", orange tinting, marked "Lucille Ball In MGM Pictures," c1940 . . . . **20.00**
Bernhardt, Sarah, cabinet photo, 4¼ x 6½", sepia portrait, c1910 . . . . **30.00**

Record Duster, Bing Crosby, yellow ground, 3½" d, $8.00.

Blyth, Ann, coloring book, 1952, some pages colored. **12.00**

Cantor, Eddie

    Big Little Book, *Eddie Cantor In An Hour With You,* Whitman, #774, 1934, 154 pgs, 4½ x 5¼". **40.00**

    Children's Book, *Eddie Cantor In Laughland,* Goldsmith Publishing Co, 1934, 5 x 5¼" soft cover, 122 page story, art by Henry Vallely, foreword with endorsement by Juvenile Educations League. **35.00**

Captain Kangaroo

    Puzzle, 10 x 14", frame tray, Captain and nursery rhyme characters, 1956 K— Enterprises copyright, Milton Bradley **18.00**

    Whisk Broom, 7" h, wood handle, blue and flesh tones, black, white, red, and yellow accents, copyright R.K.A., c1960 . . . . **35.00**

Chamberlain, Richard, book cover, 13½ x 20", stiff blue paper, black and white photos, issued by Richard Chamberlain International Fan Club, c1960, unused. **20.00**

Crawford, Joan, tin, 7", plaid design, young MGM Studios portrait. **235.00**

Dionne Quintuplets

    Advertisement, 5 x 7", Quintuplet Bread, Schulz Baking Co, diecut cardboard, loaf of bread, brown crust, bright red and blue letters, named silhouette portraits, text on reverse **60.00**

    Fan, 8¼ x 8¾" diecut cardboard, titled "Sweethearts Of The World," full color tinted portraits, light blue ground, 1936 copyright, name of funeral director. **20.00**

Douglas, Donna, exhibit card, 3¼ x 5¼", cardboard, black and white photo, signature, early 1960s **15.00**

Evans, Dale

    Jewelry Set, child's, orig wrist watch **20.00**

    Ring, litho tin, Post's Raisin Bran premium, copyright 1952. . . . . **25.00**

Flynn, Erroll, pin, 1" d, litho tin disk, black and white photo, silver rim, reverse with name and fold over tab with straight pin, English, c1950 . . . . . . **20.00**

Garland, Judy, sheet music, *On The Atchison, Topeka, and the Santa Fe,* from 1945 MGM movie *The Harvey Girls,* sepia photo on purple, light pink, and brown cov **20.00**

Gleason, Jackie

    Display Card, 10½ x 15", "Jackie Gleason Buttons," stiff cardboard, blue tone photo, copyright 1955 VIP Corp. **25.00**

    Game, Jackie Gleason's TV Fun Game, Transogram, copyright 1956 VIP Corp, orig box **75.00**

    Magazine, *TV Guide,* May 21, 1955, Philadelphia edition, three page article on Honeymooners. **15.00**

Godfrey, Arthur, sheet music, *Dance Me Loose,* 3 pgs, black and white photo on cov, Irwin—Howard Music Co, copyright 1951 . . . . **18.00**

Haley, Bill, pinback button, ⅞" d, light blue litho, brown tone portrait, marked on back "A Decca Recording Star". . **35.00**

Houdini, Harry, big little book, *Houdini's Big Little Book Of Magic,* Whitman, 1927, premium for American Oil and Amoco Gas, 192 pgs. **20.00**

Kaye, Danny, nodder, 5" h, composition, green base, 1950s. **100.00**

Leigh, Vivian, pin, 1" d, litho tin disk, black and white photo, silver rim, reverse with name and fold over tab with straight pin, English, c1950 . . . . **20.00**

Lloyd, Harold, playing card, 2½ x 3½", white, black, red, and flesh tone image as Jack of Hearts, white lady, black maid playing card game, promoting comedy movie *Dr Jack,* 1922 . . . . . . **15.00**

Marx Brothers

    Book, *Beds,* hardbound **40.00**

    Sheet Music, 9½ x 12¼", *Alone,* MGM musical *A Night At The Opera,* 1935, orange, blue, and white cover, blue photos of Groucho, Chico, Harpo, Allan Jones, and Kitty Carlisle. **20.00**

Maynard, Ken

    Big Little Book, *Ken Maynard & The Gun Wolves of the Gila.* **25.00**

    Pinback Button, 1¾" d, "Cole Bros Circus/Ken Maynard," black, white, and gray, c1930. . . . . **90.00**

Monroe, Marilyn

    Calendar, 1953, colorful, complete . **225.00**

    Magazine, *Life,* April 7, 1952, cover article, black and white photo cover, 172 pgs. **35.00**

Peck, Gregory, pin, 1" d, litho tin disk, black and white photo, silver rim, reverse with name and fold over tab with straight pin, English, c1950 . . . . **20.00**

Presley, Elvis

    Charm Bracelet, 6" l, gold colored metal link, four metal charms, picture frame, guitar, hound dog, and heart, c1956 . . . . **150.00**

    Pin, 1¾" l brass guitar, simulated white mother–of–pearl inlay on face, yellow paint, six tiny green rhinestones, small brass frame with black and white photo inscribed "Best Wishes From Elvis Presley," c1950 . . . . **125.00**

Radnor, Gilda, paper doll book, 8½ x
11″, 12 pgs, Avon Books, copyright
1979 Above Average Productions,
Inc, unused. 40.00
Rogers, Roy
Bank, Roy on reared Trigger, porce-
lain, sgd "Roy Rogers and Trigger"   250.00
Clothing, sweatshirt, child's, Roy and
Trigger graphics, c1950 . . . .   65.00
Toy, Roy Fit It Stagecoach, figure,
Bullet, two horses, and complete
accessories. 75.00
Yo–Yo, illus of Roy and Trigger on
side, unplayed with. 15.00
Rogers, Will, rolled penny, portrait, star
designs, issued c1935 to commemo-
rate death in plane crash 20.00
Rooney, Mickey
Post Card, showing home, c1940   .   7.50
Washboard, wood and tin 20.00
Sinatra, Frank, pin, 2½″ h, diecut wood,
brass pin, black-and-white face, red
accents, c1940, minor wear 25.00
Temple, Shirley
Children's Book, *Shirley Temple's
Birthday Book,* Dell Publishing Co,
c1934, soft cover, 24 pgs, unused
condition. 100.00
Handkerchiefs, Little Colonel, boxed
set of three 195.00
Magazine, Hollywood, June 1936, full
color cov of Shirley holding bouquet
of flowers, article titled "Is Shirley A
Poor Little Rich Girl," 74 pgs, other
mid 1930s movie stars 35.00
Turner, Lana
Autograph, black and white glossy
photo, 8 x 10″, c1940, black ink
inscription 35.00
Pin, 1″ d, litho tin disk, black and white
photo, silver rim, reverse with name
and fold over tab with straight pin,
English, c1950. . . . .   18.00
Vallee, Rudy, adv, clapper, wood   . . .   50.00
Valentino, Rudy, book, *Sons of the
Sheik,* Photo Play movie edition, orig
dust jacket 50.00
Young, Alan, photo, 8 x 10″, black and
white glossy, boldly sgd "Our Best To
Patricia Ann/Alan Young," early
1960s. 50.00

CHELSEA

History: Chelsea is a fine English porcelain designed to compete with Meissen. The factory be-

gan operating in the Chelsea area of London, England, in the 1740s. Chelsea products are divided
into four periods: (1) early period, 1740s, with incised triangle and raised anchor mark; (2) the
1750s, with red raised anchor mark; (3) the 1760s,
the gold anchor period; and (4) The Derby period
from 1770–83. In 1924 a large number of the molds
and models of figurines were found at the Spode-
Copeland Works, and many items were brought
back into circulation.

Reference: Susan and Al Bagdade, *Warman's
English & Continental Pottery & Porcelain, 2nd Edition,* Wallace-Homestead, 1991.

Figurine, 6½″ h, $500.00.

Bowl, 8¾″ d, swirled ribs, scalloped,
floral and foliage dec. 575.00
Candlesticks, pr, 7½″, figural, draped
putti, sitting on tree stump holding
flower, scroll molded base encircled in
puce, gilt, wax pan. 825.00
Cup and Saucer, multicolored exotic
birds, white ground gold anchor mark,
c1765. . . . .   750.00
Dish
6³⁄₁₆″, flower sprays and leaves, silver
form molded edge, red anchor
mark, c1755, price for pair 350.00
6½″, Flying Dog, Kakiemon style, ten
sided, red anchor mark, c1755 . . .   1,250.00
Figure, 14″ h, fruit and flower sellers with
animals,   multicolored   clothing,
shaped socles, gold anchor mark, late
18th C, price for pair 600.00
Plate
8½″ d, multicolored floral design, scalloped rim, gold anchor mark 450.00
9″ d, botanical, Hans Sloane type, red
anchor period, c1756, price for set
of six. 4,675.00
Scent Bottle, 3″ h, cupid at altar, applied
florals, c1760 . . . .   2,400.00

Soup Plate, 9⅜", octagonal, center painted with iron–red and gold phoenix in flight, yellow breasted blue and iron–red pheasant, turquoise rock, iron–red, blue, turquoise, and gold flowering tree, ridged rim, iron–red floral border, red anchor mark, c1753 **2,000.00**

Teapot, 6¼" h, multicolored floral dec, D and anchor mark. **750.00**

"CHELSEA" GRANDMOTHER'S WARE

History: "Chelsea" Grandmother's ware identifies a group of tableware with raised reliefs of either grapes, sprigs of flowers, or thistles on a white ground. Some examples are lustered.

The ware was made in the first half of the 19th century in England's Staffordshire district by a large number of manufacturers. The "Chelsea" label is a misnomer but commonly accepted in the antiques field.

Pitcher, Scrolls and Medallions pattern, light purple dec, white ground, 6¾" h, $65.00.

Bowl, 8" d, Grape **30.00**
Butter Pat, 4" d, Sprig **12.00**
Cake Plate
  9" d, Sprig **35.00**
  10" d, Grape **40.00**
Creamer
  Grape **30.00**
  Sprig **50.00**
Cup
  Grape **22.50**
  Thistle **20.00**
Egg Cup, Grape **25.00**
Milk Pitcher, Sprig **50.00**
Plate
  7" d, Sprig **18.00**
  8" d, Grape **20.00**
  9" d, Sprig **30.00**

Ramekin, blue, underplate, Sprig . . . **12.00**
Sauce Dish, Sprig **5.00**
Saucer, Thistle **7.50**
Sugar, cov, 7½" w, Sprig **110.00**
Teapot, 10" h, octagonal, Grape luster **125.00**

CHILDREN'S BOOKS

History: Because there is a bit of the child in all of us, collectors always have been attracted to children's books. In the 19th century, books were popular gifts for children, with most of the children's classics written and published during this time. These books were treasured and often kept throughout a lifetime.

Developments in printing made it possible to include more attractive black-and-white illustrations and colorplates. The work of artists and illustrators has added value beyond the text itself.

References: Barbara Bader, *American Picture Books From Noah's Ark To The Beast Within,* Macmillan, 1976; E. Lee Baumgarten, *Price Guide For Children's & Illustrated Books For The Years 1880–1950, 1993 Edition, Sorted by Artist,* published by author, 1993; Margery Fisher, *Who's Who In Children's Books: A Treasury of the Familiar Characters of Childhood,* Holt, Rinehart and Winston, 1975; Virginia Haviland, *Children's Literature, A Guide To Reference Sources,* Library of Congress, 1966, first supplement 1972, second supplement 1977, third supplement 1982; Bettina Hurlimann, *Three Centuries Of Children's Books In Europe,* translated and edited by Brian W. Alderson, World, 1968; Cornelia L. Meigs (ed.), *A Critical History of Children's Literature,* 2nd ed., Macmillan, 1969.

Periodicals: *Book Source Monthly,* PO Box 567, Cazenovia, NY 13035; *Martha's KidLit Newsletter,* PO Box 1488, Ames, IA 50010.

Libraries: Free Library of Philadelphia, PA; brary of Congress, Washington, D.C.; Pierpont Morgan Library, New York, NY; Toronto Public Library, Toronto, Ontario, Canada.

Advisor: Joyce Magee.

Additional Listings: See *Warman's Americana & Collectibles* for more examples and an extensive listing of collectors' clubs.

Note: Abbreviations: dj = dust jacket; wraps = paper covers; pgs = pages; unp = unpaged; n.d. = no date; teg = top edges gilt.

Alexander, Lloyd, *The Castle of Llyr,* Evaline Ness, illus, Holt, Rinehart & Winston, 1966, 201 pgs, dj, 1st ed, sgd by author **35.00**
Annie & Willie's Prayer Book, Snow, 1885, leather cov. **12.00**
Appleton, Victor, *Tom Swift Among the Fire Fighters,* Grossett & Dunlap, 1921, 214 pgs. **9.00**
Bancroft, Laura, *Sugar–Loaf Mountain,* 1906 . . . . **125.00**

Kellogg's Funny Jungleland Moving Pictures, fold out, three sections, movable flaps, © 1909, published by W. K. Kellogg, $18.00.

Bartman, Mark, *Yank in France,* Albert Whitman, 1946, dj 28.00

Bobbsey Twins at Meadowbrook, 1915 . . . . . . 12.00

Brandeis, Madeline, *Mitz and Fritz of Germany,* Grossett & Dunlap, 1933, 160 pgs 4.00

Brown, Margaret Wise, *The Indoor Noisy Book,* Scott, 1942, 44 pgs 14.00

Burgess, Thornton W, *A Merry Coasting Party,* Platt & Munk, 1940 . . . . 25.00

Chadwick, Lester, *Baseball Joe, Champion of the League,* Cupples & Leon, 1925, 246 pgs, dj 9.00

Chapman, Allen, *Fred Fenton the Pitcher,* Cupples & Leon, 1913, 206 pgs, dj 7.00

Clarde, J Erskine, *Chatterbox,* J, Esxes & Lauriat, 1896, 412 pgs 16.00

Cyr, Ellen M, *The Children's Second Reader,* Ginn, 1894, 197 pgs 12.00

Curtis, Alice Turner, *Little Maid of Quebec,* Penn Publishing Co, 1936, 224 pgs, dj 8.00

Denslow, W. W., *New Wizard of Oz,* 1904 . . . . 130.00

Drake, Robert L, *The Boy Allies At Jutland,* A L Burt, 1917, 255 pgs, dj, Navy series 6.00

Elson, William H & William S Gray, *Elson–Gray Basic Readers–Book Two,* Scott, Foresman, 1936, 240 pgs . . . 5.00

Finley, Martha, *Elsie Dinsmore,* Donohue, c1920, 395 pgs 10.00

Fryer, Jane Eayre, *The Mary Frances Storybook,* Edwin John Prittie, illus, Winston, 1921, 328 pgs 45.00

Garis, Howard R, *The Curly Tops and Their Playmates,* Cupples & Leon, 1922, 246 pgs 3.00

Grimm, Jacob and Wilhelm, *Grimm's Fairy Tales,* Koerner & Hayes, 1896, full page of litho plates 30.00

Gruelle, Johnny
Little Brown Bear, 1920 . . . . 40.00
Magical Land of Noom, 1922 . . . . . 225.00

Hughes, Thomas, *Tom Brown's School Days,* Dodd Mead, 1900, 339 pgs . . . 10.00

Irwin, Ihez Haynes, *Marda's Little Houseboat,* Grossett & Dunlap, 1943, 207 pgs 13.00

James, Will, *Sun Up, Tales of the Cow Camps,* Junior Literary Guild, 1931, 342 pgs 40.00

Keene, Carolyn, *Mystery of the Brass Bound Trunk,* Russell H Tandy, illus, Grossett & Dunlap, 1940, 220 pgs, dj 10.00

Lenski, Lois, *The Little Farm,* Oxford University Press, 1942, unp, dj, 1st ed 18.00

Mayhew, Ralph and Johnston Burooes, *The Pie Party Book, the 5th Bubble Book,* Rhoda Chase, illus, Harper & Columbia Graphophone Co, 1919, 15 pgs, 3 records 30.00

Miller, Olive Beaupre, *Nursery Friends from France,* Maud & Miska Petersham, illus, Book House for Children, 1927, 191 pgs 35.00

Montgomery, Frances Trego, *Billy Wiskers' Kids,* W H Fry, illus, Saalfield, 1903, 134 pgs, dj 25.00

Mother Goose, Mary Lafetya Russell, illus, Sam Gabriel, 1911, unp 15.00

Newberry, Clare Turlay, *Mittens,* Harper, 1936, dj, 1st ed, unp 50.00

Only True Mother Goose, Boston, 1905, 100 pgs, 1st ed 37.50

Packer, Eleanor Lewis, *A Day with Our Gang,* Whitman, 1929, unp 18.00

Perkins, Lucy Fitch, *The Puritan Twins,* Houghton Mifflin, 1921, 178 pgs 16.00

Peter Pan & Wendy, Scribner, 1911, 1st ed 40.00

Pyle, Howard, *Otto of the Silver Hand,* Scribner, 1906, 173 pgs 30.00

Pyle, Katherine, *The Christmas Angel,* Little, Brown, 1900, 136 pgs, 1st ed . 40.00

Sidney, Margaret, *Five Little Peppers Grown Up,* Mente, illus, D Lathrop, 1892, 527 pgs, 1st ed 75.00

Spyri, Johanna, *Heidi,* Frances Brundage, illus, Saalfield, 1924, 307 pgs . 18.00

Sutton, Margaret, *The Name on the Bracelet,* Pelagie Doane, illus, Grossett & Dunlap, 1940, 216 pgs, dj 10.00

Thompson, Ruth, *Hungry Tiger of Oz,* Reilly & Lee, 1926 . . . . 125.00

Ungerer, Tomi, *The Mellops Strike Oil,* Harper, 1958, 32 pgs, dj, 1st ed 23.00

Watson, Jane Werner, *The True Story of Smokey the Bear,* Feodor Rojankovsky, illus, Golden Press, 1955, unp, 1st ed **10.00**

Waugh, Ida, *Holly Berries,* 1881, 40 color prints **30.00**

White, Stewart Edward, *Daniel Boone: Wilderness Scout,* James Daugherty, illus, Garden City, 1922, 274 pgs ... **15.00**

Wiggin, Kate Douglas, *The New Chronicles of Rebecca,* F C Yohn, illus, Houghton Mifflin, 1907, 278 pgs, 1st ed **22.00**

CHILDREN'S FEEDING DISHES

History: Unlike toy dishes meant for play, children's feeding dishes are the items actually used in the feeding of a child. Their colorful designs of animals, nursery rhymes, and children's activities are meant to appeal to the child and make mealtimes fun. Many plates have a unit to hold hot water, thus keeping the food warm.

Although glass and porcelain examples from the late 19th and early 20th centuries are most popular, collectors are beginning to seek some of the plastic examples from the 1920s to 1940s, especially those with Disney designs on them.

References: Doris Lechler, *Children's Glass Dishes, China and Furniture,* Vol. I (1983), Vol. II (1986, 1993 value update), Collector Books; Dana G. Morykan and Harry L. Rinker, *Warman's Country Antiques & Collectibles, Second Edition,* Wallace–Homestead, 1994; Margaret and Kenn Whitmyer, *Collector's Encyclopedia of Children's Dishes: An Illustrated Value Guide,* Collector Books, 1993.

Bone China, multicolored decal dec, white ground, marked "BCM/Nelson Ware, Made in England," 5¾" d, $20.00.

Baby Dish, Little Bo Peep, Liverpool . **60.00**

Bowl
6¾" d, Beach Baby, marked "P. K. Unity, Germany" **40.00**
9" d, Sing A Song of Sixpence **45.00**

Breakfast Set, plate, bowl, and creamer, white, blue design of children playing **75.00**

Christening Mug, sterling silver, hallmarked, "R. Redgrave, R. A.," London, c1865 .... **500.00**

Creamer
Bunnykins, marked "Royal Doulton" **40.00**
Buster Brown **50.00**

Creamer, elephant juggling **35.00**

Cup, swan, milk glass, white **35.00**

Cup and Saucer
Boy, girl, and bunny, red mark, Germany.................. **12.00**
Century of Progress, nursery rhyme dec, marked "Shenango China," 1933..................... **48.00**
Old Mother Hubbard, marked "Royal Doulton" **50.00**
Sand Baby, marked "Royal Bayreuth" **75.00**

Egg Cup, Bunnykins, marked "Royal Doulton". **10.00**

Feeding Dish
Buddy Tucker with bear **100.00**
Little girl with two puppies, marked "Royal Baby Plate, Patd 2–1905" . **75.00**
Two girls dancing with butterflies, sgd "Nippon". **105.00**

Mug, 3" h, Farmer's Arms, God Speed the Blough, marked "B & L, England" **65.00**

Plate
Kate Greenaway illus, children playing, 4½" d **75.00**
Little Bo Peep, marked "Shenango China" **40.00**
Sunbonnet Babies, Royal Bayreuth, blue mark, babies sewing, 6½" d.. **165.00**
Uncle Wiggily, 8½" d **50.00**

Sugar, Bunnykins, marked "Royal Doulton". **20.00**

Warming Dish, 8" d, red circus decals, white ground, divided, marked "Hazel Atlas". **20.00**

CHILDREN'S NURSERY ITEMS

History: The nursery is a place where children live in a miniature world. Things come in two sizes. Child scale designates items actually used for the care, housing, and feeding of the child. Toy or doll scale denotes items used by the child in play and for creating a fantasy environment which copies that of an adult or his own.

Cheap labor and building costs during the Victorian era enabled the nursery to reach a high level of popularity. Most collectors focus on items from the 1880 to 1930 period.

References: Marguerite Fawdry, *An International Survey of Rocking Horse Manufacture,* New Cavendish Books, 1992; Gene Florence, *The Collector's Encyclopedia of Akro Agate Glassware, Revised Edition,* Collector Books, 1975, 1992 value update; Roger and Claudia Hardy, *The Complete Line of Akro Agate: Marbles, General Line and Children's Dishes, With Prices,* published by authors, 1992; Doris Lechler, *Children's Glass Dishes, China and Furniture,* Vol. I (1983), Vol. II (1986, 1993 value update), Collector Books; Doris Lechler, *English Toy China,* Antique Publications, 1989; Doris Lechler, *French and German Dolls, Dishes and Accessories,* Antique Publications, 1991; Doris Lechler, *Toy Glass,* Antique Publications, 1989; Anthony and Peter Miall, *The Victorian Nursery Book,* Pantheon Books, 1980; Patricia Mullins, *The Rocking Horse: A History of Moving Toy Horses,* New Cavendish Books, 1992; Lorraine May Punchard, *Child's Play,* published by author, 1982; Lorraine May Punchard, *Playtime Kitchen Items and Table Accessories,* published by author, 1993; Tony Stevenson and Eva Marsden, *Rocking Horses: The Collector's Guide To Selecting, Restoring, and Enjoying New and Vintage Rocking Horses,* Courage Books, 1993; Margaret and Kenn Whitmyer, *Collector's Encyclopedia of Children's Dishes,* Collector Books, 1993.

Additional Listings: Children's Books, Children's Feeding Dishes, Children's Toy Dishes, Dolls, Games, Miniatures, and Toys.

Bed, 29 x 48 x 30½", turned posts and legs, four rails with lattice slats, solid board bottom, old green paint over red	75.00
Bonnet, crocheted, white, Popcorn Stitch pattern	18.00
Book, *A Rabbit's Tale,* Nister, four color lithos	22.00
Booties, Victorian, leather, blue	30.00
Carriage, Victorian, ornate, blue and cream paint, orig upholstery, fringe around top, 1860.	330.00
Chair, wooden, Kutztown adv on seat	175.00
Chamber Pot, 8" d, 4¾" h, blue and white Oriental scene	165.00
Christening Dress, white, 19th C	65.00
Coat, 25" l, baby, 1902	75.00
Cradle, 37" l, walnut, dovetailed, cutout rockers, shaped sides, hand holds	225.00
Dress, child's, Mary Hartline tag	10.00
Highchair, Victorian, oak, pressed back, cane seat, converts to stroller.	400.00
Mug, glass, raised alphabet, girl looking at Christmas tree, and boy at desk scene.	125.00
Nursing Bottle, glass, blue	20.00
Quilt	
40 x 58", nursery rhyme characters, embroidered names	100.00
45 x 37", crib, Amish, cotton, appliqued, four geometric cross motifs, chain, foliate vine, and vertical bar quilting, pale gray and black, Ohio, c1930	350.00
Rattle	
Celluloid, bell shape	15.00
Wood, 14" l, turned, carved "A T Junior"	60.00
Record Book, baby, eight color lithos, Nister, 1912	40.00
Rocker, 26" h, ladder back, three slats, turned arms and finials, old dark finish	150.00

Rocking Horse, wood head and legs painted red, red burlap covered straw filled body, red felt and leather saddle, hair mane, Cebasco, Germany, $975.00.

Rocking Horse, 40" h, 34" l, wood head, straw filled body with red burlap cov, wood legs, red paint, red felt and leather saddle, hair mane, marked "Cebasco, Made in Germany"	975.00
Sled, 27½" l, Victorian, maple and steamed oak, red center board with stenciled flowers and transfer portrait of Indian, marked "No 52, Paris Mfg Co, So Paris Maine"	1,000.00
Slop Jar, blue, Dutch children dec	75.00
Suitcase, Little Miss Muffet	60.00
Tea Set, 14 pcs, three 5¾" plates, 5⅝" teapot, 3¾" waste bowl, sugar, and four cups and saucers, ironstone, red transfer of Punch and Judy.	170.00
Toy	
Doll Baby Carriage, 28" l, 31" h, wood, wire, and wicker, red finish, black leatherized hood	110.00
Doll Cradle, 19" l, pine, painted dec, old brown graining	165.00
Pull, 14" l, Scrappy & Margy, wood and metal, musical, figures with full color litho paper image	250.00
Tricycle, wood frame and wheels, black striping, orig red paint	500.00

Tumbler, aluminum, colored dec	12.00
Wash Bowl, blue, Dutch children dec	60.00

CHILDREN'S TOY DISHES

History: Dishes made for children often served a dual purpose—playthings and a means of learning social graces. Dish sets came in two sizes. The first was for actual use by the child when entertaining friends. The second, a smaller size than the first, was for use with dolls.

Children's dish sets often were made as a sideline to a major manufacturing line either as a complement to the family service or as a way to use up the last of the day's batch of materials. The artwork of famous illustrators, such as Palmer Cox, Kate Greenaway, and Rose O'Neill, can be found on porcelain sets.

References: Gene Florence, *The Collector's Encyclopedia of Akro Agate Glassware, Revised Edition,* Collector Books, 1975, 1992 value update; Roger and Claudia Hardy, *The Complete Line of Akro Agate: Marbles, General Line and Children's Dishes, With Prices,* published by authors, 1992; Doris Lechler, *Children's Glass Dishes, China and Furniture,* Vol. I (1983), Vol. II (1986, 1993 value update), Collector Books; Doris Lechler; *English Toy China,* Antique Publications, 1989; Doris Lechler, *French and German Dolls, Dishes and Accessories,* Antique Publications, 1991; Doris Lechler, *Toy Glass,* Antique Publications, 1989; Lorraine May Punchard, *Child's Play,* published by author, 1982; Lorraine May Punchard, *Playtime Kitchen Items and Table Accessories,* published by author, 1993; Margaret and Kenn Whitmyer, *Collector's Encyclopedia of Children's Dishes,* Collector Books, 1993.

Collectors' Club: Toy Dish Collectors, PO Box 351, Camilus, NY 13031.

Porcelain, Japanese tea set, 11 pcs, $45.00.

Akro Agate
Tea Set, large octagon, closed handles, blue creamer, teapot, and sugar, white lids, green plates and cups, yellow saucers, price for seventeen piece set	110.00
Water Service, Stippled Band, amber, price for pitcher and six tumblers	125.00

China
Tea Set
Nippon, white and pink trim, black silhouette of children playing, teapot, creamer, sugar, three cups, four saucers and plates, rising sun mark, price for sixteen piece set	210.00
Japanese, white ground, gold trim, little girl wheeling doll carriage, dog at side, teapot, four plates, cups and saucers, creamer, and sugar, price for seventeen piece set	170.00
Luster Ware, oval shaped pink luster, pink florals, raised scrolling, teapot, creamer, sugar, two cups and saucers, German, price for eight piece set	95.00

Depression Glass
Set
Homespun, pink, complete, orig box	375.00
Laurel, red trimmed ivory, complete, orig box	335.00
Enameled Glass, lemonade set, multicolored enameled flowers, pitcher, six tumblers	400.00
English Softpaste, tea set, Sprig pattern, 4" h teapot, sugar, creamer, four cups and saucers, imp mark "Adams," 19th C, price for eleven piece set	200.00

Milk Glass
Punch Set, White Rose, lemon stain, price for punch bowl and six cups	200.00
Stein, Monk	20.00

Table Set, cov butter, creamer, cov sugar, and spooner
Cloud Band, worn dec, minor chips, sugar lid missing	150.00
Tappan	90.00

Pattern Glass
Berry Set, Lacy Daisy, price for seven piece set	65.00
Cake Stand, Baby Thumbprint, 3" d	185.00
Candlesticks, pr, Star, Cambridge	25.00

Condiment Set
English Hobnail, emerald green, cruet, open salt, cloverleaf tray	75.00
Hickman, clear, cruet with stopper, open salt, pepper shaker, cloverleaf shaped tray	75.00
Punch Bowl, Oval Star	35.00
Punch Set, Thumbelina, bowl, four cups, sun colored	85.00

Sugar, cov, Oval Star	25.00
Table Set, cov butter, creamer, cov sugar, spooner	
Oval Star	125.00
Whirligig	95.00
Water Set, Rex, (Fancy Cut), sun colored, price for pitcher and six tumblers	85.00

Tin

Baking Set, Sunny Suzy, #260, Wolverine	150.00
Dinner Set, four dinner plates, dessert plates, cups, and saucers, strawberry dec, white ground, marked "J Chein"	35.00
Tea Set, blue and white Dutch scene, six cups, saucers, plates, teapot, and tray, Wolverine	50.00

CHRISTMAS ITEMS

History: The celebration of Christmas dates back to Roman times. Several customs associated with modern Christmas celebrations are traced back to early pagan rituals.

Father Christmas, believed to have evolved in Europe in the 7th century, was a combination of the pagan god Thor, who judged and punished the good and bad, and St. Nicholas, the generous Bishop of Myra. Kris Kringle originated in Germany and was brought to America by the Germans and Swiss who settled in Pennsylvania in the late 18th century.

In 1822 Clement C. Moore wrote "A Visit From St. Nicholas" and developed the character of Santa Claus into what we know today. Thomas Nast did a series of drawings for *Harper's Weekly* from 1863 until 1886 and further solidified the character and appearance of Santa Claus.

References: Robert Brenner, *Christmas Past,* Schiffer Publishing, 1986; Robert Brenner, *Christmas Through The Decades,* Schiffer Publishing, 1993; George Johnson, *Christmas Ornaments, Lights & Decorations,* Collector Books, 1987, 1990 value update; Helaine Fendelman and Jeri Schwartz, *The Official Price Guide To Holiday Collectibles,* House of Collectibles, 1991; Polly and Pam Judd, *Santa Dolls & Figurines Price Guide: Antique to Contemporary,* Hobby House Press, 1992; Robert M. Merck, *Deck The Halls,* Abbeville Press, 1992; Mary Morrison, *Snow Babies, Santas and Elves: Collecting Christmas Bisque Figures,* Schiffer Publishing, 1993; Dana G. Morykan and Harry L. Rinker, *Warman's Country Antiques & Collectibles, Second Edition,* Wallace–Homestead, 1994; Lissa Bryan–Smith and Richard Smith, *Christmas Collectibles: A Guide To Selecting, Collecting, and Enjoying The Treasures of Christmas Past,* Chartwell Books, 1993; Margaret and Kenn Whitmyer, *Christmas Collectibles, Second Edition,* Collector Books, 1994.

Periodicals: *Golden Glow of Christmas Past,* 6401 Winsdale St., Golden Valley, MN 55427; *Ornament Collector,* RR #1, Canton, IL 61520.

Additional Listings: See *Warman's Americana & Collectibles* for more examples.

Advisors: Lissa L. Bryan–Smith and Richard M. Smith.

Candy Container, Belsnickle, papier mâché, light blue mica coat, black base, missing feather tree, 5″ h, $375.00.

Candy Container, 4″ h, Santa	
Composition, red felt suit, rabbit fur beard, sitting on log pile, bottom opens, Germany	150.00
Glass, metal closure on bottom ...	100.00
Children's Books	
Denslow's Night Before Christmas, MA Donohue & Co, Chicago, 1902, hardback.................	30.00
Old Saint Nicholas, unknown publisher and author, color hard cover, black-and-white illus..........	15.00
The Night Before Christmas, Father Tuck's Nursery Tale Series, soft cover, color lithograph pictures ...	25.00
Figure	
Deer, 4½″ h, composition, brown wood legs, metal antlers, Germany	45.00
Santa	
2″ h, chenille, green, composition face, Japan	10.00
5½″ h, red suit, composition face, on chimney	70.00
8¼″ h, felt coat, composition legs and boots, standing, basket on back	400.00
18″ h, three dimensional, wood, painted red and white	250.00
Game, Game of Christmas Jewel, McLoughlin Bros, full color litho box, 1899	400.00

Light Bulb
  House, 2½″ h, pink and blue, Japan   **10.00**
  Santa, 3″ h, leg in chimney, Japan . **25.00**
  Street Lamp, 2″ h, Japan **12.00**
Light Set, celluloid, assorted figures,
  large string **150.00**
Navitity Scene
  German, paper scene, each figure
    mounted on wood **40.00**
  Italian, 4″ h, wooden scene **18.00**
  Swedish, 6″ h, lithograph paper fold-
    out, 1930s. **15.00**

**Glass Beads, multicolored, various
shapes and sizes, 100″ l strand, $60.00.**

Ornament
  Angel
    Chromolithograph, 7″ h, Dresden
      wings. **80.00**
    Wax, large **85.00**
  Basket, 3″ h, metal **35.00**
  Basket of Fruit, art glass, oranges . **85.00**
  Boy, 4″ h, cotton batting, white, com-
    position face, brown cotton shoes,
    Germany. **120.00**
  Clown Head, glass, ruffled collar . . **45.00**
  Doll Carriage, 3″ h, three dimensional,
    gold, Dresden **125.00**
  Father Christmas, 9″ h, chromolitho-
    graph, cotton batting coat **150.00**
  Fish, 5″ h, glass, blue, red trim . . . **90.00**
  Girl, 4″ h, Kewpie type, composition
    face, white legs, orange skirt. **150.00**
  House, glass, elf peeking out door,
    gold, red trim. **50.00**
  Indian, 3¾″ h, blown glass, black hair,
    red and yellow clothing. **130.00**
  Kugel, bunch of grapes, purple and
    blue **85.00**
  Parrot, glass, blue, red, and silver . **45.00**

Santa, 4″ h, cotton batting, tomato red
  suit, black trim, legs, and boots . . . **40.00**
Slipper, 5″ h, flat, gold, netting and tin-
  sel trim, Dresden **40.00**
Snake, 7″ l, glass, orange, silvered **20.00**
Windmill, glass, blue **8.00**
Wine Keg, glass, red and silver, flower
  dec. **20.00**
Pinback Button
  Health for All, ½″ d, National Tuber-
    culosis Assoc symbol and Santa
    head. **5.00**
  Joe The Motorists Friend, 1½″ d,
    Santa head, pack of toys, sus-
    pended red ribbon and bell **10.00**
  Merry Christmas, Butler Bros Co, 1¼″
    d, Santa head, star background. . . **8.00**
Putz Items
  Animal
    Camel, 7″ h, composition, brown,
      wood legs, stamped "Germany" **30.00**
    Cow, 4″ h, celluloid, brown, Japan **10.00**
    Donkey 3″ h, composition, hide cov,
      wood legs, German. **25.00**
    Sheep, 3″ h, composition, wool
      fleece, wood legs, paper collar,
      German **35.00**
  Fence
    Cast iron, ten sections, dark green,
      gate. **185.00**
    Wood, four sections, blue, picket
      type, gate. **45.00**
  Log Cabin, 5″ h, white mica roof,
    marked "Germany". **18.00**
  Village, 5″ h, lithograph paper, five
    buildings, USA. **25.00**
Puzzle
  Santa Claus Picture Puzzle, Parker
    Bros, color litho box **280.00**
  Santa Claus Scroll Puzzle, Mc-
    Loughlin Bros, full color litho box,
    1899. **350.00**
Roly Poly, 6″ h, Santa, red, green belt **250.00**
Tree
  4″ h, brush, green, white snow, red
    wood base. **5.00**
  8″ h, paper, green, USA **15.00**
  50″ h, feather, painted wood base,
    mounted on clockwork revolving
    platform, stenciled "Hohner Har-
    monicas" on each side **200.00**
  76″ h, feather, mounted on wood base **400.00**

CIGAR CUTTERS

History: Counter and pocket cigar cutters were
used at the end of the 19th and the beginning of
the 20th centuries. They were a popular form of
advertising. Pocket-type cigar cutters often were a
fine piece of jewelry attached to a watch chain.

COUNTERTOP

Advertising
    East Rock Cigars, glass top, mountain
      scene **80.00**
    Gentlemen's Preference, El Santo,
      glass base. **115.00**
    Great Ohio 5¢ Cigar, cast iron, pig
      shape **425.00**
    Plug Tobacco, iron, star, dated 1885   **65.00**
    Strauss & Hamburger, Chicago, oak,
      match holder, lighter, cigar cutter,
      and container, 7½ x 11" **100.00**
Figural
    Bulldog, cast iron, desk type **40.00**
    Donkey, cast iron, tail plunger cutter   **200.00**
    Horse's head, bridle, flowing mane,
      SP, 5¾" **100.00**

**Pocket, pistol, nickel plated, gutta–per-
cha handle, English, 3⅜" l, $150.00.**

POCKET

Advertising
    New Bachelor, brass **20.00**
    Swift & Co, watch chain **45.00**
Figural
    Bakelite, log, wood grain design   . .   **20.00**
    Silver metal, dog's head, 5¾" l   . . .   **65.00**
Knife Type
    Brass
      Girl on potty **90.00**
      Revolver, black onyx handle, 3½"   **150.00**
    Ivory, boar tusk, sterling silver mount   **200.00**
    Scissors Type, sterling silver, floral   . .   **25.00**

CIGAR STORE FIGURES

History: Cigar store figures were familiar sights
in front of cigar stores and tobacco shops from
about 1840. Figural themes included Sir Walter Ra-
leigh, sailors, Punch figures, and ladies, with Indians being the most popular.

Most figures were carved in wood, although figures also were made in metal and papier–mâché

for a short time. Most carvings were life size or
slightly smaller and brightly painted. A coating of
tar acted as a preservative against the weather. Of
the few surviving figures, only a small number have
their original bases. Most replacements are due to
years of wear and usage by dogs.

Use of figures declined when local ordinances
were passed requiring shopkeepers to move the
figures inside at night. This soon became too much
trouble, and other forms of advertising developed.

Reference: A. W. Pendergast and W. Porter
Ware, *Cigar Store Figures,* Lightner Publishing
Corp., 1953.

**Indian, carved and painted wood,
$770.00. Photograph courtesy of Skin-
ner, Inc.**

Black Boy, 56" h, wood, carved tobacco
    leaf skirt, one movable arm, other held
    display, tar pitch covered, 1870–1900   **8,500.00**
Indian
    Chief, 72" h, papier mache, detailed,
      bold colors, iron bracket in upraised
      hand, sq base **5,000.00**
    Maiden, 28" h, pine, carved and
      painted, wearing three feathered
      headdress, standing on circular
      base, missing one arm, c1870. . . .   **3,575.00**
    Princess, 79" h, pine, carved and
      painted, feathered headdress and
      sash, red and green costume,
      carved and yellow painted fringe,
      blue leggings and moccasins, one
      foot raised on tobacco block, holds

tobacco leaves and pink rose in
right hand, platform base, c1875 . . **10,450.00**
Warrior, 108" h, holding staff in left
hand, hatchet in right, polychrome
dec. **11,100.00**
Punch, 50" h, pine, carved and painted,
holds bunch of cigars in one hand,
other hand raised, circular base, early
20th C **2,750.00**
Racetrack Tout, 78" h, holds can in left
hand, offers race sheets in right, four
cigars in jacket pocket, black top hat,
repainted, stood in front of Opera
House Restaurant, Nantucket, 19th C **42,500.00**

CINNABAR

History: Cinnabar is a ware made of numerous
layers of a heavy mercuric sulfide and is often referred to as vermillion, the red hue in which it is
most commonly found. It was carved into boxes,
buttons, snuff bottles, and vases. The best examples were made in China.

Reference: Gloria and Robert Mascarelli, *Warman's Oriental Antiques,* Wallace-Homestead,
1992.

**Snuff Bottle, lapis lazuli top, late 19th
C, 2¾" h, $300.00.**

Box, cov, 12" d, 6½" h, compressed
globular, deeply carved scene of gentlemen in garden, pavilion, rocky out-
croppings and trees, base with roundel scenes of children in landscapes,
peonies and foliate meander ground,
raised foot with key fret pattern below
band of stylized lotus lappets, 19th C **880.00**
Cigarette Case, 6⅛" l, rect hinged top,
cinnabar lacquer and ivory, carved
courtly scene, key fret band border . . **350.00**
Dish, 14½" l, carved, three maidens in

palace courtyard scene, lotus scrolls
on sides, barbed and lobed rim. **225.00**
Ginger Jar, 9" h, ivory, marked "China,"
price for pair **650.00**
Plate, 7" d, carved village scene **185.00**
Snuff Bottle, 3½" h, carved scene, figures in garden, carved matching stop-
per, c1825 . . . . **250.00**
Sweetmeat, 4½ x 9 x 9", carved, open-
work cov, eight Buddhist Emblems,
latticework platform galleried base,
diaper ground **1,320.00**
Table Screen, 22¼" h, figural scene with
monk rowing boat, reverse with three
dragons above rock, flower scroll bor-
der, stand. **300.00**
Vase, 12¼" h, six lobed pear shape,
carved with flowering plants, flower
scrolls at neck, 19th C **200.00**

CLAMBROTH GLASS

History: Clambroth glass is a semiopaque, gray-
ish-white glass which resembles the color of the
broth from clams. Pieces are found in both a
smooth finish and a rough sandy finish. The Sandwich Glass Co. and other manufacturers made
clambroth glass.

Pickle Dipper, 9½" l, $28.00.

Barber Bottle, "Witch Hazel" in red
letters. **65.00**
Candlesticks, pr
7¼" h, hexagonal petal top, Sandwich **225.00**
8¾" h, reeded, scalloped base . . . **100.00**
Ewer, 10⅞" h, green applied handle and
band, pewter fittings **55.00**
Ladle, 9½" l **40.00**
Lamp Shade, sgd "Northwood" **30.00**
Mug, Lacy Medallion pattern, souvenir **35.00**
Pomade Jar, 3¾" h, bear, made for F B
Strouse, NY **375.00**

Salt, master, Sawtooth pattern, Sandwich, c1850 .... **50.00**
Soap Dish, cov, orig insert, Robin and Wheat pattern.................. **100.00**
Talcum Shaker **25.00**
Toothpick Holder, souvenir **35.00**

CLARICE CLIFF

History: Clarice Cliff, born on January 20, 1899, in Tunstall, Staffordshire, England, was one of the major pottery designers of the 20th century. At the age of thirteen, she left school and went to Lingard, Webster and Company, where she learned freehand painting. In 1916 Cliff was employed at A. J. Wilkinson's Royal Staffordshire Pottery, Burslem. She supplemented her in–house training by attending a local school of art in the evening.

In 1927 her employer sent her to study sculpture for a few months at the Royal College of Art in London. Upon returning, she was placed in charge of a small team of paintresses at the Newport Pottery, taken over by Wilkinson in 1920. Cliff designed a series of decorative motifs which were marketed as "Bizarre Ware" at the 1928 British Industries Fair.

Throughout the 1930s Cliff added new shapes and designs to the line. Her inspiration came from art magazines, books on gardening, and plants and flowers. Cliff and her Bizarre Girls gave painting demonstrations in the stores of leading English retailers. The popularity of the line increased.

World War II halted production. When the war ended, the hand painting of china was not renewed. In 1964 Midwinter bought the Wilkinson and Newport firms.

The original pattern names for some patterns have not survived. It is safe to rely on the hand-written or transfer printed name on the base. The Newport Pattern books in the Wilkinson's archives at the Hanley Library also are helpful.

Bizarre and Fantasque are not patterns. Rather, they are range names, Bizarre being used from 1928 to 1937 and Fantasque used from 1929 to 1934.

References: Susan and Al Bagdade, *Warman's English & Continental Pottery & Porcelain, 2nd Edition,* Wallace–Homestead, 1991; Leonard R. Griffin and Louis Meisel, *Clarice Cliff & The Bizarre Affair,* Thames and Hudson, 1988; Howard Watson, *Collecting Clarice Cliff,* Kevin Francis Publishing, 1988; Howard and Pat Watson, *The Colourful World of Clarice Cliff,* Kevin Francis Publishing, 1991.

Collectors' Club: Clarice Cliff Collectors Club, Fantasque House, Tennis Drive, The Park, Nottingham, NG7 1AE, England.

Reproduction Alert: In 1986 fake *Lotus* vases appeared in London and quickly spread worldwide. Very poor painting and patchy, uneven toffee–colored Honeyglaze are the clues to spotting them.

Collectors also must be alert to patterns being added to plain items bearing the "Clarice Cliff" backstamp.

In the summer of 1985, Midwinters produced a series of limited-edition reproductions to honor Clarice Cliff. They are clearly dated 1985 and contain a special amalgamated backstamp.

Ashtray, Tonquin pattern, Royal Staffordshire Pottery, Wilkinson, Ltd **35.00**
Biscuit Jar, 8" h, Honolulu **1,700.00**
Bowl, 10" d, Umbrellas pattern **900.00**
Condiment Set, Cabbage Flower pattern, conical shape **300.00**
Cracker Jar, 9¼" h, Bizarre ware, My Garden pattern, rattan handle. **355.00**
Creamer and Sugar, Bizarre ware, ovoid, hp landscape scene........ **250.00**
Cup and Saucer, Crows pattern **75.00**
Dinner Set
Service for six, Coral Fir pattern, includes candleholders **1,850.00**
Service for twelve, black, red, orange, and yellow dec bands on ivory. . . . **3,400.00**
Flower Frog, Autumn Crocus pattern . **340.00**
Honey Pot, Beehive, stripes **300.00**
Jam Pot, Melon cylindrical **400.00**

Jar, cov, Bizarre, yellow top, orange base, $200.00.

Marmalade Jar, cov, Capri pattern, orange dec **300.00**
Plaque, 13" d, Bizarre, orange, yellow, and lavender flowers **595.00**
Plate
6" d, Bizarre ware, stylized branches and foliage center design, black concentric rings **100.00**
10" d, Citrus Delicia **300.00**
Sugar Sifter, Crocus, conical **300.00**
Teapot, cov, Tonquin pattern, reddish brown..................... **100.00**
Vase
7" h, Geometric, cylinder **1,000.00**
8" h, Oranges, triangle **1,200.00**

12¼" h, Lovebirds, yellow ground, Newport Pottery mark. **225.00**
Vegetable Bowl, Tonquin pattern, reddish brown **35.00**

CLEWELL POTTERY

History: Charles Walter Clewell was first a metalworker and second a potter. In the early 1900s he opened a small shop in Canton, Ohio, to produce metal overlay pottery.

Metal on pottery was not a new idea, but Clewell was perhaps the first to completely mask the ceramic body with copper, brass, and "silvered" and "bronzed" metals. One result was a product whose patina added to the character of the piece over time.

Most of the wares are marked with a simple incised "CLEWELL" along with a code number. Because Clewell used pottery blanks from other firms, the names "Owens" or "Weller" are sometimes found.

Since Clewell operated on a small scale with little outside assistance, only a limited quantity of his artwork exists. He retired at the age of 79 in 1955, choosing not to reveal his technique to anyone else.

References: Paul Evans, *Art Pottery of the United States, 2nd Edition,* Feingold and Lewis Publishing Corp., 1987; Ralph and Terry Kovel, *The Kovels' Collector's Guide To American Art Pottery,* Crown Publishers, 1974.

Vase, relief floral design, twisted flask body, marked "Z/Owens/120," 4¾" h, $400.00.

Bowl, 8" d, blue–green patina **135.00**
Box, cov, round, riveted, imp "Clewell, Canton, OH". **275.00**
Flask, 4¾" h, twisted body, relief flower design, marked "Z/Owens/120" **425.00**
Pitcher, 5¾" h, copper clad Owens blank, green patina **165.00**
Punch Bowl Set, 12" pedestal bowl,

matching cups, riveted design, brown patina. **1,250.00**
Vase, 3¾" h, bronze over bisque, mat green patina, incised "Clewell 343," bronze cracks. **165.00**

CLIFTON POTTERY

History: The Clifton Art Pottery, Newark, New Jersey, was established by William A. Long, once associated with Londhuna Pottery, and Fred Tschirner, a chemist.

Production consisted of two major lines: Crystal Patina, which resembled true porcelain with a subdued crystal-like glaze, and Indian Ware or Western Influence, an adaptation of the American Indians' unglazed and decorated pottery with a high glazed black interior. Other lines included Robin's Egg Blue and Tirrube. Robin's Egg Blue is a variation of the crystal patina line but in blue-green instead of straw-colored hues and with a less prominent "crushed crystal" effect in the glaze. Tirrube is on a terra-cotta ground; features brightly colored, slip decorated flowers; and is often artist signed.

Marks are incised or impressed. Early pieces may be dated and shape numbers impressed. Indian wares are identified by tribes.

References: Paul Evans, *Art Pottery Of The United States, 2nd Edition,* Feingold & Lewis Publishing Corp., 1987; Ralph and Terry Kovel, *The Kovels' Collector's Guide To American Art Pottery,* Crown Publishers, 1974.

Bowl, Indian Ware, feather design, red clay body, glazed black int., c1906, 3½" d, $135.00.

Bowl, 8″ d, 5″ h, Indian Ware, small neck and rim, squatty bulbous body, dark brown bands, redware ground, Four Mile Ruin, AZ, inspired design, stamped. 150.00

Oil Lamp, 12″ h, bulbous, brass fixture, earth tones, geometric pattern, sgd in script, numbered, initials. 770.00

Teapot, cov, Indian Ware, small 45.00

Vase

2½ x 3½″, Indian Ware, squatty, bulbous shoulder, matte red, tan, and black S–curve dec, base inscribed "Mississippi," and numbered. 50.00

5 x 7½″, bulbous, earth tones, bisque clay, banded geometric dec, die stamped, numbered, marked "Little Colorado, Ariz" 250.00

8 x 10″, Indian Ware, wide short neck, squatty bulbous body, geometric Indian motifs, brown and beige glazes, Homolobi Tribe, sgd "Clifton 233," c1910. . . . . 360.00

CLOCKS

History: The sundial was the first man–made device for measuring time. Its basic disadvantage is well expressed in the saying: "Do like the sundial, count only the sunny days."

With a need for greater dependability, man developed the water clock, oil clock, and the sand clock, respectively. All these clocks worked on the same principle—time was measured by the amount of material passing from one container to another.

The wheel clock was the next major step. These clocks can be traced back to the 13th century. Many improvements on the basic wheel clock were made and continue to be made. In 1934 the quartz crystal movement was introduced.

Recently, an atomic clock has been invented that measures time by the frequency of radiation and only varies one second in a thousand years.

Identifying the proper model name for a clock is critical in establishing price. Condition of works also is a critical factor. Examine the works to see how many original parts remain. If repairs are needed, try to include this in your estimate of the purchase price. Few clocks are purchased purely for decorative value.

References: Robert W. D. Ball, *American Shelf and Wall Clocks: A Pictorial History for Collectors,* Schiffer Publishing, 1992; Philip Collins, *Pastime: Telling Time From 1879 to 1969,* Chronicle Books, 1993; Roy Ehrhardt, *Clock Identification And Price Guide: Book I,* rev. ed., Heart of America Press, 1979; Roy Ehrhardt, *Clock Identification And Price Guide: Book II,* Heart of America Press, 1979; Roy Ehrhardt (ed.), *The Official Price Guide To Antique Clocks, Third Edition,* House of Collectibles, 1985;

Tran Duy Ly, *American Clocks: A Guide To Identification and Prices,* Arlington Book Co., 1989, 1991 value update; Rick Ortenburger, *Vienna Regulators And Factory Clocks,* Schiffer Publishing, 1990; Derek Roberts, *Carriage and Other Traveling Clocks,* Schiffer Publishing, 1993; Robert W. & Harriett Swedberg, *American Clocks and Clockmakers,* Wallace–Homestead, 1989.

Collectors' Club: National Association of Watch and Clock Collectors, Inc., 514 Poplar St., Columbia, PA 17512.

Museums: American Clock & Watch Museum, Bristol, CT; Museum of National Association of Watch and Clock Collectors, Columbia, PA.

Carriage, brass, four beveled glass panels, French, 2½ x 3¼ x 4½″, $450.00.

MISCELLANEOUS

Alarm

Ansonia Clock Co, Ansonia, CT, patented April 23, 1878, nickel plated case, beveled glass, bell on top, 30 hour time and alarm movement with winding mechanism, sgd dial and case, 4″ h 75.00

Gilbert Clock Co, Winsted, CT, 1890, nickel plated case, top mounted with rolling bell swings back and forth causing hammer to strike, paper dial, 30 hour time and alarm lever movement, 10¾″ h 75.00

Parker Clock Co, Meriden, CT, 1900, Model #60, brass case mounted on brass bell, beveled glass, painted dial, inscribed, 5″ h 140.00

Terry Clock Co, Terryville, CT, 1875, ebonized cast iron case, paper on zinc dial, 30 hour time and alarm movement, fixed pendulum, paper label, 6″ h 30.00

Thomas, Seth, Thomaston, CT, 1885, student lever model, nickel plated and gilded case, paper on zinc dial, 30 hour time and alarm lever movement, 7″ h 75.00

Unmarked, Germany, c1920, animated, carved chapel, Friar ringing bell, 30 hour lever movement, simulated porcelain dial with gilt center, 13¼″ h 500.00

Westclox, American, c1925, Art Deco white metal case, silvered dial, 30 hour time and alarm movement, 3″ h 30.00

Automated, Thomas Armstrong & Bros, Manchester, England, 1880, ship's hull cross section shape revealing engine room, crankshaft powered by spring movement, deck mounted with timepiece with inscribed silvered dial, aneroid barometer, thermometer, compass and cannons, brass and nickel plated brass case, 8 day time lever movement, carved stone base, 17¼″ h 8,800.00

Blinking Eye, figural

Dog, Bradley & Hubbard cast iron case, orig paint, paper on zinc dial, 20 hour movement, fixed pendulum, 8½″ h 1,430.00

John Bull, Chauncey Jerome, Bristol, CT, 1870, 30 hour time and movement, paper on zinc dial, 16″ h . . . 880.00

Lion, Bradley & Hubbard cast iron case, orig paint, 30 hour time movement, fixed pendulum, 8″ h 1,950.00

Monkey, German, 1900, multicolored white metal, animated mouth, 9¾″ h 440.00

Organ Grinder, Waterbury Clock Co, Waterbury, CT, 1870, painted cast iron case, eyes move up and down, paper on zinc dial, 30 hour lever movement, 17¼″ h 1,700.00

Owl, German, c1900, nickel plated front, green eyes, paper dial, 30 hour lever movement, 6½″ h 465.00

Sambo, balance wheel, 30 hour time movement, 16″ h 630.00

Topsy, Waterbury Clock Co, Waterbury, CT, 1870, balance wheel, 30 hour time movement, 17″ h 600.00

Figural, Gilbert Clock Co, Preacher & Drunk, cast and painted white metal, 30 hour time lever movement, paper dial, 9″ h 230.00

Gravity

Europe, 37″ h, 1875, ebonized case, pitched head and bracket, 30 hour movement with crown wheel escapement, white porcelain dial with Arabic numerals surrounded with gilded shelled shape dial, inlaid oak board behind sawtooth track 3,740.00

Germany, carved base, 30 hour time movement, sawtooth bar driven, porcelain dial inscribed "Anno 1750," 26½″ h 360.00

Night Light

Arfandaux, Paris, France, c1850, cast iron base, gilt brass mounts, lacy style clear glass, frosted glass dial, 30 hour fusee verge escapement movement, pierced and engraved balance cock, 14″ h 770.00

Standard Novelty Co, NY, c1885, nickel plated case, revolving milk glass shade, 30 hour time lever movement, 6½″ h 250.00

Unknown Maker, 1880, gas, milk glass dial, cast brass rim and dec, 30 hour time movement, unsigned, 6″ h 80.00

Novelty

Dog, cast metal case, revolving eyes indicate hour and minute, 5¼″ h . . 550.00

Commemorative, Admiral Dewey, gilded iron case, 30 hour lever movement, 10″ h 165.00

Train, Ansonia Clock Co, NY, pat 1878, white metal train front case, includes engineers and amber reflector, 30 hour balance wheel movement with paper dial, gilt highlights, 8″ h 600.00

Woman, Junghans Clock Co, Germany, c1920, mounted on turned base, cast figure supports brass case, 30 hour lever movement, inscribed white porcelain dial, 15½″ h 600.00

Paperweight, E N Welch Mfg Co, amber glass case, octagon, porcelain dial, 30 hour lever movement, 4″ h 155.00

Ship

Ashcroft Mfg Co, NY, c1920, cast brass case mounted on walnut base, engraved brass dial, seconds indicator, 8 day double wind time lever movement, chipped bezel glass, 12½″ h 355.00

Thomas, Seth, Thomaston, CT, 1900, brass case, silvered dial inscribed, "Kelvin White & Co Nautical Instruments Boston–New York, Seth Thomas," 30 hour lever movement, bell strike, later mahogany base, 10¼″ h 330.00

Waterbury Clock Co, Waterbury, CT, 1940, cast brass case, ship's wheel bezel, silvered dial, 8 day jeweled lever movement, bell strike, 8″ d . . 250.00

Stick, Japan, 19th C, rosewood, brass

numerals, small drawer holds winding key, pierced and engraved plates, crown wheel escapement with hairspring and balance, strike mechanism with weight powers time train movement, 19″ h. **3,300.00**

Stove, cast iron, 30 hour time and alarm hair spring movement, 9¾″ h, c1900 **100.00**

Table, Lalique, frosted glass, lily of the valley motif, white enamel highlights, sgd, c1931, 7″ h, $4,620.00. Photograph courtesy of William Doyle Galleries.

SHELF

Acorn
Brown, J C, and Forestville Mfg Co, laminated rosewood veneered case, painted tablet with floral dec and geometric designs, painted zinc dial, 8 day time and strike double fusee movement with pendulum, 19″ h **5,000.00**
Forestville Manufacturing Co, Bristol, CT, c1850, fusee movement, 24″ h **4,125.00**
Animated
Cathedral shape, Germany, c1900, carved case, door opens to Friar ringing the bell in steeple, 30 hour movement with pendulum striking two hammers on single bell, 31″ h **1,100.00**
The Steam Hammer, France, 1880, cast brass case, marble base, hammer attached to escapement, 8 day time and strike movement, black metal dial with applied brass numerals, 18″ h. **2,750.00**
Beehive
Beals, J J, Boston, MA, 1860, mahogany veneered case, enameled zinc dial, J C Brown 8 day time, strike, and alarm movement, 18¾″ h **200.00**
Brewster & Ingraham, Bristol, CT, 1850, mahogany veneered case,

cut glass tablet, painted zinc dial, 8 day time and strike movement with orig brass springs and pendulum, 19″ h. **440.00**
Brown, J C and Forestville Mfg Co, Bristol, CT, 1850, rosewood veneered case, ripple molding, cut glass tablet, painted zinc dial, 8 day time and strike movement with pendulum, 19″ h **880.00**
Ingraham, E & A, Bristol, CT, 1850, mahogany veneered case, etched glass tablet, enameled zinc dial, 8 day time and strike movement with pendulum, 19″ h. **220.00**
Unknown Maker, England, c1906, electric, mahogany case, satinwood banding, engraved silvered dial, balance wheel mounted with coil, dated and numbered 2769, 10¾″ h **850.00**
Welch, E N, Forestville, CT, mahogany veneered case, rippled door, cut glass tablet, painted zinc dial, 8 day time and strike movement with pendulum, 19″ h. **500.00**
Box or Cottage
Atkins Clock Co, Bristol, CT, 1870, rosewood veneered case, black and gold tablet, enameled zinc dial, paper label, 30 hour time movement, pendulum, 10″ h **250.00**
Favnor, German, c1940, oak case, stained glass insert on door, silvered dial, 8 day three–train movement with Westminster chimes and pendulum, 28″ h. **55.00**
Gilbert Mfg Co, Winsted, CT, 1875, rosewood veneered case, gilded moldings, dec tablet, enameled zinc dial, paper label, 8 day time and strike movement, pendulum, 13½″ h **80.00**
Jerome, Chauncey, New Haven, CT, 1850, rosewood veneer case, painted zinc dial, 8 day time and strike fusee movement, 13½″ h . . . **250.00**
New England Clock Co, Bristol, CT, 1850, painted tablet, painted zinc dial, 30 hour time and alarm movement with pendulum, 11″ h **425.00**
Terry, S B, Terryville, CT, 1860, applied dec paper on case surface, frosted glass tablet, enameled zinc dial, 30 hour ladder movement with pendulum, 10½″ h **825.00**
Bracket
Kienzle Clock Co, NY and Germany, c1930, mahogany case, engraved silvered brass dial, 8 day time and strike three–train movement, Westminster chimes, pendulum, brass plaque on back, 15¾″ h **200.00**

Pashler, Edward, London, c1800, George III, mahogany, four gilt flame finials, two winged lions surmount top, ring handles on side, scalloped apron with gilt feet, elaborate scrolled gilt dec on face, strike and chime movement, plays six musical selections, 24″ h **5,500.00**

Quosig, S, Germany, c1850, walnut case, brass carrying handle, glazed doors and case sides, pewter and brass engraved hands, pierced brass hands, 8 day movement with crown wheel escapement, 19¾″ h. **2,200.00**

Unknown Maker

China, 19th C, rosewood, revolving base, cabriole legs, glazed door with inlaid mother–of–pearl, porcelain dial with engraved brass, 8 day time and strike fusee movement, crown wheel escapement, sweep seconds, and pendulum, 18½″ h. **1,000.00**

Japan, 1850, rosewood case, 30 hour time and strike pillar movement with engraved front and back plates, time train fusee, vertical crown wheel escapement, revolving hour dial, two zodiac sign apertures, 10″ h **5,500.00**

Calendar

Ansonia Brass & Copper Co, Ansonia, CT, 1870, rosewood veneered case, drop finials, painted tablet, enameled zinc dial, 8 day time and strike movement with iron weights and pendulum, 32¾″ h **660.00**

Burwell Mfg Co, Bristol, CT, c1860, rosewood veneered case, laminated and turned bezels, black and gold tablet, upper paper on zinc dial, lower enameled zinc dial, 8 day time and strike movement with rolling pinions, two iron weights and pendulum, 36″ h. **660.00**

Davis Clock Co, Texarkana, AK, 1890, pressed and carved oak case, two black and gold tablets, paper on zinc dial, 8 day time and strike movement, simple calendar mechanism, pressed brass pendulum, 27½″ h. **600.00**

Gilber, William L, Winsted, CT, c1870, rosewood veneered case, black and gold tablet, painted zinc dial, 8 day time and strike movement with pendulum, 17½″ h **1,155.00**

Ingraham, E Clock Co, Bristol, CT, rosewood veneered case, laminated bezels, painted tablet, enameled zinc dial, 8 day time and strike

movement with pendulum, Josiah K Seem calendar dial, 22″ h. **925.00**

Ithaca Calendar Clock Co, Ithaca, NY, c1870

No 10 Farmers model, carved walnut case, paper on zinc dial, inscribed lower dial, 8 day time and strike movement, nickel plated pendulum, 26″ h **880.00**

No 11 Octagon model, walnut case, inscribed paper on zinc dial, 8 day time and strike movement by E N Welch, pendulum, 21″ h . . . **550.00**

Seth Thomas Clock Co, Thomaston, CT, c1875

Fashion #2, walnut case, three turned finials, paper on zinc dials, 8 day time and strike movement with pendulum, 31½″ h **880.00**

Fashion #5, walnut case, three turned finials, painted zinc dials, 8 day time and strike movement, cathedral gong, damascene dec nickel plated pendulum, gold inscribed tablet, 31½″ h **1,590.00**

Waterbury Clock Co, C W Feishtinger Patent Calendar, Waterbury, CT, 1895, walnut case, registers date and month, day of week on bottom case, 8 day time, strike, and alarm movement with pendulum, painted zinc dials, gold dec glass, 22″ h. . . **660.00**

Welch, E N Mfg Co, Forestville, CT, c1880, Arditi model, date, day, and month indicators, 8 day time and strike movement, paper on zinc dials, pendulum, 27″ h **600.00**

Carriage

H & H, France, 1890, beveled glass panels, porcelain dial, gold five minute markers, 8 day lever time movement, leather covered carrying case, 4″ h **340.00**

Unknown Maker, French, repeater movement, made for Shreve, Crump & Low, 7¾″ h **2,100.00**

Commemorative

Admiral George Dewey, E Ingraham & Co, Bristol, CT, flags, cannonballs, stars, and anchors, oak case, orig gold tablet, gilded lead pendulum, 8 day time and strike movement with steel plates, 23″ h, 1899 **300.00**

Capitol, E Ingraham, Bristol, CT, c1900, oak case, dome pressed on crest, gold dec tablet, paper on zinc dial, 8 day time and strike movement with calendar mechanism and pendulum, paper label on reverse of case, 22″ h **275.00**

President McKinley, E Ingraham & Co, Bristol, CT, flags, cannonballs, stars, and anchors, oak case, orig gold tablet with ship and flags, gilded lead pendulum, 8 day time and strike movement with steel plates, 23″ h, 1900 . . . . **300.00**

President Theodore Roosevelt, E N Welch, Forestville, CT, 1900, pressed oak case, crest portrait, soldiers on side brackets, patriotic glass, paper on zinc dial, 8 day time and strike movement, pendulum, 24¼″ h **250.00**

Cuckoo

Frankfield, A & Co, NY, c1890, carved oak case, grapes and grape leaves, 8 day time and strike movement, paper label on case int., pendulum, 17½″ h **465.00**

Unknown Maker, Germany, c1900, carved oak case, 30 hour time and strike movement, pendulum, 16½″ h **275.00**

Garniture, French, 3 pcs, marble, black, cast brass mounts surmounted by urn, dial engraved and gilded with Roman numerals, 8 day time and strike movement with pendulum, two conforming dec vases, 19″ h clock, dial inscribed "Shreve, Crump & Low," c1880 . . . . **550.00**

Gingerbread (Kitchen)

Ansonia Clock Co, Ansonia, CT, 1890, carved and pressed walnut case, paper on zinc dial, silver dec glass, 8 day time and strike movement with pendulum, 22″ h **100.00**

Welch, E N, Forestville, CT, c1900, Admiral Sampson bust pressed on crest with nautical motifs, gold dec tablet with warship, paper on brass dial, 8 day time and strike movement with pendulum cast of lead with eagle and shield, 24½″ h **275.00**

Lantern

Forman, Francis, St Paules, England, 17th C, engraved brass dial, single hand, pierced engraved fret, 30 hour time and strike movement, orig balance escapement, 14″ h **3,850.00**

Hitchman, Henry, Pickadilley, London, 1775, engraved dial and nameplate surrounded with spandrels, 30 hour pull–up time and alarm movement, crown wheel escapement, short pendulum and single hand, brass weight, 9″ h **2,970.00**

Mantel . . . .

Birge and Fuller, Bristol, CT, c1840, Gothic, double steeple, fusee movement, 27½″ h **1,210.00**

Bulle, France, 1920, engraved silver and gilt dial, battery movement with

pendulum oscillating over curved magnet, ebonized base, round glass dome, 10½″ h **170.00**

Eureka Clock Co, London, c1906, electric, mahogany case, quarter column inlaid with brass banding, porcelain dial, bimetallic balance wheel mounted with coil, dated and numbered 7945, 15½″ h **1,100.00**

Jungans Clock Co, Germany, c1930, mahogany case, three–train movement, silvered dial with attached brass numerals, pendulum, 10½″ h **45.00**

Marshall and Adams, Seneca Falls, NY, c1825, Classical, carved mahogany, 40½″ h **990.00**

McInnes, J, Bunbarton, England, c1790, gothic, mahogany veneered case, ebony banding, pierced brass inserts, engraved brass dial, 8 day time and strike movement, 18″ h . . **880.00**

Poole Mfg Co, New York City, 1940, battery operated brass movement with round movement support column, engraved silvered dial with seconds indicator, turned wood base, glass dome, 10¾″ h **200.00**

Sozet, Mereville, France, 1890, black marble case, incised gold dec, figure mounted on top, black and gold dial, 8 day time and strike movement with pendulum, discolored, 19¼″ h **30.00**

Unknown Maker

Charles X, c1830, figural, ormolu, reading woman reclining beneath pagoda form canopy, wreath and torch surmounts circular clock, white enameled face, Roman numerals, octagonal base with additional ormolu, imperfections, 18″ h **4,125.00**

Classical, Paris, c1815, ormolu, enamel dial inscribed "Made for Mr. Nathan Appleton by Isidore Grenot Paris," minor imperfections, 14″ w, 4½″ d, 19″ h **5,100.00**

Egyptian Revival, French, 19th C, black marble, bronze, and onyx, 17″ h clock with movement marked Vincent et Cie and H. & P.B., circular clock flanked by onyx columns, winged beasts, Sphinx on rect top, pr of conforming obelisks with incised dec, price for three piece garniture set **4,125.00**

Late Charles X, Gothic Revival, second quarter 19th C, ormolu, cathedral form, time and strike movement, pendulum, replaced key, rosette missing, 24½″ h . . . **1,760.00**

Louis XVI, late 18th C, bronze and

ormolu, figural, J Roque, Paris, two women with floral urn, white marble base, dial, and movement, sgd "Roque a Paris," patina rubbed, lacking pendulum and key, 17" h **1,980.00**

Neoclassical, Austrian, early 19th C, mahogany and gilt bronze, circular dial supported by caryatids, rect base, pendulum missing, 12½" h. **770.00**

Massachusetts Shelf

Hubbard, Daniel, Medfield, MA, c1820, Federal, mahogany and eglomise, shaped crest, urn and foliate form finial, rect eglomise door dec with lyres and foliate motifs, gold painted dished dial, hinged eglomise door with mill and waterfall scene, molded base, gilt wood ball feet, 36" **42,000.00**

Willard, Aaron, Boston, c1820, Federal, mahogany and eglomise, shaped crest, brass eagle finial, door dec with polychrome foliate and lyre motifs, white painted dished dial above eglomise panel painted with corner lyre motifs, oval mirror, brass ball feet, 34½" **9,500.00**

Metal, Terry, S B, Terryville, CT, 1852, iron, ebonized, mother–of–pearl inlay, painted gold dec, enameled zinc dial, 30 hour time movement, torsion balance, marked "Oct 5th 1852," 8½" h **1,000.00**

Ogee

Ansonia Clock Co, Ansonia, CT, 1850, mahogany veneered case, black and silver dec tablet, enameled zinc dial, 30 hour time and strike movement with iron weights and pendulum, 25½" h **90.00**

Atkins & Porter, Bristol, CT, c1845, mahogany veneered case, glass tablet, painted zinc dial, 30 hour time and strike movement with cast iron weights, missing pendulum and key, 26" h **470.00**

Beals, J J, Boston, MA, 1840, mahogany veneered case, frosted glass tablet, enameled wood dial, 30 hour time and strike wood movement with iron weights and pendulum, 26" h **75.00**

Birge & Fuller, Bristol, CT, 1840, mahogany case, frosted tablet, painted wood dial, 8 day time and strike strap brass movement with pendulum and iron weights, 29¾" h **220.00**

Brewster, E C & Co, Bristol CT, 1850, veneered, mirror tablet, Charles Kirk cast iron backplate 8 day time and strike spring driven movement,

rack and snail strike, orig finish, 28" h **275.00**

Brown, J C, Bristol, CT, c1850, mahogany and rosewood veneered case, painted wood dial, 8 day time and strike movement with iron weights and pendulum, 29" h **330.00**

Forestville Mfg Co, Bristol, CT, mahogany veneered case, Boston Harbor view on glass tablet, inscribed 8 day time and strike movement with two iron weights and pendulum, enameled wood dial, 28½" h, 1850 . . . . **275.00**

Gilbert, Jerome & Grant, Bristol, CT, 1840, mahogany veneered case, two painted tablets, brass dial, 30 hour time and strike movement with pendulum and iron weights, 25" h . **330.00**

Gilbert, William, Winsted, CT, c1860, veneered case with matching figured mahogany veneered panels, frosted tablet, 30 hour time and strike fusee movement with pendulum, 17" h **220.00**

Ives, Joseph, Plainville, CT, c1840, mahogany, veneered case, glazed door, painted tablet, paper label, 8 day time and strike movement, iron weights, roller pinions and pendulum, carved and gilded crest, 31" h **940.00**

Jerome, Chauncey, New Haven, CT, 1850, mahogany veneered case, painted tablet, enameled wood dial, 8 day time and strike movement with iron weights and pendulum, 30" h **500.00**

Jones, Jacob, Concord, NH, 1820, mahogany veneered case, one painted tablet, one mirror tablet, enameled iron dial, 8 day time and strike movement with lead weights and pendulum, 31¾" h **2,310.00**

Smith & Goodrich, Bristol, CT, 1850, rosewood veneered case, floral tablet, painted zinc dial, 30 hour time and strike fusee movement with pendulum, 15½" h **385.00**

Smith, Philip L, Marcellus, NY, c1830, mahogany veneered case, mounted print behind lower glass, enameled wood dial, 8 day time and strike movement with strap brass plates, iron pendulum and stamped brass pendulum bob, two iron weights, 36" h **500.00**

Terry, Silas B, Plymouth, CT, 1840, rosewood and mahogany veneered case, wood dial with brass seconds disc, 8 day time and strike movement, 34½" h **440.00**

Thomas, Seth, Thomaston, CT, 1863,

mahogany veneered case, colorful floral tablet, enameled zinc dial inscribed "Patented May 19, 1863," paper label, 30 hour time and strike lyre movement with pendulum, 16½" h **250.00**

Union Manufacturing Co, Bristol, CT, 1845, mahogany veneered case, painted tablet, wood dial with winged cherubs and floral dec, 30 hour time and strike movement, 26" h **165.00**

Waterbury Clock Co, Waterbury, CT, 1850, rosewood veneered case, dec glass tablet, enameled zinc dial, 30 hour time and strike movement with iron weights and pendulum, 25¾" h. **90.00**

Welch, E N, Forestville, CT, 1850, rosewood veneered case, Baltimore Cemetery scene on tablet, painted zinc dial, paper label, 8 day time and strike movement with iron weights and pendulum, 29" h **140.00**

Pillar and Scroll

Downes, Ephraim, Bristol, CT, 1820–30, Federal, broken arch scroll pediment, three brass urn finials, glazed and eglomise hinged door, white painted dial with Roman numerals, turned tapering columns, French feet, 31" h, 16½" w **2,090.00**

Neal, Elisha, New Hartford, CT, 1830, mahogany, scrolled crest, turned columns, painted tablet, painted wood dial, 30 hour time and strike wood movement, iron weights and pendulum, three brass finials, 29¼" h **1,100.00**

Stow, Solomon, mahogany veneered case, inlaid maple plinths, painted tablet, enameled wood dial, 30 hour time and strike wood movement, iron weights and pendulum, three brass finials, 29" h **710.00**

Terry, Eli and Sons, Plymouth, CT, c1820, Federal, mahogany, scrolled crest, columns, and feet, three brass finials

30¼" h, scrolling dec dial, reverse painted glass tablet, old refinish **1,870.00**

31¼" h, reverse painted glass tablet, paper label **2,200.00**

Thomas, Seth, scrolled top with finials, reverse painted glass door, fret work, orig label, 30½" h **900.00**

Porcelain, Royal Bonn, France, 8 day time and strike movement with pendulum, 13¾" h **500.00**

Shelf

Birge & Ives, Bristol, CT, 1832, triple decker, carved mahogany eagle splat, columns, and feet, gilded columns painted tablet, mirror tablet, enameled wood dial, strap brass time and strike movement with iron weights and pendulum, 36½" h . . . **935.00**

Birge, John & Co, Bristol, CT, c1848, mahogany, gilded plaster crest, painted dec columns, painted tablet, enameled wood dial, 8 day time and strike brass movement with iron weights and pendulum, 35" h . **440.00**

Blakeslee, E Jr, NY, c1845, mahogany veneered case, painted tablet, enameled wood dial, Davies Patent lever strike mechanism marked on 30 hour movement with iron weights and pendulum, refinished case, 26" h **250.00**

Boardman & Wells, Bristol, CT, 1840, split column, stenciled splat, painted tablet, enameled wood dial, 30 hour time and strike wood movement, iron weights and pendulum, 31½" h **220.00**

Brewster, N L, Bristol, CT, c1860, rosewood veneered case with turned columns, painted tablet with coat of arms, painted zinc dial, pendulum, Joseph Ives tin plate 30 hour movement, squirrel cage rolling pinion escapement, tin plates, and roller pinions, 17½" h **1,870.00**

Brown, J C and Forestville Mfg Co, Bristol, CT, 1850, rosewood veneered case, painted tablet, painted zinc dial, 8 day time and strike movement, orig finish, 15" h **500.00**

Conant, William S, NY, 1860, mahogany and rosewood veneered case, molded crest and base, four turned columns, enameled wood dial, 30 hour time and strike weight driven movement, 25¾" h. **500.00**

Connecticut Clock Co, 1850, rosewood veneered case, glass tablet, painted zinc dial, Miles Morse 8 day time and strike movement with pendulum, 15" h **440.00**

Crane, A D, rosewood and mahogany veneered case, orig cut and frosted glass door, glass and paper dial, 8 day time and strike movement with torsion suspension and three ball pendulum, iron weights, 20½" h. . . **3,300.00**

Downs, Ephraim, mahogany veneer, ebonized pilaster and crest with gold stenciled dec, wooden works, painted wooden face and printed label "Patent Clocks made & sold by Ephraim Downs, Bristol, Conn," carved paw feet, old finish, minor veneer loss, replacements, and touch–ups, 28″ h **250.00**

Dutton, David, Mount Vernon, NH, c1830, strawberry dec on dial, 30 hour wood time and strike movement, 33¾″ h. **140.00**

Forestville Mfg Co, Bristol, Ct, Empire, mahogany flame grain veneer, brass works, worn painted face, veneer damage, 27¾″ h. **415.00**

Gains, John, Portsmouth, NH, c1800, Federal, mahogany, inlaid, eight day weight driven brass movement, shaped carved cornice with three fluted and acorn capped finials over semicircular bonnet with conforming glazed door, flanked by reeded columns, white painted faceplate with maker's name, short waisted case over base flanked with reeded pilasters and urn shaped finials, 41″ h **22,000.00**

Goodwin, E O, Bristol, CT, 1852, mahogany veneered case, three painted tablets, painted zinc dial, Brewster & Ingraham 8 day time and strike movement, refinished, 20½″ h **710.00**

Hotchkiss, Spencer & Co, Salem Bridge, CT, 1830, mahogany veneered case, stenciled half round columns, molded cornice, gold leaf dec dial, 8 day Salem Bridge time movement with pendulum and lead weight, turned feet, 28″ h **1,485.00**

Ingraham, E & Co, Bristol, CT, 1875, rosewood veneered case, gold dec tablet, paper on zinc dial, 8 day time and strike movement with pendulum, 16½″ h **120.00**

Ives, C & L C, Bristol, CT, 1835, triple decker, mahogany and veneer case, enameled wood dial, ebonized ball feet and columns, eagle dec crest, 8 day time and strike strap brass movement with pendulum, refinished case, 36½″ h **2,640.00**

Jerome & Co, New Haven, CT, 1875, rosewood veneered case, gutta percha panels behind glass, 8 day time and strike movement with pendulum, 16″ h **165.00**

Jerome & Darrow, c1830, stenciled half columns and splat, carved pineapple finial and paw feet, 30″ h **770.00**

Kroeber, F, NY, 1875, carved poplar case, porcelain dial, 8 day time and strike movement with glass pendulum, refinished case, 20″ h **200.00**

Manross, Elisha, Bristol, CT, 1850, rosewood veneered case, line inlay, painted zinc dial, 30 hour time and

strike movement with pendulum, 14″ h. **355.00**

Marsh, George, Bristol, CT, 1835, split stenciled column, glazed door with mirror, painted tablet, enameled wood dial, 8 day time and strike movement, ivory bushings, iron weights, pendulum, 35½″ h **660.00**

Morse, Miles, Plymouth, CT, 1825, mahogany veneered case with inlaid satinwood panels, turned columns, enameled dial, painted tablet with mustard background, 8 day Salem Bridge movement with iron weights, 26½″ h. **7,700.00**

New Haven Clock Co, New Haven, CT, 1860, Empire style, mahogany veneered case, painted dec columns, enameled zinc dial, two tablets, 8 day time, strike, and alarm movement with pendulum, 20½″ h **440.00**

Pratt, Daniel, Jr, Reading, MA, 1843, mahogany veneered case, mirror tablet, enameled wood dial, 30 hour time and strike movement with weights and pendulum, 28″ h **330.00**

Seymour, Williams & Porter, Unionville, CT, c1835, mahogany case, carved basket of fruit crest, columns, and paw feet, enameled wood dial, 8 day time and strike wood movement, with weights and pendulum, 37¼″ h **600.00**

Smith & Goodrich, Bristol, CT, 1850, mahogany veneer, painted tablet with eagle, shield, and arrows, 30 hour time and strike fusee movement with pendulum, 14¾″ h **355.00**

Sperry & Shaw, NY, 1845, mahogany veneered case, painted floral dec tablet, enameled wood dial, 30 hour time and strike movement with lead weights and pendulum, 19¾″ h . . . **135.00**

Spring, S C & Co, Bristol, CT, c1865, rosewood veneered case, ebonized columns, black and gold tablet, painted zinc dial, 8 day time and strike strap movement with iron weights and pendulum, 30½″ h . . . **440.00**

Terry, Eli, Empire, mahogany case, flame veneer, carved detail, eagle crest, acanthus pilasters, wooden works, painted wooden face, paw feet, paper label "Patent Clocks made & sold by Eli Terry Jun'r," orig reverse painted glass, veneer repairs and touch–ups, 37″ h **660.00**

Terry, Silas B, Terryville, CT, 1840, mahogany veneered case, molded door, painted tablet, 30 hour weight driven brass time and strike movement with orig iron weights and pendulum, 24" h **2,530.00**

The Year Clock Co, NY, 1888, ebonized case with brass mounts, cut glass tablet, green paper label, glass dial with paper back, Aaron Crane patent torsion suspension with six ball pendulum and one year fusee time and strike movement, 21½" h **6,000.00**

Thomas, Seth, mahogany veneer case, brass works with alarm, worn painted metal face and reverse decorated glass, 15 ½" h **250.00**

Unknown Maker

Classical, mahogany, triple decker, strap movement, 16¼" w, 38½" h **470.00**

Gothic Revival, rosewood veneer and mahogany case, enameled face with brass trim, ornate pendulum, minor damage and repairs, 18¾" h **275.00**

Votti, G, Philadelphia, PA, c1885, elaborate case, raised gilded and silvered gesso dec, 8 day movement with escapement and pendulum, silvered brass dial with applied numerals and damascene dec, 29½" h **1,430.00**

Welch, E N, Forestville, CT, 1880, carved walnut case with three turned finials, paper on zinc dial, 8 day time and strike movement with emb pendulum, 26" h **330.00**

Williams, Orton, Prestons & Co, Farmington, CT, 1835, mahogany case, stenciled columns and splat, painted tablet, 30 hour time and strike wood movement with iron weights and pendulum, 32" h **110.00**

Skeleton

Bolt, Thomas & Co, Liverpool, England, 1870, silvered and engraved pierced brass dial, 8 day time and strike fusee movement with recoil escapement, ebonized wood base, glass dome, pendulum, 15" h **1,870.00**

Ithaca Calendar Clock Co, Ithaca, NY, 1890, nickel plated cast frames and dials, black and silver paper day and month indicators, 8 day time and strike movement, walnut base, ball feet, glass dome, pendulum, 14½" h **2,975.00**

Lamport, W H, Plymouth, England, 1860, glass dome, rosewood veneered base, engraved silvered dial, 8 day time fusee movement, 14" h. **1,430.00**

Terry Clock Co, Waterbury, CT, 1875, glass dome, porcelain dial, pressed brass dial, 8 day double wind time

movement, painted dec on base, 11½" h **990.00**

Steeple

Birge & Fuller, Bristol, CT, 1845, mahogany veneered case, four turned candles, painted tablet, painted zinc dial, 8 day time and strike movement with lever spring, pendulum, 26" h. **1,760.00**

Boardman, Chauncey, Bristol, CT, 1845, mahogany veneered case, painted zinc dial, 30 hour time and strike movement, Joseph Ives patent lever spring, pendulum, 21¾" h **4,125.00**

Brewster & Ingraham, Bristol, CT, 1865, mahogany veneered case, turned columns, cut glass tablet, paper label, enameled zinc dial, 8 day time and strike movement, pendulum, 20" h **550.00**

Brown, J C, Forestville, CT, c1850, rosewood veneered case, etched glass tablet, enameled zinc dial, 8 day time and strike fusee movement with pendulum, 20" h **825.00**

Forestville Hardware & Clock Co, Forestville, CT, 1853–55, mahogany veneered case, frosted glass tablet, turned finials, painted zinc dial, 30 hour time movement with pendulum and key, 12¼" h. **440.00**

Ingraham, E & A, Bristol, CT, c1855, mahogany veneered case, cut glass tablet, painted zinc dial, 30 hour time, strike, and alarm movement with pendulum, 20" h **500.00**

Jerome, Chauncey, New Haven, CT

Mahogany veneered case, frosted glass tablet, enameled zinc dial, 8 day time and strike fusee movement with pendulum, 19¾" h, 1840 . . . . **440.00**

Rosewood veneered case, glass tablet, enameled zinc dial, 30 hour time and strike movement with pendulum, 20" h. **220.00**

Johnson, William S, NY, c1850, steeple on steeple, mahogany veneered case, turned finials, orig painted tablets, painted zinc dial, 8 day brass spring driven time and strike movement with pendulum, 23½" h **440.00**

Manross, Elisha, Bristol, CT, 1845, rosewood veneered vertically, painted zinc dial, 8 day time and strike movement strap brass fusee movement with pendulum, 24" h . . **1,980.00**

Platt, A S & Co, Bristol, CT, 1850, mahogany veneered case, mirror tablet, enameled zinc dial, 30 hour time and strike fusee movement, 20" h . **220.00**

Smith & Goodrich, Bristol, CT, mahogany veneer, brass double fusee works, reverse dec glass with Presidents house, old finish, 20″ h **300.00**

Terry & Andrews, Bristol, CT, 1850, mahogany veneered case, painted tablet, painted zinc dial, 8 day time and strike lyre movement with pendulum, 19½″ h **575.00**

Terry, Silas B, Terryville, CT
Mahogany and rosewood case, painted wood dial, 30 hour time and strike with two wood fusee cones, wood winding drums, 25″ h **6,600.00**

Mahogany veneered case, four finials, frosted glass tablet, enameled zinc dial, 30 hour time and strike movement with pendulum, 19¾″ h **275.00**

Terry & Andrews, Ansonia, CT, c1850, rosewood veneered vertically, painted zinc dial, 8 day time, strike, and alarm lyre movement, orig brass springs and pendulum, 20″ h **355.00**

Terryville Manufacturing Co, Terryville, CT, 1860, rosewood veneered case, nautical dec tablet, 30 hour time and strike movement with pendulum, 20″ h **410.00**

Unknown Maker, rosewood veneered case, applied rippled molding, etched glass tablet, painted zinc dial, converted Waterbury 8 day time and strike movement with pendulum, 20″ h **1,265.00**

Welch, E N, Forestville, CT, 1860, rosewood veneered case, enameled zinc dial, 8 day time, strike, and alarm movement with pendulum, 23½″ h **940.00**

Triple Decker, Empire, mahogany veneer, grained and gilded pilasters, carved crest and turned feet, brass works, painted wooden face, paper label "Birge Mallory & Co Bristol, Conn," refinished and repainted, orig reverse painting, 38½″ h **880.00**

TALL-CASE CLOCKS

Allsop, London, mid 18th C, George II, japanned, rounded arched hood, three brass spike finials, engraved brass arched dial, calendar aperture, raised colored and gilt chinoiseries dec, molded plinth base, 88½″ h **5,225.00**

Balch, Daniel, Newbury, MA, c1760, walnut, molded stepped pediment hood with three ball and eagle brass finials, engraved brass dial mounted with foliate spandrels, waisted case

Pillar and Scroll, Eli Terry & Sons, Plymouth, CT, brass urn finials, French feet, 8 day movement, $875.00.

with arched hinged door, molded base with shaped pendant, bracket feet, stylized gilt highlights, 93½″ h, 20″ w, 10½″ d **5,500.00**

Bevan, Thomas, Marlborough, England, c1780, oak case, cross banded mahogany veneers, flat top, glazed door with turned columns, shaped waist door with quarter columns, straight bracket feet with central drop, inscribed engraved dial, 8 day time and strike movement plays musical tone on nest of bells on quarter hour, pendulum and three weights, 81½″ h . . . **4,075.00**

Blondel, Nicholas, Guernsey, c1760, George III, blue japanned, pagoda hood, brass arched dial, calendar aperture, molded plinth base, colored and gilt chinoiseries dec, 8 day time and hour strike with alarm, 91″ h **3,025.00**

Brokaw, Issac, NJ, c1780, cherry, molded swan's neck crest, brass urn finials, arched glazed door flanked by reeded pilasters, engraved brass dial, Roman numerals, arched waist door, molded base, ball feet, 88″ h **3,300.00**

Cheney, Asahel, Northfield, CT, c1800, Federal, cherry, arched molded hood with center ball finial, white painted dial, reeded pilasters on hood and body with painted capitals, diamond inlaid on molded door and base, paint flakes to dial, very worn finish, 84″ h **5,225.00**

Cheney, Benjamin, East Hartford, CT, c1760, Queen Anne, maple, key shaped bonnet over semicircular molded cornice, shaped engraved brass dial, Roman numerals, brass hands, slender molded body with shaped door, brass knob, stepped molded base, 89½″ h **15,400.00**

Cole, R, Rochester, NH, early 19th C, grained and painted to simulate rosewood, stringing, inlay, stencil motifs, wooden works, early surface, sgd "R. Cole Painter" on skirt, 83″ h **5,500.00**

Crane, William, Stoughton, MA, Federal, tiger maple, arched pediment with whale's tail type scrolling, center brass ball finial, two eagles mounted on ball finials, arched glazed door flanked by reeded pilasters with brass capitals, engraved brass dial with moon phase, Roman numerals, waist door with string inlay, bracket feet, 88″ h **5,225.00**

Fouche, Bastide, St Savin, France, 1860, Morbier, pine grain painted case, 8 day time and strike movement with alarm, porcelain dial with brass dec, gridiron pendulum, two iron weights and one brass alarm weight, 94″ h **500.00**

Gere, Isaac, Northampton, MA, c1795, cherry carved and inlaid, weight driven movement, strike, seconds dial, calendar, and moon phase, restoration, 89½″ h. **13,200.00**

Hallett, James, NY, c1790, Chippendale, mahogany, shaped crest hood, three brass ball and steeple finials, arched glazed door, white painted dial, waisted case with arched hinged door, bracket feet, 96½″ h, 19″ w, 9½″ d **6,655.00**

Haneye, Nathaniel, Bridgewater, MA, 18th C, pine, flat molded top, brass engraved dial, rect door, ogee bracket feet, wooden movement, 82″ h **3,025.00**

Keim, John, Reading, PA, 1790, walnut case, molded flat top, glazed door, inscribed enameled dial, rect waist door with incurvate upper corners, inset base panel, turned feet, 30 hour time and strike pull–up movement with one iron weight and pendulum, 91¼″ h . . **880.00**

Lock, William, Taunton, England, 1780, carved oak case, arched hood, glazed doors with turned columns with gilded capitals, rect waist door, cutout feet, 8 day time and strike movement, lead weights and pendulum, engraved silver and gilt dial with calendar aperture and month indicator, 80½″ h **1,200.00**

Mulliken, Samuel, Bradford, MA, 1750, cherry, hood with broken arch crest, applied dentil moldings, turned hood columns, engraved brass dial, tombstone waist door, flat fluted columns,

straight bracket feet, 30 hour time and strike pull–up posted movement, iron weight and pendulum, 89½″ h **2,500.00**

Newton, Edward, Grantham, c1760, George III, black japanned, caddy style hood, brass arched dial, calendar aperture, molded plinth base, gilt chinoiseries dec, 8 day time and hour strike, 92½″ h **2,750.00**

Penny, George, third quarter 18th C, George III, mahogany, broken scrolled pediment, fluted center tablet, brass urn finial, engraved brushed steel arched dial, bracket feet, 92″ h **2,750.00**

Pyke, Joseph, London, England, 1840, Victorian, mahogany, engraved silvered dial, 8 day time movement with dead beat escapement, brass tubular pendulum and weight, case with sloping pediment, glazed door, applied bracket, 78½″ h. **1,700.00**

Rittenhouse, David, Philadelphia, PA, c1765, walnut case, flat molded top, glazed hood door with turned columns, tombstone waist door, high bracket feet, 30 hour pull–up time and strike movement, iron weight and pendulum, engraved brass dial with pewter spandrels and inscribed nameplate, 90″ h. **12,100.00**

Smith, James, London, last quarter 18th C, George III, mahogany, musical, broken scroll pediment, three vasiform finials, fluted disengaged columns, brass arched dial with moon phase, arched door with molded edge, fluted quarter round columns, applied paneled base, ogee bracket feet, hour strike, tune played on ten nested bells, 91″ h. **6,600.00**

Spencer, Elisha, central MA, c1795, Federal, mahogany, inlaid, arched molded hood with three ball finials, arched glazed door flanked by freestanding columns, waisted case with thumb molded door, molded base, short bracket feet, painted dial with moon phase, sgd "Elisha Harrington Spencer, Ma 1795," 95″ h **24,200.00**

Unknown Maker

Country, cherry, broken arch pediment, dovetailed bonnet with columns, dial with moon phases, paneled base with wide cone moldings and chamfered corners, turned feet, refinished, 93½″ h. **1,100.00**

George III, Provincial, oak, flat top hood, engraved brass dial, scalloped shaped top door, conforming applied paneled base, eight day strike, 80″ h. **2,200.00**

Napoleon III, fourth quarter 19th C,

mahogany and ornate ormolu mounts, movement incised Juveanux, enameled dial over waisted case, wheel barometer and thermometer, 104″ h, 23″ w. **9,350.00**

Urletig, Valentin, Reading, PA, c1770, walnut case, broken arch hood, three carved finials, turned hood columns, tombstone waist door with inlaid initials, inlaid waist with turned and fluted quarter columns, flaring French feet, inscribed engraved brass dial with moon phase, 8 day time and strike movement, brass weights and pendulum, 96½″ h **4,675.00**

Vandelle, C, Paris, France, 1880, Morbier, walnut case with inset panels, round pendulum opening, three–train 30 hour movement, three bells, porcelain dial, three iron weights, 96½″ h **1,760.00**

Wilder, Joshua, Hingham, MA, c1810, Federal, inlaid mahogany, hood with two brass ball and steeple finials, white painted dial, turned columns, waisted case with hinged door, cross banded base above shaped skirt, bracket feet, 41½″ h, 10½″ w, 5½″ d **25,850.00**

Williams, Dan, Neath, England, c1760, japanned case, arched hook, tombstone waist door, bracket feet, gilded and painted dec case, brass dial with calendar indicator and engraved boss, 8 day time and strike movement with weights and pendulum, 91¾″ h . **1,430.00**

WALL

Alarm, Elnathan Taber, Roxbury, MA, c1820, mahogany, scrolled broken pediment cornice, rect case, white painted dial, Roman numerals, 32″ h **770.00**

Banjo

Brewster & Ingraham, Bristol, CT, mahogany, painted zinc dial, black and gold glasses, 8 day time movement with pendulum, 31½″ h. **600.00**

Howard, E & Co, Boston, MA, 1870, cherry grained case, two black and gold glasses, paper on zinc dial, 8 day time movement with damascene dec on front plate, orig iron weight and pendulum, 29¼″ h. . . . **5,000.00**

Howard & Davis, Boston, MA, 1850, cherry grained case, black and gold glasses, paper on zinc dial, 8 day time movement with damascene dec front plate, iron weight and pendulum, 32″ h **1,980.00**

New Haven Clock Co, 1920s, mahogany case, 8 day spring–driven movement, triple wind time, 41½″ h **410.00**

Sawin, John, Federal, Boston, gilt-

wood and mahogany, brass weight driven full striking movement, imperfections, 33½″ h **3,575.00**

Taber, E, Boston, MA, 1820, mahogany, two painted tablets, brass finial, enameled iron dial, 8 day time movement with lead weight and pendulum, 34½″ h **2,035.00**

Tift, Horace, Attleboro, MA, 1840, mahogany, finial on top, figured panels, enameled iron dial, 8 day time movement, iron weight and pendulum, 33¼″ h **550.00**

Tower, Reuben, Hingham, MA, 1820, 8 day time and alarm movement, inscribed enameled iron dial, replaced bell on top, lead weight, 29½″ h **3,500.00**

Unknown Maker, Federal, attributed to MA, c1815, giltwood and mahogany, restored, 38″ h **1,430.00**

Waterbury Clock Co, 1920–30, miniature, 8 day jeweled time movement, 15″ h **240.00**

Willard, Aaron, Federal, 1815, giltwood and mahogany

Dial inscribed "A. A. Cheney Brookline, Mass," eagle finial over circular dial, painted lyre section, reverse painted tablet, molded ball drops over scalloped bracket, 42½″ h. **6,820.00**

Dial sgd "Willard Jr. Boston No. 3668," imperfections, 33½″ h. . . . **1,650.00**

Calendar

Atkins Clock Co, Bristol, CT 1875, rosewood veneered and grain painted case, B B Lewis perpetual calendar indicates day, date, month, and time, painted zinc dial, 8 day time movement with pendulum, black and gold tablet, 24½″ h **825.00**

Gilbert, William L, Winsted, CT, 1875, carved and pressed oak case, dec glass panel with day, month, and date apertures, paper on zinc dial, 8 day time and strike movement, Thomas McCabe patent calendar mechanism with three revolving sheet metal discs, lever connected to strike train activates day and date discs, month disc moved manually, pendulum, 35½″ h **1,875.00**

Maranville, Galusha, rosewood veneered case, carved side arms, black and gold tablet, painted zinc dial, William L Gilbert 8 day time weight driven movement with dead beat escapement, pendulum and iron weight, 34″ h. **1,925.00**

Thomas, Seth, mahogany, arched top with three finials, old dark varnish, veneer damage, patent date 1876, 30½" h 990.00

Welch Spring & Co, Forestville, CT, c1885, Gale Drop Calendar, astronomical calendar with time, date, moon phase, sunrise, and sunset, and day of week, rosewood veneered and grain painted case, black and gold tablet, black paper label, 8 day time and strike movement marked "E N Welch" with pendulum, 30" h 3,850.00

Cuckoo

Black Forest

23" h, bird crest, 8 day time and strike movement, 1870–80. ..... 110.00

26½" h, eagle crest, 8 day time and strike movement, c1880 .... 410.00

Germany

19" h, carved case, bird with glass eyes on top, 30 hour three–train movement, single cuckoo bird and two doors open to dancing figures, 1940 .... 110.00

22½" h, carved deer, trumpet, powder flask, and guns, 30 hour time and strike movement, paper instruction label, two weights and carved pendulum, c1890 ...... 275.00

24½" h, carved case, bird with glass eyes on top, 30 hour three–train movement, double striking cuckoo birds, three weights and pendulum, 1940. .... 385.00

Figure Eight, E Howard & Co, Boston, MA, c1870, mahogany, regulator, 34" l. 2,860.00

Gallery

Ansonia Brass & Copper Co, Ansonia, CT, 1880, rolled brass case, paper label, painted zinc dial, 30 hour lever movement, 8½" d 80.00

Brewster & Ingraham, Bristol, CT, 1850, laminated and turned mahogany bezel, convex enameled wood dial, 8 day horizontal movement with upside–down pendulum suspension, 19¼" d. 1,430.00

Clark, J, Manchester, England, 1930, mahogany case, enameled dial, 8 day time and strike movement, two chime rods, 15½" d 120.00

Jerome, S B, New Haven, CT, 1865, ebonized canvas covered wood case, brass trim, enameled zinc dial, paper label, 30 hour lever movement, 9" d 165.00

Marine Clock Mfg Co, New Haven, CT, c1850, rosewood veneered case, enameled zinc dial, 20 hour time and strike movement, Charles

Kirk Patent double wheel escapement, 11" h 3,660.00

Pomeroy, N, Bristol, CT, 1850, rippled octagon, rosewood veneered case, applied rippled moldings, painted zinc dial with balance wheel aperture, 8 day time lever movement, 10½" h 500.00

Terryville Mfg Co, Terryville, CT, 1855, rosewood veneered case, enameled zinc dial, torsion pendulum, 8 day time movement, refinished 600.00

Waterbury Clock Co, NY, 1880, laminated and turned walnut case, paper label, painted zinc dial with seconds indicator, 8 day time, double wind lever movement, 12" d 220.00

Welch, E N Mfg Co, Forestville, CT, 1870, rosewood veneered octagon case, enameled zinc dial, 30 hour lever movement, 8¾" h. 120.00

Lyre

Sawin, John, Boston, MA, 1830, carved mahogany case, brass bezel, painted iron dial inscribed "Sawin," eagle finial, painted tablet, 8 day weight driven time movement, replaced finial and plinth, refinished and reglued, some replacements, 36½". 1,100.00

Unknown Maker, New England, c1820, Classical, carved mahogany, Roman numerals, second hand, 36" h 2,200.00

Willard, Aaron, Roxbury, MA, 1820, carved mahogany case, painted tablet, wood panel, enameled iron dial inscribed "Aaron Willard, Patent, Roxbury," 8 day time movement with iron weight and pendulum, 38" h 1,480.00

Miscellaneous

Dutch, oak case, removable arched hood with ball finials, applied split columns and gilded capitals, applied brass dec on lower case, enameled iron dial, 30 hour time, strike, and alarm pull–up movement with pendulum and brass weights, 50" h. 880.00

Marine Lever, E N Welch, 1860, octagon, rosewood veneered case, 8 day brass time movement, second bit, 8¾" d 110.00

Metal, Gilbert, c1875, iron, filigree, 8 day brass spring driven time and strike movement, 28" h. 660.00

Mission Oak, National Clock & Mfg Co, Chicago, IL, 1920, brass plated numerals and hands, 8 day time and strike movement with pendulum, 26" h 55.00

Morbier, France
53" h, Stolz, 1880, 8 day time, strike, and alarm movement, three weights and brass pendulum, gridiron and lyre dec, porcelain dial. 410.00

58½" h, 1860, 8 day time and strike movement, calendar mechanism fitted with strike mechanism, iron weights, repousse pendulum, white porcelain dial inscribed "Barennes fils de l'aine'a Clairac" 690.00

Oriental, Japan, 1800, engraved brass case and dial, 30 hour time, strike, and alarm movement with foliate escapement, cast iron weight and four lead counterweights, 9" h 2,475.00

Ogee, George Hills, Plainville, CT, 1850, mahogany veneered case, mirror tablet, enameled zinc dial, 20 hour time and strike movement, 36½" h 600.00

Regulator
Atkins Clock Co, Bristol, CT, 1860, rosewood veneered case, black and gold glass, enameled zinc dial, 8 day double wind time only weight driven movement with two brass weights and pendulum, 36½" h . . . 660.00

Becker, Gustave, Germany, 1890, walnut veneered case with ebonized carved dec, turned finials, 30 day time and strike movement, porcelain dial, two brass weights, pendulum, 59" h 3,300.00

Brewster & Ingraham, Bristol, CT, 1860, rosewood veneered case, applied rippled molding, enameled zinc dial, 8 day time and strike movement with pendulum, 22" h . . 275.00

Ingraham, E & Co, Bristol, CT, 1880, poplar case, grain painted dec, paper on zinc dial, 8 day time movement with calendar mechanism and pendulum, 24" h. 220.00

Jerome, Chauncey, 1850, octagon, 8 day time and strike movement, 24" h 330.00

Juguns, c1900, walnut case, eagle pediment, 8 day time and strike spring driven movement, 38" h . . . 275.00

Kroeber, F & Co, NY, 1880, Vienna Regulator #51, glazed sides, porcelain dial with seconds indicator, 8 day time movement with brass weight and pendulum, 44" h 500.00

National Clock & Mfg Co, Chicago, IL, 1900, mahogany case, black and gold tablets, paper on tin dial, 8 day time movement with calendar mechanism, brass pendulum, 39½" h 600.00

Sessions, Model #2, 1910, oak case, 8 day time spring driven movement, 38½" h 300.00

Sexty, Grantham, 1875, mahogany rosewood veneered case, carved twisted rope columns and bezel, enamel iron dial, 30 day time movement with brass weight and pendulum, 68½" h 1,100.00

Sperry, Henry & Co, NY, c1850, mahogany veneered case, cross banding, carved brackets, painted tablet, enameled zinc dial, 8 day time movement with pendulum, 24½" h 330.00

Terry, Silas B, Terryville, CT, 1840, rosewood veneered case, black and gold tablet, enameled zinc dial, 8 day time movement with dead beat escapement, gilded pendulum rod, lead weight, 37½" h. 550.00

Seth Thomas, Thomaston, CT, Model #30, mahogany case, 8 day time only movement, second bit, 50" h, 1900. . . . . 1,540.00

Unknown Maker, Empire, mahogany, flame grain veneer, enameled face with brass trim, brass and steel pendulum, gilded letters on glass door, marked "Standard Time," refinished, 66¼" h 965.00

Waltham, 1900–10, oak case, 8 day time movement, 34" h. 500.00

Waterbury, Waterbury, CT, 1900, mahoganized poplar case, regular tablet, paper on zinc dial, seconds indicator, paper label on reverse, 30 day time movement, pendulum, 31" h 550.00

Welch, E N, c1870, octagon, mahogany veneered case, 8 day time and strike movement, 24½" h 275.00

Schoolhouse
New Haven, New Haven, CT, 1880, pressed oak case, gold dec tablet, paper on tin dial, 8 day time movement, calendar mechanism, 27½" h 360.00

Sessions Clock Co, Forestville, CT, c1900, oak case, paper on tin dial, 8 day time movement with pendulum, 19¼" h 500.00

Thomas, Seth, rosewood veneer frame, brass works, reverse gilded glass in base, paper label, replaced cardboard face glued over metal face, key and pendulum, 25¼" h . . 165.00

Wag on Wall
Dutch, 18th C, enameled dial with painted nautical motifs, gilded cast lead crest and side brackets, back-

board and bracket painted with mermaids, canopy with gilded cast lead dec, 30 hour time and alarm movement with turned pillars, verge escapement and outside count wheel, pendulum, 27" h **770.00**

Germany, 1890, enameled wood dial, 30 hour time and strike three–train Black Forest type movement activates animated Friar bows when strikes, pendulum and three tin weights, 16½" h **2,750.00**

CLOISONNÉ

History: Cloisonné is the art of enameling on metal. The design is drawn on the metal body. Wires, which follow the design, are glued or soldered on the body. The cells thus created are packed with enamel and fired; this step is repeated several times until the level of enamel is higher than the wires. A buffing and polishing process brings the level of enamels flush to the surface of the wires.

This art form has been practiced in various countries since 1300 B.C. and in the Orient since the early 15th century. Most cloisonné found today is from the late Victorian era, 1870–1900, and was made in China and Japan.

Beaker, 19½" h, spheroid, long flaring neck, galleried rim, stepped foot, brocade dec, green ground, Japanese, mid 19th C, price for pair **650.00**

Bowl, 12" d, 3½" h, turned in rim, marine blue, variety of large lotus blossoms, clusters of small circle cloisonnes, cobalt border with silkworm cloisonnes, overlapping pomegranates on bottom, Chinese **500.00**

Plate, Japan, 5" d, $85.00.

Box, cov

6½" d, 3½" h, pink and brown dec, Chinese **335.00**

12" d, steep sloping sides, high splayed foot, int. polychrome enameled medallion of Buddha flanked by two arhats, lotus pond, two kinnara flying through cloud scrolls, turquoise ground, ext. with sinuous dragons winding through flowering lotus plants and Chinese characters of longevity and happiness, two character base mark of "Daimin," Chinese, Meiji period **600.00**

Brush Pot, 5" h, asters and butterfly dec, light blue ground, sgd "Takeuchi," Japanese, c1875. . . . . **200.00**

Buckle, two panels with mountains, flowers, birds, and butterflies **135.00**

Charger

17⅞" d, int. dec of large writhing dragon, blue ground, geometric patterned band, eight petal shaped reserves of ho–o alternating with suspended jewels, black ground, floral patterned rim band, warped, drilled, Meiji period **440.00**

23½" d, birds and butterfly hovering over peonies, chrysanthemums, morning glories, wisteria, and hydrangea, sky blue ground, brocade floral rim border, Meiji/Taisho period, price for pair **4,400.00**

Cigarette Case, green, three dragons, multicolored, Chinese **150.00**

Dish, 25⅜" d, shallow, circular, raised ring foot, int. dec of blue, green, pink, purple, orange, yellow, brown, and gilt enameled peacocks perched on reticulated rocks, two songbirds perched on flowering magnolia branches, flowering roses and magnolias, underside enameled pale blue and gilt florets, two ruyi–lappet bands **660.00**

Figure, animal, Chinese, teakwood base

3" h, 6" l, running boars, ridged back, price for pair **275.00**

3" h, 7½" l, fantailed goldfish, removable eyes, price for pair **330.00**

5" h, 8" l, lounging, gold horned and bearded beasts, sgd, price for pair **412.50**

Libation Cup, 5½" l, figural ram's head, blue, multicolored swirl and dragon design **250.00**

Plate, 9¾" d, marine blue, two white cranes, scenic terrain, peonies, foliage, etc., Japanese **300.00**

Potpourri Jar, cov, 4¼" h, 4⅛" d, multicolored flowers and butterflies, black, gold, and blue flowers, Japanese . . . **275.00**

Ruyi–Scepter, 22" l, carved wood and enamel, two long sinuous quilong with applied enamel ruyi–lappet heads, central cloisonne medallion, lotus flowers, pomegranates, antique objects, and interwoven floral scrolls, reverse carved with geometric diaper pattern, price for pair **770.00**

Vase

7½" h, dragon dec, blue ground . . . **100.00**

18" h, slender ovoid, tall waisted neck, slightly flaring rim, coral–red oval shaped reserves of birds and flowers, long undulating dragon and phoenix among stylized blossoms, green ground. **715.00**

19¾" h, quadrangular, two sinuous dragons chasing flaming jewel, band of taotie masks, archaistic motifs, waisted neck with stylized archaistic ruyi–lappet band, gilt rims, four character Xuande mark, minor restorations, price for pair . . **770.00**

CLOTHING

History: While museums and a few private individuals have collected clothing for decades, it is only recently that collecting clothing has achieved a widespread popularity. Clothing reflects the social attitudes of a historical period.

Christening and wedding gowns abound and, hence, are not in large demand. Among the hardest items to find are men's clothing from the 19th and early 20th centuries. The most sought after clothing is by designers, such as Fortuny, Poirret, and Vionnet.

Note: Condition, size, age, and completeness are critical factors in purchasing clothing. Collectors divide into two groups: those collecting for aesthetic and historic value and those desiring to wear the garment. Prices are higher on the West Coast; major auction houses focus on designer clothes and high-fashion items.

References: C. Willett Cunnington, *English Women's Clothing in the Nineteenth Century*, Dover Publications, 1990 (reprint of 1937 book); C. Willett and Phillis Cunnington, *The History of Underclothes*, Dover Publications, 1992; Maryanne Dolan, *Vintage Clothing 1880–1960*, Second Edition, Books Americana, 1987; Dover Publications, Inc., *Women's Fashions of the Early 1900s: An Unabridged Republication of New York Fashions*, National Clock & Suit Co, Dover Publications, 1992; Cynthia Giles, *The Official Identification And Price Guide To Vintage Clothing*, House of Collectibles, 1989; Carol Belanger Grafton, *Fashions of the Thirties*, Dover Publications, 1993; Tina Irick-Nauer, *The First Price Guide to Antique and Vintage Clothes*, E. P. Dutton, 1983; Terry McCormick, *The Consumer's Guide To Vintage Clothing*, Dembner Books, 1987; Diane McGee, *A Passion For Fashion: Antique, Collectible, and Retro*

Clothes, Simmons–Boardman Books, 1987; Jo-Anne Olian (ed.), *Everyday Fashions of the Forties As Pictured in Sears Catalogs*, Dover Publications, 1992; Merideth Wright, *Everyday Dress of Rural America: 1783–1800*, Dover Publications, 1992.

Periodical: *Vintage Clothing Newsletter*, PO Box 1422, Corvallis, OR 97339.

Collectors' Club: The Costume Society of America, 55 Edgewater Dr., PO Box 73, Earleville, MD 21919.

Museums: Los Angeles County Museum (Costume and Textile Dept.), Los Angeles, CA; Metropolitan Museum of Art, New York, NY; Museum of Costume, Bath, England; Philadelphia Museum of Art, Philadelphia, PA; Smithsonian Institution (Inaugural Gown Collection), Washington, D.C.

Additional Listings: See *Warman's Americana & Collectibles* for more examples.

Bathing Suit, man's, black wool, $18.00.

Baby Christening Outfit, cotton batiste, white, lace tiers, dress and matching cap **40.00**

Bathing Tunic, sateen, 1915 . . . . **35.00**

Blouse

Lace, black, long sleeves, 1920s . . **25.00**

Nylon, white, satin trim, long sleeves, 1930s. **15.00**

Silk, taffeta, pale green, handmade bobbin lace trim, 1900 . . . . **400.00**

Bodice, satin, beige, fully lined, nine satin lace cov buttons, pleated tail back, 22" fitted waist line, 9½" ruffled cuff trim, lace overlay. **25.00**

Bolero, 18" l, fur, leopard **225.00**

Cape

Gauze, black, stenciled foliate scrolls, tied at shoulders, hem threaded with striped Venetian glass beads, Fortuny, 36" l. **400.00**

Satin, evening, semicircular, hip

length, ivory, brocade poppies, pink satin lining, ruffled pink and ivory silk organdy trim, ivory ostrich feather neck dec **200.00**

Velvet, black, white fur collar and sleeves, 1930s. **75.00**

Chemise, silk, cream, Valenciennes lace trim, garlands of flowers embroidered in French knots, V neck, pale yellow ribbon. **275.00**

Coat, lady's
Crepe, black, dots, fox trim, fringed neck, 1920s. **225.00**

Gabardine, lavender–gray, flaring form, panels of blue and gray silk, floral embroidery, gray rabbit fur collar. **120.00**

Leather, wrap style, lavender, long, tie belt, cuffed dolman sleeves, slash pockets, irid taffeta lining **125.00**

Wool twill, blue, single breasted, wide lapels, slightly fitted waist, two clear plastic buttons, two false pockets, 15″ w at shoulders, 40″ l, designed by Galanos **25.00**

Collar, velvet, black, rhinestones, beads and pearls, 1930s **30.00**

Dress
Day
Cotton, turquoise, high neck, lace inserts, ruffled sleeves, 1895 . . . **200.00**

Rayon, pink, blue piping, padded shoulders, 1935–45. . . . . **35.00**

Silk, irid green, lace trim, hand-made, 1890–1900. . . . . **225.00**

Evening
Gauze, white work, Empire style, c1815 . . . . **115.00**

Gabardine, royal blue, net and silk satin, matching piping, white lace, black velvet trim, 1890–1900 . . . . **225.00**

Lace, silk, 2 piece, nile green, long waisted, snug fitting bodice, layered rows of ruffled skirt, hip length jacket, 1928 . . . . **50.00**

Satin, red, ruffled edge, 1920s . . **65.00**

Taffeta, black, sequin flowers, label "Jeanne Lanvin, Paris Hiver," 1938–39 . . . . **325.00**

Housecoat, mandarin style, blue silk brocade, brown silk lining, black velvet trim **45.00**

Jacket
Fur, fox, brown, label "Henry Marshall, Brooklyn," 1940–50 . . . . **250.00**

Silk, irid blue moire, full length sleeves and cording, c1855. . . . . **70.00**

Wool, pinstripe, black and white, silk lined, 1910–20. . . . . **55.00**

Nightgown, silk, lace edge neckline, embroidered, 1930s. **85.00**

Pantaloon, cotton, white, eyelet embroidery trim and tucking, hand sewn . . . **25.00**

Robe
Gauze, black, gilt foliate scrolls and medallions, Fortuny, 44″ l **1,000.00**

Silk, blue ground, eight couched gold dragons chasing flaming pearls, stylized clouds and bats, boashan haishui band at hem, Chinese, mid 19th C. **1,700.00**

Romper, child's, cotton, white, hand tucking and embroidery **18.00**

Skirt, felt, gray, velvet embroidered border, c1880 . . . . **40.00**

Smoking Jacket, velvet, brown, silk quilted collar, cuffs, and pockets, silk lined, 1900–10 . . . . **75.00**

Suit, lady's
Rayon, white and black print, padded shoulders, peplum, 1935. . . . . . . **65.00**

Wool Gabardine, double breasted jacket, straight skirt, Adrian, 1940s **150.00**

Sweater
Knit, cream, pastel floral embroidery and beads, 1960–65. . . . . **45.00**

Wool, bolero style, lilac and gray . . **12.50**

Teddy, French lace yoke, rose print on white background **35.00**

Tuxedo, wool, black, cutaway coat, pants button in front, 1900–10 . . . . . **100.00**

Waistcoat, gentleman's, late 18th C, silk
Chain stitch embroidery, polychrome silk threads, two lower pockets, minor discoloration, let out at back . . **660.00**

Embroidered silk threads, chenille yarns, and ribbons, shades of blue, yellow, and taupe, upper vest type pockets, c1820 . . . . **470.00**

CLOTHING ACCESSORIES

References: Joanne Dubbs Ball and Dorothy Hehl Torem, *The Art of Fashion Accessories,* Schiffer Publishing, 1993; Kate E. Dooner, *A Century of Handbags,* Schiffer Publishing, 1993; Kate E. Dooner, *Plastic Handbags: Sculpture To Wear,* Schiffer Publishing, 1992; Rod Dyer and Ron Spark, *Fit To Be Tied: Vintage Ties Of The Forties And Early Fifties,* Abbeville, 1987; Roseann Ettinger, *Handbags,* Schiffer Publishing, 1991; Evelyn Haetig, *Antique Combs & Purses,* Gallery Graphics Press, 1983; Richard and Teresa Holiner, *Antique Purses,* Second Edition, Collector Books, 1987, 1990 value update; Mary Trasko, *Heavenly Soles: Extraordinary Twentieth–Century Shoes,* Abbeville Press, 1989.

Additional Listings: See *Warman's Americana & Collectibles* for more examples.

Belt, turquoise links spaced with silver
gilt links, large turquoise clasp, Russian hallmarks, 29″ l. 165.00
Bonnet, baby
  Crochet, ribbon insert, newborn . . . 15.00
  Organdy, white, blue ribbon and trim 18.00
Camisole, crochet 25.00
Change Purse, 14 kt yg, flat engine—
  turned shield shape, mesh bag and
  handle, cabochon sapphires and seed
  pearls, 49.3 dwt. 550.00

**Handbag, gold colored mesh, Whiting
& Davis Co., 7″ w, 6″ h, $65.00.**

Handbag, evening
  Art Deco, brocade, engraved gold
    filled frame 75.00
  Mesh, 14 kt yg
    Engraved frame, herringbone pattern, cabochon blue stone closure, 108.7 dwt. 1,100.00
    Pierced frame, cabochon sapphire
     closure, chain, seed pearl tassel,
     71.8 dwt. 660.00
Hat
  Felt, skull cap, black, elaborate ostrich
    trim, French, label "Lorelei
    Designs". 25.00
  Milan Braid, garden, black, ecru appliques, black feather edged ribbon
    trim. 25.00
  Silk, black, ruched crown with bow
    trim, large brim, ribbons, flowers
    and chartreuse feather trim. 65.00
  Velvet, black, 1939, MIB 28.00
Motorcycle Cap, boy's, embroidered
  blue wheel with silver wings 15.00
Parasol
  Child's, silk, black 85.00
  Girl's, lace, black, Victorian 40.00
  Lady's, white, embroidered, 1910 . 60.00

Pocket
  14″ l, quilted chintz, block printed plum
    tree and pheasant pattern, madder,
    blue, and drab, chintz tape binding,
    lined with printed sepia feather and
    star patterned cotton, America,
    c1825, two small fold slits 880.00
  16″ l, linen, yellow, green, blue and
    umber crewel embroidery, homespun backing, bound with various
    printed cotton fabrics, America, late
    18th C, some fiber loss. 990.00
Shawl
  Gauze, embroidered metallic threads,
    c1815. 95.00
  Kashmir, paisley, rose 225.00
  Lace, black, 12 x 66″, 1925 . . . . . . 45.00
  Wool, black, black satin embroidery,
    silk fringe. 75.00
Shoe
  High Button
    Leather, black 55.00
    Satin, white 75.00
  Pumps, sling back, lavender and blue
    floral, matching rosette on toe,
    Schiaparelli, 1940s. 30.00
Stockings, white, stamped "Imperial
  Lisle". 10.00

COALPORT

History: In the mid 1750s Ambrose Gallimore
established a pottery at Caughley in the Severn
Gorge, Shropshire, England. Several other potteries, for example, Jackfield, developed in the area.

About 1795 John Rose and Edward Blakeway
built a pottery at Coalport, a new town founded
along the right–of–way of the Shropshire Canal.
Other potteries located adjacent to the canal were
those of Walter Bradley and Anstice, Horton, and
Rose. In 1799 Rose and Blakeway bought the
"Royal Salopian China Manufactory" at Caughley.
In 1814 this operation was moved to Coalport.

A bankruptcy in 1803 led to refinancing and a
new name, John Rose and Company. In 1814 Anstice, Horton, and Rose was acquired. The South
Wales potteries at Swansea and Nantgarw were
added. The expanded firm made fine-quality,
highly decorated ware. The plant enjoyed a renaissance in the 1888 to 1900 period.

World War I, a decline in trade, and a shift of the
pottery industry away from the Severn Gorge
brought hard times to Coalport. In 1926 the firm,

now owned by Cauldon Potteries, moved from Coalport to Shelton. Later owners included Crescent Potteries, Brain & Co., Ltd., and finally, in 1967, Wedgwood.

References: Susan and Al Bagdade, *Warman's English & Continental Pottery & Porcelain, 2nd Edition,* Wallace–Homestead, 1991; Michael Messenger, *Coalport 1795–1926,* Antique Collectors' Club, 1990.

Additional Listings: Indian Tree Pattern.

Cup and Saucer, demitasse, Indian Tree pattern, $25.00.

Bough Pot, 11½″ h, hp landscape scene with two British soldiers, gilt floral dec, yellow ground, c1809.	350.00
Cup and Saucer, Harebell pattern . . .	25.00
Dish, leaf shape, apple green, garden flower bouquet, gilt foliage, c1820. . .	90.00
Ginger Jar, cov, Blue Willow pattern .	70.00
Plate, 9″ d, pink roses, green garlands, heavy gold, artist sgd, made for Davis Collamore, NY	90.00
Spill Vase, 5″ h, pink, garden flowers and gilt scroll bands, bird's head handles with gilt rings, flared rim, sq base, c1830, price for three piece set. . .	875.00
Teapot, cov, oval, first quarter 19th C 5½″ h, four lattice filled roundels, meandering bead chain, scattered floral sprig ground, polychrome enamels, conforming domed cov and knop.	330.00
6½″ h, sepia monochrome landscape scene, conforming conical cov. . . .	440.00
Tureen, cov, 12½″ l, iron red, yellow and gilt scattered flower sprays, gilt handles, flowerhead finial, c1850	400.00
Vase, 7″ h, waisted, pierced lip dec with leaf sprays and applied flowerheads, body with gilt highlighted leaf scrolls which form pierced handles, painted butterflies and floral sprays, magenta glazed lower section, scroll molded foot, quatrefoil base, underglaze blue mark	185.00

COCA–COLA ITEMS

History: The originator of Coca–Cola was John Pemberton, a pharmacist from Atlanta, Georgia. In 1886 Dr. Pemberton introduced a patent medicine to relieve headaches, stomach disorders, and other minor maladies. Unfortunately, his failing health and meager finances forced him to sell his interest.

In 1888 Asa G. Candler became the sole owner of Coca–Cola. Candler improved the formula, increased the advertising budget, and widened the distribution. Accidentally, a "patient" was given a dose of the syrup mixed with carbonated water instead of still water. The result was a tastier, more refreshing drink.

As sales increased in the 1890s, Candler recognized that the product was more suitable for the soft drink market and began advertising it as such. From these beginnings, a myriad of advertising items have been issued to invite all to "Drink Coca–Cola."

Dates of interest: "Coke" was first used in advertising in 1941. The distinctively shaped bottle was registered as a trademark on April 12, 1960.

References: Deborah Goldstein Hill, *Price Guide to Coca–Cola Collectibles,* Wallace–Homestead, 1991; Allan Petretti, *Petretti's Coca-Cola Collectibles Price Guide, 8th Edition,* Wallace–Homestead, 1992; *Goldstein's Coca–Cola Collectibles,* Collector Books, 1991, 1993 value update; Al Wilson, *Collectors Guide To Coca–Cola Items, Volume I,* (revised: 1987, 1993 value update) and *Volume II,* (1987, 1993 value update), L–W Book Sales.

Collectors' Club: The Coca–Cola Collectors Club International, PO Box 49166, Atlanta, GA 49166.

Museum: Coca–Cola Memorabilia Museum of Elizabethtown, Inc., Elizabethtown, KY.

Additional Listings: See *Warman's Americana & Collectibles* for more examples.

Ashtray, glass, 1940s	10.00
Baseball Scorekeeper, perpetual counter.	400.00
Bell, 2¼″ h, enameled printing, c1920	200.00
Blotter	
1929, man and woman toasting with Coke bottles	75.00
1936, 50th Anniversary 1886–1936	40.00
Bookends, pr, bottle shape, bronze, 1963	130.00
Bookmark, pretty lady	300.00
Bottle Carrier, wood, holds six bottles, 1939	45.00
Bottle Opener	
Bone handle, 1930–40	20.00
Nashville 50th Anniversary, gold plated, 1952	40.00
Wall mount, toothed, c1930	75.00
Calendar, 1922, lady wearing hat hold-	

Advertising Trade Card, 1896, 3½ x 5½", $2,500.00. Photograph courtesy of Alan Petretti.

ing glass, active baseball field background, 12 x 30"	1,210.00
Catalog, 1936–41 Replacement Parts, The Reconditioning of Coolers for Coca–Cola	12.00
Chair, child's, folding	25.00
Change Purse, triangle shape, snap closure, c1908	90.00
Change Tray	
1909, 5½ x 3", oval	750.00
1910, oval, red borders, artist Hamilton	100.00
1914, Betty, 6 x 4¼"	70.00
1916, Elaine	135.00
1917, Elaine	90.00
Cigar Band, bottle in center, 1930s . .	75.00
Clicker, metal, 1930s	60.00
Coaster	
Cardboard, round, 1950s	4.00
Rubber, set of 4, orig envelope, 1940s	15.00
Convention Badge, 1959	35.00
Cooler, unusual shape and size	300.00
Dispenser, porcelain, German	400.00
Door Push, 24" l, stenciled steel, red lettering, white background	90.00
Envelope, unused, 1908	10.00
Festoon, Autumn Leaves, 1922	600.00
Flag, German	65.00
Flyswatter, net with wood handle, Coca–Cola, Helena, Ark	10.00
Game	
Cribbage Board, 1940s	45.00
Paddle Ball, c1950	35.00
Punching Ball Game, mask and ball, orig box, 1930	400.00
Ice Pick, opener on one end	30.00
Ice Tongs, wood handle with Coca–Cola adv, 1920s	150.00

Knife, opens on each end	220.00
Letterhead, used, handwritten and sgd, 1912	100.00
License Plate, red	20.00
Menu Board, tin	40.00
Mirror, pocket, woman with flowing hair	130.00
Notebook, 2¾ x 4½", Compliments The Coca–Cola Co, 1905	150.00
Pencil Box, includes contents, 1930s .	30.00
Pencil Holder, ceramic, 1960s	150.00
Playing Cards, double deck, 100th Anniversary, sealed.	18.00
Poster, 50th Anniversary 1886–1936, two ladies sitting, each holding bottle	170.00
Radio, cooler shape, 7 x 12 x 9½", 1950	450.00
Ruler, wood, 1950s	5.00
Sign	
10 x 27½", litho tin, "Delicious and Refreshing," emb, Christmas bottle, dated 1931	365.00
12 x 20", paper, color litho, metal strip top and bottom	
"Pause A Minute Refresh Yourself," woman with bottle.	440.00
"That Taste–Good Feeling," boy eating hot dog holding bottle . . .	275.00
"Treat Yourself Right," man opening bottle	355.00
12 x 28", Fountain Service Drink Coca–Cola, porcelainized sheet metal, green, red, and white	145.00
String Holder, 16" h, convex stenciled tin, red, white, and yellow.	330.00
Syrup Container	
Can, paper label, 1950s	75.00
Jug, ceramic, paper label, early 1900s	100.00
Thermometer, litho tin, 16" h	
1937, Christmas bottle, red background.	145.00

Serving Tray, 1910, 10½ x 13¼", $650.00.

1940, girl, silhouette, green, red, and gold	220.00
1941, emb, two bottles	230.00
Thimble, 1920s	28.00
Toy, Buddy L	
Racer	25.00
Truck	60.00
Tray	
1904, lovely girl, 13″	1,320.00
1914, Betty, 15 x 12¼″	90.00
1917, Elaine, 19 x 8½″	80.00
1938	85.00
1941	85.00
1942, 13 x 10½″	50.00
1950	20.00
Uniform Button,¾″ d, c1910	45.00
Vienna Art Plate, topless lady, Western Bottling Co, 1905	450.00
Watch Fob, "Drink Coca–Cola in Bottle–5¢," brass, emb, girl with product, 1905	250.00
Whistle, wood, 1920s	50.00

COFFEE MILLS

History: Coffee mills or grinders are utilitarian objects designed to grind fresh coffee beans. Before the advent of stay-fresh packaging, coffee mills were a necessity.

The first home-size coffee grinders were introduced about 1890. The large commercial grinders designed for use in stores, restaurants, and hotels often bear an earlier patent date.

Reference: Terry Friend, *Coffee Mills,* Collector Books, 1982, out of print.

Landers, Frary & Clark, New Britain, CT, No. 2, cast iron, two wheels, 12″ h, $450.00.

COUNTERTOP (COMMERCIAL)

Coles Mfg, No 7, cast iron, patented 1887, 27″	475.00
Elgin National, No 40, cast iron, two wheels	325.00
Enterprise, No 12, two wheels, eagle, patented 1898	625.00
Parker, No 5000, cast iron, patented 1897	275.00
S & H, cast iron, drawer, 12″	425.00

FLOOR MODEL (COMMERCIAL)

Enterprise, eagle on top, patented 1873, 72″	3,500.00
Fairbanks Morse, cast iron, brass hopper, 72″	1,300.00
Starr, cast iron, 72″	975.00

LAP (DOMESTIC)

A Kendrick & Sons, No 1, cast iron, brass hopper	100.00
Arcade	
Favorite, cast iron top and hopper	100.00
Imperial, wood and cast iron, 11″	75.00
Common, wood, box joints, cast iron hopper	75.00
Delmew, Simons Hardware, St Louis	75.00
J Fisher, Warranted, walnut, dovetailed, brass hopper	150.00
Landers, Frary & Clark, cast iron, corset shape, round sculpted cup and hopper, curved crank handle with wood knob	220.00
New Model, cast iron, drawer, 5½ x 4½ x 5½″	75.00
Unmarked, cherry, dovetailed, brass hopper, 4″	155.00
W W Weaver, walnut, dovetailed, pewter hopper	155.00

TABLE (DOMESTIC)

Sheet and wrought steel, brass finials, tin hopper, wide flat handle with engraved foliage, marked "Zur Erinnerung," 10″ h	105.00
Tin and wood, cast iron hopper labeled "The Bronson–Walton Co, Cleveland, O," red and blue lithography on pale green tin sides, calvary officers, crossed flags, wear, some paint loss, 8″ h plus handle	550.00
Wooden	
Cherry	
6¼″ h plus handle, dovetailed case, nailed drawer, iron hopper and handle, branded label "J Fisher Warranted"	200.00
10″ h, dovetailed, scalloped base,	

drawer with porcelain handle, pewter hopper, wrought iron handle, marked "E Nagle, Maker" . . **165.00**
11¼" h, cylindrical, cast iron handle and grinder arm, well made replacement drawer **135.00**

WALL (DOMESTIC)

Lunbrack, Czechoslovakia **70.00**
National Specialty Co, Philadelphia, cast iron, orig red scroll, gilt dec. **85.00**
Unmarked, funnel hopper, made by blacksmith, c1790 . . . . **180.00**

COIN-OPERATED ITEMS

History: Coin-operated items include amusement games, pinball machines, jukeboxes, slot machines, vending machines, cash registers, and other items operated by coins.

The first jukebox was developed about 1934 and played 78 RPM records. Jukeboxes were an important part of teenage life before the advent of portable radios and television.

The first pinball machine was introduced in 1931 by Gottlieb. Pinball machines continued to be popular until solid-state games came on the scene in 1977, along with advanced electronic video games.

The first three–reel slot machine, the Liberty Bell, was invented in 1905 by Charles Fey in San Francisco. In 1910, Mills Novelty Company copyrighted the classic fruit symbols. Improvements and advancements have led to the sophisticated machines of today.

Vending machines for candy, gum, and peanuts were popular from 1910 until 1940 and can be found in a wide range of sizes and shapes.

Because of the heavy usage these coin-operated items received, many are restored and at the very least have been repainted by either the operator or manufacturer. Using reproduced mechanisms to restore pieces is acceptable in many cases, especially when the restored piece will be able to perform as originally intended.

References: Jerry Ayliffe, *American Premium Guide To Jukeboxes And Slot Machines, Gumballs, Trade Stimulators, Arcade,* Books Americana, 1985; Richard Bueschel, *Pinball I: Illustrated Historical Guide To Pinball Machines, Volume I,* Hoflin Publishing, 1988; Richard Bueschel, *Slots 1: Illustrated Guide to 100 Collectible Slot Machines, Volume 1,* Hoflin Publishing, 1989; Richard Bueschel and Steve Gronowski, *Arcade 1, Illustrated Historical Guide to Arcade Machines, Volume I,* Hoflin Publishing, 1993; Nic Costa, *Automatic Pleasures: The History Of The Coin Machine,* Kevin Francis Publishing, 1988; Bill Enes, *Silent Salesmen: An Encyclopedia Of Collectible Gum, Candy & Nut Machines,* published by author, 1987; Bill Kurtz, *Slot Machines and Coin–Op Games,* Chartwell Books, 1991; Stephen K. Loots, *The Official Victory Glass Price Guide To Antique Jukeboxes, 1988 (Third) Edition,* Jukebox Collector Newsletter, 1988; Eiden, Heirbert, and Jurgen Lukas, *Pinball Machines,* Schiffer Publishing, 1992; Vincent Lynch, *American Jukebox The Classic Years,* Chronicle Books, 1990; Scott Wood, *A Blast From the Past Jukeboxes: A Pictorial Price Guide,* L–W Book Sales, 1992.

Periodicals: *Classic Amusements,* 12644 Chapel Road, PO Box 315, Clifton, VA 22024; *Coin Machine Trader,* 569 Kansas SE, PO Box 602, Huron, SD 57350; *Coin–Op Newsletter,* 909 26th Street NW, Washington, DC 20037; *Gameroom Magazine,* 1014 Mt. Tabor Rd., New Albany, IN 47150; *Jukebox Collector Newsletter,* 2545 SE 60th Street, Des Moines, IA 50317; *Loose Change,* 1515 S. Commerce St., Las Vegas, NV 89102.

Additional Listings: See *Warman's Americana & Collectibles* for separate categories for Jukeboxes, Pinball Machines, Slot Machines, and Vending Machines.

Advisor: Bob Levy.

Columbus Vendor, Columbus, OH, 1¢ gum ball, clear glass globe, green enameled base, $135.00.

GAME

Bally Fireball, pinball **1,700.00**
Challenger, target practice, 10 shots for 1¢, ABT Mfg Corp, Chicago, USA, orange, black, and gold, key **275.00**
Foxhunt, pinball, 5¢, 65 x 21 x 51", Pat 1936, orig instruction card, 1940. . . . **200.00**
Mutascope 2¢ Hockey, orig marquee **1,200.00**
Over the Top 1¢ Skill Game, penny push–up, 8 x 20". **400.00**
Play Football, arcade, Chester Pollard Amusement Co, c1924 . . . . **1,500.00**
Select–Em, dice game, Exhibit Supply Co, Chicago **275.00**

JUKEBOX

AMI, Model C	800.00
Mills Throne of Music	750.00
Rockola, #1422, 1946	1,700.00

Seeburg
Model P148, light up side columns, top changes colors with revolving lights, blue glass mirrored tile front, 5 plays for a quarter, 1948 ..... 1,450.00
Wurlitzer, Model 1015, bubble tubes framing glazed front, veneered wood case, 50" h, c1947. .... 2,700.00

SLOT MACHINE

Buckley, 10¢, 3 reel, metal case, chrome dec, green 800.00
Caille Commander Streamline, yellow case, 1930s 900.00
Figural, Indian, holding Bursting Cherry slot machine, 3 reel, carved wood with headdress, restored. 2,500.00
Jennings, Standard Chief, 10¢, 3 reel, wood and chrome case 1,000.00

Mills
High Top, jackpot, 1947–62 ...... 1,100.00
Mystery Castle, 1933 .... 1,200.00
The Owl, 5¢, one wheel upright, oak cabinet carved with owl and foliage below color wheel, 5 way cast metal coin head, 64", c1905, restored... 6,000.00
Vest Pocket, 1938 .... 300.00
Pace, Comet, Deluxe twin jackpots, 3 reel, restored, 1940's. 900.00
Watling, Rol–A–Top, 5¢, coin front .. 3,000.00

VENDING

Acorn, 5¢, all purpose, Oak Mfg, 1940 65.00
Advance, 1¢, peanuts, football style globe, c1923. .... 140.00
Dean, 1¢, gum, metal case, glass panels, 13 x 7 x 8". 60.00
Eat 'Em Hot Nuts, orig glass cup dispenser, 1934. .... 375.00
Jacob's, 5¢, cigars, 36" w, patent 1907 1,400.00
Mansfield, 5¢, gum, 12" h, 10½" sq, etched glass front, glass sides 400.00
Master, 1¢, peanuts, 16" h, 8" sq, cast metal, red and black paint, complete with orig keys, c1930s 120.00
Pulver Yellow Kid, 1¢, gum, clockwork movement of Yellow Kid with insertion of penny. 700.00
Zeno, collar buttons 750.00

MISCELLANEOUS

Cash Register, National, Model 542, brass, keys up to $99.99, receipt machine at side, running totals at other side, crank operated, brass cash drawer, 24" h 600.00
Fare Box, Jonson, hand crank, patent 1914, restored. 225.00
Piano, Seeburg style A, mandolin attachment, oak case, art glass panel . 6,750.00
Radio, hotel, "25 for 2 hours," gray metal case, Corado, c1940, 14 x 8 x 7½". . 65.00
Scale, 1¢, porcelain and steel, mirror top with info guide, Watling Scale, Chicago 250.00
Telephone, Western Electric, wall type, oak, uses dimes, nickels, and quarters, c1920 .... 475.00

COMIC BOOKS

History: Shortly after comics first appeared in newspapers of the 1890s, they were reprinted in book format and often used as promotional giveaways by manufacturers, movie theaters, candy stores, and stationery stores. The first modern format comic was issued in 1933.

The magic date is June 1938, when DC issued Action Comics No. 1, marking the first appearance of Superman. Thus began comics' "Golden Age," which lasted until the mid 1950s and witnessed the birth of the major comic book publishers, titles, and characters.

In 1954 Fredric Wertham authored *Seduction of the Innocent*, a book which pointed a guilt–laden finger at the comic industry for corrupting youth, causing juvenile delinquency, and undermining American values. Many publishers were forced out of business while others established a "comics code" to assure parents that their comics were compliant with morality and decency censures upheld by the code authority.

Comics' "Silver Age," the mid 1950s through the end of the 1960s, witnessed the revival of many of the characters from the Golden Age in new comic formats. The era began with *Showcase No. 4* in October 1956, which marked the origin and first appearance of the Silver–Age Flash.

While comics survived in the 1970s, it was a low point for the genre. In the early 1980s a revival occurred. In 1983 comic book publishers, aside from Marvel and DC, issued more titles than existed in the past forty years. The mid and late 1980s were a boom time, a trend which appears to be continuing into the 1990s.

References: Mike Benton, *Crime Comics: The Illustrated History,* Taylor Publishing, 1992; Mike Benton, *Superhero Comics of the Golden Age: An Illustrated History,* Taylor Publishing, 1992; Mike Benton, *The Comic Book In America, An Illustrated History,* Taylor Publishing, 1989; Mike Benton, *Science Fiction Comics: The Illustrated History,* Taylor Publishing, 1992; Mike Benton, *Superhero Comics of the Silver Age: The Illustrated History,* Taylor Publishing, 1992; *Comic Buyer's Guide 1994 An-*

nual, *Third Edition,* Krause Publications, 1993; Ernst and Mary Gerber (compilers), *Photo–Journal Guide To Comics, Volume 1 (A–J)* and *Volume 2 (K–Z),* Gerber Publishing, 1990; John Hegenberger, *Collector's Guide To Comic Books,* Wallace–Homestead, 1990; D. W. Howard, *Investing in Comics,* The World of Yesterday, 1988; Duncan McAlpine (comp.), *The Official Comic Book Price Guide For Great Britain,* Price Guide Productions, 1992; Alex G. Malloy (ed.), *Comic Book Artists,* Wallace–Homestead, 1993; Alex G. Malloy (ed.), *Comic Values Annual: 1993–94, The Comic Books Price Guide,* Wallace–Homestead, 1993; Robert Overstreet, *The Overstreet Comic Book Price Guide, No. 24,* Avon Books, 1994; Robert M. Overstreet, *The Overstreet Comics and Cards Price Guide,* Avon Books, 1993; Robert Overstreet and Gary M. Carter, *The Overstreet Comic Book Grading Guide,* Avon Books, 1993; Don and Maggie Thompson (eds.), *Comic Book Superstars: Who is Who Among Comics Creators,* Krause Publications, 1993; Don and Maggie Thompson (eds.), *Marvel Comics Checklist & Price Guide: 1961 to Present,* Krause Publications, 1993; Jerry Weist, *Original Comic Art: Identification and Price Guide,* Avon Books, 1992.

Periodicals: *Overstreet Comic Book Marketplace,* 801 220th St., NW, Suite 3, Cleveland, TN 37320; *The Comics Buyer's Guide,* 700 East State Street, Iola, WI 54990; *The Comics Buyer's Guide Price Guide,* 700 East State Street, Iola, WI 54990; *Comic Values Monthly,* Attic Books, 15 Danbury Road, Ridgefield, CT 06877; *Wizard: The Guide To Comics,* PO Box 6782, Syracuse, NY 13217.

Museums: International Museum of Cartoon Art, 300 SE 5th Ave., #5150, Boca Raton, FL 33432; Museum of Cartoon Art, Rye, NY.

Reproduction Alert: Publishers frequently reprint popular stories, even complete books, so the buyer must pay strict attention to the title, not just the portion printed in outsized letters on the front cover. If there is any doubt, look inside at the fine print on the bottom of the inside cover or first page. The correct title will be printed there in capital letters.

Also pay attention to the size of the comic. Reprints often differ in size from the original.

Note: The comics listed below are in near mint condition, meaning they have a flat, clean shiny cover that has no wear, only tiny corner creases; no subscription creases, writing, yellowing at margins, or tape repairs; staples are straight and rust free; pages are supple and like new; and generally just-off-the-shelf quality.

PRE-GOLDEN AGE

Detective Comics, No. 35, Batman appears, National Periodical Publications–DC Comics **1,750.00**
Fighting Yank, No. 1, Mystico, the Wonder Man appears. **650.00**

Tarzan, #137, August 1963, Edgar Rice Burroughs, GK Publications, $5.00.

Plastic Man, No. 9, Quality Comics . . **300.00**
Red Ryder Comics, No. 7, Dell Publishing **85.00**
Shadow Comics, No. 2, The Avenger begins, Street & Smith Publications. . **350.00**

GOLDEN AGE

Abbott and Costello, No. 8, St. John Publishing Co. **60.00**
Adventures of Mighty Mouse, No. 4, St. John Publishing Co. **40.00**
Archie's Pal, Jughead, No. 23, Archie Publications **65.00**
Billy the Kid, No. 24, Toby Press **20.00**
Classic Comics, Gilberton Publications
No. 1, Three Musketeers, sixth edition, 1946 . . . . **65.00**
No. 18, The Hunchback of Notre Dame, first Gilberton edition, March 1944. **450.00**
No. 98, The Red Badge of Courage, eighth edition, June 1964 . . . . **4.00**
Cowgirl Romances, No. 8, Wild Beauty, Fiction House, 1952. . . . . **45.00**
Crackajack Funnies, No. 5, Naked Women, Dell, 1938 . . . . **275.00**
Donald and Mickey Merry Christmas, No. 8, Donald in Toyland, 1948, Firestone Tire giveaway. **400.00**
Fawcett Movie Comic
No. 12, "Rustlers on Horseback," Rocky Lane. **165.00**
No. 20, "Ivanhoe," Liz Taylor **125.00**
First Romance Magazine, No. 8, Home Comics (Harvey Publications). **4.00**
Flaming Love, No. 7, Fighting Yank, Nedor Publications, 1942 . . . . **150.00**

Frankenstein Comics, No. 19, Prize
Publications **75.00**
Gabby Hayes Western, No. 16, Fawcett **50.00**
Girls in Love, No. 1, May 1950,
Fawcett **35.00**
Hopalong Cassidy, No. 40, Fawcett . . **42.00**
Intimate Confessions, No. 3, Realistic
Comics. **60.00**
Jungle Jim, Four Color, No. 10, Dell
Publishing. **15.00**
Little Audrey, No. 6, St. John Publishing **75.00**
Looney Tunes and Merrie Melodies
Comics, No. 73, Dell Publishing **25.00**
Lovers Lane, No. 8, Lev Gleason Pub-
lishing, 1949. . . . . **15.00**
MAD, No. 34, Berg starts as a regular,
E. C. Comics **70.00**
March of Comics, Western Publishing
No. 58, Henry **30.00**
No. 171, Oswald the Rabbit **20.00**
No. 240, Tarzan **45.00**
No. 334, Lassie (TV) **10.00**
No. 421, Tweety & Sylvester **3.00**
Mister Mystery, No. 14, SPM Publishing **80.00**
Phantom Lady, No. 3, Fox Features
Syndicate. **200.00**
Rin Tin Tin, Four Color, No. 14, Dell
Publishing. **35.00**
Roy Rogers, No. 46, Dell Publishing . **50.00**
Secret Loves, No. 2, Comics Maga-
zines, 1949. . . . . **75.00**
Sergeant Preston of the Yukon, No. 13,
origin of Sergeant Preston, Dell
Publishing. **30.00**
Silver Streak, No. 5, Dickie Dean, Lev
Gleason. **750.00**
Smitty, No. 2, Dell Publishing **35.00**
Star Studded, Blue Beetle, Cambridge
House **250.00**
Strange Suspense Stories, No. 28 . . . **22.00**
Tell It To The Marines, No. 2, Madame
Cobra appears, Toby Press
Publications **45.00**
U.S. Marines In Action, No. 3, Avon
Periodicals **25.00**
Wild Boy Of The Congo, No. 10, Ziff–
Davis. **35.00**
Zago, Jungle Prince, No. 3, Fox Fea-
tures Syndicate. **125.00**

SILVER AGE

Adam–12, No. 4, Gold Key **4.50**
Amazing Spiderman, No. 94, origin re-
told, Marvel. **35.00**
Astonishing Tales, No. 12, Man Thing,
Marvel. **8.00**
Beatles, No. 1, Dell Publishing **400.00**
Bomba, The Jungle Boy, No. 5, DC . . **10.00**
Casper, The Friendly Ghost, No. 43,
Harvey Publications. **6.00**
Daredevil, No. 19, Marvel **50.00**

Dark Shadows, No. 6, Gold Key **45.00**
Doctor Strange, No. 14, Marvel **6.00**
Fantastic Four, Marvel
No. 6, Sub–Mariner and Dr. Doom
team up **800.00**
No. 91 . . . . **18.00**
No. 217, Dazzler **4.50**
No. 340 . . . . **2.50**
Girl from U.N.C.L.E., No. 3, Gold Key **22.00**
Hawkman, No. 20, National Periodical
Publications **28.00**
Iron Man, No. 64, Marvel **10.00**
Korak, Son Of Tarzan, No. 9, Gold Key **30.00**
Lucy Show, No. 3, Gold Key **40.00**
Magnus, Robot Fighter, No. 22, origin,
Gold Key **3.50**
Metal Men, No. 52, DC Comics **8.00**
Movie Comics, The Love Bug, Gold Key **11.00**
Nick Fury, Agent Of SHIELD, No. 7,
Marvel. **11.00**
Planet Of The Apes, No. 10, Marvel . **2.50**
Powerman, No. 19, Marvel **7.50**
Ripley's Believe It Or Not, No. 27, Gold
Key **3.50**
Space Ghost, No. 1, 1967, Gold Key . **6.00**
Star Trek, No. 11, Gold Key **50.00**
Sub–Mariner, No. 10, Marvel **1.50**
Tomahawk, No. 4, DC, 1950 . . . . **150.00**
Tower Of Shadows, No. 7, Marvel . . . **8.00**
Twilight Zone, No. 6, Gold Key **25.00**
X–Men, No. 112, Marvel **20.00**

POST–SILVER AGE

Adventures Of The Fly, No. 21, Fly Girl,
Archie Comics. **25.00**
Alien Nation: The Spartans, No. 2, Ad-
venture Comics. **2.50**
Aztec Ace, No. 6, Eclipse **3.00**
Barbie and Ken, No. 4, Dell **125.00**
Battletech, No. 4, Blackthorne **1.75**
Blood Sword Dynasty, No. 1, J. C.
Productions **2.00**
Captain Victory, No. 7, Pacific **1.00**
Death Rattle, No. 2, Kitchen Sink . . . **2.00**
Duck Tales, No. 14, Planet Blues, Walt
Disney. **1.75**
E–Man, No. 20, First **1.25**
FemForce, No. 6, AC Comics **2.50**
Howard Chaykin's American Flagg, No.
8, First **1.75**
Mr. Monster, No. 3, Eclipse **3.50**
Robotech Masters Comics, No. 10, Zor **2.50**
Speed Racer, No. 1, Now **3.50**
Spooky Haunted House, No. 6, Harvey **2.00**
Teenage Mutant Ninja Turtles, Mirage
No. 1, fourth printing **9.00**
No. 9 . . . . **3.00**
No. 30 . . . . **1.25**
Three Stooges, No. 2, Dell **50.00**
Transformers, No. 3 . . . . **2.00**

Unusual Tales, No. 13, Charlton Comics, 1950 . . . . **20.00**
Walt Disney Showcase, No. 19, That Darn Cat, Gold Key **7.00**
Zot, No. 2, Eclipse **3.00**

COMPACTS

History: In the first quarter of the 20th century attitudes regarding cosmetics changed drastically. The use of makeup during the day was no longer looked upon with disdain. As women became "liberated" and as more and more of them entered the business world, the use of cosmetics became a routine and necessary part of a woman's grooming. Portable containers for cosmetics became a necessity.

Compacts were made in a myriad of shapes, styles, combinations, and motifs, all reflecting the mood of the times. Every conceivable natural or man–made medium was used in the manufacture of compacts. Commemorative, premium, souvenir, patriotic, figural, combination compacts, Art Deco, and enamel compacts are a few examples of the compacts that were made in the United States and abroad. Compacts combined with cigarette cases, music boxes, watches, hatpins, canes, lighters, and so on, also were very popular.

Compacts were made and used until the late 1950s, when women opted for the "au naturel" look. The term "vintage" is used to distinguish the compacts from the first half of the 20th century from contemporary examples.

References: Roseann Ettinger, *Compacts and Smoking Accessories*, Schiffer Publishing, 1991; Roselyn Gerson, *Ladies' Compacts of the 19th and 20th Centuries*, Wallace–Homestead, 1989; Laura M. Mueller, *Collector's Encyclopedia of Compacts, Carryalls & Face Powder Boxes*, Collector Books, 1994.

Collectors' Club: The Compact Collectors Club, PO Box Letter S, Lynbrook, NY 11563.

Advisor: Roselyn Gerson.

Additional Listings: See *Warman's Americana & Collectibles* for more examples.

American Maid, heart shape, goldtone, brocade lid, c1930. . . . . **40.00**
Amita, damascene with inlaid gold and silver Mt Fuji scene, black matte finish lid, Japan, c1920. . . . . **125.00**
Cartier, 18 kt yg, circular outline, center black enamel medallion accented by green beryl terminal and closure, reeded case with black enamel edge, marked "Cartier, Paris," 56.6 dwt . . . **1,650.00**
Coro, enamel, black, horseshoe shape, case and watch, snap closure, powder and rouge compartments, c1920 **150.00**
Coty
Flying Colors, gilt metal, spread eagle

14K yellow gold, rect, ornate mongram dec, mirror, 39 dwt, $242.00. Photograph courtesy of Freeman/Fine Arts of Philadelphia.

   shape, red, white, and blue lipstick tube center, orig presentation box, c1940 . . . . **225.00**
Octagonal, polished nickel finish . . **75.00**
Croco, sq, leather, white, zippered, multicolored cord in lid, Israel. **50.00**
D F Briggs Co, vanity case, gold filled, engine turned, enamel disk on lid, carrying chain **90.00**
Delettrez, Wildflower, pale blue paper compact, floral spray on lid, 1940s . . **50.00**
Dorette, snakeskin, vanity purse, zipper compartments for powder, lipstick in lid **225.00**
Dunhill vanity, silvered, cigarette lighter shape, sliding lipstick, c1920 . . . . . . **125.00**
E A Bliss Co, compact/bracelet, vermeil nickel silver, etched floral dec on lid, applied cutout leaf shape metal band **150.00**
Eastern Star, enameled, jeweled **45.00**
Elizabeth Arden, harlequin shape, light blue, c1940. . . . . **75.00**
Evans, bronzed metal, compact and cigarette case, engine turned design, white cloisonne disk on lid, c1930. . . **75.00**
Girey, Kamra–Pak, confetti plastic case, camera shape, compartments and slide–out lipstick, 1930–40 . . . . **65.00**
Fuller, plastic, comb sleeve mounted on lid **40.00**
Harmony, Boston, box shape, tan, snap closure, 1920s **50.00**
Harriet Hubbard Ayer, engine turned, goldtone, center compartments. **60.00**
Illinois Watch Co, compact and watch, goldtone, engraved design on lid, 1930–40. **125.00**
K & K, mother–of–pearl, gray, faux sapphires and rhinestones, 1930–40 . . . **50.00**

LaMode, heart shape, silverplated	55.00
Marathon, goldtone, heart on lid, lid reveals locket	60.00
Mary Dunhill, satin goldtone, hinged, rhinestones and green stones set in thumbpiece.	75.00
Mireve, enamel, black, sliding lipstick, perfume bottle, France.	75.00
Rex, mesh, vanity pouch, white plastic beads, c1930	50.00
Richard Hudnut, vanity clutch, fabric, white and gold, Tree of Life motif with green stones, 1940s	100.00
Tiffany & Co, 14 kt yg, octagon shaped outline, engine turned design, chased edge, engraved center initials, marked "Tiffany & Co," 17.7 dwt.	250.00
Timepact, enamel, black, elongated horseshoe shape, case and watch, powder and rouge compartments	175.00
Unknown Maker	
Alligator, pull–out mirror	80.00
Girl Scout, satin goldtone, insignia on top	60.00
Hand Mirror shape	
Goldtone, dec and engraved lid	90.00
Plastic, ivory color, Germany, 1920s	60.00
Horseshoe shape, gilt metal, tolled leather inserts on lid and back.	100.00
Wadsworth, Compakit, plastic, black, camera shape, compartment on front, lipstick and cigarette lighter on top, cigarette compartment on bottom, c1940.	200.00
Whiting & Davis, vanity bag, silvered mesh, etched and engraved lid, braided carrying chain, 1920s.	400.00
Zell Fifth Avenue, goldtone, poodle motif with red cabochon stones, lipstick fitted black grosgrain case, 1940–50	110.00

CONSOLIDATED GLASS COMPANY

History: The Consolidated Lamp and Glass Company resulted from the 1893 merger of the Wallace and McAfee Company, glass and lamp jobbers of Pittsburgh, and the Fostoria Shade and Lamp Company of Fostoria, Ohio. When the Fostoria plant burned down in 1895, Corapolis, Pennsylvania, donated a seven–acre tract of land near the center of town for a new factory. In 1911 the company was the largest lamp, globe, and shade works in the United States, employing more than 400 workers.

In 1925 Reuben Haley, owner of an independent design firm, convinced John Lewis, president of Consolidated, to enter the giftware field utilizing a series of designs inspired by the 1925 Paris Exposition Internationale des Arts Decoratifs et Industriels Modernes and the work of Rene Lalique. Initially, the glass was marketed by Howard Selden through his showroom at 225 Fifth Avenue, New York, New York. The first two lines were Catalonian and Martele.

Additional patterns were added in the late 1920s: Florentine (January 1927), Chintz (January 1927), Ruba Rombic (January 1928), and Line 700 (January 1929). On April 2, 1932, Consolidated closed it doors. Kenneth Haley moved thirty–five to forty molds to Phoenix. In March 1936 Consolidated reopened under new management. The "Haley" molds were returned. During this period the famous Dancing Nymph line, based on an 8″ salad plate in the 1926 Martele series, was introduced.

In August 1962 Consolidated was sold to Dietz Brothers. A major fire damaged the plant during a 1963 labor dispute. In 1964 the company closed its doors for good.

References: Ann Gilbert McDonald, *Evolution of the Night Lamp*, Wallace–Homestead, 1979; Jack D. Wilson, *Phoenix & Consolidated Art Glass, 1926–1980*, Antique Publications, 1989.

Collectors' Club: Phoenix and Consolidated Glass Collectors, PO Box 81974, Chicago, IL 60681.

Bowl, Olive pattern, Martele Line, green	60.00
Butter Dish, cov, Guttate, white, gold trim	45.00
Candlestick	
Five Fruits pattern, Martele Line, green	25.00
Hummingbird pattern, Martele Line, green frosted.	95.00
Celery Tray, Florette, pink	35.00
Compote, Fish	
Amber stain	60.00
Green	90.00

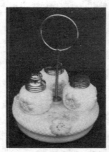

Condiment Set, salt and pepper shakers and mustard, Cosmos pattern frame with pink band, metal ring handle, $325.00.

Cruet
Cone, 5¼″ h, pink, applied clear
frosted handle, facet cup stopper. . 300.00
Florette, pink, orig stopper 70.00
Cup and Saucer, Dance of the Nudes,
clear, frosted nudes. 60.00
Goblet, Russet Fruits, Martele Line, 9 oz 25.00
Ice Tea Tumbler, Catalonian Line, ame-
thyst, ftd. 18.00
Lamp, 13″ h, amber Ruba Rombic shade
flanked by two nude women, Art Deco
base 1,500.00
Pickle Castor, Cone, pink, SP frame
marked "Tufts," resilvered 200.00
Pitcher
Five Fruits, clear and frosted 350.00
Guttate, 9½″ h, pink satin, applied
clear handle. 175.00
Plate
10″ d, Dance of the Nudes 75.00
12″ d, Bird of Paradise, Martele Line,
pink—orchid 95.00
Puff Box, Lovebirds, blue 95.00
Salt Shaker, orig top
Cone, blue 25.00
Guttate, green 30.00
Snack Set, Five Fruits, amber stain . . 60.00
Sugar, cov
Florette, pink 40.00
Ruba Rombic, jungle green, 3″ h . . 150.00
Sugar Shaker, Cone, green, glossy fin-
ish, orig top. 85.00
Sundae, Russet Fruits, Martele Line . 27.00
Tumbler
Cone, pink 45.00
Dance of the Nudes, 3½″ h 45.00
Five Fruits, green stain 20.00
Russet Fruits, Martele Line, ftd,
5¾″ h 27.00
Vase
2¾″ h, Ruba Rombic, jade green . . 250.00
5″ h, Dance of the Nudes, fan, clear
and frosted 125.00
6¾″ h, Ruba Rombic, green cased to
opal, slight irid surface, c1928. . . . 770.00
9½″ h, Ruba Rombic, jade green,
base drilled for lamp fittings. 1,250.00
10¾″ h, Love Bird pattern, Martele
Line, green stain 275.00
11″ h, Dancing Nudes, blue figures,
custard ground. 500.00
Violet Vase, 3½″ h, Catalonian Line,
amethyst 40.00
Water Pitcher, Guttate, pink cased . . 395.00

CONTINENTAL CHINA AND PORCELAIN (GENERAL)

History: By 1700, porcelain factories existed in
large numbers throughout Europe. In the mid 18th

century, the German factories at Meissen and
Nymphenburg were dominant. As the century
ended, French potteries assumed the leadership
role. The "golden age" of Continental china and
porcelains was from the 1740s to the 1840s.

Americans living in the last half of the 19th century eagerly sought the masterpieces of the European porcelain factories. In the early 20th century,
this style of china and porcelain was a "blue chip"
among the antiques collectors.

References: Susan and Al Bagdade, *Warman's
English & Continental Pottery & Porcelain, 2nd Edi-
tion,* Wallace–Homestead, 1991; Rachael Feild,
*Macdonald Guide To Buying Antique Pottery &
Porcelain,* Wallace–Homestead, 1987; Judith and
Martin Miller (eds.), *Miller's Antiques Checklist:
Porcelain,* Viking Studio Books, 1991.

Additional Listings: France—Haviland, Limoges, Old Paris, Sarreguemines, and Sevres; Germany—Austrian Ware, Bavarian China, Carlsbad
China, Dresden/Meissen, Rosenthal, Royal Bayreuth, Royal Bonn, Royal Rudolstadt, Royal Vienna, Schlegelmilch, and Villeroy and Boch; Italy—
Capo–di–Monte.

**Figure, gold accents on white ground,
light blue tufted sleigh int. with gold
buttons, marked "Chantilly," c1860,
$1,400.00.**

FRENCH

Faience, figure, 21″ h, bisque, nymph,
standing, polychrome, curled pale
brown hair, wreath of fruiting sprigs,
blue sash, floral print drape, tree
trunk, mound base, imp factory mark,
c1900. . . . . 1,000.00
Jacob Petit
Clock Case, 15¾″ h, portrait of French
courtesan, sgd, c1840, chips. 1,000.00
Vase, 7″ h, cornucopia shape, multicolored floral garland, green
ground, molded foliate scrollwork,
shaped rect base with scroll mold-

ing and emb floral sprigs and gilt highlighting, underglaze blue "J. P." mark, price for pair **400.00**

Mennecy, figure, 9" h, lady, seated, polychrome and gilt dec, c1755, minor damage **3,300.00**

Orlik, breakfast set, small 5¾" h coffeepot, creamer, cov sugar, cup and saucer, bowl, two plates, gilt floral sprays, pink ground, overglaze red mark "Orlik/Made In France/Hand–painted," price for eight piece set **200.00**

St. Cloud
Bonbonniere, cov, cat form, SS mountings, late 19th C **225.00**
Cup and Saucer, trembleuse, c1750 **600.00**

Samson
Jardiniere, bisque, tapering cylindrical body, relief molded continuous frieze of dancing putti holding floral garland, white foliate scroll border, blue ground, gilt ram's heads, pseudo interlaced L's enclosing AA mark, late 19th C, price for pair . . . **6,000.00**
Plate, 9" d, octagonal, porcelain, armorial center, floral dec cavetto, gilded rim, Chinese Export, late 19th C, price for set of eight **1,700.00**

Vieux Paris
Clock, 13" h, vase form, yellow ground, minor chips, c1820. . . . . . **950.00**
Tray, 13½" sq, mythological dec, iron red factory mark, Duc d'Angouleme factory, c1800 . . . . **450.00**
Vase, 14¾", floral medallion, lavender ground, handles, sq marble plinth base, mounted as lamp, c1815, price for pair **3,125.00**

GERMAN

Berlin, plaque, 10½ x 14¼", domestic int. scene, painted in the manner of Felix Schlesinger, c1870 . . . . **3,750.00**

Frankenthal, tea service, teapot, milk jug, four cups and saucers, polychrome dec of two lovers, rococo garden ornament, floral sprays, underglaze blue crowned monogram, modeler's, gilder's, and artist's marks, c1762–95, price for ten piece set . . . **3,200.00**

Furstenberg
Cup and Saucer, purple dec, underglaze blue "F" mark, c1765. . . . . . **500.00**
Plate, 9½" d, underglaze blue script "F" mark, painted by C G Albert, c1770, price for pair **1,200.00**

Hochst
Figure, 11" w, group of lovers, rococo arbor entwined with grapes, underglaze wheel mark, incised triangle, c1765, minor restoration. **9,250.00**

Platter, 17½" l, oval, scrolling handles, pierced border, polychrome floral spray, underglaze blue wheel mark **1,700.00**

Sugar Bowl, 6¼" d, Meissen type dec, polychrome village scene, randomly scattered sprigs and sprays, underglaze blue crowned wheel mark. **600.00**

Hutschenreuther
Portrait Plate, 9⅝" d, Princess de Lamballe, yellow roses and pink ribbons in hair, white ruffled dress, gray ground, imp factory mark, blue "lamb Dresden 135.K," artist sgd "Vorberger". **800.00**
Service Plate, 10⅞" d, central dec, summer flowers within heavily gilt cavetto, rim worked with scrolling acanthus, textured ground, underglaze green factory marks, minor rubbing, price for twelve piece set . **1,320.00**

Ludwigsburg
Figure, 5" h, peasant, modeled by Pierre Francois Lejeune, painted by D Chr Sausenhofer, underglaze blue crowned interlaced C's, c1765 **1,100.00**
Teapot, cov, 3½" h, painted, green, brown, blue, and iron–red, underglaze blue crowned interlaced C's, c1765. . . . . **1,100.00**

Nymphenburg, cup and saucer, painted large bouquet and scattered sprays, brown rims, imp shield mark, c1765 . **200.00**

Potshcappel, urn, 28" h, ovoid, figures in garden listening to music, white ground, scattered floral sprays and sprigs, scrolled handles with partially draped female figure and applied flowerheads and leaves, gadrooned, floral encrusted cov, cartouche shaped shield flanked by two cupids, circular stand painted with four figural vignettes, shell and scroll molded borders, four spreading scroll feet with applied flowerheads, underglaze blue crossed lines mark with T, minor losses to flowers, firing cracks, price for pair. **8,250.00**

Saxony
Butter Pat, 2⅞" h, shaped rect, central painted spray of bright colored flowers, one corner surmounted by brightly painted figure of 18th C lady or gentleman, underglaze blue or gilt monogram over "Dresden, Saxony," price for set of thirteen **1,210.00**
Vase, cov, 21½", polychrome floral dec, applied flowers and putti, gilt dec, massive floral finial, blue mark, 19th C, slight damage, price for pair **1,250.00**

Volkstedt, teapot, swelled circular, faint ridging, dome cov, applied purple berry finial, purple floral sprigs, applied scroll handle, underglaze blue crossed pitchforks mark, handle restored, mid 18th C. **250.00**

ITALIAN

Doccia

Charger, 15¾" d, Imari style, cobalt blue, iron–red, and gold, branches of flowering prunus and peonies, trellis, diaper, and floral panel borders, c1755 . . . . **300.00**

Tea Bowl, 3¼" d, chinoiserie figures, c1770 . . . . **450.00**

Naples

Ewer, 20" h, relief dec, bacchic scene in orchard, female rising from leaf ornaments handle, late 19th C. **350.00**

Vase, 13½", Francis I of Bourbon and his consort portraits, rubbed gilding, sgd "Raffaele Giovine, 1823," price for pair **6,000.00**

COOKIE JARS

History: Cookie jars, colorful and often whimsical, are now an established collecting category in their own right. Do not be misled by the high prices released at the 1988 Andy Warhol auction. Many of the same cookie jars that sold for more than $1,000 each can be found in the field for less than $100.

Many cookie jar forms were manufactured by more than one company and, as a result, can be found with different marks. This resulted from mergers or splits by manufacturers; for example, Brush–McCoy is now Nelson McCoy. Molds also were traded and sold among companies.

Cookie jars often were redesigned to reflect newer tastes. Hence, the same jar may be found in several different style variations.

References: John W. Humphries, *Humphries Price Guide To Cookie Jars,* published by author, 1992; Dana G. Morykan and Harry L. Rinker, *Warman's Country Antiques & Collectibles, Second Edition,* Wallace–Homestead, 1994; Harold Nichols, *McCoy Cookie Jars: From The First To The Last, Second Edition,* Nichols Publishing, 1991; Fred and Joyce Roerig, *Collector's Encyclopedia of Cookie Jars,* Book I, (1991, 1993 value update), Book II (1994), Collector Books; Mike Schneider, *The Complete Cookie Jar Book,* Schiffer Publishing, 1991; Ermagene Westfall, *An Illustrated Value Guide To Cookie Jars,* Book I (1983, 1993 value update), Book II (1993), Collector Books.

Periodicals: *Cookie Jarrin',* RR 2, Box 504, Walterboro, SC 29488; *Crazed Over Cookie Jars,* PO Box 254, Savanna, IL 61074.

ABC

Cat	65.00
Chick, yellow	65.00
Churn Boy	225.00
Cookie Truck	65.00
Kittens on Yarn	65.00
Pig–in–Poke	65.00
Pig, strawberries	95.00
Poodle, maroon	95.00
Recipe Jar	135.00

Abingdon

Wigwam	950.00
Windmill	425.00

American Bisque

Dutch Boy with sailboat, gold buttons	200.00
Jack in the box	95.00

Applause, 57 Chevy **60.00**

Brush

Davy Crockett	250.00
Hen on Nest	120.00
Lantern	65.00
Squirrel on Log	85.00

California Originals, Muppets, set of 6 **950.00**

Enesco

Betsy Ross	165.00
Betty Boop	395.00
Cinderella	250.00
Little Bo Peep	225.00
Little Red Riding Hood	225.00
Snow White	775.00

F & F, Keebler Elf **125.00**

Hoan, Mickey Mouse **60.00**

Lefton, Santa **75.00**

McCoy

Cat on black coal bucket	275.00
Coke Jug	75.00
Cylinder	26.00
Engine	190.00
Grandfather Clock	115.00
Hocus Rabbit	45.00
Indian	195.00
Jack–O–Lantern	450.00
Koala Bear	85.00

Clown, Morton Pottery, $25.00.

Mammy	175.00
Mickey Mouse, leather ears	395.00
Mugsey	395.00
Puppy with Sign	85.00
Rooster, yellow and brown	125.00
Superman, brown	395.00
Tepee	195.00
Touring Car	75.00
Metlox	
Clown	85.00
Lion	350.00
Scottie	
Black	150.00
White	275.00
Morton, hen with chick	50.00
Mosaic Tile, Mammy, blue	450.00
Napco, Little bo Peep	195.00
Ransburg, Davy Crockett	125.00
Red Wing, Chef, yellow	60.00
Regal China Co, majorette	375.00
Robinson Ransbottom Pottery	
Hootie Owl	75.00
Sheriff Pig	125.00
Sierra Vista, Humpty Dumpty	345.00
Shawnee	
Koala Bear	185.00
Kraft Marshmallow Bear	175.00
Puss N' Boots	150.00
Treasure Craft	
Cookie Chef	65.00
Hobo	65.00
Monk	60.00
Stagecoach	95.00
Twin Winton, Mammy	95.00
Vandor, Popeye	475.00

COPELAND

COPELAND AND SPODE

History: In 1749 Josiah Spode was apprenticed to Thomas Whieldon and in 1754 worked for William Banks in Stoke–on–Trent. In the early 1760s Spode started his own pottery, making cream-colored earthenware and blue-printed whiteware. In 1770 he returned to Banks's factory as master, purchasing it in 1776.

Spode pioneered the use of steam-powered pottery-making machinery and mastered the art of transfer printing from copperplates. Spode opened a London shop in 1778 and sent William Copeland there circa 1784. A number of larger London locations followed. At the turn of the century, Spode introduced bone china. In 1805 Josiah Spode II and William Copeland entered into a partnership for the London business. A series of partnerships between Josiah Spode II, Josiah Spode III, and William Taylor Copeland resulted.

In 1833 Copeland acquired Spode's London operations and the Stoke plants seven years later. William Taylor Copeland managed the business until his death in 1868. The business remained in the hands of Copeland heirs. In 1923 the plant was electrified; other modernizations followed.

In 1976 Spode merged with Worcester Royal Porcelain to become Royal Worcester Spode, Ltd.

References: Susan and Al Bagdade, *Warman's English & Continental Pottery & Porcelain, 2nd Edition,* Wallace–Homestead, 1991; D. Drakard & P. Holdway, *Spode Printed Wares,* Longmans, 1983; L. Whiter, *Spode: A History Of The Family, Factory, And Wares, 1733–1833,* Barrie & Jenkins, 1970.

Teapot, cream colored cameos, dark green ground, marked, c1890, 9½" h, $250.00.

Bowl, 10⅝" d, 4½" h, sculptured white floral dec, marked "Spode, Impl. England," c1930	125.00
Creamer, 4" h, Spode's Tower pattern, blue transfer	48.00
Cup and Saucer, Rosalie pattern	8.00
Dinner Set	
51 pcs, Indian Tree, service for eight, cov butter dish, vegetable bowl, 12" d pedestal cake plate, Spode marks	375.00
95 pcs, Felspar, royal blue border outlined with gilt, puce printed Spode Felspar marks, iron–red Pat #3951, c1810	1,600.00
Dish, 11½" w, two handles, mushroom	

ground, gilt foliage, gilt scroll molded handles, puce Spode Felspar mark, c1800. . . . . 125.00

Figure, 17″ l, 17½″ h, bisque, seated young woman bending over to mend fishing net draped over her lap, oval base inscribed "Mending The Net, Edward W. Lion, Sculptor, 1873, Art Union of London Copyright Reserved, Copeland L74". 1,750.00

Jar, cov, 10″ h, globular, handled, Oriental style, apple green, birds on flowering peony branches, iron–red, pink, and gilt, gilt knob finial, Spode mark, Pat #3086, c1820. . . . . 700.00

Jardiniere, 14 x 10¼″, rect gilt bronze frame inset with four porcelain panels, rose ground, transfer printed and enameled reserves of two ladies in 17th C costume, cartouche shaped border, gilt foliate C scrolls with polychrome floral festoons, four gilt bronze bun feet, brass liner, circular factory mark imprinted on each panel "Copeland & Garrett/Late Spode," c1833–47, price for pair. 4,400.00

Jug, 6 /12″ d, 8¼″ h, bright blue ground, raised ivory figures on front and back, raised leaf trim around top, Copeland marks, made for Columbian Expo, 1893 . . . . 200.00

Milk Pitcher, 6″ h, Spode's Tower pattern, blue 135.00

Plaque, 5″ w, turquoise, printed multicolored sporting trophy, gilt scroll and foliage surround, green Copeland mark, late 19th C. 30.00

Plate
8½″ d, Imari pattern, c1900, price for set of eight 330.00
8¾″ d, creamware, pink shell motif, gilt flowering foliage, brown net pattern ground, gilt rim, imp Spode mark, c1820 . . . . 80.00
9½″ d, bird perched on snowy branch, holly leaves and berries 100.00
10¼″ d
Rosalie 13.00
Rose Briar 12.00

Platter
9½″ l, oval, birds on gnarled tree trunk issuing Oriental flowers, peonies, chrysanthemums, and foliage border, imp Copeland Spode oval mark, pat #4639, 19th C. 100.00
10½″ l, oval, creamware, pierced rim, Spode, marked, c1820 . . . . 75.00

Potpourri Jar, 10″ h, pierced cov, flared rim and foot, Imari style, flowering plants, gilt knop finial, Spode mark, Pat #967, c1810. . . . . 600.00

Relish Tray, Italian pattern, blue 45.00

Soup Plate, black transfer printed, multicolored insert and flowering plants, scrolling floral foliage borders, Spode mark, pattern #2148, c1810, price for twelve piece set 450.00

Soup Tureen, cov, matching stand, 13″ h, compressed baluster, loop handles and finials, three peonies and fowl, rocky landscape, marked "Spode Stone China," mid 19th C. 350.00

Spill Vase, 4¾″ h, flared rims, pale lilac, gilt octagonal panels with portrait of bearded man, band of pearls on rims and bases, Spode, c1820, price for pair 400.00

Teapot, cov, 4¼″ d, 4¾″ h, spherical body, cream ground, wide deep blue band dec with white relief classical figures, Dancing Hours pattern. 125.00

Tray, 11½″ w, sq, rose spray center, floral bouquet in corners, blue ground with gilt scale pattern, Pat #1163, iron–red Spode mark, c1800 . . . . . . 350.00

COPPER

History: Copper objects, such as kettles, tea kettles, warming pans, measures, and so on, played an important part in the 19th-century household. Outdoors, the apple butter kettle and still were the two principal copper items. Copper culinary objects were lined with a thin protective coating of tin to prevent poisoning. They were relined as needed.

Great emphasis is placed by collectors on signed pieces, especially those by American craftsmen. Since copper objects were made abroad as well, it is hard to identify unsigned examples.

References: Mary Frank Gaston, *Antique Brass & Copper: Identification & Value Guide,* Collector Books, 1992; Henry J. Kauffman, *Early American Copper, Tin, and Brass,* Medill McBride Co., 1950.

Additional Listings: Arts and Crafts Movement and Roycroft.

Reproduction Alert: Many modern reproductions also exist.

Bedwarmer, 43½″ l, copper pan, tooled brass lid, turned wooden handle with old brown graining, basket of flowers design on lid 330.00

Bowl, 6½″ d, hand hammered, scalloped rim, brown patina, stamped "Harry Dixon San Francisco," c1920 . . . . . . 335.00

Cigar Box, 10¼″ l, 5⅜″ w, 4″ h, shaped bronze handle, two polychrome enamel dec cedar lined compartments, ext. dec with raised, organic, and geometric Arts and Crafts devices 600.00

Coal Bucket, 10″ d, 12″ h, swing and side handles, German, late 19th C. 70.00

Colander, 10¾″ d, punched star design 75.00

Measure, strap handle, 1 gallon, $85.00.

Compote, 5¾″ d, 6¼″ h, enameled, red with white reserves, well detailed scenes on all surfaces, Cupid and Psyche in bowl, old repair 360.00
Dipper, wrought iron handle
   7″ l, 3¾″ d bowl 70.00
   20¾″ l 45.00
   23½″ l 45.00
Fish Poacher, cov, 20½″ l, oval, rolled rim, iron swing bail handle, C–shaped handle on lid, 19th C 330.00
Food Mold, turk's head, decorative detail, dovetailed seams, dents, 10″ d . . 125.00
Fruit Cooler, 15″ h, hammered, applied spherical handle, shallow cone shaped lid, bulbous body, geometric detail, four cutout and stepped feet, c1905. . . . . 350.00
Kettle, cov, 9½″ d, cylindrical, dovetailed construction, iron loop handles, domed cov, button finial, marked "Range Co, Cini, O" 95.00
Ladle, 17¾″ l, wrought iron handle . . 135.00
Lantern, 15″ h, hexagonal beveled glass panels, circular handle, 19th C 250.00
Milk Pail, 12″ h, swing handle, stamped "1870," Dutch. 500.00
Mug, 7½″ h, wrought iron handle, 18th C 55.00
Pitcher, 7½″ h, hammered pattern, sq strap handle, brown–green patina, imp AG Barton marks 85.00
Planter, 9¼″ d, 3″ h, hammered, flaring bowl, applied ivy dec, brown and green patina, orig liner, imp metal L LaGatta tag 550.00
Sauce Pan, dovetailed construction
   5″ d, 6½″ l wrought iron handle, tinned int. 55.00
   5½″ d, 7¼″ h to handle, heavy, wrought copper handle, some edge damage. 75.00

Scoop, turned wooden handle, lip split, old soldered reinforcement, 14½″ l . . 75.00
Skillet
   10½″ d, wrought steel handle, stamped "Colony RI" 85.00
   12¼″ d, cov, flared, riveted iron handled, marked "NN". 75.00
Tea Kettle
   6½″ h, dovetailed construction, gooseneck spout, domed cov on raised rim, brass knob finial. 70.00
   10½″ h, dovetailed construction, gooseneck spout, brass trim, acorn, finial, well shaped stationary handle, maker's mark of intertwined initials "W.C. & S." 95.00
   11″ h, gooseneck spout, brass band 65.00
Umbrella Stand, 25″ h, hand hammered, flared rim, cylindrical body, two strap work loop handles, repousse medallion, riveted flared foot, c1910. . . . . . 665.00
Vase, 11¾″ h, hand hammered, baluster form, waisted neck, flared mouth, brown patina, imp "Jauchens, Old Copper Shop, 36," c1915. . . . . 400.00
Wall Sconce, 12¼″ h, concave crimped tops, c1830, price for pair. 650.00
Watering Can, long spout, labeled "Joseph Breck & Sons, Boston" 145.00
Weathervane, 24″ l, fish, iron mount, 20th C 500.00

CORALENE

History: Coralene is a glass or china object which has the design painted on the surface of the piece and tiny colorless glass beads applied with a fixative. The piece is placed in a muffle which fixes the enamel and sets the beads.

Several American and English companies made glass coralene in the 1880s. Seaweed or coral was the most common design. Other motifs were "Wheat Sheaf" and "Fleur–de–Lis." Most of the base glass was satin finished.

China and pottery coralene, made from the late 1890s to the post–World War II era, is referred to as Japanese coralene. The beading is opaque and inserted into the soft clay. Hence, it is only half to three–quarters visible.

Reproduction Alert: Reproductions are on the market, some using an old glass base. The beaded decoration on new coralene has been glued and can be scraped off.

CHINA

Condiment Set, open salt, cov mustard, pepper shaker, white opaque ground, floral coralene dec, SP stand 245.00
Pitcher, 4½″ h, 1909 pattern, red and

Vase, white shading to blue, yellow seaweed coralene dec, white cased int., c1880, 6¼″ h, $250.00.

brown ground, beaded yellow daffodil
dec 950.00
Vase
4¾″ h, yellow shading to burnt orange,
yellow, green, and orange beaded
flowers, Japanese patent mark . . . 345.00
5½″ h, bisque, lavender ground, pink
and yellow flowers 175.00
8″ h, 6¾″ w, melon ribbed, sq top, yellow drape coralene, rose shaded to
pink ground, white int. 800.00

GLASS

Bowl, 5½″ d, blue MOP satin, Herringbone pattern, pink seaweed coralene,
deeply crimped top, applied rim 615.00
Cruet, pink satin, yellow coralene, orig
stopper. 400.00
Pickle Castor, 10½″ h, cranberry, In-
verted Thumbprint pattern, butterflies
and flowers coralene dec, ornate SP
marked "Meriden" frame 450.00
Pitcher, 6¼″ h, shaded yellow, white int.,
seaweed coralene. 350.00
Sweetmeat Jar, cov, 3½″ d, 4¾″ h, white
Bristol body, orange seaweed
coralene. 325.00
Tumbler, 3¾″ h, satin glass, medium to
light pink, white int., gold seaweed
coralene, gold rim 225.00
Vase
4½″ h, flared rim, peachblow opal
body, yellow seaweed coralene. . . 175.00
5½″ h, ovoid, short wide cylindrical
neck, clear shaded to cobalt blue
body, yellow seaweed coralene. . . 375.00

CORKSCREWS

History: The corkscrew is composed of three
parts: (1) the handle, (2) the shaft, and (3) the worm

or screw. The earliest known reference to "a Steele
Worme used for drawing corks out of bottles" is
1681. Samuel Henshall, an Englishman, was
granted the first patent in 1795.
Elaborate mechanisms were invented and patented from the early 1800s onward, especially in
England. However, three basic types emerged: "T"
handle (the most basic, simple form), lever, and
mechanism. Variations on these three types run
into the hundreds. Miniature corkscrews, employed
for drawing corks from perfume and medicine bottles between 1750 and 1920, are among the most
eagerly sought by collectors.
Nationalistic preferences were found in corkscrews. The English favored the helix worm and
tended to coppertone their steel products. By the
mid 18th century, English and Irish silversmiths
were making handles noted for their clean lines and
practicality. Most English silver handles were hallmarked.
The Germans preferred the center worm and
nickel plate. The Italians used chrome plate or
massive solid brass. In the early 1800s the Dutch
and French developed elaborately artistic silver
handles.
Americans did not begin to manufacture quality
corkscrews until the late 19th century. They favored the center worm and specialized in silver-
mounted tusks and carved staghorn for handles.
Collectors' Club: Canadian Corkscrew Collectors Club, 670 Meadow Wood Rd., Mississaugua,
Ontario, L5J 2S6 Canada.

**Turned wood handle with brush,
$25.00.**

LEVER

Chrome plated steel, Italian (Vogliotti–
Torino), double, wire helix, marked
"Japan" and "Christian–Brothers–
San Francisco 1908". 125.00
Nickel plated steel
Helical worm, stamped "Patent,

Weir's Patent 1280425 Sept, 1884/
J. Helley & Son Maker". 75.00
Hinged, retractable, scalloped casing,
marked "The Handy" and "Patented Feb 24, 1891," round shaft
with center worm 35.00

MECHANISM

Brass, four triangular posts, open cage,
uncyphered solid cutworm, probably
Italian, c1890 . . . .   220.00
Bronze, rosewood handle with brush,
marked "G. Twigg's Patent," c1868. .   400.00
Nickel plated steel, open cage, swivel
over collar on handle to raise shaft,
hanging ring, cyphered center worm,
German Pat 1892 . . . .   40.00
Steel, cylindrical sheath, wood barrel
handle with metal caps, metal rim
stamped "Magic Cork Extractor Pat
March 4–79, May 10–92," Mumford .   300.00

MINIATURE

Brass, 2″ l, figural, elephant, tail corkscrew, marked "Perage England,"
c1930.   30.00
Chrome, two finger pull, wire helix,
enamel City of Clacton. 25.00
Meissen, head of Johann Von Schiller,
poet and philosopher, uncyphered
center worm, head marked with
crossed swords under glaze, c1870 .   385.00
Nickel plated steel, cut, 3″ peg and
worm, fluted wire helix, mid 18th C . .   80.00

NOVELTY

Boar's head, silver, carved, scroll mount,
monogrammed, Archimedean screw,
nickel plated bell cap 265.00
Old Snifter, Senator Volstead standing,
brass corkscrew and bottle opener,
helical worm, fixed hat 200.00
Lady, figural, celluloid, white, folding
type, helical worm, stamped "Ges.
Gech," Germany. 525.00

T–HANDLE

Brass, Thomason type, bone handle
with brush, helical worm. 150.00
Figural, 5½″, horse head, carved, flowing mane, spirited glass eyes, tapered
shaft, staghorn handle, center worm
with point, c1880. . . . .   250.00
Steel, scrolled handle, Archimedean
screw. 55.00

COWAN POTTERY

History: R. Guy Cowan founded the Cowan Pottery in 1913 in Cleveland, Ohio. The establishment
remained in almost continuous operation until
1931, when financial difficulties forced closure.

Early production was redware pottery. Later a
porcelainlike finish was perfected with special emphasis placed on glazes. Lustreware is one of the
most common types. Commercial wares marked
"Lakeware" were produced from 1927 to 1931.

Early marks include an incised "Cowan Pottery"
on the redware (1913–17), an impressed "Cowan,"
and an impressed "Lakewood." The imprinted stylized semicircle, with or without the initials R. G.,
came later.

References: Paul Evans, *Art Pottery of the
United States, 2nd Edition,* Feingold & Lewis Pub-
lishing Corp., 1987; Ralph and Terry Kovel, *The
Kovels' Collector's Guide to American Art Pottery,*
Crown Publishers, 1974; Tim and Jamie Saloff,
*The Collector's Encyclopedia of Cowan Pottery:
Identification and Values,* Collector Books, 1993.

Museums: Cowan Pottery Museum, Rocky
River Public Library, Rocky River, OH; Everson
Museum of Art, Syracuse, NY.

Bowl, 3¼″ d, Lakeware 18.00
Candleholders, pr, 2 x 5″, handles on
side 25.00
Centerpiece Bowl, 6½″ h, figural nude
flower frog 175.00
Cigarette Holder, figural, seahorse, ivory   50.00

**Candleholder, triple light, ivory col-
ored, 8½″ w, 4⅞″ h, $35.00.**

Compote, 7" d, 2½" h, diamond shape 22.00
Cup and Saucer, melon dec, tan glaze 30.00
Flower Frog
  6½" h, nude dancer with scarf 135.00
  11¼" h, 6" d, flamingo, perforated base, white glaze, die stamped twice. 300.00
Soap Dish, 4 x 7", white and pink matte, seahorses at base. 40.00
Trivet, 6½" d, scalloped rim, bust of young girl framed by flowers, sgd ... 275.00
Vase
  5½" h, blue luster, fluted, ftd 100.00
  6" h, blue and green glaze, hp mushrooms................. 365.00
  8½" h, irid blue 65.00

CRANBERRY GLASS

History: Cranberry glass is transparent and named for its color, achieved by adding powdered gold to a molten batch of amber glass which then is reheated at a low temperature to develop the cranberry or ruby color. The glass color first appeared in the last half of the 17th century but was not made in American glass factories until the last half of the 19th century.

Cranberry glass was blown, mold blown, or pressed. Examples often are decorated with gold or enamel. Less expensive cranberry glass was made by substituting copper for gold and can be identified by its bluish–purple tint.

Reference: William Heacock and William Gamble, *Encyclopedia Of Victorian Colored Pattern Glass: Book 9, Cranberry Opalescent from A to Z,* Antique Publications, 1987.

Additional Listings: See specific categories, such as Bride's Baskets, Cruets, Jack–in–the–Pulpit Vases, and so on.

Reproduction Alert: Reproductions abound. These pieces are heavier, off–color, and lack the quality of older examples.

Bowl, 5¼" d, 2½" h, elaborate enamel dec, gold tracery insects, butterflies, dragonflies, and foliage, price for set of six 800.00
Butter Dish, cov, round, Hobnail pattern 100.00

Bowl, cranberry cut to clear, flaring sides, diamond and dot cutting, Pairpoint, 12" d, $66.00. Photograph courtesy of Leslie Hindman Auctioneers.

Cologne Bottle, 7" h, dainty blue, white, and yellow flowers, green leaves, gold outlines and trim, orig clear ball stopper...................... 180.00
Cruet, Hobnail pattern, matching stopper...................... 350.00
Cup and Saucer, gold bands, enameled purple and white violets, gold handle 125.00
Decanter, 11½" h, cranberry shaded to clear rubena, cut grape, leaf, and vine design, sterling silver basketweave and stylized urn overlay, orig matching clear stopper.............. 350.00
Finger Bowl, scalloped, matching underplate 125.00
Jam Dish, 4½" d, applied clear rim, SP holder 100.00
Miniature Lamp, 7¼" h, lily of the valley dec on shade and base 1,075.00
Perfume Bottle, 5½" h, enameled, beveled glass house shape casket, gilt brass fittings, price for pair 335.00
Pickle Castor, 11" h, baby thumbprint, floral enameling, ornate ftd frame, saucer type base. 425.00
Pitcher
  6" h, Diamond Quilted pattern, clear applied handle, ground pontil. 125.00
  7" h, 5¼" w, water, bulbous, enameled purple–blue pansies and leaves, floral dec, applied clear glass loop handle. 475.00
  7½" h, Inverted Thumbprint pattern, clear applied handle, ruffled rim. .. 80.00
  11½" h, tankard shape, clear applied handle, orig label, Dorflinger Glass Co 385.00
Rose Bowl, 4¾" h, egg shape, applied clear swags, scroll feet, berry pontil. . 250.00
Salt, master
  Clear pedestal base 125.00
  Footed, enamel dec 200.00
  Two vaseline rigaree rows, ftd handled metal frame 165.00
Salt Shaker, Chevarie Pillar, round pillar, wide int. ribbing, two brown speckled game birds enamel dec, two piece lid 250.00
Sugar Shaker
  Coinspot, nine panels 275.00
  Diamond Quilted, orig screw on lid . 235.00
Toothpick, 3¾" h, applied vaseline rigaree...................... 115.00
Tumble–Up Set, Inverted Thumbprint pattern.................... 85.00
Tumbler, Inverted Thumbprint pattern 35.00
Urn, cov, 12½" h, allover cutting, raised diamonds, bands of bull's eyes, cut clear glass stem, sq pedestal base, cut dome cov, clear acorn finial. 275.00
Vase
  2⅞" h, white enameled scrolls and dot dec, gold trim. 40.00

4¾" h, ovoid, gold leaves, white enamel trees 375.00

5¼" h, boat shape, amber rigaree rim and feet, strawberry pontil 195.00

5¾" h, sanded white enameled dec, Roman Key design, gold trim, ormolu feet, price for pair 275.00

6¾" h, sanded gold leaf dec outlined with white enamel, pedestal foot . . 85.00

7½" h, emb ribs, applied clear feet, three swirled applied clear leaves around base 100.00

8⅞" h, bulbous, white enameled lilies of valley dec, cylinder neck 100.00

10" h, pedestal, sterling silver overlay of daisies, leaves, and stems 1,350.00

CROWN MILANO

History: Crown Milano is an American art glass produced by the Mt. Washington Glass Works, New Bedford, Massachusetts. The original patent was issued in 1886 to Frederick Shirley and Albert Steffin.

Normally, it is an opaque white satin glass finished with light beige or ivory-color ground embellished with fancy florals, decorations, and elaborate heavy raised gold. When marked, pieces carry an entwined CM with crown in purple enamel on the base. Sometimes paper labels were used. The silver-plated mounts often have "MW" impressed or a Pairpoint mark as both Mount Washington and Pairpoint supplied mountings.

Advisors: Clarence and Betty Maier.

Vase, Diamond Quilted body, ruffled rim, gold enamel floral dec, crown and mark, 4" d, 4⅝" h, $625.00.

Bowl, cov, 9" w, 5¾" h, Aladdin lamp shape, pigtail handles, tiny lid, gleaming white ground, four enameled fully opened roses, tulips, and other spring flowers, raised gold dec, red signature and number "1013" 1,850.00

Condiment Set, cream pitcher, cov jam jar, and sugar, glossy finish, pink blush, gold chrysanthemums, ormolu mounts, sgd, price for three piece set 1,100.00

Creamer and Sugar, 3½" h creamer, 4¼" d sugar, lusterless white, pink edge blush, gold trim, lavender violets, paper label on sugar, price for pair 920.00

Cream Pitcher, petticoat shape, wide flattened pouring spout, pansy dec, gold accents on rim and applied reeded handle, numbered in polished pontil 485.00

Jewel Box, cov, 8" l, gold dec, cartouche with summer floral bouquet, sgd "The Pairpoint Corp" on base. 950.00

Pickle Castor, 8½" h, 5" d, dec insert shaded blue to white, Timothy Canty blue and white enameled flowers, orig SP Pairpoint frame, cov, and tongs, sgd "Pairpoint Mfg Co, New Bedford, MA 664". 800.00

Rose Bowl, 5⅛" d, ten pansies, pastel enamel white, purple, brown, and blue, foliage, gold blossoms, and random dec, washed enamel background shaded to simulate Mt Washington Burmese. 585.00

Salt and Pepper Shakers, pr, tall, ribbed, white satin ground, pink floral dec. . . 195.00

Sweetmeat Jar, cov, 6" d, bulbous, raised swirl band, raised design, beige swirls, six gold and silver spider chrysanthemums, SP cov and handle, C.M. monogram and number, "M.W. 4416" with raised turtle 1,100.00

Syrup, 6½" h, Burmese coloring painted on white opaque body, honeybee hovering above flowering branches, ornate SP fittings, flip top lid with emb florals and insects 1,250.00

Trinket Box, cov, 3½" d, 2½" h, shiny finish, round, swirl pattern, enameled pansies, gold accents 275.00

Tumbler, 3¾" h, shiny finish, several shades of raised gold floral swags, ribbons, and bows, numbered "1026" . . 745.00

Vase

4½" h, bulbous, eight pulled up ribs, beige ground, deeper beige tracery, heavy raised gold enameled petit point iris, leaves, and scrolls 875.00

11½" h, cream ground, spider mums dec, gold trim. 900.00

Water Set, 9" h pitcher, four 3¾" h tumblers, glossy white ground, gold enameled floral sprays and bows, laurel wreath and crown mark, numbered 1026, gilt handle worn, price for five piece set **1,450.00**

CRUETS

History: Cruets are small glass bottles used to hold oil, vinegar, wine, and so on, for the table. The high point of cruet use was during the Victorian era when a myriad of glass manufacturers made cruets in a wide assortment of patterns, colors, and sizes. All cruets had stoppers; most had handles.

References: Elaine Ezell and George Newhouse, *Cruets, Cruets, Cruets, Volume I*, Antique Publications, 1991; William Heacock, *Encyclopedia of Victorian Colored Pattern Glass: Book 6, Oil Cruets From A To Z*, Antique Publications, 1981.

Additional Listings: Pattern Glass and specific glass categories, such as Amberina, Cranberry, and Satin.

Pattern Glass, Cathedral, amber, Bryce Bros., $125.00.

Amberina, 6″ h, 4½″ w, Expanded Inverted Thumbprint pattern, orig amber stopper, Mt Washington. **750.00**
Art Glass, red, gold trim, "God Bless America," capitol. **75.00**
Burmese, 6¼″ h, ribbed, orig stopper, Mt Washington **710.00**
Cranberry, 6″ h, 4″ w, Diamond Quilted pattern, blown molded, clear applied handle, cut stopper **125.00**
Custard Glass, Louis XV pattern, gold trim, no stopper. **175.00**
Opalescent Glass
    Coin Dot pattern **70.00**
    Intaglio pattern, blue and white . . . **125.00**
    Jackson pattern, vaseline, no stopper **135.00**
    Reverse Swirl pattern, blue, heat checked handle, bruised stopper. . **100.00**
Pattern Glass, orig stopper
    Broken Column pattern **65.00**

Cape Cod pattern **40.00**
Daisy and Button with Amber Panels pattern, no stopper. **175.00**
Paneled Thistle pattern **65.00**
Peachblow, 6½″ h, Wheeling, petticoat shape, deep coloring, applied reeded handle, faceted amber stopper **1,750.00**
Rubina Verde, 6¾″ h, 4″ w, Inverted Thumbprint pattern, petticoat shape, orig cut vaseline stopper, Wheeling. . **385.00**
Satin Glass
    Apricot shading to white, MOP int., Diamond Quilted pattern, white thorny knobby stopper, triangular white handle **1,540.00**
    Cranberry Moire, frosted handle, frosted orig stopper **300.00**
Silver Overlay, 7¼″ h, cut green over crystal overlay body, star cut bottom, cut panels, heavy floral and scroll sterling silver overlay, orig conforming stopper with sterling silver overlay. . . **750.00**

CUP PLATES

History: Many early cups and saucers were handleless, with deep saucers. The hot liquid was poured into the saucer and sipped from it. This necessitated another plate for the cup, the "cup plate."

The first cup plates made of pottery were of the Staffordshire variety. In the mid 1830s to 1840s, glass cup plates were favored. The Boston and Sandwich Glass Company was one of the main contributors to the lacy glass type.

It is extremely difficult to find glass cup plates in outstanding (mint) condition. Collectors expect some marks of usage, such as slight rim roughness, minor chipping (best if under rim), and in rarer patterns a portion of a scallop missing.

Reference: Ruth Webb Lee and James H. Rose, *American Glass Cup Plates*, published by author, 1948, reprinted by Charles E. Tuttle Co., in 1985.

Collectors' Club: Pairpoint Cup Plate Collectors of America, PO Box 890052, East Weymouth, MA 02189.

Notes: The numbers used are from the Lee–Rose book in which all plates are illustrated.

Prices are based on "average" condition.

GLASS

LR 22–B, 3⁷⁄₁₆″ d, clear, pontil, New England origin, slight roughage. **90.00**
LR 26, 3⁵⁄₁₆″ d, clear, attributed to Sandwich or New England Glass Co **150.00**
LR 37, 3¼″ d, opalescent, attributed to Sandwich or New England Glass Co, two heat checks in rim, light roughage **150.00**
LR 45, 3⁹⁄₁₆″ d, pale opalescent, attributed to Sandwich or New England

Glass Co, mold overfill, slag deposit near center. **100.00**

LR 51, 3¾″ d, clear, pontil, eastern origin, moderate rim roughage, few shallow flakes. **175.00**

LR 58, 3⅜″ d, clambroth, unlisted, eastern origin **275.00**

LR 61, 3⅛″ d, opalescent, attributed to New England Glass Co **250.00**

LR 75–A, 3¹³/₁₆″ d, clear, attributed to New England Glass Co, one tiny rim flake. **70.00**

LR 80, 3¾″ d, opalescent, New England origin **250.00**

LR 81, 3¾″ d, fiery red opalescent, New England origin. **350.00**

LR 88, 3¹¹/₁₆″ d, deep opalescent opaque, attributed to Sandwich or New England Glass Co, two minute flakes under rim **175.00**

LR 95, 3⅝″ d, opalescent opaque, attributed to New England, tiny nick under rim. **150.00**

LR 100, 3¼″ d, clear, attributed to Philadelphia area, normal mold roughness **95.00**

LR 121, 3⅛″ d, clear, lacy, midwestern, slight rim roughage, two minor nicks, mold overfill **100.00**

LR 242–A, 3½″ d, black amethyst, lacy, eastern origin, mold underfill and overfill **650.00**

LR 247, 3⁷/₁₆″ d, emerald green, lacy, attributed to Sandwich or New England Glass Co, small chip on one scallop. **750.00**

LR 253, 3⁹/₁₆″ d, blue–green, Roman Rosette, midwestern origin, two very small rim nicks **300.00**

LR 259, 3⁷/₁₆″ d, clear, eastern origin, small chip on one point and one scallop, normal mold roughness **85.00**

LR 276, 3⁷/₁₆″ d, blue, lacy, Boston and Sandwich Glass Co, slight opalescence bloom. **325.00**

LR 279, 2⅞″ d, light green, lacy, eastern origin, two chipped scallops **250.00**

LR 319, 3⁵/₁₆″ d, clear, one scallop missing, five have small flakes, normal mold roughness **100.00**

LR 399, 3⁵/₁₆″ d, clear, eastern origin, normal mold roughness **60.00**

LR 433, 4⅛″ d, clear, two chips, mold roughness **75.00**

LR 445, 3⁷/₁₆″ d, cloudy, midwestern origin, four bull's eyes missing, five chips, mold roughness. **265.00**

LR 459M, jade opaque, twelve hearts, near mint **450.00**

LR 516, 3¼″ d, amethyst, attributed to Sandwich, rim chip on underside, surface spalls, and rim roughage. **425.00**

Historical Staffordshire, Castle Garden Battery, New York, Enoch Wood, dark blue transfer, 3⅝″ d, $300.00.

GLASS HISTORICAL

LR 568, 3⁷/₁₆″ d, clear, attributed to Sandwich, one scallop tipped, mold roughness **50.00**

LR 586–B, clear, Ringgold, Palo Alto, stippled ground, small letters, Philadelphia area, 1847–48, trace of mold roughness **650.00**

LR 595, 3¼″ d, amber, attributed to Sandwich, three small mold spalls, one scallop missing, six scallops tipped, one spall on underside, average mold roughness **265.00**

LR 615–A, 3⅜″ d, clear, unknown origin, Constitution **650.00**

LR 695, 3″ d, clear, midwestern origin, two scallops tipped, normal mold roughness **125.00**

PORCELAIN OR POTTERY

Gaudy Dutch, Butterfly pattern **750.00**

Leeds, 3¾″ d, softpaste, gaudy blue and white floral dec, very minor pinpoint edge flakes. **240.00**

Staffordshire, Historical
Franklin Tomb, 3½″ d, dark blue, Wood, faint hairline **600.00**

Landing of Lafayette, 4⅝″ d, dark blue, full border, Clews. **425.00**

The Tyrants Foe...Lovejoy, 4″ d, light blue, unknown maker, minute pinpoint on foot rim **275.00**

Unidentified View of Country Estate, 4⅝″ d, grapevine border series, dark blue, Wood. **60.00**

Staffordshire, Romantic
Alcock, J, Balantyre, twelve sided . **50.00**

Mayer, Garden Scenery, twelve
sided, pink. 30.00
Wood & Sons, canary, emb rim, ma-
hogany striping, black transfer of fat
child eating, imp "Enoch Wood &
Sons," 4½″ d. 350.00

CUSTARD GLASS

History: Custard glass was developed in England in the early 1880s. Harry Northwood made
the first American custard glass at his Indiana,
Pennsylvania, factory in 1898.

From 1898 until 1915, many manufacturers pro-
duced custard glass patterns, such as Dugan
Glass, Fenton, A. H. Heisey Glass Co., Jefferson
Glass, Northwood, Tarentum Glass, and U.S.
Glass. Cambridge and McKee continued the pro-
duction of custard glass into the Great Depression.

The ivory or creamy yellow custard color is
achieved by adding uranium salts to the molten hot
glass. The chemical content makes the glass glow
when held under a black light. The higher the
amount of uranium, the more luminous the color.
Northwood's custard glass has the smallest
amount of uranium, creating an ivory color; Heisey
used more, creating a deep yellow color.

Custard glass was made in patterned tableware
pieces. It also was made as souvenir items and
novelty pieces. Souvenir pieces are marked with
place names or hand-painted decorations, such as
flowers. Patterns of custard glass often were highlighted in gold, enamel colors, and stains.

References: William Heacock, *Encyclopedia Of
Victorian Colored Pattern Glass, Book IV: Custard
Glass From A to Z*, Peacock Publications, 1980;
William Heacock, James Measell, and Berry Wig-
gins, *Harry Northwood: The Early Years 1881–
1900*, Antique Publications, 1990.

Reproduction Alert: L. G. Wright Glass Co. has
reproduced pieces in the Argonaut Shell and Grape
and Cable patterns. It also introduced new patterns, such as Floral and Grape and Vintage Band.
Moser reproduced toothpicks in Argonaut Shell,
Chrysanthemum Sprig, and Inverted Fan and
Feather.

Additional Listings: Pattern Glass.

Banana Boat, Geneva, 11″ l, oval . . . 125.00
Berry Bowl
  Individual
    Fan 40.00
    Louis XV, gold trim 40.00
    Ring Band, gold and rose dec . . 40.00
  Master
    Chrysanthemum Sprig, blue 595.00
    Geneva 135.00
    Intaglio, green 195.00
    Louis XV 160.00
Bowl, Grape and Cable, 7½″ d, basket
weave ext., nutmeg stain, Northwood 50.00

Butter Dish, cov
  Argonaut Shell 375.00
  Beaded Circle 485.00
  Intaglio, green 295.00
  Louis XV 175.00
  Maple Leaf 375.00
  Victoria 280.00
Celery
  Georgia Gem 175.00
  Ring Band 300.00
Cologne Bottle, Grape, nutmeg stain,
orig stopper, marked "N" 400.00
Compote, jelly
  Argonaut Shell 160.00
  Intaglio, green trim 100.00
Condiment Set, Creased Bale, 4 pcs . 180.00
Creamer
  Beaded Circle 190.00
  Chrysanthemum Sprig, blue 385.00
  Intaglio, green 135.00
  Louis XV 85.00
  Maple Leaf 160.00
Cruet
  Argonaut Shell, orig stopper 425.00
  Chrysanthemum Sprig, clear stopper,
    goofus dec 60.00
  Louis XV, no stopper 175.00
Dresser Tray, Winged Scroll, hp dec . 165.00
Goblet, Grape and Gothic Arches, nut-
meg stain 65.00
Hair Receiver, Winged Scroll 125.00
Hat, Grape and Gothic Arches 60.00
Humidor, Winged Scroll 175.00
Ice Cream Set, Fan, master bowl, six
serving dishes, 7 pcs. 500.00
Jelly Compote, Geneva 80.00
Lamp, finger, 3¾″ to top of burner, slight
greenish cast, emb tulip design, ap-
plied handle, orig burner and chimney 190.00
Nappy
  Northwood Grape 50.00
  Prayer Rug, 6″ d 50.00
Plate, 7½″ d
  Prayer Rug 20.00

**Sugar, cov, chrysanthemum sprig dec,
sgd, 6½″ h, $175.00.**

Three Fruits	22.00
Punch Bowl, matching base, Grape and Cable, pink stain dec	6,000.00
Punch Cup	
Diamond with Peg	60.00
Inverted Fan and Feather	250.00
Northwood Grape	48.00
Rose Bowl, Grape and Gothic Arches	75.00
Salt and Pepper Shakers, pr	
Geneva	225.00
Vine with Flowers	50.00
Spooner	
Beaded Circle	190.00
Chrysanthemum Sprig, blue	275.00
Geneva	100.00
Intaglio, green	135.00
Maple Leaf	160.00
Sugar, cov	
Chrysanthemum Sprig, blue	465.00
Everglades	150.00
Fluted Scrolls	150.00
Maple Leaf	235.00
Sugar, open, Beaded Swag	45.00
Syrup	
Ring Band	300.00
Winged Scroll	350.00
Table Set, cov butter, creamer, cov sugar, spooner, Ring Band, rose dec	470.00
Toothpick Holder	
Chrysanthemum Sprig, blue	300.00
Diamond with Peg	55.00
Geneva	300.00
Maple Leaf	550.00
Ring and Beads, souvenir	45.00
Tumbler	
Beaded Circle	45.00
Chrysanthemum Sprig, blue	225.00
Diamond Peg, dec	75.00
Geneva	55.00
Intaglio, green	85.00
Maple Leaf	95.00
Ribbed Thumbprint, dec	77.00
Vermont	80.00
Water Pitcher	
Argonaut Shell	475.00
Chrysanthemum Sprig	475.00
Diamond Peg, dec	395.00
Geneva	265.00
Intaglio, green	475.00
Inverted Fan and Feather	650.00
Jackson, undecorated	275.00
Louis XV	195.00
Maple Leaf	395.00
Winged Scroll	
Bulbous	375.00
Tankard, gold trim, heat check	225.00

CUT GLASS, AMERICAN

History: Glass is cut by the process of grinding decoration into the glass by means of abrasive–carrying metal wheels or stone wheels. A very ancient craft, it was revived in 1600 by Bohemians and spread through Europe to Great Britain and to America.

American cut glass came of age at the Centennial Exposition in 1876 and the World Columbian Exposition in 1893. The American public recognized American cut glass to be exceptional in quality and workmanship. America's most significant output of this high-quality glass occurred from 1880 to 1917, a period now known as the "Brilliant Period."

About the 1890s some companies began adding an acid–etched "signature" to their glass. This signature may be the actual company name, its logo, or a chosen symbol. Today, signed pieces can command a premium over unsigned pieces since the signature clearly establishes the origin.

However, caution should be exercised in regard to signature identification. Objects with forged signatures have been in existence for some time. To check for authenticity, run your fingertip or fingernail lightly over the area with the signature. As a general rule, a genuine signature cannot be felt; a forged signature exhibits a raised surface.

Many companies never used the acid–etched signature on the glass and may or may not have affixed paper labels to the items originally. Dorflinger Glass and the Meriden Glass Co. made cut glass of the highest quality yet never acid–etched a signature on the glass. Furthermore, cut glass made before the 1890s was not signed. Many of these wood-polished items, cut on blown blanks, were of excellent quality and often won awards at exhibitions.

Consequently, if collectors restrict themselves to signed pieces only, many beautiful pieces of the highest quality glass and workmanship will be missed.

References: E. S. Farrar & J. S. Spillman, *The Complete Cut & Engraved Glass Of Corning,* Crown Publishers [Corning Museum of Glass monograph], 1979; John Feller, *Dorflinger: America's Finest Glass, 1852–1921,* Antique Publications, 1988; J. Michael Pearson, *Encyclopedia Of American Cut & Engraved Glass,* Volumes I to III, published by author, 1975; Albert C. Revi, *American Cut & Engraved Glass,* Schiffer Publishing, 1965; Martha Louise Swan, *American and Homestead Glass of the Brilliant Period,* Wallace–Homestead, 1986, 1994 value update; H. Weiner & F. Lipkowitz, *Rarities In American Cut Glass,* Collectors House of Books, 1975.

Collectors' Club: American Cut Glass Association, 36 Crosstie Lane, Batesville, IN 47006.

Museums: The Corning Museum of Glass, Corning, NY; High Museum of Art, Atlanta, GA; Huntington Galleries, Huntington, WV; Lightner Museum, St. Augustine, FL; Toledo Museum of Art, Toledo, OH.

Atomizer, 6" h, De Vilbiss, allover cutting, Brilliant Period **125.00**

Banana Bowl, 11½ x 8", American Brilliant Period, Royal pattern **550.00**

Basket

7" w, 6½" h, American Brilliant Period, geometric and floral cutting, twisted handle. **150.00**

12" w, 17" h, large butterfly, smaller one with flowers and leaves, elaborate sterling silver handle **1,100.00**

Bell, 5½" d, American Brilliant Period, hobstar diamond point fan **225.00**

Berry Set, master bowl, six serving bowls, Eggington, cluster pattern, hobnail, hobstar, star, and strawberry diamond, price for seven pc set **495.00**

Bonbon, 8" d, 2" h, Huntly, American Brilliant Period, Broadway pattern, minor flakes **125.00**

Bottle, 12½" h, attributed to Tuthill, American Brilliant Period, large intaglio cut tulips **175.00**

Bowl, Clark, sgd, 8⅛" d, 3⅜" h, $165.00.

Bowl

7¾" d, 4" h, fluted, well cut border of flowers and leaves, 1¾" w diamond border. **125.00**

8" d, hobstar diamond point fan, blown out **525.00**

8¼" d, Hawkes, American Brilliant Period, Panel pattern, sgd. **1,000.00**

9" d, tricornered, Sinclaire, flutes, panel border, two small rim flakes . **90.00**

12" d, two handles, sectional, low, Russian hobstar diamond cut buttons **225.00**

Bread Tray, 11 x 5", Clark, hobstars, sgd **275.00**

Butter Dish, cov

8" d, 5" h, Libbey, hobstars and fans **425.00**

8" d, 5½" h, American Brilliant Period, heavy brilliant cutting, star and punty design **150.00**

Buttermilk Jug, 8" h, allover geometric pattern, notched handle **300.00**

Buttermilk Pitcher, 8" h, American Brilliant Period, notched handle **250.00**

Candelabra, 17" h, American Brilliant Period, five silverplate arms and base, Prism and Flute pattern stem, full length double teardrop, silverplate marked "Simpson Hall & Miller" **400.00**

Candlesticks, pr, 12" h, Pairpoint, Adelaide, amber **365.00**

Candy Dish, cov

Hawkes, Devonshire pattern, pedestal base, sgd **245.00**

Pairpoint, lift off lid, vintage cutting, dark canary **150.00**

Carafe

7¼" h, 6" w, American Brilliant Period, expanding stars and notched prism neck **125.00**

8" h

Hawkes, Cypress pattern, large hobstars separated by smaller fans, clear centers, blown blank, wood polished, sgd **145.00**

J Hoare, American Brilliant Period, Carolyn pattern. **200.00**

Celery Tray

10½" l, American Brilliant Period, Harvard pattern sides, two large flowers and leaves on base **95.00**

10½" l, 5" w, Hawkes, American Brilliant Period, Festoon pattern **150.00**

Champagne, Dorflinger, cranberry cut to clear, Panel and Flute cut bowl, clear stem with ring in center **160.00**

Cheese and Cracker Dish, 9" d, cross cut diamond, fan, and large star **140.00**

Cigar Jar, Hoare, Monarch pattern, hobstar base, hollow for sponge in lid. . . **625.00**

Cologne Bottle, 7½ x 2¾", Dorflinger, Parisian pattern, sq, price for pair . . . **620.00**

Compote

8" d, 6¾" h, Hoare, hobstars, buttons, crosshatching, fans, sgd. **235.00**

8" d, 7" h, American Brilliant Period, scalloped rim

Fine hobstar cutting, notched teardrop stem, scallop cut base, four sections. **300.00**

Hobstar and diamond cutting, tear drop rim, round ray cut base . . . **250.00**

8½" d, 3⅝" h, Sinclaire, Forty and Grapes pattern, amber, faceted horizontally stepped cutting, engraved leaf and vine border, price for pair **200.00**

9" d, 8" h, American Brilliant Period, four sections **300.00**

Compote Serving Set, master compote, seven matching smaller compotes, American Brilliant Period allover cutting, pointed rims, price for eight pc set 325.00

Cordial Bottle, 9" h, Boston and Sandwich, American Brilliant Period, square base 175.00

Creamer and Sugar, 2½" h
American Brilliant Period, hobstars, nailhead, and fan, triple cut handles 250.00
Jewel Cut Glass Co, Aberdeen pattern, chain of hobstars and clear undecorated motifs 250.00

Cream Pitcher, 5¼" h, Persian pattern, bulbous, notched fluted rim, clear hobstar center, triple notched handles 150.00

Cruet
6" h, Hawkes, Chrysanthemum pattern, tri–pour spout, cut handle and stopper 350.00
7½" h, American Brilliant Period, Harvard and Band pattern, orig cut stopper 90.00
8½" h, Tuthill, wild roses, leaves, and thorns, dec body, handle, and stopper, stone engraved 225.00

Decanter
11½" h, American, Russian pattern, three ringed faceted neck, bulbous body, starred base, conforming teardrop stopper 935.00
13" h, American Brilliant Period, alternating hobstar and fan cutting, notched handle and neck 400.00

Dessert Set, Hawkes, American Brilliant Period, Chrysanthemum pattern, early wood polished blanks, 9" d master bowl, eight 5" d matching sauces, price for nine piece set 900.00

Dish, Swirled Primrose, Tuthill, sgd, 1912, 8¼" d, 3¼" h, $500.00.

Dish, 6 x 8", Hawkes, American Brilliant Period, Grecian pattern, leaf shape . . 500.00

Dresser Tray, 12 x 8", American Brilliant Period, hobstar and diamond, fan border 325.00

Eggnog Punch Set, bowl, stand, four matching punch cups, American Brilliant Period, hobstars 2,750.00

Finger Bowl and Underplate, 4½" d bowl, 6" d underplate, Dorflinger, blown blank, wood polished 150.00

Flower Center
10" d, 7½" h, American Brilliant Period, hobstars in diamond shaped fields, fans, strawberry diamond, honeycomb neck 750.00
10" w, 8½" h, Strauss, American Brilliant Period, large pinwheel pattern, notched stepped neck, sgd 800.00

Ice Bucket, 6" d, 6" h, expanding star design, American Brilliant Period. . . . 135.00

Ice Cream Tray
8" w, 13½" l, American Brilliant Period, two large twenty–four point rosettes cut in center, wood polished blank, some edge chips 250.00
10" w, 18" l, American Brilliant Period, heavy blank, intricate cutting 650.00

Ice Tub
American Brilliant Period, 5½" d, 5½" h, heavy brilliant blank, band of hobstars and diamond cutting, two tab ears, slight rim roughage 195.00
Mount Washington, c1870, Russian pattern, single star, Russian pattern tab handles, blown blank wood polished 425.00

Jar, cov, 5½" h, Hawkes, Venetian pattern, barrel shaped, matching cov, faceted finial, small nicks to cov 300.00

Juice Tumbler, 3½" h, Russian pattern, American Brilliant Period, price for three piece set 145.00

Knife Rest, 5" l, barbell shape, pinwheel cut ends 90.00

Mayonnaise, 6" d x 2¾" h bowl, 7¼" d underplate, Propeller pattern, scalloped rim, small nicks 575.00

Milk Pitcher, 7" h, Prism pattern, sterling silver rim and spout, American Brilliant Period, small heat fracture at applied handle 120.00

Napkin Ring, cut thistle and leaf design, minor roughage on one, price for pair 110.00

Nappy, 11" w, 8½" h, American Brilliant Period, Harvard pattern, step cut pedestal, double applied handles 400.00

Orange Bowl, 7½" d, Eggington, Lotus pattern 275.00

Pitcher, 10¼" h, American Brilliant Period, sterling silver top, notched handle 300.00

Boudoir Lamp, American Brilliant period, dome shaped shade hung with beaded pendants, faceted standard, 13" h, $550.00. Photograph courtesy of William Doyle Galleries.

Plate
7" d, swirls of notched prisms and
hobstars 125.00
7" w, sq, Arcadia type pattern 225.00
8" d, Hawkes, Gladys pattern, American Brilliant Period, sgd 85.00
10" d, brilliant cut expanding star . . 100.00

Punch Bowl, bowl and base
12" d, Hunt, Royal pattern 1,500.00
15" d, 14" h, Ideal Glass Co, Corning, NY, c1902, American Brilliant Period, large hobstar cutting, heavy Pairpoint blank. 3,000.00

Punch Cup, 3" d, 2¼" h, double lozenge pattern, American Brilliant Period, price for six piece set. 200.00

Relish, 13" l, Russian pattern, clear buttons, leaf shape 315.00

Salad Fork, 12" l
Hobstar and allover brilliant period cutting, silver bowl marked "Gorham & Company". 295.00
Hobstar cut handle, metal bowl . . . 100.00

Salad Set, Russian pattern, starred buttons, silver mountings by Gorham and Sons, c1890 . . . . 375.00

Salt, open
Dorflinger, wood polished, price for six piece set. 175.00
J Hoare, Monarch pattern, blown blank, wood polished 95.00

Spooner, 4 x 8", Eggington, Lotus pattern. 80.00

Syrup Pitcher, Russian pattern, hinged silverplate top, cut handle. 770.00

Tankard Pitcher
11" h, Averbeck, Genoa pattern . . . 395.00
14" h, American Brilliant Period, Harvard pattern, notched handle. 625.00

Tazza
6" d, 4" h, Tuthill, Vintage pattern . . 225.00
6" d, 7½" h, American Brilliant Period, expanding star, fan, and strawberry diamond pattern, teardrop stems, price for pair 300.00
7" d, 5" h, Tuthill, Evening Primrose pattern, allover delicate intaglio cuttings, unsigned 325.00
9" d, 10½" h, American Brilliant Period, alternating band of finely cut hobstars, extremely heavy blank . . 800.00

Teapot, 10" l, 6½" h, Pyrex, floral and line engraving, matching Pyrex underplate 250.00

Tray, 8" l, 5" w, Tuthill, Wild Rose pattern, allover heavy brilliant and floral pattern 250.00

Tumbler
Dorflinger, Renaissance Exact, price for six piece set 180.00
Hawkes, 4" h, strawberry diamond and fan, some edge flakes, price for seven piece set 125.00
Unknown maker, Russian pattern, cut buttons, price for nine piece set. . . 325.00

Vase
5" h
Hawkes, Brazilian pattern, trumpet 175.00
Libbey, corset shape, punty and strawberry diamond and fan cutting, Masonic signature 125.00
8" h, American Brilliant Period, trumpet. 150.00
8½" h, green cut to clear, price for pair 350.00
11" h, Tuthill, urn shape, vintage cutting, two handles, Brilliant Period. . 475.00
11½" h, emerald green intaglio cut to clear, engraved floral repeating design, base border. 470.00
12" h, Libbey, Wisteria pattern, corset shape, brilliant deep crystal, two naturalistic colored lovebirds. 800.00
12½" h, Tuthill, American Brilliant Period, heavily sculpted Intaglio pattern, three fruits combined with intricate geometric motifs, ftd, unsigned. 600.00
14" h, American Brilliant Period, Brunswick pattern 550.00
18¼" h, American Brilliant Period, allover hobstar and sunburst cutting, fine heavy blank. 1,000.00

Water Set, pitcher, matching tumbler, Greek Key with hobstars, caning. . . . 595.00

Whiskey, Russian pattern, single star centers, wood polished, attributed to Hawkes 85.00

Wine
  Dorflinger
    Cranberry cut to clear, Old Colony
      pattern. **195.00**
    Solid green cut to clear, strawberry,
      diamond, and fan cutting, clear
      stem **275.00**
  Libbey, cranberry bowl cut to clear,
    concentric circle in single stars,
    clear knob stem, c1890. . . . . **210.00**
  New England Glass Co, Rhine, apri-
    cot cut to clear, canes, fans, oval
    vesicias, nailhead diamonds, clear
    stem, rayed base, c1890. . . . . **225.00**

CUT VELVET

History: Several glass manufacturers made cut velvet during the late Victorian era, c1870–1900. An outer layer of pastel color was applied over a white casing. The piece then was molded or cut in a ribbed or diamond shape in high relief, exposing portions of the casing. The finish had a satin velvety feel, hence the name "cut velvet."

Vase, pink, ribbed, undulating crimped top, white int., 7½" h, $225.00.

Biscuit Jar, pink, SP mountings and lid. **265.00**
Celery Vase, 6½" h, DQ, box pleated
  top, deep blue over white, Mt
  Washington **725.00**
Creamer, 3½" h, DQ, cranberry, applied
  multicolored enamel dec **365.00**
Ewer, 4¾" h, DQ, deep blue, applied
  frosted handle. **165.00**
Finger Bowl, 4½" d, DQ, blue **135.00**
Pitcher, 10¾" h, DQ, blue **220.00**
Toothpick, 3⅝" h, DQ, yellow, sq mouth **190.00**

Vase
  8½" h
    Green, DQ, cased, ruffled top,
      raised pattern, price for pair. . . . **300.00**
    Pink, raised criss–cross lattice de-
      sign, attributed to Mt Washington **275.00**
  8¾" h, elongated neck, DQ, robin's
    egg blue, daisy blossom like base **385.00**
  11" h, DQ, deep purple, white int., ruf-
    fled top, raised pattern **825.00**

CZECHOSLOVAKIAN ITEMS

History: Objects marked "Made in Czechoslovakia" were produced after 1918 when the country claimed its independence from the Austro–Hungarian Empire. The people became more cosmopolitan and liberated and expanded their scope of life. Their porcelains, pottery, and glassware reflect many influences.

A specific manufacturer's mark may be identified as being much earlier than 1918, but this only indicates the factory existed in the Bohemian or Austro–Hungarian Empire period.

References: Dale and Diane Barta and Helen M. Rose, *Czechoslovakian Glass & Collectibles,* Collector Books, 1992; Ruth A. Forsythe, *Made in Czechoslovakia,* Richardson Printing Corp., 1982; Ruth A. Forsythe, *Made in Czechoslovakia, Book 2,* Antique Publications, 1993; Jacquelyne Y. Jones–North, *Czechoslovakian Perfume Bottles and Boudoir Accessories,* Antique Publications, 1990.

Canister Set, pearl luster ground, gold letters, marked, price for five pc set, $135.00.

Ashtray, figural glass, cowboy **120.00**
Bowl, 3" d, Mrazek peasant art **18.00**
Cologne Bottle, 4" h, porcelain, glossy
  blue, bow front **12.00**
Demitasse Service, partial, hp, red

Geisha teahouse scene, 17½ x 9½"
oval tray, cov sugar, five cups and
saucers 90.00
Lamp Shade, glass, beaded, Forsythe
"659". 35.00
Mantel Lusters, 12½" h, pr, ruby and
white overlay glass, cup form waisted
top, scalloped rim, cylindrical stem,
faceted knop, domed spreading foot,
polychrome floral sprays, gilt trim . . .   360.00
Perfume Bottle, 3½" h, glass, yellow,
clear top.   70.00
Plate
9" d, Bartered Bride, hp, price for pair   50.00
10" d, Art Deco, maiden, black and
yellow, 1920s. 50.00
Powder Box, cov, round, glass, yellow,
black knob top 55.00
Tea Kettle, 6¼" h, earthenware, carved
and polychrome dec, stamp and imp
Eleanor mark, c1925 . . . .   220.00
Vase
5" h, bulbous, black ground, multicolored coralene daisies. 45.00
6" h, opaque, enameled birch trees,
house, and barn with red roof 45.00
8¼" h, bubbly green glass, hp, fox
hunt scene, ftd. 145.00
10½" h, flared cylinder, colorless
blown glass shading to cobalt blue,
strong gold irid oil spot surface dec,
smoothed pontil with acid stamp
"Made in Czechoslovakia" 550.00

DAVENPORT
LONGPORT
STAFFORDSHIRE

DAVENPORT

History: John Davenport opened a pottery in
Longport, Staffordshire, England, in 1793. His ware
was of high quality, of light weight, and cream colored with a beautiful velvety texture.

The firm made soft–paste (Old Blue), luster-
trimmed ware, and pink luster with black transfer.
There have been pieces of Gaudy Dutch and Spatterware found with the Davenport mark. Later Davenport became a leading maker of ironstone and
early flow blue. His famous "Cyprus" pattern in
mulberry became very popular. His heirs continued
the business until the factory closed in 1886.

Reference: Susan and Al Bagdade, *Warman's
English & Continental Pottery & Porcelain, 2nd Edition,* Wallace-Homestead, 1991.

**Cup and Saucer, flow blue, Amoy pat-
tern, incised anchor mark, 6" d saucer,
3¾" d cup, $75.00.**

Compote, 2½" h, 8½" d, turquoise and
gold band, tiny raised flowers, hp
scene with man fishing, cows at edge
of lake, c1860, pr 195.00
Creamer, tan, jasperware, basket-
weave, incised anchor mark. 50.00
Cup and Saucer, Amoy pattern, flow
blue, 3¾" h cup, 6" d saucer, incised
anchor mark 70.00
Cup Plate, Teaberry pattern, pink luster   30.00
Dish, ftd, tricorn, Belvoir Castle dec . .   85.00
Ewer, 9" h, floral dec, multicolored,
c1830. . . . .   185.00
Mustard Pot, 3½" h, hinged SP cov, tur-
quoise, gilt foliage and florals, 1870–
86 . . . .   85.00
Pitcher, 8" h, black transfer print of ca-
thedral, pink luster trim. 200.00
Plate
8" d, octagonal, floral dec, gold rim   40.00
9⅛" d, Legend of Montrose, transfer,
1850–70 . . . .   50.00
Platter
17¼" l, Tyrol Hunter, brown transfer   100.00
18" l, white, blue border, anchor mark,
c1820 . . . .   200.00
20" l, rect, blue and white, transfer
printed exotic bird and flower pat-
tern, c1840 . . . .   300.00
Punch Bowl, 14" d, int. painted iron–red,
blue, and gilt, chrysanthemum and
rockwork, iron–red trellis border, rim
with flowering foliage on blue ground,
ext. with band of seaweed pattern in
gilt on pale blue ground between
bands of dark blue foliage, puce mark
"Davenport, Manufacturers To Their
Majesties, Long Port, Staffordshire,"
c1830. . . . . 2,200.00
Sauce Dish, cov, ladle, creamware,
molded leaves, lime green veining,
early 425.00
Soup Plate, 8⅛" d, pearlware, green
feather edge, stylized orange, brown,
and yellow house dec, imp "Daven-
port," tiny flakes 425.00

Tazza, 9½" d, octagonal, ftd, Imari pattern, c1860 . . . . **110.00**

Teapot, cov, 6" h, compressed ovoid form, bouquet of garden flowers on each side, polychrome enamel, gilt highlights, anchor and inscribed banner mark. **440.00**

Tea Set, teapot, creamer, and ftd sugar, blue and white, marked "Davenport," c1880. **100.00**

Tureen, 10" h, 11½" d, ogee shape body, round foot, underglaze blue dec, Chinese walled garden with crane and flowers, dec rim int., cobalt blue upturned bracket handles, domical cov with applied flowerhead knob, 1805–20, price for pair. **1,100.00**

Vegetable Dish, Berry pattern, imp sgd, anchor mark **50.00**

DECOYS

History: Carved wooden decoys, used to lure ducks and geese to the hunter, have become widely recognized as an indigenous American folk art form in the past several years.

Many decoys are from the 1880–1930 period when commercial gunners commonly hunted using rigs of several hundred decoys. Many fine carvers also worked through the 1930s and 1940s.

The value of a decoy is based on several factors: (1) fame of the carver, (2) quality of the carving, (3) species of wild fowl—the most desirable are herons, swans, mergansers, and shorebirds, and (4) condition of the original paint (o.p.).

The inexperienced collector should be aware of several facts. The age of a decoy, per se, is usually of no importance in determining value. Since very few decoys were ever signed, it will be quite difficult to attribute most decoys to known carvers. Anyone who has not examined a known carver's work will be hard pressed to determine if the paint on one of his decoys is indeed original.

Repainting severely decreases a decoy's value. In addition, there are many fakes and reproductions on the market, and even experienced collectors are occasionally fooled.

Decoys listed below are of average wear unless otherwise noted.

References: Joe Engers (gen. ed.), *The Great Book of Wildfowl Decoys,* Thunder Bay Press, 1990; Henry A. Fleckenstein, Jr., *American Factory Decoys,* Schiffer Publishing; Ronald J. Fritz, *Michigan's Master Carver Oscar W. Peterson, 1887– 1951,* Aardvark Publications, 1988; Bob and Sharon Huxford, *Collector's Guide To Decoys, Volume II,* Collector Books, 1992; Gene and Linda Kangas, *Decoys,* Collector Books, 1992; Linda and Gene Kangas, *Collector's Guide To Decoys,* Wallace–Homestead, 1992; Art, Brad, and Scott Kimball, *The Fish Decoy,* Aardvark Publications, 1986;

Carl F. Luckey, *Collecting Antique Bird Decoys: An Identification & Value Guide,* Books Americana, 1983.

Periodicals: *Decoy Geographer,* 4532 Old Leeds Rd., Birmingham, AL 21673; *Decoy Hunter Magazine,* 901 North 9th, Clinton, IN 47842; *Decoy Magazine,* PO Box 277, Burtonsville, MD 20866; *Decoy World,* RFD 1, Box 5, Trappe, MD 21673; *North America Decoys,* PO Box 246, Spanish Fork, UT 84660; *Sporting Collector's Monthly,* RW Publishing, PO Box 305, Camden, DE 19934; *Wildfowl Art,* Ward Foundation, 909 South Schumaker Dr., Salisbury, MD 21801; *Wildfowl Carving & Collecting,* PO Box 1831, Harrisburg, PA 17105.

Collectors' Clubs: New England Decoy Collectors Association, 2320 Main St., West Barnstable, MA 02668; Ohio Decoy Collectors and Carvers Association, PO Box 499, Richfield, OH 44286; Minnesota Decoy Collectors Association, PO Box 130084, St. Paul, MN 55113.

Museums: Harve de Grace Decoy Museum, Harve de Grace, MD; Museum of Stony Brook, Stony Brook, NY; Peabody Museum of Salem, Salem, MA; Refuge Waterfowl Museum, Chincoteague, VA; Shelburne Museum, Inc., Shelburne, VT; Ward Museum of Wildfowl Art, Salisbury, MD.

Bluebill Drake, Lake Ontario, hollow carved, c1920, $175.00.

Black–breasted Plover, George Boyd, Seabrook, NH, orig paint, minor wear **1,000.00**

Black Duck

Baldwin, Willard, C, Stratford, CT, orig paint, small neck repair. **550.00**

Crowell, Elmer A, East Harwich, MA, orig paint, rect brand mark, minor wear. **3,500.00**

Down East Decoy Company, Freeport, ME, swimming position, orig paint, minor wear. **200.00**

Hart, Charles, Gloucester, MA, carved wing detail, orig paint, c1900. . . . . **3,750.00**

Hendrickson, Gene, NY, orig paint, good condition. **125.00**

Sullivan, Gene, orig paint, carved Salisbury style **385.00**

Updike, John, orig paint, worn 110.00
Bluebill Drake
  Elliston, Robert, Bureau, IL, round
  body style, c1880. . . . . **14,000.00**
  Nichol, Addie, Smith Falls, Ontario,
  professionally restored **275.00**
Bluebill, mated pair, Mason, challenge
  grade, orig paint **1,600.00**
Bluewing Teal Drake
  Serigny, Joseph, LA, hand carved, cy-
  press root, raised detail and tail
  feathers, orig paint **210.00**
  Stevens Decoy Factory, Weedsport,
  NY, excellent condition, stencil
  mark. **8,250.00**
Bluewing Teal Hen, Charles Spiron,
  Winston-Salem, NC, carved, head
  and bill, raised detail, branded name
  on bottom. **200.00**
Bluewing Teal, mated pair, orig paint,
  minor wear. **1,750.00**
Brant
  Cobb, Nathan, Cobb's Island, VA,
  swimming position, V tail, old
  repaint **80,000.00**
  Corliss, Rube, old repaint, good
  condition. **175.00**
  Hudson, Ira, Chincoteague, VA, hol-
  low carved, bold orig paint, minor
  wear. **3,600.00**
  Predmore, Cooper, NJ, repainted, re-
  placed bill **90.00**
Broadbill Drake
  Barnegat Bay Decoy Company, Point
  Pleasant, NJ, orig paint **210.00**
  Corliss, Rube, orig paint, gouges to
  body. **60.00**
Bufflehead, mated pair, D K Nichol,
  Smith's Falls, Ontario, drake sgd,
  unused. **750.00**
Canada Goose
  Horner, Rowley, West Creek, NJ, orig
  paint, restored bill, minor wear. . . . **4,500.00**
  Wheller, Charles, Stratford, CT, cork
  and pine, orig paint, minor wear. . . **10,000.00**
Canvasback Drake
  Anderson, Andy, Chillicothe, IL, orig
  paint. **450.00**
  Barnes, Samuel T., MD, orig paint, mi-
  nor defects, c1910 . . . . **900.00**
  Crowell, Elmer, carved primary feath-
  ers, glass eyes, orig paint, oval
  brand **3,500.00**
  Mason, premier grade, orig paint . . **700.00**
Canvasback Hen, Ken Anger, missing
  most of paint. **300.00**
Coot, Ben Schmidt, Detroit, MI, orig
  paint, minor wear, c1940 . . . . **900.00**
Curlew, Elmer Crowell, MA, turned neck,
  orig paint, maker's stamp on base. . **16,500.00**
Dowitcher, spring plumage, orig paint,
  minor wear. **1,700.00**

Goldeneye Drake, Orel LaBoeuf, Quebec, branded on bottom, two fine hair-
  line cracks **660.00**
Loom, Byron Bruffee, orig paint, name
  stamped on base **330.00**
Green Winged Teal, D W Nichol, On-
  tario, mated pair, orig condition. . . . **1,325.00**
Mallard Drake
  Mason Decoy Company, premiere
  grade, orig paint. **610.00**
  Verdin, Joseph, LA, hand carved, cy-
  press root **220.00**
Mallard Hen, Illinois River, feeding position, inletted tail, glass eyes, carved
  underbill, orig paint **300.00**
Mallard, mated pair, Mason Decoy Fac-
  tory, Detroit, MI, premier grade, slope
  breasted. **12,000.00**
Merganser Drake, hooded
  Hamilton, John, hollow and hand
  carved, inletted weight bottom,
  branded on bottom. **125.00**
  Sprankle, James, NY, orig blue ribbon
  carving, sgd on bottom **200.00**
  Unknown Maker, preening, carved
  pine, orig painted dec, c1870, 10⅛″
  h, 20¼″ l, 8¼″ w **6,000.00**
Pintail Drake
  Mason Decoy Factory, Detroit, MI,
  premier grade, slope breasted. . . . **6,000.00**
  Reineri, Lou, VA, c1960s, flying
  position. **330.00**
Pintail Hen, Charles Perdew, Henry, IL,
  sleeping position, orig paint, two shot
  marks. **28,000.00**
Redbreasted Merganser, mated pair
  Conklin, Harry, NJ, orig paint, some
  exposed wood. **1,210.00**
  Meekens, Alvin, VA, orig paint, shot
  scarring, and bare wood. **385.00**
Redbreasted Merganser Drake, un-
  known maker, bare wood. **825.00**
Redhead Drake, John Holly, Havre De
  Grace, MD, orig paint with varnish fin-
  ish, c1870. . . . . **1,600.00**
Sanderling
  Crowell, Elmer, MA, preening posi-
  tion, raised wing carving, orig paint,
  maker's stamp under base **4,400.00**
  Shourds, Harry V, Tuckerton, NJ, repainted head, minor wear **1,125.00**
Surf Scoter, Gus Wilson, South Portland, ME, preening position, old re-
  paint, minor wear. **4,250.00**
Widgeon Drake, Wildfowler Decoy Com-
  pany, CT, orig paint, normal wear. . . **150.00**
Yellowlegs
  Boyd, George, Seabrook, NH, orig
  paint, minor age splits. **900.00**
  Gelston, Thomas, Quogue, NY, feed-
  ing position, orig paint, minor wear **2,750.00**

DEDHAM POTTERY

History: Alexander W. Robertson established the Chelsea Pottery in Chelsea, Massachusetts, in 1860. In 1872 it was known as the Chelsea Keramic Art Works.

In 1895 the pottery moved to Dedham, and the name was changed to Dedham Pottery. Their principal product was gray crackleware dinnerware with a blue decoration, the rabbit pattern being the most popular. The factory closed in 1943.

The following marks help determine the approximate age of items: (1) Chelsea Keramic Art Works, "Robertson" impressed, 1876–1889; (2) C.P.U.S. impressed in a cloverleaf, 1891–1895; (3) Foreshortened rabbit, 1895–1896; (4) Conventional rabbit with "Dedham Pottery" stamped in blue, 1897; (5) Rabbit mark with "Registered," 1929–1943.

References: Lloyd E. Hawes, *The Dedham Pottery And The Earlier Robertson's Chelsea Potteries,* Dedham Historical Society, 1968; Dana G. Morykan and Harry L. Rinker, *Warman's Country Antiques & Collectibles, Second Edition,* Wallace–Homestead, 1994.

Reproduction Alert: Several rabbit pattern pieces have been reproduced.

Bowl
   5¼″ d, Rabbit pattern, blue rabbit
     stamp on bottom and Davenport
     mark. **55.00**

Plate, Snow Tree pattern, 10″ d, $175.00.

5¾″ d, cov, Rabbit pattern, blue rabbit
   stamp on bottom **165.00**
5⅞″, Rabbit pattern, blue stamp on
   bottom **90.00**
6⅛″ d, Rabbit pattern, blue registered
   mark on bottom **140.00**
7½″ d, flared rim, Rabbit pattern, blue
   rabbit stamp on bottom. **140.00**
8″ sq, Rabbit pattern **300.00**
Candle Snuffer, 2″ h, Rabbit pattern . **660.00**
Celery Tray, 10″ l, Rabbit pattern . . . **300.00**
Chop Platter, 12″ d
   Lobster pattern, imp marks and
     stamp, glaze bursts **880.00**
   Rabbit pattern, imp mark twice and
     stamp **275.00**
Coffeepot, 8″ h, Rabbit pattern, blue rab-
   bit stamp on bottom. **165.00**
Creamer and Sugar, Rabbit pattern, No.
   1, stamped mark, 4¾″ h bowl **360.00**
Cup and Saucer
   Azalea pattern, blue rabbit stamp . . **50.00**
   Elephant pattern, stamp registered
     mark, 6″ d saucer. **770.00**
Cup Plate, 4⅜″ d, Rabbit pattern, blue
   rabbit stamp on bottom **140.00**
Egg Cup, 2½″ h, Rabbit pattern, blue
   rabbit stamp on bottom, price for set
   of six **360.00**
Flower Arranger, 4⅝″ d, Rabbit pattern,
   blue rabbit stamp on bottom **30.00**
Humidor, 7″ h, two elephants, inscribed
   "Dedham Pottery/May 1917/#79". . . **1,980.00**
Mug, 6″ h, Rabbit pattern, incised and
   stamped. **330.00**
Pitcher
   8⅜″ h, No. 3, Rabbit pattern, one rab-
     bit leaping over lower handle, ini-
     tialed "P," imp and stamp mark. . . **1,320.00**
   8½″ h, Rabbit pattern, stamped twice,
     imp mark, peppering, bursts **360.00**
Plate
   6″ d, slightly raised Snow Tree pat-
     tern, blue rabbit stamp on bottom . **70.00**
   6⅛″ d, Swan pattern, blue rabbit
     stamp and two incised rabbits mark **250.00**
   6¼″ d, Moth pattern, imp and stamped
     mark. **365.00**
   6½″ d, Iris pattern, blue rabbit stamp **45.00**
   7½″ d
     Horse Chestnut pattern, stamped,
       imp twice, base chip **125.00**
     Swan pattern, blue rabbit stamp
       and two incised rabbits **255.00**
   7⅝″ d, Rabbit pattern, blue rabbit
     stamp **75.00**
   8¼″ d, Horse Chestnut pattern, blue
     rabbit stamp **50.00**
   8⅜″ d
     Magnolia pattern, blue rabbit stamp
       and one incised rabbit mark. . . . **25.00**
     Poppy pattern, blue rabbit stamp,

incised rabbit and underlined X
mark 45.00
8½" d
Poppy pattern, imp mark, stamp
and inscribed cross. 495.00
Turkey pattern, stamped and imp,
minor imperfections. 135.00
8⅝" d
Duck pattern, imp and stamped
mark 365.00
Rabbit pattern, blue 150.00
8¾" d
Butterfly pattern, crackleware, blue
ink mark, imp bunny 415.00
Lobster pattern, imp and stamped
mark, foot chip, price for set of
five 1,650.00
8⅞" d, Magnolia pattern, blue rabbit
stamp and two impressed mark. . . 70.00
9¾" d
Azalea pattern, blue rabbit mark on
bottom. 40.00
Rabbit pattern, blue rabbit stamp on
bottom. 40.00
9⅞" d
Rabbit pattern, blue mark and two
incised rabbits on bottom. 80.00
Turkey pattern, blue rabbit mark . 35.00
10" d
Golden Gate, SF, inscribed on reverse to "M Sheperd," artist's
cipher for Hugh C Robertson, imp
mark, enhanced blue stamp, chip
on one foot, glaze bursts 2,750.00
Lion and Owl pattern, bisque, dark
pattern, imp mark, artist initials of
Hugh C Robertson, c1900 . . . . . 1,540.00
Moth pattern, blue rabbit mark on
bottom. 40.00
Turkey pattern, stamped 245.00
Sugar Bowl, cov, 4¼" h, Rabbit pattern,
blue rabbit mark on bottom. 55.00
Tea Stand, 6" d, Rabbit pattern,
stamped, early 20th C 165.00
Tile, 5½" d, Rabbit pattern 250.00
Tumbler, 3⅜" h, Rabbit pattern, blue
stamp on bottom. 30.00
Vase
4½" h, bisque, c1880, imp "CKAW"
Eight recesses framed and ac-
cented by incising. 275.00
Rounded shoulder, incised shad-
owing, four sq sides, circular ftd
base 275.00
6⅝" h, center cylindrical neck surrounded by four smaller necks, bulbous body, circular foot, mustard
glaze, imp mark of Hugh C Robertson, Chelsea Keramic Art Works,
c1880 . . . . 825.00
6¾" h, gray crackle glaze, imp Chel-

sea Keramic Art Works mark,
c1886, peppering. 165.00
9½" h, dragon's blood and olive green
irid gloss glaze, imp "CKAW,"
c1888, crazing, base pulls. 1,540.00

DELFTWARE

History: Delftware is pottery of a soft red clay
body with tin enamel glaze. The white, dense,
opaque color came from adding tin ash to lead
glaze. The first examples had blue designs on a
white ground. Polychrome examples followed.

The name originally applied to pottery made in
the region around Delft, Holland, beginning in the
16th century and ending in the late 18th century.
Tin came from the Cornish mines in England. By
the 17th and 18th centuries, English potters in London, Bristol, and Liverpool were copying the glaze
and designs. Some designs unique to English potters also developed.

In Germany and France, the ware is known as
Faience and in Italy as Majolica.

Reference: Susan and Al Bagdade, *Warman's
English & Continental Pottery & Porcelain, 2nd Edition,* Wallace–Homestead, 1991.

Reproduction Alert: Much souvenir Delft-type
material has been produced in the late 19th and
20th centuries to appeal to the foreign traveler.
Don't confuse these modern pieces with the older
examples.

Bottle, 10" h, globular, flared garlic neck,
blue and white, stylized baskets of
flowers and trailing branches, Liver-
pool, c1770. . . . . 500.00
Bowl, 12" d, blue and white, bird on flow-

**Charger, stylized basket of flowers cen-
ter, 13½" d, $300.00.**

ering foliage and insert, int. with flower spray, yellow rim, band of stylized flowerheads, Liverpool, c1740 . . . . . **275.00**

Charger
13⅝″ d, broad cavetto with flowers and geometric dec, bird and flowers in center, late 17th C, one faint age crack **600.00**
21″ d, broad cavetto, plain center, scenes of Chinese at tea, shades of blue, mid 18th C. **850.00**

Coffeepot, cov, de Porceleyne Fles, blue parsley dec. **135.00**

Creamer and Sugar, cov, de Porceleyne Fles, blue parsley dec **45.00**

Dinner Service, de Porceleyne Fles, blue parsley dec, 10″ d dinner plates, 8½″ d soup plates, 8″ d salad plates, 6″ d bread and butter plates, 8 oz cups and saucers, demitasse cups and saucers, price for service for ten. . . . **1,200.00**

Ewer, 8½″ h, floral dec, zigzag band, blue, purple, and yellow ochre **250.00**

Fish Plate, 14½″ l, de Porceleyne Fles, blue parsley dec **60.00**

Flower Brick, 5″ l, rect, blue and white scene, buildings in landscape on long side, figure in boat on short sides, pierced top with blue dot pattern, four ogee feet, English, c1750. . . . . **375.00**

Inkwell, 4¼″ h, handle, stylized floral dec, multicolored, Lambeth, English, c1700. . . . . **350.00**

Jar, cov, 17¼″ h, ribbed octagonal baluster, blue and white, four cartouches with seashore landscapes, two panels with amorous couples, upper border of flowerheads and scrollwork, densely painted ground, lion form knob, inscribed "AL" **550.00**

Plaque, 15″ h, polychrome scrolled border, blue and white figural landscape, Dutch Rococo style, 19th C **330.00**

Plate
9″ d, blue and white, floral design, late 18th C. **185.00**
10¾″ d, floral design, chipped rim . **350.00**

Platter, de Porceleyne Fles, blue parsley dec
11½″ d, round **35.00**
12 x 8″ rect **35.00**

Relish, 9½ x 5½″, de Porceleyne Fles, blue parsley dec **20.00**

Shoe, 6¾″ l, blue and white, high heel, pointed toe, molded buckle, band of trellis pattern ribbon, Bristol, c1760 . . **600.00**

Soup Plate, 8¾″ d, blue and white, fisherman on pier, boat, buildings, and trees in background, pine cones and foliage border, Bristol, c1760, price for pair **375.00**

Stein
7½″ h, blue and white florals, sponged purple dec, pewter lid and base, marked "BP". **450.00**
8½″ h, Oriental motif, pewter base and lid, 1719 . . . . **1,500.00**

Tile, 17 x 12″, river, boat, and horse scene, manganese, Dutch **400.00**

Vegetable Dish, cov, 9½″ l, de Porceleyne Fles, blue parsley dec. **46.00**

DEPRESSION GLASS

History: Depression glass is a glassware made during the period of 1920–40. It was an inexpensive machine–made glass, produced by several companies in various patterns and colors. The number of pieces within a pattern also varied.

Depression glass was sold through variety stores, given as premiums, or packaged with certain products. Movie houses gave it away from 1935 until well into the 1940s.

Like pattern glass, knowing the proper name of a pattern is the key to collecting. Collectors should be prepared to do research.

References: Gene Florence, *Collectible Glassware from the 40's, 50's, 60's: An Illustrated Value Guide, Second Edition,* Collector Books, 1994; Gene Florence, *The Collector's Encyclopedia of Depression Glass, Eleventh Edition,* Collector Books, 1994; Gene Florence, *Elegant Glassware of the Depression Era, Fifth Edition,* Collector Books, 1993; Gene Florence, *Very Rare Glassware of the Depression Era,* First Series (1988, 1991 value update), Second Series (1991), Third Series (1993), Collector Books; Carl F. Luckey and Mary Burris, *An Identification & Value Guide to Depression Era Glassware, Third Edition,* Books Americana, 1993; Hazel Marie Weatherman, *1984 Supplement & Price Trends for Colored Glassware Of The Depression Era, Book 1,* published by author, 1984.

Periodical: *The Daze,* 10271 State Rd., Box 57, Otisville, MI 48463.

Collectors' Clubs: National Depression Glass Association, Inc., PO Box 69843, Odessa, TX 79769; 20–30–40 Society, Inc., PO Box 856, LaGrange, IL 60525.

Reproduction Alert: Send a self-addressed, stamped business envelope to *The Daze* and request a copy of its glass reproduction list. It is one of the best bargains in the antiques business.

Additional Listings: See *Warman's Americana & Collectibles* for more examples.

AUNT POLLY, U. S. Glass Co, late 1920s. Made in blue, green, and iridescent.

	Blue	Green	Iridescent
Berry Bowl			
Individual, 4¾″ d	17.50	8.00	8.00
Master, 7⅛″ d	20.00	17.00	17.00
Bowl			
4¾″ d, 2″ h	19.00	10.00	9.00
5½″ d, one handle	20.00	14.00	12.00
8⅜″ l, oval	80.00	35.00	35.00
Butter Dish, cov	190.00	225.00	225.00
Candy, cov	—	60.00	60.00
Creamer	40.00	25.00	25.00
Pickle, 7¼″ l, oval, handle	35.00	10.00	10.00
Pitcher	150.00	—	—
Plate			
6″ d, sherbet	10.00	5.00	5.00
8″ d, luncheon	16.00	—	—
Salt & Pepper Shakers, pr	180.00	—	—
Sherbet	9.00	8.00	5.00
Sugar, open	20.00	22.50	24.00
Tumbler	25.00	—	12.00
Vase, 6½″ h	35.00	25.00	25.00

AVOCADO, No. 601, Indiana Glass Co, 1923–33. Made in crystal, green, and pink. Limited production in white. Reproductions.

	Crystal	Green	Pink
Bowl			
5¼″ d, 2 handles	10.00	30.00	25.00
8″ l, oval, 2 handles	9.50	24.00	20.00
9½″ d, 3¼″ h	20.00	110.00	90.00
Cake, 10¼″ d, two handles	14.00	45.00	35.00
Creamer, ftd	12.00	37.50	30.00
Cup, ftd	—	30.00	30.00
Plate			
6⅜″ d, sherbet	5.00	15.00	14.00
8¼″ d, luncheon	6.50	18.00	16.50
Preserve, 7″ d, 1 handle	8.00	25.00	18.00
Relish, 6″ d, ftd	9.00	20.00	24.00
Salad Bowl, 7½″ d	12.00	48.00	32.00
Saucer, 6⅜″ d	—	25.00	22.00
Sherbet	—	50.00	47.50
Sugar, ftd	12.00	30.00	32.00
Tumbler	24.00	215.00	195.00

BEADED BLOCK, Imperial Glass Co, 1927–30s. Made in amber, crystal, green, ice blue, iridescent, milk white, opalescent, pink, red, and vaseline.

	Amber	Crystal	Green	Pink
Bowl				
5½″ sq	7.00	7.00	7.00	7.00
6¼″ d	7.00	7.00	7.00	7.00
6¾″ d	7.50	7.00	7.50	8.00
7¼″ d, flared	10.00	9.00	10.00	10.00
7½″ d, fluted	18.00	15.00	15.00	18.00
7½″ d, plain	16.00	15.00	25.00	25.00

	Amber	Crystal	Green	Pink
Celery, 8¼″ d	12.00	12.00	12.00	12.00
Creamer	15.00	12.00	15.00	17.00
Jelly Bowl, 4⅞″ d, two handles	7.50	7.50	7.50	7.50
Pickle, 6½″ d	15.00	15.00	15.00	15.00
Pitcher	110.00	100.00	115.00	110.00
Plate				
7¾″ sq	7.50	7.00	10.00	9.00
8¾″ round	16.00	15.00	18.00	18.00
Sugar	14.00	12.00	15.00	15.00
Vase, 6″ h	18.00	12.00	18.00	20.00

CHINEX CLASSIC, MacBeth-Evans, late 1930s–early 1940s. Made in ivory and ivory with decal decorations.

	Browntown	Plain Ivory	Decal Dec	Castle Decal
Bowl, 11″ d	17.00	16.00	30.00	35.00
Butter Dish, cov	55.00	5.00	70.00	120.00
Cake Plate, 11½″ d	7.50	7.50	12.50	19.50
Cereal Bowl, 5¾″ d	5.50	5.50	7.00	12.50
Creamer	5.50	5.50	8.50	10.00
Cup	4.50	4.50	8.00	12.00
Plate				
6¼″ d, sherbet	7.00	6.00	3.50	5.50
9¾″ d, dinner	4.50	4.50	8.00	9.50
Saucer	2.25	2.25	2.00	2.00
Sherbet	7.00	7.50	9.50	19.50
Soup Bowl, 7¾″ d	11.50	11.50	18.00	27.50
Sugar, open	5.50	5.00	9.00	17.50
Vegetable Bowl				
7″	12.00	10.00	20.00	27.50
9″	12.00	10.00	18.00	30.00

DORIC, Jeannette Glass Co, 1935–38. Made in green and pink. Limited production in delphite and yellow.

	Delphite	Green	Pink
Berry Bowl			
Individual, 4½″ d	36.00	7.00	6.00
Master, 8¼″ d	110.00	17.00	12.00
Bowl, 9″ d, two handles	—	15.00	15.00
Butter Dish, cov	—	75.00	60.00
Cake Plate, 10″ d	—	21.00	20.00
Candy Dish, 3 part	8.00	6.00	5.00
Cereal Bowl, 5½″ d	—	50.00	42.00
Coaster	—	18.00	21.00
Creamer	—	12.00	10.00
Cup	—	8.00	7.50
Pitcher			
5½″ h	900.00	36.00	32.00
7½″ h	—	750.00	425.00
Plate			
6″ d, sherbet	—	4.00	2.50
7″ d, salad	—	16.00	15.00
9″ d, dinner	—	14.50	15.50
9″ d, grill	—	15.00	13.50

Left: Beaded Block, plate, 7¾″ sq, green, $10.00. **Center:** Princess, pitcher, 8″ h, 60 oz, pink, $55.00. **Right:** Sharon, plate, 9½″ d, dinner, amber, $10.00.

	Delphite	Green	Pink
Platter, 12″ oval	—	22.00	20.00
Relish Tray			
4 x 4″	—	15.00	13.50
4 x 8″	—	16.00	10.00
Salt and Pepper, pr	—	32.00	30.00
Saucer	—	3.50	2.75
Sherbet, ftd	5.00	12.00	9.50
Sugar, cov	—	20.00	16.00
Tray			
8 x 8″	—	26.00	24.00
10″, handle	—	15.00	14.00
Tumbler			
4″ h, 10 oz, ftd	—	70.00	45.00
4½″ h, 9 oz	—	80.00	50.00
5″ h, 12 oz, ftd	—	95.00	65.00
Vegetable Bowl, 9″ l, oval	—	32.00	30.00

FLOWER GARDEN WITH BUTTERFLIES, Butterflies and Roses, U. S. Glass Co, late 1920s. Made in amber, black, blue–green, canary yellow, crystal, green, and pink.

	Amber Crystal	Black	Blue Canary	Green	Pink
Ashtray	175.00	—	185.00	75.00	80.00
Bonbon, cov, 6⅜″ d	—	250.00	—	—	—
Candlesticks, pr					
4″	40.00	—	90.00	65.00	65.00
6″	—	350.00	—	—	—
8″	80.00	275.00	120.00	125.00	125.00
Candy, cov					
6″, flat	125.00	—	—	150.00	155.00
7½″, cone shape	75.00	—	150.00	130.00	130.00
Cheese and Cracker	—	—	325.00	—	—
Cigarette Box, cov	—	150.00	—	—	—
Cologne Bottle, 7½″ h	—	—	225.00	175.00	175.00
Compote					
2⅞″ h	—	200.00	25.00	24.00	24.00
3″ h	20.00	65.00	25.00	24.00	24.00
4¼″ h, 4¾″ w	—	225.00	50.00	50.00	50.00
4¾″ h, 10¼″ w	45.00	—	80.00	80.00	80.00

	Amber Crystal	Black	Blue Canary	Green	Pink
5⅞" h, 11" w	55.00	225.00	90.00	—	—
7¼" h, 8¼" w	60.00	185.00	—	80.00	80.00
Console Bowl					
8½" d	—	150.00	—	—	—
12" d, rolled edge	—	200.00	—	—	—
Creamer	—	—	—	70.00	70.00
Cup	—	—	—	65.00	65.00
Mayonnaise, ftd	60.00	—	65.00	80.00	80.00
Plate					
7" d	13.00	—	30.00	20.00	20.00
8" d	15.00	—	32.00	24.00	24.00
10" d	—	100.00	45.00	40.00	40.00
Powder Jar					
3½", flat	—	—	—	75.00	75.00
6¼" h, ftd	75.00	—	150.00	95.00	95.00
7½" h, ftd	80.00	—	175.00	120.00	120.00
Sandwich Server	50.00	125.00	90.00	65.00	65.00
Saucer	—	—	—	25.00	25.00
Sugar	—	—	—	70.00	70.00
Tray					
5½ x 10", oval	50.00	—	—	55.00	55.00
11¾ x 7¾", rect	50.00	—	80.00	75.00	75.00
Tumbler, 7½" h	175.00	—	—	—	—
Vase					
6¼" h	70.00	145.00	125.00	125.00	125.00
10½" h	—	350.00	185.00	125.00	125.00
Wall Vase, 9" h	—	325.00	—	—	—

FORTUNE, Hocking Glass Co, 1937–38. Made in crystal and pink.

	Crystal	Pink		Crystal	Pink
Berry Bowl, 4" d	4.00	5.00	Juice Tumbler, 3½" h, 5 oz	9.00	9.00
Bowl			Plate		
4½" d, handle	5.00	5.00	6" d, sherbet	3.00	3.00
5¼" d, rolled edge	6.00	6.00	8" d, luncheon	3.00	3.00
Candy Dish, cov	20.00	20.00	Salad Bowl, 7¾" d	12.00	12.00
Cup	3.50	4.00	Saucer	2.00	2.00
Dessert Bowl, 4½" d	4.50	4.50	Tumbler, 4" h, 9 oz	8.00	8.00

JUBILEE, Lancaster Glass Co, early 1930s. Made in pink and yellow.

	Pink	Yellow		Pink	Yellow
Bowl			Fruit Bowl		
8" d, 5⅛" h, 3 ftd	250.00	200.00	9" d, handle	—	110.00
11½" d, 3 ftd	250.00	250.00	11½" d, flat	200.00	170.00
13" d, 3 ftd	250.00	225.00	Goblet, 7½" h, 11 oz	—	38.00
Cake Plate, 11" d	85.00	50.00	Iced Tea Tumbler, 6⅛" h,		
Candlesticks, pr	190.00	200.00	12½ oz	—	115.00
Candy Jar, cov	—	300.00	Juice Tumbler, 5" h, 6 oz, ftd	—	85.00
Champagne, 5½" h, 7 oz	—	75.00	Mayonnaise, Underplate,		
Cheese and Cracker	250.00	225.00	ladle	320.00	300.00
Cordial, 4" h, 1 oz	—	225.00	Plate		
Creamer	35.00	20.00	7" d, salad	24.00	13.00
Cup	40.00	17.50	8¾" d, luncheon	30.00	15.00

	Pink	Yellow		Pink	Yellow
Sandwich Plate, 13½″ d	185.00	200.00	Tray, 11″ l, 2 handles	85.00	50.00
Saucer	12.00	6.00	Tumbler, 6″ h, 10 oz	75.00	45.00
Sherbet, 3″ h	—	65.00	Wine, 4⅞″ h, 3 oz	—	125.00
Sugar	40.00	20.00			

MANHATTAN, Horizontal Ribbed, Anchor Hocking Glass Co, 1938–43. Made in crystal and pink. Limited production in green, iridescent, and ruby.

	Crystal	Pink		Crystal	Pink
Ashtray			Plate		
4″ d, round	10.00	—	6″ d, sherbet	4.75	45.00
4½″ d, sq	8.00	—	8½″ d, salad	11.00	—
Berry Bowl			10¼″ d, dinner	16.00	100.00
Individual, 5⅜″ d	15.00	15.00	Relish Tray, 14″ d, with		
Master, 7½″ d	13.00	13.00	inserts	42.00	45.00
Bowl, 8″ d, closed handles . .	20.00	21.00	Relish Tray Insert	5.00	4.00
Candlesticks, pr, 4½″ h	15.00	—	Salad Bowl, 9″ d	20.00	24.00
Candy Dish, cov	—	10.00	Salt and Pepper, pr	25.00	45.00
Cereal Bowl, 5¼″ d	15.00	—	Sandwich Plate, 14″ d	20.00	—
Coaster, 3½″ d	14.00	—	Sauce Bowl, 4½″ d	8.50	—
Compote, 5¾″	27.00	26.00	Saucer, 6″ d	4.00	45.00
Creamer	8.00	10.00	Sherbet	7.00	15.00
Cup	18.00	120.00	Sugar, oval	20.00	18.00
Fruit Bowl, 9½″ d	35.00	32.00	Tumbler, 10 oz, ftd	13.00	9.00
Pitcher			Vase, 8″ h	15.00	—
24 oz	25.00	—	Wine, 3½″ h	5.00	—
80 oz, tilted	28.00	50.00			

NEWPORT, Hairpin, Hazel Atlas Glass Co, 1936–40. Made in amethyst, cobalt blue, fired-on colors, pink, and platonite.

	Amethyst	Cobalt Blue	Fired-On Colors	Platonite White
Berry Bowl				
Individual, 4¾″ d	11.00	15.00	5.00	2.50
Master, 8¼″ d	30.00	32.00	12.00	10.00
Cereal Bowl, 5¾″ d	23.00	37.50	—	
Creamer	12.00	17.50	7.50	4.50
Cream Soup, 4¾″ d	15.00	20.00	7.50	5.50
Cup	10.00	10.00	6.00	4.00
Plate				
5⅞″ d, sherbet	4.00	5.00	1.50	
8½″ d, luncheon	10.00	13.00	4.50	3.00
9″ d, dinner	20.00	25.00	12.00	4.00
Platter, 11¾″ l, oval	32.00	40.00	17.50	12.50
Salt and Pepper Shakers, pr .	45.00	48.00	20.00	8.50
Sandwich Plate, 11¾″ d	30.00	35.00	12.00	10.00
Saucer	3.75	3.50	1.00	1.00
Sherbet	11.00	16.50	6.00	1.00
Sugar	15.00	17.50	5.00	4.00
Tumbler, 4½″ h, 9 oz	28.00	40.00	10.00	—

OLD CAFE, Hocking Glass Co, 1936–40. Made in crystal, pink, and royal ruby.

	Crystal	Pink	Royal Ruby
Berry Bowl, 3¾″ d	3.00	3.00	5.00
Bowl			
5″ d	5.00	10.00	—
9″ d	10.00	12.00	15.00
Candy Dish, 8″ d, low	10.00	10.00	12.00
Cereal Bowl, 5½″ d	6.00	6.50	10.00
Cup	5.00	5.00	10.00
Juice Tumbler, 3″ h	10.00	10.00	9.00
Lamp	17.50	20.00	22.00
Olive Dish, 6″ l, oblong	5.00	5.00	—
Pitcher			
36 oz	60.00	65.00	—
80 oz	75.00	175.00	—
Plate			
6″ d, sherbet	2.00	2.50	8.00
10″ d, dinner	25.00	27.50	30.00
Saucer	3.00	3.00	8.00
Sherbet	6.00	7.00	10.00
Tumbler, 4″ h	10.00	10.00	17.50
Vase, 7¼″ h	12.00	13.00	18.00

PRINCESS, Hocking Glass Co, 1931–35. Made in apricot yellow, blue, green, pink, and topaz yellow.

	Apricot	Green	Pink	Topaz
Ashtray, 4½″ d	85.00	65.00	85.00	85.00
Berry Bowl, 4½″ d	40.00	20.00	22.00	40.00
Bowl, 9½″ d	26.00	39.00	35.00	26.00
Butter Dish, cov	600.00	85.00	85.00	600.00
Cake Stand	—	22.50	25.00	—
Candy Dish	—	55.00	55.00	—
Cereal Bowl, 5″ d	26.50	20.00	20.00	26.50
Coaster	85.00	32.00	60.00	85.00
Cookie Jar, cov	—	50.00	55.00	—
Creamer, oval	10.00	14.00	15.00	10.00
Cup	8.00	15.00	10.00	9.00
Iced Tea Tumbler, 5¼″ h, 13 oz	85.00	35.00	35.00	85.00
Juice Tumbler, 3″ h, 5 oz . . .	24.00	25.00	25.00	23.00
Pitcher				
6″ h, 37 oz	500.00	40.00	45.00	500.00
8″ h, 60 oz	80.00	50.00	55.00	80.00
Plate				
5½″ d, sherbet	4.00	9.50	9.00	4.00
8″ d, salad	9.00	13.50	13.00	9.00
9½″ d, dinner	12.00	22.50	19.00	12.00
9½″ d, grill	15.00	11.00	11.00	15.00
10½″ d, grill, handles	6.50	9.00	10.00	6.50
Platter, 12″ l	35.00	22.00	20.00	35.00
Relish, 7½″ l				
Divided	90.00	22.00	22.00	90.00
Plain	130.00	90.00	150.00	135.00
Salad Bowl, 9″ d, octagonal .	110.00	35.00	30.00	110.00
Salt and Pepper Shakers, pr .	60.00	50.00	50.00	60.00
Sandwich Plate, 10¼″ d, handles	12.00	15.00	19.00	12.00

	Apricot	Green	Pink	Topaz
Saucer	8.00	9.00	4.00	8.00
Sherbet	30.00	20.00	18.00	30.00
Sugar, cov	15.00	12.00	16.00	12.00
Tumbler				
4" h, 9 oz	20.00	25.00	22.50	20.00
4¾" h, 9 oz, ftd	—	60.00	55.00	—
5¼" h, 10 oz, ftd	18.00	30.00	25.00	18.00
6½" h, 12½ oz, ftd	95.00	24.00	24.00	95.00
Vase, 8" h	—	31.00	30.00	—
Vegetable Bowl, 10" oval . . .	50.00	28.00	26.00	50.00

SHARON, Cabbage Rose, Federal Glass Co, 1935–1939. Made in amber, crystal, green, and pink. Reproduced.

	Amber	Green	Pink
Berry Bowl			
Individual, 5" d	8.50	14.00	12.50
Master, 8½" d	6.50	25.00	27.50
Butter Dish, cov	23.00	80.00	47.50
Cake Plate, 11½" d, ftd	24.00	55.00	35.00
Candy Jar, cov	45.00	150.00	50.00
Cereal Bowl, 6" d	18.00	24.00	22.00
Cheese Dish, cov	180.00	—	—
Creamer, ftd	10.00	20.00	25.00
Cream Soup, 5" d	27.50	45.00	40.00
Cup	9.00	18.00	17.50
Fruit Bowl, 10½" d	21.00	35.00	35.00
Jam Dish, 7½" d	35.00	40.00	160.00
Pitcher, 80 oz			
Ice Lip	100.00	350.00	150.00
Plain	120.00	400.00	130.00
Plate			
6" d, bread and butter	4.00	8.00	7.50
7½" d, salad	15.00	20.00	24.00
9½" d, dinner	10.00	21.00	17.50
Platter, 12½" l, oval	18.00	27.50	27.50
Salt and Pepper Shakers, pr	40.00	65.00	45.00
Saucer	6.00	5.00	5.00
Sherbet, ftd	12.00	25.00	13.00
Soup Bowl, 7¾" d	45.00	—	40.00
Sugar, cov	30.00	45.00	28.00
Tumbler			
4⅛" h, 9 oz, thick	23.00	40.00	37.50
4⅛" h, 9 oz, thin	25.00	37.50	30.00
5¼" h, 12 oz, thick	25.00	37.50	37.50
5¼" h, 12 oz, thin	28.00	40.00	48.00
6½" h, 15 oz, ftd	90.00	—	50.00
Vegetable Bowl, 9½" d, oval	20.00	30.00	24.00

TEA ROOM, Indiana Glass Co, 1926–31. Made in amber, some crystal, green, and pink.

	Green	Pink		Green	Pink
Banana Split, 7½"			Celery Bowl, 8¼" d	30.00	25.00
Flat	75.00	75.00	Creamer		
Footed	80.00	80.00	3¼" h	25.00	25.00
Candlesticks, pr	60.00	56.00	4½" h, ftd	22.00	25.00

	Green	Pink		Green	Pink
Rectangular	20.00	18.00	Sugar, cov		
Cup	50.00	50.00	3″ h	75.00	120.00
Finger Bowl	45.00	35.00	4½″ h, ftd	28.00	26.00
Goblet	70.00	60.00	Rectangular	20.00	18.00
Ice Bucket	55.00	65.00	Sundae, ftd, ruffled	85.00	75.00
Lamp, 9″ h	55.00	45.00	Tray		
Marmalade, notched lid	175.00	150.00	Center handle	185.00	195.00
Mustard, cov	135.00	120.00	Rectangular	50.00	45.00
Parfait	65.00	60.00	Tumbler		
Pitcher, 64 oz	200.00	175.00	6 oz, ftd	35.00	35.00
Plate			8 oz, flat	30.00	28.00
6½″ d, sherbet	25.00	25.00	8 oz, ftd	35.00	35.00
8¼″ d, luncheon	32.00	30.00	11 oz, ftd	65.00	65.00
Relish, divided	24.00	20.00	12 oz, ftd	55.00	55.00
Salad Bowl, 8¾″ d	75.00	72.00	Vase		
Salt and Pepper Shakers, pr .	55.00	55.00	6½″ h, ruffled	145.00	85.00
Sandwich Plate, 10½″ d	50.00	48.00	9½″ h, ruffled	140.00	80.00
Saucer	25.00	25.00	9½″ h, straight	65.00	60.00
Sherbet			11″ h, ruffled	185.00	200.00
Low	28.00	25.00	11″ h, straight	90.00	85.00
Low, flared edge	35.00	32.00	Vegetable Bowl, 9½″ l,		
Tall, ftd	45.00	40.00	oval	60.00	55.00

DISNEYANA

History: Walt Disney and the creations of the famous Disney Studios hold a place of fondness and enchantment in the hearts of people throughout the world. The release of *Steamboat Willie* featuring Mickey Mouse in 1928 heralded an entertainment empire.

Walt and his brother, Roy, showed shrewd business acumen. From the beginning they licensed the reproduction of Disney characters in products ranging from wristwatches to clothing. In 1984 Donald Duck celebrated his 50th birthday, and collectors took a renewed interest in material related to him.

The market in Disneyana has been established by a few determined dealers and auction houses. Hake's Americana and Collectibles of York, Pennsylvania, offers several hundred Disneyana items in each of its bimonthly mail and phone bid auctions. Sotheby's and Christie's New York auctions offer original art and cels several times each year.

References: David Longest and Michael Stern, *The Collector's Encyclopedia of Disneyana*, Collector Books, 1992; Richard Schickel, *The Disney Version: The Life, Times, Art and Commerce of Walt Disney*, Avon Books, 1968; Michael Stern, *Stern's Guide to Disney Collectibles, First Series*, (1989, 1992 value update), *Second Series*, (1990, 1993 value update), Collector Books; Tom Tumbusch, *Tomart's Illustrated Disneyana Catalog and Price Guide*, Vols. 1, 2, 3, and 4, Tomart Publications, 1985; Tom Tumbusch, *Tomart's Illustrated Disneyana Catalog and Price Guide, Condensed Edition*, Wallace–Homestead, 1989; Walton Rawls,

Disney Dons Dogtags: The Best of Disney Military Insignia From World War II, Abbeville Press, 1992.

Archives: Walt Disney Archives, 500 South Buena Vista Street, Burbank, CA 91521.

Collectors' Clubs: Mouse Club East Newsletter, PO Box 3195, Wakefield, MA 01880; National Fantasy Fan Club for Disneyana Collectors and Enthusiasts, PO Box 19212, Irvine, CA 92713; The Mouse Club, 2056 Cirone Way, San Jose, CA 95124.

Museum: Walt Disney Archives, Burbank, CA.

Additional Listings: See *Warman's Americana & Collectibles* for more examples.

Advisor: Ted Hake.

Alice in Wonderland	
Figure, Alice, 5½″ h, painted and glazed, green leaves and brown mushrooms on base, Shaw, c1951	225.00
Marionette, composition, blue dress, white apron, yellow hair, black felt hair bow, 14″, by Peter Puppet Playthings, 1950s.	75.00
Postcard, 3½ x 5½″, color illus, unused, 1951	15.00
Bambi	
Alarm Clock, animated, Flower and Thumper on dial, second hand is butterfly on Bambi's tail, light blue metal case, 2½ x 4½ x 5″, orig box, Bayard of France, 1972	125.00
Bowl, cereal, 5″ d, Bambi on bottom, butterfly on tail, flowers, Walt Disney Productions, c1940	20.00
Handkerchief, 9 x 10″, fabric, red,	

blue, yellow, and green image of Bambi and Thumper, Walt Disney Productions copyright, c1950 .... **20.00**

Picture, framed, "Bambi and Mother," c1942, Courvoisier Galleries sticker, c1940 .... **150.00**

Planter, 3½ x 7 x 6", ceramic, painted and glazed, Bambi standing alongside tree stump, Thumper in front, incised Disney copyright, Leeds, c1949 .... **55.00**

Cinderella

Doll, 18" h, hp, dressed, Madame Alexander, 1950 .... **125.00**

Handkerchief, 8 x 8½", fabric, red, yellow, green, blue, and pink image, c1950 .... **20.00**

Toy, wind–up, dancing Cinderella and Prince, orig box, 1940s **175.00**

Davy Crockett, toy, "Walt Disney's Official Davy Crockett Western Prairie Wagon," red litho tin, full color scene, Mouseketeer symbol on side, orig brown carton with red illus, Adco–Liberty Mfg Co, c1950 .... **175.00**

Donald Duck, riding tricycle, bisque, marked "Japan," 3¼" h, $35.00.

Donald Duck

Book, *How To Draw Donald Duck Character Model Guide,* from Art Corner at Disneyland, spiral bound, 32 pgs, 8½ x 11", late 1950s. **50.00**

Camera, Herbert George Co **50.00**

Comic Book Art, orig 8 panel strip, pen and ink by Al Taliaferro, Walt Disney Comics #55, page 29, 19 x 13" **600.00**

Doll, 16", leatherette, angry Donald, by Richard G. Krueger, c1935. .... **400.00**

Planter, figural, sitting on top of ABC blocks, 5½", Leeds, c1940 ...... **35.00**

Pocket Watch, Ingersoll, 1939 .... **450.00**

Toy, wooden, Donald playing xylophone, paper labels, Fisher Price #177, 6 x 11 x 13", c1940. ...... **125.00**

Dumbo

Figure, 5½" h, Baby Weems, seated, baby bonnet, incised No 41, Vernon Kilns, c1940. .... **300.00**

Sketch Pad, 24 ink drawings in sequence, stamped Disney Studios, c1940, 13 x 17" **300.00**

Goofy

Plate, china, Goofy seated on a crate, brick wall and flowers in back, cameos of Bambi, Thumper, Flower, two butterflies, and bluebird around edge, marked "Beswick, England, 7" **35.00**

Wristwatch, "Backwards," 17 jewels, leather band, MIB. **350.00**

Mickey Mouse, Slate Dancer toy, $29,150.00. Photograph courtesy of James D. Julia, Inc.

Mickey Mouse

Alarm Clock, 4" h, green metal case, Ingersoll, c1930 .... **300.00**

Bank, treasure chest, red leatherette, brass trim, emb Mickey and Minnie on top, marked "Zell Products" ... **175.00**

Book

Mickey Mouse Crusoe, Whitman Publishing Co, 1936, 72 pgs, 7 x 9½" . **75.00**

Mickey Mouse Stories, 1931, David McKay Co, 64 pgs, 6¼ x 8½" **75.00**

Button, 1¼" celluloid, red, black, white, Good Teeth, Mickey brushing Big Bad Wolf's teeth **150.00**

Coloring Book, Mickey Mouse Explorers Club Coloring Book, Kroger, 64 pgs, 8 x 10¾", 1965. .... **15.00**

Game, Mickey Mouse Coming Home Game, Marks Brothers, 2 x 9 x 20" cardboard box, 16 x 16" board, multicolored. **150.00**

Guitar, plastic, 6½ x 21", yellow front, large paper label, six plastic strings, Walt Disney copyright, c1970 . . . . **15.00**

Handkerchief, 7½" sq, small black figure of Mickey in one corner, 1930s **20.00**

Hot Pad, fabric, beige, 6 x 6", 3" center stripe depicts Mickey images in black, white, and red, c1930 . . . . . **25.00**

Marionette, 13" h, composition head and feet, wood body and legs, stuffed velveteen arms and hands, Hestwood Marionettes, mid 1930s **1,000.00**

Painting, Mickey and Minnie on country lane, Mickey pointing to moon, tempera on card, sgd "Walt Disney," c1935, 15½ x 10½" **2,500.00**

Sheet Music, *What! No Mickey Mouse? What Kind Of A Party Is This?*, 9½ x 13", Irving Caesar Inc, copyright 1932 . . . . **100.00**

Toothbrush Holder, 5" h, bisque, one movable arms **200.00**

Umbrella, two silk screen poses of Mickey, Minnie on satinlike cloth, 20" l, Walt Disney Enterprises, c1930 . . . . **150.00**

Minnie Mouse

Ashtray, 3 x 3", china, holding sheet music and singing, marked "Authorized By Walter E Disney/Made In Bavaria" **200.00**

Book, *Minnie Mouse And The Antique Chair*, Whitman, No 845, hard cov, 5 x 5½", 1948 . . . . **20.00**

Figure, 3½" h, bisque, carrying first-aid kit, c1930. . . . . **50.00**

Mug, Minnie brushing hair, marked "Salem China". **75.00**

Peter Pan

Book, *Walt Disney's Peter Pan*, Simon & Schuster, 1952, 28 pgs, 9½ x 13" **15.00**

Overnight Case **25.00**

Pinocchio

Bank, 7" h, composition, Pinocchio riding on turtle, missing metal trap, Crown. **175.00**

Celluloid, Jiminy Crickett standing behind the eight ball with fists raised, titled "I'll Teach You," applied to airbrushed ground, 1939, 10½ x 8" . . **1,400.00**

Doll, 7½" h, wood body, composition head, jointed arms and legs, Ideal, c1940. **150.00**

Figure

Figaro, 3½" h, ceramic, painted and glazed, Shaw, c1946. . . . . **100.00**

Gepetto, 5" h, wood composition, blue shirt, red pants, and yellow socks . **60.00**

Plaque, wood, Jiminy Crickett and Pinocchio seated on Gepetto's sideboard, Blue Fairy holding wand, brown finish, blue dress, yellow hair, white wings, and yellow hat, 4 x 5", c1940 . . . . **75.00**

Postcard, 3¼ x 5¼", color illus, unused, marked "Walt Disney's Pinocchio," c1940. . . . . **25.00**

Sheet Music, *Wish Upon A Star* . . **15.00**

Valentine, 5 x 5", mechanical, heart shape, diecut, copyright 1939 . . . . **25.00**

Pluto

Big Little Book, *Pluto the Pup*, #1467, Whitman Publishing Co, 1938 . . . . **25.00**

Celluloid, Sheep Dog, Pluto walking across desert with bone in mouth, 1949, 9 x 27". **250.00**

Figure, 3⅓" h, 6⅓" l, painted and glazed, American Pottery sticker, 1948. **100.00**

Mug, glazed china, Pluto on one side, seated Mickey Mouse on other, 3", c1930. **60.00**

Planter, glazed china, multicolored, 4 x 8 x 6½", c1940 . . . . **30.00**

Salt Shaker, glazed china, Disney copyright on base, 4" h, c1960 . . . **10.00**

Snow White and the Seven Dwarfs

Doll, Snow White, 14" h, orig felt, Molly–O **150.00**

Glass, set of 8, 4½" h, full figures, poems on each, Libbey, c1930 . . . **150.00**

Handkerchief, small image of Snow White, deer, rabbits, and birds, red, white, blue, and brown, 8½" sq, c1938. **15.00**

Lamp, figural, composition, Walt Disney Enterprises, dated 1938 . . . . . **175.00**

Pin, molded celluloid, multicolored, Snow White surrounded by dwarfs with musical instruments, orig 3½ x 4" white, blue, and yellow card, pin 1¾ x 2". **25.00**

Pitcher, glazed china, raised figures, multicolored, large handle with two bluebirds and squirrel, music box base plays "Whistle While You Work," Wade Heath, England, 7½" h, 6" d, c1938 . . . . **250.00**

Premium, game, Walt Disney's Snow White Game, Johnson & Johnson Tek Toothbrushes, copyright 1937 **75.00**

Rug, 21 x 45", velvet type finish, brown fringe, Snow White, dwarfs, animals, and cottage scene, c1938 **150.00**

Sheet Music, *Whistle While You Work*, Irving Berlin Inc, 1937, 9 x 12", 4 pgs **15.00**

Three Little Pigs

Bisque Set, litho box, 2 x 3½ x 5", top

shows wolf puffing at brick house,
3½" figures, c1930. . . . . **175.00**
Toothbrush Holder, bisque, pigs
shown with fife, fiddle, and orange
bricks, 2 x 3½ x 4". **75.00**
Toy, 4" h, wind–up, celluloid, pale orange, pig with silver drum, reverse
with patent number and "Made In
Japan," c1930. . . . . **210.00**
Watch, silvered metal case and link
band, dial illus of wolf's head and
pigs, Ingersoll, c1934. . . . . **400.00**
20,000 Leagues Under The Sea, toy,
Nautilus, submarine, tin, orig box . . . **175.00**
Zorro
Activity Set, Walt Disney's Zorro Activity Box, 9 x 12 x 1½" box, paper
layout sheet, ten figures, building,
stable, gate, wall section, and accessory pieces, Whitman, copyright
1965. . . . . **75.00**
Dominoes, Zorro on horseback on
back, Halsman, 1950s **35.00**
Hat, straw, felt trim, orig fabric chin
strap, brim with fabric "Zorro"
patch, 1950s **55.00**
Lunch Box, litho tin, raised figures,
thermos, c1950 . . . . **75.00**
Mask, 12 x 12½", felt, black, white
string chin strap, Benay Albee Cre-
ation, 1950s. **75.00**
Mug, 4½" h, boot shape, plastic, yel-
low, "Zorro" sticker, Productions
copyright, 1950s **50.00**

DOLLHOUSES

History: Dollhouses date from the 18th century
to modern times. Early dollhouses often were
handmade, sometimes with only one room. The
most common type was made for a young girl to
fill with replicas of furniture scaled especially to fit
into a dollhouse. Specially sized dolls also were
made for dollhouses. All types of accessories and
styles allowed a dollhouse to portray any historical
period.
References: Caroline Clifton–Mogg, *The Dollhouse Sourcebook,* Abbeville Press, 1993; Nora
Earnshaw, *Collecting Dolls' Houses and Miniatures,* Pincushion Press, 1993; Caroline Hamilton,
Decorative Dollhouses, Clarkson Potter, 1990;
Flora Bill Jacobs, *Dolls' Houses in America: Historic Preservation in Miniature,* Charles Scribner's
Sons, 1974; Donald and Helene Mitchell, *Dollhouses, Past and Present,* Collector Books, 1949,
out of print; Eva Stille, *Doll Kitchens 1800–1980,*
Schiffer Publishing, 1988; Margaret Towner, *Dollhouse Furniture: The Collector's Guide To Selecting and Enjoying Miniature Masterpieces,* Courage
Books, 1993; Blair Whitton (ed.), *Bliss Toys And
Dollhouses,* Dover, 1979.

Periodicals: *Doll Castles News,* PO Box 247,
Washington, NJ 07882; *International Dolls' House
News,* PO Box 79, Southampton, England S09
7EZ.
Museums: Margaret Woodbury Strong Museum, Rochester, NY; Washington Dolls' House
and Toy Museum, Washington, D.C.

Bliss, litho on wood
10 x 13 x 13" h, Wild Rose Cottage,
Little Red Riding Hood at the front
door **1,100.00**
20 x 13 x 9", two story, front door
opens, four eisenglass windows,
lace curtains, metal porch rail, two
chimneys, ext. stair **2,225.00**
27 x 18 x 11", Victorian, two rooms,
two story, high steepled roof, dormer windows, spindled porch rail-
ings, second floor balcony. **1,000.00**
Converse
15 x 17", cottage, red and green litho
on redwood, painted bay window,
stone base, roof dormer **450.00**
19½ x 17", Red Robin Farm, cupola,
double barn doors, six stalls, nine
orig animals, 1912 . . . . **475.00**
Gearhart, Nita, 10 x 25", house, seven
rooms, wallpapered cov walls, handmade wood furniture, ten handmade
bisque dolls, c1976 . . . . **675.00**
German, Victorian style, litho on cardboard, one room, three sided, hinged,
wood furniture, marked "Made in Ger-
many," c1880 . . . . **295.00**
McLoughlin, house with garden, two
story, two rooms, orig box, c1911 . . . **800.00**
Schoenhut
12¾ x 11 x 9", bungalow, one story,
yellow and green, red roof, orig
decal **400.00**
29 x 26 x 30", mansion, two story,
eight rooms, attic, tan brick design,
red roof, large dormer, twenty glass
windows, orig decal, c1923. . . . . . **1,800.00**

DOLLS

History: Dolls have been children's play toys for
centuries. Dolls also have served other functions.
During the 14th through 18th centuries, doll making
was centered in Europe, mainly in Germany and
France. The French dolls produced in this era represented adults and were dressed in the latest cou-
turier designs. They were not children's toys.
During the mid 19th century, child and baby
dolls, made in wax, cloth, bisque, and porcelain,
were introduced. Facial features were hand
painted; wigs were made of mohair and human
hair. They were dressed in baby or children's fashions.

Marks from the various manufacturers are found on the back of the head, neck, or back area. These marks are very important in identifying the doll and date of manufacture.

Doll making in the United States began to flourish in the 1900s with names such as Effanbee, Madame Alexander, Ideal, and others.

References: Johana Gast Anderton, *More Twentieth Century Dolls From Bisque to Vinyl, Volumes A–H, Volumes I–Z, Revised Edition,* Wallace–Homestead, 1974; John Axe, *The Encyclopedia of Celebrity Dolls,* Hobby House Press Inc., 1983; Julie Collier, *The Official Identification And Price Guide To Antique & Modern Dolls, Fourth Edition,* House of Collectibles, 1989; Carol Corson, *Schoenhut Dolls: A Collector's Encyclopedia,* Hobby House Press, 1993; Nora Earnshaw, *Collecting Dolls,* Pincushion Press, 1992; Jan Foulke, *11th Blue Book Dolls and Values,* Hobby House Press, 1993; Caroline Goodfellow, *The Ultimate Doll Book,* Hobby House Press, 1993; R. Lane Herron, *Herron's Price Guide To Dolls,* Wallace–Homestead, 1990; Judith Izen, *A Collector's Guide To Ideal Dolls,* Collector Books, 1994; Polly Judd, *Cloth Dolls: Identification and Price Guide,* Hobby House Press, 1990; Polly and Pam Judd, *Composition Dolls: 1928–1955,* Hobby House Press, 1991; Wendy Lavitt, *American Folk Dolls,* Alfred A. Knopf, 1982; Wendy Lavitt, *Dolls,* Alfred A. Knopf, 1983; A. Glenn Mandeville, *Glenn Mandeville's Madame Alexander Dolls Value Guide,* Hobby House Press, 1993; Edward R. Pardella, *Shirley Temple Dolls and Fashion: A Collector's Guide To The World's Darling,* Schiffer Publishing, 1992; Lydia and Joachim F. Richter, *Bru Dolls,* Hobby House Press, 1989; Lydia Richter and Karin Schmelcher, *Heubach Character Dolls and Figurines,* Hobby House Press, 1992; Lydia Richter, *China, Parian, and Bisque German Dolls,* Hobby House Press, 1993; Patricia R. Smith, *Antique Collector's Dolls,* Vol. I (19875, 1991 value update), Vol. II (1976, 1991 value update), Collector Books; Patricia R. Smith, *Madame Alexander Collector's Dolls Price Guide # 18,* Collector Books, 1993; Patricia R. Smith, *Madame Alexander Dolls 1965–1990,* Collector Books, 1991; Patricia R. Smith, *Modern Collector's Dolls, Volumes I, II,III, IV, V,* Collector Books, 1973, 1975, 1976, 1979, 1984, 1993 value updates; Patricia R. Smith, *Modern Collector's Dolls, Sixth Series,* Collector Books, 1994; Patricia R. Smith, *Shirley Temple Dolls and Collectibles,* Vol. I (1977, 1992 value update), Vol. II (1979, 1992 value update), Collector Books; Patricia R. Smith, *Patricia Smith's Doll Values Antique to Modern, Ninth Series,* Collector Books, 1993; Florence Theriault, *More Dolls: The Early Years 1780–1910,* Gold Horse Publishing, 1992.

Periodicals: *Doll Collector's Price Guide,* 306 East Parr Rd., Berne, IN 46711; *Doll Reader,* 6405 Flank Dr., Harrisburg, PA 17112; *Dolls—The Collector's Magazine,* 170 Fifth Avenue, 12th Floor,

New York, NY 10010; *Doll World,* 306 East Parr Rd., Berne, IN 46711.

Collectors' Clubs: Madame Alexander Fan Club, PO Box 330, Mundeline, IL 60060; United Federation of Doll Clubs, 8B East St., PO Box 14146, Parkville, MO 64152.

Museums: Margaret Woodbury Strong Museum, Rochester, NY; Yesteryears Museum, Sandwich, MA.

Additional Listings: See *Warman's Americana & Collectibles* for more examples.

Tete Jumeau, #15 bebe, marked body, 32″ h, $5,500.00. Photograph courtesy of Cobb's Doll Auction.

Alabama Doll Co, 22½″ h, rag face, stuffed body, arms, legs, and hands, neck, and bust sewn to torso, ears sewn to head, flesh colored waterproof paint, features painted over, painted black shoes and white socks, orig clothes c1900, marks: Mrs S. S. Smith Manufacturer and Dealer to The Alabama Indestructible Doll, Roanoke, Ala, Patented Sept 26, 1905 . . . **2,500.00**

Alt Beck Gottshcalk

22″ h, bisque solid dome turned shoulderhead, kid body, gusseted joints, bisque forearms, blond wig, blue glass inset eyes, closed mouth, well dressed, c1885, marks: 639 Made In Germany **1,150.00**

26″ h, Sweet Nell, bisque socket head, composition wood ball jointed body, brunette human hair wig, gray glass sleep eyes, real lashes, painted features, open mouth, four porcelain teeth, old clothes, c1910, marks: 1362 Made In Germany . . . **875.00**

AM

8/0, bisque, Indian **295.00**

12½″ h, Just Me, bisque, marks: 310 **700.00**

13″ h, Dream Baby, replaced cloth body, nicely dressed. **115.00**

Arranbee Doll Co

12″ h, My Dream Baby, bisque solid dome head, painted hair, glass sleep eyes, open mouth, old baby clothes, c1924, marks: A.M. 341 or 351 or ARRANBEE **400.00**

13″ h, Bottletot, all composition, baby body, bent arms and legs, molded painted hair, blue sleep eyes, open mouth, celluloid hands, orig clothes, right holds bottle marked Arranbee/ Pat Aug. 10, 26, doll is unmarked . **195.00**

16″ h, Nancy, all composition, body jointed at neck, shoulders and hips, molded hair, painted eyes, closed mouth, marks: Arranbee **250.00**

20″ h, Debu Teen, all composition swivel head, shoulder plate, composition body, jointed at neck, shoulders and hips, mohair wig, sleep eyes with lashes, closed mouth, orig clothes, c1938, marks: R & B **250.00**

Averill

10″ h, Topsy & Eva, double–ender cloth doll, hp faces, one black with yarn hair, other white with painted hair, orig polka–dot cotton flip dress, red/white to blue/white, c1930, marked: paper tag, Georgene Novelties. **135.00**

13″ h, Rag Doll, all stuffed cloth head, body, arms, and legs, yarn hair, painted mask faces, orig costume, c1930, marks: A/GENUINE/ (script)GEORGENE/DOLL/A PRODUCT OF GEORGENE NOVELTIES INC. NEW YORK/ MADE IN U.S.A.. . . . . **135.00**

16½″ h, Bonnie Babe, celluloid head, stuffed cloth body, movable arms and legs, molded painted hair, brown set glass eyes, smiling open closed mouth, two teeth, fine old clothing, c1926, marks: BONNIE BABE/Reg. U.S. PAT OFF/Copyright by Georgene Averill/Germany 34 (turtle mark) **650.00**

19″ h, Baby Hendren, composition swivel head, stuffed cotton body, cry box, composition arms and legs, molded painted hair, blue tin decal sleep eyes, painted upper and lower lashes, open mouth, two teeth, nicely dressed, c1930, marks: BABY HENDREN on head **245.00**

23″ h, Baby Georgene, composition head, arms and legs, cloth body, curly blond mohair wig, blue sleep eyes, closed mouth, undressed, orig shoes and socks, c1935. . . . . **3,500.00**

Bahr & Proschild

12″ h, Character Baby, bisque solid dome socket head, composition baby bent limb body, blue glass sleep eyes, open mouth, two upper teeth, well dressed, c1910, marks: BP 585 Germany. **525.00**

22″ h, Character Baby, bisque socket head, composition baby bent limb body, brunette human hair wig, brown glass sleep eyes, open mouth, two upper teeth, nicely dressed, c1915, marks: BP 585 Germany. **775.00**

Bebe Le Parisien, 23″ h, composition body, bisque socket head, blue paperweight eyes, painted lashes, closed mouth, pierced ears, blond wig, chemise trimmed with lace and pink ribbons, orig undergarments, pink satin undress, lace and eyelet overdress, matching pink silk bonnet, marks: Au Nain Bleu–Paris, A–15/Paris, and Le Parisien/Bte SGDG/A–15, body with Bebe Le Parisien/Medaille D'Or/Paris **5,500.00**

Belton Type, 14″ h, child, bisque socket head, solid flat top with holes for stringing, composition and wood ball jointed body, straight wrists, blue paperweight eyes, closed mouth, pierced ears, c1875 French style clothing, incised 137 . . . . **2,700.00**

Bergmann, C. M., 15″ h, bisque socket head, composition bent limb baby body, brunette mohair wig, almond shaped small gray glass sleep eyes, open mouth, two porcelain upper teeth, nicely dressed, marks: Simon & Halbig, C. M. Bergmann 612 Germany **1,400.00**

Borgfeldt, George

12½″ h, Hug Me Kiddie, round all composition mask face, pink felt body, fleecy brunette hair, inset large round glass googlie side glancing eyes, closed watermelon mouth, pug nose, orig clothes, c1911, marks: paper label. **850.00**

24″ h, Character Baby, bisque socket head, blond mohair wig, brown glass sleep eyes, open smiling mouth, two upper porcelain teeth, tongue, nicely dressed, c1913, marks: G 327B Germany A. M. . . . **800.00**

Bru

9″ h, wood and composition body, bisque socket head, blond wig, blue paperweight eyes, closed mouth, pierced ears, blue satin dress, blue satin French shoes, marks: Bru Jne/2/0 . . . . **8,800.00**

19″ h, bisque swivel head, leather body, bisque hands, blue paperweight eyes, closed mouth, tongue behind upper lips, dressed, marks: impressed circle, dot, and crescent and Bru Jne/6 . . . . **7,100.00**

Cameo Doll Company

10″ h, Margie, composition head, wooden segmented spool like body, arms and legs, molded painted hair, painted eyes, nose, and mouth, undressed, c1929, marks: red triangular decal label on chest reads MARGIE Des. & Copyright by Jos. Kallus. **250.00**

12″ h, Betty Boop, composition swivel head, wooden segmented spool type arms and legs, molded painted black hair, side glancing eyes, tiny closed mouth, composition torso with molded and painted swim suit, wearing old cotton print dress, c1932, marks: heart shaped label on chest, BETTY BOOP Des. & Copyright by Fleischer Studios . . . **600.00**

13″ h, Black Scootles, all composition, toddler body, jointed at neck, shoulders, and hips, molded painted hair, painted eyes, closed smiling mouth, wrist tags **725.00**

15″ h, Scootles, all composition, toddler body, jointed at neck, shoulders, and hips, molded painted hair, painted side glancing eyes, smiling closed mouth, undressed, c1925, wrist tags **600.00**

Chase, Martha, 16″ h, boy, stockinet and cloth, jointed at shoulders, hips, elbows, and knees, molded and painted bobbed hair, oil painted facial features, nicely dressed, c1893–1930, marks: Chase Stockinet Doll stamped on left leg, Martha Chase, Pawtucket, Rhode Island **1,000.00**

Daniel et Cie, 26″ h, Paris Bebe, bisque socket head, French composition and wood jointed body, blond human hair wig, amber/brown paperweight inset eyes, closed mouth, pierced ears, costumed, c1885, marks: Paris Bebe Depose 11 Eiffel Tower symbol on body **4,700.00**

Dressel, Cuno & Otto, 7″ h, toddler, bisque socket head, five piece composition toddler body, hair wig, almond shaped blue glass sleep eyes, open mouth, painted shoes and socks, nicely dressed, c1914, marks: Jutta 1914 8 . . . . **550.00**

Effanbee

2½″ h, Wee Patsy, all composition, one piece body and head, jointed at hips and shoulders, molded and painted bobbed hair style, painted eyes, closed mouth, molded Mary Jane style shoes and socks, orig clothes, pin, and box, c1930, marks: Effanbee Wee Patsy on back **325.00**

14″ h

First Patsy, all composition, well defined molded hair, unusual painted eyes glance to side, open closed smiling type mouth, nicely dressed, old fabric clothes, c1926, marks: Effanbee/Patsy . . **650.00**

Patsy, composition head and shoulder plate, cloth body with cry box, composition slightly bent arms and legs, rosy knees, molded hair, glued reddish–brown mohair wig, blue–gray tin sleep eyes, open mouth with four teeth, painted rosy cheeks, molded dimples, orig blue and white gingham dress, matching panties, shaded blue silk socks with diamond design, red imitation leather shoes, celluloid Effanbee button, red with gold heart and red silk bow, c1926, marks: Effanbee/Patsy **750.00**

20″ h, Charlie McCarthy, composition head, hands, and feet, cloth body and limbs, painted hair and eyes, open and closed ventriloquist mouth, strings at back of head, orig clothes, top hat, and book, c1937, marks: Edgar Bergan's Charlie McCarthy, An Effanbee Product . . **780.00**

24″ h, Dy–Dee Baby, hard plastic head, soft rubber jointed body, molded painted hair, open drinker mouth, soft rubber inset ears, orig coat and hat outfit, marks: Effanbee/Dy–Dee Baby/U. S. Pat. 1–857–485/England 880–00/France 723–980/Germany 5–85–647/Other Pat. Pending. **350.00**

Fulper, 16″ h, toddler, bisque socket head, five piece composition toddler body, short bobbed brown curly tousled hair wig, set eyes, open mouth, nicely dressed, c1918–21, marks: CMU (in triangle) Fulper, (vertically) Made in USA **550.00**

Gaultier, 11″ h, bisque swivel head, kid lined bisque shoulder plate, kid fashion body with gusset jointing at hips, orig hair, blue paperweight inset eyes, closed mouth, pierced ears, well costumed, fancy straw bonnet, c1880, marked: F. G. on side of shoulder. . . **1,750.00**

Gaultier and Gesland, 30″ h, bisque

socket head, composition shoulder plate, stockinet body with composition lower arms and legs, blond human hair wig over cork pate, brown paperweight inset eyes, closed mouth, dimpled chin, pierced ears, nicely dressed, c1875, marks: F14G, body stamped E. Gesland on shoulder . . . **6,250.00**

Greiner, Ludwig, 25″ h, papier-mâché shoulder head, muslin body, brown leather arms, stitched fingers, painted hair, painted blue upper glancing eyes, closed mouth, partially exposed ears, well dressed, c1860, marks: Greiner Improved Patent Heads, Pat. March 30th '58 . . . . **750.00**

Handwerck, Heinrich
20″ h, bisque socket head, composition and wood ball jointed body, brunette human hair wig, brown glass sleep eyes, open mouth, four porcelain teeth, pierced ears, well dressed, c1900, marks: Handwerck 109–11 Germany **725.00**
22″ h, bisque socket head, fully jointed composition body, blond wig, brown glass sleep flirty eyes, open mouth, four teeth, pierced ears, nice old red dress, lace trim overcoat, c1855, marks: Germany, Heinrich Handwerck, Simon & Halbig **550.00**

Handwerck–Halbig, 28″ h, old wig, old clothes **750.00**

Hertel, Schwab & Co., 12″ h, bisque socket head, composition bent limb baby body, blond mohair wig, blue glass side glancing googlie eyes, closed mouth, watermelon smile, well dressed, c1910, marks: 165 . . . . **3,000.00**

Heubach, Ernst
14″ h, Character Baby, bisque socket head, composition bent limb baby body, blond human hair wig, blue glass sleep eyes, open mouth, two upper teeth, wobbly tongue, nicely dressed, c1910, marks: Heubach Koppelsdorf 300.14/0 Germany . . . **475.00**
23″ h, Child, bisque socket head, fully jointed composition body, brown wig, brown glass sleep eyes, open mouth, four teeth, well dressed, c1888, marks: Heubach Koppelsdorf 250 Germany **525.00**

Heubach, Gebruder
8¾″ h, skier, candy box body, bisque hands, bisque shoulder head, intaglio blue eyes, closed mouth, orig outfit with skis and poles, replaced sweater and knitted hat, marks: 66–88/Germany **330.00**
9½″ h, five piece composition body, starfish hands, bisque socket head,

blue glass google eyes, painted lashes, closed smiling mouth, brown wig, orig clothing, marks: 10720/0/Heu/bach/Germany **660.00**
11″ h, cloth body, mitten hands, bisque shoulder head, molded blond hair, blue intaglio eyes, closed smiling mouth, pants, jacket, shirt, and shoes, marks: 2/0 D/Heubach sunburst/7644/Germany. **165.00**
12″ h, composition body, fully jointed, bisque socket head, blond wig with pigtails, blue intaglio eyes, closed mouth, dressed with matching hat, shoes, marks: 1307/3/Germany, indistinct green Heubach number. . . **950.00**
14″ h, composition body, jointed, bisque socket head, painted blue eyes, open mouth, dimples, molded blond hair, long dress baby outfit, marks: 4/Heu/Bach/1911/Germany **990.00**
14¾″ h, Whistling Jim, bisque head, straw and felt body, composition hands, molded and painted hair, intaglio painted blue eyes, whistle mouth with center hole, striped outfit, marks: Heu/bach/Germany. . . . **550.00**
17″ h, bisque head
Composition body, full jointed, blond molded hair, blue intaglio eyes, closed mouth, romper suit, marks: Heubach in sunburst 7602/6/Germany. **770.00**
Leather body, button jointed, composition lower legs, bisque hands, molded hair, blue intaglio eyes, smiling mouth with six molded teeth, dressed, marks: head with Heu/111/5/Germany, body with Imperial paper label . . **990.00**

Horsman, E. I. and Co., 12″ h, Tynie Baby, solid dome infant head, flanged neck, muslin body, composition hands, brown painted hair, blue glass sleep eyes, pouty type mouth, nicely dressed, marks: copyright 1924 E. I. Horsman Inc., Made In Germany . . . **650.00**

Ideal Novelty Co., 13″ h, Shirley Temple, all composition, socket head, composition body jointed at shoulders and hips, blond curly mohair wig, green tin sleep eyes, hair lashes, open smiling mouth, six upper teeth, orig clothing labeled "Genuine Shirley Temple Doll, Reg US Patent Off, Ideal Novelty & Toy Co., Made In USA," orig celluloid fan club pin, c1934, marks: Shirley Temple 13, Ideal on head and body . **650.00**

Jumeau, Emile
9½″ h, bisque socket head, body with jointed wrists, light brown wig, brown eyes, stroked eyebrows,

Ideal, Miss Revlon, vinyl, jointed, rooted honey blonde hair, high heel feet, marked "Ideal Doll/VT," 10½" h, $60.00.

closed mouth, orig lavender pierced earrings, dressed, orig Jumeau shoes, marks: head with Depose/Tete Jumeau/Bte SGDG/1, sole with 2 E Jumeau Med Dor Paris Depose.................. **3,000.00**

12" h, bisque socket head, ball jointed body, blond wig, gray–blue threaded eyes, closed mouth, pierced ears, marks: incised Jumeau on back of head, blue Jumeau stamp on body.......... **1,550.00**

13" h, bisque socket head, composition body, jointed shoulders and elbows, orig blond mohair wig, blue glass threaded eyes, painted lashes, orig pierced earrings, ecru silk dress, pantalets, chemise petticoat, orig maroon armband and bonnet, marks: head with Brevette SGDG/Jumeau, shoes with Bebe Jumeau Med or 1878/Paris Depose, body with blue Jumeau stamp **7,500.00**

15" h, boy, bisque flange head, mechanical body, bisque right hand, composition left hand, blue paperweight eyes, closed mouth, moves head and plays violin when wound, music box base, marks: Depose/Tete Jumeau................ **2,750.00**

17½" h, bisque socket head, composition body, blonde hair, brown thread eyes, painted upper and lower lashes, closed mouth, applied pierced ears, white dress with layers of pleating and lace, pink bows, orig cream satin shoes, marks: 6 EJ on head, shoe with Bebe Jumeau Med Or 1878/Paris/Depose...... **7,700.00**

19" h, body with walking mechanism, orig blonde wig, blue glass paperweight eyes, closed mouth, dressed, marks: head with Tete Jumeau 8 and body with blue Jumeau stamp.................... **3,300.00**

24" h, bisque socket head, jointed body, brown long curl wig, brown eyes, painted lashes, brushed eyebrows, closed mouth, pierced ears, dress, matching bonnet, marks: Depose/Tete Jumeau/Bte SGDG/11. . **2,900.00**

32" h, bisque socket head, orig body, jointed wrists, brown wig, brown paperweight eyes, closed mouth, applied pierced ears, one orig Jumeau earring, green outfit, matching bonnet, marks: Depose/Tete Jumeau/SDGD/15............. **5,500.00**

Kammer & Reinhardt

7" h, Hans, bisque head, ten piece composition body, orig brown wig, blue painted eyes, closed pouty mouth, knitted outfit, marks: K * R/114........................ **990.00**

11" h, bisque head, composition body, brown sleep eyes, closed pouty mouth, pudgy cheeks, brown wig, dressed, marks: K * R/115A . . **2,750.00**

19½" h, Peter, bisque socket head, jointed body, short blond mohair wig, painted blue eyes, pouty mouth, plaid wool suit, marks: K * R/101/50.................. **775.00**

Kestner

12" h, bisque socket head, brown body, jointed hips, knees, elbows, and shoulders, black wig, brown sleep eyes, pierced ears, closed mouth, brushed eyebrows, marks: impressed 7................. **3,250.00**

15" h, bisque socket head, leather body, bisque hands, blond wig, gray–blue sleep eyes, closed mouth, dressed, marks: indistinct number.................... **650.00**

Kley and Hahn, 16" h, Walkure, bisque socket head, jointed composition body, straight wrists, glass sleep eyes, open mouth, nicely dressed, c1925, marks: K + H, Walkure Made In Germany **550.00**

Konig & Weinicke, 13" h, bisque head, jointed composition body, dark hair, brown sleep eyes, open mouth with two cut teeth, marks: Made in Germany/99/4 on head, body with K & W **275.00**

Kruse, Kathy, 15" h, celluloid socket head, celluloid jointed body, blond human hair wig, blue inset eyes, closed mouth, orig clothes, c1958, marks: turtle mark, Modell Kathy Kruse T40 **425.00**

Lanternier & Cie, 18″ h, Lady, bisque socket head with adult look, French composition and wood jointed lady body, brunette human hair wig, almond shaped brown glass inset eyes, open/closed mouth, row of molded teeth, pierced ears, nicely dressed, c1915, marks: Fabrication Francasie IL E Cie Limoges **950.00**

Lenci, 15″ h, cloth body, felt limbs, jointed neck, hips, and shoulders, blond wig, painted blue eyes, closed mouth, brown felt jumper, striped shirt, shoes, holding red and white felt ball **250.00**

Madame Alexander, Scarlet O'Hara, green print dress, $650.00.

Madame Alexander

14″ h, Snow White, all hard plastic, socket head, five piece body jointed at shoulders and hips, black saran wig, green plastic sleep eyes, real lashes, painted features, closed mouth, orig tagged ivory satin gown, gold leaf patterned brocade vest, c1952, marks: Walt Disney Snow White Madam Alexander U.S.A.. . . . . **500.00**

16″ h

David Copperfield, all cloth, one piece body and head, cloth arms and legs, mitted type hands, blond human hair wig, molded felt face mask, painted facial features, brown side glancing eyes, closed mouth, orig blue flannel trousers, black felt jacket and top hat, white shirt and bow tie, orig labels sewn in seams marked "Madam Alexander" and "David Copperfield," early 1930s, marks: Alexander **650.00**

Snow White, all composition, socket head, five piece body jointed at shoulders and hips, black mohair or human hair wig, brown sleep eyes, real lashes, closed mouth, all orig clothes tagged "Snow White, Madam Alexander," c1937, marks: Princess Elizabeth Alexander Doll Co. **500.00**

Marseille, Armand

9″ h, bisque socket head, chubby composition body, jointed at shoulders, brown wig, gray google eyes, closed smiling mouth, check dress and shoes, marks: Armand Marseille/Germany/323 A 6/O M **330.00**

18″ h, bisque socket head, jointed composition body, dark hair, sleep eyes, open mouth with four upper teeth, marks: Armand Marseille/390 D./A 2½ M. **225.00**

22″ h, bisque socket head, composition fully jointed body, orig brown long curl wig, blue tricolored eyes, painted lashes and eyebrows, open mouth with four upper teeth, orig dress, marks: Made in Germany/Armand Marseille/390/DRGM 246/61/A7M **300.00**

Mason and Taylor, 12″ h, all wooden, sculpted and painted, dowel body jointed at shoulders, elbows, hips, and knees, spoon shaped hands, short blond hair, painted facial features, blue eyes, c1880. . . . . **850.00**

Ohlhover, Gebruder, 20″ h, Baby Type, bisque socket head, composition bent limb baby body, auburn human hair baby style wig, blue glass sleep eyes, real hair lashes, open mouth, two upper molded teeth, old fabric christening dress, petticoat, and bonnet, c1915, marks: Revalo Germany 22—12 . . . . **750.00**

Putnam, Grace S., Bye—Lo Baby, 14″ h, closed eyes, marks: 1923 by/Grace S Putnam/Made in Germany **330.00**

Raggedy Ann and Andy

15½″ h, all cloth, movable arms and legs, brown yarn hair, button eyes, painted features, striped fabric stockings and black for socks, orig clothes, marks: Patented Sept. 7, 1915, pr **850.00**

18″ h, all cloth, red yarn hair, painted features, striped fabric and black cloth shoes, all orig clothing, c1938–63, marks: cloth label sewn in side seam of bodies, pr. **375.00**

Revalo, 12″ h, Character, bisque socket head, composition body, molded short brown curly hair, molded blue ribbon with rosette trim, gray painted eyes and other features, open/closed mouth, nicely dressed, c1915 . . . . . **725.00**

Schoenau and Hoffmeister, 21″ h, Child, bisque socket head, composition ball jointed body, brunette human hair wig, brown glass sleep eyes, real hair lashes, open mouth, four porcelain teeth, old fabric clothing, c1901, marks: S (star with PB) H 1909 Germany **550.00**

Shansen, Walter, 16″ h, bisque head, jointed composition body, dark hair, sleep eyes, open mouth with four upper teeth, marks: Walter Shansen/Germany/1916a/O. **110.00**

Schoenhut

14″ h, boy, orig pin, clothes, hat . . . **850.00**

16½″ h, wood, articulated, molded brown braided hair with blue bow, blue intaglio eyes, closed mouth, pensive expression, dressed, marks: Schoenhut Doll/Pat Jan 17 '11 USA/& Foreign Countries. **1,500.00**

18½″ h, boy, wood, articulated, wire strung, auburn wig, blue decal eyes, closed mouth, dressed, straw hat, oval Schoenhut label **550.00**

19″ h, wood, articulated, blond wig, intaglio eyes, closed mouth, dressed, marks: Schoenhut/Jan 17 '11 USA/& Foreign Countries **770.00**

Simon & Halbig

7¾″ h, bisque socket head, peg jointed arms and legs, blond mohair wig, brown sleep eyes, open mouth with upper teeth, dress, blue stockings, and black molded five strap shoes, marks: SH. **250.00**

13″ h, bisque socket head, composition body, jointed hips and knees, light brown wig, blue sleep eyes, closed mouth, underclothing and dress, marks: 1469/Simon & Halbig/2. . . . . **1,750.00**

15″ h, boy, bisque socket head, jointed composition body, blue sleep eyes, open mouth with two upper teeth, marks: Simon Halbig/121. . . . . **660.00**

Societe Francaise de Bebes et Jouets

19″ h, Character Toddler, bisque socket head, French composition toddler body, side hip jointing, socket wrists, blond human hair wig, blue glass sleep eyes, closed pouty type mouth, nicely dressed, c1910, marks: S. F. B. J. 252 Paris 8 . . . . **7,000.00**

27″ h, Character Toddler, bisque socket head, composition and wood hip jointed toddler body, human hair wig, half moon shaped brown glass sleep eyes, open mouth, beaded upper teeth, wobbler tongue, orig clothes, orig paper label on body, c1915, marks: 21 S.F.B.J. 251 Paris 12 . . . . **2,800.00**

Steiner, E. U., 16″ h, Child, bisque socket head, kid body with bisque lower arms and legs, blond mohair wig, brown glass inset eyes, open mouth, four teeth, nicely dressed, c1900, marks: E. U. Steiner (in diamond), Made In Germany **275.00**

Steiner, Jules, 13″ h, bisque socket head, composition body, jointed hips, knees, shoulders, and elbows, blond wig, blue paperweight eyes, closed mouth, pierced ears, redressed, marks: J Steiner/Bte SGDG/Paris/Fre A5 . . . . **2,700.00**

Unidentified Maker

Puzzy, orig, slight crazing **220.00**

Trudy, three faces, undressed **220.00**

DOOR KNOCKERS

History: Before the advent of the mechanical bell or electrical buzzer and chime, a door knocker was considered an essential door ornament to announce the arrival of visitors. Metal was used to cast or forge the various forms; many cast-iron examples were painted. Collectors like to find knockers with English registry marks.

BRASS

Atlantis, head, dolphin, and seashells   **75.00**

Cast Iron, owl, brown, yellow eyes, green ribbon, $75.00.

Devil, head, serpent striker ring	45.00
Flower basket	75.00
Oval, ring knocker, monogram	30.00
Pheasants	45.00
Scottie Dog, English	48.00
Shakespeare, bust, 4″ h	75.00

BRONZE

Grecian, bust, 4½″ h	80.00
Hand, ruffled sleeve, 5″ h	75.00
Maenad, bust, fruit vines in hair, 7″ h, Continental, 19th C	385.00
Parrot, hp multicolored dec	75.00

CAST IRON

Basket, white and blue, pink bow and flowers.	45.00
Betty Boop, figural	45.00
Cherub, head, acorn finial, 8¼″ h . . .	100.00
Fox, head, ring in mouth, 5½″ h	75.00
Lady's hand, holding ball, matching strike plate, pitted surface, 19th C, 6½″ h.	150.00
Parrot, Hubley	125.00
Rooster	65.00
Woodpecker, Hubley	145.00

DOORSTOPS

History: Doorstops became popular in the late 19th century. They can be found flat or three dimensional and were made in cast iron, bronze, wood, and other material. Hubley, a leading toy manufacturer, made many examples.

References: Jeanne Bertoia, *Doorstops: Identification And Values,* Collector Books, 1985; Marilyn Hamburger and Beverly Lloyd, *Collecting Figural Doorstops,* A. S. Barnes and Company, 1978.

Collectors' Club: Doorstop Collectors of America, 2413 Madison Ave., Vineland, NJ 08630.

Reproduction Alert: Reproductions are proliferating as prices on genuine doorstops continue to rise. There is usually a slight reduction in size in a reproduced piece unless an original mold is used, at which time size remains the same. Reproductions have less detail, lack smoothness to the overall casting, and lack detail in the paint. If there is any bright orange rusting, this is strongly indicative of a new piece. Beware. If it looks too good to be true, it usually is.

Notes: Pieces described below contain at least 80% or more of the original paint and are in very good condition. Repainting drastically reduces price and desirability. Poor original paint is preferred over repaint.

All listings are cast iron and flatback castings unless otherwise noted.

Doorstops marked with an asterisk are currently being reproduced.

B + H = Bradley and Hubbard.
Advisor: Craig Dinner.

Basket, 11″ h, rose, ivory wicker basket, natural flowers, handle with bow, sgd "Hubley 121"	135.00
Bear, 15″ h, holding and looking at honey pot, brown fur, black highlights	1,000.00
Bellhop, black, 7½″ h, carrying satchel, facing sideways, orange–red uniform and cap	375.00
Bowl, 7 x 7″, green–blue, natural colored fruit, sgd "Hubley, 456"	100.00
Boy	
9⅜″, "The Tiger," hands at side, riding outfit, cartoon like eyes, "FISH" on front, sgd "Hubley 269"	785.00
10⅝″ h, wearing diapers directing traffic, police hat, red scarf, brown dog at side	575.00
11″ h, full figure, Dutch, hands in pocket, blue jumpsuit and hat, red belt and collar, brown shoes, blonde hair.	395.00
12¾″ h, native wearing turban and leopard skin, one hand extended. .	500.00
Caddie, 8″ h, carrying brown and tan bag, white, brown knickers, red jacket.	475.00
Camel, 7″ h, 9″ l, full figure, brown, two humps	350.00
Cat	
6″ h, wedge, black and white body, green eyes and base	250.00
*7″ h, male and female holding each other's waist, dressed.	195.00
*8″ h, black, red ribbon and bow around neck, on pillow.	125.00
9½″ h, 7″ w, full figure, Persian, sitting, gray, light markings, sgd "Hubley" inside casting.	145.00

Cast Iron, fraternal, red base, white bird, gold chain, $85.00.

Child, 17″ h, reaching, naked, flesh color, short curly brown hair **625.00**

Clown, 10″ h, full figure, 2 sided, red suit, white collar, blue hat, black shoes. . . **675.00**

Cottage
6⅜″ h, three dimensional garden, tan roof, 3 red chimneys, flowers, 2 pc casting, Ann Hathaway. **275.00**
8⅝″ l, 5¾″ h, Cape type, blue roof, flowers, fenced garden, path, sgd "Eastern Speciality Mfg Co 14". . . **135.00**

Dancer
8⅞″ h, Art Deco couple doing Charleston, pink dress, black tux, red and black base, "FISH" on front, sgd "Hubley 270". **485.00**
11⅛″ h, black woman doing Rhumba, red, yellow, and blue dress, red kerchief. **425.00**

Dog
Boston Bull
9″ h, full figure, facing left, black, tan markings **85.00**
10½″ h, facing right, black, white markings **55.00**
Boxer, 8½ x 9″, full figure, facing forward, brown, tan markings **225.00**
Doberrman Pinscher, 8″ h, full figure, black, brown markings, Hubley . . . **385.00**
German Shephard, Hubley **110.00**
Japanese Spaniel, 9″ h, black and white, long curly hair, sgd "1267". . **185.00**
Pekingese, 14½″ l, 9″ h, full figure, life-like size and color, brown, sgd "Hubley". **1,000.00**
*Puppies, 7″, three puppies in basket, natural colors, sgd "Copyright 1932 M Rosenstein, Lancaster, PA, USA" **325.00**

Drum Major, 12⅝″, full figure, ivory pants, red hat with feather, yellow baton in right hand, left hand on waist, sq base **225.00**

Duck
7½″, white, green bush and grass . **375.00**
7¾″ h, full body, dressed in pants and top hat, orig polychrome paint **425.00**

Elephant, 14″, pulling coconut out of palm tree, natural color **145.00**

Fisherman, 6¼″ h, standing at wheel, hand blocking sun over eyes, rain gear. **165.00**

Fish, 9¾″ h, three, fantail, orig paint, sgd "Hubley 464" **125.00**

Flower
Goldenrods, 7⅛″ h, natural color, sgd "Hubley 268". **225.00**
Jonquil, 7″ yellow flowers, red and orange cups, sgd "Hubley 453" **185.00**

Frog, 3″, full figure, sitting, yellow and green. **40.00**

Giraffe
12½″ h, full figure, brown, black spots and hoofs, pink ears, Hubley. **950.00**
20¼″ h, tan, brown spots, squared off lines to casting. **1,250.00**

Girl
8¾″ h, dark blue outfit and beanie, high white collar, black shoes, red hair, incised "663" **350.00**
9″
French, holding skirt out at sides, hat, sgd "Hubley 23". **125.00**
Sunbonnet, blue hat, pink dress . . **225.00**
10⅞″, bathing, yellow and red swimsuits, green and yellow bathing caps under umbrella, "FISH" on front, sgd "Hubley 250" **375.00**
*13¾″ h, 9¾″ l, white hat, flowing cape, holding orange jack–o–lantern with red cutout eyes, nose, and mouth . **1,000.00**

*Golfer, 10″ h, overhead swing, hat and ball on ground, Hubley. **395.00**

Grandpa Rabbit, 8⅝″ h, croched down, sitting with hands on knees, brown skin, red jacket, white shirt, cream colored pants and collar, watch hanging out of vest **525.00**

Guitar Player, 11⅞″ h, flatback, yellow hat and pants, red jacket with green trim and waist band, brown guitar . . . **335.00**

Horse, 7⅞″ h, jumping fence, jockey, sgd "Eastern Spec Co #790". **325.00**

House
5½″ h, 8¼″ l, 2 story, attic, path to door, shutters, sgd "Sophia Smith House". **225.00**
6″ h, woman walking up front stairs, grapevines, sgd "EasternSpec Co" **165.00**

*Kitten, 7″ h, 3 kittens in wicker basket, sgd "M Rosenstein, c1932, Lancaster, PA" **335.00**

Indian Chief, 9¾″ h, flatback, orange and tan headdress, yellow pants with blue stripes and red patches at ankles, green grass, sgd "A A Richardson," copyright 1927 . . . . **395.00**

Lighthouse, 14″ h, flatback, green rocks, black path, white lighthouse, red window and door trim **250.00**

*Mammy
8½″ h, full figure, red dress, white apron, blue kerchief with white spots, sgd inside "Hubley 327" . . . **150.00**
10″ h, white scarf and apron, very dark blue dress, red kerchief on head, full figure, one pc casting **375.00**
12″, full figure, blue dress, white apron, red kerchief with white spots, sgd "copyright Hubley" inside **410.00**

Messenger Boy, 10″ h, bouquet in hand, cap, rosy checks, front sgd "FISH" . . **365.00**

Monkey, 14⅜" h, hand reaching up, brown, tan, and white. 550.00

Musician, 6⅞" h
  Black man playing saxophone, white pants, red jacket 425.00
  Black man playing drums, black paint 410.00

Old Mill, 6¼" h, brown log mill, tan roof, white path, green bushes. 225.00

Pan, 7" h, with flute, sitting on mushroom, green outfit, red hat and sleeves, green grass base 155.00

Parrot, 13¾" h, in ring, two sided, heavy gold base, sgd "B & H" 215.00

Penguin, 10" h, full figure, facing sideways, black, white chest, top hat and bow tie, yellow feet and beak, unsgd Hubley. 275.00

*Pheasant, 8½", brown, bright markings, green grass, sgd "Fred Everett" front, sgd "Hubley" back. 285.00

Policeman, 9½" h, leaning on red fire hydrant, blue uniform and tilted hat, comic character face, tan base, "Safety First" on front 625.00

Popeye, 9" h, full figure, pipe in mouth, white hat, blue pants, black and red shirt, sgd "Hubley, 1929 King Features Syn, Made in USA". 1,000.00

Owl, 9½" h, sits on books, sgd "Eastern Spec Co" 375.00

*Quail, 7¼" h, 2 brown, tan, and yellow birds, green, white, and yellow grass, Fred Everett on front, sgd "Hubley 459". 285.00

Rabbit
  8⅛" h, eating carrot, red sweater, brown pants 300.00
  15¼" h, sits on hind paws, tan, green grass, detailed casting, sgd "B & H 7800" 485.00

Ringmaster, 10½" h, full figure, hands clasped behind back, red jacket, green pants, top hat 1,000.00

Rooster
  7", standing, black, colorful detail . . 135.00
  12", full figure, black, red comb, yellow claws and beak 295.00
  13" h, red comb, black and brown tail and chest, yellow stomach 325.00

Ship
  5¼" h, clipper, full sails, American flag on top mast, wave base, two rubber stoppers, sgd "CJO" 50.00
  11¼", three masts, full sail 25.00

Skier, 12½" h, full figure, woman, red scarf, gloves, and belt, blue ski suit and beret, wood skis at side. 385.00

Squirrel, 9", sitting on stump eating nut, brown and tan. 185.00

Stork, 13¾", white, yellow beak, orange feet, black markings, flowers and grass 335.00

Storybook
  Huckleberry Finn, 12½" h, floppy hat, pail, stick, Littco Products label . . . 410.00
  Humpty Dumpty, 4½", full figure, sgd "661" inside. 285.00
  Little Miss Muffet, 7¾" h, siting on mushroom, blue dress, blonde hair 165.00
  Little Red Riding Hood
    7½" h, 9½" w, sgd "NUYDEA" . . 450.00
    9½", basket at side, red cape, tan dress with blue pattern, blonde hair, sgd "Hubley". 385.00
  Mary Quite Contrary, 11⅜" h, blue hat, yellow dress and socks, green watering can, "Littco Products" label 545.00
  Puss in Boots, flat back, head sticking out of boot, sgd "Creations Co 1930" 325.00

Whistler, 20¼" h, flatback, boy, hands in tan knickers, yellow striped baggy shirt, lips rounded as if to whistle, two rubber stoppers, sgd "B & H" 1,350.00

Windmill, 6¾" h, 6⅞" w, ivory, red roof, house at side, green base 95.00

Woman
  8" h, Colonial, sgd "Hubley" 115.00
  8½" h, minuet, one hand on hip . . . 175.00
  8¾" h, peasant, blue dress, black hair, fruit basket on head 125.00
  *11" h, flowers and shawl 145.00
  12" h, carrying parasol and hat box in left hand, satchel with "Phoebe" in right hand, flowered hat 285.00

Zinnias, 11⅝" h, multicolored flowers, blue and black vase, detailed casting, two rubber stoppers, sgd "B & H". . . 175.00

1727

Dresden
1883-93

Dresden
MODERN MARK

DRESDEN/MEISSEN

History: Augustus II, Elector of Saxony and King of Poland, founded the Royal Saxon Porcelain

Manufactory in the Albrechtsburg, Meissen, in 1710. Johann Frederick Boettger, an alchemist, and Tschirnhaus, a nobleman, experimented with kaolin clay from the Dresden area to produce porcelain. By 1720 the factory produced a whiter hardpaste porcelain than that from the Far East. The factory experienced its golden age in the 1730s–50s period under the leadership of Samuel Stolzel, kiln master, and Johann Gregor Herold, enameler.

Many marks were used by the Meissen factory. The first was a pseudooriental mark in a square. The famous crossed swords mark was adopted in 1724. A small dot between the hilts was used from 1763 to 1774 and a star between the hilts from 1774 to 1814. Two modern marks are swords with a hammer and sickle and swords with a crown.

The Meissen factory was destroyed and looted by forces of Frederick the Great during the Seven Years' War (1756–63). It was reopened but never achieved its former greatness.

In the 19th century, the factory reissued some of its earlier forms. These later wares are called "Dresden" to differentiate them from the earlier examples. Further, there were several other porcelain factories in the Dresden region, and their products also are grouped under the "Dresden" designation of collectors.

Reference: Susan and Al Bagdade, *Warman's English & Continental Pottery & Porcelain, 2nd Edition,* Wallace–Homestead, 1991.

DRESDEN

Compote, 4½" h, ftd, gilt beaded banding, floral garlands, gilt scrolls, white ground, price for set of eighteen **475.00**
Cup, 3½" d, white, relief prunus dec, two handles, attributed to Boettger, unmarked, 1715 . . . .   **250.00**

Demitasse Cup and Saucer, floral reserves, blue ground. **250.00**
Dessert Plate, 9" d, central female portrait, heavily gilt, green ground, marked, c1910, price for set of twelve   **1,000.00**
Ewer, 5½" d, 12" h, flattened oval, maroon bands top and bottom, heavy gold trim, center scene of two ladies and cupid in garden, obverse with four children playing blind man's bluff, ornate gold handle, Wissmann mark, c1890. . . . .   **800.00**
Figure
7" h, Ballerina, young girl, white and pink lace dress, pink shoes, red hair, applied flowers on dress **225.00**
8 x 10½", Gypsy Lady with Goat, seated, sandals, red kerchief, young goat, crown mark **450.00**
Jardiniere, 14½" d, painted and transfer print, central cartouche, courting couple in landscape, pale yellow borders, relief floral garlands, gilt highlights, scrolled feet late 19th C **385.00**
Tea Caddy, 5¼" h, 3½" w, sq, lacy gold flowers on two panels, scene of courting boy and girl, crossed swords mark, "H" and "Dresden" **175.00**
Urn, cov, 12" h, two panels of lovers, garden setting, red ground, floral dec, c1860–1920 . . . .   **400.00**
Vase, 8½" h, portrait scene, cobalt blue ground, raised gold dec, artist sgd . .   **375.00**

MEISSEN

Bowl, 10" d, gold and pink, raised leaf dec, c1920 . . . .   **175.00**
Candelabra, five light, shaped sq base,

Figural Group, crinoline porcelain, two girls with young man playing pipe (left), two girls and tree stump (right), late 19th C, 9″ w, price for pair, $402.50. Photograph courtesy of Leslie Hindman Auctioneers.

waisted plinth, applied cartouches with arms of Saxony and Poland, putti, seated maiden, floral dec tunic, purple drape, foliate stem spreading as light branch, foliate molded drip pan and nozzle, pink, turquoise, and gilt highlights, underglaze blue crossed swords mark, late 19th C, minor restoration, price for pair. **4,675.00**

Clock, 9½" l, 9" h, mantel, figural, putto reading, 19th C, minor damage. **1,980.00**

Coffee Service, cov 10½" h coffeepot, creamer, cov sugar, twelve 6½" d cups and saucers, white ground, foliage gilt highlights, orig fitted case, underglaze blue crossed swords mark, early 20th C, price for sixteen piece set. **2,750.00**

Figure
7½" h, Pluto with pink drape and gilt crown, carrying struggling Proserpine, oval base with molded and applied gilt scrolls, underglaze blue crossed swords, incised and imp numbers, after model by J J Kaendler, c1900 . . . . **600.00**

7¾" h, kissing couple, lady in white dress with scattered polychrome floral sprays, white cap, gentleman in gilted purple overcoat, black breeches, shaped oval base with applied flowerheads and leaves, underglaze blue crossed swords mark, iron–red inscribed numerals, imp numerals, after model by J J Kaendler, c1900. . . . . **775.00**

8¼" h, cavalier and lady, standing side by side, lady in black dress dec with iron–red, purple, and blue floral sprays, white ruffled neckline and cap, holding fan, gentleman in orange and pale blue coat, dark puce breeches, oval base with applied flowerheads, underglaze blue crossed swords, incised and imp numbers, after model by J J Kaendler, c1900 . . . . **900.00**

8½" d, Europa and The Bull, two attendants, 19th C, restoration. **825.00**

12" h, Diana, seated on sq socle, quiver at side, white, clear glaze, blue underglaze mark. **875.00**

Garniture, 12" h centerpiece, Baroque style basket, three applied cherubs with rose blossoms, matching pair of four light candelabra formed as seated women holding infants, similar rose dec, blue underglaze mark **700.00**

Plate, 9¾" d, molded scrolls and flowers, white ground, blue enameled floral sprigs, underglaze blue factory mark **100.00**

Soup Plate, floral dec, canceled under-

glaze factory mark, price for set of twelve **650.00**

Sugar Box, cov, 4½ x 3¼ x 3", oval, yellow tiger, brown rim, rabbit finial, crossed swords mark, c1730 . . . . . **185.00**

Teacup and Saucer, Kakiemon style birds and flowers, brown ground on cup, white ground saucer, underglaze blue crossed swords mark, price for pair **275.00**

Wine Bottle Stand, 9" h, 6¾" d, flattened ovoid form, scalloped rim, pierced flowerhead and C scroll frieze, molded and painted pink grisaille body, storks and swans, raised shell molded foot, oval base, underglaze blue crossed swords mark, price for pair. **2,750.00**

DUNCAN AND MILLER

History: George Duncan, Harry B. and James B., his sons, and Augustus Heisey, his son–in–law, formed George Duncan & Sons in Pittsburgh, Pennsylvania, in 1865. The factory was located just two blocks from the Monongahela River, providing easy and cheap access by barge for materials needed to produce glass. The men, from Pittsburgh's southside, were descendants of generations of skilled glassmakers.

The plant burned to the ground in 1892. James E. Duncan, Sr., selected a site for a new factory in Washington, Pennsylvania, where operations began on February 9, 1893. The plant prospered, producing fine glassware and table services for many years.

John E. Miller, one of the stockholders, was responsible for designing many fine patterns, the most famous being "Three Face." The firm incorporated, using the name Duncan and Miller Glass Company until its plant closed in 1955. The company's slogan was "The Loveliest Glassware in America." The U.S. Glass Co. purchased the molds, equipment, and machinery in 1956.

References: Gene Florence, *Elegant Glassware Of The Depression Era, Revised Fifth Edition*, Collector Books, 1993; Gail Krause, *The Encyclopedia Of Duncan Glass*, published by author, 1984; Gail Krause, *A Pictorial History Of Duncan & Miller Glass*, published by author, 1976; Gail Krause, *The Years Of Duncan*, published by author, 1980.

Collectors' Club: National Duncan Glass Society, PO Box 965, Washington, PA 15301.

Additional Listings: Pattern Glass.

Animal
Goose, fat **220.00**
Heron **90.00**
Swan, 7" h **20.00**
Ashtray, cigarette holder, Spiral Flutes **27.00**
Banana Boat, Mardi Gras, oval **40.00**

Basket
Hobnail, pink opalescent, 10″ h	75.00
Sandwich, loop handle, 6½″ h	90.00

Boat Bowl, Viking ... 95.00
Bonbon, Lotus, black dec, ftd ... 17.50

Bowl
Diamond, apricot, oval	25.00
Early American Hobnail, flared, 12″ d	25.00
Murano, white milk glass, oval, 10½″ l, 7″ w, 4″ h	155.00
Sandwich, clear, crimped, 11½″ d	30.00
Terrace, 5″ d	12.50

Cake Plate, rolled edge, pedestal, 11½″ d ... 145.00

Candlestick
Early American Hobnail, price for pair	25.00
First Love, two light style	40.00
Sandwich, 4″ h, price for pair	30.00

Candy Dish, Sylvan, white milk glass, red handle, 7 x 5″ ... 110.00
Celery, Early American Hobnail, oval, 12″ l ... 22.00

Centerpiece bowl with candleholders, pink opalescent, 13½″ l, $45.00.

Champagne
Caribbean, blue	45.00
Teardrop	6.75

Cigarette Box, Canterbury, silver lid ... 25.00
Claret, Teardrop ... 20.00
Coaster, Sandwich, 4½″ d ... 13.00

Cocktail
Astaire	6.00
Early American Hobnail	10.00
First Love	18.00
Mallard Duck	6.00
Plaza, crystal	12.00
Spiral Flutes, yellow flashed rim, ftd	9.00

Compote
Early American Hobnail	20.00
Indian Tree	45.00
Teardrop, 5″ d, 3″ h	35.00

Cordial, Terrace ... 45.00
Cornucopia, chartreuse, 13″ l ... 85.00
Creamer and Sugar, matching tray, Early American Hobnail ... 20.00

Cream Soup, Spiral Flutes ... 15.00

Cup and Saucer
Radiance, light blue	25.00
Teardrop	35.00

Decanter, First Love, 32 oz ... 175.00
Deviled Egg Plate, Sandwich ... 85.00
Egg Cup, Mardi Gras ... 20.00

Goblet
Caribbean, blue	38.00
Early American Hobnail	10.00
Sandwich, clear, 9 oz, 6″ h	12.00
Teardrop, dinner	9.75

Grapefruit, Spiral Flutes, green, ftd, 6¾″ 10.00
Hat, top, Early American Hobnail, 4″ h 25.00
Mayonnaise, Language of Flowers ... 25.00
Milk Pitcher, Caribbean, blue ... 350.00
Mint Dish, Sylvan, white milk glass, red handle, 8 x 7″ ... 125.00

Nappy
Early American Hobnail, 6″ d	8.00
Murano, ruffled, 6″ d	20.00

Nut Bowl, Spiral Flutes, green, individual size ... 14.00
Olive Dish, Teardrop, 7″ l ... 15.00

Plate
Caribbean, blue, 6″ d	18.00
Indian Tree, 8½″ d	16.00
Plaza Punties, amber, 6″ d	5.00
Sanibel, blue opalescent, 8½″ d	28.00
Terrace, cobalt blue, two handles, 5″ d	30.00
Teardrop, 11″ d	45.00

Punch Bowl Set
King Arthur, price for ten piece set	140.00
Radiance, clear, red handles, price for boxed set	175.00

Relish
Caribbean, blue, round, two parts, 6″ d	30.00
First Love, two parts, 8″ l	30.00

Rose Bowl, Canterbury, Copenhagen Blue, four toes ... 75.00
Salt and Pepper Shakers, pr, orig tops, Teardrop ... 45.00

Sherbet
Early American Hobnail	8.00
Teardrop	7.00

Sugar, Radiance, light blue ... 20.00

Tumbler
First Love, ftd, 5 oz	24.00
Indian Tree, ftd	24.00
Plaza Punties, amber, cone, ftd, 3¾″ h	10.00

Urn, Grecian, sq, ftd, ring handle, 5⅜″ h 37.50

Vase
First Love, cornucopia, 8″ h	60.00
Sandwich, ftd, 10″ h	65.00
Three Feather, blue opalescent, cornucopia, 8″ h	140.00

Water Pitcher
Caribbean, blue	950.00
Sandwich, ice lip	165.00

Wine
Sandwich	....	**15.00**
Teardrop	....	**16.75**

DURAND

History: Victor Durand (1870–1931), born in Baccarat, France, apprenticed at the Baccarat glassworks, where several generations of his family worked. In 1884 Victor came to America to join his father at the Whitall–Tatum & Co. in New Jersey. In 1897 father and son leased the Vineland Glass Manufacturing Company in Vineland, New Jersey. Products included inexpensive bottles, jars, and glass for scientific and medical purposes. By 1920 four separate companies existed.

When Quezal Art Glass and Decorating Company failed, Victor Durand recruited Martin Bach, Jr., Emil J. Larsen, William Wiedebine, and other Quezal men and opened an art glass shop at Vineland in December 1924. Quezal-style iridescent pieces were made. New innovations included cameo and intaglio designs, geometric Art Deco shapes, Venetian Lace, and Oriental-style pieces. In 1928 crackled glass, called Moorish Crackle and Egyptian Crackle, was made.

Much of Durand glass is not marked. Some bear a sticker labeled "Durand Art Glass" while some have the name "Durand" scratched on the pontil or "Durand" inside a large "V." Etched numbers may be part of the marking.

Durand died in 1931. The Vineland Flint Glass Works was merged with Kimble Glass Company a year later, and the art glass line was discontinued.

Lamp, Moorish Crackle, orange with green highlights, 9¼″ h, $110.00.

Box, cov, 5″ d, 4″ h, King Tut, coiled green dec on ambergris cased to opal, irid gold int., cut star at pontil on matching lid **770.00**
Compote, 7½″ d, 6¼″ h, gold, stretched irid surface, baluster stemmed foot, inscribed "V Durand 5002," price for pair **660.00**
Lamp
  Mantel, 13¼″ h, gold irid flared trumpet, green heart and vine design, gilt metal socket fixture **315.00**
  Table, 12½″ h art glass, 28″ h overall, coiled King Tut green dec, gold irid lamp shaft, heavy gold and green enameled metal platform base, two socket lamp fittings **615.00**
  Torchere, floor
    61″ h, 12″ d shade, red amber crackle shade, gilt metal floor lamp base, price for pair **880.00**
    67″ h, 8″ h bulbed ruffled rim crackle shades, blue, opal white, and irid gold, gilt metal lamp bases, molded floral swags, knights in armor and heraldic elements, stepped onyx platform bases, price for pair **2,310.00**
Lamp Base, 20″ h, gold, irid, classic baluster shape, random threading, ormolu mounts **300.00**
Powder Box, 4¾″ d, 3½″ h, cut glass, mirror bright ambergris cov jar, wheel engraved blossom on cov, base inscribed "Durand" **330.00**
Rose Bowl, 4″ h, trapped bubble symmetrical design, colorless blown glass, inscribed "Durand V 1995–4" . **220.00**
Tumbler, 5½″ h, red and white crackle, ambergris **300.00**
Vase
  7¼″ h, 4½″ w, irid peacock blue, gold and pink shades, sgd "V Durand 18122/7" **400.00**
  8″ h, classic form, flared vertically ribs, shaded emerald green cased to opal, int. gold irid, sgd "Durand 1710–8" **1,100.00**
  8½″ h, flared rim, ten ribbed ruby red body cased in opal and amber, gold irid int.. . . . . **1,540.00**
  9¼″ h, cobalt blue cased to white, irid gold heart and vine design, inscribed "Durand" **1,100.00**
  9½″ h, 4″ w, irid peacock blue, threaded, sgd "Durand 1707" **525.00**
  9¾″ h, 10″ d, beehive, ambergris, smooth gold irid surface, sgd "V Durand 10–8" **825.00**
  10″ h, 3¼″ w, irid peacock blue, orig Ovington label **250.00**
  12½″ h, Lady Gay Rose, deep rose

red irid ext., gold irid int., vertical
ribs. **2,750.00**
14″ h, flared amber oval, gold irid sur-
face, inscribed "V Durand 1982–14" **660.00**
Wall Sconce, 8¾″ h, deep irid teardrop
shaped glass, alligator skin texture,
Art Nouveau bronze floral motif fix-
tures, price for pair **1,350.00**

ENGLISH CHINA AND PORCELAIN (GENERAL)

History: The manufacture of china and porcelain
was scattered throughout England, with the majority of the factories located in the Staffordshire district. The number of potteries was more than one
thousand.

By the 19th century English china and porcelain
had achieved a worldwide reputation for excellence. American stores imported large amounts for
their customers. The special-production English
pieces of the 18th and early 19th centuries held a
position of great importance among early American
antiques collectors.

References: Susan and Al Bagdade, *Warman's
English & Continental Pottery & Porcelain, 2nd Edition,* Wallace–Homestead, 1991; John A. Bartlett,
British Ceramic Art: 1870–1940, Schiffer Publishing, 1993; John Bartlett, *English Decorative Ceramics,* Kevin Francis Publishing, 1989; David Bat-
tie and Michael Turner, *The Price Guide to 19th
and 20th Century British Porcelain,* Antique Collectors' Club; Peter Bradshaw, *18th Century English
Porcelain Figures, 1745–1795,* Antiques Collectors' Club; John and Margaret Cushion, *A Collector's History of British Porcelain,* Antique Collectors' Club, 1992; Rachael Feild, *Macdonald Guide
To Buying Antique Pottery & Porcelain,* Wallace–
Homestead, 1987; Geoffrey A. Godden, *Godden's
Guide To Mason's China And The Ironstone
Wares,* Antique Collectors' Club; Geoffrey A. Godden, *Godden's Guide To English Porcelain,* Wallace–Homestead, 1992; Pat Halfpenny, *English
Earthenware Figures 1740–1840,* Antique Collec-
tors' Club, 1992; R. K. Henrywood, *Relief Molded
Jugs, 1820–1900,* Antique Collectors' Club; Kathy
Hughes, *A Collector's Guide to Nineteenth–Cen-
tury Jugs,* Routledge & Kegan Paul, 1985; Kathy
Hughes, *A Collector's Guide to Nineteenth–Cen-
tury Jugs, Volume II,* Taylor Publishing, 1991; Llew-
ellyn Jewitt, *The Ceramic Art of Great Britain,* Ster-
ling Publishing, 1985 (reprint of 1883 classic);
Griselda Lewis, *A Collector's History Of English
Pottery,* Antique Collectors' Club; Donald C.
Peirce, *English Ceramics: The Frances and Emory
Cocke Collection,* High Museum of Art, 1988.

Additional Listings: Castleford, Chelsea, Coalport, Copeland and Spode, Liverpool, Royal Crown
Derby, Royal Doulton, Royal Worcester, Historical
Staffordshire, Romantic Staffordshire, Wedgwood,
and Whieldon.

BOW

Bowl, 4½″ d, blue trailing vine, white
ground, c1770. . . . . **170.00**
Egg Cup, 2½″ h, two half flower panels,
powder blue ground, pseudooriental
mark, c1760 . . . . **850.00**
Figure
5½″ h, sportsman, seated, gun on
arm, tricorn hat, white sq mound
base, c1752 . . . . **310.00**
9½″ h, gardener, puce jacket, under-
glaze blue hat, turquoise breeches,
black shoes, blue, puce, and gilt
base, c1765. . . . . **750.00**
Pickle Dish, 4″ l, leaf shape, painted
flowers and grapes, molded veins,
serrated edge, c1760. . . . . **140.00**
Plate, 7⅛″ d, octagonal, center reserve
Oriental island scene panel, circular
and fan shape panels of landscapes
and flowers border, pseudooriental
mark, c1765 . . . . **440.00**

CAUGHLEY

Custard Cup, cov, 3⅛″ d, Oriental river
scene, blue printed buildings **25.00**
Jug, 7¼″ h, cabbage leaf mold, gilt entwined "JPM" in oval gilt and blue cartouche, gilt and blue flowers from pink
ribbon swags, mask spout, c1795. . . **290.00**
Tea Caddy, 5¼″ h, blue printed bou-
quets and butterflies, c1770 . . . . **70.00**

COALBROOKDALE

Cologne Bottle, 7½″ h, raised floral dec,
c1820, price for pair. **750.00**
Inkstand, 10″ l, floral encrusted, molded
asters, leafy ground, scrolling handle,
early 19th C **200.00**
Vase, cov, 15″ h, pear shape, raised
floral dec, gilt rim and cov, flower
spray finial, c1840, price for pair. . . . **800.00**

DERBY

Butter Dish, cov, 7″ d, blue, iron–red,
and gilt, flowering scrolling foliage
bands, matching stand, c1800, price
for pair. **250.00**
Figure, 8″ h and 8½″ h, pastoral, boy
resting against tree stump playing
bagpipe, black hat, bleu–du–roi
jacket, gilt trim, butter yellow
breeches, girl with green hat, bleu–
du–roi bodice, pink skirt, white apron
with iron–red flowerheads, gilt centers, leaves, scroll molded mound
base, crown and incised iron–red D
mark, price for pair **2,000.00**

Jar, cov, 22″ h, octagonal, iron red, bottle green, and leaf green, alternating cobalt blue and white grounds, gilding, grotesque sea serpent handles, now fitted as lamp with carved base, 19th C, price for pair **10,000.00**

Plaque, cluster of fruit, carved giltwood frame, c1830, price for pair. **2,000.00**

FLIGHT, BARR, & BARR

Crocus Pot, 9″ w, 4″ d, 6¼″ h, D form, molded columns and architrave, peach ground panels, ruined abbey landscape reserve, gilding **2,200.00**

Plate, 8″ d, armorial, iron–red, gold, blue, and black arms and crest, Abbot quartering Bryan impaling Harris quartering another, iron–red and gray mantling, pink banderole, motto "Toujours Prest," gilt edged rim and salmon ground border, incised letter mark, crowned and plumed brown "Barr Flight & Barr Royal Porcelain Works, Worcester" oval mark, c1804–09 . . . . **975.00**

Hicks & Meigh, tureen and undertray, blue and orange Oriental pattern, gold trim, marked, 7″ l, 7½″ h, $375.00.

HICKS, MEIGH & JOHNSON

Sugar, cov, 8¼″ d, printed and painted transfer, famille rose type dec, gilted, molded rim, handles, and finial, stand, c1860, price for pair. **425.00**

Tureen, 11″ l, octagonal, flaring rim, applied acanthus tip handle, underglaze blue and white, gilt, iron–red, dark red, and underglaze blue flowerheads, scrolling foliage, and vases, c1813–30 . . . . **350.00**

JACKFIELD

Creamer, 4¼″ h, bulbous, emb grapes design, leaves, and tendrils, gilt highlights, three paw feet, ear shape handle **150.00**

Sugar, cov, 4½″ h, 3¾″ d, scalloped SS rims, SS mounted cov and ornate pierced finial. **225.00**

Teabowl and Saucer, plain **100.00**

LOWESTOFT

Coffeepot, cov, 9″ h, dark blue, underglaze river scene, Chinese man fishing, trellis diaper border, c1770–75 . . **910.00**

Demitasse Cup and Saucer, blue underglaze. **120.00**

Milk Jug, 3¼″ h, dark blue underglaze, Chinese river scene, diaper border, brown rim, c1775. . . . . **200.00**

MASON

Creamer, 4″ h, Oriental style shape, marked "Mason's Patent Ironstone" . **75.00**

Ice Cooler, 14½″ h, straight sides, two applied molded twig form handles, liner with dished gilt rimmed border, fluted high domed cov, inverted pear shaped knob, underglaze blue and enamel iron–red and gold florals, foliage, and vase shapes, imp "Mason's Patent Ironstone China," price for pair **2,750.00**

Jug, 8″ h, octagonal, Hydra pattern, waisted straight neck, green enameled handle, lion head terminal, underglaze blue and iron–red flowers and vase, two imp marks and printed rounded crown mark, c1813–30 . . . . **300.00**

Pitcher, 11¼″ h, octagonal, serpent handle, polychrome and gilt dec transfer printing, underglazed mark, late 19th C. **220.00**

Platter, 13½ x 10¾″, Double Landscape pattern, Oriental motif, deep green and brick red, c1883 . . . . **250.00**

Potpourri Vase, cov, 25¼″ h, hexagonal body, cobalt blue, large gold stylized peony blossom, chrysanthemums, prunus, and butterflies, gold and blue dragon handles and knobs, trellis diaper rim border, c1820–25, price for pair **1,650.00**

Punch Bowl, 14⅛″ h, ironstone, famille rose type dec, c1825. . . . . **825.00**

NEALE

Salt Cellar Group, 8¼″ h, male and female figures holding baskets, seated,

rocky base, polychrome dec, late 18th
C, minor leaf chips. 935.00
Vase, 8¼″ h, porphyry creamware,
speckled brown and blue glaze, central portrait and floral medallions
above floral garlands, molded mask
handles, gilt accents, mounted on
black basalt plinth, imp wafer mark,
c1780, cover missing, gilt wear, nicks 1,100.00

NEW HALL

Creamer, Chinese figure on terrace,
c1790. . . . . 170.00
Dessert Set, two oval dishes, eight
plates, bat printed and colored named
views, lavender–blue borders, light
blue ground, c1815 . . . . 425.00
Dish, deep blue underglaze, orange
flowers and leaves dec, gilt, c1825 . . 120.00
Sugar, cov, multicolored bands of flowering foliage, puce rims, two handles,
c1790. . . . . 125.00

WOODS

Coffeepot, 9⅝″ h, cauliflower form, overlapping leaves, green glaze, foliage
molded spout and handle, c1770 . . . 375.00
Figure, 7¼″ h, squirrel, seated on
haunches, eating nut, splashed manganese and yellow, grass mound
base, c1760 . . . . 2,550.00
Jug, 5¾″ h, ovoid, cameos of Queen
Caroline, pink luster ground, beaded
edge, molded and painted floral bor-
der, c1820 . . . . 395.00
Plate, 10″ d, blue feather edge, marked
"E Wood & Sons" 55.00
Stirrup Cup, 5½″ l, modeled hound's
head, translucent shades of brown,
c1760. . . . . 1,900.00
Whistle, 3⅞″ h, modeled as seated
sphinx, blue accents, oval green
base, c1770 . . . . 500.00

WORCESTER

Bowl
6″ d, underglazed Oriental landscape
scene, open crescent mark, c1780,
int. glaze wear. 300.00
8¼″ d, blue and white, Oriental
coastal village scene, crescent
mark, late 18th C, surface wear. . . 550.00
Fruit Bowl, 10¼″ d, scalloped rim, un-

derglazed blue floral dec, crescent
mark, c1775, chip, rim line 300.00
Plate, 6¼″ d, scalloped rim, blue floral
and berry design, crescent mark, late
18th C, chips, price for set of three . . 200.00
Teabowl, 2⅞″ d, blue Oriental figural
cartouches, "W" mark, late 18th C . . 100.00

ENGLISH SOFTPASTE

History: Between 1820 and 1860 a large number of potteries in England's Staffordshire district
produced decorative wares with a soft earthenware
(creamware) base and a plain white or yellow
glazed ground.

Design or "stick" spatterware was created by
cut–sponge (stamp), hand painting, or transfer.
Blue was the dominant color. The earliest patterns
were carefully arranged geometrics and generally
covered the entire piece. Later pieces had a decorative border with a center motif, usually a tulip.
In the 1850s Elsmore and Foster developed the
Holly Leaf pattern.

King's Rose features a large, cabbage–type rose
in red, pale red, or pink. The pink rose often is
called "Queen's Rose." Secondary colors are pastels of yellow, pink, and occasionally green. The
borders vary: a solid band, vined, lined, or sectional. The King's Rose exists in an oyster motif.

Strawberry China ware comes in three types:
strawberries and strawberry leaves (often called
strawberry luster), green featherlike leaves with
pink flowers (often called cut–strawberry, primrose,
or old strawberry), and a third type with the decoration in relief. The first two types are characterized
by rust-red moldings. Most pieces have a creamware ground. Davenport was one of the many potteries that made this ware.

Yellow–glazed earthenware (canary luster) has
a canary yellow ground, transfer design which is
usually in black, and occasional luster decoration.
The earliest pieces date from the 1780s and have
a fine creamware base. A few hand-painted pieces
are known. Not every piece has luster decoration.

Marked pieces are uncommon. Because the
ground is softpaste, the ware is subject to cracking
and chipping. Enamel colors and other types of
decoration do not hold well. It is not unusual to see
a piece with the decoration worn off.

Reference: Susan and Al Bagdade, *Warman's
English & Continental Pottery & Porcelain, 2nd Edition,* Wallace–Homestead, 1991.

Additional Listings: Adams Rose, Gaudy
Dutch, Salopian Ware, Staffordshire Items.

DESIGN SPATTERWARE

Bowl, 7½″ d, 4″ h, polychrome stripes   75.00
Creamer, 4⅜″ h, Gaudy Floral pattern,
red, green, blue, and black, marked
"Baker & Co, England" 65.00

Cup and Saucer
 Floral pattern, red, blue, green, and
  black. 45.00
 Peony, red and green 175.00
Jug
 5½" h, Holly Leaf, red and green . . 150.00
 7" h, barrel shape, blue, rosettes and
  fern prongs 180.00
Pitcher, 10¾" h, red, green, and purple
 floral wreaths, red borders 160.00
Plate, 8½" d, red and blue flower center,
 green leaves, black stick spatter
 border 175.00
Platter, 15⅝" l, Rosebud and Thistle pat-
 tern, red stripe and columbine, green
 spatter. 235.00
Sugar, cov, 5" h, white, blue, and red
 flowers, green leaves, closed ring and
 shell handles. 100.00
Teapot, cov, rose dec, pink and blue . 200.00

KING'S ROSE

Coffeepot, pink, green, yellow, and red
 dec 800.00
Creamer, helmet shape, brick red rose 225.00
Cup and Saucer, handleless
 Applied yellow, red, pink, and green
  enamel dec. 100.00
 Line border, minor enamel wear . . 130.00
Plate
 6½" d, yellow puff balls, vine border 140.00
 8⅜" d, emb feather edge border, red,
  green, brick–red, and yellow center
  flower dec, imp "Rogers" 75.00
 8⅞" d, brown and purple stick spatter,
  green stripes 65.00
Soup Plate, 9¼" d, broken band border,
 puff balls 145.00
Sugar, scalloped rim, ribbed, vine bor-
 der, pink rose 165.00
Teapot Caddy, 8¼" h, enameled red,
 green, blue, and purple flowers, rust
 line border 50.00
Teapot, Queen Anne shape, minor chips
 on cov 450.00

STRAWBERRY CHINA

Bowl, 4" d 150.00
Cup and Saucer, pink border, scalloped
 edge 220.00
Plate
 5¾" d, strawberry center, strawberry
  and vine border, chipped 60.00
 8¼" d, Cut Strawberry 190.00
Relish Dish, 8¾" d, shell shape 120.00
Sugar, cov, raised strawberries, straw-
 berry knob 130.00
Teabowl and Saucer, vine border . . . 225.00
Vegetable Dish, cov, octagonal 375.00

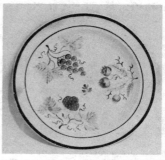

Strawberry China, plate, 5⅝" d, $85.00.

YELLOW GLAZED

Creamer
 4" h, fluted, red and green floral
  enamel, chips and short hairlines. . 75.00
 4½" h, white reserves with black
  transfer scene of milkmaid, and
  cows, polychrome enamel, wear
  and hairlines 85.00
Cup and Saucer, red transfer of fisher-
 man, imp "Sewell," poorly repaired
 rim chip on cup 110.00
Jug
 4⅞" h, black transfer bust with verse
  "The determined enemy of corruption and the constitutional friend of
  his sovereign," polychrome
  enamel, wear, chips, and hairlines,
  repair to spout 140.00
 6" h, molded basketweave, vintage
  and double mask spout, polychrome enamel, wear, professional
  repair to spout 115.00
Mug, 2½" h, red transfer, two children
 and beehive, pink luster band, wear
 and chips 170.00
Plate, 8½" d, black transfer of Hotel de
 Ville d'Amsterdam, French, some
 wear 50.00
Saucer, black transfer of outdoor tea
 party, imp "Adams," rim hairlines . . . 215.00
Sugar Bowl, 4½" h, silver luster floral
 dec, intertwined handles, floral finial,
 imp "Leeds Pottery," wear and small
 chips 560.00
Waste Bowl, 5⅞" d, 3" h, red transfer of
 woman and child in classical attire, minor wear and short rim hairline 300.00

FAIRINGS, MATCH-STRIKERS, AND TRINKET BOXES

History: Fairings are small, charming china objects which were purchased or given away as prizes at English fairs in the 19th century. Although fairings are generally identified with England, they actually were manufactured in Germany by Conte and Boehme of Possneck.

Fairings depicted amusing scenes of courtship and marriage, politics, war, children, and animals behaving as children. More than four hundred varieties have been identified. Most fairings bore a caption. Early examples, 1860–70, were of better quality than later ones. After 1890 the colors became more garish, and gilding was introduced.

The manufacturers of fairings also made match–strikers and trinket boxes. Some were captioned. The figures on the lids were identical to those of the fairings. The market for the match–strikers and trinket boxes was identical to that for the fairings.

Reference: Susan and Al Bagdade, *Warman's English & Continental Pottery & Porcelain, Second Edition,* Wallace–Homestead, 1991.

Advisors: Barbara and Melvin Alpren.

Trinket Box, white ground, blue dec, girl putting on stockings, imp marks, 3½ × 4 ×2″, $145.00.

FAIRINGS

After the Race, cats in a basket	200.00
Five O'Clock Tea, group of cats	200.00
God Save The Queen, children singing around piano	350.00
Opportunity Creates Thieves, child and pig	150.00
Peep Through A Telescope, sailor and child	150.00
You Dirty Boy, mother scrubbing boy's ears	200.00

MATCH–STRIKERS

Button Hole Sir? young lady flower seller	300.00
Penny Please, Sir? young lad match seller	275.00
Safe Messenger, dog carrying basket	275.00
Two children and teacher	200.00

TRINKET BOXES

Clock and anchor on dresser	175.00
Paddling His Own Canoe, child on dresser in canoe	250.00
Pins Madame? dog in a cape	250.00
Swansea to Bristol, train engine	250.00
Windsor Castle	200.00

FAIRY LAMPS

History: Fairy lamps, originating in England in the 1840s, are candle-burning night lamps. They were used in nurseries, hallways, and dim corners of the home.

Two leading candle manufacturers, the Price Candle Company and the Samuel Clarke Company, promoted fairy lamps as a means to sell candles. Both contracted with other manufacturers of glass, porcelain, and metal to produce the needed shades and cups. For example, Clarke used Worcester Royal Porcelain Company, Stuart & Sons, and Red House Glass Works in England, plus firms in France and Germany. Clarke's trademark was a small fairy with a wand surrounded by the words "Clarke Fairy Pyramid, Trade Mark."

Fittings were produced in a wide variety of styles. Shades ranged from pressed to cut glass, from Burmese to Nailsea. Cups are found in glass, porcelain, brass, nickel, and silver plate.

American firms selling fairy lamps included Diamond Candle Company of Brooklyn, Blue Cross Safety Candle Co., and Hobbs–Brockunier of Wheeling, West Virginia.

Fairy lamps are found in two pieces (cup and shade) and three pieces (cup with matching shade and saucer). Married pieces are common.

References: John F. Solverson, *Those Fascinating Little Lamps,* Antique Publications, 1988; John F. Solverson (comp.), *Those Fascinating Little Lamps, Miniature Lamps Value Guide,* Antique Publications, 1988.

Periodicals: *Light Revival,* 35 West Elm Ave., Quincy, MA 02170; *Night Light Newsletter,* 38619 Wakefield Ct., Northville, MI 48167.

Reproduction Alert: Reproductions abound.

Baccarat, 5¾″ d, 3⅞″ h, Sunburst pattern, matching saucer base	165.00
Bisque, 4″ h, figural, owl, cat, and dog, glass eyes, clear glass base marked "Clarke"	250.00

Vaseline, ribbed dome, green pressed Clarke base, 2⅞ x 3½", $200.00.

Burmese
   5½" h, Webb, dome shaped shade, droopy crimped edge base, turned up at applied Burmese leaf, unsigned clear glass candle cup, orig unused wax candle sgd "The Burglar's Horror" **1,450.00**
   6" h, 4½" d, Mt Washington, prunus blossom dec, dec ruffled skirted base, clear Clarke base **1,200.00**
   7½" d, Webb, floral dec on shade and open saucer ring, crystal Clarke base and candle cup, minimal chips to saucer base. **1,430.00**
Cranberry
   2⅞" d, 3½" h, Diamond Quilted pattern, clear glass base marked "Clarke" **95.00**
   4½" h, crown shaped overshot shade, clear glass base marked "Clarke," c1887 . . . . **200.00**
Nailsea
   5¼" h, cranberry frosted verre moire, white loopings, clear glass base marked "Clarke" **200.00**
   6½" h, red verre moire, white loopings, dome shaped shade, six pinched pleated bowl shaped base, clear glass candle cup marked "Clarke Fairy Patent Trade Mark" . **850.00**
Opalescent, 2⅞" d, 4" h, Swirl pattern, amber ground, clear glass base marked "Clarke" **95.00**
Peachblow, 3⅞" h, acid finished rose shaded to pink shade, black lacy flower and leaf dec, cream lining, clear glass base marked "Clarke," gold washed metal stand **325.00**
Satin Glass
   2⅞" d, 3½" h, yellow, emb ribs, clear glass base marked "Clarke" **125.00**
   3⅞" d, 5" h, blue, Swirl pattern, MOP int., clear glass base marked "Clarke" **195.00**
   6" d, lavender ruffled dome top, three

gold inset jeweled medallions, matching ruffled base **330.00**
   7½" h, cased pink house shaped shade, molded roof, bricks, and window details, upturned ruffled base, crystal holder, small candle cup **955.00**
Spatter Glass, 2⅞" d, 3½" h, yellow and white spatter, clear glass base marked "Clarke" **125.00**

FAMILLE ROSE

History: Famille Rose is a Chinese export of enameled porcelain in which the pink color predominates. It was made primarily in the 18th and 19th centuries. Other porcelains in the same group are Famille Jaune (yellow), Famille Noire (black), and Famille Verte (green).

Decorations include courtyard and home scenes, birds, and insects. Secondary colors are yellow, green, blue, aubergine, and black.

Mid- to late-19th-century Chinese export wares similar to Famille Rose are identified as Rose Canton, Rose Mandarin, and Rose Medallion.

Reference: Gloria and Robert Mascarelli, *Warman's Oriental Antiques*, Wallace–Homestead, 1992.

Bowl
   8" d, scalloped, floral dec, yellow ground **220.00**
   10" d, floral and scrolled border int., figural cartouche on gilt ground ext., 19th C. **600.00**
   11½" d, bouquet of flowers int., floral chain, elaborate rim borders, floral trellis ext. band and border, late 18th C. **1,000.00**
Box, cov, 4½" d, figural and floral dec **80.00**
Brush Washer, 7½" l, lotus pad shape, ducks, lotus blossoms, and pads int., 19th C **625.00**
Charger, 12" d, central figural dec, brocade border **250.00**
Creamer, cov, pear shape, ladies and child at play with landscape scene, Qianlong **410.00**
Dish, 8½" l, oval, central figural garden scene, foliated piercework basketry rim, multicolored flowers **700.00**
Flask, 19" h, Moon, turquoise ground, repairs **330.00**
Garden Seat, 18¾" h, hexagonal, animals and cranes beneath ruyi borders with bats and fruit, pierced top and sides **1,800.00**
Ginger Jar, cov, 8½" h, cockerel and floral dec **110.00**

Jar, cov

12″ h, pseudo tobacco leaf dec, mounted as lamps, price for pair . . 550.00

18½″ h, ovoid, scattered peony sprays and flowers, peacocks and exotic birds on rockwork, cloud collar band, domed lid, c1900, price for pair. 2,475.00

Jardiniere, 21½″ h, ovoid, continuous scene of maidens on pavilion terrace with landscape scene, lappet band at neck, stiff leaf lappets around base, flattened rim with scrolling lotus tendril dec 330.00

Mug, 5″ h, Mandarin Palette, Qianlong, 1790 . . . . 425.00

Plate, 10″ d, floral dec, ribbed body, Tongzhi mark, price for pair 275.00

Sauce Boat, 7″ l, Meissen style harbor scene, c1750 . . . . 600.00

Table Screen

14½ x 8″ each panel, four fold, hardwood frame. 330.00

31″ h, wood stand 440.00

Tea Caddy, 5½″ h, Mandarin Palette, arched rect form, painted front, figures and pavilion reverse, c1780 . . . . 550.00

Teapot, cov, 4½″ h, drum form, floral dec, sepia garland with flowers on shoulder and cov, strawberry finial, c1790. . . . . 770.00

Tea Service, Millefleur pattern, teapot, cov sugar, creamer, six dessert plates, coffee cups, saucers, eight tea cups and saucers, price for 37 pc set 1,000.00

Tray, 8″ l, oval, multicolored center armorial crest, underglaze blue diaper and trefoil borders, reticulated rim, late 18th C 550.00

Vase, Mandarin, figures in reserves, c1820, 10½″ h, $500.00.

Tureen, 15″ l, goose form, relief feathers, detailed feet, neck, and iron red beak 800.00

Umbrella Stand, medallions with hunting scenes surrounded by gilt scrolling foliate dec, black ground 275.00

Vase

6½″ h, bird perched on flowering prunus tree dec 115.00

10″ h, bird in flowering tree dec, Rouleau 200.00

16⅝″ h, baluster form, trumpet neck, eight flowering chrysanthemum branches, pale yellow, blue, violet, and iron–red blooming flowers, six–character Guangxu mark 1,210.00

17½″ h, sq sectioned bottle, each face dec with seasonal flowers, brilliant enamels, shiny black ground, 19th C 1,300.00

FANS

History: Today, people tend to think of fans as fragile, frivolous accessories wielded by women; yet the origin of the fan was no doubt highly practical. Early man may have used it to winnow his grain, shoo flies, and cool his brow. This simple tool eventually became a symbol of power: ancient lore maintains that Emperor Hsien Yuan (c2697 B.C.) used fans; the tomb of Egypt's Tutankhamen (1350 B.C.) yielded two ostrich feather fans with gold mounts. Fans also began to assume religious significance and were used to whisk flies from altars. Early Christians recognized the practicality of this practice and included a flabellum, or fixed fly–whisk, in their early services. Meanwhile, the Chinese and Japanese continued to use fans in their courts, often incorporating precious materials such as ivory, gold, and jade.

Until the seventh century A.D., fans were non–folding. Then, according to Japanese legend, Emperor Jen–ji noticed the logic of a bat's folded wings and applied it to a new fan design. Later, European traders returned from the East with samples of these wonders. By the sixteenth century sophisticated Italian women had appropriated the fans, which soon became *de rigueur* throughout Europe. Now primarily feminine fashion accessories, their styles came to complement the ever–changing dress styles. The popularity of fans led to experimentation in their production and merchandising. They also became popular as a way for artists to test their skills—a fan leaf's curved, folding surface offered challenges in perspective.

World War I was the end of slower eras; the 1920s raced at a frenetic pace. The modern woman set aside her ubiquitous fan, freeing both hands to drive her roadster or carry her political banner. Fans became more an advertising tool than a fashion statement.

Some basic guidelines are:
— 19th C artisans copied 18th C styles. True Georgian figures should have gray hair; if the wigs are white, the fan is more recent. The later fans will often have a "heavier" appearance and anachronistic costuming.
— Empire fans were also copied. The period ones have sequins made by flattening circles of wire; a tiny line shows where the wire ends meet. Later sequins were stamped whole out of sheet metal and have no joining line.
— Ivory, bone, celluloid, and plastic may look somewhat alike. Ivory often has a subtle, textureless graining pattern and may feel smooth and buttery; bone frequently reveals channels. Look for mold marks in plastic.
— Many leaves became damaged with wear and were replaced. These "marriage" fans can still be delightful collectibles, but beware of dating a fan merely based on one component.
— Loops are rarely found on fans before 1830.
— Framing a fan often causes its sticks to warp and its leaf to lose its elasticity and ability to fold. It is also difficult to tell if a fan has been sewn or glued to its backing, making its removal difficult.
— The number of degrees a folding fan opens is a key to dating.
— Handle fans gently, unfolding from left to right.

Fan Terminology:
Brisé—fan with no leaf, but made of rigid, overlapping sticks held together at base by a rivet and at the other end by a ribbon.
Cockade—pleated fan opening to form complete circle.
Folding fan—fan with a flexible, pleated leaf mounted on sticks.
Fontange—shape of folding fans c1890–1935, with center of leaf longer than guards.
Guard—the outermost sticks, usually the height of fan.
Leaf or mount—flexible, pleated material which unites the upper parts of a folding fan's sticks.
Lithograph—printing process invented in 1797, often subsequently hand-colored.
Loop—often "u" shaped finger holder attached to rivet at base of fan; rare before 1830.
Medallion—pictorial representation, usually circular or oval, in leaf.
Piqué-point—decorative small gold or silver points or pins set flush with surface of sticks or guards.
Rivet—pin about which sticks of a folding fan pivot.
Sticks—rigid framework of a folding fan.
Studs—exposed end of rivet, sometimes shaped as decorative paste "gem."
Washer—small disk to prevent friction between end of rivet and fan.

References: Helene Alexander, *Fans,* Batsford, 1984; Nancy Armstrong, *A Collector's History of Fans,* Clarkson N. Potter, 1974; Nancy Armstrong, *The Book of Fans,* Mayflower Books, Inc.; Nancy Armstrong, *Fans: A Collector's Guide,* Souvenir Press, 1984; Anna Gray Bennett, *Fans In Fashion,* San Francisco Art Museum, 1981; Anna Gray Bennett, *Unfolding Beauty,* Thames and Hudson, 1988; Braintree Historical Society, *Hunt and Allen Fans,* Braintree Historical Society, 1988; Reiko Chiba, *Painted Fans of Japan,* Charles E. Tuttle Co., 1962; Debrett's Peerage, *Fans From The East,* Debrett's Peerage, Ltd., 1978; Francoise DePerthuis and Vincent Meylan, *Eventails,* Hermé, 1989; Bertha DeVere Green, *A Collector's Guide To Fans Over The Ages,* Frederick Muller Ltd., London, 1975; Tseng Yu–ho Ecke, *Poetry on the Wind,* Honolulu Academy of Arts, 1981; M. A. Flory, *A Book About Fans,* Macmillan, 1895; Julia Hutt and Helene Alexander, *Ogi,* Dauphin Publishing, 1992; Neville John Irons, *Fans of Imperial China,* Kaiserreich Ltd., 1981; Neville John Irons, *Fans of Imperial Japan,* Kaiserreich Ltd., 1981; Christl Kammerel, *Der Facher,* Himmer Verlag, Munich, 1989; Susan Mayor, *A Collector's Guide To Fans,* Wellfleet Books, 1990; Susan Mayor, *Collecting Fans,* Mayflower Books, 1980; Susan Mayor, *Fans,* Vancouver Museum, 1983; Musee de la Mode et du Costome, *L'Eventail,* 1985; McIver Percival, *The Fan Book,* T Fisher Unwin Ltd., London, 1920; G. W. Woolliscroft Rhead, *The History Of The Fan,* Kegan Paul, Trench, Trubner & Co., London, 1910; Mary E. G. Rhoads, *The Fan Directory,* Fan Collectors, Press, 1993; Maryse Volet, *L'Imagination au Service de L'Eventail,* 1986.

Collectors' Club: FANA, Fan Association of North America, 6138 Deacon Rd., Windermere, FL 34786.

Advisor: Wendy Hamilton Blue.

Note: Abbreviations:
chlth–chromolithograph
gl–Guard Length
MOP–mother of pearl

1893, paper, folding, Chicago Columbian Exposition, three color litho scenes of buildings, 14 wood sticks, 2 wood guards, metal loop, 24″ w open, $150.00.

AMERICAN AND EUROPEAN

Mid 18th C, paper, ivory, German or English, double, paper, hp, front: China blue background with multicolored floral garlands, central scene of courting couple in period costume, lady seated on garden bench, standing gentleman with hands in supplicating gesture, right gold edged round reserve showing gentleman offering flower in his left hand, topped with stylized double bow, left reserve with woman, eyes demurely lowered; reverse: ecru paper, rough central painting of gazebo atop small hill, 12 ivory sticks, painted and carved with floral baskets, urns, and two women, gilt highlights, both ivory guards roughly carved with male in short Oriental costume, same floral motif painting as sticks, metal rivet, MOP washer, 11″ gl, 20¾″ op, 140 degrees **250.00**

Early 19th C

    Horn brisé, c1810–20, English Regency or Biedermeier style, 19 greenhorn sticks plus guards, Gothic arch finials, each stick pierced in trailing vine motif, hp floral band½″ below plus pink ribbon, brass rivet, MOP washer, 6⅛″ gl, 11¼″ op, 145 degrees **135.00**

    Ivory brisé, 26 fine ivory sticks, tips dec with birds, insects, and flowers of applied feathers, insect wings, and velvet, finer hp details, 2 plain guards notched at top and gently tapered through head, clear paste stud, 6¾″ gl, 11½″ op, 145 degrees **200.00**

    Swanskin (fine paper), horn, c1810–20, double hp in gouache, one side with Bay of Naples looking across volcano to far right, foreground fashionable couple strolling, group of musicians and dancers, fisherman pulling boats ashore, soft blue, green, gray, and rosy hills, reverse labeled "Nobile Sepol Cro. A Pompeiano," depicting massive sepulcher, man rolling lawn, front and back bordered on 3 sides by decorative frieze, orange on black, 17 horn sticks, 2 plain guards, 6¾″ gl, 13″ op, 155 degrees **900.00**

Mid 19th C

    French for Export market double, litho, hand colored

        Paper, bone, front: extended scene of 3 family groups, left: scholarly father looks as wife plays with toddler on lap, daughter kneels by her side; center: woman presents infant to noble couple seated on terrace, young girl entertains another infant in canopied cradle; right: mother and 3 young children looking at bay, full masted sailing ship, blue and gilt decorative borders, reverse: courtiers playing cards, observer reclining in canopied bed as woman brings refreshment tray, other courtiers rest nearby or stroll castle grounds, "Belleville" printed lower left edge, intricate fruit/floral garlands, urns, 14 bone sticks, 2 intricately carved guards, silver and gold foil dec, brass rivet, MOP washer, 10⅜″ gl, 20″ op, 180 degrees **175.00**

    Paper, lacquered wood, front: romantic scene, 11 young people enjoying day in country, gilt borders, reverse: small applied scene of kneeling man presenting basket of flowers to 2 wealthy young women, 12 heavily black lacquered sticks, gilt scene of man seated under tree offering nest with 3 singing birds to young woman, 2 guards continue gilded floral motif, front guard with flirting mirror, brass rivet, loop, MOP washer, 10½″ gl, 19⅝″ op, 180 degrees **125.00**

    Paper, lacquered wood, double, deep blue foil, gilt garlands, applied litho, hand colored, front: central scene of 5 young people in 18th C costume picking cherries, left reserve: courtier bows to 2 young women; right reserve: man displays jewelry to 2 uncertain young women; reverse: 4 wealthy young women, sketching and reading in garden, 12 lacquered sticks widen½″ below leaf to form 2″ shield, each dec in oil and varnish with scene from Aesop's fables, each guard has scene on the shield, second one at tip, brass rivet, shaped and etched loop, double MOP washers, orig pink cardboard box labeled "Bailey & Co., Jewellers, 136 Chestnut Street, Philadelphia," 10⅝″ gl, 20¼″ op, 170 degrees **250.00**

Mid to late 19th C

    Gauze, bone, ecru gauze edged and inset with Carrickmacross lace, entire leaf set with silver sequins, approx 36 per fold, 16 serpentine bone sticks and 2 guards dec with pique–point, steel rivet, celluloid loop and washer, 9⅝″ gl, 18″ op, 175 degrees **150.00**

Ivory brisé, 13 very thin ivory sticks, 2 guards, front with intricate carved monogram "M" attached with 2 small silver nails, brass rivet, ivory loop, ivory washer, 8″ gl, 14⅜″ op, 155 degrees **140.00**

Ivory, MOP, ecru handmade Point de Gaze lace with multicolored roses and geometric forms on honeycomb net, 16 MOP sticks, 2 guards, gentle slightly pink irid, brass rivet, loop, MOP washer, 10″ gl, 18¾″ op, 155 degrees **180.00**

Linen, wood cockade, wooden handles cov in textured paper with gold fan design, holding one handle at base, user lifts other handle, up and around hinge, until it again meets first handle, small metal loop fastens handles together, leaf unfolds out of hollowed handles forming circle, white leaf, cut into star shapes at outer edge, strung by yellow ribbon, 9¼″ l closed, 9⅝″ unfolded diameter **55.00**

c1860, black silk, gilded wood, "Jenny Lind," brisé fan named for singer who reportedly popularized style, black silk pieces cut in feather shapes, gold sequins and stars dec, top of gilded sticks carved in floral motif, 12 sticks, 2 guards, brass rivet, loop, MOP washer, orig cardboard box in shape of closed fan, 7½″ gl, 14¼″ op, 145 degrees. . . . **45.00**

Fourth Quarter 19th C, linen, leather cockade, brown leather casing, gold paint edge, red linen fan, brass knob slides to top of channel, fan pushes out of case and unfolds in circle, small turned leather cov handle and ring, maroon cord, tassel, 8″ l from ring to top of closed case, 9″ d open leaf **65.00**

Late 19th C

Gauze, MOP, pale green gauze topped with 2½″ pale green lace, lace descents into leaf at 4 points, framing hp pink floral sprays and center group of 3 chickadees, 16 sticks, 2 guards of irid ecru MOP, clear paste stud, brass loop, pale green silk cord, tassel, 13¾″ gl, 26⅛″ op, 175 degrees **140.00**

Gauze, wood, black gauze inset with black net and soutache, top edged with black lace which dips at 9 points 4″ into leaf, hp cream, mauve, gray, and moss green roses, dogwood blossoms, and butterflies, smooth black wood sticks, painted in gilt and deep black enamel floral motif, small red flower centers, right guard edges carved to look like tree branch, center guard hollowed to display floral carving, reverse guard repeats stick motif, 16 sticks, 2 guards, shaped brass rivet, loop, 13¾″ gl, 26″ op, 170 degrees **100.00**

Net, gauze, wood, black net, 3 hp scenes: woman sitting at twilight lake shore, center: romantic scene of buxom young woman suspended as if on swing among dogwood blossoms; right: darker small scene of woman at foot of stairs leading to tower, black lace, embroidered autumn toned stalks and berries surround scenes, 16 sticks, 2 guards, dark brown wood serpentine sticks, incised and painted gold flowers, center 2 sticks doubled so that carved, painted floral motif continues into leaf, 4 other single thickness sticks in front of lace, guards carved like tree branches blossoming into gilded floral sprays, brass rivet, loop, MOP washer, 12⅝″ gl, 24¼″ op, 175 degrees **130.00**

Paper, wood, Spanish, double paper, chlth on front, Spaniards enjoying party on verandah, women's dresses and men's boleros with glitter accents, reverse: plain salmon colored paper, gold band edge, 16 wood sticks with silver leaf design, 2 guards topped by figure of man painted in silver, brass rivet, washer, 14¼″ gl, 27½″ op, 180 degrees. **50.00**

Satin, wood, double golden taupe satin, central hp scene of 4 lively chicks examining empty shell, framed by wisps of grasses, daisies, plain reverse, 12 undecorated highly varnished sticks, 2 beveled top guards, brass rivet, loop with ring, MOP washer, 13″ gl, 24¼″ op, 160 degrees **125.00**

c1901–02, celluloid, mechanical, "The Zephyr," patent date, slender ⅜″ column of celluloid, 8″ 1⅝″ long, narrows in middle to 1″ to fit palm of hand, thumb resting atop celluloid button, when user pumps button, 3 celluloid blades near tip revolve, brass pin marked "Paris" atop blades. **60.00**

c1905–10, net, lace, horn, black net completely edged in white handmade lace, 3 groups of lace daffodils with sequin accents, 16 sticks, 2 reprocessed horn guards, single row of pique point on each stick, top half of guard serpentine, pierced, with pique–point in 4 curving rows, steel rivet, celluloid washer, lace extends ⅜″ above guard, 10¾″ gl, 21¾″ op, 170 degrees **200.00**

AMERICAN AND EUROPEAN SOUVENIR, COMMEMORATIVE, AND ADVERTISING

1880, paper, wood, folding, double paper, chlth, painted by Donaldson Brothers, Five Points, NY, advertises ladies hats for summer 1880, I. S. Custer Son & Co, Philadelphia, offers 7 models on front and 12 on back, each style named, decorative paisley lower border, 12 pierced balsa wood sticks, 2 solid guards, steel rivet, brass washer, metal loop, 11¼″ gl, 20½″ op, 160 degrees **200.00**

1883, paper, wood, folding, double paper, dated Tues, Dec 11, commemorates anniversary of Boston's Bijou Theatre opening, chlth souvenir program of *The Beggar Student,* playbill centered among play scenes, reverse: putti fly kite and balloon, display banner with theatre's managers, 13 pierced balsa sticks, 2 pierced balsa guards, brass rivet, washer, and loop, 12″ gl, 22″ op, 165 degrees . . . **175.00**

1885, cardboard brisé, folding, chlth, four heart shaped sections, each shows "girl of the period," from "100 years ago" to "today" showing dress with exaggerated bustle, back: adv C. Aultman & Co, Canton, OH, farm equipment, thresher, and Phoenix straw burning engine, 5½″ h, 3⅞″ w . **125.00**

c1891, wood brisé, folding, autograph, hp violets, strung with purple ribbon, 40 signatures, dates from Oct 31 1891 to Nov 24, 1911, 9⅜″ gl, 17½″ op, 155 degrees **45.00**

1892, cardboard, celluloid, folding brisé, souvenir of 1,200th performance of *Men and Women,* Demille and Belasco play, April 12, 1892, Hollis St Theatre, Boston, front: 16 shaped celluloid sticks, each printed with gold character name, fascimile signature of actor, back: 16 shaped cardboard sticks, each sgd in pencil, brass loop, gold satin ribbon, 9¾″ gl, 15″ op, 150 degrees **150.00**

1893
Paper, wood, folding, double paper, front: right ⅔ chlth aerial view of Chicago Columbian Exposition,

buildings, and canals, left ⅓ with dozen sepia tone trompe l'oeil cards, each depicting building, made in Italy, plain orange paper reverse, 14 wood sticks, 2 guards, brass rivet, washer, loop, 13⅜″ gl, 24½″ op, 155 degrees **150.00**

Wood, linen, assorted fabrics, cockade, closed fan looks like nosegay of fabric flowers atop green wooden handle stem, by pulling center flower, blue tube appears, then blue linen cockade fan rises, banner reads "Souvenir of the Chicago Columbian Exposition, 1893," Columbus and date 1740 on bottom left, new world landing scene on bottom right, 6¾″ h, 7⅞″ d cockade **200.00**

1895, cardboard, wood, flat, palmette shape, chlth, trompe l'oeil of trade card of young woman modeling corset, violets, ribbon, red seal proclaiming "Highest Award and Diploma, 1893 World's Fair," copyright by Donaldson Brothers, reverse: muted ecru, moss green leaves, award repetition, 8½″ h cardboard, 7⅞″ w, ½″ w x 7″ wood stick with rounded edges, slotted to hold fan. **90.00**

Late 19th C, paper, wood, folding, double paper, chlth, front: 5 circular pictures of people enjoying holiday sites, Dieppe, Etretat, Dinard, Le Harve, Mont St Michel, carnations, sweet williams, bird, foliage, and ladybug frame circles, sgd in print "E Nerm..." rest cov by guard, reverse touts mail service between New York and Paris, Paris Terminus Hotel, and express service to Paris to London, boat speeds, horsepower, and tonnage, French, British, US, and naval flags frame each side, Eventail Monte par Ganne, Paris, 14 balsa wood sticks, 2 guards, 12¾″ gl, 23½″ op, 160 degrees **200.00**

1904, paper, cockade, World's Fair, St Louis, red, white, blue, and yellow, 5 leaf clover shape, Pylonic Gateway at top, US flag and seal to left and right, other nation flags at base, reverse: Uncle Sam at top, 4 US flags, 2 shields, 11¾″ l, 12″ w, two 9⅝″ l gold painted cardboard sticks **125.00**

1921, cardboard, flat, fan shaped cardboard, chlth, singers dressed in costumes from various operas, posing on stairs, large record in background, "All–Star Concert In Your Own Home on Your Own Victrola," dog with "His Master's Voice" logo at bottom, reverse: people dancing, camping, picnicing, reinforced handle, copyright 1921, Reinecke–Ellis Co, 8½″ h, 12½″ op **80.00**

1920s to 1930s, cardboard, wood stick, flat, bright red diecut tomato shape, can of tomato soup on front, reverse: Campbell's New Toronto, Canada, plant, list of 21 soups, 6½″ h cardboard, 9⅛″ d, 6″ l front wood stick, 9½″ l in back **100.00**

1930s, cardboard, flat, stickless, balloon shape narrowing to self handle, full color front of mother, father, young son, toddler daughter ready to enjoy glasses of Pur–Ox, back depicts 6 places to enjoy product, 2 recipes, reinforced bottom, 11³⁄₁₆″ h, 8¼″ w. . . . **30.00**

1929, cardboard, wood stick, flat, Rolf Armstrong illus "Queen of the Ball," full color, sgd in print, Oklahoma Free State Fair adv on back, 8¾″ h x 8⅞″ w cardboard, slotted 5½″ l front wood stick, 10¾″ l in back. **60.00**

1936, cardboard, flat

Front: sepia tone photo of "Three Little Daisies," young actors from *The Green Pastures*, stickless, reinforced bottom, thumbhole, 9⅝″ h, 10⅝″ w **45.00**

Front: full color print of Dionne Quintuplets as toddlers, playing in sand, copyright 1936, reverse: plain adv of local Dodge–Plymouth distributor, 8⅝″ l cardboard, 8¼″ w, 6″ l front wood stick, 11″ l in back **40.00**

1937, cardboard, wood stick, red banner reads "Our President and His Cabinet," soft blue background, black and white photos of Franklin D Roosevelt and first term cabinet, VP Garner, back: electrical repair shop adv, 8⅛″ l cardboard, 9½″ w, 6″ l front wood stick, 11″ in back. **70.00**

1940s, cardboard, wood stick, Boy Scout, Norman Rockwell illus, scout standing in front of Lincoln and Washington, eagle flying in background, full color, shield shape, reverse: war savings bonds and stamps and laundry adv, 9⅜″ l cardboard, 8⅛″ w, 6″ l front wood stick, 11″ l in back. **65.00**

ORIENTAL, PACIFIC

c1800, ivory brisé, single side carved, bird and flower motif finials, central cartouche of 5 tiered pagoda in landscape, floral ground with baskets of flowers, flower and vine gorge, 6½″ gl, 9½″ op, 150 degrees. **350.00**

c1840

Lacquer brisé, each finial depicts man sitting or standing by building, feathery, swirled, floral borders rim middle design of people in tiled central courtyard, gorge echoes main design with group of 4 people centered against floral background, 20 sticks, 2 guards each 6 persons in middle, 2 below, trees, flowers, and butterflies, clear paste stud, shaped and engraved silver loop, contemporary box, 8⅕″ gl, 14½″ op, 140 degrees. **450.00**

Paper, sandalwood, MOP, tortoise shell, ivory, Cantonese Mandarin or Thousand Faces, 14 carved sticks alternating in order listed above, each stick carved with scenes of Chinese life, front tortoise shell guard, reverse ivory guard, double paper, hp blue and green dec, 25 figures on front, including emperor and empress, ivory faces, appliqued silk robes, 14 figures hold fans, reverse: 24 court figures with ivory faces, appliqued silk robes, 10¼″ gl, 19¼″ op, 175 degrees . . . **550.00**

c1860, silk and ivory, 6¼″ h silk mount, intricately embroidered in muted moss, ivory, beige, four herons by pond, birds and butterflies above nearby flowers, reverse: 3 ducks frolicking in stream overhung by graceful trees, flower border, 14 central subtly notched sticks, 2 intricately carved ¼″ guards, multilayers with figures on staircases, walking in fields, brass rivet, MOP washer, etched silver loop, silk tassel, 12¼″ gl, 22⅝″ op, 180 degrees **400.00**

Late 19th C

Folding Mai Ogi or Japanese dancing fan style, 8 thin, widely spaced wood sticks, 2 tri–part guards (each guard single at bottom, spreads and separates into 3 parts to reinforce and support leaf), triple strands of cord crisscross top half of each guard, double paper, subtly painted in green and beige, white flowers, front: central printed photograph of Japanese style bridge leading to park area with statue, reverse: 5 simple floral stalks, hp, brass loop, rivet, 12½″ gl, 23¼″ op, 140 degrees. **35.00**

Sandalwood brisé, 19 pierced sticks, carved on both sides with scenes of daily life, scholars reading, farmers, men navigating, flowers in gorge, both guards carved approx ¼″ with more detailed scene, dark blue ribbon, brass rivet, loop, MOP washer, 10⅝" gl, 18¼" op, 145 degrees. . . **45.00**

Silk, ivory, Ogi Sensu, c1870, deep gray silk leaf, 10" hp scene of Japanese man, woman with umbrella, young boy standing on verandah watching rain storm move across lake, deep greens, blues, grays, ecru, and white, painted pine cones scattered around outside edge of scene; reverse: group of wild flowers to left of center, 3 small birds in flight to right, top and bottom of leaf metallic banded, 28 slender, notched ivory sticks, 2 ivory guards dec with hiramaki–e (low relief) and takmaki–e (high relief) of tree branches and birds, 11¼" gl, 20⅜" op, 150 degrees. **260.00**

c1960, paper, bamboo, double paper leaf, identical front and back, red background, silver waves, sailing ship in gold circle, imprinted "Japan–U. S. Centennial 1860–1960" and "Japan Tourist Association," 8 bamboo sticks, 2 bamboo guards, metal rivet, 10⅞" gl, 18⅞" op, 145 degrees. **35.00**

FENTON GLASS

History: The Fenton Art Glass Company began as a cutting shop in Martins Ferry, Ohio, in 1905. In 1906 Frank L. Fenton started to build a plant in Williamstown, West Virginia, and produced the first piece of glass in 1907. Early production included carnival, chocolate, custard, and pressed plus mold-blown opalescent glass. In the 1920s stretch glass, Fenton dolphins, jade green, ruby, and art glass were added.

In the 1930s boudoir lamps, "Dancing Ladies," and various slags were produced. The 1940s saw crests of different colors being added to each piece by hand. Hobnail, opalescent, and two–color overlay pieces were popular items. Handles were added to different shapes, making the baskets they created as popular today as then.

Through the years Fenton has added beauty to its glass by decorating it with hand painting, acid etching, color staining, and copper-wheel cutting. Several different paper labels have been used. In 1970 an oval raised trademark also was adopted.

References: Shirley Griffith, *A Pictorial Review Of Fenton White Hobnail Milk Glass,* published by author, 1984; William Heacock, *Fenton Glass: The First Twenty–Five Years,* O–Val Advertising Corp., 1978; William Heacock, *Fenton Glass: The Second Twenty–Five Years,* O–Val Advertising Corp., 1980; William Heacock, *Fenton Glass: The Third Twenty–Five Years,* O–Val Advertising Corp., 1989; Ferill J. Rice (ed.), *Caught In the Butterfly*

Net, Fenton Art Glass Collectors of America, Inc., 1991.

Collectors' Clubs: Fenton Art Glass Collectors Of America, Inc., PO Box 384, Williamstown, WV 26187; National Fenton Glass Society, PO Box 4008, Marietta, OH 45750.

Museum: Fenton Art Glass Co, Williamstown, WV.

Additional Listing: Carnival Glass.

Advisor: Ferill J. Rice.

Ashtray
   Black Crest, 7" d **65.00**
   Mandarin Red, pipe **115.00**
Banana Boat, Open Edge, milk glass **70.00**
Basket
   Ivory Crest, 10", #1922 . . . . **150.00**
   Plum Opalescent Hobnail **120.00**
   Turquoise, Hobnail, 4½" **50.00**
   Twin Ivy, etched, 10" metal handle **140.00**
Batter Set, #1639, Jade Green, price for
   five piece set **350.00**
Beverage Set, Fenton Rose, Ming, black
   handles, price for jug and six tumblers **450.00**
Bowl
   Burmese, maple leaf decal **45.00**
   Mandarin Red, #1663, 11" d **140.00**
   Periwinkle Blue, 11" d, flared **90.00**
   Shell, Cranberry Opalescent, Coin
     Dot. **130.00**
Candelabra
   Jade Green, Pineapple **60.00**
   Mandarin Red, Pineapple **110.00**
Candlesticks, pr
   Chinese Yellow **80.00**
   Mandarin Red **110.00**
   Silver Crest, cornucopia **50.00**
Compote
   #10
     Jade Green **50.00**
     Lilac **190.00**
   #260, Marigold, 7" **110.00**
Condiment Set, Tear Drop, Turquoise **125.00**
Cruet, orig stopper
   Burmese, hp
     Rose **125.00**
     Violets **150.00**
   Cranberry Opalescent, #3869 Oil . **145.00**
Cup and Saucer
   Silver Crest **35.00**
   Square Blue Opalescent Hobnail . . **60.00**
Decanter Set, #1934, flower stopper,
   amber, silver overlay, price for eight
   piece set **180.00**
Epergne, Silver Crest, large, single lily **150.00**
Fairy Lamp
   Rose Satin **45.00**
   Ruby Hobnail **25.00**
Flower Pot, Six Ring, Lilac, price for pot
   and saucer. **195.00**
Ginger Jar, Wistaria, satin etched crystal, price for three piece set **125.00**

Cruet, Hobnail, vaseline, clear stopper,
4¾" h, $45.00.

Goblet
Plymouth, ruby	18.00
Silver Crest, ftd	45.00

Hat
Burmese, hp butterfly	125.00
Cranberry Opalescent, Coin Dot, 4"	55.00

Jam Set, Block and Star, ftd tray, tur-
quoise, price for set 250.00
Mug, child's, milk glass, Hobnail 55.00
Powder Jar, Antique Green, Hanging
Heart 450.00

Plate, 12" d
Emerald Crest	50.00
Silver Crest	45.00

Rose Bowl
Burmese, hp rose	95.00
Green Opalescent, milk glass base	90.00

Salt and Pepper Shakers, pr
D. O. Ruby	250.00
Lincoln Inn, royal blue	200.00

Sherbet
Georgian, royal blue	20.00
Silver Crest	20.00

Tid Bit Tray, Emerald Crest 75.00

Tumbler
Blue Opalescent, Coin Dot	45.00
Ming Crystal	20.00

Vase
Mandarin Red, Peacock, 10"	320.00
Milady, Kitchen Green	225.00
Mongolian Green, Peacock, 8"	75.00
Vessel of Gems, milk glass	45.00

FIESTA

MADE IN
U.S.A

History: The Homer Laughlin China Company
introduced Fiesta dinnerware in January 1936 at

the Pottery and Glass Show in Pittsburgh, Pennsylvania. Fredrick Rhead designed the pattern; Arthur Kraft and Bill Bensford molded it. Dr. A. V.
Bleininger and H. W. Thiemecke developed the
glazes.

The original five colors were red, dark blue, light
green (with a trace of blue), brilliant yellow, and
ivory. A vigorous marketing campaign took place
between 1939 and 1943. In mid 1937 turquoise
was added; red was removed in 1943 because of
the war effort and did not reappear until 1959. In
1951 light green, dark blue, and ivory were retired
and forest green, rose, chartreuse, and gray were
added to the line. Other color changes took place
in the late 1950s, including the addition of a medium green.

Fiesta ware was redesigned in 1969 and discontinued in 1972–73. In 1986 Fiesta was reintroduced
by the Homer Laughlin China Company. The new
china body shrinks more than the old semivitreous
and ironstone pieces, thus making the new pieces
slightly smaller than the earlier pieces. The modern
colors are also different in tone or hue. The cobalt
blue is darker than the old blue. Other modern
colors are black, white, apricot, and rose.

References: Linda D. Farmer, *The Farmer's
Wife Fiesta Inventory and Price Guide,* published
by author, 1984; Sharon and Bob Huxford, *The
Collector's Encyclopedia of Fiesta, Revised Seventh Edition,* Collector Books, 1992; Dana G. Morykan and Harry L. Rinker, *Warman's Country Antiques & Collectibles, Second Edition,* Wallace–
Homestead, 1994.

Periodical: *Fiesta Collector's Quarterly,* 19238
Dorchester Circle, Strongsville, OH 44136.

Reproduction Alert.

Additional Listings: See *Warman's Americana
& Collectibles* for more examples.

Ashtray
Red	35.00
Yellow	25.00

Carafe, cov, yellow, 10" h, $110.00.

Bowl
4¾″ d, light green 15.00
5½″ d, fruit
    Light Green 15.00
    Yellow 18.00
6″ d, dessert
    Gray 50.00
    Light Green 22.00
    Turquoise 50.00
8½″ d, cobalt blue 30.00
Cake Plate, yellow, Kitchen Kraft ... 30.00
Candlesticks, pr
    Pink, tripod 85.00
    Yellow, tripod 415.00
Carafe, yellow 115.00
Casserole, cov, 8½″ d, Kitchen Kraft
    Light Green 40.00
    Turquoise 90.00
    Yellow 200.00
Chop Plate, 13″ d
    Cobalt Blue 50.00
    Light Green 20.00
    Turquoise 20.00
    Yellow 35.00
Coffeepot, cov
    Ivory 90.00
    Turquoise 135.00
Compote, 12″ d
    Cobalt Blue 135.00
    Turquoise 110.00
Creamer
    Ivory, side handle 15.00
    Red, stick handle 16.00
Cream Soup
    Cobalt Blue, cov 35.00
    Red 40.00
    Turquoise 35.00
    Yellow 30.00
Demitasse Cup and Saucer, cobalt blue 50.00
Eggcup
    Cobalt Blue 35.00
    Light Green 30.00
Gravy Boat
    Cobalt Blue 50.00
    Green 20.00
    Light Blue 35.00
Grill Plate
    10½″ d, cobalt blue 40.00
    12″ d, yellow 30.00
Jug
    Cobalt Blue, two pint 75.00
    Green, cov, Kitchen Kraft ... 170.00
Juice Pitcher, yellow 32.00
Juice Tumbler
    Cobalt Blue 30.00
    Green 15.00
    Rose 35.00
Marmalade
    Green 150.00
    Turquoise 160.00
Mixing Bowl
    #1, turquoise 95.00

#3, ivory 65.00
#5, cobalt blue 85.00
#7, green 150.00
Mug, rose 40.00
Mustard, cov
    Light Green 50.00
    Red 145.00
Nappy
    8½″ d, red 32.00
    9½″ d, cobalt blue 60.00
Pie Baker, green, Kitchen Kraft 35.00
Pitcher, red, disc 145.00
Plate
6″ d
    Ivory 6.00
    Rose 9.00
    Turquoise 5.00
7″ d
    Gray 10.00
    Yellow 7.00
9″ d
    Cobalt Blue 18.00
    Dark Green 10.00
    Red 12.50
Platter
    12″ l, oval, medium green 45.00
    15″ d, red 55.00
Refrigerator Dish, cov, round, green,
    Kitchen Kraft. 25.00
Salt and Pepper Shakers, pr
    Dark Green 40.00
    Red, Kitchen Kraft 75.00
Sauce Boat, chartreuse 55.00
Saucer, cobalt blue 4.00
Sugar, cov, cobalt blue 25.00
Syrup, ivory 195.00
Teacup and Saucer, chartreuse 35.00
Teapot, red, large, pinpoint flake on rim 100.00
Tray, figure 8, cobalt blue 55.00
Tumbler
    Cobalt Blue 40.00
    Red 55.00
Vase
    8″ h, turquoise 300.00
    10″ h, cobalt blue 500.00

FIGURAL BOTTLES

History: Figural bottles, made of porcelain either in glaze or bisque form, achieved popularity in the late 1800s and remained popular to the 1930s. The majority of figural bottles were made in Germany, with Austria and Japan accounting for the balance. They averaged in size from three to eight inches.

Figural bottles were shipped to the United States empty and filled upon arrival. They were then given away to customers by brothels, dance halls, hotels, liquor stores, and taverns. Some were lettered with the names and addresses of the establishment; others had paper labels. Many were used for holidays, such as Christmas and New Year's Day.

Figural bottles also were made in glass and other materials. The glass bottles held perfumes, foods, or beverages.

References: Ralph and Terry Kovel, *The Kovels' Bottle Price List, 9th Edition,* Crown Publishers, 1992; Otha D. Wearin, *Statues That Pour,* Wallace–Homestead, 1965, out of print.

Periodicals: *Antique Bottle And Glass Collector,* PO Box 187, East Greenville, PA 18041; *Bottles & Extras,* PO Box 154, Happy Camp, CA 96039.

Collectors' Clubs: Federation of Historical Bottle Clubs, 14521 Atlantic Ave., Riverdale, IL 60627; New England Antique Bottle Club, 120 Commonwealth Rd., Lynn, MA 01904.

Museums: National Bottle Museum, Ballston Spa, NY; National Bottle Museum, Barnsley, S. Yorkshire, England.

Owl, transparent orange glass, painted face and feet, 8″ h, $60.00.

GLASS

Acorn, 2¾″ h, clear	25.00
Barrel, 9¾″ h, sapphire blue	750.00
Bear, aqua, applied facial details	35.00
Clock, 4½″ d, 5″ h, clear, paper dial under glass, metal cap, marked "US"	85.00
Dice, milk glass	250.00
Dog, 10″ h, amber	32.00
Eiffel Tower, 14¾″ h, clear, pontil	55.00
Fish, 6″ h, amber	30.00
Girl, 4¼″ h, reading book, milk glass	150.00
Grant's Tomb, 11⅛″ h, milk glass, metal bust of Grant	300.00
John Bull, 11⅜″ h, golden amber	225.00
Kummel Bear, 11″ h, black amethyst	55.00
Monkey, 4½″ h, sitting, milk glass	145.00
Monument, 5⅛″ h, purple tint	15.00

Moses, 11″ h, honey amber, Poland Springs Water	85.00
Oyster, clear, screw cap, ground lip	50.00
Parrot, 8″ h, opaque white	55.00
Pineapple, 8½″ h, deep olive yellow, iron pontil, W & Co, NY	550.00
Santa Claus, 12¼″ h, clear, sq collared mouth	125.00
Shoe, 3½″ h, black amethyst	50.00
Violin, 10″ h, light green	12.00

POTTERY AND PORCELAIN

Book, 10¾″ h, brown and cream glaze	300.00
Dog, 9″ h, sitting, tan and white, Germany	20.00
Camel, 4″ h, mother–of–pearl glaze, stopper	35.00
Fox, reading book, beige, brown mottled dec	45.00
Mermaid, 7¾″ h, brown glaze	80.00
Monkey, 5½″ h, olive green glaze	75.00
Pig	
6½″ h, tan glaze, 1850–80	220.00
7″ h, "We Trust G A R," salt glazed, blue slip	245.00
Pretzel, brown	30.00
Skeleton, 8″ h, brown and white glaze, marked "Poison," stopper	90.00
Wolf, 4⅞″ h, sitting reading book, brown/beige glaze, marked "Germany"	55.00
Woman, 8¾″ h, Rockingham type glaze	150.00

FINDLAY ONYX GLASS

History: Findlay onyx glass, produced by Dalzell, Gilmore and Leighton Company, Findlay, Ohio, was patented in 1889 for the firm by George W. Leighton. Due to high production costs resulting from a complex manufacturing process, the glass was made only for a short time.

Layers of glass were plated to a bulb of opalescent glass through repeated dippings into a glass pot. Each layer was cooled and reheated to develop opalescent qualities. A pattern mold then was used to produce raised decorations of flowers and leaves. A second mold gave the glass bulb its full shape and form.

A platinum luster paint, producing pieces identified as silver or platinum onyx, was applied to the raised decorations. The color was fixed in a muffle kiln. Other colors, such as cinnamon, cranberry, cream, raspberry, and rose, were achieved by using an outer glass plating which reacted strongly to reheating. For example, a purple or orchid color came from the addition of manganese and cobalt to the glass mixture.

Reference: James Measell and Don E. Smith, *Findlay Glass: The Glass Tableware Manufacturers, 1886–1902,* Antique Publications, 1986.

Collectors' Club: Collectors of Findlay Glass, PO Box 256, Findlay, OH 45839.

Bowl, 7½" d, rose	425.00
Celery, 6" h, cream	265.00
Creamer, 4½" h, raspberry	275.00
Dresser Box, cov, 5" d, cream	650.00

Spoon Holder, tulip, daisy, and thistle motif, cinnamon ground, 4¼" h, $650.00.

Mustard, cov, raspberry	550.00
Pitcher, 8" h, amber florals and handle, minor bubbles in inner liner	660.00
Spooner, cream, platinum blossoms	265.00
Sugar Shaker, 5½" h, raspberry	350.00
Syrup, cov, cream, hinged metal thumb lift lid, applied opalescent handle.	450.00
Toothpick, 2½" h, cinnamon	400.00

FINE ARTS

Notes: There is no way a listing of a hundred paintings or less can accurately represent the breadth and depth of the examples sold over the last year. To attempt to make such a list would be ludicrous.

In any calendar year, tens if not hundreds of thousands of paintings are sold. Prices range from a few dollars to millions. Since each painting is essentially a unique creation, it is difficult to establish comparables.

An essential purpose of *Warman's Antiques and Their Prices* is to assist its users in finding information about a category, so this "Fine Arts" introduction has been written primarily to identify the reference books that you will need to find out more about a painting in your possession.

Artist Dictionaries: Emmanuel Benezit, *Dictionnaire Critique et Documentaire des Peintres, Sculpteurs, Dessinateurs et Graveurs*, 10 volumes, Third Edition, Grund, 1976; Peter Hastings Falk, *Dictionary of Signatures & Monograms of American Artists*, Sound View Press, 1988; Mantle Fielding, *Dictionary of American Painters, Sculptors and En-*gravers, Apollo Books, 1983; J. Johnson and A. Greutzner, *Dictionary of British Artists, 1880–1940: An Antique Collector's Club Research Project Listing 41,000 Artists*, Antique Collector's Club, 1976; Les Krantz, *American Artists*, Facts on File, 1985.

Introduction: Alan Bamberger, *Buy Art Smart*, Wallace–Homestead Book Company, 1990; Alan S. Bamberger, *How To Buy Fine Art You Can Afford*, Wallace–Homestead, 1994.

Price Guide References, Basic: *Art At Auction in America, 1993 Edition*, Krexpress, 1993; William T. Currier (comp.), *Currier's Price Guide To American Artists 1645–1945 at Auction, Fifth Edition*, Currier Publications, 1991; William T. Currier (comp.), *Currier's Price Guide To European Artists 1545–1945 at Auction, Third Edition*, Currier Publications, 1991; Huxford's *Fine Art Value Guide*, Vol. II (1991), Vol. III (1992), Collector Books; Rosemary and Michael McKittrick, *The Official Price Guide To Fine Art, Second Edition*, House of Collectibles, 1993; Susan Theran, *Fine Art: Identification and Price Guide, Second Edition*, Avon Books, 1992.

Price Guide References, Advanced: Peter Hastings Falk (ed.), *Art Price Index International '94*, Sound View Press, 1993; Richard Hislop (ed.), *The Annual Art Sales Index*, Weybridge, Surrey, England, Art Sales Index, since 1969; Enrique Mayer, *International Auction Record: Engravings, Drawings, Watercolors, Paintings, Sculpture*, Paris, Editions Enrique Mayer, since 1967; Judith and Martin Miller (comps. and eds.), *Miller's Picture Price Guide, 1993, Vol. I*, Millers Publications, 1993; Susan Theran (ed.), *Leonard's Price Index of Art Auctions*, Auction Index, since 1980.

Museum Directories: *American Art Directory*, R. R. Bowker Co.; American Association of Museums, *The Official Museum Directory: United States and Canada*, updated periodically.

FIREARM ACCESSORIES

History: Muzzle-loading weapons of the 18th and early 19th centuries varied in caliber and required the owner to carry a variety of equipment with him, including a powder horn or flask, patches, flints or percussion caps, bullets, and bullet molds. In addition, military personnel were responsible for bayonets, slings, and miscellaneous cleaning equipment and spare parts.

In the mid 19th century, cartridge weapons replaced their black powder ancestors. Collectors seek anything associated with early ammunition, from the cartridges themselves to advertising material. Handling old ammunition can be extremely dangerous due to the decomposition of compounds. Seek advice from an experienced collector before becoming involved in this area.

Military-related firearm accessories generally are worth more than their civilian counterparts. See "Militaria" for additional listings.

References: John Delph, *Firearms and Tackle Memorabilia,* Schiffer Publishing, 1991; Jim and Vivian Karsnitz, *Sporting Collectibles,* Schiffer Publishing, 1992.

Reproduction Alert: The amount of reproduction and fake powder horns is large. Be very cautious!

Canteen, painted, cheesebox style, dark red paint overall, one side painted in gold with a large primitive eagle with shield breast, the top of the shield red with cream lettering "No. 37", the other side painted in gold letters "Lt Rufus Cook," pewter nozzle, square nail construction, 7" d, 2⅝" deep, strap loops missing **1,600.00**

Cartridge Belt

   Civilian, American, early 19th C, 15" long pouch with 25 tin cylinders for paper cartridges, pouch mounted on the inside of the 2½" leather belt, pouch flap fits over the belt when tied, a vent prick and brass chain tied to the small simple buckle. . . . **500.00**

   Military, belt and plate, Kerksis #160, embossed with 5 pointed star, spread winged eagle, etc., on the orig tan Moroccan leather belt, shoulder strap and frog for sword, strong traces of light gilt finish to plate, forward suspension for the frog restitched, faint gold embossing at edges **200.00**

Cartridge Boxes

   Hall & Hubbard, .22 Caliber, green and black label, "100 No.½ 2–100/ PISTOL CARTRIDGES," 3⅞ x 2 x 1", cov with molted cream and black paper, empty, missing about half green side label **$300.00**

   Phoenix Metallic Cartridge Co., early green and black label, "50 CARTRIDGES/32–100 CALIBER LONG," 3⅞ x 2⅛ x 1¼", opened but full, three–quarter raised "P" headstamped cartridges **250.00**

   Smith, Hall & Farmer, .22 Caliber, green and black label, large view of Smith & Wesson 1st Model 2nd Issue, "100 No. 1 PISTOL CARTRIDGES...Successors to SMITH & WESSON in the manufacture of Cartridges," 3⅞ x 1⅞ x ¹³⁄₁₆", cov with marbled paper, empty, light age. **400.00**

   Union Metallic Cartridge Company .32 Caliber, cream and black label "FIFTY .32 CALIBER/No. 2/PISTOL CARTRIDGES," engraving of Smith & Wesson 1st Model 3rd Issue, 4 x 2⅛ x 1¼", checkered covering, orange and black side labels, unopened **200.00**

   .32–100 Short, orange and black label, "FIFTY No. 2 or 32–100 SHORT," large illus of Smith & Wesson 1st Model 2nd Issue, 4 x 2 x 1", checkered wrapping, opened but full, missing about 20% of the side label. **275.00**

   Winchester, .32 Caliber, green and black label, "50 No. 32/Extra Short" and "FOR REMINGTON RIDER PISTOL," opened, missing some cartridges **375.00**

Epaulets, pr, military, gilt, officer, large "MASSACHUSETTS" buttons with standing Indian warrior, orig purple carton with green edging, orig label "MILITIA ESTABLISHMENT/BENT & BUSH/BOSTON". **250.00**

Flask, Powder

   Brass, 7⅝" l, threaded brass top marked "A.M. FLASK & CAP Co.," fitted with four carrying rings, orig green carrying cord, brass body emb on one side with crossed revolvers, stars, eagle with shield breast, cannon with large American flag to each side, ground with various military weapons and accessories, missing spout screw, body with 90% orig dark lacquer **450.00**

   Copper, Colt Dragoon flask, emb on both sides with stand of flags over crossed rifles and crossed pistols, "COLTS PATENT" in ribbon below, cover for the balls compartment stamped "COLTS PATENT," the top inspected "WAT" and "K", the dispensing nozzle stamped "35/ Grs," missing one of the three screws that holds the top to the body, strong traces of orig gold colored lacquer, retains 40 to 50% of orig dark lacquer finish **500.00**

   Iron, military, 10¼" l, turned wooden plug for spout, body made of molded or stamped sheet iron with rolled over seam and two steel carrying rings on each side, orig black paint, complete with orig carrying cord, early 19th C. **75.00**

Flask, Shot, leather

   7" l, black pigskin body stamped "SYKES/EXTRA/lb/1," fitted with carrying ring, 2" German silver top with bright steel dispenser stamped "SYKES EXTRA". **70.00**

   8½" l, emb on both sides with a Highland scene showing a Scottish hunter alongside a fallen stag with 2 hounds, brass top **50.00**

Gorget, British, engraved with the Royal
Cipher over large "GR," 1790–1820 . **275.00**
Holster, Western, Colt Action Holster,
tooled dec along borders on both
sides, brown leather **125.00**

Powder Horn, scrimshaw, eagle, man with pipe, dog, and deer, 1858, 8½" l, $200.00.

Horn, Powder
10½" l, orig oak spout plug carved in
the shape of an eagle's head, plain
wood base fitted with a large brass
stud, body with raised carving of a
large eagle, an Indian Head, grape
vines, a flying pheasant, the American shield, flowers, and the name
"Paul/Bohret," late 19th C **300.00**
11" l, spout carved with a faceted pattern ending in scallops, scalloped
pattern repeated about ⅓ down toward pine base, body engraved
with 2 pecking chickens and a large
marine scene showing a 3 masted
warship flying the English flag plus
2 smaller large boats and 2 row-
boats with a man in each, the carving primitive but well done, base
with a brass button for carrying
cord, c1800 with nice age patination **400.00**
14¼" l, engraved, nearly entire surface cov with floral designs along
with fish, bird, and animal, long
panel outlined with a ropelike border engraved "JAMES BOUING
1756," neat scalloping just before
the recessed portion 3½" from the
spout, wooden stopper, flat pine
plug with period brass carrying ring,
base rim originally drilled with 2
holes for carrying cord, rim of horn
and plug chipped during use **3,250.00**
16" l, King George's War style, engraved, inscribed "JAMES

WAUGHT/HIS HORN Sye:11:1748"
in two ribbon banners with fancy
shaded letters, much geometric and
floral engraving, stag with "A BU/
CK" below, a doe with "DO" below,
the name "WILLIAM" in shaded letters, also inscribed "Ebenezer
Woods of Groton October ye 7
1748" all with a fine line beneath,
below this the numbers 1 through
12, flat pine plug with copper carrying ring, raised ring carved 3" from
spout, rim of horn at base drilled
with 2 net holes and bottom for a
carrying cord during use **5,500.00**
Powder Keg, 9¼" h, 6¼" d, wood, stan-
dard construction, wooden plugged
end with black painted number 56,
3¼" black and white "ORIENTAL
POWDER MILLS" label, plus 2"
"EASTERN SPORTING FFG GUN-
POWDER," the other end with 5"
"ORIENTAL POWDER MILLS BOS-
TON FF WESTERN SPORTING
POWDER G" purple and gold label,
orig wooden screw plug with slight
chips **500.00**
Target Ball, Bogardus, approx. 2¾" d,
molded, amber glass, surface with
overall net pattern, bottom with raised
sunburst pattern, middle with a ½"
band "BOGARDUS GLASS BALL
PATd APRIL '10 1877," unusual chips
at neck **200.00**
Uniform Button Mold, 9" l, brass, Amer-
ican, 18th C, casting 6 round buttons
with central raised letter "I" for infantry, one 25mm, one 18mm, and four
14.5mm d, the casting each including
the eyelet, wooden handles missing . **550.00**
Water Can, military, American, late 19th
C, tinned, 13" h with the folding handle
upright, 17" overall to tip of spout
which has holder for cup or glass on
each side, painted a dark maroon
overall with tan–yellow striping, one
side lettered "N.H.N.G.," the other
"Co. H," some chipping of paint, about
80 to 85% remaining **425.00**
Water Keg, 9 x 7½ x 9", wooden, Amer-
ican, late 18th or early 19th C, oval
cross section with flattened bottom,
held together by two Shaker style
wide tongued wooden straps, large
hand forged nail on each end for car-
rying cord, orig wood stopper **350.00**

FIREARMS

History: The 15th-century Matchlock Harque-
bus was the forerunner of the modern firearm. The

Germans refined the wheelock firing mechanism during the 16th and 17th centuries. English settlers arrived in America with the smoothbore musket; German settlers had rifled arms. Both used the new flintlock firing mechanism.

A major advance was achieved when Whitney introduced interchangeable parts into the manufacturing of rifles. The warfare of the 19th century brought continued refinements in firearms. The percussion ignition system was developed by the 1840s. Minie, a French military officer, produced a viable projectile. By the end of the 19th century cartridge weapons dominated the field.

Two factors control the pricing of firearms—condition and rarity. The value of any particular antique firearm covers a very wide range. For instance, a Colt 1849 pocket model revolver with a 5″ barrel can be priced from $100 to $700, depending on whether or not all the component parts are original, whether some are missing, how much of the original finish (bluing) remains on the barrel and frame, how much silver plating remains on the brass trigger guard and back strap, and the condition and finish of the walnut grips. Be careful to note any weapon's negative qualities. A Colt Paterson belt revolver in fair condition will command a much higher price than the Colt pocket model in very fine condition. Know the production run of a firearm before buying it.

References: Ralf Coykendall, Jr., *Coykendall's Second Sporting Collectibles Price Guide*, Lyons and Burford, 1992; Ralf Coykendall, Jr., *Coykendall's Sporting Collectilbes Price Guide*, Lyons and Burford, 1991; Norman Flayderman, *Flayderman's Guide To Antique American Firearms And Their Values, Fifth Edition*, DBI Books, 1990; *Gun Trader's Guide, Fifteenth Edition*, Stoeger Publishing, 1992; Joseph Kindig, Jr., *Thoughts On The Kentucky Rifle In Its Golden Age*, 1960, available in reprint; Russell and Steve Quetermous, *Modern Guns Identification & Values, Revised Ninth Edition*, Collector Books, 1993; L. Gordon Stetser, Jr., *The Compleat Muzzleloader*, Mountain Press, 1992; Paul Wahl (comp.), *Paul Wahl's Big Gun Catalog, Volume One, A to L*, Paul Wahl Corporation, 1988; Paul Wahl (comp.), *Paul Wahl's Big Gun Catalog, Volume Two, M to Z*, Paul Wahl Corporation, 1988; Frederick Wilkinson, *Handguns: A Collector's Guide To Pistols And Revolvers From 1850 To The Present*, New Burlington Books, 1993.

Periodicals: *Gun List*, 700 E. State Street, Iola, WI 54990; *Gun Tests*, PO Box 2626, Greenwich, CT 06836–2626; *Historic Weapons & Relics*, 2650 Palmyra Rd., Palmyra, TN 37142; *Man at Arms*, PO Box 460, Lincoln, RI 02865; *Sporting Gun*, PO Box 301369, Escondido, CA 92030–9957; *The Gun Report*, PO Box 38, Aledo, IL 61231.

Collectors' Clubs: American Society of Military History, Los Angeles Patriotic Hall, 1816 S. Figuerora, Los Angeles, CA 90015; Winchester Arms Collectors Assoc., Inc., PO Box 6754, Great Falls, MT 59406.

Museums: Battlefield Military Museum, Gettysburg, PA; National Firearms Museum, Washington, D.C.; Remington Gun Museum, Ilion, NY.

Colt Model 1855, Sidehammer Pocket Revolver, Model 3A, .31 caliber, 3½″ octagonal barrel, walnut grips, $485.00.

FLINTLOCK PISTOLS—SINGLE SHOT

English, East India Co, military, 9″ barrel, London proofs, 15¾″ overall, captive ramrod, lock stamped "Crown/S" and with standing lion mark of East India Company, walnut full stock with heavy brass mounts, forend missing 1¾ x ½″ chip of wood broken out by ramrod, tip of forend and brass forend cap repaired **325.00**

English, officer's pistol, .64 caliber, smoothbore, octagonal barrel with London proofs, 14½″ overall, beveled lock with sliding half cock safety, sgd "S. Wallis," lightly engraved steel trigger guard, plain walnut stock with shield shape silver wrist escutcheon, full stock with shield shape silver wrist escutcheon, barrel rebrowned **500.00**

English, pistol, 2½″ screw–off barrel with London proofs, 6¾″ overall, iron box-lock frame sgd "Saunder" and "Liverpool," typical slab walnut grip. **400.00**

Kentucky, .45 caliber, 9½″ octagonal barrel, unmarked, fitted with open sights, 14¼″ overall, lockplate with roller frizzen spring and goose neck hammer with some light engraved decoration, sgd "JOHN WALKER/ WARRANTED," full stock with applied trigger strips, orig heavy reddish varnish finish with brass mounts, plain forend cap, 2 faceted ramrod pipes, two engraved escutcheons for the lockplate screws, trigger guard with simple engraved pineapple finial and engraved bow, stock dec with several silver inlays. **8,650.00**

Kentucky, 10″ octagonal iron barrel, .48 caliber, full curly maple stock with brass forend cap, brass trigger guard and ramrod pipes, lock marked "Ashmore/Warranted". **3,000.00**

New York State Militia, .50 caliber, 9″ octaglon Birmingham proved brass barrel, smoothbore, engraved "ALBANY" on top flat, 15″ overall, engraved locked sgd "POND & CO.," full stock with lightly engraved brass mounts, barrel key escutcheon possibly old pewter replacement, stock broken from trigger to rear of barrel, poor repair, antique brass tipped ramrod a short replacement. **700.00**

U.S. Model 1808, Navy, Simeon North, Berlin, CT, c1808–10, 10⅛″ round barrel, .64 caliber, smoothbore, unmarked barrel, lock marked with spread eagle above U. STATES ahead of hammer and vertically at rear S. NORTH/BERLIN/CON., hickory ramrod with swelled tip, full walnut stock, pin–fastened, iron belt hook attached to left side of stock **3,000.00**

U.S. Model 1813, Army and Navy, Simeon North, CT, c1813–15, 9¹⁄₁₆″ round barrel, .69 caliber, smoothbore, breech of barrel marked P/US on left side and inspector marking H.H.P. above touchhole, lock marked ahead of hammer S. NORTH over an American eagle motif with letters U and S at either side over bottom line MIDLN CON., hickory ramrod with swelled tip at one end and metal ferrule at other, iron mountings **2,400.00**

U.S. Model 1819, Simeon North, Middletown, CT, c1819–23, 10″ round barrel, .54 caliber, smoothbore, barrel marked at breech J/P/US, lock marked ahead of hammer S. NORTH over American eagle and shield motif with letters U and S at either side over bottom line MIDLTN CONN., date of production marked at rear of lock below safety bolt, swivel type ramrod, iron mountings, sliding safety bolt, brass blade front sight, oval shape rear sight on tang **1,000.00**

PERCUSSION PISTOLS—SINGLE SHOT

Note: Conversion of flintlock pistols to percussion was common practice. Most English and U.S. military flintlock pistols listed above can be found in percussion. Values for these percussion-converted pistols are from 40 to 60% of the flintlock values as given.

Clement, underhammer pistol, .36 caliber, 7¾″ half round barrel, stamped "Wm T. CLEMENT/GREENFIELD/MASS./CAST STEEL," walnut grip with small silver escutcheon on each side, grip with old glued break **400.00**

Elgin Cutlass Pistol, Morrill, Mosman & Blair, Amherst, MA, 4″ round barrel rifled with six grooves, .34 caliber, a bowie blade 10″ long and 1½″ wide fastened to the barrel and etched with a vase containing fruit surmounted by "ELGIN'S PATENT" in script in a rect and an eagle holding a pennant in his beak (right), vase containing fruit surmounted by "Morill/Mosman/& Blair/Amherst Mass" and eagle holding pennant in beak (left), leather scabbard **3,000.00**

English, pair, .60 caliber, 10″ octagonal barrel, smoothbore, 2 gold bands at breach, sunken gold maker's stamp "T. KETLAND/& Co/LONDON," finely engraved lock with same maker's mark, period conversion to percussion, engraved silver forend caps, silver barrel key plates, opposite locks inlaid a small silver rectangle, engraved steel trigger guards, butt caps engraved "J. Read/US Marines" (commissioned a 2nd Lt. in U.S. Marines in 1848, later resigned and became Captain in C.S. Marine Corps), straight walnut stocks, checkered, ramrods replaced **5,000.00**

European, target pistols, pair, .50 caliber, deeply rifled, 9½″ octagonal watered steel barrels, Crown "V" proofed and inlaid in silver "l.h.DAMM in ELBERFELD," blade front sights, adjustable rear sights on profusely engraved tang, profusely engraved back action locks, engraved steel butt caps and trigger guards, single set trigger, grained burl walnut stocks, checkered wrists, engraved steel sideplate **3,500.00**

U.S. Model 1842, Henry Aston, Middletown, CT (also by Ira N. Johnson of Middletown, CT, and Palmeto Armory of Columbia, SC), c1845–52, 8½″ round barrel, .54 caliber, smoothbore, proof stamps on breech of barrel beneath which are inspector's initials, date stamping on barrel tang, lockplate marked US/H. ASTON forward of hammer, marked vertically at rear MIDDTN/CONN., swivel type steel

ramrod, all brass mountings, brass
blade front sight **650.00**

Waters, Single Shot, A. H. Waters & Co.,
Millbury, MA, mid 1840s to 1849,
round barrel, .54 caliber, smoothbore,
flat flush fitted lockplate, marked "A.
H. WATERS & Co./MILLBURY
MASS." in center of lock, side lug nipple, iron furniture, brass blade front
sight, oval shape rear sight on tang. . **500.00**

PERCUSSION PISTOLS—MULTISHOT

Colt
Dragoon, Second Model, 7½″ part
round, part octagonal barrel, .44
caliber, 6 shot, barrel stamped "AD-
DRESS SAML COLT NEW–YORK.
COLT'S/PATENT" with "U.S." centered beneath, one piece walnut
grip, squareback trigger guard and
rect cylinder stop slots, Texas
Ranger and Indian fight scene roll
engraved on cylinders **4,500.00**

Navy, Model 1861, 7½″ round barrel,
.36 caliber, 6 shot, creeping style
loading lever, barrel stamped AD-
DRESS COL. SAML COLT NEW–
YORK, U.S. AMERICA–.36 CAL,"
cylinder roll scene depicts battle between Texas Navy and that of Mex-
ico, one piece walnut grip **1,400.00**

Pocket, Model 1849, barrel lengths of
3″, 4″, 5″, and 6″, .31 caliber, 5 or 6
shot, octagonal barrel with attached
loading lever, barrel stamped "AD-
DRESS COL SAML COLT NEW–
YORK U.S. AMERICA," cylinder
engraved with stagecoach holdup
scene, round trigger guard, walnut
grips **675.00**

Remington
Belt, New Model, 6½″ octagonal barrel, .36 caliber, 6 shot, barrel
stamped "PATENTED SEPT. 14,
1856/E. REMINGTON 7 SONS, IL-
ION, NEW YORK U.S.A./NEW
MODEL," round cylinder, threads
visible at breech end, safety
notches on cylinder shoulders be-
tween nipples **600.00**

Navy, 1861, 7⅜″ octagonal barrel, .36
caliber, 6 shot, barrel stamped
"PATENTED DEC 17, 1861/MAN-
UFACTURED BY REMINGTON'S
ILION, N.Y.," round cylinder, walnut
grips **650.00**

Remington–Beals 3rd Model Pocket
Revolver, cased, 4″ octagonal barrel, .31 caliber, 5 shot, barrel
stamped "BEAL'S PATENT 1856 7
57 758/MANUFACTURED BY

REMINGTON'S ILION, N.Y.," orig
cardboard box with brass bullet
mold, quantity of bullets, eagle and
shield flask, mushroom shape
cleaning rod with screw–in type extension, extra pawl spring, can of
Eley percussion caps **2,250.00**

Other
Deringer and Deringer Type
Deringer, Henry, Philadelphia, PA,
c1830–60, medium pocket
model, 3½″ barrel, .41 caliber,
barrel stamped "DERINGER/
PHILADELA," identical marking
appears on lockplate, checkered
walnut stock, German silver trigger guard and butt cap (Flayder-
man 7D–002) **800.00**

Robertson, Philadelphia, PA,
pocket, 4½″ barrel, approx. .41
caliber, barrel stamped "ROB-
ERTSON, PHILA.," forends have
double wedges and escutcheons
and double ramrod pipes (Flay-
derman 7D–022). **550.00**

Pepperboxes
Bacon, Thomas K., Norwich, CT,
c1852–58, 4″ ribbed barrel, .31
caliber, 6 shot, barrel stamped
"BACON & CO., NORWICH, CT"
and "CAST STEEL," single action, underhammer, engraved
nipple shield, blued finish, walnut
grips (Flayderman 7B–001) **350.00**

Pecare & Smith, Ten–Shot, Jacob
Pecare and Joseph Smith, NY,
late 1840s to early 1850s, 4″ barrel, .28 caliber, 10 shot barrel
cluster, dec scroll engraving on
frame and barrel shield, semicon-
cealed hammer visible from top,
trigger folds down, brass frame,
walnut grips (Flayderman 7B–
013). **1,750.00**

Stocking & Co, Worcester, MA, late
1840s to early 1850s, .31 caliber,
6″ barrel cluster, barrel stamped
"STOCKING & CO., WORCES-
TER" and "CAST STEEL WAR-
RANTED," dec scroll engraving
on iron frame and nipple shield,
trigger spur guard (Flayderman
7B–017). **350.00**

REVOLVERS (CARTRIDGE)

Colt
Bisby, .38 Colt caliber, Serial Number
30XXXX (1907 production), 7½″
barrel, Rampant Colt checkered
grips, 95% orig glassy blue finish on
barrel (Flayderman 5B–149) **3,200.00**

Remington, New Model, Navy Revolver, .44 caliber, $450.00.

Border Patrol Revolver, .357 Magnum, Serial Number J859XX, 4″ barrel, target sights, oversize checkered walnut "COLT" medallion grips, blued 250.00

Model 1911, Auto, Serial Number 55XXXX, "UNITED STATES PROPERTY" marking above no., orig commercial style blue finish rather than usual WWI pasty blue finish, checkered walnut grips, with "US" issue holster made by "GRATON & KNIGHT CO./1943". 650.00

Sheriff's Model, .45 caliber, Serial Number SA4XXXX, orig shipping carton, orig Colt Factory display case for the pistol and extra cylinder, orig tabs and papers 700.00

Woodsman, caliber .22LR, Serial Number 15XXXX, 4½″ barrel, 99.5% orig prewar blue finish, orig carton missing one–half of end label   550.00

Harrington & Richardson, blue Jacket No. 2, caliber .32RF, Serial Number 5XX, full factory engraved, deeper cuts highlighted with black paint or enamel, checkered hard rubber grips with head of dog at top, 99% plus orig nickel plate. 175.00

High Standard, Supermatic Trophy Auto, caliber .22LR, Serial Number 23XXXX, 7¼″ barrel, spare 5½″ barrel, orig foam plastic carton, blued, 99.9% brand new 450.00

Hopkins & Allen XL Navy, Serial Number 9XX, caliber .38RF, 6½″ round barrel, varnished grips, orig brown leather holster, leather flap replaced during period with a piece of black oil cloth, cylinder with 80% nickel, blued trigger and case colored hammer (Flayderman 8A–065) 550.00

Luger, Model S/42, 9mm caliber, chamber date 1937, Serial Number 6XXX, all matching except the magazine with correct aluminum base, Nazi Eagel proofs 600.00

Mauser, Banner Luger, 9mm caliber,

1942 chamber date, Serial Number 3XXX, all matching, orig issue black leather holster with spare matching magazine, slight wear on holster. . . .   1,450.00

Remington, Police Revolver, factory conversion to .38RF, Serial Number 4XXX, 3½″ barrel, nickel plated brass trigger guard, varnished walnut grips (Flayderman 5E–029) 1,000.00

Savage, Model 1917 Auto, caliber .32, Serial Number 25XXXX, visible spur type hammer, ten–shot magazine, 3¾″ barrel, dull blue–black finish, later production with model designation on left side of frame, 99% plus dull blue–black finish (Flayderman 8B–019). . .   200.00

Smith & Wesson

Model 1½ Old, Serial Number 10XXX, caliber .32RF, 5–shot nonfluted cylinder, rosewood grips, 80% orig blue, left grip missing a small chip at rim (Flayderman 5G–027) 350.00

Model 90–1, .32 S & W Long caliber, Serial Number H40XXX, 3″ barrel, holster.   200.00

32 Safety 1st Model DA, Serial Number 77XXX, caliber .32 S & W, 3″ barrel, 5–shot fluted cylinder, bottom of left grip stamped with number 6304, black hard rubber "S & W" grips, over 95% orig blue, only hints of bright wear at edge (Flayderman 5G–043) 100.00

38 Double Action Perfected, Serial Number 9XXX, caliber .38 S&W, 6″ barrel, 5–shot fluted cylinder, "S&W" checkered hard rubber grips, about mint with bright case colored trigger and hammer, blued release catch at top of frame, balance of steel parts with 99.9% orig nickel plate (Flayderman 5G–080)   300.00

Stevens Diamond Model, .22 caliber, Serial Number 47XXX, 6″ barrel, orig cardboard carton, cov with dark brown small diamond pattern lightly embossed in surface, orig black and gold end label (Flayderman 5H–016) 700.00

FLINTLOCK LONG ARMS

Concord Light Infantry Musket, .75 caliber, 42″ round barrel, stamped with various marks including "7,M,I" or "JH" plus several others that again were struck at angle, full stocked with brass mounts, a sheet silver Indian, Massassoit, inlaid on right side of butt, left side with silver eagle, both inlays surrounded by silver wire inlay, additional silver wire inlay at barrel tang, sideplate, silver shield to rear of lock screws, trigger guard marked "Concord Lt. Infantry," very good reconversion to flint. **3,750.00**

Kentucky, .48 caliber, 40½" three–inch part round and part octagonal barrel, sgd "JOHN RUP," 55½" overall, converted to percussion during period of use, engraved and scalloped patchbox with pierced and flowing C–scroll carving on both sides of cheekpiece, inlaid with a stylized engraved silver star, further extensive carving around tang and tailpipe, forward of trigger guard tangs with incised Indian head, engraved trigger guard bow, faceted ramrod pipes, 8 engraved silver pointed oval barrel key plates on each side of forend, engraved silver wrist escutcheon with script initials "H.J.," early 19th C **45,000.00**

Kentucky, .52 caliber, 45" part round barrel, unmarked, smoothbore, thick walls at muzzle probably rifled, full stock with 3 brass ramrod pipes, brass trigger guard, fine raised sideplate with beveled and scalloped edges, wide brass buttplate with faceting at top, brass patchbox, maple stock with simple carved area at wrist, simple raised carved scroll at barrel tang, late 18th C, flintlock period but not orig to piece, other minor restorations **1,800.00**

New England Flower, 53" barrel, unmarked, flat beveled lockplate signed in block letters "WHITE/& ELY," brass mounts including a raised oval wrist escutcheon, early Brown Bess style long tailed sideplate, full cherry stock, reconverted to flint using correct style original hammer, 41" of forend restored, right side of butt with long grain crack **1,250.00**

New England Flower, 54½" round barrel, .75 caliber, shallow raised rib running to the front sight and light engraved dec at breech and tang, lightly engraved flat beveled lockplate sgd "T. Earl," full cherry stock with brass mounts, cloud shape sideplate, ornate buttplate, orig flint, 4 ramrod pipes, broken at wrist, poor repair. **4,000.00**

U.S. Model 1803, Harpers Ferry Armory, later production, c1814–20, .54 caliber, single shot, muzzleloader, 33" part octagonal and part round 36" barrel, blade front sight, open rear sight, lock with integral forged iron flashpan with fence at rear, brass mountings, walnut half stock of 30½" with small cheekrest, brass patchbox on right side of butt (Flayderman 9A–114). . . **4,000.00**

U.S. Model 1808, Thomas French, Canton, MA, Contract Musket, Harpers Ferry pattern, tail of lock stamped "CANTON/1810," below the pan with the eagle and "US" over "FRENCH" (well struck with no trace of "T."), barrel stamped "US/V" with sunken eagle head CT proof (Flayderman 9A–131) **1,500.00**

U.S. Model 1819, Hall, breech loading, second production type, Harpers Ferry Armory, John Hall's patents, .52 caliber, single shot, 32⅝" round barrel, three barrel bands, breechblock deeply stamped "J. H. HALL/ H.FERRY/1836" (Flayderman (A– 249). **1,800.00**

PERCUSSION LONG ARMS

Note: Conversion of flintlock long arms to percussion was common practice. Most English, French, and U.S. military flintlock model long arms listed in the previous section can be found in percussion. Values for these percussion-converted long arms are from 40 to 60% of the flintlock values previously noted.

Kentucky, .40 caliber, 38¼" rifled octagonal barrel, sgd "G. KOPP," 53" overall, full stock with applied tiger stripes and brass mounts, forend cap, 3 ramrod pipes, trigger guard with double set triggers, long single screw sideplate with two small retaining screws, buttplate and toeplate, oval patchbox, cheekpiece with 2½" thin oval German silver inlay engraved with American Eagle, engraved orig percussion lock sgd "THE DAISY" within a banner, ramrod replaced with old cleaning rod. **1,200.00**

Tennessee Mountain Rifle, .50 caliber, 45½" heavy octagonal barrel, pinprick marking on top of flat "H 35," right flats cov with old sheet of copper at the nipple drum, old too small percussion lock appears to have been on gun for long time, full stock with pewter forend cap and two simple brass pipes, hand forged trigger guard with double set triggers, iron buttplate with brass toeplate, basic oval patchbox with inlaid German silver arrow in front, cheekrest with large crudely engraved German silver blossom, replaced ramrod, damage to forend of stock **600.00**

U.S. Model 1842, Springfield Armory, c1844–55, .69 caliber, single shot, muzzleloader, 42" round barrel, three barrel bands, lockplate stamped with American eagle motif above "US" forward of hammer, stamped vertically behind hammer "Springfield/1852," inspector initial cartouche stamped on left side of stock, steel ramrod with trumpet head, bayonet lug on bottom of barrel at muzzle, walnut stock with comb (Flayderman 9A–291) **800.00**

Model 1863, Rifle Musket, Type II (a.k.a. Model 1864), Springfield Armory, c1864–65, .58 caliber, single shot, muzzleloader, 40″ round barrel, three barrel bands, lock stamped with eagle motif to right of hammer, "U.S./ SPRINGFIELD" beneath nipple bolster, "1864" at angle at rear section of lock, single leaf rear sight, walnut stock (Flayderman 9A–341) **850.00**

RIFLES

Garand, Model M–1, made at Springfield Armory, near mint welded receiver, Elmer balance **300.00**

Griffin & Howe Rifle, .416 Rigby caliber, 26″ barrel engraved "No. 1954 GRIFFIN & HOWE INC. NEW YORK," ramp front sight, 3 leaf rear sight (50, 100, and 150 yards), "POLDI ANTI– CORRO" barrel with caliber marking "416 RIGBY," magnum square bridge Mauser action, walnut stock with checkered wrist and forend, large horn forend tip, orig swing swivels, cheekrest, orig rubber recoil pad. . . . **5,750.00**

Lee Enfield Carbine, .303 caliber, left side of receiver stamped "No 5MKI-ROF(F)5/45/N202," good to very good condition **200.00**

Marlin, Model 1893 Carbine, .32 Special caliber, 20″ barrel, 2 barrel bands, carbine style buttplate, no provision for saddle ring (Flayderman 5D–034). . . **400.00**

Mauser Commercial Sporter, 9.3 x .62 caliber, front of receiver checkered and with "MAUSER" banner, button release floor plate, grained orig Mauser stock missing buttplate. **500.00**

Remington

Hepburn, .40–.70 caliber, 28″ half round barrel with adjustable wind gauge peep front sight (period but not Remington), no provision for rear sight, tang with Long Range Remington sight missing the elevation screw, nickel plated Swiss buttplate (Flayderman 5E–105) . . . **900.00**

U.S. Model 1917, .30–.06 caliber, barrel stamped "R" over Ordnance bomb and "9–18," 99% plus orig blue **750.00**

Ruger, No. 1, .308 Winchester caliber,

mounted with a scope block, about new **500.00**

Winchester

Model 1892, .25–.20 caliber, 23″ round barrel, full magazine, checkered steel shotgun style buttplate, fitted with later sling swivels, barrel and tube with 98% orig blue (Flayderman 5K–075) **500.00**

Model 1894, Sample, Serial No. 12XXXX, .30 caliber, full factory scroll engraved, left side with a large panel showing a ram, the right with a stag, light scroll work at rear of round barrel, bit more on forend cap, deluxe varnished wood, checkered hard rubber shotgun buttplate, first shipped from warehouse on January 4, 1904, exhibited for 24 years **18,000.00**

SHOTGUNS

Beretta S–2, .12 gauge, 30″ barrels, vent rib, engraved action, single trigger, 14¼″ pull, rubber pad, Browning trunk case, slight handling marks only **1,800.00**

Beretta Silver Snipe, .20 gauge, top lever break open, box lock, hammerless, 30″ barrel, full choke, blued, nickel receiver, checkered walnut pistol grip stock and forearm. **350.00**

Fox Super Fox, .12 gauge, top lever break open, box lock, hammerless, double trigger, automatic ejector, 32″ double barrel, full choke, blued, checkered walnut pistol grip stock and forearm **450.00**

High Standard Flite–King Trophy, .410 gauge, hammerless, slide action, repeating, 5–shot tubular, 27″ barrel, adjustable choke, ventilated rib, blued, checkered wood, plain walnut semipistol grip stock and grooved slide handle **200.00**

Ithaca Model 37T (Trap), .16 gauge, hammerless, extended slide handle, repeating, 4–shot tubular, 26″ barrel, blued ventilated rib, trap stock, recoil pad **250.00**

Mauser Model 620, .12 gauge, top lever break open, box lock, hammerless, automatic ejectors, single trigger, 28″, over and under double barrel, modified and full choke, ribbed, blued, paint walnut pistol grip stock and forearm, recoil pad **750.00**

Noble Model 70, .410 gauge, hammerless, slide action, 5–shot tubular, 26″ barrel, full choke, blued, checkered walnut pistol grip stock and slide handle **175.00**

Parker Super Grade, .10 gauge, 32″
double barrels with standard address
on matted rib, action with very deeply
sculpted bolsters and totally covered
in extremely fine scroll engraving with
two small panel scenes on each side
and a small "PARKER BROS." with a
ribbon, bottom of action also with two
scenes, trigger guard with scene, barrel and water table stamped with "6,"
Parker skeleton type buttplate, light
pitting from poor storage, reblued . . . **3,000.00**

Remington Model 17, .20 gauge, hammerless, slide action, bottom ejection,
repeating, 3–shot tubular, 30″ steel
barrel, full bore, matted sighting
groove on receive, blued, plain walnut
pistol grip stock and forearm. **225.00**

J. P. Sauer & Son, 26″ double barrel,
ejector, bored ¾ choke and improved
cylinder, rib marked "Abercrombie &
Fitch Co., New York, N.Y. U.S.
Agents," double trigger, 14½″ pull,
prewar leather trunk case with clean-
ing tools **1,200.00**

FIREHOUSE COLLECTIBLES

History: The volunteer fire company has played
a vital role in the protection and social growth of
many towns and rural areas. Paid professional fire-
men usually are found only in large metropolitan
areas. Each fire company prided itself on equipment and uniforms. Conventions and parades gave
the fire companies a chance to show off their equipment. These events produced a wealth of fire-
house-related memorabilia.

References: Chuck Deluca, *Firehouse Memorabilia: A Collectors Reference,* Maritime Antique
Auctions, 1989; James Piatti, *Firehouse Memorabilia: Identification and Price Guide,* Avon Books,
1994; Mary Jane and James Piatti, *Firehouse Collectibles,* The Engine House, 1979.

Periodicals: *Fire Apparatus Journal,* PO Box
141205, Staten Island, NY 10314; *The Fire Mark
Circle of the Americas,* 2859 Marlin Dr., Chamblee,
GA 30341.

Collectors' Club: Fire Collectors Club, PO Box
992, Milwaukee, WI 53201.

Museums: American Museum of Fire Fighting,
Corton Falls, NY; Fire Museum of Maryland, Lu-
therville, MD; Hall of Flame, Scottsdale, AZ; Insurance Company of North America (INA) Museum,
Philadelphia, PA; New England Fire & History Museum, Brewster, MA; New York City Fire Museum,
Inc., New York, NY; Oklahoma State Fireman's Association Museum, Oklahoma City, OK; San Francisco Fire Dept. Memorial Museum, San Francisco,
CA.

Additional Listings: See *Warman's Americana
& Collectibles* for more examples.

Sheet Music, *The Midnight Fire Alarm,*
© 1907, 10½ x 13¼″, $15.00.

Alarm Box, Gamewell, 1880s **75.00**
Badge
  Bucks County, PA Fireman's Assoc,
    two goat heads **40.00**
  Newburgh, NY Fire Dept **75.00**
  Volunteer Fireman's Assoc, City of
    Brooklyn **55.00**
Bell, 11″ h, brass, iron back **100.00**
Belt, 52″ l, red, black, and white, marked
  "Director" **125.00**
Cake Board, 11″ l, carved wood, double
  sided, fireman sounding trumpet,
  floral medallions on reverse, sgd "PE
  Coon" **715.00**
Catalog, American La France No. 10,
  black and white photo illus **110.00**
Ephemera, invitation, hand colored en-
  graving on wove paper, Alert Eagle
  Fire Society Meeting, Boston, Feb 25,
  1800, sgd in plate "D Staniford Del"
  and "S. Hill SC 1800," sgd in ink "Daniel Staniford" as society secretary, 7⅝
  x 6½″, slight loss, discoloration, foxing **880.00**
Fire Bucket, leather
  11½″ h, J Card 1829, gilt letters, black
    ground, red band, New England,
    imperfections. **150.00**
  11¾″ h
    Jeffers Fire Society, Thomas Pike,
    Charlestown, 1807, old worn
    black paint, polychrome dec of
    eagle and banner, handle
    missing **300.00**

T Ropes 1807 No. 2, polychrome dec of clasping hands, name inscribed, craquelure, minor pigment loss **850.00**

12½" h, Amasa Breck 1835, paint dec, losses, imperfections **300.00**

13½" h
  N Lufkin Green St, name in black letters, green ground, varnished, losses to handle **900.00**
  W F Clob and E P Pike, 1829, gilt cornucopias and American eagle, handle **2,500.00**
  18" h, Waltham Fire Club 1824 Townsend, gilt lettering on black ground, red band, imperfections . . **360.00**

Fire Extinguisher
  Hazelton's High Pressure Chemical Fire Keg, 11½" h, amber glass, bail handle, c1890 . . . . **125.00**
  Red Comet, red, metal canister, red glass bulb **45.00**

Fire Mark
  4 x 5", tin, Sun of London, sun illus, gold lettering and illus, black ground **125.00**
  7¼ x 11½", oval, cast iron, hose and "F.A.," worn old green repaint **75.00**
  8 x 12", black, gold eagle and banner, marked "Eagle Ins Co Cin C" **950.00**

Helmet, oil cloth, blue, tin shield inscribed "Niagara 3 Brunswick," red underbrim, early 19th C **1,100.00**

Painting, *The Great Boston Fire*, Frederick A Shaw, oil on canvas, signed and dated "F Shaw/75" in lower right, period frame, 10¼ x 16" **935.00**

Parade Fire Hat, top hat style
  Composition, painted bust portrait of Thomas Jefferson, gilt bordered banners inscribed "Independent Hose Co" and "JH" in script on back, shield with initials "JH," 7½" h **8,250.00**
  Pressed felt, painted and gilt dec, gilt inscribed "South Work" and "FA," black ground, red brim, imperfections. **1,870.00**

Presentation Trumpet, 20½" h, silverplate, engraved "Presented to their Foreman E. P. Buffinten, Esq, by the members of the Niagara Fire Co, No. 4 of Fall River...," minor imperfections **1,540.00**

Print
  "Hunneman & Co., Builders, Boston, Mass, A Fire Engine," John H Bufford, lithographer, identified in the matrix, chromolithograph on paper, sheet size 17 x 23¾", framed **412.00**
  "Prairie Fires of the Great West," Currier and Ives, publishers, 1871, identified in inscriptions in lower margin, hand colored lithograph, sheet size 10 x 13¼", framed **715.00**

Sheet Music
  Quick Step, 1949, Diligent Hose Comp, hose cart, parade uniforms, stovepipe hats, Sarony litho **200.00**
  The Fireman's Heart Is Bold And Free, 1855, Sarony litho **150.00**

Sign, sheet metal, fire pumper shape, from steam fitter's shop in Worcester, MA, 36" l **550.00**

Toy, 31" l, hook and ladder truck, carved and painted wood, metal meetings, rubber tires, America, c1930, minor imperfections **880.00**

FIREPLACE EQUIPMENT

History: The fireplace was a gathering point in the colonial home for heat, meals, and social interaction. It maintained its dominant position until the introduction of central heating in the mid 19th century.

Because of the continued popularity of the fireplace, accessories still are manufactured, usually in an Early American motif.

References: Dana G. Morykan and Harry L. Rinker, *Warman's Country Antiques & Collectibles, Second Edition,* Wallace–Homestead, 1994; George C. Neumann, *Early American Antique Country Furnishings: Northeastern America, 1650–1880's,* L–W Book Sales, 1984, 1993 reprint.

Reproduction Alert: Modern blacksmiths are reproducing many old iron implements.

Additional Listings: Brass and Iron.

Kettle Stand, reticulated brass top, wrought iron base, turned wood handle, 12" h, $185.00

Andirons, pr
11½" h, brass, acorn finial, faceted plinth, spurred arched legs, penny feet, American, c1800. . . . . **440.00**
13½" h
  Bell metal, lemon finial, round plinth, slipper feet, American, 19th C **220.00**
  Wrought iron, goose neck finials, penny feet, old black repaint over rust **50.00**
15¼" h, brass and iron, ball finial, spurred legs, slipper feet, 19th C . . **200.00**
17" h, brass and iron, ball finial, slipper feet, American, 19th C **525.00**
18" h, brass, lemon finial, conforming log stops, American, early 19th C . **440.00**
19" h, wrought iron, knife blade, brass urn shaped finials, penny feet, old repairs **385.00**
20½" h, iron, goose neck, American **660.00**
Bellows
17" l, turtle back, brass nozzle, orig red paint, green, gold, black, and yellow stenciled and brushed fruit and foliage dec, worn old leather, back handle damaged **75.00**
17¾" l, orig red and black rosewood graining, yellow striping, gold and black stenciled border, yellow, green, gold, and black basket of stylized fruit and foliage, brass nozzle, some wear, old releathering . . **250.00**
Crane, 24" l, sawtooth trammel, primitive wrought iron **210.00**
Fire Fender Set, brass, Art Nouveau, European, c1900
  Mushroom finials, scrolling center design on linear 54" l x 12" h fire fender, matching tools **470.00**
  Scrolling dec, 19½" h andirons, 53¼" l fire fender, and matching tools. . . **1,100.00**
Fire Screen
  Copper, 18¼ x 28½" h, wrought-iron frame, center blue glazed ceramic insert, England, c1900 . . . . **330.00**
  Leaded Glass, 48½" w, 32" h, three panels, clear glass top, hammered white glass lower half, central applied Art Nouveau floral design, green bull's eye highlights. **2,750.00**
Fire Tongs, 15½" l, brass, dolphin head jaws. **55.00**
Fireside Broiler, 28" h, wrought iron, tripod base, penny feet, adjustable heart shaped rack with five sets of tines to hold small game, decorative diamond shaped rivet on sprint. **1,100.00**
Fireplace Crane, 26" l, wrought iron . . **100.00**
Jamb Hooks, brass, steeple top, England, early 19th C, price for pair . . . **440.00**

Kettle Shelf, 16½" h, hanging type, wrought iron, very pitted. **65.00**
Lighting Stand, 20½" h, wrought iron, primitive, tripod base, adjustable octagonal pan with candle socket, hanger finial, corner spouts, one foot old replacement **385.00**
Roaster, 30" l, screen mesh, wooden handle, tin lid, emb eagle **60.00**
Skewer, 11½" l, wrought iron, four twisted skewers. **150.00**
Skimmer, 25¼" l, wrought iron and brass, large flat bowl, shaped handle **182.00**
Spit Rack, 13½ x 19½", wrought iron, spike end, three hooks to adjust end of spit, good detail. **55.00**
Stove Plate, 25½" w, 23½" h, cast iron, H. W. Stiegel Foundry, stylized floral designs with hearts in double arch, emb "Henrich Wilhelm, Elisabeth Furnace," very pitted, crack in right side **225.00**
Toaster, 26" l, wrought iron, double jaws end in scrollwork, turned wooden handle **140.00**
Toasting Fork, adjustable, brass, weighted conical base, stamped "Patent No.—," dents in base. **165.00**
Trammel, sawtooth
  Brass, simple detail, adjusts from 18" l **305.00**
  Wrought Iron
    With grease lamp with four spouts, 15" h **330.00**
    With three prong hook at end, adjusts from 23" l **115.00**
Trivet
  Brass, 6½" d, octagonal, four short feet, engraved star design. **60.00**
  Wrought Iron, primitive, fork rest, pitted **95.00**
Wafer Iron, 26" l, round iron with lyre design, wrought-iron handles **80.00**

FISCHER J. BUDAPEST.

FISCHER CHINA

History: In 1893 Moritz Fischer founded his factory in Herend, Hungary, a center of porcelain production from the 1790s.

Confusion exists about Fischer china because of its resemblance to the wares of Meissen, Sevres, and Oriental export. It often was bought and sold as the product of these firms. Forged marks of other potteries are found on Herend pieces. The mark "MF," often joined, is the mark of Moritz Fischer's pottery.

Fischer's Herend is hardpaste ware with luminosity and exquisite decoration. Pieces are designated by pattern names, the best known being Chantilly Fruit, Rothschild Bird, Chinese Bouquet, Victoria Butterfly, and Parsley.

Fischer also made figural birds and animal groups, Magyar figures (individually and in groups), and Herend eagles poised for flight.

Reference: Susan and Al Bagdade, *Warman's English & Continental Pottery & Porcelain, Second Edition,* Wallace–Homestead, 1991.

Jar, cov, multicolored floral motif, white ground, raised relief medallions with reticulated fleur–de–lis, reticulated oval finial, 7¼″ h, $275.00.

Cachepot, 5″ h, Rothchild Bird pattern, handled	160.00
Charger, 13″ d, multicolored enamel floral dec, gold trim	325.00
Ewer	
7½″ h, enameled floral dec	200.00
16½″ h, reticulated body, rose, blue, green, and gold enamel floral dec .	275.00
Jar, cov, 7¼″ h, multicolored floral motif, raised relief medallions with reticulated fleur–de–lis, white ground, matching oval reticulated finial	250.00
Nappy, 4½″ w, triangular shape, Victoria Butterfly pattern, gold trim	125.00
Pitcher, 12″ h, reticulated, multicolored floral dec	285.00
Plate, 7½″ d, luncheon, Chantilly Fruit pattern	90.00
Sauce Boat, underplate, matching china ladle	
Parsley pattern	225.00
Victoria Butterfly pattern	250.00
Tureen, cov, 8½″ l, Chantilly Fruit pattern, natural molded fruit finial, handled	300.00

Urn, 12″ h, reticulated, blue floral dec, shield mark.	**325.00**
Vase	
8″ h, reticulated, blue flowers and green leaves, gold handles, shield mark.	**230.00**
10½″ h, reticulated, pink, blue, green, and white floral dec	**200.00**

FITZHUGH

History: Fitzhugh, one of the most recognized Chinese Export porcelain patterns, was named for the Fitzhugh family for whom the first dinner service was made. The peak period of production was from 1780 to 1850.

Fitzhugh features an oval center medallion or monogram surrounded by four groups of flowers or emblems. The border is similar to that on Nanking china. Occasional border variations are found. Butterfly and honeycomb are among the rarest.

Blue is the common color. Color is a key factor in pricing with rarity in ascending order of orange, green, sepia, mulberry, yellow, black, and gold. Combinations of colors are scarce.

Reference: Gloria and Robert Mascarelli, *Warman's Oriental Antiques,* Wallace–Homestead, 1992.

Reproduction Alert: Spode Porcelain Company, England, and Vista Alegre, Portugal, currently are producing copies of the Fitzhugh pattern. Oriental copies also are available.

Basket, 11″ l, oval, reticulated, handles, blue, matching undertray	1,500.00
Bowl	
6¼″ d, blue	200.00
10″ w, sq, blue	325.00
Brush Box, 7¾″ l, blue, China, imperfections	275.00
Creamer, 5½″ h, helmet shape, blue .	450.00
Cup and Saucer, blue, price for set of 6	350.00
Dish	
5⅛″ l, 5¼″ w, scallop shell shape, c1770.	275.00
7⅞″ d, sq shape, rounded corners, blue	600.00
9½″ d, sq, fluted, scalloped rim, blue	850.00
Garden Seat, 18¼″ h, hexagonal, blue	5,000.00
Gravy Boat, blue, plain sides	100.00
Jug, 12½″ h, blue	800.00
Pitcher	
7½″ h, blue	850.00
8½″ h, cov, blue	900.00
Plate, 10¼″ d, Armorial, unicorn crest, reticulated, China, 19th C.	470.00
Platter, oval	
17″ l, China, 19th C	660.00
17¾″ l, pierced inset liner, gilt highlights, China, 19th C.	1,100.00
Rice Bowl, blue, price for pair	75.00

Plate, orange dec, white ground, 9⅝″ d, $300.00.

Soap Dish, 5½″ l, blue, orig drain . . .	375.00
Sugar Bowl, cov, blue, gold highlights, matching undertray	750.00
Teapot, cov, 6½″ h, blue	450.00
Tureen, cov, blue, matching undertray, price for pair	2,750.00
Vase, 13¼″ h, beaker shape, blue, teakwood stand.	1,250.00
Vegetable Dish, cov	
9½″ l, oblong, blue	325.00
12½″ l, rect, blue, liner	1,500.00
13″ l, cov, oval, liner	1,050.00
Wine Bottle, 10⅞″ h, blue	900.00

FLASKS

History: A flask is a container for liquids, usually having a narrow neck. Early American glass companies frequently formed them in molds which left a relief design on the front and/or back. Historical flasks with a portrait, building, scene, or name are the most desired.

A chestnut is hand blown, small, and has a flattened bulbous body. The pitkin has a blown globular body with vertical ribs with a spiral rib overlay. Teardrop flasks are generally fiddle shaped and have a scroll or geometric design.

Dimensions can differ for the same flask because of variations in the molding process. Color is important, with scarcer colors demanding more money. Aqua and amber are the most common colors. Bottles with "sickness," an opalescent scaling which eliminates clarity, are worth much less.

Reference: George L. and Helen McKearin, *American Glass,* Crown Publishers, 1941 and 1948.

Periodicals: *Antique Bottle & Glass Collector,* PO Box 187, East Greenville, PA 18041; *Bottles & Extras,* PO Box 154, Happy Camp, CA 96039.

Collectors' Clubs: Federation of Historical Bottle Clubs, 14521 Atlantic Ave., Riverdale, IL, 60627; The National Early American Glass Club, PO Box 8449, Silver Spring, MD 20907.

Blown Three Mold, clear, rolled mouth, pontil scar, pint, McKearin GI–22 . . .	1,100.00
Chestnut, light green, collared lip, half pint	75.00
Freeblown, 4⅝″ h, olive green, white flecks, wide flared mouth, pontil scar	400.00
Historical	
Adams–Jefferson, golden amber, ½ pint, McKearin GI–114	55.00
Baltimore Monument/Corn For The World, pale cornflower blue, sq collared mouth, smooth base, quart, McKearin GVI–4	50.00
Clasped Hands–Eagle, golden amber, double collared mouth, iron pontil, quart, 1845–60, McKearin GXII–43	220.00
Columbia–Eagle, aquamarine, sheared mouth, pontil scar, pint, McKearin GI–117	625.00
Double Eagle, olive green, sheared mouth, pontil scar, pint, McKearin GII–70.	145.00
Eagle/Anchor, medium orange amber, applied double collared mouth, smooth base, ½ pint, New London Glass Works, McKearin GII–67 . . .	425.00
Eagle/Cornucopia, olive amber, McKearin GII–72	75.00
Eagle/Horse and Cart, yellowish olive, sheared mouth, pontil scar, pint, McKearin GV–9	240.00
Eagle/Masonic	
Amber, ½ pint, McKearin GIV–24	100.00
Clear, pint, McKearin GIV–2	350.00

Pocket, cobalt blue, 25 swirls to right, $275.00.

Eagle/Medallion, aquamarine, sheared mouth, pontil scar, pint, McKearin GII–23 .... 450.00

Eagle/Morning Glory, aquamarine, sheared mouth, pontil scar, pint, McKearin GII–19 .... 195.00

Eagle/Railroad, gold amber, pint, McKearin GV–9 .... 110.00

Franklin/Dyott, aquamarine, sheared mouth, pontil scar, pint, McKearin GI–95 .... 220.00

General Jackson, aquamarine, sheared mouth, pontil scar, pint, McKearin GI–65 .... 325.00

General Washington/Eagle, aquamarine, sheared mouth, pontil scar, pint, McKearin GI–16 .... 120.00

Hard Cider, cabin, ice blue, sheared mouth, pontil scar, pint 1,300.00

Jenny Lind, light powder blue, applied round collared mouth, iron pontil, quart, Mckearin GI–104 .... 360.00

Kossuth/Sloop, aquamarine, sheared mouth, pontil scar, pint, McKearin GI–111 .... 180.00

Kossuth/Tree, grayish blue, applied sloping collared mouth, pontil scar, quart, McKearin GI–113 .... 450.00

Lafayette–DeWitt Clinton, yellow olive, sheared mouth, pontil scar, pint, McKearin GI–80 .... 500.00

Lafayette–Liberty, olive,½ pint, McKearin GI–86 .... 220.00

Masonic–Eagle, blue green, tooled mouth, pontil scar, pint, 1815–30, McKearin GIV–1 .... 270.00

Seeing Eye Masonic, medium amber, sloping collared mouth, smooth base, pint, McKearin GIV–43. .... 110.00

Success to The Railroad/Eagle, olive green, pint, McKearin GV–8 ..... 110.00

Washington–Jackson, yellow olive, sheared mouth, pontil scar ½ pint, 1830–48, McKearin GI–34 ...... 320.00

Washington–Sailing Ship, amber, double collared mouth, pontil scar, pint, 1847–50, McKearin GI–28 ... 600.00

Washington–Taylor, bluish–green, sheared mouth, pontil scar, quart, 1840–60, McKearin GI–39 ...... 160.00

Pattern Molded, flattened chestnut form, golden amber, sheared mouth, pontil scar, 5″ h 190.00

Pictorial
Cornucopia–Urn
Emerald Green
½ pint, McKearin GIII–14 .... 110.00
Pint, McKearin GIII–17 ...... 325.00
Golden Amber, McKearin GIII–12 ... 55.00
Olive Green, pint, McKearin GIII–4 .. 45.00
Fish, amber, 9¾″ l 15.00
Flora Temple, horse, medium puce,

applied mouth, smooth base, pint, 1860–80, McKearin GXIII–21 .... 150.00

Horseman–Hound, yellow amber, applied double collared mouth, smooth base, pint, McKearin GXIII–17. .... 150.00

Rampant Lion, cobalt blue, German ... 75.00

Sheaf of Wheat, deep yellow olive, sheared mouth, pontil scar, half pint, McKearin GXIII–37 .... 825.00

Sheaf of Wheat/Grapes, aquamarine, sheared mouth, pontil scar, half pint, McKearin GX–3 .... 130.00

Soldier–Ballet Dancer, deep yellow olive, applied collared mouth with ring, smooth base, pint, McKearin GXIII–13 .... 750.00

Will You Take A Drink?/Will A Duck Swim?, aquamarine, applied mouth ring, smooth base, quart, McKearin GXIII–27 .... 110.00

Pitkin
5⅛″ h
Bluish Green, sheared mouth, pontil scar 260.00
Yellow Olive, sheared mouth, pontil scar. 460.00
5¹/₁₆″ h, olive green, sheared mouth, pontil scar 325.00
5½″ h, yellowish olive, sheared mouth, pontil scar. 400.00
6⅜″ h, yellowish olive, sheared mouth, pontil scar. 310.00
6⅝″ h, medium green, ribbed and swirled, sheared mouth, pontil scar, 1800–30 .... 425.00
7¼″ h, yellowish olive green, slightly flared sheared mouth, pontil scar. . 325.00

Pocket, Bininger's Traveler's Guide, flattened teardrop form, golden amber, double collared mouth, smooth base, 6½″ h. 220.00

Scroll
Aquamarine, McKearin GIX–10 ... 30.00
Golden Amber, sheared mouth, pontil scar, pint, McKearin GIX–10 ..... 320.00
Medium Olive Green, crudely sheared mouth, pontil scar, pint, McKearin GIX–12. .... 550.00
Moonstone, sheared mouth, pontil scar, half pint, Bakewell, Page & Bakewell Mfg, McKearin GIX–39 .. 250.00

Stoneware, dark brown glaze, half pint 45.00

Sunburst
Half pint
Medium Bluish Green, tooled mouth, pontil scar, McKearin GVIII–29 .... 150.00
Yellowish Olive, sheared mouth, pontil scar, McKearin GVIII–18. . 275.00

Pint
Clear, sheared mouth, pontil scar,
McKearin GVIII–2 . . . . **290.00**
Yellowish Olive, sheared mouth,
pontil scar, Keene Marlboro
Street Glassworks, McKearin
GVIII–8 . . . . **225.00**

FLOW BLUE

History: Flow blue or flowing blue is the name applied to china of cobalt and white whose color, when fired in a kiln, produced a flowing or smudged effect. The blue varies in color from dark cobalt to a grayish or steel blue. The flow varies from very slight to a heavy blur where the pattern cannot be easily recognized. The blue color does not permeate through the china.

Flow blue was first produced around 1835 in the Staffordshire district of England by a large number of potters, including Alcock, Davenport, J. Wedgwood, Grindley, New Wharf, Johnson Brothers, and many others. The early flow blue, 1830s to 1870s, was usually of the ironstone variety. The late patterns, 1880s to 1910s, and modern patterns, after 1910, usually were made of the more delicate semiporcelain variety. Approximately 95% of the flow blue was made in England, with the remaining 5% made in Germany, Holland, France, and Belgium. A few patterns also were made in the United States by Mercer, Warwick, and Wheeling Pottery companies.

References: Susan and Al Bagdade, *Warman's English & Continental Pottery & Porcelain, Second Edition,* Wallace–Homestead, 1991; Mary F. Gaston, *The Collector's Encyclopedia Of Flow Blue China,* Collector Books, 1983, 1991 value update; Ellen R. Hill, *Mulberry Ironstone: Flow Blue's Best Kept Little Secret,* published by author, 1993; Dana G. Morykan and Harry L. Rinker, *Warman's Country Antiques & Collectibles, Second Edition,* Wallace–Homestead, 1994; Thomas Nix, *Abbie's Flow Blue Price Guide Survey,* Centennial Publishing, 1992; Jeffrey Snyder, *Flow Blue: A Collector's Guide to Pattern, History and Values,* Schiffer Publishing, 1992; Petra Williams, *Flow Blue China: An Aid To Identification, Revised Edition,* Fountain House East, 1981; Petra Williams, *Flow Blue China II, Revised Edition,* Fountain House East, 1981; Petra Williams, *Flow Blue China and Mulberry Ware: Similarity and Value Guide, Revised Edition,* Fountain House East, 1993.

Collectors' Club: Flow Blue International Collectors' Club, PO Box 205, Rockford, IL 61105.

EARLY PATTERNS: c1825–1850

Berry Bowl
Pelew, E Challinor, c1840 . . . . **100.00**
Whampoa, Mellor & Venables, c1840 **80.00**

Butter Dish, cov
Chusan, Podmore, Walker & Co,
c1845 . . . . **125.00**
Pelew, E Challinor, c1840 . . . . **125.00**
Coffeepot, Temple, Wood & Brownfield,
c1845 . . . . **795.00**
Creamer
Amoy, Davenport, c1844 . . . . **225.00**
Cashmere, Ridgway & Morley, c1840 **275.00**
Hindustan, Wood & Brownfield,
c1845 . . . . **275.00**
Manilla, Podmore Walker, c1845 . . **550.00**
Temple, Wood & Brownfield, c1845 **550.00**
Cup and Saucer, handleless
Amoy, Davenport, c1844 . . . . **90.00**
Jeddo, Adams & Co, c1840 . . . . . . **90.00**
Scinde, J & G Alcock, c1840 . . . . . **145.00**
Cup Plate
Amoy, Davenport, 1844 . . . . **110.00**
Oregon, T J & J Mayer, c1845, 4″ d **125.00**
Rhine, Thomas Dimmock, c1844 . . **75.00**
Dessert Bowl, Chen–Si, John Meir,
c1835, 5″ d **135.00**
Gravy Boat
Daliah, E Challinor, c1850 . . . . **100.00**
Scinde, J & G Alcock, c1840 . . . . . **575.00**
Honey Dish, Manilla, Podmore Walker,
c1845 . . . . **135.00**
Pitcher
Formosa, Thomas, John & Joseph
Mayer, c1850, 7″ h **695.00**
Shell, Wood & Challinor, 1840 . . . . **465.00**
Temple, Wood & Brownfield, c1845,
9″ h **850.00**
Plate
Amoy, Davenport, 1844, 7¼″ d . . . **100.00**
Bamboo, Thomas Dimmock, c1845,
10¼″ d **135.00**
Hong Kong, Charles Meigh, c1845
7″ d **95.00**
10⅜″ d **175.00**
Indian Jar, Jacob & Thos Furnival,
c1843, 10½″ d **115.00**
Manilla, Podmore Walker, c1845
9″ d **125.00**
9⅞″ d **135.00**
Pelew, E Challinor, c1840 . . . . **105.00**
Sabroan, unknown maker, c1845,
10¾″ d **175.00**
Scinde, J & G Alcock, c1840 . . . . . **155.00**
Platter
Bamboo, Thomas Dimmock, c1845,
16¾ x 13⅞″ **595.00**
Beauties of China, Mellor, Venables &
Co, 1845, 10″ l **295.00**
Chen–Si, John Meir, c1835, 16 x
12¼″ **775.00**
Hong Kong, Charles Meigh, c1845,
16″ l **350.00**
Indian Jar, Jacob & Thomas Furnival,
1843, 12″ **215.00**
Manilla, Podmore Walker, c1845

16" l 795.00
18" l 895.00
Oregon, T J & J Mayer, c1845, 13⅜"
l 375.00
Potato Bowl, Oregon, T J & J Mayer,
c1845. .... 735.00
Relish Dish, Tonquin, Heath, c1850 . 270.00
Sauce Dish
Amoy, Davenport, c1844, 5" d 60.00
Indian Jar, Jacob & Thos Furnival,
c1843 .... 50.00
Shell, Wood & Challinor, c1840 ... 40.00
Tulip and Sprig, Thomas Walker,
c1845 .... 40.00
Sauce Tureen, Manilla, Podmore
Walker, c1845, three pc 1,595.00
Soup Plate
Amoy, Davenport, 1844, 9" d 110.00
Arabesque, T J & J Mayer, c1945 . 75.00
Sobraon, unknown English maker,
c1945, 9" d, flange rim 100.00
Soup Tureen
Chusan, Podmore Walker & Co,
c1845, open 200.00
Scinde, J G Alcock, c1840, cov ... 600.00
Sugar, cov
Amoy, Davenport, 1844, slight rim
wear..................... 495.00
Manilla, Podmore Walker, c1845 .. 850.00
Teapot, Rhine, Thomas Dimmock,
c1844. .... 650.00
Undertray, Manilla, Podmore Walker,
c1845, 7" l 275.00
Vegetable, cov, Manilla, Podmore
Walker, c1845, 10⅞" l........... 795.00
Wash Bowl and Pitcher, Whampoa, Mel-
lor & Venables, c1840 .... 2,250.00
Waste Bowl, Chen–Si, John Meir,
c1835, 8½" d 125.00

MIDDLE PATTERNS: c1850–1870

Charger, Tyrolean, Wm Ridgway & Co,
c1850, 12¼" d 125.00
Coffeepot, Simila, Elsmore & Forster,
c1860. .... 175.00
Creamer, Honc, Petrus Regout, c1858 150.00
Cup and Saucer, handleless, Rhoda
Gardens, Hackwood, 1850........ 165.00
Dish, Blossom, G L Ashworth & Bros,
c1865, 9½" d 35.00
Milk Pitcher, Tonquin, Joseph Heath,
1850, 10½" h 1,100.00
Pitcher
Coburg, John Edwards, c1860, 8" h 795.00
Flora, Davenport, 1850 .... 435.00
Plate
Carlton, Samuel Alcock, 1850, 7¼" d 85.00
Cashmere, Francis, Morley, c1850,
9½" d 250.00
Coburg, John Edwards, c1860, 10¼"
d 150.00

Sugar, cov, Holland, Johnson Bros.,
England, 5⅝" h, $85.00.

Platter
Chapoo, John Wedgwood, c1850, 16"
l 400.00
Hindustan, Wood & Brownfield, 12 x
16". 220.00
Shanghae, J Furnival, c1860, 13½" l 175.00
Relish Dish, Coburg, John Edwards,
c1860. .... 220.00
Soup Plate
Cashmere, Francis, Morley, c1850,
10½" d 260.00
Gothic, Jacob Furnival, c1850, flange
rim 75.00
Soup Tureen, Willow, Ashworth Bros,
1862, two pc. 775.00
Sugar, cov, Temple, Podmore Walker &
Co, c1850. .... 250.00
Toddy Plate, Tonquin, W Adams & Son,
c1845. .... 75.00
Vegetable Bowl, Cashmere, Francis,
Morley, c1850, 8⅝ x 6⅝"........ 775.00
Waste Bowl, Cashmere, Francis, Mor-
ley, c1850, ... 875.00

LATE PATTERNS: c1880–1900s

Biscuit Jar, Watteau, Doulton, 1896–
1930, metal top................ 325.00
Bone Dish
Agra, F Winkle & Co, c1891 ..... 40.00
Touraine, Stanley Pottery Co, c1898 85.00
Bouillon Cup, underplate, Irdis, WH
Grindley, c1910, two handles 45.00
Butter Dish, cov
Colonial, J & G Meakin, c1891, orig
insert 115.00
Kyber, W Adams & Co, c1891 .... 475.00
Linda, John Maddock & Sons, Ltd,
c1896 .... 80.00
Butter Pat
Blue Danube, Johnson Bros, c1900 25.00

Touraine, Stanley Pottery Co, c1898	60.00
Chamber Pot, Glenwood, Johnson Bros, c1900, 8½ x 5¼"	170.00
Chocolate Cup and Saucer, Kyber, W Adams & Co, c1891	135.00
Creamer	
Non Pariel, Burgess & Leigh, c1891	350.00
Seville, New Wharf Pottery, 1891	210.00
Cup and Saucer	
Kyber, W Adams & Co, c1891	120.00
Verona, Wood & Son, 1891	95.00
Demitasse Cup and Saucer, Lorne, WH Grindley, 1900	75.00
Gravy Boat	
Dainty, John Maddock & Son, 1896	145.00
Holland, Johnson Bros, c1891, attached undertray	150.00
Mongolia, Johnson Bros, c1900, double spouts, attached underplate	165.00
Ladle, Vermont, Burgess & Leigh, c1895	85.00
Milk Pitcher	
La Belle, WH Grindley, c1893	450.00
Pitcher, Non Pariel, Burgess & Leigh, c1891	
6" h	275.00
8" h	325.00
Plate	
Corinthian Flute, Cauldon, 1905	72.00
Fairy Villas, W Adams & Co, c1891, 9" d	90.00
Lakewood, Wood & Sons, c1900, 9½" d	75.00
Lorne, WH Grindley, 1900, 10" d	90.00
Waldorf, New Wharf Pottery, c1892, 9" d	75.00
Wild Rose, George Jones, c1910, 10½" d	85.00
Platter	
Argyle, WH Grindley, 1896	
17¼ x 12"	395.00
19 x 13¼"	545.00
Gainsborough, Ridgway, c1905, scalloped, 16 x 12"	235.00
Lorne, WH Grindley, 1900	
12" l	165.00
16" l	335.00
18" l	395.00
Lucerne, New Wharf Pottery, 1891, 19" l	435.00
Sauce Dish, Non Pariel, Burgess & Leigh, c1891, 5¼" d	40.00
Saucer, Tokio, Johnson Bros, c1891, 6" d	25.00
Soup Plate	
Lancaster, New Wharf Pottery, c1891, 9" d, flange rim	50.00
Rose, Ridgway, c1910, 9" d, flange rim	25.00
Tulip, Johnson Bros, c1900, 9" d, gilt trim	65.00
Soup Tureen	
Clarence, WH Grindley, 1900	495.00
Messina, Alfred Meakin, 1891, matching ladle	1,600.00
Soup Plate	
Kyber, W Adams & Co, c1891	120.00
Touraine, Stanley Pottery Co, c1898	95.00
Soup Tureen, cov, Linda, John Maddock & Sons, Ltd., c1896	150.00
Sugar, cov, Non Pariel, Burgess & Leigh, c1891	265.00
Teapot, Arabesque, G Kent	895.00
Vegetable Bowl, Landscape, WT Copeland & Sons, c1891	225.00
Wash Bowl, Doreen, WH Grindley, 1891, octagonal	400.00
Waste Bowl, Touraine, Stanley Pottery Co, c1898	250.00

FOLK ART

History: The definition of what constitutes folk art is still being vigorously debated among collectors, dealers, museum curators, and scholars. Some want to confine folk art to nonacademic, handmade objects. Others are willing to include manufactured material. In truth, the term is used to cover objects ranging from crude drawings by obviously untalented children to academically trained artists' paintings of "common" people and scenery.

The folk art market is subject to hype and manipulation. Neophyte collectors are encouraged to read Edie Clark's "What Really Is Folk Art?" in the December 1986 *Yankee*. Clark's article provides a refreshingly honest look at the folk art market.

Finally, the folk art market is extremely trendy and fickle. What is hot today can become cool and passé tomorrow. Collecting folk art is not for the weak of heart or the cautious investor.

References: Kenneth L. Ames, *Beyond Necessity: Art In The Folk Tradition*, W. W. Norton, 1978; Robert Bishop and Judith Rieter Weissman, *Folk Art: The Knopf Collectors' Guides To American Antiques*, Alfred A. Knopf, 1983; George H. Meyer, *American Folk Art Canes: Personal Sculpture*, Sandringham Press, Museum of American Folk Art, and University of Washington Press; Dana G. Morykan and Harry L. Rinker, *Warman's Country Antiques & Collectibles, Second Edition*, Wallace–Homestead, 1994; Henry Niemann and Helaine Fendelman, *The Official Identification and Price Guide To American Folk Art*, House of Collectibles, 1988; Beatrix T. Rumford and Carolyn J. Weekley, *Treasures of American Folk Art from The Abby Aldrich Rockefeller Folk Art Center*, Little, Brown and Company, 1989.

Museums: Abby Aldrich Rockefeller Folk Art Center, Williamsburg, VA; Daughters of the American Revolution Museum, Washington, D.C.; Landis Valley Farm Museum, Lancaster, PA; Museum of American Folk Art, New York, NY; Museum of Early Southern Decorative Arts, Winston–Salem, NC; Museum of International Folk Art.

Bank, 2¼ x 3⅞ x 2⅛", wooden, stylized village scene, peg construction, Continental................... 150.00

Bed, decorated, hardwood, orig red and brown graining, turnings, applied moldings, harlequin scratch carving, zigzag detailed picked out in black paint with white striping, some wear and age cracks, removable plates cover holes for bed bolts (one orig, others old replacements), expertly replaced finials, replaced side rails, Harrisburg, PA, orig, sgd "Biekman," 45" w, 74" l mattress size, 78" h....... 2,700.00

Boat Scraper, 12¾" l, iron, dragon, arc welded, good detail, pitted........ 215.00

Diorama, 4 x 27", Kalevala, carved by Alfred Johnson, c1910.......... 225.00

Doll, 10" h, rag, whisk broom, black woman, embroidered face, hand-sewn clothes.................. 30.00

Embroidery, 13½ x 14½", crewel, still-life, pink, yellow, white, blue, and green bouquet of garden blossoms arranged in crocheted basket, mounted on white cotton ground, framed, PA, early 19th C................ 660.00

Figure
4¼" h, black native, wood, carved, orig polychrome paint......... 75.00
5¼" h, woman sitting in chair, articulated arms, wood, carved, orig polychrome paint............ 250.00

6" h, bust of Lincoln, wood, carved, orig polychrome paint, pedestal base..................... 110.00

7⅜" h, log cabin with frog int., stone carving, intricate open work detail . 330.00

Fire Bucket, 13½" h, leather, painted and stitched, gilt cornucopias and American eagle, inscribed "E P Pike" and "W F Clob," dated 1829...... 2,500.00

Marble Shooter, 12" h, soldier, wood, metal fittings, orig polychrome paint, tin shoe damaged.............. 75.00

Miniature Portrait, American School, 19th C
2¾ x 2⅝", young woman, watercolor on ivory, framed............. 1,000.00
4¾ x 3¼", lady in eyelet cap and collar, gentleman in black frock coat, pencil on paper, sgd and dated on verso "J M Crowley, Delineator, Valatie, Jany 28–1836"........ 1,320.00

Painting
4 x 3", watercolor, profile of man, sitting on Chippendale chair, orig frame with gold leaf striping, c1840 500.00
7 x 9", American School, watercolor and ink, The Charter Oak, paper label, marked on back "Drawn and colored by Maria Kellogg, sister of Amanda Kellogg"............ 935.00
14½ x 10½", watercolor, two lovebirds and butterflies garland, c1858.... 110.00

Plaque, 7" h, 5⅞" w, wooden, carved, profile of man, orig polychrome paint, sgd "Carved by John W Saur, Newark, O Aug"................. 55.00

Quilt, 76½ x 75", applique, brown plumes, yellow birds, blue shirt pattern ground, paisley fabric backing, PA, c1890..................... 350.00

Scherenschnitte, 11½ x 16", one with church in landscape of houses and trees, mill and fisherman, second with manor house with swan pond and garden gate, scissor–cut white paper, turquoise blue paper ground, PA German, 19th C, price for pair........ 1,100.00

Sculpture, 23½" w, sea gull, wooden, tin wings, sheet metal tail feathers, upholstery tack eyes, New England, c1910..................... 850.00

Shelf, 13 x 24 x 6", wood, owl and half moon motif, early 20th C........ 55.00

Sign, 25" d, Holyoke Water Heater adv, galvanized sheet metal, large center heart, painted, orig weathered surface 55.00

Theorem, American
9½ x 13¾", bowl of fruit, early 19th C 715.00
16½ x 19½", velvet, painted basket of flowers, gilt frame............ 350.00

Theorem, "A Primrose," watercolor and ink on paper, sgd "Painted by Sally Stearns 1857," light staining, tears lower edge, 6¾ x 8¼", $825.00. Photograph courtesy of Skinner, Inc.

Weather Vane, 28″ l, 35½″ h, airplane,
wood and metal, worn and weathered
gray, red, and black paint, modern
base, American, 20th C **425.00**

FOOD BOTTLES

History: Food bottles were made in many sizes,
shapes, and colors. Manufacturers tried to make
an attractive bottle that would ship well and allow
the purchaser to see the product, thus assuring him
that the product was as good and as well made as
home preserves.

Reference: Ralph and Terry Kovel, *The Kovels'
Bottle Price List, 9th Edition,* Crown Publishers,
Inc., 1992.

Periodicals: *Antique Bottle and Glass Collector,*
PO Box 187, East Greenville, PA 18041; *Bottles &
Extras,* PO Box 154, Happy Camp, CA 96039.

Catsup
  Cuyuga County Tomato Catsup, 10″
    h, aqua, swirl design. **60.00**
  Pioneer Catsup, 9¼″ h, amber,
    hexagonal **175.00**
Extract
  A & P Extract **4.00**
  Baker's Flavoring Extracts, 4¾″ h,
    aqua, sq ring lip. **15.00**
  L C Extract, label, orig box **180.00**
  Red Dragon Extract, emb dragon . .   **10.00**
Horseradish
  Bunker Hill, aqua, label **12.00**
  Lake Horseradish **10.00**
Lime Juice, 10¼″ h, dark olive amber,
  arrow design, applied top **125.00**
Milk
  Alta Crest Farms, green, paper cap   **700.00**
  Bernard Dairy,½ pt, sq, red, cow illus   **8.00**
  Cloverleaf Creamery Co, qt **80.00**
  Cream Top Dairy, qt, sq, green . . .   **20.00**
  Dellinger Dairy Farm, Jefferson, IN   **15.00**
  Golden State Brand Dairy Products,½
    pt, red pyroglazed dec **12.00**
  Holsgern Farms Dairy, qt, clear, tin
    top and closure **85.00**
  Olin Hill, Providence, RI, 7″ h, clear,
    cylindrical, tooled mouth. smooth
    base, tin top **160.00**
  Purity Dairy, pt **55.00**
  Red Top, qt, emb top **10.00**
  Scott's Dairy, qt, emb **25.00**
  Taylor's Dairy,½ pt, sq, amber **35.00**
  Wagner Bros Dairy, qt, round **18.00**
Mustard
  Blossom Brand Prepared Mustard,
    wire bail, label **18.00**
  Crosse & Blackwell Mustard, 4⅜″ h,
    pottery, coat–of–arms dec. **50.00**
  Giessen's Union Mustard, 4⅝″ h,
    clear, eagle **80.00**

Old Style Mustard, clear, label **5.00**
Olive Oil
  Bertin Brand Pure Olive Oil, 7½″ h,
    dark green. **15.00**
  Elwood Cooper Pure Olive Oil, 11″ h,
    aqua. **40.00**
  T H McGruder & Co, Extra Superfine
    Olive Oil, 11″ h, olive green. **20.00**
Peppersauce
  Cathedral, 10¾″ h, hexagonal, aqua,
    applied double collared mouth, pon-
    til scar.   **260.00**
  C L Stickney, 9″ h, aqua, open pontil   **75.00**
  G Miller, 10″ h, aqua, vertical fluted
    dec, open pontil. **125.00**
W & E Peppersauce, 8⅞″ h, sq, aqua   **150.00**
Pickle
  Cathedral
    11⅞″ h, sq, aqua, arched panels
      rolled mouth, smooth base, Wil-
      lington Glass Works, CT **225.00**
    13⅝″ h, sq, medium green, tooled
      collared mouth, pontil scar, Wil-
      lington Glass Works, CT **2,100.00**
  Wine Cured Pickles, Manhattan Pic-
    kle Co, qt, clear **5.00**
Syrup
  Boston Cooler, 12¼″ h, clear, blue
    and gold label, tooled mouth, metal
    cap, smooth base, c1900 . . . .   **310.00**
  Golden Tree Maple Syrup, 20 oz,
    clear, screw top **2.00**
Vinegar, Maple Sap & Boiled Cider Vi-
  negar, 11¼″ h, cobalt blue **600.00**

FOOD MOLDS

History: Food molds were used both commercially and in the home. For the most part, pewter
ice cream molds and candy molds were used on a
commercial basis; pottery and copper molds were
used in homes. Today, both types are collected
largely for decorative purposes.

Pewter ice cream molds were made primarily by
two American companies: Eppelsheimer & Co.
[molds marked E & Co., N.Y.] and Schall & Co.
[molds marked S & Co.]. Both companies used a
numbering system for their molds. The Krauss Co.
bought out Schall & Co., removed the S & Co. from
some but not all the molds, and added more designs [marked K or Krauss].

The majority of pewter ice cream molds are individual serving molds. When used, one quart of
ice cream would make eight to ten pieces. Scarcer,
but still available, are banquet molds which used
two to four pints of ice cream per example. European pewter molds [CC is a French mold mark] are
available.

Chocolate mold makers are more difficult to determine. Unlike the pewter ice cream molds, makers' marks were not always on the mold or were

covered by frames. Eppelsheimer and Company of New York marked many of its molds either with name or with a design resembling a child's toy top with "Trade Mark" and "NY." Many chocolate molds were imported from Germany and Holland and were marked with the country of origin and, in some cases, the mold maker's name.

Reference: Judene Divone, *Chocolate Moulds: A History & Encyclopedia,* Oakton Hills Publications, 1987.

Museum: Wilbur's Americana Candy Museum.

Additional Listing: Butter Prints.

Chocolate Mold, rabbit playing drum, tin, three cavities, Anton Reiche, Dresden, #26024, 10⅝″ w, 6″ h, $45.00.

CHOCOLATE MOLDS

Boy on bicycle, 8¾″ h, two parts	375.00
Chick and egg, 3½″ h, two parts, folding, marked "Allemagne", Germany.	40.00
Circus Peanuts, 28 x 13″, tray type, 105 cavities.	50.00
Elephant, tin, three cavities	75.00
Heart, 6½ x 6″, two cavities	65.00
Hen, folding, 2½″ h, tin, two part	105.00
Rabbits, 10½″ l, sitting, three, tin plated steel, folding, two part	50.00
Skeleton, 5½″ h, pressed tin	60.00
Teddy Bear, two pcs, clamp type, marked "Reiche".	275.00
Turkey, 14 x 10″, tray type, eight cavities	45.00
Two Eggs, 3¼″ h, alligatored relief design	35.00
Witch, 4½ x 2″, four cavities	55.00

ICE CREAM MOLDS

Banquet Size	
Owl, four pints, marked "S & Co/7″	550.00
Pear, marked "S & Co, #17″	250.00
Ship, two quarts	225.00
Individual Size, pewter	
Asparagus, 3⅝″ h	25.00
Basket, replaced hinge pins	18.00
Cherub riding Easter Bunny, 4″ h . .	25.00

Circle with cupid, 4″ d	50.00
Duck, 4″ l	50.00
Egg, 2¾″ d, marked "E & Co, NY" .	25.00
Flag, thirteen stars	50.00
Fruit, 2¾″ d, marked "E & Co, NY"	25.00
Heart with cupid, 4″ h	60.00
Hen, 3¾″ h	85.00
Man in the Moon, 5½″ h, marked "E & Co, copyright 1888"	75.00
Playing Cards with diamond, marked "E & Co, NY".	25.00
Possum, 5″ l	115.00
Potato, 4″ h, pewter	65.00
Shoe, lady's, 5¾″ l	25.00
Steamboat	90.00
Tulip, 4⅛″ h, marked "E & Co, NY"	35.00

MISCELLANEOUS

Butter, 4½ x 6⅞″, rect cased, cherry, deep carved geometric design	110.00
Cake, rabbit, Griswold	245.00
Maple Candy, wood	
Fruit and foliage design, 5½ x 8″, two part.	28.00
Two hearts, 3⅛″, varnished	125.00
Food	
Copper and tin, 6½″ l, pears, battered, minor repair.	35.00
Rockingham, 9″ d, tulip design on bottom of bowl, brown sponged glaze, wear and minor hairlines.	30.00
Tin, 5¼″ l, oval, lion	45.00
Pudding	
5 x 5 x 6½″, oval, pineapple, tin and copper	65.00
12½″ h, tin, rabbit form, late 19th C, early 20th C.	125.00

POTTERY (Center Design Indicated)

Ear of Corn, 6″ l, yellow ware, oval . .	40.00
Grapes and leaf, 3 x 5 x 7″, oval, Wedgwood Creamware	110.00
Rose, ironstone, marked "Alcock" . . .	50.00
Strawberries, 4″ d	55.00
Turk's Head, 9″ d, redware, swirled fluting, brown sponged rim	45.00

FOSTORIA GLASS   FOSTORIA

History: Fostoria Glass Company began operations at Fostoria, Ohio, in 1887 and moved to Moundsville, West Virginia, its present location, in 1891. By 1925 Fostoria had five furnaces and a variety of special shops. In 1924 a line of colored tableware was introduced. Fostoria was purchased by Lancaster Colony in 1983 and continues to operate under the Fostoria name.

References: Gene Florence, *Elegant Glassware Of The Depression Era, Revised Fifth Edition,* Collector Books, 1993; Robert E. Foster, *Fostoria American Pattern,* published by author, 1984; Ann Kerr, *Fostoria: An Identification and Value Guide of Pressed, Blown, & Hand Molded Shapes,* Collector Books, 1994; JoAnn Schleismann, *Price Guide To Fostoria, The Popular Years, Third Edition,* Park Avenue Publications; Ellen T. Schroy, *Warman's Glass,* Wallace-Homestead, 1992; Sidney P. Seligson, *Fostoria American, A Complete Guide,* published by author, 1992; Hazel M. Weatherman, *Fostoria, Its First Fifty Years,* published by author, 1972.

Collectors' Club: Fostoria Glass Society of America, PO Box 826, Moundsville, WV 26041.

Periodical: *The Daze,* 10271 State Rd., Box 57, Otisville, MI 48463.

Museums: Fostoria Glass Museum, Moundsville, WV; Huntington Galleries, Huntington, WV.

Plate, Heather, crystal, 9½" d, $15.00.

Ashtray, Coin, light blue, frosted coins	24.50
Baker, Versailles, yellow, oval, 9" l	60.00
Bonbon, Lido, three toes, handles, 7" d	16.00
Bowl	
Buttercup, handle, 10" d	45.00
Lido, handled, 8½" d	21.00
Versailles, yellow, 5½" d	20.00
Butter Dish, cov	
Baroque, blue	275.00
Fairfax, orchid	350.00
Cake Plate, Fairfax, blue, handle, 10" d	37.50
Candlesticks, pr	
Lafayette, wisteria, 2" h	65.00
Lido, 5½" h	30.00
Candy Dish, cov	
Baroque, blue, ftd, 9½" h	70.00
Coin, red, frosted	50.00
Candy Jar, cov, Camillia, 7" h	65.00
Champagne	
Chintz	16.00
Fairfax, orchid	25.00
Cheese and Cracker Set, Versailles, yellow, #2375.	75.00
Cocktail, Versailles, pink	25.00
Cordial	
Fairfax, orchid	55.00
Lafayette, wisteria	150.00
Willowmere	18.00
Creamer and Sugar, Lido	28.00
Cream Soup, Kashmir, blue	60.00
Cruet, orig stopper, Fairfax, pink	125.00
Cup and Saucer	
Colony	10.00
Fairfax, blue	12.50
Navarre	27.50
Versailles, green	22.00
Demitasse Cup, Fairfax, blue	15.00
Fruit Bowl and Stand, American, 16" d	175.00
Goblet	
Jamestown, crystal	9.00
Lido	11.00
Mayflower	22.50
Willowmere	19.00
Grapefruit, liner, Fairfax, orchid	75.00
Ice Bucket	
American, 6½" d, metal handle and tongs	48.00
Sunray	40.00
Versailles, yellow	75.00
Iced Tea Tumbler	
Argus, crystal	18.00
Jamestown, crystal	10.00
Lido	10.00
Iced Tea, ftd	
America, 12 oz	13.00
Baroque, blue, 6" h	75.00
Chintz	21.00
Jamestown, blue	19.00
Juice Tumbler	
Colony	16.00
Jamestown, crystal	8.00
Lemon Plate, Fairfax, blue	20.00
Mayonnaise, liner, ladle, Buttercup	55.00
Mint Tray, Baroque, yellow, ftd, 4¼" d	18.00
Nappy	
American, 8" d	30.00
Coin, red	20.00
Olive Dish, Colony, 5½" d	20.00
Oyster Cocktail	
Lido	5.00
Willowmere	6.00
Parfait, Fairfax, blue	31.00
Pitcher, Acanthus, amber	300.00
Plate	
Jamestown, blue	18.00
Lido, 7¼" d	6.00
Navarre, 7½" d	14.00
Versailles, yellow, 7½" d	9.00

Platter
American, oval, 12" l	32.00
Minuet, yellow, 11" l	35.00
Punch Bowl, Baroque, crystal	400.00

Relish
Baroque, blue, sq, two parts, 6" w	35.00
Lido, three parts, 10" d	25.00
Midnight Rose, four parts	37.50
Salt and Pepper Shakers, pr, Versailles, pink	150.00
Server, center handle, Romance	35.00

Sherbet
Jamestown, crystal	12.00
Lido	7.00
Sugar, cov, June, yellow	225.00
Sweetmeat, Fairfax, blue, two handles	22.50

Torte Plate
American, red, 14" d	40.00
Lido, 14" d	30.00

Tumbler
Jamestown, blue	20.00
Lafayette, wisteria	35.00

Vase
America, sq, ftd, 10" h	40.00
Buttercup, ftd, 7" h	135.00
Whipped Cream Bowl, Fairfax, blue	24.00
Whiskey, Fairfax, orchid	30.00

Wine
America, hex foot	15.00
Chintz	40.00

FRAKTUR

History: Fraktur, the calligraphy associated with the Pennsylvania Germans, is named for the elaborate first letter found in many of the hand-drawn examples. Throughout its history, printed, partially printed–hand drawn, and fully hand-drawn works existed side by side. Frakturs often were made by the schoolteachers or ministers living in rural areas of Pennsylvania, Maryland, and Virginia. Many artists are unknown.

Fraktur exists in several forms—geburts and taufschein (birth and baptismal certificates), vorschrift (writing example, often with alphabet), haus sagen (house blessing), bookplates and marks, rewards of merit, illuminated religious text, valentines, and drawings. Although collected for decoration, the key element in fraktur is the text.

Fraktur prices rise and fall along with the American folk art market. The key market place is Pennsylvania and the Middle Atlantic states.

References: Dana G. Morykan and Harry L. Rinker, *Warman's Country Antiques & Collectibles, Second Edition*, Wallace–Homestead, 1994; Donald A. Shelley, *The Fraktur–Writings Or Illuminated Manuscripts Of The Pennsylvania Germans*, Pennsylvania German Society, 1961; Frederick S. Weiser and Howell J. Heaney (comp.), *The Pennsylvania German Fraktur Of The Free Library Of Philadelphia*, Pennsylvania German Society, 1976, two volumes.

Museum: The Free Library of Philadelphia, Philadelphia, PA.

HAND DRAWN

Blowsy (Flying) Angel Artist, birth letter, dated 1796, watercolor and pen and ink, wove paper, red and yellow flying angels with tulips and hearts for Anna Maria Zollner, 13 x 15½"	3,575.00
Crossed Legged Angel Artist, birth and baptismal certificate, Lancaster County, dated 1812, watercolor and pen and ink on laid paper, block format, floral motif on side borders, crossed legged angel in center of top panel, star burst in center of bottom panel, birth of Michael Klop, 14 x 17¼"	2,500.00
Eyer, Johann Adam, bookplate, dated 1781, 4¼ x 2½", watercolor and pen and ink, red and yellow peacock perched on flowering tulip tree	4,125.00
Geburts und Taufschein, birth record, pen and ink and watercolor, wove paper, primitive angel in brown ink, green polka dots, holding upside-down rose, Wullimann family births from 1840 to 1877, wear, stains, and fading, framed, 15½" h, 13½" w	440.00
Gottschall, M., baptismal certificate, Bucks County, dated 1827, watercolor and pen and ink, hearts, birds, pinwheels, and flying angels, Rakel Stahr, 12¾ x 16"	24,200.00
Heydrich, Baltzer, drawing, Montgomery County, 1845, pen and ink and water-	

Birth and Baptismal, hand drawn, Daniel Peterman, York County, PA, 15¾" × 12½", $3,000.00.

color drawing on wove paper, checkerboard border, center with wall (altar) flanked by stylized flowers in a semicircular motif, bird on branch of two of flowers, PA German inscription, "Baltzer Heydrich. . . 1845. . . in his 83rd year," tones of red, black, green, blue, and yellow, minor stains, tears and damage at fold line, beveled frame with red graining, 16¼ x 20¼" **7,600.00**

Kern, Amandas, drawing, pen and ink and watercolor, laid paper, stylized flowers, foliage, and three birds, back inscribed "Sarah Ann Mohr, Upper Milford Township, Lehigh County PA, August the 21st AD 1864, Amandas Kern Painter 1858," black frame with yellow corners. **990.00**

Otto, Daniel (The Flat Tulip Artist), birth and baptismal certificate, Northumberland County, dated 1788, watercolor and pen and ink on paper, central heart text, flanked at bottom by two large parrots with checkered wings facing outward and at top by two smaller parrots with plain wings facing inward, heart with border of attached flowers, red and yellow tones, birth of Catharina Lotz, 11½ x 14¾" . **13,250.00**

Seller, H., birth certificate, Dauphin County, PA, 1807, pen and ink and watercolor on laid paper, central heart flanked at base by large parrots above which are a tulip and peacock, tulip flanked by starburst across top, geometric circles along bottom with "H./ Seiler," shades of red, green, blue, brown, yellow, and black, text is primarily in red ink, minor stains, short tears, large tulips have some holes caused by acid ink, bottom edge a bit ragged, 16¼ x 19¼" **12,000.00**

Spanenberg, John, double bookplate for Catharina Haupt, pen and ink and watercolor on laid paper, stylized horizontal floral bands across top and bottom, tones of red, blue, green, yellow, and brown, some stains, fading, and damage on fold line, 5¾ x 6¼", gilt frame 8½ x 10½" **3,500.00**

Unknown Artist
  Birth Record, 1814, Jacob Becter, pen and ink and watercolor, geometric border design, compass stars and designs, orange, yellow, and olive green, curly maple frame, 14 x 17¾". **1,320.00**
  Bookplate, pen and ink and watercolor on paper
    10½" h, 7½" w, black and red, dated 1849, framed, red has bled and stained paper **110.00**

11" h, 11" w, red, yellow, and green roses, black ink inscription, dated 1854, matted and framed. **95.00**

Drawing, 1793, pen and ink and watercolor, birds, flowers, and "Anno 1793," brown paper, framed, stained, 7⅜ x 11⅝" **880.00**

Reward of Merit, southeastern PA, c1820–40, wove paper, stylized vining plant with flowers and birds, initials "F/Z," green, brown, blue, and faded red, old damage and repairs, 8 x 12¾", framed **1,600.00**

Song Book, southeastern PA, c1800–10, possibly Bucks County, dated 1804, bookplate has circular text flanked by vertical flower with multileaf stem, checkered border, belongs to "Abraham Landes," cover pulled loose from string binding but is not damaged, 6⅜ x 3¾" **3,000.00**

HAND DRAWN–PRINTED

Brechall, Martin, birth and baptismal, printed form by Hütter, Easton, 1821, central heart, borders hand painted with filigree and flowers in red, yellow, blue, and green, for Lea Schull, 13 x 16". **950.00**

Dulheur, Henrich, birth and baptismal, 13 x 15¾". **950.00**

Ebner, Henrich, birth record, Allentown, PA, Cumberland County, 1818, hand colored, olive, yellow, and purple, matted and framed, 20 x 16½" **220.00**

Geburts und Taufschein, birth record, hand colored, recording 1823 Montgomery County, PA birth, printed by "H. Ebner, Allentown," faded colors, creases, and tears, modern painted frame, 19¼ x 16¼" **115.00**

Otto, Heinrich, The Great Comet Of 1769, decorated with parrots and shooting stars. **2,500.00**

Peters, birth record, Harrisburg, Berks County, PA, hand colored, molded walnut frame, 19¼ x 16" **165.00**

Unknown Artist, birth certificate, Northampton County, 1821, German calligraphy, inscription within a keystone device, hand painted paired birds and large flowering tulip plants, birth of Maria Margaretha Scherner, 7¾" x 12". **750.00**

PRINTED

Adam and Eve
  Bruckman, C. A., Reading **300.00**
  Dahlem, M., Philadelphia **400.00**

Birth and Baptismal
Baumann, S., Ephrata	400.00
Blumer, A. & W., Allentown	175.00
Hartman, Joseph, Lebanon	250.00
Hanesche, J. G., Baltimore	150.00
Herschberger, Johann, Chambersburg.	325.00
Lepper, Wilhelm, Hanover	300.00
Lippe, G. Ph., Pottsville	150.00
Puwelle, A., Reading	125.00
Saeger and Leisenring, Allentown, early form	150.00
Sage, G. A., Allentown	175.00
Scheffer, Theo. F., Harrisburg	75.00
Wiestling, Johann S., Harrisburg . .	200.00

Note: If signed by a scrivener, increase value by 25% to 40%.

FRANKART

History: Arthur Von Frankenberg, artist and sculptor, founded Frankart, Inc., in New York City in the mid 1920s. Frankart, Inc., mass-produced practical "art objects" in the Art Deco style into the 1930s. Pieces include aquariums, ashtrays, bookends, flower vases, lamps, and so on. Although Von Frankenberg used live female models as his subjects, his figures are characterized by their form and style rather than specific features. Nudes are the most collectible; caricatured animals and other human figures were also produced, no doubt, to increase sales.

With few exceptions, pieces were marked Frankart, Inc., with a patent number or "pat. appl. for."

Pieces were cast in a white metal composition in the following finishes: cream—a pale iridescent white; bronzoid—oxidized copper, silver, or gold; french—a medium brown with green in the crevices; gun metal—art iridescent gray; jap—a very dark brown, almost black, with green in the crevices; pearl green—pale iridescent green; and verde—a dull light green. Cream and bronzoid were used primarily in the 1930s.

Note: All pieces listed are all original in very good condition unless otherwise indicated.

Aquarium, 10½″ h, three kneeling nude figures encircle 10″ d crystal glass aquarium bowl	675.00

Ashtray
5″ h, stylized duck with outstretched wings supports green glass ash receiver.	90.00
6″ h, nude figure kneels on cushion, holding 3″ d removable pottery ashtray.	210.00
7″ h, caricatured monkey supports 3″ d glass ash receiver in tail.	85.00
9½″ h, seated nude figure on 3″ h column, leg extends over 5″ sq ceramic ashtray.	385.00

12″ h, acrobatic nude figure balances 3″ d glass ball shaped ash container on toes	365.00
25″ h, nude figure grows from tobacco plant to hold scalloped glass tray overhead.	625.00

Bookends, pr
5″ h, horse heads with flowing manes	45.00
6″ h, seated cubist styled bears . . .	70.00
8″ h, nude figures peek around edge of books	245.00
10″ h, nude figures sit atop metal books	235.00
Candlesticks, pr, 12½″ h, nude figures standing on tiptoes, holding candle cup over heads.	365.00
Cigarette Box, 8″ h, back to back nudes support removable green glass box. .	425.00
Incense Burner, 10″ h, draped figure holds tray and cover for incense. . . .	250.00

Lamp, No. L22OX, two inverted figures balance glass globe on raised toes, 8″ d gold irid globe with green leaves dec, Patented Design No. D77202, 1928, 18″ h, $850.00.

Lamp
8″ h, nude figure kneels before 4″ d crystal bubble ball	585.00
10½″ h, two nude figures stand on either side of geometrically shaped plate glass panel	1,150.00
13″ h, two back to back dancing nude figures support 11″ sq glass cylinder satin finished shade	750.00
18″ h, standing nude figure holds 6″ d round crackled rose glass globe . .	395.00
Wall Pocket, 12″ h, seated nude figure supported by wrought iron metal frame work, metal pan for flowers . . .	285.00

FRANKOMA POTTERY

History: John N. Frank founded a ceramic art department at Oklahoma University in Norman and taught there for several years. In 1933 he established his own business and began making Oklahoma's first commercial pottery. Frankoma moved from Norman to Sapulpa, Oklahoma, in 1938.

A fire completely destroyed the new plant later the same year, but rebuilding began almost immediately. The company remained in Sapulpa and continued to grow. Frankoma is the only American pottery to be permanently exhibited at the International Ceramic Museum of Italy.

In September 1983 a disastrous fire struck once again, destroying 97% of Frankoma's facilities. The rebuilt Frankoma Pottery reopened on July 2, 1984. Production has been limited to 1983 production molds only. All other molds were lost in the fire.

Prior to 1954 all Frankoma pottery was made with a honey–tan colored clay from Ada, Oklahoma. Since 1954 Frankoma has used a brick red clay from Sapulpa. During the early 1970s the clay became lighter and is now pink in color.

There were a number of early marks. One most eagerly sought is the leopard pacing on the FRANKOMA name. Since the 1938 fire, all pieces have carried only the name FRANKOMA.

References: Phyllis and Tom Bess, *Frankoma Treasures,* published by authors, 1983, 1990 value update; Susan N. Cox, *Collectors Guide To Frankoma Pottery,* Book I (1979), Book II (1982), published by author.

Leaf Dish, Gracetone, green and brown, ftd, #226, 12¼″ l, 6⅛″ w, 1⅞″ h, $15.00.

Bookends, pr, 5¾″ h, Mountain Girl	60.00
Bottle Vase, V–2, 1970, sgd "John Frank"	50.00
Bowl, 10″ d, Cactus, carved	40.00
Candleholder, Oral Roberts	8.00
Christmas Card	
1952, Donna Frank	45.00
1960, The Franks	55.00
1975, Grace Lee & Milton Smith	85.00
Coin, 1¾″ d, Elect John Frank	15.00
Decanter, Fingerprint, stopper, 2 qt	25.00
Dish, leaf shape, Gracetone	15.00
Jar, carved, #70	25.00

Jewelry, earrings, clip, pr	20.00
Match Holder, 1¾″ h, #89A	15.00
Mask	
Comedy	5.00
Tragedy	5.00
Mug	
American Airlines Eagle	35.00
Donkey, red and white, 1976	18.00
Elephant, gold and white, 1973	50.00
Pitcher	
Thunderbird, 5″ h	50.00
Wagon Wheel, 2 qt	20.00
Plate	
Christmas, 1972	20.00
Jesus The Carpenter, 1971	20.00
Liberty, 1986	15.00
Madonna of Love, 1978	15.00
Salt and Pepper Shakers, pr, wagon wheels	10.00
Sculpture	
Amazon Woman, 6¼″ h	225.00
Buffalo, 3½″ h	225.00
Clydesdale, 6¾″ h, rearing position	55.00
Colt, 8″ h, prancing	250.00
Fan Dancer, red clay	150.00
Greyhound, 14″ l, peach glow	125.00
Indian Chief, Ada clay, brown high glaze	65.00
Mountain Girl, Ada clay, prairie green	210.00
Toby Mug	
Cowboy, 4½″ h	8.00
Uncle Sam, 4½″ h	8.00
Trivet	
Cattle Brands	10.00
Lazybone	30.00
Vase	
Fireside, 17″ h	30.00
Flowerabrum, #58, 11½″ h	70.00
Hobby Horse, 3½″ h	75.00
Wall Pocket	
Boot	15.00
Leaf, 8½″ l	35.00
Ram's Head	50.00
Wreath, "With Our Love, Frankoma" on back	40.00

FRATERNAL ORGANIZATIONS

History: Benevolent and secret societies played an important part in American society from the late 18th to the mid 20th centuries. Initially the societies were organized to aid members and their families in times of distress or death. They evolved from this purpose into important social clubs by the late 19th century.

In the 1950s, with the arrival of civil rights, an attack occurred on the secretiveness and often discriminatory practices of these societies. The fraternal movement, with the exception of the Masonic organizations, suffered serious membership loss. Many local chapters closed and sold their lodge halls. This resulted in many fraternal items arriving in the antiques market.

Museums: Knights of Columbus Headquarters Museum, New Haven, CT; Museum of Our National Heritage, Lexington, MA; Odd Fellows Historical Society, Caldwell, ID 83661.

Additional Listings: See *Warman's Americana & Collectibles* for more examples.

MASONIC

Apron
  12½" h, 14" w, white satin, blue velvet, silver metallic embroidery and trim, tassels, fringe, and cording **25.00**
  23¾" h, 19½" w, painted satin, applied faded blue ribbon edging, wear and damage, framed. **40.00**
  71 x 15", printed, early 19th C, some discoloration **110.00**
Book, *History of the Most Ancient & Honorable Fraternity of Free & Accepted Masons in New York from the Earliest Date,* Charles T McClenachan, 1888, Grand Lodge, New York. **20.00**
Certificate, Amos and Elias A Galloupe, ornate carved frame, gilt liner, c1872, 22" w, 31" l **935.00**
Creamer, Ruby Thumbprint pattern, engraved "Masonic Temple 1893" **30.00**
Jewelry
  Pendant, 2⅞" h, silver, engraved inscriptions, insignia and "Wm Faulkner Geneva, Royal Arch Chapt No 36" **500.00**
  Pin, 14K gold, Masonic emblem centered by a carved moonstone depicting man in the moon, elaborate frame, 6.4 dwt **220.00**
Ring, platinum and diamond, center old mine–cut diamond, five point star set with colored stones, pierced diamond set top. **1,100.00**
Medal, 3¼" h, silver, engraved "Ira E Finfrock 1893," orig case **125.00**
Shelf, 15½" h, folding, walnut, old varnish finish, good carved detail, incomplete bottom bracket **55.00**
Sign, 29" d, wrought iron, hammered wreath mounted with ribbon, encircling calipers and triangle, three hanging bells, 19th C **440.00**

OTHERS

American Legion, cane, wood, Milwaukee, 1941.   **25.00**
Benevolent & Protective Order of the Elks, BPOE
  Badge, 1920 Chicago 56th Annual Reunion **15.00**
  Beaker, 5" h, cream, black elk head, marked "Mettlach, Villeroy & Boch"   **100.00**
  Book, *National Memorial,* 1931, color illus. **30.00**
  Plaque, 10½" d, hp, elk head, Sioux City Lodge #112, c1895. . . . .   **110.00**
  Plate, tin, litho Elk lodge, Mt Hood and elk by river scene, 1912 . . . .   **75.00**
  Shaving Mug, pink and white, gold elk head, crossed American flags and floral dec, marked "Germany" on bottom **70.00**
  Tumbler, engraved "Philadelphia 1907" **15.00**
Eastern Star
  Demitasse Cup and Saucer, porcelain   **18.00**
  Jewelry, ring, gold, Past Matron, star shape stone with diamond in center   **135.00**
Grand Army of the Republic, GAR
  Badge, Wisconsin State Encampment, May 20–22, 1896 . . . .   **20.00**
  Flask, 2½ x 2¾", china, Encampment at Trenton, NJ, June 22 and 23, 1905, cork closure **150.00**
  Souvenir Spoon, Philadelphia Encampment, 1899 . . . .   **20.00**
Independent Order of Odd Fellows, IOOF
  Sign, 29½" h, 100" l, Phillipstown Lodge 815, carved, painted, gilt lettering, three interlacing ropes, c1830 . . . .   **2,640.00**
  Watch Fob, 94th Anniversary, April 12, 1913 . . . .   **25.00**
Knights of Columbus
  Matchbook holder, 1919 . . . .   **24.00**
  Sword, dress, scabbard, detailed

Independent Order of Odd Fellows, pinback button, Temple, Philadelphia, ⅞" d, $5.00.

blade, marked "The McLilley Co, Columbus, OH" **50.00**

Knights Templar
Plate, 8″ d, china, Pittsburgh Commandery, 1903 . . . . **45.00**
Tumbler, 3½″ h, metal, 1901 Conclave **70.00**

Shrine
Cup and Saucer, china, Los Angeles, 1906 . . . . **70.00**
Goblet, St Paul 1908, ruby stained glass, pedestal foot **65.00**
Ice Cream Mold, 4¼″ l, pewter, crescent with Egyptian head, marked "E & Co, NY" **25.00**
Liquor Measurer, cranberry and clear, symbols and officers names, St Louis, 1909 . . . . **295.00**
Mug, Syria Temple, Pittsburgh 1895, Nantasket Beach, gold figures **120.00**

FRUIT JARS

History: Fruit jars are canning jars used to preserve food. Thomas W. Dyott, one of Philadelphia's earliest and most innovative glassmakers, was promoting his glass canning jars in 1829. John Landis Mason patented his screw-type canning jar on November 30, 1858. This date refers to the patent date, not the age of the jar. There are thousands of types of jars in many colors, types of closures, sizes, and embossings.

References: Alice M. Creswick, *The Red Book No. 6: The Collector's Guide To Old Fruit Jars*, published by author, 1990; Dick Roller, *Standard Fruit Jar Reference*, published by author, 1987; Dick Roller, *Supplementary Price Guide To Standard Fruit Jar Reference*, published by author, 1987; Bill Schroeder, *1000 Fruit Jars: Priced And Illustrated*, 5th Edition, Collector Books, 1987.

Periodicals: *Bottles & Extras*, PO Box 154, Happy Camp, CA 96039; *Fruit Jar Newsletter*, 364 Gregory Ave., West Orange, NJ 07052.

Collectors' Clubs: Ball Collectors Club, 22203 Doncaster, Riverview, MI 48192; Midwest Antique Fruit Jar & Bottle Club, PO Box 38, Flat Rock, IN 47234.

Additional Listings: See *Warman's Americana & Collectibles* for more examples.

Advance, Pat Apld For, aqua, ground lip, qt **80.00**
Atlas Mason's Patent, medium yellow–green, ABM lip, qt **45.00**
Ball, Mason, yellow–green, amber striations, qt **75.00**
BBGMCO, aqua, ground lip, insert, zinc band, qt **70.00**
Belle, Pat Dec 14th 1869, aqua, three raised feet, ground lip, lid, metal neck band, wire bail, qt **750.00**

Atlas E–Z Seal, blue, 1 quart, $10.00.

Clarke Fruit Jar Co, Cleveland, OH, aqua, ground lip, lid, metal cam lever closure, 1½ pt **160.00**
Cohansey, aqua, ground lip, lid, wire clamp, pt **55.00**
Crystal Jar, Patd Dec 17, 1878, clear, ground lip **70.00**
Dodge Sweeney & Co's, California, Butter, aqua, ground lip, glass insert, zinc band, 1½ qt **425.00**
Eagle, aqua, applied mouth, lid, cast iron yoke, qt **120.00**
Excelsior, aqua, ground lip, insert, zinc band, qt **575.00**
Fahnestock Albree & Co, aqua, applied mouth, qt **35.00**
Flaccus Bros, yellow–amber, ground lip, steer head motif **350.00**
Franklin Fruit Jar, aqua, ground lip, zinc lid **210.00**
Fruit Keeper, pale green aqua, ground lip, orig lid, GCCO monogram, pt . . . **35.00**
Gem aqua, ground lip, zinc band, CFJCO monogram **80.00**
Gilberds Improved Jar, aqua, ground lip, wire band, qt **150.00**
Globe, yellow–amber, ground lip, lid, metal closure, half gallon **100.00**
C K Halle & Co, 121 Water St, Cleveland, OH, aqua, applied mouth, qt . . **50.00**
Helme's Railroad Mills, amber, ground lip, insert, zinc band, pt **70.00**
High Grade, aqua, ground lip, zinc lid, qt **150.00**
Howe, Scranton, PA, aqua, ground lip, lid, wire bail, qt **40.00**
Johnson & Johnson, New York, cobalt blue, ground lip, orig insert, screw band, qt **325.00**
Lafayette, aqua, tooled lip, orig 3 pc glass and metal stopper, qt **190.00**
Mason
Cross, patent Nov 30th 1858, yellow–amber, qt **160.00**
Improved, aqua, ground lip, zinc band **40.00**

Patent Nov 30th 1858, medium yellow–green, ground lip, qt 210.00
Star, medium amber, ground lip, zinc lid, pt 300.00
Union, shield, aqua, ground lip, qt . 100.00
McMechens Always The Best Old Virginia Wheeling, WV, clear, black woman holding box, screw band, pt . 55.00
Millville–Hitall's Patent, aqua, applied mouth, iron yoke, half pt. 140.00
Ne Plus Ultra Airtight Fruit Jar, aqua, applied mouth, missing lid, half gallon. . 575.00
Peerless, aqua, applied mouth, iron yoke, half gallon 80.00
Phoenix Surgical Dressing Co, Milwaukee, WI, amber, ground lip, wire closure, qt. 275.00
Potter & Bodine, Air–tight Fruit Jar, Philada, aqua, pontil scar base, applied wax seal ring, half gallon 400.00
Protector, aqua, ground lip, orig metal lid, half gallon 40.00
Star, aqua, emb star, ground lip, zinc insert and screw band, qt. 300.00
The Magic Fruit Jar, pale green, ground lip, metal clamp, qt 160.00
The Pearl, aqua, ground lip, screw band, qt. 35.00
The Schaffer Jar, Rochester, NY, aqua, orig domed lid, qt 160.00
Tillyer, aqua, ground lip, lid, wire clamp, qt. 55.00
Union N1, Beaver Falls Glass Co, Beaver Falls, PA, aqua, applied wax seal ring, half gallon 30.00
Whitmore's Patent, Rochester, NY, 3, aqua, ground lip, wire closure, qt . . . 425.00

FRY GLASS

History: The H. C. Fry Glass Co. of Rochester, Pennsylvania, began operating in 1901 and continued until 1933. Their first products were brilliant period cut glass. They later produced Depression tablewares. In 1922 they patented heat-resisting ovenware in an opalescent color. This "Pearl Oven Glass" was produced in a variety of oven and table pieces, including casseroles, meat trays, pie and cake pans, and so on. Most of these pieces are marked "Fry" with model numbers and sizes.

Fry's beautiful art line, Foval, was produced only in 1926-27. It is pearly opalescent, with jade green or delft blue trim. It is rarely signed, except for occasional silver overlay pieces marked "Rockwell." Foval is always evenly opalescent, never striped like Fenton's opalescent line.

Reference: Fry Glass Society, *Collector's Encyclopedia of Fry Glass*, Collector Books, 1989, 1990 value update.

Collectors' Club: H. C. Fry Glass Society, PO Box 41, Beaver, PA 15009.

Reproduction Alert: In the 1970s, reproductions of Foval were made in abundance in Murano, Italy. These pieces, including candlesticks, toothpicks, and so on, have teal blue transparent trim.

Butter Dish, cov, Pearl Oven Ware . . 65.00
Canape Plate, 6¼" d, 4" h cobalt blue center handle, Foval 160.00
Candlesticks, pr, 9" h, Foval, blue threads, cobalt blue neck and base rings 250.00
Casserole, cov, Pearl Oven Ware . . . 25.00
Compote, 6¾" d, Foval, jade green stem 115.00
Creamer, Foval, blue tinted loopings, applied Delft blue handle 150.00
Cruet, Foval, cobalt blue handle, orig stopper. 115.00
Cup and Saucer, Foval, cobalt blue stripe, pale blue opaline ground 60.00

Custard Cups, marked "Fry/Ovenglass," left: 3⅝ x 2¾", 1927–26 patent dates, $8.00; right: 3½ x 2", 1936–41 patent dates, $10.00.

Decanter, 9" h, ftd, Foval, applied Delft blue handle. 165.00
Ice Cream Tray, 14" l, 7" w, cut glass, Nelson pattern variation, allover cutting, sgd "Fry". 270.00
Plate, 9½" d, Foval, Delft blue rim . . . 72.00
Platter, Pearl Oven Ware, etched rim 20.00
Punch Cup, Crackle, clear, cobalt blue ring handle 42.00
Reamer, canary, fluted 200.00
Salad Bowl, 9¼" d, 5½" h, opalescent pearl, jade green rim and pedestal foot, Catalog No. 2504, accompanied by Fry Co. Catalog No. 12 . . . . 275.00
Sherbet, 4" h, cut glass, Chicago pattern 72.00
Teapot, Foval, cobalt blue spout, handle and knob 215.00
Tumbler, 5¼" h, Crackle, green handle 65.00
Vase
    7½" h, Foval, jade green, rolled rim and foot 200.00
    10" h, Foval, bud, cobalt blue foot . 125.00
Water Pitcher, Foval, alabaster body, jade green base and handle. 275.00

FULPER POTTERY

History: The American Pottery Company of Flemington, New Jersey, made pottery jugs and housewares from the early 1800s. They made Fulper Art Pottery from approximately 1910 to 1930.

Their first line of art pottery was called Vasekraft. The shapes were primarily either rigid and controlled, being influenced by the arts and crafts movement, or of Chinese influence. Equal concern was given to the glazes which showed an incredible diversity.

Pieces made between 1910 and 1920 were of the best quality because less emphasis was put on production output. Almost all pieces are molded.

References: Robert Blassberg, *Fulper Art Pottery: An Aesthetic Appreciation,* Art Lithographers, 1979; John Hibel et al., *The Fulper Book,* published by authors, n.d.

Bottle, music box, 10″ h, $300.00.

Bowl
  11½″ d, No. 559, blue, ivory, and
    brown flambe glaze, imp mark. . . .   220.00
  11¾″ d, double handles, matte rose
    and green flambe glaze, stamp
    mark. 240.00
  15″ d, No. 472L, verte antique, green
    and ivory flambe glaze, Vasekraft
    label remnants, stamp mark 285.00
Dresser Box, cov, 8½″ h, bisqueware,
  figural Egyptian Revival woman on
  cov, hp accessories, imp marks 315.00

Jar, 6¼″ h, No. 564, matte green glaze,
  obscured mark 260.00
Jug, 7¾″ d, 12¼″ h, ovoid, wide shoulder,
    short cylindrical neck, high
    arched loop handle, copper dust
    glaze, raised vertical mark, paper
    label. 2,310.00
Lamp, 16″ h, 14″ d pottery mushroom
    shaped shade, soft olive green,
    pierced heraldic form openings with
    inset colored leaded glass, tall waisted
    trumpet form pottery base,
    printed company logo, numbers, and
    "Fulper Patents Pending in United
    States and Canada, England, France
    and Germany" 11,000.00
Vase
  6¾″ h, 2″ d, bud, slender ovoid body,
    flared rim, short pedestal, domed,
    ringed foot, wisteria matte glaze,
    vertical ink mark. 90.00
  8″ h, 5¾″ d, squatty, narrow bulbous
    ftd base narrowing to cylindrical
    body, four molded buttress handles,
    mirrored black and apple green
    flambe glaze, vertical box ink mark   350.00
  10″ h, 7½″ d, Pilgrim flask form, ftd
    round flattened body, short cylindrical
    neck, flared rim, C-scroll handles,
    apple green and gunmetal
    brown flambe glaze, small vertical
    ink mark 450.00
  10″ h, 8″ d, compressed bulbous form,
    thick foot, tapering to wide short cylindrical
    banded neck, flaring rim,
    crystallized gunmetal gray glaze
    over tiger's eye base, vertical ink
    mark. 1,650.00
  12″ h, 11½″ d, wide bulbous ftd body,
    very short wide cylindrical neck,
    heavy rolled rim, two molded loop
    handles, crystalline celadon and
    dusty pink glaze, incised vertical
    mark. 880.00
  17″ h, No. 56M, hand thrown, crystalline
    green glaze, partial paper Vasekraft
    label and stamp, drilled . . .   360.00
  18″ h, vasiform, circular ftd base,
    white glazed, imp Fulper–Stangl
    mark, crazing. 220.00

FURNITURE

History: Two major currents dominate the American furniture marketplace—furniture made in Great Britain and furniture made in the United States. American buyers continue to show a strong prejudice for objects manufactured in the United States. They will pay a premium for such pieces and accept them above technically superior and more aesthetic English examples.

Until the last half of the 19th century formal American styles were dictated by English examples and design books. Regional furniture, such as the Hudson River Valley [Dutch] and the Pennsylvania German styles, did develop. A less formal furniture, often designated as the "country" or vernacular style, developed throughout the 19th and early 20th centuries. These country pieces deviated from the accepted formal styles and have a genre charm that many collectors find irresistible.

America did contribute a number of unique decorative elements to English styles. The American Federal period is a reaction to the English Hepplewhite period. American designers created furniture which influenced, rather than reacted to, world taste in the Gothic Revival style, Arts and Craft Furniture, Art Deco, and Modern International movement.

FURNITURE STYLES [APPROX. DATES]

William and Mary	**1690–1730**
Queen Anne	**1720–1760**
Chippendale	**1755–1790**
Federal [Hepplewhite]	**1790–1815**
Sheraton	**1790–1810**
Empire [Classical]	**1805–1830**
Victorian	
French Restauration	**1830–1850**
Gothic Revival	**1840–1860**
Rococo Revival	**1845–1870**
Elizabethan	**1850–1915**
Louis XIV	**1850–1914**
Naturalistic	**1850–1914**
Renaissance Revival	**1850–1880**
Neo-Greek	**1855–1885**
Eastlake	**1870–1890**
Art Furniture	**1880–1914**
Arts and Crafts	**1895–1915**
Art Nouveau	**1896–1914**
Art Deco	**1920–1945**
International Movement	**1940–Present**

Furniture is one of the few antiques fields where regional preferences is a factor in pricing. Victorian furniture is popular in New Orleans but unpopular in New England. Oak is in demand in the Northwest but not so much in the Middle Atlantic states.

Prices vary considerably on furniture. Shop around. Furniture is plentiful unless you are after a truly rare example. Examine all pieces thoroughly. Too many furniture pieces are bought on impulse. Turn furniture upside down; take it apart. The amount of repairs and restoration to a piece has a strong influence on price. Make certain you know about all repairs and changes before buying.

Beware of the large number of reproductions. During the twenty–five years following the American Centennial of 1876, there was a great revival in copying furniture styles and manufacturing techniques of earlier eras. These centennial pieces now are more than one hundred years old. They confuse many dealers and collectors.

The prices listed below are "average" prices. They are only a guide. High and low prices are given to show the market range.

References: Henri Algoud, Leon LeClerc, and Paul Baneat, *Authentic French Provincial Furniture From Provence, Normandy, and Brittany,* Dover Publications, 1993; *American Manufactured Furniture, Furniture Dealers' Reference Book,* reprint by Schiffer Publishing, 1988; John Andrews, *Victorian and Edwardian Furniture Reference and Price Guide,* Antique Collectors' Club, 1992; Sam Burchell, *A History Of Furniture: Celebrating Baker Furniture 100 Years Of Fine Reproductions,* Harry N. Abrams, 1991; Joseph T. Butler, *Field Guide To American Furniture,* Facts on File Publications, 1985; Robert Judson Clark et al., *Design In America: The Cranbrook Vision, 1925–1950,* Harry N. Abrams, Detroit Institute of Arts, and the Metropolitan Museum of Art, 1983; Wendy Cooper, *Classical Taste In America: 1800–1840,* Abbeville Press, 1993; Eileen and Richard Dubrow, *Furniture, Made In America, 1875–1905,* Schiffer Publishing, 1982; Eileen and Richard Dubrow, *American Furniture of the 19th Century, 1840–1880,* Schiffer Publishing, 1983; Rachael Feild, *Macdonald Guide To Buying Antique Furniture,* Wallace–Homestead, 1989; Benno M. Forman, *American Seating Furniture, 1630–1730,* Winterthur Museum, W. W. Norton & Company, 1988; Phillipe Garner, *Twentieth–Century Furniture,* Van Nostrand Reinhold, 1980; Myrna Kaye, *Fake, Fraud, Or Genuine, Identifying Authentic American Antique Furniture,* New York Graphic Society Book, 1987; Constance King, *Country Pine Furniture,* Chartwell Books, 1989; *Knopf Collectors' Guides To American Antiques: Furniture,* 2 vols., Alfred A. Knopf, 1982; Ralph Kylloe, *Rustic Traditions,* published by author, 1993; Lew Larason, *Buying Antique Furniture: An Advisory,* Scorpio Publications, 1992; David P. Lindquist and Caroline C. Warren, *Colonial Revival Furniture With Prices,* Wallace–Homestead, 1993; David P. Lindquist and Caroline C. Warren, *English & Continental Furniture With Prices,* Wallace–Homestead, 1994; L–W Book Sales (ed.), *Furniture Of The Arts & Crafts Period,* L–W Book Sales, 1992; Karl Mang, *History of Modern Furniture,* Harry N. Abrams, 1978; Robert F. McGiffin, *Furniture Care and Conservation, Revised Third Edition,* AASLH, 1992; Kathryn McNerney, *American Oak Furniture,* Book I (1984, 1994 value update), Book II (1994), Collector Books; Kathryn McNerney *Pine Furniture, Our American Heritage,* Collector Books, 1989; Kathryn McNerney *Victorian Furniture,* Collector Books, 1981, 1994 value update; Dana G. Morykan and Harry L. Rinker, *Warman's Country Antiques & Collectibles, Second Edition,* Wallace–Homestead, 1994; Milo M. Naeve, *Identifying American Furniture: A Pictorial Guide To Styles and Terms, Colonial to Contemporary, Second Edition,* American Association for State and Local History, 1989; George C. Neumann, *Early American Antique Country Furnishings: Northeastern America, 1650–1880's,* L–W Book Sales, 1984, 1993 reprint; Peter Philip, Gillian Walkling, and John Bly, *Field Guide To Antique Furniture,* Houghton Mifflin, 1992; Ellen M. Plante, *Country Furniture,* Wallace–Homestead, 1993; Don and Carol Raycraft, *Collector's Guide to Country Furniture,* Book I (1984, 1991 value update), Book II (1988), Collector Books; Harry L. Rinker (ed.), *Warman's Furniture,* Wallace–Homestead, 1993; Charles Santore, *The Windsor Style in America, 1730–1830, Revised,* Volumes I and II, Running Press, 1992; Tim Scott, *Fine Wicker Furniture, 1870–1930,* Schiffer Publishing, 1990; Dominic R. Stone, *The Art of Biedermeir,* Chartwell Books, 1990; Robert W. and Harriett Swedberg, *American Oak Furniture Styles and Prices,* Book I, Third Edition (1992), Book II, Second Edition (1991), Book III, Second Edition (1991), Wallace–Homestead; Robert W. and Harriett Swedberge, *Collector's Encyclopedia of American Furniture,* Vol. 1 (1990, 1993 value update), Vol. 2 (1992), Vol. 3 (1994), Collector Books; Robert W. and Harriett Swedberg, *Furniture of the Depression Era,* Collector Books, 1987, 1992 value update; Robert W. and Harriett Swedberg, *Swedberg's Price Guide To Antique Oak Furniture, First Series,* Collector Books, 1994; Robert W. and Harriett Swedberg, *Victorian Furniture, Book III,* Wallace–Homestead, 1985; Norman Vandal, *Queen Anne Furniture,* The Taunton Press, 1990; Gerald W. R. Ward, *American Case Furniture,* Yale University Art Gallery, 1988; Velma Susanne Warren, *Golden Oak Furniture,* Schiffer Publishing, 1992; Derita Coleman Williams and Nathan Harsh, *The Art and Mystery of Tennessee Furniture,* Tennessee Historical Society, 1988; Christopher Wilk, *Marcel Breuer: Furniture and Interiors,* The Museum of Modern Art and Harry N. Abrams, 1981; Ghenete Zelleke, Eva B. Ottillinger, and Nina Stritzler, *Against The Grain: Bentwood Furniture From The Collection Of Fern And Manfield Steinfield,* The Art Institute of Chicago, 1993.

There are hundreds of specialized books on individual furniture forms and styles. Two examples of note are: Monroe H. Fabian, *The Pennsylvania–German Decorated Chest,* Universe Books, 1978, and Charles Santore, *The Windsor Style In America, 1730–1830, Revised,* Vols. I and II, Running Press, 1992.

Additional Listings: Arts and Craft Movement, Art Deco, Art Nouveau, Children's Nursery Items, Orientalia, Shaker Items, and Stickley.

BEDS

Arts and Crafts, Gustav Stickley, three–quarter size, seven slats, butterfly joints, orig medium finish, branded mark, 45½″ w, 48″ h **2,100.00**
Chinese, 19th C, opium bed, ivory and

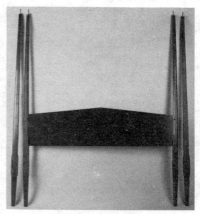

Federal, pencil post, maple, peaked headboard, New England, c1800, 53¾″ w, 75″ d, 76″ h, $1,045.00. Photograph courtesy of Skinner, Inc.

wood floral and figural inlay, 80½″ l, 50″ w, 92½″ h **2,200.00**
Chippendale, New England, c1770, daybed, carved mahogany, shaped crest, molded ears, pierced baluster splat, molded seat frame, cabriole legs joined by turned stretchers, pad feet, 74″ l **5,775.00**
Classical, American, recamier, scrolled upholstered support, exposed seat rail, scrolled legs, ball feet, 77″ l **1,980.00**
Colonial Revival, Regency Style, inlaid rosewood, upholstered head and footboard, shaped framework, brass inlay and mounts, double mattress size, 56″ h **600.00**
Continental, 19th C, sleigh, fruitwood, shaped headboard, footboard, and side rails, 83″ l, 47″ d, 45″ h **385.00**
Daybed, rattan, mid 20th C, swept back ends, wraparound skirt, spring seat support, natural finish, 79″ w, 30″ h . . **615.00**
Federal
New England, c1800, carved mahogany, tall post, tester, two fluted, vasiform, and ring turned posts, two plain posts, 82″ h **1,980.00**
New England, c1810, country, carved maple, turned and fluted, urn finials, 71″ h **1,320.00**
New England, c1820, maple, turned and carved tester, old finish, some restoration, 78″ l, 54″ w, 84″ h **1,210.00**

Pennsylvania, c1810, carved and turned mahogany, four fluted posts over carved vase shape sections, straight tapered legs terminating in block feet, brass medallions, 86" h   **3,685.00**

Salem, MA, c1805, carving attributed to Samuel McIntire, carved mahogany, four post, tapered birchwood headposts, arched pine headboard with cyma–shaped cutout, baluster form footposts with upper section reeded over acanthus leaf and waterleaf carved vase form midsection with draped grapes and leaves tied with bowknots against punchwork ground, turned feet, later tester, 58" w, 77" h. **7,425.00**

German, pine, panel shaped headboard with painted landscape of lady and gentleman, floral and leaf motifs, inscribed "Johann and Maria Katharina" and "1824," turned footposts, overhead tester panel with medallions of painted landscapes, 50½" w, 72½" h   **4,675.00**

Neoclassical, Italian, 19th C, sleigh, walnut and ebonized wood, applied scrolled dec on sides, applied turned posts on legs, 52" w, 69" l, 47" h. . . .   **1,540.00**

Rope, refinished maple with some curl, turned posts with bottlelike finials, replaced footboard, replaced side rails, 56 x 74" mattress size, 52" h **990.00**

Sheraton, c1825, rope, maple, goblet finials, side rails, 57" h, 54" w **350.00**

Victorian, Renaissance Revival, American, c1872, stained maple and burled maple, tester, arched headboard with center carved rosette above panel dec with opposed winged griffins and floral scrolls, panel of suspended palmettes below, gilt incised half round pilasters flanking the conforming footboard, side rails, posts, and rounded quarter canopy, minor restorations, 67" w, 72" h headboard **6,600.00**

BENCHES

Bucket, Ohio, Amish, ash, three shelves, old varnish finish, 37" w, 14" d, 32" h **250.00**

Cobbler, country, pine, top divided shelf, drawers, old nut brown patina, old repairs, 44" l **450.00**

Dresser, French style, carved wood frame, reupholstered gold plush seat, blonde finish, 35" l. **150.00**

Garden, Gothic Revival, American, Philadelphia, mid 19th C, cast iron, scrolled back and arms, slat seat, marked "Wood & Perot, Makers Philad".   **2,100.00**

Settle Bench, pine, New England, 54" l, 52" h, $850.00.

Hall, George IV, English, c1850, mahogany, rect seat, turned legs, 42" l, 11¾" d, 17¼" h **770.00**

Kneeling, walnut, old dark finish, 39" l   **50.00**

Primitive, pine, legs mortised through top, old worn finish, traces of paint, 61" l, 12" d, 18" h **85.00**

Settle

  Arts and Crafts, Gustav Stickley, No. 225, five side slats, one broad horizontal back slat, orig color and finish, branded mark, 78" l, 31" d, 28" h **5,225.00**

  Country, scrolled arms, spindle back with turned posts, plank seat, plain turned tapering legs, old black repaint, minor repairs, 72½" l **250.00**

  English, early 18th C, pine, shaped sides, plank seat, U–shape base, old refinish, 24" w, 14" d, 64" l . . .   **950.00**

  Plank seat, arrow back, simple turnings, curved arms, brown refinishing, 90" l **610.00**

Water Bench, country, poplar, old worn olive gray repaint, 48½" w, 41" d, 29" h. **450.00**

Window

  Federal, mahogany, S–scroll end, brass inlaid crest above pierced cornucopia slat, molded supports, plain seat rail foliage stenciled with gilt highlights, rect drop–in seat, saber legs, 45 x 32½" **4,950.00**

  Italian, Neoclassical, pierced foliate carved overscrolled sides, carved apron, gold textured upholstered seat, toupie feet, 41" l **835.00**

Regency style, stained wood, carved sides, needlepoint upholstered seat, circular turned legs, 52" l, 16" d, 30" h. **210.00**

BENTWOOD

In 1856, Michael Thonet of Vienna perfected the process of bending wood by using steam. Shortly after, Bentwood furniture became popular. Other manufacturers of Bentwood furniture were Jacob and Joseph Kohn; Philip Strobel and Son; Sheboygan Chair Co.; and Tidoute Chair Co. Bentwood furniture is still being produced today by the Thonet firm and others.

Bed, c1900, scrolled and carved headboard, conforming footboard, double mattress size, 60" h. **750.00**
Chair
  Armchair, Thonet, c1900, scrolled back and arms, cane seat, splayed legs, orig label and stamp. **300.00**
  Desk, c1890, arched crest rail, tightly woven cane back and rounded seat, scrolled bentwood arms, X–form base, adjustable pedestal . . .   **450.00**
  Side, J & J Kohn, c1900, oak, pressed wood seat insert, branded and paper label remnants, 36" h **110.00**
Cradle, c1900, oval bentwood basket, shaped cradle, extended ornate scrolled support, 52" l, 36" h. **750.00**
Easel, artist's **75.00**
Rack, spindle back, central mirror, overhead spindle shelf, bentwood hook on outside rails, spindle containers flank horizontal rack, bentwood frame, natural color, 48½" w, 17" d, 74¼" h . . .   **1,320.00**
Rocker, Thonet, sleigh type, sgd . . .   **850.00**
Settee, Kohn, three part scrolled back and arms, cane back and seat, splayed legs, 47" l. **700.00**
Table, Austria, c1900, center, shaped oblong white marble top, narrow frieze, elaborate bentwood cruciform base with interlocking and overlapping scrolls centering on turned standard, 45½" l, 28½" h **300.00**

BLANKET CHESTS

Chippendale, Pennsylvania, c1774, dower, walnut, inlaid initials and date, rect, dovetailed, two drawers, bracket feet, 49" w, 23½" d, 27" h. **1,540.00**
Federal, Central Massachusetts, c1820, grain and putty dec, lid top, brass escutcheon, two drawers, glass knobs, bracket feet, 38" w, 17½" d, 41" h. . . .   **4,290.00**
Grain Painted
  American, pine, orig flame graining, dovetailed case, lid edge molding, turned feet, 38" w, 20¼" d, 24½" h   **500.00**
Massachusetts, c1750, maple and pine, painted salmon, lift rect top, two faux drawers, single base drawer, 41¾" w, 18" d, 34½" h . . .   **1,540.00**
Maine, c1830, pine, oblong top, outset corners, till, well grained painted, front panel with two convex pilasters above dentil carved shaped skirt, bracket feet, painted brown and ocher on cream ground, 45" w, 19¼" d, 25¾" h **6,000.00**
New England, late 18th C, pine, painted salmon, 42" w, 18" d, 37" h   **1,650.00**
New England, c1800, pine, red and black paint dec, rect lift top, scalloped bracket feet, 42½" w, 20½" d, 28" h .   **1,760.00**
New England, c1820, grain painted, rect lift top, two faux drawers, two long drawers, wooden knobs, ring turned urn shaped feet 37½" w, 18" d, 44" h. **1,540.00**
Pennsylvania
  Pine, attributed to Centre County, dovetailed case, bracket feet, and till, orig wrought-iron bear trap lock and strap hinges, worn orig painted dec, central panel of eagle, shield, banner, pinwheels, tulips, and compass stars, banner reads "Catarine Klinglibe 1816," traces of compass dec on lid and ends, replaced escutcheon, minor edge damage, 51½" w, 22½" d, 27" h. **3,500.00**
  Pine, rect hinged lid, painted front with arch centered with flowers in urn, floral motifs and 1828, sides painted with geometric and diaper designs, molded base, bracket feet, blue, green, yellow, and tan, 43½ x 19¾ x 24½". . . .   **11,000.00**
  Poplar, early 19th C, paint dec, 35½" w, 18½" d, 23" h. **7,700.00**
Vermont, six board, pine and poplar, orig brown graining simulating figured wood with inlay, till with lid and secret drawer, scalloped apron, cutout feet, orig hinges reset, some damage, 43¾" w, 17½" d, 43¼" h   **1,700.00**
George III, early 19th C, mahogany, hinged rect top, storage well, front with two false drawers over deep drawer, ogee bracket feet, 37½" l, 33" h.   **1,980.00**
Pilgrim Century, carved, painted, and ebonized oak, attributed to Peter Blin, Wethersfield, CT, c1675–1710, rect hinged lid, well with till, front of case carved with two rect inset panels of stylized tulips and leaves, center oc-

tagonal panel carved with sunflowers, ebonized split balusters, mid molding, two long drawers with egg appliques, stiles form reduced feet, replaced lid, traces of orig red and black pigment, 47½" w, 20 3 /4" d, 34¼" h. **9,900.00**

Queen Anne, Massachusetts, c1740, pine, old red paint, 36" w, 17" d, 31¾" h **1,980.00**

William and Mary, New England, early 18th C, pine and turned maple, molded lift top, well above case with two mock drawers over two working molded drawers, turned feet, 39¼" w, 18½" d, 37½" h. **1,760.00**

BOOKCASES

Art Deco, American, early 1900s, polished aluminum, tin plate, pr of leaded glass doors, bird's eye maple back panels, 58" w, 17" d, 65" h . . . **7,500.00**

Art Nouveau, Majorelle, c1900, carved walnut, molded crest, carved splayed leaves, glazed door mounted with central textured purple glass panel, silvered bronze branch form spandrels, pr of narrow cupboards, molded base, carved feet, 64¼" w, 79" h . . . **3,500.00**

Arts and Crafts, Gustav Stickley, similar to No. 542, c1912, oak, medium light finish, two doors, three fitted int. shelves, hammered copper hardware, branded mark, varnished, 35¼" w, 13" d, 56" h **3,190.00**

Eastlake, American, c1870, carved walnut and burl walnut, three sections, broken pediment with architectural center ornament, plinth base with drawers **1,750.00**

Empire, mahogany, reeded top molding, three pairs of doors with Winthrop style glass dividers, rope twisted columns, paw feet. **2,950.00**

Federal, New York, c1810, inlaid mahogany, two parts, upper section with flat top, molded cornice, pr of hinged glazed doors, int. with three adjustable shelves, projecting lower section with four cockbeaded inlaid drawers, shaped skirt, bracket feet, patches of molding and veneers, 46½" w, 22" d, 92" h **4,400.00**

George III, English, c1800, mahogany, stepped molded and Greek key carved cornice, blind–fret carved frieze, pr of geometrically glazed doors over sloping fall, fitted int. of drawers and pigeonholes, blind–fret carved cupboard flanked by document drawers, four long graduated

drawers, ogee bracket feet, restorations, 37½" w, 84" h. **2,750.00**

Georgian Style, mahogany, rect top, ovolo molded edge, straight frieze, canted glazed doors, four shelves, fluted stiles, plinth base, 47" w, 37" h **825.00**

Neoclassical, Italian, walnut, projected cavetto molded cornice, two grilled cupboard doors with shelf int., two paneled cupboard doors below, sq tapered legs, 62" w, 82" h **4,675.00**

Syrian, late 19th C, mother–of–pearl and bone inlaid, shaped rect top over case fitted with arched glass doors, int. shelves, series of drawers, 66½" w, 23" d, 95" h. **3,300.00**

Victorian, American

Gothic Revival, c1830, carved rosewood, architectural pediment, two glass doors, 45¾" w, 13¾" d, 86" h **3,800.00**

Renaissance Revival, c1865, walnut, highly carved, three glass doors enclosing shelves, three cupboard doors below, 90" w, 17½" d, 118½" h **3,900.00**

BOXES

Ballot

Maple, dovetailed, sliding top, 8" w, 6" d, 12" h. **185.00**

Walnut, wide dovetails, carved wooden handles, 7½" w, 7" d, 18¼" h **125.00**

Band, New England, printed paper, rural country scene, 10½" w, 15" h **375.00**

Bible, Continental, late 17th C, oak chip work, rect molded top slanting above deep well, floral carved dec, 25" w, 16" d, 10" h **250.00**

Blanket, attributed to Pennsylvania, early 19th C, painted, stylized heart on front, six board, imperfections, 15" w, 12" d, 20½" h **1,100.00**

Bonnet Box, PA, late 18th C, bentwood, fitted lid, dower chest type dec, green ground, large central red, yellow, black, and white stellate device, two large sprouting dark green feathered leaf forms, foliate and vines on lid, 21" oval, 11¾" h **5,775.00**

Bride's, 7¾" h, 18" w, 11¼" d, dome cov, carved frieze and landscape painting, orig polychrome paint, 1790–1810 . . **3,750.00**

Candle, Georgian, British, 18th C, mahogany, sliding lid, tapered, scalloped bottom, 13¼" h **250.00**

Cigar, mahogany, striped inlay on lid and base, zinc lined, nickel plated hardware, 7½" w, 4" d, 12" h **150.00**

Document, New England, early 18th C,

found in Charlestown, MA, pine, painted green, 10½″ w, 7½″ d, 7″ h . . **825.00**

Dressing
Federal, America, early 19th C, mahogany, inlaid, mirror, 17″ w, 19″ h **275.00**
Hepplewhite, England, c1800, mahogany, inlaid, mirror, 16½″ w, 8″ d, 23″ h. **880.00**

Hat, Georgian, walnut and walnut veneer, arched top, handle, 18″ l, 8″ w, 15¼″ h. **110.00**

Knife, inlaid mahogany, England or American, c1780, minor imperfections, 9″ w, 11″ d, 14½″ h, price for pair **1,980.00**

Pantry, set of 3, graduated sizes, swing handles, orig red, gray, and blue-green paint, price for set of three . . . **1,125.00**

Pipe, cherry, well scalloped top edge, heart cutout in front, circular crest, dovetailed overlapping drawer, dovetailed base, applied edge molding, refinished, 22¼″ h **4,000.00**

Salt, hanging, oak, dovetailed, cutout opening, 6½″ w, 7½″ d, 15″ h **150.00**

Seaman's Chest, New England, c1850, rect lid, fitted well with tiers of small drawers, incised "C. B. Fisher," top dec with compass star motifs and center rect panel, underside of top painted with compass star motifs, American flag, and applied paper engraving of man and machinery, front with recessed panel painted with compass star, center applied American shield, sides with applied shields and carrying handles, painted in shades of red, white, and blue, some restoration to paint, 39½″ w, 20½″ d, 19¾″ h . . . **3,300.00**

Spice, American, 19th C, grained, round, locking top, 9¾″ h **195.00**

Storage, American, mid 19th C, painted black, gold stenciled dec, eagle on front, compass rose on lid, dove on each end, imperfections, 11″ w, 8″ d, 6″ h **165.00**

Trinket, New England, smoke grained, basket of flowers motif on lid, brass feet, 4½″ h **600.00**

Wall, American, 19th C, carved, painted red, scrolled crest, lift lid, single sectioned drawer, mustard and green floral dec, imperfections to paint, 9½″ w, 6⅜″ d, 14½″ h. **880.00**

CABINETS

Cellarette, Classical Revival, attributed to NY, c1825, mahogany and mahogany veneer, shaped base with canted corners, flattened ball shaped feet, 16½″ w, 15″ d, 33″ h **1,045.00**

Side Cabinet, Adam style, demilune, walnut and marquetry, central frieze drawer above door enclosed shelf and pair of doors, square tapered legs, brass capped caster feet, 46¼″ w, 17½″ d, 32¾″ h, $2,750.00. Photograph courtesy of C. G. Sloan & Co., Inc.

Chime, eastern US, c1840, painted, poplar, heart and scrolled cutouts, molded curved top with ball finial, molded base, 15″ w, 7″ d, 48″ h **660.00**

China
Arts and Crafts, New York state, c1912, oak, medium brown, two doors, applied framing, three removable int. shelves, brass hardware, remnants of paper label, minor burn marks, 40″ w, 16″ d, 61″ h **1,210.00**
Colonial Revival, Chippendale Style, c1940, walnut veneer, breakfront, scrolled broken pediment, center urn finial, pr of glazed doors and panels, long drawer over two cupboard doors, 44″ w, 15″ d, 76″ h . . **600.00**
Hepplewhite, inlaid mahogany, leaded glass, velvet lined int., 63″ w, 21″ d, 75½″ d **650.00**
Victorian, oak, bow front, leaded glass, amber glass diamonds in top panels, 37½″ w, 14½″ d, 61¾″ h . . **450.00**

Console, French Restoration, New York, c1820, mahogany and mahogany veneer, rect marble top, center swell front drawer over pair of molded cupboard doors flanked by plain columns capped with gilt capitals terminating in turned squatty bulbed feet, 42″ w, 17½″ d, 36″ h **1,870.00**

Curio, French style, figured veneer, ormolu trim, curved crylic panels on

doors and ends, lighted, 40¾" w,
17½" d, 71¼" h. **300.00**
Display, Baroque Style, Dutch, 19th C,
marquetry, arched molded cornice
over two glazed doors above long
drawer, raised on sq tapering legs,
bun feet, joined by double "Y" stretch-
ers, 61" w, 16½" d, 96" h **8,250.00**
Dressing, Neoclassical, North German,
c1820, mahogany and ormolu, brass
fitted triangular top, two small drawers, rotating/tilting mirror section, cabinet door, and six drawers, over two
drawers, top drawer opening to fitted
writing surface, 20" w, 154" d, 36½" h **2,750.00**
Library, George IV, English, c1825, mahogany, superstructure of four graduated bookshelves on either side,
stand with two frieze drawers on one
side, false drawers on reverse, trestle
support with concentric bosses, down
swept legs joined by turned cylinder
stretcher, casters, 36" w, 59" h **5,225.00**
Parlor
Aesthetic Movement, American,
c1880, inlaid and ebonized cherry,
superstructure with arrangement of
shelves with floral pierced galleries
on turned baluster supports, beveled rect mirror panel surrounded
by floral emb red velvet, pr of glazed
doors below flanked by inlaid stylized floral sprigs, over two cupboard doors carved with large flowerheads, flanked by inlaid sprigs,
single shelf int., stylized bracket
feet, 36" w, 72½" h. **2,200.00**
French Provincial, c1800, pine, rect
top, fielded door enclosing shelves
to one side, two glazed doors to the
right enclosing grilled shelf, two
drawers, and three cupboard doors
base, stiles continuing to form feet,
84" l, 81" h. **3,300.00**
Pedestal, Empire, c1825, mahogany,
circular gray marble top, cylindrical
body, door enclosing shelves, plinth
base, 16" d, 29" h **770.00**
Side
Napoleon III, ebonized, breakfront
top, door with central oval medallion, gilt metal mounted pilasters,
plinth base, 40" w, 38½" h. **610.00**
Regency Style, rosewood and brass
inlaid, three frieze drawers over two
grill inset cupboard doors, saber
feet, 40" w, 13" d, 36" h **1,430.00**
Rococo Style, Dutch, 19th C, marque-
try, rect top with inlaid central oval
medallion reserved on trellis
ground, tambour slide, inlaid bell-

flower pendants, exaggerated cab-
riole legs, 27¾" w, 18" h **610.00**
Vitrine
Art Nouveau, Galle, c1900, marquetry, shaped rect top, chamfered corners, molded edge, rect cabinet,
glazed door and sides, back inlaid
with tall stalks of cow parsley, door
inlaid with cow parsley and butterfly,
reeded legs, 25¾" w, 18" d, 47¾" h **5,225.00**
Louis XV, ormolu mounted amaranth
marble top, glass shelves, stamped
on back "BOUDIN," capital inter-
twined script "ME," 37½ x 15". . . . **3,750.00**
Louis XVI style, bow front, shaped incurved molded top, swag dec,
glazed sides and door, pale lime silk
lined shelf int., fluted tapered legs,
60 x 30¼ x 17" **1,900.00**

CANDLE SHIELDS

Country, cherry, replaced maple
scrolled shield, turned column, snake
feet, refinished, minor repairs, 15½"
w, 15" d, 26½" h **300.00**
George III, mahogany, walnut and sat-
inwood, shield form screen fitted with
later embroidered and painted satin
panel, adjusting on rect standard, entwined C–scroll base with ball feet, pr **8,500.00**
Hepplewhite, mahogany, embroidered
floral motif, 53" h. **600.00**

CANDLESTANDS

Chippendale
Country, cherry, one board top, stout
turned column with chip carving, tri-

**Candlestand, walnut, Zoar, OH, c1840,
18¾" w top, 25½" h, $425.00.**

pod base, scimitar feet, 17¾ x 18",
27¾" h **330.00**
Philadelphia, c1750, carved mahogany, circular dished tilt and revolving top, bird cage support, ring turned and compressed ball standard, cabriole legs, claw and ball feet, repairs to three legs, 24¼" d, 27¾" h **7,700.00**
Salem, MA, c1785, mahogany, tilt top with serpentine sides, urn standard, cabriole legs, snake feet, 20" w, 19½" d, 27½" h **2,860.00**
Classical Revival, Massachusetts, c1815, mahogany, tip top, acanthus carved post, 23 x 18¾" top, 29½" h . **1,210.00**
Empire Style, country, curly maple, tilt top, scrolled legs, turned column, two board top, refinished, repairs, 19" d, 26¾" h **600.00**
Federal
  Connecticut, c1800, inlaid cherry, 12½" x 12¼" rect top, 27¼" h **3,190.00**
  New England, c1800, birch and tiger maple, inlaid, cut corner top with center tiger maple oval inlay, tripod spider leg base, 14¼ x 16" top, 29" h **935.00**
  New England, c1810, mahogany and cherry, tilt top, 19¾" d, 29½" h . . . **1,320.00**
George III, mahogany, circular dished top, baluster turned standard, three cabriole legs, snake feet, 28 x 18". . . **610.00**
Hepplewhite, walnut, coffin shape top, spider leg, American, 18th C **350.00**
Hepplewhite Style, country, birch, tilt top, turned column, spider legs, repairs, 16" w, 28½" h **450.00**
Queen Anne
  Cherry, circular top, vasiform standard, arched legs, snake feet, American, 18th C, 16½" d, 28½" h **1,600.00**
  Mahogany, coffin shape top, turned standard, spider legs, American, late 18th C, 28⅝" h **350.00**
  Pine, sq top, turned standard, arched legs, paw feet, American, 18th C, 27" h. **440.00**
Sheraton, mahogany, hexagonal one board top, turned column, tripod base, spider legs, 17¾" sq top, 28½" h . . **350.00**
Victorian, maple, circular tilt top with foliate marquetry and penwork, ring and baluster turned standard, tripod base, toupie feet, 16" d, 30" h **410.00**

CHAIRS

Adam Style, armchair, fruitwood, shaped crest rail, pierced splat, cane seat, dec seat rail, dec tapered leg, price for pair **1,050.00**

Neo–Classical style, Italian, hall chairs, ivory and specimen marble inlaid, ebonized, price for pair, $2,200.00. Photograph courtesy of William Doyle Galleries.

Art Deco, Paimio, armchair, designed by Alvar Aalto, c1932, birch plywood seat suspended in continous laminated wood frame, 24½" w, 34½" d, 25" h . **3,300.00**
Art Moderne
  Armchair and side chair, Luigi Tagliabue, light wood, vertical ebony stripes, black seats, 39" h, price for pair. **500.00**
  Lounge
    Black wire frame seat and back, dec wooden arm rests, coiled spring seat support, four prong shaped splayed legs, c1955, 32½" h, price for pair. **990.00**
    Jens Risom, curvilinear seat frame, angular arm and leg supports, 1952, 26" d, 30" h. **165.00**
    Russel Wright, horizontal slatted back, deep seat, flat angular arm and leg supports, striped linen seat cushions, c1955, 32" d, 29¾" h. **330.00**
  Side, Charles Eames, manufactured by Herman Miller, natural finish laminated wood, backrest on metal frame, rod shape legs, paper label, 17½" d, 30" h, price for set of six. . **500.00**
Art Nouveau, side, carved walnut, rounded crest rail over solid vertical splat, carved poppy sprigs, nail studded light brown simulated leather bow front seat, channeled cabriole legs, pointed toes, price for pair **800.00**

Arts and Crafts
  Arm
    Harden Co, oak, medium–dark finish, bent arm over four vertical slats, spring cushion seat, refinished, 29¼" w, 38¼" h **715.00**
    Quaint Furniture Co, No. 916½, c1905, oak, orig dark finish, oval paper label, replaced upholstery, 27⅝" w, 38" h. **330.00**
  Dining
    Limbert, c1910, oak, orig medium finish, branded mark, 17¼" w, 38" h, price for set of six **1,980.00**
    Quaint Furniture Co, No. 377 and 377½, c1910, oak, orig medium finish, leather upholstery, metal tag, 17¾" w, 37½" h, price for set of four side chairs and one armchair **825.00**
  Gustav Stickley
    No. 370, c1912, oak, orig medium brown finish, leather upholstery, drop seats, branded mark, paper label, 17" w, 37" h, price for set of six **2,860.00**
    No. 2618, c1902, oak, medium finish, orig rush seats, red decal, 16" w, 34¾" h **550.00**
  Morris
    Lifetime, No. 584, c1910, oak, orig medium brown finish, box spring and cushion, hinged back, remnant of paper label, retailer's metal tag, 29⅜" w, 40½" h. **360.00**
  L & J G Stickley
    No. 412, c1910, oak, orig worn finish, adjustable back, wide shaped flat arms, elongated corbels, decal, 34¾" w, 42" h   **825.00**
    No. 471, c1915, oak, orig medium finish, shaped flat arms, six vertical slats, branded mark, missing bar and knobs, 31¾" w, 41½" h. **1,650.00**
    Recliner, L & J G Stickley, No. 830, c1912, oak, orig leather upholstery, box spring and cushion, remnants of "The Work of..." decal, 29¼" w, 40" h. **1,045.00**
  Chinese Export, early 19th C, armchair, bamboo, rect back, down swept arms, caned seat, columnar legs joined by stretchers, fitted with cushion, minor losses, 34" h. **880.00**
  Chippendale
    Boston, 1755–95, side, mahogany, Roman numerals "IIII" and "IIIII" inscribed in top edge and front seat rail, delicately carved vasiform back, early surface, minor imperfections, provenance descended from

John Hancock to present owner, price for pair **46,200.00**
    Connecticut, Eliphalet Chapin, c1780, side, carved cherry, solid vasiform spat, slip seat, front cabriole legs, back extends into shaped legs, turned shaped stretchers, spoon feet, 37" h. **3,630.00**
    Middle Atlantic States, c1780, side, ladderback, mahogany, minor imperfections, 38" h. **315.00**
    Newport, RI, 1770–90, armchair, mahogany, reupholstered in silk brocade, 15" h seat rail, 44½" h **11,000.00**
    Philadelphia
      Armchair, c1780, carved mahogany, ladderback of four strapwork slats, shaped arms, scrolled handholds, molded seat rail, slip seat, sq legs joined by stretchers, minor patches and repairs **1,750.00**
      Side, 1755–80, carved mahogany, acanthus carved crest, seven lobed central shell above tassel carved splat, gadrooned shoe over shell carved seat rail, acanthus carved cabriole legs, ball and claw feet, red brocade seat, 17⅛" h seat, 41½" h **45,100.00**
      Portsmouth, NH, c1780, side, carved mahogany, shaped crest with incised edge, pierced vase form splat with Gothic arch, overupholstered seat, sq molded legs joined by stretchers, price for pair **6,600.00**
  Chippendale Style
    Side, 19th C, mahogany, pierced splat, sq legs joined by stretchers, slip seat, old finish, price for set of five **2,350.00**
    Wing, late 19th C, walnut, upholstered, claw and ball feet, 44½" h, 33¼" w, 31" d **250.00**
  Classical Revival
    Massachusetts, 1809, dining, carved mahogany, semicircular drapery type back, reupholstered seat, carving at knees, reeded tapering slightly outswept legs, each carved with date, price for set of five. **1,870.00**
    New England, c1810–15, side, child's, carved and inlaid exotic woods, whale ivory, bone, and mother-of-pearl, name "Sylvia" inlaid on crest for Sylvia Howland (1806–65), old finish, minor imperfections, 13¾" h seat, 29" h. **11,000.00**
  Eastlake, American, c1870
    Lady's, walnut, Minerva head carving on crest, incised lines, applied burl veneer panels and roundels dec, shaped hip brackets with conform-

ing dec, shaped reupholstered back
and seat, turned front legs, 36″ h. . **400.00**
Side, walnut, small arms, cane seat **225.00**
Edwardian, English, c1900, side, rect
pierced carved splat with Gothic
arches, rect figural painted panel, foliate and fluted circular stiles, rect
caned seat, turned tapering legs,
price for pair.................. **660.00**
Elizabethian Revival, George Hunzinger, NY
Armchair, arched crest with spindles,
inlay cloth cov woven metal back
and seat, marked "Hunzinger Ny
Pat March 20, 1869, Pat April 18,
1876," 18″ w, 17½″ d, 38″ h **1,250.00**
Side, ebonized, back stamped "Hunzinger, NY, pat March 30, 1869,"
34″ h.................. **175.00**
Empire, American, 1825–35
Armchair, mahogany, upholstered
rect back, bowed seat, sq tapering
legs, 23″ w, 20½″ d, 35″ h, price for
pair..................... **2,750.00**
Dining, mahogany, carved crest rail,
shaped splat, needlepoint - seats,
shaped legs, price for set of four . . **550.00**
Federal
Maryland, c1820, side, rect crest rail
with painted sailing vessel and landscape, cane seat, turned tapering
legs, classical motifs and gilt on
pale yellow ground, price for pair.. **725.00**
Massachusetts, 1790–1800, dining,
six side chairs and two armchairs,
mahogany, inlaid, shield back with
rays terminating in sunset type
carving, upholstered seats with
decorative tacks, straight tapered
legs and cross stretchers, 17½″
seat rail, 37″ h, price for set of eight **13,200.00**
New England, c1810, lolling, mahog-
any, arched crest, rect back,
shaped arms, molded supports,
frontal ring turned tapering legs,
brass casters................ **2,750.00**
Philadelphia, c1805, side, carved and
satinwood inlaid mahogany,
molded shield back, pierced flowerhead and bellflower carved splat,
satinwood inlaid fan, overupholstered seat, sq molded tapering legs,
feet extended, price for pair...... **4,125.00**
Portsmouth, NH, Boston or North
Shore, MA, 1800, side, square
back, refinished, reupholstered,
17⅜″ h seats, 36″ h, price for set of
seven.................... **8,800.00**
Rhode Island, Newport or Providence,
c1880, side, carved mahogany,
molded back, pierced splat carved
at the center with calyx and swags,

upholstered seat with serpentine
front, molded sq legs joined by H–
stretcher, minor repair to shoe. **4,400.00**
George I Style, armchair, open waisted
back with inset acanthus and tassel
carved vase form splat, shepherd's
crook arms, balloon seat, acanthus
carved molded legs, claw and ball feet **720.00**
George II Style
Armchair, mahogany, carved vase
shaped splat back, drop in seat,
cabriole legs, ball and claw feet, 40″
h, price for pair **770.00**
Side, English, late 19th C, carved mahogany, foliate and ruffle carved
crest rail over interlaced and
pierced baluster splat, flared rect
seat, cabriole legs carved at knees
with ruffles and foliage, hairy animal
paw feet **425.00**
George III
English, third quarter 18th C
Armchair, beechwood, molded
crest rail, shaped upholstered
back, serpentine seat, molded
cabriole legs, scrolled feet, repairs, 37″ h................ **660.00**
Dining, mahogany, serpentine
molded crest rail, pierced splat,
bowed upholstered seat, sq tapering legs joined by stretchers,
36″ h, price for pair.......... **715.00**
Library, armchair, mahogany, rect
upholstered back, blind–frét
carved arms, sq blind–fret carved
legs joined by pierced stretchers,
extensive restoration, 37″ h, price
for pair................... **1,650.00**
Provincial, oak, arched crest rail,
strapwork splat, plank seat, sq tapering legs joined with stretcher,
price for pair **450.00**
George III Style
Armchair, English, mahogany, shield
form backrest, pierced carved splat,
Prince of Wales feathers above
outscrolled arms, red velvet upholstered serpentine seat, sq tapering
fluted legs, spade feet **440.00**
Dining, mahogany, two armchairs, six
side chairs, serpentine top rail,
pierced splat, carved wheat motif,
upholstered seat, sq tapering legs,
21″ w, 16½″ d, 37½″ h, price for set
of eight **1,650.00**
Library, English, mahogany, sq upholstered back, blind–fret carved
arms, sq upholstered seat, blind–
fret carved legs joined by stretch-
ers, distressed upholstery, 38½″ h **1,760.00**
Gothic Revival, American, mid 19th C,

armchair, walnut, carved, upholstered
arms and seat. **5,250.00**

Hepplewhite

Armchair, Martha Washington, string
inlay, upholstered back and seat . . **3,600.00**

Side

American, cherry, curved crest,
pierced splat with urn detail, slip
seat, sq tapering legs, H–
stretcher, refinished, price for pair **1,150.00**

Connecticut, c1780, mahogany,
pierced vase splat, urn finial, upholstered seat, straight tapering
legs, replaced rear corner braces **650.00**

Hitchcock, dining, two arm and four side,
turned crest rail, two horizontal slats,
plank seat, turned legs, turned front
H–form stretcher, price for set of six . **660.00**

International Movement

Alvar Aalto, c1954, reclining, armchair, birch frame supports laminated bentwood frame, back rest attached by wrought iron bar,
unmarked, restoration, 24½″ w,
30¾″ h **400.00**

Norman Chernier, designed for Plycraft, Lawrence, MA, c1958, bent
plywood seat–back, orig zipped–
back orange upholstery, Plycraft labels, 25½″ w, 30⅞″ h, price for set
of two armchairs and two side
chairs **825.00**

Ladderback, child's high chair, Middle
Atlantic States, 18th C, maple and
ash, old refinish, 18″ h seat, 34″ h
overall **825.00**

Louis XV, armchair, upholstered oval
back with carved dec, partially upholstered arm rests, upholstered seat,
carved shaped seat rail, carved
French cabriole legs, price for pair . . **330.00**

Louis XVI Style, oval shape back with
elaborate dec, balloon shape seat,
carved seat rail, fluted legs, gold finish **250.00**

Neoclassical

Italian, c1800, armchair, walnut,
caned back, molded frame above
down swept arms, scrolled terminals, bow front seat raised on stop
fluted tapering cylindrical legs, price
for set of four. **7,150.00**

Swedish, side, parcel gilt, oval upholstered back, beaded ribbon dec,
bow front seat, leaf tip carved,
fluted, tapering legs, peg feet **440.00**

Plank Seat, decorated, old yellow–green
repaint over earlier colors, striping,
stenciled, free hand fruit and foliage,
minor damage, 33″ h, price for set of
six **575.00**

Prairie School, designed by Purcell,
Feick and Elmslie for Merchants Bank

of Winona, Minnesota, c1911, flat
even arm over vertical side spindles
separated by bands of cubes at top
and bottom, recessed and framed in
stepped molding, ball feet, orig green
leather upholstery, brass tacks, un-
signed, 24⅛″ w, 23″ d, 36¾″ h **14,300.00**

Queen Anne

American, 18th C, wing, maple frame,
shaped back, out curved wings,
walnut cabriole legs, stretchers,
pad feet over flattened ball feet, 46″
h **27,250.00**

Hudson River Valley, c1750–80, armchair, maple and ash, shaped crest,
solid vase form splat, shaped arms,
rush seat, turned tapering legs
joined by stretchers, pad feet, later
brass platforms **1,760.00**

Massachusetts, c1750, wing, carved
walnut, arched upholstered back,
ogival wings, out scrolled arms, upholstered bowed seat, loose cushion, cabriole legs joined by turned
stretchers, pad feet **30,250.00**

New England

Corner, c1775, maple, shaped
arms, turned supports, turned
legs, two turned box stretchers,
red paint traces, 19″ h **450.00**

Side, c1780, painted, vase back,
Spanish foot, 41″ h **360.00**

Philadelphia, c1740, armchair, walnut, molded and scrolled carved
crest rail, vase form splat, cyma–
curved rounded stiles, scooped
arms ending in knuckle terminals,
shaped arm supports, cyma–
curved balloon seat, cabriole legs
carved with shells and C–scrolls at
knees, shaped pad feet, rear legs
flaring outward ending in sq pad
feet, repairs to arms, rear legs
pieced. **22,000.00**

Regency, French, early 19th C, armchair, ebonized and parcel gilt, caned
crest rails and seats, saber legs, orange velvet seat cushions, 23″ w, 19″
d, 35″ h, price for pair **8,250.00**

Renaissance Revival, American, attributed to John Jelliff, c1870, armchair,
walnut and burl walnut, heavily
carved, upholstered back, arms, and
seat. **600.00**

Rococo Revival

Armchair, oak, twisted arm supports
and stretchers, intricate designed
apron, striped upholstery, 46¾″ h . **200.00**

Side, walnut, balloon back, mounted
scroll and foliate carved crest,
carved splat, serpentine front seat
rail, acanthus carved hipped saber

legs, burgundy velvet upholstery, price for pair **250.00**

Rococo Style, armchair, walnut, green and cream upholstered shaped back and seat, cabriole legs, bun feet, joined by cross stretchers, 27″ w, 21½″ d, 39″ h, price for pair **1,210.00**

Sheraton

American, armchair, turned detail, shaped arms, gold striping dec, orig dark paint **210.00**

Middle Atlantic States, c1815–25, grained and paint dec, Grecian style, side, simulated rosewood, gold striping, rush seat, old surface, minor imperfections, 18″ h seat, 33½″ h overall, price for set of four **450.00**

William and Mary

Boston, Massachusetts, c1720, painted and carved, shaped back with shaped slender cane section in back, caned seat, scalloped apron, turned and block carved legs, bulbous turned stretchers, elongated Spanish feet, 19¼″ h, 45″ h overall **660.00**

Connecticut, early 18th C, armchair, turned and carved, banister back, damaged, 49″ h **880.00**

Massachusetts, 18th C, side, painted, banister back, rush seat, 45″ h . . . **525.00**

New England, 18th C, armchair, painted, rush seat, 50¼″ h **4,675.00**

Windsor

Bow Back, New England, c1805–15

Child's, plank seat on raking and baluster turned legs joined by stretchers, painted green **650.00**

Side

Bowed crest, bamboo turned posts, shaped plank seat, bamboo turned splayed legs joined with turned stretchers, stamped "E Tebbets" under seat, c1820, price for set of six **2,475.00**

Maple and pine, seven turned spindles, horseshoe shaped seat, bamboo turned legs, H-stretcher, painted red over old black paint, price for pair **500.00**

Brace Back, armchair

New England, 19th C, continuous arm, restoration, 16″ h seat **990.00**

New York, 1790–1810, continuous arm, painted, labeled "W Mac-Bride N. York," 18″ h seat, 37″ h overall **2,100.00**

Comb Back, New England, c1785, armchair, shaped crest, eight tapering spindles, U–shaped back continuing to scroll handholds, elliptical plank seat, turned legs joined by stretchers, later black paint **2,475.00**

Fan Back, American, c1790, side, shaped crest, seven tapering spindles and plank seat, turned legs joined by turned stretchers **1,000.00**

Rod Back, Massachusetts, side, painted, imp "I. C. Tuttle," 17¼″ h seat, 34¼″ h, price for set of six . . **8,250.00**

Sack Back, New England, c1780, knuckle arm, old red varnish, 28″ h **3,850.00**

Thumb Back, Pennsylvania, c1830, child's, side, polychrome dec, 29″ h **470.00**

Chippendale, carved walnut, serpentine front, molded rect top, five graduated cockbeaded drawers, cabriole legs, claw and ball feet, New England, probably MA, late 18th C, 35″ w, 21¼″ d, 33½″ h, $11,000.00. Photograph courtesy of Freeman/Fine Arts of Philadelphia.

CHESTS OF DRAWERS

Arts and Crafts, L. & J. G. Stickley, two small drawers over four large drawers, paneled sides, 30 x 37½″ w mirror, new medium finish, 37½″ w, 19½″ d, 47″ h **1,375.00**

Baroque, South Germany, mid 18th C, oak, serpentine molded top, conforming case, three drawers, molded base, flattened bun feet, 41″ w, 29½″ d, 31″ h **1,320.00**

Chinese, mid 19th C, campaign, teakwood, two pr of brass carrying handles, two part construction, foldout writing desk with pigeonholes, marble top (later addition), as found, 37½″ w, 19¾″ d, 45″ h **3,250.00**

Chippendale
American, country
Maple, dovetailed case, six overlapping dovetailed drawers, molded cornice, cutout feet, replacements and refinishing, backboard dated 1801, 36¼″ w, 58¾″ h . . . **1,600.00**
Poplar, old red repaint, molded cornice, five overlapping dovetailed drawers, applied base moldings, cutout feet, 37″ w **2,900.00**
Massachusetts, c1780, cherry, serpentine, four graduated drawers, old refinish, minor imperfections, 33¾″ w, 18″ d, 34″ h. **26,400.00**
New England, c1780, butternut and maple, six graduated drawers, ogee bracket feet, 36″ w, 18″ d, 59½″ h . **4,400.00**
New England, c1780, maple, painted red, molded cornice, six graduated long drawers, eagle brasses, scalloped bracket foot, 36″ w, 17¾″ d, 53″ h. **7,150.00**
New Hampshire, c1780, birch, molded cornice, six graduated long drawers, eagle brasses, scalloped long bracket foot, 36″ w, 18″ d, 51″ h **3,300.00**
Pennsylvania, c1780, tall, walnut, carved, molded cornice, canted sides, three small drawers over two drawers over four graduated drawers, ogee bracket feet, eagle brasses, 42½″ w, 21¼″ d, 69½″ h . **3,575.00**
Empire, country
Cherry, curly maple facade with cherry drawer edge beading, seven dovetailed drawers, paneled ends, turned pilasters and feet, refinished, 41⅜″ w, 21½″ d, 49″ h **950.00**
Curly maple, cherry, and figured walnut, seven dovetailed drawers and three step back handkerchief drawers, orig crest finials, turned feet and pilasters, alligatored varnish, 45″ w, 46¼″ h **675.00**
Curly maple, poplar secondary wood, four dovetailed drawers, cock beading, turned quarter columns, solid ends, turned feet, replaced brasses, old refinishing, 41″ w, 18″ d, 35¾″ h **1,950.00**
Mahogany, serpentine front, rect ovolo corner marble top, four graduated drawers, reeded three–quarter columns, turned feet, casters, 48″ w, 43½″ d, 24″ h **880.00**
Federal
American
Cherry, bow front, figured walnut veneer drawers, reeded front edge, four dovetailed drawers,

figured mahogany rails and shaped apron, reeded stiles, turned feet, replaced brasses, old refinishing, 40½″ w, 23½″ d, 41½″ h. **1,150.00**
Cherry, walnut, and curly maple, reeded edge top, three short and three long dovetailed drawers with applied edge beading, paneled ends, scalloped apron, turned feet, inlaid escutcheons, replaced brasses, old refinishing, 45″ w, 21½″ d, 49″ h **1,950.00**
Maryland, c1810, mahogany, oblong top, bow front, bookend inlaid edge, four diamond and line inlaid graduated drawers, shaped skirt with fan inlaid pendant, bracket feet, 39½″ w, 19″ d, 36″ h **4,400.00**
Massachusetts
Inlaid mahogany, c1810, bow front, four cockbeaded graduated and crossbanded long drawers, reeded three–quarter round stiles, turned feet, 44″ w, 21″ d, 40″ h **2,420.00**
Inlaid mahogany and branch satinwood, c1805, bow front, top with inlaid edge, four beaded and bowed long drawers inlaid with oval feathered birch panels, ivory knobs, base with central sq inlaid pendant, flaring bracket feet, 39½″ w, 20¾″ d, 38½″ h **6,500.00**
New England, c1800
Cherry, bow front, oblong top with inlaid edge, four graduated line and fan inlaid drawers, flared bracket feet, 41½″ w, 22″ d, 37″ h. **4,400.00**
Mahogany, bow front, four graduated long drawers, scalloped apron, French bracket feet, refinished, imperfections, 41½″ w, 16¾″ d, 39¼″ h **1,320.00**
Maple, bow front, old refinish, minor imperfections, 40″ w, 22″ d, 35½″ h. **1,430.00**
Northern Connecticut River Valley, c1800, cherry, bombe front, rect top with line inlay, four graduated drawers, oval brasses and escutcheons, scalloped apron, flaring bracket feet, 37″ w, 20″ d, 32½″ h . . . **5,100.00**
Pennsylvania, c1790, cherry, molded cornice, five short and five long molded graduated long drawers, quarter columns, ogee bracket feet, 43″ w, 22″ d, 70¼″ h **5,225.00**
Piedmont Area, NC or VA, c1810, walnut, inlaid, rect top, four graduated drawers with delicate scribing and

inlay, corners inlaid, teardrop inlaid
escutcheons, oval brasses, scalloped apron with stylized floral inlay,
French bracket feet, 38″ w, 21″ d,
40″ h. **3,575.00**
Southern, early 19th C, inlaid walnut,
four cockbeaded and graduated
long drawers flanked by inlaid
canted corners, shaped apron, flar-
ing bracket feet, 40″ w, 18″ d, 42″ h   **3,960.00**
George II, walnut, crossbanded rect top,
three short and three long graduated
drawers, shaped bracket feet, 38½ x
42½″ **3,025.00**
George III, mahogany, serpentine,
molded top, three graduated drawers,
swept bracket feet, replaced top, re-
pairs, 48″ w, 23¼″ d, 34″ h. **6,600.00**
George III Style, mahogany, bow front,
rect top with rounded front and
molded edge, four graduated cockbeaded drawers, shaped bracket feet,
34″ w, 36″ h **1,100.00**
Hepplewhite
Cherry, bow front, three board replaced top, pull–out shelf under top,
four overlapping dovetailed drawers
with applied edge beading, well
shaped French feet, orig brasses,
mellow refinishing, 34¾″ w, 22¼″ d,
41″ h. **2,550.00**
Cherry, poplar secondary wood, five
overlapping dovetailed drawers,
fluted inlaid stile, molded cornice,
inlaid banded base, French feet,
orig brasses, refinished, 36 x 43¾″   **2,700.00**
Cherry and curly maple, country, po-
plar secondary wood, seven dovetailed drawers, applied edge beading, veneered top, curly maple
cross banding, French feet, old refinishing, replaced brasses, 43¾″ w   **1,400.00**
Jacobean, late 17th C, oak, rect top, two
over three drawers, bun feet, 38½″ w,
21″ d, 34″ h. **1,100.00**
Louis XV, French, Provincial, walnut,
rect molded top, conforming case,
three short drawers over two long
drawers, fluted sides, cabriole legs,
restoration, 44″ l, 20¼″ d, 33″ h. **1,650.00**
Louis XIV, French, Provincial, early 18th
C, walnut, rect top, rounded corners,
molded edge, three drawers flanked
by foliate carved scrolled stiles continuing to form bracket feet, 50″ w, 33″ h   **6,600.00**
Neoclassical, marquetry
Milanese, c1800, rect top with central
oval reserve inlaid with scene of
Abraham about to slay Isaac, angel
above holding his arm, flanked by
diamond reserves inlaid with marine scenes, three long drawers,

sides with conforming dec, tapering
sq legs, 48½″ w, 34½″ h. **30,250.00**
North Italian, early 19th C, rect top,
molded edge, inlaid central trophy
surrounded by foliate scroll cartouche with flowering urns and
perched birds, sides with similar inlay within rect reserves, slight serpentine front, two short over three
long drawers, shallow bracket feet,
age cracks to top, 54″ w, 37½″ h . . **12,100.00**
Queen Anne, Massachusetts, c1760,
walnut, block front, thumbmolded
edge, four graduated blocked long
drawers with cockbeading, shaped
pendant, blocked bracket feet, 34¼″
w, 20″ d, 29¼″ h **33,000.00**
Rococo, Dutch, mid 18th C, marquetry,
bombe, serpentine front and top,
molded edge, elaborate flowering urn,
butterflies, and birds perched in foliate
scrolls, sides dec en suite, four graduated cockbeaded drawers, scrolled
feet, minor losses to top, age splits to
side, minor repairs, 36″ w, 31¾″ h. .   **5,500.00**
Sheraton
Country, curly maple, pine secondary
wood, paneled ends, four overlapping dovetailed drawers, inlaid
stiles, turned feet, refinished, replaced brasses, 43¼″ w, 44¾″ h . .   **1,800.00**
Curly maple, butternut, pine, and poplar secondary wood, four cockbeaded dovetailed drawers,
paneled ends, turned feet, eagle
brass handles, 41½″ w, 43¼″ h . . .   **2,700.00**
Victorian, American, 19th C, mahogany,
bowed top, two short drawers, three
graduated drawers, shaped apron,
turned legs. **385.00**
William and Mary, late 17th C, oak, two
part, paneled sides, two paneled
frieze drawers over geometrically
molded cushion double fronted
drawer, restored turnip feet, 38″ w,
34½″ h. **3,300.00**

CHESTS, OTHER

Apothecary, pine, forty dovetailed drawers, replaced frame to create freestanding drawers from former built–in
unit, sponged red repaint, white
painted labels, 51½″ w, 10″ d, 47½″ h   **500.00**
Bachelor, George III Style, walnut,
molded rect top, writing slide, two
short and three long graduated cockbeaded drawers, bracket feet, 30½ x
30″. **1,430.00**
Butler's, Empire, American, c1835, ma-
hogany, five drawers with brass es-

cutcheons, fall front, fitted int., pr of cupboard doors, finely carved acanthus leaf and scroll designed columns, hairy paw feet, 53¼" w, 22¾" d, 53" h **1,700.00**

Chest on Chest

Chippendale

Connecticut, c1770, cherry, bonnet top, three flame finials, two small drawers with larger center drawer with carved sunrise, top with four graduated drawers, base with three graduated long drawers, scalloped bracket feet, eagle brasses, 38½" w, 17½" d, 85" h **6,600.00**

Philadelphia, c1760, carved mahogany, bonnet top, two parts, upper section with molded swan's neck crest, three urn and flame finials on fluted plinths, central short cockbeaded drawers with carved concave shell, applied leafage above five short cockbeaded drawers, four cockbeaded graduated long drawers, fluted canted corners, lower section with two short cockbeaded drawers over two long gradated cockbeaded drawers, fluted canted corners, molded base, canted ogee bracket feet, orig brasses, stamped "J. Stow," also inscribed "J. A. Alston," minor repair to feet and finial support, 46" w, 24" d, 101¾" h **41,800.00**

George III, English, early 19th C

Mahogany, rect molded top over pair of drawers, three graduated long drawers, case with two drawers simulated as three, bracket feet, repairs, 43½" w, 22¼" d, 76¾" h **1,870.00**

Oak, rect molded cornice over two short and three graduated long drawers, base with three graduated drawers, bracket feet, 40½" w, 21½" d, 68" h **1,760.00**

Late George III, English, early 19th C

mahogany, molded and dentil cornice, two short drawers and three long graduated drawers above base with three long drawers, cockbeaded borders, top lower drawer fitted with later leather inset writing slide, concealed swiveling drawer on right side, bracket feet, drawers partially relined, handles replaced, 40¼" w, 70" h **2,750.00**

Chest on Frame

Chippendale, c1755, walnut, flat top, molded cornice top with three short and four long molded graduated drawers, bottom with one long

molded drawer, shaped skirt, cabriole legs, claw and ball feet, c1755, 43" w, 22" d, 65" h **6,600.00**

Queen Anne, Pennsylvania, c1760

Walnut, two parts, upper section with molded cornice, five short and four long molded graduated drawers, lower section with projecting molding, shaped skirt, short angular cabriole legs, stylized trifid feet, 43½" w, 24¾" d, 70" h **4,950.00**

Walnut, poplar and oak secondary woods, molded cornice, dovetailed case, nine dovetailed overlapping drawers, base with scalloped apron, wide molding, cabriole legs, and trifid feet, old worn varnish finish, some drawer edge damage, insect damage, loose back boards, 39¼" w, 21¾" x 42¼" cornice, 69¼" h **5,500.00**

William and Mary, Philadelphia, c1715, carved and turned walnut, two parts, upper section with molded cornice, two short and three graduated long drawers, lower section with mid–molding above long drawer, arched apron, six baluster and trumpet turned legs joined by shaped stretcher, ball feet, ink inscription on top board of lower section "Robert Pascall, Philadelphia, PA," repairs to four legs, two legs restored, 42" w, 22½" d, 61" h. . . . **12,650.00**

Commode

Baroque Style, South German, 19th C, walnut and inlaid, serpentine front, four fitted long drawers, bun feet, 42¼" w, 26¼" d, 33" h. **3,025.00**

Louis XV Style

Bombe style, marquetry, variegated Sienna marble top, central frieze drawer, three drawers, gilt metal mask form design on corners, foliate cast feet, 64" w, 38½" h . . . **3,025.00**

Rosewood, crossbanded serpentine top, gilt metal banded edge, three line inlaid long drawers, sq cabriole legs, 22" w, 32½" h. . . . **550.00**

Louis XVI, Provincial, walnut, rect thumbmolded top, three drawers, sq legs, 43" w, 21" d, 33½" h. . . . **2,900.00**

Neoclassical, North Italian, late 18th C, walnut and parquetry, rect top, two drawers, sq tapering legs, 45½" w, 22¾" d, 34" h **5,500.00**

Highboy

Chippendale, PA, c1760, carved walnut, flat top, two sections, upper section with molded cornice, five short and three long graduated molded drawers, fluted quarter columns flanking, lower section with projecting mid–molding above three short molded drawers, center drawer shell and volute carved, fluted quarter columns flanking, shaped skirt, center carved shell, scroll cut cabriole legs, claw and ball feet, some losses to feet and drawer lips, 42¼" w, 24" d, 66½" h .**14,850.00**

George I, Provincial, oak and walnut, top with projecting molded cornice, two short and three long crossbanded drawers, base with one short and two deep crossbanded drawers, cockbeaded scalloped apron, sq cabriole legs, 40 x 66" . . **1,540.00**

Queen Anne

American, country, curly maple, pine secondary wood, mismatched dovetailed top case with five drawers and molded cornice, base with four overlapping dovetailed drawers and scrolled apron, cabriole legs with duck feet and pads, refinished, 35¾" w, 66½" h **2,900.00**

Connecticut, attributed to Stonington Area, c1750, tiger maple, flat top, two parts, upper section with molded cornice, convex secret drawer, two short and three molded graduated long drawers, projecting molding, lower section with three short molded drawers, scroll cut shaped skirt, cabriole legs, pad feet, minor repair to front leg, 39¼" w, 21½" d, 96" h **37,400.00**

Connecticut, c1765, carved cherry, flat top, two parts, upper section with projecting molded cornice, five molded and graduated long drawers, lower section with one long and three short molded drawers, center fan carved, shaped skirt, scrolled center pendant, cabriole legs, pad feet, repair to rear leg and some moldings, 43¾" w, 19¼" d, 73½" h . . **6,600.00**

Massachusetts, 1730–50, maple and pine, flat top with molded cornice, two short and three long graduated molded drawers in upper section, lower section with three short molded drawers, allover japanned Chinoiserie motifs with gilt highlights, shaped skirt, cabriole legs, pad feet. **41,250.00**

New England, 18th C, carved maple, flat top, two sections, upper section with molded cornice, four graduated long drawers, lower section with one long drawer over triple fronted drawers, double carved fan, shaped apron, short cabriole legs, repairs, top and base may be married, 40½" w, 74½" h. **2,200.00**

Newport, RI, Goddard–Townsend School, c1750, mahogany, flat top, two parts, upper section with molded cornice over three short and three long graduated molded drawers, projecting molding below, lower section with one long and three short molded drawers, scalloped skirt, removable angular cabriole legs, pointed slipper feet, orig brasses, incised initials "TB," 38¾" w, 20½" d, 71½" h. . **34,100.00**

Lowboy, Queen Anne

Connecticut, c1765, cherry, rect molded top, one long and three short molded drawers, central fan carving, shaped skirt, cabriole legs, pad feet, 34⅞" w, 21⅛" d, 34" h . . **41,250.00**

Pennsylvania

c1750, carved cherry, rect thumbmolded top, notched front corners, case with one long drawer faced to simulate three short molded drawers over two short molded drawers, flanking fluted quarter columns, pierced and scroll cut skirt, scroll cut cabriole legs, paneled trifid feet, 40¼" w, 25½" d, 29⅛" h **38,500.00**

c1750, curly maple, oblong top, thumbmolded edge, notched corners, one long and three short molded drawers, stop fluted pilasters, shaped skirt, shell carved cabriole legs, paneled pad feet, 34¼" w, 19¾" d, 29" h. **7,150.00**

c1760, walnut, rect thumbmolded top, one long and three short molded drawers, shaped skirt, cabriole legs, trifid feet, repairs and losses, 34" w, 8¼" d, 28½" h **4,400.00**

c1770, cherry, rect molded top, notched corners, four molded small drawers, scroll cut skirt, cabriole legs, trifid feet, 34¾" w, 22" d, 30" h **15,400.00**

Mule, decorated

Pine, two dovetailed drawers, hinged lid with molded edge, orig red and black graining with brown vinegar painting, green and yellow striping, gilt stenciled floral designs, 42" w, 35¾" h **750.00**

Pine and poplar, two dovetailed drawers, hinged lid, orig reddish brown flame graining, turned wood pulls, 38 x 36½" **800.00**

Spice

Chippendale, Pennsylvania

1763, walnut, projected molding, arched paneled door with inlaid flower head and initials "MF" and date 1763, opens to eleven small drawers, ogee bracket feet, 18¾ x 13 x 9½" **60,500.00**

c1765, miniature, cherry, molded cornice above two short and two long drawers, scroll cut base, 6⅛" w, 4¾" d, 7¾" h **4,675.00**

William and Mary, MA, early 18th C, grain painted, single hinged door, int. drawers arranged as two over three over single base drawer, ball feet, molded top and base, 18¾" w, 12½" d, 18" h **10,450.00**

Tall

Chippendale, New England, late 18th C, carved curly maple, molded cornice, seven thumbmolded long drawers, bracket feet, 40½" w, 17½" d, 65½" h **8,250.00**

Neoclassical style, Dutch, 19th C, marquetry, rect top, out–set drawer over five conforming long drawers, inlaid lyres, flowering vines, and birds grasping floral sprigs, saber legs, losses to veneer, 38½" w, 64" h **3,575.00**

CRADLES

Birch, hooded, dovetailed, cutout rockers, scalloped ends, 41" l **500.00**

Cherry, mortised sides, scrolled detail, sq corner posts, turned finials, scrolled rockers, old dark finish, nailed repairs, 40" l **200.00**

Mahogany, dovetailed, scrolled sides and ends, old dark finish, 49½" l **500.00**

Pine, American, late 18th or early 19th C, pine, scalloped hood sides, plain bonnet top, orig finish **400.00**

Poplar, open, central cutout sides and ends, hand holds, trestle rockers, old dark finish, 41" l **250.00**

Walnut, dovetailed, scalloped sides, hand holds, brass knobs, heart cutout in headboard, large rockers, 43½" l . . **375.00**

CUPBOARDS

Armoire

Biedermeier, first quarter 19th C, elm and ebonized, triangular cornice,

Crib, Victorian, tubular brass, projecting canopy, on casters, pink satin bedding, late 19th C, 49" l, 65" h, $550.00. Photograph courtesy of Butterfield & Butterfield.

Corner Cupboard, Georgian, pine, projecting molded cornice, two pairs of paneled cupboard doors, c1800, 53" w, 23" d, 92" h, estimated price $2,000.00 to $3,000.00. Photograph courtesy of Leslie Hindman Auctioneers.

two glazed short doors, lower cabinet door and drawer, 39¾" w, 20" d, 81" h **1,980.00**

Louis XV, French, Provincial, walnut, molded cornice, frieze with center stylized flowerhead in oval reserve, two doors with asymmetrically scroll carved panels, apron with center carved flowerhead, scrolled feet, 56" w, 94½" h **3,300.00**

Corner

Country, Pennsylvania, one piece construction

Cherry, molded cornice, double doors with three panes of glass, one dovetailed drawer, paneled cupboard doors, simple scalloped feet, renailed backboards, rebuilt drawer, minor repairs, refinished, 46¾" w, 80¾" h **1,700.00**

Curly Maple, poplar secondary wood, crown molded cornice, double top doors each with six panes of old glass, tapered mullions, arched top lights, two dovetailed overlapping drawers, orig brass thumb latches, arched panel doors, scalloped apron, cutout feet, old golden color refinishing, 57¼" w, 84" h **6,500.00**

Pine cleaned down to traces of old blue paint, perimeter molding with unusual applied scalloping, double top doors with eight panes of old glass, reeded and relief carved midsection panel, single paneled door flanked by two stationary panels, butterfly scalloped top int. shelves, int. with arched baffle with cutout pinwheels, minor edge damage, 54½" w, 89¼" h **6,500.00**

Country, two pieces, dovetailed cases

Curly maple, cove molded cornice, single top door with twelve panes of old wavy glass, base with paneled doors, scalloped apron, orig turned cherry feet, refinished, 40¼" w, 88" h **7,250.00**

Pine and tulip poplar, PA or NY, c1820, upper section with molded cornice, glazed cupboard door, shelved int., half round ring and spirally turned colonettes flanking, lower section with paneled cupboard door, ogee bracket feet, 50¾" w, 27¼" d, 82" h **1,980.00**

Federal

American, walnut, top with molded cornice above carved arch with line and flower inlaid panel, line inlaid arched and glazed doors

opens to shelved int., line inlaid pilasters, bottom with two short drawers, and pr doors, bracket feet, 96 x 58½ x 26¼" **9,075.00**

Pennsylvania, c1795, inlaid cherry, upper section with triglyph inlaid molded pitched pediment, turned urn finial, arched glazed hinged door, blue painted shelved int., lower section with three cockbeaded line inlaid drawers, pr of hinged paneled cupboard doors opening to shelf, scroll cut faceted bracket feet, 46" w, 27¼" d, 97" h **19,800.00**

George III, late 18th C, pine, two cabinet doors over two cabinet doors, 43½" w, 24" d, 80½" h **825.00**

Court, Jacobean, English, carved oak, flat molded cornice above frieze, flanked at ends with block and turned pendants, recessed upper segment of two cupboard doors on each side of a panel, base of two doors, sq feet, 50" w, 21¼" d, 70" h **1,870.00**

Credenza, Renaissance Style, Italian, walnut, two parts, rect molded cornice, two wrought iron grill doors over two small drawers, frieze drawer over two cabinet doors, paw feet, 33½" w, 15" d, 67" h **1,100.00**

Hanging

Country, one piece, poplar, orig red paint, dovetailed case with base and cornice molding, board and batten door, two int. nailed drawers, added turnbuckle latch, 22" w, 11½ x 23¼" cornice, 36½" h **1,125.00**

New York, Victorian, early 19th C, country, pine, shaped crest with three turned urn form finials, pr of hinged paneled cupboard doors, applied block corners, shelved int., geometric designs painted and dec in dark green and red, yellow ground, initials "JC," and date 1836 on top board, 28½" w, 9½" d, 42½" h **4,675.00**

Pennsylvania, c1755, walnut, molded cornice, paneled hinged door with rattail hinges, shelved int., scroll cut sides, molded open transverse shelf, 27" w, 14" d, 36" h **4,070.00**

Southern States, 19th C, walnut, glazed door with four panes, two int. shelves, old refinish, 25¼" w, 11" d, 34" h **470.00**

Jelly

Country, Pennsylvania, pine, shaped splashboard, two drawers, pr hinged doors, painted and grained, bracket feet, 41½″ w, 22½″ d, 47″ h   **1,650.00**

Empire, poplar, pine secondary wood, double door top with molded cornice and four dovetailed spice drawers, base with paneled doors, molded center stiles, paneled ends, and two dovetailed drawers, replaced brass drawer handles, 47″ w, 18¾″ d, 85½″ h **2,600.00**

Kas, country, pine, orig red paint, molded edge base, paneled doors set in beaded frames, one board ends, molded 21½″ x 64″ cornice, open int. with cast iron hooks, 62″ w, 76¾″ h . .   **1,500.00**

Linen Press

George III, English, late 18th C, oak, rect molded cornice, pr of paneled doors, base with three false drawers over two working drawers **2,800.00**

George III Style, bird's eye maple, projecting molded cornice with dentil frieze, two paneled doors above writing slide, two cockbeaded drawers, bracket feet, 61½ x 32″ . .   **1,900.00**

Pewter, New England, c1820, grain painted, orig simulated burnt sienna mahogany and mustard graining, four open shelves, three small drawers over two banks of two graduated drawers, wooden knobs, 61″ w, 14⅛″ d, 71¼″ h **3,850.00**

Wall

Country, one piece

Pine, reeded frame, paneled doors, scrolled base, refinished, repairs, replaced 15¾ x 39¾″ crown mold cornice, 84¾″ h **400.00**

Pine and poplar, old green and red paint, primitive, six small shelves, age cracks in backboards, 10″ w, 6″ d, 41¼″ h **525.00**

Poplar, red repaint, four paneled doors, two nailed drawers, one board cornice, damage to base, one nailed on back foot, edge damage to one drawer, 40½″ w, 20″ d, 71″ h **1,210.00**

Victorian, Renaissance Revival, American, c1872, parcel gilt and stained burled maple, arched cornice dec and stained with opposed winged griffins flanked by foliate scrolls, canted corners with flanneted urn form finials, frieze incised and stained with stylized suspended palmettes, rounded rect beveled mirror door flanked by parcel gilt fluted columns dec with leafy bands, base fitted with single drawer, circular disc feet, back in-

scribed in pencil "Mr. Latham," 48″ w, 97½″ h **6,600.00**

Wardrobe

Classical Revival, carved mahogany and mahogany veneer, molded cornice, arched pediment, two paneled doors flanked by columns, ornate feet, labeled "Manufactured...at Mathews Cabinet and Chair Factories...New York," c1820, 35″ w, 24″ d, 86″ h **4,400.00**

Georgian Style, late 19th C, mahogany, breakfront, molded projecting cornice, paneled doors, two small and two large drawers, two paneled doors on each side, plinth base, 82 x 92 x 24″ **2,750.00**

Welsh Dresser, George III, Provincial, third quarter 18th C, oak, flat molded cornice over frieze, wrought iron hooks, three open shelves, base: three frieze drawers supported by four columns, low open shelf, sq feet, lacking back boards, 66½″ w, 17″ d, 84″ h   **2,100.00**

DESKS

Art Nouveau, Austrian, gilt metal, repousse panels of country scenes,

Canterbury Desk, Victorian, walnut, hinged pen drawer, sloping writing surface, fitted int., single long drawer, pair of front doors, bank of three side drawers, raised panels, c1870, estimated price $1,000.00 to $2,000.00. Photograph courtesy of Morton M. Goldberg Auction Galleries., Inc.

glass top, brocade lining, matching armchair. **1,200.00**

Arts and Crafts
Quaint Furniture, No. 2806, c1910, oak, single drawer flanked by side bookshelves over two vertical side slats, decal and branded marks, refinished, replaced hardware, 40" l, 28" d, 30" h **250.00**
Unknown Maker
c1910, oak, secretary top with central open compartment flanked by doors, dec inset portrait of Dutch folk, fitted int., flip writing surface over single drawer, round tapering legs, pad feet, unsgd, 25" w, 14¼" d, 41½" h **385.00**
c1915, oak, flat top, central drawer flanked by short drawer, side bookshelves below with flat slats front and back, unsgd, replaced hardware, 43" w, 24¾" d, 30¼" h **330.00**
Baroque Style, Italian, mid 19th C, ebony and inlaid ivory, top with drawers and cabinet doors, base frieze drawer opens to fitted writing surface, turned and sq tapering legs joined by pierced X–form stretcher, 48" w, 20½" d, 69" h **3,575.00**
Chippendale
Massachusetts, c1770, carved mahogany, serpentine, stepped int. with compartments and drawers, four graduated drawers, claw and ball feet, orig brasses, refinished, 41½" d, 22" d, 43" h **9,350.00**
Massachusetts, c1780, carved mahogany, ox bow, slant front, fitted int., four graduated drawers, brass escutcheons, bail handles, molded apron, claw and ball feet, 42" w, 24" d, 44" h **2,750.00**
New England
c1760, curly maple, slant front, hinged rect lid opens to fitted int., four graduated drawers, bracket feet, 36¼" w, 19¼" d, 41¼" h . . **4,675.00**
c1775, Massachusetts or Rhode Island, carved mahogany, rect top, thumbmolded edge, hinged front flap above hinged fall front faced to simulate two working drawers, opening to pullout stepped int. of three fan carved and blocked drawers, center valanced pigeonholes and small drawers below, case with one long drawer with incised edges, molded skirt, pierced leg brackets, stop fluted sq legs, some restoration to plain drawers, replaced pierced brackets, 42½" w, 24¾" d, 41½" h . . . **15,400.00**

c1780, maple and cherry, thumb-molded edge slant front, fitted int. compartment with six valanced pigeonholes, two center document drawers, two stepped shelves of eight short drawers above four thumbmolded graduated long drawers, lamb's tongue chamfered corners, molded bracket feet, restored int. and feet, 40¼" w, 42" h **3,025.00**
Colonial Revival
Chippendale Style, c1930, block front, solid walnut case, walnut veneered slant front lid, fitted int. with secret drawer, paw feet, 32" w, 18" d, 42" h **450.00**
Governor Winthrop Style, c1920, mahogany veneer, serpentine front, solid mahogany slant front, fitted int. with two document drawers, shell carved center door, four long drawers, brass pulls and escutcheons **400.00**
Queen Anne Style, c1940, walnut veneer top, sides, and front, crotch walnut veneer on two side drawers, shell carved cabriole legs, 44" w, 20" d, 31" h **450.00**
Edwardian, late 19th C
Mahogany and satinwood, lady's, reticulated galleried shelf and two drawers, rect tooled leather inset writing surface, frieze drawer, reeded edges, fluted sq tapered legs, inlaid and finished front, 42" l, 20¾" d, 37½" h **1,900.00**
Satinwood, Carlton House, U–shaped superstructure with drawers, pigeonholes, and letter slots, felt lined writing surface, floral inlay, two frieze drawers, sq tapering legs, spade feet, 39¼" l, 22" d, 40" h . . . **4,950.00**
Federal
Massachusetts, c1800, mahogany and mahogany veneer inlaid, rect top, two cupboard doors with fitted int. over two long drawers, straight tapered legs, 38" w, 20" d, 45" h . . **2,100.00**
Mid Atlantic States, c1820, curly maple, three sort drawers above retracting cylinder lid opening to short drawers over valanced pigeonholes, center tambour slide, retractable baize lined writing surface, two short drawers and long drawers, turned feet, 40½" w, 22" d, 50" h . . **5,000.00**
New York, butler's, mahogany, oblong top, oval inlaid drawer, fall front opening with fitted int., three line inlaid long drawers on bottom, shaped skirt with central inlaid fan,

splayed bracket feet, c1805, 42" w, 22½" d, 46¼" h **3,850.00**

George I, English, early 18th C, slant front, walnut, rect crossbanded top, canted lid, shaped and stepped int. with small drawers and conforming cubbyholes, center prospect door, rect case with three short, two short and two full cockbeaded and cross-banded drawers, bracket feet, 37" w, 21" d, 40" h. **6,500.00**

George III, English, c1800–1810
Partner's, mahogany, gold tooled olive brown leather inset top, frieze drawer and two deep drawers, shallow arched kneehole, opposing with similar arrangement, replaced lion mask ring handles, ring turned tapering legs, inverted baluster feet, 42" l, 29" h. **2,750.00**

Slant front, oak, valanced pigeonholes and drawers, four cockbeaded drawers, shaped bracket feet, c1800, 36" w, 39½" h **1,045.00**

Louis XV Style, attributed to RJ Horner & Co, NY, early 20th C, bureau plat, mahogany and marquetry, rect top, serpentine sides, rounded corners, hidden frieze drawer, tapering cabriole legs, ormolu chutes, 51" l, 32" w, 30" h **4,125.00**

Napoleon III, fourth quarter 19th C, Bureau en Pente, walnut and marquetry, rect galleried open shelf, fall front writing surface, frieze drawer, tapering fluted legs joined by shaped stretchers, 25½" w, 16" d, 46" h **2,530.00**

Neoclassical
Dutch, early 19th C, Bonheur du Jour, mahogany and Chinoiserie dec, inset lacquer panels, 32¼" l, 19½" d, 49" h. **1,760.00**

German, early 19th C, walnut, rect top, two drawers, top drawer opens to fitted int. and writing surface, sq tapering legs, 33½" w, 21" d, 34" h, losses, damage to top **2,475.00**

Queen Anne, New England, c1760, maple, slant lid, high back with whale's tail pediment, circular inlay, and rect beveled glass mirror, row of five small drawers, fitted int. of valanced pigeonholes and drawers, four graduated drawer base, bracket feet, 35¼" w, 19" d, 66¾" h **9,350.00**

Regency, c1815, Davenport, rosewood, sliding sq writing surface, tooled brown leather inset, rect three quarter brass gallery, pullout writing slide on either side fitted with pen and ink drawer, four long drawers, false drawers on other side, turned cylindrical feet, minor losses to molding, 30" h. . **3,600.00**

Restoration, American, c1835–40, carved rosewood, fall front, well fitted line inlaid int., 30½" w, 57" h. **2,400.00**

Rococo Style, German, 19th C, walnut and inlaid, slant front, three small drawers, knee hole flanked by two small drawers, sq tapering saber legs, brass sabots, lock inscribed "Danl. Mann, Frankfurt," 38" w, 17½" d, 40" h **1,540.00**

Victorian, Derby Desk Co, Boston, late 19th C, cherry, tambour roll top, fitted int., rect top, pedestals with drawers, plinth base, 54" l, 33" d, 50½" h **2,310.00**

William and Mary, Boston area, 1710–30, burled walnut, slant front, int. with end blocked serpentine small drawers, valanced compartments flanking veneered prospect door and document drawers with pilasters, three graduated long drawers, eagle brasses, ball feet, 38¾" w, 20½" d, 39¾" h. **12,100.00**

DOUGH TROUGHS

Cherry, dovetailed, turned feet, white porcelain knobs, name "Hardin" scratched on base. **265.00**

Decorated, pine, American, late 18th C
Orig blue paint, early train painted on one side in black, white, and faded red, sq nail construction, curved tin bottom, unpainted inner lid, worn leather hinges, 21 x 31" breadboard top, 15¼ x 25¾ x 28½" **700.00**

Orig red paint, stretcher base, 46½ x 23 x 27⅜". **750.00**

Maple, dovetailed, old replacement lid, traces of old red paint, 38 x 19¼ x 28¾" **450.00**

Poplar, old red paint, heart cutouts in ends, age cracks, some edge damage, 33½" l. **300.00**

Walnut, dovetailed, splayed legs, 20 x 27 x 39". **450.00**

DRY SINKS

Chippendale, cherry two paneled doors on top, rect sink over two paneled doors in base, 46" l, 23½" w, 77" h . . **1,100.00**

Country
Pine, two raised panel doors set in reeded frames, apron drop on center stile, central well flanked by two dovetailed drawers, cutout feet, interiors and well painted blue, old mellow refinishing, 58¾" w, 22" d, 32" h. **935.00**

Poplar, old dark finish, well shaped cutout feet, two paneled doors, two dovetailed drawers in base, zinc lined well, hutch top with top shelf and two dovetailed drawers, 61¾" w, 21½" d, 51" h **2,200.00**

Poplar and Walnut, old worn red repaint with black brushed graining, black door panels over darker blue, 39¼" w, 19" d, 36" h. **635.00**

Grain Painted
Poplar, one piece, hutch top, original brown flame graining, four paneled doors, three dovetailed drawers, damaged zinc lined well, chamfered corners, cutout feet, castiron and brass thumb latches, whit porcelain pulls, wire nail construction, 36" w, 19" d, 74¼" h **1,650.00**

Poplar, one secondary wood, original red vinegar graining on yellow ground, sunbursts, fans, X's, etc., well shaped bracket feet, paneled doors, one dovetailed drawer, open well, worn int. shelf, 42" w, 19¼" d, 31¾" h **11,500.00**

HAT RACKS AND HALL TREES

Art Nouveau
French, c1900, carved walnut, thumb-molded cornice over shaped mirror plate, molded tendril border, serpentine projecting shelf, panel carved at sides with tendrils and leafy sprays, shaped feet, 50" w, 85" h. **1,500.00**

Galle, c1900, oak, arched superstructure inlaid with three divided panels, sheep gracing scene, buildings, and rolling hills, paneled back with relief carving of branch, leaf, and pod motifs, flanked by glazed cupboard doors, int. shelves, rect seat above panels inlaid with floral sprigs, insects, and waterlilies, molded base, block feet, 77½" w, 79½" h **5,000.00**

Arts and Crafts, Gustav Stickley, double, orig light finish, six black iron hooks, small version of Stickley No. 53, from Cleveholm Manor, CO, 13" w, 22" d, 66" h **1,870.00**

Classical, New England, maple, turned and acanthus carved post, fifteen clothes supports, ball finial, scrolled legs, 79" h **1,320.00**

Federal, New England, 1820–30, maple, single post, acorn shaped final, fourteen shaped pegs descending full length of post, ring turned shaped

vase base, three scrolled legs, 70½" h **1,320.00**

Victorian, American
Gothic Revival, c1855, oak, ornate arched open cut upper frame, hooks at side, white marble shelf, ornate open cut base flanked by umbrella racks **10,000.00**

Renaissance Revival, c1870, walnut, orange carved cresting, shaped mirror within molded framework, drop columns at each side, candle sockets and candle shelves, white marble shelf, single drawer flanked by umbrella racks, orig brass pans **2,000.00**

Rococo Revival, walnut, intricate carving, six small and two large shelves, stained, mirror back, 46" w, 14" d, 90" h. **700.00**

MAGAZINE RACKS

Arts and Crafts
Derby Co., oak, vertical double side stretchers, five shelves, rect legs, dark finish, remnants of paper label "Derby . . . Boston" **140.00**

Michigan Chair Co, oak, sq overhanging top, four open shelves, sides with two vertical slats, lower shelf with keyed tenons, 33⅛" h, c1910 **500.00**

Stickley, Gustav No. 547, c1902, oak, sq top, beveled edge over three shelves, two closed sides with recessed panel, painted white, unsgd, 15½" w, 34⅞" h **1,430.00**

Tobey Company, beveled overhanging top, slatted sides, orig dark finish, 16½" sq, 33" h. **550.00**

George III, late 18th C, upper portion divided into three sections, full frieze drawer, turned legs, 18" w, 13½" d, 19" h **1,500.00**

Regency Style, mahogany, rect, four partitions, one drawer, ring turned tapered legs, caster feet, 19½" w, 13¾"d, 20" h. **425.00**

Victorian
Mahogany, c1840, divided top, turned cylindrical center posts, base with single drawer, turned tapered cylindrical legs on casters, 18" l, 21½" h **2,100.00**

Rosewood
American, c1850, single short drawer, turned feet, brass caps and casters, 18" w, 16" d, 19" h **1,250.00**

English, early 19th C, upper portion divide into four sections, turned supports at corners, apron with full drawer, ring turned legs, 20" w, 15" d, 21"h. **2,400.00**

William IV, c1835, rosewood, X–form dividers, baluster turned rails, bellflower wreaths above single long drawer, baluster turned legs, casters, 20" l, 19¾" h.................... **1,800.00**

MIRRORS

Adams Style, 57 x 35", oval, carved, urn and bellflower cartouche, leaf scroll supports, two griffins, garland apron . **1,200.00**
Baroque Style
Continental
    Mahogany and parcel gilt, carved, rect mirror plate, conforming molded frame with floral and foliate spray, 61½" l, 35" h...... **725.00**
    Oak, rect plate, carved pierced foliate mounted with cartouche and two putti, late 19th C, 44" l, 26½" h.................... **1,870.00**
Italian, mid 19th C, parcel gilt, ebonized, rect mirror plate, elaborate fruit and floral carved frame surmounted by figure of infant blackamoor holding large drapery swag aloft, polychromed blue, red, silver, and gilt foliate and floral scrolls, knotted at corners and interlacing the frame, corners with carved high relief blackamoor winged cherub heads, 42½" w, 62" h......... **6,050.00**
Chippendale, American, c1770
    Parcel gilt mahogany, surmounted by giltwood phoenix finial flanked by swan's neck crest, rect mirror plate with gilt slip, shaped pendant, replaced finial, 19¾" w, 39" h..... **2,650.00**
    Parcel gilt walnut, shaped crest, pierced gilt leaf reserve, shaped pendant, 24¼" w, 45" h...... **5,775.00**
    Parcel gilt mahogany on pine, gilded phoenix in crest, molded frame, gilded liner, old refinishing, some damage to gilding, worn mirror plate, 20¼" w, 36½" h......... **3,960.00**
Classical Revival, America, 1830, giltwood
    Architectural style, carved upper tablet, rect mirror plate, gilding retouched, 39" h.............. **660.00**
    Convex, mounted spread eagle cartouche, two candle arms, 40 x 30" **3,600.00**
Mantel
    c1795, wirework crest, central urn, scrolling vines, rect mirror plate, pierced flowerhead pendant, c1795, 28½" d, 59½" h....... **2,750.00**
    c1820, mounted eagle flanked by C–scrolls, mirror plate surrounded with molded and pierced scroll carved border, shell carved pendant, 31½" d, 49" h....... **3,410.00**

Continental, 31 x 37½", rect, knight and reeded columns sides, sailing ships scene, 19th C................. **500.00**
Empire, New England, c1830
Architectural
    Giltwood, split baluster, crest with cornucopia in relief, 19" w, 33" h **715.00**
    Mahogany, acorn drop cornice, turned and acanthus carved pilasters, reeded trim, orig reverse painting of house, trees, and sailboat, old finish, one brass corner rosette missing, 18" w, 32¾" h. . **250.00**
    Mahogany, molded ball cornice, turned pilasters, reverse glass painting of ship, brass corner rosettes, old finish, some damage to cornice, 19" w, 30" h....... **275.00**
    Split baluster, reverse painted tablet with child and dog, imperfections, 13¼" w, 29¼" h....... **330.00**
Dressing, 1820, swing, mahogany, rect, shaped cornice, half columns on sides, fitted single drawer, 1820, 17½" w, 10" d, 29" h.......... **275.00**
Mantle
    Giltwood, triptych panels, block and ring turned supports, 25½ x 63½" **210.00**
    Mahogany, rect, gilt and ebonized dec, triptych, 31 x 60"........ **675.00**
Federal
American
    1820, gilded frame, semicircular crest, eagle shield and banner, old gilding with some sear, 27¼" w, 40¼" h.............. **1,650.00**
    1830, mahogany, eglomise panel of patriotic American eagle stencil, 25½" w, 51" h.......... **385.00**
    Mantle, early 19th C, mantle, gilt and gesso, carved, molded gadrooned cornice, rect triptych mirror flanked by half Ionic columns, brass paw feet, 22 x 58"............. **325.00**
New England, early 19th C
    Rectangular, carved, gilt and gesso, flat molded cornice with acorn drops, geometric and landscape eglomise panel, double column sides, 55 x 34"...... **2,800.00**
    Tabernacle, eglomise tablet, 15¾" w, 36½" h.............. **500.00**
Federal Style, mahogany, crested with urn filled with wheat sheaves and flowerheads, scrollboard with inlaid eagle, eglomise panel with landscape below, 22¾" w, 52" h.......... **1,650.00**
George I, Continental, c1725, walnut, beveled two section rect plate
    Raised molded border, scroll cut pierced cresting, carved giltwood

foliage and scrolls, pomegranate, conforming apron, 16¾" w, 38¾" h **2,200.00**

Shaped upper border, tall arched pierced scroll cut cresting, circular aperture inset with gilt plume, matching plume on apron, regilt, 20" w, 55" h. **3,300.00**

George II Style, 19th C, carved giltwood, vertical beveled plate, eared and mitered frame, interrupted scrolled pediment with center acanthus carved cartouche, applied molded cornucopia, C–scroll, husks, and foliage border on raised ovolo carved frame with applied pendant acorns and oak leaves, apron with center basket of flowers, minor loss to gesso, repaired cresting, 35½" w, 72" h. **3,575.00**

George III, American, late 18th C, inlaid mahogany, rect mirror plate tilting between two ring turned canted uprights, case with three drawers flanked by cruciform dies, turned ivory ball feet, knobs, and mounts, 29½" w, 9" d, 28" h. **880.00**

Hepplewhite Style, 56" h, oval mirror, urn crest with garlands, phoenix birds and leaves, putti rosettes, garlands, and two side brackets on bottom. . . . **1,100.00**

Louis XV Style, 19th C, rect carved giltwood and gesso frame, raised outer edge, mirrored oval reserves, center carved floral crest surrounded by sectioned inner mirrors, 66" w, 86" h, pr **26,500.00**

Louis XVI, Provincial, late 18th C, giltwood, pierced scrolled crest, rect mirror plate, 17" w, 28" h, repairs. **935.00**

Neoclassical
Dutch, early 19th C, shaving, inlaid satinwood, arched mirror, demilune case, inset verre eglomise panels, 26" h. **1,870.00**

Scandinavian, second quarter 19th C, mahogany and parcel gilt, relief swan scene above rect plate, flanked by columns, 23½" w, 60" h **1,210.00**

Queen Anne, England, c1750, walnut and gilt, Prince of Wales Plumes centered in scrolling crest, two piece shaped beveled mirror plate, 22" w, 48" h **2,200.00**

Regency, early 19th C, giltwood, pierced floral crest, replacements, losses, 38 x 25" **1,760.00**

Renaissance, American, Herter Bros, NY, c1872, for Thurlow Lodge, Menlo Park, CA
Carved walnut, arched architectural pediment, center carved mask of Mercury flanked by seated putti, over central medallion of caduceus flanked by frieze of lionhead me-

topes and stylized flowering sprigs, large rect mirror plate with canted upper corners, flanked by simulated veined green marble columns with Ionic capitals, palmette carved bases, lower section with shaped simulated marble top over palmette carved frieze, tapering urn form supports with Ionic capitals joined by laurel swags, flanked by opposed winged lions, shaped plinth base, 130" w, 186" h **22,000.00**

Ebonized and inlaid maple, shaped cornice with central rounded section inlaid with opposed griffins, center urn over divided stylized sprig inlaid frieze, rounded rect mirror plate, flanked by palmette inlaid spandrels and stiles, outset platform with simulated gold veined marble top over conforming plinth base, 80" w, 155" h **15,400.00**

Rococo, Italian, c1770, giltwood, rect mirror plate, molded frame surmounted by pierced C–scroll, ruffle, and flowerhead crest and mirrored cartouche, sides with similar pendants, scrolled pendant below, 40" w, 58" h **4,950.00**

Sheraton, American, c1800, architectural pediment, upper panel with incised black and gold Gothic arches, foliage, and rosettes, turned columned sides, 39½" h. **800.00**

Ladderback, turned ball finials, three shaped slats, replaced woven splint seat, turned front stretcher and legs, $150.00.

ROCKERS

Arrowback, bamboo turnings, red and black graining, stenciled floral designs on slats **200.00**

Art Furniture, Adirondack, American, early 20th C, bent rustic twigs and branches, interwoven latticework back and down swept arms, round seat, curlicue skirt **250.00**

Arts and Crafts, American

Harden Co, c1910, oak, orig medium finish, three slats under each arm, paper label, wear to finish, 28½″ w, 38¼″ h **330.00**

Limbert, c1910, No. 518, open flat arms, elongated corbels, adjustable back, orig upholstered spring cushion, branded mark, 36¾″ h **1,200.00**

Quaint Furniture Co, No. 806, c1910, oak, orig medium finish, shaped crestrail over four vertical slats, shaped arms, decal and branded mark, 27½″ w, 36¾″ h **250.00**

Boston, American, mid 19th C, grain painted, gilt stencil dec, scenic dec rest, rosewood grained seat **600.00**

Eastlake, American, late 19th C, mahogany platform, incised and pierced cresting over sq panel back, center, padded reeded arms, velvet seat upholstered, reeded supports. **225.00**

Ladderback

Armchair, short scrolled arms, turned supports, old woven splint seat, old worn dark graining, yellow striping, traces of floral dec, 38″ h **400.00**

Child's, armchair, old dark alligatored varnish, replaced blue and white tape seat, 27¼″ h **225.00**

Mission, L. & J. G. Stickley, c1910, arm, vertical back and side slats, decal mark **625.00**

Shaker, Mt Lebanon, NY, c1900, No. 7, arms, old brown wash finish, rush seat, 41½″ h **500.00**

Wicker, loom woven fiber, padded back, flattened down swept arms, loose cushion seat, turned and fiber wrapped legs, painted white **200.00**

Windsor, New England, c1810, bamboo turned, bird cage back, 41″ h **350.00**

SECRETARIES

Art Nouveau, attributed to Walter Gropius, Austria, c1900, oak and oak veneer, secretary top, adjustable shelves, slant lid, butterfly spines and shaped vertical straps, fitted int., paneled sliding doors, conforming wall shelf, unsgd, remnants of Holland

Secretary Bookcase, carved cherry, two sections, upper: molded broken pediment bonnet, pair of arched raised panel cupboard doors, and shelved int.; lower: thumbmolded rect hinged writing surface, fitted int., four thumbmolded graduated drawers, bracket feet; feet reduced in height, brasses replaced, 36″ w, 85″ h, $8,800.00. Photograph courtesy of Butterfield & Butterfield.

American Line label, veneer loss, 50¾″ w, 16½″ d, 115″ h **550.00**

Chippendale

Massachusetts, c1770, cherry, block front, top with molded cornice above pr arched and paneled doors, fitted int., carved pilaster with stylized scrolls, molded base with thumbmolded hinged lid opens to fitted int., four blocked and graduated drawers, bracket feet, 40½″ w, 21¾″ d, 96″ h **11,550.00**

Pennsylvania, c1765, walnut, bonnet top, two parts, upper section with swan's neck crest, carved rosettes, pr of arched hinged doors, int. adjustable shelves, small drawers, and pigeonholes, candle slides, lower section with hinged molded lid, int. with small pigeonholes and drawers, center prospect door opening to small drawer and pigeonhole, four molded graduated long drawers below, bracket feet, staining to int. drawers, 37½″ w, 21″ d, 96″ h. **18,700.00**

Directorie, early 19th C, mahogany, rect gray marble top over frieze drawer, fall front writing surface, fitted int., base with three drawers, sq tapering legs, brass sabots, 37¾″ w, 16″ d, 56″ h . . **1,650.00**

Empire, American, c1830, mahogany, straight plain top, two paned glass doors with three shelf int., three small drawers below, three drawer base with rope turned frontal posts, shaped apron, turned feet, replaced hardware, 45″ w, 20¾″ d, 78¼″ h **825.00**

Federal

Massachusetts, c1800, mahogany, top with cornice centering inlaid rect reserve, three ball and steeple finials, pr glazed hinged doors opens to shelf int. over valanced pigeonholes, bottom with hinged flap opening to lined writing surface, four graduated long drawers, shaped skirt, slightly flared bracket feet, 42¼″ w, 19″ d, 75″ h **8,100.00**

New England, c1820, tiger maple, shaped cornice with block finials, two glazed cupboard doors with diamond shaped mullions, shelved and fitted int. with drawers, document shelves, and valanced pigeonholes, over three small drawers, base with pullout drawer supports, three graduated long drawers, reeded legs, scalloped apron, 39½″ w, 19″ d, 70″ h. **3,960.00**

George III, lacquer, scarlet japanned ground, Chinoiserie dec of people pursing various pursuits, animals, and foliage, broken triangular cornice over pair of doors, shelved int., base with hinged slant front, fitted int., two short and two long drawers, bun feet, restorations, 37″ w, 21¾″ d, 89″ h **6,100.00**

Neoclassical

Austrian, c1790, carved and inlaid walnut, two parts, superstructure with rect top, slant front opening to three suspended drawers flanked by shaped drawers with Gothic arch fret carved panels, two long drawers with corresponding fret carved panels, sides with brass handles, cabriole legs, pointed pad feet, 46″ l, 39½″ h **7,700.00**

Italian, c1780, carved walnut, two parts, upper section with scrolled crest, center shell finial over pr of paneled doors, int. shelves, lower section with cylinder front opening, pullout writing slide, drawers, and fitted compartments, three long

drawers below flanked by shaped cupboard doors, shaped bracket feet, 62½″ w, 108½″ h **77,000.00**

Regency, English, early 19th C, mahogany, two sections, flat top, molded Greek Key cornice, two glazed mullioned doors, shelved int., one short drawer over three long drawers, bracket feet, 44½″ w, 22½″ d, 89″ h . **2,860.00**

Rococo

Dutch, c1725, marquetry, two parts, upper section with double arched top over two doors inlaid with elaborate flowering urns and birds, cherubs among foliate scrolls, sides with putti holding foliate sprigs over flowering urns, int. shelves over floral sprig inlaid sharply serpentine drawers, lower section with slant front inlaid with foliate scrolls, flowering urns, and cornucopia, valanced compartments over floral sprig inlaid concave drawers, sliding compartment below flanked by stepped drawers, secret drawer on one side, over two short and two long drawers, later bun feet, minor losses to molding, 42″ w, 86″ h . . . **33,000.00**

German, 1775, parquetry, two parts, upper section with C–scroll molded arched crest over central rounded rect cupboard door with penwork dec of classical walkway and arches, single drawer below flanked by banks of four drawers, lower section with tambour opening to pullout writing slide and four drawers, two serpentine long drawers below, cabriole legs, 38½″ w, 69½″ h. . . . **7,150.00**

Rococo Style, Venetian, c1900, scrolled broken pediment, silver giltwood crest, two shaped foliate painted paneled doors, foliate painted paneled slant front with fitted int., three drawers center frieze drawer and kneehole, bracket feet, 38″ w, 77″ h. **3,850.00**

Victorian, American, J & JW Meeks, c1845, mahogany and satinwood, molded cornice, pr of glazed doors, enclosing shelves, lower section with roll top, fitted compartments, pr of cabinet doors, molded block feet, stenciled inside drawer. **3,850.00**

Wooton, American, c1880, walnut, standard grade, pierced three–quarter gallery above two arched doors opening to fall front secretary, door int. fitted on one side with pigeonholes, compartments on other, fall front, fitted compartments over four drawers flanked by horizontal and vertical file

SETTEES

Arts and Crafts, No. 334A, c1910, oak, crest rail over ten canted vertical back slats, arm over six sq cutouts, five vertical slats, framed recessed panel, orig laced cushion on rounded and slotted slats, casters, unsgd, veneer splitting and loss, caps, finish loss, 83" w, 30¼" d, 39" h **1,210.00**

Charles X, early 19th C, meridienne, mahogany, serpentine back, outscrolled arms, rect seat, bracket feet, reupholstered, 58" l, 27" d, 27½" h . . **825.00**

Classical Style, well shaped crest, plank seat, scrolled arms, turned spindles and legs, refinished, repairs, 80" l . . . **450.00**

Federal, country, c1835, polychrome rose painted crest, spindle back, scrolling arms, turned legs, box stretcher, 72" l **2,000.00**

George III, Provincial, early 19th C, oak, rect top rail, triple chairback, stylized baluster splats, drop in seat, sq legs joined by stretchers, 50" l **2,125.00**

Hepplewhite, four shield shape chair back, upholstered seat, sq tapered legs **1,500.00**

Jacobean style, walnut, carved, high back, short cabriole legs, boldly scrolled acanthus feet, green velvet upholstery, 40" l **440.00**

Regency, English, second quarter 18th C, walnut, rect back, serpentine seat, carved cabriole legs, upholstered in 17th C verdure tapestry, repairs, 59" w, 30" d, 42½" h **4,125.00**

Rococo, Venetian, 18th C, painted, serpentine crest rail, open back, single pierced baluster splat, cabriole legs, paw feet, 70" w, 19" d, 33½" h **3,300.00**

Victorian, American, c1860, floral dec, triple chair back, shaped crest, scrolling arms, caned back and seat, turned legs, 72" l **1,600.00**

Windsor

American, c1810, arched crest, thirty–one bamboo turned spindles, plank seat, bamboo turned legs joined by stretchers, 77" l **5,500.00**

Windsor, Philadelphia, 1760–80, painted, 47" w, 17½" h seat, 28" h back, wear, minor damage **1,540.00**

SIDEBOARDS

Arts and Crafts

Limbert, Grand Rapids, MI, c1903, gallery top, three short drawers over three cabinet doors, single long drawer, round copper and brass pulls, mirrored backboard with cutouts flanked by elongated corbels, 59¼" w, 22½" d, 56" h . . . **1,760.00**

Quaint Furniture Co, c1910, oak

No. 8820, gallery top over mirror flanked by arched corbels, two short drawers, long drawer, two cabinet doors below, copper hardware, orig medium finish, metal tag and paper label, 48" l, 22" d, 53¾" h **1,100.00**

Shaped plate rail, two banks of short drawers with cabinet doors on each side, metal tag, refinished, restoration, 66" l, 23" d, 46" h **2,100.00**

L & J G Stickley, No. 745, c1912, oak, orig medium finish, copper hardware, wooden knobs on cabinet doors, decal "The Work of . . .," watermark, 54" w, 24" d, 48" h **2,530.00**

Sideboard, pine, scalloped backsplash with bracket shelf, three short drawers over two paneled cupboard doors, turned feet, English, 57" w, 20" d, 52½" h, $750.00.

Classical Revival, Massachusetts, c1825, mahogany, wavy birch and mahogany veneer, inlaid, scrolled backsplash, rect top, three small drawers over pair of cupboard doors flanked by drawers, center swell front drawer over two long drawers, glass knobs, brass escutcheons, small brass knobs, carved pilasters, brass medallions on turned feet, lower drawer sgd in pencil "James Banks, Boston," 46½" w, 21½" d, 50¼" h. . . . **1,430.00**

Edwardian, English, c1900, Neoclassical taste inlaid and penwork dec, mahogany, inverted broken outline, maple crossbanded top with boxwood strung edges, dart and line inlaid border, concave fronted frieze drawer inlaid with ribbon tied swags of husks and flanked by simulated fluted end drawers and cupboards, each with penwork dec of classically robed maiden representing summer and music, left-hand cupboard enclosing three fitted drawers, plinth base, 83½" l, 33" h **4,675.00**

Empire, mahogany, elaborate carved backsplash, shaped rect top, two cushion molded drawers, three paneled doors, Corinthian columns, acanthus carved paw feet, 73" l, 22¾" d, 55½" h **700.00**

Federal

Maine, York, 1810, flame birch inlaid mahogany, bow front, oblong top, bowed front, conforming shaped case, three convex drawers, two pr of hinged cupboard doors, center bottle drawers, rect inlaid dies on intersecting line, bellflower, and dot inlaid sq double tapering legs, crossbanded cuffs, orig brass knobs, penciled inscription "Made by Thomas Chandler, York, July 25 1810," 69" w, 26" d, 41½" h **38,500.00**

Massachusetts, c1790, mahogany, inlay, refinished, imperfections, 69½" w, 26" d, 40" h **5,000.00**

New England (southern tier), 1790–1810, cherry, inlaid, trapezoidal shaped top, center long drawer over pair of large inverted cupboard doors, flanked by smaller doors, smaller drawers over single cupboard doors on each end, oval and circular inlays, oval brasses, ivory shield shaped escutcheons, bellflower inlay on straight tapering cross banded legs, 72" w, 15¼" d, 42½" h **13,200.00**

New York, c1800

Bow front, painted and inlaid mahogany, oblong top, bowed front, case with two convex cupboard doors, two center convex drawers, bookend and line inlaid dies, line inlaid sq tapering legs, crossbanded cuffs, front painted in 19th C polychrome with classical motifs including griffins, bacchanalic figures, masks, and garlands,

repair and losses to veneer, 68" w, 27½" d, 39¼" h **4,125.00**

Serpentine front, inlaid mahogany, oblong top, two convex small drawers, pr cupboard doors and bottle drawers, central hinged door, tombstone inlaid dies, line inlaid sq tapered legs, crossbanded cuffs, 73" l, 28" d, 44" h **16,500.00**

George III, mahogany and tulipwood, shaped top, frieze drawer flanked by cabinet doors, sq tapering legs, spade feet, restorations, 60" l, 22¾" d, 36½" h **1,980.00**

George III Style, late 19th C, mahogany, bow front, central frieze drawer flanked by deep drawer and cabinet door, sq tapering legs, spade feet, 42" w, 22" d, 34" h **1,870.00**

Hepplewhite, country, Southern, decorated, poplar and yellow pine, orig blue paint, black, red, and white geometric dec on drawer fronts, molded edge top, three dovetailed drawers, sq tapering legs, wear, replaced brasses, minor repairs, 50⅛" w, 21¼" d, 47¾" h **9,500.00**

Louis XV, French, Provincial

Pine, molded cornice over frieze with center carved fruit and flower filled basket, two glazed doors opening to shelves, lower section with pr of cupboard doors, cabriole feet, restorations, 50½" w, 90" h **2,200.00**

Walnut, rect top, pair of frieze drawers, two cabinet doors, shell carving on scalloped, molded apron, scrolled feet, 53¾" w, 21" d, 42" h **1,540.00**

Victorian, c1860, walnut, carved, serpentine Carrara marble top with molded edge, mirrored splash board with carved eagle, three paneled mirrored cupboard doors, scalloped plinth, 61" w, 98" h **1,870.00**

SOFAS

Chippendale, NY, c1770, mahogany, camelback, shaped crest, outward scrolling arm supports and seat, sq molded legs, flat stretchers, 80" l . . . **10,000.00**

Classical

Boston, MA, 1820s, carved mahogany veneer, rolled brass trim outlines leafage cravings, punch work ground, red velvet upholstery, old refinish, minor imperfections, 84" l, 35" h **1,870.00**

New York, c1815–20, box style, carved mahogany and rosewood, carved eagle brackets, brass inlay, paw feet, cherry and pine second-

ary woods, slightly reduced, orig damaged brocade upholstery **2,000.00**
English, Adams, stylized foliage designs on base, sq tapered leg, mortised stretchers, brass casters, blue and white Apotheosis of Franklin print reupholstery, 78" l **750.00**

Empire

American, c1830, mahogany, carved cornucopias, acorns, oak leaves, and acanthus leaves, basket of flowers finial, refinished, gold brocade reupholstery, 83" l **1,750.00**
New York, c1835, mahogany, acanthus carved shaped crest continuing to carved scrolled arms, rounded base, acanthus carved hairy paw feet, gilt feather returns, 78" l **1,500.00**

Federal

Massachusetts, attributed to, c1815, mahogany, carved, minor imperfections, 77" w, 29" d, 35" h **1,870.00**
New England, c1815, mahogany, reeded arm supports, gently bowed seat rail, square tapering molded legs, no upholstery, 79" w, 25½" h, 14½" seat h, 36½" h **2,150.00**
Philadelphia, c1815, carved mahogany, slightly arched crest, upholstered back flanked by leaf carved terminals, semiexposed seatrail with flowerhead carved dies,

Stand, circular top with marble insert, carved floral motif, carved cabriole legs, X–form stretcher, price for pair, $1,000.00.

reeded tapering legs, restoration to legs and crest, 74¾" l **2,420.00**
Salem, MA, c1800, carved and inlaid mahogany, molded serpentine exposed crest rail, center carved basket of flowers and fruit, upholstered arms with acanthus carved front panels, serpentine overupholstered seat, line inlaid sq tapering legs, crossbanded cuffs, feet extended, repairs to legs, 89" l **16,500.00**
George III, 18th C, mahogany, camelback, upholstered serpentine crest, upholstered back flanked by outscrolling arms, serpentine upholster seat, molded sq tapered legs, casters, 83" l **3,300.00**
Mission, L. & J. G. Stickley, c1910, oak, decal mark, 72" l **1,450.00**
Restauration, American, NY, c1835–40, carved mahogany, scrolling back extends to form arms, orig upholstery removed. **1,200.00**
Victorian, American, mid 19th C, carved mahogany, shaped crest rail, arched pediment, acanthus carved arm supports, later velvet upholstery. **1,000.00**

STANDS

Chinese, mother–of–pearl inlaid hardwood, sq inset marble top, 18" d, 32" h **385.00**
Coffin
  21¾" h, folding sawhorse type, turned legs, old black paint, pr. **95.00**
  29¾" h, tripod, turned wooden legs and stretchers, old worn red and black paint, set of four **200.00**
Easel, Victorian, Gothic style, American, c1872, oak, swiveling pierced stand, tracery–carved top rail, rotating on platform base, molded sq legs joined by stretchers, adjustable racks missing, stamped 1738, 31" w, 87" h, pr. . **4,950.00**
Etagere, Victorian
  American, Gothic Revival, c1850, corner, mahogany, three arched fret carved shelves, base with doors and int. shelves, shaped plinth base **4,125.00**
  English, late 19th C, turned maple, five galleried rect shelves flanked by brass capped ring turned supports, 10½" w, 53" h, pr **3,025.00**
Music
  Arts and Crafts, Stickley, c1907, No. 670 type, four tapering posts, four shelves, gallery, 19¾" w, 14¾" d, 39" h **1,100.00**
  Eastlake, late 19th C, ebonized, rect top over floral inlaid fall front, folio compartment, sq legs, medial shelf

above single drawer, 22½″ w, 15½″
d, 39″ h **325.00**
George III, English, early 19th C, ma-
hogany
    Lyre form angled music rests, ad-
justable brass support, hexagonal shaft, three downswept legs,
minor repairs and losses, 13½″
w, 56½″ h **770.00**
    Rect top, adjustable support, two
swing candle holders, columnar
form standard, three cabriole
legs, snake feet, 24″ w, 43″ h . . . **550.00**
Night
    Arts and Crafts, Gustav Stickley, one
drawer, one door, sq wooded faceted pulls, orig light finish, minor
varnish alligatoring, red decal, from
Cleveholm Manor, CO, 20″ w, 16″
d, 33½″ h **2,530.00**
    Country, refinished curly maple,
square tapered legs with turned detail, two dovetailed drawers, 19½ x
20″, 28¾″ h **770.00**
Plant
    Arts and Crafts, Paine Furniture Co,
pedestal, circular top with orig leatherette cov, sides tacked, four long
corbels, four slender legs, orig dark
finish, metal tag, 12½″ d, 31″ h . . . **450.00**
    Edwardian, c1900, mahogany, hex-
agonal top with inlaid satinwood
edge, paneled baluster form standard with bellflower inlay, three
down scrolled supports, acanthus
carved centerpiece, cylindrical feet,
15″ w, 42″ h **770.00**
    Folk Art, wood, beaded trim, old gold
repaint with black and red dec, repaired break on leg, 15¾″ sq, 31″ h **125.00**
    George III Style, late 19th C, mahog-
any, octagonal dish top, acanthus
carved ogee molded edge, baluster
form reeded standard and fluted
knop, foliate carved flaring plinth
base, 16″ d, 64″ h **990.00**
    Victorian, wire, three tiers, semicircu-
lar, wheels, old worn white paint,
some damage and rust, 42″ w,
37½″ h **275.00**
Pool Rack, Arts and Crafts, Brunswick–
Balke–Collender, c1912, inlaid mahogany, central mirror over ball rack,
flanked by cue racks, linear and geometric wood and mother of pearl inlay,
48¼″ w, 61″ h **1,760.00**
Shaving, Victorian, walnut, canted rect
top with molded edge, foliate carved
crest and adjustable support, single
tier with drawer, fluted standard supports bowl, tripod base, paw feet, 15″
d, 62″ h **550.00**

**Washstand, Victorian, walnut, shaped
three quarter gallery, rect top with bowl
cutout, two frieze drawers, turned legs,
shaped base shelf, turned feet, $275.00.**

Washstand
    Empire, country, pine, elaborately
scrolled gallery, single oval front
drawer, base shelf, S–curved and
turned legs, reeded apron, repainted, old dark varnish stain, gold
striping, 22½″ w, 15″ d, 39¾″ h . . . **275.00**
Federal
    Mahogany, dovetailed gallery, cut-
out for bowl, scalloped front with
two small drawers, shaped sides,
base with one drawer, turned
legs, worn finish, 18″ w, 15½″ d,
37¾″ h **425.00**
    Mahogany, shaped crest, scalloped
top drawer, shelf, bottom drawer,
wood knob handles, rope legs,
American, first quarter 19th C . . **355.00**
Grain Painted, New England, c1830,
bowed high back with shelf, scalloped supports, rect top with outset
corners, two drawers, bamboo legs,
shaped medial shelf, 39″ w, 23″ d,
46″ h **415.00**
George III, 19th C, mahogany, corner,
quarter round top with basin hole,
circular splash board, lower tier with
line inlaid drawer, down curved legs
with shaped stretcher, 23″ w, 44″ h **330.00**
Regency Style, rect marble top, beveled mirror, shelf over marble backsplash, two raised panel doors,
turned legs, caster feet, 42¼″ w,
20¼″ d, 59″ h **375.00**

Victorian, walnut, marble top, shaped rect backsplash, two applied shelves, two short and one long drawer, cabinet door, 30¾" w, 15¾" d, 41" h.................. **325.00**

What–Not, Victorian, English, third-quarter 19th C, burl walnut, rect top, leather (distressed) inset over two shelves, spiral carved end supports, tapering cylindrical legs, later casters, 29" l, 30½" h................. **1,320.00**

Wig, Queen Anne, English, washbowl holder, mahogany, pine and oak secondary woods, turned ring supporting blue transfer Copeland Spode bowl, turned and carved columns, two dovetailed drawers, tripod base, snake feet, 31½" h............ **700.00**

Work

American, country, drop leaf, curly maple, walnut and poplar secondary wood, one board top, two dovetailed drawers, turned legs, old mellow refinishing, minor age cracks, 17½" w, 25" d, 10¾" leaves, 29" h............... **1,200.00**

New England, c1800, mahogany veneer, two small drawers, glass knobs, two small "D" shaped drop leaves, old refinish, 17" w, 17½" d, 29" h.................. **715.00**

STEPS

Bed

Regency, early 19th C, mahogany, three treads, inset tooled morocco leather surfaces, paneled risers, drawer, turned tapering fluted legs, 20½" w, 29" d, 28" h......... **2,400.00**

Victorian, English, c1840, mahogany, rect platforms with tooled red leather inset, two platforms open to storage area, turned cylindrical legs, 28¾" l, 28" h........... **1,870.00**

Library, Georgian, English, early 19th C, mahogany, four steps

Bench folds to steps, reupholstered seat.................... **1,050.00**

Table folds to steps, emb green leather top, as found.......... **700.00**

STOOLS

Bar, International Movement, Alvar Aalto, designed for Artek, c1954, "X," each leg of five laminated ash pieces jointed at seat, leather upholstery, traces of orig label, 18½" w, 18" h, price for pair................ **385.00**

Choir, Louis XV, Provincial, oak, molded

D–shaped top, sq legs joined by stretchers, 25¼" h, pr **440.00**

Foot

Chippendale, carved mahogany, rect upholstered top, shaped skirt, cabriole legs, claw and ball feet, 19¼" l, 8¼" h.................. **990.00**

Continental, walnut, carved, scroll feet, black velvet upholstery, 13" l, 6½" h **150.00**

English, oak, foliate and scroll carved cabriole legs, shell carved knees, claw and ball feet, green damask upholstery, nailhead trim, 30" l, 18" d, 19" h.................. **725.00**

Louis XVI Style, wood, petit–point upholstery, 4" h.............. **175.00**

Neoclassical, Italian, c1800, carved walnut, tan suede upholstered sq feet, rail carved sides, elongated cartouche flanked by foliate dies, fluted tapering sq legs **1,980.00**

Victorian, Renaissance Revival, American, green velvet upholstery, 18" l, 13" h.................. **170.00**

William and Mary, English, late 17th C, ebonized, rect upholstered wool crewelwork seat, turned feet, joined by H–form stretcher, 20" l, 15½" d, 16" h.................... **1,100.00**

Gout, American, c1880, walnut, upholstered, rocking top, 19" l, 21" h..... **250.00**

Hinged, George III Style, mahogany, rect padded top, inlaid recessed panel sides, sq tapered legs, 18½" l, 20" h **225.00**

Milking, country, primitive, three legs, heart cutout handle, relief carving of cow, old dark finish............ **275.00**

Organ, Victorian, circular, three fancy metal legs, ebonized stem, upholstered top.................. **175.00**

Piano, Classical, late, American, c1840, rosewood, columnar, swivel top **250.00**

TABLES

Altar, Chinese, rosewood, carved, inset marble top, 49½" l, 21" w, 31½" h... **850.00**

Banquet

Empire, American, c1840, mahogany, two sections, rect top, rounded corners, rect drop leaf, cushion molded frieze, ring turned tapering legs, 76" l extended, 30" h **935.00**

Sheraton, country, cherry, curly maple drop leaf top, figured cherry veneer shaped aprons, turned and rope carved legs, casters, refinished, 44½" w, 82" l extended, 30½" h, price for pair **4,000.00**

Breakfast

Classical Revival, attributed to NY,

c1820, mahogany and mahogany veneer, 38½" w, 47" d, 29" h **880.00**

Empire, mahogany, rect top, two shaped drop leaves, single molded edge drawer, four turned drops at each corner, foliate carved pedestal, four down curving acanthus and lion paw carved legs, 38" l, 28" h . . **660.00**

George III, English, c1800, mahogany, sq tilt top, reeded edge, ring turned vase form standard, high arched molded quadruple base, foliate and shell cast gilt bronze caps on casters, restored, 50½" l, 27" h **1,650.00**

George IV, English, c1825, mahogany, rect top with molded edge, multiring turned shaft, incised tripod base, plain brass cappings and casters, 28¾" w, 49" h **1,050.00**

Hepplewhite, walnut, drop leaf, rect round cornered top, line inlaid frieze, sq tapering legs, 46½" l, 27½" h **550.00**

Regency

Continental, mahogany, rect molded top, turned and reeded pedestal, four splayed legs, paw feet, casters, 59½" l, 43" w, 27¾" h. **1,045.00**

English, mahogany, round tilt top, turned column, tripod base, scroll carved legs, old finish, 52½" d, 30¾" h. **1,250.00**

Card

Chippendale

Newport, RI, 1780–1800, mahogany, shaped top with slightly outset corners, single center long drawer, straight reeded legs, branded "N Hoyt", 35½" w, 17¼" d, 28¼" h. **4,730.00**

Philadelphia, c1780, carved mahogany, rect top, skirt with cockbeaded frieze drawer, bracketed sq legs, Marlborough feet, orig brasses, brackets restored, 33¼" l, 17½" w, 28¾" h **2,750.00**

Classical Revival, Massachusetts, c1820, mahogany and veneer, D-shaped tops with outset corners, ring turned and fluted legs, 38" w, 17" d, 29¼" h, price for pair. **2,200.00**

Federal

Boston, attributed to Seymour Workshop, c1800, mahogany, inlaid, small drawer behind one of two hinged fly rails, old surface, minor imperfections, 39¾" w, 19⅛" d, 28¾" h **7,150.00**

Maryland, c1800, mahogany, D-shaped hinged top, conforming apron, oval and floral inlaid dec

Pembroke, Country Federal, cherry, oblong top, shaped drop leaves, recessed frieze with end drawer, square tapered legs, wavy X–form stretcher, 36" w, 20" d, 27½" h, $1,430.00. Photograph courtesy of William Doyle Galleries.

on straight tapering legs, 36" w, 17" d, 29¼" h **2,310.00**

North Shore, MA, c1805, flame birch and inlaid mahogany, oblong top with serpentine front and sides, conforming shaped hinged leaf, crotch figured frieze, inlaid dies, reeded tapering legs, elongated vase form feet, minor repair to two legs, 37½" l, 18" w, 29¾" h. **3,850.00**

George II Style, burl walnut, carved, serpentine shape folding top with cable molded edge, acanthus carved cabriole legs, claw and ball feet, 31" w, 31" h **1,100.00**

George III, late 18th C, satinwood and inlaid, hinged D–shaped top, conforming frieze, sq tapering legs, 36" w, 18" d, 29¼" h **1,540.00**

George IV, English, c1825, carved mahogany, hinged rect top, rounded front corners, lotus carved baluster support with gadrooned border, four down swept reed legs, brass animal paw feet on casters, 37" w, 29" h. **1,760.00**

Hepplewhite, English, late 18th C, walnut, line inlaid folded top, bellflower inlaid sq tapering legs, shell inlaid medallions, 35¼" l, 17" w, 29¼" h **625.00**

Queen Anne, mahogany, carved, folding rect top, straight frieze, four shell carved cabriole legs, trifid feet, 29″ w, 29″ h **1,870.00**

Sheraton, Country, cherry, curly maple and mahogany veneer apron, hinged top with D–shape leaf, turned legs, reeded detail, 18¾ x 36¼″, 29″ h **990.00**

Center

Arts and Crafts, walnut, sq molded edge top, reeded reticulated frieze, shaped X–form base, turned stretcher, floral carved legs, caster feet, 26″ w, 31″ h **300.00**

Biedermeier, 19th C, walnut, circular top, tripod base, reduced height, 36″ d, 22″ h **550.00**

Louis XV, Provincial, walnut, shaped top, frieze drawer, scrolled apron, cabriole legs, 32½″ l, 26¾″ w, 29″ h **1,320.00**

Renaissance Revival, American, third-quarter 19th C, walnut and marquetry, 42″ l, 29″ w, 30½″ h . . . **1,100.00**

Victorian, Italian, 19th C, central medallion micromosaic of Roman forum, malachite border, Renaissance Revival walnut stand, 26½″ d, 31″ h **3,960.00**

Queen Anne, Boston, 1730–50, carved walnut, rect marble top, shaped corners, projecting molding and apron with pendant on front and back rails, cabriole legs, platform pad feet, repairs to marble top, repairs to bracket returns and rear molding, 50″ l, 26¼″ w, 31½″ h . . . **52,250.00**

Victorian, Gothic Revival, New York, 1840–50, rosewood, carved, hexagonal marble top, six standards on shaped base, casters, 41¾″ l, 31″ h **27,000.00**

William and Mary, oak, rect top, straight frieze, baluster turned legs joined with fluted box stretcher, 38½″ l, 29″ h **1,540.00**

Console

Empire

American, early 19th C, carved mahogany, circular tilt top, radiating crotch mahogany veneers, tapering triangular paneled pedestal, trefoil concave base, three winged eagle and lion paw feet, restoration to veneers, 47″ d, 28½″ h **2,750.00**

Dutch, early 19th C, marquetry, circular top, inlaid elaborate flowering vines, border of alternating floral sprigs and butterfly roundels, three foliate inlaid scrolled legs joined by shaped triangular platform stretcher, age cracks to top, 46½″ d, 28″ h **6,150.00**

George III, English, c1800, inlaid mahogany, D–shaped top, inset rounded corners inlaid with double banded borders of satinwood and rosewood, ebonized double stringing lines, inlaid frieze, fluted and reeded turned tapering legs, slender tapered plain feet, 36″ l, 33¾″ h **3,575.00**

Gothic Style, wrought iron, gray marble rect top, arched plate within scrollwork, scrolled frieze, trestle base, 76″ l, 43″ h **1,650.00**

Louis XVI, late 18th C, oak, semioval marble top with molded edge, carved apron, tapering fluted legs, pendant swags, D–shaped platform base, 34½″ l, 24″ h **1,650.00**

Louis XVI Style, rect marble top with floral inlay, guilloche carved edge, frieze centers angel's head on front, rosettes on sides, fluted trumpet legs, 59″ l, 28″ h **3,750.00**

Regency Style, 19th C, giltwood, carved, rect rouge marble top with molded edge, acanthus carved frieze, foliate carved scroll legs joined with X–shape stretcher mounted with bouquet, 41½″ l, 33½″ h **4,675.00**

Rococo, Italian, c1775, parcel–gilt, silvered, false marble top, serpentine molded edge over elaborate ruffled C–scroll and foliate carved apron, ruffled C–scroll legs, conforming stretcher, 60″ l, 35″ h **6,600.00**

International Movement, Gilbert Rohde, designed for Herman Miller Furniture Co, cloud, rosewood veneer irregular top, leather cov legs, brass tacks, metal tag, minor dents and abrasions, 27″ w x 27¼″ h end table, 41″ w x 15¼″ coffee table, price for pair **1,870.00**

Corner, Chinese, rosewood, bow front, inset marble top with scalloped edge, reticulated floral and foliate carved frieze, carved cabriole legs joined with shaped medial shelf, claw and ball feet, 25″ w, 18″ d, 32″ h **700.00**

Dining

Anglo–Indian, rosewood, circular top, carved and reticulated base, mythical reptile feet with casters, 54″ l, 32½″ h **1,600.00**

Arts and Crafts

Limbert Oak, c1910, No. 418, oak, orig medium finish, five sq legs, wide corbels, branded mark, edge surface recess, 48″ d, 29″ h **1,980.00**

Quaint Furniture, c1910, oak, round top, four sq legs, sq crossed stretchers, exposed tenons, orig medium finish, two boxed leaves,

metal tag, paper lbel, 48″ d, 28¾″ h **935.00**
Chippendale, PA, 1770–90, walnut, two end thumb molded drawers, squared legs, block feet, 49¼″ w, 52¼″ d, 29¾″ h **4,290.00**
Federal
Massachusetts, c1815, mahogany, three parts, center drop leaf, two matching D–shaped extensions, old refinish, imperfections, label on underside reads "3 piece dining table belonging to Com. Oliver Hazard Perry," 48″ w, 110″ l, 28½″ h **15,400.00**
Virginia, c1800, walnut, inlaid, three parts, center drop leaf, two matching D–shaped extensions, straight tapering legs, 46″ w, 92″ d open, 29″ h **2,640.00**
George II Style, late 19th C, mahogany, rect top with rounded corners, ring and baluster turned standard, four fluted down swept legs, brass cuffs and casters, 80″ l extended, 28½″ h **2,200.00**
George III, English, c1800, mahogany, three parts
Drop leaf table, two D–shaped consoles, shaped top, molded sq legs, 47″ w, 107″ l extended, 28½″ h **3,300.00**
Rect top, rounded ends, reeded edges, three pedestals, baluster turned supports, four down swept legs, brass caps on casters, two leaves, 126″ extended, 29″ h . . . **9,350.00**
George III Style, mahogany, two D–shaped ends, central section, restorations, 72″ l, 45″ d, 30″ h **715.00**
Louis XVI Style, mahogany, oval top, brass band, round tapering fluted legs, brass casters, two leaves, 80½″ l, 41½″ d, 30″ h **2,200.00**
Queen Anne
Long Island, NY, c1770, mahogany, rect top, D–shaped hinged leaves, cabriole legs, pad feet, 40½″ w, 51½″ d, 28″ h **4,400.00**
New England, c1760, cherry, rect top, D–shaped hinged leaves, cabriole legs, pad feet, 54″ l, 53″ w open, 28″ h **7,150.00**
Rhode Island, c1770, mahogany, rect top and leaves, cabriole legs, slipper feet, 47¾″ l, 46½″ w open, 27″ h **5,500.00**
Rococo, Italian, carved walnut, serpentine top, molded edge, scalloped apron, cabriole legs, 58″ l, 29¼″ h **1,430.00**

Victorian, American
Gothic Revival, c1840, mahogany, hinged rect top with rounded corners and molded edge, four baluster turned swivel supports, reeded down swept legs, baluster turned stretchers, foliate cast brass feet, tapered sq and ball supports, 28½″ h **3,300.00**
Renaissance Revival, walnut, carved, rect plank top, gadrooned frieze, two foliate and scroll carved trifid supports, 100″ l, 30″ h **1,430.00**
William and Mary, PA, c1740, walnut, oblong top, two hinged D–shaped leaves, molded frieze fitted at each end with a drawer, vase and reel turned gate legs joined by stretchers, flattened ball feet, top and frame restored, 48¾″ l, 56″ w extended, 29″ h **4,400.00**
Dressing
George II, English, mid 18th C, oak, rect molded top, three drawers, cabriole legs, stylized pad feet, 28¼″ l, 18½″ d, 26½″ h **1,210.00**
George II Style, English, walnut, rect top, molded edge, frieze drawer over small blind drawer, recessed cupboard flanked by three crossbanded drawers on either side, bracket feet, 28½″ w, 30″ h **1,100.00**
Neoclassical, Italian, early 19th C, burl walnut, parcel gilt, superstructure with retractable mirror, door flanked by four drawers over rect top, frieze fitted with slide, drawer, and basket, flanked by columns, shaped base, ball feet, 23″ l, 17¼″ w, 38½″ h . . . **2,640.00**
Drop Leaf
Classical Revival, New England, c1820, mahogany, rope turned legs, 41¾″ l, 48″ w open, 28½″ h . . **330.00**
Empire, American, first-quarter 19th C, mahogany, two shaped drop leaves, plain frieze with one drawer, rope turned legs, 39⅝″ l, 51¾″ extended, 28¾″ h **440.00**
Federal, New England, early 19th C, mahogany, old refinish, imperfections, 48″ w, 49½″ l, 29″ h **1,210.00**
Sheraton, American, 1800–1810
Cherry, D–shape drop leaves, shaped frieze, scissorlike supports, fluted legs, 39″ l, 51½″ extended, 28″ h **1,650.00**
Mahogany, rect top with two D–shape drop leaves, flute d legs, 40″ l, 55″ w extended, 28¾″ h . . **385.00**
Drum
Federal, mahogany and maple, cir-

cular star inlaid top, four frieze drawers, foliate carved vase form standard, reeded out swept legs, brass hairy paw caster feet, 22" d, 28" h. **5,000.00**

Victorian, English, mahogany, circular top, four drawers alternating with false drawers, plain standard, four down swept reeded legs, casters, replaced top, 42" d, 30" h **770.00**

End

Arts and Crafts, American, Charles Rohlfs, rect top, four sq legs, sgd and dated 1905, 23¾" l, 18" w, 28½" h **880.00**

Napoleon III Style, mahogany, ormolu mounted marquetry, shaped green marble top, floral marquetry one drawer frieze, sq fluted supports joined by medial shelf, cabriole legs ending with sabots, 24¾" l, 13" w, 29¾", price for pair. **1,700.00**

Games

George II, English, mid 18th C, mahogany, rect hinged top, leather lined surface with wells, plain frieze, cabriole legs with foliate knees, ball and claw feet, 33" l, 16" d, 28½" h **2,200.00**

George III, English, c1800, rect folding top, shaped outset corners, int. with center painted checkerboard, four oval counter wells, plain frieze, end drawer, straight tapering legs, circular ovoid feet, later japanned and gilt work, cloud shaped reserves, landscape vignettes, scrollwork and bamboo sprays, black ground, 31½" l, 29½" h **990.00**

Louis XV Style, French, Provincial, oak, sq top, gilt dec red leather inset surface, shallow gallery, scalloped apron, cabriole legs, 32¼" l, 28¾" h **1,980.00**

Neoclassical, Dutch, early 19th C, satinwood, rect top, painted floral swags and bows dec, felt lined surface, sq tapering legs, 37" w, 18¼" d, 31" h **2,200.00**

Regency Style, English, c1830, kingwood, rect top with central reversible slide with crossbanded and inlaid chessboard, crossbanded frieze, ring turned trestle legs, down swept feet, 22" d, 29" h **1,430.00**

Gateleg

George III, English, first-quarter 19th C, mahogany, rect top, cylindrical and block turned legs joined with turned stretchers, ball feet, 28" w, 31" h. **2,200.00**

William and Mary, New England,

c1725, maple, oblong top, two D–shaped hinged leaves, single drawer frieze, ring and vase and block turned legs, flattened ball feet, ring and vase turned stretcher, 28½" w, 41¾" h. **13,200.00**

Hutch, PA, early 18th C, pine and maple, oval top, turned columns, box stretcher, 39½" l, 29½" w, 27½" h . . . **660.00**

Lamp, Arts and Crafts, American, L. & J. G. Stickley, No. 575, round top, lower shelf, arched and pegged cross–stretchers, orig finish, decal, 29" h, 24" d. **1,210.00**

Library

Arts and Crafts, Gustav Stickley, No. 655, c1907, oak, orig medium–light finish, spindle sides, paper label, top separation, 36" l, 24" d, 29" h. . **3,410.00**

Continental, rosewood, carved detail, conforming molded edge top, one dovetailed drawer, serpentine apron with carved shells, cabriole legs, old worn finish, 45¼" l, 27" d, 31½" h **2,025.00**

French Provincial, walnut, rect molded edge top, recessed panel two drawer frieze, block and vase turned legs, disk feet, 70" l, 30½" d, 34" h. **850.00**

Neoclassical, Italian, marquetry, walnut, rect egg and dart carved edge top, mythical figures above inlaid one drawer frieze, animal inlaid ring and tapering block legs joined by X–shape stretcher with urn finial, turnip feet, 30" l, 45" w, 27" h **2,750.00**

Renaissance Revival, American, third-quarter 19th C walnut, felt inset top, 38" l, 23½" w, 28½" h **440.00**

Victorian, English, top c1840, base c1820, mahogany, oval top with red leather writing surface, frieze fitted with drawer on both sides, ends with short drawers, ring turned support, four reeded down swept legs, brass animal paw feet on casters, leather distressed, 60" l, 30¼" h . . **3,850.00**

Occasional, Neoclassical

Austrian, early 19th C, mahogany, rect top, ormolu mounted frieze, ring turned legs joined by lower open shelf, 21" w, 16½" d, 30½" h **2,200.00**

German, 19th C, walnut and parquetry, oval top, frieze drawer, sq tapering incurved legs joined by open shelf, 23¼" l, 17½" w, 31" h **1,100.00**

Pembroke

Chippendale, Philadelphia, c1775, mahogany, rect top, two hinged leaves, single drawer frieze, molded skirt, sq legs, X–form

stretcher, Marlborough feet, 31" l,
29" h **3,850.00**

Federal, New England
c1800, mahogany, inlaid, old refinish, minor imperfections, 15½" w,
32" d, 28" h **1,980.00**

c1806, mahogany and veneer inlaid, D–shaped hinged leaves,
single drawers with illegible inscription and date, 32" l, 38" w
open, 28" h **1,980.00**

George II, English, mid 18th C, mahogany, rect top, frieze drawer,
Marlborough legs, 34¼" w, 30½" l,
28" h **660.00**

Sheraton, Country, cherry and curly
maple, drop leaf, shaped leaves,
turned legs, 18 x 35½", 12" leaves,
28¾" h **440.00**

Pier, Classical Revival
Boston, c1820–35, mahogany veneer, carved, rect white marble top,
gilt carvings include flowers tied
with ribbon and center carving of
cupids and wreath, mirrored back,
columns with gilded gaps and base,
shaped base, 45½" w, 16⅞" d,
19¼" h **4,125.00**

Pennsylvania, c1830, mahogany veneer, carved, rect marble top,
carved doric capitals on columns as
supports, D–shaped shelf with conforming apron, plain back, reeded
bulbed feet, 40" w, 22" d, 40" h . . . **1,430.00**

Quartetto, George III, English, c1800,
mahogany, graduated rect top, shallow galleried border, simulated bamboo turned and blocked double standards, rect plinth base over ringed
feet, 20" w, 30" h, nested set of four . **3,300.00**

Refectory, Italian Renaissance Style,
walnut, rect top, lozenge carved
molded edge, trestle supports carved
with lion form monopodia, center
carved cartouche, mask and foliate
carved stretcher, 74" l, 33" h **3,300.00**

Sewing

Federal
American, curly maple and mahogany, octagonal crossbanded top,
frieze drawer, sq tapering ebony
inlaid legs, 20" l, 14½" w, 29½" h **6,000.00**

Massachusetts, c1820, mahogany,
oblong top, rounded outset corners, single cockbeaded drawer,
sewing bag drawer, carved flowerheads on each corner, reeded
tapering legs, ball feet, 18" l,
20¾" w, 28½" h **2,750.00**

George III, English, c1800, rosewood,
tulipwood, and satinwood, c1790,
octagonal top, three hinged compartments, slender sq tapering saber legs joined by X–form stretcher,
16" l, 12" w, 30¾" h **1,320.00**

Side
Baroque, Dutch, seaweed marquetry,
rect top, molded edge, inlaid central
foliate medallion surrounded by
similar roundels and spandrels, single drawer, later spiral carved legs
joined by inlaid stretcher, later bun
feet, age cracks to top, 36¾" l, 28¼"
h **4,675.00**

Classical Revival, New England,
c1825, mahogany and mahogany
veneer, circular marble top, top
supported by center pedestal and
three C–shaped supports, scrolled
shaped base, casters, 24" d, 30" h **6,050.00**

Federal, Mid Atlantic States, c1820,
curly maple, sq top, single cockbeaded drawer, sq tapering legs,
19½" l, 19½" w, 29¾" h **1,320.00**

George III, Provincial, c1800, oak,
rect top with canted corners and
molded edge, crossbanded and
cockbeaded frieze drawer, scalloped apron, canted sq legs, 32" l,
27" h **2,750.00**

Late George III, English, c1810, penwork and brown japanning, octagonal top, Chinese figures with border of flowers and leaves dec, ring
turned baluster shaft, tripod base
dec with chains of leaves, minor
losses to borders, 14" w, 28" h . . . **825.00**

Queen Anne
Pennsylvania, c1750, walnut, rect
top, plain skirt, splayed turned tapering legs, pad feet, 20½" l,
19¾" w, 28½" h **6,700.00**

Rhode Island, c1760, mahogany,
molded oblong top, shaped skirt,
turned tapering legs, pad feet,
40¼" l, 21" w, 26" h **6,600.00**

William and Mary, late 17th C, walnut,
rect top with molded edge, frieze
drawer, ring and baluster turned
legs joined with waved cross
stretcher, ball feet, 27" l, 26" h **3,300.00**

Sofa
Classical Revival, attributed to NY,
c1820, mahogany and mahogany
veneer, drawer with orig escuthesons, 36" w, 21" d, 28¾" h **3,025.00**

George IV, mahogany, rosewood inlay, rect crossbanded rounded corner top, two frieze drawers, baluster
form standard, four out swept legs,
brass paw caster feet, 34½" l, 29¾"
w, 29" h **2,200.00**

Regency, early 19th C, mahogany,

rect hinged top, pair of frieze drawers, splayed legs joined by stretcher, some veneer loss, 34" l, 26¾" w, 27½" h **1,540.00**

Tabouret, Arts and Crafts, American, L. & J. G. Stickley, round top, through tenon cross–stretchers, orig finish, light water stain, conjoined "Craftsman" and "Handcraft" decal, 20" h, 18" d **825.00**

Tavern

Chippendale, New England, c1780, country, cherry and pine, painted, slight warp to two board top, 37¾" w, 25½" d, 25¾" h **1,540.00**

Queen Anne, New England, c1750–75, maple and birchwood, oval top, arched skirt, turned legs, pad feet, 33¾" l, 26¾" h **5,500.00**

Spanish, wrought iron, marble top, shaped rect top with beveled edge, foliate trestle base, 30½" l, 21" w, 29" h **325.00**

William and Mary

New England, c1760, pine, 33½ x 24¾" top, 27" h **715.00**

Pennsylvania, 1780–1810, walnut, rect top, molded skirt, three molded drawers, ring turned legs, box stretcher, flattened ball feet, 29" w, 30" h **5,500.00**

Tea

Chippendale

Attributed to MA, c1780, cherry, scalloped top, turned vasiform standard, tripod base terminating in claw and ball feet, 33 x 30½" top, 27¾" h **935.00**

Attributed to RI, c1780, mahogany, tilt top, vasiform standard, tripod base, slipper feet, 32¾" d, 28½" h **1,650.00**

Lancaster County, PA, 1750–70, carved walnut, molded tilt top, bird cage with baluster support, leafage carved pedestal with punch work and gadrooning over similar carved cabriole legs, webbed ball and claw feet, old refinish, 33" d, 27⅜" h **45,100.00**

Federal, New England, c1805, birchwood and mahogany, octagonal top with inlaid edge, petal carved urn standard, inlaid and shaped down curving legs, 16" w, 30½" h **9,900.00**

George II Style, mahogany, circular dished top, columnar standard, baluster knop on three down scrolled fluted legs, 16" d, 25" h **375.00**

George III, Irish, 18th C, mahogany, dished rect top, scrolled and carved shell apron, cabriole legs, pad feet, 29½" l, 19" w, 27½" h **2,100.00**

Oriental, black lacquer, gilded chinoiserie dec, bird cage support, turned column, tripod base, paw feet, 23½" d, 30½" h **650.00**

Tip, Arts and Crafts, L & J G Stickley, No. 589, c1915, oak, round top, sq post base, elongated reverse corbels, branded "The Work of L & J G Stickley," screw holes under feet, varnish, 20" d, 24" h **715.00**

Trestle

Mission, oak, rect top, three corbels at sides, applied belt and vertical rect cut out, unsgd, refinished top, 50" w, 28" d, 29" h **770.00**

William and Mary, Hudson River Valley, early 18th C, pine, rect cleated top, scroll upright supports join with molded board stretcher, trestle feet, 96" l, 30¾" h **8,250.00**

Work

Chippendale, country, New England, late 18th C, 30¼" w, 22¾" d, 27½" h, imperfections **1,760.00**

Classical Revival, New York, upstate, 1830–40, mahogany veneer, drawers, 27" w, 15¾" d, 29" h **770.00**

Empire, early 19th C

American, country, figured mahogany veneer, drop leaf top, two dovetailed drawers, four clear lacy glass pulls, tapered pedestal with edge beading, four legs, acanthus carved knees, brass paw feet with casters, minor repairs, two replaced pulls, old refinishing, 17" w, 20½" d, 8¾" l leaves, 29¼" h **400.00**

New York, carved mahogany, rect top, two drawers, twisted scroll carved pedestal, four acanthus carved curved hairy lion paw feet, casters, repairs to side, veneer missing, repairs to two feet, 22½" w, 30½" h **550.00**

Federal

Boston, c1800, mahogany, flame birch veneer, shaped octagonal top, single drawer, straight tapered legs, spade foot, X–shaped stretcher, casters, 20 x 18¼" top, 28½" h **2,420.00**

New York, c1815, mahogany veneer, carved, astragal end, hinged top, fitted int., two working and two false drawers, gilded animal paw feet with casters, 26½" w, 13½" d, 32" h **1,760.00**

Hepplewhite, work, walnut, pine secondary wood, removable three board top, two cockbeaded drawers with replaced turned drawer pulls, square tapered legs, old mellow refinishing, replaced top is well-made replacement, 33¼" w, 59" l, 29" h .   660.00

Neoclassical, Austrian, early 19th C, walnut, rect top, canted corners, frieze drawer, sq tapering incurved legs joined by open shelf, 25" w, 16" d, 31" h 615.00

Writing

George II Style, walnut, brown tooled leather top, scalloped frieze with two drawers, fluted canted corners, carved trailing acanthus molded cabriole legs, claw and ball feet. . .   3,575.00

George III, English, c1800, mahogany, rect leather inset top, frieze fitted with drawers, false drawers on reverse, sq tapering legs, 51" l, 41¾" d, 30" h. 2,530.00

Late George III, English, c1810, mahogany, gold and blind tooled faded green leather top, boxwood strung border, long frieze drawer, two short drawers flanking kneehole, sq tapering legs, brass caps and casters, 48" l, 31" h 4,675.00

Renaissance Style, Italian, walnut, rect carved edge top, two aligned foliate carved frieze drawers, foliate and mask carved trestle base, 53" l, 20" w, 24½" h 225.00

Tea, Queen Anne, mahogany, circular dished tilting top, bird cage support, pillar and compressed urn standard, cabriole tripod base, club feet, 1725–50, 24¾" d, 28¼" h, $1,430.00. Photograph courtesy of William Doyle Galleries.

William IV, mahogany, tooled green leather sq top, single drawer, four spiral twist columns, rect platform base, reeded scroll feet, 30" w, 31¾" h 1,540.00

TEA WAGONS

Black lacquer finish, raised Chinese figures, landscape, D–shaped drop leaves, turned legs, support, two wheels 200.00

Victorian, brass, glass top and shelf .   700.00

Wicker, serpentine edge, scrolled handle, removable glass serving tray top   325.00

WAGON SEATS

Wagon seats cannot be classified with seats from a wagon. Early wagon seats were usually constructed with a double frame and a basketry–type seat. They served a dual purpose: in the house and in the family wagon for additional seating.

Hickory spindle back and arms, leather basketweave seat, six legs, 18th C . .   750.00

Maple and oak, double chair back, flame turned finials, scrolled arms, rush seat, turned supports, box stretchers, 33" l 1,200.00

Painted

Ladderback, two slat back, turned stiles, splint seat, red paint, 35" l . .   600.00

Spindle, two seater, turned arms, open back, five vertical turned spindles, double stretchers, red and green paint, 36" l 800.00

Pine, Windsor, primitive, shoe feet, 30¾" l 500.00

Walnut, Windsor, one board seat, trestle feet, natural finish, 33" l, 28½" h 250.00

WICKER

Bookcase, four oak shelves, turned wood frame, reed and wood fancy sunburst back, natural finish, c1890 .   550.00

Carriage, c1890, serpentine edges, natural finish, orig velvet upholstery. . . .   475.00

Chair

Armchair, Gustav Stickley, No. 88, c1913, high flat topped back, rect piercings, shallow wings continue to wide flat arms, conforming skirt, 39½" h 800.00

Armchair and Ottoman, Heywood Brothers and Wakefield, Chicago, IL, early 20th C, rounded back crestrail continues to arms, woven sides and apron, circular feet, upholstered pad seat, matching ottoman   825.00

Corner, elaborate scrolling, bird cage arms and supports, natural finish. . **650.00**

Highchair, c1880, shell design back, set in cane seat, wooden footrest, turned wooden legs, natural finish **285.00**

Side, Heywood Brothers and Wakefield Co, c1890, closely woven back panel with center scalloped design, closely woven shields over legs, natural finish **350.00**

Foot Stool, upholstered seat, painted **165.00**

Pedestal, 34½" h, 13" d top, sq top, conforming tapered column, flared base, natural, Heywood Wakefield **220.00**

Piano Chair, Heywood Brothers and Wakefield Co, Wakefield, MA, No. 3901, tall arched back with ornate scrolls and loops, round tightly woven seat, cabriole front legs trimmed with graduated scrolls, joined by stretchers with center turned drop, orig label, 43½" h **825.00**

Rocker, Wakefield Rattan Co, serpentine edges, braided trim, wooden rockers, painted white **250.00**

Settee, rect back, upholstered section on back and seat, woven arms, scalloped skirt. **425.00**

Stand, music, Wakefield Rattan Co, c1883, three shelves, orig paper label **265.00**

Table, Karpen Guaranteed Construction Furniture, library, oval, orig paper label. **325.00**

GAME PLATES

History: Game plates, popular between 1870 and 1915, are specially decorated plates used to serve fish and game. Sets originally included a platter, serving plates, and a sauce or gravy boat. Many sets have been divided. Today, individual plates are used for wall hangings.

Reference: Susan and Al Bagdade, *Warman's English & Continental Pottery & Porcelain, Second Edition,* Wallace–Homestead, 1991.

BIRDS

Plate

9¼" d, wild geese, Buffalo Pottery, 1908. . . . . **60.00**

9½" d, bird, scalloped edge, mauve ground, gold trim, sgd "Vitet Limoges". **125.00**

10" d, pheasant, Limoges, sgd "Max" **90.00**

10½" d, game bird and two water spaniels, crimped gold rim, sgd "RK Beck" **75.00**

12½" d, flying game, hp, heavy gold,

rococo border, Limoges, artist sgd "Rogin". **210.00**

13¼" d, game bird and pheasant, heavy gold scalloped, emb rococo border, Coronet Limoges, sgd "Brussillon" **245.00**

Platter

16" l, quail, two handles, hp gold trim, Limoges, France **125.00**

18 x 14¼", harvest scene, turkey center, floral border, brown dec, Royal Staffordshire **55.00**

Set

7 pcs, wild game birds, pastoral scene background, molded edges, shell dec, Fazent Mehlem, Bonn, Germany. **220.00**

9 pcs, eight 9¼" d plates, large platter, hp, various birds, gold scalloped edge, Haviland and Co **350.00**

12 pcs, ten 10½" plates, platter, sauce boat, game birds in natural habitat, sgd "I Bubedi". **3,300.00**

DEER

Plate, 9" d, buck and doe, forest scene **50.00**

Set

5 pcs, four plates, large platter, Buffalo Pottery, artist sgd "Beck" **275.00**

13 pcs, twelve plates, platter, deer, bear, and game birds, yellow ground, scalloped border, Haviland China, sgd "MC Haywood" **3,000.00**

ELK

Plate, 9" d, two elk in natural setting, Buffalo Pottery **45.00**

Fish, green border, blue flowers, brown fish, marked "Austria," 8⅜" d, $20.00.

FISH

Plate
8″ d, bass, scalloped edge, gray—
green trim, fern on side of fish,
Limoges 50.00
8½″ d, colorful fish swimming on
green shaded background, scalloped border, gold trim, pierced for
hanging, sgd "Biarritz, W. S. or S.
W. Co., Limoges, France". 35.00
9″ d, Limoges, hp dec, price for set of
six luncheon plates. 275.00
Platter
14″ l, bass on lure, sgd "RK Beck" . 90.00
23″ l, hp, Charoone, Haviland 200.00
Set
8 pcs, four plates, 24″ platter, sauce
boat with attached plate, cov tur-
een, Rosenthal 350.00
11 pcs, ten plates, serving platter, sgd
"Limoges". 350.00
13 pcs, twelve 8″ d plates, 23″ l platter,
colorful hp fish, gold scalloped
edges, artist sgd, Limoges 475.00
14 pcs, twelve plates, platter, gravy
boat, bass, blue beehive mark. . . . 250.00
15 pcs, twelve 9″ plates, 24″ platter,
sauce boat with attached plate, cov
tureen, hp, raised gold design edge,
artist sgd, Limoges. 750.00

GAMES

History: Mass production of board games did
not take place until after the Civil War. Firms such
as McLoughlin Brothers, Milton Bradley, and Selchow and Righter were active in the 1860s, followed by Parker Brothers, who began in 1883. Parker Brothers bought out the rights to the W. & S.
B. Ives Co., who had produced some very early
games in the 1840s, including the "first" American
board game, The Mansion of Happiness. All except
McLoughlin Brothers are giants in the game industry today.

McLoughlin Brothers' games are a challenge to
find. Not only does the company no longer exist
[Milton Bradley bought it out in 1920], but the lithography on its games was the best of its era.
Most board games are collected because of the
bright, colorful lithography on their box covers. In
addition to spectacular covers, the large Mc-
Loughlin games often made lead playing pieces and
fancy block spinners, thus making them even more
desirable.

Common games such as Anagrams, Authors,
Jackstraws, Lotto, Tiddledy Winks, and Peter Coddles do not command high prices nor do the games
of Flinch, Pit, and Rook, which still are being produced.

Games, with the exception of the common ones

stated above, generally are rising in price. However, interesting to note is the fact that certain
games dealing with good graphics on popular subject matter, for example, trains, planes, baseball,
Christmas and others, often bring higher prices because they are also sought by collectors in those
particular fields.

Condition is everything when buying. Do not buy
games that have been taped or that have price tags
stickered on the face of their covers. Also, beware
of buying games at outdoor flea markets where
weather elements can cause fading and warping.

References: Avedon and Sutton–Smith, *The
Study of Games,* Wiley and Son, 1971; R. C. Bell,
The Board Game Book, Knapp Press, 1979; Lee
Dennis, *Warman's Antique American Games,
1840–1940,* Wallace–Homestead, 1991; Caroline
Goodfellow, *A Collector's Guide To Games and
Puzzles,* Apple Press, 1991; Brian Love, *Great
Board Games,* 1895–1935, Macmillan Publishing
Co., 1979; Brian Love, *Play The Game: Over 40
Games From The Golden Age Of Board Games,*
Reed Books, 1978; Norman E. Martinus and Harry
L. Rinker, *Warman's Paper,* Wallace–Homestead,
1994; Rick Polizzi and Fred Schaefer, *Spin Again:
Board Games from the Fifties and Sixties,* Chroni-
cle Books, 1991; Harry L. Rinker, *Collector's Guide
To Toys, Games, and Puzzles,* Wallace–Home-
stead, 1991; Bruce Whitehill, *Games: American
Boxed Games and Their Makers, 1822–1992,* Wal-
lace–Homestead, 1992.

Periodicals: *Toy Shop,* 700 E. State St., Iola,
WI 54990; *Toy Trader,* 100 Bryant St., Dubuque,
IA 52001.

Collectors' Clubs: American Game Collectors
Association, 49 Brooks Ave., Lewiston, ME 04240;
American Toy Collectors of America, Inc., c/o
Carter, Ledyard & Milburn, Two Wall St., 13th
Floor, New York, NY 10005; Games Alliance, PO
Box 197, East Meadow, NY 11554.

Museums: Checkers Hall of Fame, Petal, MS;
Essex Institute, Salem, MA; University of Waterloo
Museum & Archive of Games, Waterloo, Ontario,
Canada; Washington Dolls' House and Toy Mu-
seum, Washington, D.C.

Additional Listings: See *Warman's Americana
& Collectibles* for more examples.

Aero–Chute Target Game, American
Toy Airship Co, sky and target game
board, 1930s, 19⁹⁄₁₆ x 13³⁄₁₆″, eight
playing pieces 35.00
An Exciting Motor Boat Race, No. 112,
American Toy Manf'g Co, boxed
board game, 1925, 11½ x 9¼″, instructions on back of box cover, four
colored wood counters, multicolored
lithographed board with spinner superimposed, track game. 75.00
Bottoms Up, The Embossing Company,
© 1934, 6½ x 3″, instructions on back
of box cover, pair of dice and nine

Peg Top, Parker Brothers, 12 x 10¾", $18.00.

round domino–type counters with pigs' bottoms on their backs **15.00**

Cats and Mice, Gantlope, and Lost Diamond, McLoughlin Bros, c1890, 7½ x 14", wood "book" board game with slipcase, three different multicolored lithographed boards, instruction book, box of playing pieces including block spinner, 32 wood counters of assorted shapes **120.00**

Colors, Game Of, McLoughlin Bros, boxed board game, c1888, 8 x 15½", Gem Series, instructions on back of box cover, 23 pcs (spinner, red token, white token, ten red counters, ten white counters), multicolored lithographed board, pooling game **100.00**

Comic Conversation Cards, J. Ottmann Lith Co, card game, c1905, 5 x 7", instruction sheet, numerous question and answer cards **40.00**

Game of Advance and Retreat, Milton Bradley, boxed board game, c1900, 19½ x 10¼", instructions on back of box cover, lithographed, red and blue checker board **95.00**

Glider Racing Game, Milton Bradley, boxed board game, 1930s, 14½ x 8¼", instructions printed on center of board, multicolored lithographed board pasted on box bottom, spinner, four round wood colored counters, track game **40.00**

Glydor, #423, All-Fair, 1931, 15½ x 12½", instructions on back of box cover, multicolored lithographed board with attached spinner and four gliders, track game **45.00**

Honey Bee Game, Milton Bradley, boxed board game, c1913, 12¼" sq, instructions on back of box cover, multicolored lithographed board, colored

metal disks, revolving metal disk, and magnet **45.00**

Jack Straws, Crandall (of Montrose, PA), skill game, c1869, covered wood cylinder 6¼" h, 39 wood paddle letters, two hooks, Anagram game as well **100.00**

Jolly Darkie Target Game, Milton Bradley, skill game, c1905, 8 x 15½", instructions on back of box cover, multicolored lithographed board on platformed box, three wood balls, same picture on board, Black theme **200.00**

Leap For Life Game, Milton Bradley, boxed board game, 1930s, 8¼ x 14", instructions printed in center of board, four wood counters and spinner, multicolored lithographed board **25.00**

Limited Mail And Express Game, Parker Brothers, boxed board game, © 1894, 21 x 14", wood box, instructions on back of box cover, pack of route cards, four colored wood counters, four colored flat metal train tokens, board is multicolored lithographed map of U.S. pasted on box bottom . . **300.00**

Little Boy Blue, Milton Bradley, 1905–10, boxed board game, multicolored lithographed board with instructions printed on bottom, four wood markers, spinner **40.00**

Meteor Game, A C Gilbert, skill game, 1916, 7½ x 5", metal board with sixty–one holes, clay marbles, metal forceps, instruction booklet **18.00**

Militac, Parker Brothers, card game, 1910, 5½ x 4", 52 cards, instruction card, and advertising card, cards show photographs of pre–WWI NCOs, Officers, and weaponry, red backs state "Tactics–The Military Game" **35.00**

New Game Of Red Riding Hood, The, McLoughlin Bros, card game, c1888, 6¼ x 4½", 42 multicolored lithographed cards, instruction booklet . . **25.00**

New Premium Game of Logomachy, The, McLoughlin Bros, card game, 1887, 8½ x 6", wood box, 56 multicolored lithographed alphabet cards with bird on backs, instruction booklet, invented by F. A. Wright in 1874 . . . . **25.00**

Ocean To Ocean Flight Game, Wilder Mfg Co, boxed board game, c1927, 7½ x 12¼", spinner and six counters, multicolored lithographed board of U.S. map, directions in lower left corner of board **65.00**

Owl And The Pussy Cat, The, E. O. Clark, Tokalon Series, boxed board game, c1890, 19¼ x 10½", wood box, instructions on back of box cover, spinner with four wood counters, multicolored lithographed board with turkey and pig. 85.00

Parker Brothers Post Office Game, educational play acting game, c1910, 9 x 12", contains postman's mask, cancel stamp, sheets of stationery, envelopes, postcards, etc. 125.00

Quartette Union War Game, E. G. Selchow, Civil War card game, 1874, 2½ x 3½", 48 cards, instruction card, cards black on white, involves battles and Union generals 45.00

Round The World, Milton Bradley, boxed board game, c1912, 21¼ x 14¼", spinner with four round wood counters, multicolored lithographed board with instructions printed on it, track game. 195.00

Rummy, manufacturer unknown, card game, c1910, 5½ x 7½", 48 cards, instruction sheet 12.00

Setto, Game Of Syllables, Selchow and Righter, © 1882, 6 x 4", 51 black and white cards, five illustrated "prize" cards, instruction booklet, invented by Charles P. Goldey 25.00

Ski–Hi New York To Paris, Cutler & Saleeby Co., #2117, boxed board game, c1927, 12½ x 7½", one die with four metal planes, multicolored lithographed board showing ocean, NYC, and Eiffel Tower, track game based on Lindbergh's crossing of the Atlantic 85.00

Snake Eyes, Selchow & Righter, card game, c1930s, 11 x 7½", 185 pcs (120 cards, dice cup, two wood dice, 62 chips), instructions on back of box cover, multicolored lithographed cards with "craps" expressions printed on them. 55.00

Teddy Bear's Trip, J. Ottmann Lith Co, card game, c1910, 7¼ x 11¼", storybook, instructions on bottom of box cover together with legend of the storybook, numerous printed cards, played like Peter Coddles. 28.00

Telephone Game, The, J. H. Singer, card game, © 1898, 7½ x 6", numerous question and answer cards, two black wood "receivers" connected to each other by a string 55.00

Tiny Town Bank, The, Spear, boxed play acting game, c1910, 10½ x 7½", instructions on back of box cover, two bank books, deposit slips, withdrawal slips, fake paper money and change 85.00

Uncle Wiggily's New Airplane Game, Milton Bradley, board game with matching box of playing pieces, 1920s, instructions on back of box cover, numerous playing cards and

counters, multicolored lithographed board opens to 16" sq, track game . . 45.00

Ups And Downs Of School Life, Spear, boxed board game, c1910, 12½ x 6½", instructions on back of box cover, 10 pcs (folding board, dice cup, two dice, six wood counters), multicolored lithographed board featuring amusing pictures of school life 45.00

When My Ship Comes In, Parker Brothers, card game, © 1888, 5¼ x 4", 84 nonillustrated cards, instruction sheet 25.00

Whirlpool, McLoughlin Brothers, c1899, No. 408, boxed board game, 7¼" sq, instructions on cover, multicolored lithographed board, twelve wood counters, and spinner 20.00

Who Do You Love Best, J Jay Gould, 1876, card game, 7½ x 5", instructions of box cover, 70 cards, four wood pegs, two pencils. 25.00

Wings, Parker Brothers, card game, © 1928, 5½ x 4", 99 cards, instruction booklet, card backs are pink and white picturing airmail planes 20.00

Yankee Pedlar, McLoughlin Brothers, 1865–70, 4⅛ x 5⅝", twelve lithographed handpainted merchant cards, instruction booklet 65.00

GAUDY DUTCH

History: Gaudy Dutch is an opaque, soft–paste ware made between 1790 and 1825 in England's Staffordshire district. Most pieces are unmarked; marks of various potters, including the impressed marks of Riley and Wood, have been found on pieces.

The pieces first were hand decorated in an underglaze blue, fired, and then received additional decoration over the glaze. Many pieces today have the overglaze decoration extensively worn. Gaudy Dutch found a ready market within the Pennsylvania German community because it was inexpensive and intense with color. It had little appeal in England.

References: Susan and Al Bagdade, *Warman's English & Continental Pottery & Porcelain, 2nd Edition,* Wallace–Homestead, 1991; Eleanor and Edward Fox, *Gaudy Dutch,* published by authors, 1970, out of print; John A. Shuman III, *The Collector's Encyclopedia of Gaudy Dutch & Welsh,* Collector Books, 1990, 1991 value update, out of print.

Reproduction Alert: Cup plates, bearing the impressed mark "CYBRIS," have been reproduced and are collectible in their own right. The Henry Ford Museum has issued pieces in the single rose pattern, although they are of porcelain and not soft–paste.

Advisor: John D. Querry.

Plate, Butterfly pattern, 9¾″ d, $775.00.

Butterfly
Coffeepot, high domed cov	10,000.00
Creamer	1,200.00
Cup Plate	975.00

Plate
7¼″ d	775.00
9⅞″ d	850.00
Platter, oval, 14″ l	1,800.00
Sugar Bowl, rect	1,350.00
Tea Bowl and Saucer, Butterfly center position	875.00
Teapot, spout repair	650.00
Wash Basin, 13¾″ d, marked "Adams"	10,000.00

Carnation
Coffeepot, high domed cov	2,500.00
Creamer	750.00
Cup and Saucer, handleless	355.00
Cup Plate	975.00

Plate
9¾″ d	725.00
10″ d	1,100.00
Soup Plate	775.00
Sugar Bowl	850.00
Tea Bowl and Saucer	600.00
Teapot	850.00

Dahlia
Creamer	850.00
Plate, 8⅜″ d, double border	1,200.00
Sugar Bowl	1,200.00
Tea Bowl and Saucer	975.00

Double Rose
Creamer	850.00
Cup Plate	750.00
Jug, mask spout	1,550.00
Pitcher, 8¼″ h	1,300.00
Plate, 8¾″ d	775.00

Platter
10½″ l	2,700.00
11⅝″ l	3,300.00
15″ l	3,300.00

Tea Bowl and Saucer	600.00
Teapot	1,800.00
Toddy Plate	625.00
Waste Bowl	675.00

Dove
Creamer	675.00
Plate, 8¼″ d	675.00
Sugar Bowl	750.00
Tea Bowl and Saucer	650.00
Teapot, knop restored on lid	625.00
Toddy Plate	675.00

Grape
Creamer	450.00
Cup Plate	725.00
Plate, 9¾″ d	525.00
Pitcher, 8″ h	2,200.00
Soup Plate, 8¾″ d	675.00
Teapot	650.00
Toddy Plate	450.00

Leaf
Bowl, unusual shape	975.00
Tea Bowl and Saucer	775.00

Oyster
Coffeepot, high domed lid	1,900.00
Creamer	375.00

Plate
4½″ d	450.00
8½″ d	525.00
10″ d	650.00
Tea Bowl and Saucer	425.00
Teapot	625.00
Toddy Plate	625.00
Waste Bowl, rim chips	350.00

Primrose
Plate
8¾″ d, imp "Riley"	650.00
9⅞″ d	2,400.00
Sugar Bowl	850.00
Tea Bowl and Saucer	675.00

Rose
Coffeepot, high domed cov	5,200.00
Creamer	550.00
Cup Plate	1,075.00

Plate
7½″ d, imp mark	325.00
9½″ d	425.00
Sugar Bowl	650.00
Tea Bowl and Saucer	325.00
Waste Bowl	300.00

Straw Flower
Plate, 9¼″ d	2,500.00
Soup Plate	975.00

Sunflower
Coffeepot, high domed cov, restored spout	1,500.00
Creamer	775.00

Plate
6½″ d	750.00
9¾″ d	1,050.00
Tea Bowl and Saucer	775.00

Urn
Creamer	375.00

Cup Plate	1,075.00
Plate	
5½" d	775.00
9⅞" d	600.00
Soup Plate	525.00
Tea Bowl and Saucer	375.00
Teapot	650.00
Waste Bowl	350.00
War Bonnet	
Creamer	575.00
Cup Plate	950.00
Pitcher, 5¾" h, rim repair	200.00
Plate	
6⅜" d	575.00
8¼" d	675.00
Soup Plate	775.00
Tea Bowl and Saucer	550.00
Water Lily, tea bowl and saucer, pink luster border	1,100.00
Zinnia, plate	
6⅜" d	550.00
8½" d	575.00

GAUDY IRONSTONE

History: Gaudy Ironstone was made in England around 1850. Most pieces are impressed "Ironstone" and bear a registry mark. Ironstone is an opaque, heavy body earthenware which contains large proportions of flint and slag. Gaudy Ironstone is decorated in patterns and colors similar to Gaudy Welsh.

Reference: Susan and Al Bagdade, *Warman's English & Continental Pottery & Porcelain, Second Edition,* Wallace–Homestead, 1991.

Butter Dish, cov, octagonal, Seaweed pattern, three color, luster dec, orig insert	90.00

Soup Plate, unmarked, 7⅝" d, $45.00.

Creamer, Morning Glory pattern, underglaze blue and luster dec	75.00
Cup and Saucer, handleless	
Floral design, underglaze blue, polychrome enamel and luster, wear and chip on cup	95.00
Morning Glory and Berries pattern, underglaze blue, red, green, and yellow enamel, hairline in cup, chips on table ring	95.00
Mug, underglaze blue stripes, luster, and red wavy lines	35.00
Plate	
8⅜" d, Morning Glory pattern, underglaze blue and luster	105.00
8½" d	
Floral design, underglaze blue, polychrome enamel and luster, imp registry mark and "E. Walley, Niagara Shape," wear and flaking	125.00
Strawberry pattern, underglaze blue, polychrome enamel and luster, wear and chip on table ring	150.00
8⅝" d, Morning Glory pattern, underglaze blue, red and two shades of green enameling, chip on table ring	105.00
8¾" d	
Florals, underglaze blue and polychrome enamel and luster, imp "Ironstone," wear	115.00
Tulips and berries dec, underglaze blue, red, green, and black enamel, stains	150.00
8⅞" d, Urn pattern, underglaze blue, polychrome enameling and luster, wear and flaking	200.00
9" d, Vintage pattern, underglaze blue, red and green enameling and luster	115.00
9½" d, florals, underglaze blue and polychrome enamel and luster, imp "Ironstone," wear	180.00
Sugar, cov, Urn of Flowers pattern, underglaze blue and luster, red and green enamel, emb lion head handles	85.00
Tea Set, Morning Glory pattern, 9¼" h cov teapot, 6¼" h creamer, 8¼" h cov sugar, minor wear, price for set	400.00

GAUDY WELSH

History: Gaudy Welsh is a translucent porcelain that was originally made in the Swansea area of England from 1830 to 1845. Although the designs resemble Gaudy Dutch, the body texture and weight differ. One of the characteristics is the gold luster on top of the glaze.

In 1890, Allerton made a similar ware. These wares are heavier opaque porcelain and usually bear the export mark.

References: Susan and Al Bagdade, *Warman's*

English & Continental Pottery & Porcelain, Second Edition, Wallace–Homestead, 1991; John A. Shuman III, *The Collector's Encyclopedia of Gaudy Dutch and Welsh,* Collector Books, 1990, 1991 value update, out of print; Howard Y. Williams, *Gaudy Welsh China,* Wallace–Homestead, out of print.

Cup and Saucer, Shan Wa See, peppermint transfer, $65.00.

Daisy and Chain
Creamer	80.00
Sugar, cov	125.00
Teapot, cov	165.00

Feather
Cake Plate	45.00
Cup and Saucer	40.00

Flower Basket (also known as Urn or Vase)
Bowl, 10½" d	175.00
Creamer	75.00
Cup and Saucer, handleless	65.00
Plate, 8½" d	45.00
Sugar, cov	90.00

Lotus
Creamer, 4¾" h	125.00
Cup and Saucer	110.00
Plate, 9" d	85.00

Morning Glory
Creamer	85.00
Cup and Saucer	50.00
Plate, 8" d	70.00

Oyster
Bowl, 6¼" d	50.00
Creamer, 4½" h	105.00
Cup and Saucer	75.00
Plate, 8½" d, wear	100.00

Peach, teapot, cov, 6" h, crow's foot . 330.00

Shanghai
Plate, 5½" d	75.00
Sugar, cov, ftd	100.00

Strawberry
Creamer	95.00
Mug, 4⅛" h	125.00
Plate, 8½" d	75.00
Spill Holder, 4⅜" h	110.00

Teapot, cov	185.00

Tulip
Creamer, 5¼" h	75.00
Cup and Saucer	60.00
Milk Pitcher	110.00
Plate, 9" d	45.00
Waste Bowl, 6¾" d	50.00

Vine, teapot, cov, 9¼" h, stains, chips, and short hairlines. 220.00

Wagon Wheel
Bowl, 7½" d	60.00
Cup and Saucer	75.00
Pitcher, 8" h	175.00
Plate, 7½" d	50.00
Platter	100.00

GEISHA GIRL PORCELAIN

History: Geisha Girl porcelain is a Japanese export ware whose production commenced during the last quarter of the 19th century and continued heavily until World War II. The ware features kimono–clad Japanese ladies and children amidst Japanese gardens and temples. There are more than 125 brightly colored scenes depicting the premodern Japanese life-style. More than 140 marks and almost 200 patterns and variations have been identified on pieces.

Geisha Girl ware may be totally hand painted, hand painted over a stenciled design, or occasionally decaled. The stenciled underlying design is usually red–orange but also is found in brown, black, and green (rare).

All Geisha Girl items are bordered by one or a combination of blues, reds, greens, rhubarb, yellow, black, browns, or gold. The most common is red–orange. Borders may be wavy, scalloped, or banded and range from¹⁄₁₆″ to¼″. The borders themselves often are further decorated with gold, white, or yellow lacings, flowers, dots, or stripes. Some examples even display interior frames of butterflies or flowers.

Geisha Girl is found in many forms, including tea, cocoa, lunch, and children's sets, dresser items, vases, serving dishes, and so on. Large plates or platters, candlesticks, miniatures, and mugs are hardest to locate. Geisha Girl advertising items add to a collection.

Reference: Elyce Litts, *The Collectors Encyclopedia Of Geisha Girl Porcelain,* Collector Books, 1988.

Additional Listings: See *Warman's Americana & Collectibles* for more examples.

Reproduction Alert: Geisha Girl porcelain's popularity continued after Wordl War II and it is being reproduced today. Chief reproduction characteristics are a red–orange border, very white and smooth porcelain, and sparse coloring and detail. Reproduced items include dresser, tea and sake sets, toothpick holders, small vases, table plates, and salt-and-pepper shakers.

Cup and Saucer, after dinner, three geisha in reserves, diaper background with stylized chrysanthemums and florals, sgd in Japanese Dai Nihon Tashiro Zo, c1925, $15.00.

Bowl
6½" d, lobed, red, gold lacing, Flag	23.00
9½" d, octagonal, Geisha in Sampan E, red–orange, gold buds, Nippon	43.00

Celery Set, child's, master and five salts, Flower Gathering A, pine green, Made in Japan, price for six piece set **40.00**

Child's Dishes
Demitasse Set, pot, creamer and sugar, six cups and saucers, Parasol C, price for fifteen piece set . . . **65.00**
Pitcher, 3⅝ x 1¾", cylindrical slenderizing towards top, almost indistinguishable pouring lip, Parasol B, red, Japan **15.00**

Chocolate Pot, Parasol & Lesson, blue and gold, floral and butterfly ground . **100.00**

Creamer, cov, Garden Bench, hp, black, beige, and red–orange geometric border with gold diaper patterns, red–orange lid and spout with stylized chrysanthemums and gold lacings, marked "Ozan" **25.00**

Cup and Saucer
After dinner, Parasol B, red–orange, gold buds, celadon ground, Japan **25.00**
Tea, Kite A, brown and gold **12.00**

Dresser Tray, Flower Gathering A, pine green, Made in Japan **35.00**

Hair Receiver
Geisha in Sampan, sq, red, marked "t't' Japan" **18.00**
Spider Puppet, round, blue and gold, fluted rim, marked **40.00**

Nut Bowl, 6" d, nine lobed, three feet, Basket A, dark apple green **30.00**

Olive Dish, 7" l, oval, Mother and Son C, red–orange, Kutani **25.00**

Plate
6" d, Chinese Coin	15.00
8½" d, Geisha in Sampan A, brown and gold	25.00

Rice Bowl, Samurai Dance, red and gold **20.00**
Sake Cup, Garden Bench B, red rim . **6.00**

Salt and Pepper Shaker, pr
Pointing, sq, pine green **18.00**
Visiting with Baby, individual, bulbous, blue and gold. **20.00**

Salt
Temple A, floral and turquoise border, pedestal, marked **25.00**
To The Teahouse, red, fluted, handled, Kutani. **20.00**

Stein, 7½" h, Chrysanthemum Garden, red, gold buds, marked "Japan" **100.00**

Sugar Bowl, Flower Gathering B, green, gold lacing **15.00**

Teapot, Butterfly, apple green and gold, ftd, hairline on bottom **30.00**

GIRANDOLES AND MANTEL LUSTRES

History: A girandole is a highly elaborate branched candleholder, often featuring cut glass prisms surrounding the mountings. A mantel lustre is a glass vase with attached cut glass prisms.

Girandoles and mantel lustres usually are found in pairs. It is not uncommon for girandoles to be part of a large garniture set. Girandoles and mantel lustres achieved their greatest popularity in the last half of the 19th century both in the United States and Europe.

Mantel Lustres, ruby glass, enameled floral dec, 14" h, price for pair, $450.00.

GIRANDOLES, pr

11¾", gilt bronze, French, 19th C . . .	630.00
13", tulip shape, cranberry, rect prisms, gilt dec, circular foot, Bohemian, c1875.	310.00
15", Victorian, pink, enameled and colored wild flowers, notched prisms . . .	275.00
16", two branch, cut glass, Regency ormolu, bell shaped sockets, bobeches hung with beads, stepped oval base	1,000.00
18", oval base, ormolu mounted, gilt brass foliage, porcelain flowers, maroon parrots, Oriental birds as girandoles, electrified	350.00
27", gilt bronze and cut glass, scrolling candle arms, faceted glass beads and pendant ropes, electrified, French, early 20th C	850.00

MANTEL LUSTRES

9", pr, blue, enameled florals, gold trim, white beading, Waterford crystal prisms	225.00
10½", green, cut to crystal, ten cut glass prisms	285.00
12", opalene, green fold over top, white satin glass bodies, gold trim	225.00
13", pr, white cut to cranberry, scalloped flaring bowl, facet cut prisms	575.00
14", double cut overlay, white to emerald green, prisms of alternating lengths. .	250.00
15¾", cobalt blue, gilt scrollwork dec, colored floral sprigs, two rows of clear prisms, Bohemian, late 19th C	325.00

GLASS ANIMALS

History: It did not take glass manufacturers long to realize that there was a ready market for glass novelties. In the early 19th century, walking sticks and witch balls were two dominant forms. As the century ended, glass-covered dishes with an animal theme were featured.

In the period between World War I and II, glass manufacturers such as Fostoria Glass Company and A. H. Heisey & Company created a number of glass animal figures for the novelty and decorative accessory markets. In the 1950s and early 1960s, a second glass animal craze swept America led by companies such as Duncan and Miller Glass Company and New Martinsville—Viking Glass Company. A third craze struck in the early 1980s when companies such as Boyd Crystal Art Glass, Guernsey Glass, Pisello Art Glass, and Summit Art Glass began offering the same animal figure in a wide variety of collectible glass colors, with some colors in limited production.

There are two major approaches to glass animal collecting: (a) animal type and (b) manufacturer.

Most collectors concentrate on one or more manufacturer, grouping their collections accordingly.

References: Lee Garmon and Dick Spencer, *Glass Animals of the Depression Era*, Collector Books, 1993; Everett Grist, *Covered Animal Dishes*, Collector Books, 1988, 1993 value update; Frank L. Hahn and Paul Kikeli, *Collector's Guide to Heisey and Heisey By Imperial Glass Animals*, Golden Era Publications, 1991; Evelyn Zemel, *American Glass Animals A to Z*, A to Z Productions, 1978.

Price Note: Prices are for animal figures in clear (crystal) glass unless otherwise noted.

Angel Fish, bookends, pr, Heisey, clear, wave base, 7" h	175.00
Bear, New Martinsville, clear, 3½" h .	45.00
Bull, Heisey, 4" h	1,100.00
Cat, animal covered dish, milk glass, blue body, white head	75.00
Cockerel, frosted, circular base, block sgd "R Lalique, France," 8" h	800.00
Deer, Fostoria, blue, standing, 4½" h .	35.00
Dog	
Animal Covered Dish, milk glass, wide rib base.	45.00
Scottie, caramel slag, Heisey by Imperial.	200.00
Donkey, Heisey by Imperial, caramel slag	90.00
Eagle, Westmoreland, frosted, brown mist base	85.00
Elephant, Heisey	245.00
Fish	
Bookends, pr, Viking	55.00
Vase, Fostoria, red	90.00
Frog, animal covered dish, amethyst slag, 5" d	55.00
Giraffe, Heisey, head turned, clear, 11" h	175.00
Goose, Heisey	75.00
Hen	
American Hen, milk glass	58.00
Atterbury, milk glass	
Blue and marble, lacy base	185.00
White body, blue head, lacy base	145.00
Yellow and marble, lacy base . . .	150.00
Vallerystahl, milk glass, white, 5¾" w base.	65.00
Westmoreland, milk glass, white, green trim, 1" h	20.00
Hen and Chicks, New Martinsville, rooster, hen, and five chicks	175.00
Horse, rearing, bookends, pr, LE Smith, green.	65.00
King Fish, LE Smith, green, 10" h . . .	250.00
Mallard Duck, Heisey, wings down . .	30.00
Owl	
Doorstop, green slag	35.00
Paperweight, cobalt carnival, Summit Art Glass.	15.00
Penguin, decanter, Heisey, 8½" h . . .	185.00

Horse, automobile mascot, "Cinq Cheveaux," clear and frosted glass, marked "R. Lalique, France," c1925, $7,975.00. Photograph courtesy of William Doyle Galleries.

Pigeon, Pouter, bookends, pr, Fenton	175.00
Pony, balking, caramel slag, Heisey by Imperial	135.00
Ringed Neck Pheasant, Heisey	95.00
Robin, on nest, milk glass	
Mint Green	65.00
White	50.00
Rooster, head, cocktail shaker, Heisey	85.00
Swan	
Cambridge, amber, 3½"h	25.00
Lalique, double, frosted, hand sgd, "Lalique, France," 3 x 3½"	120.00
Milk Glass, white	
Block, glass eyes, 8" h	195.00
Raised wing, eye sockets	140.00
New Martinsville, ebony, crystal neck, 11" h.	60.00
Turtle, milk glass, white	105.00

GLASS, EARLY AMERICAN

History: Early American glass covers glass made in America from the colonial period through the mid 19th century. As such, it includes the early pressed glass and lacy glass made between 1827 and 1840.

Major glass-producing centers prior to 1850 were Massachusetts with the New England Glass Company and the Boston and Sandwich Glass Company, South Jersey, Pennsylvania with Stiegel's Manheim factory and Pittsburgh, and Ohio with Kent, Mantua, and Zanesville.

Early American glass was collected heavily during the 1920 to 1950 period. It has now regained some of its earlier popularity. Leading sources for the sale of early American glass are the auctions of Early Auction Company, Garth's, Glass–Works, Heckler & Company, James D. Julia, and Skinner, Inc.

References: William E. Covill, *Ink Bottles and Inkwells*, 1971; Lowell Inness, *Pittsburgh Glass: 1797–1891*, Houghton Mifflin Company, 1976; George and Helen McKearin, *American Glass*, Crown, 1975; George and Helen McKearin, *Two Hundred Years of American Blown Glass*, Doubleday and Company, 1950; Helen McKearin and Kenneth Wilson, *American Bottles And Flasks*, Crown, 1978; Adeline Pepper, *Glass Gaffers of New Jersey*, Scribners, 1971; Jane S. Spillman, *American and European Pressed Glass*, Corning Museum of Glass, 1981; Kenneth Wilson, *New England Glass And Glassmaking*, Crowell, 1972.

Periodicals: *Antique Bottle & Glass Collector*, PO Box 187, East Greenville, PA 18041; *Glass Collector's Digest*, Antique Publications, PO Box 553, Marietta, OH 45750–0553.

Collectors' Clubs: Early American Glass Traders, RD 5, Box 638, Milford, DE 19963; Glass Research Society of New Jersey, Wheaton Village, Glasstown Rd, Millville, NJ 08332; The National Early American Glass Club, PO Box 8489, Silver Spring, MD 20907.

Museums: Bennington Museum, Bennington, VT; Chrysler Museum, Norfolk, VA; Corning Museum of Glass, Corning, NY; Glass Museum, Dunkirck, IN; Glass Museum Foundation, Redlands, CA; New Bedford Glass Museum, New Bedford, MA; Sandwich Glass Museum, Sandwich, MA; Toledo Museum of Art, Toledo, OH; Wheaton Historical Village Assoc. Museum of Glass, Millville, NJ.

Additional Listings: Blown Three Mold, Cup Plates, Flasks, Sandwich Glass, and Stiegel-Type Glass.

Bakewell	
Lamp, fluid, 11¾" h, clear, blown pear shaped font, typical cut Pittsburgh pattern, large bulbous knops, heavy pressed ftd base, pewter collar	600.00
Window Pane, 6⅞ x 4⅞", clear,	

Sandwich, salt shaker, Christmas, yellow ground, green leaves, brown accents, December 25, 1877 patent date, 2¾" h, 1¾" d, $85.00.

church, gothic arch design, sgd "Bakewell" on reverse, Innes Fig 303–2 . . . . **2,000.00**
Boston and Sandwich Glass Works, Sandwich, MA
Inkwell, 1⅞″ h, 1⅞″ d, cylindrical, vertical ribs, dark cherry puce, ground mouth, smooth base. **325.00**
Toilet Water Bottle, 7⅛″ h, blown three mold, cobalt blue, tooled mouth, stopper, pontil scar **260.00**
Coventry Glass Works, Coventry, CT
Flask, double eagle, yellow olive, sheared mouth, pontil scar **150.00**
Inkwell, blown three mold, cylindrical, dark olive amber, disc mouth, pontil scar **120.00**
Keene Marlboro Street Glassworks, Keene, NH, 1815–30, inkwell, blown three mold, green, 1¾″ w, 1½″ h. . . . **150.00**
Lockport
Creamer, 4⅞″ h, blue, free blown, solid applied handle and foot, folded rim, wide flaring mouth, pontil **600.00**
Vase, 3½″ d, 7⅛″ h, blue, free blown, three part vase, flared mouth, round base set onto solid baluster stem, thick solid circular foot, 5¼″ d witch ball cov **600.00**
Midwestern
Candlesticks, pr, 7⅛″ h, clear, free blown sockets, lacy hairpin pattern base. **5,250.00**
Flask, cornucopia and medallion, pale yellowish green, inward rolled mouth, pontil scar, ½ pint **375.00**
Sugar, cov, clear, lacy, Peacock Feather pattern, one foot scallop chipped. **500.00**
Mount Vernon Glass Works, Vernon, NY
Decanter, 6¾″ h, light yellow green, flared mouth, pontil scar **6,000.00**
Salt, aqua, lacy, price for pair **150.00**
New Jersey, South
Creamer, 5⅞″ h, cobalt blue, applied crimped foot and solid curled handle, tooled rim, int. spall on side of spout **650.00**
Pitcher, 7⅝″ h, aqua, opaque white loopings, double ribbed applied handle crimped at base, tooled lip, heavy circular applied foot **650.00**
New York, bowl, 4½″ d, aqua, free blown **75.00**
Pittsburgh
Bowl, 4⅞″ d, 2⅝″ h, sapphire blue, pattern molded, broken swirl, sixteen ribs to the right, folded rim, tooled foot, lead glass, pontil scar . **335.00**
Candlesticks, pr, 9¾″ h, clear, flint, large sockets. **100.00**
Compote, cov, 6½″ d, 7″ h, lacy, Hairpin pattern, two large rim chips . . . **2,750.00**
Creamer, 5⅛″ h, opalescent blue, eight rib pillar molded, short circular stem, circular foot, applied handle **4,500.00**
Inkwell, 5½″, clear, free blown, egg shaped body, two reservoirs, applied rounded well, small cup for seals, short knop stem, circular foot, nine applied rosettes. **1,000.00**
Pitcher, 8″ h, eight pillar molded, blown, applied handle. **350.00**
Plate
5 15/16″ d, octagonal, clear, lacy, steamboat, Lee 170–3, minute roughage on upper rim **1,800.00**
6⅛″ d, octagonal, clear, lacy, Constitution "Union," Lee 170–4, small rim flakes. **1,400.00**
Salt, divided, sapphire blue **500.00**

Redwood or Redford Glass Works, NY
Bowl, 14″ d, 5 7/16 to 5⅞″ h, brilliant aquamarine, wide flaring rim, heavy out–folded edge, applied circular foot, superimposed lily pad dec, similar to McKearin Plate 15, c1831–50 . . . . **4,000.00**
Compote, 9″ d, 4½″ h, brilliant aquamarine, blown, circular bowl flaring to wide out–folding rim, short cylindrical stem, circular stepped foot, superimposed of lily pad dec. **9,000.00**
Vase, 4¾″ h, free blown, brilliant aquamarine, urn form, two applied miniature handles. **700.00**

Saratoga, NY
Creamer, 4″ h, olive–green, yellow tones, applied solid handle and foot, attributed to Morris Holmes **575.00**
Sugar Bowl, cov, 7⅝″ h, green–aqua, flaring lip, applied threading extending to mid body, thick strap handles, large medial ribs, blown ball shaped cov, pontil scar, two small pieces of threading missing, McKearin Plate 69, lower right **2,900.00**

South Boston
Decanter, 9″ h, clear, free blown, two bands of chain dec around bodies and two around necks, period stoppers, price for pair **700.00**
Sugar, cov, 5⅞″ h, clear, free blown, galleried rim, one band of applied chain dec on base and one on cover **3,250.00**

Stourbridge Flint Glass Works, salt, dark blue, lacy, Innes Color Plate 6 . . . . . **1,200.00**
Unknown
Freeblown
Bowl, 4¾″ d, milk glass, red amethyst shaded tint, cylindrical, flared rim, plain tooled circular foot, tooled rim, pontil scar. **100.00**
Creamer and Sugar, 3½″ h, clear,

cobalt rim, engraved monogram on open sugar, pontil scar 450.00

Decanter, 7⅝" h, yellowish olive, elongated tapered form, flared mouth, pontil scar 240.00

Fruit Bowl, 7¾" d, 9" h, light yellow green, cylindrical inverted cone base, tooled flared rim, pontil . . . 275.00

Inkwell, 2¾" h, olive–green, cylindrical, slightly conical, pontil scar 275.00

Jar, 5¾" d, 14¼" h, yellowish–olive, cylindrical, sheared mouth, pontil scar 280.00

Miniature Bottle, 2¾" h, light yellow–olive, tooled collared mouth, pontil scar 500.00

Mortar and Pestle, 4¾" d, 4⅜" h, green, slight flared rim, tooled spout and rim, solid pestle, ground pontil scar 350.00

Mug, 4¼" h, clear, cylindrical, enamel red, white, yellow, blue, black, and green dec, flared foot, applied strap handle 375.00

Snuff Bottle, 6¼" h, olive–amber, rect with beveled corners, tooled mouth, pontil scar 125.00

Wine Glass, 3½" h, greenish–aquamarine, sheared and ground rim, pontil scar 180.00

Whiskey Jug, 8" h, dark puce amber, applied sloping collared mouth, pontil scar 110.00

Pattern Molded

Salt Cellar, 2½" d, 3" h, sapphire blue, swirled ribs, tooled rim, applied circular foot, pontil scar . . . 375.00

Tumbler, 4¾" h, golden amber, twenty ribs with broken pattern, sheared rim, pontil scar 5,400.00

Witch Ball, 3½" d, clear, twelve vertical ribs 160.00

Pillar Molded, decanter, clear, orig stopper, quart 50.00

Wheeling

Compote, 7¼" d, 4¼" h, octagonal, Oak Leaf pattern, bull's eye rim, Roman Rosette pattern base. 1,200.00

Window Pane, 7 x 5", clear, portrait of steamboat in center with name "J & C Ritchie" above, c1833. . . . . . . 5,000.00

Whitney Works, Glassboro, NJ, pitcher, 6¹⁵⁄₁₆" h, medium sapphire blue, free-blown, horizontal threading around neck, folded rim, small pinched lip, heavy circular applied foot, solid applied handle crimped at lower end, Joel Duffield, South Jersey c1835–40, McKearin Plate 60, No. 6 . . . . 1,300.00

Zanesville, OH

Bowl, 8½" d, 3¾" h, amber, blown, folded rim, minor broken blisters . . 450.00

Pan, 6⅝" d, light green, blown, faint impression of twenty four ribs, folded rim 250.00

GOLDSCHEIDER

History: Friedrich Goldscheider founded a porcelain and faience factory in Vienna, Austria, in 1885. Upon his death, his widow carried on operations. In 1920 Walter and Marcell, Friedrich's sons, gained control. During the Art Deco period, the firm commissioned several artists to create figural statues, among which were Pierrettes and sleek wolfhounds. During the 1930s, the company's products were most traditional.

In the early 1940s, the Goldscheiders fled to the United States and reestablished operations in Trenton, New Jersey. The Goldscheider Everlast Corporation is listed in Trenton City directories between 1943 and 1950. Goldscheider Ceramics, located at 1441 Heath Avenue in Trenton, was listed in the *1952 Crockery and Glass Journal Directory*. The firm was not listed in 1954.

Ashtray, 7½" l, German Shepherd . . . 45.00

Bust

7" h, Madonna, crown 75.00

26" h, finely molded face, downcast eyes, long light brown hair looped into chignon, narrow mauve head band with oval irid glass jewel, gilt draped gown, narrow mauve straps set with matching jewel, incised "Montenave," Goldscheider seal molded in relief, imp "Reproduction/ Reservee" and numerals 2,750.00

Figure, dancer, Art Deco, Dakon artist, marked "7195/374/2," 14½" h, $1,375.00.

Figure
 Boy and girl, #7844 and #7845, price
  for pair 1,500.00
 Black sailor and girl, #7958, price for
  pair. 850.00
 Chinese Teahouse, kneeling figures,
  6¾" h, Helen Lindoff, price for pair 60.00
 Duck, 13" h, flying, modeled by E
  Straub. 100.00
 Gentleman, 14⅛" h, Negro, sitting on
  rock, top hat and cane, brown suit 325.00
 Girl
  11⅝" h, Butterfly Girl, winged cape
   with butterfly wing dec, burnt orange, cream, and brown, standing beside vase of flowers, imp
   "Goldscheider–Wien–Lorenzi,"
   and "Made in Austria," factory
   numbers, c1930 . . . . 1,550.00
  12" h, summer hat, sgd "Bakon,"
   #6940. 1,050.00
  12½" h, sailor suit, #6748 . . . . . 1,050.00
  13" h, dress parted to hip, sgd
   "Loring". 1,150.00
 Juliet with Doves, 12¼" h 225.00
 Lady, 8½" h, muff, plumed hat, incised
  "BCV". 90.00
 Old Virginia, 8½" h, sgd "Peggy
  Porcher". 125.00
Head, 8" l, red/orange hair and lips, yel-
 low blossom, green accents, stamped
 and incised marks, c1926. . . . . 360.00
Music Box, 7" h, Colonial girl 100.00
Plaque, 13½" w, 25⅛" h, earthenware,
 rect, molded, maiden in profile, gar-
 land of blossoms and berries in hair,
 large blossom and cluster on left,
 earth tones, designer sgd "Lamassi,"
 Goldscheider mark, c1900 . . . . 1,000.00
Plate, mermaid pattern, multicolored . 150.00
Wall Mask, 13½" h, girl, curly green hair,
 red lips, black mask. 365.00

GONDER POTTERY

History: Lawton Gonder established Gonder Ceramic Arts, Inc., at Zanesville, Ohio, in 1941. He gained experience while working for other factories in the area. Gonder experimented with glazes, including Chinese crackle, gold crackle, and flambé. Lamp bases were manufactured under the name Eglee at a second plant location.

Gonder pieces are clearly marked. The company ceased operation in 1957.

Reference: Ron Hoppes, *The Collector's Guide and History of Gonder Pottery*, L–W Book Sales, 1992.

Periodical: *Gonder Pottery Collectors' Newsletter*, PO Box 3174, Shawnee, KS 66203.

Bowl, 6½" d, ribbed, yellow 8.50
Candlestick, pr, 4¾" h, ext. turquoise
 ext., pink coral int., marked "E–14,
 Gonder". 18.00
Creamer and Sugar, dark brown drip
 and brown spatter. 24.00
Ewer
 6" h, mottled blue, pink int. 20.00
 9" h, light green, matte finish, marked
  "Gonder, USA H34". 25.00
 13" h, Shell and Star, green 50.00

Vase, green–blue, 6½" h, $8.00.

Figure
 7" h, swan, shaded blue 12.00
 10 1/12" h, elephant with raised trunk,
  rose and gray 40.00
Flower Frog, 7¾ x 7", swirl pattern, blue
 and brown glossy glaze. 18.00
Vase, 7½" h, flower shape, pink and
 mottled blue glaze. 15.00

GOOFUS GLASS

History: Goofus glass, also known as Mexican Ware, Hooligan glass, and Pickle glass, is a pressed glass with relief designs. The back or front was painted. The designs are usually in red and green with a metallic gold ground. It was popular from 1890 to 1920 and was used as a premium at carnivals.

It was produced by several companies: Cresent Glass Company, Wellsburg, West Virginia; Imperial Glass Corporation, Bellaire, Ohio; LaBelle Glass Works, Bridgeport, Ohio; and Northwood Glass Co., Indiana, Pennsylvania, Wheeling, West Virginia, and Bridgeport, Ohio. Northwood marks include "N," "N" in one circle, "N" in two circles, and one or two circles without the "N."

Goofus glass lost its popularity when people found the paint tarnished or scaled off after re-

peated washings and wear. No record of its manufacture has been found after 1920.

References: Carolyn McKinley, *Goofus Glass,*
Collector Books, 1984, out of print; Ellen T. Schroy,
Warman's Glass, Wallace-Homestead, 1992.

Bowl
9″ d, carnations	25.00
10½″ d, red roses, molded, gold ground	35.00
Cake Plate, 11″ d, Dahlia and Fan, red dec, gold ground	32.00
Candle Holder, red and gold	18.00
Candy Dish, red strawberries and green leaves, molded applied ring handle	12.00
Compote, 9½″ d, strawberries and leaves, red and green dec, gold ground, ruffled	45.00
Dish, 11″ d, chrysanthemum sprays, red and gold, scalloped rim	70.00
Jar, butterflies, red and gold	20.00
Pickle Jar, aqua, molded, gold, blue, and red painted floral design	25.00
Pitcher, red rose bud, gold leaves	45.00

Plate, gold, red flowers, 10¾″ d, $20.00.

Plate
7½″ d, apples, red dec, gold ground	18.00
8½″ d, red apples, molded, gold ground	20.00
11″ d, roses, red and gold, scalloped rim	25.00
Salt and Pepper Shakers, pr, 3″ h, Poppy	35.00
Syrup, Strawberry	32.50

Vase
7½″ h, brown, red bird	18.00
8″ h, red roses, molded, gold ground	15.00
12″ h, red roses, molded, gold ground	40.00
13″ h, Statue of Liberty	175.00

MARK

W H GOSS

GOSS CHINA AND CRESTED WARE

History: In 1858 William H. Goss opened his
Henley factory and produced terra–cotta ware. A
year later he moved to Stoke–on–Trent and added
Parian ware to his line. In 1883 Adolphus, William's
son, expanded on his father's idea of decorating
small ivory pots and vases with the coat of arms of
schools, hospitals, colleges [especially Oxford and
Cambridge], and other motifs to appeal to the sou-
venir-seeking English "day–tripper." The forms
used were copied from ancient artifacts in museums.

William died in 1906, his son in 1913. Following
business setbacks, the firm was sold in 1929 to
Geo. Jones and Sons, Ltd., who had previously
acquired Arcadian, Swan, and other firms that
made crested wares. As late as 1931 the Goss
name was still being used. In 1936–37 Cauldon
Potteries purchased the Goss assets. Production
ceased in 1940. In 1954 Ridgeway and Adderley
acquired all Goss assets [molds, patterns, designs,
and right to use the Goss name and trademark].

From 1883 to 1931 pieces carry the mark of
GOSHAWK, with W. H. Goss beneath, and "England" on later pieces. Many early examples carry
an impressed "W. H. Goss," either with or without
the printed mark.

Other manufacturers of crested ware in England
were: Arcadian, Carlton China, Grafton China, Sa-
voy China, Shelley, and Willow Art. Gemma in Germany also made crested wares.

Crests are of little value unless they match, for
example, Shakespeare's jug with Shakespeare's
crest. Collectors tend to collect one form (vase,
ewer, jug, and so on), one particular crest, or one
type of object (boat, cat, dog, and so on). Price is
determined not by crest but size, condition, and
bottom mark.

References: Sandy Andrews, *Crested China:
The History of Heraldic Souvenir Ware,* Milestone
Publications [England]; John Galpin, *A Handbook
Of Goss China,* Milestone Publications; Nicholas
Pine, *The 1984 Price Guide To Goss China,* Mile-
stone Publications, 1984; Nicholas Pine and Sandy
Andrews, *The 1984 Price Guide To Crested China*
(including revisions to *Crested China*), Milestone
Publications; Roland Ward, *The Price Guide To
The Models Of W. H. Goss,* Antiques Collectors'
Club.

Collectors' Clubs: Crested Circle, 75 Cannon
Grove, Fetcham, Leatherhead Surrey, England

KT22 9LP; Goss Collectors Club, 4 Khasiaberry, Walnut Tree, Milton Keynes, England MK7 7DP.

GOSS

Bottle
Sunderland	25.00
Waterlooville Army Water	45.00
Bucket, Norwegian, Maldon	25.00

Building
First and Last House	145.00
Look Out House	150.00
St Nicholas Chapel	200.00
Bust, parian, Dickens, 8" h	150.00

Creamer, Sir William Wallace, marked
"W. H. Goss"	25.00
Can, Welsh Mills	20.00
Carafe, Goodwin Sands	19.00

Ewer
Arundel, 4½" h	20.00
Chichester, Roman, Beaulieu Abbey	20.00
Jug, Spanish, Eddyston	30.00
Lamp, Hamworthy, Reigate Poole	30.00
Night Light, Manx Cottage	200.00
Nogen, Irish, wood	22.00

Pitcher
Cambridge	18.00
Leiston, Abbey	22.00
Pot, Roman, Painswick	20.00
Salt, Glastonbury, Wickford	30.00

Urn
Laxey, Huntington	28.00
Tewkesbury Saxon, Lizard	24.00

Vase, Mary Queen of Scots crest, 2¾" h, $28.00.

OTHER CRESTED WARE MANUFACTURERS

Arcadian
Bathing Wagon, Stockbridge	30.00
Ewer, Wembley, handled	20.00
Toby Jug, Wantage	30.00
Warming Pan, Tesbury	30.00

Carlton
Bank, bell shape	20.00
Pot, cov, handled	25.00
Urn, Bourne	25.00

Coronet
Cottage, Tony Panda	25.00
Pot, Arms of Weymouth, two handles, three legs	15.00

Gemma
Cup, Aberystwyth	18.00
Helmet	30.00

Shelley
Fish Basket, Fleetwood	30.00
Olive Jar, Sussex	25.00
Rose Bowl, Stafford, silver, #147	35.00
Tea Caddy, Abbey of Glastonbury	25.00
Tray, 4 x 4", Royal visit to Canada, 1959	35.00
Urn, #118, Roman, Chester	25.00
Victoria, Cheshire Cat, matching crest	25.00

Willow Art
Anvil, Saltash	25.00
Shakespeare Cottage	150.00

GOUDA POTTERY

History: Gouda and the surrounding areas of Holland have been one of the principal Dutch pottery centers for centuries. Originally the potteries produced a simple utilitarian Delft-type earthenware with a tin glaze and the famous clay smoker's pipes.

When the pipe-making portion declined in the early 1900s, the Gouda potteries turned to art pottery. Influenced by the Art Nouveau and Art Deco movements, artists expressed themselves with free-form and stylized designs in bold colors.

Reference: Susan and Al Bagdade, *Warman's English & Continental Pottery & Porcelain, Second Edition*, Wallace–Homestead, 1991.

Periodical: *The Dutch Potter*, 47 London Terrace, New Rochelle, NY 10804.

Reproduction Alert: With the Art Nouveau and Art Deco revivals of recent years, modern reproductions of Gouda pottery currently are on the market. They are difficult to distinguish from the originals.

Bowl, 12" d, 3¼" h, flattened rim, emb Art Deco style black flowerhead dec, blue, orange, white, and gold geo-

Chamberstick, matte green ground, yellow, blue, and cream dec, marked "0139 DAM III Holland," c1885, 6½" d, 3" h, $125.00.

metric ground, matte finish, center flower holder, marked 175.00
Box, cov, 4¼" l, carved, black, gold, and white, glazed, Regina mark 160.00
Candlestick, 17" h, dark glaze 450.00
Charger, 12" d, white magnolias, teal petals, black stems, orange and amber speckled ground, marked "NV Kon Plazuid Unique Gouda Holland," artist's monogram "JVS" (J W Van Schaik), c1930 . . . . 440.00
Creamer, Verona pattern 45.00
Decanter, 10½" h, stopper, handle, Nadra pattern, orange, brown, and ocher floral dec, black base. 150.00
Dish, 13" d, 7" h, ftd, shallow, polychrome foliage int., five black branched base supports, circular foot, painted factory marks, 1921 . . . . 440.00
Dutch Shoe, high glaze 75.00
Ewer, 6½" h, cobalt blue, rust, and bright yellow design, marked "2960" 125.00
Inkwell, attached undertray, Kelat house mark 150.00
Jar, cov, 5½" h, Areo pattern, glossy finish, Royal Zuid mark 55.00
Lantern, 6" h, Art Nouveau, Palzuid house mark 145.00
Pitcher, 9½" h, orange, turquoise, and ocher stylized animal dec, ivory ground, marked "Distel Goedewaagen". 200.00
Planter, 5 x 7", Art Nouveau, Royal Zuid mark, 1917. . . . . 100.00
Plate, 12" d, Nadra pattern 110.00
Powder Box, cov, 6" d, round, stylized brown and rose florals, black ground, glossy finish, house mark. 60.00
Tobacco Jar, cov, 5" h, Verona pattern 90.00

Trivet, 4" w, Damascus, c1895 . . . . . 185.00
Tumbler, 4⅜" h, Art Deco style multicolored flowers and leaves, cream ground, black trim, wide flaring rim, matte finish, house mark 60.00
Vase
7¼" h, baluster, flared rim, brightly colored flowers, gray ground. 80.00
12½" h, Art Nouveau, blue and gold iris, green ground. 330.00

GRANITEWARE

History: Graniteware is the name commonly given to iron or steel kitchenware covered with enamel coating.

The first graniteware was made in Germany in the 1830s. Graniteware was not produced in the United States until the 1860s. At the start of World War I, when European manufacturers turned to the making of war weapons, American producers took over the market.

Colors commonly marketed were white and gray. Each company made its own special color, including shades of blue, green, brown, violet, cream, and red.

Older graniteware is heavier than new graniteware. Pieces with cast-iron handles date from 1870 to 1890; wood handles date from 1900 to 1910. Other dating clues are seams, wood knobs, and tin lids.

References: Helen Greguire, *The Collector's Encyclopedia of Granite Ware: Colors Shapes and Values*, Book 1 (1990, 1992 value update), Book 2 (1993), Collector Books; Dana G. Morykan and Harry L. Rinker, *Warman's Country Antiques & Collectibles, Second Edition*, Wallace–Homestead, 1994.

Collectors' Club: National Graniteware Society, PO Box 10013, Cedar Rapids, IA 52410–0013.

Reproduction Alert: Graniteware still is manufactured in many of the traditional forms and colors.

Additional Listings: See *Warman's Americana & Collectibles* for more examples.

Baking Pan, cobalt blue and white swirl 100.00
Bowl, 7" d, blue and white mottled . . . 25.00
Bucket, 9 x 11", gray, iron bail, wood handle 30.00
Canister Set, 4 pcs, robin egg blue . . . 130.00
Chamber Pot, cobalt blue and white swirl. 180.00
Coffeepot
Blue and white marbleized, 8 cup . 80.00
White, large 35.00
Dipper, dark brown and white mottled, Onyxware. 40.00
Flask, gray, missing lid 70.00
Food Mold, melon ribbed, gray, tin bottom with ring, marked "Extra Agate, etc" 70.00

Grater, mottled gray, marked "Ideal"	345.00
Kettle, 12½" w, gray, iron bail, wood handle	25.00
Loaf Pan, gray	25.00
Lunch Box, mottled gray, tray and cup, bail handle	75.00
Measure, qt, gray, emb "For Household Use Only"	40.00
Milk Pan	
Crystolite green, swirled, small	32.00
Turquoise, swirl	25.00
Muffin Pan, six sections, gray	12.00
Pan, cov	
9" d, blue and white swirl	80.00
10¼" d, dark blue and white swirl, white int., black trim	45.00
Pie Pan	
Cobalt blue and white swirl, 6" d	25.00
Crystolite green, swirled	18.00
Pitcher	
7⅝" h, blue and white swirl	115.00
11" h, gray, ice lip	110.00
Plate	
8½" d, mottled gray	12.00
10" d, blue and white swirl	8.00
Preserving Kettle	
9" d, blue and white swirl, two handles	65.00
10½" d, shaded blue	50.00
Roaster, cov, 15" l, mottled gray	40.00
Salt Box, hanging, white, navy trim	125.00
Skimmer, blue and white swirl	70.00
Spoon, 9" l, mottled gray	15.00
Strainer, squatty, light blue and white mottled, black handles and trim	275.00
Tea Kettle, cobalt and white swirl, gooseneck spout	125.00
Teapot, cov	
Bulbous, blue speckled, ornate pewter lid, collar, and spout, marked "Manning–Bowman"	175.00
Lighthouse shape, tapered, mottled gray, pewter rim, spout, and bracket handle with knob finial, domed cov with pointed finial, copper band around base, late 19th C	285.00
Vegetable Pan, 13" l, Chrystolite green	80.00

GREENAWAY, KATE **K. G.**

History: Kate Greenaway, or "K.G." as she initialed her famous drawings, was born in 1846 in London. Her father was a prominent wood engraver. Kate's natural talent for drawing soon was evident, and she began art classes at the age of 12. In 1868 she had her first public exhibition.

Her talents were used primarily in illustrating. She did cards for Marcus Ward, which are largely unsigned. China and pottery companies soon had her drawings of children appearing on many of their wares. By the 1880s she was one of the foremost children's book illustrators in England.

Reference: Ina Taylor, *The Art of Kate Greenaway: A Nostalgic Portrait of Childhood*, Pelican Publishing, 1991.

Collectors' Club: Kate Greenaway Society, PO Box 8, Norwood, PA 19074.

Reproduction Alert: Some Greenaway buttons have been reproduced in Europe and sold in the United States.

Book	
Marigold Garden, illus and rhymes by Kate Greenaway, Frederick Warne & Co, 56 pgs	30.00
Toyland	100.00
Butter Pat, boy and girl transfer print	35.00
Button, ¾" d, girl with kitten on fence	10.00
Children's Dishes, tea set, multicolored scenes, gold trim, price for fifteen piece set	450.00
Cup and Saucer, girl doing laundry in wooden tub	35.00
Dish, 11" l, oval, Jack Sprat and Sunbonnet girl dec	50.00
Figure	
8½" h, boy with basket, satin, gold, pink, and blue trim, marked "1893"	525.00
9" h, girl with tambourine beside tree, marked "Royal Worcester"	400.00
Hat, bisque, three girls sitting on brim, flowers	90.00
Inkwell, bronze, two children, emb	200.00
Jewelry Box, wooden, stenciled children on front	45.00
Match Safe, pocket, SP, children, emb	50.00
Mug, pink, children playing	60.00
Napkin Ring, SS	
Boy holding books	165.00
Girl feeding yearling	150.00
Pencil Holder, porcelain	18.00

Soap Dish, hanging, gray mottled, $30.00.

Book, *Under the Window,* Kate Greenaway illus, $65.00.

Perfume Bottle, 2″ l, SS, girls in low relief, orig stopper	200.00
Pin Tray, children playing seesaw	65.00
Plate	
5″ d, two girls playing ball	60.00
7″ d, boy chasing rabbits	65.00
Stickpin, figural, bronze, children playing ring around the rosy, c1900	25.00
Tape Measure, figural, girl holding muff	45.00
Tapestry, 14½ x 56″, children playing outdoors	265.00
Teaspoon, SS, figural, girl handle, bowl engraved with Lucy Locket verse	50.00
Tile, 6⅛″ d, transfer print, four seasons, one spacer, brown and white dec, blue border, stamped mark, produced by T & R Boote, 1881, price for set of five	325.00
Toothpick Holder, bisque, German	
4″ h, boy beside tree stump	60.00
5½″ h, girl, playing	75.00
Tray, boy with hoop and girls playing, silver frame	150.00

GREENTOWN GLASS

History: The Indiana Tumbler and Goblet Company, Greentown, Indiana, produced its first clear, pressed glass table and bar wares in late 1894. Initial success led to a doubling of plant size in 1895 and other subsequent expansions, one in 1897 to allow for the manufacture of colored glass. In 1899 the firm joined the combine known as the National Glass Company.

In 1900, just before arriving in Greentown, Jacob Rosenthal developed an opaque brown glass, called "chocolate," which ranged in color from a dark, rich chocolate to a lighter "cream" coffee hue.

Production of chocolate glass saved the financially pressed Indiana Tumbler and Goblet Works. The Cactus and Leaf Bracket patterns were made almost exclusively in chocolate glass. Other popular chocolate patterns are Austrian, Dewey, Shuttle, and Teardrop and Tassel. In 1902 the National Glass Company bought Rosenthal's chocolate glass formula so other plants in the combine could use the color.

In 1902 Rosenthal developed the Golden Agate and Rose Agate colors. All work ceased on June 13, 1903, when a fire of suspicious origin destroyed the Indiana Tumbler and Goblet Company Works.

After the fire, other companies, such as, McKee and Brothers, produced chocolate glass in the same pattern design used in Greentown. Later reproductions also have taken place, with Cactus among the most heavily copied pattern.

References: Brenda Measell and James Measell, *A Guide To Reproductions of Greentown Glass,* 2nd ed., The Printing Press, 1974; James Measell, *Greentown Glass: The Indiana Tumbler & Goblet Co.,* Grand Rapids Public Museum, 1979, 1992–93 value update, distributed by Antique Publications.

Collectors' Club: National Greentown Glass Assoc., 19596 Glendale Ave., South Bend, IN 46637.

Museums: Grand Rapids Public Museum, Ruth Herrick Greentown Glass Collection, Grand Rapids, MI; Greentown Glass Museum, Greentown, IN.

Additional Listings: Holly Amber and Pattern Glass.

Animal Covered Dish	
Dolphin, chocolate, chip on tail fin	195.00
Rabbit, dome top, amber	250.00
Bowl, 7¼″ d, Herringbone Buttress, green	130.00
Butter, cov	
Cupid, chocolate	575.00
Herringbone Buttress, green	200.00
Celery Vase, Beaded Panel, clear	90.00

Butter, cov, chocolate, Geneva pattern, tripod feet, $425.00.

Compote, Geneva, 4½″ d, 3½″ h,
chocolate 145.00
Cookie Jar, Cactus, chocolate 250.00
Cordial, Austrian, canary 125.00
Creamer
Cactus, chocolate 70.00
Cupid, Nile green 400.00
Indian Head, opaque white 450.00
Shuttle, tankard, clear 35.00
Cruet, orig stopper, Dewey, vaseline . 165.00
Goblet
Overall Lattice 36.00
Shuttle, chocolate 500.00
Mug
Elf, green 75.00
Herringbone Buttress 65.00
Overall Lattice 40.00
Mustard, cov, Daisy, opaque white . . 75.00
Nappy, Masonic, chocolate 85.00
Novelty, hairbrush, clear 55.00
Paperweight, Buffalo, Nile green 600.00
Pitcher, 8¾″ h, Squirrel, clear 82.50
Plate, Serenade, chocolate 85.00
Punch Cup
Cord Drapery, clear 20.00
Shuttle, chocolate 75.00
Relish, Leaf Bracket, 8″ l, oval,
chocolate 75.00
Salt and Pepper Shakers, pr, Cactus,
chocolate 150.00
Sauce, Cactus, chocolate, ftd 48.00
Stein, 4⅜″ h, outdoor drinking scene,
Nile green. 135.00
Sugar, cov
Cupid, opaque white 100.00
Dewey, cobalt blue 125.00
Syrup
Cactus, chocolate 125.00
Indian Feather, green 165.00
Toothpick
Cactus, chocolate 65.00
Indian Head, chocolate 140.00
Tumbler
Cactus, chocolate 55.00
Dewey, canary 60.00

GRUEBY POTTERY

History: William Grueby was active in the ceramic industry for several years before he devel-

oped his own method of producing matte glazed pottery and founded the Grueby Faience Company in Boston, Massachusetts, in 1897.

The art pottery was hand thrown in natural shapes, hand molded, and hand tooled. A variety of colored glazes, singly or in combinations, was produced, with green being the most prominent. In 1908 the firm was divided into the Grueby Pottery Company and the Grueby Faience and Tile Co., the latter making art pottery until bankruptcy forced closure shortly after 1908.

References: Paul Evans, *Art Pottery of the United States, 2nd Edition,* Feingold and Lewis Publishing, 1987; Ralph and Terry Kovel, *The Kovels' Collector's Guide to American Art Pottery,* Crown Publishers, 1974.

Tile, Prancing Horses, blue ground, white horses, green earth, 6¼ x 6″, $475.00.

Bowl, 8½″ d, 3¼″ h, Model No. 119, bisque, carved and incised overlapping leaves, high relief, shaped rim, incised artist's initials of Wilhelmina Post, imp mark, nicks, staining 825.00
Lamp Base, 16″ h, wide cylindrical neck, ribbed bulbous base, mottled green glaze, sgd with logo and paper label "World's Fair St Louis 1904," artist initials of Ruth Erickson, undrilled 5,200.00
Paperweight, 4″ l, scarab, green matte glaze, imp mark, orig paper label and Society of Arts and Crafts, Boston, base chip 360.00
Pot
2½″ h, matte green glaze, paper label 440.00
3¼″ h, matte green glaze, incised rings, imp mark, paint traces 305.00
Tile, Faience
8″ sq, polychrome matte glazed tile, masted ship dec, red clay body, imp "82," price for pair 495.00

8½" sq, seascape, matte blue, green,
ivory, and brown glaze, artist ini-
tialed, price for set of three 1,760.00
Vase
2¾" h, matte green glaze, imp mark,
remnants of paper label 270.00
3" h, 5" d, squatty, teal blue glaze,
relief naturalistic segments, imp
mark, paper label, minor rim nicks,
crazing 605.00
5⅞" h, matte navy blue glaze, incised
alternating floral and leaf dec, imp
mark, artist's cipher for Gertrude
Stanwood, glaze bursts 990.00
7" h
Matte green glaze, carved and incised repeating dec, incised artist's cipher for Ruth Erickson, imp
mark 770.00
Model No. 85, matte green glaze,
bud and stem alternate with relief
leaf, imp mark and model no., pa-
per label 660.00
7½" h, matte green glaze, imp mark
and paper label 450.00
8⅝" h, cucumber green glaze, relief
stylized and repeating foliate de-
sign, imp marks 1,210.00
10" h, belted rim, cylindrical neck,
squatty body, imp concentric horizontal rings, green glaze, unsigned,
base chip 440.00
11¼" h, matte green glaze, five mod-
eled leaves, five scrolled handles,
imp mark, attributed to Wilhelmina
Post, base chip, handle nick 7,150.00
12½" h, matte green glaze, imp mark 1,760.00
13" h, matte dark green glaze
Imp mark, glaze miss 615.00
Imp mark, paper label 1,650.00

HAIR ORNAMENTS

History: Hair ornaments, one of the first accessories developed through primitive man, were used to
remove tangles and keep hair out of one's face.
Remnants of early combs have been found in many
archaeological excavations.

As fashion styles changed through the centuries,
hair ornaments kept pace through design and use
changes. Hair combs and other hair ornaments are
made in a wide variety of materials, such as precious metals, ivory, tortoiseshell, plastics, and
wood.

Combs were first made in America during the
Revolution when imports from England were restricted. Early American combs were made of horn
and treasured as valued toiletry articles.

Reference: Evelyn Haetig, *Antique Combs and
Purses*, Gallery Graphics Press, 1983.

Collectors' Club: Antique Fancy Comb Collectors Club, 4901 Grandview, Ypsilanti, MI 48197.

Museums: Leominster Historical Society, Field
School Museum, Leominster, MA; Miller's Museum
of Antique Combs, Homer, AK.

**Comb, sterling silver, serpent motif,
double pronged, 4" l, $40.00.**

Back Comb, Art Nouveau, tortoiseshell,
gilt brass and turquoise glass accents 125.00
Barrette, 4" l, bar type, faux tortoiseshell
with rhinestones 10.00
Bodkin
Art Nouveau, celluloid, imitation tortoiseshell, sinuous contours, pique,
rhinestones 8.00
Sterling Silver, emb Greek Key type
design. 40.00
Comb, ivory
Art Nouveau, paste stones, French,
c1910 . . . . 45.00
Oriental, Victorian, c1860 . . . . 145.00
Hairpin, Victorian, tortoiseshell and 14K
gold pierced work, c1870 . . . . 125.00
Ornament
4½", plastic, simulated stones, c1935 65.00
4¾", rhinestones and simulated
pearls, c1925. . . . . 45.00
Ornamental Comb, 7¼ x 6", Art Nou-
veau, plastic pierced work, imitation
blue stones. 75.00
Pompadour Comb, Art Nouveau, faux
tortoiseshell, gilt brass and turquoise
glass accents, price for pair 75.00

HALL CHINA COMPANY

History: Robert Hall founded the Hall China
Company in 1903 in East Liverpool, Ohio. He died
in 1904 and was succeeded by his son, Robert
Taggart Hall. After years of experimentation, Robert T. Hall developed a leadless glaze in 1911,

opening the way for production of glazed household products.

The Hall China Company made many types of kitchenware, refrigerator sets, and dinnerware in a wide variety of patterns. Some patterns were exclusive, such as Heather Rose for Sears.

One of the most popular patterns was Autumn Leaf, an exclusive premium designed in 1933 for the Jewel Tea Company by Arden Richards. Still a Jewel Tea property, Autumn Leaf has not been listed in catalogs since 1978 but is produced on a replacement basis with the date stamped on the back.

References: Harvey Duke, *Hall: Price Guide Update,* ELO Books, 1992; Harvey Duke, *Superior Quality Hall China,* ELO Books, 1977; Harvey Duke, *Hall 2,* ELO Books, 1985; Harvey Duke, *The Official Price Guide To Pottery And Porcelain,* Collector Books, 1989; Dana G. Morykan and Harry L. Rinker, *Warman's Country Antiques & Collectibles, Second Edition,* Wallace–Homestead, 1994; Margaret and Kenn Whitmyer, *The Collector's Encyclopedia of Hall China,* Collector Books, 1989, 1992 value update.

Periodical: *The Daze,* 10271 State Rd., Box 57, Otisville, MI 48463; *The Hall China Encore,* 317 N. Pleasant St., Oberlin, OH 44074.

Collectors' Clubs: Autumn Leaf Reissues Assoc., 19238 Dorchester Circle, Strongsville, OH 44136; National Autumn Leaf Collectors Club, 7346 Shamrock Dr., Indianapolis, IN 46217.

Additional Listings: See *Warman's Americana & Collectibles* for more examples.

MISCELLANEOUS

Bowl, cov, 7″ d, blue, Westinghouse	25.00
Coffeepot, Cube, ivory	30.00
Roaster, cov, canary, Westinghouse	20.00
Water Server, cov, blue, Westinghouse	45.00

PATTERNS

Autumn Leaf. Premium for Jewel Tea Co. Produced from 1933 until 1978.

Ball Jug	25.00
Bean Pot	90.00
Cake Plate	14.00
Clock, electric	345.00
Coffeepot, electric	240.00
Mixing Bowl, price for three piece set	40.00
Pitcher, ear shaped handle	18.00
Plate	
7¼″ d	4.00
9″ d	7.50
Platter, 13½″ l	15.00
Range Set, salt and pepper shakers and drip jar, price for three piece set	30.00
Sifter, metal	140.00
Vegetable, cov, oval	36.00

Orange Poppy, pitcher, 6⅜″ h, $65.00.

Heather Rose. Produced during the 1940s.

Bowl, oval	8.00
Coffeepot, Terrace	30.00
Fruit Dish, 5¼″ d	3.00
Platter, 15½″ l	14.00
Pitcher	12.00

Orange Poppy. Premium for Great American Tea Co. Produced from 1933 through 1950s.

Ball Jug	32.00
Bean Pot	55.00
Drip Jar, cov	17.00
Salad Bowl	13.00
Teapot, Boston	55.00

Rose Parade. Kitchenware line introduced in the 1940s.

Baker, French	15.00
Bean Pot, tab handle	35.00
Bowl, 7½″ d, straight–sided #4	14.00
Drip Jar, tab handle	16.00
Jug, 7½″ h, Pert	25.00

Springtime. Premium for Standard Tea Co. Limited production.

Ball Jug, #3	27.00
Batter Bowl, Chinese red	47.00
Bowl	
6″ d, cereal	6.00
9″ d, round	14.00
Casserole, thick rim	25.00
Drip Coffee	75.00
Gravy Boat	18.00
Jug, Radiance, #6	25.00
Plate, 8¼″ d	4.00
Platter, 14″ l	9.00
Soup, flat	9.00

TEAPOTS

Aladdin, black and gold	40.00
Doughnut, ivory	125.00
French, cadet, 4 cup	25.00
Globe, dripless, cadet and gold	175.00
Los Angeles, canary, 4 cup	30.00
Nautilus, yellow, 6 cup	65.00
New York, maroon, 4 cup	30.00
Philadelphia, pink, gold label	35.00
Plume, pink	25.00
Windcrest, yellow	55.00

HAMPSHIRE POTTERY

History: In 1871 James S. Taft founded the Hampshire Pottery Company in Keene, New Hampshire. Production began with redwares and stonewares, followed by majolica decorated wares in 1879. A semiporcelain, with the recognizable matte glazes plus the Royal Worcester glaze, was introduced in 1883.

Until World War I the factory made an extensive line of utilitarian and art wares, including souvenir items. After the war the firm resumed operations but only made hotel dinnerware and tiles. The company was dissolved in 1923.

Reference: Joan Pappas and A. Harold Kendall, *Hampshire Pottery Manufactured by J. S. Taft & Company, Keene, New Hampshire,* published by author, 1971.

Bowl, 6½" d, 2½" h, blue, molded cattails	65.00
Chamberstick, mottled blue–gray and green, black glaze	175.00
Chocolate Pot, 9½" h, cream, holly dec	265.00
Compote, 13¼" d, ftd, two handles, Ivy pattern, light green highlights, cream ground, red decal mark	150.00
Inkwell, 4⅛" d, 2¾" h, round, large center well, three pen holes	90.00
Lamp, table	
7⅞" h base, 12¼" d flaring green slag glass shade, irregular border of red stylized tulips, pottery base with rolled rim, stylized repeating relief leaves, matte green glaze, inscribed "Hampshire Pottery 93" in circle, canister insert	950.00
19" h, matte green glaze, bent panel green slag glass shade, imp marks, designed by Cadmon Robertson, Keene, drilled	615.00
Lamp Base, 19" h, matte green glaze, canister lamp insert, imp marks "03," designed by Cadmon Robertson, Keene	600.00
Mug, East Hampton Library, scenic design	50.00
Nappy, 9" d, violet dec, ivory ground, artist sgd	75.00

Pitcher, 11¾" h, stein type, unglazed, imp mark	150.00
Pot, 2 x 5½", styled Greek Key, glossy cream with red glaze	225.00
Tankard, 8¼" h, cylindrical, imp abstract floral design, green matte, imp "Hampshire"	165.00

Vase, dandelion motif, green over white ground, imp mark, 5⅞" h, $195.00.

Vase	
3½" h, narrow mouth, spherical body, four raised leaves, mottled brown matte glaze, imp mark, c1910	260.00
6" h, opalescent green glaze, raised petal motif, marked "M" in circle	90.00
8" h, narrow rim, large bulbous body, wavy leaf dec, mottled blue glaze, imp marks, c1905	375.00
11" h, ribbon, matte green finish, imp Hampshire and "M" within circle mark	325.00

HAND-PAINTED CHINA

History: Hand painting on china began in the Victorian era and remained popular through the 1920s. It was considered an accomplished art form for women in the upper- and upper-middle-class households. It developed first in England but spread rapidly to the Continent and America.

China factories in Europe, America, and the Orient made the blanks. Belleek, Haviland, Limoges, and Rosenthal are among the European firms. American firms include A. H. Hews Co., Cambridge, Massachusetts; Willetts Mfg. Co., Trenton, New Jersey; and Knowles, Taylor and Knowles, East Liverpool, Ohio. Nippon blanks from Japan were used heavily during the early 20th century.

The quality and design of the blank is a key factor in pricing. Some blanks were very elaborate. Many pieces were signed and dated by the artist.

Aesthetics is critical. Value is added to a piece when a decorator goes beyond the standard forms and creates a unique and pleasing design.

Collectors' Club: World Organization of China Painters, 2641 NW 10th St., Oklahoma City, OK 73107.

Museum: World Organization of China Painters, Oklahoma City, OK.

Bread Tray, 12" l, oval, rose dec, open handles, artist sgd	50.00
Compote, 8⅞" d, 5½" h, shallow, pink roses and green leaves dec, artist sgd, dated 1907	125.00
Cup and Saucer, floral dec, marked "Clairon Ohme, Silesia," c1870.	35.00

Vegetable Dish, floral dec, 9¼" d, $75.00.

Dish, 6½ x 10½", oval, strawberries and leafy vines dec, gold trim, loop handle on one edge, marked "Selb, Bavaria"	55.00
Hair Receiver, violet dec, blue and white, Limoges blank	50.00
Jug, 5¾" h, green and purple grapes and green leaves dec, gold trim	90.00
Milk Pitcher, 7" h, white, basketweave design, yellow flowers, green leaf handle	17.50
Plate	
8½" d, pink roses dec, green ground, gold border, Limoges	40.00
9⅜" d, cavalier and lady scene, artist sgd "D.L.R.L.," marked "Limoges, France".	100.00
9½" d, rose dec, Elite, France	20.00
Platter, 23½" l, yellow roses and green leaves dec, gold trim, artist sgd, marked "Haviland"	240.00
Sugar Shaker, 3½" d, 4½" h, blue and white, pink roses and green leaves dec, gold top and feet	45.00
Tankard, 14½" h, green and purple grapes and green leaves dec, Lenox blank	175.00
Teapot, 5" h, purple violets and green leaves dec, gold trim, Lenox blank . .	125.00
Tobacco Jar, 7¼" h, multicolored Indian bust, gold trim and finial, artist sgd "Florence Weaver, 1925," blank marked "Favorite, Bavaria"	200.00
Tray, 8⅝" l, floral dec, two handles, artist sgd, marked "L. Haviland, France" . .	55.00
Trinket Box, 4½ x 3½ x 1½", yellow, couple and woodland setting, marked "JBH #121815, France"	75.00
Vase, 5" h, white orchids dec, black ground, artist sgd, marked "Rosenthal"	100.00

HATPINS AND HATPIN HOLDERS

History: When the vogue for oversized hats developed around 1850, hatpins became popular. Designers used a variety of materials to decorate the pin ends, including china, crystal, enamel, gem stones, precious metals, and shells. Decorative subjects ranged from commemorative designs to insects.

Hatpin holders are porcelain containers which set on a dresser to hold these pins. The holders were produced by major manufacturers, among which were Meissen, Nippon, R. S. Germany, R. S. Prussia, and Wedgwood.

Reference: Lillian Baker, *Hatpins & Hatpin Holders: An Illustrated Value Guide,* Collector Books, 1983, 1994 value update.

Collectors' Clubs: American Hatpin Society, 28227 Paseo El Siena, Laguna Niguel, CA 92677; International Club for Collectors of Hatpins and Hatpin Holders, 15237 Chanera Avenue, Gardena, CA, 90249.

Museum: Los Angeles Art Museum, Costume Dept., Los Angeles, CA.

Rhinestones, 1¼" d top, $10.00.

HATPINS

Art Deco, plique–a–jour, two baroque pearls.	385.00
Bakelite, black fluted disc, rhinestone dec and silver accents	35.00

Black Glass, faceted ball, painted top, 8″
l. 25.00
Brass, openwork, amber setting 45.00
Carnival Glass, figural, rooster, amber 35.00
Garnet, round, Etruscean granulation,
c1860. . . . . 85.00
Hand Painted China, violets, gold trim 25.00
Ivory, ball shape, carved design 65.00
Jet, faceted top 25.00
Mercury Glass, elongated cased
teardrop 70.00
Plique–a–jour, dome shape, green . . 675.00
Satsuma, Geisha girl dec 245.00
Schafer & Vater, pink relief molded
lady's head on top and sphinx on
base, tan ground. 185.00
Silver
Plated, tennis racquet shape 25.00
Sterling, Art Nouveau, four sided, 12″
l. 85.00
Studded Rhinestone, 1½″ d 25.00

HATPIN HOLDERS

Bavarian
Irid luster, white ground, gold handles
rising from bottom, marked "H & C
Selb, Bavaria". 85.00
Mother–of–Pearl dec, marked "H & C
Bavaria". 65.00
Twist Ribs, floral dec, marked "Z S &
Co". 65.00
Belleek, 5¼″ h, relief pink and maroon
floral dec with green leaves, gold top,
marked "Willets Belleek," dated 1911 125.00
Hand Painted China
4″ h, violets, gold trim and beading 75.00
5″ h, blue forget–me–not dec, marked
"Austria". 35.00
Limoges, grapes, pink roses, matte fin-
ish, artist sgd 60.00
Nippon, hp
Clover dec 45.00
Pink florals, gold trim 75.00
Royal Bayreuth
Figural, owl 400.00
Tapestry, portrait of lady wearing hat,
blue mark 575.00
Schlegelmilch, R S Germany, lily dec 75.00

H&C°   H&C°
L   L
         FRANCE

HAVILAND CHINA

History: In 1842, American china importer David
Haviland moved to Limoges, France, where he began manufacturing and decorating china specifically for the U.S. market. Haviland is synonymous
with fine, white, translucent porcelain, although
early hand-painted patterns were generally larger
and darker colored on heavier whiteware blanks
than are later ones.

David revolutionized French china factories by
both manufacturing the whiteware blank and decorating it at the same site. In addition, Haviland and
Company pioneered the use of decals in decorating china.

David's sons, Charles Edward and Theodore,
split the company in 1892. Theodore opened an
American division in 1936 which continues until today. In 1941 Theodore bought out Charles Edward's heirs and recombined both companies under the original name of H. and Co. The Haviland
family sold its interests in 1981.

Charles Field Haviland, cousin of Charles Edward and Theodore, worked for, and then ran, the
Casseaux Works after his marriage in 1857 until
1882. Items continued to carry his name as decorator until 1941.

Haviland patterns were not consistently named
until after 1926. Pattern identification is difficult because of the similarity found in the more than
66,000 patterns that have been made. Numbers
assigned by Arlene Schleiger and illustrated in her
books have become the identification standard for
matching.

References: Mary Frank Gaston, *Haviland Collectibles & Art Objects*, Collector Books, 1984, out
of print; Arlene Schleiger, *Two Hundred Patterns
of Haviland China, Books I–V*, published by author,
1950–77.

Collectors' Club: Haviland Collectors Internationale Foundation, PO Box 423, Boone, IA 50036.

Bouillon, Rajah pattern, matching saucer, marked "Theo Haviland" 20.00
Bowl
6″ d, oatmeal, scalloped edge with
gold 18.00
7½″ d, soup, blue scroll, pink flower
border. 16.00
8″ d, hp, yellow roses, marked
"Haviland". 35.00
Butter Dish, Gold Band, Theo Haviland 45.00
Butter Pat, sq, rounded corners, gold
trim 10.00
Cake Plate, 10″ d, gold handles and
border 35.00
Celery Dish, scalloped edge, green flow-
ers, pale pink scroll 45.00
Chocolate Set, chocolate pot, six cups
and saucers, Baltimore Rose pattern 1,500.00
Cream Soup and Saucer, cranberry and
blue scroll border. 30.00
Creamer and Sugar
Gold Band, 1930s, Theo Haviland . 45.00

Rajah pattern, marked "Theo Haviland" **20.00**
Scalloped, small pink flowers, gold trim. **65.00**
Cup and Saucer
  Coffee, scalloped gold edge, deep pink flowers. **30.00**
  Tea, small blue flowers, green leaves **25.00**
Demitasse Cup and Saucer, 1885 . . . **30.00**
Dinner Set
  Service for 8, pink flowers, H and Co, price for 55 piece set **900.00**
  Service for 12, Gold Band, Theo Haviland, price for 77 piece set **1,200.00**
Gravy Boat
  Oval, pink flowers, blue ribbon, H and Co **45.00**
  Round, navy and rust, double handles and lips, matching tray, Theo Haviland **35.00**
Ink Blotter, hp violets and foliage dec, marked "Haviland" **35.00**
Oyster Plate, 9″ d, blue and pink flowers, marked "Haviland & Co" **80.00**

Plate, green outer band, gold trim, white ground, 7⅜″ d, $15.00.

Plate
  Bread and Butter
    6″ d, Rajah pattern, marked "Theo Haviland" **5.00**
    7½″ d, gold scalloped edge, pink flowers. **16.00**
  Dinner
    Athena pattern **45.00**
    Princess, 9½″ d, H and Co **22.00**
  Luncheon, 9″ d
    Frontenac **18.00**
    Whiteware, hp, pink rose, sgd H and Co **22.00**
  Salad, 7″ d, Rajah pattern, marked "Theo Haviland". **9.00**

Platter
  12″ l, turquoise morning glories, gold scalloped edge **35.00**
  14″ l, Athena pattern **195.00**
  16″ l, gold band, scalloped end handles, Theo Haviland **55.00**
  22″ l, deep pink flowers, two wells, fancy gold edges **75.00**
Relish Dish, blue and pink flowers **25.00**
Sandwich Plate, 11½″ d, Drop Rose pattern. **275.00**
Soup Plate
  7½″ d, Eden pattern, marked "Theo Haviland" **15.00**
  9½″ d, olive and rust flowers, 1885 mark. **22.00**
Vegetable Bowl, Athena pattern **45.00**

HEISEY GLASS

History: The A. H. Heisey Glass Co. began producing glasswares in April 1896 in Newark, Ohio. Heisey was not a newcomer to the field, having been associated with the craft since his youth.

Many blown and molded patterns were produced in crystal, colored, milk (opalescent), and Ivorina Verde (custard) glass. Decorative techniques of cutting, etching, and silver deposit were employed. Glass figurines were introduced in 1933 and continued until 1957, when the factory ceased production. All Heisey glass is notable for its clarity. Not all Heisey glassware is marked with the familiar "H" within a diamond.

References: Neila Bredehoft, *The Collector's Encyclopedia of Heisey Glass, 1925–1938,* Collector Books, 1986, 1993 value update; Neila M. and Thomas H. Bredehoft, *Handbook of Heisey Production Cuttings,* Cherry Hill Publications, 1991; Mary Louise Burns, *Heisey's Glassware of Distinction,* 2nd edition, published by author, 1983; Lyle Conder, *Collector's Guide To Heisey's Glassware for Your Table,* L–W Books, 1984, 1993–94 value update; Tom Felt and Bob O'Grady, *Heisey Candlesticks, Candelabra, and Lamps,* Heisey Collectors of America, Inc., 1984; Gene Florence, *Elegant Glassware Of The Depression Era, Revised Fifth Edition,* Collector Books, 1993; Frank L. Hahn and Paul Kikeli, *Collector's Guide to Heisey and Heisey by Imperial Glass Animals,* Golden Era Publications, 1991; Ellen T. Schroy, *Warman's Glass,* Wallace–Homestead, 1992.

Collectors' Clubs: Heisey Collectors of America, 169 W. Church St., Newark, OH, 43055; National Capital Heisey Collectors, PO Box 23, Clinton, MD 20735.

Museum: National Heisey Glass Museum, Newark, OH.

Reproduction Alert: Some Heisey molds were sold to Imperial Glass of Bellaire, Ohio, and certain items were reissued. These pieces may be mistaken for the original Heisey. Some of the reproductions were produced in colors which were never made by Heisey and have become collectible in their own right.

Examples include: the Colt family in Crystal, Carmel Slag, Ultra Blue, and Horizon Blue; the mallard with wings up in Carmel Slag; Whirlpool (Provincial) in crystal and colors; and Waverly, 7" oval-footed compote in Carmel Slag.

Salt, clear, tub shape, $28.00.

Bonbon, Lariat, hp, 7½" d	95.00
Bowl	
Crystolite, 12" d	30.00
Empress, crystal, dolphin ftd, sterling	
floral overlay, 11" d.	60.00
Lariat, centerpiece, crimped, 11" d .	30.00
Orchid, 12" d	60.00
Queen Ann, orchid etch, 9" d	70.00
Waverly, tea rose, 13" d	70.00
Butter Dish, cov	
Orchid, sq, horsehead finial	178.00
Rose, etched	175.00
Cake Plate, Crystolite	325.00
Cake Stand, Plantation	80.00
Candlesticks, pr	
Charter Oak, Flamingo pink, three	
light	155.00
Heisey Rose, three light	225.00
New Era, crystal, two light, bobeche	110.00
Orchid, three light	85.00
Plantation, two light	190.00
Windsor, 7" h	125.00
Candy Basket, Lariat, Moonglo cutting	45.00
Candy Dish, cov	
Continental	195.00
Crystolite, three toes	50.00
Celery Tray	
Greek Key, 9" l	24.00
King Arthur, diamond optic, hand dec,	
11" l.	24.00
Marigold	25.00
Champagne	
Fairacre, Flamingo pink stem and foot	25.00
Peacock Etch	27.50

Saturn	20.00
Stanhope, zircon blue–green	55.00
Cheese Dish, Empress, etched, pink, 6"	
d	15.00
Cheese Server, Rose, 14" d	150.00
Cigarette Set, Ridgeleigh, box, two	
matching ashtrays, price for three	
piece set	35.00
Coaster	
Colonial	10.00
Lariat	8.00
Cocktail	
Chintz	18.00
Moonglo	
Lariat stem, blown, cut #5040 ..	25.00
Rooster tail stem	75.00
Old Sandwich, Sahara	20.00
Cocktail Shaker, Ipswich	275.00
Cologne Bottle, Winged Scroll, emerald	75.00
Cordial, Colonial	15.00
Creamer and Sugar	
Empress, Moongleam, matching tray	195.00
Old Dominion, Sahara	65.00
Orchid	65.00
Queen Ann, Minuet etching, dolphin	
feet.	75.00
Cruet, stopper	
Crystolite, clear	25.00
Plantation	125.00
Provincal, clear	45.00
Victorian, diagonal cut stopper	30.00
Yeoman, Moongleam	85.00
Cup and Saucer, Empress, Sahara ..	43.00
Custard, Colonial	5.00
Egg Cup, Raised Loop	25.00
Flower Bowl, Twist, Sahara	60.00
Flower Holder, figural, kingfisher, Flam-	
ingo pink	200.00
Goblet	
Carcassone, Sahara	35.00
Colonial	9.00
Everglades	20.00
Peacock Etch	32.50
Ice Bucket, Twist, Moongleam, orig	
tongs	100.00
Iced Tea Tumbler	
Everglades	20.00
Moonglo, Lariat stem, blown, cut	
#5040.	25.00
Jelly Compote	
Empress, Sahara, 6" h	30.00
Prince of Wales Plumes, crystal, gold	
trim.	50.00
Waverly, 6½" d	40.00
Jug, Greek Key, three pints	175.00
Juice Tumbler	
Carcassone, Sahara	30.00
Moonglo, Lariat stem, blown, cut	
#5040.	20.00
Mayonnaise, liner, Rose	85.00
Mint Dish, Empress, etched, pink, 6" d	15.00
Oyster Cocktail, Ipswich, crystal, 4 oz	15.00

Parfait, Plantation 45.00
Plate
    Colonial, 4½" d 8.00
    Queen Anne, Sahara, 7½" d 25.00
Preserves Bowl, Empress, Sahara, two
    handles, 5" d. 30.00
Punch Bowl Set, Lariat, punch bowl, six
    cups, matching underplate, price for
    eight piece set 385.00
Relish
    Crystolite, five part, round, 10" d . . 40.00
    Lariat, three part, Moonglo cutting, 10"
    d 35.00
    Orchid, three part 60.00
    Ridgeleigh, two part 24.00
Salt and Pepper Shakers, pr
    Empress, Sahara, ftd 130.00
    Provincial, crystal 30.00
Server, center handle, King Arthur, dia-
    mond optic, hand dec 40.00
Sherbet
    Carcassone, Sahara 35.00
    Moonglo, Lariat stem, blown cut
    #5040. 25.00
Sherry, Colonial 11.00
Soup, Pleat and Panel, green 18.00
Sugar, Crystolite, individual 12.00
Toothpick, Sunburst 60.00
Torte Plate, Lariat, rolled edge, 12" d 28.00
Tumbler
    Chintz, ftd, 12 oz 20.00
    Old Sandwich 25.00
    Orchid 50.00
    Peacock Etch 32.50
    Spanish Cut, ftd, 12 oz 25.00
Water Bottle, Greek Key 200.00

HOLLY AMBER

History: Holly Amber, originally called Golden
Agate, was produced by the Indiana Tumbler and
Goblet Works of the National Glass Co., Greentown, Indiana. Jacob Rosenthal created the color
in 1902. Holly Amber is a gold-colored glass with a
marbleized onyx color on raised parts.

A new pattern, Holly [No. 450], was designed by
Frank Jackson for Golden Agate. Between January
1903 and June 1903, more than 35 items were
made in this pattern; the factory was destroyed by
fire in June.

References: Brenda Measell and James Mea-
sell, *A Guide To Reproductions of Greentown
Glass, 2nd Edition,* The Printing Press, 1974;
James Measell, *Greentown Glass, The Indiana
Tumbler & Goblet Co.,* Grand Rapids Public Mu-
seum, 1979, 1992–93 value update, distributed by
Antique Publications.

Collectors' Club: National Greentown Glass
Assoc., 19596 Glendale Ave., South Bend, IN
46637.

Museums: Grand Rapids Public Museum, Ruth

Herrick Greentown Glass Collection, Grand Rapids, MI; Greentown Glass Museum, Greentown, IN.
    Additional Listing: Greentown Glass.

Berry Bowl, 8½" d 375.00
Butter, cov, 7¼ x 6¼" 1,200.00
Cake Stand 2,000.00

Compote, 6¾" h, 7⅜" d, $875.00.

Compote
    4¾" d, jelly, open 450.00
    8½" d, 12" h, cov 1,800.00
Creamer and Sugar 1,550.00
Cruet, 6½" h, orig stopper 2,100.00
Match Holder 400.00
Mug, 4½" h, several heat lines on rim 330.00
Nappy 375.00
Parfait 575.00
Relish, oval 275.00
Salt and Pepper Shakers, pr 500.00
Sauce Dish 225.00
Spooner 425.00
Syrup, 5¾" h, silverplated hinged lid . 2,000.00
Toothpick, 2½" h, deep amber, fiery
    opalescence. 685.00
Tumbler 350.00

HORN

History: For centuries horns from animals have
been used for various items, such as drinking cups,
spoons, powder horns, and small dishes. Some
pieces of horn have designs scratched in them.
Around 1880 furniture made from the horns of
Texas longhorn steers was popular in Texas and
the southwestern United States.
    Additional Listings: Firearm Accessories.

Calling Card Case, horn and ivory, floral
    design 40.00

Chair, steer horns, $2,250.00.

Chair, arm, curled horn crest, arms, and legs, black leather reupholstery, 29½" w, 21" d, 41" h.	470.00
Comb Case, 7½ x 9", pocket type, diamond shape mirror	35.00
Inkwell, 1½" h, turned banded dec, c1810.	35.00
Shoehorn, scratch carved, 1756	65.00
Spoon, 5½" l, thistle, monogrammed "MBL, 1907," hallmarked.	45.00
Stand, Victorian, four horns form legs, American Southwest, 19th C	275.00
Tea Caddy, 12¼ x 9¼ x 7½", tapering ribbed sides and cov, wide plain border, claw and ball feet, lobed domical flowerhead knop, dark stain, Anglo–Indian, c1815	900.00

HULL POTTERY

History: In 1905 Addis E. Hull purchased the Acme Pottery Company, Crooksville, Ohio. In 1917 the A. E. Hull Pottery Company began making a line of art pottery, novelties, stoneware, and kitchenware, later including the famous Little Red Riding Hood line. Most items had a matte finish with shades of pink and blue or brown predominating.

After a disastrous flood and fire in 1950, J. Brandon Hull reopened the factory in 1952 as the Hull Pottery Company. New, more modern style molds, mostly with glossy finish, were produced. The company currently produces pieces, such as the Regal and Floraline lines, for sale to florists.

Hull pottery molds and patterns are easily identified. Pre–1950 vases are marked "Hull USA" or "Hull Art USA" on the bottom. Many also retain their paper labels. Post–1950 pieces are marked "Hull" in large script or "HULL" in block letters.

Each pattern has a distinctive number, such as Wildflower with a "W" and number, Waterlily with

an "L" and number, Poppy with 600 numbers, Orchid with 300 numbers, etc. Early stone pieces have an H.

References: Barbara Loveless Gick–Burke, *Collector's Guide To Hull Pottery: The Dinnerware Lines: Identification & Values,* Collector Books, 1993; Joan Hull, *Hull: The Heavenly Pottery, Revised Third Edition,* published by author, 1993; Brenda Roberts, *The Collectors Encyclopedia Of Hull Pottery,* Collector Books, 1980, 1993 value update; Brenda Roberts, *Roberts' Ultimate Encyclopedia of Hull Pottery,* Walsworth Publishing Co., 1992; Brenda Roberts, *The Companion Guide to Roberts' Ultimate Encyclopedia of Hull Pottery,* Walsworth Publishing, 1992.

Periodicals: *Hull Pottery Newsletter,* 11023 Tunnel Hill NE, New Lexington, OH 43764; *The Hull Pottery News,* 466 Foreston Place, St. Louis, MO 63119.

Additional Listings: See *Warman's Americana & Collectibles* for more examples.

Advisor: Joan Hull.

Woodland, ewer, post–1950, W–3–5½", $40.00.

PRE–1950 (MATTE)

Bowknot	
Bowl, B–18, 5¾" d	165.00
Ewer, B–1, 5½" h, green to blue . .	165.00
Teapot, B–20, 6" h	400.00
Vase, B–8, 8½" h	85.00
Calla Lily	
Cornucopia, 570/33, 8" h, turquoise and cream.	100.00
Vase, 560/33, 8" h	250.00
Dogwood	
Bowl, 521, 7" h, cream	35.00
Jardiniere, 514, 4¾" h, blue to pink, orig label.	75.00
Vase, 516, 4¾" h, turquoise to cream	55.00

Little Red Riding Hood

Bank, 7" h	650.00
Cookie Jar, 13" h	300.00
Mustard, spoon, 5¼" h	350.00
Pitcher, open head, 8" h	300.00

Magnolia

Basket, 10, 10½" h	300.00
Creamer and Sugar, 24 and 25, 3¾" h, brown to yellow	100.00
Lamp Base, 12½" h	400.00
Teapot, H–20, 6½"	150.00
Vase, 8½" h, blue to pink	125.00

Mardi Gras/Granada

Basket, 65, 8" h	40.00
Vase, 215, 9" h	45.00

Novelty

Bank, Piggy, emb florals, 14"	40.00
Casserole, Cinderella, 7½" d	25.00
Shaving Mug, Old Spice, 3" h	25.00

Orchid

Bookends, pr, 316, 7" h	800.00
Bowl, 314, 13" d	300.00
Vase, 308, 4¼" h	75.00

Poppy

Bowl, 608, 4¾" d	75.00
Ewer, 610, 4¾" d	100.00
Wall Pocket, 609, 9" h	350.00

Rosella

Cornucopia, R–13, 8½" h	75.00
Creamer and Sugar, R–4, 5½" h	100.00
Wall Pocket, R–10, 6½" h	85.00

Tulip

Vase

100–33–10, 10" h	250.00
104–44–6, 6½" h, bud	95.00
110–33–6, 6" h	605.00

Wildflower

Teaset, 8" h teapot, 72; 4¾" h creamer, 73; 4¾" h cov sugar, 74; price for three piece set	1,500.00
Pitcher, W–2, 5½" h	65.00
Vase, W–15–10½, 10½" h	150.00

Woodland

Basket, W–9	185.00
Console Bowl, W–29	275.00
Cornucopia, W–10	130.00
Flowerpot, 5¾" h, W–11	150.00

POST–1950

Blossom Flite

Basket, T–8, 8¼" h	115.00
Creamer, 15	40.00
Cornucopia, T–6, 10½" l	85.00
Planter, T–12, 10½" l	75.00

Butterfly

Ashtray, B–3, 7" w	50.00
Basket, B–13, 8"	125.00
Bonbon, B–4, 6" d	35.00
Pitcher, 8¾" h	95.00
Teapot, B–18	135.00

Capri

Pitcher, C–87, 12" h	75.00
Twin Swan, C–81	65.00

Ebb Tide

Basket, E–5	95.00
Console Bowl, E–12	150.00
Creamer, E–15	45.00
Sugar, cov, E–16	45.00
Vase, E–6, fish	95.00

Imperial

Madonna, F–7, 7" h	35.00
Planter, F–475, praying hands, 6" l	35.00

Royal

Basket, W9, 8¾" h	50.00
Vase, W–4, 6½" h	35.00

Serenade

Ashtray, S–23	95.00
Planter, S–3	35.00
Vase, S–11, 10½" h	95.00

Tuscany/Tokay

Candy Dish, 8½" d	95.00
Leaf Dish, 13" l	55.00

Woodland, glossy glaze

Candleholder, pr, W–30	50.00
Console Bowl, W–29	175.00
Jardiniere, W–7, 5½" h	75.00
Pitcher, W–6, 6½" h	75.00

HUMMEL ITEMS

History: Hummel items are the original creations of Berta Hummel, born in 1909 in Massing, Bavaria, Germany. At age 18, she was enrolled in the Academy of Fine Arts in Munich to further her mastery of drawing and the palette. Berta entered the Convent of Siessen and became Sister Maria Innocentia in 1934. In this Franciscan cloister, she continued drawing and painting images of her childhood friends.

In 1935 W. Goebel Co. in Rodental, Germany, began reproducing Sister Maria Innocentia's sketches into three–dimensional bisque figurines. The Schmid Brothers of Randolph, Massachusetts, introduced the figurines to America and became Goebel's U.S. distributor.

In 1967 Goebel began distributing Hummel items in the United States. A controversy developed between the two companies involving the Hummel family and the convent. Lawsuits and countersuits ensued. The German courts finally effected a compromise. The convent held legal rights to all works produced by Sister Maria Innocentia from 1934 until her death in 1946 and licensed Goebel to reproduce these works. Schmid was to deal directly with the Hummel family for permission to reproduce any preconvent art.

All authentic Hummels bear both the signature M. I. Hummel and a Goebel trademark. Various trademarks were used to identify the year of production. The Crown Mark (trademark 1) was used from 1935 until 1949; Full Bee (trademark 2) 1950–59; Stylized Bee (trademark 3) 1957–72; Three Line Mark (trademark 4) 1964–72; Last Bee Mark (trademark 5) 1972–79; Missing Bee Mark (trademark 6) 1979–90; and the Current Mark or New Crown Mark (trademark 7) from 1991 to the present.

References: Carl F. Luckey, *Luckey's Hummel Figurines and Plates: A Collector's Identification and Value Guide, 10th Edition,* Books Americana, 1993; Robert L. Miller, *The No. 1 Price Guide to M. I. Hummel: Figurines, Plates, More . . ., Fifth Edition,* Portfolio Press, 1992; Lawrence L. Wonsch, *Hummel Copycats With Values,* Wallace–Homestead, 1987, out of print.

Collectors' Clubs: Hummel Collector's Club, Inc., PO Box 257, Yardley, PA 19067; M. I. Hummel Club, Dept. O, Goebel Plaza, PO Box 11, Pennington, NJ 08534.

Museum: The Hummel Museum, New Branufels, TX.

Additional Listings: See *Warman's Americana & Collectibles* for more examples.

Chicken Licken, #385, trademark 5, $100.00.

Bookends, pr
Apple Tree Boy and Apple Tree Girl, #252A&B, trademark 3	250.00
Bookworms, #14/A&B, trademark 3	300.00
Strolling Along, #5, trademark 7 . .	275.00

Candleholder
Silent Night, #54, trademark 5	175.00
Watchful Angel, #194, trademark 2	400.00

Candy Box
Happy Pastime, #III/69, trademark 4	125.00
Joyful, #III/53, trademark 4	115.00

Figurine
Adoration, #23/II, trademark 7	750.00
Auf Widersehen, #153/0, trademark 5	130.00
Baker, #128, trademark 3	85.00
Band Leader, #129, trademark 5 . .	120.00
Be Patient, #197/2/0, trademark 2 .	125.00
Bird Duet, #169, trademark 4	90.00
Boy With Toothache, #217, trademark 4	110.00
Celestial Musician, #188	80.00
Chick Girl, #57/0, trademark 2 . . .	100.00
Chicken Licken, #385, trademark 4	100.00
Chimney Sweep, 122/0, trademark 5	70.00
Close Harmony, #336	100.00
Congratulations, #17/0 (no socks), trademark 2.	225.00
Doll Bath, #319, trademark 4	130.00
Easter Time, #384, trademark 5 . .	85.00
Farewell, #65, trademark 5	80.00
Feathered Friends, #344	80.00
Going To Grandma's, #51/0, trademark 2	175.00
Heavenly Angel, #21/0, trademark 3	75.00
Heavenly Lullaby, #262, trademark 5	110.00
Joyful, #52/0, trademark 4	135.00
Just Resting, #112/3/0, trademark 5	85.00
Kiss Me, #311, trademark 4	145.00
Knitting Lessons, #256, trademark 4	350.00
Little Goat Herder, #200/0, trademark 3	120.00
Little Hiker, #16/2/0, trademark 2 .	80.00
Little Pharmacist, #322, trademark 2	2,500.00
March Winds, #43, trademark 5 . .	75.00
Mother's Darling, #175, trademark 2	225.00
Not For You, #317, trademark 5 . .	130.00
Playmates, #58/I, trademark 3 . . .	150.00
Postman, #119, trademark 2	145.00
Puppy Love, #1, trademark 7	425.00
School Girls, #177/I, trademark 5 .	900.00
She Loves Me, She Loves Me Not, #174, trademark 2.	175.00
Smart Little Sister, #346, trademark 4	100.00
Stargazer, #132, trademark 5	50.00
Surprise, #94/3/0, trademark 2 . . .	165.00
The Artist, #304, trademark 4	350.00
The Builder, #305, trademark 4 . . .	140.00
The Photographer, #178, trademark 3	140.00
To Market, #49/3/0, trademark 2 . .	195.00
Umbrella Boy, #152/A/II, trademark 7	2,000.00
Village Boy, #51/3/0, trademark 7 .	115.00

Wayside Devotion, #28/III, trademark
7 . . . . 1,300.00
Which Hand?, #258, trademark 3 . 350.00
Font
Angel Cloud, #206, trademark 5, 2¼
x 4¾" 40.00
Child With Flowers, #36/I, trademark
3 . . . . 100.00
Child Jesus, #26/0, trademark 4 . . 30.00
Guardian Angel, #248, trademark 4,
2¼ x 5½" 50.00
Holy Family, #246, trademark 3, 3 x
4" 65.00
Seated Angel, #167, trademark 2, 3¼
x 4¼" 75.00
Music Box, Little Band, #388M, trade-
mark 4 . . . . 250.00
Plaque
Ba–Bee Rings, #30/OA&B, trade-
mark 2 . . . . 250.00
Madonna, #48/0, trademark 7, 3 x 4" 250.00
Mail Coach, #140, trademark 5, 4½ x
6¼" 135.00
Merry Wanderer, #92, trademark 2,
4¾ x 5⅛" 185.00
Table Lamp, Culprits, #44/A, trademark
2 . . . . 350.00

IMARI

History: Imari derives its name from a Japanese
port city. Although Imari ware was manufactured in
the 17th century, the wares most commonly encountered are those made between 1770 and
1900.

Early Imari was decorated simply, quite unlike
the later heavily decorated brocade pattern commonly associated with Imari. Most of the decorative
patterns are an underglaze blue and overglaze
"seal wax" red supported by turquoise and yellow.

The Chinese copied Imari ware. Important differences of the Japanese type include grayer clay,
thicker glaze, runny and darker blue, and deep red
opaque hues.

The pattern and colors of Imari inspired many
English and European potteries, such as Derby
and Meissen, to adopt a similar style of decoration
for their wares.

Reference: Gloria and Robert Mascarelli, *Warman's Oriental Antiques,* Wallace–Homestead,
1992.

Reproduction Alert: Reproductions abound,
and many manufacturers continue to produce
pieces in the traditional style.

Bowl
7¼" d, steep sides, low ring foot, central medallion of garden setting surrounded by reserves of phoenix in
flight and diaper patterns alternat-

Platter, iron–red and cobalt blue border, c1875, 12⅜" l, $125.00.

ing with blue and gilt painted bands
and floral shaped reserves, 19th C 385.00
8" d, scalloped 140.00
9½" d, figural dec, brocade ground 275.00
Charger
17¾" d, painted underglaze blue and
polychrome enamels, landscape
scene, reserve ground of scattered
floral and geometric pattern roundels, linked diamond rim band, 19th
C 715.00
18⅛" d, shaped reserve character encircled with radiating panels with alternating dragon, floral, and geometric motifs, precious emblems on
underside, 19th C. 1,210.00
25¾" d, sloping int., randomly scattered book and fan shape reserves
int., cobalt blue flowers and scrolling tendrils ext., lappet band around
ring foot, Meiji period 3,850.00
Creamer and Sugar, 5½" h creamer,
5⅞" h cov sugar, ovoid, dragon form
handles, gilt and bright enamels,
shaped reserves, dragonlike beasts,
stylized animal medallions, brocade
ground, high dome lid, knob, cipher
mark of Mount Fuji and Fukagama
Studio marks, Meiji period 500.00
Jar, 10½" h, cov, ribbed, red and blue
floral dec, 19th C. 625.00
Jardiniere, 10" h, hexagonal, bulbous,
short flared foot, alternating bijin figures and immortal symbols, stylized
ground 250.00
Plate
9" d, wide everted rim, central medallion of Chinese scholars seated
on garden terrace, blossoming
plum tree, gilt highlights, Chinese,
early 19th C. 300.00

9⅝" d, gilt, multicolored enamels, and underglaze blue, irregular ho–o and floral reserves, blue ground, foliate and cloud design, foliate edge, price for set of six. **500.00**

Platter, 14" l, hexagonal, central reserve of flowers in vase, cavetto with floral reserves, scrolling branches, narrow blue band, Meiji period, price for pair **1,000.00**

Punch Bowl, 11" d, red and blue floral dec, scalloped rim, 19th C **375.00**

Urn, 21" h, gilt bronze mounts, deep bowl, red, blue, and gilt floral dec, everted pierced collar, S scroll arms of leaves and cattails, mid band of plaited reeds, flaring porcelain base banded in bronze, pierced skirt interspersing four foliate clasps, price for pair **14,000.00**

Vase, 22" h, ovoid, fan design **880.00**

IMPERIAL GLASS

History: Imperial Glass Co., Bellaire, Ohio, was organized in 1901. Its primary product was pattern (pressed) glass. Soon other lines were added, including carnival glass, NUART, NUCUT, and NEAR CUT. In 1916 the company introduced "Free–Hand," a lustered art glass line, and "Imperial Jewels," an iridescent stretch glass that carried the Imperial cross trademark. In the 1930s the company was reorganized into the Imperial Glass Corporation and continues to produce a great variety of wares.

Imperial recently has acquired the molds and equipment of several other glass companies— Central, Cambridge, and Heisey. Many of the "retired" molds of these companies are once again in use. The resulting reissues are marked to distinguish them from the originals.

References: Margaret and Douglas Archer, *Imperial Glass,* Collector Books, 1978, 1993 value update; Gene Florence, *Elegant Glassware Of The Depression Era, Revised Fifth Edition,* Collector Books, 1993; Frank L. Hahn and Paul Kikeli, *Collector's Guide to Heisey and Heisey by Imperial Glass Animals,* Golden Era Publications, 1991; National Imperial Glass Collector's Society, *Imperial Glass 1966 Catalog,* reprint, 1991 price guide, Antique Publications; Ellen T. Schroy, *Warman's Glass,* Wallace–Homestead, 1992; Mary M. Wetzel, *Candlewick: The Jewel of Imperial,* published by author, 1981; Mary M. Wetzel, *Candlewick: The Jewel of Imperial Price Guide II, Revised 2nd Edition,* published by author, 1993.

Collectors' Club: National Imperial Glass Collectors Society, PO Box 534, Bellaire, OH 43906.

Additional Listings: See Carnival Glass, Pattern Glass, and *Warman's Americana & Collectibles* for more examples of Candlewick.

Vase, Drag Loop, pedestal base, cobalt blue with yellow, c1915, 6" d, 6½" h, $575.00.

ENGRAVED OR HAND CUT

Bowl, 6½" d, flower and leaf, molded star base **20.00**

Candlesticks, pr, 7" h, Amelia **32.00**

Celery Vase, three side stars, cut star base **25.00**

Nut Dish, 5½" d, Design No. 112 . . . **15.00**

Pitcher, tankard form, Design No. 110, flowers, foliage, and butterfly cutting **50.00**

Plate, 5½" d, Design No. 12 . . . . **12.00**

JEWELS

Bowl, 6¼" d, purple Pearl Green luster, marked. **75.00**

Candlesticks, pr, blue luster **50.00**

Compote, 7½" d, irid teal blue **60.00**

Rose Bowl, amethyst, green irid **75.00**

Vase, 6" h, irid pearl green and purple luster **135.00**

LUSTERED (FREE-HAND)

Candlesticks, pr, 10¾" h, cobalt blue, white vine and leaf dec **325.00**

Hat, 9" w, ruffled rim, cobalt blue,
  embedded irid white vines and leaves ... 100.00
Pitcher, 10" h, applied clear handle, pale
  yellow luster, white pulled loops 225.00
Rose Bowl, 6" d, irid orange, white floral
  cutting 75.00
Vase
  10" h, translucent cobalt blue, balus-
    ter, free-hand opaque white heart
    and vine dec 495.00
  11½" h, expanded tooled trefoil rim,
    dark ground, orange heart and vine
    dec, bright luster 660.00

NUART

Ashtray 18.00
Lamp Shade, marigold 50.00
Vase, 7" h, bulbous, irid green 125.00

NUCUT

Bowl, 4½" d, berry, handles 15.00
Celery Tray, 11" l 18.00
Creamer 17.50
Fern Dish, 8" l, brass lining, ftd 32.00
Orange Bowl, 12" d, Rose Marie 48.00
Punch Set, 13" d bowl, base, six cups,
  Rose Marie, price for eight piece set 175.00
Tumbler, flared rim, molded star 15.00

PRESSED

Ashtray, Cathay, jade 65.00
Bonbon, 5¼" d, D'Angelo, green, handle 18.00
Bowl, 9" d, satin irid, handles 20.00
Butter Dish, cov, Colonial, rose 50.00
Cheese Dish, cov, Monticello 35.00
Cordial, Wakefield, amber 20.00
Creamer and Sugar
  Cape Cod, clear 20.00
  Flora, rose 15.00
Goblet, Cape Cod, red 15.00
Mayonnaise, Monaco, amber, matching
  underplate and orig spoon, price for
  three piece set 20.00
Salt and Pepper Shakers, pr, Huckabee,
  aluminum tops 25.00
Sandwich Tray, black handle 25.00
Sweet Pea Vase, 4" h 15.00
Toothpick, ivory, orig label 18.00

INDIAN ARTIFACTS, AMERICAN

History: During the historic period there were
approximately 350 tribes of Indians grouped into
the following regions: Eskimo, Northeast and
Woodland, Northwest Coast, Plains, and West and
Southwest.

American Indian artifacts are quite popular. Currently the market is in a period of stability following
a rapid increase of prices during the 1970s.

References: John W. Barry, *American Indian
Pottery, 2nd Edition,* Books Americana, 1984, out
of print; C. J. Brafford and Laine Thom (comps.),
Dancing Colors: Paths of Native American Women,
Chronicle Books, 1992; Harold S. Colton, *Hopi Ka-
china Dolls, Revised Edition,* University of New
Mexico Press, 1959, 1990 reprint; Robert Edler,
Early Archaic Indian Points & Knives, Collector
Books, 1990; Larry Frank, *Indian Silver Jewelry of
the Southwest, 1868–1930,* Schiffer Publishing,
1989; Lar Hothem, *Arrowheads & Projectile Points,*
Collector Books, 1983, 1993 value update; Lar
Hothem, *Indian Artifacts of the Midwest,* Collector
Books, 1992; Lar Hothem, *North American Indian
Artifacts, 5th Edition,* Books Americana, 1993; Lar
Hothem, *North American Indian Points,* Books
Americana, 1984; Noel D. Justice, *Stone Age
Spear And Arrow Points Of the Midcontinental and
Eastern United States,* Indiana University Press,
1987; Allan Lobb, *Indian Baskets Of The Pacific
Northwest and Alaska,* Graphic Arts Center Pub-
lishing Co., 1990; Evan M. Maurer, *Visions Of The
People: A Pictorial History Of Plains Indian Life,*
University of Washington Press, 1992; Robert M.
Overstreet and Howard Peake, *The Official Over-
street Price Guide to Indian Arrowheads, Second
Edition,* House of Collectibles, 1991; Robert M. Ov-
erstreet and Howard Peake, *The Overstreet Indian
Arrowheads Identification and Price Guide, Third
Edition,* Avon Books, 1993; Dawn E. Reno, *The
Official Identification and Price Guide To American
Indian Collectibles,* House of Collectibles, 1988;
Laine Thom, *Becoming Brave: The Path To Native
American Manhood,* Chronicle Books, 1992; Sarah
and William Turnbaugh, *Indian Baskets,* Schiffer
Publishing, 1986.

Periodicals: *American Indian Art Magazine,*
7314 E. Osborn Dr., Scottsdale, AZ 85251; *American Indian Basketry Magazine,* PO Box 66124,
Portland, OR 97266; *Indian–Artifact Magazine,* RD
#1, Box 240, Turbotville, PA 17772; *Prehistoric
Antiquities & Archaeological News,* PO Box 88,
Sunbury, OH 43074; *The Indian Trader,* PO Box
1421, Gallup, NM 87305.

Collectors' Club: Indian Arts and Crafts Assoc.,
Suite B, 122 Laveta NE, Albuquerque, NM 87108.

Museums: Colorado River Indian Tribes Museum, Parker, AZ; Indian Center Museum, Wichita,
KS; Maryhill Museum of Art, Goldendale, WA; Museum of Classical Antiquities & Primitive Arts, Medford Lakes, NJ; Museum of the American Indian,
Heye Foundation, New York, NY; U.S. Deptartment
of the Interior Museum, Washington, D.C.; Wheel-
wright Museum of the American Indian, Santa Fe,
NM.

Note: American Indian artifacts listed below are
objects made on the North American continent during the prehistoric and historic periods.

Necklace, Zuni, squash blossom in needlepoint, Bisby blue turquoise, 13¾″ l, $1,750.00.

ESKIMO

Basket
    4³⁄₁₆″ l, 2½″ h, oval, different colored baleen bands, carved ivory walrus finial and bottom disk, Inuit **660.00**
    5⅞″ d, 4⅞″ h, woven grass, beaded design, red and black, cov **95.00**
Belt, hunter's, 37″ l, caribou hide, caribou teeth dec, black and white beaded dec, 19th C **775.00**
Doll, 21″ l, carved wood head, seagrass stuffed body, red hair, sealskin clothing, late 19th C **775.00**
Moccasins, hide, black cotton and velvet panels, puckered toe and floral beadwork, red, green, blue, yellow, and translucent beads, Iroquois, c1890 . . **330.00**
Necklace, 26″ l, twenty–two fossilized ivory tooth pendants, blue and orange glass trade beads, 19th C **825.00**
Saddle Blanket, 32 x 55″, blue wool trade cloth, floral beadwork dec, white, red, pink, green, yellow, and mustard beads, green twisted wool fringe, Cree, c1880 . . . . **1,210.00**

NORTHEAST AND WOODLANDS

Bag, black velvet cloth, beaded dec, stag branches, and floral design, green, pink, red, yellow, pumpkin, and white beads, faceted black bead fringe, Chippewa, c1920. . . . . **225.00**
Bandolier Bag, 44″ l, black velvet and red trade cloth, floral beadwork, red, green, pink, yellow, blue, and white beads, Chippewa, c1900 . . . . **1,100.00**
Bowl, 10½ x 20″, wood, stylized abstract face effigy, 1780–1820. . . . . **3,300.00**
Knife, 9½″ l, wood, carved, file attached to handle with lead inlay and brasswork, 19th C. **1,650.00**
Mask, 14 x 12″, corn husk, braided and detailed, attached pouch of tobacco and corn seed. **440.00**
Moccasins, pr, child's
    5¼″ l, hide and cloth, blue, yellow, pink, translucent, and white beaded floral motif, Iroquois, c1900 . . . . . . **75.00**
    5½″ l, hide, black velvet tongue and cuff, red, white, pink, translucent, green, yellow, and blue beaded floral design, Cree, late 19th C . . . **165.00**
Strap, 28¼″ l, loom woven, quillwork, horizontal diamond pattern, blue, red, white, and purple quills, Cree, late 19th C **990.00**

NORTHWEST COAST

Bag
    9⅜ x 8¼″, cornhusk, geometric yarn designs, maroon, blue, and green, leather handles **165.00**
    15 x 19″, cornhusk, weave, triangle in star design, aniline dyes, green, purple, yellow, orange, and red, Nez Perce, late 19th C **1,155.00**
Basket, cov, 9 x 9½ x 18″, rect, imbricated stepped zigzag design, c1915 **725.00**
Dress, 44″ l, 56″ w, sinew sewn elkskin, pink, blue, yellow, and maroon beaded geometric patterns, fringes with glass and trade beads dec, Nez Perce, late 19th C **4,675.00**
Hat, 7 x 7″, woven cornhusk, black, red, and purple handspun wool embroidery, hide tassel with brass bells, dentil shells, and trade beads, Nez Perce, late 19th C **1,980.00**
Ladle, 11″ l, mountain sheep horn bowl, carved totem style handle, copper brads, c1890. . . . . **660.00**
Totem Pole, 72″ h, wood, carved and painted, bear, human head, beaver, two winged creatures, frog, and wolf design, c1890. . . . . **13,750.00**
Tunic, 38½″ l, wool, green trade cloth, red trade cloth octopus cutout dec, white and blue beaded floral dec, Tlingit, c1880 . . . . **9,350.00**

PLAINS

Awl Case, 20″ l, hide, blue, yellow, and red beadwork, quill wrapped fringe suspensions, tin cones and dyed feathers, 1890s. **330.00**

Belt, 30″ l, hide, loom beaded panels, blue, yellow, orange, and red beads, c1940. . . . . **225.00**

Bonnet, 8″ l, blue, red, green, and yellow beaded geometric design, white background, purple ribbon, Sioux, late 19th C. **770.00**

Club, 27″ l, stone head, rawhide wrapped handle, fur attachment, late 19th C. **330.00**

Cradleboard, 40″ l, yellow painted wood boards with brass tacks, cover with red, white, blue, and green geometric design, Cheyenne, c1880. . . . . **6,600.00**

Dress, 53″ l
Cheyenne, hide, white, blue, red, pink, and green beaded dec on yoke, red, white, and blue beads on bottom, beaded rosettes, ribbons, and sequins, 1890s **2,475.00**
Sioux, hide, blue, white, brown, yellow, green, and red beaded geometric pattern, fringe dec, c1910 . . **4,950.00**

Jacket, 22 x 35″, hide, fringed, white, yellow, green, orange, and blue beaded floral motif, fur trim, 1870s . . **6,325.00**

Knife Sheath
6⅜″ l, beaded front with white heart red and yellow, green background, tin dangles, beaded tip tassel and cones, Sioux **355.00**
12″ l, canvas panel with white, blue, red, and green classic design, tin cone and dyed horsehair suspensions, Cheyenne, c1890. . . . . **1,430.00**

Leggings, pr, 13½″ l, hide and muslin cloth, blue, white, red, and green beaded design, Sioux, c1910 . . . . . . **610.00**

Moccasins, pr
3⅞″ l, baby, red, gold, and dark blue beaded design on toe and heel . . . **150.00**
8½″ l, hide, white, blue, pink, green, and red beaded floral design, yellow cloth piping, Crow, late 19th C. . . . **550.00**
9″ l, hide, dark blue, crimson, and yellow beaded design, Blackfoot, late 19th C. **330.00**
10½″ l, hide, blue, red, pink, white, green, and faceted steel beaded design, Sioux, c1880 . . . . **2,530.00**
11″ l, hide, blue, yellow, red, and green beaded geometric design, Arapaho, 1880s **770.00**
17″ h, hightop, sinew sewn buckskin, yellow ocher, red, blue, yellow, and green beaded geometric pattern, white background, Arapaho, c1890 **2,310.00**

Necklace, 21″ l, hide, braided sweetgrass and bead design, dark and light blue and yellow beads, hide fringes, late 19th C **440.00**

Parfleche, 8 x 14½″, hide and red stroud cloth, geometric designs, red, yellow, blue, and green, Sioux, 19th C **330.00**

Pipe Bag
22″ l, hide, gold, blue, green, red, and pink geometric beadwork panel on one side, reverse with blue, green, red, and white beaded dec, blue, black, and pumpkin beaded edge, Blackfoot, c1920 . . . . **425.00**
25″ l, geometric beaded designs, dark blue, yellow, green, and white heart red, Cheyenne blue background, quilled tassel and parfleche slats. . **2,420.00**

Pouch
6¾ x 4¾″, Blackfoot design, spot stitch beading, lazy stitch in central design, maroon, green, dark blue, yellow, pink, and white heart red, light blue background **300.00**
11″ l, hide, painted yellow ocher, red, yellow, and blue beadwork designs, quill wrapped fringe, Sioux, late 19th C. **775.00**
16″ l, buckskin, beaded yellow, white, and blue geometric designs, hide fringe, attached strap with white, blue, and red beaded ends, c1870 **1,100.00**

Rattle, 14″ l, wood hoop with hide covering, painted cross design, hide wrapped handle, tin cone suspensions, late 19th C **330.00**

Saddlebag, 14 x 70″, buffalo hide and canvas, geometric beadwork dec, blue, yellow, red, and green beads, white background, long hide fringe, Sioux, late 19th C **3,575.00**

Stick Game, 9″ l, buffalo ribs, painted and dec, hide pouch with red, white, and blue geometric beaded design, Blackfoot, c1910 . . . . **1,210.00**

Vest, child's, 15″ l, calico cloth, gold, silver, green, white, and translucent floral beadwork, pale blue background, Sioux, c1900. . . . . **1,100.00**

WEST AND SOUTHWEST

Basket
4¹¹⁄₁₆″ d, 4⁷⁄₁₆″ h, corn seed, aniline design, red, green, and faded purple, Hopi **65.00**
13″ d, coiled, four Crow Mother Kachinas, brown stitching, cream background, Hopi, c1920 . . **1,100.00**
14½″ d, geometric pattern, Pima, c1920 . . . . **385.00**

Blanket, Navajo
32½ x 46″, child's, wool, serrated interlocking diamonds and cross mo-

tifs, indigo blue, aniline red and green, natural white, c1880s **5,500.00**

45" sq, wool, natural black and white, aniline red, c1915. . . . . **715.00**

56 x 75", wool, interlocking concentric stepped diamonds, aniline orange and red, natural white and brown, c1890 . . . . **1,320.00**

Bowl

6½" d, ceramic, blackware, carved Avanyu, Santa Clara **440.00**

7⅜" d, pottery, white slip, umber design, incised rim. **75.00**

7⅞" d, 3¾" h, pottery, red ocher floral design, umber geometric design, chalk white slip **75.00**

8⅜" d, 3½" h, basketry, yucca, five martynia female figures, Papago . . **110.00**

8⅝" l, 3⅝" h, basketry, yucca, oval, eight martynia male figures, Papago. **135.00**

10" d, basketry, twined, half twist overlay design, Pomo **95.00**

11¼" l, 4" h, basketry, oval, three rod coil, martynia design. **195.00**

11½" d, brown geometric and bird motifs, orange slip, Hopi, early 20th C **610.00**

13" d, 3½" h, basketry, stepped geometric design, black martynia and willow, Apache. **495.00**

Doll, Kachina, Hopi

9" h, carved and painted wood, 1920s **1,100.00**

12½" h, cottonwood, painted, pop eyes, ears, and snout, red, white, and black, early 20th C. **3,850.00**

Dough Bowl, ceramic

14" d, bold black geometric design, cream slip, Santo Domingo, late 19th C. **1,650.00**

15" d

Acoma, brown, geometric and foliate designs, white slip, 1940s . . **1,375.00**

Zia, brown and black floral motifs, cream slip, scalloped rim, late 19th C **1,650.00**

Dress, 39" l, woven black wool, red and royal blue bands with embellished serrated diamonds, shoulder with stepped crosses, Navajo, 1920s **550.00**

Drum, 9" d, hide with painted image of Thunderbird, black, green, white, and brown. **1,045.00**

Jar

6" h, ceramic, blackware, black on black design of Avanyu and serpent, San Ildefonso, c1950 . . . . . . **1,650.00**

7⅜" h, 8¾" d, pottery, creamy buff slip over red slip bottle bottom, black design, Santo Domingo. **300.00**

7⅜" h, 9¾" d, pottery, white slip, red umber bottle bottom, umber geometric design, Acoma. **375.00**

9½" h, 10" d, pottery, cream slip, polychrome design, red ocher and black, redware bottle bottom with red band, San Ildefonso. **1,400.00**

Kilt, Kachina, 20 x 23½", handspun cotton, fringed, Germantown wool embroidery, red, black, blue–green, and indigo blue yarn, Hopi **1,320.00**

Manta, 28" sq, child's, wool, natural brown and white handspun yarn, alternating brown and white bars. **1,320.00**

Olla

10¼" d, coiled wood and willow, geometric designs, horses, dogs, and arrowhead motifs, Apache. **2,475.00**

10½" d, ceramic, white slip, brown geometric painted designs, Acoma, 1920s **770.00**

12" h, ceramic, black geometric designs, cream field, Acoma, c1910 . **5,500.00**

16" h, geometric designs, Papago, 1920s **165.00**

21" h, interlocking diamonds and checkerboard design, Apache, late 19th C. **7,700.00**

Plate, 6¼" d, ceramic, blackware, black on black feather design, 1950s **725.00**

Pot

5¾" d, ceramic, polychrome dec, brown and red, cream slip, sgd "Adelle L Nampeyo," Hopi **330.00**

7½" d, ceramic, geometric design and deer with heart lines, Zuni, 1950s . **385.00**

Rasping Stick, pr, 14" l, carved wood, bird effigies dec, Pueblo, early 20th C **550.00**

Rug, Navajo

33 x 72", serrated design, aniline red and orange, carded brown and natural handspun wool **440.00**

35 x 61", bold storm pattern, double dye red, orange, dark brown, and natural hand carded and spun wool, c1920 . . . . **1,320.00**

45 x 72", six Yei figures holding dance rattles, rainbow bars, corn plants, feather motifs, and glyphs, red, orange, green, turquoise, and green aniline yarns, c1915 . . . . **2,200.00**

49 x 73", cross and serrated diamond design, dark brown, red, airbrush tan, and natural and carded and spun wool **685.00**

50 x 65", handspun wool, wove serrated zigzags and stepped squares, red, blue, and white aniline dyes, c1880 . . . . **2,145.00**

57 x 98", wool, three columns of interlocking serrated diamonds, natural black and white, aniline red, and orange, c1930 . . . . **1,100.00**

66 x 106", wool, natural black, gray, brown, white, and aniline red, two

central diamond motifs, angular hooks, four red crosses, c1930 . . .	1,650.00
Saddle Blanket, 31 x 50″, hand carded and spun wool, dark brown and red star corners	385.00
Sash, Kachina, 43″ l, Germantown and cochineal dyed wool on cotton, native wool weft, two fringed panels, brocaded, red, green, indigo blue, and black, Hopi, late 19th C	610.00
Serape	
53 x 82″, wool, white, blue, and green stepped open diamond design, salmon red background, handspun natural and aniline dyes	7,700.00
68 x 71″, wool, natural and aniline dyes, red, blue, black, and white yarns, Navajo, c1880	17,050.00
Tapestry, 21½ x 28″, wool, six Yei figures, natural white, beige, gray, yellow, pink, brown, and turquoise, gold brown field, mounted and framed, c1960s.	330.00
Tray, basketry	
10″ d, martynia star design	195.00
11½″ d, stepped lines, attached leather thong, Pima, 1920s	220.00
12″ d, eight small dogs, three arrowhead motifs, and central whirlwind design, Apache, late 19th C	610.00
13⅝″ d, geometric fret design, martynia and willow, Pima	165.00
14″ d, cactus motifs, Papago, c1920	165.00
15½″ d, six crosses and zigzag, mounted triangle designs, Apache, c1890	3,300.00
20″ d, three dogs, four whirling logs, and whirlwind design, Apache, late 19th C.	1,925.00

INDIAN TREE PATTERN

History: The Indian Tree pattern is a popular pattern of porcelain made from the last half of the 19th century until the present. The pattern, consisting of an Oriental crooked tree branch, landscape, exotic flowers, and foliage, is found in predominantly greens, pinks, blues, and oranges on a white ground. Several English potteries, including Burgess and Leigh, Coalport, and Maddock, made wares with the Indian Tree pattern.

Reference: Susan and Al Bagdade, *Warman's English & Continental Pottery & Porcelain, Second Edition,* Wallace–Homestead, 1991.

Berry Set, 10″ d master bowl, six 5″ d serving bowls, Maddox, price for seven piece set.	165.00
Bowl, 8½″ d, ftd, Minton	48.00
Butter Dish, cov, Johnson Bros	45.00
Cake Plate, 10½″ d, Coalport	40.00

Plate, 10¼″ d, Copeland–Spode, $25.00.

Creamer	
Breakfast, Coalport	15.00
Large, semi scalloped, Coalport . . .	25.00
Cup and Saucer, full scallop, Coalport	25.00
Egg Cup, 4″ h, Maddock & Sons	20.00
Fruit Bowl, full scallop, Coalport	12.00
Gravy Boat, Brownfield & Sons, c1856	35.00
Plate	
6″ d, bread and butter, full scallop, Coalport	8.00
9½″ d, dinner, KPM	15.00
Relish Dish, semi scalloped, Coalport	20.00
Salt and Pepper Shakers, pr, Coalport	50.00
Sauce Dish, 5″ d, Johnson Bros	8.00
Soup Plate, 7½″ d, Coalport	20.00
Soup Tureen, 10″ w, matching cov and ladle, Maddock & Sons	150.00
Sugar, open, semi scalloped, Coalport	20.00
Vegetable Bowl, oval, smooth edge, Coalport.	60.00

INK BOTTLES

History: Ink was sold in glass or pottery bottles in the early 1700s in England. Retailers mixed their own formula and bottled it. The commercial production of ink did not begin in England until the late 18th century and in America until the early 19th century.

Initially, ink was supplied in pint or quart bottles, often of poor manufacture, from which smaller bottles could be filled. By the mid 19th century, when writing implements were improved, emphasis was placed on making an "untippable" bottle. Shapes ranging from umbrella style to turtles were tried. Since ink bottles were displayed, shaped or molded bottles became popular.

The advent of the fountain pen relegated the ink bottle to the back drawer. Bottles lost their decorative design and became merely functional items.

References: Ralph and Terry Kovel, *The Kovels'*

Bottle Price List, Ninth Edition, Crown Publishers, 1992; Carlo and Dot Sellari, *The Standard Old Bottle Price Guide,* Collector Books, 1989.

Periodical: *Antique Bottle and Glass Collector,* PO Box 187, East Greenville, PA 18041.

Additional Listings: See *Warman's Americana & Collectibles* for more examples.

Aquamarine, applied lip and collar, c1880s, 3″ h, $15.00.

Allings High School Ink, 1⅞″ h, aqua	150.00
Bertinguoit, 2″ h, 2⅜″ d, cylindrical, domed, olive amber, sheared mouth, pontil scar	140.00
Blackwood & Co, 2½″ h, pottery, rect base	50.00
Carter's, ½ pt, emerald green	25.00
Cone shape, octagonal, cobalt blue	750.00
Davids & Black, 4¾″ h, emerald green, open pontil	110.00
Dunbars Black Ink, 6¾″ h, aqua	55.00
E Waters Troy, NY, aqua, pint	325.00
Farley's, 3½″ h, octagonal, olive amber, pontil	165.00
Figural, 5½″ l, barrel, aqua, ftd	100.00
G H Gilbert Co, West Brookfield, MA, octagonal cone shape, orig label	140.00
Gross & Robinson's American Writing Fluid, 3⅞″ h, aqua, pontil	385.00
Harrison's Columbian Ink, octagonal, light green	60.00
Hill's Pennsylvania Writing Ink, 4⅛″ h, twelve sided, aqua	80.00
Lynn Burnishing Ink, 7½″ h, honey amber	18.00
NE Plus Ultra Fluid, 2⅝″ h, sq, house form, aqua, sheared mouth, pontil	350.00
Parker Quink, 2 oz, orig box	5.00
Pitkin Type, 1⅜″ h, 2¼″ w, sq, beveled corners, ribbed and swirled, olive amber, disc mouth, pontil	650.00
Robert Keller Inks & Mucilage, qt, aqua, spout	45.00
S Fine Black Ink, 2⅞″ h, cylindrical,	

bright medium green, inward rolled mouth, pontil scar	425.00
Shaeffer's Skript, 2 oz, orig box	5.00
T & M Ink, 2⅜″ h, aqua, dark green swirl, rolled lip, pontil	95.00
Umbrella, 2¼″ h, 2⅜″ d, octagonal, yellow olive, sheared mouth, pontil	220.00
Waterlow & Sons, 7½″ h, pottery	25.00
Winslow's Improved Chemical Indelible Ink, 5″ h, olive amber, label	330.00

INKWELLS

History: The majority of commonly found inkwells were produced in the United States and Europe from the early 1800s to the 1930s. The most popular materials were glass and pottery because these substances resisted the corrosive effects of ink.

Inkwells were a sign of the office or a wealthy individual. The common man tended to dip his ink directly from the bottle. The period from 1870 to 1920 represented a "golden age" when inkwells in elaborate designs were produced.

References: William E. Covill, Jr., *Inkbottles and Inkwells,* William S. Sullwold Publishing, 1971; Betty and Ted Rivera, *Inkstands and Inkwells: A Collector's Guide, Second Edition,* Crown Publishers, 1973.

Collectors' Club: The Society of Inkwell Collectors, 5136 Thomas Avenue So., Minneapolis, MN 55410.

Additional Listings: See *Warman's Americana & Collectibles* for more examples.

Art Pottery, 3″ d, figural, artichoke, matching loose lid, natural colors, art pottery insert, artichoke blossom on lid	125.00
Gilt Bronze, 12″ w, 6⅞″ h, Art Nouveau, two nude women in surf, inkwell lid in form of crab, brown composition base, Vve Leonie Ledru, France, c1900	525.00
Glass	
1½″ h, 2¼″ d, blown three mold, cylindrical, medium olive amber, disc mouth, pontil	130.00
1⅝″ h, 2⅛″ d, pitkin type, cylindrical, forest green, thirty–six swirled ribs, funnel mouth, pontil	500.00
1⅞″ h, 2″ d, pitkin type, cylindrical, aquamarine, ribbed and swirled, sheared mouth, pontil	1,100.00
2″ h, 2⅝″ d, melon form, yellowish olive mouth, pontil	1,800.00
2″ sq, vaseline, Daisy and Button, matching loose lid	175.00
2½″ d, clear, dome shaped, sixteen point star on base, round brass hinged lid	95.00

4" d, round, irid, fluted, ribbed, brass
hinged lid, orig glass insert **395.00**
4" h, fountain, yellow and white striped
well, brass and marble base,
ground mouth with metal ring,
smooth base **350.00**
Blue, brass hinged lid, fitted pierced
brass tray, hp floral dec **225.00**
Marble, 9½" l, Sienna, modeled after
sarcophagus of Lucius Seipio, Italian,
19th C **1,980.00**
Metal, figural, tree stump, whippet,
painted white, orig insert **125.00**

**Pot Metal, WWI helmet shape, 2½" h,
$65.00.**

Porcelain
1¼" sq inkwell, attached sq white saucer, dainty floral dec, hinged lid . . . **95.00**
2½" sq inkwell, hp, round lid, marked
"Herend Hungary" **135.00**
3" d, bird's nest, large bird, three eggs,
and snake, multicolored coleslaw
on inkwell, Staffordshire **195.00**
Oriental Boy, figural, sitting on flat
stand, groove for pen, hat as lid,
colorful costume. **80.00**
Sterling Silver, allover engraved motifs
set with various faceted and buff top
agates, top faceted citrine, vermeil
int., Scottish hallmarks, c1899 . . . . . **1,430.00**
Stone, 2½" d, tan marbleized, curling,
hinged lid **75.00**

IRONS

History: Ironing devices have been used for
many centuries, with the earliest references dating
from 1100. Irons from the Medieval, Renaissance,
and early industrial era can be found in Europe but
are rare. Fine brass-engraved irons and hand-
wrought irons dominated the period prior to 1850.
After 1850 irons began a series of rapid evolution-
ary changes.

Between 1850 and 1910 irons were heated in
four ways: 1) a hot metal slug was inserted into the
body, 2) a burning solid, such as coal or charcoal,
was placed in the body, 3) a liquid or gas, such as
alcohol, gasoline, or natural gas, was fed from an
external tank and burned in the body, and 4) con-
duction heating, usually drawing heat from a stove
top.

Electric irons are just beginning to find favor
among iron collectors.

References: Esther S. Berney, *A Collectors
Guide To Pressing Irons And Trivets,* Crown Pub-
lishers, 1977; A. H. Glissman, *The Evolution Of
The Sad Iron,* published by author, 1970; Brian
Jewell, *Smoothing Irons, A History And Collector's
Guide,* Wallace–Homestead, 1977, out of print;
Judy (author) and Frank (illustrator) Politzer, *Early
Tuesday Morning: More Little Irons and Trivets,*
published by authors, 1986; Judy and Frank Pol-
itzer, *Tuesday's Children,* published by authors,
1977.

Collectors' Clubs: Friends of Ancient Smoothing Irons, PO Box 215, Carlsbad, CA 92008; Midwest Sad Iron Collectors Club, 2828 West Ave.,
Burlington, IA 52601.

Museums: Henry Ford Museum, Dearborn, MI;
Shelburne Museum, Shelburne, VT; Sturbridge Village, Sturbridge, MA.

Additional Listings: See *Warman's Americana
& Collectibles* for more examples.

Advisors: David and Sue Irons.

Charcoal
Acme, lift off top **130.00**
Bullet Nose European, L shape
handle. **95.00**

**Goffering, brass, cast iron insert, En-
glish, c1700, $500.00.**

Children's
- Block grip type, ACW 70.00
- Enterprise, various sizes, holes in handle. 120.00
- Swan
  - Painted red, white, and blue, pint striping 150.00
  - Unpainted, iron, various sizes, mold mark 95.00

Electric, Deco, Sauders, "Silver Streak," pyrex, red or blue 60.00

Fluter
- Combination, hinged front, wire clip closure 140.00
- Machine, brass rolls, black patent with stenciled star 250.00

Goffering, missing heater
- Brass, miniature, 2½" barrel, figured base, S shape stand 150.00
- Wrougth Iron, spider base, four feet 350.00

Liquid Fuel
- Coleman, gasoline, porcelain, blue . 65.00
- Vulcan, Wm Crane Co, natural gas 115.00

Slug
- Brass Box English, trap door, various sizes. 150.00
- L F Dean's, removable top, 6¾" l . . 175.00

Specialty
- Hat, brass, curved ridges on bottom, wood handle 125.00
- Sleeve, Ober, detachable handle . . 85.00

IRONWARE

History: Iron, a metallic element that occurs abundantly in combined forms, has been known for centuries. Items made from iron range from the utilitarian to the decorative. Early hand–forged ironwares are of considerable interest to Americana collectors.

References: Frank T. Barnes, *Hooks, Rings & Other Things: An Illustrated Index of New England Iron, 1600–1860,* The Christopher Publishing House, 1988; *Griswold Cast Iron: A Price Guide,* L–W Book Sales, 1993; Kathryn McNerney, *Antique Iron Identification and Values,* Collector Books, 1984, 1993 value update; Dana G. Morykan and Harry L. Rinker, *Warman's Country Antiques & Collectibles, Second Edition,* Wallace–Homestead, 1994; George C. Neumann, *Early American Antique Country Furnishings: Northeastern America, 1650–1880's,* L–W Book Sales, 1984, 1993 reprint; Herbert, Peter, and Nancy Schiffer, *Antique Iron,* Schiffer Publishing, 1979.

Periodicals: *Cast Iron Cookware News,* 28 Angela Ave., San Anselmo, CA 94960; *Griswold Cast Iron Collectors' News & Marketplace,* PO Box 521, North East, PA 16428.

Collectors' Club: Griswold and Cast Iron Cookware Assoc., PO Box 8, Perrysburg, NY 14129.

Additional Listings: Banks, Boot Jacks, Doorstops, Fireplace Equipment, Food Molds, Irons, Kitchen Collectibles, Lamps, and Tools.

Andirons, pr, wrought, knife blade shaft, brass urn finial and detail, penny feet, marked "IC" 550.00

Boot Scraper, 10¼" w, 17½" h, wrought, outward curved ends, pitted 115.00

Bottle Opener
- Advertising, Bishop & Babcock, 6⅝" h, cast, nickel finish, cork screw. . . 95.00
- Cockatoo on perch, 5½" h, cast, polychrome dec 75.00

Broiler
- 14" d, 26½" l, twistwork grill, 18th C 225.00
- 15" d, 22¾" l, elaborate serpentine grillwork, 18th C. 330.00

Candleholder, miner's, 7½" l, Sticking Tommy, wrought 70.00

Candle Stand, 33" h, wrought, adjustable candle arm, two sockets 30.00

Candlestick
- 7⅛" h, adjustable, wide spiral stem, turned wood base 165.00
- 7¼" h, pushup marked "Fisher," lip hanger, brass ring 140.00
- 7¾" h, adjustable, thin spiral stem, turned wood base 75.00
- 9" h, pushup, lip hanger, brass ring 275.00

Clothing Hook, 9" w, cast, eagle shape, snake in talons forms hook, gold paint 40.00

Dipper, 4¼" d, 12" l, cast, swivel lid, wrought handle 85.00

Door Knocker, 3¾" l, cast, basket of flowers, orig polychrome paint 30.00

Doorstop, cast
- 8" h, cat with bow, black paint 75.00
- 12½" l, greyhound, red paint 150.00

Door Stop, Wild Roses, multicolored pastel flowers, yellow ribbon and basket, Hubley No. 475, 7¼" h, $125.00.

Fireplace Crane, 24″ l, 16″ h, wrought, scroll work and three hooks **50.00**

Figure, hat, 7″ h, cast **125.00**

Fork, 19½″ l, wrought, two tines with turned down ends **30.00**

Frame, 19 x 11½″, reticulated scroll crest, Cluette Peabody and Co. **45.00**

Garden Urn, 16″ h, cast, rebolted bowl, white repaint. **275.00**

Herb Grinder, 16″ h, cast, 18th C **450.00**

Hitching Post, cast, horsehead, stylized detail, black repaint, repair, 15″ h . . . **415.00**

Jug, 7″ h, barrel shape, handle, enamel coated int., marked "OSIPIS" on side, early 19th C **90.00**

Kettle, 5″ d, cast, caldron style, three short legs, late 18th–early 19th C . . . **75.00**

Ladle, 19⅜″ l, wrought **55.00**

Lamp

Crusie, 12½″ l, double, scrollwork, delicate hanger **330.00**

Pan, 15″ l, orig trammel **165.00**

Lock, 4¼ x 7″, box, cast **40.00**

Meat Hook, 8″ d, 13½″ h, wrought, crown shape, four hooks **210.00**

Nut Cracker, 11″ l, cast, figural, dog, nickel finish, marked "The L A Althoff Mfg Co, Chicago" **45.00**

Paperweight, 9″ l, cast, souvenir of Bonney–Floyd Company **55.00**

Peel

37½″ l, large blade, knob finial on handle. **75.00**

44″ l, 18th C **110.00**

Roaster, 22¾″ l, hooks fasten to open fire grate, adjustable tin pan with hood, wood handle **175.00**

Rotary Broiler, 13″ d, 24″ l, wrought, shaped handles **110.00**

Rush Light

29½″ h, simple design, penny feet . **275.00**

36⅛″ h, adjustable, tripod base, penny feet. **550.00**

39″ h, wrought, tripod base, twisted detail and hooks, late 19th c **470.00**

41½″ h, graceful base, penny feet, attached wood yarn box **1,800.00**

Sewing Clamp, 4″ l, table type, wrought **25.00**

Shooting Gallery Target, cast

4¼″ l, bird **40.00**

5½″ l, duck **65.00**

Skillet

5¼″ d, cast, three short legs, handle, late 18th–early 19th C **70.00**

6½″ d, wrought, three legs, 11″ l handle with hook end. **220.00**

8½″ d, cast, 9″ l handle, American, 19th C. **75.00**

12″ d, wrought, three legs, 19″ l handle **275.00**

Spatula, wrought, keyhole end

15¾″ l **30.00**

19″ l **110.00**

Tea Kettle, cov, cast, swing–out lid, sloped spout, South Co–Op Foundry Co, Rome, GA **50.00**

Tether, 44″ h, figure, standing, wearing black pants and white shirt, right arm holding tether ring, yellow sq plinth base, 19th C. **1,650.00**

Toaster, 16″ l, wrought, down–hearth, stylized tree designs with spiral arches **275.00**

Trammel, wrought

12¾″ l **95.00**

19½″ l, sawtooth **150.00**

Trivet, 7¼″ l, wrought, heart shape . . **150.00**

Utensil Rack, 12½″ l, wrought, tooled bar, tooled finials, spike ends, marked "JB". **385.00**

Waffle Iron, 13¾″ l, hand wrought, heart design, c1835. . . . . **175.00**

IVORY

History: Ivory, a yellowish–white organic material, comes from the teeth or tusks of animals and lends itself well to carving. It has been used for centuries by many cultures for artistic and utilitarian items.

Ivory from elephants shows a reticulated crisscross pattern in a cross section. Hippopotamus teeth, walrus tusks, whale teeth, narwhal tusks, and boar tusks also are ivory sources. Vegetable ivory, bone, stag horn, and plastic are ivory substitutes which often confuse collectors.

For information on how to identify real ivory, see Bernard Rosett's "Is It Genuine Ivory" in Sandra Andacht's *Oriental Antiques & Art: An Identification and Value Guide* (Wallace–Homestead, 1987).

Reference: Gloria and Robert Mascarelli, *Oriental Antiques*, Wallace–Homestead, 1992.

Periodical: *Netsuke and Ivory Carving Newsletter*, 3203 Adams Way, Ambler, PA 19002.

Note: Dealers and collectors should be familiar with the Endangered Species Act of 1973, amended in 1978, which limits the importation and sale of antique ivory and tortoiseshell items.

Bottle, 5½″ h, baluster type, carved continuous mountain scene and figures, mother–of–pearl plaque sgd "Shiun Kore–o Saku". **825.00**

Box, 4¼″ h, bust form with floral headdress, carved, Chinese **110.00**

Brush Pot, 4″ h, carved, figures and pavilions, Chinese, c1885 . . . . **1,000.00**

Bust, 8″ h, Madame Recamier, curly hair with wrapped band, arms hold shawl, raised on ebonized ivory fitted pedestal with crowned initial "R" & "J G," France, late 19th C **1,650.00**

Cane, 36½″ l, bamboo form, horse foreleg shape handle, 19th C **250.00**

Elephant Figurine, 1⅜ x 1¾″, $40.00.

landscape pines and figures, two
ring handles 475.00
18½″ h, flattened cylindrical, indented
neck, raised rect panel with figures
above continuous scene of women
and children in gardens, domed cov
with Foo lion finial, ring handles,
China, c1900, price for pair 1,050.00

JACK-IN-THE-PULPIT VASES

History: Jack–in–the–Pulpit glass vases, made
in the trumpet form, were in vogue during the late
19th and early 20th centuries. The vases were
made in a wide variety of patterns, colors, and
sizes.

Additional Listings: See specific glass categories.

Loetz type, olive green, 12″ h, $165.00.

Card Case, 4⅛″ l, carved, figures and
pavilions, Chinese, 19th C 500.00
Ceremonial Drum, oval, carved, cords
with stone beads 220.00
Cigarette Holder, carved 25.00
Crochet Hook, 6¼″ l, hand shape finial 45.00
Figure, carved
  5½″ h, Quan Yin holding bowl of fruit 80.00
  9″ h, peasant, low relief, hunched
    back, holding fishing rod and pipe,
    mounted on pedestal 880.00
  11″ l, five elephants ascending in size
    on curved bridge, carved base, sgd
    "Yoneyama" 190.00
Frame, 5¼″ h, oval, easel style, carved
dragon, scroll, and heart 60.00
Gavel, 8¼″ l, engraved scribe lines . . 250.00
Jagging Wheel, 4¾″ l, carved, heart
shape handle, mid 19th C 170.00
Ladle, 7⅛″ l, African 100.00
Memo Pad, 1½ x 2¾″, silver fittings . 25.00
Model, 15¾″ l, boat, carved zoomorphic
figures on ends, wood oars on each
side, cockswain in bow, Dutchman at
stern, diaper pattern hull, carved
cabin, 19th C 360.00
Napkin Ring, 2″ h, relief carved bird . 12.00
Pendant, 1 x 1½ x 2¼″, double dragon
design, orig silk chord 150.00
Pie Crimper, 6¼″ l, pewter wheel, wood
handle 30.00
Shoehorn, 8½″ l, maiden and child . . 150.00
Snuff Bottle, bottle shape, carved vase
of flowers dec, repair, Chinese 55.00
Stand, 7″ h, pierced relief, pink and
cream flowers, peony and lotus flow-
ers, green stones 425.00
Vase
  4″ h, carved, four vertical ribs,
    Chinese, 18th C 500.00
  10″ h, ovoid, carved court ladies in
    musical pursuits, domed cov with

Amberina, 7″ h, honey amber stem and
applied wafer base, ruby red top 475.00
Burmese, Mt Washington
  6¾″ h, ruffled, yellow pastel rust and
    tan ground, autumn leaves, blue
    berries, and tendrils dec 485.00
  8″ h, flesh tone to yellow, pink top,
    yellow refired border 585.00
Cased
  6½″ h, white ext., shaded maroon int.,
    ruffled 120.00
  7¼″ h, creamy opaque ext., white and
    yellow flowers, green leaves, gold
    trim, deep rose pink int., amber
    edge, ormolu leaf feet 125.00
Iridescent amethyst and gold luster,
feather veining 200.00
Loetz, 13½″ h, freeblown floriform, colorless, striated gold amber pulled
feather dec, gold and blue irid surface 1,430.00
Opalescent, 7½″ h, chartreuse green,
ruffled 75.00

Peachblow, 7½″ h, blue–gray, cherry blossom pink ruffled edge	2,450.00
Spatter, 8½″ h, white, green, and cranberry	110.00
Stevens & Williams, 6¾″ h, rainbow swirl, trefoil crimped top	485.00
Vaseline, 6″ h, clear bulging opalescent body, cranberry flared rim, ftd.	145.00

JADE

History: Jade is the generic name for two distinct minerals, nephrite and jadeite. Nephrite, an amphibole mineral from Central Asia and used in pre–18th-century pieces, has a waxy surface and ranges in hues from white to almost a black green. Jadeite, a pyroxene mineral found in Burma and used from 1700 to the present, has a glassy appearance and comes in various shades of white, green, yellow–brown, and violet.

Jade cannot be carved because of its hardness. Shapes are achieved through sawing and grinding with wet abrasives, such as quartz, crushed garnets, and carborundum.

Prior to 1800 few pieces are signed or dated. Stylistic considerations are used for dating. The Ch'ien Lung period (1736–95) is considered the "golden age" of jade.

Reference: Gloria and Robert Mascarelli, *Warman's Oriental Antiques,* Wallace–Homestead, 1992.

Periodical: Bulletin of the Friends of Jade, 5004 Ensign St., San Diego, CA 92117.

Museum: Avery Brundage Collection, de Young Museum, San Francisco, CA.

Floral Centerpiece, 21½″ w, 12½″ h, $325.00.

Bowl	
5″ d, translucent ivory to mottled white, russet striations, everted rim, ring foot	500.00
8¾″ d, spinach green, hemispherical, ftd, polished surface, sgd "H Wolf"	1,045.00
Box, cov, 3½ x 5½″, rect, translucent dark gray–green, pale white streaking, ftd, wood stand, incised six–character Quianlong mark	2,090.00
Brush Pot, 4¼″ h, scrolling cloud pattern, Chinese, 19th C.	310.00
Candlestick, pr, 12⅞″ h, dark green, carved low relief goose with outspread wings, stands on tortoise, head supports three tiered pricket, tripod bowl with int. carving, reticulated wood base with carved keyscroll motifs and floral scrolls	525.00
Cup, 4½″ h, white, boat shape, curved spout, dragon handles, Chinese	350.00
Dish, 5½″ d, octagonal, green spinach	140.00
Figure	
6¾″ h, grotto, wrinkled elephant and attendant on ledge beneath rocky outcropping and pine trees on front, reverse with gnarled pine and sage on flight of stairs with climbing monkey, China, late 17th C.	16,500.00
7⅛″ h, Meiren, standing, holding peach bough and hoe, mint green, China	1,980.00
Inkstone, 3⅝″ l, oval depression to one side, black and white mottling, incised rim band.	175.00
Knife Handle, 4½″ l, spinach green, archaistic form, Chinese, price for two piece set	525.00
Lamp, 29″ h, Goddess, Kuan Yin, standing, flowing cowl, robes, and jewels, child on one upraised arm, rosary and fly whisk in other.	1,600.00
Letter Opener, 10¾″ l, carved interlocking C scrolls between keyfret bands handle, SS knife	250.00
Pitcher, 5⅜″ h, spiral and whirl circle bands, rope borders, angular strap handle.	525.00
Saucer, 4¼″ d, flared rim, deep green, brown mottling, short ring foot.	200.00
Snuff Bottle	
Grayish–white, mottled russet skin on one side, rose quartz stopper	550.00
Greenish–white, sloping shoulder, oval foot, 1800–80, pr.	600.00
Ovoid, carved leafy fruiting melon vines and rat, mottled grayish–white, russet inclusions, green glass twig and leaf form stopper, late 19th C	660.00
Urn, 8″ h, ovoid form, incised taotie mask dec, narrow neck, handles, domed lid with suspending carved chains, yoke shape hanger.	700.00
Vase	
7″ h, ovoid, nephrite, animal headed ring handles, stork and lotus scroll on cov.	500.00
8½″ h, dark green, spade form, carved	

low relief dec, keyscroll band, russet inclusions, natural fissure cracks. **610.00**

JAPANESE AND CHINESE CERAMICS

History: The Chinese pottery tradition has existed for thousands of years. By the sixteenth century, Chinese ceramic wares were being exported to India, Persia, and Egypt. The Ming dynasty (1368–1643) saw the strong development of glazed earthenwares and shapes. During the Ch'ing dynasty, the Ch'ien Lung period (1736–95) marked the golden age of interchange with the West.

Trade between China and the West began in the sixteenth century when the Portuguese established Macao. The Dutch entered the trade early in the seventeenth century. With the establishment of the English East India Company, all of Europe was seeking Chinese–made pottery and porcelain. Styles, shapes, and colors were developed to suit Western tastes. The tradition continued until the late nineteenth century.

Like the Chinese, the Japanese spent centuries developing their ceramic arts. Each region established its own forms, designs, and glazes. Individual artists added to the uniqueness.

Japanese ceramics began to be exported to the West in the mid 19th century. Their beauty quickly made them a favorite of the patrician class. The ceramic tradition continues into the 20th century. Modern artists enjoy equal fame with older counterparts.

Reference: Gloria and Robert Mascarelli, *Warman's Oriental Antiques,* Wallace–Homestead, 1992.

Periodical: *Orientalia Journal,* PO Box 94, Little Neck, NY 11363.

Museums: Art Institute of Chicago, Chicago, IL; Asian Art Museum of San Francisco, San Francisco, CA; George Walter Vincent Smith Art Museum, Springfield, MA.

Additional Listings: Canton, Fitzhugh, Imari, Kutani, Nanking, Rose Medallion, and Satsuma.

CHINESE

Bowl, 5½" d, red and gold dragon, bird and cloud dec, blue floral int., late 18th C. **450.00**
Brush Pot, cov, 3½" d, blue landscape design, 18th C **160.00**
Charger, 10¾" d, blue and white, crane and floral dec, Ming Dynasty **300.00**
Cup, 4⅜" h, inverted bell form, tapered cylindrical foot, copper red glaze, orange peel texture, six character Qianlong mark **1,045.00**

Creamer, Sumida Guwa, figural, black robe, unglazed clay face, 4½" h, $160.00.

Dish
  6" d, flowers and butterfly, polychrome dec. **220.00**
  6¼" d, flaring sides, cream glaze . .   **220.00**
Figure
  7" h, green and yellow bird, gray rocky plinth, price for pair. **425.00**
  15¼" h, rooster, white, early 19th C   **1,450.00**
Fishbowl, 20" d, powder blue and white, figural scenes, Kangxi style, 19th C, minor damage. **660.00**
Fruit Bowl, 9½" d, floral spray dec, blue border **75.00**
Jar, 7½" h, blue and white dec **55.00**
Plate, 8½" d, blue and white, Ming Dynasty **375.00**
Punch Bowl, 14½" d, flared sides, painted chrysanthemums with yellow ground int. and ext., early 19th C . . .   **850.00**
Vase
  8½" h, cov, flattened spherical form, butterflies flying over plants and flowers, green, yellow, and blue enamel, orange ground. **675.00**
  15" h, baluster shape, flaring rim, blue and white, early 19th C. **80.00**
  20" h, cov, ovoid, gold floral sprays, blue ground, carved teak base, rim chip, early 19th C. **440.00**

CHINESE EXPORT

Bowl
  5⅝" d, crest and floral spray dec, early 19th C. **275.00**
  8" d, Oriental figures in various activities, polychrome dec **125.00**
  10" d, Nanking dec **260.00**
  10⅜" d, three cov urns with flowers around side, polychrome dec. **110.00**

14⅛" d, floral center with paneled floral border. 950.00

Candlestick, 6⅜" h, armorial dec, blue, red, and gold 440.00

Charger, 13⅝" d, two sheep and rose bush dec, three floral panels on rim. . 1,400.00

Dish, 6¼" d, grapes, staff, hat, horn, locket, and flag, polychrome dec. . . . 75.00

Figure, 6½" h, pigeon, white, price for pair 750.00

Mug, gold floral dec and striping 75.00

Plate, 7⅝" d, romantic landscape dec, sloop, manor house, and two figures with dog, sepia and gold 275.00

Platter
13¼" l, oblong serpentine form, floral spray dec, early 19th C. 675.00
13½" l, oval, center floral spray, red, green, and blue star border, c1800 220.00
14¾" l, Canton dec, first half 19th C 400.00
15¼" l, oval, reticulated border, yellow inner border, first quarter 19th C . . 425.00
16" l, octagonal, Nanking dec, ornate floral border, early 19th C 550.00
16¾" l, octagonal, blue and white floral dec, 18th/19th C 275.00
17¼" l, mandarin rose medallion, landscape dec border, veritas vincitomnia crest, early 19th C. 1,600.00
19½" l, oval, Canton dec, first half 19th C. 770.00

Punch Bowl
11¼" d, teahouse dec, ornate Nanking border 290.00
12" d, dragon and cloud dec, floral int., red scrolled border. 425.00
16" d, mandarin figural reserves on aqua ground, int. with figural reserve and floral border 2,300.00

Punch Pot, two figural reserves, blue, gold, green, and red floral background, early 19th C 550.00

Sauceboat, 7¼" l, molded oval reserves, floral sprays, horn with blossoms, multicolored enamel dec, diaper and floral border int. and ext., applied double strap handle, lozenge form saucers, price for pair 725.00

Soup Tureen, cov
14" l, blue chantilly dec, white ground, molded basketwork borders, strapwork handles, fruit finial, matching undertray, late 18th C, price for pair 3,300.00
16½" l, oval, serpentine, blue flowers, trees, and leaves dec, plume finial, 18/19th C 1,050.00

Teabowl and Saucer, floral int., chocolate brown glaze ext., handleless, 18th C 110.00

Teapot, cov
Drum shape, shield with "ITW" monogram, blue border, gilt berry finial, 18th/19th C 325.00

Garden scene with family, gilt handle and spout, 18th C 350.00

Tureen, 8" l, cov, oval, Fitzhugh dec, rustic strap handle. 425.00

Vase, 18⅛" h, cov, rect urn shape, rich mandarin dec, gilt dragon handles . . 2,600.00

Waste Bowl, 5½" d, floral dec, fluted sides, early 19th C. 165.00

JAPANESE

Bowl, 6¾" d, painted iron–red, green, deep turquoise, black, gray, and gold int., chrysanthemum spray tied with tasseled gilt ribbon, molded base with incised petal border on ext., gold highlights, Arita, 18th C 1,150.00

Dish, 10" d, blue and white dec, 18/19th C. 100.00

Ewer, 10½" h, red and gilt motif, riverscape and figure dec, loop handle, dragon finial, Kaga, late 19th C. 525.00

Nodder, 5½" h, Fukujurojin, seated figure, robe with knotted tie cord on chest, polychrome dec, Banko 450.00

Plate
8½" d
Kakiemon style, blue and white, dragons among clouds dec, Karakusa and Fugu mark, 19th C, price for pair. 310.00
Nabeshima style, relief and underglaze blue hibiscus dec, c1900. . 210.00
9¾" d, one relief carp and one underglaze blue carp dec, Fugu mark, c1900 . . . . 285.00

Sake Bottle, 7¼" h, rect, underglaze blue, two pine trees and three pavilions, stylized landscape scene, sq top with leaf and cloud dec, sq spout and pierced hole, Arita, late 17th C 675.00

KOREAN

Bowl
8¾" d, round, gray crackle glaze . . 130.00
9½" d, flaring sides, four blue panel dec. 75.00

Jar, 5" h, squat form, four loop handles, short spout 55.00

JASPERWARE

History: Jasperware is a hard, unglazed porcelain with a colored ground, varying from the most common blues and greens to lavender, yellow, red, or black. The white designs are applied in relief and often reflect a classical motif. Jasperware was first produced at Wedgwood's Etruria Works in 1775.

Josiah Wedgwood described it as "a fine terra–cotta of great beauty and delicacy proper for cameos."

Many other English potters, in addition to Wedgwood, produced jasperware. Two of the leaders were Adams and Copeland and Spode. Several continental potters, such as, Heubach, also produced the ware.

References: Susan and Al Bagdade, *Warman's English & Continental Pottery & Porcelain, 2nd Edition,* Wallace–Homestead, 1991; R. K. Henrywood, *Relief–Moulded Jugs, 1820–1900,* Antique Collector's Club.

Reproduction Alert: Jasperware still is made today, especially by Wedgwood.

Note: This category includes all pieces of jasperware which were made by companies other than Wedgwood. Wedgwood jasperware is found in the Wedgwood listing.

Cheese Dish, tan and white, marked "Adams," c1820, $400.00.

Box, 6" d, gray–green ground, white cameos of cherubs and lovebirds on cov . . . **175.00**

Casserole, 11⅛" l, oval, light blue dip, white applied classical angelic figures between male masks, unmarked, England, late 18th C, base hairlines . . . **1,100.00**

Cheese Dish, 11" d, 11¼" h, high domed blue cov, panels of white relief figures of classical ladies, rolled rim base with white relief flower and leaf band, acorn finial, Dudson Bros, England . . **550.00**

Creamer, 2½" h, sage green ground, pale pink frolicking Kewpies, sgd "O'Neill" **175.00**

Hatpin, 4½" l, star form, multifaceted steel beading surrounded by blue jasper dip button, white floret in relief, England, late 18th C **440.00**

Jewelry, brooch, 1⅝ x 2⅛", oval, pale blue jasper dip, white classical figure,

Turner imp mark, late 18th C, 14K gold frame **275.00**

Jug, 4⅞" h, 4⅜" d, blue ground, white relief hunting scene with men on horses, dogs, and stag, white relief rim band, Copeland **75.00**

Pitcher, 7⅛ h, 5" d, dark blue ground, cylindrical, band of white relief floral swags around rim, band of small white classical figures at base, angled white handle, Copeland **110.00**

Plaque, oval
2½ x 3¼", dark steel blue, white applied portraits of Lord Howe and Napoleon Bonaparte, brass frames, imp marks, England, c1800, price for pair **385.00**

3⅜ x 4½", solid blue, white classical relief figures, Enoch Wood imp marks, late 18th C, brass frame, price for set of three **375.00**

5¾" d, sage green ground, white relief angel beside two children, white relief floral border, Germany, late 19th or early 20th C **75.00**

6" d, sage green ground, white relief of Cupid shooting arrow at seated lady, Germany. **75.00**

Tea Set, 5¾" h cov teapot, 4¾" h cov teapot, cylindrical hot water pitcher with metal lid, open sugar, cylindrical creamer, bulbous spherical bodies, dark blue ground, white relief bands of classical dancing figures, garland bands around tops, Copeland–Spode, price for seven piece set **250.00**

Tobacco Jar, cov, 6¼" h, cylindrical, dark blue ground, white relief band around base, silverplated rim, bail handle and cov, ivory finial, imp "Adams, Tunstall, England". **100.00**

Vase, 7½" h, green, white, and pink ground, white relief Indian chief and owls, Germany **165.00**

JEWEL BOXES

History: The evolution of jewelry was paralleled by the development of boxes in which to store it. Jewel box design followed the fashion trends dictated by furniture styles. Many jewel boxes are lined.

Cast Iron and Brass, 9" w, 7" d, 6" h, Napoleon III, relief scrollwork, birds, and emperor silhouette on cov, paw feet **75.00**

Ebony, 11¾" l, allover scrolling flowering foliage dec, inlaid ivory, 19th C **300.00**

German Silver, 6½" l, 13 oz, rect, heavily

Wood, double book shape, hinged cov with Victorian lady dec, 5¼″ l, 3¼″ w, 2⅞″ h, $18.00.

JEWELRY

History: Jewelry has been a part of every culture. It was a way of displaying wealth, power, or love of beauty. In the current antiques marketplace, it is easiest to find jewelry dating between 1800 to 1950.

Jewelry items were treasured and handed down as heirlooms from generation to generation. In the United States, antique jewelry is any jewelry one hundred or more years old, a definition linked to U.S. Customs law. "Heirloom/estate" jewelry, that is, jewelry at least twenty–five years old and acquired new, used, or through inheritance, is used for old jewelry that does not meet the "antique" definition.

The jewelry found in this listing fits either the antique or "heirloom/estate" definition. The list contains no new reproduction pieces. The jewelry is made of metals and gemstones proven to endure over time. Inexpensive and mass–produced costume jewelry is covered in *Warman's Americana & Collectibles*.

Several major auction houses, especially Christie's, Doyle's, Sotheby's, Skinner's, and Butterfield and Butterfield, hold specialized jewelry auctions several times each year.

Note: The first step in determining the value of a piece of old jewelry is to correctly identify the metal and gemstones. Take into account the current value of the metal and gemstones plus the piece's age, identifying marks, quality, condition, construction, and so on.

References: Lillian Baker, *Art Nouveau & Art Deco Jewelry: An Identification & Value Guide,* Collector Books, 1981, 1992 value update; Lillian Baker, *Fifty Years of Collectible Fashion Jewelry, 1925–1975,* Collector Books, 1986, 1992 value update; Lillian Baker, *100 Years of Collectible Jewelry, 1850–1950,* Collector Books, 1978, 1993 value update; Lillian Baker, *Twentieth Century Fashionable Plastic Jewelry,* Collector Books, 1992; Vivienne Becker, *Antique & Twentieth Century Jewellery, Second Edition,* N.A.G. Press, 1987; Vivienne Becker, *Fabulous Costume Jewelry: History of Fantasy and Fashion in Jewels,* Schiffer Publishing, 1993; Jeanenne Bell, *Answers to Questions About 1840–1950 Old Jewelry, Third Edition,* Books Americana, 1992; David Bennett and Daniela Mascetti, *Understanding Jewellery,* Antique Collectors' Club, 1989; Matthew L. Burkholz and Linda Lichtenberg Kaplan, *Copper Art Jewelry: A Different Lustre,* Schiffer Publishing, 1993; Shirley Bury, *Jewellery 1789–1910: The International Era,* Antique Collectors' Club, 1991; Deanna Farnetti Cera (ed.), *Jewels of Fantasy: Costume Jewelry of the 20th Century,* Harry N. Abrams, 1992; Franco Cologni and Ettore Mocchetti, *Made By Cartier: 150 Years of Tradition and Innovation,* Abbeville Press, 1993; Maryanne Dolan, *Collecting Rhinestone & Colored Jewelry: A Collector's ID & Value Guide, Third Edition,* Books

molded and bellied sides, winged dolphin form feet, early 19th C	850.00
Gilt Bronze, 16″ w, 9½″ h, elaborate Moorish design, semiprecious stones, enamel dec.	900.00
Glass	
Amethyst, 6 x 4⅞″, enameled floral dec, silverplated rim and base. . . .	125.00
Cranberry, 4½ x 2¾″, enameled floral dec, silverplated rim	150.00
Opaque, 3½″ h, 6¼″ w, floral dec, satin finish, sgd "Nakara OFM Company," c1910	500.00
Ivory, 8¾ x 5½ x 4¾″, rect, hinged lid, delicate engraved and repousse mounts.	200.00
Malachite, 4½ x 2½″, veneer, rect, raised feet, satin lining, Russian, 19th C.	225.00
Ormolu, 10 x 8 x 7″, Art Nouveau, raised figural and floral dec, plaque dated 1903	225.00
Pewter, 5½ x 9½″, engraved brass framelike ornament on top, oval mosaic work, purple velvet lining, marked "Marshall & Sons, Edinburgh, Scotland".	250.00
Russian Silver, 4¾ x 8¾″, rect, sky blue, deep red, and white enamel diapering pattern and stylized flower heads, raised studded bands, swing handles on lid and sides, pale blue padded satin lining, four bun feet	2,475.00
Silverplated	
8″ l, rococo floral design	85.00
8 x 5 x 3″, oval, hinged lid, ftd emb cupids, daisy chain and roses, velvet lining, marked "Wilcox"	75.00
Sterling Silver, 13 x 5 x 4″, repousse sides, small petallike beaded edges, fancy feet, red velvet lining, marked "Meridan".	150.00
Wave Crest, 6 x 3″, pale blue painted flowers, red banner mark	570.00

Americana, 1993; Roseann Ettinger, *Popular Jewelry, 1840–1940,* Schiffer Publishing, 1990; Gabriele Greindl, *Gems of Costume Jewelry,* Abbeville Press, 1991; Susan Jonas and Marilyn Nissensor, *Cuff Links,* Harry N. Abrams, 1991; Arthur Guy Kaplan, *The Official Identification Price Guide To Antique Jewelry, Sixth Edition,* House of Collectibles, 1990; Elyse Zorn Karlin, *Jewelry and Metalwork in the Arts and Crafts Tradition,* Schiffer Publishing, 1993; Antoinette Matlins and A. C. Bonanno, *Jewelry & Gems: The Buying Guide,* Gemstone Press, 1987; Patrick Mauries, *Jewelry By Chanel,* Bulfinch Press, 1993; Anna M. Miller, *Cameos Old and New,* Van Nostrand Reinhold, 1991; Harrice Simons Miller, *Costume Jewelry: Identification and Price Guide, Second Edition,* Avon Books, 1994; Michael Poynder, *The Price Guide to Jewellery 3000* BC– 1950 AD, Antique Collectors' Club, 1990 reprint; Penny Proddow, Debra Healy, and Marion Fasel, *Hollywood Jewels: Movies, Jewelry, Stars,* Harry N. Abrams, 1992; Dorothy T. Rainwater, *American Jewelry Manufacturers,* Schiffer Publishing, 1988; Nancy N. Schiffer, *Rhinestones! A Collector's Handbook & Price Guide,* Schiffer Publishing, 1993; Nancy N. Schiffer, *Silver Jewelry Treasures,* Schiffer Publishing, 1993; Walter Schumann, *Gemstones of the World,* Sterling Publishing Co., 1988; Sheryl Gross Shatz, *What's It Made Of? A Jewelry Materials Identification Guide,* published by author, 1991; Doris J. Snell, *Antique Jewelry With Prices, Updated Edition,* Wallace–Homestead, 1991; Ulrike vonHase–Schmundt et al., *Theodor Fahrner, Jewelry...between Avant–Garde and Tradition,* Schiffer Publishing, 1991; Janet Zapata, *The Jewelry and Enamels of Louis Comfort Tiffany,* Harry N. Abrams, 1993.

Periodical: *Vintage Fashion and Costume Jewelry Newsletter,* PO Box 265, Glen Oaks, NY 11004.

Collectors' Club: National Cuff Link Society, PO Box 346, Prospect Heights, IL 60070.

Advisor: Christie Romero.

Dates:

Georgian	1714–1830
Victorian	1830–1900
Edwardian	1900–1910
Art Nouveu	1880–1920
Arts and Crafts	1895–1915
Art Deco	1920–1930
Retro Modern	1940–1950

Bracelet

Art Deco

Diamond–set double row spaced by four collet–set diamonds accented with foliate and X links, approx 4.00 cts, some solder . . . **4,400.00**

Openwork "S" shaped flexible links, round diamonds, 7.00 cts total weight, platinum, French hallmarks **9,350.00**

Arts and Crafts

Opal and pearl, oval opal doublet plaques alternating with blister pearls, 18K gold foliate mounts, 14K plunger, sgd "Oakes," for Edward Everett Oakes **4,100.00**

Sea Glass, mixed metal, center panel set with green glass within silver, copper, and gold mount flanked by brown glass, foliate design clasp, marked "HBF" for Hazel B French. **1,760.00**

Edwardian

Bangle

Center oval 1.30 cts sapphire surrounded by old mine cut diamonds, 18K yg solid top mount set with old mine cut and rose cut diamonds, 1.75 cts tw, Austrian hallmarks **2,860.00**

Center pierced diamond—set foliate plaque, seed pearl and platinum wire bracelet, some wire breaks, French hallmarks **1,980.00**

Seed pearls strung with platinum chain, diamond bar clasp, 0.28 ct **3,025.00**

Mexican Silver, William Spratling, sterling, naturalistic segments linked by alternating single and double dome links, imp oval mark "Spratling Silver," circle mark "Spratling, Made in Mexico," c1940, 8″ l **825.00**

Victorian, 14K yg

Bangle

Hinged, black enamel, center star set diamond, some enamel damage **550.00**

Hinged, snake, designed as knot set with turquoise and seed pearl, some dents and solder . **500.00**

Woven, 18K yg, mesh design, two sphere terminals, turquoise and beadwork, tiny pearls, minor dents, two turquoise missing, 11.3 dwt **825.00**

Link, center lion's head holding diamond in mouth, red stone eyes, joined by tapering oval plaques, solder, 7.8 dwt **165.00**

Brooch

Art Deco

Circle, approx 1.75 cts round diamonds, calibré cut sapphires, platinum mount, marked "JEC & Co," for JE Caldwell, No. K5609 **6,100.00**

Flower and ribbon design, 1.15 cts diamond frame, four corners accented by emeralds **1,650.00**

Art Nouveau

Center faceted amethyst, pierced mounting, enamel highlights . . . **770.00**

Floral, enamel flowers each with center prong set diamond, sgd "Tiffany and Co".............. **1,210.00**

Opal, oval shaped opal, gold frame, fresh water pearl suspended from base.................... **440.00**

Serpent holding freshwater pearl in mouth, articulated seaweed tail accented with freshwater pearls **1,980.00**

Arts and Crafts, Murle Bennett, England, c1900, oval turquoise flanked by pearls, gold finished setting, imp conjoined mark........ **990.00**

Edwardian, faceted amethyst, pavé–set rose cut diamond rider and horse, seed pearl frame with rose cut diamonds, 14K yg setting, minor solder to clasp.............. **2,310.00**

Retro, 14K rose gold, double circle design, engine turned finish, channel–set ruby dome, 15.9 dwt........ **715.00**

Victorian

Cameo

Onyx, profile of woman, architectural style mount, wire twist and bead details, 14K yg....... **880.00**

Shell, full figure, classical female, 18K yg mount, wire twist and beadwork frame......... **1,870.00**

Hand, 14K yg, holding 1.10 ct old mine cut diamond, black enamel tracery cuff.............. **1,430.00**

Micromosaic, quatrefoil, turquoise color mosaic background, 18K yg twist wire frame, Castellani mark after 1861................. **2,310.00**

Scrolled openwork 14K yg, frame centered by cabochon amethyst suspending pin and drop set with pear shaped amethyst, minor damage and solder......... **550.00**

Shield, black enamel, center oval diamond cluster, 14K yg mount, some enamel scratches....... **615.00**

Victorian, Mid, 15K gold, quatrefoil and tassel motif, center 1.75 cts emerald–cut emerald, four smaller emeralds and pearls, wire twist detail.................... **3,850.00**

Victorian, Late, rose–cut garnets surrounding center cabochon, swags of garnets, silver gilt frame...... **1,210.00**

Charm Bracelet, silver gilt, five hardstone intaglios, two locks, star and moon motif bracelet............ **275.00**

Chatelaine, 18K tricolor gold, natural motif, includes matching pocket watch, dust cov sgd "A Bolle," Case No. 42188, jeweled nickel movement, display crystal, white porcelain dial, black Roman numerals, yellow gold hands accented with diamonds..... **2,200.00**

Clip

Arts and Crafts, Mary Gage, silver, leaf and crystal berry, foliate shaped cluster, maker's tag, 2⅜" l **385.00**

Retro, 18K yg, stylized hand with two bangles, white and yellow fringed glove, 11.4 dwt.............. **880.00**

Coin Pendant Necklace, ten dollar Liberty coin, 14K yg link chain, 5.0 mm gold bead accents, 18.1 dwt....... **360.00**

Cufflinks, pr, Art Nouveau, 18K yg, lion holding bezel set diamond, 6.9 dwt.. **550.00**

Earpendants, pr

Etruscan Revival, 18K yg, spheres, applied wire and beadwork, slight wear.................... **880.00**

Victorian

Black enamel, oval shaped black onyx suspended from geometric enameled mount, disc accented with cultured pearl and wire twist, 14K yg mounts, some enamel loss.................... **770.00**

Kite shaped, pierced under–bezels and pear shaped garnet mounted on top, wire twist detail and beadwork, suspending gold tassels, 14K yg, some holes on bottom.. **1,650.00**

Micromosaic, dragon within navette shaped mounts suspending pear shaped elements, all suspended from round top with mythological face, 18K yg mounts, hallmarks **3,575.00**

Earrings, pr

Art Nouveau, enameled flowering lily pad, center 4.0 mm cultured pearl, 14K yg screwbacks, marked "Krementz," minor enamel loss...... **440.00**

Victorian, 14K yg, textured spheres, black enamel tracery floral motif.. **275.00**

Hairpin, Art Deco, diamond–set top accented with onyx set in platinum, yg pin, marked "BB&B," (Bailey Banks & Biddle), no. 45008.............. **935.00**

Locket, Victorian, 15K yg, pavé–set turquoise boss, wire twist and bead frame, gold chain............. **385.00**

Lorgnette

Art Deco, platinum

Old European cut diamond, 1.90 cts, geometric onyx and diamond mount enhanced by calibré–cut onyx, can be used as a clip, clasp needs repair.............. **5,775.00**

Onyx and diamond handle suspended from seed pearl chain, onyx bead spacers, navette shaped links, 41" l........ **1,760.00**

Art Nouveau, 14K yg, polished gold finish, scrollwork handles and top, 14.9 dwt................. **440.00**

Necklace

Art Nouveau, 14K yg and enamel, gold pendant with collet–set opals and green and yellow enamels, suspended from chain with enamel bar links, hallmarked, 26" l 990.00

Arts and Crafts

Hale, Frank Gardner, Boston, nine faceted teardrop amethysts each set in gold foliate frame, gold chain, largest frame inscribed "F. G. Hale," 15" l 3,850.00

Kalo, center oval coral, acid finish foliate mount, paper clip chain, sgd "Kalo," 20" l, minor lead solder 1,540.00

Edwardian, festoon, white and pink freshwater pearls, bezel set diamond highlights 1,650.00

Victorian, festoon, 15K yg, chain suspending three oval etched plaques set with rhodolite garnets, each suspending urn shaped elements, 18" l 990.00

Pendant

Art Deco, 3.84 cts tw old European cut diamonds suspended from black cord, diamond set platinum slide, 15" l 4,125.00

Art Nouveau

14K yg, lady with flowing hair, repeating floral motif, amethyst top 330.00

18K yg, three oval collet–set opals, foliate openwork frame suspending pear shape pendant, minor cracks to gold, slight crazing to opals................... 1,100.00

Arts and Crafts

Enamel and silver, shades of green and blue enamel highlighted by foliate silver design, joined by split silver chain, single trace chain, marked "MB" for Murrle Bennett & Co 360.00

Silver, openwork design, dyed green onyx and mother of pearl 85.00

Pin

Art Deco

Bow shape, pave set diamond center, channel set emerald and onyx border, 14K yg pen stem, European hallmarks, two diamonds and one emerald missing 2,310.00

Lozenge shape pierced design, rose cut and old mine cut diamonds (approx 2.75 cts), 14K gold brooch attachment suspended from platinum and cultured pearl chain, 30" l 3,300.00

Navette shape, fluted crystal, center platinum set diamond within onyx and blue enamel frame, flanked by row of diamonds, green and black enamel border, 14K yg mount, minor enamel loss 1,045.00

Arts and Crafts, Kalo Shop, Chicago, sterling, central amethystine, radiating scrolls and reticulation, imp marks and pouch, 1¼" d 615.00

Ring, silver, Atlas cameo, Wedgwood, $195.00.

Ring

Art Deco

Jade, central jade 19.5 mm x 13.5 mm cabochon, three 0.80 ct baguettes, platinum mount 7,700.00

Platinum, center 1.50 cts old European cut diamond, platinum navette shaped pierced mount, wire shank 4,180.00

Sterling silver, naturalistic design, animal head, signed "Delon," French hallmarks 2,640.00

Art Nouveau, cultured pearl, rose cut diamonds and rubies, 14K yg mount................... 275.00

Edwardian, old European cut 1.50 ct

Pin, 1½" w, Art Nouveau, sterling silver, woman with flowing hair, $95.00.

diamond, diamond set quatrefoil foliate mounts 3,575.00

Egyptian Revival, 14K yg, center scarab locket, set on swivel, flanked by twisted rope detail, maker's mark, 5.0 dwt. 1,210.00

Retro, large 30.00 mm x 21.00 mm rect–cut citrine flanked by cabochon rubies, scrolled 14K yellow gold mount 330.00

Victorian, citrine seal, rampant lion, 14K yg chased floral mount. 420.00

Slide and Chain, Victorian

14K yg, gold slide, gold plated fob as hand clasping bar, some solder, 15.2 dwt 200.00

15K yg, fancy links, bead terminals, removeable slide enhanced with applied textured leaf dec, 60" l, 46.7 dwt. 1,320.00

Suite

Brooch and Necklace, Victorian, coral, double strand of coloral beads, cluster brooch suspending three pear shaped drops. 480.00

Brooch and Earrings, Victorian, 14K yg, geometric brooch, black and white enamel, gold plated earrings with black enamel tracery, floral dec 165.00

Locket and Necklace, Victorian, vulcanite, oval locket with gold monogram, necklace: gold overlay links alternating with plain links 310.00

Necklace and Earrings, Etruscan Revival, lapis beads, wire twist and beadwork finials suspended from 18K yg foxtail chain, marked "Roma," 15½" l necklace, conforming 14K earrings 2,750.00

Watch Chain, Victorian, 15K yg, alternating round and oval shaped links with wire twist and bead detail, 14" l, 19.4 dwt, minor dents 660.00

Watch, pendant, Bulova, Swiss, 18K, openface, gold dial, abstract chapters and hands, rubbed and polished gold mount, pendant loop 315.00

Watch, pocket, 14K yg, red guillouché enamel with fleur–de–lis diamond cover, matching watch pin, suspended from chain of scrolled links, enamel loss 660.00

JUDAICA

History: Throughout history, Jews have expressed themselves artistically in both the religious and secular spheres. Most Jewish art objects were created as part of the concept of "Hiddur Mitzva," that is, adornment of implements involved in performing rituals both in the synagogue and home.

For almost 2,000 years, since the destruction of the Jerusalem Temple in 70 A.D., Jews have lived in many lands. The widely differing environments gave traditional Jewish life and art a multifaceted character. Unlike Greek, Byzantine, or Roman art, which has definite territorial and historical boundaries, Jewish art is found throughout Europe, the Middle East, North Africa, and other areas.

Ceremonial objects incorporated not only liturgical appurtenances but also ethnographic artifacts, such as amulets and ritual costumes. The style of each ceremonial object responded to the artistic and cultural milieu in which it was created. Although diverse stylistically, ceremonial objects, whether for Sabbath, holidays, or the life cycle, still possess a unity of purpose.

Judaica has been crafted in all media, though silver is the most collectible. Sotheby's, Christie's, and Swann's hold several Judaica auctions in the United States, England, Amsterdam, and Israel.

References: Abraham Kanof, *Jewish Ceremonial Art,* Harry N. Abrams, n.d.; Cecil Roth, *Jewish Art—An Illustrated History,* Graphic Society of New York, 1971; Geoffrey Wigoder (ed.), *Jewish Art and Civilization,* Chartwell Books, 1972.

Museums: B'nai B'rith Klutznick Museum, Washington, D.C.; H.U.C., Skirball Museum, Los Angeles, CA; Judah L. Magnes Museum, Berkeley, CA; Judaic Museum, Rockville, MD; Spertus Museum of Judaica, Chicago, IL; Morton B. Weiss Museum of Judaica, Chicago, IL; National Museum of American Jewish History, Philadelphia, PA; Plotkin Judaica Museum of Greater Phoenix, Phoenix, AZ; The Jewish Museum, New York, NY; Yeshiva University Museum, New York, NY.

Box, charity, 5" d, cylindrical, sheet copper, Germany, 1800s. 250.00

Chalice, 13" h, Continental silver, Herman Lang, Augsburg, 17th C, 29 oz . 2,325.00

Charger, 23" d, Continental silver, repousse floral and figural dec, c1780, 48 oz 1,650.00

Circumcision Cup, 5" h, German, double, silver gilt, marked "Johanna Becker, Augsburg," c1755–57 . . . . . 13,200.00

Circumcision Knife

6¾" l, Continental brass handle, 1700s 700.00

7" l, tortoiseshell, sterling silver, and steel, Continental, late 18th C 1,650.00

Comb, 6" w, Burial Society, brass, Hungarian, 1881 . . . . 5,775.00

Esther Scroll, 10½" l, cased, Austro–Hungarian silver, Vienna, 1846. . . . . 1,650.00

Presentation Goblet, 4" h, German silver, c1850 . . . . 660.00

Hanukkah Lamp, 9¾" h, Austrian 800 fine silver, scroll edge backplate surmounted by crown, facing emb with pair of tablets flanked by pair of griffins, Star of David cartouche, rect plat-

Diecut, © Heb. Pub. Co., 1909, 3¼" w, 4" h, $8.00.

8" d, tower shape, pewter, mounted
wood, lion top, German, 1700s . . . **1,300.00**
Torah Binder, linen, embroidered silk,
German, 1809. . . . . **650.00**
Torah Pointer, 10½" l, Polish silver, worn
on index finger, 18th C. **825.00**
Wall Sconce, 10½" l, Menorah style,
Continental silver, heraldic repousse
back shield, c1858, 18 oz. **2,860.00**

JUGTOWN POTTERY

History: In 1920 Jacques and Julianna Busbee
left their cosmopolitan environs and returned to
North Carolina to revive the state's dying craft of
pottery making. Jugtown Pottery, a colorful and
somewhat offbeat operation, was located in Moore
County, miles away from any large city and accessible only "if mud permits."

Ben Owens, a talented young potter, turned the
wares. Jacques Busbee did most of the designing
and glazing. Julianna handled promotion.

Utilitarian and decorative items were produced.
Although many colorful glazes were used, orange
predominated. A Chinese blue glaze that ranged
from light blue to deep turquoise was a prized glaze
reserved for the very finest pieces.

Jacques Busbee died in 1947. Julianna, with the
help of Owens, ran the pottery until 1958, when it
was closed. After long legal battles, the pottery was
reopened in 1960. It now is owned by Country
Roads, Inc., a nonprofit organization. The pottery
still is operating and using the old mark.

form, continuous row of eight urn form
lamps on wire frame, four scrolled
supports, servant's lamp missing, late
19th C, 22 oz, 10 dwt **1,800.00**
Kiddush Cup
5¼" h, silver gilt, Polish, mid 18th C **3,850.00**
5½" h, silver, tulip form, engraved, Polish, c1800. . . . . **950.00**
Knife, 3¾" l, Burial Society, wood, brass,
and steel **2,200.00**
Mezuzah Case, 4½" d, American silver,
Ludwig Wolpert, NY, stamped "Toby
Pascher Workshop, The Jewish Museum, NY" **650.00**
Passover Dish, 15¼" d, pewter, German, maker's initials "D.V.D.," c1768 **3,750.00**
Passover Plate
8¾" d, ceramic, Continental, 18th C **500.00**
14" d, pewter, Continental, c1800 . **225.00**
Plaque, 2¾ x 2", SS, rabbi, inscribed,
after engraving by Boris Schatz,
framed **500.00**
Sabbath Candlesticks, pr, 16¼" h,
Aaron Katz, London, 1894, Polish
style. **1,000.00**
Spice Box
4¾" d, SS, Scandinavian, fish form,
blurred marks on tail, articulated
body, hinged head, green jeweled
eyes, 19th C, 1 oz 10 dwt **385.00**
5¼" d, SS, filigree, Bohemian, sgd "R.
G., Prague, 1815" **1,200.00**

Bowl, 6" d, 2" h, crimped, Chinese
Translation, Chinese blue and red
glaze **85.00**
Candlesticks, pr, 3" h, Chinese Translation, Chinese blue and red, marked **75.00**
Creamer, cov, 4¾" h, yellow **50.00**
Finger Bowl, Chinese Translation,
Chinese blue and red. **115.00**
Jar, cov, 6¾" h, bulbous, flaring rim,
eared handles, redware, bright orange glaze **75.00**

Pie Plate, 9½" d, orange ground, black concentric circles dec 70.00
Pitcher, 5" h, gray and cobalt blue salt glaze 85.00
Rose Jar, cov, 4½" h, blended olive green glaze 50.00

Platter, oval, orange wash glaze, 12¾" l, 11½" w, 1½" h, $25.00.

Teapot, cov, 5¼" h, Tobacco Spit glaze, sgd, c1930 . . . . 60.00
Vase
  Bulbous, Chinese blue 700.00
  Ovoid, frogskin, Ben Owen, 4" h . . 135.00

KPM

History: The mark, KPM, has been used separately and in conjunction with other symbols by many German porcelain manufacturers, among whom are the Königliche Porzellan Manufactur in Meissen, 1720s; Königliche Porzellan Manufactur in Berlin, 1832–1847; and Krister Porzellan Manufactur in Waldenburg, mid 19th century.

Collectors now use the term "KPM" to refer to the high-quality porcelain produced in the Berlin area in the 18th and 19th centuries.

Reference: Susan and Al Bagdade, *Warman's English & Continental Pottery & Porcelain, Second Edition,* Wallace–Homestead, 1991.

Cup and Saucer, hunting scene, filigree, 18th C 50.00
Dinner Service, Art Deco style, gilt and jeweled in turquoise and pink, flowering plants on speckled gilt and iron red ground, sea green borders with molded gilt swags, blue scepter, iron red orb, KPM mark, c1880 . . . . 8,000.00
Dish, 9½" l, leaf shape, painted, birds on flowering branch, burgundy border, gilt drapery, blue scepter, iron red KPM and orb mark, c1860 . . . . 250.00
Figure, 9" h, hurdy–gurdy woman, 19th C. 285.00
Plaque
  6 x 7", three children, style of Van Dyke, imp KPM and scepter marks, inscribed verso "Fr. Till/Dresden". . 3,575.00
  8½ x 5½", Ruth, pierced foliate frame, slightly reduced, mark partially removed 1,210.00
  9 x 6½", Empress Louise, bust length portrait, sgd "H. Bork," imp KPM and scepter marks, framed 1,870.00

Figure, woman wearing turquoise shawl with red flowers and purple skirt, marked, c1913, 7" h, $595.00.

Plate
  9" d, hp, gold dec, wide scroll reticulated rims, orb mark, price for set of four. 125.00
  10½" d, Princess Royal 30.00
Scent Bottle, molded scrolls, multicolored painted bouquets of flowers, gilt trim, gilt metal C–scroll stopper, marked, mid 19th C 150.00
Teapot, 6" h, oval, medallion with figural dec, gilt ground 70.00
Urn, cov, cobalt blue and gilt, floral and cherub dec, price for pair 300.00

Vase, cov, blue, painted floral bouquets
with gilt foliage, flared foot, two loop
handles, blue scepter and KPM mark,
c1860. . . . .   **1,150.00**

KAUFFMANN, ANGELICA

History: Marie Angelique Catherine Kauffmann
was a Swiss artist who lived from 1741 until 1807.
Her paintings were copied by many artists who
hand decorated porcelain during the 19th century.
The majority of the paintings are neoclassical in
style.

Reference: Susan and Al Bagdade, *Warman's
English & Continental Pottery & Porcelain, Second
Edition,* Wallace–Homestead, 1991.

**Plate, cranberry colored scalloped rim
with gold dec, three maidens dancing
center, sgd "Kaufmann," beehive mark,
8½" d, $65.00.**

Bowl, scenic portrait, gold, jeweled
enamel edge, sgd, Limoges **78.00**
Cake Plate, 10" d, ftd, classical scene,
two maidens and cupid, beehive mark   **85.00**
Compote, 8" d, classical scene, beehive
mark, sgd. **80.00**
Cup and Saucer, classical scene, heavy
gold trim, ftd **90.00**
Inkwell, pink luster, classical lady   . . .   **75.00**
Pitcher, 8½" h, garden scene, women,
children, and flowers, sgd. **100.00**
Plaque, 8¾" d, classical scene, three
maidens dancing. **75.00**
Plate, 8" d, classical scene with two figures, cobalt blue border, reticulated
rim. **55.00**
Tobacco Humidor, women and cupid,
green ground, SP cov with pipe finial   **400.00**
Tray, 16½" d, round, classical figures in
reserve, sgd, beehive mark **175.00**

KEW BLAS

History: Amory and Francis Houghton established the Union Glass Company, Somerville, Massachusetts, in 1851. The company went bankrupt
in 1860 but was reorganized. Between 1870 and
1885 the Union Glass Company made pressed
glass and blanks for cut glass.

Art glass production began in 1893 under the
direction of William S. Blake and Julian de Cor-
dova. Two styles were introduced. A Venetian style
consisted of graceful shapes in colored glass, often
flecked with gold. An iridescent glass, labeled Kew
Blas, was made in plain and decorated forms. The
pieces are close in design and form to Quezel products but lack the subtlety of Tiffany items.

The company ceased production in 1924.

Museum: Sandwich Glass Museum, Sandwich,
MA.

**Vase, urn shape, squatty bulbous top,
pulled feather dec, dark glazed int., sgd,
7" h, $1,200.00.**

Bowl, 14" d, pulled feather, red ground,
sgd **1,200.00**
Candlesticks, pr, 8½" h, irid gold, twisted
stems. **725.00**
Compote, 7" h, twisted stem, ribbed
bowl, irid gold, pink highlights **375.00**
Creamer, 3¼" h, irid gold, applied
handle **225.00**
Finger Bowl and Underplate, 5" d bowl,
6" d plate, ribbed, scalloped border,
metallic luster, gold and platinum
highlights **465.00**
Pitcher, 4½" h, green pulled feather pat-
tern, deep gold irid int., applied swirl
handle, sgd "Kew–Blas". **800.00**
Rose Bowl, 3½" h, green and gold
hooked dec, butterscotch ground,
gold int. **525.00**

Salt, irid gold	200.00
Sherbet, 5" h, irid gold	200.00
Tumbler, 4" h, pinched sides, irid gold, sgd	185.00
Vase	
7" h, flared oval, gold irid and green diagonally striped design, engraved "Kew Blas"	615.00
10" h, manipulated rim, flared irid gold body, repeating green pulled leaf form dec, inscribed "Kew Blas" . . .	300.00
Wine Glass, 4¾" h, curving stem, irid gold	185.00

KITCHEN COLLECTIBLES

History: The kitchen was a central focal point in a family's environment until the 1960s. Many early kitchen utensils were handmade and prized by their owners. Next came a period of utilitarian products made of tin and other metals. When the housewife no longer wished to work in a sterile environment, color was added through enamel and plastic and design served both an aesthetic and functional purpose.

The advent of home electricity changed the type and style of kitchen products. Many items went through fads. The high-technology field already has made inroads into the kitchen, and another revolution seems at hand.

References: Ronald S. Barlow, *Victorian Houseware: Hardware and Kitchenware,* Windmill Publishing, 1992; Linda Campbell Franklin, *300 Years of Housekeeping Collectibles,* Books Americana, 1992; Linda Campbell Franklin, *300 Years of Kitchen Collectibles, Third Edition,,* Books Americana, 1991; *Griswold Cast Iron: A Price Guide,* L–W Book Sales, 1993; Garry Kilgo et al., *A Collectors Guide To Anchor Hockings "Fire–King" Glassware,* K & W Collectibles Publisher, 1991; Kathryn McNerney, *Kitchen Antiques 1790–1940,* Collector Books, 1991, 1993 value update; Gary Miller and K. M. Mitchell, *Price Guide To Collectible Kitchen Appliances,* Wallace–Homestead, 1991; Dana G. Morykan and Harry L. Rinker, *Warman's Country Antiques & Collectibles, Second Edition,* Wallace–Homestead, 1994; Ellen M. Plante, *Kitchen Collectibles: An Illustrated Price Guide,* Wallace–Homestead, 1991; Susan Tobier Rogove and Marcia Buan Steinhauer, *Pyrex By Corning: A Collector's Guide,* Antique Publications, 1993; Diane Stoneback, *Kitchen Collectibles: The Essential Buyer's Guide,* Wallace–Homestead, 1994; April M. Tvorak, *Fire–King II,* published by author, 1993; April M. Tvorak, *History & Price Guide To Fire–King,* AL Enterprises, 1992; April M. Tvorak, *Pyrex Price Guide,* published by author, 1992.

Periodicals: *Cast Iron Cookware News,* 28 Angela Ave., San Anselmo, CA 94960; *Kettles 'n' Cookware,* PO Box B, Perrysburg, NY 14129;

Kitchen Antiques & Collectible News, 4645 Laurel Ridge Drive, Harrisburg, PA 17110.

Collectors' Clubs: Cookie Cutter Collectors Club, 1167 Teal Rd., SW, Dellroy, OH 44620; Griswold & Cast Iron Cookware Assoc, PO Box B, Perrysville, NY 14129; National Reamer Collectors Association, 405 Benson Rd. N, Frederic, WI 54837–8943; The Glass Knife Collectors Club, PO Box 342, Los Alamitos, CA 90720.

Museums: Corning Glass Museum, Corning, NY; Kern County Museum, Bakersfield, CA; Landis Valley Farm Museum, Lancaster, PA.

Additional Listings: Baskets, Brass, Butter Prints, Copper, Fruit Jars, Food Molds, Graniteware, Ironware, Tinware, and Woodenware. See *Warman's Americana & Collectibles* for more examples, including electrical appliances.

Ezy Raisin Seeder, removable cup, clamp grip, May 21, 1895 patent date, 5" h, $110.00.

Apple Peeler, 7 x 31½", wood, hand crank, old dark finish	140.00
Broiler, 9" d, 16" l, wrought iron, rotary	125.00
Butter Churn, 24" h, stave constructed, steel bands, lid and dasher, old red paint	175.00
Butter Paddle	
9½" l, maple, curl and key type handle, refinished	165.00
12¼" l, curl and circle end handle, old soft finish	150.00
Butter Scoop, 11½" l, burl, large blade, curved handle	585.00
Coffee Roaster, 51" l, down–hearth, sheet metal, iron rod, wood handle, late 18th–early 19th C	125.00
Cookie Board	
6¾ x 5¼", rect, nine carved designs, dark patina	250.00
19 x 23", poplar, round, cutout handle, old patina	160.00
19¼ x 3½", hardwood, elongated, four carved bunches of grape, dark patina	425.00

20 x 5", elongated, fourteen carved animals, fish, fruit, birds, man, and mermaid, dark patina 360.00

25½" l, poplar, round, handle, old finish. 210.00

Cookie Cutter, tin
Bird, 5" h, long neck 40.00
Horse, 6½" l 175.00
Stag, 6½" l, stylized 95.00

Corn Stick Pan, seven cavities, Griswold #79 . . . . 35.00

Cutting Board, 17½" h, 10" w, butternut, worn surface. 75.00

Dough Box, 19 x 35", 27" h, poplar, turned legs, mortised and pinned frame, dovetailed box 660.00

Dough Scraper, 4" l, wrought iron, heart cutout in blade, minor damage to iron handle 110.00

Drying Rack, 20" w, 33" h, pine, two mortised and pinned bars, block feet with some damage, old dark green repaint 150.00

Food Chopper
8" w, wrought iron, wood handles, one blade signed, primitive, price for pair. 80.00
9" w, crescent blade, turned double handles, orig maker's label 60.00

Food Mold
3½ x 5¼", pear 75.00
4 x 6", ear of corn, tin and copper, tin wash. 110.00
4½ x 6", sheaf of wheat, tin and copper, tin wash 95.00
5" d, 5½" l, copper, marked "Temple & Crook, Ironmongers". 40.00
6⅝" d, copper, swirl design 85.00

Fork, 23" l, wrought, three tine, tooling, brass handle, slightly battered 160.00

Grater, 4½ x 12½", brass, scratched initials and mark 165.00

Kraut Cutter, 19¼" l, pine, red finish, scratch carved date "1801" 95.00

Meat Tenderizer, 9½" l, stoneware, wood handle, marked "Pat'd Dec 25, 1877". 75.00

Muddler
7" l, turned maple 35.00
12½" l, wood, turned 40.00

Pell, 33½" l, poplar, old refinishing . . 95.00

Raisin Seeder, 6" l, cast iron, marked "Ezy Raisin Seeder, Pat May 21, 1895" and "Scald the Raisins" 110.00

Roasting Spit, 12" l, brass and wrought iron 40.00

Rolling Pin
15¼" l, curly maple 50.00
21" l, curly maple 150.00

Skillet, down–hearth, iron, long handle, hook hanger. 165.00

Skimmer, 12" d, wrought iron, large flat bowl. 40.00

Spoon Rack, 15¼" h, pine, orig rose dec 110.00

Sugar Bucket
8¾" h, wood, stave constructed, old dark patina 100.00
9¾" h, wood, stave constructed, paint layers, light green top. 45.00

Sugar Nippers, wrought steel
8¼" l 200.00
9" l, tooled designs 100.00

Toaster, 15" l, wrought iron, shaped handle 110.00

Trivet, 10½" l, wrought iron, penny feet 175.00

Waffle Iron
22" l, cast iron, double handles . . . 45.00
28" l, cast iron, long wrought handles, one reattached. 140.00
29½" l, down–hearth, heart shape, late 18th–early 19th C 325.00

KUTANI

History: In the mid 1600s Kutani originated in the Kaga province of Japan. Kutani comes in a variety of color patterns, one of the most popular being Ao Kutani, a green glaze with colors such as green, yellow, and purple enclosed in a black outline. Wares made since the 1870s for export are enameled in a wide variety of colors and styles.

Reference: Gloria and Robert Mascarelli, *Warman's Oriental Antiques,* Wallace–Homestead, 1992.

Beaker, 17½" h, rakan, sgd "H Senda," Komatsu, Japan 385.00

Plate, cream and beige ground, multi-colored poppy center, four section border dec in gold, black, and red, marked, 8¼" d, $95.00.

Biscuit Jar, Geisha Girl, c1890 . . . . . 165.00
Bowl, 6⅝″ d, gilt and bright enamel design, figural, animal, and floral reserves, kinrande ground, base inscribed "Kutani–sei," price for set of ten. 385.00
Charger, 18⅜″ d, pomegranate tree, chrysanthemums, and two birds on int., birds and flowers between scrolling foliate bands, irregular floral and brocade border, 11 character inscription. 525.00
Dish, 10½″ d, central scene, magpies in bamboo forest. 250.00
Figure
  12″ h, Bodhidharma, standing, long red robe, flywisk in right hand 175.00
  14¼″ h, Kannon, standing, polychrome and gilt dec, dragon mount, high coiffure, wind–swept robe, inscribed "Kutani–sei". 500.00
Garden Seat, 19″ h, barrel shape, two large circular reserves of courtly figures in garden, small reserves with florals and landscape scenes, spiraling brocade ground, top pierced with circular florets, price for pair 2,000.00
Jar, 20½″ h, ovoid, fan shaped reserves of warriors, molded ribbon tied tasseled ring handles, shippo–tsunagi ground, multicolored brocade patterned dome lid, price for pair. 1,350.00
Mustard Pot, attached saucer, Nishikide diapering, figural raised gold reserves, marked. 65.00
Tea Caddy, 6″ h, bulbous, hexagonal, Nishikide diapering, figural raised gold reserves of children, red script mark 75.00
Teapot, cov, bulbous, One Thousand Faces. 225.00
Tray, 14″ l, polychrome and gilt, figural scene, red, orange, and gold border 325.00
Vase, 9¾″ h, ovoid, waisted neck, recessed ring foot, upper portion with enameled reddish–brown wave pattern, underglaze blue wide band of archaistic keyfret design, raised borders, lower section with gilt painted stylized lotus blossoms, green enamel scrolling leafy tendrils, bluish–black ground 360.00

LALIQUE

LALIQUE

A.LALIQUE

History: Rene Lalique (1860–1945) first gained prominence as a jewelry designer. Around 1900 he

began experimenting with molded glass brooches and pendants, often embellishing them with semiprecious stones. By 1905 he was devoting himself exclusively to the manufacture of glass articles.

In 1908 Lalique began designing packaging for the French cosmetic houses. He also produced many objects, especially vases, bowls, and figurines, in the Art Noveau style in the 1910s. The full scope of Lalique's genius was seen at the 1925 Paris International Exhibition of Decorative Arts. He later moved to the Art Deco form.

The mark "R. LALIQUE FRANCE" in block letters is found on pressed articles, tableware, vases, paperweights, and mascots. The script signature, with or without "France," is found on hand-blown objects. Occasionally a design number is included. The word "France" in any form indicates a piece made after 1926.

The post–1945 mark is "Lalique France" without the "R"; there are exceptions to this rule.

References: Hugh D. Guinn (ed.), *The Glass of Rene Lalique At Auction*, Guindex Publications, 1992; Katherine Morrison McClinton, *Introduction to Lalique Glass*, Wallace–Homestead, 1978, out of print; Tony L. Mortimer, *Lalique*, Chartwell Books, 1989; Ellen T. Schroy, *Warman's Glass*, Wallace–Homestead, 1992.

Periodical: *Lalique Magazine*, 400 Veterans Blvd., Carlstadt, NJ 07072.

Collectors' Club: Lalique Society of America, 400 Veterans Blvd., Carlstadt, NJ 07072.

Reproduction Alert: Much faking of the Lalique signature occurs, the most common being the addition of an "R" to the post–1945 mark.

Auto Mascot
  7″ h, Vitesse, frosted gray, nude woman, selectively polished, sgd in raised block letters at lower sides "R. Lalique/France" 5,500.00
  8¼″ h, Grande Libellule, gray–crystal, dragonfly, wings aloft, faint mold mark, script engraved "R. Lalique France". 4,400.00
Bonbonniere, 10″ d, 2″ h, Cigales, fiery opalescent cov molded with twelve cicada flies, orig satin lined composition box, imp "R Lalique" 1,100.00
Bowl
  7¾″ d, 3⅛″ d, Ondines Refermee, molded opalescent, blue–opal inverted rim, six nude mermaids on ext., lower edge engraved block sgd "R. Lalique/France No. 381". . 1,870.00
  8⅛″ d, 3⅛″ h, Ondines Ouverte, molded opalescent, flared rim, six nude mermaids on bubbling background, ext., side molded "R. Lalique". 1,100.00
  10″ d, 4¼″ h, Nemours, heavy walled colorless crystal, graduated recessed blossoms, black enameled

dot centers, etched base "Lalique" mark. **770.00**

Center Bowl, 14¼" d, 2½" h, flattened flared rim, eight full-length nude women, different poses, base inscribed "R. Lalique". **1,320.00**

Display Plaque, 7½" h, molded "Cristal Lalique Paris," 3¾" sq black plastic stand marked "Lalique Society of America" **250.00**

Goblet, fifteen champagnes, fifteen highball glasses, Marc Lalique Marjorque design, price for set of thirty . . **385.00**

Paperweight, 4½" h, St Christophe, intaglio molded, frosted medallion, mold inscribed "R. Lalique France". **715.00**

Pendant
Fioret, roundel, molded seated nude among flowers, rose patina, mold pierced for silk cord, sgd in mold . . **385.00**

Sauterelles, oval, crystal, lilies and three grasshoppers, green foil, metal mount with ring, imp "Lalique". **1,320.00**

Scrolled, roundel, crystal, molded curvilinear motif, sienna patina, mold pierced for silk cord, script inscribed "R. Lalique". **415.00**

Perfume
3½" h, Fougeres, sq, bottle form, molded fern motif, center portrait medallion insert on front and back, sq green stopper, base molded "R. Lalique". **4,675.00**

3⅞" h, Quatre Coeur, frosted vial, gilt metal screw cap, molded signature, orig blue leather pouch. **200.00**

4¼" h, Dans La Nuit, Worth, sphere, blue, star motif, quarter moon stopper, sgd **715.00**

5¼" h, Molinard, flattened oval, molded twelve nude dancing women, floral border, sienna patina, gilt metal atomizer marked "Le Provencal," base inscribed "R Lalique/Molinard/France" **250.00**

5⅜" h, Fleurs de Pommier, molded, scalloped, reticulated apple blossoms on tiara stopper, molded signature "R. Lalique," stress lines, tiny edge chip **4,400.00**

5½" h, Ambre d'Orsay, rect, polished black glass, frosted caryatids at corners, conforming floral stopper, sgd in mold **1,320.00**

6¾" h, Sirenes, Brule, opal perfume burner, allover green patina, ten full-length mermaids, ocean wave motif on cov. **1,320.00**

Statue, 9¼" h, Danseuse Bras Leves, frosted nude, polished crystal stan-

Vase, clear and frosted, flaring, molded stylized bird head handles, inscribed "R. Lalique," 6¾" h, $550.00. Photograph courtesy of William Doyle Galleries.

dard inscribed "Lalique France," attributed to Marc Lalique **330.00**

Vase
5¼" h, Rampillon, conical, golden amber, deeply molded protrusions, floral surround, inscribed block letters "R. Lalique France". **2,420.00**

7" h, 10¼" d, Farandole, flared, bright blue, wide frieze of cherubic naked dancing children, floral ground, base inscribed "R. Lalique France" **15,400.00**

7½" h, Alexandrite Graines, reactive glass, blue–green in shadow, bright pink in light, molded graduated rows of seed pod devices, etched "R. Lalique" on base, worn base edge . . **2,860.00**

8¼" h, Marguerites, Catalog No. 922, opaque white glass, molded daisy blossoms, inverted centers, molded sgd "R. Lalique". **990.00**

8½" h, Domremy, bulbous fiery opal ovoid, molded thistle design, acid stamped "R. Lalique France" **1,210.00**

8¾" h, Actina, press molded spiraled and swirled opalescent crystal, orig blue wash, sgd in block stamp "R. Lalique" **3,100.00**

9¼" h, Monnaie du Pape, bright red–amber, selective frosted and polished leaves, inverted molded signature. **3,850.00**

10½" h, Archers, smoky topaz, frosted and selectively polished motif, ten male hunters aiming bows at wide border of birds in flight, imp molded sgd "R. Lalique". **4,675.00**

11¼" h, 10" d, Milan, colorless sphere, orig applied green patina, symmet-

rical repeating leaf design, inscribed "R. Lalique" block letters,
script "France". **3,575.00**

LAMPS AND LIGHTING

History: Lighting devices have evolved from
simple Stone Age oil lamps to the popular electrified models of today. Aim Argand patented the first
oil lamp in 1784. Around 1850 kerosene became a
popular lamp burning fluid, replacing whale oil and
other fluids. In 1879 Thomas A. Edison invented
the electric light bulb, causing fluid lamps to lose
favor and creating a new field for lamp manufacturers to develop. Companies such as Tiffany and
Handel developed skills in the manufacture of electric lamps, having their decorators produce beautiful aesthetic bases and shades.

References: James Edward Black (ed.), *Electric
Lighting of the 20s–30s*, L–W Book Sales, 1988,
1993 value update; James Edward Black (ed.),
*Electric Lighting of the 20s & 30s, Volume 2 with
Price Guide*, L–W Book Sales, 1990, 1993 value
update; J. W. Courter, *Aladdin Collectors Manual
& Price Guide #2*, published by author, 1993; J.
W. Courter, *Aladdin Collectors Manual & Price
Guide #14*, published by author, 1992; J. W.
Courter, *Aladdin Electric Lamps*, published by au-
thor, 1987; J. W. Courter, *Aladdin Electric Lamps
Price Guide #1*, published by author, 1989; J. W.
Courter, *Aladdin, The Magic Name in Lamps*, Wal-
lace–Homestead, 1980; J. W. Courter, *Angle
Lamps: Collectors Manual & Price Guide*, pub-
lished by author, 1992; Robert De Falco, Carole
Goldman Hibel, and John Hibel, *Handel Lamps*, H
& D Press, 1986; Larry Freeman, *New Light on Old
Lamps*, American Life Foundation, 1984; L–W
Book Sales (ed.), *Quality Electric Lamps: A Picto-
rial Price Guide*, L–W Book Sales, 1992; Edward
and Sheila Malakoff, *Pairpoint Lamps*, Schiffer
Publishing, 1990; Nadja Maril, *American Lighting:
1840–1940*, Schiffer Publishing, 1989; Richard
Miller and John Solverson, *Student Lamps of the
Victorian Era*, Antique Publications, 1993; Bill and
Linda Montgomery, *Animated Motion Lamps 1920s
To Present*, L–W Book Sales, 1991; Leland and
Crystal Payton, *Turned On: Decorative Lamps of
the 'Fifties*, Abbeville Press, 1989; *Quality Electric
Lamps*, L–W Book Sales, 1992; Catherine M. V.
Thuro, *Oil Lamps*, Wallace–Homestead, 1976,
1992 value update; Catherine M. V. Thuro, *Oil
Lamps II*, Thorncliffe House, 1983.

Periodical: *Light Revival*, 35 West Elm Ave.,
Quincy, MA 02170.

Collectors' Clubs: Aladdin Knights of the Mystic
Light, RR #1, Simpson, IL 62985; Historical Light-
ing Society of Canada, 9013 Oxbow Rd., North
East, PA 16428; The Incandescent Lamp Collec-
tors Assoc., Museum of Lighting, 717 Washington
Place, Baltimore, MD 21201; The Rushlight Club,

Inc., Suite 196, 1657 The Fairway, Jenkintown, PA
19046.

Museums: Kerosene Lamp Museum, Winchester Center, CT; Pairpoint Lamp Museum, River
Edge, NJ.

**Aladdin, reverse painted, three colorful
jungle birds against green foliage
ground, bronzed metal Art Nouveau
base with floral molded design, sgd,
No. 1763, 16″ d shade, 20″ h, $1,100.00.
Photograph courtesy of James D. Julia,
Inc.**

AMERICAN, EARLY

Argand
    Clark and Cargill, NY, mid 19th C, pa-
    tinated bronze, single arm, shades
    missing, imperfections, 18¾″ h,
    price for pair **1,320.00**
    Unknown American Maker, early 19th
    C, single arm, orig prisms, shade,
    electrified, 21″ h, price for pair. . . . **1,200.00**
Astral, American, third quarter 19th C,
brass
    22″ h, frosted and cut glass shade,
    electrified **360.00**
    27″ h, brass, acid etched and wheel
    cut glass shade, acanthus dec
    shaft, marble base, electrified **4400.00**
Candlelamp, 19½″ h, Handel, 9″ h Ter-
oma flared hurricane shade, chipped
ice textured finish, hp ext. with green
and white birch trees, yellow int.,
mounted to brass rim, mahogany
candlestick base **550.00**

BOUDOIR

Handel, 14″ h, 7″ d ribbed basketweave
    dome shade, reverse painted tropical

Boudoir, Chicago Mosaic Co., leaded glass, orange floral design on green variegated ground, irregular borders, bronzed metal open root style tree trunk base, 10″ d shade, 18″ h, $1,430.00. Photograph courtesy of James D. Julia, Inc.

isle moonlight scene with sailing ships, Treasure Island, sgd "Handel 7165D" on edge, bronzed metal basketweave base, imp "Handel" in mold **2,310.00**

Pairpoint

13″ h, 10″ d flared reverse painted Art Deco floral, swag and urn motif, stylized umbrella top, stamped "The Pairpoint Corp," mahogany base, gilt metal trim, marked "Pairpoint" **1,100.00**

14″ h, 9″ d blown out ribbed Stratford shade, reverse painted pink and yellow roses, stylized trees, blue ground, black border, gilt metal lappet base marked "Pairpoint" **2,530.00**

CHANDELIERS

Austrian, 19th C, six light, gilt wood, flowering basket design, regilt. **1,870.00**

Daum Nancy, 20″ h, three light, oval gilt metal drop, orange and amethyst glass bell art glass shades, inscribed "Daum Nancy" **615.00**

Quezal

14″ h, two light, bell form opal glass shades, pulled feathers and irid, collet rim inscribed "Quezal," burnished gilt metal mount and chain . **355.00**

16″ h, three light, shouldered flared opal shades, rib mold design, gold irid int., collet rim inscribed "Quezal," classic gilt metal sockets, wheel with chain drop. **440.00**

Steuben

14″ h, two light, flared rib molded gold Aurene shade, sgd collet rim inscribed "Steuben," urn form burnished gilt metal hanger and chain **305.00**

22½″ h, three light, rib molded trumpet form gold Aurene shades, vasiform hanger, burnished gilt metal scrolled fittings and ceiling mount . **715.00**

Tiffany

23″ h, four 7½ x 6″ green turtleback tiles, wrought bronze frame, openwork crown dec with three coiled wire circles, massive ring, hook and chain bronze fittings **2,710.00**

46″ h, four 6¼″ d leaded favrile dome shades, green and orange–amber dichroic segments, heart shaped acorn medial belt, each tag imp "Tiffany Studios New York," elaborate metal cased light bowl, cast butterflies, women, and Art Nouveau floral elements, chains and mounts in Tiffany manner. **5,170.00**

Unknown Maker, leaded, 14″ h, 21″ d, two part fixture, caramel slag brickwork pagoda top, purple iris blossom flared oval drop below, three socket light fixture **1,870.00**

Desk, Bradley & Hubbard, double student lamp, brass, kerosene burners sgd "Stern Bro's. New York," replaced 10″ d white milk glass shades, 21″ h, $1,100.00. Photograph courtesy of James D. Julia, Inc.

DESK

Handel, Arts and Crafts, 16″ h, 8″ d conical shade of three caramel slag glass
panels, hammered metal strap and
floral frame, brass finish, cast metal
base, hammered metal patina, Handel shade tag   **660.00**

Tiffany Studios
13½″ h, double bulbed amber and
opal shade, five pulled feathers, inscribed "L.C.T." on rim, adjustable
swivel socket between bronze harp,
ribbed cushion base, imp "TG & D
Co" mark **1,430.00**
14″ h, Nautilus, shell form green
leaded glass segments, swivel two
arm shaft, lappet base, imp "Tiffany
Studios New York S 1543," and TG
& D Co mark **4,290.00**
14″ h, 7″ d bronze shade cut with
stars, six opal glass bent panel liners, bronze cantilever base
stamped "Tiffany Studios New York
417" **2,530.00**
14½″ h, Zodiac, emerald green turtle-
back tiles, dark bronze adjustable
shade, swivel holder, Zodiac patterned platform base, imp "Tiffany
Studios New York 541" **4,290.00**
16″ h, 7″ d cased gold and amber
wave irid damascene shade, sgd
"L.C.T." on rim, arched gilt bronze
base with counterlever ball weight,

**Gone With The Wind Lamp, electrified,
hp mermaids riding large fish, seagulls,
and crashing waves on gray ground,
Tam–O–Shanter shade with 10″ d fitter
ring, 26″ h, $550.00. Photograph cour-
tesy of James D. Julia, Inc.**

imp "Tiffany Studios New York
415," orig wiring removed **3,190.00**
Wedgwood, 15″ h, green glazed ceramic
shade, brass arm, copper base, imp
and printed marks, c1933, hairline . .   **275.00**

FLOOR

Bradley and Hubbard, 56″ h, 7″ d small
domed leaded glass shade, green
slag glass, gold key border, open
framework, adjustable standard,
domed circular foot **375.00**
Durand, 67″ h, 8″ h bulbed ruffled rim
blue, opal white, and irid gold glass
shades, elaborate gilt metal lamp
bases, molded floral swags, knights–
in–armor and heraldic elements,
stepped onyx platform base, price for
pair **2,310.00**
Handel, harp base, bronze finish, two
parrots on yellow ground shade, sgd
"Handel #7073 GA" **8,000.00**
Tiffany Studios, 54″ h, counterbalance,
gold dore finish, bulbed five ftd base,
adjustable ball lever socket, sgd "Tif-
fany Studios" on foot **825.00**

FLUID

Bristol Glass, 27″ h, Victorian, high relief
foliate and cherub head dec, polychrome enamel painted floral
reserves **425.00**
New England Glass Co, Acorn and Dra-
pery pattern, stepped pressed base,
three ring knob, free blown font, pew-
ter collar **265.00**
Ripley, 14½″ h, opaque white and blue,
double fonts **475.00**
Sandwich, Onion pattern, opaque white,
c1840 . . . .   **650.00**
Tiffany, 16″ h, 9½″ d gourd form opal
glass shade, gold irid combed surface, ten green pulled vertical elements, inside rim inscribed "534," oil
font collar, conforming bronze gourd
form base, five ball feet, Tiffany Glass
and Decorating Co mark, converted to
electricity **2,860.00**

STUDENT

Double, 22½″ h, 27″ w, yellow brass,
green cased shades, electrified **400.00**
Tiffany
29″ h, 10″ d translucent green favrile
glass shade, blown into two bronze
shade frames, numbered 22503,
adjustable fluid burner arms, central
fuel canister, orig bronze frame-

work, twist and beaded dec, frame
imp 25574 . . . . **12,100.00**
30″ h, 9¾″ d, green and irid gold Da-
mascene ribbed opal white lined favrile glass shades, marked "L.C.T."
at rim, ring holders, Manhattan
Brass Co fluid burners, bronze
framework, Pine Needle pattern
fuel canister, stepped pedestal
base, converted to electricity **11,000.00**
Wild & Wessel, Berlin, Germany, brass,
cast foliage design, green shades, retailed by Shreve, Crump & Low, price
for pair **2,750.00**

TABLE

Astral Style, 31″ h, gilded brass and marble, cut prisms, frosted and cut to
clear shade, electrified **375.00**
Bradley and Hubbard, Prairie School,
c1908
20″ h, 16″ d octagonal shade, linear
and geometric grid work over green
slag glass panels, red ripple glass
highlights, hexagonal metal base,
imp mark and "216" **1,320.00**
22½″ h, 16″ d conical shade, for car-
amel slag glass panels, blue and
red slag glass border, linear and
geometric gridwork, four light sockets, conforming design on base,
marked "B & H 222" **2,090.00**
Handel
14¼″ h, 10″ d domed chipped ice scenic shade, reverse painted naturalistic landscape, sgd on edge
"2709," single socket bronzed
metal base imp "Handel" at back
edge **1,870.00**
18″ h, 11″ d mushroom cap dome
shade, reverse painted green,
bright enameled dragon and sunburst, ext. gold and black highlights,
sgd on rim "Handel Co. 2186," 10″
ring, bronzed base, eight coiled wire
dec, imp "Handel" **1,650.00**
20″ h, 14″ d conical glass shade, reverse
painted wide yellow and pink
tea roses border, yellow ground,
applied ext. accents, sgd "Handel
6300," artist initial "A," two socket
bronzed foliate molded metal Han-
del base **2,310.00**
21″ h, 15″ d dome shade, reverse
painted strong sunset forest scene,
full length evergreens, red–orange
sky, amethyst fields, sgd at rim
"Handel 7045," lappet molded
bronzed two socket base, imp
"Handel" **2,970.00**
22″ h, 16″ d dome shade, reverse

painted full blossom pink, maroon,
and white ball shaped hydrangeas,
green leafy ground, sgd at edge
"Handel 6739," two socket bronzed
metal Handel base **9,625.00**
24½″ h, 18″ d dome
Chipped ice textured shade, reverse painted three polychromed
exotic parrots, floral and confetti
type ground, sgd "Handel 7128
Bedigie," three socket triparte
bronzed metal base, marble dish
foot **9,900.00**
Exterior painted dome, stylized
red–brown and yellow floral motif,
green textured surface, opal
glass int., sgd "Handel 6374" on
edge, three socket bronze base
imp "Handel" **1,870.00**
Jefferson
22″ h, 14″ d Art Deco style shade, reverse painted four repeating elements, stylized double blossom motif in bright primary colors, ring
mount marked "Jefferson," orig
vasiform two socket metal base . . . **990.00**
22½″ h, 18″ d shaped dome, reverse
painted pastoral scene, meadow
with pond, earthtone browns and
greens, boldly signed at rim "1885
Jefferson F," bronzed metal two
socket base with molded foliate
paneled elements **1,320.00**
Moe Bridges, 21″ h, 16″ d mesh textured
dome shade, hp int., riverside country
scene, autumn trees, yellow sky, rim
sgd "Moe Bridges Co," bronzed metal
two socket standard, four applied
blossom scrolls, quatreform base . . . **1,100.00**
Pairpoint
23″ h, 19½″ d flared domical Berkeley
shade, reverse painted tropical
waterfront scene, palm trees, tran-
quil sailboats, stamped "The Pairpoint Corp," gilt metal urn form
three light base, imp "Pairpoint
D2035" **3,025.00**
24″ h, 18″ d Copley flared shade, re-
verse painted expansive mountain
and meadow scene with shepherd
and sheep, artist sgd "N Gifford,"
gilt metal standard, mahogany
base, both inscribed "The Pairpoint
Corp" **3,575.00**
Salterini, John B, c1925, 26½″ h,
wrought iron and mica, skyscraper
type, brown patina, metal tag, loss to
finial **1,980.00**
Tiffany
Acorn, 17″ h, 12″ d favrile glass leaded
shade, mottled yellow, band of
green–blue heart shaped elements,

two socket bronze base, imp "Tiffany Studios New York" 6,050.00

Apple Blossom, 22" h, 16" d leaded favrile segments, yellow centered pink and opal pink apple blossoms, dark and light green leaves and branches, mottled and striated green and white background, rim imp "Tiffany Studios New York 1455–11," three arm spider, three socket coiled wire and ribbed cushion base, imp marks, some segments cracked. 6,325.00

Damascene, 21½" h, 16" d cased opal favrile glass shade, green pulled ripped gold irid dec, early three arm and socket bronze base, wire twist and cast turtleback dec, imp "Tiffany Studios New York 25882" and "TG&D Co" logo 4,400.00

Grapevine, 16" h, 14" d bronze dome shade, eight green favrile bent panels, rim tag reads "Tiffany Studios New York," three arm spider over Tiffany spun bronze tobacco leaf fluid lamp 5,225.00

Lily, 22" h, seven gold irid eight–rib lily blossom shades marked "L.C.T," porcelain socket decumbent arms, bronze lily pad base, broad alligatored dark patina, base plate imp "Tiffany Studios New York 385," some restoration to arms 1,870.00

Lotus, 21" h, 15½" d bell form shade, green and white favrile glass leaded segments, rib reinforcements, bronze bell frame, ribbed five ftd base, numbered and imp "Tiffany Studios New York," some segments cracked. 19,800.00

Pansy, 23" h, 16" d leaded favrile glass segments, four repeating clusters of gold centered yellow, opal, pink slag, and fiery amber pansy blossoms, dark green and striated green amber leaves, green and white slag background, horizontal tag "Tiffany Studios New York 1448–3," three arm spider base, three socket ribbed and scrolled shaft, four ftd cushion platform base, imp "Tiffany Studios New York 9939". 11,000.00

Pomegranate, 18" h, 16" d leaded glass dome shade, deep green favrile segments, yellow border belt, spun bronze converted fluid lamp base, conforming three arm shade supports, imp "Tiffany Studios New York" 4,400.00

Wilkinson, 29" h, 22" d conical leaded shade, four repeating yellow, orange,

and green blossom motifs, brown and white glass segments border and background, bent glass tuck–under edge, later three socket gilt metal standard. 2,530.00

LAMP SHADES

History: Lamp shades were made to diffuse the harsh light produced by early gas lighting fixtures. These early shades were made by popular Art Nouveau manufacturers, including Durand, Quezal, Steuben, Tiffany, and others. Many shades are not marked.

References: Dr. Larry Freeman, *New Lights on Old Lamps,* American Life Foundation, 1984; Jo Ann Thomas, *Early Twentieth Century Lighting Fixtures,* Collector Books, 1980, out of print.

Blue frosted glass, ribbed, emb flowers, 2" d fitter ring, $15.00.

Aladdin, satin, white, dogwood dec . .	50.00
Bigelow Kennard, 12¼" d, leaded, brickwork, matching pearl pink slag glass segments, tag on rim "Bigelow–Kennard & Co./Boston," 3⅝" d fitter rim .	770.00
Bradley and Hubbard, 18" d, leaded glass, geometric mottled green pattern.	350.00
Cameo Glass, 8⅜" d, 5" h, white leaves, yellow ground	225.00
Custard Glass, 2" d fitter ring, brown nutmeg stain	45.00
Durand, 9½" h, Gold Egyptian Crackle, blue and white overlay, bulbous, ruffled rim, sgd	175.00
Fostoria, 5½" d, zipper pattern, green pulled dec, opal ground, gold lining. .	175.00
Imperial, NuArt, marigold	50.00
Loetz, 8½" d, irid green oil spot dec, ribbon work over white glass int., c1900	225.00
Monart Glass, 6½" d, white opal	85.00
Muller Fres, half round flared bowl ceiling type 12" d, mottled yellow, orange, and	

blue, three chains affixed for
hanging. **415.00**
15½" d, mottled orange, blue, and red,
hanging ring mount, sgd **825.00**
Pairpoint, 7" h, puffy, flower basket, reverse painted pink and yellow poppies
and roses **400.00**
Quezal, feather pattern, irid gold ground,
sgd **110.00**
Steuben, 5" h, 2¼" d rim, aurene, gold,
ten ribs, flared trumpet shape, silver
fleur de lis mark, price for set of three **360.00**
Tiffany
6" h, 2⅛" d rim, Moorish, octagonal
bubbled opal shade, eight green
and gold pulled feather elements,
inscribed at rim "L. C. Tiffany
Favrile". **880.00**
7¾" h, 3⅞" d rim, gas, ribbed, closed
top
Opal white translucent, numbered
S4612, price for set of five. **300.00**
Pink–amber, numbered S624 . . . **150.00**
10" h, 5¾" d opening, ruffled rim, Favrile aquamarine and opal oval, inscribed and labeled "TG & D Co,
Tiffany Favrile Glass Registered
Mark" **420.00**
22" d, 11" drop, shaded green and
white Favrile leaded segments arranged as bamboo stalks and
leaves, imp "Tiffany Studios New
York 1509," three socket generic
electrical and hanging fittings **45,100.00**
Unknown Maker
4" d fitter, 5½" h, blue cased glass
shading dark to light, candy ribbon
edge, enameled birds and flowers **300.00**
10" d, 5½" d fitter, 8¾" h, gas hall type,
vaseline opal, fleur–de–lis pattern . **90.00**
22" d, 9½" h, leaded, fiery caramel
slag rippled glass segments, irregular edge of yellow centered pink
poppies, three socket ceiling mount **1,045.00**

LANTERNS

History: A lantern is an enclosed, portable light
source, hand carried or attached to a bracket or
pole to illuminate an area. Many lanterns can be
used both indoors and outdoors and have a protected flame. Fuels used in early lanterns included
candles, kerosene, whale oil, coal oil, and later
gasoline, natural gas, and batteries.

References: Anthony Hobson, *Lanterns That Lit
Our World,* published by author, 1991; Dana G.
Morykan and Harry L. Rinker, *Warman's Country
Antiques & Collectibles, Second Edition,* Wallace–
Homestead, 1994.

**Miner's, brass, label reads "Patterson
Lames, Ltd., Gateshead on Tyne,"
$50.00.**

Astronomical, 12" l, tole ware, orig black
and gold paint, two candle sockets,
frosted glass, thirteen cards punched
with constellations, orig wooden box,
labeled "Clarke's Astronomical Lantern, Manufactured by D. C. Heaty &
Co, Boston," unused condition **385.00**
Barn, 11" h, wood, four glass sides,
hinged door **145.00**
Campaign, 48" l, tin, two spouts, re-
placed bamboo handle, wire wrap,
wire cradle **30.00**
Candle
6" h, tin, pierced conical vent top, horn
glazing **240.00**
11½" h, tin, square, tapered, deep
reddish cobalt glass in four sides,
damage, soldered repairs, black
paint. **115.00**
18" h, tin, hexagonal, turned finials,
good detail, old worn silver, red, and
gold repaint, fastened on pole, 78"
h overall **140.00**
21½" h, tin, hexagonal, old black and
gold repaint, finial incomplete,
wooden pole, 63" h overall **110.00**
Dark Room, 17" h, Carbutt's Dry Plate
Lantern, orig black paint, white striping, tin kerosene font and burner,
name and patent date of April 25,
1882 on label **65.00**
Folding, 10" h, tin, glass sides, emb
"Stonebridge, 1908" **65.00**
Kerosene
12¼" h, tin, brass trim, clear glass
globe **130.00**
24½" h, orig black paint and kerosene
burner, mercury reflector, stenciled
label "C. T. Ham Mfg Co's New No.
8 Tubular Square Lamp, Label Reg-
istered 1886". **175.00**

Miner's, tin, three part, leather fitting for head, adapter with brass plate for pole, two wire loop handles, adjustable reflector, hinged tin door, emb "Ferguson, NY 1878". **150.00**

Railroad, 16" h, tin, wide reflector, kerosene burner, marked "Buhol No. 100". **75.00**

Skater's, 13½" h, cast iron, lacy base, bulbous clear globe, pierced tin top and wire bail handle. **225.00**

Whale Oil, 13½" h, tin, clear blown glazed globe, worn brown japanning, pierced star and diamond vent holes, removable font with whale oil burner, attributed to New England Glass Co, ring handle, minor damage to base ring **200.00**

Figure

12½" h, creamware, Hamlet, c1775, damages. **770.00**

17½" h, pearlware, horse, underglazed polychrome enamel dec, raised rect base, one ear reglued, c1830 . . . .**17,600.00**

Jar, cov, 4¼" h, blue and yellow dec . **175.00**

Jug

5¾" h, sponge dec in shades of gray and blue, entwined strap handle, flower head and foliage terminals . **400.00**

8¾" h, creamware, Mary and Elizabeth/William and Joseph, floral terminal on handle. **3,500.00**

Miniature

Cup and Saucer, handleless, multicolored enameled flowers **125.00**

Pitcher, 2" h, softpaste, multicolored dec, emb leaf handle **85.00**

Mug, pearlware, floral dec **160.00**

Nut Dish, 4¾" l, leaf shape, blue Oriental dec **140.00**

LEEDS CHINA

History: The Leeds Pottery in Yorkshire, England, began production about 1758. Among its products was creamware that was competitive with that of Wedgwood. The initial factory closed in 1820, but various subsequent owners continued until 1880. They made exceptional cream-colored ware, either plain, salt–glazed, or painted with colored enamels, and glazed and unglazed redware.

Early wares are unmarked. Later pieces bear marks of "Leeds Pottery," sometimes followed by "Hartley–Green and Co." or the letters "LP." Reproductions also have these marks.

Reference: Susan and Al Bagdade, *Warman's English & Continental Pottery & Porcelain, Second Edition,* Wallace–Homestead, 1991.

Bowl, cov, floral panels dec, swan finial **160.00**

Candlestick, 10" h, spreading sq pedestal pierced shaft, stylized flowers, balustrade nozzle, sq leaf sprig molded bobeche, sq coved leaf sprig molded and foliate reticulated base, imp "Leeds Pottery" **225.00**

Charger, 15⅝" d, multicolored urn of flowers dec, blue feather edge **450.00**

Creamer, 4½" h, gaudy flowers and leaves, creamware **325.00**

Cup and Saucer, handleless, pearlware, four color dec, small flakes. **275.00**

Cup Plate, 3¾" d, gaudy blue and white floral dec **250.00**

Egg Cup, 2¾" h, creamware, reticulated **145.00**

Plate, multicolored mayfly in center, scalloped edge outlined in black with blue fleur–de–lis at indentations, red flowerheads, c1800, 9½" d, $145.00.

Plate

6⅜" d, multicolored house scene, sponged trees, blue feather edge . **325.00**

7½" d, multicolored strawberry dec, blue feather edge. **300.00**

8⅛" d, pearlware, Chinoiserie dec, small edge chips, short rim hairline **350.00**

Platter, 19¼" l, blue flowers and leaves, blue feather edge, minor staining . . . **235.00**

Sugar, softpaste

4¾" h, fluted ribs, multicolored floral dec. **200.00**

6" h, gaudy floral, blue bands **250.00**

Teapot, 5½″ h, gold, blue, green, and
brown garlands, spout repaired,
discolored. 75.00

LENOX CHINA

History: In 1889 Jonathan Cox and Walter Scott
Lenox established the Ceramic Art Co. at Trenton,
New Jersey. By 1906 Lenox formed his own com-
pany, Lenox, Inc. Using potters lured from Belleek,
Lenox began making an American version of this
famous ware.

Older Lenox china has two marks: a green
wreath and a palette. The palette mark appears on
blanks supplied to amateurs who hand painted
china as a hobby. The Lenox Company still exists
and currently uses a gold stamped mark.

Reference: Mary Frank Gaston, *American Belleek,* Collector Books, 1984.

Additional Listings: Belleek.

**Salt, swan, light coral, green mark, 3″ l,
2″ h, $25.00.**

Bowl, Art Deco, ftd, sterling silver overlay, blue glazed ground 115.00
Chocolate Set, chocolate pot, cov, six
cups and saucers, Golden Wheat pattern, cobalt ground, price for thirteen
piece set 275.00
Cigarette Box, white apple blossoms,
green ground, wreath mark 40.00
Cream Soup, Tuxedo, green mark   . .   35.00
Cup and Saucer, Golden Wreath   . . .   20.00
Honey Pot, 5″ h, ivory beehive, gold bee
and trim, matching underplate 75.00
Jug, 4″ h, hp, grapes and leaves, shaded
brown ground, sgd "G Morley" 240.00

Mug
5¼″ h, Harvard College dec, dated
1910. . . . .   85.00
6¼″ h, monk, smiling, holding up glass
of wine, shaded brown ground, SS
rim 150.00
Perfume Lamp, 9″ h, figural, Marie An-
toinette, bisque finish, dated 1929. . .   650.00
Plate
Dinner, Alden 15.00
Salad, Tuxedo, gold mark 10.00
Salt, 3″ d, creamy ivory ground, molded
seashells and coral, green wreath
mark 35.00
Salt and Pepper Shakers, pr, hp, green
and gold bird dec 65.00
Shoe, white, bow trim 185.00
Tea Set, teapot, creamer, and sugar,
wide gold borders, old mark, price for
set. 135.00
Tea Strainer, hp, small roses dec   . . .   65.00
Toby, William Penn, pink handle 150.00
Vase
6″ h, roses dec, sgd "W Morley"   . .   165.00
8″ h, tree stump, robin, glazed white   125.00
9¼″ h, hp, woodland scene, shaded
brown ground, marked "Ceramic
Art Co" 100.00

LIBBEY GLASS

History: In 1888 Edward Libbey established the
Libbey Glass Company in Toledo, Ohio, after the
closing of the New England Glass Works of W. L.
Libbey and Son in East Cambridge, Massachusetts. The new Libbey company produced quality
cut glass for the "Brilliant Period."

In 1930 Libbey's interest in art glass production
was renewed. A. Douglas Nash was employed as
a designer in 1931.

The factory continues production today as Libbey Glass Co.

References: Carl U. Fauster, *Libbey Glass
Since 1818: Pictorial History & Collector's Guide,*
Len Beach Press, 1979; Ellen T. Schroy, *Warman's
Glass,* Wallace–Homestead, 1992.

Additional Listings: Amberina Glass and Cut
Glass.

Bon Bon, 7″ d, 1½″ h, amberina, wavy
six pointed 1½″ fuchsia rim shading to
pale amber, sgd 600.00
Bowl
8″ d, Regis pattern 230.00
9″ d, saber, hobstars, and crosshatch-
ing, notched prism, sgd. 220.00
10″ d, 4″ h, amberina, fold down rim,
sgd. 825.00
Compote, 10″ h, amberina, deep color,
Joseph Locke, Toledo, 1917, sgd . . .   2,310.00

Cordial, 5" h, crystal, green jade knop inserts, engraved Empire pattern bowls, marked "Libbey" in circle, price for set of eight.	385.00
Ice Cream Tray, 10 x 14", Gloria pattern	275.00
Pitcher, 10" h, copper wheel cut leaves and butterfly design, sgd	140.00
Plate, 7" d, Gloria pattern	165.00
Sherbet, silhouette stem, black rabbit, sgd	135.00
Tray, 15" l, oval, saber, hobstars, cane, and central feather design, sgd.	610.00
Tumbler, Maize pattern, blue leaves .	195.00
Vase	
8" h, oviform, ribbed, waisted neck, wafer and ball stem	715.00
8¼" h, tapered, optic fern and pink threaded design, clear foot, sgd. . .	310.00
9" h, bud, elongated, ribbed	610.00
12" h, trumpet	
Amberina, fuchsia, ribbed	415.00
Cut glass, floral pattern, flutes and horizontal ladder, precise cutting, clear blank, 1906–19 trademark	295.00
13½" h, baluster, emerald green cut flower panels, ftd, sgd base.	700.00
14" h, amberina, tapered, ribbed, fuchsia flared rim, ftd	880.00

LIMITED-EDITION COLLECTOR PLATES

History: Bing and Grondahl made the first collector plate in 1895. Royal Copenhagen issued its first Christmas plate in 1908.

In the late 1960s and early 1970s, several potteries, glass factories, mints, and artists began issuing plates commemorating people, animals, events, etc. Christmas plates were supplemented by Mother's Day plates, Easter plates, etc. A sense of speculation swept the field, fostered in part by flamboyant ads in newspapers and flashy direct-mail promotions.

Collectors often favor the first plate issued in a series above all others. Condition is a prime factor. Having the original box also increases price.

Limited-edition collector plates, more than any other object in this guide, should be collected for design and pleasure and only secondarily as an investment.

References: Susan Elliott and K. Samara, *The Official Price Guide To Limited Edition Collectibles*, House of Collectibles, 1994; Diane Carnevale Jones, *Collectors' Information Bureau's Collectibles Market Guide & Price Index, Eleventh Edition*, Collectors' Information Bureau, 1994, distributed by Wallace–Homestead; Diane Carnevale Jones, *Collectors' Information Bureau's Collectibles Price Guide 1994, Fourth Edition*, Collectors' Information Bureau, 1994, distributed by Wallace–Homestead;

Diane Carnevale Jones, *Collectors' Information Bureau's Directory To Limited Edition Collectible Stores*, Collectors' Information Bureau, 1993, distributed by Wallace–Homestead; Diane Carnevale Jones, *Collectors' Information Bureau's Directory To Secondary Market Retailers: Buying And Selling Limited Edition Artwork*, Collectors' Information Bureau, 1992, distributed by Wallace–Homestead; Carl Luckey, *Luckey's Hummel Figurines & Plates: A Collector's Identification and Value Guide, 10th Edition*, Books Americana, 1993; Paul Stark, *Limited Edition Collectibles, Everything You May Ever Need To Know*, New Gallery Press, 1988.

Periodicals: *Collector Editions*, 170 Fifth Ave., 12th Floor, New York, NY 10010; *Collectors Mart Magazine*, PO Box 12830, Wichita, KS 67277; *Collectors News*, 506 Second St., PO Box 156, Grundy Center, IA 50638; *Insight On Collectibles*, 193 Lakeshore Rd., Suite 202, St. Catharines, Ontario, Canada L2N 2T6; *International Collectible Showcase*, One Westminster Place, Lake Forest, IL 60045; *Plate World*, 9200 N. Maryland Ave., Niles, IL 60648; *Toybox Magazine*, 8393 East Holly Rd., Holly, MI 48442.

Collectors' Clubs: Franklin Mint Collectors Society, The Franklin Mint, U.S. Route 1, Franklin Center, PA 19091; International Plate Collectors Guild, PO Box 487, Artesia, CA 90702; M. I. Hummel Club, Goebel Plaza, Dept. O, PO Box 11, Pennington, NJ 08534.

Museum: Bradford Museum, Niles, IL.

Additional Listings: See *Warman's Americana & Collectibles* for more examples of collector plates plus many other limited edition collectibles.

BAREUTHER (Germany)

Christmas Plates, Hans Mueller artist, 8" d

1967 Stiftskirche, FE	90.00
1969 Christkindlmarkt	20.00
1971 Toys For Sale	20.00
1973 Christmas Sleigh Ride	20.00
1975 Snowman	25.00
1977 Story Time (Christmas Story)	30.00
1979 Winter Day	40.00
1981 Walk In The Forest	40.00
1983 The Night Before Christmas .	45.00
1985 Winter Wonderland	42.50
1987 Decorating The Tree	46.50
1989 Sleigh Ride	50.00
1990 The Old Forge in Rothenburg	52.50
1991 Christmas Joy	56.50
1992 Market Place in Heppenheim	59.50

Father's Day Series, Hans Mueller artist, 8" d

1969 Castle Neuschwanstein	48.00
1971 Castle Heidelberg	24.00
1973 Castle Katz	30.00
1975 Castle Lichtenstein	35.00
1977 Castle Eltz	30.00
1979 Castle Rheinstein	30.00

1981 Castle Gutenfels	40.00
1983 Castle Lauenstein	40.00

Mother's Day

1969 Mother & Children	75.00
1971 Mother & Children	20.00
1973 Mother & Children	22.00
1975 Spring Outing	25.00
1977 Noon Feeding	28.00
1979 Mother's Love	38.00
1981 Playtime	40.00

Bing & Grondahl, 1964, The Fir Tree and Hare, 7¼" d, $50.00.

BING AND GRONDAHL (Denmark)

Christmas Plates, various artists, 7" d

1895 Behind The Frozen Window	3,400.00
1896 New Moon Over Snow Covered Trees	1,975.00
1897 Christmas Meal Of The Sparrows	725.00
1898 Christmas Roses And Christmas Star	700.00
1899 The Crows Enjoying Christmas	900.00
1900 Church Bells Chiming In Christmas	800.00
1901 The Three Wise Men From The East	450.00
1902 Interior Of A Gothic Church	285.00
1903 Happy Expectation Of Children	150.00
1904 View Of Copenhagen From Frederiksberg Hill	125.00
1905 Anxiety Of The Coming Christmas Night	130.00
1906 Sleighing To Church On Christmas Eve	95.00
1907 The Little Match Girl	125.00
1908 St Petri Church Of Copenhagen	85.00
1909 Happiness Over The Yule Tree	100.00
1910 The Old Organist	90.00
1911 First It Was Sung By Angels To Shepherds In The Fields	80.00
1912 Going To Church On Christmas Eve	80.00
1913 Bringing Home The Yule Tree	85.00
1914 Royal Castle Of Amalienborg, Copenhagen	75.00
1915 Chained Dog Getting Double Meal On Christmas Eve	120.00
1916 Christmas Prayer Of The Sparrows	85.00
1917 Arrival Of The Christmas Boat	75.00
1918 Fishing Boat Returning Home For Christmas	85.00
1919 Outside The Lighted Window	80.00
1920 Hare In The Snow	70.00
1921 Pigeons In The Castle Court	55.00
1922 Star Of Bethlehem	60.00
1923 Royal Hunting Castle, The Hermitage	55.00
1924 Lighthouse In Danish Waters	65.00
1925 The Child's Christmas	70.00
1926 Churchgoers On Christmas Day	65.00
1927 Skating Couple	110.00
1928 Eskimo Looking At Village Church In Greenland	60.00
1929 Fox Outside Farm On Christmas Eve	75.00
1930 Yule Tree In Town Hall Square Of Copenhagen	85.00
1931 Arrival Of The Christmas Train	75.00
1933 The Korsor–Nyborg Ferry	70.00
1935 Lillebelt Bridge Connecting Funen With Jutland	65.00
1937 Arrival Of Christmas Guests	75.00
1939 Ole Lock–Eye, The Sandman	150.00
1941 Horses Enjoying Christmas Meal In Stable	345.00
1943 The Ribe Cathedral	155.00
1945 The Old Water Mill	135.00
1947 Dybbol Mill	70.00
1949 Landsoldaten, 19th Century Danish Soldier	70.00
1951 Jens Bang, New Passenger Boat Running Between Copenhagen And Aalborg	115.00
1953 Royal Boat In Greenland Waters	95.00
1955 Kalundborg Church	115.00
1957 Christmas Candles	155.00
1959 Christmas Eve	120.00
1961 Winter Harmony	115.00
1963 The Christmas Elf	120.00
1965 Bringing Home The Christmas Tree	65.00
1967 Sharing The Joy Of Christmas	48.00
1969 Arrival Of Christmas Guests	30.00
1971 Christmas At Home	20.00
1973 Country Christmas	25.00
1975 The Old Water Mill	24.00
1977 Copenhagen Christmas	25.00
1979 White Christmas	30.00
1981 Christmas Peace	50.00

1983 Christmas In Old Town	55.00
1985 Christmas Eve At The Farmhouse	55.00
1987 The Snowman's Christmas Eve	60.00
1989 Christmas Anchorage	65.00
1990 Changing of the Guards	75.00
1991 Copenhagen Stock Exchange	85.00
1992 Christmas At the Rectory . . .	69.50
1993 Father Christmas in Copenhagen.	69.50

Mother's Day Plates, Henry Thelander, artist, 6″ d

1969 Dog And Puppies	400.00
1971 Cat And Kitten	24.00
1973 Duck And Ducklings	20.00
1975 Doe And Fawns	20.00
1977 Squirrel And Young	25.00
1979 Fox And Cubs	30.00
1981 Hare And Young	40.00
1983 Raccoon And Young	45.00
1985 Bear And Cubs	40.00
1987 Sheep With Lambs	42.50
1989 Cow With Calf	48.00
1990 Hen with Chicks	65.00
1991 The Nanny Goat and her Two Frisky Kids	75.00
1992 Panda With Cubs	59.50
1993 St. Bernard Dog and Puppies	59.50

HAVILAND & PARLON (France)

Christmas Series, various artists, 10″ d

1972 Madonna And Child, Raphael, FE	80.00
1974 Cowper Madonna And Child, Raphael	55.00
1976 Madonna And Child, Botticelli	50.00
1978 Madonna And Child, Fra Filippo Lippi.	65.00

Lady And The Unicorn Series, artist unknown, 10″ d

1977 To My Only Desire, FE	60.00
1978 Sight	40.00
1980 Touch	110.00
1982 Taste	80.00

Tapestry Series, artist unknown, 10″ d

1971 The Unicorn In Captivity	145.00
1972 Start Of The Hunt	70.00
1974 End Of The Hunt	120.00
1976 The Unicorn Is Brought To The Castle.	55.00

LALIQUE (France)

Annual Series, lead crystal, Marie–Claude Lalique, artist, 8½″ d

1965 Deux Oiseaux (Two Birds), FE	800.00
1966 Rose de Songerie (Dream Rose).	215.00

1968 Gazelle Fantaisie (Gazelle Fantasy).	70.00
1970 Paon (Peacock)	50.00
1972 Coquillage (Shell)	55.00
1974 Sous d'Argent (Silver Pennies)	65.00
1976 Aigle (Eagle)	100.00

LENOX (United States)

Boehm Bird Series, Edward Marshall Boehm, artist, 10½″ d

1970 Wood Thrush, FE	175.00
1972 Mountain Bluebird	65.00
1974 Rufous Hummingbird	50.00
1976 Cardinal	58.00
1978 Mockingbirds	60.00
1979 Golden–Crowned Kinglets . . .	75.00
1980 Black–Throated Blue Warblers	75.00
1981 Eastern Phoebes	92.50

Boehm Woodland Wildlife Series, Edward Marshall Boehm, artist, 10½″ d

1973 Raccoons, FE	80.00
1974 Red Foxes	50.00
1976 Eastern Chipmunks	60.00
1979 Squirrels	76.00
1978 Whitetail Deer	60.00
1980 Bobcats	90.00
1981 Martens	150.00
1982 River Otters	100.00

LLARDO (Spain)

Christmas, 8″ d, undisclosed artists

1971 Caroling	30.00
1973 Boy & Girl	50.00
1975 Cherubs	60.00
1977 Nativity	70.00
1979 Snow Dance	80.00

Mother's Day, undisclosed artists

1971 Kiss Of The Child	75.00
1973 Mother & Children	35.00
1975 Mother & Child	55.00
1977 Mother & Daughter	60.00
1979 Off to School	90.00

REED & BARTON (United States)

Christmas Series, Damascene silver, 11″ d through 1978, 8″ d 1979 to present

1970 A Partridge In A Pear Tree, FE	200.00
1971 We Three Kings Of Orient Are	65.00
1973 Adoration Of The Kings	75.00
1975 Adoration Of The Kings	65.00
1977 Decorating The Church	60.00
1979 Merry Old Santa Claus	65.00
1981 The Shopkeeper At Christmas	75.00

ROSENTHAL (Germany)

**Christmas Plates, various artists, 8½"
d**

1910 Winter Peace	550.00
1911 The Three Wise Men	325.00
1912 Shooting Stars	250.00
1913 Christmas Lights	235.00
1915 Walking To Church	180.00
1917 Angel Of Peace	210.00
1919 St Christopher With The Christ Child.	225.00
1921 Christmas In The Mountains .	200.00
1923 Children In The Winter Wood	200.00
1925 The Three Wise Men	200.00
1927 Station On The Way	200.00
1929 Christmas In The Alps	225.00
1931 Path Of The Magi	225.00
1933 Through The Night To Light .	190.00
1935 Christmas By The Sea	185.00
1937 Berchtesgaden	195.00
1939 Schneekoppe Mountain	195.00
1941 Strassburg Cathedral	250.00
1943 Winter Idyll	300.00
1945 Christmas Peace	400.00
1947 The Dillingen Madonna	975.00
1949 The Holy Family	185.00
1951 Star Of Bethlehem	450.00
1953 The Holy Light	185.00
1955 Christmas In A Village	190.00
1957 Christmas By The Sea	195.00
1959 Midnight Mass	195.00
1961 Solitary Christmas	225.00
1962 Christmas Eve	195.00
1963 Silent Night	185.00
1965 Christmas In Munich	185.00
1967 Christmas In Regensburg . . .	185.00
1969 Christmas In Rothenburg . . .	220.00
1971 Christmas In Garmisch	100.00
1973 Christmas In Lubeck–Holstein .	110.00
1974 Christmas in Wurzburg	100.00

ROYAL COPENHAGEN (Denmark)

**Christmas Plates, various artists, 6" d
1908, 1909, 1910; 7" 1911 to present**

1908 Madonna And Child	1,750.00
1909 Danish Landscape	150.00
1910 The Magi	120.00
1911 Danish Landscape	135.00
1912 Elderly Couple By Christmas Tree.	120.00
1913 Spire Of Frederik's Church, Copenhagen	125.00
1914 Sparrows In Tree At Church Of The Holy Spirit, Copenhagen.	100.00
1915 Danish Landscape	150.00
1916 Shepherd In The Field On Christmas Night.	85.00
1917 Tower Of Our Savior's Church, Copenhagen	90.00
1918 Sheep and Shepherds	80.00

**Royal Copenhagen, 1920, Christmas
Series, Mary with the Child Jesus,
$75.00.**

1919 In The Park	80.00
1920 Mary With The Child Jesus . .	75.00
1921 Aabenraa Marketplace	75.00
1922 Three Singing Angels	70.00
1923 Danish Landscape	70.00
1924 Christmas Star Over The Sea And Sailing Ship	100.00
1925 Street Scene From Christianshavn, Copenhagen.	85.00
1926 View Of Christmas Canal, Copenhagen	75.00
1927 Ship's Boy At The Tiller On Christmas Night.	140.00
1928 Vicar's Family On Way To Church	75.00
1929 Grundtvig Church, Copenhagen	100.00
1930 Fishing Boats On The Way To The Harbor	80.00
1931 Mother And Child	90.00
1932 Frederiksberg Gardens With Statue Of Frederik VI	90.00
1933 The Great Belt Ferry	110.00
1934 The Hermitage Castle	115.00
1935 Fishing Boat Off Kronborg Castle.	145.00
1936 Roskilde Cathedral	130.00
1937 Christmas Scene In Main Street, Copenhagen	135.00
1938 Round Church In Osterlars On Bornholm	200.00
1939 Expeditionary Ship In Pack–Ice Of Greenland.	180.00
1940 The Good Shepherd	300.00
1941 Danish Village Church	250.00
1943 Flight Of Holy Family To Egypt	425.00
1945 A Peaceful Motif	325.00
1947 The Good Shepherd	210.00
1949 Our Lady's Cathedral, Copenhagen.	165.00

1951 Christmas Angel	300.00
1953 Frederiksborg Castle	120.00
1955 Fano Girl	185.00
1957 The Good Shepherd	115.00
1959 Christmas Night	120.00
1961 Training Ship Danmark	155.00
1963 Hojsager Mill	80.00
1965 Little Skaters	60.00
1967 The Royal Oak	45.00
1969 The Old Farmyard	35.00
1971 Hare In Winter	80.00
1973 Train Homeward Bound For Christmas	85.00
1975 Queen's Palace	85.00
1977 Immervad Bridge	75.00
1979 Choosing The Christmas Tree	60.00
1981 Admiring The Christmas Tree	55.00
1983 Merry Christmas	60.00
1985 Snowman	55.00
1987 Winter Birds	58.00
1989 The Old Skating Pond	50.00
1990 Christams at Tivoli	76.00
1991 The Festival of Santa Lucia	69.50
1992 The Queen's Carriage	69.50
1993 Christmas Guests	69.50

Mother's Day Plates, various artists, 6¼" d

1971 American Mother	125.00
1973 Danish Mother	60.00
1975 Bird In Nest	50.00
1977 The Twins	50.00
1979 A Loving Mother	30.00
1981 Reunion	40.00

SCHIMD (Japan)

Disney Christmas Series, undisclosed artists, 7½" d

1973 Sleigh Ride, FE	400.00
1975 Caroling	20.00
1977 Down The Chimney	25.00
1979 Santa's Surprise	20.00
1981 Happy Holidays	22.00
1982 Winter Games	29.00

Disney Mother's Day Series

1974 Flowers For Mother, FE	80.00
1976 Minnie Mouse And Friends	20.00
1978 Flowers For Bambi	20.00
1980 Minnie's Surprise	20.00
1981 Playmates	35.00
1982 A Dream Come True	20.00

Peanuts Christmas Series, Charles Schulz, artist, 7½" d

1972 Snoopy Guides The Sleigh, FE	90.00
1974 Christmas Eve At The Fireplace	65.00
1976 Woodstock's Christmas	30.00
1978 Filling The Stocking	20.00
1980 Waiting For Santa	50.00
1981 A Christmas Wish	17.50
1982 Perfect Performance	35.00

Mother's Day Series

1972 Playing Hooky	15.00

1974 Bumblebee	20.00
1976 Devotion For Mother	30.00
1978 Afternoon Stroll	32.50
1980 Mother's Little Helpers	52.00
1982 The Flower Basket	47.50
1984 A Joy to Share	45.00
1986 Home From School	55.00
1989 Pretty as a Picture	75.00
1990 Mother's Little Athlete	53.00
1991 Soft & Gentle	55.00

WEDGWOOD (Great Britain)

Christmas Series, jasper stoneware, 8" d

1969 Windsor Castle, FE	225.00
1970 Christmas In Trafalgar Square	30.00
1972 St Paul's Cathedral	40.00
1974 The Houses Of Parliament	40.00
1976 Hampton Court	46.00
1978 The Horse Guards	55.00
1980 St James Palace	70.00
1982 Lambeth Palace	80.00
1984 Constitution Hill	80.00
1986 The Albert Memorial	80.00
1987 Guildhall	85.00
1988 The Observatory/Greenwich	90.00
1989 Winchester Cathedral	88.00

Mothers Series, jasper stoneware, 6½" d

1971 Sportive Love, FE	25.00
1972 The Sewing Lesson	20.00
1974 Domestic Employment	30.00
1976 The Spinner	35.00
1978 Swan and Cygnets	35.00
1980 Birds	48.00
1982 Cherubs With Swing	55.00
1984 Musical Cupids	55.00
1986 Cupids Fishing	55.00
1988 Tiger Lily	59.00
1991 Peonies	65.00

Queen's Christmas, A Price artist

1980 Windsor Castle	30.00
1981 Trafalgar Square	25.00
1982 Piccadilly Circus	35.00
1983 St Pauls	32.50
1984 Tower Of London	35.00
1985 Palace Of Westminister	35.00
1986 Tower Bridge	35.00

LIMOGES

History: Limoges porcelain has been produced in Limoges, France, for more than a century by numerous factories other than the famed Haviland. One of the most frequently encountered marks is "T. & V. Limoges," which is the ware made by Tressman and Vought. Other identifiable Limoges marks are A. L. (A. Lanternier), J. P. L (J. Pouyat, Limoges), M. R. (M. Reddon), and Elite and Coronet.

References: Susan and Al Bagdade, *Warman's English & Continental Pottery & Porcelain, Second Edition,* Wallace–Homestead, 1991; Mary Frank Gaston, *The Collector's Encyclopedia Of Limoges Porcelain, 2nd Edition,* Collector Books, 1992.

Additional Listings: Haviland China.

Loving Cup, maroon ground, gilt trim, marked "J. P. France," dated 1905, 6¾" w, 5¾" h, $175.00.

Bowl, 4½" h, ftd, hp, wild roses and leaves, sgd "J E Dodge, 1892". . . . . | 75.00

Box, 4¼" sq, cobalt and white ground, cupids on lid, pate–sur–pate dec. . . . | 170.00

Cachepot, 7½" w, 9" h, male and female pheasants on front, mountain scene on obverse, gold handles and four ball feet . . . . | 225.00

Cake Plate, 11½" d, ivory ground, brushed gold scalloped rim, gold medallion, marked "Limoges T & V" . . . . | 70.00

Chocolate Pot, 13" h, purple violets and green leaves, cream ground, gold handle, spout, and base, sgd "Kelly, JPL/France" . . . . | 325.00

Chocolate Set, 9½" h chocolate pot, four cups and saucers, light green, floral dec, gold trim . . . . | 250.00

Creamer, 3¼" h, purple flowers, white ground, gold handle and trim . . . . . . | 40.00

Cup and Saucer, hp, flowers and leaves, gold trim, artist sgd . . . . | 75.00

Dresser Set, pink flowers, pastel blue, green, and yellow ground, large tray, cov powder, cov rouge, pin tray, talc jar, and pr candlesticks, price for seven piece set. . . . . | 395.00

Dinner Service, twelve dinner plates, eleven salad plates, eight dessert plates, ten tea cups, eleven saucers, gilt geometric panels, white ground, stamped factory mark "J P, L France," incised numbers, price for 52 piece set. . . . . | 365.00

Figure, 25" h, 13" w, three girls, arms entwined, holding basket of flowers, books, and purse, marked "C & V" and "L & L". . . . . | 450.00

Fish Service, twelve sq plates, six different fishing scenes in center, gilt dec cobalt blue border, matching rect two handled sauce boat, underglaze green mark "CFH/GDM," Gerad Defraissein et Morel, late 19th C, price for 13 piece set. . . . . | 275.00

Hair Receiver, blue flowers and white butterflies, ivory ground, gold trim, marked "JPL". . . . . | 75.00

Lemonade Pitcher, matching tray, water lily dec, sgd "Vignard Limoges" . . . . | 335.00

Mug, corn motif, sgd "T & V Limoges France" . . . . | 60.00

Nappy, 6" d, curved gold handle, gold scalloped edges, soft pink blossoms, blue–green ground . . . . | 30.00

Oyster Plate, 8" d, six wells, ribbed molded, gold tracery, cream and yellow ground . . . . | 85.00

Plaque, 13¼" d, facing pair, two stags on one, two deer on other, heavy gold rococo border, artist sgd "DuBois," price for pair. . . . . | 850.00

Perfume Tray, 9½" d, hp, apple blossoms, blue shaded to pink to gray ground, pierced handles. . . . . | 50.00

Pitcher, 8 x 6½", hp, russet yellow apples, multicolored shaded ground, beaded handle, artist sgd "JPL" . . . . | 115.00

Plate

7½" d, hp, pink and gold roses, gold rim . . . . | 30.00

8½" d, hp, pink roses, leaves, gold trim, scalloped rim . . . . | 25.00

9" d, hp, pastel florals, Art Nouveau enameled gold dec, ornate gold scalloped rim. . . . . | 30.00

Presidential China, 8½" d plate, cup, and saucer, William Henry Harrison, made for firm of M W Beveridge, Washington, DC, marked "Harrison 1892," price for three piece set. . . . . | 1,150.00

Punch Bowl, 13" d, scalloped gold rim, fruit blossom dec, gold band pedestal base . . . . | 225.00

Sauce Bowl, hp, fish, baskets, and sailing ships, shell motif, c1895 . . . . | 95.00

Snuff Box, hp, wildflowers and gold tracery, pink ground, artist sgd, dated 1800 . . . . | 200.00

Tankard Set, 14" h tankard, four mugs, hp, grape dec, gold and green ground, price for five piece set . . . . | 300.00

Tray, 14⅛" d, scenic, thatched cottages, bridge, and stream, two people on path, emb leaf border, pink and gold trim . . . . | 225.00

Vase, 12¼" h, flattened cylindrical form,

iris bouquet, luster and gilt ground, polychrome enamel dec, handles, four ball feet, sgd "Steve," printed green mark. **250.00**

LINENS

History: The term linen now has become a generic designation for household dressings for table, bed, or bath, whether made of linen, cotton, lace, or other fabrics.

Linen, as a table cover, is mentioned in the Bible and other writings of an early age. We see "borde cloths" in early drawings and paintings with their creases pressed in sharply. It was a sign of wealth and social standing to present such elegance.

During the period before the general use of forks, when fingers were the accepted means of dining, napkins were important. They usually were rectangular and large in size. In the early 18th century, napkins lost their popularity. The fork had become the tool of the upper classes, who apparently wished to show off their newfound expertise in the use of the fork. After diners did much damage to tablecloths, finicky hostesses decided that the napkin was a necessity. It soon reappeared on the table.

The Victorian era gave us the greatest variety of household linens. The lady of the house had time to sit and sew a fine seam. Sewing became a social activity. Afternoon callers brought their handwork with them when they came to gossip and take tea. Every young girl was expected to fill her hope chest with fine examples of her prowess. In the late 19th century these ladies made some very beautiful "white work," using white embroidery of delicate stitchery, lace insertions, and ruffles on white fabrics. These pieces are highly sought after today.

The 20th century saw a decline in that type of fine stitchery. The social pace quickened. Household linens of that period show more bright colors in the embroidery, the designs become more lighthearted and frivolous, and inexpensive machine–made lace was used. Kitchen towels were decorated with animals or pots and pans. Vanity sets dominated the bedroom; the Bridge craze put emphasis on tablecloths and napkin sets. To fill the desire for less-expensive lace cloths and bedspreads, women of the Great Depression started crocheting. Many examples of this craft are available.

With the advent of World War II, more women went to work. The last remnant of fine stitchery quickly diminished. Technological advances in production and fibers lessened the interest in handmade linens.

Collecting And Use Tips: Most old linens are fragile; some are age stained from being stored improperly for years. Unless you have a secret for removing these stains without damaging the fabric, look for those items in very good or better condition.

Linens which are not used frequently are best stored unpressed, rolled Boy Scout style, and tucked away in an old pillowcase out of bright light. Be sure the linens and pillowcases have been rinsed several times to remove all residue of detergent.

For laundered pieces which are used often, wrap in acid–free white tissue or muslin folders. If the tissue is not acid free, it will cause the folded edges to discolor. If possible, store on rollers to prevent creasing. Creased areas become weak and disintegrate in laundering. Acid–free wrapping material can be purchased from Talas, 104 Fifth Avenue, New York, NY 10011.

References: Virginia Churchill Bath, *Lace*, Henry Regnery Co., 1974; Maryanne Dolan, *Old Lace & Linens Including Crochet: An Identification and Value Guide*, Books Americana, 1989; Alda Horner, *The Official Price Guide Linens, Lace and Other Fabrics*, House of Collectibles, 1991; Frances Johnson, *Collecting Antique Linens, Lace, and Needlework*, Wallace–Homestead, 1991; Lois Markrich and Heinz Edgar Kiewe, *Victorian Fancywork*, Henry Regnery Co., 1974; *McCall's Needlework Treasury*, Random House, 1963; Francis M. Montgomery, *Textiles In America, 1650–1870*, W. W. Norton & Co. (A Winterthur/Barra Book); Dana G. Morykan and Harry L. Rinker, *Warman's Country Antiques & Collectibles, Second Edition*, Wallace–Homestead, 1994; Patricia Esterbrook Roberts, *Table Settings. Entertaining And Etiquette. A History And Guide*, Viking Press, 1967.

Periodical: *The Lace Collector*, PO Box 222, Plainwell, MI 49080.

Collectors' Club: International Old Lacers, PO Box 481223, Denver, CO 80248.

Museums: Metropolitan Museum of Art, New York, NY; Museum of Early Southern Decorative Arts (MESDA), Winston–Salem, NC; Museum of Fine Arts, Boston, MA; Rockwood Museum, Wilmington, DE; Shelburne Museum, Shelburne, VT; Smithsonian Institution, Washington, D.C.

Bedspread

    Crochet, double size, small medallion motif, crocheted together with fine webbing, pale green, green fringed, three sides **250.00**

    Embroidered, white, embroidered with red thread, squares of birds and flowers, 1920s. **95.00**

    Victorian, 104 x 112", white work, bleached muslin, one third tucking and embroidered eyelet dec, eyelet edges, c1890. . . . . **225.00**

Bolster Case, white linen, ends open, embroidered garland of white flowers with script letter "P" in center, crocheted edging, c1920 . . . . **50.00**

Bridge Set

    Irish Linen, double damask, allover

floral and swirl pattern, wide hand hemstitched border, four matching napkins, price for set **35.00**

Madeira, white linen, drawn and embroidery work, embroidered flower basket corners, scalloped edges, four matching napkins, price for set **25.00**

Curtain Panel, each panel 36 x 84″, pr, appliqued linen and reembroidered floral and scroll pattern, scalloped outer edge and bottom, net background, machine made **75.00**

Doily
Crochet, 10 x 13″, rooster center, white. **24.00**
Filet Net, 14″ d, ecru, reembroidered flowers and leaves. **3.50**

Dresser Scarf
Madeira, cut work, hand embroidered satin stitch, pointe lace insets each end, filet lace borders on four sides, c1930. **30.00**
Victorian, 122 x 36″, white linen, white work, floral design ends, heavy padded satin stitch, scalloped edges, c1890. . . . . **25.00**

Napkin
Cocktail, cotton, pale yellow, one corner elephant embroidered, fringed edges, c1930, set of eight. **7.50**
Dinner, linen
20″ sq, double damask, ½″ hand hemstitched border, wreath motif center, price for set of four. **24.00**
22″ sq, double damask, rose pattern, hand rolled hem, price for set of 8 . . . . **36.00**
24″ sq, double damask, satin stripe border, hand hemstitched, price for set of eight **40.00**
Luncheon, 14″ sq, white Swiss linen, one corner flower basket embroidered, c1920, price for set of four . **12.00**

Pillowcase
Cotton, embroidered girl with umbrella, bright colors, machine made lace edge, from stamped kit, c1935, price for pair **15.00**
Linen, 22 x 15″, cut work and embroidery, filet lace showing mythological marine theme in center and filet lace corner, edged in machine made lace, button back. **65.00**
Madeira, linen, pointe lace surrounded by embroidered cut work, pale blue floral and swirl design, scalloped end opening, price for pair. **45.00**
Percale, 19 x 12″, scalloped and eyelet border. **15.00**

Pillow Sham
48 x 34″, white muslin, wide border of machine tucking, machine made lace edge **35.00**
50 x 35″, muslin, Victorian white work, narrow machine tucking on border, cut and embroidered edges, c1890 **65.00**

Placemat Set, cotton, white, Battenberg, lavish corners and edging, napkins to match, c1940, price for set of eight . . **75.00**

Runner
10½ x 105″, Pointe de Venise, cartouche and circle design, handmade, early 20th C. **275.00**
16 x 50″, cotton, white, Chinese hand drawn work, early 20th C **18.00**
26 x 148″, Irish linen, white, double damask, allover small flower design, hand rolled ends, early 20th C **75.00**

Sheet, linen, white
44 x 100″, floral and spray motif cut work top, scalloped sides, machine hemmed bottom. **100.00**
86 x 101″, Madeira, bridal, 18″ deep embroidered cut work, filet lace insets, 2″ filet lace border top, narrow hemstitching bottom, pr matching pillow cases, price for set **250.00**

Tablecloth
50″ sq, white, printed multicolored dec
Mexican, minor repairs **22.50**
Strawberries **25.00**
54″ sq, tea cloth, Chinese cotton, hand drawn central star motif, deep drawn work borders sides, hand hemstitched border **15.00**

Tablecloth, natural color linen, Richelieu, all handmade cutwork and embroidery, floral and scroll motif, early 20th C, 68 x 100″, $575.00.

55 x 64", red and white, leaf design ... 72.00
56 x 66", white, printed multicolored floral and fruit dec, 1940s 26.00
56 x 96", linen, white, red Greek key design borders. 40.00
60" d, white linen, heavy padded satin stitch, roses and open work, 4" machine made lace border 50.00
68 x 98", Irish linen, double damask, Queen Victoria Royal Jubilee 1887, portrait of Queen circular motif center, surrounded by symbols of countries of Realm interspersed with thistles motif, Royal Jubilee and 1887 ribbon motif, fleur–de–lis, Maltese crosses, and small bellflowers background border, 19th C ... 950.00
72 x 58", crochet, tobacco string, filet lace sq motifs, c1930–40 ...... 50.00
92 x 105", cotton, cut work with blue apenzell type cut work and embroidery design center, scalloped edges 75.00
Table Set, tablecloth and twelve napkins
66 x 128", banquet cloth, ecru, allover handmade Pointe de Venise lace, central five medallions motif with floral and foliate design set in panel, bordered swirls of medallion of flowers, interspersed flower vase forms with flowers, floral design outside border, scalloped edge, napkins with motif in one corner and 1" matching lace edge, pre–1935, napkins unused 3,500.00
68 x 100", hemstitched, lavish blue Madeira embroidery 225.00
76 x 116", linen, cut work and filet lace inserts. 325.00
Towel, hand
23 x 15", linen, cut work and filet lace inserts on both ends, late 19th C .. 8.00
24 x 40", white linen, double damask, gold color woven border leaf pattern, satin stitch monogram "MW", 6" hand tied fringe 18.00
Tray Cover, two matching napkins, pale blue linen, embroidered small pink flowers, "Good Morning" upper left corner, price for three piece set 12.00

LITHOPHANES

History: Lithophanes are highly translucent porcelain panels with impressed designs. The design is formed by the difference in thickness of the plaque. Thin parts transmit an abundance of light while thicker parts represent shadows.

Lithophanes were first made by the Royal Berlin Porcelain Works in 1828. Other factories in Germany, France, and England later produced them.

The majority of lithophanes on the market today were made between 1850 and 1900.

Wall Lamp, brass, four woodland scene panels, 2½" h panels, price for pair, $280.00.

Cup and Saucer, blue Oriental lady with nude lady 150.00
Fairy Lamp, 9" h, three panels, lady leaning out of tower, rural romantic scenes 1,200.00
Lamp
Night, 5¼" h, sq, four scenes, irid green porcelain base, gold trim, electrified 600.00
Table
8" h, 8" d five panel shade, 4½ x 6¼" panels with scenes of children, lovers, emb floral brass frame, panels sgd "PPM" 400.00
20¾" h, colored umbrella style shade, four panels of outdoor Victorian scenes, bronze and slate standard, German...... 675.00
Lamp Shade, 13" d, dome, three genre scenes, scrolling designs 425.00
Panel
KPM
2½ x 3¼", view from West Point . 175.00
3⅞ x 5¼", lake setting, ship and windmill 150.00
4¾ x 6½", man kneeling, mosque type building. 225.00
PPM
3¼ x 5¼", view of Paterson Falls 175.00
4 x 6", boy with drum 400.00
P.R. Sickle, 4¼ x 5"
Cupid and girl fishing 150.00
Scene of two women in doorway, dog, and two pigeons, sgd, #1320................... 115.00

Unmarked
  6 x 7½", Madonna and Child . . . **175.00**
  7¾ x 6", Paul and Virginia, scene of
    young man holding bird's nest
    and lemon, young woman, tropi-
    cal setting **100.00**
Pitcher, puzzle type, Victorian scene,
  nude on bottom. **165.00**
Stein, ½ liter
  Floral front, soldier bidding farewell on
    reverse. **150.00**
  Negro Boy, 5" h **175.00**
  Regimental **190.00**
Tea Warmer, 5⅞" h, one pc cylindrical
  panel, four seasonal landscapes with
  children, copper frame, finger grip and
  molded base. **225.00**

Teabowl and Saucer, multicolored, Pennington, c1768–75, $675.00.

LIVERPOOL CHINA

History: Liverpool is the name given to products made at several potteries in Liverpool, England, between 1750 and 1840. Among the early potters who made tin enameled earthenwares were Seth and James Pennington and Richard Chaffers.

By the 1780s tin–glazed earthenware gave way to cream-colored wares decorated with cobalt, enamel colors, and blue or black transfers.

The Liverpool glaze is characterized by bubbles and most often there is clouding under the foot rims. By 1800 about 80 potteries were working in the town producing not only creamware but soft-paste, soapstone, and bone porcelain.

Reference: Susan and Al Bagdade, *Warman's English & Continental Pottery & Porcelain, Second Edition,* Wallace–Homestead, 1991.

Creamer
  3½" h, underglaze blue floral dec, red
    enamel, gilt, very minor flakes on
    table ring. **150.00**
  4" h, polychrome enamel Chinoiserie
    dec, gilt trim. **225.00**
Jug, creamware
  6" h, orange transfer print, compass
    with label "Come box the compass"
    on one side, sailor's farewell scene
    on other, three rim chips and minor
    roughage. **300.00**
  8" h, orange transfer print, ship on one
    side, Britannia weeping loss of Lord

Nelson and banner "Trafalgar" on
  other, repaired around top. **415.00**
8⅞" h, black transfer print, The Farm-
  ers Arms, The Hatters Arms, and
  Thomas Dulson/1799 . . . . **550.00**
10¼" h, black transfer print of frigate,
  Poor Jack the Sailor poem, En-
  gland, c1870 . . . . **140.00**
10¾" h, black transfer print of three
  American images, Great Seal,
  Washington crowned with laurels,
  and allegorical scene, eagle trans-
  fer under spout, c1800 . . . . **3,300.00**
Mug, creamware
  Black transfer of children playing, pint **165.00**
  Brown transfer print, Hope, allover
    luster trim, c1820–30 . . . . **125.00**
Pitcher, creamware, transfer print
  5¼" h, brown transfer print of two clas-
    sical women in large oval, brown
    transfer print of flowers on ext. rim,
    pseudo brown transfer Fitzhugh
    border on int. rim, floral transfer on
    handle, highlighted with applied
    green, red, blue, and magenta,
    small base chip, minor restoration
    to spout. **195.00**
  8" h
    Independence, reverse with Wash-
      ington and Justice, Liberty and
      Victory, American eagle under
      spout, c1800 . . . . **1,650.00**
    Washington Apotheosis, grieving
      Liberty and Indian seated in fore-
      ground, Father Time raises
      Washington from his tomb toward
      rays emanating from heaven,
      words on tomb "Sacred to the
      Memory of Washington Ob 14
      Dec AD 1799 Ae 68," United
      States seal and ribbon under
      spout, transfer of frigate, waving
      American flag, three pinhead size
      flakes. **3,650.00**

9⅛″ h, L'Enfant's Plan of the City of Washington, reverse with "Peace, Plenty, and Independence" under spout, American eagle, c1790, small flakes at base, glaze wear at spout **2,860.00**

10″ h, three masted ship *Amelia,* flying American flag, green, yellow, red, blue, and black enamel, inscription "Amelia, of New York, William S. Brooks, Commander of New–York," reverse with portrait of Washington and inscription "First President of the United States of America," wreathed monogram under spout, early 19th C **4,950.00**

11½″ h, black transfer print, Boston Fusilier, red, yellow, and blue enameled accents, reverse with allegorical figures, inscription "United We Stand and Divided We Fall," surmounted by American eagle, vestiges of gilt dec, c1790, damaged, glued **5,225.00**

Plaque, 5″ h, creamware, transfer print, George Washington medallion, early 19th C, scratched **1,540.00**

Teapot, 10″ h, creamware, black transfer print of romantic scene **175.00**

LOETZ

History: Loetz is a type of iridescent art glass made in Austria by J. Loetz Witwe in the late 1890s. Loetz was a contemporary of L. C. Tiffany and worked in the Tiffany factory before establishing his own operation; therefore, much of the wares are similar in appearance to Tiffany. Some pieces are signed "Loetz," "Loetz, Austria," or "Austria." The Loetz factory also produced ware with fine cameos on cased glass.

Bowl

5″ d, 3″ h, ruffled and folded rim, opal cased threaded vessel, irid dusty pink ground, spot dec **300.00**

8″ d, 4½″ h, ruffled quatrefoil rim, jardiniere form, basketweave irid surface **715.00**

Compote, 11″ d, 10½″ h, ruffled rim, hobnailed bowl, mottled irid rose red and pale green, gilt metal Vienna Secessionist style triparte frame **250.00**

Cracker Jar, 7¾″ h, irid green–blue, brown oil spot dec, blown–out teardrops, silverplate lid and mountings . . **625.00**

Decanter, 11¼″ h, bottle form, cobalt blue ground, silver blue luster, silver overlay carved as foliate and scrolling dec, monogrammed, conforming silver overlaid stopper **2,420.00**

Inkwell

Amethyst, 3½″ h, sq, irid, web design, bronze mouth **100.00**

Cobalt and irid gold, angular quatreform, conforming Art Nouveau hinged metal cov, ceramic well **360.00**

Jack in the Pulpit Vase, 13½″ h, freeblown floriform, colorless, striated gold amber pulled feather dec, gold and blue irid surface **1,430.00**

Lamp, table, 17¾″ h, irid mushroom glass shade, pinched and tooled dec, hexagonal bronze base **4,000.00**

Pitcher, 8⅝″ h, pinched bulbous body, purple green irid, applied handle, gilt metal mount with cast foliate motif . . **600.00**

Rose Bowl, 6½″ d, ruffled purple irid raindrop dec **200.00**

Sweetmeat Jar, cov, 5″ h, irid silver spider web dec, green ground, sgd **400.00**

Urn, 9¼″ h, ovoid, irid, blue oil spot dec, inscribed "Loetz, Austria" **1,500.00**

Vase, melon shaped, straight collar, tortoise shell irid, unsgd, 6½″ d, 4¼″ h, $185.00.

Vase

4″ h, amber body, random vertical threading, applied rim, gold irid full form fruits, leaves, and stems **470.00**

5½″ h, squat bulbous dimpled body, flattened rim, irid deep red and purple irid, subtle gold floral tracery . . **200.00**

5½″ h, 8½″ l, frosted opalescent conch shell form, threaded ext., green simulated sea grasses and platform base, minor damage to applied dec **200.00**

5¾″ h, conical amber body, three areas of irid orange, gold, swirled green, silver overlay of Art Nouveau swirls and foliage design stamped "L Sterling" base inscribed "Loetz Austria" **1,760.00**

7¼″ h, 5″ d, melon ribbed, Art Nouveau design, sterling silver overlay, pale green ground, highly irid swirls and raindrops **800.00**

8¾″ h, 3½″ w, gooseneck, gold peppering, irid raindrop finish, highly irid pink and blue highlights, Art Nouveau style irid sterling silver overlay, silver rim **1,000.00**

9¼″ h, broad trefoil rim, pinched oval body, pale green, wavy combed blue–green irid dec, polished pontil base **550.00**

9½″ h
Baluster, pale bronze colored ground, highly irid purple, gold, rainbow raindrops, heavy sterling silver overlay of bleeding hearts **2,050.00**
Rect, crimped rim, waisted body, royal purple, swirled and coiled at surface, silver blue irid, polished pontil mark **305.00**

10½″ h, allover papillon design with raindrops, Art Nouveau floral sterling silver overlay dec, irid peacock blue **2,450.00**

11¼″ h, oval, cobalt blue, textured lustrous surface, applied amber polished pontil **525.00**

LOTUS WARE CHINA

History: Knowles, Taylor, and Knowles Co., East Liverpool, Ohio, made a translucent, thinly potted china between 1891 and 1898. It compared favorably to Belleek. It first was marked "KTK." After being exhibited at the 1893 Columbian Exposition in Chicago, Col. John T. Taylor, company president, changed the marking to Lotus Ware because the body resembled the petals of the lotus blossom.

Blanks also were sold to amateurs who hand painted them. Most artist–signed pieces fit this category.

Bowl
7½″ d, boat shape, pink and gold openwork, cherry blossoms, marked "KTK" **500.00**
9″ w, 5″ h, twig handles, floral dec, artist initials **1,300.00**
Creamer, 3¾″ h, white ground, undecorated **200.00**

Tea Set, pink blossoms, gold trim, white ground, marked "KTK," price for three pc set, $550.00.

Cup and Saucer, hp violets, white ground, marked "KTK" **100.00**
Dish, shell shape, shell pink and pale green, small green florals, gilt coral feet, marked "KTK" **400.00**
Ewer, 7½″ h, pierced, jeweled, pastel panels, Lotus mark **500.00**
Pitcher, 7″ h, bulbous, fishnet dec, gold, marked "KTK" **450.00**
Sugar, 4″ d, fishnet dec, florals, white ground, handles **350.00**
Teapot, emb flowers, gold trim, white ground, marked "KTK" **350.00**
Vase
4¼″ h, white Belleek bowl, reticulated medallions, green Knowles, Taylor, and Knowles mark **360.00**
8″ h, cylinder, ball feet, green fishnet pattern, orange flowers **520.00**

LUSTER WARE

History: Lustering on a piece of pottery creates a metallic, sometimes iridescent, appearance. Josiah Wedgwood experimented with the technique in the 1790s. Between 1805 and 1840 luster earthenware pieces were created in England by makers such as Adams, Bailey and Batkin, Copeland and Garrett, Wedgwood, and Enoch Wood.

Luster decorations often were used in conjunction with enamels and transfers. Transfers used for luster decoration covered a wide range of public and domestic subjects. They frequently were accompanied by pious or sentimental doggerel as well as the humors of everyday life.

Copper luster was created by the addition of a copper compound to the glaze. It was very popular in America during the 19th century and experienced a collecting vogue from the 1920s to the 1950s. Today it has a limited market. The market stagnation can partially be attributed to the large number of reproductions, especially creamers and the "polka" jug, which fool many new buyers. Reproductions are heavier in appearance and weight than the earlier pieces.

Pink luster was made by using a gold mixture. Silver luster was first covered completely with a thin coating of a "steel luster" mixture containing a small quantity of platinum oxide. An additional coating of platinum, worked in water, was applied before firing.

Sunderland is a coarse type of cream-colored earthenware with a marbled or spotted pink luster decoration which shades from pink to purple. A solution of gold compound applied to the white body developed the many shades of pink.

The development of electroplating in 1840 created a sharp decline in the demands for metal–surfaced earthenware.

Reference: Susan and Al Bagdade, *Warman's English & Continental Pottery & Porcelain, Second Edition,* Wallace–Homestead, 1991.

Additional Listings: English Softpaste.

Copper Luster, teapot, turquoise enamel dec, 11½″ w, 7½″ h, $135.00.

COPPER

Creamer
  3⅛″ h, two rect panels, Hope transfers, red, green, blue, and purple enamel highlights, pink luster dec handle and mouth int.. . . . . 70.00
  3⅝″ h, three bands of copper luster alternating with two bands of mustard, round blue flowers 25.00
  4″ h, polychrome floral dec, French, 19th C. 75.00
Figure, 8″ h, spaniels, pr 110.00
Goblet, 4½″ h, 3½″ d, pink luster band, floral resist dec, copper luster int. . . . 45.00
Jug, 8″ h, three transfers of mother and child playing badminton and writing letters on canary yellow band 175.00
Mug
  4″ h, raised green and white flowers on tan luster band 50.00
  4¾″ h, leaves and berries on orange luster band 60.00

Pepper Shaker, 4¼″ h, cream colored band 40.00
Pitcher
  5″ h, compressed baluster, polychrome floral band, white ground. . 75.00
  6″ h, two narrow white bands with pink luster house and trees dec, wide copper luster bands 50.00
  7″ h, green and white raised floral dec on broad blue band 90.00
  10″ h, wide blue band around body, emb greyhound, bull, and urn of flowers in polychrome enamel, pink and purple luster 200.00
Teapot
  5½″ h, oblong, blue enamel band, relief molded gadrooning 50.00
  6″ h, emb ribs, polychrome enameled floral dec. 125.00

PINK

Creamer, 4⅜″ h, stylized flower band, pink luster highlights and rim, ftd. . . . 55.00
Cup and Saucer, magenta transfers, Faith, Hope, and Charity, applied green enamel highlights, pink luster line borders. 45.00
Dish, 12⅝ x 7½″, shell shape, imp "Wedgwood–DUF–I–R," black underglaze "R. PHOLAS EASTATUS". . . . 85.00
Jug
  5½″ h, bulbous, gadrooned rim, molded berry vine border highlighted in purple–pink and lime green luster. 75.00
  5¾″ h, bulbous, applied scroll handle, green glazed ground, luster spotted tracking dogs, luster spout, rim, and handle. 85.00
  8″ h, church, white toned to tan . . . 150.00
Mug, 2⅞″ h, overall pink splash luster dec, handled. 35.00
Pitcher, 4½″ h, Vintage, blue striping, chips 220.00
Plate
  6¼″ d, relief figures of dogs running on rim, highlighted with green, red, and pink luster, red, green, and blue stylized floral dec in center 50.00
  7⅝″ d, King's Rose pattern, red, green, and yellow, double pink luster band border 25.00
Teapot, 12″ h, House pattern, Queen Anne style, repaired finial on lid 275.00
Toddy Plate, 5 1/16″ d, pink luster House pattern, emb flower sprigs border . . . 40.00
Waste Bowl, 6½″ d, 3¾″ h, canary, floral dec, pink luster, polychrome enameling. 125.00

SILVER

Bowl, 9¼" d, 4¼" h, Vintage, wear and hairlines in foot	165.00
Creamer, 4⅝" h, bird in tree	130.00
Jug, 4½" h, ribbed, Staffordshire, 19th C	75.00
Mug, 3⅜" h, floral, stains, hairlines, and small flakes	12.00
Mustard Pot, 3⅞" h, vertical ribbed design, emb body, matching cov, ftd.	70.00
Pepper Pot, 5" h, standing toby form, round hollow base, pouring holes	85.00
Pitcher	
5¼" h, Vintage and Grain, wear and hairlines	50.00
5⅜" h	
Canary ground, foliage, worn luster	310.00
Ivory ground, black transfer of English country scenes, minor wear and short hairline	105.00
5½" h	
Bird and flowers, minor wear	140.00
Vintage and farmer's arms, wear	140.00
6¼" h, floral, wear and small flakes	245.00
Shaker, 3⅝" h, ringed circumference, pedestal base	48.00
Tea Set, pot, dome cov, sugar and creamer, oval, bulbous body, standard handles	135.00
Tray, 8¼" l, canary band, white center and rim	200.00
Vase, 5¼" h, flared top, painted red and silver luster nasturtium vine, c1810	110.00

SUNDERLAND

Bowl, 10" d, House pattern	125.00
Celery Dish, scene of couple courting, sgd "Bucher"	120.00
Cup and Saucer, black transfer, farm scene, handleless	85.00
Dish, pink splash, black transfer, mother playing with son	22.00
Gravy Boat, House pattern	150.00
Jug	
5½" h, black and white transfer of Mariners Arms on front, Cast Iron Bridge on back	140.00
9" h, black transfer, "A Frigate in Full Sail," verse, sailor and maid, French and English coats of arms joined with "Cremea"	200.00
17¼" h, heroic, pink luster int. and ext.	850.00
Mug, 5" h, Foresters Arms transfer on front, Mariner's Compass on back	175.00
Pitcher	
6¾" h	15.00
9⅛" h, black transfer, farmer's arms, "Cast Iron Bridge over the River Wear at Sunderland...," polychrome enameling, marked "Dixon Austin & Co, Sunderland"	475.00

Plate	
7" d, pink splash	15.00
8" d, floral center, luster border	50.00
Salt, master	60.00
Sugar, House pattern	75.00
Syrup, cov, 5" h	100.00
Tumbler, 2¾" h	60.00
Vase, 7" h, trumpet shape	100.00

LUTZ-TYPE GLASS

History: Lutz-type glass is an art glass attributed to Nicholas Lutz. He made this type of glass while at the Boston and Sandwich Glass Company from 1869 until 1888. Since Lutz-type glass was popular, copied by many capable glassmakers, and unsigned, it is nearly impossible to distinguish genuine Lutz products.

Lutz is believed to have made two distinct types of glass, striped and threaded glass. This style often is confused with a similar style of Venetian glass. The striped glass was made by using threaded glass rods in the Venetian manner. Threaded glass was blown and decorated by winding threads of glass around the piece.

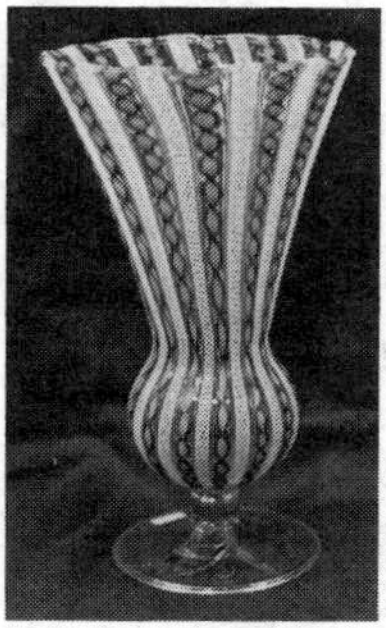

Vase, white lattice, pink with goldstone edges, pedestal base with gold highlights, 11¼" h, $315.00.

Compote, 8⅞ x 6½", DQ, threaded, amberina, clear hollow stem	500.00
Epergne, pink threads, price for three pieces	250.00
Finger Bowl, 7" d, ruffled edge, amber swirls, amethyst latticino, gold metallic borders, matching underplate, price for set	150.00
Lamp Shade, 8" sq, 6¼" h, 2½" fitter, sq top, opaque white loopings, applied cranberry threading, ribbon edge	175.00

Punch Cup, 3 x 2⅝", cranberry threading, clear ground, circular foot, applied
clear handle **85.00**
Tumbler, 3¾" h, white and amethyst lat-
ticino, goldstone highlights **75.00**

MAASTRICHT WARE

History: Maastricht, Holland, is where Petrus
Regout founded the De Sphinx Pottery in 1836.
The firm specialized in transfer-printed earthenwares. Other factories also were established in the
area, many employing English workmen and their
techniques. Maastricht china was exported to the
United States in competition with English products.

Reference: Susan and Al Bagdade, *Warman's
English & Continental Pottery & Porcelain, Second
Edition,* Wallace–Homestead, 1991.

Periodical: *The Dutch Potter,* 47 London Terrace, New Rochelle, NY 10804.

Bowl
5¾" d, red, green, and blue agate pattern, "Petrus Regout, Maastricht"
with lion mark **30.00**
6" d, Sana pattern, black Oriental
transfer, orange wash, marked "Pe-
trus Regout Maastricht, Sana". . . . **15.00**
7¾" d, Panama pattern, marked "Pe-
trus Regout & Co" **60.00**
Creamer and Sugar, 2¼" h, yellow,
green, and blue gaudy stick spatterware floral design, marked
"Maastricht" **165.00**
Pitcher, 5" h, red transfer rooster, iris,
and leaves, marked "Regout & Co
Haan" **65.00**

**Bowl, Honc pattern, marked "Maas-
tricht, Petrus Regoulec Co., Made in
Holland," 6⅛" d, 3⅛" h, $75.00.**

Plate
8½" h, blue and white floral design,
marked "P. Regout & Co
Maastricht". **20.00**
9" d, polychrome floral dec, marked
"Maastricht". **25.00**
Platter, 11⅝" l, polychrome floral dec,
wear and stains, marked
"Maastricht" **75.00**
Vegetable Dish, 8¼" sq, polychrome
floral dec, wear and stains, marked
"Maastricht" **75.00**

MAJOLICA

History: Majolica, an opaque, tin-glazed pottery,
has been produced by many countries for centuries. It originally took its name from the Spanish
island of Majorca, where figuline (a potter's clay) is
found. Today majolica denotes a type of pottery
which was made during the last half of the 19th
century in Europe and America.

Majolica frequently depicted elements in nature:
leaves, flowers, birds, and fish. Human figures
were rare. Designs were painted on the soft clay
body using vitreous colors and fired under a clear
lead glaze to impart the rich color and brilliance
characteristic of majolica.

Among English majolica manufacturers who
marked their works were Wedgwood, George
Jones, Holdcraft, and Minton. Most of their pieces
can be identified through the English Registry mark
and/or the potter–designer's mark. Sarreguemines
in France and Villeroy and Boch in Baden, Germany, produced majolica that compared favorably
with the finer English majolica. Most Continental
pieces had an incised number on the base.

Although 600 plus American potteries produced
majolica between 1850 and 1900, only a handful
chose to identify their wares. Among these manufacturers were George Morely, Edwin Bennett, the
Chesapeake Pottery Company, the New Milford–
Wannoppee Pottery Company, and the firm of Griffen, Smith, and Hill. The others hoped their unmarked pieces would be taken for English examples.

References: Susan and Al Bagdade, *Warman's
English & Continental Pottery & Porcelain, Second
Edition,* Wallace–Homestead, 1991; Nicholas M.
Dawes, *Majolica,* Crown Publishers, 1990; Marilyn
G. Karmason and Joan B. Stacke, *Majolica: A
Complete History And Illustrated Survey,* Harry N.
Abrams, 1989; Mariann Katz–Marks, *The Collec-
tor's Encyclopedia of Majolica,* Collector Books,
1992; Mike Schneider, *Majolica,* Schiffer Publish-
ing, 1990.

Collectors' Club: Majolica International Society,
1275 First Ave., Suite 103, New York, NY 10021.

Bowl
7" d, Shell and Seaweed, Griffen,

Smith & Hill Potteries, Phoenixville,
PA, c1880 . . . . 200.00
10″ d, large center maple leaf, rose,
cream, and green edges, marked
"G.H.S." 135.00
10″ d, 5″ h, ftd, Bird and Fan, Wedg-
wood, c1870, price for pair 850.00
Butter Pat, multicolored leaves 25.00
Cake Stand
9″ d, 3″ h, Bird and Fan, Wedgwood,
c1870 . . . . 225.00
9″ d, 5″ h, Fruit, Wedgwood, c1870 250.00
Charger, 12″ d, central geometric reserve, berry and vine border, 19th C 250.00
Cheese Dish, cov, 8″ d, 4″ h, floral dec,
pale blue ground, lavender int., vine
handle, 19th C 385.00
Creamer, 4¼″ h, Bamboo pattern, imp
marks, Griffen, Smith & Hill Potteries,
Phoenixville, PA, c1880, chip 200.00
Decanter, allover floral, rose bud stop-
per, price for pair. 285.00
Dish, leaf shape 75.00
Figure, 31″ h, Whippet, seated, amber
and white glaze, repairs. 1,870.00
Garden Seat, 19″ h, hexagonal, cobalt
blue ground, polychrome enamels,
pierced floral and geometric side
panels, imp mark and date code, Minton, England, 1871, surface wear,
price for pair 3,300.00
Ink Stand, 6″ h, 11″ w, Art Nouveau
brass ormolu mounts. 500.00
Jardiniere, 9½″ h, relief molded fruit and
foliage dec on sides, paw feet, 19th
C. 330.00
Pitcher
6¾″ h, Shell and Seaweed, Griffen,
Smith & Hill Potteries, Phoenixville,
PA, c1880. . . . . 300.00

7¼″ h, relief song bird dec,
Wedgwood 200.00
7¼″ h, 5½″ d, allover light green
leaves and flowers, beige ground,
pink int., imp "Etruscan". 245.00
8½″ h, hound handle, hanging game
dec, shades of brown, blue, and
green 440.00
9″ h, ear of corn, yellow and green
glaze, 19th C. 135.00
Plaque, 19½″ l, 12″ h, portrait of Art Nouveau lady, long flowing hair, overlook-
ing pond with water lilies, lily pads,
setting sun, self frame, grapes trim,
pierced for hanging 475.00
Plate
6″ d
Fern and Picket 135.00
Grape Leaf, Wedgwood, c1870 . 90.00
7″ d, Fruit, Wedgwood, c1870 . . . . 80.00
7½″ d, Black Forest, grapes, leaves,
Erphila 65.00
8″ d
Bird and Fan, blue fans, Wedg-
wood, c1870. . . . . 150.00
Blackberry, Wedgwood, c1870 . . 100.00
8¼″ d, plumed bird on branch, cherries, leaves, some damage 40.00
9″ d
Bird and Fan, Wedgwood, c1870 150.00
Grape Leaf, Wedgwood, c1870 . 135.00
Serving Plate, 7″ d, center well, Strawberry, Wedgwood, c1870 . . . . 100.00
Syrup Jug, 7½″ h, hexagonal, bamboo
framed sides and handle, imp marks,
Griffen, Smith & Hill Potteries, Phoenixville, PA, c1880. . . . . 245.00
Toby Jug, ugly woman, pig under arm,
umbrella and doctor's bag in hands. . 290.00
Umbrella Stand, 23″ h, stork and ostrich
dec, blue ground, pink int. 750.00
Urn, 27″ h, globular, mermaid handles,
spreading foot, armorial dec, Italian,
19th C 500.00
Vase, 13″ h, classical shape, multico-
lored floral dec, price for pair 330.00
Wall Bracket, 9⅜″ h, standing cupid supporting drapes below shelf, Wedgwood, imp marks and date letters,
c1877, restorations, chips, and hair-
lines, price for pair. 770.00

MAPS

History: Maps provide one of the best ways to
study the growth of a country or region. From the
16th to the early 20th century, maps were both
informative and decorative. Engravers provided ornamental detailing which often took the form of
bird's-eye views, city maps, and ornate calligraphy

**Plate, blue center portrait, pink raised
border, Germany, 6½″ d, $30.00.**

and scrolling. Many maps were hand colored to enhance their beauty.

Maps generally were published in plate books. Many of the maps available today result from these books being cut apart and the sheets sold separately.

In the last quarter of the 19th century, representatives from firms in Philadelphia, Chicago, and elsewhere traveled the United States preparing county atlases, often with a sheet for each township and a sheet for each major city or town. Although mass-produced, they are eagerly sought by collectors. Individual sheets sell for $25 to $75. The atlases themselves can usually be purchased in the $200 to $400 range. Individual sheets should be viewed solely as decorative and not as investment material.

References: Norman E. Martinus and Harry L. Rinker, *Warman's Paper,* Wallace–Homestead, 1994; Dana G. Morykan and Harry L. Rinker, *Warman's Country Antiques & Collectibles, Second Edition,* Wallace–Homestead, 1994.

Periodical: *Antique Map & Print Quarterly,* PO Box 290–681, Wethersfield, CT 06129.

Collectors' Clubs: The Association of Map Memorabilia Collectors, 8 Amherst Road, Pelham, MA 01002; The Chicago Map Society, 60 West Walton St., Chicago, IL 60610.

Museum: Hermon Dunlap Smith Center for the History of Cartography, Newberry Library, Chicago, IL.

Africa, Homann Heirs, c1737, 495 x 570 mm, double page, engraved, hand colored, letterpress key labels mounted in lower margin 355.00

Asia, Aaron Arrowsmith, 1801, 1245 x 1465 mm, engraved, hand colored, 28 section, linen back. 660.00

Canada, "Plan of City of Quebec," Andrews, c1771, 33 x 24 cm, engraved, vignettes. 125.00

England, "Lower Saxony...Tho. Kitchin, Geographer," 14½" h, 15" w, hand colored, matted and framed 85.00

Ireland

"A New Map of Ireland," Herman Moll, 1714, 1040 x 630 mm, engraved, hand colored in outline, folds reinforced on reverse. 465.00

"The Kingdom of Ireland," Robert Morden, c1695, 410 x 345 mm, double page, engraved, hand colored, trimmed 525.00

Mexico, "Hispaniae Novae," Ortelius, 1579, 53 x 42 cm, uncolored, Latin text 350.00

Moscow, "Plan of Moscow," Ivan Michruin, 1739, 510 x 540 mm, double page, engraved, minor browning, framed. 440.00

Scotland, published by Samuel Lewis, engraved by I Dower, 1915 x 1315 mm, six sheets, hand colored, linen back. 725.00

South America, Thomas Kitchin, 1794, double page, engraved, hand colored, browned 90.00

United States

Florida, "A Map of Part of West Florida, from Pensacola to the Mouth of the Iberville River with a View to show the Proper Spot for a Settlement on the Mississippi," J Lodge, 1772, 7½ x 13½", engraved, hand colored, Plan for a New Settlement inset 250.00

Idaho, "Railroad And County Map Of Idaho," Cram, 1880, 19¾ x 16¾", lithograph, outline color. 100.00

Maryland, Robert de Vaugondy, "Gilles, Carte de la Virginie et du Maryland," 1755, 490 x 660 mm, double page, engraved, hand colored 1,100.00

New Hampshire, "An Accurate Map of New Hampshire," c1795, 335 x 295 mm, folding, engraved, hand colored, allover browning 200.00

New York, "The Empire State," 1851, 555 x 745 mm, engraved, hand colored, ... 330.00

North Carolina, "Map of the State of North Carolina," G W and C B Colton, 1866, two folding maps, lithographed, picture one half of state, orig cloth folder 525.00

South Carolina, "State of South Carolina From The Best Authorities," Samuel Lewis, 15 x 18" 475.00

Texas, c1840, engraved, hand colored 125.00

Venezuela, Willem Blaeu, c1638, 375 x 485 mm, double page, engraved, Latin text on reverse, hand colored . . 355.00

World, "A Chart Of The World According To Mercator's Projection Showing The Latest Discoveries Of Capt. Cook," Dilly and Robinson, 1785, 14½ x 19", colored borders and outlines . . 100.00

MARBLEHEAD POTTERY

History: This hand-thrown pottery had its beginning in 1905 as a therapeutic program introduced by Dr. J. Hall for the patients confined to a sanitarium located in Marblehead, Massachusetts. In 1916 production was removed from the hospital to another site. The factory continued under the directorship of Arthur E. Baggs until it closed in 1936.

Most pieces found today are glazed with a smooth, porous, even finish in a single color. The most desirable pieces are decorated with conventionalized design in one or more subordinate colors.

Candlestick, rose matte glaze, imp ship stamp, 4" h, $50.00.

Bookends, pr, 5¾" h, sq tile form side, stylized cutback and incised panel of galleon on sea, dark blue glaze, incised mark and paper label	200.00
Bowl, 6¼" d, beige matte glaze	90.00
Candlestick, 7⅝" h, green matte glaze, stylized turnings, imp mark.	305.00
Honey Pot, 3½" h, light yellow–green ground, painted stylized grapevine, clusters of blue grapes, green leaves, and vines, marked.	475.00
Pitcher, 6⅛" h, scenic band, brown bands, designed by Arthur Baggs, imp artist's marks, c1915	1,760.00
Tile	
4¾" sq, high relief, oyster white sailing ship, blue ground, imp mark	300.00
6" sq, deep brown border of long dashes, green ground, solid dark brown edge band, matte glaze, imp mark, minor nicks.	660.00
6⅛" sq, incised woodland scene, shades of green glaze, imp mark, paper label, chips.	385.00
Vase	
3" h, flared, green	230.00
3¾" h, ovoid	
Blue	225.00
Lavender	245.00
4½" h, trumpet, blue	235.00

5¼" h, 6¼" d, bulbous, banded dec of brown abstract geometric patterns, smooth matte green glaze, imp ship mark, incised artist initials, stilt pull on base.	2,310.00
5⅝" h, bud, blue matte glaze	150.00

MARY GREGORY TYPE GLASS

History: The use of enameled decoration on glass, an inexpensive imitation of cameo glass, developed in Bohemia in the late 19th century. The Boston and Sandwich Glass Co. copied this process in the late 1880s.

Mary Gregory (1856–1908) was employed for two years at the Boston and Sandwich Glass Co. factory when the enameled decorated glass was being manufactured. Some collectors argue that Gregory was inspired to paint her white enamel figures on glass by the work of Kate Greenaway and a desire to imitate pate–sur–pate. However, evidence for these assertions is very weak. Further, a question can be raised whether or not Mary Gregory even decorated glass as part of her job at Sandwich.

The result is that "Mary Gregory Type" is a better term to describe this glass. Collectors should recognize that most examples are either European or modern reproductions.

Reference: R. and D. Truitt, *Mary Gregory Glassware: 1880–1990,* published by authors, 1992.

Museum: Sandwich Glass Museum, Sandwich, MA.

Box, cov	
3½" d, 2¼" h, round, amethyst ground, white enameled young girl holding sack of flowers, standing in garden	375.00
3½" d, 2½" h, sapphire blue ground, white enameled boy with hat on lift off lid, white enameled floral sprays around sides	200.00
4½" d, 4½" h, cranberry ground, white enameled young girl on lid	275.00
5" d, 3⅜" h, lime green ground, white enameled young boy with hat on hinged lid, white enameled sprays around sides	200.00
7" d, 3¼" h, dark amethyst ground, white enameled two girls making rose wreaths, detailed basket and trees, floral band on base	1,100.00
Cordial, 2½" h, cylindrical cranberry bowl, clear stem and base, white enameled Victorian girl on one, boy on other, facing pair.	220.00
Cruet, 8" h, ovoid body, slender neck, applied clear handle, clear ground,	

white enameled boy in forest meadow, orig ball stopper **380.00**

Decanter, 9½″ h, cranberry ground, white enameled young lady standing beside lake, swan in water, orig clear stopper. **425.00**

Dresser Set, tray, two perfume bottles, powder box, ring tree, pin tray, cranberry ground, white enameled dec, price for six piece set. **1,100.00**

Mug, 4½″ h, amber ground, ribbed, white enameled praying girl **65.00**

Perfume, 2½″ h, 2⅜″ w base, 1⅜″ deep, trapezoid, jet black body, white enameled little girl, hands tucked beneath apron, lamb standing in front, stylized floral dec on other sides, emb floral on hinged lid, brass colored metal fittings **485.00**

Pitcher, sapphire blue, white enamel young child, 10″ h, $345.00.

Pitcher

2″ h, sapphire blue, white enameled girl **225.00**

7½ x 9½″, medium green ground, white enameled boy with bird and trees, girl with bowl and brush dec, facing pair. **250.00**

Plate, 6¼″ d, cobalt blue ground, white enameled girl with butterfly net **120.00**

Salt Shaker, 5″ h, blue, paneled, white enameled girl in garden, brass top . . **175.00**

Tumbler, 1¾″ d, 2¼″ h, cranberry ground, white enameled boy on one, girl on other, facing pair **100.00**

Vase

5″ h, robin's egg blue, white enameled girl running through field of flowers, holding butterfly neck **125.00**

5¼″ h, wide ovoid body, short neck,

flared rim, short ringed pedestal on cushion foot, black ground, white enameled girl on one, boy on other, facing pair. **250.00**

7¾″ h, deep amethyst–black ground, young girl in garden, leaning forward, arms sweeping up skirt, reverse floral spray, figural base of two storks joined by leaves and vines. **750.00**

12½″ h, medium green, white enameled woman holding hoop around her, birds perched on hoop **330.00**

Water Set, tankard with hinged pewter lid, six goblets, white enameled dec of children at play, price for seven piece set. **680.00**

MATCH HOLDERS

History: After 1850 the friction match achieved popular usage. The early matches were packaged and sold in sliding cardboard boxes. To facilitate storage and to eliminate the clumsiness of using the box, match holders were developed.

The first examples were cast iron or tin, the latter often having advertising on them. A patent for a wall hanging match holder was issued in 1849. By 1880 match holders also were being made from glass and china. Match holders lost popularity in the late 1930s and 1940s with the advent of gas and electric heat and ranges.

Advertising,

American Manure Spreader, litho tin, 5″ h. **380.00**

Advertising, Milwaukee Binders and Mowers, C. W. Shonk Co. Lith, Chicago, 5 x 3½″, $32.00.

Bliss Native Herbs, litho tin, Capitol building illus, 6½" h 85.00
Compliments of F H Ohaus Grocer, litho tin, figural, arrowhead with Indian bust, emb, 5½" h 145.00
Dockash Stove Factory, litho tin, 5" h 25.00
Dr Shoops Health Coffee Imitation, litho tin, blue, white, and red design, yellow ground, 5" h. 220.00
Dutch Boy Paint, litho tin, emb, diecut, Dutch boy, 6½" h 275.00
Ellwood Steel Fences, litho tin, red, white, and blue, 5" h. 35.00
Gale Manufacturing Co, Agriculture Implements, litho tin, aerial view of factory, 5" h. 300.00
Garland Stoves and Ranges, litho tin, red, yellow, and white, 5" h 35.00
Milwaukee Harvesting Machines, litho tin, 5½" h 125.00
Newberry Shoe, litho tin, gold dec, black ground, 4¼" h. 75.00
Old Judson, J C Stevens, litho tin, 4¾" h 185.00
Sharples Tubular Cream Separators, litho tin, 6¾" h 425.00
Smith–Wallace Shoe Co, Best of Everything In Shoes, litho tin, 5" h 125.00
Solarine Metal Polish, litho tin, 5" h 90.00
T H Coal & Lime Co, cast iron, figural, coal scuttle, painted, 5¼" h. 100.00
Topsy, Quality Shows in Topsy Hose, litho tin, 5" h 100.00
Universal Stoves and Ranges, litho tin, blue globe dec, red lettering, tan ground, 4¾" h 200.00
Brass, 2¾" h, cast, owl, glass eyes . . 60.00
Cast Iron, painted, swing lid, C Parker, pat Sept 14, 1867, May 3, 1870, repainted, 5¾" h 110.00
Glass, 4¼" h, cylindrical, cobalt blue, SP brass trim. 40.00
Porcelain, seated girl feeding dog on table, sgd "Elbogen" 125.00
Sterling Silver, 1¾ x 2½", diecut striking area, cigar cutter on one corner, hinged lid with inscription "H R" and diamond, int. marked "Made For Tiffany & Co/Pat 12, 09/Sterling" 75.00
Tin, Victorian, emb, litho, 7¼" h 55.00

MATCH SAFES

History: Match safes are small containers used to safely carry matches in one's pocket. They were first used in the 1850s. Match safes are often figural with a hinged lid and striking surface.
Reference: Audrey G. Sullivan, *A History of Match Safes In The United States,* published by author, 1978.

Note: While not all match safes have a striking surface, this is one test, besides size, to distinguish a match safe from a calling card case.

Advertising
Buster Brown Bread, litho tin, Buster, Tige, and children 925.00
DeLaval, cream separator shape . . 100.00
Ka–Noo–No, litho tin, Indian and tepees dec. 25.00
National Supply Co, Boston, silvered brass, horse head illus, black and white design and text, early 1900. . 45.00
Old Judson Whiskey 145.00
Old Reliable Elwood Steel Fences, litho tin 45.00
San Felice Cigars, "For Gentlemen of Good Taste," man and woman, dated 1912 . . . . 65.00
Brass
Dragon, Chinese 175.00
Metamorphic, skull changes to rooster 275.00
Walnut 200.00
Lapis, cylindrical, hinged top, brass accents, 2 ⅝ x ⅞". 350.00
Nickel Plated, figural, shoe 125.00
Pewter, figural, pig, silvered 175.00

Silverplated, relief hunting scene, 2¼ x 1¾", $55.00.

Silver
800 Silver
Art Nouveau, stylized flowers, loop, 1⅜ x 1⅝". 75.00
Four enamel plaques depicting vices 200.00
Repousse, allover floral motif, sgd "Jacob & Jenkins" 230.00
Sterling, Art Nouveau, woman with flowing hair, repousse. 225.00

Tin, decorated, 7½" h **300.00**
Wood, carved, shoe form, painted yellow, black, red, and ochre, 19th C, 5¼" l, 2¼" h **615.00**

Vase, red, handled, imp daisy design, #619, 9" h, $12.00.

McCOY POTTERY

History: The J. W. McCoy Pottery Co. was established in Roseville, Ohio, in September 1899. The early McCoy Co. produced both stoneware and some art pottery lines, including Rosewood. In October 1911, three potteries merged, creating the Brush-McCoy Pottery Co. This company continued to produce the original McCoy lines and added several new art lines. Much early pottery is not marked.

In 1910, Nelson McCoy and his father, J. W. McCoy, founded the Nelson McCoy Sanitary Stoneware Co. In 1925, the McCoy family sold its interest in the Brush-McCoy Pottery Co. and started to expand and improve the Nelson McCoy Co. The new company produced stoneware, earthenware specialities, and artware. Most of the pottery marked McCoy was made by the Nelson McCoy Co.

References: Sharon and Bob Huxford, *The Collectors Encyclopedia of McCoy Pottery,* Collector Books, 1980, 1993 value update; Dana G. Morykan and Harry L. Rinker, *Warman's Country Antiques & Collectibles, Second Edition,* Wallace–Homestead, 1994; Harold Nichols, *McCoy Cookie Jars: From The First To The Last, Second Edition,* Nichols Publishing, 1991; Steve and Martha Sanford, *The Guide To Brush–McCoy Pottery,* published by authors, 1992.

Periodicals: *Our McCoy Matters,* PO Box 14255, Parkville, MO 64152.

Additional Listings: *See Warman's Americana & Collectibles* for more examples.

Bank, Cookie Cabin **78.00**
Cookie Jar, cov
  Basket of Eggs **80.00**
  Chilly Willy, MIB **90.00**
  Frontier Family **30.00**
  Grandma **150.00**
  Penguin **230.00**
  Raggedy Ann **125.00**
  Rocking Chair Dalmations **650.00**
  Tepee **250.00**
  Traffic Light **75.00**
  Wren House **195.00**
Cuspidor, floral dec, dark brown ground, Loy–Nel–Art **65.00**
Jardiniere
  7 x 8", Onyx Line, floral emb band,

vertical ribbed panels, mottled black brown, and blue glaze, c1832 . . . . **35.00**
12" h, Florastone Line, c1923 . . . . **95.00**
Mug, WC Fields **60.00**
Pitcher, Buccaneer, waisted cylindrical body, relief molded pirate. **60.00**
Planter
  Dog with spinning wheel **18.00**
  Pine Cone pattern **65.00**
  Wishing Well, brown and green glaze **15.00**
Soup Tureen, cov, El Rancho pattern, sombrero shape **50.00**
Teapot, cov, Pine Cone pattern **25.00**
Vase, 8" h, tulips, brown–green leaves, c1948. . . . . **48.00**
Wall Pocket, mailbox **45.00**

McKEE GLASS

History: The McKee Glass Co. was established in 1843 in Pittsburgh, Pennsylvania. In 1852 it opened a factory to produce Pattern Glass. In 1888 the factory was relocated to Jeannette, Pennsylvania, and began to produce many types of glass kitchenwares, including several patterns of Depression Glass. The factory continued until 1951 when it was sold to the Thatcher Manufacturing Co.

McKee named its colors Chalaine Blue, Custard, Seville Yellow, and Skokie Green. McKee glass may also be found with painted patterns, e.g., dots and ships. A few items were decaled. Many of the canisters and shakers were lettered in black to show the purpose for which they were intended.

References: Gene Florence, *Kitchen Glassware of the Depression Years, 4th Edition,* Collector Books, 1990, 1992 value update; Gene Florence, *Very Rare Glassware of the Depression Years, Third Series,* Collector Books, 1993; M'Kee and

Brothers, *M'Kee Victorian Glass*, Dover Publications, 1871, 1981 reprint.

Additional Listings: See *Warman's Americana & Collectibles* for more examples.

Bowl
4½" d, custard 10.00
5" d
    Laurel, green 6.50
    Rock Crystal pattern 12.00
6" d, Laurel, French Ivory, scalloped 9.00
9" d, Ships, red dec 16.00
Canister, Seville Yellow, labeled "Cereal," orig glass cov, 40 oz 48.00
Cheese Dish, cov, Laurel, French Ivory 58.00
Creamer, Laurel, French Ivory, tall . . 12.00
Cup, Laurel, green 7.50
Custard Cup, custard 5.00

Candy Dish, cov, orange body, gold trim and finial, clear pedestal base, 7¾" h, $25.00.

Dresser Tray, heart shaped, Poudre Blue. 25.00
Goblet, 8" h, Rock Crystal 14.00
Mayonnaise Bowl and Underplate, Rock Crystal, ruby, price for two piece set 50.00
Mixing Bowl, 11½" d, Skokie Green . . 24.00
Percolator, Range–Tec, clear, multicolored concentric rings. 65.00
Pitcher, 9" h, Rock Crystal, tankard . . 200.00
Plate
  6" d, Serenade, milk white 150.00
  9⅛" d, Laurel, French Ivory, grill . . 12.00
Radium Eminator Filter, two bottle set, vaseline, orig carton 350.00
Reamer, 6" d, milk white, Sunkist . . . 35.00
Refrigerator Dish, cov, rect, 4 x 5", Skokie Green. 15.00
Salt and Pepper Shakers, pr, 4¼" h, Roman Arch pattern, black lettering "Salt" and "Pepper," orig metal tops 32.00
Sugar, Laurel, French Ivory, tall 11.00
Tom and Jerry Bowl, French Ivory . . . 25.00
Toothpick
  Aztec 24.00

Toltec 40.00
Tumbler, Plutec 15.00
Whiskey Tumbler, Rock Crystal, ruby 45.00
Wine
  Plutec 16.00
  Rock Crystal, ruby 50.00
  Sunbeam 32.00
Wren's Honeymoon Hut, hanging birdhouse. 75.00

MEDICAL AND PHARMACEUTICAL ITEMS

History: Medicine and medical instruments are well documented for the modern period. Some instruments are virtually unchanged since their invention. Others have changed drastically.

The concept of sterilization phased out decorative handles. Early handles of instruments were often carved and can be found in mother–of–pearl, ebony, and ivory. Today's sleekly designed instruments are not as desirable to collectors.

Pharmaceutical items include items commonly found in a drugstore and pertain to the items used to store or prepare medications.

References: Bill Carter, Bernard Butterworth, Joseph Carter, and John Carter, *Dental Collectibles & Antiques*, Dental Folklore Books of K.C., 1984; Douglas Congdon–Martin, *Drugstore and Soda Fountain Antiques*, Schiffer Publishing, 1991; Don Fredgant, *Medical, Dental & Pharmaceutical Collectibles*, Books Americana, 1981; Patricia McDaniel, *Drugstore Collectibles, A Wallace-Homestead Price Guide*, Wallace-Homestead, 1994; Lillian C. and Charles G. Richardson, *The Pill Rollers: Apothecary Antiques And Drug Store Collectibles, Second Edition*, Old Fort Press, 1992; Keith Wilbur, *Antique Medical Instruments: Revised Price Guide*, Schiffer Publishing, 1987, 1993 value update.

Periodical: *Scientific, Medical & Mechanical Antiques*, 11824 Taneytown Pike, Taneytown, MD 21787.

Collectors' Clubs: Maryland Microscopical Society, 8621 Polk St., McLean, VA 22102; Medical Collectors Association, 1300 Morris Park Ave., Bronx, NY 10461.

Museums: Dittrick Museum of Medical History, Cleveland, OH; International Museum of Surgical Science & Hall of Fame, Chicago, IL; National Museum of Health & Medicine, Walter Reed Medical Center, Washington, DC; National Museum of History and Technology, Smithsonian Institution, Washington, DC; Schmidt Apothecary Shop, New England Fire & History Museum, Brewster, MA; Waring Historical Library, Medical University of South Carolina, Charleston, SC.

Amputation Saw, bow blade, ebony handle 125.00

Catalog Proof Sheet, medicine bottle labels, 1908, 12 x 15½" matted size, $45.00.

Apothecary Case, rect, mahogany, fitted with eighteen bottles and mixing implements, 19th C.............. 925.00

Book
Gunn's New Family Physician, 1884, illus, 1,230 pgs.............. 25.00
Mould Guide For Trubyte New Hue Teeth, The Dentist's Supply Company of New York, American, 1920s.................... 125.00
The Physician Hand Book, 1879, American, leather bound........ 500.00

Bottle, 9" h, Lithuanian Stomach Bitters, milk glass, colorful litho labels on three sides.................... 45.00

Box, wood, black print, stenciled
Dr Greene's Nervura Nerve Tonic, 10½ x 11 x 8½"............... 60.00
Goff's Cough Syrup, 16½ x 14⁹⁄₁₆ x 9".................... 55.00

Cabinet
Dr Frost's Homeopathic Remedies Build Health, wood, stained, litho tin door panel, lists 38 ailment remedies, 19" h.................... 425.00
Dr M A Simmons Liver Medicine, wood, stained, impressed lettering in panels, 30½" h............. 625.00

Capsule Filler, 8 x 16", Sharp and Dohme, chrome, orig wood box and instruction book, 1920–30........ 150.00

Cough Drop Container, Lutted's S P Cough Drops, figural, cabin, clear, amethyst tin dec, 1910–20........ 260.00

Door Push, porcelainized steel
Dr Caldwell's, yellow and black, 9½" h...................... 110.00

Ex–Lax, red, white, and blue design, blue and yellow background..... 95.00
Foley Kidney Pills, yellow and black, 6½ x 3".................... 75.00
Vicks Vaporub, shades of blue, green, and red, 7½ x 4".............. 130.00

Dose Glass, clear, American, 1900–10
Royal Pepsin Stomach Bitters 40.00
Todd's Best Tonic In The World ... 50.00

Drug Store Interior, four apothecary units, twenty–two drawers in each unit, unfinished ends, 48 x 108".... 1,325.00

Eyelid Retractor, ivory handle, marked "Hills King St," c1853.......... 125.00

Forceps, dental, extracting, SP, handle design, F Arnold.............. 50.00

Jar, clear, label under glass
Dr Kings New Light Pills 325.00
Dr Mills Anti Pain Pills Cures Headaches................. 375.00

Mortar and Pestle, 9" h, ash burl, turned.................... 125.00

Nasal Douche Cup, The Ideal Nasal Douche Cup, emb, handle........ 225.00

Opthalmoscope, cased, Morton 100.00

Optician's Instruments, graduated lenses, frames, measures, eyeglasses, cased..................... 425.00

Pill Maker, 12" l, brass, iron, and wood, American, c1900............. 130.00

Pliers, dental, nerve canal 15.00

Scale, chemist's, brass and steel, oak box with drawers, glazed top and sides, Becker's Sons, Rotterdam, c1920.................... 225.00

Scalpel, ebony, c1860, price for set of 3........................ 400.00

Sign
Dr D Jaynes Family Medicines, glass, emb silver and gold foil lettering, gold border, black background, framed, 11½" h, 21¾" w........ 110.00
Dr Harter's Iron Tonic, Beautifies The Complexion Purifies the Blood, litho paperboard, man and woman, shades of brown and white, wood frame, 12 x 7½"............. 75.00
Medical Center Pharmacy Drugs, Perfumes, and Rubber Goods, reverse painted glass, gilt lettering, black background, 11½ x 30½"....... 250.00
Pepto Bismol, figural, bottle, diecut cardboard, red and black lettering . 50.00

Stethoscope, monaural, metal 110.00

Surgical Instrument Set
Codman and Shurtleff Surgical and Dental Instruments, 13 Tremont St, Boston, leather case.......... 3,400.00
G Tiemann & Co Manufacturers, 67 Chatham St, NY, mahogany case . 3,000.00

Thermometer, Exlax, porcelain, black

and white lettering, dark blue ground, 36⅛" h. **100.00**

Vaporizer, Vapo–Cresolene, 6½" h, metal stand with glass oil burning lamp, orig box and instructions, American, c1900. . . . . **130.00**

MEDICINE BOTTLES

History: The local apothecary and his book of formulas played a major role in early America. In 1796 the first patent for a medicine was issued by the United States Patent Office. Anyone could apply for a patent. As long as the dosage was not poisonous, the patent was granted.

Patent medicines were advertised in newspapers and magazines and sold through the general store and by "medicine" shows. In 1907 the Pure Food and Drug Act, requiring an accurate description of contents of medicine on the label, put an end to the patent medicine industry. Not all medicines were patented.

Most medicines were sold in distinctive bottles, often with the name of the medicine and location in relief. Many early bottles were made in the glass manufacturing area of southern New Jersey. Later companies in western Pennsylvania and Ohio manufactured bottles.

References: Joseph K. Baldwin, *A Collector's Guide To Patent And Proprietary Medicine Bottles Of The Nineteenth Century,* Thomas Nelson, 1973; Ralph and Terry Kovel, *The Kovels' Bottle Price List, 9th Edition,* Crown Publishers, 1992; Carlo and Dot Sellari, *The Standard Old Bottle Price Guide,* Collector Books, 1989.

Periodicals: *Antique Bottle And Glass Collector,* PO Box 187, East Greenville, PA 18041; *Bottles & Extras Magazine,* PO Box 154, Happy Camp, CA 96039.

Apothecary Jar, emerald green, ground stopper, recessed label, 8″ h, $45.00.

Abner Royce Co, 5½″ h, clear **5.00**
Atlas Medicine Co, Henderson, NC, 9¼″ h, amber. **15.00**
Baker's Celery Kola, 10″ h, amber . . . **45.00**
Begg's Diarrhea Balsam **12.00**
Blodgett's Persian Balm, 4⅞″ h, aqua, pontil **125.00**
C A Newman Druggist, aqua, pontil . . **12.00**
Cantrell's Pectoral Or Cough Syrup, 6″ h, open pontil **185.00**
Compound Extract of Hops & Boneset, 4⅝″ h, aqua, pontil **50.00**
Craig Kidney Cure Company, 9½″ h, amber **125.00**
Davis Vegetable Pain Killer, 6⅝″ h . . **45.00**
Dr Adolf Hommel's Haematogen, aqua **15.00**
Dr Lindsey's Blood Searcher, 8½″ h, clear **20.00**
Dr Nywall's Family Medicine, 7½″ h, amber **15.00**
Dr S Feller's Lung Balsam, 6¾″ h, aqua, iron pontil **145.00**
Elliman's Embrocation, yellowish–aqua **20.00**
Farrell's Arabian Liniment, aqua, open pontil **45.00**
Flagg's Good Samaritans Relief, 3⅞″ h, five sided, pale cornflower blue. **125.00**
Gardner's Liniment, 3⅞″ h, aqua, open pontil **65.00**
Gibb's Bone Liniment, 6½″ h, olive–green. **450.00**
Ginseng Panacea, 4⅜″ h, aqua, open pontil **75.00**
H G & Co, Philadelphia, 3⅞″ h, cylinder, clear **10.00**
H H Warner & Co, Tippe Canoe, dark amber, pint. **50.00**
Himalaya The Kola Compound Natures, 7¼″ h, yellow–amber. **40.00**
H Lake's Indian Specific, aquamarine, pint **200.00**
Hop Tonic, 9¾″ h, amber **60.00**
Jewett's Nerve Liniment, 3″ h, aqua, open pontil **50.00**
J Paul Liebe, golden–yellow **15.00**
Kemp's Balsam For Throat & Lungs, 8″ h, light blue–green. **18.00**
Keough's Foul Remedy **50.00**
Langenbach's Dysentary Cure, aqua, label. **25.00**
Lehman's Nerve & Bone Liniment, 4½″ h, aqua, open pontil. **125.00**
Lockyeer's Sulphur Hair Restorer, 7½″ h, green–aqua, oval. **30.00**
MB Robert's Vegetable Embrocation, blue–green, open pontil **90.00**
Mendenhall's Cough Remedy, 4⅜″ h, aqua, open pontil. **100.00**
Moores Revealed Remedy, 9″ h, amber **45.00**
Nature's Remedy, 6½″ h, amber **15.00**

Nelson's Chill Cure, Natchez, MI, 6" h,
clear 20.00
Oldridge's Balm of Columbia, 5¼" h,
aqua, open pontil 45.00
Paine's Vegetable Pain Curer, 5⅜" h,
aqua, open pontil 100.00
Phillip's Emulsion Cod Liver Oil, amber 10.00
Porter's Cure of Pain, 5¼" h, aqua, open
pontil 145.00
Querus Cod Liver Oil Jelly, 5½" h,
aqua 100.00
Radway's Ready Relief, One Dollar,
New York, 8" h, rect with beveled cor-
ners, aquamarine, applied sloping collared mouth, pontil scar 160.00
Reed, Carnrick & Andrus Chemists, 8⅞"
h, cobalt blue 250.00
Robert Gibson & Son Lozenge Makers,
13" h, clear. 110.00
Rohrer's Wild Cherry Tonic Expectoral,
10½" h, golden–amber. 145.00
Sanford's Radical Cure, 7⅝" h, cobalt
blue 30.00
Shecut's Southern Balm For Coughs, 6"
h, aqua. 150.00
Smith Green Mountain Renovator, 7¾"
h, aqua, oval, smooth base 75.00
Swaims Panacea, 8" h, olive–green . 80.00
T B Smith Kidney Tonic, 10½" h, aqua 12.00
Thomas Electric Oil, 4¼" h, clear . . . 10.00
Thorn's Hop & Burdock Tonic, 6⅜" h,
yellow. 40.00
Turner's Balsam, 4⅞" h, aqua, eight
sided 60.00
USA Hospital Dept, 6" h, forest green,
sq collar 240.00
Vaughn's Vegetable Lithontriptic Mix-
ture, 8" h, aqua 130.00
Warner's Safe Cure, 9½" h, amber . . 125.00
Web's Cathartic A No. 1 Tonic, 9½" h,
amber 55.00
Westlake's Vegetable Ointment, 2⅞" h,
light cornflower blue. 55.00
Wishart's Pine Tree Cordial, 9¾" h,
clear 60.00

Master Salt, applied floral dec, gold gilt int., 2⅝" h, $35.00.

Bowl, 4¾" d, gold, enameled floral dec 50.00
Cake Stand, 8" d, pedestal base, emb
floral dec 75.00
Candlestick, 10½" h 110.00
Cologne Bottle, 4¼ x 7½", bulbous,
flashed amber panel, cut neck, etched
grapes and leaves, corked metal stop-
per, c1840 . . . . 160.00
Creamer, 6½" h, etched ferns, applied
clear handle, attributed to Sandwich . 125.00
Curtain Tie Back, 2⅝" d, pewter fitting,
star flower dec 60.00
Goblet, 5" h, gold, white lily of the valley
dec 35.00
Pitcher, 5½ x 9¾" h, bulbous, panel cut
neck, engraved lacy florals and
leaves, applied clear handle, c1840. . 220.00
Salt, 2¾" d, 2¼" h, master, gold, vintage
etching, pedestal base. 85.00
Sugar, cov, 4¼ x 6¼", low foot, enameled white foliage dec, knob finial . . . 55.00
Vase, 9¾" h, cylindrical, raised circular
foot, everted rim, bright enameled yellow, orange, and blue floral sprays
and insects, price for pair. 225.00
Wig Stand, 10½" h, large sphere applied
to baluster pedestal continuing to flaring round foot, 19th C 225.00

MERCURY GLASS

History: Mercury glass is a light-bodied, double-walled glass that was "silvered" by applying a solution of silver nitrate to the inside of the object through a hole in the base of the formed object.

F. Hale Thomas, London, patented the method in 1849. In 1855 the New England Glass Co. filed a patent for the same type of process. Other American glassmakers soon followed. The glass reached the height of its popularity in the early 20th century.

Reference: Ellen T. Schroy, *Warman's Glass,* Wallace–Homestead, 1992.

METTLACH

History: In 1809 Jean Francis Boch established a pottery at Mettlach in Germany's Moselle Valley.

His father had started a pottery at Septfontaines in 1767. Nicholas Villeroy began his pottery career at Wallerfanger in 1789.

In 1841 these three factories merged. They pioneered in underglaze printing on earthenware, in using transfers from copper plates, and in using coal-fired kilns. Other factories were developed at Dresden, Wadgassen, and Danischburg.

The castle and Mercury emblems are the two chief marks. Secondary marks are known. The base also contains a shape mark and usually a decor mark. Pieces are found in relief, etched, prints under the glaze, and cameo.

Prices are for print under glaze unless otherwise specified.

References: Susan and Al Bagdade, *Warman's English & Continental Pottery & Porcelain, Second Edition,* Wallace–Homestead, 1991; Gary Kirsner, *The Mettlach Book, Second Edition,* Glentiques, 1987; R. H. Mohr, *Mettlach Steins, Ninth Edition,* published by author, 1982.

Collectors' Club: Stein Collectors International, 3530 Mimosa Court, New Orleans, LA 70131–8305.

Additional Listings: Villeroy & Boch.

Charger, 1044, 12½" d, discolored glaze	50.00
Creamer, 2947, 4" h, etched	75.00
Flagon, 2270, 18" h	615.00
Jar, cov, 1324, 4½" h, mosaic, floral design	175.00
Mug, 5" h, "Join Health and Cheer, Drink Hires Root Beer," tan ground, marked "Mettlach Made in Germany"	145.00

Pitcher
8" h, applied brown floral and leafy vine dec, gray shell motif body, ftd, brown seal on base	120.00
12½" h, 2893, cylindrical, figures by the sea, hinged pewter lid	200.00

Plaque
1044, 18" d, geese in flight and wildflowers	350.00
2013, 27" d, German eagle, names and crests of cities, eye bolts, chain hanger, imp castle mark	6,600.00
2112 and 2113, 16" d, gnome sitting in tree drinking from goblet, holding wine bottles, etched, relief gold border, sgd "H S Schlitt," price for pair	1,800.00
2625, 7½" d, mandolin player, etched	300.00
7048, 20¾" d, white cameo of man riding dolphin, two seated females, and flying mallards, c1900	2,500.00
Punch Bowl, 3149, 16" h, white cameo relief, classical women and children, blue ground, castle mark	850.00
Relish Tray, 3363, 7" l, Art Nouveau design, etched	500.00

Stein
1005, 1 L, drinking scene, relief dec, grape arbor, pewter lid with figural thumbpiece	385.00
1452, ¼ L, mosaic, blue and beige floral dec, inlaid lid	300.00
1467, ½ L, harvest scene, relief	225.00
1526/598, 1 L, man with rifle scene	310.00
1863, ½ L, Scene of Stuttgart, etched, inlaid lid	595.00
1940, 3 L, keeper of the wine, etched, sgd "Warth"	1,500.00
2035, ½ L, Bacchus party, inlaid lid	445.00
2057, ½ L, peasants dancing, etched, inlaid lid	490.00

Stein, #2090II/10/94, matte finish, $625.00.

2192, ½ L, student joke, Etruscan style, etched, inlaid lid, sgd "Schlitt"	785.00
2278, ½ L, sporting scenes, rust ground, relief, pewter lid	300.00
2530, ½ L, boar hunt	850.00
2893/1197, 2 L, PUG, Hessen shield	450.00
2922, ¼ L, etched, hunters drinking by campfire, etched, inlaid lid	300.00
3253, ½ L, card players, dog, etched, pewter thumb grip	495.00
Sugar, 3321, 4½" h, etched	75.00
Tile, 3¼ x 5¾", blue warrior	225.00
Tobacco Jar, 1231, 7" h, cattle, etched	350.00
Toothpick Holder, 1461, incised floral design	60.00

Vase
1591, 11" h, four scenes of boy	470.00
1897, 11" h, mosaic, geometric design	345.00

MILITARIA

History: Wars always have been part of history. Until the mid–19th century, soldiers often had to fill their own needs, including weapons. Even in the 20th century, a soldier's uniform and some of his gear are viewed as his personal property, even though issued by a military agency.

Conquering armed forces made a habit of acquiring souvenirs from their vanquished foes. They brought their own uniforms and accessories home as badges of triumph and service.

Saving militaria may be one of the oldest collecting traditions. Militaria collectors tend to have their own special shows and view themselves outside the normal antiques channels. However, they haunt small indoor shows and flea markets in hopes of finding additional materials.

References: Thomas Berndt, *Standard Catalog of U. S. Military Vehicles: 1940–1965,* Krause Publications, 1993; Ray A. Bows, *Vietnam Military Lore 1959–1973,* Bows & Sons, 1988; Robert Fisch, *Field Equipment of the Infantry 1914–1945,* Greenberg Publications, 1989; *North South Trader's Civil War Collector's Price Guide, 5th Edition,* North South Trader's Civil War, 1991; Harry Rinker, Jr. and Robert Heistand, *World War II Collectibles: The Collector's Guide To Selecting And Enjoying Military And Home Front Items,* New Burlington Books, 1993; Jack H. Smith, *Military Postcards 1870–1945,* Wallace–Homestead, 1988; Sydney B. Vernon, *Vernon's Collectors' Guide To Orders, Medals, and Decorations,* published by author, 1986.

Periodicals: *Military Collector Magazine,* PO Box 245, Lyon Station, PA 19536; *Military Collector News,* PO Box 702073, Tulsa, OK 74170; *North South Trader's Civil War,* PO Drawer 631, Orange, VA 22960.

Collectors' Clubs: American Society of Military Insignia Collectors, 526 Lafayette Ave., Palmerton, PA 18071; Association of American Military Uniform Collectors, PO Box 1876, Elyria, OH 44036; Company of Military Historians, North Main Street, Westbrook, CT 06498; Imperial German Military Collectors Association, 82 Atlantic St., Keyport, NJ 07735; Orders and Medals Society of America, PO Box 484, Glassboro, NJ 08028.

Reproduction Alert: Pay special attention to Civil War and Nazi material.

Additional Listings: Firearms, Nazi, and Swords. See World War I and World War II in *Warman's Americana & Collectibles* for more examples.

WAR OF 1812

Cartridge Box, leather, white cloth strap, very worn, missing plate. **65.00**
Lancer's Cap, 8th Chevau Legers Lanciers, Polomais, black leather skull and visor, brass visor trim, "N" emb on front plate, chin chain, green cloth top. **800.00**
Military Drum, large eagle painted on sides, red, and blue stripes, one drum head, good condition, 22" h, 17" d. . .   **750.00**
Officer's Sabretach, dark blue, silver cord trim, large crowned cypher "FWR," German **500.00**
Shoes, leather, pegged sole, brass buckle, stitching reads "H. S. Shawner, CT". **150.00**

Civil War, Confederate cap box, found at Antietam, $275.00.

CIVIL WAR

Bowie Fighting Knife, 9" blade, single edged, crossguard of iron, brass eagle head pommel, made by Roby of West Chelmsford, MA **1,000.00**
Enlisted Man's Artillery Hat, black felt, broad brim, cloth trim, turned upward at right side, brass "US Arms" device, brass crossed cannons on front, black ostrich feather. **375.00**
Epaulets, Navy Commander's, raised edges, gold lace strap, crossed metal anchors, bullion crescent design. . . .   **350.00**
Field Binoculars, good optics, fair condition, 7" l **45.00**
Musician's Sword, 32" blade, Ames Mfg marks, dated 1864, leather scabbard   **200.00**
Socket Bayonet, cross section blade, ring lock. **50.00**
Surgeon's Kit, ivory handled tools in fitted case, portable brass microscope in fitted box, imperfections **2,970.00**

SPANISH AMERICAN

Bayonet, US Krag, steel scabbard, 12" blade dated 1901, wood grips in fair condition **45.00**

Hat Badge, infantry, brass, crossed Krag rifles, 2" l 25.00
Leggings, Army, canvas, worn, price for pair 25.00

WORLD WAR I

Bayonet
  British, MK II, No. 4, spike, scabbard 20.00
  Imperial Germany, long triangular cross blade, socket style, metal scabbard 65.00

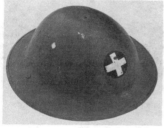

World War I, divisional helmet, American, orig liner, $50.00.

Helmet
  Austrian, Pattern 1916, riveted lower head 150.00
  British, MK I Pattern, rough liner, khaki finish 35.00
  German, Pattern 1916, painted gray/green 80.00
Knife, French, British, brass hilt, knuckle duster, marked "Made by Robert Kelley & Sons, Liverpool," leather scabbard 220.00
Luger Breakdown Tool 15.00
Medal, Bulgarian, bronze gilted, ribbon, frontline combatant, marked "1915–18" 25.00
Overcoat, US Army officers, Melton, olive drab, wool, double breasted, ten bone buttons 60.00
Service Medal, British, Pakistan, green and white ribbon 10.00
Stickpin, German EKI and EKII, enameled and silver 15.00
Tunic, German Army, plain field gray wool, two upper and two lower pockets, crown design buttons, good condition 180.00
Wound Badge, Imperial German, gold, solid back 15.00

WORLD WAR II

Belt Buckle, USMC, dress, brass . . . 20.00
Belt of 1000 Stitches, Japanese, tie strings, red and white silk, 42" l 65.00
Blouse, Canadian NCO's, battle dress style, brown wool 350.00
Boots, US Army, double buckle, brown leather, worn 100.00
Cap, US Woman's Army Corps, tan, gold braid trim, tropical 10.00
Collar Tabs, Japanese, Private First Class, price for pair 8.00
Compass, German, Lensatic, black painted 50.00
Entrenching Tool, British, tan canvas cov 45.00
Flight Jacket, US Pilot's, bomber style, leather, fur liner 450.00
Gas Mask, German, canister style, rubber mask, canvas straps, carrying container, price for mask, two canister filters, and case 80.00
Gas Mask Glass Lens Inserts, German, silk bands, gray painted tin case, marked "Masen–Brille" 45.00
Helmet
  Canadian Paratrooper's, canvas chin strap, olive drab color 250.00
  Italian, steel, leather chin strap . . . 98.00
ID Tag
  British, pressed paper, red, price for pair with cloth cord 25.00
  US Army, oval pattern, instruction envelope, price for pair with chain . . . 25.00
Immunization Records, soldier's, US, Form 81, Medical Department USA (Revised Sept 23, 1942) 10.00
Manual, Canadian Army, First Aid, Training Pamphlet No. 14 . . . . 7.00
Officer's Visor Hat, Japanese, red band on dark green, red Infantry piping, gold star attached to front 75.00
Overcoat, German, enlisted, late war style, gray wool, double breasted, twelve buttons 150.00
Pack, German, fur covered front flat, green canvas, metal D–rings, leather straps, Tornister 100.00
Ribbon, Great Britain, "The 1939–43 Star," three colored striped ribbon, bronze star 20.00
Rucksack, US Army, tan canvas, aluminum tubular frame, designed for mountain troops 65.00
Telescope, Australian, MKI, 14" l, heavy leather case and carrying straps, covers 45.00
Tunic, German Officer's, mountain troops, dark green wool, silver piping, pebble front buttons, edelweiss and silver wire Bevo eagle patches 175.00

VIETNAM

Hand Grenade, practice, Viet Cong, 9",
wooden handle, canister, olive green **25.00**
Helmet
US Army, M1, canvas straps and
camouflage cover, peace sign
painted on front, happy face on
back, marked "P.F.C. Hart". **25.00**
Viet Cong, Officer's, pith, pressed
cardboard, green cloth covering. . . **35.00**

MILK GLASS

History: Opaque white glass attained its greatest popularity at the end of the 19th century. American glass manufacturers made opaque white tablewares as a substitute for costly European china and glass. Other opaque colors, e.g., blue and green, were made. As the Edwardian era began, milk glass expanded into the novelty field.

The surge of popularity in milk glass subsided after World War I. However, milk glass continues to be made in the 20th century. Some modern products are reissues and reproductions of early forms. This presents a significant problem for collectors, although it is partially obviated by patent dates or company markings on the originals and by the telltale signs of age.

Collectors favor milk glass from the pre–World War I era, especially animal-covered dishes. The most prolific manufacturers of these animal covers were Atterbury, Challinor–Taylor, Flaccus, and McKee.

References: E. McCamley Belknap, *Milk Glass,* Crown Publishers, 1949, out of print; Regis F. and Mary F. Ferson, *Yesterday's Milk Glass Today,* published by author, 1981; Regis F. and Mary F. Ferson, *Today's Prices For Yesterday's Milk Glass,* privately printed, 1985; Myrna and Bob Garrison, *Imperial's Vintage Milk Glass,* published by authors, 1992; Everett Grist, *Covered Animal Dishes,* Collector Books, 1988, 1993 value update; Lorraine Kovar, *Westmorelane Glass, 1950–1984,* Antique Publications, 1991; Lorraine Kovar, *Westmoreland Glass, 1950–1984, Volume II,* Antique Publications, 1991; S. T. Millard, *Opaque Glass,* Wallace–Homestead, 1975, 4th edition, out of print; Ellen T. Schroy, *Warman's Glass,* Wallace–Homestead, 1992.

Collectors' Club: National Milk Glass Collectors Society, 46 Almond Dr., Hersey, PA 17033.

Museum: Houston Antique Museum, Chattanooga, TN.

Notes: There are many so–called McKee animal-covered dishes. Caution must be exercised in evaluating pieces because some authentic covers were not signed. Further, many factories have made, and many still are making, split-rib bases with McKee–like animal-covers or with different animal covers. There also is disagreement among

collectors on the issue of flared versus unflared bases. The prices for McKee pieces as given are for authentic items with either the cover or base signed.

Pieces are cross-referenced to the Ferson and Belknap books by the (F—) or (B—) marking at the end of a listing.

Plate, Trumpet Vine, lattice border, Challinor/Taylor, 10⅝" d, $45.00.

Bowl
"H" pattern, Atterbury, 7" d **55.00**
Wicket, Atterbury, 8" d, 2½" h **65.00**
Cake Plate, "H" pattern, Atterbury, 8" d **45.00**
Compote, pedestal base
Basketweave pattern, Atterbury . . . **140.00**
Fleur–de–lis border, low pedestal . **75.00**
Jenny Lind pattern **80.00**
Covered Dish
Automobile, sgd "Portieux, France" **175.00**
Battleship *Maine,* 7½" l **50.00**
Beehive, pyramidal cov, bees on hive
and lid. **40.00**
Duck, wavy base, glass eyes, painted
beak. **125.00**
Hen, baby chicks around base,
Flaccus. **45.00**
Moses in Bulrushes, 5½" l **175.00**
Rabbit, domed, split rib base **65.00**
Swan, arched neck, raised wings, lattice base, McKee. **220.00**
Creamer
Blackberry pattern **40.00**
Paneled Wheat pattern **30.00**
Dresser Tray, Actress pattern **45.00**
Glove Box, Shell on Beach pattern . . **160.00**
Goblet
Beaded Jewel pattern **55.00**
Ivy in Snow pattern **65.00**
Jar, cov, eagle (Old Abe) **120.00**
Match Holder, wall type, Indian head, 5"
l. **65.00**

Perfume Bottle, dec, 9″ h 160.00
Pitcher, owl, glass eyes, 7½″ h 150.00
Plate
  Anchor and Belaying Pin (M42) . . . 45.00
  Angel and Harp (B11c) 40.00
  Bear (F543) 140.00
  California Bears, 9″ d 125.00
  Chick and Eggs, 7¼″ d 35.00
  Contrary Mule (B12b) 40.00
  Cupid & Psyche (B6b) 35.00
  Eagle, flag, fleur de lis (B271) 25.00
  Eagle, flat and stars (B6d) 25.00
  Easter Sermon, preacher under tree,
    rabbits listening, 7½″ d 80.00
  Forget Me Not, 7″ d 40.00
  Owl Lovers, 7″ d 50.00
  Rising Sun, 4⅜″ d 65.00
  Three Kittens (B10c) 30.00
  Wicket, Atterbury
    8″ d 35.00
    9″ d 40.00
  Woof Woof (B13f) 85.00
  Yacht and Anchor (B13a) 35.00
Relish, figural, fish, emb "Pat June 4
  1872," 4½ x 11″ 40.00
Salt Dip, Strawberry pattern, ftd 40.00
Spooner
  Blackberry pattern 35.00
  Sunflower pattern, Atterbury 85.00
Sugar, cov
  Basketweave pattern, dated 1874 . 100.00
  Trumpet Vine pattern, fired on dec,
    melon ribbed body, three leaf spring
    feet, imp "S. V. France" 65.00
Sugar Shaker, orig top
  Forget Me Not pattern, Challinor . . 110.00
  Netted Oak pattern, Northwood . . . 115.00
Syrup
  Chain and Bead pattern, Atterbury . 85.00
  French Primrose pattern 55.00
  Tree of Life pattern, Challinor–Taylor 70.00
Table Set, cov butter, creamer, cov
  sugar, and spooner, Versailles pat-
  tern, exc dec. 110.00
Whimsey, canoe, enameled flowers and
  gold trim, 6″ l. 15.00

**Box, cov, royal blue and white, 2¾″ d,
2½″ h, $250.00.**

Bowl, 8″ d, tricorn, scalloped, folded
  sides, amethyst and silver deposit. . . 125.00
Creamer, 4¼″ h, white and cobalt blue
  canes, yellow centers, satin finish . . . 100.00
Cruet, bulbous, multicolored canes, applied camphor handle, matching
  stopper. 100.00
Cup and Saucer, white and cobalt blue
  canes, yellow centers, satin finish . . . 85.00
Doorknob, 2½″ d, paperweight, center
  cane dated 1852, New England Glass
  Co 375.00
Goblet, 7½″ h, multicolored canes, clear
  stem and base 150.00
Lamp, boudoir, 11½″ h, red, blue, turquoise, and white closed cane dome
  top, brass collar and three arm spider
  fittings, Bryant socket. 275.00
Pitcher, 6½″ h, multicolored canes, applied candy cane handle 165.00
Rose Bowl, 6″ d, crimped top, cased,
  white lining 145.00
Slipper, 5″ l, camphor ruffle and heel . 135.00
Sugar, cov, 3½″ h, white canes, yellow
  centers, satin finish 115.00
Vase, 3½″ h, waisted, ruffled top, light
  blue, cobalt blue, medium blue, and
  white canes, four applied knob
  handles 65.00

MILLEFIORI

History: Millefiori (thousand flowers) is an ornamental glass composed of bundles of colored
glass rods fused to become canes. The canes were
pulled while still ductile to the desired length, sliced,
arranged in a pattern, and again fused together.
The Egyptians developed this technique in the first
century B.C.; it was revived in the 1880s.

Reproduction Alert: Millefiori items, such as
paperweights, cruets, toothpicks, etc., are being
made by many modern companies.

MINIATURE LAMPS

History: Miniature oil and kerosene lamps, often
called "night lamps," are diminutive replicas of
larger lamps. Simple and utilitarian in design, miniature lamps found a place in the parlor (as "courting" lamps), hallway, children's rooms, and sick-
rooms.

Miniature lamps are found in many glass types,
from amberina to satin glass. Miniature lamps measure 2½ to 12 inches in height, with the principal
parts being the base, collar, burner, chimney, and

shade. In 1877 both L. J. Atwood and L. H. Olmsted patented burners for miniature lamps. Their burners made the lamps into a popular household accessory.

Study a lamp carefully to make certain all parts are original; married pieces are common. Reproductions abound.

References: Frank R. & Ruth E. Smith, *Miniature Lamps*, Schiffer Publishing, 1981, 6th printing; Ruth E. Smith, *Miniature Lamps–II*, Schiffer Publishing, 1982; John F. Solverson, *Those Fascinating Little Lamps: Miniature Lamps and Their Values*, Antique Publications, 1988, includes prices for Smith numbers.

Collectors' Club: Night Light, 38619 Wakefield Ct., Northville, MI 48167.

Note: The numbers given below refer to the figure numbers found in the Smith books.

Satin Glass, red, emb design, $300.00.

Figure III, artichoke lamp, white milk glass, pink and green painted dec, nutmeg burner, 7¾" h, fish scale flakes on shade.	150.00
#5–I, rainbow, DQ, MOP, satin finish	550.00
#11–I, milk glass pedestal base and shade, clear pressed font, Sandwich, 6¾" h.	250.00
#12–I, amber, emb, all orig	95.00
#29–I, cobalt blue glass font, emb "Nutmeg," narrow base band forming handle, nutmeg burner, clear glass chimney, 2¾" d base	110.00
#34–I, crystal, upside down cup and saucer lamp, 3" h	60.00
#49–I, cobalt blue, Little Butter Cup, 2" h	125.00
#52–I, white milk glass, match holder, 7¾" h, surface stress crack under handle	100.00
#59–II, clear, emb "Vienna"	125.00
#68–I, pewter base, emb rococo de-	

sign, burner marked "Stellar, E M & Co," 3½" h	85.00
#87–I, double student, brass, white milk glass shades, log emb "OCT 28 79," nutmeg burners, 12¼" h.	600.00
#109–I, green, Beaded Heart pattern, acorn burner, orig clear glass chimney, 5" h.	100.00
#111–I, white milk glass, emb bull's eye pattern, acorn burners, 5" h, nick to one foot	225.00
#112–I, emb "Daisy," 4¾" h	
Amber, acorn burner	135.00
Blue, nutmeg burner	65.00
Green, acorn burner	95.00
#125–I, ball shaped shade, red paint, emb flowers and designs, acorn burner, clear glass chimney, 7¼" h.	135.00
#186–I, white milk glass, painted satin eggshell finish, orange and brown floral dec, acorn burner, 7¼" h, inside edge flake	50.00
#190–I, milk glass, Block and Dot pattern, 7¾" h	135.00
#204–II, blue, camphor shade	100.00
#213–I, Chrysanthemum and Swirl pattern, red dec, hornet burner, 9" h	425.00
#219–I, Nellie Bly, white milk glass, pink ground, multicolored daisy dec, 8⅝" h	70.00
#229–I, green	570.00
#230–I, milk glass, Acanthus pattern, fired on yellow dec, base marked "Buc. PA/1898," 8½" h	175.00
#248–II, white milk glass, emb ribbed chimney shade, green, blue, and gold painted dec, hornet burner, 8" h, wear to paint	100.00
#262–I, apple green, beaded panels, enamel dec.	285.00
#267–II, Pairpoint, all orig, sgd "Dresden" on base	400.00
#284–I, red satin, nutmeg burner, 8¾" h, minor flakes at top edge of shade	115.00
#288–I, orange	550.00
#292–I, camphor glass, emb design, goofus dec, nutmeg burner, 8¼" h, some wear to painted dec	100.00
#293–I, camphor glass, spiral melon ribbing, painted blue, yellow, burgundy, and green pansy dec, nutmeg burner, 6¼" h, small manufacturing defect in back.	115.00
#317–I, milk glass, pink and yellow flowers, shaded green ground	300.00
#337–I, white milk glass, painted brown, orange, and gray farm scene, nutmeg burner, 9" h.	175.00
#378–II, hanging, dark pink shading to light cased satin glass shade, yellow brass frame, bottom of frame missing	45.00

#388–I, blue **575.00**
#389–I
  Blue **575.00**
  Pink **575.00**
#403–I, Beaded Drape pattern, white opalescent, ruby thumbprints, nutmeg burner, 9¾″ h **140.00**
#459–II, satin, red shaded to pink, emb scrolled leaves and swirls, 10″ h **1,650.00**
#490–I, skeleton, white bisque, blue and orchid trim, green glass eyes, foreign burner, 6½″ h **5,000.00**
#497, owl, milk glass, painted shades of gray and black, orange eyes, acorn burner, 7½″ h **600.00**
#523–II, blue milk glass, medallion pattern filigreecoppery–gold cov, 7½″ h **500.00**
#545–I, amber, swirled base, amber glass cigar lighter shade, foreign burner and ring, 8″ h, roughness to one foot **25.00**

MINIATURES

History: There are three sizes of miniatures: dollhouse scale (ranging from ½ to 1″), sample size, and child's size. Since most earlier material is in museums or extremely expensive, the most common examples are 20th century.

Many mediums were used for miniatures: silver, copper, tin, wood, glass, and ivory. Even books were printed in miniature. Prices are broadly ranged, depending on scarcity and quality of workmanship.

The collecting of miniatures dates back to the 18th century. It remains one of the world's leading hobbies.

References: Caroline Clifton–Mogg, *The Dollhouse Sourcebook,* Abbeville Press, 1993; Nora Earnshaw, *Collecting Dolls' Houses and Miniatures,* Pincushion Press, 1993; Caroline Hamilton, *Decorative Dolls Houses,* Clarkson Potter, 1990; Flora Gill Jacobs, *Dolls Houses in America: Historic Preservation in Miniature,* Charles Scribner's Sons, 1974; Flora Gill Jacobs, *History of Dolls Houses,* Charles Scribner's Sons; Constance Eileen King, *Dolls and Dolls Houses,* Hamlyn; Eva Stille, *Doll Kitchens, 1800–1980,* Schiffer Publishing, 1988; Margaret Towner, *Dollhouse Furniture,* Courage Books, Running Press, 1993; Von Wilckens, *Mansions in Miniature,* Tuttle.

Periodicals: *Doll Castle News,* PO Box 247, Washington, NJ 07882; *Miniature Collector,* PO Box 631, Boiling Springs, PA 17007; *Miniatures Showcase,* 21027 Crossroads Circle, PO Box 1612, Waukesha, WI 53187; *Nutshell News,* 21027 Crossroads Circle, PO Box 1612, Waukesha, WI 53187.

Collectors' Clubs: International Guild Miniature Artisans, PO Box 71, Bridgeport, NY 18080; National Association of Miniature Enthusiasts, PO Box 69, Carmel, IN 46032.

Museums: Margaret Woodbury Strong Museum, Rochester, NY; Mildred Mahoney Jubilee Doll House Museum, Fort Erie, Canada; Museums at Stony Brook, Stony Brook, NY; Toy and Miniature Museum of Kansas City, Kansas City, MO; Toy Museum of Atlanta, Atlanta, GA; Washington Dolls' House and Toy Museum, Washington, DC.

Additional Listings: See Doll House Furnishings in *Warman's Americana & Collectibles* for more examples.

ACCESSORIES

Birdcage, brass, bird and stand, 7″ h . **60.00**
Box, lacquered, cockerel and hen form, naturalistic coloring, feather and plumage, nashiji int., 19th C, price for pair **1,000.00**
Cabinet, lacquered, Japanese, 18″ h, 12″ w **150.00**
Chamber Pot, 1¾″ h, yellow ware, white and brown stripes **55.00**
Chest of Drawers, Hepplewhite, walnut, four dovetailed drawers, scalloped apron, French feet, missing one foot, edge damage and wear........... **5,995.00**
Cigarette Box, silver and enamel, rect, painted bull elk **125.00**
Clock, table, rect, enamel, blue **55.00**
Coffeepot, brass **20.00**
Desk, Hepplewhite style, cherry, slant front, inlay dec, dovetailed drawers, handmade, 21″ w, 14″ d, 28¾″ h **440.00**
Dresser, 12½″ w, 7¼″ d, 15¾″ h, walnut, rect top, adjustable mirror, raised panel ends, three drawers with white porcelain pulls, high cutout feet, wire nail construction **220.00**
Dust Pan and Broom, pewter, German, c1890. .... **30.00**
Figure, Staffordshire
  5″ h, lady **90.00**
  5½″ h, dog, price for pair **145.00**
Mandolin, 5½″ l, tortoiseshell **200.00**
Painting
  Ivory
    Boy, wearing brown jacket, oval, framed, sgd "Amy Otis," 4¼ x 2¾″.................... **150.00**
    Gentleman, oval, gilt metal frame, late 19th C............... **210.00**
    Lady Louisa Manner, oval, gilt frame, sgd "Stopford," 3¼ x 2¼″ **440.00**
    Napoleon, oval, gilt metal frame, sgd "Hagab" **550.00**
    Woman, wearing red dress, gilt frame, mid 19th C. **110.00**
  Porcelain, portrait of maiden with daisies, oval, 5¼ x 4″ **495.00**

Sauce Pan, cov, Queen Anne, turned
ebony handle, knob finial 385.00
Settee, Victorian, out curved armrests,
turned carved feet, c1880, 19″ h, 36½″
w, 18″ d 495.00
Telephone, wall, oak, speaker and bell,
German, c1890. . . . . 30.00
Vase
3½″ h, Satsuma 35.00
4½″ h, blue and white, price for pair 40.00

CHILD SIZE

Barber Chair, 29″ l, hand carved and
painted horse's head with glass eyes,
horsehair mane, metal frame, orig
leather harness and upholstered seat,
leather covered hanging hooks 550.00
Bed, turned walnut, tester frame, American, c1830, minor imperfections, 24″
w, 29″ h 2,200.00
Blanket Chest, walnut, poplar secondary
wood, dovetailed case, molded edge
of lid and till, inlaid diamond escutcheon, bracket feet, old soft finish, 13″ l 615.00
Chair
Bamboo, green decorative strapwork 75.00
Ladderback, arm, damaged woven
splint seat, old dark finish, 25½″ h 220.00
Windsor
Bamboo, yellow striping and stenciled flowers on crest, worn old
dark repaint, 26″ h. 250.00
Birdcage, blue paint, seven spindle
back, plank seat, New England,
c1825, 26¾″ h 440.00
Chest of Drawers
Federal style, maple, straight front,
four drawers, oval brass bail handles and escutcheons, shaped
apron, French bracket feet, 22½″ h,
19½″ w, 12″ d 625.00
Grain painted, stepped back top with
two small drawers, base with two
long drawers, sides carved with
concentric circles, wooden knobs,
New England, 1830, 8″ l, 6″ d, 9½″
h, some wear. 660.00
Desk, Federal style, mahogany, drop lid,
fitted int., four drawers in base, brass
bail handles and escutcheons,
shaped apron, French bracket feet,
28″ h, 21¾″ w, 15″ d 500.00
Pedal Car, sheet metal, convertible,
cream colored, red stripe, plated
bumpers, headlights, gear shift, red
seat, 44″ l, 17″ w, 19″ h 475.00
Piano, Falconer, 22 keys, orig adjustable stool, 22¾″ w, 11″ d, 20⅞″ h 225.00
Potty Chair, Windsor, bamboo, old worn
red paint, 19¼″ h. 80.00

Rocker
Empire style, mahogany, vase
shaped splat, rush seat, scrolled
arms, 22″ h 200.00
Victorian, American, late 19th C,
wooden arms, caned back and
seat, painted black. 300.00
Sleigh, Victorian, painted dec, 21″ h, 34″
l 600.00
Wagon, 21″ l, pine, four metal rimmed
spoked wheels, S shape pull handle,
mid 19th C 450.00
Wall Box, 2½″ h, grain painted, sides
carved with concentric circles, American, 19th C, minor age cracks 250.00

**Doll House Size, bathtub, painted tin,
white int., light blue ext. with gold trim,
three gold legs, c1890, $55.00.**

DOLLHOUSE SIZE

Bathroom, wood, painted white,
Strombecker. 35.00
Bedroom, Victorian style, metal, veneer
finish, bed, nightstand, commode, armoire, cradle, Biedermeier clock, and
metal washstand, faux marble tops on
nightstand and commode 650.00
Buffet, stenciled, three shelves, column
supports, Biedermeier, 6″ h 400.00
Chair, oak, upholstered seat, German,
c1875, price for pair. 70.00
Cradle, cast iron, painted green, 2″ l,
2½″ h. 40.00
Desk and Chair, roll top, oak, drawers
open 75.00
Dining Room, French style, gilded wood,
round pedestal table, six matching
chairs, damask upholstered settee,
pier mirror, fireplace, table with faux
marble top 800.00
Doll
4¾″ h, woman, bisque, brown molded
hair. 80.00
5½″ h, woman, china head, bisque
hands, arms, and legs, worn and
faded dress and jacket 115.00

6" h, woman, articulated wooden body, arms, and legs, hair, worn silk dress	275.00
6¼" h, man, bisque, brown molded hair.	50.00
6½" h, boy, bisque, molded gimp and sailor hat, blond molded hair, undressed.	110.00

Living Room

Empire style, sofa, fainting couch, two side chairs, tapestry upholstery, matching drapery.	350.00
Victorian style, red velvet upholstered settee and two parlor chairs, foot-stool, two plant stands, two gilt fili-gree tables, three panel screen, Gone with the Wind style lamp . . .	500.00
Piano, grand, wood, eight keys, 5" h .	30.00
Sewing Table, oak, one drawer, c1880	100.00
Table, tin, ornate, white top, floral design, painted brown, 1½" l, ¾" h. . . .	20.00
Tea Cart, Petite Princess	20.00

DOLL SIZE

Bed

Brass, orig mattress and pillow, 18" l	25.00
Wood, tapered legs, old black paint, 12 x 21 x 15".	330.00

Carriage

Leather and metal, painted white, rubber tires, collapsible, marked "Doucet/Made in France," 12½" l, 9½" h	175.00
Metal, orig lining and parasol, 5" l, 3½" h	90.00
Victorian, wicker trim, metal rimmed wheels, steel springs, missing umbrella connector, 33" l.	225.00

Cradle

Poplar, hooded, old dark finish, 25" l	440.00
Walnut, dovetailed, shaped rockers, old mellow refinish, 22½" l	275.00

SALESMAN'S SAMPLES

Boots, pr, leather, 4½" h	100.00
Loom, wood, "Miniature Loom" paper label, "NRA" (National Recovery Act) ink stamp, 9½ x 12½ x 15½"	25.00
Lunch Pail, Lisk, metal, nickel plated, cup and two liners, 4" h	275.00
Pitchfork, True Temper, wood and cast iron, 30" l	350.00
Plow, cast iron, painted, 13" l	125.00
Sofa, oak, carved lion's head, orig upholstery, replaced foot, 16" l.	425.00

Stove, cast iron

Novelty, 7 x 9"	175.00
Triumph, 10 x 13"	200.00

Table

Drop Leaf, walnut, turned legs, 9¼" h	175.00
Victorian, ornate design, 10" h	225.00
Thrasher, wood and tin, 19 x 9 x 8¾"	110.00
Trash Canister, galvanized tin, hp panels, 12" h.	100.00
Windmill, Aero Mfg Co, Model 12B, aluminum, 16¾" h	130.00
Wringer, Gem, American Wringer Co, cast iron and wood, 16" l	90.00

MINTON CHINA

History: In 1793 Thomas Minton and others formed a partnership and built a small pottery at Stoke–on–Trent, Staffordshire, England. Production began in 1798 with blue-printed earthenware, mostly in the Willow pattern. In 1798 cream-colored earthenware and bone china were introduced.

A wide range of styles and wares was produced. Minton introduced porcelain figures in 1826, Parian wares in 1846, encaustic tiles in the late 1840s, and Majolica wares in 1850. Many famous designers and artists in the English pottery industry worked for Minton.

Many early pieces are unmarked or have a Sevres-type marking. The "ermine" mark was used in the early 19th century. Date codes can be found on tableware and Majolica. Between 1873 and 1911 a small globe signed Minton with a crown on top was used.

In 1883 the modern company was formed and called Mintons Limited. The "s" was dropped in 1968. Minton still produces bone china tablewares and some ornamental pieces.

References: Paul Atterbury and Maureen Batkin, *The Dictionary of Minton,* Antique Collectors' Club; Susan and Al Bagdade, *Warman's English & Continental Pottery & Porcelain, Second Edition,* Wallace–Homestead, 1991.

Biscuit Jar, teal dec, gray–blue ground, gold trim knobs, rim, and base, orig woven handle, Imperial mark	200.00

Pitcher, salt glazed, raised Arabic design, scalloped base, 11½″ h, $315.00.

Dessert Plate, 8¾″ d, wide border, pink morning glories and roses swags, price for twelve piece set 285.00

Dresser Set, pin box, 5½″ h pitcher, 11″ d tray, pink roses dec, gold trim, incised maker and potter marks, c1898, price for four piece set 250.00

Ewer, 21¼″ h, majolica, heron and fish, after model by J Protat, imp mark, 1869 date code 2,300.00

Figure, 7½″ h, two nude children holding oval trays, pierced baskets, circular base, white, imp mark, c1882. . . . . . 225.00

Flask, 16¾″ h, circular body, cherub seated on apple branch, brown ground, reverse with kingfisher flying beside large yellow irises, green ground, molded ring handles, flared rect feet, 1883 imp marks and date code 825.00

Garden Seat, 19″ h, majolica, hexagonal, cobalt blue ground, polychrome enamels, pierced floral and geometric side panels, imp mark and 1871 date code, surface wear, price for pair . . . 3,300.00

Jug, 9⅞″ h, majolica, bright yellow, green, blues, aubergine, and white, imp mark "437," and 1873 date code 2,345.00

Oyster Stand, 10″ d, majolica, revolving base, glazed green, brown, and white, imp mark, 1869. . . . . 2,225.00

Pitcher, 5″ h, relief molded cupid and vintage motif, blue and white matte finish, white glazed int., c1830–40 . . . . 125.00

Plate
9″ d, gold band, emb Grecian urns and palm fronds, white ground. 25.00
9½″ d, cobalt blue transfer, Washington's Headquarters, Valley Forge. . 30.00
10″ d, cobalt blue transfer, Girard College. 30.00

10¼″ d, portrait, Clare, rust, orange, and black paneled border, 1878 . . 75.00

Scent Bottle, 4″ h, baluster, encrusted colored flowers and foliage, gilded bulbous neck, floral cluster stopper, c1830, price for pair. 1,100.00

Soup Plate, 10⅜″ d, ironstone, printed and painted famille rose style, Orientals, molded floral band border, c1825. 50.00

Sweetmeat Dish, 8″ d, majolica, blue titmouse on branch, leaf shaped dish, imp mark, 1868. . . . . 665.00

Teapot, 3½″ h, applied trailing colored flowers, gilt accents, rustic handle and spout, c1830, blue crossed swords mark 400.00

Vase, 5″ h, lily of the valley dec, overlapping green leaves, three applied sprigs of white biscuit blossoms, three dark green leaves, scroll molded dotted base, gilt edge, c1830, price for pair 1,925.00

MOCHA

History: Mocha decoration usually is found on utilitarian creamware and stoneware pieces and is produced through a simple chemical action. A color pigment of brown, blue, green, or black is made acidic by an infusion of tobacco or hops. When the acidic colorant is applied in blobs to an alkaline ground, it reacts by spreading in feathery, seaplant like designs. This type of decoration usually is supplemented with bands of light-colored slip.

Types of decoration vary greatly, from those done in a combination of motifs, such as "Cat's Eye" and "Earthworm," to a plain pink mug decorated with green ribbed bands. Most forms of mocha are hollow, e.g., mugs, jugs, bowls, and shakers.

English potters made the vast majority of the pieces. Marked pieces are extremely rare. Collectors group the ware into three chronological periods: 1780–1820, 1820–1840, and 1840–1880.

References: Susan and Al Bagdade, *Warman's English & Continental Pottery & Porcelain, Second Edition*, Wallace–Homestead, 1991; Dana G. Morykan and Harry L. Rinker, *Warman's Country Antiques & Collectibles, Second Edition* Wallace–Homestead, 1994.

Reproduction Alert.

Bowl
5⅛″ d, 3⅛″ h, orange band with white, brown, and blue cat's eye dec, black stripes 200.00
11″ d, 5″ h, yellow ware, East Liverpool, brown, white, and green earthworm dec, wear and stains . . 690.00

Caster, 4½″ h, cat's eye dec 425.00

Pitcher, chocolate brown stripes, mint green incised arrowhead bands, 5¾" h, $475.00.

Chamber Pot, 8¾" d, 5½" h, ironstone, two tone blue band with black stripes, black earthworm dec, leaf handle, wear, glaze flakes to rim 275.00

Creamer, 3⅝" h, ironstone, blue band, black stripes, white and black cat's eye dec, leaf handle, chips and edge wear 80.00

Cup and Saucer, handleless, cup with black and white checkerboard band around rim, white fluted band around base, and medium blue ground, matching saucer 125.00

Flowerpot, 7¼" h, flared lip, black seaweed dec, black stripes, pale salmon ground, detachable saucer, imp "Creil," wear and chips 600.00

Jug, 8¼" h, chocolate brown seaweed dec, gray band, blue bands at top and bottom 350.00

Measure, 4¾" h, black seaweed dec, emb black stripe at rim, emb leaf handle, applied crest "Imperial" 145.00

Mug
2¾" h, pearlware, emb blue and white checkerboard design, dark brown stripes, molded handle 165.00

4⅞" h, blue and teal bands, black stripes and seaweed, marked "Pint" 360.00

6" h, orange–tan bands, black stripes and seaweed, incised green rim, molded leaf handle, wear and small flakes 415.00

Mustard Pot, cov, 3⅝" h, orange, chocolate brown, and white stripes, emb green band and leaf handle, chips and repair 465.00

Pepper Pot, 4½" h, seaweed dec, dark brown stripes, ftd 550.00

Pitcher
6" h, cat's eye and dot dec, some

roughness on spout, hairline crack in handle 400.00

7" h, marbleized, white spout and handle, old restoration to handle, int. hairline cracks 2,475.00

8" h, baluster, incised green bands enclosing central butternut, brown, and white bands, twig, wave, and cat's eye dec, molded foliate spout and handle, imperfections 2,750.00

Salt, 2¾" d, blue and brown bands, worm dec, ochre ground, flake to rim 140.00

Shaker, 4¼" h, tan cat's eye dec on chocolate brown band, slate blue, tan, olive gray, and chocolate brown stripes, white ground, damage and repair 325.00

Spill Holder, 4⅜" h, machine tooled, chocolate brown stripes, green glaze, short hairline, small chips, glued flake 160.00

Sugar Bowl, 2⅜" h, miniature, brown, tan, and white marbleizing, stains, small edge chips, short hairline 425.00

Tea Canister, 4" h, blue, black, and white band at shoulder, white fluted band around base, medium blue ground . . 95.00

Teapot, 5½" h, globular body with black and white checkerboard band around shoulder, medium blue ground, acorn finial 200.00

Waste Bowl, 6¼" d, 3¼" h, pearlware, blue, tan, white, and dark brown earthworm dec, emb beaded bands, small int. blister, rim flake 350.00

MONART GLASS

History: Monart glass is a heavy, simple-shaped art glass in which colored enamels are suspended in the glass during the glassmaking process. This technique was originally developed by the Ysart family in Spain in 1923. John Moncrief, a Scottish glassmaker, discovered the glass while vacationing in Spain, recognized the beauty and potential market, and began production in his Perth glassworks in 1924.

The name "Monart" is derived from the surnames Moncrief and Ysart. Two types of Monart were manufactured: a "commercial" line which incorporated colored enamels and a touch of aventurine in crystal and the "art" line in which the suspended enamels formed designs, such as feathers or scrolls. Monart glass, in most instances, is not marked. The factory used paper labels.

Basket, brown to light tan opal vertical striations, Cluthra type 585.00

Bowl, 11½" d, mottled orange and green 185.00

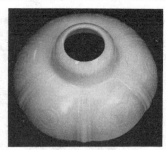

Lamp Shade, white, opal finish, 6¼″ d, $75.00.

Candlestick, two shades of green, goldstone and mica flecks, paper label . .   95.00
Lamp Shade, 6½″ d, white opal 85.00
Vase
  6½″ h, mottled shades of red and
    blue, white lining 190.00
  8½″ h, blue, silver, mica, and orange
    streaks, small bubbles 250.00
  9¼″ h, Art Deco style, brilliant opaque
    red overlaid in clear crystal, crac-
    kled black int. dec, circular mark
    "Moncreiff Scotland V. SA.91,"
    c1930 . . . .   385.00

MONT JOYE GLASS

History: Mont Joye is a type of glass produced
by Saint–Hilaire, Touvier, de Varreaux & Company
at their glassworks in Pantin, France. Most pieces
were lightly acid etched to give them a frosted appearance and decorated with enameled floral decorations. All pieces listed are frosted unless otherwise noted.

Pitcher, 10″ h, amethyst, enameled
  aqua, blue, pink, and gold flowers,
  sgd 295.00
Rose Bowl, 3¾″ h, 4¼″ d, pinched sides,
  acid etched, enameled purple violets,
  gold stems, and dec 195.00
Vase
  4½″ h, 4½″ d, heavily enameled flow-
    ers, light green ground 125.00
  10″ h, opalescent rib molded body,
    polychrome enamel blossom
    and scrolling ribbon dec, Mont
    Joye stamp on base 220.00
  10¾″ h, cylindrical, enameled green
    and gold floral dec, raisin brown
    ground, patterned gold band rim . .   900.00

15¾″ h, cameo, trumpet, emerald
  green ground, carved border,
  etched surface of oak leaves and
  acorns, heavily enameled and
  gilded 900.00
19″ h, cameo, tall slender stick neck
  tapering to bulbous base, acid textured brown ground, green overlay,
  large horse chestnut leaf clusters
  and blossoms, gold trimmed, gilt
  sgd. 825.00
20″ h, etched grapevine motif, gold
  outlines and enameled scrolling
  devices 750.00

MOORCROFT

History: William Moorcroft was first employed as
a potter by James Macintyre & Co., Ltd., of Burslem
in 1897. He established the Moorcroft pottery in
1913. The company initially used an impressed
mark, "Moorcroft, Burslem"; a signature mark, "W.
Moorcroft," followed.

The majority of the art pottery wares were hand
thrown, resulting in a great variation among simi-
larly styled pieces. Color and marks are keys to
determining age.

Walker, William's son, continued the business
upon his father's death and made the same style
wares. Modern pieces are marked simply "Moorcroft" with export pieces also marked "Made in England."

Reference: Susan and Al Bagdade, *Warman's
English & Continental Pottery & Porcelain, Second
Edition,* Wallace–Homestead, 1991.

Basket, Pomegranate pattern, multico-
  lored dec, dark ground, SP holder,
  MIE mark 350.00
Bowl, 9″ d, Eventide pattern 2,450.00
Candlesticks, pr, Orchid pattern, low,
  flambe 375.00
Coffeepot, cov, Sicilian pattern, sgd
  "Moorcroft–MacIntyre". 265.00
Cologne Bottle, Orchid pattern, orig
  stopper. 385.00
Ginger Jar, cov, 11½″ h, Pomegranate
  pattern 525.00
Jar, cov
  5½″ h, Claremont pattern, blue–green
    ground, cov missing, 20th C 180.00
  6″ h, Hibiscus pattern, green ground,
    20th C. 250.00

Lamp

    10½" h, Leaf and Berry pattern, red
flambe. **1,250.00**

    12" h, Orchid pattern, deep blue–
black flambe **1,150.00**

    14¼" h, Eventide pattern, landscape,
brass fittings, sgd and imp mark,
paper label, c1930 . . . . **2,420.00**

Loving Cup, 4¼" h, tulip and cornflower
dec, green, blue, and red, three handles, printed and painted signature,
c1900. . . . . **350.00**

Marmalade Jar, blue flowers, attached
stand, sgd "MacIntyre" **185.00**

Plate, 12" d, large floral design, orig
label. **165.00**

Urn, 3½" h, red and purple berries, large
green, yellow, and red leaves, dark
teal shading to green ground, blue
sgd **185.00**

**Vase, Florian Ware, four color, yellow
flower on base, 12¼" h, $1,025.00.**

Vase

    3½" h, Anemone pattern **95.00**

    4½" h, Wisteria pattern, applied ster-
ling silver rim **265.00**

    7¼" h, Tudric Ware, trumpet, wisteria
design, dark blue ground, hammered pewter mounted base
marked "Made in England, Tudric,
Moorcroft, 01358, Made by Liberty
& Co," c1925. . . . . **495.00**

    8" h, Bramble pattern **300.00**

    11½" h, Tulip pattern, black ground,
sgd on bottom **325.00**

    12¼" h, Anemone pattern, dark blue
ground, 20th C. **235.00**

    12½" h, chestnut leaves dec, brown
ground **750.00**

    14¾" h, agave plant dec, dark blue
ground **800.00**

MORIAGE, JAPANESE

History: Moriage refers to applied clay (slip) relief motifs and decorations used on certain classes
of Japanese pottery and porcelain.

This decorating was done by three methods: 1)
hand rolling and shaping, which was applied by
hand to the biscuit in one or more layers—the design and effect required determined thickness and
shape; 2) tubing or slip trailing, which applied decoration from a tube, like decorating a cake; and 3)
hakeme, which is reducing the slip to a liquid and
decorating the object with a brush. Color was applied either before or after the process.

**Biscuit Jar, green ground, maroon
band, maroon shaded flowers, white
moriage, gold trim, 3 ftd, 6" d, 7¼" h,
$325.00.**

Bowl, 7" d, orange flowers and leaves,
green wreath mark **135.00**

Chocolate Pot, 9" h, green ground, four
floral medallions, heavy moriage. . . . **225.00**

Demitasse Set, pot, two ftd cups and
saucers, white wisteria flowers, green
trim, price for set **400.00**

Manicure Set, three tools, buffer, and
cov trinket box, heavy dec, price for
set. **175.00**

Planter, 3¾" h, 3¾" l, swan, figural, multicolored enamel dec **95.00**

Powder Box, 5" d, light green, raised turquoise beading, hp flowers. **75.00**

Tea Set, teapot, creamer, cov sugar, five
cups and saucers, mauve ground, red
roses, delicate white slipwork, un-
marked, price for set **650.00**

Vase

    9¼" h, pedestal base, green ground,
white allover slipwork, floral
medallions. **250.00**

    12½" h, tan ground, light green bands,
pink and blue flowers, three panels
of multicolored Bird on Limb dec,
Japanese **250.00**

Moser *Moser Karlsbad*

MOSER GLASS

History: Ludwig Moser (1833–1916) founded his polishing and engraving workshop in 1857 in Karlsbad (Karlovy Vary), Czechoslovakia. He employed many famous glass designers, e.g., Johann Hoffmann, Josef Urban, and Rudolf Miller. In 1900 Moser and his sons, Rudolf and Gustav, incorporated Ludwig Moser & Söhne.

Moser art glass included clear pieces with inserted blobs of colored glass, cut colored glass with classical scenes, cameo glass, and intaglio cut. Many inexpensive enameled pieces also were made.

In 1922 Leo and Richard Moser bought Meyr's Neffe, their biggest Bohemian rival in art glass. Moser executed many pieces for the Wiener Werkstätte in the 1920s. The Moser glass factory continues to produce new items.

References: Gary Baldwin and Lee Carno, *Moser—Artistry In Glass: 1857–1938,* Antique Publications, 1988; Mural K. Charon and John Mareska, *Ludvik Moser, King of Glass: A Treasure Chest of Photographs And History,* published by authors, 1984.

Automobile Hood Ornament, 2½" h, kissing doves, sgd "Moser, Carlsbad"	125.00
Beverage Set, 10¼" h frosted and polished smoky topaz decanter, four cordials, molded nude women, price for five piece set	250.00
Centerpiece, 5 x 9", green, intaglio cut flowers	425.00
Compote, 7" d, 6¾" h, bright purple bowl, wide engraved band of Amazon female warriors, faceted stem and pedestal foot	360.00
Cup and Saucer, amber, gold scrolls, multicolored enameled flowers	295.00
Dish, 7½" l, 7" w, leaf shaped, eighteen points, shaded amethyst to clear, heavy raised yellow–orange enameled tiny flowers and stems, matching enameled "World's Fair 1904 St Louis"	375.00
Perfume	
3¾" h, amethyst, angular faceted bottle, conforming crystal stopper, unsgd, edge nick	165.00
4¼" h, pink–lavender Alexandrift, faceted panels, matching stopper, sgd in oval	250.00
Pitcher, 6¾" h, amberina, IVT, four yellow, red, blue, and green applied glass beaded bunches of grapes, pinched in sides, three-dimensional bird beneath spout, allover enamel and gold leaves, vines, and tendrils.	3,025.00
Rose Bowl, 3¼" h, black amethyst, faceted panels below cut peacock frieze, gold enamel accents	215.00

Vase, deep amethyst, classic warrior frieze, gilded, German script signature "Moser, Karlsbad," 11" h, $285.00.

Vase	
4½" h, cranberry, heavy enamel flowers, berries, scrolls, price for pair.	625.00
5" h, Malachite, faceted bright green body, six nude woman molded in high relief below fruit laden grape vines, selectively polished.	525.00
6½" h, apple green Radion, faceted, cut and enameled medial frieze of Amazon women, inscribed "Made in Czecho–Slovakia Moser Carlsbad"	300.00
7" h, flattened aquamarine oval, slit flared rim, four applied snakes, polychrome spots, and blossoms.	420.00
7¼" h, marbleized green faceted form, gilded cameo cut medial frieze of female Amazon warriors.	275.00
8" h	
Angelfish, acid cut back, clear, gold trim, c1950, sgd	235.00
Art Deco, amber, acid cut back Greek warriors, sgd.	675.00
8½" h, urn form, faceted amber, broad engraved band of Amazon female warriors, some on horseback, base script inscribed "Made in Czechoslovakia Moser Carlsbad"	470.00
16" h, brilliant cobalt blue faceted ground, etched and engraved wide	

medial frieze of Art Deco whimsical costumed characters in outdoor scene under Japanese lanterns and trees, monkey, cat, dog, turtle, and rabbit watching party, gold enamel accents, sgd "Moser" in scene, base stamped "Made in Czechoslovakia Moser Carlsbad" **1,980.00**

MOSS ROSE PATTERN CHINA

History: Several English potteries manufactured china with a Moss Rose pattern in the mid–1800s. Knowles, Taylor and Knowles, an American firm, began production of a Moss Rose pattern in the 1880s.

The moss rose was a common garden flower grown in English gardens. When American consumers tired of English china with Oriental themes, they purchased the Moss Rose pattern as a substitute.

Cup, 3¼" d, 2⅞" h, $15.00.

Butter Pat, sq, marked "Meakin"	15.00
Coffee Mug and Saucer, marked "Meakin"	40.00
Coffeepot, marked "Haviland, Limoges," small repair	75.00
Cup and Saucer, marked "Haviland, Limoges"	20.00
Dessert Set, 28 pcs, cake plate, eight 7½" plates, eight cups and saucers, creamer and sugar, marked "Fr Haviland," price for set	250.00
Gravy Boat, matching underplate, marked "Green & Co, England," price for two pieces	40.00
Nappy, 4½" d, marked "Edwards" . . .	10.00
Plate	
7½" d, Haviland, Limoges	15.00
8½" d, marked "KTK"	20.00
9½" d, marked "Haviland"	12.00
Platter, 10" w, 14" l, rect, marked "Meakin"	26.00
Salt and Pepper Shaker, pr, 5" h, sterling silver top and base, marked "Rosenthal"	50.00
Sauce Dish, 4½" d, marked "Haviland"	15.00
Soup Plate, 9" d, marked "Meakin" . .	18.00
Sugar, cov, marked "Haviland, Limoges"	65.00
Syrup, 8½" h, pewter top, marked "KTK," c1872	165.00
Tea Service, teapot, 5½" h creamer, and 6¼" h sugar bowl, marked "Meakin," price for set	200.00
Teapot, 8½" h, bulbous, gooseneck spout, basketweave trim, marked "T & V"	40.00
Tureen, cov, 12" l, gold trim	75.00

MOUNT WASHINGTON GLASS COMPANY

History: In 1837 Deming Jarves, founder of the Boston and Sandwich Glass Company, established for George D. Jarves, his son, the Mount Washington Glass Company in Boston, Massachusetts. In the following years the leadership and the name of the company changed several times as George Jarves formed different associations.

In the 1860s the company was owned and operated by Timothy Howe and William L. Libbey. In 1869 Libbey bought a new factory in New Bedford, Massachusetts. The Mount Washington Glass Company began operating again there under its original name. Henry Libbey became associated with the company early in 1871. He resigned in 1874 during the general depression, and the glassworks was closed. William Libbey had resigned in 1872 to work for the New England Glass Company.

The Mount Washington Glass Company opened again in the fall of 1874 under the presidency of A. H. Seabury and the management of Frederick S. Shirley. In 1894 the glassworks became a part of the Pairpoint Manufacturing Company.

Throughout its history the Mount Washington Glass Company made a great variety of glass, including pressed glass, blown glass and art glass, lava glass, Napoli, cameo, cut glass, Albertine, and Verona.

References: George C. Avila, *The Pairpoint Glass Story,* Reynolds–DeWalt Printing, Inc., 1968, out of print; Edward and Sheila Malakoff, *Pairpoint Lamps,* Schiffer Publishing, 1990; Leonard E. Padgett, *Pairpoint Glass,* Wallace—Homestead, 1979, out of print; John A. Shuman III, *The Collector's Encyclopedia of American Art Glass,* Collector Books, 1988, 1991 value update.

Collectors' Club: Mount Washington Art Glass Society, 60 President Ave., Providence, RI 02906.

Museum: The New Bedford Glass Museum, New Bedford, MA.

Additional Listings: Burmese, Crown Milano, Peachblow, and Royal Flemish.

Beverage Set, 8″ h Rose Amber pitcher, four matching tumblers, price for five piece set **395.00**

Biscuit Jar, 9″ w, Napoli, clear petticoat shaped body with pinched in sides, four Palmer Cox Brownies, one dressed as policeman, one seated, two running, white and black duck, all-over gold netting, fancy emb floral design and butterfly finial on cov, sgd in pontil "Napoli 538," stamped "M.W. 4418". **5,500.00**

Bowl, Diamond Quilted, white shading to apricot, painted and enameled floral dec, rect top, 4⅛″ d, 2¼″ h, $160.00.

Bowl, 13″ d, 3″ h, Ambero, broad flared flat rim, textured bowl, reverse painted pink, yellow, and white water lilies, yellow amber ground, centrally sgd "Ambero/W".   **880.00**

Bride's Bowl, 12″ l, 7½″ w, 5″ h, satin, pale blue shading to pink, melon ribbed **175.00**

Candle Light, 3¾″ h, set of eight, two each of white, pink, blue, and yellow, tumbler shape, DQ satin glass, clear glass candle cups, brass covers, price for set **220.00**

Creamer and Sugar, satin finish, opaque white lid on sugar, silverplated mountings. **115.00**

Ewer, 9¼″ h, satin, MOP, rainbow, deep rose, yellow, blue, apricot, green, and lavender, applied frosted handle, ruffled top.   **1,750.00**

Flower Frog, 5″ w, 2¾″ h, mushroom shape, white lusterless body, enameled floral dec. **375.00**

Lamp, table, 17″ h, bulbous base, pansy dec, satin finish, 10″ d shade **725.00**

Mustard Jar, 2″ h, 2½″ w, melon ribbed, opal glass, moss, rose dec, yellow ground, orig spoon, pagoda cov **350.00**

Pitcher, Verona, bulbous, maiden hair fern dec, gold highlights, applied clear reeded D–shaped handle. **225.00**

Rose Bowl, Verona, brown and gold pond lilies.   **300.00**

Sugar Shaker, 4″ h, egg shape, satin, pink flowers, green ground. **150.00**

Sweetmeat Jar, 6″ d, squatty, oak leaves and acorns dec, yellow ground, ornate gold rim, bail, and cov, marked "MW #4417" **550.00**

Talc Shaker, 3″ h, Erie Twist, gray florals, blue and gold scrolls, pink ground.   **450.00**

Tumbler, 3⅝″ h, shiny opaque white body, delft blue Dutch windmill scene, blue tinted rim. **165.00**

Vase

4¾″ h, 6″ d, 1½″ wide rim, Napoli, int. dec of dark purple and rust chrysanthemums, gold webbed ext., molded swirls, six dents, bright gold rim edge, sgd "Napoli 837". **1,475.00**

7½″ h, satin peachblow shading from deep rose to pale pink, yellow crystal coralene beads in seaweed pattern, gold trim top, polished pontil, c1896.   **625.00**

11¾″ h, Napoli, allover chrysanthemum dec, gold highlights, thumbprint design with slight yellow tint, allover gold sponging and black enamel, sgd "Napoli" and "814" . .   **1,600.00**

MULBERRY CHINA

History: Mulberry china, made primarily in the Staffordshire district of England between 1830 and 1850, is porcelain whose transfer pattern is the color of mulberry juice. The potters that manufactured Flow Blue also made Mulberry china; the ware often has a flowing effect similar to Flow Blue.

References: Susan and Al Bagdade, *Warman's English & Continental Pottery & Porcelain, Second Edition*, Wallace–Homestead, 1991; Ellen R. Hill, *Mulberry Ironstone: Flow Blue's Best Kept Little Secret*, published by author, 1993; Petra Williams, *Flow Blue China and Mulberry Ware—Similarity and Value Guide*, Revised Edition, Fountain House East, 1981.

Coffeepot, Jeddo, William Adams, c1849.   **175.00**

Cream Pitcher, Jeddo, William Adams, c1849, 5¼″ h **275.00**

Creamer

Beehives in Garden, unknown maker   **140.00**

Foliage, J Edwards or Walley, c1846   **85.00**

Jeddo, William Adams, c1849 . . . .   **100.00**

Marble, Wedgwood, c1850 . . . . . .   **65.00**

Tavoy, Walker or Brougham & Mayer, c1850 . . . .   **100.00**

Temple, Podmore, Walker, c1849 . **125.00**
Cup and Saucer, handled cup
  Genoa, William Davenport, c1840 . **40.00**
  Roselle, J M & Son, England, c1850 **40.00**
Cup and Saucer, handleless
  Abbey, Adams, c1849 . . . . **75.00**
  Bochara, James Edwards, c1847 . . **85.00**
  Castle Scenery, Jacob Furnival, c1850. **50.00**
  Washington Vase, Podmore Walker, c1849. . . . . **95.00**
Cup Plate
  Allegheny, Thomas Goodfellow, c1840. **45.00**
  Bochara, James Edwards, c1847 . . **85.00**
  Jeddo, William Adams, c1849 . . . . **68.00**
Dessert Bowl, Jeddo, William Adams, c1849, 5″ d. **45.00**
Gravy Boat
  Jeddo, William Adams, c1849 . . . . **65.00**
  Pelew, Edward Challinor, c1847 . . **85.00**
Pitcher, 9½″ h, Vincennes, J & G Alcock, c1844. . . . . **135.00**
Plate
  7½″ d, Pelew, Edward Challinor, c1847. **42.00**
  8″ d, Temple, Podmore Walker, c1849. **25.00**
  9⅞″ d, Pelew, Edward Challinor, c1847. **42.00**
  10½″ d
    Cyprus, William Davenport, c1840 **60.00**
    Vincennes, J & G Alcock, c1844 . **45.00**
Platter
  Corean, Podmore Walker, c1849, 10¾″ w, 13⅞″ l **325.00**
  Jeddo, William Adams, c1849, 12″ w, 15½″ l. **425.00**
  Vincennes, J & G Alcock, c1844, 11¾″ w, 15½″ l **350.00**
Relish, unidentified Oriental pattern . . **55.00**

Platter, Cyprus pattern, Davenport, c1850, 13½ x 10¼″, $125.00.

Sauce Dish, 5″ d, Corea, Joseph Clementson, c1840. . . . . **18.00**
Sauce Tureen, cov, Bochara, James Edwards, c1847 . . . . **125.00**
Soup Bowl, 10½″ d, Scinde, Thomas Walker, c1848. . . . . **30.00**
Sugar, cov, Jeddo, William Adams, c1849. . . . . **75.00**
Teapot, Strawberries, unknown maker **175.00**
Vegetable Bowl, cov, octagonal, pedestal base
  Cyprus, William Davenport, c1840 . **75.00**
  Jeddo, William Adams, c1849 . . . . **100.00**

MUSIC BOXES

History: Music boxes were invented in Switzerland around 1825 and include a broad field of automatic musical instruments, from a small box to a huge circus calliope.

A cylinder box consists of a comb with teeth which vibrate when striking a pin in the cylinder and producing music, from light tunes to opera and overtures.

The first disc music box was invented by Paul Lochmann of Leipzig, Germany, in 1886. It used an interchangeable steel disc with pierced holes bent to a point which hit the star–wheel as the disc revolved and thus produced the tune. Discs were easily stamped out of metal, allowing a single music box to play an endless variety of tunes. It reached the height of its popularity from 1890 to 1910. The phonograph replaced it.

Music boxes also were put into many items, e.g., clocks, sewing and jewelry boxes, steins, plates, toys, perfume bottles, and furniture.

References: Gilbert Bahl, *Music Boxes: The Collector's Guide To Selecting, Restoring, and Enjoying New and Vintage Music Boxes,* Courage Books, Running Press, 1993; H. A. V. Bulleid, *Cylinder Musical Box Design and Repair,* Almar Press, 1987.

Collectors' Clubs: Musical Box Society International, 1062 Alber St., Wabash, IN 46992; Music Box Society of Great Britain, 102 High St., Landbeach, Cambridge CB4 4DT England.

Museums: Bells ,Cars and Music of Yesterday, Sarasota, FL; Lockwood Matthews Mansion, Norwalk, CT; Miles Musical Museum, Eureka Springs, AR; The Musical Museum, Deansboro, NY; The Musical Wonder House Museum, Iscasset, ME.

Additional Listings: See *Warman's Americana & Collectibles* for more examples.

CYLINDER–TYPE

3⅝″ cylinder, mahogany, glass lid int., four tune. **500.00**
4½″ cylinder, grained case, inlay dec, lever wind, six tune **475.00**

5″ cylinder, France, simple case, four tune 425.00

5⅛″ cylinder, Junod, rosewood case with inlaid musical motif, glass lid int., four tune, two bells 1,100.00

6¼″ cylinder, Abrahams, grained case, transfer dec on lid, three bells. 550.00

7″ cylinder, Bremond, simple case, tune card, four tune 525.00

7½″ cylinder, simple case, crank wind, ten tune 800.00

8″ cylinder, burled walnut case, glass lid int., eight tune. 800.00

9″ cylinder, inlaid bird and flowers motif on lid, single comb, eight tune, six bells. 1,250.00

10½″ cylinder, Paillard, rosewood case with inlaid dec, six tune, zither attachment, matching table 2,750.00

10¾″ cylinder, Swiss, rosewood case, boxwood brass and enamel inlay, key wind, four tune, c1850 . . . . 3,000.00

11″ cylinder, Baker & Co, maple case, glass lid int., Sublime–Harmonie combs, tune sheet. 1,500.00

11¼″ cylinder, Ducommon Girod, walnut case, three control levers, six tune, c1840. . . . . 800.00

12″ cylinder, Thibouville–Lamy, simple case, glass lid int. 1,000.00

13″ cylinder, rosewood, inlaid dec, single comb, thirty tune, stand 4,180.00

13½″ cylinder, walnut veneer case, inlaid musical motifs, crank wind on side, eight tune, zither attachment, c1900. . . . . 1,100.00

15″ cylinder, burl walnut on ebony and rosewood case, Sublime–Harmonie double comb, matching table with cabriole legs, c1870. . . . . 7,000.00

17″ cylinder, Baker–Troll, walnut case, brass inlaid dec, six bells, three part comb, matching storage table. 2,750.00

DISC–TYPE

Adler, 14¾″ disc, walnut inlaid case, crank wind, lithograph cov int. 1,850.00

Britannia, 9″ disc, upright, walnut case, transfer and inlaid dec, double comb 1,200.00

Criterion, 8¾″ disc, table model, mahogany case, figural lithograph lid int. . . . 625.00

Edelweiss, 4½″ disc, table model, simple case, hand crank 300.00

Euphonia, 15¾″ disc, mahogany case, metal corners, lithograph female on int. cov. 1,100.00

Intona, twelve discs 425.00

Kalliope, 7″ disc, walnut, four bells, zither attachment. 800.00

Lochmann, 21″ disc, counter model . . 3,400.00

Monopol, 8¼″ disc, walnut, lithograph lid int. 550.00

Orphenion, 11″ disc, ornate case, two combs 1,100.00

Perfection, 10½″ disc, table model, mahogany case, zinc discs. 1,250.00

Regina, 15½″ disc, oak case with impressed pattern, double comb, litho card under lid, 22″ l, No. 52455. . . . . 3,400.00

Stella, 25½″ disc, upright, mahogany veneer case, damaged comb, 25 discs 6,050.00

Symphonion, 6¼″ disc, rosewood case, winding lever, four bells 500.00

Troubadour, 9″ disc, case with gold dec, crank wind 750.00

MISCELLANEOUS

Birdcage, 9″ h, domed cage on sq base, cast and enameled geometric dec. . . 275.00

Coin Operated
  Regina, 22″ l, table top, double comb,

Reginaphone, style 140, floor model, 15½″ disc, serpentine front case, cabriole legs, 22 discs, 23″ w, 40½″ h, $7,700.00. Photograph courtesy of Butterfield & Butterfield.

oak case with impressed pattern,
includes one disc. **3,900.00**
Sirion, 14½" disc, walnut case **3,000.00**
Figural, 13½" h, man, heavily carved,
elaborate bow tie, bowler hat, hands
in pockets, whistles "How Dry I Am,"
c1920. **525.00**
Organette, Amorette, ebony finished
case, metal discs **425.00**
Organ-Grinder, Uniflute Caveou & Cie,
SCDG, Paris, oak case **4,125.00**
Roller Organ
Chautauqua, walnut case, glass lift–
up door. **500.00**
Concert, walnut case, gold stencil
dec, glass doors. **600.00**
Gem, black painted case **400.00**
Organita, table model, walnut case,
rounded segmented top, multiple
tune paper strip **400.00**

MUSICAL INSTRUMENTS

History: From the first beat of the prehistoric
drum to the very latest in electronic music makers,
musical instruments have provided popular modes
of communication and relaxation.

The most popular antique instruments are violins, flutes, oboes, and other instruments associated with the classical music period of 1650 to
1900. Many of the modern instruments, such as
trumpets, guitars, drums, etc., have value on the
"used" rather than antiques market.

The collecting of musical instruments is in its
infancy. The field is growing very rapidly. Investors
and speculators have played a role since the
1930s, especially in early string instruments. Skinner's, Sotheby's, and Christie's hold annual auctions of fine musical instruments.

References: George Gruhn and Walter Carter,
*Acoustic Guitars And Other Fretted Instruments: A
Photographic History,* GPI Books, 1993; George
Gruhn and Walter Carter, *Gruhn's Guide To Vin-
tage Guitars,* GPI Books, 1991; *The Official Price
Guide To Music Collectibles, Sixth Edition,* House
of Collectibles, 1986, out of print.

Periodicals: *Concertina & Squeezebox,* PO Box
6706, Ithaca, NY 14851; *Piano & Keyboard,* PO
Box 767, San Anselmo, CA 94979–0767.

Collectors' Clubs: Automatic Musical Instru-
ment Collectors Association, 919 Lantern Glow
Trail, Dayton, OH 45431–2915; Fretted Instrument
Guild of America, 2344 South Oakley Avenue, Chi-
cago, IL 60608; Musical Box Society International,
1062 Alber St., Wabash, IN 46992; Reed Organ
Society, Inc., PO Box 901, Deansboro, NY 13328;
The American Musical Instrument Society, 414
East Clark St., Vermillion, SD 57069.

Museums: C. F. Martin Guitar Museum, Naza-
reth, PA; International Piano Archives at Maryland,
Neil Ratliff Music Library, College Park, MD; Miles

Musical Museum, Eureka Springs, AR; Streitwieser
Foundation Trumpet Museum, Pottstown, PA; The
Museum of the American Piano, New York, NY;
The Musical Museum, Deansboro, NY; University
of Michigan, Stearns Collection of Musical Instru-
ments, Ann Arbor, MI; Yale University Collection of
Musical Instruments, New Haven, CT.

Accordion
Concertone, ten keys, fourteen fold
bellows, rosewood finish, white
enameled pressed borders, steel
bronze reeds. **150.00**
Kalbe Imperial, ten nickel plated keys,
two sets of reeds, ebonized mold-
ing, twin bellows. **450.00**
Banjo
Bacon Banjo Co, Style C, 17 fret neck,
hardshell case. **175.00**
Edgemere Banjo, 17 nickel plated
hexagonal brackets, nickel shell,
wood lined, birch neck with faux
mahogany finish, c1900 . . . . **300.00**
Gibson Tenor, 17 fret neck, hardshell
case, 1920s. **275.00**
Bassoon, 48¼" l, pearwood, eight keys,
brass mounts and keys, Milliam Mil-
house, branded "Milhouse/London". . **525.00**
Bugle, artillery, brass, c1900 . . . . **140.00**
Cello
American, bass, four string, iron head,
1895–1905 . . . . **600.00**
German, 29½" l, single piece back,
burnt rust–red varnish, Leopold
Widhalm, dated 1768 . . . . **1,250.00**
Clarinet, 11½" l, stained maple, brass
mounts, ten brass keys, stamped "F
Muss/Wien" **425.00**
Cymbals, 10" d, leather handles, Amer-
ican, c1900. . . . . **90.00**
Drums
Acme Professional
Bass, 24" d, c1900 . . . . **175.00**
Snare, 16" d, eight rawhide snares,
c1900 . . . . **210.00**
German, bass, foot pedal, c1860 . . **550.00**
Flute
American, cherrywood, first quarter
19th C. **3,100.00**
German, cocoa wood, silver trim, one
key, late 19th/early 20th C **65.00**
Guitar
Cambridge, rosewood back and
sides, spruce top, ebony finger-
board, nickel plated head, 1905–
10. . . . . **145.00**
Meyer Model, ten keys, c1900 . . . . **275.00**
Oxford, mahogany back and sides,
spruce top, inlaid sound hole, rosewood inlaid head, metallic frets on
fingerboard, 1905–10 . . . . **150.00**
University, rosewood back and sides

with vine and leaf pattern dec, spruce top, ebony guard plate, mahogany neck, mother-of-pearl trim, 1905–10 .... **250.00**

Harmonica
  Bohm's Jubilee, ten single holes, 20 brass reeds, c1900 .... **25.00**
  Doerfel's International, celluloid, ten double holes, 40 reeds **15.00**
  Hohner, 20 double holes, 80 reeds, c1900 .... **30.00**
  Sousa's Band, 20 holes, 40 brass reeds, c1900 .... **45.00**
Harp, Italian, walnut, carved base, gilt traces, partially restored, restrung, c1620 .... **3,400.00**
Mandolin
  Ballinger, mahogany and maple, black wood strips, rosewood cap, faux tortoiseshell guard plate, 1905–10 .... **50.00**
  Werjmann, fiber case with inlaid dec, parchment sounding board, eight string **110.00**
Oboe, German, mid 18th C **5,000.00**

Piano, Clementi & Co., London, England, c1800, needs restoration, $1,600.00.

Piano
  Baldwin, baby grand, 5' 3", early 1900s **600.00**
  Fisher, grand, 5' 1", ebony **4,250.00**
  Hallet and Davis, baby grand, 5' 2" **4,750.00**
  Schiller Cabinet Grand, upright model, 1890s **1,750.00**
  Sears Roebuck American Home Parlor Grand, upright, mahogany finish **1,750.00**
  Steinway, grand, richly ornamented, late 19th C **75,000.00**
Piccolo, Atlas, cast metal, c1900 .... **45.00**
Reed Organ
  Beatty Golden Tongue, ornate walnut

case, ten stops, two ranks of reeds, octave coupler **650.00**
  Crown Parlor Organ, ornate walnut case, high top, ten stops, two sets of reeds, octave coupler **500.00**
  Farrand Organ Company, style S 3–B, oak case, twelve stops, two sets of reeds, restained **325.00**
  Miller Parlor Organ, walnut case, beveled mirror, ten stops, two ranks of reeds, octave coupler **575.00**
Saxophone
  Bantone, three valves, bell front **1,200.00**
  Dupont, B–flat, baritone, highly polished brass **350.00**
  Marceau, B–flat, alto, silverplated, satin finish **175.00**
  Tourville & Co, tenor, silver **350.00**
Tambourine, English, third quarter 19th C **100.00**
Trombone
  Concertone, silverplated, gold plated bell, satin finish **300.00**
  Lamoureaux Freres Slide, brass, bell ornament, polished, c1905 ..... **250.00**
Trumpet, Holton, B–flat, nickel finish . **550.00**
Tuba
  Dupont, E–flat, bass, nickel plated . **475.00**
  Marceau, B–flat, bass, brass **250.00**
  Sousaphone, B–flat, brass, lacquer bore **2,750.00**
Violin
  Adani, Pancrazio, Modena, 1770–1830 .... **7,250.00**
  John Justice Hull, PA, two piece back, orange–brown varnish, label "Made by John Justice Hullin Kingston, Pa. 1926/USA" **750.00**
Zither, Columbia, 47 strings, c1900 .. **275.00**

MUSIC RELATED

Banjo Bag, cloth, green, button closure **10.00**
Book
  Burgh, A, *Anecdotes of Music*, London, 1814, three volumes **100.00**
  Davey, *History of English Music*, London, 1895 .... **12.00**
Guitar Case, canvas, brown, leather bound edges, strap, buckle, and handle, 1890–1900 .... **15.00**
Music Rack, brass, three prongs, plate for bass drum **25.00**
Pick, gutta–percha, oval **4.00**
Sheet Music
  Circus Parade, E T Paull, color litho, 1904 .... **25.00**
  I'm On My Way Home, Irving Berlin, 1926 .... **3.00**
Stand, 34" h, teak, shaped platform, tripod base with flaring legs, Wendell

Castle, dated 69 and numbered 11/
12 . . . . **1,500.00**
Tuning Hammer, zither, ivory handle,
early 1900s. **8.00**
Violin Case, wood, flannel lining, nickel
plated lock, hook clasp, varnished. . . **40.00**
Violin Chin Rest, Becker's, ebonite and
nickel, 1900 . . . . **25.00**

MUSTACHE CUPS AND SAUCERS

History: Mustache cups and saucers were popular in the late Victorian era, 1880–1900. They
were made by many companies in porcelain and
silver plate. The cups have a ledge across the top
of the bowl of the cup to protect a gentleman's
mustache from becoming soiled while drinking.
Reference: Susan and Al Bagdade, *Warman's
English & Continental Pottery & Porcelain, Second
Edition,* Wallace–Homestead, 1991.

**Bone China, Continental, rib molded,
leaf motif, gold trim, $45.00.**

PORCELAIN

Bavarian, Victorian transfer scene,
shaded blue–green ground, gold trim **60.00**
German, pink and green florals and
"Papa," gold trim. **40.00**
Hand Painted, floral design, artist sgd on
base, France. **75.00**
Haviland, white, gold trim **90.00**
Limoges, hp pastel flowers, rococo
molded scrolls, allover gold dec **45.00**
Majolica, shell and seaweed, pink and
gray, Estruscan. **265.00**
Nippon, hp Oriental design, gold dec,
blue leaf mark. **45.00**
Onion Meissen, c1890 . . . . **85.00**
Pink Luster, gold leaves, beaded
edges. **65.00**
Royal Worcester, hp flowers, peach
ground. **125.00**
Schlegelmilch, R S Prussia, rose cas-
cade dec, gold trim **210.00**

SILVER PLATED

Barbour Bros Co, cut floral design . . . **60.00**
Derby Silver Co, engraved floral design,
crimped rim. **50.00**
Pairpoint, engraved florals **65.00**
Tufts, engraved flowers, inscribed
"1887". **75.00**

NAILSEA TYPE GLASS

History: Nailsea type glass is characterized by
swirls and loopings, usually white, on a clear or
colored ground. One of the first areas where this
glass was made was Nailsea, England, 1788–
1873, hence the name. Several other glasshouses,
including American factories, made this type of
glass.
Reference: Ellen T. Schroy, *Warman's Glass,*
Wallace–Homestead, 1992.

**Fairy Lamp, pink and white, ruffled
base, Clarke sgd insert, $275.00.**

Bottle
8″ h, gemel, flattened ovoid body, two
necks, white casing, red, white, and
blue loopings. **400.00**
10½″ l, bellows, white, rose loopings,
applied rigaree, stand. **250.00**
Candlestick, 10″ h, clear, white loopings,
folded socket rim, hollow blown socket
drawn out to a double knop, bulb
shaped stem, and two additional
knops, inverted cone shaped base,
early 19th C **375.00**
Fairy Lamp, 6″ h, blue shade, matching
ruffled trifold rim base, clear pressed
insert. **710.00**
Finger Bowl and Underplate, clear, white
loopings, satin finish, ruffled rim, price
for two pieces. **150.00**
Flask, cranberry, white zigzag allover
loopings. **165.00**
Lamp, 11½″ h, pink and white loopings

on font and ruffled shade, applied
clear feet, berry prunt **2,475.00**
Pitcher, 4″ d, 6½″ h, clear, white loop-
ings, ftd, solid applied base, triple
ribbed solid handle with curled end,
flaring formed mouth, attributed to
South Jersey, c1840–60 . . . . **1,125.00**
Powder Horn, 13″ l, clear, white loopings
and red stripes, stand **250.00**
Rolling Pin, 17″ l, knobbed handle, red
and white loopings, attributed to New
Jersey **500.00**
Tumbler, white, blue loopings **115.00**
Vase, 5″ d, 8″ h, cylindrical, flared mouth
and base, clear, white loopings, plain
sheared rim–pontil, attributed to
South Jersey. **175.00**
Witch Ball, 5¼″ d, clear, opaque white
casing, red loopings, attributed to
Pittsburgh. **250.00**

NANKING

History: Nanking is a type of Chinese porcelain
made in Canton, China, from the early 1800s into
the 20th century for export to America and England. It is often confused with the Canton pattern.

Three elements help distinguish Nanking from
Canton. Nanking has a spear-and-post border, as
opposed to the scalloped-line style of Canton. The
blues may tend to be darker on the Nanking ware.
Second, in the water's edge or Willow pattern, Canton usually has no figures. Nanking features a
standing figure with open umbrella on the bridge.
Finally, Nanking wares often are embellished with
gold.

Green and orange variations of Nanking survive,
although scarce.

Reference: Gloria and Robert Mascarelli, *Warman's Oriental Antiques,* Wallace–Homestead,
1992.

Reproduction Alert: Copies of Nanking ware
currently are being produced in China. They are of
inferior quality and decorated in lighter rather than
the darker blues.

Bottle, 10″ h, 19th C **200.00**
Bowl, 10″ w, shaped, 19th C **880.00**
Candlesticks, pr, 9½″ h **770.00**
Cider Jug, 10″ h, gilt highlights, 19th C,
price for pair **825.00**
Cup and Saucer, loop handle **60.00**
Ewer, 11″ h, small spout, blue and white,
mid 19th C **300.00**
Jug, 9½″ h, blue and white, c1800 . . **450.00**
Pitcher, cov, 9½″ h, blue and white, Liv-
erpool shape. **550.00**
Plate, 9½″ d, water's edge scene,
c1780–1800 . . . . **85.00**
Platter
14½″ l, rect, 19th C **200.00**

Platter, 14½ x 11½″, $400.00.

15¾″ l, 19th C
Oval **250.00**
Rectangular **800.00**
Rice Bowl, 19th C **100.00**
Serving Dish, cov, 19th C
12¼″ l **615.00**
14½″ l **250.00**
Teapot, 19th C
7″ h **300.00**
7½″ h **220.00**
Tray, 9¾″ l, 19th C **500.00**
Tureen, cov, 19th C
12″ l **385.00**
13½″ l **1,210.00**

NAPKIN RINGS, FIGURAL

History: Gracious home dining during the Victorian era meant each household member had his
or her personal napkin ring. Figural napkin rings
were first patented in 1869. The remainder of the
19th century saw most plating companies, e.g.,
Cromwell, Eureka, Meriden, Reed and Barton, etc.,
manufacturing figural rings, many copying with
slight variations the designs of other companies.

Values are determined today by the subject matter of the ring, the quality of the workmanship, and
the condition.

Reference: Victor K. Schnadig, *American Victorian Figural Napkin Rings,* Wallace–Homestead,
1971, out of print.

Reproduction Alert: Quality reproductions do
exist.

Additional Listings: See *Warman's Americana
& Collectibles* for a listing of nonfigural napkin rings.

Barrel, two cherubs holding dolls, Meri-
den Britannia Co. **135.00**
Bird, wings spread over nest of eggs . **145.00**
Boy
Holding baseball bat behind back . **190.00**

Boy lugging ring, Rogers Bros., #223, $275.00.

Sitting on bench, holding drumstick	180.00
Brownie, climbing up side of ring, Palmer Cox	175.00
Butterfly, perched on pair of fans ...	100.00
Cat, glass eyes, ring on back	260.00
Cherries, stems, leaf base, ball feet .	70.00
Cherub, sitting crosslegged on base, candleholder and ring combination ..	175.00
Chicken, nesting beside ring	160.00
Dachshund, supporting ring on back .	160.00
Deer, standing next to fence	175.00
Dog, pulling sled, emb sides, engraved name, Meriden	165.00
Eagle, one on each side of ring	110.00
Fox, standing erect, dressed	225.00
Frog, holding drumstick, pushing drum-like ring	300.00
Girl, holding stick above begging dog, Kate Greenaway.............	240.00
Goat, pulling wheeled flower cart ...	245.00
Horse, standing next to ornate ring ..	175.00
Man, walking uphill, ring on shoulders	190.00
Owl, sitting on leafy base, owls perched on upper limbs	250.00
Parrot, on wheels, Simpson, Hall Miller & Co	175.00
Rabbit, alert expression, sitting next to ring	175.00
Roman Centurion, sword drawn, standing next to ring	130.00
Runner, male nude, holding torch, sq base	150.00
Sailor Boy, anchor	210.00
Schoolboy, holding books, feeding begging puppy	225.00
Sheep, resting on base near ring ...	165.00
Squirrel, eating nut, log pile base ...	125.00
Swan, one on each side of ring, separate bases	110.00

NASH GLASS

History: Nash glass is a type of art glass attributed to Arthur John Nash and his sons, Leslie H. and A. Douglas. Arthur John Nash, originally em-ployed by Webb in Stourbridge, England, came to America and was employed in 1889 by Tiffany Furnaces at its Corona, Long Island, plant.

While managing the plant for Tiffany, Nash designed and produced iridescent glass. In 1928 A. Douglas Nash purchased the physical facilities of Tiffany Furnaces. The A. Douglas Nash Corporation firm remained in operation until 1931.

Reference: Ellen T. Schroy, *Warman's Glass,* Wallace–Homestead, 1992.

Cologne Bottle, Chintz, wide pale green stripes separated by wide clear stripes with thin blue centers, clear stopper, marked "Nash/1008/JJ," 5″ h, $485.00.

Bowl	
10″ d, 3½″ h, red Chintz, silver dec	550.00
13″ d, 4″ h, ftd, clear, overall blue and turquoise vines, sgd...........	425.00
Candlestick, 4″ h, red and gray Chintz, sgd	450.00
Compote, 6 x 2″, fold over rim, green–blue Chintz bowl, clear pedestal foot, sgd........................	200.00
Cordial, 5½″ h, green–blue Chintz ...	90.00
Goblet, 6¾″ h, feathered leaf motif, gilt dec, sgd	275.00
Plate, 8″ d, green–blue Chintz	195.00
Tumbler, 5″h, conical, blue and silver Chintz, low pedestal foot, sgd......	165.00
Vase	
4¼″ h, inverted pear shape, ftd, purple and gold, sgd on base	385.00
9¼″ h, vertical orange and clear striped body, pale green knob, ftd .	250.00
13″ h, gold irid ribbed body, blue pedestal foot, sgd "Nash 532"	525.00
15½″ h, flared ovoid, red Chintz, alternating wide and narrow vertical silver stripes, applied double pedestal foot, minor bubble blemishes	990.00

NAUTICAL ITEMS

History: The seas that surround us have fascinated man since time began. The artifacts of sailors have been collected and treasured for years. Because of their environment, merchant and naval items, whether factory or handmade, must be of quality construction and long lasting. Many of these items are aesthetically designed as well.

References: Alan P. Major, *Maritime Antiques*, A. S. Barnes & Co., 1981; Jean Randier, *Nautical Antiques*, Doubleday and Co., 1977.

Periodical: *Nautical Brass*, PO Box 3966, North Fort Myers, FL 33918; *Nautical Collector*, PO Box 16734, Alexandria, VA 22304.

Collectors' Club: Nautical Research Guild, 62 Marlboro St, Newburyport, MA 01950–3130.

Museums: Kittery Historical & Naval Museum, Kittery, ME; Lyons Maritime Museum, St Augustine, FL; Museum of Science and Industry, Chicago, IL; Mystic Seaport Museum, Mystic, CT; National Maritime Museum, San Francisco, CA; Peabody Museum of Salem, Salem, MA; The Mariners' Museum, Newport News, VA; U.S. Naval Academy Museum, Naval Academy, MD.

Depth Gauge, Moving Coil Armature, George Kent, London, England, mounted on board, $300.00.

Barograph, 14½″ l, 9″ w, 8¾″ h, SS *Port Bowen*, oak case.	440.00
Bell, 8″ d, ship's, *Alister Hardy*, brass, dated 1953.	135.00
Binnacle	
Arctic Queen, brass, 1905	600.00
Small Vessel, 9″ h, brass, compass, missing lamp.	110.00
Book	
A Complete Epitome of Practical Navigation, London, 1825.	35.00
The Seaman's Friend, Richard Henry Dana, Jr, Boston, 1856.	25.00
Catalog, Plymouth Cordage Co, Plymouth, MA, Rope for the Boatman, 1929, 32 pgs, 6 x 9″.	10.00
Chair, saloon, SS *Mapourika*	165.00
Chart, 17 x 24″, Boston Harbor, George W Eldridge, 1876.	175.00
Chronometer, 6″ sq, Hamilton Watch Co, cased.	550.00
Clock, 7″ d, SS *Kaponga*, engine room bulkhead, brass.	330.00
Compactum, 19¾″ w, 10¾″ d, 55¼″ h, SS *Willochra*, shelves, drawers, sink, soap dishes, catch basin, early 1900s.	1,100.00
Compass, lifeboat, 8″ sq, 7¼″ h, boxed, 20th C.	165.00
Diorama, 33″ l, 5″ d, 24″ h, shadowbox, 3–masted schooner, last quarter 19th C.	550.00
Diver's Helmet, Navy, copper and brass.	550.00
Document, bark *Fanny*, sgd by crew, framed.	135.00
Foghorn, brass, hand crank	220.00
Harness Cask, 21″ d, 28¾″ h, vessel *Fifeshire*, oak, brass bound	1,100.00
Inclinometer, ship's, 4½″ d, brass, cased, bubble type, Kelvin Bottomley & Baird Ltd.	55.00
Lamp, ship's riding, 13″ h, onion shape globe, painted green, orig oil burner.	110.00
Lantern, ship's	
Cargo, 14″ h, brass, orig lamp, British, 20th C.	300.00
Port, 21½″ h, copper, hinged lid	275.00
Lithograph, folio, clipper ship *Mirage*, Victorian frame	165.00
Medicine Chest, 50″ l, 24″ w, 27″ h, *Halcione*, hinged top, compartment int., contains bottles, ceramic jars, and other accessories	1,300.00
Model	
Bark, sailor's model, last half 19th C, 35¾″ l, 12″ w, 23½″ h.	550.00
Ship, sailor's model, full rigged ship, ivory and bone dec, wood case with plywood bottom, 35¾″ l, 12″ w, 23¼″ h	2,400.00
Sloop, black hull, sails, 10″ l, 16¾″ h	440.00
Speedboat	
Chris–Craft, mahogany, 1930s, 35″ l	2,475.00
Dixie II, mounted on mahogany table with inlaid design, 83″ l, 17″ w, 52″ h.	3,300.00
Yacht, *Ranger*, planked deck with winches, bollards, skylights, wheel, binnacle, and hatches, mounted on mahogany case with rope design inlay, 25″ l, 8″ w, 30″ h	1,100.00

Nameplate, 31" l, SS *Rangatira* 110.00

Octant, Walker, Liverpool, ebony, brass fittings, ivory plates, orig case bears label "John Bliss & Co. 110 Wall Street," pencil inscription "John A. Ryder South Orrington Maine" 412.00

Painting

Bailey, T, American, 20th C, *Putting Out To Seas,* oil on canvas, full rigged ship sailing away from land, lighthouse background, sgd lower right 330.00

Hanson, W, American, 20th C, *Clipper Ship in Rough Seas,* 24 x 36", oil on canvas, sgd lower left, orig gold frame 550.00

Jacobsen, Antonio, American, 1850–1921, *Lightning 1854 Don McKay, 244F Australia Trade,* 12 x 20", oil on panel, sgd lower right, title lower left 6,000.00

Norton, William Edward, American, 1843–1916, *Bark Sailing Near Thatcher's Island Lighthouses,* oil on canvas, bark, schooner, and two lighthouses, sgd lower left, framed 4,950.00

Salmon, Robert, British–American, 1775–1842, *Shipping Off Liverpool,* 13½ x 17", oil on canvas, several figures on shore watching ships, orig gilt frame. 3,300.00

Plaque

6¼" d, china, "Gloucester Fishing Schooner," 9½" d mounting board 110.00

7½" d, copper and wood, flagship *Foudroyant* 330.00

Porthole, 13½" l, 9" h, *Edwin Fox,* rect, brass 80.00

Print, 11 x 32", The Naval Review At Spithead, T G Dutton lithographer, published by Ackermann & Co, London. 350.00

Quadrant

Ebony, cased, marked "D Booth" and "New Zealand" 330.00

Sea captain's, cased, ivory label "H Duren–New York," orig case 400.00

Sea Chest, 30" w, 16½" d, 15" h, SS *Mapourika,* splayed construction, carved crest, restored and refinished 650.00

Sextant

Frodsham & Keene, Liverpool, brass, cased 465.00

Spencer, Browning & Rust, London, brass, orig box bears label of "J Sewell 61, South Castle Street, Liverpool," 19th C 525.00

Telegraph, SS *Kumea,* engine room, painted green, 1927. .... 400.00

Textile, 29 x 38", woolwork, medallion center with British ship, pearl studded

crown, colorful flags, drapery across the top, last half 19th C 2,100.00

Water Filter, 14½" h, SS *Cyrena,* ceramic, Slack & Brownlow, Manchester, England, 1913. .... 75.00

Wheel, ship's

26" d, wood

Brass hub, c1900 .... 220.00

Brass inlaid ring on each side, brass capped king spoke, John Hastie & Co, Greenock 330.00

42" d, brass 412.00

NAZI ITEMS

History: The National Socialist German Workers Party (NSDAP) was created on February 24, 1920, by Anton Drexler and Adolf Hitler. Its twenty–five-point nationalist program was designed to renovate the depressed German economy and government.

In 1923, after the failed Beer Hall Putsch, Hitler was sentenced to a five-year term in Landsberg Prison. He spent only a year in prison, during which time he wrote the first volume of *Mein Kampf.*

In the late 1920s and early 1930s the NSDAP developed from a regional party into a major national party. In Spring 1933 Hitler became Reich chancellor. Shortly after the death of president von Hindenberg in 1934, Hitler combined the offices of president and chancellor into a single position, giving him full control over the German government as well as the NSDAP. From that point until May 1945, the National Socialist German Workers Party dominated all aspects of German life.

In the mid–1930s Hitler initiated a plan, from rearming to territorial acquisition, designed to unite the German speaking peoples of Europe in a single nation. Germany's invasion of Poland in 1939 triggered the hostilities that led to the Second World War. The war in Europe ended on V-E (Victory in Europe) Day, May 7, 1945.

References: John M. Kaduck, *World War II German Collectibles,* published by author, 1978, 1983 price update; Sydney B. Vernon, *Vernon's Collectors' Guide To Orders, Medals, and Decorations (With Valuations),* published by author, 1986.

Periodicals: *Der Gauleiter,* PO Box 721288, Houston, TX 77272; *Military Collector Magazine,* PO Box 245, Lyon Station, PA 19536; *Military History,* 602 S. King St., Suite 300, Leesburg, VA 22075.

Note: The objects that appear below are associated with the NSDAP as a political party. See **Militaria** for objects associated with the German military prior to and during World War II.

Armband, 20½" l, Ortsgruppenleiter, metal pip, Bevo NSDAP patch, gold oak leaves wrapped around band, red wool, blue piping. 200.00

Banner, 7 x 38", double sized 30.00

Bayonet, police, dress, 13″ blade, stag handle, attached police insignia, black leather scabbard, silvered fittings, orig black frog, guard marked "S. MG. 415" and matching numbers. 165.00

Belt, NSCAP, political officer's, light tan leather belt, clawed buckle. 35.00

Belt Buckle

Prison Official's, round, eagle holding sword and bolts, swastika on breast. 50.00

SA, rotated swastika, brass body, SP faceplate, 2 pcs 45.00

Cap Badge, RAD, silver finish, enameled, wreath 25.00

Car Pennant, 8½ x 11½″, Teno, printed on both sides, white eagle on blue field, two tie strings 75.00

Cigarette Case, presentation, steel, painted, brass plate, emb heads of Mussolini and Hitler, "Vincere" above heads, eagle embracing wreath of swastikas, wreath with emblem of Italy 175.00

Collar Tabs, NSDAP, Hauptgemeinschaftsleiter rank, four gold pips, gold eagle, double rows of gold ribbon, dark brown, white piping 100.00

Correspondence Card, 5 x 8″, raised gold eagle and Adolf Hitler, Mujnchen, Den address, orig gilt stamped, 2 pcs 45.00

Dagger, orange and yellow celluloid grip, SP fittings and scabbard, marked "E & F Horstaer". 110.00

Document, 6 x 8″, Kriegsurlaubsschein, seal, unissued. 10.00

Membership Pins, white metal, top: NSKOV, WW I veteran, 1¼″ l, $55.00; bottom: RDB, state official's organization,⅞″ l, $85.00.

Emblem, 27 x 16″, train engine, eagle with swastika 250.00

Fez, SS 175.00

Flag, sport, 58 x 31″, double sided, sports eagle and swastika 50.00

Flagpole Top, 8½″ h, nickel plated, round gear with swastika int. 45.00

Hat, police officer, black visor, bright eagle and wreath device, green blue wool, silver cord, leather chin strap, pebbled side buttons 150.00

Holster, P–38, black leather, Nazi acceptance mark, pouch for extra clip. . 50.00

Invitation, 4½ x 7″, gold gilt heading, black printed German script, engraved Hitler, orig 35.00

Lamp, table, 16″ h, figural, eagle, Munich party headquarters, plaster, gold leaf, marbleized stand 100.00

Magazine, NSDAP *Der Schulungsbrief*, 1940, official periodical of Nazi Party 35.00

Medal

Eastern People's, 2nd Class, silver metal, ribbon 25.00

Shooting, Kreisschiessen Kofstein, 1942, silver finish. 25.00

Membership Pin, swastika in circle, winged NSFK figure. 15.00

Passbook, D. R. Arbeitsbuch, Weimer eagle, dated 1936, some entries. . . . 15.00

Pennant, 54″ l, 11″ h, NSDAP, triangular, painted swastika, double sided. 35.00

Postcard, commemorating Hitler's birthday, Austria, April 20, 1941 . . . . 15.00

Poster

9½ x 14″, slogan by Hitler, multicolored, published by NSDAP of Munich, 1940. . . . . 55.00

12 x 20″, Mein Kampf, portrait of Hitler, black and white 25.00

Shoulder Boards, police, Wachtmeister Rank, black and silver cord, pink piping, removable style. 10.00

Stationery, 8½ x 11½″, NSDAP eagle and Der Fuhrer in raised gold, orig single sheet 40.00

Stickpin, SS, NSDAP, swastika 20.00

Street Sign, "Juden Gasse," enameled metal, historical piece 650.00

Sword

Dress, eagle and Swastika, engraved brass handle, black wire wrapped plastic grip, black painted scabbard. 100.00

Officer's, dove head, scabbard, NSDAP eagle on guard 65.00

Tinnie, Ten Years Of The Nazi Party In Weimer, silver, Standart. 20.00

Tunic, police, green piping, removable shoulder boards, Bevo collar tabs, Bevo green police eagle arm shield on

left sleeve, silver pebbled buttons, tailored cuffs, dark brown trim **185.00**
Wine Glass, 4″ h, white Nazi eagle on side **70.00**

NETSUKES

History: The traditional Japanese kimono has no pockets. Daily necessities, such as money, tobacco supplies, etc., were carried in leather pouches or *inros* which hung from a cord with a netsuke toggle. Netsuke comes from "ne" (to root) and "tsuke" (to fasten).

Netsukes originated in the 14th century and initially were associated with the middle class. By the mid–18th century all levels of Japanese society used them. Some of the most famous artists, e.g., Shuzan and Yamada Hojitsu, worked in the netsuke form.

Netsukes average 1 to 2 inches and are made from wood, ivory, bone, ceramics, metal, horn, nutshells, etc. The subject matter is broad based but always portrayed in a lighthearted, humorous manner. A netsuke must have no sharp edges and balance so that it hangs correctly on the sash.

Value depends on artist, region, material, and skill of craftsmanship. Western collectors favor *katabori*, pieces which represent an identifiable object.

Reference: Gloria and Robert Mascarelli, *Warman's Oriental Antiques,* Wallace–Homestead, 1992.

Periodical: *Netsuke & Ivory Carving Newsletter,* 3203 Adams Way, Ambler, PA 19002.

Collectors' Club: Netsuke Kenkyukai Society, PO Box 31595, Oakland, CA 94604.

Reproduction Alert: Recent reproductions are on the market. Many are carved from African ivory.

Horn
Lotus leaf, stag horn, 19th C **100.00**

Carved ivory, popping eyes, $225.00.

Shishi form, pressed, 19th C **45.00**
Ivory
Bamboo Shoot, aperture of feasting mice, sgd "Ashu Tadayoshi No Saku," early 19th C **600.00**
Boy
Fighting giant carp, deeply carved, torrent and rock background, sgd "Mitsushige," 19th C. **550.00**
Wearing leafy cloak, holding brush and chrysanthemum leaf, sgd "Tomochika," early 19th C. **275.00**
Coiled Dragon, sgd "Tomoto," c1800 **525.00**
Gamma Sennin, standing figure wearing cloak, holding three toed frog, 18th C. **425.00**
Monkey, holding chestnut, unsigned, late 18th C **230.00**
Oni, standing on one leg, wearing tiger skin loincloth, carrying large pouch on back, leaf shaped reserve sgd "Hidekazu," 19th C **240.00**
Shishi, seated female with open mouth, 18th C **180.00**
Tigers, roaming bamboo grove, bun form, sgd "Ashu Tadayoshi No Saku," 19th C **375.00**
Wrestling Group, man and oni arm wrestling on top of lotus leaf, rectangular reserve sgd "Tomotada," 18th C. **1,000.00**
Porcelain
Fruit and leaves, red, brown, and celadon, 19th C. **55.00**
Hotei, sgd "Masakazu," 19th C . . . **50.00**
Two puppies, 19th C **80.00**
Wood
Boy, boxwood
Leaning on millstone, sgd "Ryukei," 19th C **175.00**
Seated, reading scroll, sgd "Masayuki," 19th C **180.00**
Geisha, seated, wearing flowing robe, holding tray, sgd "Toshikazu," 19th C **225.00**
Karasu Tengu, seated figure with beaked and fanged face, holding cucumber, sgd "Jugyoko," 19th C **800.00**
Monkey, seated, clasping raised left knee, unsigned, first half 19th C . . **425.00**
Monkey and Nut, carved, early 19th C **130.00**
Mother and Child, woman feeding infant with chopsticks, sgd "Gyokkei," 19th C. **250.00**
Noblewoman, wretched beggar form, dying by roadside, sgd "Ichihyo," first half 19th C **525.00**
Ox, recumbent, sgd "Sukenaka," 19th C **280.00**
Persimmon, stippled skin and leaves, unsigned, 19th C **275.00**

Reichi Fugus Group, three fungi,
stained, unsigned, 19th C **275.00**
Scribe, sitting, holding writing slip and
brush, sgd "Shinsai," 19th C **275.00**
Shishi, beast crouching over bro-
caded ball, sgd "Shozan," 19th C . **550.00**
Snail, boxwood, crawling from shell,
19th C **475.00**
Trainer, wrestling monkey to ground,
sgd "Miwa" and seal, 19th C **250.00**
Woman, boxwood, nude, seated by
basin, wringing towel, first half 19th
C **340.00**

NEWCOMB POTTERY

History: William and Ellsworth Woodward, two
brothers, were the founders of a series of businesses which eventually merged into the Newcomb pottery effort. In 1885 Ellsworth Woodward,
a proponent of vocational training for women, organized a school from which emerged the Ladies
Decorative Art League. In 1886 the brothers
founded the New Orleans Art Pottery Company,
with the ladies of the league serving as decorators.
The first two potters were Joseph Meyer and
George Ohr. The pottery closed in 1891.

William Woodward was on the faculty at Tulane.
Ellsworth taught fine arts at the Sophie Newcomb
College, a women's school which eventually
merged with Tulane. In 1895 Newcomb College
developed a pottery course in which the wares
could be sold. Some of the equipment came from
the old New Orleans Art Pottery.

Mary G. Sheerer joined the staff to teach decoration. In 1910 Paul E. Cox solved many of the
technical problems connected with making pottery
in a southern environment. Other leading figures
were Sadie Irvine, Professor Lota Lee Troy, and
Kathrine Choi. Pottery was made until the early
1950s.

Students painted a quality art pottery with a distinctive high glaze. Designs have a decidedly
southern flavor, e.g., myrtle, jasmine, sugarcane,
moss, cypress, dogwood, and magnolia motifs.
Later matte glazed pieces usually are decorated
with carved back floral designs. Pieces depicting
murky, bayou scenes are most desirable.

References: Suzanne Ormond and Mary E. Ir-
vine, *Louisiana's Art Nouveau: The Crafts Of The
Newcomb Style,* Pelican Publishing, 1976; Jessie
Poesch, *Newcomb Pottery: An Enterprise for
Southern Women,* Schiffer Publishing, 1984.

Collectors' Club: American Art Pottery Association, 125 E. Rose Ave., St. Louis, MO 63119.

Museum: Newcomb College, Tulane University,
New Orleans, LA.

Candlestick, 9½" h, flaring, band of stylized white blossoms at top, long green
stems, semimatte glaze, blue ground,
Sadie Irvine, incised "NC" **825.00**
Mug, 4½" h, 5" d, devil's mask dec, high
glaze, blue motto "Pile up the coals/
Fill the red bowl/Drink every one,"
neutral ground, decorated by Gertrude Roberts Smith, painted initials
and die stamped "Newcomb
College". **2,530.00**
Plaque, 5¾" w, 9¾" l, scenic, Palms,
matte glaze, blue/green foliage and
trees, blue border, pale pink lower sky
changing to light blue, framed, incised
and painted "NC" on lower right, imp
registration number 84, incised artist's
cipher, shape number 514, paper label, kiln particles, decorated by Anna
Frances Connor Simpson. **4,400.00**
Pot, 3" d, 2" h, flaring body, circular ftd
base, stylized foliate relief design,
blue ground, mauve, green, and gray
matte glaze, incised "NC, Sa 14, 12,"
artist's ciphers. **715.00**
Tile, 4" sq, floral dec, high gloss, sgd "L
Nicholson" **550.00**

**Vase, blue tones, tree motif repeated
three times, marked "NC/AE/HU58,"
3¼" h, $725.00.**

Vase
3¾" h
Twilight landscape, pink background moss draped oak, low relief, blue, green, and pink, decorated by Anna Frances Connor
Simpson, marked "N" within "C"
cypher and initials "AFS, QG83,"
c1927 . . . . **1,050.00**

Vertical leaf design, low relief, blue, green, and cream, Kenneth Smith, decorated by Henrietta Bailey, 1930s **1,100.00**

4″ h, Oriental stick neck form, incised geometric design, cream, brown glossy glaze, Joseph Meyer potter, decorated by Sabina Wells, 1902–04. . . . . **990.00**

5⅞″ h, hexagonal form, metallic mottled black, applied copper rim, white body, Leona Nicholson, c1900. . . . **1,150.00**

6⅛″ h, corset, band of green bats and yellow crescent moons, sgd "FP," painted "AQ44" **4,400.00**

7⅞″ h, moonlit landscape, low relief, blue, green, and yellow, matte glaze, Kenneth Smith potter, decorated by Sadie Irvine, c1933 . . . . . **1,800.00**

10¼″ h, incised orange iris blossoms, green leaves, neutral and deep blue ground, high glaze, decorated by Sabina Elliot Wells **18,700.00**

NILOAK POTTERY, MISSION WARE

History: Niloak Pottery was made near Benton, Arkansas. Charles Dean Hyten experimented with native clay, trying to preserve its natural colors. By 1911 he perfected Mission Ware, a marbleized pottery in which the cream and brown colors predominate. The pieces were marked Niloak (kaolin spelled backward).

After a devastating fire, the pottery was rebuilt and named Eagle Pottery. This factory included the space to add a novelty pottery line which was introduced in 1929. This line usually was marked Hywood–Niloak until 1934, when the name Hywood was dropped from the mark. Hyten left the pottery in 1941. In 1946 operations ceased.

Reference: David Edwin Gifford, *Collector's Encyclopedia of Niloak,* Collector Books, 1993.

Collectors' Club: Arkansas Pottery Collectors Society, 12 Normandy Rd., Little Rock, AR 72207.

Additional Listings: See *Warman's Americana & Collectibles* for more examples, especially the novelty pieces.

Note: Prices listed below are for Mission Ware pieces.

Bowl, 7½″ d, marbleized swirls, cream, brown, and blue **65.00**

Planter, elephant balancing on circus drum, pink and gray, 6″ h, $35.00.

Candlesticks, pr, 8″ h, marbleized swirls, blue, cream, terra cotta, and brown. . **250.00**

Pot, 2¾ x 3¾″, marbleized swirls, red, brown, and chocolate, early **125.00**

Toothpick Holder, marbleized swirls, tan and blue. **100.00**

Urn, 4½″ h, marbleized swirls, brown and blue. **35.00**

Vase

4½″ h, marbleized swirls, red and brown **55.00**

5½″ h, bulbous, marbleized swirls, rust, blue, and cream **65.00**

6″ h, marbleized swirls, cream, turquoise blue, rust, and brown **70.00**

6½″ h, marbleized swirls, cream, brown, and blue. **135.00**

NIPPON CHINA, 1891–1921

History: Nippon, Japanese hand-painted porcelain, was made for export between 1891 and 1921. In 1891, when the McKinley tariff act proclaimed that all items of foreign manufacture be stamped with their country of origin, Japan chose to use "Nippon." In 1921 the United States decided the word "Nippon" no longer was acceptable and required that all Japanese wares be marked with "Japan." The Nippon era ended.

There are over 220 recorded Nippon backstamps or marks. The three most popular are the wreath, maple leaf, and rising sun marks. Wares with variations of all three marks are being reproduced today. A knowledgeable collector can easily spot the reproductions by the mark variances.

The majority of the marks are found in three different colors: green, blue, and magenta. Colors indicate the quality of the porcelain used: green for first-grade porcelain, blue for second grade, and magenta for third grade. Marks were applied by two methods, decal stickers under glaze and imprinting directly on the porcelain.

References: Gene Loendorf, *Nippon Hand Painted China,* McGrew Color Graphics, 1975; Joan Van Patten, *The Collector's Encyclopedia Of Nippon Porcelain,* First Series (1979, 1991 value updte), Second Series (1982, 1991 value update), Third Series (1986, 1991 value update), Collector Books; Kathy Wojciechowski, *The Wonderful World of Nippon Porcelain, 1891–1921,* Schiffer Publishing, 1992.

Collectors' Clubs: ARK–LA–TEX Nippon Club, 112 Ascot Drive, Southlake, TX 76092; Dixieland Nippon Club, 700 E. High St., Hicksville, OH 43526; International Nippon Collectors Club, 112 Ascot Drive, Southlake, TX 76092; Lakes & Plains Nippon Collectors Club, PO Box 230, Peotone, IL 60468; Long Island Nippon Collectors Club, 145 Andover Place, W. Hempstead, NY 11552; MD–PA Collectors' Club, 920 B Collings Ave., Collingswood, NY 08107; New England Nippon Collectors Club, 64 Burt Rd., Springfield, MA 01118.

Additional Listings: See *Warman's Americana & Collectibles.*

Advisor: Kathy Wojciechowski.

Teapot, hexagonal, hp floral dec, yellow, purple, and green, gold trim, marked "Imperial Nippon, Hand Painted," 5½" h, $95.00.

Ashtray, triangular	
5¼" w, multicolored Art Deco scene	80.00
5½" w, Mt Fuji scene, gold beading, "Hand Painted Mt Fujiyama Nippon" mark	65.00
Basket, hp, blown out, peanuts	85.00
Bowl, 10" d, hp, flowers, scrolls, and center medallion dec, open handles, green "M" in wreath mark	85.00
Bread Tray, Gaudy style, green and gold, pink asters	225.00
Butter Dish, cov, floral band, "Hand Painted RC Nippon" mark	40.00

Calling Card Tray, 7¾ x 6", mythical dragon and bird, blue maple leaf mark	45.00
Candlesticks, pr	
6" h, Wedgwood and rose nosegay design, Jasperware, wreath mark	235.00
10" h, Galle scene, moriage trees, maple leaf mark	400.00
Candy Dish, scalloped edge, pink roses, gold trim, twisted handle	50.00
Celery Set, 11½" l tray, four matching salts, hp, garland of red wild roses and daisies dec, lime green border, blue rising sun mark	75.00
Chocolate Pot, 11" h, hp, pale pink, rose, violet, lavender, and yellow, gold beaded dec, turquoise jewels, blue maple leaf mark, wear to handle	75.00
Compote, 4¾" h, 8½" d, Wedgwood and rose nosegay dec, wreath mark	200.00
Cracker Jar, melon ribbed, bisque background, Indian in canoe shooting moose on river edge, ftd, wreath mark	425.00
Doll, 11" h, boy, bisque head, brown hair and eyes, teeth, composition body, FY Nippon mark	275.00
Dresser Set, woodland scene, tray, hatpin holder, powder box, and hair receiver, maple leaf mark, price for set	950.00
Egg Warmer, holds four eggs, stopper, sailboat scene, rising sun mark	110.00
Ferner, 6" w, floral dec, gold beading, four handles, green "M" in wreath mark	125.00
Hair Receiver, 5" d, yellow and red roses, black ground, blue maple leaf mark	60.00
Hatpin Holder, 5" h, serpent in relief, mottled ground	165.00
Humidor, sailing ships, palm trees, small flake on lid, "Hand Painted Nippon" M in wreath mark	45.00
Jam Jar, cov, matching underplate, deep cobalt blue, heavily raised gold cartouches, allover gold dec, pink and pale apricot flowers, two handles, blue leaf mark, price for three pieces	135.00
Lazy Susan, 10" d, floral dec, pastel shades, heavy gold overlay, orig papier mache box	175.00
Mayonnaise Dish, 4½" d, ladle, multicolored floral dec, gold trim, price for two pieces	60.00
Mug, 5½" h, gray bisque background, moriage dragon, blue enameled eyes, green "M" in wreath mark	225.00
Napkin Ring, 4" h, figural, owl on tree stump, wreath mark	375.00
Nappy, 6½" d, lake scene, forest in distance, moriage trim, gold beading	55.00
Nut Set, 7" d, master bowl, six cups, re-	

lief molded, nut shell shape, price for
seven piece set. **225.00**
Pitcher, 7" h, slate gray ground, moriage
sea gulls, leaf mark. **250.00**
Plaque, hanging
7¾" d, brown sailing ship, shaded
beige and orange sunset, "Hand
Painted Nippon" M in wreath mark **95.00**
9" d, palm trees in foreground, sailing
ship and mountains in distance,
moriage dec, "Hand Painted Nip-
pon" M in wreath mark. **150.00**
10" d
Harbor scene, boats in full sail,
shades of beige and brown,
"Hand Painted Nippon" M in
wreath mark. **175.00**
Hunting dog scene, multicolored,
"Hand Painted Nippon" M in
wreath mark. **250.00**
10½" w, hp, blown out, shaded brown
Indian warrior, feather in hat, bow
and arrow, sgd "N" in wreath **450.00**
10¾" w, hp, blown out, brown elk,
shaded blue ground, pale green,
brown, and purple scene, "N" in cir-
cle mark **350.00**
Plate
8½" d, lake, house, and roses scene,
cobalt and gold trim, leaf mark . . . **185.00**
10" w, gold center, cobalt and gold
trim, maple leaf mark **150.00**
Powder Box, cov, 5¼" d, portrait on cov,
green and white base, heavy gold
scrolling, gold feet, blue maple leaf
mark **125.00**
Punch Bowl and Stand, 12½" d, 6½" h,
bisque, bouquet of roses scene, wide
rim decorated with gold and jewels,
wreath mark **315.00**
Scent Bottle, 4¼" h, cream, pink and red
roses, green raised lattice with white
dots **125.00**
Serving Tray, 11" d, gold and burgundy
medallions inside gold fluted rim, multicolored roses and leaves center,
gold open pierced handles, Royal Kin-
ran mark. **195.00**
Shaving Mug, shaded green, floral dec,
gold beading, gold handle **225.00**
Spittoon, lady's hand, violets, turquoise
beading, green "M" in wreath mark. . **150.00**
Stein, relief molded, dog heads, leash
handle, green "M" in wreath mark. . . **950.00**
Sugar Shaker, 4¼" h, cobalt, floral, ma-
ple leaf mark. **145.00**
Tankard
11" h, deep cobalt blue trim, bright
pink floral dec, turquoise banded
flute, green leaves, yellow ground,
blue leaf mark **150.00**
11½" h, oval body, ornate gold rim

and base bands, gold handle, large
blown out shaded green roses and
foliage, pale green satin ground. . . **245.00**
Tea Set, teapot, creamer, and sugar,
melon ribbed shape, gold handles and
trim, gold overlay design, pink roses,
leaf mark, price for set. **250.00**
Tea Strainer, pink roses **50.00**
Trivet, octagonal, portrait, Egyptian lady,
shaded red ground, blue trim **140.00**
Urn
9½" h, white flowers, gold outline,
fancy handles, dome lid, pedestal
base, Royal Kinran mark. **425.00**
10" h, Gaudy style, ornate shoulder
handles, ftd, large red poppies, cobalt blue ground, heavy gold trim,
Royal Nishiki mark. **175.00**
Vase
6½" h, high sq handles, relief molded
scene of stag and hunting dogs, forest setting, green "M" in wreath
mark. **675.00**
8½" h, 8" w, hp, double handles, cen-
tral cartouche of yellow and red
roses, blue and green leaves, elaborate moriage design of leaves and
pine cones, blue leaf mark **325.00**
9¼" h, 4" w, scenic, deep cobalt blue
band at top and base, landscape
with pond of swans, pink and green
trees and mountains, green "R & C
Nippon" mark **225.00**
9½" h, cylindrical, gold collared neck,
relief molded autumn colored foli-
age, gold beading **525.00**
9¾" h, Rose Tapestry, double han-
dles, bright pink and yellow roses,
buds, and leaves, blue, green, and
white ground, gold handles and
trim, bottom mark removed **250.00**
10½" h, tapering cylindrical body,
small mouth, gold loop shoulder
handles, pink roses, gold beading . **375.00**
12" h, red flowers, gold neck and
base, jeweling, blue maple leaf
mark. **275.00**
13" h, medallions of chrysanthemums,
gold handles, blue maple leaf mark **225.00**
Whiskey Jug, 6½" h, cylindrical, short
slender neck, wide flat shoulder, stylized dragons and jewels, orig stopper,
green "M" in wreath mark **300.00**

NODDERS

History: Nodders are figurines with heads and/
or arms attached to the body with wires to enable
them to move. They are made in a variety of ma-

terials—bisque, celluloid, papier–mâché, porcelain, and wood.

Most nodders date from the late 19th century, with Germany being the principal source of supply. Among the American-made nodders, those of Disney and cartoon characters are most eagerly sought.

Man, white and blue costume, gold trim, holding cane and bottle, wire glasses, $150.00.

African Couple, pr, bisque, black man and woman.	575.00
Brownie, 10″ h, policeman, blue, Palmer Cox	275.00
Bulldog, 10 x 6½″, brown, sanded finish	60.00
Buttercup, bisque, German	175.00
Colonial Woman, 7½″ h, bisque	185.00
Daddy Warbucks, bisque	100.00
Elephant, 8½ x 6½″, gray felt, canvas blanket, wood base	150.00
Happy Hooligan, 4½″ h, bisque, seated, painted, 1920s	125.00
Hawaiian Girl	30.00
Indian Princess, 3¾″ h, bisque, seated, holding fan, pale blue, gold trim	115.00
Japanese Boy and Girl, pr, 5½″ h, papier mâché	35.00
Kayo, bisque, marked "Germany" . . .	125.00
Monk, 5¾″ h, bisque, standing, holding wine pitcher, German.	140.00
Oriental Couple, 8¾″ h, pr, bisque, pink robes, gilding, seated before keyboard and music book, Continental, 19th C	500.00
Orphan Annie, bisque, German	100.00
Rabbit, 8″ h, papier mâché, sitting, light brown.	80.00
Santa Claus, 10″ h, papier mâché, candy container, mica glitter trim, German	100.00

Schoolboy, 5½″ h, bisque, black boy seated in chair, white shirt, blue, white, and tan plaid pants, holding slate.	125.00
Shriner, 7″ h, papier mâché	85.00
Turkish Girl, 6 x 6″, bisque, white beading	300.00

NORITAKE CHINA

History: Morimura Brothers founded Noritake China in 1904 in Nagoya, Japan. They made high-quality chinaware for export to the United States and also produced a line of china blanks for hand painting. In 1910 the company perfected a technique for the production of high-quality dinnerware and introduced streamlined production.

During the 1920s the Larkin Company of Buffalo, New York, was a prime distributor of Noritake China. Larkin offered Azalea, Briarcliff, Linden, Modjeska, Savory, Sheridan, and Tree in the Meadow patterns as part of its premium line.

The factory was heavily damaged during World War II; production was reduced. Between 1946 and 1948 the company sold its china under the "Rose China" mark, since the quality of production did not match the earlier Noritake China. In 1948, expansion saw the resumption of quality production and the use of the Noritake name once again.

There are close to 100 different marks for Noritake, the careful study of which can determine the date of production. Most pieces are marked "Noritake" and have a wreath, "M," "N," or "Nippon." The use of the letter "N" was registered in 1953.

References: Joan Van Patten, *Collector's Encyclopedia of Noritake*, First Series (1984, 1994 value updte), Second Series (1994), Collector Books.

Periodical: *Noritake News*, 1237 Federal Ave. East, Seattle, WA 98102.

Additional Listings: See *Warman's Americana & Collectibles* for price listings of the Azalea pattern.

Ashtray, 3½ x 3″, hexagon, Art Deco dancing couple in center, tan luster. .	125.00
Bowl, 10″ l, oval, Rosewin #6584 pattern.	26.00
Cake Plate, 8″ d, handle, tree, boat, water, purple sage, and mountain, orange sunset, wreath with M mark . . .	45.00
Candlesticks, pr, 8¼″ h, gold flowers and bird, blue luster ground, wreath with M mark	125.00
Creamer and Sugar, Art Deco, pink Japanese lanterns, cobalt blue ground, basket type handle on sugar, wreath with M mark, price for pair	40.00
Cup and Saucer, Florola #83374 pattern.	22.00
Gravy Boat, Florola #83374 pattern .	28.00

Bowl, orange ground, white floral motif, green band on rim, gold edge, three open handles, red M in wreath mark, 8½″ d, 2″ h, $30.00.

Hair Receiver, 3¼″ h, 3½″ w, Art Deco, geometric designs, gold luster, wreath with M mark	50.00
Jam Jar, cov, 5½″ h, pink rose finial, floral dec on side, wreath with M mark	45.00
Match Holder, underplate, camel scene, wreath with M mark	35.00
Mug, white, 1″ w border of purple iris, wreath with M mark	60.00
Napkin Ring, Art Deco man and woman, wreath with M mark, price for pair . . .	60.00
Placecard Holder, figural	
Bluebird with butterfly, gold luster, white stripes, wreath with M mark, price for pair	35.00
Flower, orange luster, white stripe, wreath with M mark, price for pair .	35.00
Platter, 11″ l, Rosewin #6584 pattern	22.00
Relish, divided, orange center bird, wreath with M mark	95.00
Salt, 3″ l, swan, white, orange luster, price for pair	25.00
Sauce Dish, underplate, cream, black, gold dec, wreath with M mark	30.00
Serving Dish, cov, 9″ l, Art Deco, orange and black floral dec, luster, wreath with M mark	40.00
Soup Bowl, Florola #83374 pattern . .	12.00
Tray, Art Deco, brunette, white dress with blue design, spray of pink flowers, orange luster ground, blue trim, wreath with M mark	165.00
Vegetable Bowl, cov, 9″ d, round, Rosewin #6584 pattern	35.00
Waffle Set, handled serving plate, sugar shaker, Art Deco flowers, wreath with M mark, price for set	45.00

Wall Pocket	
Blue luster	
Art Deco vase of flowers	65.00
Butterfly, applied, wreath with M mark	65.00
White and orange luster, Art Deco flower	65.00

NORITAKE: TREE IN THE MEADOW PATTERN

History: Tree in the Meadow is one of the most popular patterns of Noritake china. Since the design is hand painted, there are numerous variations of the scene. The basic scene features a large tree (usually in the foreground), a meandering stream or lake, and a peasant cottage in the distance. Principal colors are muted tones of brown and yellow.

The pattern is found with a variety of backstamps and appears to have been imported into the United States beginning in the early 1920s. The Larkin Company distributed this pattern through its catalog sales in the 1920–30 period.

Reference: Joan Van Patten, *Collector's Encyclopedia of Noritake*, First Series (1984, 1994 value updte), Second Series (1994), Collector Books.

Periodical: *Noritake News,* 1237 Federal Ave. East, Seattle, WA 98102.

Salt and Pepper Shakers, pr, marked "Made in Japan," $35.00.

Ashtray, 5¼″ d, green mark	35.00
Berry Set, large bowl with pierced handles, six small bowls, price for seven pieces	72.00
Bowl, 6½″ d, green mark	25.00
Cake Plate, 7½″ sq	25.00
Centerpiece Bowl, 7½″ d, wreath with M mark	105.00
Compote	80.00
Condiment Set, mustard pot, ladle, salt and pepper shakers, tray	40.00
Creamer and Sugar, scalloped, price for pair	85.00

Cruet, vinegar and oil, price for pair	140.00
Demitasse Cup and Saucer	35.00
Demitasse Pot	245.00
Dish, 6″ d, pierced handles, blue luster border	40.00
Gravy Boat	52.50
Jam Jar, underplate, and spoon, price for three pieces	65.00
Lemon Dish, 5½″ d, center ring handle	15.00
Plate	
6½″ d	10.00
7½″ d	12.00
8½″ d	15.00
Platter	
12″ l	30.00
14″ l	35.00
Relish, divided	48.00
Salt and Pepper Shakers, marked "Made In Japan," pr	30.00
Shaving Mug, 3¾″ h, green mark	85.00
Tea Set, teapot, creamer, and cov sugar, six cups and saucers, price for set	135.00
Tea Tile, 5″ w, chamfered corners, green mark	25.00
Toothpick Holder	75.00
Vase, 7″ h, fan shape	120.00
Vegetable Dish, 9⅜″ l, oval, Noritake mark	30.00
Wall Plaque, 8½″ l, green mark	75.00
Waste Bowl	37.50

NORTH DAKOTA SCHOOL OF MINES

History: The North Dakota School of Mines was established in 1890. Earle J. Babcock, an instructor in chemistry, was impressed with the high purity of North Dakota potter's clay. In 1898 Babcock received funds to develop his finds. He tried to interest commercial potteries in North Dakota clay but had limited success.

In 1910 Babcock persuaded the school to establish a Ceramics Department. Margaret Cable, who studied under Charles Binns and Frederick H. Rhead, was appointed head. She remained until her retirement in 1949.

Decorative emphasis was placed on native themes, such as flowers and animals. Art Nouveau, Art Deco, and fairly plain pieces were made.

The pottery is marked in cobalt blue underglaze with "University of North Dakota/Grand Forks, N.D./Made at School of Mines/N.D. Clay" in a circle. Some earlier pieces only are marked "U.N.D." or "U.N.D./Grand Forks, N.D." Most pieces are numbered (they can be dated with university records) and signed by both the instructor and student. Cable-signed pieces are most desirable.

Reference: *University Of North Dakota Pottery, The Cable Years,* Knight Publishing, 1977.
Collectors' Club: North Dakota Pottery Collectors Society, PO Box 14, Beach, ND 58621.

Vase, dark purple, blue flecks, stamped "U.N.D.," 2¾″ d, $100.00.

Bowl	
4″ d, carved turkeys, shaded green to brown, sgd "Mattson"	275.00
5½″ d, carved florals, gray–green matte	150.00
Curtain Pull, Indian head, turquoise, marked "Homecoming 1939," orig box	115.00
Paperweight, 3½″ d, "Parent's Day, 1938," deep blue	100.00
Tile, 5″ d, round, incised oxen pulling covered wagon, matte green, brown glaze, stamped and incised artist's mark of Flora Huckfield	250.00
Vase, 3½″ h, 3¾″ d, band of coyotes, ivory ground, blue semimatte glaze, ink stamp and "934," "JM"	550.00

NUTTING, WALLACE

History: Wallace Nutting (1861–1941) was one of America's foremost photographers in the first third of the 20th century. Between 1897 and his death, he took over 50,000 pictures, kept approximately 10,000, destroyed the rest because they did not meet his standards, and commercially marketed over 2,500 of the 10,000 that he retained. Of the remaining 7,500 views, some were sold in limited numbers and the others used personally for lectures, research, or simply for entertaining friends.

Millions of Nutting's hand–colored platinotype pictures were sold. Nutting opened his first studio in New York City in 1904. In 1905 he moved to a larger studio in Southbury, Connecticut. A Toronto branch office followed in 1907. In 1911–12 Nutting sold his business and house, Nuttinghame, in Southbury. The person who purchased the business backed out, leaving Nutting without a home.

Nutting moved his entire operation, including twenty employees, to Framingham, Massachusetts. His business blossomed. At its peak, it provided employment for over two hundred people in positions ranging from colorists and support staff to salesmen and framers.

Wallace Nutting began actively collecting antiques sometime around 1912. In 1917 he published his first book on furniture, *American Windsor*. In 1928 the first two volumes of *The Furniture Treasury* appeared. Volume 3 followed in 1933.

In 1917–18 Wallace Nutting began offering reproduction furniture for sale. During the early 1920s the business prospered. However, by 1927–28 the business was in decline. The Depression brought further decline. Nutting laid off employees but refused to allow the business to fold. It was operating on a very limited basis at the time of his death.

During his lifetime Nutting had a close relationship with Berea College in Kentucky. Upon his wife's death, Berea was given the remains of the furniture business. After copying the blueprints and patterns at the Framingham factory for its records, Berea sold the business to Drexel Furniture Company.

References: Michael Ivankovich, *The Alphabetical & Numerical Index to Wallace Nutting Pictures*, Diamond Press, 1988; Michael Ivankovich, *The Guide To Wallace Nutting Furniture*, Diamond Press, 1990; Michael Ivankovich, *The Guide To Wallace Nutting–Like Photographers of the Early 20th Century*, Diamond Press, 1991; Michael Ivankovich, *The Price Guide To Wallace Nutting Pictures, Fourth Edition*, Diamond Press, 1989; Wallace Nutting, *Colonial Reproductions* (reprint of 1921 catalog), Diamond Press, 1992; Wallace Nutting, *The Wallace Nutting Expansible Catalog* (reprint of 1915 catalog), Diamond Press, 1987; Wallace Nutting, *Wallace Nutting General Catalog, Supreme Edition* (reprint of 1930 catalog), Schiffer Publishing, 1977; Wallace Nutting, *Windsors* (reprint of 1918 catalog), Diamond Press, 1992.

Collectors' Club: Wallace Nutting Collectors Club, 186 Mountain Ave., North Caldwell, NJ 07006.

Museum: Wadsworth Atheneum, Hartford, CT.

BOOKS

Furniture Treasury, first edition	30.00
Ireland Beautiful	180.00
Massachusetts Beautiful	40.00
Pathways of the Puritans	150.00
Pennsylvania Beautiful	45.00
Photograph Art Secrets	220.00
The Clock Book	80.00
The Cruise of the 800	115.00
Wallace Nutting's Biography	75.00

Book, *Old New England Pictures*, 64 pgs, 32 sgd, titled, and matted hand colored pictures, marked "Copy #4," 18 x 13", $10,175.00. Photograph courtesy of Clinton–Ivankovich Auction Co., Inc.

FURNITURE

Chair	
#390, ladderback	500.00
#464, Carver armchair	425.00
#476, Flemish	600.00
Chest, oak, single drawer	2,585.00
Tavern Table, pine top, turned maple	
legs, block branded signature	1,250.00

PICTURES

A Checkered Road	280.00
Almost Home	55.00
A Pause at the Bridge	165.00
Blossom Landing, 11 x 17"	105 00
Brookside Blooms, 10 x 12"	65.00
Calling on Priscilla, 10 x 16"	120.00
Comfort and a Cat, 14 x 15"	270.00
Cutting A Silhouette, 12 x 16"	205.00
Grandfather's Clock, 14 x 17"	130.00
Grandmother's China, 11 x 17"	125.00
Hollyhock Cottage, 12 x 16"	165.00
Honeymoon Drive	65.00
Hospitable Preparations, 10 x 12"	135.00
Joy Path, 11 x 14"	115.00
Larkspur, 16 x 20"	150.00
Old Senate Chamber	275.00
Pine Landing, 13 x 16"	145.00
Sewing The Rag Rug	125.00
Summer Opulence	425.00
Summer Wind, 13 x 22"	110.00
The Natural Bridge, 14 x 17"	260.00
The Quilting Party, 14 x 17"	40.00
The Way Through the Orchard, 11 x 14".	55.00
The Work Basket, 9 x 11"	95.00
Untitled Interior, 8 x 10"	90.00
Where Trout Lie, 13 x 16"	75.00
Wisteria Gate, 10 x 18"	235.00

SILHOUETTES

Alden, John and Priscilla, price for pair	130.00
Girl, playing piano, 7 x 8″	65.00
Lincoln, Abe and Mary Todd, 4 x 5″, price for pair	200.00
Nutting, Mr and Mrs, Christmas card type, 6 x 8″	110.00

OCCUPIED JAPAN

History: At the end of World War II, the Japanese economy was devastated. To secure needed hard currency, the Japanese pottery industry produced thousands of figurines and other knickknacks for export. From the beginning of the American occupation until April 28, 1952, these objects were marked "Japan," "Made in Japan," "Occupied Japan," and "Made in Occupied Japan." Only pieces marked with the last two designations are of strong interest to Occupied Japan collectors. The first two marks also were used at other time periods.

The variety of products is endless—ashtrays, dinnerware, lamps, planters, souvenir items, toys, vases, etc. Initially it was the figurines which attracted the largest number of collectors; today many collectors focus on nonfigurine material.

References: Florence Archambault, *Occupied Japan For Collectors,* Schiffer Publishing, 1992; Gene Florence, *The Collector's Encyclopedia Of Occupied Japan Collectibles,* First Series (1976, 1992 value update), Second Series (1979, 1993 value update), Third Series (1987), Fourth Series (1990, 1993 value update), Fifth Series (1992), Collector Books; David C. Gould and Donna Crevar–Donaldson, *Occupied Japan Toys With Prices,* L–W Book Sales, 1993.

Collectors' Club: The Occupied Japan Club, 29 Freeborn Street, Newport, RI 02840.

Additional Listings: See *Warman's Americana & Collectibles* for more examples.

Bisque
Ashtray, 2¼″ w, heart shape, hp, floral sprays, white ground	15.00
Creamer, figural cow	20.00
Figure	
3″ h, girl, bright dress	10.00
3½″ h, girl sitting on bench	10.00
6½″ h, boy standing by fence . . .	20.00
8″ h, Victorian man, playing instrument	40.00
Miniature, pitcher, multicolored applied floral spray, pink ground	8.00
Planter, figural, peasant girl standing beside leaf covered planter	35.00
Shelf Sitter, 4¾″ h, Oriental girl, green	12.00
Vase, 7″ h, ftd, emb floral dec	18.00

Figures, couple, man with tan coat, blue vest, and brown pants, lady with yellow skirt, blue bustle, and rose blouse, price for pair, 5½″ h, $30.00.

Wall Pocket, 5″ h, cuckoo clock, orange luster, pine cone weights . . .	12.00
Celluloid	
Doll Carriage, 2¾″ h, pink and blue, movable hood, Acme	24.00
Figure, 6″ h, Betty Boop, blond hair, movable arms	24.00
Toy, monkey, playing banjo	165.00
Metal	
Ashtray, 6¾″ d, chrome plated, pierced floral rim	10.00
Binoculars, Egyptian figures, emb .	32.00
Candy Dish, pedestal base	10.00
Cigarette Lighter, 4″ h, cowboy, head flips back.	25.00
Harmonica, butterfly shape	20.00
Nut Dish, 6″ d, floral borders	10.00
Pincushion, figural, shoe, silver finish, red velvet cushion	15.00
Plate, 4½″ d, pierced scalloped fancy rim, silvered.	12.00
Vase, 6″ h, SP, Art Deco style, stylized blossoms, ftd	25.00
Papier Mâché	
Nodder, rabbit, sitting	35.00
Tray, 10½″ l, rect, floral dec	50.00
Plastic, necklace, 25″ l, hp, football and baseball players, other figural charms.	65.00
Porcelain	
Child's Tea Set, white, floral dec, price for twenty–four piece set.	100.00
Creamer and Sugar, rose, pink, and white, price for pair.	24.00
Dish, 5″ d, triangular, handle, gold trim.	20.00
Figure	
3″ h, cherub, playing drum, pierced pedestal base.	10.00

6¾" h, lady, Art Deco style dress . 25.00
Honey Pot, 4½" h, black Mammy, head lifts off, spoon as tongue, holding spoon and frying pan 35.00
Incense Burner, cobalt blue, floral dec, gold trim. 18.00
Lamp, figural, Colonial man and woman, price for pair 65.00
Planter, figural, shoe, floral dec . . . 18.00
Plaque, ducks in flight 18.00
Plate, 7½" d, Ambassador pattern . 8.00
Rice Bowl, 6" d, emb dragon 25.00
Salt, master, figural, swan 18.00
Salt and Pepper Shakers, pr, Negro chefs 30.00
Tea Set, cov teapot, four cups and saucers, white, small pink roses, green leaves, price for set. 65.00
Toby Mug, 5½" h
Blinker man 45.00
Grinning man, prominent white teeth, black bow tie, green cap. . 45.00
Old gent with gray beard, mustache, green cap. 45.00

OHR POTTERY

History: Ohr pottery was produced by George E. Ohr in Biloxi, Mississippi. There is some discrepancy as to when he actually established his pottery. Some suggest 1878, but Ohr's autobiography indicates 1883. In 1884 Ohr exhibited 600 pieces of his work, indicating that he had been working for some time.

Ohr's techniques included twisting, crushing, folding, denting, and crinkling thinwalled clay into odd, grotesque, and sometimes graceful forms. Much of his early work is signed with an impressed stamp of his name and location in block letters. His later work, often marked with the flowing script designation "G E Ohr," was usually left unglazed.

In 1906, Ohr closed the pottery and stored over 6,000 pieces as his legacy to his family. He hoped it would be purchased by the U.S. government, which never happened. The entire collection remained in storage until it was rediscovered in 1972.

Today Ohr is recognized as one of the leading potters in the American Art Pottery movement. Some greedy individuals have taken the later unglazed pieces and covered them with poor-quality glazes in hopes of making them more valuable. These pieces, usually with the flowing script mark, do not have "stilt marks" on the bottom.

Reference: Garth Clark, Robert Ellison, Jr., and Eugene Hecht, *The Mad Potter of Biloxi: The Art & Life of George Ohr,* Abbeville Press, 1989.

Chamberstick, olive green, script signature "G. E. Ohr," 3¾" h, 3⅞" d, $315.00.

Candlestick
3⅞" h, dark and light green mottled glaze, marked 175.00
4½" h, twisted body, handles, gunmetal black 425.00
Creamer, 5" h, pinched cylinder, open handle, deep violet and mottled blue glaze, imp "G. E. OHR Biloxi, Miss" . 5,000.00
Inkwell, 2" h, 5½" l, 5" w, artist's palette, green high glaze inkwell, brown high glaze base, die–stamped mark. 1,980.00
Jug, 5" h, bisque, tapered, script sgd . 350.00
Mug
Single handle, gunmetal gray 350.00
Three handles, green, brown, and gray 700.00
Pitcher
5" h, bulbous, brown irid, off center handle, imp mark 415.00
8¼" h, black speckled dark mustard, handle, imp mark 600.00
9½" h, molded body, Battle of New Orleans scene, green, buff int., glossy glaze, incised script on bottom 2,300.00
Puzzle Mug
3¼" h, brown, glossy glaze, incised script on bottom. 350.00
3½" h, mottled green high glaze, pressed rope and leaf handle, screw under handle, script sgd "G E Ohr" 375.00
Shelf, 6" h, 6" w, 3" d, corner, ceramic, curving sides, beehive pattern, two factory holes for hanging, khaki–green high glaze, die–stamped mark, imp "JHP," minor chip at base 525.00

Teapot, 4⅛" h, unglazed bisque, shading orange to cream, marked **85.00**

Vase

3" h, 4¼" d, bulbous, deep in–body twist, fired red clay, incised mark, dated "06". **525.00**

3½" h

2½" d, pedestal base, flared rim, metallic green and black high glaze, die–stamped twice. **385.00**

2¾" d, cylindrical, bulging center, green and brown high glaze flambe, die–stamped mark. **330.00**

4½" h

2¼" d, bud, rose–pink high glaze, band of purple sponged pattern at top and base, die–stamped mark, small kiln bruise on side . . **550.00**

3" d, flaring neck, hammered shoulder, black lustrous glaze, die–stamped twice **600.00**

5½" h, 2" d, bud, pinched waist, semi-imatte lapis blue glaze, die–stamped mark **440.00**

6" h, 4½" h, bulbous base, cylindrical neck, bulbous rim, bisque fired, script mark **300.00**

12½" h, 4" d, bulbous top, flared circular base, bisque fired, die–star.,ped mark **470.00**

Water Jug, 8" h, 6½" d, bulbous, two spouts, ring handle, bisque fired, unmarked. **300.00**

OLD IVORY
84

OLD IVORY CHINA

History: Old Ivory derives its name from the background color of the china. It was made in Silesia, Germany, during the second half of the 19th century. Marked pieces usually have a pattern number (pattern names are not common) and the crown Silesia mark.

Reference: Susan and Al Bagdade, *Warman's English & Continental Pottery & Porcelain, Second Edition,* Wallace–Homestead, 1991.

Periodical: *Old Ivory Newsletter,* PO Box 1004, Wilsonville, OR 97070.

Berry Set, 9½" d master bowl, six 5" d berry bowls, No. 15, marked "Silesia,"

Plate, Pattern VIII, floral dec, 8" d, $45.00.

some wear to gold, price for seven piece set **110.00**

Butter Pat, 3" d, No. 16, price for set of six **450.00**

Cake Plate, 11" d, No. 15, marked "Clarion," slight wear to gold trim **100.00**

Celery Dish, 11½" l, No. 15, marked "Silesia & Ohme". **50.00**

Chocolate Set, No. 16, chocolate pot and five cups and saucers, marked "Ohme & Silesia," price for set **400.00**

Chop Platter, No. 15, marked "Silesia & Clarion" **120.00**

Creamer and Sugar, No. 84, marked "Ohme & Silesia" **300.00**

Cup and Saucers, No. 84, marked "Silesia," nicks, price for twenty pieces . **250.00**

Hair Receiver **100.00**

Mayonnaise and Tray, No. 16, marked "Silesia" **120.00**

Oyster Bowl, No. 16, marked "Ohme & Silesia," 2" crack on side **55.00**

Plate, 8½" d, marked "Silesia & Ohme," minor wear to gold trim, price for set of five. **100.00**

Salad Plate, 7½" d, No. 15, marked "Ohme & Silesia," price for set of three **55.00**

Toothpick, No. 16, marked "Silesia" . **200.00**

Waste Bowl, marked "Silesia & Ohme" **225.00**

OLD PARIS CHINA

History: Old Paris china is fine-quality porcelain made by various French factories located in and about Paris during the 18th and 19th centuries. Some pieces were marked, but the majority was not. Characteristics of this type of china include fine porcelain, beautiful decorations, and gilding. Favorite colors were dark maroon, deep cobalt blue, and a deep green.

Reference: Susan and Al Bagdade, *Warman's English & Continental Pottery & Porcelain, Second Edition,* Wallace–Homestead, 1991.

Additional Listings: Continental China and Porcelain (General).

Candlestick, 12″ h, figural, young girl, landscape base, gilt metal candle stand with white porcelain candle cup	**185.00**
Clock, mantle, floral dec, giltwood base, 19th C	**425.00**
Corbeille, 7½″ h, 10″ d, basket of fruit, white, reticulated stand, 19th C.	**165.00**
Creamer, boy portrait, pink and blue .	**150.00**
Cup and Saucer, sailboats and shore dec, gilt base rim on saucer	**80.00**

Figure
- 8½″ h, chinoiserie man, wearing green robe, 19th C. **110.00**
- 19″ h, Diane and Hercules, Diane as Goddess of the Hunt, Hercules wearing leopard watch, gilt dec circular stands, painted hunt trophies, Greek Key form feet, price for pair **1,210.00**

Garniture Vase, 15¼″ h, figural, woman wearing pastoral dress standing against painted bayou landscape, gentleman and dog against evergreen branches and river landscape, relief molded cascading waterfall, gilt dec scrolled base, c1840, price for pair . .	**2,475.00**
Jar, 10½″ h, laurel branch dec, gilt highlights, 1825–40, price for pair	**75.00**
Perfume Bottle, 9″ h, rect, floral motif and gilt scrolled dec, green ground, oval stopper, rect foot, late 19th C, price for pair	**375.00**

Punch Bowl, 11″ d, oval reserve with British bark, gold dec, ftd, 19th C . . .	**210.00**
Sugar, cov, 5½″ h, painted scene with shepherd, gilt handles, mid 19th C . .	**75.00**
Urn, 9¾″ h, classical form, George and Martha Washington portraits and stylized floral reserves, gold ground, handled, price for pair	**675.00**

Vase
- 6½″ h, floral dec **325.00**
- 6¾″ h, flatted oval shape, floral and bird reserve, 19th C, price for pair **355.00**
- 9″ h, floral dec, yellow–orange ground **250.00**
- 10″ h, ovoid, spreading foot, landscape scenes, blue celeste ground, 19th C, price for pair. **500.00**
- 14½″ h, floral painted reserves, handles with gilt dec, scalloped top, pale green painted base, mid 19th C, price for pair **425.00**
- 16″ h, painted floral reserves, gilt dec, scrolling vine handles, mid 19th c . **250.00**

Wine Cooler, 6″ d, 5″ h, courtiers in landscape scene, price for pair.	**300.00**

OLD SLEEPY EYE

History: Sleepy Eye, a Sioux Indian chief who reportedly had a droopy eye, gave his name to Sleepy Eye, Minnesota, and one of its leading flour mills. In the early 1900s Old Sleepy Eye Flour offered four Flemish gray heavy stoneware premiums, decorated in cobalt blue: a straight–sided butter crock, curved salt bowl, stein, and vase. The premiums were made by Weir Pottery Company, later to become Monmouth Pottery Company and finally to emerge as the present–day Western Stoneware Company of Monmouth, Illinois.

Additional pottery and stoneware pieces were issued. Forms included five sizes of pitchers (4, 5½, 6½, 8, and 9 inches), mugs, steins, sugar bowls, and tea tiles (hot plates). Most were cobalt blue on white, but other glaze hues, such as browns, golds, and greens, were used.

Old Sleepy Eye also issued many other items, including bakers' caps, lithographed barrel covers, beanies, fans, multicolored pillow tops, postcards, trade cards, etc. Production of Old Sleepy Eye stoneware ended in 1937.

In 1952 Western Stoneware Company made a 22- and 40-ounce stein in chestnut brown glaze with a redesigned Indian head. From 1961 to 1972 gift editions, dated and signed with a Maple Leaf mark, were made for the board of directors and others within the company. Beginning in 1973, Western Stoneware Company issued an annual limited-edition stein, marked and dated, for collectors.

Urns, pr, Italinate Village, deep rose ground, gold trim, 9½″ h, $1,250.00.

Reference: Elinor Meugnoit, *Old Sleepy Eye*, published by author, 1979.

Collectors' Club: Old Sleepy Eye Collectors Club, PO Box 12, Monmouth, IL 61462.

Reproduction Alert: Blue-and-white pitchers, crazed, weighted, and often with a stamp or the word "Ironstone," are the most copied. The stein and salt bowl also have been made. Many reproductions come from Taiwan.

A line of fantasy items, new items which never existed, includes an advertising pocket mirror with miniature flour barrel label, small glass plates, fruit jars, toothpick holders, glass and pottery miniature pitchers, and salt and pepper shakers. One mill item has been made, a sack marked as though it were old but of a size that could not possibly hold the amount of flour indicated.

Pitcher, pottery, blue and white, 9″ h, $225.00.

MILL ITEMS

Bread Board Scraper	625.00
Calendar, 1904	200.00
Cookbook, loaf of bread shape	120.00
Demitasse Spoon	130.00
Postcard	
Monument	45.00
Picture of mill	17.50
Stationery, envelope	65.00
Teaspoon, silverplate	90.00

POTTERY AND STONEWARE

Creamer, #1, all white, pottery	900.00
Mug	
Brush–McCoy, green and brown, cream ground	255.00
Stoneware	420.00
Pitcher, pottery	
#2, blue rim	580.00
#4, blue rim	425.00
#5, blue rim	420.00
Standing Indian, blue dec, gray ground	850.00

Salt Bowl, stoneware	465.00
Stein	
Blue dec, white ground	475.00
Directors, 1968	185.00
Stoneware, 7¾″ h, brown, Western Stoneware, 1950s	350.00
Sugar Bowl, blue dec, white ground	510.00
Vase, cattail dec	295.00

ONION MEISSEN

History: The blue onion or bulb pattern is of Chinese origin and depicts peaches and pomegranates, not onions. It was first made in the 18th century by Meissen, hence the name Onion Meissen.

Factories in Europe, Japan, and elsewhere copied the pattern. Many still have the pattern in production, including the Meissen factory in Germany.

Note: Prices given are for pieces produced between 1870 and 1930. Many pieces are marked with a company's logo; after 1891 the country of origin is indicated on imported pieces. Early Meissen examples bring a high premium.

Soup, flat, scalloped edge, marked Meissen with star, late, 9¾″ d, $42.00.

Bowl	
6″ d	40.00
9″ d	135.00
Butter Dish, cov	40.00
Butter Pat	90.00
Candle Snuffer, 10¼″ l, SP handle	62.00
Cheese Dish, cov	150.00
Coffeepot, 9½″ h	160.00

Compote, 9" h, 9" d, reticulated rim	350.00
Creamer, 3½" h	50.00
Cup and Saucer	
Coffee	40.00
Tea	30.00
Darner, wooden handle	75.00
Dinner Set, blue, price for 66 piece set	375.00
Dipper, wood handle	100.00
Dish, 10½" d, round, deep, imp mark	55.00
Egg Cup	225.00
Fish Plate, pierced drain insert	225.00
Fruit Knives, price for set of six	85.00
Funnel, 4¾" l	85.00
Knife Rest	30.00
Ladle, 4 x 2", wood handle	135.00
Lemon Dish	35.00
Match Holder	35.00
Mustache Cup	85.00
Pastry Wheel	135.00
Pitcher, 7" h, rococo molded, c1860	225.00
Plate	
6" d	35.00
9" d	48.00
10½" d	70.00
Platter	
12" l, oval, marked	160.00
17" l	225.00
19" l	250.00
Pot de Creme	50.00
Relish Dish	
6½ x 4¾", oblong, octagonal	45.00
11¾ x 7¼", scalloped edge	85.00
Rolling Pin	150.00
Salt Box	135.00
Salt Dip, crossed swords mark	48.00
Sauce Dish, 4¾" d	30.00
Soup Bowl, 9" d	60.00
Soup Tureen, cov, 10½ x 14", rose finial.	250.00
Spill Vase, 5½" h, scroll feet	65.00
Stein, ½ liter, matching conical lid, dwarf thumb lift	500.00
Sugar, cov, melon ribbed, late 19th C	100.00
Tea Strainer, 5" l, handle	65.00
Teapot, 10" h, rose finial, 19th C	200.00
Vegetable Dish	
8½" d, cov	90.00
10" d, cov, sq	130.00
14" d, divided	225.00

OPALESCENT GLASS

History: Opalescent glass is a clear or colored glass with milky white decorations which shows a fiery or opalescent quality when held to light. The effect was achieved by applying bone ash chemicals to designated areas while a piece was still hot and then refiring it at tremendous heat.

There are three basic categories of opalescent glass: (1) Blown (or mold blown) patterns, e.g., Daisy & Fern and Spanish Lace; (2) Novelties, pressed glass patterns made in limited pieces which often included unusual shapes, such as Corn or Trough; and (3) Pattern (pressed) glass.

Opalescent glass was produced in England in the 1870s. Northwood began the American production in 1897 at its Indiana, Pennsylvania, plant. Jefferson, National Glass, Hobbs, and Fenton soon followed.

References: Bill Edwards, *The Standard Opalescent Glass Price Guide,* Collector Books, 1992; William Heacock, *Encyclopedia of Victorian Colored Pattern Glass, Book II, Opalescent Glass from A to Z, Second Edition,* Antique Publications, 1977; William Heacock and William Gamble, *Encyclopedia of Victorian Colored Pattern Glass, Book 9, Cranberry Opalescent from A to Z,* Antique Publications, 1987; William Heacock, James Measell, and Berry Wiggins, *Dugan/Diamond: The Story of Indiana, Pennsylvania, Glass,* Antique Publications, 1993; William Heacock, James Measell, and Berry Wiggins, *Harry Northwood: The Early Years 1881–1900,* Antique Publications, 1990; William Heacock, James Measell, and Berry Wiggins, *Harry Northwood: The Wheeling Years, 1901–1925,* Antique Publications, 1991; Ellen T. Schroy, *Warman's Glass,* Wallace–Homestead, 1992; Ellen T. Schroy (ed.), *Warman's Pattern Glass,* Wallace–Homestead, 1993.

Bowl, white, Inverted Feather pattern, ruffled, three ftd, 8¼" d, 4" h, $50.00.

BLOWN

Berry Bowl, master	
Bubble Lattice, blue satin	50.00
Ribbed Opal Lattice, cranberry	250.00
Biscuit Jar, Spanish Lace, vaseline	275.00
Bowl	
10" d, Christmas Snowflake, green, ruffled rim	80.00
11" d, 4½" h, Poinsettia, white, ruffled brilliant blue rim	185.00
Butter Dish, cov, Hobbs Hobnail, vaseline	245.00
Celery Vase	
Daffodils, blue	100.00

Spanish Lace, blue 80.00
Creamer, Reverse Swirl, blue 80.00
Cruet, Christmas Pearls, orig stopper 250.00
Finger Bowl, Hobbs Hobnail, cranberry 50.00
Lamp, oil
  Finger, Polka Dot, white, #0 burner
    and chimney, 5″ h 450.00
  Stem
    Coinspot, white, crystal fan base,
      #1 burner, 7½″ h 100.00
    Hobbs Snowflake, blue, glass
      sleeve and clear glass foot, 8¾″
      h, minor foot flakes 300.00
    Inverted Thumbprint, white, amber
      fan base, #0 burner and chim-
      ney, 7¼″ h, foot flakes. 125.00
    Sheldon Swirl, blue, 8½″ h, fish
      scale flake on foot rib 325.00
Mustard, cov, Reverse Swirl, vaseline 60.00
Pitcher
  Button and Braids, green 175.00
  Swirl, blue, sq ruffled rim 175.00
Rose Bowl, 4½″ h, 3½″ d, Reverse Swirl,
  white, white bottom rim 40.00
Salt Shaker, orig top
  Consolidated Criss–Cross, cranberry 85.00
  Ribbed Opal Lattice, cranberry . . . 95.00
Spooner
  Hobbs Hobnail, blue 80.00
  Spanish Lace, canary yellow 80.00
Sugar Shaker, Reverse Swirl, cranberry,
  orig top. 450.00
Syrup
  Daisy and Fern, WV optic mold, blue 165.00
  Reverse Swirl, blue, orig top 235.00
Tumbler
  Acanthus, blue 90.00
  Arabian Nights, blue 140.00
  Bubble Lattice, cranberry 145.00
  Button and Braids, cranberry 135.00
  Christmas Snowflake, blue, ribbed . 125.00
  Chrysanthemum Swirl, blue 90.00
  Maze, swirling, green 65.00
  Poinsettia, blue 95.00
  Reverse Swirl, cranberry 58.00
  Scroll, blue 90.00
  Stripe, blue 95.00
  Swirl
    Blue 85.00
    Cranberry 95.00
Waste Bowl, Hobbs Hobnail, vaseline 70.00

NOVELTIES

Barber Bottle, Stars and Stripes,
  cranberry 150.00
Basket, Old Man Winter, vaseline, ftd,
  applied handle 145.00
Bowl
  Grape and Cherry, blue 80.00
  Ruffles and Rings, white 30.00
  Scheherezade, blue 65.00

Winter Cabbage, white 30.00
Bushel Basket, blue 75.00
Chalice, Maple Leaf, vaseline 35.00
Hat, ruffled rim, one side turned up,
  white swirled stripes, blue, 6¼″ w, 4″
  h 145.00
Lamp, oil, Gay, opalescent stripes,
  vaseline, matching chimney, 9″ h, 3⅜″
  d fitter 175.00

PRESSED

Berry Bowl, master
  Flora, blue 60.00
  Tokyo, green 55.00
Butter Dish, cov
  Inverted Fan and Feather, blue . . . 550.00
  Water Lily and Cattails, blue 300.00
Creamer
  Inverted Fan and Feather, blue . . . 125.00
  Swag with Brackets, green 60.00
Cruet, Tokyo, green, orig stopper . . . 190.00
Jelly Compote, Intaglio, blue 45.00
Salt and Pepper Shakers, pr, Jewel and
  Flower, canary yellow, orig tops 250.00
Sauce Dish
  Palm Beach, blue 50.00
  Shell, white 25.00
Spooner
  Swag with Brackets, blue 50.00
  Wreath and Shell, canary yellow . . 80.00
Toothpick
  Ribbed Spiral, blue 90.00
  Wreath and Shell, white 125.00
Tumbler
  Drapery, blue 85.00
  Iris with Meander, blue 85.00
  Jackson, green 45.00
  Jeweled Heart, blue 85.00
  Water Lily and Cattails, blue 70.00

OPALINE GLASS

History: Opaline glass was a popular mid- to
late-19th-century European glass. The glass has a
certain amount of translucency and often is found
decorated in enamel designs and trimmed in gold.
    Reference: Ellen T. Schroy, *Warman's Glass,*
Wallace–Homestead, 1992.

Biscuit Jar, white ground, hp, florals and
  bird dec, brass lid and bail handle. . . 150.00
Bouquet Holder, 7″ h, blue opaline cornucopia shaped gilt dec flower holders
  issuing from bronze stag heads, Belgian black marble base, English, Victorian, early 19th C, price for pair . . . 715.00
Chalice, white ground, Diamond Point
  pattern 25.00
Cheese Dish, cov, white ground, gold
  enamel dec. 180.00

Box, brass band and clasp, 5½ x 3⅝ x 4¼", $125.00.

Dresser Jar, 5½" d, egg shape, blue
  ground, heavy gold dec **200.00**
Ewer, 13¼" h, white ground, Diamond
  Point pattern. **125.00**
Lamp, table
  21" h, hexagonal glass shade, floral
    painted edge, floraform base with
    bronze finish, sgd "Handel". **1,200.00**
  22½" h, octagonal glass shade, spi-
    derweb frame, tree form base with
    bronze finish, fabric label, sgd
    "Handel". **1,150.00**
Perfume, 3⅛" d, 7¾" h, tapering cylin-
  der, flat flared base, white, ring of
  white opaline around neck and match-
  ing teardrop stopper, gold trim **110.00**
Pitcher, 4¼" h, pink ground, applied
  white handle. **70.00**
Salt, boat shaped, blue dec, white
  enamel garland and scrolling **75.00**
Urn, 13" h, flared rim, blue ground,
  enameled blue flowers, gilt trim, price
  for pair **335.00**
Vase, 15½" h, blue fluted body, slender
  neck, reticulated handles, floral and
  Indian reserves, c1840, price for pair **1,250.00**

ORIENTAL RUGS

History: The history of Oriental rugs or carpets dates back to 3000 B.C.; but it was in the 16th century that they became prevalent. The rugs originated in the regions of Central Asia, Iran (Persia), Caucasus, and Anatolia. Early rugs can be classified into basic categories: Iranian, Caucasian, Turkoman, Turkish, and Chinese. Later India, Pakistan, and Iraq produced rugs in the Oriental style.

The pattern name is derived from the tribe which produced the rug, e.g., Iran is the source for Hamadan, Herez, Sarouk, Tabriz, and others.

When evaluating an Oriental rug, age, design, color, weave, knots per square inch, and condition determine the final value. Silk rugs and prayer rugs bring higher prices.

References: Murray Eiland, *Oriental Rugs: A New Comprehensive Guide*, Little, Brown and Company, 1981; Linda Kline, *Beginner's Guide To Oriental Rugs*, Ross Books, 1980; Ivan C. Neff and Carol V. Maggs, *Dictionary of Oriental Rugs*, Van Nostrand Reinhold, 1979; Joyce C. Ware, *The Official Price Guide to Oriental Rugs*, House of Collectibles, 1992.

Periodicals: *HALI*, PO Box 4312, Philadelphia, PA 19118; *Rug News*, 34 West 37th St., New York, NY 10018; *The Decorative Rug*, PO Box 709, Meredith, NH 03253.

Reproduction Alert: Beware! There are repainted rugs on the market.

Mohtashem Kashan, West Persia, midnight blue and ivory medallion on red field, ivory spandrels, midnight blue border, even wear, reovercast edges, new fringes added, last quarter 19th C, 9' 10" x 7' 6", $9,350.00. Photograph courtesy of Skinner, Inc.

Baktiari, 13' 3" x 9' 5", multicolored stylized floral motif, dark blue ground, red
  band border **5,750.00**
Baluch, Northeast Persia, late 19th/early
  20th C, 5' 5" x 3' 4", red and aubergine palmettes, navy blue ground, red
  border **330.00**
Bidjar, Northwest Persia, late 19th/early
  20th C, 24' 6" x 3', runner, navy blue
  field with overall red, rose, sky blue,
  gold, brown, and blue–green Herati
  design, ivory rosette and blossoming
  vine border, outer guard stripe missing, small areas of wear, slight moth
  damage **1,210.00**
Gendje, South Central Caucacus, last

quarter 19th C, 7′ x 4′ 5″, three red, gold, and blue–green medallions, blue field, ivory border, slight moth damage, small hole, small crease **660.00**

Gorovan, 9′ 9″ x 6′ 7″, stylized blue center medallion, red stylized ground, blue corner pockets, band border . . . **650.00**

Hamadan, Northwest Persia, second quarter 20th C
  8′ 4″ x 6′ 10″, multicolored geometric design, red ground, blue corner pockets and stylized floral band border. **770.00**
  9′ 4″ x 3′ 2″, three diamond medallions surrounded by curved leaves and floral motifs, navy blue, red, red–brown, and green, deep rose field, dark red turtle variant border, good pile, slight moth damage. . . . **450.00**

Heriz, Northwest Persia, early 20th C
  10′ 4″ x 8′ 10″, bold multicolored geometric design, dark blue ground, geometric red band border **650.00**
  10′ 10″ x 7′ 9″, bold multicolored geometric design, brick red ground, blue geometric band border. **3,600.00**
  11′ 4″ x 7′ 6″, multicolored geometric design, brick red ground, ivory corner pockets, band border **1,450.00**
  11′ 4″ x 8′ 6″, abrashed blue–green rosette medallion, terra-cotta red field, ivory spandrels, navy blue border, small area of moth damage. **2,530.00**
  12′ 1″ x 9′ 4″, multicolored geometric center medallion, red ground, ivory corner pockets, blue geometric band border. **2,100.00**

Indian, early 20th C, 17′ 4″ x 11′ 10″, navy blue and coral cartouches inset with dragon and phoenix combat scenes, birds and floral motifs, gold field, coral border with navy blue cartouches, slight moth damage **4,100.00**

Karaja, Northwest Persia
  6′ 10″ x 2′ 7″, early/mid 20th C, three rose, blue, and camel hexagonal medallions, terra-cotta red ground, tan–gold border **495.00**
  11′ 7″ x 7′ 6″, bold multicolored geometric medallions, dark blue ground, wide conforming border . . **990.00**

Kazak, Southwest Caucasus, third quarter 19th C, 6′ 4″ x 4′ 7″, three red, blue, and blue–green squares, red ground, ivory border **440.00**

Keshan, 23′ 4″ x 10′, floral spray design, burgundy ground, one wide and six narrow borders with floral sprays . . . **10,000.00**

Khamseh, Southwest Persia, late 19th C, 6′ 9″ x 4′ 7″, three ivory diamond medallions, midnight blue field, gold border, even wear to center, slight moth damage, minor end fraying. . . . **990.00**

Kirman
  9′ 2″ x 5′ 10″, multicolored floral sprays, ivory ground. **440.00**
  12′ x 8′ 11″, multicolored floral medallion, celadon ground, wide conforming border. **1,100.00**
  13′ x 9′ 11″, red, tan, and blue floral center medallion, blue ground, floral corner pockets, tile pattern border **2,975.00**
  13′ 3″ x 9′, red and blue medallion design, dark blue floral ground, one wide and four narrow borders **16,000.00**
  13′ 3″ x 9′ 6″, pastel green, tan, and blue floral center medallion, ivory ground, floral band border. **1,800.00**
  13′ 3″ x 11′ 10″, central floral medallion, ivory ground, floral corner pockets, wide floral band border . . **2,200.00**
  19′ 5″ x 9′ 10″, multicolored floral sprays, salmon ground, wide floral band border. **8,250.00**
  21′ x 11′ 10″, pastel floral sprays, ivory field, green floral band border **3,200.00**

Kuba, Northeast Caucasus
  Early 20th C, 5′ 5″ x 3′ 7″, column of five red, sky blue, and ivory diamond medallions, slate blue field, four narrow borders, good pile, rewoven corner, small repairs. **2,530.00**
  Last quarter 19th C, 5′ 8″ x 3′ 8″, four ivory, red, and light blue Lesghi stars, midnight blue field, blue border, even wear, moth damage, repaired crease. **440.00**

Kurd, Northwest Persia, early 20th C, 8′ 8″ x 5′ 3″, rows of dark red, gold, dark brown, and blue–green boteh, navy blue field, rust flowerhead border, slight even wear **935.00**

Lilihan, 17′ 8″ x 11′ 9″, multicolored floral motif, midnight blue ground, floral wine border. **4,400.00**

Mahal, West Persia, early 20th C, 12′ 8″ x 2′ 6″ runner, red, blue, ivory, and dark blue–green diamond medallion, olive border, moth damage. **770.00**

Oushak, 14′ 9″ x 12′, pastel green and yellow medallion, pale red ground, yellow corner pockets, sgd band border **1,550.00**

Sarouk, West Persia, early 20th C
  11′ 9″ x 8′ 10″, red, blue, green, and tan floral motif, wine ground, floral band border. **6,600.00**
  11′ 11″ x 8′ 5″, blue, red, and ivory floral design, brick red field, wide band border. **1,500.00**
  13′ 6″ x 10′ 4″, blue, tan–gold, and beige, floral sprays, serrated leaves, and vines, wine field, mid-

night blue palmette border, small
areas of slight wear **3,100.00**
14' x 10', multicolored floral sprays,
wine ground, broad floral band
border. **5,250.00**
Savonnerie, 13' 10" x 9' 11", mauve and
yellow floral design, old ivory ground,
column and garden border **13,000.00**
Senneh, Northwest Persia, last quarter
19th C, 6' 2" x 4' 3", small tan, gold,
and ivory palmettes surrounded by
flowering vines, dark brown field, ivory
spandrels, palmette and rosette bor-
der, faded colors, slight even wear . . **990.00**
Shiraz, 11' x 8' 2", three blue, red, and
ivory geometric medallions, red ani-
mal dec ground, banded border **1,100.00**
Shirvan, East Caucasus, late 19th C, 4'
9" x 3' 10", two red and tan–gold stars,
medium blue ground, tan–gold
border **385.00**
Tabriz
9' 4" x 6' 2", multicolored floral design,
red ground, pale green corner pock-
ets, banded border. **2,200.00**
10' 5" x 7' 1", round central medallion,
ivory ground, intricate repeating
floral trellis pattern, russet border,
ivory corner quadrants, indigo,
salmon, and gold secondary colors **2,310.00**
11' 8" x 9', multicolored floral design,
ivory ground, red band border, moth
damage. **1,950.00**
13' 10" x 10' 9", blue and gold floral
sprays, ivory ground, wide floral
band border. **1,325.00**
Tekke, West Turkestan
5' x 3' 6", early 20th C, twenty–seven
midnight blue, apricot, and ivory
carpet guls, rust ground, similar
border and elems. **550.00**
9' 4" x 6' 7", last quarter 19th C, five
columns of midnight blue and apricot carpet guls, rust ground, similar
border and elems. **660.00**
Turkish, 9' 10" x 7', geometric and stylized bird motif, red ground, ivory corner pockets, minor wear. **550.00**
Turkoman, 10' 3" x 6' 6", multicolored
guls design, brown ground, ivory multicolored geometric band border **4,500.00**

ORIENTALIA

History: Orientalia is a term applied to objects
made in the Orient, which encompasses the Far
East, Asia, China, and Japan. The diversity of cultures produced a variety of objects and styles.

References: Lea Baten, *Japanese Animal Art:
Antique & Contemporary,* Charles Tuttle, 1989;
Carl L. Crossman, *The Decorative Arts of The*

China Trade, Antique Collectors Club, 1991; John
Esten (ed.), *Blue and White China,* Little, Brown,
and Company, 1987; Gloria and Robert Mascarelli,
Warman's Oriental Antiques, Wallace–Homestead,
1992.

Periodical: *The Orientalia Journal,* PO Box 94,
Little Neck, NY 11363.

Museums: Art Institute of Chicago, Chicago, IL;
Asian Art Museum of San Francisco, San Francisco, CA; George Walter Vincent Smith Art Museum, Springfield, MA; Pacific Asia Museum, Pasadena, CA.

Additional Listings: Canton, Celadon, Cloisonné, Fitzhugh, Nanking, Netsukes, Rose Medallion, Japanese Prints, and other categories.

Belt Buckle, rect, ivory and silver, carved
horses on both sides **110.00**
Bowl
4⅞" d, flared with inverted lip, white
glaze, raised on ring foot, Sung Dy-
nasty, 13th C. **350.00**
7" d, ceramic, flared sides, orig stand
and case, Sung Dynasty, 12th C . . **660.00**
8" d, bronze, Han Dynasty style, triple
lobed form, two loop handles, three
round feet, Chinese **275.00**
8⅛" d, flared body, cream, inverted
rim, with grayish–blue green glaze
rolls to ext., splashed streaks int.
slightly tinged red, flaring ring foot,
Sung Dynasty, 13th C. **3,500.00**
Box
2½ x 4½ x 3½", lacquered, three
tiered rect form, huts, flowing
stream, and trees dec, landscape
dec tray int., Japanese, 18th C . . . **3,400.00**
5¼" d, cov, copper and gilt, repousse
lid with bird and floral dec **110.00**
7½" l, lacquered, open fan form with
three tiers, figure, river, and mountainous landscape dec, temple and

**Dish, cov, Chinese enamel on brass,
brass Foo dog finial, 1891–1921, 6" d, 4"
h, $110.00.**

trees dec on sides, landscape dec tray int., Japanese, 18th C **4,600.00**

Cabinet Vase, 6″ h, ivory, silver, and stone, columnar neck, bulbous base, appliqued, floral and bug dec, Chinese **660.00**

Candlestick, 9½″ h, bronze, gull and wave base, wide circular dish form holder, Japanese, 19th C **250.00**

Ceremonial Drum, ivory, oval, carved, cords with stone beads **220.00**

Chest, 44 x 40 x 19″, camphor wood, carved, rect, hinged top, four drawers, paw feet. **700.00**

Cigarette Case, gilt and appliques dec, yellow silk tassel, Japanese Export, c1900. . . . . **175.00**

Compote, 7¼″ d, bronze, circular tray, cloud dec, tripod base, Japanese . . . **55.00**

Dish, 12½″ d, Celadon, fluted lip molded with simple ribs, sea–green glaze, thick ring foot, wood stand, Ming Dynasty, 14th C **750.00**

Document Box, 9¾ x 8¾″, Suzuribako style, stylized birds and autumn flowers dec, dense nashiji int. with flowers dec **375.00**

Figure
6½″ h, Sage carrying staff, ivory, carved, Chinese. **250.00**
9¼″ h, wood, dignitary, wearing court robe, seated on raised dais, Chinese, 18th/19th C **180.00**
13″ h, male and female warriors, ivory, carved, holding lances and swords, flanked by flags, Chinese, price for pair. **2,200.00**
28″ h, gilt bronze, Indian ruler, octagonal stepped plinth, 19th C **210.00**

Floor Screen, decoupage, six panels, each panel 48 x 18″, fan dec, calligraphy and watercolor drawings, Chinese **250.00**

Frame, 10⅞″ h, 8⅜″ w, stone, pale green, teak dec, marked "China" . . . **140.00**

Furniture
Altar Table, 80 x 44 x 15″, rect, teak, carved, flared ends, scroll supports, block legs, Chinese, 19th C **330.00**
Cabinet, 50½ x 27 x 20″, teakwood, rect, two paneled doors, molded base, Chinese **660.00**
Chair
Arm, open
Rosewood, bowed crest rail, flaring arms, plank seat, block supports **275.00**
Teak, carved, dragon dec, paw feet, late 19th C **950.00**
Side, rosewood, carved, slightly arched crest, rect splat with relief

carved mask suspending tassels, plank seat, block legs, Chinese, early 18th C **650.00**

Desk
Pedestal, black lacquer, rect top, three pedestals, three drawers and cupboard doors, gilt floral dec, matching chair, Chinese. . . **550.00**
Writing, teak, carved dragon motif, lift lid, fitted int., three side drawers, lattice carved legs, matching stool, Chinese, 19th C **425.00**

Table
Coffee, 25¾″ d, 17¾″ h, teak and burlwood, carved, round, fitted with four small occasional tables, claw and ball feet, Chinese, late 19th C **575.00**
Library, 46 x 29½ x 32″, ebonized, rect, carved dragon on apron, cabriole legs, scroll feet, Chinese. **550.00**
Sofa, 44 x 27 x 23″, rosewood, rect paneled top, shaped mother–of–pearl inlaid apron, inlaid block legs. **400.00**

Game Board, chess and backgammon, folding, black and gold lacquered dec, Japanese, 19th C **180.00**

Ginger Jar, 9¾″ h, enameled floral dec, dark blue ground, price for pair. **110.00**

Jar, cov, 5¾″ h, bronze, spherical form, raised dragon on body, dragon head finial, three feet, Chinese **110.00**

Kimono Stand, 58″ h, 64″ l, black lacquer, gilt dec, Japnese. **175.00**

Lantern
13″ h, ivory, carved, columned standard holds trellis pierced lantern flanked by young scholar holding scepter, Chinese **225.00**
14½″ h, porcelain, paneled with figures and pierced dec, mounted as lamp, Chinese **220.00**
17″ h, wedding, porcelain, pagoda form, gilt highlights, Ch'ing Dynasty, price for pair **880.00**
20″ h, blue and white porcelain, section added, Hirado, late 19th C, price for pair **1,760.00**

Mirror
20 x 15″, rect, giltwood, carved and pierced frieze of flowers and scrolls, columns, flame finial, drawer, carved feet, Chinese, 19th C **160.00**
63 x 21″, inlaid hardwood, mother of pearl dec, carved bats and medallions, Chinese **500.00**

Netsuke, Japanese
Dog and skeleton, carved, 1¼″ h . . **325.00**
Foo Dog, ivory, carved, reclining . . **200.00**

Man, ivory, carved
  Holding crooked cane, seated, 1½"
    h. **275.00**
  Sitting, howling, wood, carved, ivory
    teeth and eyes, 1½" h **250.00**
    With fish, 1½" h **195.00**
  Priest, sitting, wood, carved, 1¼" h **200.00**
  Two rabbits, ivory, carved, 1½" h . . **165.00**
  Woman with children, ivory, carved,
    1½" h. **280.00**
  Wrestlers, two men, ebony, carved,
    1½" h. **175.00**
Panel, 112 x 67", embroidered, figural
  and geometric design, linen backing,
  Japanese, 19th C **2,700.00**
Pipe, 9" l, silver and bamboo,
  Japanese. **110.00**
Planter and Stand, 9¾" h, impressed oc-
  tagonal shape, peony sprays dec,
  blue and white, Japanese. **275.00**
Robe, embroidered, exotic bird and
  floral dec, gold, black, red, and green,
  Japanese **330.00**
Rose Petal Jar, porcelain, blue and
  white, figural dec, Chinese **220.00**
Sculpture, 11" h, contorted dragon, hold-
  ing crystal ball. **425.00**
Serving Tray, 7¾ x 6½", lacquered, gold
  chrysanthemums dec, massed foliage
  ground, Meiji period. **425.00**
Sewing Box, octagonal, bombe sides,
  lacquered, black and gold, brass bail
  handles, landscape triptych on cov
  with figural border, Japanese, mid
  19th C **260.00**
Sign, 35½" l, wood, polychrome, seven
  humorous masks dec, Japanese. . . . **525.00**
Snuff Bottle
  3" h, agate, carved, Foo dog, bird,
    cricket, and poem dec, Chinese,
    19th C. **3,800.00**
Stand, 32" h, 17" d, hardwood, carved,
  scalloped top, marble insert, open
  shelf, Chinese. **660.00**
Tall Case Clock, 86" h, teak, carved, bird
  and blossom painted circular dial,
  eight stepped fret open shelves with
  mother-of-pearl inlaid door and single drawer, two bronze dragon supports, bracket feet, Chinese, late 19th
  C **1,900.00**
Tapestry, 81 x 54½", silk, embroidered,
  battle scene dec, green floral border,
  gold bullion thread, Japanese, 19th
  C **1,400.00**
Tea Caddy, oblong serpentine shape, fi-
  gural panels, black and gold lacquer,
  pewter liner, Japanese, mid 19th C . . **400.00**
Tobacco Box, rect, bone, carved, ojime
  and pipe holder, Japanese. **275.00**
Urn, cov, 11" h, flattened baluster, ring
  bat handles, foo dog finial, Chinese. . **180.00**

Vase
  5" h, silver, hexagonal, flared wall
    pocket form, pierced floral, bird, and
    scroll dec, Chinese. **330.00**
  7½" h, bronze, ovoid, relief butterfly,
    enameled and gilt highlights, rust
    patina, Japanese **1,400.00**
  11" h, green quartz, flattened baluster,
    floral handles, relief figural dec,
    Chinese **220.00**
  20½" h, bronze, urn form, two floral
    handles, raised bird and branch dec
    on scroll feet, circular plinth, stand,
    Japanese, late 19th C. **110.00**

OVERSHOT GLASS

History: Overshot glass was developed in the
mid-1800s. A gather of molten glass was rolled
over the marver upon which had been placed
crushed glass to produce overshot glass. The
piece then was blown into the desired shape. The
finished effect was a glass that was frosted or iced
in appearance.

Early pieces were mainly made in clear. As the
demand for colored glass increased, color was
added to the base piece and occasionally to the
crushed glass.

Pieces of overshot generally are attributed to the
Boston and Sandwich Glass Co., although many
other companies also made it as it grew in popularity.

Reference: Ellen T. Schroy, *Warman's Glass,*
Wallace-Homestead, 1992.

Museum: Sandwich Glass Museum, Sandwich,
MA.

Basket, 5" d, 6¼" h, amethyst ground
  shading to clear, crimped rim, bulbous

**Compote, clear, flint glass, attributed to
Sandwich, 7¾" d, 5⅞" h, $175.00.**

flaring base, applied clear twist handle 120.00
Cheese Dish, dome cov, 8" d, 7" h, cranberry ground, enameled crane and cattails, applied clear faceted finial . . 425.00
Compote, 10" d, 10¼" h, cranberry ground, wide rounded bowl, scalloped crown gilt trimmed rim, compressed knop on cylindrical pedestal, wide flaring foot, late 19th C 300.00
Epergne, 9½" d, 17" h, single lily, clear ground, applied green snake coiled around lily and extending to pedestal base 200.00
Ice Bucket, 7 x 5½", green ground, clear handle, yellow leaves and flowers at base of handle 165.00
Pitcher
  8¼" h, green ground, amber shell handle, Sandwich, c1875, brown age line near lip 225.00
  9" h, tankard, cranberry ground, applied clear reeded handle, hinged metal lid 175.00
  9⅜" h, bulbous, cylindrical neck, flaring pinched rim, cranberry ground, applied clear handle and wafer foot. 275.00
Vase, 7½" h, amethyst shading to clear, applied petal feet. 50.00

OWENS POTTERY

History: J. B. Owens began making pottery in 1885 near Roseville, Ohio. In 1891 he built a plant in Zanesville and in 1897 began producing art pottery. Not much art pottery was produced by Owens after 1907, when most of its production centered on tiles.

Owens Pottery, employing many of the same artists and designs of its two crosstown rivals, Roseville and Weller, can appear very similar to that of its competitors (i.e. Utopian—brown glaze; Lotus—light glaze; Aqua Verde—green glaze, etc.).

There were a few techniques used exclusively at Owens. These included Red Flame ware (slip decoration under a high red glaze) and Mission (overglaze, slip decorations in mineral colors), depicting Spanish Mission scenes. Other specialities included Opalesce (semigloss designs in lusterd

gold and orange) and Coralene (small beads affixed to the surface of the decorated vases).

References: Paul Evans, *Art Pottery of the United States, 2nd Edition,* Feingold & Lewis Publishing, 1987; Ralph and Terry Kovel, *The Kovels' Collector's Guide to American Art Pottery,* Crown Publishers, 1974.

Vase, Aborigine pattern, 6" h, $250.00.

Bowl, 5½" d, 1¼" h, lotus, five color berry dec, artist sgd 255.00
Creamer, 3½" h, Aqua Verdi, green matte, imp mark 65.00
Jardiniere, 9¼" h, orange and cream swirls, green ground, marked "JB Owens/Art Nouveau/1005" 175.00
Pitcher, 12" h, tankard style, Utopian, gooseberry dec, artist sgd 275.00
Tile, 6" sq, fourteen tiles form rect, Greek Key pattern, pale green ground, ivory design, imp "Owens," c1905, limited color variation, 23¾" w, 29⅝" l overall 660.00
Vase
  5½" h, spring flowers dec, matte glaze, imp torch mark, numbered. . 245.00
  6¾" h, incised profile of woman's head, chocolate brown ground, artist sgd "Henri Deux". 200.00
  8½" h, bulbous, hp floral dec, sgd "J B Owens" 225.00
  11" h, Lotus, morning glories dec, artist sgd "Charles Fouts". 150.00
  12" h, standard glaze, floral dec, Indian profile on back 400.00

PAIRPOINT

History: The Pairpoint Manufacturing Co. was organized in 1880 as a silver-plating firm in New

Bedford, Massachusetts. The company merged with Mount Washington Glass Co. in 1894 and became the Pairpoint Corporation. The new company produced speciality glass items, often accented with metal frames.

Pairpoint Corp. was sold in 1938 and Robert Gunderson became manager. He operated it as the Gunderson Glass Works until his death in 1952. From 1952 until the plant closed in 1956, operations were maintained under the name Gunderson–Pairpoint. Robert Bryden reopened the glass manufacturing business in 1970, moving it back to the New Bedford area.

References: Edward and Sheila Malakoff, *Pairpoint Lamps*, Schiffer Publishing, 1990; Leonard E. Padgett, *Pairpoint Glass*, Wallace–Homestead, 1979, out of print; John A. Shumann III, *The Collector's Encyclopedia of American Art Glass*, Collector Books, 1988, 1991 value update.

Collectors' Club: Pairpoint Cup Plate Collectors, PO Box 52D, East Weymouth, MA 02189.

Museum: Pairpoint Museum, Sagamore, MA.

Table Lamp, reverse painted, Carlisle shade with autumnal lakeside scene, copper finished metal vasiform base, 18″ d shade stamped "Pairpoint Corp.," base imp "Pairpoint D3034," 23½″ h, $3,530.00. Photograph courtesy of James D. Julia, Inc.

Beverage Set, 7¾″ h bulbous pitcher, applied cobalt blue handle, five cobalt blue waisted tumblers, "Pairpoint Glass" labels, price for six piece set . **150.00**

Candlesticks, pr, 10″ h, Venetti, Rosaria and white spirals, bell bottoms **1,500.00**

Creamer and Sugar, Crown Milano coloring, sprays of purple asters, blue, rose, and green leaves, gold ribbons, glass cov on sugar, gold washed metal fittings, sgd "Pairpoint–2052/140". **1,250.00**

Jug, 5½″ h, 8″ w, shiny Crown Milano ground, heavy raised gold netting, two scrolled cartouches of summer flowers, applied elaborate twisted rope handle, crown mark, sgd "Laurel, 1000". **1,200.00**

Lamp

Planter, 14″ h, 16″ d squatty mushroom cap Vienna shade, reverse painted as two landscape reserves of New England village and sailboat scene, rose bouquets on each side, extensive gold embellishments, sgd "The Pairpoint Corp" on rim, mounted on gilt metal four columned four socket base, orig glass lined planter center, imp "Pairpoint C372," metal plating worn. **3,025.00**

Table

20″ h, 17½″ d flared conical Carlisle shade, reverse painted four exotic birds among broad leafy tropical plants and flowers, silver-plated tripart scrolled base, sgd "Pairpoint D3084". **3,850.00**

21″ h, 12″ d mold blown glass shade, reverse painted large red poppy blossom, raised crown top, painted leaves and buds on sides, gold highlights on ext., three arm ring and gilt metal base with Pairpoint marks, shade stamped "The Pairpoint Corp". . **2,860.00**

21″ h, 13″ d puffy bride's bouquet shade, blown out rose blossom dome, reverse painted white rose blossoms, pink shading, yellow centers, green and yellow–green leaves, 10″ ring holder, gilt metal base with molded grape clusters, vines, and tendrils, imp "Pairpoint 3054". **8,250.00**

22″ h, 14″ d puffy bonnet deeply blown out shade, reverse painted white, pink, orange, yellow, and deep crimson red blossoms and buds, yellow, dark and light green leaves, sgd in gold "pat. applied for," 12″ d ring with four poppy blossom supports, pyramidal metal base with conforming molded poppy blossoms, imp "Pairpoint 3049". **15,400.00**

22″ h, 16″ d octagonal scalloped Murano shade, rippled surface, reverse and obverse painted, yellow–maroon orchid blossoms, blue ground, two socket gilt metal base with blue painted floral bor-

der, inscribed company marks on
shade and base **2,530.00**
Vase, 12″ h, 8″ w, Ambero, frosted ext.,
int. dec of bunches of green and purple grapes and leaves, brilliant yel-
low–green background, sgd **1,750.00**

PAPER EPHEMERA

History: Maurice Rickards, author of *Collecting
Paper Ephemera,* suggests that ephemera are the
"minor transient documents of everyday life," material destined for the wastebasket but never quite
making it. This definition is more fitting than traditional dictionary definitions that stress length of
time, e.g., "lasting a very short time." A driver's
license, which is used for a year or longer, is as
much a piece of ephemera as is a ticket to a sporting event or music concert. The transient nature of
the object is the key.

Collecting ephemera has a long and distinguished history. Among the English pioneers were
John Seldon (1584–1654), Samuel Pepys (1633–
1703), and John Bagford (1650–1716). Large
American collections can be found at historical societies and libraries across the country as well as
museums such as the Wadsworth Antheneum,
Hartford, CT, and the Museum of the City of New
York.

When used by collectors, "ephemera" usually
means paper objects, e.g., billheads and letterheads, bookplates, documents, labels, stocks and
bonds, tickets, valentines, etc. However, more and
more ephemera collectors are recognizing the transient nature of some three-dimensional material,
e.g., advertising tins and pinback buttons. Today's
specialized paper shows include dealers selling
both two- and three-dimensional material.

References: Warren R. Anderson, *Owning
Western History,* Mountain Press Publishing, 1993;
Anne F. Clapp, *Curatorial Care of Works of Art on
Paper,* Nick Lyons Books, 1987; Joseph Raymond
LeFontaine, *Turning Paper To Gold,* Betterway
Publications, 1988; John Lewis, *Printed Ephemera,*
Antique Collectors' Club, 1990; Norman E. Mar-
tinus and Harry L. Rinker, *Warman's Paper,* Wal-
lace–Homestead, 1994; Maurice Rickards, *Col-
lecting Paper Ephemera,* Abbeville Press, 1988;
Demaris C. Smith, *Preserving Your Paper Collec-
tibles,* Betterway Publications, 1989; Gene Utz,
*Collecting Paper: A Collector's Identification &
Value Guide,* Books Americana, 1993.

Periodicals: *Paper & Advertising Collector,* PO
Box 500, Mount Joy, PA 17552; *Paper Collectors'
Marketplace,* PO Box 128, Scandinavia, WI 54977-
0128; *Paper Pile Quarterly,* PO Box 337, San Anselmo, CA 94979-0337.

Collectors' Clubs: Ephemera Society, 12 Fitz-
roy Sq., London W1P 5HQ England; The Ephemera Society of America, Inc., PO Box 37, Schoharie, NY 12157; The Ephemera Society of

Canada, 36 Macauley Dr., Thornhill, Ontario L3T
5S5 Canada.

BILLHEADS

Reference: Leslie Cabarga, *Letterheads: One
Hundred Years of Design,* Chronicle Books, 1992.

B Crane & Son, Mason's Building Sup-
plies, Paterson, NJ, May 20, 1875,
black design **30.00**
Eagle Planing Mill, M Simon, Sash,
Doors, Blinds, Allegheny, PA, July
1885 . . . . **25.00**
E & L P Norton, Wholesale Prices of
Stone–Ware, Bennington, VT, Octo-
ber 14, 1870, design with blue
background. **75.00**
Francis A Fales, meat dealer, Troy, NY,
April 22, 1875, design with red
background. **20.00**
Green Sulphur Spring Cure, Green
Spring, OH, June 24, 1876, black illus
and printing. **25.00**
Hagan's Dyspepsia Bitters, John Hagan
& Co, Atlantic City, NJ, c1905, black
illus and printing, unused **20.00**
Harvey & Holden, Oyster, Fish, and
Game Depot, Washington, DC, De-
cember 21, 1877. . . . . **30.00**
James Lucas & Son, Job, Card and La-
bel Printers, March 22, 1872, full color
design with two vignettes **35.00**
Louisville Slugger Baseball Bats, J F Hil-
lerich & Son, Louisville, KY, February
9, 1909. . . . . **35.00**
Silbey & Holmwood, National Candy Co,
Buffalo, NY, October 6, 1903, full illus,
emb, and gold highlights **35.00**
William King, Manufacturer and Dealer
in Burning and Lubricating Oils, 117
Arch Street, Philadelphia, PA, De-
cember 19, 1873. . . . . **25.00**

BLOTTERS

American Family Soap, c1910, Uncle
Sam illus **15.00**

**Check, Mechanics Bank, Philadelphia,
steel engraved, black and white, 1814,
6 x 2½″, $25.00.**

Atlantic Gasoline, c1940, full color ... **15.00**

A W Anthoine, Doctor of Optics, Lewiston, ME, c1900, black printing and illus **30.00**

Buedingen Box & Lithograph Co, Rochester, NY, c1910, full color **25.00**

Defiance Home Saving & Loan Association, 1921, diecut, passbook, black, brown, and white **30.00**

F R Keens Co, Soda Fountain Foods, New Haven, CT, 1931, red, yellow and black illus **25.00**

Geo W Engle, Hazelton, PA, Dealer in Flour and Feed, Grain & Hay, Mill Agent For the Famous Ceresota Flour, c1895, full color image **25.00**

Gold Seal Champagne, Urbana Wine Co, NY, c1890, full color with gold ... **20.00**

Goodrich Zipps Shoes, G T Foltz Dept Store, Wyrheville, VA, c1935, orange, full color illus **25.00**

Gulf Refining Co, Supreme Motor Oil, c1925, full color scene **20.00**

H Gamse & Bros, Food Products Labels of Quality, full color, April, 1923 calendar **20.00**

J I Case Threshing Machine Co, Racine, WI, c1920, full color illus **25.00**

Nash Advanced 6 Sedan, Theodore J Suess, 41 Central Ave, Lancaster, NY, c1928, white, green and black illus and printing **20.00**

National Surety Co, NY, c1905, full color illus, eagle and office scene **35.00**

Red Gem Duplex Pen and Pencil Set, Laughlin Mfg Co, 234 State Street, Washington Boulevard Building, Detroit, MI, c1935, green, red, yellow, and black illus and printing **30.00**

Reo Automobile, Russell P Taber, Inc, 128 Allyn St, Hartford, CT, c1928, white, black printing and illus **20.00**

Sunoco Motor Fuel, Sun Oil Co, c1935, full color scene, man pumping gas and large Sunoco sign illus **20.00**

The Dangel Company, Lithographers, Printers, Binders, Boston, MA, c1920, green currency design **15.00**

William H Geer Co, Hudson St, NY, c1900, representative for canned goods, full color illus gold highlights .. **40.00**

BOOKLET

Buster Brown's Experiences with Pond's Extract, copyright 1904, 24 pgs, full color front cov of Buster Brown and Tige **60.00**

Daggett & Ramsdell, Perfect Cold Cream, copyright 1909, 16 pgs, full color cov of pretty woman **45.00**

Drake's Plantation Bitters, P H Drake &

Co, NY, 1871, full color cov, black and white illus **50.00**

Dr Fenner's Are Used All Over the World, People's Remedies, 1888, 26 pgs, full color cov of Statue of Liberty and ships in lake scene **35.00**

Henry's Cookbook and Household Companion, NY, 1883, 32 pgs, full color front and back cov **35.00**

Huylers Chocolate & Cocoa, copyright 1904, full color cov **20.00**

Invalids Guide to Health, Circulated for the Benefit of Suffering Humanity, Dr Kilmer's Standard Herbal Remedies, 1894, 12 pgs. **45.00**

Jell-O, Genesee Pure Food Co, Leroy, NY, copyright 1920, 14 pgs, full color cov **20.00**

Kickapoo Indian Dream Book, c1888, full color cov, testimonials, product information, and dream interpretations **50.00**

Ma-Le-Na Stomach & Liver Pills, Malena Co, Warriorsmark, PA, c1895, 12 pgs, full color cov **20.00**

No-To-Bac, Don't Tobacco Spit and Smoke Your Life Away, c1895, 32 pgs, full color cov **25.00**

Ritmeier's California Wine Bitters, Milwaukee, WI, 1891, 32 pgs, German text **30.00**

Robinson's Patent Barley For Making Infants Food & Barley Water, c1895, 8 pgs, full color illus on cov of Thumbelina and baby **20.00**

Shiloh's Medicines, Le Roy, NY, 1890, "I've Got It Mamma!" full color girl and dog on front cov **35.00**

Sulphur Bitters, Ordway & Co, Boston, MA, c1883, full color illus on front and back cov **50.00**

The Doctor's Unnecessary Visit, Tutt's Medicines, 1885, full color front cov of doctor, woman, and children. **35.00**

The Popular Songster, Rohrer's Expectoral Wild Cherry Tonic, Lancaster, PA, 1868, 32 pgs **45.00**

The Scientific American Hand Book, Munn & Co, NY, c1875, 48 pgs **20.00**

BUSINESS CARDS

References: Kit Barry, *The Advertising Trade Card, Book 1,* privately printed, 1981; Robert Jay, *The Trade Card in Nineteenth–Century America,* University of Missouri Press, 1987; Avery Pitzak, *Business Cards,* privately printed, 1989; Avery Pitzak, *Business Cards,* privately printed, 1992 (Editor's note: Although this book has the same title as Pitzak's previous book, it is entirely different); Avery N. Pitzak, *Make Your Business Card Incredibly Effective,* privately printed, 1990.

Collectors' Clubs: American Business Card

Club, PO Box 460297, Aurora, CO 80046; Business Card Collectors International, PO Box 466, Hollywood, FL 33022.

A B Davis & Co, Mortising Machines, 15th & Willow Sts, Philadelphia, PA, c1860, black illus and printing.	50.00
American Hotel, E Foster, Proprietor, State House Square, Hartford, CT, c1870.	50.00
Big Policeman Remedies, Sold by Grocers Everywhere, policeman image, blue on white	20.00
C M Moseman & Bro, 114 Chambers St, NY, c1890, full color horse vignette.	25.00
Dr W F Knowles, Dentist, Middletown, CT, c1865, black and white	25.00
Eugene Lynch Importer of Foreign Wines, Brandies and Holland Gin, Boston, MA, c1885, black, gray, and white	40.00
H F Fox, pastry, Mutton Pies, and Saratoga Chips, NY, c1885, black fox with man's head illus and printing	35.00
Island House, Charles Towns, Proprietor, Bellows Falls, VT, late 1870s	40.00
J L Ray's Livery Stable, Brattleboro, VT, c1870, emb cameo design, blue background.	75.00
John H Mann & Co, Wholesale and Retail Dealers in Teas, Coffees, Sugars, Molasses & Spices, Syracuse, NY, c1870, emb design with red background.	100.00
M A Worcester, Proprietor and Manufacturer of Worcester's World–Renowned Dry Hop Yeast, c1885, red and black printing, beige background	25.00
R Malcom, Saddles, Harness & Trunks, Toronto, Canada, c1870, emb design with red background	75.00
Riggs & Brother, Manufacturers of Chronometers and Nautical Instruments, 244 South Front St, Philadelphia, c1870, black printing	40.00
Samuel Hatz, Dealer in Tobacco, Lancaster, PA, c1870, green, white emb figured design.	100.00
The Combination Fountain Co, Col Conrad Striewing, The Soda Fountain Man, c1895, photo image, black lettering	15.00
The Island Tool Store, Ship Builders, 171 Lewis St, New York City, c1875, green, black printing	40.00

CALENDARS

1902, American Singers, bird illus, booklet type.	15.00
1904, 3 pcs, wall, Holly Berries, Ellen Clapsaddle, 9 x 14½".	65.00

1905, New York Coffee Co	5.00
1910, Benzie County Bank, 13½ x 15"	45.00
1915, American Beauty, Christmas stickers, stamps, and name tags, orig package, Successful Farming.	50.00
1926, Winchester, man shooting bear	250.00
1930, De Laval Separator Co, "Story of John & Mary," sgd Norman Price, orig mailing envelope.	150.00
1935, Central's Gold Standard Footwear	15.00
1946, Hoekstra Truck Equipment School Bus Body, Twelvetrees cov.	10.00
1948, Squirt, pinup girls	38.00

LABELS

References: Jerry Chicone, Jr., *Florida's Classic Crates*, privately printed, 1985; Joe Davidson, *Fruit Crate Art*, Wellfleet Press, 1990; Gordon T. McClelland and Jay T. Last, *Fruit Box Labels, A Collector's Guide*, Hillcrest Press, 1983; John Salkin and Lauri Gordon, *Orange Crate Art: The Story of Labels That Launched A Golden Era*, Warner Books, 1978.

Collectors' Clubs: Society of Antique Label Collectors, PO Box 24811, Tampa, FL 33623; The Citrus Label Society, 131 Miramonte Dr, Fullerton, CA 92365.

Apple	
Butterfly, foil, butterfly illus	8.00
Duckwall, wood duck by stone wall	10.00
Gosling, fluffy yellow gosling, red background.	15.00
Cigar	
La Comporita, woman holding pink rose	3.00
Round Up, cowboy smoking by campfire	5.00
Orange	
Annie Laurie, bonnie Scottish lassie, plaid background	3.00
Athlete, three runners reaching finish line.	5.00
Golden Trout, trout leaping out of water	30.00
Kings Park, Kings Park scene	8.00
Polo, polo player and pony	5.00
Reindeer, reindeer standing by lake	8.00
Strength, gray elephant with tusks	25.00
Pear	
Grand Coulee, dam scene	5.00
Violet, purple violets	6.00

LETTERHEADS

References: Leslie Carbarga, *Letterheads: One Hundred Years of Great Designs, 1850–1950*, Chronicle Books, 1992.

Letterhead, A. A. Griffing Iron Company, black and white, order acknowledgment, June 5, 1907, 8⅜ x 10⅞", $8.00.

Adam Forepaugh and Sells Brothers Circus, 1910, full color illus, gold background.	100.00
Barnum & Bailey Circus, Bridgeport, CT, 1911, full color with gold.	110.00
C D Boss & Son, Boss Crackers, New London, CT, August 11, 1896, typed letter	50.00
Chicago Engraving Company, Chicago, IL, full color, typed letter to Debois Brewing Co.	25.00
Columbian Exposition, Wisconsin State Building, Jackson Park, Chicago, 1893, unused	30.00
Columbian Pyrotechnical Co, Chicago, Fireworks, October 18, 1890, full color illus	75.00
Cooper Institute & Elevated Railroad, Third Avenue, NY, city with elevated railroad scene.	75.00
Fred W Jones, Shell, Marble & Lime Stone Quarries, Hudson, NY, April 5, 1899, handwritten letter	25.00
Geo T Chambers & Co, Hardware, Stoves and Tinware, Livingston, MT, August 21, 1889, black scene of store int.	25.00
Grass Manufacturing Co, Philadelphia, PA, April 21, 1908, black illus, mimeo copy text	20.00
Green & Daniels Mft Co, Thread & Yarn Manufactory, Pawtucket, RI, April 19, 1881, black illus of mill works, handwritten letter	35.00
Jillson & Palmer Patent Cotton Opener, Willimantic, CT, 1880s, unused.	25.00

Kickapoo Indian Medicine Co, New Haven, CT, November 9, 1896, black and white, typed letter	25.00
Pan American Exposition, Buffalo, NY, 1901, unused	12.00
Patterson Motor Car, Flint, MI, April 1, 1912, black illus and lettering, typed letter	25.00
P T Barnum & Co and The Great London Circus, New York, NY, and Bridgeport, CT, c1885, gold and black printing.	100.00
Red Raven Corporation, April 10, 1913, color illus, gold border	40.00
Ringling Bros Circus, c1911, full color with gold illus	100.00
The Century Post Co, Free Rural Delivery Mail Boxes, Tecumseh, MI, October 27, 1903, black and white, typed letter	20.00
The Park & Pollard Co, Ornamental Fowl, 46 Canal Street, Boston, MA, November 17, 1913, brown town illus	35.00
View of Madison, WI, May 31, 1857, handwritten in ink	45.00
Woolsey Garage Co, Inc, Central Valley, NY, Nash automobile, February 28, 1928, typed letter	35.00

POST CARDS

References: Diane Allmen, *The Official Price Guide to Postcards,* House of Collectibles, 1990; Janet Banneck, *The Antique Postcards of Rose O'Neill,* Greater Chicago Publications, 1992; Deborah Lengkeek (ed.), *The Postcard Collector Annual: Commemorating 100 Years Of The Postcard, Third Edition,* Jones Publishing, 1993; Joseph Lee Mashburn, *The Postcard Price Guide: A Comprehensive Listing,* World Comm, 1992; Joseph Lee Mashburn, *The Super Rare Postcards of Harrison Fisher with Price Guide,* World Comm, 1992; Frederic and Mary Megson, *American Advertising Postcards–Set and Series: 1890–1920,* published by authors, 1985; Frederic and Mary Megson, *American Exposition Postcards, 1870–1920: A Catalog and Price Guide,* The Postcard Lovers, 1992; Ron Menchine, *A Picture Postcard History of Baseball,* Almar Press, 1992; Cynthia Rubin and Morgan Williams, *Larger Than Life; The American Tall–Tall Postcard 1905–1915,* Abbeville Press, 1990; Dorothy B. Ryan, *Picture Postcards In The United States, 1893–1918,* Clarkson N. Potter, 1982, paperback edition; Jack H. Smith, *Postcard Companion: The Collector's Reference,* Wallace–Homestead, 1989; Robert Ward, *Investment Guide To North American Real Photo Postcards,* Antique Paper Guide, 1991; Jane Wood, *The Collector's Guide To Post Cards,* L–W Promotions, 1984, 1993 value update.

Periodicals: *Barr's Postcard News,* 70 S. 6th Street, Lansins, IA 52151; *Postcard Classics,* PO

Box 8, Norwood, PA 19074; *Postcard Collector,* Joe Jones Publishing, 121 N. Main St., PO Box 337, Iola, WI 54945.

Special Note: An up–to–date listing of books about and featuring post cards can be obtained from Gotham Book Mart & Gallery, Inc., 41 West 47th Street, New York, NY 10036.

Collectors' Clubs: *Barr's Postcard News* and the *Postcard Collector* publish lists of over fifty regional clubs in the United States and Canada.

Advertising

Argand Base Burning Stove, Perry & Co, Albany, NY, woman and little girl by parlor stove, July 18, 1874, text on back.	75.00
Banner Baking Co, delivery wagon	20.00
Kakenc Congress Hydraulic, barber chair, hair dresser supplies, 1909 .	8.00
Majestic Stoves	15.00
Menz Ease Elk Shoes	8.00
Pope Toledo Motor Car Building, Toledo, OH.	8.00
Sharples Tubular Cream Separator	10.00
Swift Pride Soap, rabbit	6.00
White House Teas, children having tea party	25.00

Photograph, black and white

Boy and girls playing baseball	20.00
Boy on wire wheel pedal car	12.00
Circus, horse trainer with six horses	12.00
Fisherman with trout	15.00
Loon Lake Ice Co, horse pulled saws	30.00

Political

Admiral George Dewey, USN, The Greatest Naval Hero of the War, portrait surrounded by purple wreath.	20.00
American, Undivided in the Cause of Freedom, Wilson, Lincoln, and Washington, 1917	10.00
Where Women Vote, There is No Rest	8.00
William McKinley, Late President of the US, Wrench series, No. 650	25.00

SHEET MUSIC

References: Debbie Dillion, *Collectors Guide To Sheet Music,* L–W Promotions, 1988, 1993 value update; Anna Marie Guihenn and Marie Reine A. Pafik, *The Sheet Music Reference and Price Guide,* Collector Books, 1992.

Periodicals: *New York Sheet Music Society Newsletter,* PO Box 1214, Great Neck, NY 11023; *Remember That Song,* 5623 N. 64th Ave., Glendale, AZ 85301; *Song Sheet,* 1597 Fair Park Ave., Los Angeles, CA 90041; *Sonneck Society Bulletin,* PO Box 476, Canton, MA 02021.

Collectors' Clubs: National Sheet Music Society, 1597 Fair Park Ave., Los Angeles, CA 90041; New York Sheet Music Society, PO Box 1214,

Great Neck, NY 11023; The Sheet Music Exchange, PO Box 69, Quicksburg, VA 28847.

After The War Is Over, 1917	5.00
Babes in Toyland	10.00
Father Was Crazy To Aviate, 1911	18.00
Good Ship Lollipop, Shirley Temple	12.00
Louisiana Purchase Exposition March	8.00
Son Of The South, Disney, 1946	10.00
When You Wish Upon A Star, Pinocchio	15.00
You Oughta Be In Pictures, 1934	4.00

STOCK AND BOND CERTIFICATES

Reference: Bill Yachtman, *The Stock & Bond Collectors Price Guide,* published by author, 1985.

Periodicals: *Bank Note Reporter,* 700 East State Street, Iola, WI 54990; *The Stock Press Newsletter,* 2572 Central Ave., Baldwin, NY 11510.

Collectors' Club: Bond and Share Society, 26 Broadway, New York, NY 10004.

Bond

Arlington Gas Co, NJ, 1880, $1,000, state seal vignette	20.00
Central New York & Western RR, 1892, $1,000, green, engraved, train vignette	85.00
Oakland Traction Co, 1910s, orange, engraved, two vignettes	25.00
Southern Bell Telephone & Telegraph, 1947, $1,000.	15.00
Wisconsin Interurban System, 1917, green, orange, or brown, state seal vignette, issued	45.00

Stock

American Antimony Company, 1883, eagle, Indian, and train vignette and young girl vignette	75.00
Gambrinus Brewing Co, OH, 1909–13, king vignette, issued.	25.00
Pacific Railroad of Missouri, 1875, green, train and mountains vignette, issued	75.00
Submarine Signal Co, 1940, green, ship vignette, issued.	15.00
Thomas B Jeffrey Co, CA, c1910, eagle vignette, issued and canceled .	125.00
Vallejo City Water Co, 1868, city area vignette.	15.00

TICKETS

Columbian Exposition, 1893, general admission, 5¢, 2 x 1″.	27.50
Jack Dempsey vs Tom Gibbons World's Heavyweight Championship fight, July 4, 1923, three part ticket, 7 x 2¾″.	50.00
New York Saengerrunde, Masquerade Ball, February 1, 1886, full color .	35.00

13th Regiment Drum and Bugle Corps, concert and reception, January 23, 1883, red and light purple printing. . . **25.00**

PAPERWEIGHTS

History: Although paperweights had their origin in ancient Egypt, it was in the mid–19th century that this art form reached its zenith. The classic period for paperweights was 1845–55 in France, where the Clichy, Baccarat, and Saint Louis factories produced the finest examples of this art. Other weights made in England, Italy, and Bohemia during this period rarely matched the quality of the French weights.

In the early 1850s, the New England Glass Co. in Cambridge, Massachusetts, and the Boston and Sandwich Glass Co. in Sandwich, Massachusetts, became the first American factories to make paperweights.

Popularity peaked during the classic period and faded toward the end of the 19th century. Paperweights were rediscovered nearly a century later in the mid–1900s. Contemporary weights still are made by Baccarat, Saint Louis, Perthshire, and many studio craftsmen in the United States and Europe.

References: Paul Hollister, Jr., *The Encyclopedia of Glass Paperweights,* Paperweight Press, 1969; Sibylle Jargstorf, *Paperweights,* Schiffer Publishing, 1991; Leo Kaplan, *Paperweights,* published by author, 1985; George N. Kulles, *Identifying Antique Paperweights–Lampwork,* Paperweight Press, 1987; James Mackay, *Glass Paperweights,* Facts on File, 1973; Edith Mannoni, *Classic French Paperweights,* Paperweight Press, 1984; Bonnie Pruitt, *St Clair Glass Collectors Guide,* published by author, 1992; Lawrence H. Selman, *All About Paperweights,* Paperweight Press, 1992; L. H. Selman, *Collector's Paperweights: Price Guide and Catalogue,* Paperweight Press, 1986.

Periodical: *Paperweight News,* 761 Chestnut Street, Santa Cruz, CA 95060.

Collectors' Clubs: Caithness Collectors Club, 141 Lanza Ave., Building 12, Garfield, NJ 07026; International Paperweight Society, 761 Chestnut St., Santa Cruz, CA 95060; Paperweight Collectors Assoc. Inc., PO Box 1059, Easthampton, MA 01027; Paperweight Collectors Assoc of Texas, 1631 Aguarena Springs Dr., #408, San Marcos, TX 78666.

Museums: Bergstrom–Mahler Museum, Neenah, WI; Corning Museum of Glass, Corning, NY; Degenhart Paperweight & Glass Museum, Inc., Cambridge, OH; Museum of American Glass at Wheaton Village, Millville, NJ.

Additional Listings: See *Warman's Americana & Collectibles* for examples of advertising paperweights.

Clichy, floral bouquet, three clematis type flowers in pink, purple, and white with complex cane centers, tied with blue ribbon, 1845–60, $11,000.00. Photograph courtesy of L. H. Selman Ltd.

ANTIQUE

Baccarat, 3¹⁄₁₆″ d, double overlay, six circlets of coral red, cobalt blue, white, and leaf green arrow canes and six–pointed stars, central circlet of yellow, blue, green, and white canes with florets and arrow canes, blue over white double overlay with six and one faceting **6,600.00**

Bohemian, 3⅛″ d, patterned millefiori, blue, white, green, and red stardust canes, clear ground. **330.00**

Clichy, swirled, 2⅝″ d, alternating purple and white pinwheels emanating from white, green, and pink pastry mold cane, minor bubbles **2,090.00**

Degenhart, John, 3³⁄₁₆ x 2¼ x 2¼″, window, red crystal cube with yellow and orange upright lily set in center, one top window, four side windows, bubble in center of flower's stamens. . . . **1,210.00**

Gillinder, 3¹⁄₁₆″ d, orange turtle with moving appendages in hollow center, pale orange ground, molded dome. **413.00**

Millville, 3⅛″ d, 3⅜″ h, umbrella pedestal, red, white, green, blue, and yellow int. umbrella design, bubble in sphere center directly above umbrella **770.00**

Nailsea, 6⁵⁄₁₆″ h, bottle, bullet shaped green glass dome with teardrop shaped bubbles, minor chip on top . . **220.00**

New England Glass Company, 2¾″ d, crown, red, white, blue, and green twists interspersed with white latticinio emanating from a central pink, white, and green complex floret/cog cane, minor bubbles in glass **2,200.00**

North Bohemian, 2¹³⁄₁₆″ d, 4⅛″ h, memorial, child's photograph on colored glass ground, allover geometric faceting **187.00**

Pinchbeck, 3³⁄₁₆″ d, pastoral dancing scene, man and woman dancing before a group of onlookers, two minor chips in side **523.00**

Ruby Flash Overlay, 3½″ d, circular top facet, four side windows, elaborate cutting **523.00**

Saint Louis, 3¹⁄₁₆″ d, close concentric millefiori, central silhouette with man and woman dancing, chartreuse, cadmium green, white, opaque pink, mauve, salmon, peach, powder blue, and ruby florets, cross canes, cogs, and bull's–eye canes **5,500.00**

Sandwich Glass Company, 3″ d, double poinsettia, red flower with double tier of petals, green and white Lutz rose, green stem and leaves, bubbles between petals **1,100.00**

Val St Lambert, 3½″ d, patterned millefiori, four red, white, blue, pistachio, and turquoise complex canes circlets spaced around central pink, turquoise, and cadmium green canes circlet, canes set on strips of lace encircled by spiraling red and blue torsade, minor blocking crease **825.00**

Whitefriars, 3⅝″ d, close concentric millefiori, pink, blue, purple, green, white, and yellow cog canes, 1848 date cane, minor bubble in dome **880.00**

COMMEMORATIVE

Astronauts, 3⅞″ d, sulphide, four astronauts cameo, translucent turquoise ground, eight and one faceting with fluted sides, limited edition of 1,000, 1971, D'Albret. **143.00**

Eleanor Roosevelt, 3″ d, double overlay sulphide, amethyst over white double overlay with cameo inside, five and one faceting, fancy cutting on bottom of sides and base, ftd **275.00**

Mahatma Gandhi, 2⅞″ d, sulphide, cameo on star cut ground, circular top facet with fluted sides **220.00**

Queen Elizabeth II, 2¹¹⁄₁₆″ d, coronation, sulphide, cameo on red and white jasper ground, five and one faceting, sgd and dated, 1953 . . . . **468.00**

Statue of Liberty, 3³⁄₁₆″ d, gold inclusion of statue's head encircled by pink and white stars, sky blue ground, six and one faceting, date/signature cane, 1986, Saint Louis **413.00**

MODERN

Ayotte, Rick, 2³⁄₁₆″ d, yellow finch, with yellow breast and head, black and white wings, perched on branch, faceted, sgd and dated, limited edition of 25, 1979. **550.00**

Baccarat, 3″ d, yellow carpet, twelve zodiac silhouette canes, tiny yellow florets ground, date/signature cane, limited edition of 300, 1972. . . . . **303.00**

DiNardo, Leonard, 3⁹⁄₁₆″ d, Hopi Indian, burgundy over white double overlay, traditional Indian pattern cutting, sgd and dated, 1984 . . . . **330.00**

Kaziun, Charles, 2¹⁄₁₆″ d, concentric millefiori, heart, turtle silhouette, shamrocks, six pointed stars, and floret canes encircled by purple and white torsade, turquoise ground flecked with goldstone, K signature cane. **990.00**

Manson, William, 3¹⁄₁₆″ d, compound triple butterfly, three pink, white, powder blue, green and gold aventurine, and yellow millefiori butterflies, approaching pink double clematis on bed of green leaves, encircled by garland of pink and white complex canes, date/signature cane, 1981 . . . . **330.00**

Perthshire, 3″ d, crown, central complex cane with projecting red and blue twisted ribbons alternating with latticinio ribbons, date/signature cane, limited edition of 268, 1969. . . . . **770.00**

Saint Louis, 3⅝″ l, 2⅛″ w, 2⁵⁄₁₆″ h, basket of fruit, six pears, three plums, and three red cherries, bed of green leaves, swirling latticinio basket, handle with encased lace twist, limited edition of 250, date/signature cane, 1985 . . . . **1,430.00**

Stankard, Paul, 3″ d, bouquet, yellow meadowreath, blue forget–me–nots, red St Anthony's fire, white bellflowers, and white chokeberry blossoms and buds, 1977. . . . . **2,200.00**

Tarsitano, Delmo, 3¼″ d, wasp with translucent yellow wings and striped brown and yellow abdomen, beige and amber millefiori field made to resemble wasp's nest, six and one faceting, DT signature cane **1,320.00**

Whitefriars, 3¹⁄₁₆″ d, five rows of green, yellow, aqua, and red complex canes around central quail portrait, five and one faceting, date/signature cane, 1978 . . . . **495.00**

Whittemore, Francis, 2⅜″ d, two green and brown acorns on branch with three brown and yellow oak leaves, translucent cobalt blue ground, circu-

lar top facet, five oval punties on
sides **275.00**
Ysart, Paul, 2¾″ d, pink fish with trans-
lucent red fins, sandy ground encir-
cled by ring of spaced bubbles **440.00**

PAPIER-MÂCHÉ

History: Papier–mâché is made from a mixture
of wood pulp, glue, resin, and fine sand which is
subject to great pressure and then dried. The finished product is tough, durable, and heat resistant.
Various finishing treatments are used, such as
enameling, japanning, lacquering, mother–of–pearl
inlaying, and painting.

During the Victorian era papier–mâché articles
such as boxes, trays, and tables were in high fashion. Papier–mâché also found use in the production
of banks, candy containers, masks, toys, and other
children's articles.

**Bank, black lacquered, red and gold
Oriental motif, 4¾ x 3 x 2″, $75.00.**

Candy Container
5½″ h, turkey, polychrome paint . . **40.00**
10″ h, angel, fur, wax face, German **575.00**
Figure
7″ l, grasshopper, glass eyes, poly-
chrome paint **250.00**
8″ h, cat, seated, glass eyes **25.00**
Hat Mannequin, 14½″ h, French, worn
orig polychrome paint, minor damage,
bottom marked "Mme Roland," com-
plete with old blue bonnet **850.00**
Mask, 24″ h, donkey head, brown and
white, upright ears, shoulder cutouts,
polychrome paint. **100.00**
Nodder, 9¾″ h, Easter Rabbit, oval cardboard base, orig polychrome paint . . **55.00**
Pip Squeak
4⅞″ h, rooster, orig polychrome paint,

bellows with loose leather, minor
edge damage, faint squeak. **45.00**
5″ h, bird, felt, crepe paper, and
painted dec, marked "Germany" . . **75.00**
Plate, 12″ d, painted cat, marked "Patented August 8, 1880". **35.00**
Pole Screen, 55″ h, Victorian portrait
panel, gilt stenciled pole, 19th C **660.00**
Roly Poly, 4⅛″ h, clown, orig white and
blue polychrome paint, green ribbon
around neck **60.00**
Sewing Cabinet, 10″ h, Victorian, lac-
quered, painted roundels of dogs
among gilt and mother of pearl designs, lift top, fitted compartment,
three drawers, minor losses **1,210.00**
Snuff Box
3″ d, circular, presentation of dowry
scene on top, case and bottom dec,
tortoiseshell lining, 18th C **850.00**
3⅝″ d, naval battle scene on cov,
chipped. **35.00**
Toy, pull, 4″ l, duck, wood base, card-
board wheels, polychrome paint **115.00**
Tray
17 x 15 x 12″, lacquered, gilt figures
flying kites, pavilion landscape,
black ground, later bamboo turned
stand, Chinese. **350.00**
22¼ x 28½″, Chippendale scalloped
rim, orig black lacquer, nacre inlay,
polychrome and gilt floral dec, wear,
old touch up, edge repair **450.00**

PARIAN WARE

History: Parian ware is a creamy white, translucent, marblelike porcelain. It originated in England in 1842 and was first known as "Statuary
Porcelain." Minton and Copeland have been credited with its development. Wedgwood also made it.
In America, parian ware was manufactured by
Christopher Fenton in Bennington, Vermont.

At first parian ware was used only for figures and
figural groups. By the 1850s it became so popular
that a vast range of wares were manufactured.

References: Kathy Hughes, *A Collector's Guide
to Nineteenth–Century Jugs,* Routledge & Kegan
Paul, 1985; Kathy Hughes, *A Collector's Guide to
Nineteenth–Century Jugs, Volume II,* Taylor Publishing, 1991.

Bust
8″ h, little girl, wistful expression, scarf
tied around head, inscribed "Win-
ter," and "J & T B". **95.00**
10″ h, Ulysses S Grant, civilian dress,
inscribed on back "Broome, Sculp.
1876," and "Ott and Brewer Manufacturers, Trenton, New Jersey,"
hairlines **2,640.00**

12¾″ h, Shakespeare, raised circular base, Robinson and Leadbeater mark, c1875, minor chip to hair . . . **715.00**

13¼″ h, Shakespeare, imp "R Monti SC, Crystal Palace Art Union, Copeland," raised circular base, c1860, nicks to base rim. **715.00**

15½″ h, Abraham Lincoln, raised circular base, English, c1860 . . . . . **275.00**

16″ h, maiden, garland in hair, black pedestal base **150.00**

Creamer, 5″ h, Tulip pattern, relief dec **90.00**

Ewer, 10¼″ h, blue and white, applied grapes dec, Bennington, c1850 . . . . **215.00**

Figure

14″ h, woman **175.00**

15½″ h, Columbus, young man seated atop mooring post, waves splashing at feet, imp title on base, incised on back, "copyright applied for M. F. Libby," English, mid 19th C, repair to ring on mooring **500.00**

21½″ h, barefoot boy wearing breeches and jacket, scarf tied at throat, sickle lying on ground, pointing to letter concealed in tree stump, titled "The Trysting Tree," incised "C Halse, Sc/Pubd 1874," imp Copeland/Copyright Reserved". **600.00**

21¾″ h, Maidenhood, classical style figure, standing, round base, imp Copeland mark and publishing date 1861, chips and hairline to base . . **250.00**

26″ h, The Bather Surprised, standing bather, cut-corner rect base, imp Royal Worcester mark, inscribed "T Brock, Sc, London, 1868," right arm restored **385.00**

Statue, John Bright, English orator and statesman, 1811–89, by Robinson Leadbeater, 6½″ h, $100.00.

Loving Cup, 8¾″ h, relief figures of Bacchus and woman, grapes, and vines, Charles Meigh, c1840 . . . . **300.00**

Pastile Burner, 8¼″ sq, relief molded, bird and human figures, raised on turned columns, stepped sq base, price for pair **190.00**

Pitcher

8″ h, molded foliage and medallions representing day and night **140.00**

9¾″ h, hanging game scene, flake on spout **75.00**

Statue, 18″ h, young Apollo, finely modeled. **200.00**

Vase

7⅛″ h, eagle, enameled blue and red, gilt trim, Bennington, slight hairlines in base **45.00**

10″ h, applied white monkey type figures, grape clusters at shoulders, blue ground, c1850, price for pair . **250.00**

PATE-DE-VERRE

History: Pate–de–Verre can be translated simply as glass paste. It is manufactured by grinding lead glass into a powder or crystal form, making it into a paste by adding a 2% or 3% solution of sodium silicate, molding, firing, and carving. The Egyptians discovered the process as early as 1500 B.C.

In the late 19th century, the process was rediscovered by a group of French glassmakers. Amalric Walter, Henri Cros, Georges Despret, and the Daum brothers were leading manufacturers.

Contemporary sculptors are creating a second renaissance, lead by the technical research of Jacques Daum.

Bookends, 6½″ h, Buddha, yellow amber pressed molded design, seated in lotus position, inscribed "A Walter Nancy". **2,325.00**

Bowl

2⅞″ h, ovoid, short cylindrical foot, thick clear walls, soft pink and rose streaks, imp "Decorchemont" within horseshoe, inscribed "D47," c1945 . . . . **1,980.00**

3⅞″ h, stepped and flaring ftd body, wide rim, mottled blue and white, high relief molded overlapping deep indigo stars, sgd "G Argy-Rousseau" in the mold. **6,050.00**

Center Bowl, 10⅜″ d, 3¾″ h, blue, purple, and green press molded design, seven exotic long legged birds, central multipearl blossom, repeating design on ext., raised pedestal foot, sgd "G Argy-Rousseau". **6,600.00**

Clock, 4½″ sq, stars within pentagon

Vase, rosettes, red flowers with yellow centers, purple tones throughout ground, 10¼″ h, $6,000.00.

and tapered sheaves motif, orange and black, molded sgd "G Argy–Rousseau," clock by J E Caldwell . . . **2,750.00**

Dagger, 12″ l, frosted blade, relief design, green horsehead handle, script sgd "Nancy, France" **1,100.00**

Dish, 6⅞″ l, shallow oval, molded concentric waves, case on one side with acorns and oak leaves, emerald green, lemon yellow, and mustard, modeled by Henri Mercier, molded "AWALTER–NANCY" and "HM," c1925. . . . . **1,650.00**

Jewelry
Earrings, pr
1⅜″ l, oval, mottled yellow and orange glass, molded brown and green beetles, initialed in mold, Almaric Walter, unmarked gold screw mounts. **1,000.00**
2¾″ l, teardrop form, molded violet and rose shaded tulip blossom, suspended from rose colored swirl molded circle **2,070.00**
Pendant, 1¼″ d, molded amethyst portrait of Art Nouveau woman, flowing hair, gilt metal mount **385.00**

Night Light, 5″ h, Veilleuse, Papillions, gray spherical shade, lavender and Chinese red splashes, molded shallow relief of three butterflies, stylized foliage ground in shades of Chinese red, lavender, purple, black, and chocolate brown, wrought iron mount, sgd "G Argy-Rousseau," c1926 . . . **8,800.00**

Paperweight, 2⅝″ h, Papillion de Nuit, cube, internally streaked gray, deep forest green highlights, molded full relief moths, molded "G Argy–Rousseau," c1923 . . . . **2,200.00**

Salver, 10″ d, circular, mottled amber and orange, symmetrical handles, molded "A Walter Nancy" **350.00**

Sculpture, 9⅝″ l, crab in sea grasses, lemon yellow, chocolate brown, pale mauve, and sea green, sgd "A Walter/Nancy" and "Berge/SC" **8,250.00**

Tray, 6 x 8″, apple green, figural green and yellow duck with orange beak at one end, sgd "Walter, Nancy" **800.00**

Vase
5½″ h, press molded and carved, mottled amethyst and frost ground, three black and green crabs, red eyes, naturalistic seaweed at rim, center imp "G Argy–Rousseau," base imp "France" **5,500.00**
9½″ h, ovoid, molded low relief of striding black wolves crossing snow drifts, shades of pale green mottled with purple, gray, and white, sgd "G Argy–Rousseau" and "France," c1926 . . . . **27,600.00**
11¾″ h, oval, colored body, portraits of Egyptian women carrying water jug on front and back, broad frieze repeating geometric devices, warm shades of orange, yellow, and brown, wheel cut details to gown and framing, imp "G Argy–Rousseau, France" on base **41,250.00**

PATE-SUR-PATE

History: Pate–sur–Pate, paste on paste, is a 19th-century porcelain form featuring relief designs achieved by painting successive layers of thin pottery paste one on top of the other.

About 1880 Marc Solon and other Sevres artists, inspired by a Chinese celadon vase in the Ceramic Museum at Sevres, experimented with this process of porcelain decoration. Solon migrated to England at the outbreak of the Franco–Prussian War and worked at Minton, where he perfected the pate–sur–pate process.

Centerpiece, 16″ l, elongated parian vessel, molded scroll handles and feet, pierced rim, two brown reserves, white pate–sur–pate amorini, gilding, dec attributed to Lawrence Birks, marked "Minton," retailer's marks of Thomas Goode & Co, Ltd, London, c1889. . . . . **1,300.00**

Lamp, 19″ h, Neoclassical maiden and arabesque motif, pale green ground, circular gilt bronze base, late 19th C **375.00**

Vase, cov, Meissen, ovoid, waisted socle, entwined snakes handles, reserves dec with classically dressed maiden holding a bird, 11″ h, $2,420.00.

Plaque
   5¼ x 11¼″, Victoria Ware, Wedgwood
      Rust ground, gilt florets, applied
        white figure of Adam, imp mark,
        c1880, rim chip, framed. **2,100.00**
      Teal blue ground, white applied soldier figure, imp mark, c1880,
        framed. **1,540.00**
   7⅝″ d, one with maiden and cupid
      spinning web, other with maiden
      seated on bench with whip in one
      hand, sunflowers stalked with humanistic snail in other, artist sgd
      "Louis Solin," both marked on back,
      framed, price for matching pair . . . **2,400.00**
Urn, cov
   14″ h, ovoid body, wide shoulder tapering to short neck, domed cov,
      wreath handles, ringed pedestal, sq
      plinth, gilt bands, white relief scene
      of young woman seated on pedestal holding vase, cloud of cherubs,
      deep blue–green ground, 19th C . . **1,650.00**
   16″ h, panels of putti and scrolls,
      shrimp ground, wreath molded handles, imp "Mintons," gilt crowned
      globe Mintons mark, Tiffany & Co.
      mark, c1886, price for pair **4,125.00**
Vase, 7¼″ h, 5¾″ w, 2½″ d, white flowers, green ground, gold serpent skin
   twisted handles, gold trim, price for
   pair **995.00**

PATTERN GLASS

History: Pattern glass is clear or colored glass pressed into one of hundreds of patterns. Deming Jarves of the Boston and Sandwich Glass Co. invented the first successful pressing machine in 1828. By the 1860s glass-pressing machinery had been improved, and mass production of good-quality matched tableware sets began. The idea of a matched glassware table service (including goblets, tumblers, creamers, sugars, compotes, cruets, etc.) quickly caught on in America. Many pattern glass table services had numerous accessory pieces, among which were banana stands, molasses cans, water bottles, etc.

Early pattern glass (flint) was made with a lead formula, giving it a ringing quality. During the Civil War lead became too valuable to be used in glass manufacturing. In 1864 Hobbs, Bruckunier & Co., West Virginia, developed a soda lime (nonflint) formula. Pattern glass also was produced in colors, milk glass, opalescent glass, slag glass, and custard glass.

The hundreds of companies which produced pattern glass experienced periods of development, expansions, personnel problems, material and supply demands, fires, and mergers. In 1899 the National Glass Co. was formed as a combine of nineteen glass companies in Pennsylvania, Ohio, Indiana, West Virginia, and Maryland. U.S. Glass, another consortium, was founded in 1891. These combines resulted as attempts to save small companies by pooling talents, resources, and patterns. Because of this pooling, the same pattern can be attributed to several companies.

Sometimes the pattern name of a piece was changed from one company to the next to reflect current fashion trends. U.S. Glass created the States series by issuing patterns named for a particular state. Several of these patterns were new issues, others were former patterns renamed.

References: E. M. Belnap, *Milk Glass,* Crown Publishers, 1949; Bill Edwards, *Opalescent Glass,* Collector Books, 1992; Elaine Ezell and George Newhouse, *Cruets, Cruets, Cruets, Volume I,* Antique Publications, 1991; Regis F. and Mary F. Ferson, *Yesterday's Milk Glass Today,* published by authors, 1981; William Heacock, *Custard Glass From A to Z, Book 4,* Antique Publications, 1980; William Heacock, *More Ruby Stained Glass, Book 8,* Antique Publications, 1987; William Heacock, *Oil Cruets From A to Z, Book 6,* Antique Publications, 1981; William Heacock, *Old Pattern Glass,* Antique Publications, 1981; William Heacock, *1000 Toothpick Holders: A Collector's Guide,* Antique Publications, 1977; William Heacock, *Opalescent Glass from A to Z, Book 2,* Antique Publications, 1981; William Heacock, *Rare and Unlisted Toothpick Holders,* Antique Publications, 1984; William Heacock, *Ruby Stained Glass From A To Z, Book 7,* Antique Publications, 1986; William Heacock, *Syrups, Sugar Shakers & Cruets, Book 3,* Antique Publications, 1981; William Heacock, *Toothpick Holders from A to Z, Book 1,* Encyclopedia of Victorian Colored Pattern Glass, Second Edition, Antique Publications, 1976, 1992 value update; William Heacock, *U.S. Glass From A to Z, Book 5,* Antique Publications, 1980; William Heacock and William Gamble, *Cranberry Opalescent From A to Z, Book 9,* Antique Publications, 1987; William Heacock, James Measell, and Berry Wiggins, *Harry Northwood: The Early Years 1881–1900,* Antique Publications, 1990; William Heacock, James Measell, and Berry Wiggins, *Harry Northwood: The Wheeling Years 1901–1925,* Antique Publications, 1991; Joyce Ann Hicks, *Just Jenkins,* printed by author, 1988; Kyle Husfloen, *Collector's Guide To American Pressed Glass, 1825–1915,* Wallace–Homestead, 1992.

Bill Jenks and Jerry Luna, *Early American Pattern Glass—1850 to 1910: Major Collectible Table Settings with Prices,* Wallace–Homestead, 1990; Bill Jenks, Jerry Luna, and Darryl Reilly, *Identifying Pattern Glass Reproductions,* Wallace–Homestead, 1993; Minnie Watson Kamm, *Pattern Glass Pitchers, Books 1 through 8,* published by author, 1970, 4th printing; Lorraine Kovar, *Westmoreland Glass: 1950–1984,* Volume I (1991), Volume II (1991), Antique Publications; Thelma Ladd and Laurence Ladd, *Portland Glass: Legacy of a Glass House Down East,* Collector Books, 1992; Ruth Webb Lee, *Early American Pressed Glass,* Lee Publications, 1966, 36th edition; Ruth Webb Lee, *Victorian Glass,* Lee Publications, 1944, 13th edition; Bessie M. Lindsey, *American Historical Glass,* Charles E. Tuttle, 1967; Robert Irwin Lucas, *Tarentum Pattern Glass,* privately printed, 1981; Mollie H. McCain, *The Collector's Encyclopedia of Pattern Glass,* Collector Books, 1982, 1994 value update; George P. and Helen McKearin, *American Glass,* Crown Publishers, 1941; James Measell, *Greentown Glass,* Grand Rapids Public Museum Association, 1979, 1992–93 value update, distributed by Antique Publications; James Measell and Don E. Smith, *Findlay Glass: The Glass Tableware Manufacturers, 1886–1902,* Antique Publications, Inc., 1986; Alice Hulett Metz, *Early American Pattern Glass,* published by author, 1958; Alice Hulett Metz, *Much More Early American Pattern Glass,* published by author, 1965.

S. T. Millard, *Goblets I,* privately printed, 1938, reprinted Wallace–Homestead, 1975; S. T. Millard, *Goblets II,* privately printed, 1940, reprinted Wallace–Homestead, 1975; Arthur G. Peterson, *Glass Salt Shakers: 1,000 Patterns,* Wallace–Homestead, 1970; Ellen T. Schroy, *Warman's Glass,* Wallace–Homestead, 1992; Ellen T. Schroy (ed.), *Warman's Pattern Glass,* Wallace–Homestead, 1993; Jane Shadel Spillman, *American and Euro-*pean Pressed Glass in the Corning Museum of Glass, Corning Museum of Glass, 1981; Jane Shadel Spillman, *The Knopf Collectors Guides to American Antiques, Glass,* Vol. 1 (1982), Vol. 2 (1983), Alfred A. Knopf; Doris and Peter Unitt, *American and Canadian Goblets,* Clock House, 1970; Doris and Peter Unitt, *Treasury of Canadian Glass, Second Edition,* Clock House, 1969; Peter Unitt and Anne Worrall, *Canadian Handbook, Pressed Glass Tableware,* Clock House Productions, 1983; Dina von Zweck, *The Woman's Day Dictionary of Glass,* Main Street Press, 1983.

Periodical: *Glass Collector's Digest,* Richardson Printing, PO Box 553, Marietta, OH 45750.

Collectors' Clubs: Early American Glass Traders, RD 5, Box 638, Milford, DE 19963; The National Early American Glass Club, PO Box 8489, Silver Spring, MD 20907-8489.

Museums: Corning Museum of Glass, Corning, NY; National Museum of Man, Ottawa, Ontario, Canada; Sandwich Glass Museum, Sandwich, MA; Schminck Memorial Museum, Lakeview, OR.

Additional Listings: Bread Plates, Children's Toy Dishes, Cruets, Custard Glass, Milk Glass, Sugar Shakers, Toothpicks, and specific companies.

Abbreviations:
ah—applied handle
GUTDODB—Give Us This Day Our Daily Bread
hs—high standard
ls—low standard
os—original stopper

We continue to be fortunate in assembling a panel of prestigious pattern glass dealers to serve as advisors in reviewing the pattern glass listings found in this edition. Their dedication is symbolic of those dealers and collectors who view price guides as useful market tools and contribute their expertise and time to make them better.

Research in pattern glass is continuing. As in the past, we have tried to present patterns with correct names, histories, and pieces. Catagories have been changed to reflect the most current thinking of all patterns alphabetically. Colored, opalescent, and clear patterns now are included in one listing, avoiding duplication of patterns and colors.

Pattern glass has been widely reproduced. We have listed reproductions with an *. These markings are given only as a guide and clue to the collector that some reproductions may exist in a given pattern.

Advisors: John and Alice Ahlfeld and Mike Anderton.

ACTRESS

Made by Adams & Company, Pittsburgh, PA, c1880. All clear 20% less. Some items have been reproduced in clear and color by Imperial Glass Co., including amethyst pickle dish.

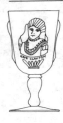

	Clear and Frosted
Bowl	
6″, ftd	45.00
7″, ftd	50.00
9½″, ftd	85.00
8″, Miss Neilson	85.00
Bread Plate	
7 x 12″, HMS Pinafore	90.00
9 x 13″, Miss Neilson	70.00
Butter, cov	90.00
Cake Stand, 10″	150.00
Candlesticks, pr	250.00
Celery Vase	
Actress Head	130.00
HMS Pinafore, pedestal	145.00
Cheese Dish, cov, The Lone Fisherman on cov, Two Dromios on base	250.00
Compote	
Cov, hs, 12″ d	300.00
Open, hs, 10″ d	90.00
Open, hs, 12″ d	120.00
Open, ls, 5″ d	45.00
Creamer	75.00

	Clear and Frosted
Dresser Tray	60.00
Goblet, Kate Claxton (2 portraits)	85.00
Marmalade Jar, cov	125.00
Mug, HMS Pinafore	50.00
Pickle Dish, Love's Request is Pickles	45.00
Pickle Relish, different actresses	
4½ x 7″	35.00
5 x 8″	35.00
5½ x 9″	35.00
Pitcher	
Milk, 6½″, HMS Pinafore	275.00
Water, 9″, Romeo & Juliet	250.00
Salt, master	70.00
Salt Shaker, orig pewter top	42.50
Sauce	
Flat	15.00
Footed	20.00
Spooner	60.00
Sugar, cov	100.00

AEGIS (Bead and Bar Medallion, Swiss)

Non-flint pattern made by McKee & Bros. Glass Co., Pittsburgh, PA, in the 1880s. Shards have also been found at the site of Burlington Glass Works, Hamilton, Ontario, Canada.

	Clear
Bowl, oval	15.00
Butter, cov	35.00
Compote	
Cov, hs	50.00
Open, hs	25.00
Creamer	25.00
Egg Cup	25.00
Goblet	30.00

	Clear
Pickle, 5 x 7″	15.00
Pitcher, water	55.00
Salt	15.00
Sauce	
Flat	7.50
Footed	10.00
Spooner	20.00
Sugar, cov	35.00

ALABAMA (Beaded Bull's Eye and Drape)

Made by U. S. Glass Co. c1898 as one of the States patterns. Also found in green (rare). Castor set ($275.00).

	Clear	Ruby Stained
Bowl, berry, master	30.00	—
Butter, cov	50.00	150.00
Cake Stand	65.00	—
Castor Set, 4 bottles, glass frame	125.00	—

	Clear	Ruby Stained
Celery Vase	35.00	110.00
Compote, cov		
7″	100.00	—
8″	125.00	—
Compote, jelly	35.00	—

	Clear	Ruby Stained		Clear	Ruby Stained
Creamer	45.00	60.00	Sauce	18.00	—
Cruet, os	65.00	—	Spooner	30.00	—
Dish, rect	20.00	—	Sugar, cov	48.00	—
Honey Dish, cov	60.00	—	Syrup	125.00	250.00
Pitcher, water	72.00	—	Toothpick	60.00	150.00
Relish	24.00	35.00	Tray, water, 10½″	50.00	—
Salt & Pepper	65.00	—	Tumbler	45.00	—

ALL-OVER DIAMOND (Diamond Splendor, Diamond Block #3)

Made by George Duncan and Sons, Pittsburgh, PA, c1891 and continued by U. S. Glass Co. It was occasionally trimmed with gold, and had at least sixty-five pieces in the pattern. Biscuit jars are found in three sizes; bowls are both crimped and non-crimped; and nappies are also found crimped and non-crimped in fifteen sizes. Also made in ruby stained.

	Clear		Clear
Biscuit Jar, cov	60.00	Nappy	
Bitters Bottle	30.00	4″	10.00
Bowl		9″	25.00
7″	20.00	Plate	
11″	35.00	6″	15.00
Cake Stand	35.00	7″	15.00
Candelabrum, very ornate, 4		Pickle Dish, long	15.00
arm with lusters	175.00	Pitcher, water, bulbous, 6	
Celery Tray, crimped or		sizes	45–60.00
straight	20.00	Punch Bowl	50.00
Claret Jug	50.00	Punch Cup	8.00
Compote, cov	60.00	Salt Shaker	15.00
Condensed Milk Jar, cov	25.00	Spooner	20.00
Cordial	35.00	Sugar	
Creamer	20.00	Cov	35.00
Cruet, patterned stopper		Open	20.00
1 oz	50.00	Syrup	55.00
4 oz	45.00	Tray	
Decanter		Ice Cream	30.00
Pint	45.00	Water	30.00
Quart	45.00	Wine	30.00
Egg Cup	20.00	Tumbler	15.00
Goblet	25.00	Water Bottle	35.00
Ice Tub, handles	35.00	Wine	15.00
Lamp, Banquet, tall stem	150.00		

ALMOND THUMBPRINT (Pointed Thumbprint, Finger Print)

An early flint glass pattern with variants in flint and non-flint. Pattern has been attributed to Bryce, Bakewell, and U. S. Glass Co. Sometimes found in milk glass.

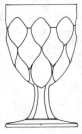

	Flint	Non-Flint		Flint	Non-Flint
Bowl, 4½″ d, ftd	—	20.00	Decanter	70.00	—
Butter, cov	80.00	40.00	Egg Cup	45.00	25.00
Celery Vase	50.00	25.00	Goblet	30.00	12.00
Champagne	60.00	35.00	Punch Bowl	—	75.00
Compote			Salt		
Cov, hs, 4¾″, jelly	60.00	40.00	Flat, large	25.00	15.00
Cov, hs, 10″	100.00	45.00	Ftd, cov	45.00	25.00
Cov, ls, 4¾″	55.00	30.00	Ftd, open	25.00	10.00
Cov, ls, 7″	45.00	25.00	Spooner	20.00	15.00
Open, hs, 10½″ ..	65.00	—	Sugar, cov	60.00	40.00
Cordial	40.00	30.00	Sweetmeat Jar, cov .	65.00	45.00
Creamer	60.00	40.00	Tumbler	60.00	20.00
Cruet, ftd, os	55.00	—	Wine	28.00	12.00

AMAZON (Sawtooth Band)

Non-flint made by Bryce Bros., Pittsburgh, PA, c1890 and by U. S. Glass Co. Mostly found in clear, either etched or plain. Heacock notes pieces in amber, blue, vaseline, and ruby stained. Over sixty-five pieces made in this pattern, including a toy set. Add 200% for color, e.g., pedestalled amber cruet with maltese cross stopper ($165.00) and pedestalled blue cruet with hand and bar stopper ($200.00). An amethyst cruet with a hand and bar stopper ($275.00) also is known.

	Etched	Plain		Etched	Plain
Banana Stand	95.00	65.00	Cordial	40.00	25.00
Bowl			Creamer	30.00	28.00
4″, scalloped	—	10.00	Cruet, os	50.00	45.00
4½″, scalloped ...	—	10.00	Egg Cup	—	15.00
5″, scalloped	—	15.00	Goblet		
6″, scalloped	—	25.00	4½″	30.00	—
6½″, cov, oval ...	—	50.00	5″	25.00	—
7″, scalloped	—	20.00	6″	30.00	—
8″, scalloped	—	25.00	Pitcher, water	60.00	55.00
9″, cov	30.00	25.00	Relish	28.00	25.00
Butter, cov	65.00	50.00	Salt & Pepper, pr ...	50.00	40.00
Cake Stand			Salt		
Large	—	50.00	Individual	—	15.00
Small	—	40.00	Master	—	18.00
Celery Vase	35.00	30.00	Sauce, ftd	10.00	10.00
Champagne	—	35.00	Spooner	25.00	20.00
Claret	35.00	30.00	Sugar, cov	55.00	45.00
Compote			Syrup	50.00	45.00
Cov, hs, 7″	—	65.00	Tumbler	25.00	20.00
Open, 4½″, jelly ..	45.00	35.00	Vase	30.00	25.00
Open, hs, 9½″,			Wine	25.00	20.00
sawtooth edge	—	45.00			

ANTHEMION (Albany)

Non-flint made by Model Flint Glass Co., Findlay, OH, c1890–1900 and by Albany Glass Co. Also found in amber and blue.

	Clear			Clear
Bowl, 7", sq, turned-in edge	20.00	Pitcher, water		50.00
Butter, cov	65.00	Plate, 10"		20.00
Cake Plate, 9½"	35.00	Sauce		8.00
Cake Stand	40.00	Spooner		25.00
Celery Vase	35.00	Sugar, cov		35.00
Creamer	30.00	Tumbler		25.00
Marmalade Jar, cov	45.00			

ARCHED FLEUR-DE-LIS (Late Fleur-De-Lis)

Made by Bryce, Higbee and Co. 1897–98. Also gilded.

	Clear	Ruby Stained		Clear	Ruby Stained
Banana Stand	35.00	150.00	Relish, 8"	15.00	—
Bowl, 9", oval	18.00	—	Salt Shaker	16.00	45.00
Butter, cov	40.00	135.00	Sauce	8.00	20.00
Cake Stand	35.00	—	Spooner, double		
Compote, jelly	20.00	—	handled	20.00	65.00
Creamer	30.00	60.00	Sugar, cov, double		
Dish, shallow, 7"	12.50	25.00	handled	35.00	100.00
Mug, 3¼"	20.00	40.00	Toothpick	30.00	100.00
Olive, handled	15.00	—	Tumbler	15.00	45.00
Pitcher, water	125.00	300.00	Vase, 10"	35.00	75.00
Plate, 7", sq	12.00	45.00	Wine	25.00	65.00

ARCHED OVALS (Concaved Almond)

Made by U. S. Glass Co., Pittsburgh, PA, c1908. Found in gilt, ruby stained, green, and rarely in cobalt blue. Popular pattern for souvenir wares, which are worth less than the prices below in the pattern glass market. A few pieces have been found in cobalt blue. They include: celery vase ($40.00), mug ($30.00), toothpick ($50.00), and a tumbler ($25.00).

	Clear	Cobalt Blue	Green	Ruby Stained
Bowl, berry	12.50	—	18.00	—
Bowl, cov, 7"	40.00	—	—	—
Butter, cov	45.00	—	50.00	80.00
Cake Stand	35.00	—	—	—
Celery Vase	15.00	40.00	20.00	—
Compote				
Cov, hs, 8", belled	42.00	—	—	—
Open, hs, 8"	30.00	—	—	—
Open, hs, 9"	35.00	—	—	—
Creamer				
Individual	20.00	—	—	—
Regular	30.00	—	—	25.00
Cruet	35.00	—	45.00	—
Goblet	20.00	—	30.00	35.00
Mug	18.00	30.00	20.00	25.00
Pitcher, water	30.00	—	40.00	—
Plate, 9"	20.00	—	25.00	—
Punch Cup	8.00	—	—	—

	Clear	Cobalt Blue	Green	Ruby Stained
Relish, oval, 9"	20.00	—	—	—
Salt & Pepper, pr ...	45.00	—	50.00	—
Sauce	7.50	—	—	—
Syrup	35.00	—	—	—
Spooner	20.00	—	25.00	35.00
Sugar, cov	35.00	—	40.00	—
Toothpick	18.00	50.00	25.00	35.00
Tumbler	12.00	25.00	18.00	30.00
Wine	15.00	—	20.00	30.00

ARGUS

Flint thumbprint type pattern made by Bakewell, Pears and Co. Pittsburgh, PA, in the early 1860s. Copiously reproduced, some by Fostoria Glass Co. with raised "H.F.M." trademark for Henry Ford Museum, Dearborn, MI. Reproduction colors include clear, red, green and cobalt blue.

	Clear		Clear
Ale Glass	75.00	* Goblet	40.00
Bitters Bottle	60.00	Lamp, ftd	100.00
Bowl, 5½"	30.00	Mug, ah	65.00
* Butter, cov	85.00	Pitcher, water, ah	225.00
Celery Vase	90.00	Salt, master, open	30.00
Champagne	65.00	* Spooner	45.00
Compote, open, 6" d, 4½" h	50.00	* Sugar, cov	65.00
* Creamer, applied handle ..	100.00	* Tumbler, bar	65.00
Decanter, qt	70.00	Whiskey, ah	75.00
Egg Cup	30.00	* Wine	35.00

ART (Jacob's Tears, Job's Tears, Teardrop and Diamond Block)

Non-flint produced by Adams & Co., Pittsburgh, PA, in the 1880s. Reissued by U. S. Glass Co. in the early 1890s. A milk glass covered compote is known.

	Clear	Ruby Stained		Clear	Ruby Stained
Banana Stand	95.00	175.00	Open, hs, 9½" d	60.00	—
Biscuit Jar	135.00	175.00	Open, hs, 10" ...	65.00	—
Bowl			Creamer		
6", 3¼" h, ftd ...	30.00	—	Hotel, large, round shape	45.00	90.00
7", low, collar base	35.00	—	Regular	55.00	100.00
8", berry, one end pointed	50.00	85.00	Cruet, os	125.00	250.00
Butter, cov	60.00	125.00	Goblet	60.00	—
Cake Stand			Pitcher		
9"	55.00	—	Milk	115.00	175.00
10¼"	65.00	—	Water, 2½ qt	100.00	—
Celery Vase	40.00	100.00	Plate, 10"	40.00	—
* Compote			Relish	20.00	65.00
Cov, hs, 7"	100.00	185.00	Sauce		
Open, hs, 9"	50.00	—	Flat, round, 4" ...	15.00	—
			Pointed end	18.50	—

	Clear	Ruby Stained		Clear	Ruby Stained
Spooner	25.00	85.00	Tumbler	45.00	—
Sugar, cov	45.00	125.00	Vinegar Jug, 3 pt	75.00	—

ASHBURTON

A popular pattern produced by Boston and Sandwich Glass Co. and by McKee & Bros. Glass Co. from the 1850s to the late 1870s with many variations. Originally made in flint by New England Glass Co. and others and later in non-flint. Prices are for flint. Non-flint values 65% less. Also reported is an amber handled whiskey mug, flint canary celery vase ($750.00), and a scarce emerald green wine glass ($200.00). Some items known in fiery opalescent.

	Clear		Clear
Ale Glass, 5″	90.00	Honey Dish	15.00
Bar Bottle		Jug, qt	90.00
Pint	55.00	Lamp	75.00
Quart	75.00	Lemonade Glass	55.00
Bitters Bottle	55.00	Mug, 7″	100.00
Bowl, 6½″	75.00	Pitcher, water	450.00
Carafe	175.00	Plate, 6⅝″	75.00
Celery Vase, scalloped top	125.00	Sauce	10.00
Champagne, cut	75.00	Sugar, cov	90.00
Claret, 5¼″ h	50.00	Toddy Jar, cov	375.00
Compote, open, ls, 7½″	65.00	Tumbler	
Cordial, 4¼″ h	75.00	Bar	75.00
Creamer, ah	210.00	Water	75.00
Decanter, qt, cut and		Whiskey	60.00
pressed, os	250.00	Whiskey, ah	125.00
Egg Cup		Water Bottle, tumble up	95.00
Double	95.00	Wine	
Single	25.00	Cut	65.00
Flip Glass, handled	140.00	Pressed	40.00
Goblet	40.00		

ASHMAN

Non-flint, c1880. Pieces are square in shape. Also made in amber and blue.

	Clear		Clear
Bread Tray, motto	55.00	Creamer	35.00
Bowl	20.00	Goblet	35.00
Butter, cov		Pitcher, water	65.00
Conventional final	38.00	Relish	15.00
Large ball-type finial, sometimes with flowers within the ball	50.00	Spooner	40.00
		Sugar, cov	45.00
Cake Stand, 9″	40.00	Tray, water	40.00
Compote		Tumbler	25.00
Cov, hs, 12″	95.00	Wine	25.00
Open hs	35.00		

ATLANTA (Clear Lion Head, Frosted Atlanta, Square Lion)

Produced by Fostoria Glass Co., Moundsville, WV, c1895. Pieces are usually square in shape. Also found in milk glass, ruby, and amber stain.

	Clear	Frosted		Clear	Frosted
Bowl			* Goblet	50.00	60.00
7", scallop rim	60.00	75.00	Marmalade Jar	75.00	85.00
8", low collar			Pitcher, water	125.00	175.00
base	55.00	85.00	Relish, oval	35.00	40.00
Butter, cov	85.00	125.00	Salt & Pepper, pr	100.00	125.00
Cake Stand, 10"	95.00	110.00	Salt		
Celery Vase	45.00	75.00	Individual	30.00	40.00
Compote			Master	50.00	70.00
Cov, hs, 7"	90.00	125.00	Sauce, 4"	22.00	25.00
Cov, hs, 8" d,			Spooner	50.00	60.00
9½" h	110.00	150.00	Sugar, cov	85.00	100.00
Open, hs, 5", jelly	55.00	65.00	Toothpick	55.00	60.00
Creamer	50.00	65.00	Tumbler	45.00	55.00
Cruet	125.00	150.00	Wine	40.00	65.00
Egg cup	25.00	30.00			

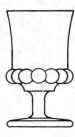

ATLAS (Bullet, Cannon Ball, Crystal Ball)

Non-flint, occasionally ruby stained and etched, made by Adams & Co.; U. S. Glass Co. in 1891; and Bryce Bros., Mt. Pleasant, PA, in 1889.

	Clear	Ruby Stained		Clear	Ruby Stained
Bowl, 9"	20.00	—	Molasses Can	65.00	—
Butter, cov, regular	45.00	75.00	Pitcher, water	65.00	—
Cake Stand			Salt		
8"	35.00	—	Master	20.00	—
9"	40.00	95.00	Individual	15.00	—
Celery Vase	28.00	—	Salt & Pepper, pr	20.00	—
Champagne, 5½" h	35.00	55.00	Sauce		
Compote			Flat	10.00	—
Cov, hs, 8"	65.00	—	Footed	15.00	25.00
Cov, hs, 5", jelly	50.00	80.00	Spooner	30.00	45.00
Open, ls, 7"	40.00	—	Sugar, cov	40.00	65.00
Cordial	35.00	—	Syrup	65.00	—
Creamer			Toothpick	20.00	50.00
Table, ah	30.00	55.00	Tray, water	75.00	—
Tankard	25.00	—	Tumbler	28.00	—
Goblet	45.00	65.00	Whiskey	20.00	45.00
Marmalade Jar	45.00	—	Wine	25.00	—

AURORA (Diamond Horseshoe)

Made in 1888 by the Brilliant Glass Works, which only existed for a short time. Taken over by the Greensburg Glass Co. who continued the pattern. Also found etched.

	Clear	Ruby Stained			Clear	Ruby Stained
Bread Plate, 10", round, large star in center	30.00	60.00	Relish Scoop		12.00	25.00
			Salt & Pepper, pr		45.00	80.00
Butter, cov	45.00	90.00	Sauce, flat		8.00	15.00
Cake Stand	35.00	85.00	Spooner		25.00	48.00
Celery Vase	35.00	60.00	Sugar, cov		45.00	65.00
Compote, cov, hs	65.00	110.00	Tray, water		45.00	60.00
Creamer	35.00	50.00	Tray, wine		35.00	60.00
Goblet	30.00	60.00	Tumbler		25.00	45.00
Mug, handle	50.00	65.00	Waste Bowl		30.00	45.00
Olive, oval	20.00	35.00	Wine		25.00	50.00
Pitcher, water	40.00	100.00	Wine Decanter, os		75.00	150.00

BANDED PORTLAND (Virginia #1, Maiden's Blush)

States pattern, originally named Virginia, by Portland Glass Co., Portland, ME. Painted and fired green, yellow, blue, and possibly pink; ruby stained, and rose-flashed (which Lee notes is Maiden's Blush, referring to the color rather than the pattern, as Metz lists it). Double-flashed refers to color above and below the band, single-flashed refers to color above or below the band only.

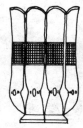

	Clear	Color-Flashed	Maiden's Blush Pink
Bowl			
4" d, open	10.00	—	20.00
6" d, cov	40.00	—	55.00
7½" d, shallow	30.00	—	55.00
8" d, cov	50.00	—	75.00
Butter, cov	50.00	165.00	85.00
Cake Stand	55.00	—	90.00
Candlesticks, pr	80.00	—	125.00
Carafe	80.00	—	90.00
Celery Tray	25.00	—	40.00
Celery Vase	35.00	—	45.00
Cologne Bottle	50.00	65.00	85.00
Compote			
Cov, hs, 7"	65.00	—	125.00
Cov, hs, 8"	75.00	—	115.00
Cov, jelly, 6"	40.00	65.00	90.00
Creamer			
Individual, oval	25.00	35.00	38.00
Regular, 6 oz.	35.00	45.00	50.00
Cruet, os	60.00	90.00	125.00
Decanter, handled	50.00	—	100.00
Dresser Tray	50.00	—	65.00
Goblet	40.00	55.00	65.00
Lamp			
Flat	45.00	—	—
Tall	50.00	—	—
Nappy, sq	15.00	55.00	65.00
Olive	18.00	—	35.00
Pin Tray	16.00	—	25.00
Pitcher, tankard	75.00	95.00	240.00
Pomade Jar, cov	35.00	45.00	65.00
Punch Bowl, hs	110.00	—	300.00

	Clear	Color-Flashed	Maiden's Blush Pink
Punch Cup	20.00	—	30.00
Relish			
6½"	25.00	30.00	20.00
8¼"	20.00	35.00	40.00
Ring Holder	75.00	—	125.00
Salt & Pepper, pr	45.00	75.00	75.00
Sardine Box	55.00	—	90.00
Sauce, round, flat,			
4 or 4½"	10.00	—	20.00
Spooner	28.00	—	45.00
Sugar, cov	48.00	75.00	75.00
Sugar Shaker, orig			
top	45.00	—	85.00
Syrup	50.00	—	135.00
Toothpick	40.00	45.00	45.00
Tumbler	25.00	35.00	45.00
Vase			
6"	20.00	—	38.00
9"	35.00	—	50.00
Wine	35.00	—	75.00

BARLEY (Sprig)

Non-flint originally made by Campbell, Jones and Co. c1882 in clear; possibly by others in varied quality. Add 100% for color, which is hard to find.

	Clear		Clear
Bowl		Honey Dish, ftd, 3½"	10.00
8", berry	15.00	Marmalade Jar	65.00
10", oval	15.00	Pickle Castor, SP frame	85.00
Bread Tray	30.00	Pitcher, water	
Butter, cov	45.00	Applied handle	100.00
Cake Stand		Pressed handle	45.00
8"	30.00	Plate, 6"	35.00
10"	35.00	Platter, 13" l, 8" w	30.00
Celery Vase	25.00	Sauce	
Compote		Flat	8.00
Cov, hs, 6"	45.00	Footed	10.00
Cov, hs, 8½"	60.00	Spooner	20.00
Open, hs, 8½"	35.00	Sugar, cov	35.00
Cordial	50.00	Vegetable Dish, oval	15.00
Creamer	30.00	Wine	30.00
Goblet	35.00		

BEADED ACORN MEDALLION (Beaded Acorn)

Made by Boston Silver Glass Co., East Cambridge, MA, c1869.

	Clear		Clear
Butter, cov, acorn finial	65.00	Creamer	40.00
Champagne	65.00	Egg Cup	25.00
Compote, cov, hs	60.00	Goblet	30.00

	Clear			Clear
Pitcher, water	125.00		Sauce, flat	12.00
Plate, 6″	30.00		Spooner	25.00
Relish	20.00		Sugar, cov	45.00
Salt, master	30.00		Wine	45.00

BEADED BAND (Thousand Eye Band)

Attributed to Burlington Glass Co., Hamilton, Ontario, Canada, c1884 as well as by an American midwestern factory. May have been made in light amber and other colors.

	Clear			Clear
Butter, cov	35.00	Relish		
Cake Stand, 7⅝″	25.00	Double	30.00
Compote, cov		Single	15.00
hs, 7″	50.00	Sauce, ftd	10.00
hs, 8″	55.00	Spooner	25.00
ls, 9″	80.00	Sugar, cov	40.00
Creamer	30.00	Syrup	95.00
Goblet	30.00	Wine	30.00
Pickle, cov	45.00		
Pitcher, water, applied strap			
handle	75.00		

BEADED GRAPE (Beaded Grape and Vine, California, Grape and Vine)

Non-flint made by U. S. Glass Co., Pittsburgh, PA, c1890. Also attributed to Burlington Glass Works, Hamilton, Ontario, and Sydenham Glass Co., Wallaceburg, Ontario, Canada, c1910. Made in clear and emerald green, sometimes with gilt trim. Reproduced in a variety of clear, milk glass, and several colors by many, including Westmoreland Glass Co.

	Clear	Emerald Green		Clear	Emerald Green
Bowl			* Goblet	35.00	50.00
5½″, sq	17.50	20.00	Olive, handle	20.00	35.00
7½″, sq	25.00	35.00	Pickle	20.00	30.00
8″, round	28.00	35.00	Pitcher		
Bread Plate	25.00	45.00	Milk	75.00	90.00
Butter, cov	65.00	85.00	Water	85.00	120.00
Cake Stand, 9″	65.00	85.00	* Plate, 8¼″, sq	28.00	40.00
Celery Tray	30.00	45.00	Salt & Pepper	45.00	65.00
Celery Vase	40.00	60.00	* Sauce, 4″	15.00	20.00
* Compote			Spooner	35.00	45.00
Cov, hs, 7″	75.00	85.00	Sugar, cov	45.00	55.00
Cov, hs, 9″	100.00	110.00	Sugar Shaker	75.00	85.00
Open, hs, 5″, sq	55.00	75.00	Toothpick	40.00	65.00
Open, hs, 8″	55.00	70.00	* Tumbler	25.00	40.00
Creamer	40.00	50.00	Vase, 6″ h	25.00	40.00
Cruet, os	65.00	125.00	* Wine	35.00	65.00

BEADED GRAPE MEDALLION

Non-flint possibly made by Boston Silver Glass Co., East Cambridge, MA, c1868. Shards have been found at Boston and Sandwich Glass Co., Sandwich, MA. Several variations are known. When bands are found on this heavily stippled pattern, it is known as Beaded Grape Medallion Banded. Also found in flint (add 40%).

	Clear		Clear
Bowl, 7″	25.00	Relish	
Butter, cov, acorn finial	75.00	Cov	140.00
Cake Stand, 11″	100.00	Open, mkd "Mould Pat'd	
Celery Vase	75.00	May 11, 1868"	45.00
Castor Set, 4 bottles	110.00	Salt	
Champagne	85.00	Individual, flat	20.00
Compote		Master, ftd	25.00
Cov, collared base	150.00	Spooner	35.00
Cov, hs	100.00	Sugar	
Cordial	55.00	Cov	60.00
Creamer, ah	50.00	Open	30.00
Egg Cup	30.00	Sweetmeat, cov	115.00
* Goblet	30.00	Syrup	150.00
Honey Dish, 3½″	10.00	* Tumbler, ftd	45.00
* Pitcher, water, ah	115.00	Vegetable, cov, ftd	75.00
Plate, 6″	30.00	Wine	55.00

BEADED LOOP (Oregon #1)

Non-flint made by U. S. Glass Co., Pittsburgh, PA, as Pattern Line No. 15,073. Reissued after the 1891 merger as one of the States series. Reproduced in clear and color by Imperial.

	Clear		Clear
Berry Set, master, 6 sauces	72.00	* Goblet	35.00
Bowl		Honey Dish	10.00
3½″	10.00	Mug	35.00
6″	12.00	Pickle Dish, boat shape	15.00
7″	15.00	Pitcher	
Bread Plate	35.00	Milk	40.00
Butter, cov		Water	60.00
English	65.00	Relish	15.00
Flanged	50.00	Salt, master	20.00
Flat	40.00	Salt & Pepper Shakers, pr	40.00
Cake Stand		Sauce	
8″	40.00	Flat, 3½ to 4″	5.00
10″	55.00	Footed, 3½″	10.00
Carafe, water	35.00	Spooner	
Celery Vase	30.00	Flat	24.00
Compote		Footed	26.00
Cov, hs, 5″, jelly	45.00	* Sugar, cov	
Cov, hs, 7″	60.00	Flat	25.00
Open, hs, 6″	30.00	Footed	30.00
Open, hs, 8″	40.00	Syrup	55.00
Creamer		Toothpick	55.00
Flat	30.00	Tumbler	25.00
Footed	35.00	Wine	50.00
Cruet	50.00		

BEADED SWIRL (Swirled Column)

Made by George Duncan and Sons, c1890. The dual names are for the two forms of the pattern. Beaded Swirl stands on flat bases and is solid in shape. Swirled Column stands on scrolled (sometimes gilded) feet, and the shape tapered toward the base. Some pieces trimmed in gold and also in milk white.

	Clear	Emerald Green		Clear	Emerald Green
Bowl			Goblet	30.00	25.00
Berry, 7"	10.00	20.00	Mug	10.00	12.00
Flat	15.00	25.00	Pitcher, water	40.00	65.00
Footed, oval	18.00	24.00	Sauce		
Footed, round	18.00	24.00	Flat	8.00	12.00
Butter, cov	35.00	45.00	Footed	10.00	14.00
Cake Stand	35.00	45.00	Spooner		
Celery Vase	30.00	55.00	Flat	25.00	40.00
Compote			Footed	30.00	45.00
Cov, hs	40.00	50.00	Sugar, cov		
Open, hs	35.00	45.00	Flat	35.00	45.00
Creamer			Footed	35.00	45.00
Flat	25.00	35.00	Sugar Shaker	35.00	60.00
Footed	30.00	40.00	Syrup	48.00	100.00
Dish	10.00	15.00	Tumbler	20.00	30.00
Egg Cup	14.00	15.00	Wine	25.00	35.00

BEAUTIFUL LADY

Made by Bryce, Higbee and Co. in 1905.

	Clear		Clear
Banana Stand, hs	30.00	Goblet	35.00
Bowl		Pitcher, water	40.00
8", low collared base	15.00	Plate	
9", flat	18.00	7", sq	15.00
Bread Plate	15.00	8"	18.00
Cake Plate, 9"	25.00	9"	25.00
Cake Stand, hs	35.00	11"	28.00
Compote		Salt & Pepper, pr	60.00
Cov, hs	35.00	Spooner	15.00
Open, hs	25.00	Sugar, cov	25.00
Open, jelly	15.00	Tumbler	15.00
Creamer	25.00	Vase, 6½"	15.00
Cruet	30.00	Wine	25.00

BLOCK AND FAN (Red Block and Fan, Romeo)

Non-flint made by Richard and Hartley Glass Co., Tarentum, PA, in the late 1880s. Continued by U. S. Glass Co. after 1891.

	Clear	Ruby Stained		Clear	Ruby Stained
Biscuit Jar, cov	65.00	150.00	Cake Stand		
Bowl, 4", flat	15.00	—	9"	35.00	—
Butter, cov	50.00	85.00	10"	42.00	—

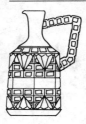

	Clear	Ruby Stained		Clear	Ruby Stained
Carafe	50.00	95.00	Pitcher		
Celery Tray	30.00	—	Milk	35.00	—
Celery Vase	35.00	75.00	Water	48.00	125.00
Compote, Open, hs,			Plate		
8″	40.00	165.00	6″	15.00	—
Condiment Set, salt,			10″	18.00	—
pepper & cruet on			Relish, rect	25.00	—
tray	75.00	—	Rose Bowl	25.00	—
Creamer			Salt & Pepper	30.00	—
Individual	—	35.00	Sauce		
Regular	25.00	45.00	Flat, 5″	8.00	—
Large	30.00	100.00	Ftd, 3¾″	12.00	25.00
Small	35.00	75.00	Spooner	25.00	—
Cruet, os	35.00	—	Sugar, cov	50.00	—
Dish, large, rect	25.00	—	Sugar Shaker	40.00	—
Finger Bowl	55.00	—	Syrup	75.00	95.00
Goblet	48.00	120.00	Tray, ice cream, rect	75.00	—
Ice Tub	45.00	50.00	Tumbler	30.00	40.00
Orange Bowl	50.00	—	Waste Bowl	30.00	—
Pickle Dish	20.00	—	Wine	45.00	80.00

BUCKLE WITH STAR (Late Buckle and Star, Orient)

Non-flint made by Bryce, Walker and Co. in 1875 and by U. S. Glass Co. in 1891. Finials are shaped like Maltese crosses.

	Clear		Clear
Bowl		Relish	15.00
6″, cov	25.00	Salt, master, ftd	20.00
8″, oval	15.00	Sauce	
10″, oval	20.00	Flat	8.00
Butter, cov	40.00	Footed	10.00
Cake Stand, 9″	35.00	Spill holder	55.00
Celery Vase	30.00	Spooner	25.00
Compote		Sugar	
Cov, hs, 7″	60.00	Cov	45.00
Open, hs, 9½″	30.00	Open	25.00
Creamer	35.00	Syrup	
Cruet	45.00	Applied handle, pewter or	
Goblet	30.00	Brittania top, man's head	
Mug	60.00	finial.	80.00
Mustard, cov	75.00	Molded handle, plain tin	
Pickle	15.00	top.	60.00
Pitcher, water, applied		Tumbler	55.00
handle.	70.00	Wine	35.00

BULL'S EYE

Flint made by the New England Glass Co. in the 1850s. Also found in colors and milk glass, which more than doubles the price.

	Clear		Clear
Bitters Bottle	80.00	Lamp	100.00
Butter, cov	150.00	Mug, 3½″, ah	110.00
Carafe	45.00	Pitcher, water	285.00
Castor Bottle	35.00	Relish, oval	25.00
Celery Vase	85.00	Salt	
Champagne	95.00	Individual	40.00
Cologne Bottle	85.00	Master, ftd	100.00
Cordial	75.00	Spill holder	85.00
Creamer, ah	125.00	Spooner	40.00
Cruet, os	125.00	Sugar, cov	125.00
Decanter, qt, bar lip	120.00	Tumbler	85.00
Egg Cup		Water Bottle, tumble up	125.00
Cov	165.00	Whiskey	70.00
Open	48.00	Wine	50.00
*Goblet	65.00		

BUTTON ARCHES (Scalloped Diamond, Scalloped Daisy-Red Top)

Non-flint made by Duncan and Miller Glass Co. c1898. Some pieces have frosted band. Some pieces, known as "Koral," usually souvenir type, are also seen in clambroth, trimmed in gold. The toothpick holder comes in both a smooth scallop and beaded scallop variety. They have the same value. In the early 1970s souvenir ruby stained pieces, including a goblet and table set, were reproduced by Westlake Ruby Glass Works, Columbus, OH. A few items documented in amethyst, including small mug. Scarce in other colors.

	Clambroth	Clear	Ruby Stained
Bowl, 8″	—	20.00	50.00
*Butter, cov	—	50.00	100.00
Cake Stand, 9″	—	35.00	180.00
Celery Vase	—	30.00	75.00
Compote, jelly	—	48.00	50.00
*Creamer	25.00	20.00	45.00
Cruet, os	—	55.00	175.00
Custard Cup	—	15.00	25.00
*Goblet	40.00	25.00	40.00
*Mug	30.00	25.00	30.00
Mustard, cov, underplate	—	—	100.00
Pitcher			
Milk	—	35.00	100.00
Water, tankard	—	75.00	125.00
Plate, 7″	—	10.00	25.00
Punch Cup	—	15.00	25.00
Salt, individual	—	15.00	—
Salt Shaker	—	15.00	30.00
*Sauce, flat	—	8.00	22.00
*Spooner	—	25.00	40.00
*Sugar, cov	—	35.00	75.00
Syrup	—	65.00	175.00
*Toothpick	30.00	20.00	35.00
Tumbler	20.00	25.00	35.00
Wine	25.00	15.00	35.00

BUTTON BAND (Umbilicated Hobnail, Wyandotte)

Non-flint made by Ripley and Co. in the 1880s and by U. S. Glass Co. in the 1890s.
Can often be found engraved, priced the same.

	Clear		Clear
Bowl, 10″	30.00	Goblet	40.00
Butter, cov	45.00	Pitcher	
Cake Stand, 10″	70.00	Milk	40.00
Castor Set, 5 bottles in glass		Water, tankard	50.00
stand	135.00	Spooner	28.00
Compote		Sugar, cov	35.00
Cov, hs, 9″	120.00	Tray, water	40.00
Open, ls	65.00	Tumbler	25.00
Cordial	35.00	Wine	35.00
Creamer	30.00		

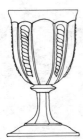

CABLE (Cable with Ring)

Flint, c1860. Made by Boston and Sandwich Glass Co. to commemorate the laying
of the Atlantic Cable. Also found with amber stained panels and in opaque colors
(rare).

	Clear		Clear
Bowl		Honey Dish	15.00
8″, ftd	45.00	Lamp, 8¾″	
9″	70.00	Glass Base	135.00
Butter, cov	100.00	Marble Base	100.00
Cake Stand, 9″	100.00	Miniature Lamp	500.00
Celery Vase	70.00	Salt, master	
Champagne	250.00	Cov	95.00
Compote, open		Ftd	45.00
hs, 5½″	65.00	Pitcher, water, rare	500.00
ls, 7″	50.00	Plate, 6″	75.00
ls, 9″	55.00	Salt, individual, flat	35.00
ls, 11″	75.00	Sauce, flat	15.00
Creamer	200.00	Spooner	40.00
Decanter, qt, ground stopper	295.00	Sugar, cov	120.00
Egg Cup		Syrup	225.00
Cov	225.00	Tumbler, ftd	200.00
Open	60.00	Wine	175.00
* Goblet	70.00		

CADMUS

Non-flint made by Beaumont Glass Co., Grafton, WV, in the mid 1880s.

	Clear		Clear
Bowl	15.00	Goblet	20.00
Butter, cov	35.00	Sauce	8.00
Compote, open		Spooner	15.00
High std	25.00	Sugar, cov	25.00
Jelly	20.00	Tumbler	20.00
Creamer	25.00	Wine	18.00

CAPE COD

Non-flint attributed to Boston and Sandwich Glass Co., Sandwich, MA, c1870.

	Clear		Clear
Bowl, 6", handled	30.00	Marmalade Jar, cov	85.00
Bread Plate	45.00	Pitcher	
Butter, cov	50.00	Milk	65.00
Celery Vase	45.00	Water	75.00
Compote		Plate	
Cov, hs, 6" d	65.00	5", handles	30.00
Cov, hs, 8"	100.00	10"	45.00
Cov, hs, 12"	175.00	Platter, open handles	45.00
Cov, ls, 6"	50.00	Sauce, ftd	12.50
Open, hs, 7"	50.00	Spooner	30.00
Creamer	35.00	Sugar, cov	35.00
Decanter	160.00	Wine	35.00
Goblet	45.00		

CARDINAL (Blue Jay, Cardinal Bird)

Non-flint attributed to Ohio Flint Glass Co., Lancaster, OH, c1875. Shards have been found at Burlington Glass Works, Hamilton, Ontario, Canada. There were two butter dishes made, one in the regular pattern and one with three birds in the base—labeled in script Red Bird (cardinal), Pewit, and Titmouse. The latter is less common. Summit Art Glass Co., OH, reproduced the goblet in clear, blue, and green.

	Clear		Clear
Bowl, berry	65.00	Pitcher, water	150.00
Butter, cov		Sauce	
Regular	65.00	Flat, 4"	10.00
Three birds in base	120.00	Footed, 4½" or 5½"	15.00
Cake Stand	75.00	Spooner	38.00
*Creamer	40.00	Sugar, cov	60.00
*Goblet	35.00		
Honey Dish, 3½"			
Cov	45.00		
Open	20.00		

CHAIN WITH STAR

Non-flint made by Bryce Bros., Pittsburgh, PA, c1882, and by U. S. Glass Co., c1891. Shards have been found at Burlington Glass Works, Hamilton, Ontario, Canada.

	Clear		Clear
Bowl, 9½"	30.00	Goblet	25.00
Bread Plate, 11", handles	30.00	Pickle, oval	10.00
Butter, cov	35.00	Pitcher, water	55.00
Cake Stand		Plate, 7"	25.00
8¾"	30.00	Relish	10.00
10½"	35.00	Salt Shaker	25.00
Celery Vase	25.00	Sauce, flat	10.00
Compote		Spooner	24.00
Cov, hs	50.00	Sugar, cov	35.00
Open, hs	30.00	Syrup	45.00
Creamer	25.00	Wine	25.00

CHANDELIER (Crown Jewel)

Non-flint made by O'Hara Glass Co., Pittsburgh, PA, c1880 and continued by U. S. Glass Co. Also attributed to Canadian manufacturer. Sauce bowls made in amber ($35.00).

	Etched	Plain		Etched	Plain
Banana Stand	—	100.00	Pitcher, water	125.00	115.00
Bowl, 8″ d, 3¼″ h . . .	35.00	37.50	Salt, master	—	30.00
Butter, cov	85.00	65.00	Salt & Pepper	75.00	65.00
Cake Stand, 10″	85.00	65.00	Sauce, flat	—	15.00
Celery Vase	40.00	40.00	Sponge Dish	—	30.00
Compote			Spooner	30.00	35.00
Cov, hs	80.00	75.00	Sugar, cov	75.00	85.00
Open, hs, 8″ . . .	70.00	68.00	Sugar Shaker	125.00	110.00
Open, hs, 9½″ . . .	70.00	68.00	Tray, water	70.00	50.00
Creamer	60.00	45.00	Tumbler	45.00	35.00
Finger Bowl	40.00	30.00	Violet Bowl	—	40.00
Goblet	60.00	65.00			
Inkwell, dated hard rubber top	—	85.00			

COLORADO (Lacy Medallion)

Non-flint States pattern made by U. S. Glass Co. in 1898. Made in amethyst stained, ruby stained, and opaque white with enamel floral trim, all of which are scarce. Some pieces found with ornate silver frames or feet. Purists consider these two separate patterns, with the Lacy Medallion restricted to souvenir pieces. Reproductions have been made.

	Blue	Clear	Green
Banana Stand	65.00	35.00	50.00
Bowl			
6″	35.00	25.00	30.00
7½″, ftd	40.00	25.00	35.00
8½″, ftd	65.00	45.00	60.00
Butter, cov	200.00	60.00	125.00
Cake Stand	70.00	55.00	65.00
Celery Vase	65.00	35.00	75.00
Compote			
Open, ls, 5″	35.00	20.00	30.00
Open, ls, 6″	45.00	20.00	42.00
Open, ls, 9¼″ . . .	95.00	35.00	65.00
Creamer			
Individual	45.00	30.00	40.00
Regular	95.00	45.00	70.00
Mug	40.00	20.00	30.00
Nappy	40.00	20.00	35.00
Pitcher			
Milk	250.00	—	100.00
Water	375.00	95.00	185.00
Plate			
6″	50.00	18.00	45.00
8″	65.00	20.00	60.00
Punch Cup	30.00	18.00	25.00
Salt Shaker	65.00	30.00	40.00
Sauce, ruffled	30.00	15.00	25.00
Sherbet	50.00	25.00	45.00

	Blue	Clear	Green
Spooner	65.00	40.00	60.00
Sugar			
Cov, regular	75.00	60.00	70.00
Open, individual . .	35.00	24.00	30.00
* Toothpick	60.00	30.00	45.00
Tray, calling card . . .	45.00	25.00	35.00
Tumbler	35.00	18.00	30.00
Vase, 12″	85.00	35.00	60.00
Violet Bowl	60.00	—	—
Wine	—	25.00	40.00

CORDOVA

Non-flint made by O'Hara Glass Co., Pittsburgh, PA. It was exhibited for the first time at the Pittsburgh Glass Show, December 16, 1890. Toothpick has been found in ruby stained (valued at $35.00).

	Clear	Emerald Green		Clear	Emerald Green
Bowl, Berry, cov . . .	30.00	—	Pitcher		
Butter, cov, handled	50.00	—	Milk	30.00	—
Cake Stand	45.00	—	Water	50.00	—
Celery Vase	45.00	—	Punch Bowl	90.00	—
Cologne Bottle	30.00	—	Punch Cup	15.00	30.00
Compote			Salt Shaker	20.00	—
Cov, hs	40.00	—	Spooner	35.00	45.00
Open, hs	35.00	—	Sugar, cov	40.00	80.00
Creamer	35.00	45.00	Syrup	125.00	40.00
Finger Bowl	18.00	—	Toothpick	15.00	20.00
Inkwell, metal lid . . .	80.00	—	Tumbler	18.00	—
Mug, handled	20.00	35.00	Vase	12.00	—
Nappy, handled, 6″					
d	12.00	—			

CROESUS

Made in clear by Riverside Glass Works, Wheeling, WV, in 1897. Produced in amethyst and green by McKee & Bros. Glass in 1899. Some pieces trimmed in gold; prices are for examples with gold in very good condition. Reproduced.

	Amethyst	Clear	Green
Bowl			
4″, ftd	60.00	10.00	30.00
6¼″, ftd	180.00	65.00	115.00
8″, flat	150.00	—	120.00
8″, ftd, cov	130.00	35.00	115.00
10″, ftd	150.00	—	120.00
* Butter, cov	160.00	85.00	170.00
Cake Stand, 10″ . . .	160.00	40.00	140.00
Celery Vase	265.00	65.00	135.00
Compote			
Cov, hs, 5″	110.00	30.00	115.00
Cov, hs, 7″	115.00	30.00	125.00

	Amethyst	Clear	Green
Open, hs, 5″	60.00	20.00	60.00
Open, hs, 7″	75.00	25.00	75.00
Compote, jelly	200.00	20.00	175.00
Condiment Set (cruet, salt & pepper on small tray)	200.00	175.00	175.00
* Creamer			
Individual	175.00	60.00	100.00
Regular	150.00	55.00	120.00
Cruet, os	300.00	125.00	150.00
Pitcher, water	325.00	80.00	200.00
Plate, 8″, ftd	75.00	20.00	65.00
Relish, boat shaped .	70.00	30.00	60.00
Salt & Pepper	115.00	40.00	125.00
Sauce			
Flat	40.00	15.00	35.00
Footed	45.00	20.00	40.00
*Spooner	80.00	60.00	70.00
*Sugar, cov	170.00	85.00	150.00
*Toothpick	100.00	25.00	85.00
Tray, condiment . . .	75.00	25.00	30.00
*Tumbler	65.00	20.00	50.00

CUPID AND VENUS (Guardian Angel)

Non-flint made by Richards and Hartley Glass Co., Tarentum, PA, in the late 1870s. Also made in vaseline, rare.

	Amber	Clear		Amber	Clear
Bowl			Goblet	—	75.00
8″, cov, ftd	—	35.00	Marmalade Jar, cov	—	85.00
9″, oval	—	32.00	Mug		
Bread Plate	75.00	40.00	Miniature	—	40.00
Butter, cov	—	55.00	Medium, 2½″	—	35.00
Cake Plate	—	45.00	Large, 3½″	—	40.00
Cake Stand	—	60.00	Pitcher		
Celery Vase	—	40.00	Milk	175.00	75.00
Champagne	—	90.00	Water	195.00	65.00
Compote			Plate, 10″, round . . .	75.00	40.00
Cov, hs, 8″	—	100.00	Sauce		
Cov, ls, 9″	—	100.00	Flat	—	10.00
Open, ls, 8½″, scalloped	135.00	35.00	Footed, 3½″, 4″ and 4½″	—	15.00
Open, hs, 9¼″ . . .	—	45.00	Spooner	—	35.00
Cordial, 3½″	—	85.00	Sugar, cov	—	65.00
Creamer	—	35.00	Wine, 3¾″	—	85.00
Cruet, os	—	135.00			

CURRIER AND IVES

Non-flint made by Bellaire Glass Co., Findlay, OH, c1889–98. Known to have been made in colors, but rarely found. A decanter is known in ruby stained.

	Clear
Bowl, oval, 10″, canoe shaped	30.00
Butter, cov	50.00
Cake Stand, 10″	75.00
Compote	
Cov, hs, 7½″	95.00
Open, hs, 7½″, scalloped	50.00
Creamer	30.00
Cup and Saucer	30.00
Decanter	35.00
Dish, oval, boat shaped, 8″	25.00
Goblet, knob stem	30.00
Lamp, 9½″, hs	75.00
Pitcher	
Milk	65.00
Water	70.00

	Clear
Plate, 10″	20.00
Relish	18.00
Salt Shaker	30.00
Sauce, oval	12.00
Spooner	30.00
Sugar, cov	45.00
Syrup	75.00
Tray	
Water, Balky Mule	65.00
Wine, Balky Mule	50.00
Tumbler	45.00
Water Bottle, 12″ h, os	55.00
Wine, 3¼″	20.00

DAHLIA

Non-flint attributed to Bryce, Higbee and Co., Pittsburgh, PA, c1885. Shards have been found at Burlington Glass Works, Hamilton, Ontario, and Diamond Flint Glass Co., Montreal, Quebec, Canada.

	Amber	Apple Green	Blue	Clear	Vaseline
Bowl	30.00	25.00	25.00	18.00	30.00
Bread Plate	55.00	50.00	60.00	45.00	55.00
Butter, cov	80.00	70.00	85.00	40.00	80.00
Cake Plate	60.00	45.00	60.00	24.00	60.00
Cake Stand, 9″	70.00	50.00	50.00	25.00	70.00
Champagne	65.00	85.00	75.00	55.00	75.00
Compote					
Cov, hs, 7″	90.00	85.00	85.00	55.00	80.00
Open, hs, 8″	60.00	45.00	45.00	30.00	60.00
Cordial	55.00	50.00	50.00	35.00	55.00
Creamer	40.00	35.00	35.00	25.00	40.00
Egg Cup					
Double	80.00	65.00	65.00	50.00	80.00
Single	55.00	40.00	40.00	25.00	55.00
Goblet	55.00	85.00	75.00	40.00	65.00
Mug					
Large	55.00	55.00	55.00	35.00	55.00
Small	50.00	45.00	40.00	30.00	50.00
Pickle	35.00	30.00	30.00	20.00	35.00
Pitcher					
Milk	70.00	55.00	55.00	45.00	70.00
Water	100.00	90.00	90.00	55.00	90.00
Plate					
7″	45.00	40.00	40.00	20.00	45.00
9″, handles	35.00	45.00	50.00	18.00	50.00
Platter	50.00	45.00	45.00	30.00	50.00
Relish, 9½″ l	20.00	20.00	20.00	15.00	25.00
Salt, individual, ftd	35.00	30.00	30.00	5.00	35.00
Sauce					
Flat	15.00	12.00	15.00	10.00	15.00
Footed	20.00	15.00	15.00	10.00	20.00
Spooner	50.00	45.00	50.00	35.00	50.00

	Amber	Apple Green	Blue	Clear	Vaseline
Sugar, cov	75.00	60.00	60.00	40.00	75.00
Syrup	75.00	—	—	55.00	—
Wine	45.00	40.00	45.00	25.00	45.00

DAISY AND BUTTON

Non-flint made in the 1880s by several companies in many different forms. In continuous production since inception. Original manufacturers include: Bryce Brothers, Doyle & Co., Hobbs, Brockunier & Co., George Duncan & Sons, Boston & Sandwich Glass Co., Beatty & Sons, and U.S. Glass Co. Reproductions have existed since the early 1930s in original and new colors. Reproductions, too, have been made by several companies, including L. G. Wright, Imperial Glass Co., Fenton Art Glass Co., and Degenhart Glass Co. Also found in amberina, amber stain, and ruby stained.

	Amber	Apple Green	Blue	Clear	Vaseline
Bowl, triangular	40.00	45.00	45.00	25.00	65.00
Bread Plate, 13″ ...	35.00	60.00	35.00	20.00	40.00
* Butter, cov					
Round	70.00	90.00	70.00	65.00	95.00
Square	110.00	115.00	110.00	100.00	120.00
Butter Pat	30.00	40.00	35.00	25.00	35.00
* Canoe					
4″	12.00	24.00	15.00	10.00	24.00
8½″	30.00	35.00	30.00	25.00	35.00
12″	60.00	35.00	28.00	20.00	40.00
14″	30.00	40.00	35.00	25.00	40.00
* Castor Set					
4 bottle, glass std	90.00	85.00	95.00	65.00	75.00
5 bottle, metal std .	100.00	100.00	110.00	100.00	95.00
Celery Vase	48.00	55.00	40.00	30.00	55.00
* Compote					
Cov, hs, 6″	35.00	50.00	45.00	25.00	50.00
Open, hs, 8″	75.00	65.00	60.00	40.00	65.00
* Creamer	35.00	40.00	40.00	18.00	35.00
* Cruet, os	100.00	80.00	75.00	45.00	80.00
Egg Cup	20.00	30.00	25.00	15.00	30.00
Finger Bowl	30.00	50.00	35.00	30.00	42.00
* Goblet	40.00	50.00	40.00	25.00	40.00
* Hat, 2½″	30.00	35.00	40.00	20.00	40.00
Ice Cream Tray,					
14 × 9 × 2″	75.00	50.00	55.00	35.00	55.00
Ice Tub	—	35.00	—	—	75.00
Inkwell	40.00	50.00	45.00	30.00	45.00
Parfait	25.00	35.00	30.00	20.00	35.00
Pickle Castor	125.00	90.00	150.00	75.00	150.00
* Pitcher, water					
Bulbous, reed					
handle	125.00	95.00	90.00	75.00	90.00
Tankard	62.00	65.00	62.00	60.00	65.00
* Plate					
5″, leaf shape ...	20.00	24.00	16.00	12.00	25.00
6″, round	10.00	22.00	15.00	6.50	24.00
7″, square	25.00	35.00	25.00	15.00	35.00
Punch Bowl, stand	90.00	100.00	95.00	85.00	100.00

	Amber	Apple Green	Blue	Clear	Vaseline
* Salt & Pepper	30.00	40.00	30.00	20.00	35.00
* Sauce, 4″	18.00	25.00	18.00	15.00	25.00
* Slipper					
5″	45.00	48.00	50.00	45.00	50.00
11½″	40.00	50.00	30.00	35.00	50.00
* Spooner	40.00	40.00	45.00	35.00	45.00
* Sugar, cov	45.00	50.00	45.00	35.00	50.00
Syrup	45.00	50.00	45.00	30.00	45.00
* Toothpick					
Round	40.00	55.00	25.00	40.00	45.00
Urn	25.00	30.00	25.00	15.00	30.00
* Tray	65.00	65.00	60.00	35.00	60.00
Tumbler	18.00	30.00	35.00	15.00	25.00
Vase, wall pocket . .	125.00	—	—	—	—
* Wine	15.00	25.00	20.00	10.00	45.00

DAISY AND BUTTON WITH V ORNAMENT (Van Dyke)

Made by A. J. Beatty & Co., Steubenville, OH, 1886–87. Reissued by U. S. Glass Co., c1892.

	Amber	Blue	Clear	Vaseline
Bowl				
9″	30.00	40.00	25.00	35.00
10″	30.00	40.00	25.00	35.00
Butter, cov	75.00	95.00	50.00	85.00
Celery Vase	50.00	55.00	30.00	55.00
Creamer	30.00	50.00	30.00	50.00
Finger Bowl	30.00	45.00	25.00	55.00
Goblet	35.00	45.00	25.00	50.00
Ice Cream Tray,				
16 x 9 x 2″	75.00	—	—	—
Match Holder	30.00	40.00	35.00	25.00
Mug	20.00	30.00	20.00	35.00
Pickle Castor	120.00	120.00	60.00	100.00
Pitcher, water	65.00	90.00	40.00	60.00
Punch Cup	12.00	20.00	12.50	25.00
Sauce, flat	20.00	20.00	12.00	30.00
Sherbet	15.00	20.00	15.00	10.00
Spooner	40.00	40.00	35.00	45.00
Sugar, cov	50.00	75.00	45.00	65.00
Toothpick	35.00	40.00	30.00	35.00
Tray, water	55.00	65.00	20.00	55.00
Tumbler	25.00	30.00	15.00	35.00
Wine	30.00	35.00	25.00	20.00

DAKOTA (Baby Thumbprint, Thumbprint Band)

Non-flint made by Ripley and Co., Pittsburgh, PA, in the late 1880s and early 1890s. Later reissued by U. S. Glass Co. as one of the States patterns. Prices listed are for etched fern and berry pattern; also found with fern and no berry, and oak leaf etching, and scarcer grape etching. Other etchings known include fish, swan, peacock, bird and insect, bird and flowers, ivy and berry, stag, spider and insect in web, buzzard

on dead tree, and crane catching fish. Sometimes ruby stained with or without souvenir markings. There is a four-piece table set available in a "hotel" variant, prices are about 20% more than the regular type.

	Clear Etched	Clear Plain	Ruby Stained
Basket, 10 x 2″	200.00	175.00	200.00
Bottle, 5½″	75.00	65.00	—
Bowl, berry	45.00	35.00	—
Butter, cov	65.00	40.00	125.00
Cake Cover, 8″ d . . .	300.00	200.00	—
Cake Stand, 10½″ . .	65.00	45.00	—
Celery Tray	35.00	25.00	—
Celery Vase	40.00	30.00	—
Compote			
Cov, hs, 5″	60.00	50.00	—
Cov, hs, 7″	70.00	55.00	—
Cov, hs, 10″	125.00	100.00	—
Open, ls, 6″	45.00	35.00	—
Open, ls, 8″	50.00	40.00	—
Open, ls, 10″	75.00	65.00	—
Condiment Tray . . .	—	75.00	—
Creamer	55.00	30.00	60.00
Cruet	90.00	55.00	135.00
Goblet	35.00	25.00	75.00
Pitcher			
Milk	100.00	80.00	200.00
Water	95.00	75.00	190.00
Plate, 10″	85.00	75.00	—
Salt Shaker	65.00	50.00	125.00
Sauce			
Flat, 4″ d	20.00	15.00	25.00
Footed, 5″ d	25.00	15.00	30.00
Spooner	30.00	25.00	65.00
Sugar, cov	65.00	55.00	85.00
* Tankard	120.00	95.00	220.00
Tray, water, 13″ d . .	100.00	75.00	—
Tumbler	35.00	30.00	55.00
Waste Bowl	65.00	50.00	75.00
Wine	30.00	20.00	55.00

DELAWARE (American Beauty, Four Petal Flower)

Non-flint made by U. S. Glass Co., Pittsburgh, PA, 1899–1909. Also made by Diamond Glass Co., Montreal, Quebec, Canada, c1902. Also found in amethyst (scarce), clear with rose trim, custard, and milk glass. Prices are for pieces with perfect gold trim.

	Clear	Green w/Gold	Rose w/Gold
Banana Bowl	40.00	55.00	65.00
Bowl			
8″	30.00	40.00	50.00
9″	25.00	60.00	75.00
Bottle, os	80.00	150.00	185.00
Bride's Basket, SP			
frame	75.00	115.00	165.00
* Butter, cov	50.00	115.00	150.00

	Clear	Green w/Gold	Rose w/Gold
Claret Jug, tankard shape	110.00	195.00	200.00
Celery Vase, flat . . .	75.00	90.00	95.00
* Creamer	45.00	65.00	70.00
Cruet, os	90.00	200.00	250.00
Finger Bowl	25.00	50.00	75.00
Lamp Shade, electric	85.00	—	100.00
Pin Tray	30.00	55.00	95.00
Pitcher, water	50.00	150.00	125.00
Pomade Box, jeweled	100.00	250.00	350.00
Puff Box, bulbous, jeweled	100.00	200.00	315.00
Punch Cup	18.00	30.00	35.00
Sauce, 5½", boat . . .	15.00	35.00	30.00
Spooner	45.00	50.00	55.00
* Sugar, cov	65.00	85.00	100.00
Toothpick	35.00	125.00	150.00
Tumbler	20.00	40.00	45.00
Vase			
6"	25.00	60.00	70.00
8"	25.00	70.00	75.00
9½"	40.00	80.00	85.00

DIAMOND THUMBPRINT (Diamond and Concave)

Flint attributed to Boston and Sandwich Glass Co. and other factories in the 1850s. Compotes, sugar bowls, and other pieces are being reproduced for Sandwich Glass Museum by Viking Glass Co., each piece embossed with the "S.M." trademark.

	Clear			Clear
Ale Glass, 6¼"	90.00	* Goblet		350.00
Bitters Bottle, orig pewter pourer, applied lip, polished pontil.	450.00	Honey Dish		25.00
		Mug, ah		200.00
		Pitcher, ah		
* Butter, cov	200.00	Milk		450.00
Celery Vase, scalloped top .	185.00	Water		500.00
Champagne	285.00	Sauce, flat		15.00
* Compote, cov, 8"	300.00	* Spooner		85.00
Cordial	325.00	* Sugar, cov		150.00
* Creamer	225.00	Sweetmeat Jar, cov		250.00
Decanter		Tray, rect, 11 × 7"		100.00
Pint, os	175.00	Tumbler, bar		125.00
Quart, os	225.00	Whiskey, ah		300.00
Egg Cup	85.00	* Wine		250.00
Finger Bowl	100.00			

EMPRESS

Made by Riverside Glass Works, Wellsburg, WV, c1898. Also found in amethyst (rare). Clear and emerald green pieces trimmed in gold; prices are for pieces with gold in very good condition.

	Clear	Emerald Green		Clear	Emerald Green
Bowl, 8½″	—	45.00	Punch Cup, ftd	20.00	35.00
Breakfast Set, individual creamer and sugar	40.00	85.00	Salt Shaker	30.00	50.00
			Sauce, 4½″ d	15.00	25.00
Butter, cov	50.00	100.00	Spooner	40.00	70.00
Celery Vase	55.00	—	Sugar, cov	45.00	125.00
Creamer	40.00	80.00	Sugar Shaker	55.00	110.00
Cruet	50.00	175.00	Syrup	60.00	300.00
Oil Lamp, atypical ..	60.00	225.00	Toothpick	—	150.00
Pitcher, water	65.00	150.00	Tumbler	32.50	55.00

ESTHER (Tooth and Claw)

Non-flint made by Riverside Glass Works, Wellsburg, WV, c1896. Some green pieces have gold trim. Also found in ruby stained and amber stained with etched or enamel decoration.

	Clear	Green	Ruby Stained
Bowl, 8″	25.00	50.00	60.00
Butter, cov	65.00	100.00	150.00
Cake Stand, 10½″ ..	60.00	80.00	95.00
Celery Vase	40.00	90.00	85.00
Cheese Dish, cov ..	85.00	135.00	125.00
Compote, jelly, hs ..	30.00	75.00	55.00
Cracker Jar	85.00	225.00	200.00
Creamer	45.00	70.00	75.00
Cruet, os	45.00	245.00	265.00
Goblet	45.00	95.00	75.00
Jam Jar, cov	40.00	125.00	75.00
Pitcher, water	65.00	165.00	250.00
Plate, 10″	25.00	60.00	60.00
Relish	20.00	25.00	40.00
Salt Shaker	20.00	35.00	25.00
Spooner	35.00	50.00	60.00
Sugar, cov	55.00	70.00	100.00
Syrup	65.00	200.00	175.00
Toothpick	45.00	85.00	100.00
Tumbler	25.00	50.00	55.00
Wine	35.00	55.00	45.00

FINECUT AND PANEL

Non-flint made by many Pittsburgh factories in the 1880s, including Bryce Bros. and Richard and Hartley Glass Co. Reissued in the early 1890s by U. S. Glass Co. An aqua wine is known.

	Amber	Blue	Clear	Vaseline
Bowl				
7″	25.00	35.00	15.00	30.00
8″, oval	40.00	—	18.00	30.00
Bread Plate	50.00	45.00	30.00	—
Butter, cov	65.00	75.00	40.00	60.00

	Amber	Blue	Clear	Vaseline
Cake Stand, 10″ . . .	50.00	75.00	30.00	50.00
Compote				
Cov, hs	125.00	135.00	75.00	130.00
Open, hs	65.00	65.00	35.00	60.00
Creamer	35.00	50.00	25.00	40.00
Goblet	40.00	48.00	20.00	35.00
Pitcher				
Milk	65.00	—	—	50.00
Water	85.00	85.00	40.00	45.00
Plate, 6″	12.00	20.00	10.00	15.00
Platter	30.00	50.00	25.00	30.00
Relish	20.00	25.00	15.00	20.00
Sauce, ftd	15.00	25.00	8.00	15.00
Spooner	35.00	45.00	20.00	30.00
Sugar, cov	37.50	42.50	30.00	32.50
Tray, water	60.00	55.00	30.00	60.00
Tumbler	25.00	30.00	20.00	38.00
Waste Bowl	30.00	35.00	20.00	35.00
Wine	30.00	35.00	20.00	35.00

FLORIDA (Emerald Green Herringbone, Paneled Herringbone)

Non-flint made by U. S. Glass Co., in the 1890s. One of the States patterns. Goblet reproduced in green and other colors.

	Clear	Emerald Green		Clear	Emerald Green
Berry Set	75.00	110.00	Pitcher, water	50.00	75.00
Bowl, 7¾″	10.00	15.00	Plate		
Butter, cov	50.00	85.00	7½″	12.00	18.00
Cake Stand			9¼″	15.00	25.00
Large	60.00	75.00	Relish		
Small	30.00	40.00	6″, sq	10.00	15.00
Celery Vase	30.00	35.00	8½″, sq	15.00	22.00
Compote, open, hs,			Salt Shaker	25.00	50.00
6½″, sq	—	40.00	Sauce	5.00	7.50
Creamer	30.00	45.00	Spooner	20.00	35.00
Cruet, os	40.00	110.00	Sugar, cov	35.00	50.00
* Goblet, 5¾″ h	25.00	40.00	Syrup	60.00	175.00
Mustard Pot, attach-			Tumbler	20.00	35.00
ed underplate, cov	25.00	45.00	Wine	25.00	50.00
Nappy	15.00	25.00			

GEORGIA (Peacock Feather)

Non-flint made by Richards and Hartley Glass Co., Tarentum, PA, and reissued by U. S. Glass Co. in 1902 as part of the States series. Rare in blue. (Chamber lamp, pedestal base, $275.00.) No goblet known in pattern.

	Clear		Clear
Bonbon, ftd	25.00	Cake Stand, 10″	50.00
Bowl, 8″	30.00	Castor Set, 2 bottles	60.00
Butter, cov	45.00	Celery Tray, 11¾″	35.00

	Clear		Clear
Children's		Decanter	70.00
Cake Stand	35.00	Lamp	
Creamer	35.00	Chamber, pedestal	85.00
Compote		Hand, oil, 7″	80.00
Cov, hs, 5″	35.00	Mug	25.00
Cov, hs, 6″	40.00	Nappy	25.00
Cov, hs, 7″	45.00	Pitcher, water	70.00
Cov, hs, 8″	50.00	Plate, 5¼″	15.00
Open, hs, 5″	20.00	Relish	15.00
Open, hs, 6″	25.00	Salt Shaker	40.00
Open, hs, 7″	30.00	Sauce	10.00
Open, hs, 8″	35.00	Spooner	35.00
Condiment Set, tray, oil cruet,		Sugar, cov	45.00
salt & pepper	75.00	Syrup, metal lid	65.00
Creamer	35.00	Tumbler	35.00
Cruet, os	55.00		

GRAPE AND FESTOON WITH STIPPLED LEAF

Non-flint made by Doyle and Company, Pittsburgh, PA, in the early 1870s.

	Clear		Clear
Bowl	15.00	Mug	20.00
Butter, cov	50.00	Pitcher	
Buttermilk Goblet	30.00	Milk, ah	75.00
Celery Vase	40.00	Water, ah	90.00
Compote		Plate, 6″	18.00
Cov, hs, 8″	115.00	Relish	15.00
Open, ls, 8″	75.00	Salt, ftd	25.00
Creamer, ah	50.00	Sauce, flat, 4″	10.00
Egg Cup	30.00	Spooner	35.00
Goblet	35.00	Sugar, cov	50.00
Lamp, oil, 7½″	65.00	Wine	45.00

HAND (Early Pennsylvania)

Made by O'Hara Glass Co., Pittsburgh, PA, c1880. Covered pieces have a hand holding bar finial, hence the name.

	Clear		Clear
Bowl		Marmalade Jar, cov	75.00
9″	30.00	Mug	40.00
10″	40.00	Pickle	20.00
Butter, cov	85.00	Pitcher, water	75.00
Cake Stand	55.00	Sauce	
Celery Vase	45.00	Flat	12.00
Compote		Footed	15.00
Cov, hs, 7″	60.00	Spooner	35.00
Cov, hs, 8″	95.00	Sugar, cov	75.00
Open, hs, 7¾″	35.00	Syrup	125.00
Cordial, 3½″	85.00	Tray	55.00
Creamer	40.00	Tumbler	85.00
Goblet	45.00	Wine	55.00
Honey Dish	10.00		

HOLLY

Non-flint, possibly made by Boston and Sandwich Glass Co. in the late 1860s and early 1870s.

	Clear		Clear
Bowl, cov, 8″ d	150.00	Pitcher, water, ah	225.00
Butter, cov	150.00	Salt	
Cake Stand, 11″	125.00	Flat, oval	65.00
Celery Vase	110.00	Ftd	60.00
Compote, cov, hs	165.00	Sauce, flat	25.00
Creamer, ah	125.00	Spooner	60.00
Egg Cup	65.00	Sugar, cov	125.00
Goblet	100.00	Tumbler	125.00
Pickle, oval	30.00	Wine	125.00

HORN OF PLENTY (Comet, Peacock Tail)

Flint and non-flint made by Bryce, McKee & Co., Pittsburgh, PA, c1850. Also produced by McKee & Bros., Pittsburgh, PA, 1850–60. Shards have been found at Boston and Sandwich Glass Co., Sandwich, MA. Applied handles. Reproductions made by Fostoria and L. G. Wright c1938.

	Clear Flint		Clear Flint
Bar Bottle, pewter spout, 8″	135.00	Egg Cup	40.00
Bowl, 8½″	145.00	* Goblet	75.00
Butter, cov		* Lamp	200.00
Conventional finial	125.00	Mug, small, applied handle	150.00
Shape of Acorn	130.00	Pepper Sauce Bottle, pewter	
Butter Pat	20.00	top	200.00
Cake Stand	395.00	* Pitcher, water	600.00
Celery Vase	185.00	Plate, 6″	100.00
Champagne	145.00	Relish, 7″ l, 5″ w	45.00
Compote		Salt, master, oval, flat	75.00
Cov, hs, 8¼″ d, 5¾″ h,		Sauce, 4½″	15.00
oval	350.00	Spill Holder	65.00
Open, hs, 7″	130.00	Spooner	45.00
Open, hs, 9¼″	200.00	Sugar, cov	150.00
Open, hs, 10½″	250.00	* Tumbler	75.00
Open, ls, 9″	85.00	Whiskey	
Cordial	150.00	Applied handle	235.00
Creamer, ah		Shot glass, 3″	100.00
5½″	225.00	Wine	125.00
7″	175.00		
Decanter, os			
Pint	475.00		
Quart	485.00		

ILLINOIS (Clarissa, Star of the East)

Non-flint; One of the States patterns made by U. S. Glass Co. c1897. Most forms are square. A few items are known in ruby stained, including a salt ($50.00), and a lidless straw holder with the stain on the inside ($95.00).

	Clear	Emerald Green		Clear	Emerald Green
Basket, ah, 11½″	100.00	—	Relish		
Bowl			7½″ x 4″	18.00	40.00
5″, round	20.00	—	8½″ x 3″	18.00	—
6″, sq	25.00	—	9 × 3″, canoe	40.00	—
8″, round	25.00	—	Salt		
9″, sq	35.00	—	Individual	15.00	—
* Butter, cov	60.00	—	Master	25.00	—
Candlesticks, pr	95.00	—	Salt & Pepper, pr	40.00	—
Celery Tray, 11″	40.00	—	Sauce	15.00	—
Cheese, cov	75.00	—	Spooner	35.00	—
Compote, open			Straw Holder, cov	175.00	400.00
hs, 5″	40.00	—	Sugar		
hs, 9″	60.00	—	Individual	30.00	—
Creamer			Table, cov	55.00	—
Individual	30.00	—	Sugar Shaker	65.00	—
Table	40.00	—	Syrup, pewter top	95.00	—
Cruet	65.00	—	Tankard, SP rim	80.00	135.00
Finger Bowl	25.00	—	Toothpick		
Marmalade Jar	135.00	—	Adv emb in base	45.00	—
Olive	18.00	—	Plain	30.00	—
Pitcher, milk			Tray, 12 x 8″, turned		
Round, SP rim	175.00	—	up sides	50.00	—
Square	65.00	—	Tumbler	30.00	40.00
Pitcher, water, sq	70.00	—	Vase, 6″, sq	35.00	45.00
Plate, 7″, sq	25.00	—	Vase, 9½″	—	125.00

JACOB'S LADDER (Maltese)

Non-flint made by Portland Glass Co., Portland, ME, and Bryce Bros, Pittsburgh, PA, in 1876 and by U. S. Glass Co. in 1891. A few pieces found in amber, yellow, blue, pale blue, and pale green.

	Clear		Clear
Bowl		Cruet, os, ftd	85.00
6″ x 8¾″	15.00	Goblet	60.00
7½″ x 10¾″	20.00	Honey Dish, 3½″	10.00
9″, berry, ornate SP holder, ftd	125.00	Marmalade Jar	75.00
		Mug	100.00
Butter, cov	65.00	Pitcher, water, ah	150.00
Cake Stand		Plate, 6¼″	20.00
8″ or 9″	50.00	Relish, 9½ x 5½″	15.00
11″ or 12″	60.00	Salt, master, ftd	20.00
Castor Bottle	18.00	Sauce	
Castor Set, 4 bottles	100.00	Flat, 4″, or 5″	8.00
Celery Vase	45.00	Footed, 4″	12.00
Cologne Bottle, Maltese cross stopper, ftd	85.00	Spooner	35.00
		Sugar, cov	80.00
Compote		Syrup	
Cov, hs, 6″	80.00	Knight's Head finial	125.00
Cov, hs, 9½″	125.00	Plain top	100.00
Open, hs, 7½″	35.00	Tumbler, bar	85.00
Open, hs, 8½″, scalloped	30.00	Wine	35.00
Creamer	35.00		

KANSAS (Jewel with Dewdrop)

Non-flint originally produced by Co-Operative Flint Glass Co., Beaver Falls, PA. Later produced as part of the States pattern series by U. S. Glass Co. in 1901 and by Jenkins Glass Co, c1915–25. Also known with jewels stained in pink or gold. Mugs (smaller and inferior quality) have been reproduced in vaseline, amber, and blue.

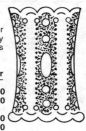

	Clear		Clear
Banana Stand	90.00	Creamer	40.00
Bowl		* Goblet	55.00
7", oval	35.00	* Mug	
8"	40.00	Regular	45.00
Bread Plate, ODB	45.00	Tall	25.00
Butter, cov	65.00	* Pitcher	
Cake Plate	45.00	Milk	50.00
Cake Stand		Water	60.00
7⅝"	45.00	Relish, 8½", oval	20.00
10"	85.00	Salt Shaker	50.00
Celery Vase	45.00	Sauce, flat, 4"	12.00
Compote		Sugar, cov	65.00
Cov, hs, 6"	50.00	Syrup	125.00
Cov, hs, 8"	85.00	Toothpick	65.00
Cov, ls, 5"	50.00	Tumbler	45.00
Open, hs, 6"	30.00	Whiskey	15.00
Open, hs, 8"	45.00	Wine	65.00

KENTUCKY

Non-flint made by U. S. Glass Co. c1897 as part of the States pattern series. The goblet is found in ruby stained ($50.00). A footed, square sauce ($30.00) is known in cobalt blue with gold. A toothpick holder is also known in ruby stained ($150.00).

	Clear	Emerald Green		Clear	Emerald Green
Bowl, 8" d	20.00	—	Plate, 7", sq	15.00	—
Butter, cov	50.00	—	Punch Cup	10.00	15.00
Cake Stand, 9½"	40.00	—	Salt Shaker, orig top	10.00	—
Creamer	25.00	—	Sauce, ftd, sq	8.00	12.00
Cruet, os	45.00	—	Spooner	35.00	—
Cup	10.00	20.00	Sugar, cov	30.00	—
Goblet	20.00	50.00	Toothpick, sq	35.00	85.00
Nappy	10.00	15.00	Tumbler	20.00	30.00
Olive, handle	25.00	—	Wine	28.00	38.00
Pitcher, water	55.00	—			

KING'S CROWN (Ruby Thumbprint, X.L.C.R.)

Non-flint made by Adams & Co. Pittsburgh, PA., in the 1890s and later. Known as Ruby Thumbprint when pieces are ruby stained. Made in clear and with the thumbprints stained amethyst, gold, green, and yellow, and in clear with etching and trimmed in gold. It became very popular after 1891 as ruby stained souvenir ware. Approximately eighty-seven pieces documented. NOTE: Pattern has been copiously reproduced for the gift-trade market in milk glass, cobalt blue, and other colors. New pieces are easily distinguished: in the case of Ruby Thumbprint, the color is a very pale pinkish red. Available in amethyst stained in goblet ($30.00) and wine ($10.00) and in green stained in goblet ($25.00) and wine ($15.00). Add 30% for engraved pieces.

	Clear	Ruby Stained		Clear	Ruby Stained
Banana Stand, ftd ..	85.00	135.00	Honey Dish, cov, sq	100.00	175.00
* Bowl			* Lamp, oil, 10″	135.00	—
9¼″ d, pointed ...	35.00	90.00	Mustard, cov, 4″ h ..	35.00	75.00
10″ d, scalloped ..	45.00	95.00	Olive Dish	25.00	45.00
Butter, cov, 7½″ d ..	50.00	90.00	Preserve, 10″ l	35.00	50.00
* Cake Stand			Pickle, lobed	18.00	40.00
9″ d	68.00	125.00	* Pitcher		
10″ d	75.00	125.00	Milk, tankard	75.00	100.00
Castor Bottle	45.00	70.00	Water, bulbous ..	95.00	225.00
Castor Set, glass			* Plate, 7″	20.00	45.00
stand, 4 bottles ..	175.00	300.00	* Punch Bowl, ftd	275.00	300.00
Celery Vase	40.00	60.00	* Punch Cup	15.00	30.00
* Champagne	25.00	35.00	Salt		
* Claret	35.00	50.00	Ind, rect	15.00	35.00
* Compote			Master, sq	30.00	50.00
Cov, hs, 8″	55.00	245.00	Salt Shaker, 3⅛″ h ..	30.00	45.00
Cov, ls, 12″	90.00	225.00	* Sauce, 4″	15.00	20.00
Open, hs, 8¼″ ...	75.00	95.00	Spooner, 4¼″ h ..	45.00	50.00
Open, ls, 5¼″ ...	30.00	45.00	* Sugar		
* Cordial	45.00	—	Ind, open, 2¾″ h .	25.00	45.00
* Creamer, ah			Table, cov, 6¾″ h .	55.00	95.00
Ind, tankard, ...	25.00	35.00	Tankard	115.00	200.00
Table, 4⅞″ h	50.00	65.00	Toothpick 2¾″ h ...	20.00	35.00
* Cup and Saucer ...	55.00	70.00	* Tumbler, 3¾″ h	20.00	35.00
Custard Cup	15.00	25.00	* Wine, 4⅜″ h	25.00	40.00
* Goblet	30.00	45.00			

KING'S #500 (Bone Stem, Parrot, Swirl and Thumbprint)

Made by King, Son & Co. Pittsburgh, PA, in 1891. Continued by U. S. Glass Co. 1891–98, and made in a great number of pieces. It was made in clear, frosted, and a rich, deep blue, known as Dewey Blue, both trimmed in gold. A clear goblet with frosted stem ($50.00) is known. Also known in dark green and a ruby stained sugar is reported ($95.00).

	Clear w/ Gold	Dewey Blue w/ Gold		Clear w/ Gold	Dewey Blue w/ Gold
Bowl			Finger Bowl	15.00	35.00
7″	10.00	30.00	Lamp		
8″	12.00	35.00	Hand	45.00	—
9″	14.00	45.00	Stand	65.00	—
Butter, cov	65.00	125.00	Pitcher, water	55.00	200.00
Cake Stand	40.00	60.00	Relish	20.00	30.00
Castor Set, 3 bottles	75.00	200.00	Rose Bowl	20.00	45.00
Celery Vase	20.00	65.00	Salt Shaker	15.00	40.00
Compote			Sauce	15.00	35.00
Cov, hs, 8″	50.00	75.00	Spooner	30.00	70.00
Open, hs, 10″ ...	25.00	40.00	Sugar, cov		
Creamer, bulbous, ah			Individual	20.00	40.00
Individual	20.00	35.00	Table	45.00	75.00
Table	30.00	50.00	Syrup	55.00	225.00
Cruet	45.00	175.00	Tumbler	25.00	35.00
Cup	10.00	15.00			
Decanter, locking					
top	100.00	—			

LILY OF THE VALLEY

Non-flint possibly made by Boston and Sandwich Glass Co., Sandwich, MA, and King, Son & Co. in the 1870s. Shards have also been found at Burlington Glass Works, Hamilton, Ontario, Canada. Lily of the Valley on Legs is a name frequently given to those pieces having three tall legs. Legged pieces include a covered butter, covered sugar, and creamer and spooner. Add 25% for this type.

	Clear		Clear
Butter, cov	70.00	Relish	15.00
Buttermilk Goblet	35.00	Salt, master	
Cake Stand	65.00	Cov	125.00
Celery Tray	40.00	Open	50.00
Celery Vase	55.00	Sauce, flat	12.00
Champagne	80.00	Spooner	35.00
Compote		Sugar	
Cov, hs, 8½″	85.00	Cov	75.00
Open, hs	50.00	Open	35.00
Creamer, ah	65.00	Tumbler	
Cruet, os	110.00	Flat	50.00
Egg Cup	40.00	Footed	65.00
Goblet	55.00	Vegetable Dish, oval	30.00
Honey Dish	10.00	Wine	100.00
Nappy, 4″	20.00		
Pickle, scoop shape	20.00		
Pitcher			
Milk	125.00		
Water	135.00		

LION (Frosted Lion)

Made by Gillinder and Sons, Philadelphia, PA, in 1876. Available in clear without frosting (20% less). Many reproductions.

	Frosted		Frosted
Bowl, oblong		* Creamer	75.00
6½ x 4¼″	55.00	Cup and Saucer, child size	45.00
8 x 5″	50.00	* Egg Cup, 3½″ h	65.00
Bread Plate, 12″	90.00	* Goblet	70.00
* Butter, cov		Marmalade Jar, rampant	
Lion's head finial	90.00	finial	90.00
Rampant finial	125.00	Pitcher	
Cake Stand	85.00	Milk	375.00
* Celery Vase	85.00	Water	300.00
Champagne	175.00	Relish, lion handles	38.00
Cheese, cov, rampant lion		* Salt, master, rect lid	250.00
finial	400.00	* Sauce, 4″, ftd	25.00
* Compote		* Spooner	75.00
Cov, hs, 7″, rampant finial	150.00	* Sugar, cov	
Cov, hs, 9″, rampant finial,		Lion head finial	90.00
oval, collared base	150.00	Rampant finial	110.00
Cov, 9″, hs	185.00	Syrup, orig top	350.00
Open, ls, 8″	75.00	Wine	200.00
Cordial	175.00		

LOG CABIN

Non-flint made by Central Glass Co. Wheeling, WV, c1875. Also available in color, but rare. Creamer, spooner, and covered sugar reproduced in clear, chocolate, and cobalt blue.

	Clear		Clear
*Bowl, cov, 8 x 5¼ x 3⅝" ..	400.00	Pitcher, water	300.00
Butter, cov	300.00	Sauce, flat	75.00
Compote, hs, 10½"	275.00	* Spooner	120.00
*Creamer	100.00	* Sugar, cov	275.00
Marmalade Jar, cov	275.00		

MAGNET AND GRAPE (Magnet and Grape with Stippled Leaf)

Flint possibly made by Boston and Sandwich Glass Co. c1860. Later non-flint versions have grape leaf in either clear or stippled. Imperial Glass began producing reproductions from new molds for the Metropolitan Museum of Art, NY, in 1971. Each lead crystal piece was marked "M.M.A."

	Flint Frosted Leaf	Non-Flint Stippled or Clear Leaf		Flint Frosted Leaf	Non-Flint Stippled or Clear Leaf
Bowl, cov, 8"	175.00	75.00	Pitcher		
Butter, cov	185.00	40.00	Milk, ah	—	75.00
Celery Vase	150.00	25.00	Water, ah	350.00	75.00
Champagne	135.00	45.00	Relish, oval	35.00	15.00
Compote			Salt, ftd	50.00	25.00
Cov, hs, 4½"	125.00	—	Sauce, 4"	20.00	7.50
Open, hs, 7½" ...	110.00	65.00	Spill	65.00	—
Cordial, 4"	125.00	—	Spooner	95.00	30.00
* Creamer	175.00	40.00	* Sugar, cov	125.00	80.00
Decanter, os			Syrup	125.00	55.00
Pint	150.00	75.00	* Tumbler, water	110.00	30.00
Quart	200.00	85.00	Whiskey	140.00	25.00
Egg Cup	75.00	20.00	* Wine	90.00	50.00
* Goblet					
Low Stem	75.00	—			
Regular stem	70.00	30.00			

MAINE (Paneled Stippled Flower, Stippled Primrose)

Non-flint made by U. S. Glass Co., Pittsburgh, PA, c1899. Researchers dispute if goblet was made originally. Sometimes found with enamel trim or overall turquoise stain.

	Clear	Emerald Green		Clear	Emerald Green
Bowl, 8"	30.00	40.00	Cake Stand	40.00	60.00
Bread Plate, oval, 10			Compote		
× 7¾"	30.00	—	Cov, jelly	50.00	75.00
Butter, cov	48.00	—	Open, hs, 7"	20.00	45.00

	Clear	Emerald Green		Clear	Emerald Green
Open, ls, 8″	38.00	55.00	Relish	15.00	—
Open, ls, 9″	30.00	65.00	Salt Shaker, single	30.00	—
Creamer	30.00	—	Sauce	15.00	—
Cruet, os	80.00	—	Sugar, cov	45.00	75.00
Mug	35.00	—	Syrup	75.00	225.00
Pitcher			Toothpick	125.00	—
Milk	65.00	85.00	Tumbler	30.00	45.00
Water	50.00	125.00	Wine	50.00	75.00

MARDI GRAS (Duncan and Miller #42, Paneled English Hobnail with Prisms)

Made by Duncan and Miller Glass Co. c1898. Available in gold trim and ruby stained.

	Clear	Ruby Stained		Clear	Ruby Stained
Bowl, 8″, berry	18.00	—	* Plate, 6″	10.00	—
Butter, cov	65.00	145.00	* Punch Bowl	200.00	—
Cake Stand, 10″	65.00	—	* Punch Cup	10.00	—
Celery Tray, curled			Relish	12.50	—
edges	25.00	—	Rose Bowl	25.00	50.00
Champagne, saucer	32.00	—	Sherry, flared or		
Claret	35.00	—	straight	35.00	—
Compote			Spooner	25.00	—
Cov, hs	55.00	—	Sugar, cov	35.00	65.00
Open, jelly, 4½″	30.00	55.00	Syrup, metal lid	65.00	—
Cordial	35.00	—	Toothpick	35.00	125.00
Creamer	35.00	60.00	Tumbler		
Finger Bowl	25.00	—	Bar	25.00	—
Goblet	35.00	—	Champagne	20.00	—
Lamp Shade	35.00	—	* Vase	35.00	—
Pitcher			Water	30.00	40.00
Milk	50.00	—	Wine	30.00	65.00
Water	75.00	200.00			

MARYLAND (Inverted Loop and Fan, Loop and Diamond)

Made originally by Bryce Bros., Pittsburgh, PA. Continued by U. S. Glass Co. as one of its States patterns.

	Clear w/ Gold	Ruby Stained		Clear w/ Gold	Ruby Stained
Banana Dish	35.00	85.00	Creamer	25.00	55.00
Berry Bowl	15.00	35.00	Goblet	30.00	48.00
Bread Plate	25.00	—	Olive, handled	15.00	—
Butter, cov	65.00	95.00	Pitcher		
Cake Stand, 8″	40.00	—	Milk	42.50	135.00
Celery Tray	20.00	35.00	Water	50.00	100.00
Celery Vase	30.00	65.00	Plate, 7″, round	25.00	—
Compote			Relish, oval	15.00	55.00
Cov, hs	65.00	100.00	Salt Shaker, single	30.00	—
Open, jelly	25.00	45.00	Sauce, flat	10.00	15.00

	Clear w/ Gold	Ruby Stained		Clear w/ Gold	Ruby Stained
Spooner	30.00	55.00	Tumbler	25.00	50.00
Sugar, cov	45.00	60.00	Wine	40.00	75.00
Toothpick	125.00	175.00			

MASSACHUSETTS (Arched Diamond Points, Cane Variant, Geneva #2, M2-131, Star and Diamonds)

Made in the 1880s, unknown maker, reissued in 1898 by U. S. Glass Co. as one of the States series. The vase ($45.00) and wine ($45.00) are known in emerald green. Some pieces reported in cobalt blue and marigold carnival glass. Reproduced in clear and colors.

	Clear		Clear
Bar Bottle, metal shot glass for cover	75.00	Pitcher, water	65.00
Basket, 4½″, ah	50.00	Plate, 8″	32.00
Bowl		Punch Cup	15.00
6″, sq	17.50	Relish, 8½″	25.00
9″, sq	20.00	Rum Jug	90.00
*Butter, cov	50.00	Salt Shaker, tall	25.00
Celery Tray	30.00	Sauce, sq, 4″	15.00
Champagne	35.00	Sherry	40.00
Cologne Bottle, os	37.50	Spooner	20.00
Compote, open	35.00	Sugar, cov	40.00
Cordial	55.00	Syrup	65.00
Creamer	28.00	Toothpick	40.00
Cruet, os	45.00	Tumbler	30.00
Goblet	45.00	Vase, trumpet	
Gravy Boat	30.00	6½″ h	25.00
Mug	20.00	7″ h	25.00
Mustard Jar, cov	35.00	9″ h	35.00
Olive	8.50	Whiskey	25.00
		Wine	40.00

MINNESOTA

Non-flint made by U. S. Glass Co. in the late 1890s as one of the States patterns. A two-piece flower frog has been found in emerald green ($46.00).

	Clear	Ruby Stained		Clear	Ruby Stained
Banana Stand	65.00	—	Creamer		
Basket	65.00	—	Individual	20.00	—
Biscuit Jar, cov	55.00	150.00	Table	30.00	—
Bonbon, 5″	15.00	—	Cruet	35.00	—
Bowl, 8½″, flared	30.00	100.00	Cup	18.00	—
Butter, cov	50.00	—	Goblet	35.00	50.00
Carafe	35.00	—	Hair Receiver	30.00	—
Celery Tray, 13″	25.00	—	Juice Glass	20.00	—
Compote			Match Safe	25.00	—
Open, hs, 10″, flared	60.00	—	Mug	25.00	—
			Olive	15.00	25.00
Open, ls, 9″, sq	55.00		Pitcher, tankard	85.00	200.00

	Clear	Ruby Stained		Clear	Ruby Stained
Plate			Spooner	25.00	—
5", turned up			Sugar, cov	35.00	—
edges	25.00	—	Syrup	65.00	—
7⅜" d	15.00	—	Toothpick, 3 handles	30.00	150.00
Pomade Jar, cov . . .	35.00	—	Tray, 8" l	15.00	—
Relish	20.00	—	Tumbler	20.00	—
Salt Shaker	25.00	—	Wine	40.00	—
Sauce, boat shape	10.00	25.00			

MISSOURI (Palm and Scroll)

Non-flint made by U. S. Glass Co. c1898 as one of the States pattern series. Also made in amethyst, blue, and canary.

	Clear	Emerald Green		Clear	Emerald Green
Bowl			Cruet	55.00	130.00
Cov, 6" d	35.00	—	Dish, cov 6"	65.00	65.00
Cov, 8" d	50.00	—	Doughnut Stand, 6"	40.00	55.00
Open, 7" d	15.00	35.00	Goblet	50.00	60.00
Open, 8" d	30.00	40.00	Mug	35.00	45.00
Butter, cov	45.00	65.00	Pickle, rect	15.00	25.00
Cake Stand, 9"	35.00	45.00	Pitcher		
Celery Vase	30.00	—	Milk	40.00	85.00
Compote			Water	75.00	85.00
Cov, hs, 5"	35.00	—	Relish	10.00	12.50
Cov, hs, 7"	45.00	—	Salt Shaker, single	35.00	45.00
Cov, hs, 8"	50.00	—	Sauce, flat, 4"	10.00	16.00
Open, hs, 6"	30.00	—	Spooner	25.00	48.00
Open, hs, 8"	45.00	—	Sugar, cov	50.00	65.00
Open, hs, 10" . . .	60.00	—	Syrup	85.00	175.00
Cordial	35.00	60.00	Tumbler	30.00	40.00
Creamer	25.00	40.00	Wine	40.00	45.00

MOON AND STAR (Palace)

Non-flint and frosted (add 30%). First made by Adams & Co., Pittsburgh, PA, in the 1880s and later by several manufacturers, including Pioneer Glass who probably decorated ruby stained examples. Also found with frosted highlights. Heavily reproduced in clear and color.

	Clear		Clear
*Banana Stand	90.00	Claret	45.00
Bowl		*Compote	
6" d	20.00	Cov, hs, 10"	68.00
* 8" d	25.00	Cov, ls, 6½"	55.00
12½" d	45.00	Open, hs, 9"	35.00
Bread Plate, rect	45.00	Open, ls, 7½"	25.00
*Butter, cov	70.00	*Creamer	55.00
Cake Stand, 10"	50.00	*Cruet	125.00
Carafe	40.00	*Egg Cup	35.00
Celery Vase	35.00	*Goblet	45.00
Champagne	75.00	Lamp, oil	140.00

	Clear			Clear
Pickle, oval	20.00	*Spooner		45.00
*Pitcher, water	175.00	*Sugar, cov		65.00
*Relish	20.00	*Syrup		150.00
*Salt, individual	10.00	Tray, water		65.00
*Salt & Pepper, pr	70.00	*Tumbler, ftd		50.00
*Sauce		Waste Bowl		65.00
Flat	8.50	*Wine		60.00
Footed	12.00			

NEW HAMPSHIRE (Bent Buckle, Modiste)

Non-flint made by U. S. Glass Co., Pittsburgh, PA, c1903 in the States pattern series.

	Clear w/ Gold	Rose Stained	Ruby Stained
Biscuit Jar, cov	75.00	—	—
Bowl			
Flared, 5½"	10.00	—	25.00
Flared, 8½"	15.00	25.00	—
Round, 8½"	18.00	30.00	—
Square, 8½"	25.00	35.00	—
Butter, cov	45.00	70.00	—
Cake Stand, 8¼"	30.00	—	—
Carafe	60.00	—	—
Celery Vase	35.00	50.00	—
Compote			
Cov, hs, 5"	50.00	—	—
Cov, hs, 6"	60.00	—	—
Cov, hs, 7"	65.00	—	—
Open	40.00	55.00	—
Creamer			
Individual	20.00	30.00	—
Table	30.00	45.00	—
Cruet	55.00	135.00	—
Goblet	25.00	45.00	—
Mug, large	20.00	45.00	50.00
Pitcher, water			
Bulbous, ah	90.00	—	—
Straight Sides, molded handle	60.00	90.00	—
Relish	18.00	—	—
Salt & Pepper, pr	35.00	—	—
Sauce	10.00	—	—
Sugar			
Individual, open	20.00	25.00	—
Table, cov	45.00	60.00	—
Syrup	75.00	—	50.00
Toothpick	25.00	40.00	40.00
Tumbler	20.00	35.00	40.00
Vase	35.00	50.00	—
Wine	25.00	50.00	—

NEW JERSEY (Loops and Drops)

Non-flint made by U. S. Glass Co., Pittsburgh, PA, c1900–08 in States pattern series. Items with perfect gold are worth more than those with worn gold. An emerald green 11" vase is known (value $75.00).

	Clear w/ Gold	Ruby Stained		Clear w/ Gold	Ruby Stained
Bowl			Molasses Can	90.00	—
8", flared	25.00	50.00	Olive	15.00	—
9", saucer	32.50	65.00	Pickle, rect	15.00	—
10", oval	30.00	75.00	Pitcher		
Bread Plate	30.00	—	Milk, ah	75.00	165.00
Butter, cov			Water		
Flat	75.00	100.00	Applied Handle	80.00	210.00
Footed	125.00	—	Pressed Handle	50.00	185.00
Cake Stand, 8"	65.00	—	Plate, 8" d	30.00	45.00
Carafe	60.00	—	Salt & Pepper, pr		
Celery Tray, rect	25.00	40.00	Hotel	50.00	115.00
Compote			Small	35.00	55.00
Cov, hs, 5", jelly	45.00	55.00	Sauce	10.00	30.00
Cov, hs, 8"	65.00	90.00	Spooner	27.00	75.00
Open, hs, 6¾"	35.00	65.00	Sugar, cov	60.00	80.00
Open, hs, 8"	60.00	75.00	Sweetmeat, 8"	70.00	90.00
Open, hs, 10½",			Syrup	90.00	—
shallow	65.00	—	Toothpick	55.00	225.00
Creamer	35.00	60.00	Tumbler	30.00	50.00
Cruet	50.00	—	Water Bottle	55.00	90.00
Fruit Bowl, hs, 12½"	55.00	110.00	Wine	40.00	60.00
Goblet	40.00	65.00			

O'HARA DIAMOND (Sawtooth and Star)

Non-flint made by O'Hara Glass Co. c1885. Reissued by U. S. Glass Co. 1891–1904.

	Clear	Ruby Stained		Clear	Ruby Stained
Bowl, berry			Pitcher, water,		
Individual	10.00	25.00	tankard	90.00	165.00
Master	25.00	75.00	Plate		
Butter, cov, ruffled			7"	20.00	—
base	45.00	125.00	8"	30.00	—
Compote			10"	40.00	—
Cov, hs	40.00	185.00	Salt, master	15.00	35.00
Open, hs, jelly	48.00	145.00	Salt Shaker	20.00	35.00
Condiment Set, pr			Spooner	20.00	55.00
salt & pepper,			Sugar, cov	35.00	90.00
sugar shaker, tray	125.00	250.00	Sugar Shaker	55.00	150.00
Creamer	30.00	60.00	Syrup	55.00	200.00
Cruet	55.00	150.00	Tray, water	30.00	45.00
Cup and Saucer	40.00	60.00	Tumbler	30.00	45.00
Goblet	25.00	50.00	Wine	25.00	35.00
Lamp, Oil	50.00	—			

PANELED THISTLE (Canadian Thistle, Delta)

Non-flint made by J. P. Higbee Glass Co., Bridgeville, PA, c1910–20. Also made by Jefferson Glass Co., Toronto, Ontario, Canada. The Higbee Glass Co. often used a bee as a trademark. This pattern has been heavily reproduced with a similar mark. Occasionally found with gilt. Rare in ruby stained, with or without gilt.

	Clear
Basket, small size	65.00
* Bowl	
8″, bee mark	25.00
9″, bee mark	30.00
Bread Plate	40.00
* Butter, cov, ...	60.00
Cake Stand, 9″	35.00
Candy Dish, cov, ftd	30.00
Celery Tray	20.00
* Celery Vase	40.00
* Champagne, bee mark . . .	40.00
* Compote	
Open, hs, 8″	30.00
Open, hs, 9″	35.00
Open, ls, 5″, jelly	30.00
* Creamer, bee mark	40.00
* Cruet, os	50.00
Doughnut Stand, 6″	25.00
* Goblet	35.00
* Honey Dish, cov, sq, bee mark.	80.00
* Pitcher	
Milk	60.00

	Clear
Water	70.00
* Plate	
7″	20.00
10″, bee mark	30.00
Punch Cup, bee mark	20.00
* Relish, bee mark	20.00
Rose Bowl, 5″	50.00
* Salt, individual	20.00
* Salt Shaker	20.00
* Sauce	
Flared, bee mark	12.00
Footed	20.00
* Spooner	25.00
* Sugar, cov	45.00
* Toothpick, bee mark	45.00
* Tumbler	25.00
Vase	
5″	25.00
9¼″	25.00
* Wine, bee mark	30.00

PAVONIA (Pineapple Stem)

Non-flint made by Ripley and Co. in 1885 and by U. S. Glass Co. in 1891. This pattern comes plain and etched.

	Clear	Ruby Stained		Clear	Ruby Stained
Bowl, 8″	25.00	55.00	Water	75.00	195.00
Butter, cov, flat	75.00	125.00	Plate, 6½″	17.50	—
Cake Stand, hs, 9″ .	55.00	100.00	Salt		
Celery Vase, etched	45.00	75.00	Individual	15.00	50.00
Compote			Master	28.00	50.00
Cov, hs, 8″	75.00	85.00	Salt Shaker	25.00	35.00
Open, jelly	35.00	—	Sauce, ftd, 3½″	15.00	20.00
Creamer			Spooner, pedestal . .	45.00	50.00
Hotel	35.00	75.00	Sugar, cov		
Table	35.00	75.00	Hotel	45.00	75.00
Cup and Saucer . . .	35.00	45.00	Table	45.00	75.00
Finger Bowl, ruffled			Tray, water, etched .	75.00	85.00
underplate	48.00	110.00	Tumbler	35.00	50.00
Goblet	35.00	60.00	Waste Bowl	60.00	55.00
Mug	35.00	50.00	Wine	35.00	40.00
Pitcher					
Lemonade	95.00	135.00			

PENNSYLVANIA (Balder)

Non-flint issued by U. S. Glass Co. in 1898. Also known in ruby stained. A ruffled jelly compote documented in orange carnival.

	Clear w/ Gold	Emerald Green
Biscuit Jar, cov	75.00	125.00
Bowl		
4"	20.00	—
8", berry	25.00	35.00
8", sq	20.00	40.00
Butter, cov	60.00	85.00
Carafe	45.00	—
Celery Tray	30.00	—
Celery Vase	45.00	—
Champagne	25.00	—
Cheese Dish, cov	65.00	—
Compote, hs, jelly	50.00	—
Creamer	25.00	50.00
Cruet, os	45.00	—
Decanter, os	100.00	—

	Clear w/ Gold	Emerald Green
Goblet	24.00	—
Juice Tumbler	10.00	20.00
Molasses Can	75.00	—
Pitcher, water	60.00	—
Punch Bowl	175.00	—
Punch Cup	10.00	—
Salt Shaker	10.00	—
Sauce	7.50	—
* Spooner	24.00	35.00
Sugar, cov	40.00	55.00
Syrup	50.00	—
Toothpick	35.00	90.00
Tumbler	28.00	40.00
Whiskey	20.00	35.00
Wine	15.00	40.00

PORTLAND

Non-flint made by several companies c1880–1900. An oval pintray in ruby souvenir ($20.00) is known and a flat sauce ($25.00).

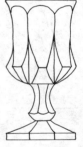

	Clear w/ Gold
Basket, ah	85.00
Biscuit Jar, cov	90.00
Bowl, berry, 7" d	20.00
Butter, cov	50.00
Cake Stand, 10½"	45.00
* Candlestick	
7" h, flared	85.00
9" h	55.00
Carafe, water	45.00
Celery Tray	25.00
Compote	
Cov, hs, 6"	60.00
Open, hs, 8¼"	40.00
Open, hs, 9½"	45.00
Open, ls, 7"	45.00
* Creamer	
Breakfast	20.00
Table	30.00
Tankard	30.00
Cruet, os	55.00
Decanter, qt, handled	50.00
Goblet	35.00

	Clear w/ Gold
Jam Jar, SP cov	35.00
Pitcher, water, straight sides	55.00
Pomade Jar, SP top	30.00
Puff Box, glass lid	35.00
Punch Bowl, 13⅝", ftd	150.00
Punch Cup	10.00
* Relish	15.00
Ring Tree	85.00
Salt Shaker	15.00
Sauce	8.00
Spooner	30.00
* Sugar	
Breakfast, open	35.00
Table, cov	45.00
Sugar Shaker	40.00
Syrup	50.00
Toothpick	25.00
Tumbler	25.00
Vase, 9" h	30.00
Water Bottle	40.00
Wine	30.00

PRINCESS FEATHER (Lacy Medallion, Rochelle)

Flint and non-flint made by Bakewell, Pears and Co. in the 1860s and 1870s. Later made by U. S. Glass Co. after 1891. Shards have been identified at Boston and Sandwich Glass Co. and several Canadian factory sites. Also made in milk glass. A rare blue opaque tumbler has been reported.

	Clear		Clear
Bowl		Goblet	45.00
7", cov, pedestal	45.00	Pitcher, water	75.00
7", oval	20.00	Plate	
8", oval	25.00	6"	30.00
9", oval	30.00	7"	35.00
Butter, cov	50.00	8"	40.00
Cake Plate, handled	35.00	9"	45.00
Celery Vase	40.00	Relish	20.00
Compote		Sauce	10.00
Cov, hs, 7"	50.00	Spooner	30.00
Cov, hs, 8"	50.00	Sugar	
Open, ls, 8"	35.00	Cov	55.00
Creamer, ah	55.00	Open	25.00
Dish, oval	20.00	Wine	45.00
Egg Cup	40.00		

QUESTION MARK (Oval Loop)

Made by Richards and Hartley Glass Co. in 1888 and later by U. S. Glass Co. in 1892. An 1888 catalog lists thirty-two pieces. Scarce in ruby stained.

	Clear		Clear
Bowl		Cordial	20.00
4", round, ftd	15.00	Creamer	30.00
7", oblong	18.00	Goblet	25.00
7", round, ftd	20.00	Nappy, ftd	20.00
8", oblong	25.00	Pickle Jar, cov	45.00
8", round, ftd	25.00	Pitcher	
9", oblong	30.00	Milk, bulbous, 1 qt	40.00
10", oblong	25.00	Milk, tankard, 1 qt	45.00
Bread Tray	30.00	Water, bulbous, ½ gal	50.00
Butter, cov	30.00	Water, tankard, ½ gal	55.00
Candlestick, chamber, finger		Salt Shaker	15.00
loop	45.00	Sauce, 4", collared	10.00
Celery Vase	28.00	Spooner	20.00
Compote		Sugar Shaker	35.00
Cov, hs, 7"	50.00	Sugar, cov	25.00
Cov, hs, 8"	65.00	Tumbler	20.00
Open, hs, 7"	25.00	Wine	20.00
Open, ls	15.00		

RED BLOCK (Late Block)

Non-flint with red stain made by Doyle and Co., Pittsburgh, PA. Later made by five companies, plus U. S. Glass Co. in 1892. Prices for clear 50% less.

	Ruby Stained		Ruby Stained
Banana Boat	75.00	Creamer	
Bowl, 8"	75.00	Individual	45.00
Butter, cov	110.00	Table	70.00
Celery Vase, 6½"	85.00	Decanter, 12", os, variant	175.00
Cheese Dish, cov	125.00	Goblet	35.00

	Ruby Stained		Ruby Stained
Mug	50.00	Salt Shaker	75.00
Mustard, cov	55.00	Sauce, flat, 4½″	20.00
Pitcher, water, 8″ h	175.00	Spooner	45.00
Relish Tray	25.00	Sugar, cov	90.00
Rose Bowl	75.00	Tumbler	40.00
Salt Dip, individual	50.00	* Wine	40.00

REVERSE TORPEDO (Bull's Eye Band, Bull's Eye with Diamond Point #2, Pointed Bull's Eye)

Non-flint made by Dalzell, Gilmore and Leighton Glass Co., Findlay, OH, c1888–90. Also attributed to Canadian factories. Sometimes found with copper wheel etching.

	Clear		Clear
Banana Stand, 9¾″	100.00	Open, hs, 7″	65.00
Basket	175.00	Open, hs, 8⅜″ d	45.00
Biscuit Jar, cov	135.00	Open, hs, jelly	50.00
Bowl		Open, ls, 9¼″, ruffled	85.00
8½″, shallow	30.00	Doughnut Tray	90.00
9″, fruit, pie crust rim	70.00	Goblet	85.00
10½″, pie crust rim	75.00	Honey Dish, sq, cov	145.00
Butter, cov, 7½″ d	75.00	Jam Jar, cov	85.00
Cake Stand, hs	85.00	Pitcher, tankard, 10¼″	160.00
Celery Vase	55.00	Sauce, flat, 3¾″	10.00
Compote		Spooner	30.00
Cov, hs, 7″	80.00	Sugar, cov	85.00
Cov, hs, 10″	125.00	Syrup	165.00
Cov, hs, 6″	80.00	Tumbler	30.00
Open, hs, 10½″ d, V shape bowl	90.00		

RIBBON CANDY (Bryce)

Non-flint made by Bryce Bros., Pittsburgh, PA, in the 1880s. Reissued by U. S. Glass Co. in the 1890s. Bowls come in a variety of sizes: open or with lids; flat or with a low collared foot. Also known in emerald green.

	Clear		Clear
Bowl		Open, hs, 8″	35.00
3½″, round	10.00	Open, ls, 3″	12.00
8″, round	25.00	Open, ls, 5″	12.00
Butter, cov		Open, ls, 7″	20.00
Flat	50.00	Cordial	55.00
Footed	55.00	Creamer	25.00
Cake Stand		Cruet, os	65.00
8″	30.00	Cup and Saucer	40.00
10½″	45.00	Goblet	65.00
Claret	65.00	Honey Dish, cov, sq	75.00
Compote		Lamp, oil	75.00
Cov, ls, 5″	30.00	Pitcher	
Cov, ls, 7″	40.00	Milk	45.00
Open, hs, 6″	25.00	Water	75.00

Plate	Clear
6″	18.00
8″	25.00
9½″	30.00
11″	35.00
Relish	10.00
Salt Shaker	35.00
Sauce	
Flat, 4″	10.00

	Clear
Footed, 4″	12.00
Spooner	30.00
Sugar, cov	40.00
Syrup	90.00
Tumbler	25.00
Wine	55.00

SAWTOOTH (Mitre Diamond)

An early clear flint made in the late 1850s by the New England Glass Co., Boston and Sandwich Glass Co., and others. Later made in non-flint by Bryce Bros. and U. S. Glass Co. Also known in milk glass, clear deep blue, and canary yellow.

	Flint	Non-Flint
* Butter, cov	75.00	45.00
* Cake Stand, 10″	85.00	55.00
Celery Vase, 10″	60.00	30.00
Champagne	65.00	30.00
* Compote		
Cov, hs, 9½″	85.00	48.00
Open, ls, 8″, saw-tooth edge	50.00	30.00
Cordial	50.00	30.00
Creamer		
Applied handle	75.00	40.00
Pressed handle	—	30.00
Cruet, acorn stopper	100.00	—
Egg Cup	45.00	25.00

	Flint	Non-Flint
* Goblet	50.00	20.00
Pitcher, water		
Applied handle	150.00	95.00
Pressed handle	—	55.00
Plate, 6½″	45.00	30.00
Pomade Jar, cov	50.00	35.00
Salt		
Cov, ftd	65.00	40.00
Open, smooth edge	25.00	20.00
Spooner	70.00	30.00
Sugar, cov	65.00	35.00
Tumbler, bar	50.00	25.00
Wine, knob stem	35.00	20.00

SNAIL (Compact, Double Snail, Small Comet)

Non-flint made by George Duncan and Sons, Pittsburgh, PA, c1880, and by U. S. Glass Co. after the 1891 merger. U. S. Glass Co. Production expanded this clear pattern by the addition of ruby staining. Add 30% for copper wheel engraved pieces.

	Clear	Ruby Stained
Banana Stand	150.00	225.00
Basket, cake		
9″	85.00	—
10″	95.00	—
Bowl		
4″	20.00	90.00
7″, cov	60.00	45.00
7″, round	28.00	45.00
8″, cov	60.00	45.00
8″, oval	28.00	45.00
9″, oval	30.00	—
10″	35.00	45.00

	Clear	Ruby Stained
Butter, cov	75.00	160.00
Cake Stand		
9″	85.00	—
10″	95.00	—
Celery Tray	35.00	—
Celery Vase	40.00	85.00
Cheese, cov	95.00	—
Compote		
Cov, hs, 7″	50.00	100.00
Cov, hs, 8″	80.00	135.00
Cov, hs, 10″	125.00	—
Open, hs, 6″	30.00	

	Clear	Ruby Stained		Clear	Ruby Stained
Open, hs, 8″	35.00	—	3″	50.00	—
Open, hs, 9″, twist-			5″	45.00	—
ed stem, scal-			7″	50.00	—
loped	75.00	—	Salt		
Cracker Jar, cov	85.00	—	Individual	35.00	40.00
Creamer	65.00	75.00	Master	35.00	75.00
Cruet, os	100.00	275.00	Salt Shaker		
Custard Cup	30.00	—	Bulbous	65.00	90.00
Finger Bowl	50.00	—	Straight sides	60.00	90.00
Goblet	65.00	95.00	Sauce	25.00	45.00
Marmalade, cov	90.00	125.00	Spooner	45.00	75.00
Pitcher			Sugar		
Milk, tankard	100.00	250.00	Individual, cov	50.00	—
Water, bulbous	125.00	—	Regular, cov	60.00	100.00
Water, tankard	135.00	250.00	Sugar Shaker	85.00	200.00
Plate			Syrup	125.00	225.00
5″	35.00	—	Tumbler	55.00	65.00
6″	35.00	—			
7″	40.00	—	Vase	50.00	90.00
Punch Cup	30.00	—	Violet Bowl, 3″	50.00	—
Relish, 7″, oval	25.00	—	Wine	65.00	—
Rose Bowl					

SPRIG (Ribbed Palm)

Non-flint made by Bryce, Higbee and Co., Pittsburgh, PA, c1880.

	Clear		Clear
Bowl, 10″, scalloped	35.00	Pitcher, water	50.00
Bread Plate	40.00	Relish	15.00
Butter, cov	65.00	Salt	
Cake Stand, 8″	35.00	Individual	35.00
Celery Vase	40.00	Master	50.00
Compote		Sauce	
Cov, hs	60.00	Flat	10.00
Open, hs	45.00	Ftd	15.00
Creamer	30.00	Spooner	25.00
Goblet	30.00	Sugar, cov	40.00
Pickle Dish	15.00	Tumbler	25.00
Pickle Jar	65.00	Wine	40.00

TENNESSEE (Jewel and Crescent, Jeweled Rosette)

Non-flint made by King, Son & Co., Pittsburgh, PA, and continued by U. S. Glass Co. in 1899 as part of the States series.

	Clear	Colored Jewels		Clear	Colored Jewels
Bowl			Cake Stand		
Cov, 7″	40.00	—	8″	35.00	—
Open, 8″	35.00	40.00	9½″	38.00	—
Bread Plate	40.00	75.00	10½″	45.00	—
Butter, cov	55.00	—	Celery Vase	35.00	—

	Clear	Colored Jewels		Clear	Colored Jewels
Compote			Pitcher		
Cov, hs, 5″	40.00	55.00	Milk	55.00	—
Cov, hs, 7″	50.00	—	Water	65.00	—
Open, hs, 6″	30.00	—	Relish	20.00	—
Open, hs, 8″	40.00	—	Salt Shaker	30.00	—
Open, hs, 10″	65.00	—	Spooner	35.00	—
Open, ls, 7″	35.00	—	Sugar, cov	45.00	—
Creamer	30.00	—	Syrup	90.00	—
Cruet	65.00	—	Toothpick	75.00	85.00
Goblet	40.00	—	Tumbler	35.00	—
Mug	40.00	—	Wine	65.00	85.00

TEXAS (Loop with Stippled Panels)

Non-flint made by U. S. Glass Co., Pittsburgh, PA, c1900, in the States pattern series. Occasionally pieces are found in ruby stained. Reproduced in solid colors by Crystal Art Glass Co. and Boyd Glass Co., Cambridge, OH.

	Clear w/ Gold	Rose Stained		Clear w/ Gold	Rose Stained
Bowl			Pickle, 8½″	25.00	50.00
7″	20.00	40.00	Pitcher, water	125.00	400.00
9″, scalloped	35.00	50.00	Plate, 9″	35.00	60.00
Butter, cov	75.00	125.00	Salt Shaker	25.00	—
Cake Stand, 9½″, hs	65.00	125.00	Sauce		
Celery Tray	30.00	50.00	Flat	10.00	20.00
Celery Vase	40.00	85.00	Footed	20.00	25.00
Compote			Spooner	35.00	80.00
Cov, hs, 6″	60.00	125.00	Sugar		
Cov, hs, 7″	70.00	150.00	* Individual, cov	45.00	—
Cov, hs, 8″	75.00	175.00	Table, cov	75.00	125.00
Open, hs, 5″	45.00	75.00	Syrup	75.00	175.00
Creamer			Toothpick	25.00	95.00
* Individual	20.00	45.00	Tumbler	40.00	100.00
Table	45.00	85.00	Vase		
Cruet, os	60.00	165.00	6½″	25.00	—
Goblet	95.00	110.00	9″	35.00	—
Horseradish, cov	50.00	—	* Wine	75.00	140.00

THOUSAND EYE

The original pattern was non-flint made by Adams & Co., Tarentum, PA, in 1875 and by Richards and Hartley in 1888. (Pattern No. 103). It was made in two forms: Adams with a three knob stem finial, and Richards and Hartley with a plain stem with a scalloped bottom. Several glass companies made variations of the original pattern and reproductions were made as late as 1981. Crystal Opalescent was produced by Richards and Hartley only in the original pattern. (Opalescent celery vase $70.00; open compote, 8″, $115.00; 6″ creamer, $85.00; ¼ gallon water pitcher, $140.00; ½ gallon water pitcher, $180.00; 4″ footed sauce, $40.00; spooner, $60.00; and 5″ covered sugar, $80.00). Covered compotes are rare and would command 40% more than open compotes. A 2″ mug in blue is known.

	Amber	Apple Green	Blue	Clear	Vaseline
ABC Plate, 6″, clock center	55.00	60.00	55.00	45.00	55.00
Bowl, large, carriage shape	85.00	—	85.00	—	85.00
Butter, cov					
6¼″	65.00	75.00	70.00	45.00	90.00
7½″	65.00	75.00	70.00	45.00	90.00
Cake Stand					
10″	50.00	80.00	55.00	30.00	85.00
11″	50.00	80.00	55.00	30.00	85.00
Celery, hat shape	50.00	65.00	60.00	35.00	55.00
Celery Vase, 7″	50.00	60.00	52.00	45.00	55.00
Christmas Light	30.00	45.00	35.00	25.00	40.00
Cologne Bottle	25.00	45.00	35.00	20.00	45.00
Compote, cov, ls, 8″, sq	—	100.00	100.00	—	—
Compote, open					
6″	35.00	40.00	40.00	25.00	40.00
7″	45.00	50.00	45.00	35.00	45.00
8″, round	40.00	50.00	45.00	35.00	50.00
8″, sq, hs	40.00	50.00	50.00	40.00	55.00
9″	50.00	60.00	55.00	40.00	55.00
10″	55.00	65.00	60.00	45.00	60.00
Cordial	35.00	55.00	40.00	25.00	60.00
Creamer					
4″	35.00	40.00	40.00	25.00	40.00
6″	40.00	75.00	55.00	35.00	75.00
Creamer and Sugar Set	—	150.00	—	100.00	—
*Cruet, 6″	40.00	60.00	50.00	35.00	60.00
Egg Cup	65.00	85.00	70.00	45.00	90.00
*Goblet	40.00	45.00	40.00	35.00	45.00
Honey Dish, cov, 6 × 7¼″	85.00	95.00	90.00	70.00	95.00
Inkwell, 2″ sq	45.00	—	75.00	35.00	80.00
Jelly Glass	25.00	30.00	25.00	15.00	25.00
Lamp, kerosene					
hs, 12″	120.00	150.00	130.00	100.00	140.00
hs, 15″	125.00	155.00	135.00	110.00	150.00
ls, handled	110.00	115.00	110.00	90.00	120.00
Mug					
2½″	25.00	30.00	25.00	20.00	35.00
3½″	25.00	30.00	25.00	20.00	35.00
Nappy					
5″	35.00	—	40.00	30.00	45.00
6″	40.00	—	45.00	35.00	55.00
8″	45.00	—	50.00	45.00	60.00
Pickle	25.00	30.00	30.00	20.00	30.00
Pitcher					
Milk, cov, 7″	85.00	110.00	115.00	70.00	105.00
Water, ¼ gal	70.00	85.00	80.00	55.00	80.00
Water, ½ gal	80.00	95.00	85.00	65.00	85.00
Water, 1 gal	90.00	100.00	95.00	85.00	95.00
*Plate, sq, folded corners					
6″	25.00	30.00	30.00	25.00	30.00
8″	30.00	30.00	30.00	25.00	30.00
10″	35.00	50.00	40.00	25.00	35.00

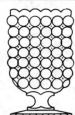

	Amber	Apple Green	Blue	Clear	Vaseline
Platter					
8 × 11″, oblong	40.00	50.00	45.00	40.00	45.00
11″, oval	75.00	80.00	55.00	40.00	75.00
Salt Shaker, pr					
Banded	60.00	70.00	65.00	60.00	65.00
Plain	50.00	60.00	55.00	40.00	60.00
Salt, ind	80.00	95.00	90.00	50.00	90.00
Salt, open, carriage shape	65.00	85.00	75.00	50.00	75.00
Sauce					
Flat, 4″	10.00	20.00	15.00	8.00	15.00
Footed, 4″	15.00	25.00	15.00	10.00	20.00
Spooner	35.00	50.00	40.00	30.00	45.00
*String Holder	35.00	60.00	45.00	30.00	45.00
Sugar, cov, 5″	55.00	75.00	60.00	50.00	60.00
Syrup, pewter top	80.00	100.00	70.00	55.00	70.00
Toothpick					
Hat	35.00	55.00	60.00	30.00	45.00
Plain	35.00	50.00	55.00	25.00	40.00
Thimble	55.00	—	—	—	—
Tray, water					
12½″, round	65.00	80.00	65.00	55.00	60.00
14″, oval	65.00	80.00	75.00	60.00	75.00
*Tumbler	30.00	65.00	35.00	25.00	30.00
*Wine	35.00	50.00	40.00	20.00	40.00

THREE PANEL

Non-flint made by Richards and Hartley Co., Tarentum, PA, c1888, and by U. S. Glass Co. in 1891. Shards have been found at Burlington Glass Works, Hamilton, Ontario, Canada.

	Amber	Blue	Clear	Vaseline
Bowl				
7″	25.00	40.00	20.00	45.00
8½″	25.00	40.00	20.00	45.00
10″	40.00	50.00	35.00	48.00
Butter, cov	45.00	50.00	40.00	50.00
Celery Vase, ruffled top	55.00	65.00	35.00	55.00
Compote, open, ls, 7″	35.00	55.00	25.00	40.00
Creamer	40.00	45.00	25.00	40.00
Cruet	250.00	—	—	—
*Goblet	30.00	40.00	25.00	35.00
Mug	35.00	45.00	25.00	35.00
Pitcher, water	100.00	125.00	40.00	110.00
Sauce, ftd	15.00	15.00	10.00	15.00
Spooner	42.50	45.00	30.00	40.00
Sugar, cov	55.00	60.00	45.00	70.00
Tumbler	35.00	40.00	20.00	30.00

U. S. COIN

Non-flint frosted, clear, and gilted pattern made by U. S. Glass Co., Pittsburgh, PA, in 1892 for three or four months. Production was stopped by the U. S. Treasury because real coins, dated as early as 1878, were used in the molds. The 1892 coin date is the most common. Lamps with coins on font and stem would be 50% more.

	Clear	Frosted
Ale Glass	250.00	350.00
* Bowl		
6"	170.00	220.00
9"	215.00	325.00
* Bread Plate	175.00	325.00
Butter, cov, dollars and halves	250.00	450.00
Cake Stand, 10"	225.00	400.00
Celery Tray	200.00	—
Celery Vase, quarters	135.00	350.00
Champagne	—	400.00
* Compote		
Cov, hs, 7"	300.00	500.00
Cov, hs, 8", quarters and dimes	—	415.00
Open, hs, 7", quarters and dimes	200.00	300.00
Open, hs, 7", quarters and halves	225.00	350.00
Open, 8⅜" d, 6½" h	—	240.00
* Creamer	350.00	600.00
Cruet, os	375.00	500.00

	Clear	Frosted
Epergne	—	1,000.00
Goblet	300.00	450.00
Goblet, dimes	—	550.00
Lamp		
Round font	275.00	450.00
Square font	300.00	—
Mug, handled	200.00	300.00
Pickle	200.00	—
Pitcher		
Milk	600.00	600.00
Water	400.00	800.00
Sauce, ftd, 4", quarters	100.00	185.00
* Spooner, quarters	225.00	325.00
* Sugar, cov	225.00	400.00
Syrup, dated pewter lid	—	525.00
* Toothpick	180.00	275.00
Tray, water, 8", round	275.00	—
* Tumbler	135.00	235.00
Waste Bowl	225.00	250.00
Wine	225.00	375.00

UTAH (Frost Flower, Twinkle Star)

Non-flint made by U. S. Glass Co., Pittsburgh, PA, and Gas City, IN, in 1901 in the States pattern series. Add 25% for frosting.

	Clear
Bowl	
Cov, 6"	20.00
Open, 8"	18.00
Butter, cov	35.00
Cake Plate, 9"	20.00
Cake Stand	
7"	35.00
8"	20.00
10"	30.00
Castor Set, 2 bottles	40.00
Celery Vase	20.00
Compote	
Cov, hs, 6"	45.00
Cov, hs, 8"	60.00
Open, hs, 7"	25.00
Open, hs, 9"	35.00
Open, hs, 10"	40.00

	Clear
Condiment Set, salt & pepper shakers, holder	45.00
Creamer	30.00
Cruet	40.00
Goblet	25.00
Pickle	12.00
Pitcher, water	45.00
Salt Shaker, orig top	20.00
Sauce, 4"	8.50
Spooner	15.00
Sugar, cov	35.00
Syrup	50.00
Tumbler	15.00
Wine	25.00

WASHINGTON (Early Washington, Leafy Panel and Thumbprint)

Flint made by New England Glass Co., East Cambridge, MA, c1869.

	Clear		Clear
Ale Glass	125.00	Goblet	110.00
Bottle, bitters	85.00	Honey Dish, 3½"	30.00
Bowl, 6 x 9", oval	45.00	Lamp	150.00
Butter, cov	175.00	Lemonade Glass	85.00
Celery Vase	95.00	Mug	85.00
Champagne	125.00	Pitcher, water	375.00
Claret	110.00	Plate, 6"	60.00
Compote		Salt, individual	20.00
Cov, hs, 6"	125.00	Sauce, 5"	25.00
Cov, hs, 10"	175.00	Spooner	75.00
Cordial	150.00	Sugar, cov	125.00
Creamer	200.00	Tumbler	85.00
Decanter, os	150.00	Wine	125.00
Egg Cup	75.00		

WESTWARD HO! (Pioneer, Tippecanoe)

Non-flint, usually frosted, made by Gillinder and Sons, Philadelphia, PA, c1879. Molds made by Jacobus who also made Classic. Has been reproduced since the 1930s by L. G. Wright Glass Co., Westmoreland Glass Co., and several others. This pattern was originally made in milk glass (rare) and clear with acid finish as part of the design. Reproductions can be found in several colors and clear.

	Clear		Clear
Bowl, 5", ftd	125.00	* Goblet	90.00
Bread Plate	175.00	Marmalade Jar, cov	200.00
* Butter, cov	185.00	Mug	
* Celery Vase	125.00	2"	225.00
* Compote		3½"	175.00
Cov, hs, 5"	225.00	* Pitcher, water	250.00
Cov, hs, 9"	275.00	* Sauce, ftd, 4½"	35.00
Cov, ls, 5"	150.00	* Spooner	85.00
Open, hs, 8"	125.00	* Sugar, cov	185.00
* Creamer	95.00	* Wine	200.00

WILDFLOWER

Non-flint made by Adams & Co., Pittsburgh, PA, c1885 and by U. S. Glass Co., c1891. This pattern has been heavily reproduced. Reproductions date as early as 1936. L. G. Wright Glass Co. and Crystal Art Glass Co. have issued items from new molds and in additional colors.

	Amber	Apple Green	Blue	Clear	Vaseline
Bowl, 8", sq	25.00	35.00	35.00	15.00	20.00
Butter, cov					
Collared base	40.00	50.00	50.00	35.00	45.00
Flat	35.00	45.00	45.00	30.00	40.00

	Amber	Apple Green	Blue	Clear	Vaseline
Cake Stand, 10½" ..	50.00	80.00	75.00	45.00	50.00
* Champagne	40.00	55.00	50.00	25.00	45.00
Celery Vase	55.00	60.00	55.00	35.00	55.00
* Compote					
Cov, hs, 8"	80.00	85.00	85.00	50.00	75.00
Cov, ls, 7"	—	—	70.00	—	—
Open, hs	80.00	—	—	—	—
* Creamer	35.00	50.00	45.00	40.00	48.00
* Goblet	30.00	40.00	40.00	25.00	40.00
Pitcher, water	55.00	95.00	65.00	40.00	70.00
* Plate, 10", sq	30.00	30.00	45.00	25.00	30.00
Platter					
10", oblong	40.00	45.00	40.00	30.00	30.00
11 x 8", deep scalloped edges ...	—	—	45.00	—	—
Relish	20.00	22.00	20.00	18.00	20.00
* Salt, turtle	45.00	50.00	50.00	30.00	40.00
Salt Shaker	35.00	55.00	40.00	20.00	45.00
* Sauce, ftd, 4", round	17.50	18.00	18.00	12.00	17.50
Spooner	30.00	35.00	30.00	20.00	40.00
* Sugar, cov	45.00	45.00	50.00	30.00	45.00
Syrup	125.00	150.00	160.00	65.00	150.00
Tray, water, oval ...	50.00	60.00	60.00	40.00	55.00
* Tumbler	40.00	35.00	35.00	25.00	35.00
* Wine	45.00	45.00	45.00	25.00	45.00

WISCONSIN (Beaded Dewdrop)

Non-flint made by U. S. Glass Co. in Gas City, IN, in 1903. One of the States patterns. Toothpick reproduced in colors.

	Clear		Clear
Banana Stand	75.00	Cup and Saucer	50.00
Bowl		* Goblet	65.00
6", oval, handled, cov ...	40.00	Marmalade Jar, straight	
7", round	42.00	sides, glass lid.........	125.00
Butter, flat flange	75.00	Mug	35.00
*Cake Stand		Pitcher	
8½"	45.00	Milk	55.00
9½"	55.00	Water	70.00
Celery Tray	40.00	Plate, 6¾"	25.00
Celery Vase	45.00	Punch Cup	12.00
Compote		Relish	25.00
Cov, hs, 5"	45.00	Salt Shaker	30.00
Cov, hs, 7"	60.00	Spooner	30.00
Open, hs, 6"	35.00	Sugar, cov	55.00
Open, hs, 8"	50.00	Sugar Shaker	90.00
Open, hs, 10"	75.00	Sweetmeat, 5", ftd, cov ...	40.00
Condiment Set, salt & pepper, mustard, horse radish,		Syrup	110.00
tray................	110.00	*Toothpick, kettle	55.00
Creamer	50.00	Tumbler	40.00
Cruet, os	80.00	Wine	75.00

WYOMING (Enigma)

Made by U. S. Glass Co., Gas City, IN, in the States pattern series in 1903.

	Clear		Clear
Bowl		Creamer	
4″	15.00	Cov	50.00
8″	45.00	Open	35.00
Butter, cov	50.00	Goblet	65.00
Cake Plate	55.00	Mug	45.00
Cake Stand, 9″, 10″, 11″	70.00	Pitcher, water	75.00
Compote		Relish	15.00
Cov, hs, 6″	60.00	Salt & Pepper Shakers, pr	45.00
Cov, hs, 7″	75.00	Spooner	30.00
Cov, hs, 8″	85.00	Sugar, cov	45.00
Open, hs, 8″	60.00	Syrup, small, glass cov	65.00
Open, hs, 9″	65.00	Tumbler	55.00
Open, hs, 10″	75.00	Wine	85.00

YALE (Crow-foot, Turkey Track)

Non-flint made by McKee & Bros. Glass Co., Jeannette, PA, patented in 1887.

	Clear		Clear
Bowl, berry, 10½″	20.00	Pitcher, water	65.00
Butter, cov	45.00	Relish, oval	12.00
Cake Stand	55.00	Salt Shaker	30.00
Celery Vase	35.00	Sauce, flat	10.00
Compote		Spooner	20.00
Cov, hs	50.00	Sugar, cov	35.00
Open, scalloped rim	25.00	Syrup	65.00
Creamer	30.00	Tumbler	20.00
Goblet	30.00		

S.E.G.
PAUL REVERE POTTERY

History: Paul Revere Pottery, Boston, Massachusetts, was an outgrowth of a club known as "The Saturday Evening Girls." The S.E.G. was a group of young female immigrants who met on Saturday nights for reading and crafts such as ceramics.

Regular production began in 1908. The name Paul Revere was adopted because the pottery was located near the Old North Church. In 1915 the firm moved to Brighton, Massachusetts. Known as the "Bowl Shop," the pottery grew steadily. In spite of popular acceptance and technical advancements, the pottery required continual subsidies. It finally closed in January 1942.

Items produced range from plain and decorated vases to tablewares to illustrated tiles. Many decorated wares were incised and glazed either in an Art Nouveau matte finish or an occasional high glaze.

In addition to the impressed mark, paper "Bowl Shop" labels were used prior to 1915. Pieces also can be found dated with P.R.P. or S.E.G. painted on the base.

References: Paul Evans, *Art Pottery of the*

United States, Second Edition, Feingold & Lewis Publishing, 1987; Ralph and Terry Kovel, *The Kovels' Collector's Guide to American Art Pottery*, Crown Publishers, 1974.

Collectors' Club: American Art Pottery Association, 125 E. Rose Ave., St. Louis, MO 63119.

Vase, mustard yellow, marked "PR" on horse, 6½" h, $75.00.

Luncheon Set, cream ground, blue and green repeating tree and sky design below rim, black outlines, sgd and numbered, five cups, luncheon, and dessert plates, price for fifteen piece set **1,650.00**

Mug
  3″ h, inscribed "John Fisk/Zueblin" below rim, dec with grass strolling rabbit, matte brown and blue, cream ground, blue band, inscribed "Xmas/1914/S.E.G.," hairline **385.00**
  4″ h, dec by Sara Galner, incised tree filled landscape, solitary nightingale over inscription "In the forest must always be a nightingale and in the soul a faith so faithful that it comes back even after it has been slain," green, brown, blue, cream, and yellow glazes, incised artist's initials and marks, c1915 . . . . **1,430.00**

Pitcher, 7¾″ h, incised and dec stylized yellow tulips, brown leaves, black outlines, yellow ground, white horizontal ring below spout, sgd "SEG/AM," spout loss, hairline. **660.00**

Plate
  3½″ d, dec by Lily Shapiro and Rose Bikini, Helen Osbourne Storrow monogram incised at center, running pigs at rim, bands of brown, yellow, and green, artists' ciphers, numbered, and marked "SEG," price for pair **3,190.00**
  8½″ d, incised central monogram, running pigs on rim, brown, yellow, and green bands, sgd "SEG/FL," numbered **1,870.00**

Tile, 5¾″ d, central cottage by lake scene, green, brown, white, and orange, black outlines, light blue ground, sgd and numbered **420.00**

Vase
  7¼″ h, flaring cylindrical, stylized trees, gray–green glaze, black outlines, sgd "SEG" **440.00**
  8⅜″ h, light blue ground, band of flying ducks over blue water, horizon of green land, yellow and blue sky, black outlines, inscribed marks, remnants of paper label, rim peppering **1,320.00**
  9⅛″ h, matte yellow glaze body, matte yellow, green, and brown stylized floral band, black outlines, matte white/yellow band at shoulder and rim, inscribed marks, two hairlines at rim **525.00**

PEACHBLOW

History: Peachblow, an art glass which derives its name from a fine Chinese glazed porcelain, resembles a peach or crushed strawberries in color. Three American glass manufacturers and two English firms produced peachblow glass in the late 1880s. A fourth American firm renewed the process in the 1950s. The glass from each firm has its own identifying characteristics:

Hobbs, Brockunier & Co., Wheeling peachblow: Opalescent glass, plated or cased with a transparent amber glass; shading from yellow at the base to a deep red at top; glossy or satin finish.

Mt. Washington "Peach Blow": A homogeneous glass, shading from a pale gray–blue to a soft rose color. Pieces may be enhanced with glass appliqués, enameling, and gilting.

New England Glass Works, New England peachblow: advertised as "Wild Rose" but called "Peach Blow" at the plant. Translucent, shading from rose to white; acid or glossy finish. Some pieces enameled and gilted.

Thomas Webb & Sons and Stevens and Williams, England: Around 1888 these two firms made a peachblow-style art glass marked "Peach Blow" or "Peach Bloom." A cased glass, shading from yellow to red. Occasionally found with cameo–type designs in relief.

Gunderson Glass Co.: About 1950 produced peachblow-type art glass to order; shades from an opaque faint tint of pink, which is almost white, to a deep rose.

Reference: John A. Shuman III, *The Collector's Encyclopedia of American Glass*, Collector Books, 1988, 1991 value update.

GUNDERSON

Creamer and Sugar	420.00
Cruet, 6½" h	175.00
Goblet	140.00
Jug, 4½" h, 4" d, acid finish, bulbous, applied white loop handle	450.00
Sugar, open, ftd	65.00
Tumbler, 4" h	125.00

MT WASHINGTON

Bowl, 3 x 4", shading from deep rose to bluish–white, MOP satin int	120.00
Pitcher, 6⅞" h, bulbous, sq handle	3,700.00
Toothpick, DQ, sq mouth, enamel floral and berry dec	6,350.00
Vase	
8" h, bulbous, blue and white enamel forget–me–not dec, acid finish	3,875.00
8¼" h, lily form, satin finish	1,800.00

NEW ENGLAND

Basket, 6½" h, 6" w, hobnail design basket, applied amber handle, attributed to Sandwich	250.00
Celery Vase, 6¼" h, 3¾" d, deep crimson blush shading to lightly tinted pink base, piecrust crimped top	545.00
Darner, 6" l, hollow blown ball shading dark pink to white handle, price for pair	220.00
Finger Bowl, 5¼" d, wide ruffled top	335.00
Salt and Pepper Shaker, pr, metal holder, orig tops	850.00
Toothpick, 2" h, tricorn, shiny finish	480.00
Vase	
5" h, matte finish, swirled, ruffled, applied camphor frosted edge, deep pink shading to white, attributed to Sandwich	250.00
5½" h, 2¼" to 3" w body, matte finish, cupped shape top, deep raspberry upper third shading to white base, polished pontil	735.00

WEBB

Cologne, 5" h, bulbous, raised gold floral branches, silver hallmarked dome top	900.00
Creamer, satin finish, Coralene dec, rolled rim, flat base	660.00
Epergne, 7½" h, three clear glass leaves, shiny finish, mirror base	785.00
Finger Bowl, 4½" d, cased	185.00

Vase	
6½" h, stick, gold prunus flowers, leaves, and insect dec, propeller mark	550.00
7" h, teardrop, satin finish	195.00
9½" h, flattened oval, cased pink to white, gold and silver enameled butterfly and foliage	330.00

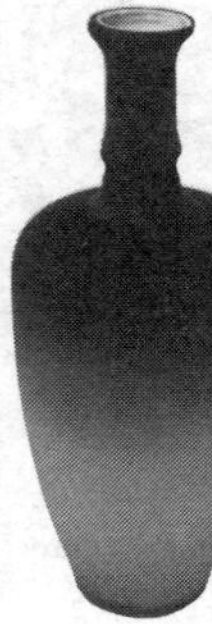

Wheeling, vase, acid finish, 7¾" h, $675.00.

WHEELING

Cruet, bulbous, amber reeded handle and cut faceted stopper	970.00
Decanter, 9" h, amber, faceted stopper, satin reeded handle	3,140.00
Ewer, 6¾" h, 4" w, glossy finish, duck bill top, applied amber loop handle	3,500.00
Mustard, SP cov and handle	450.00
Pitcher, 7¼" h, glossy, deep red shading to creamy pale green, bulbous, quatrefoil top, applied amber handle, white casing, polished pontil, c1870, Hobbs, Brockunier	850.00
Salt Shaker, 2¾" h, glossy finish, cherry red to butter yellow base	485.00
Syrup, glossy finish, fuchsia red to deep amber, deep amber handle, orig metal top	2,750.00
Tumbler, 4" h, orig glossy finish, Hobbs Brockunier	225.00
Vase	
8" h, Morgan	
Glossy, deep maroon–rose shading to amber	770.00
Satin finish, strong amberina shading	615.00
9¼" h, long slender neck	985.00

PEKING GLASS

History: Peking glass is a type of cameo glass of Chinese origin. Its production began in the 1700s and continued well into the 19th century. The background color of Peking glass may be a delicate shade of yellow, green, or white. One style of white background is so delicate and transparent that it often is referred to as the "snowflake" ground. The overlay colors include a rich garnet red, deep blue, and emerald green.

Reference: Gloria and Robert Mascarelli, *Oriental Antiques,* Wallace–Homestead, 1992.

Box, cov, turquoise, Oriental figures and dog, 4⅝" d, $200.00.

Bowl
  6¼" d, 2¼" h, shallow, opaque white ground, green overlay carved in repeating floral design, border chip. . **165.00**
  6½" d, 3" h, flared, opaque white ground
    Green overlay cut as chrysanthemum motif **135.00**
    Red overlay cut as stylized blossoming trees **125.00**
  8" d, quatrefoil, opaque sky blue ground, price for pair **880.00**
Jar, 5" h, wide ovoid sea green body, narrow short flared neck, Qianlong period, sgd. **4,400.00**
Jardiniere, 5⅛ x 7⅜" h, flaring rect ruby sides, finely carved chrysanthemum, peony, prunus, and narcissus blossoms on leafy stems, recessed rect base, four "L" shaped tab feet, 18th C. **2,750.00**
Vase
  5¼" h, bulbous ovoid, tricolor, thick applied foot, small flat mouth, center opaque cream wide band, deep raspberry overlay carved with hooks, volutes, and ruyi–heads, carved double row of overlapping

lotus petals around base, opaque blue thick neck ring and flaring base foot, four character mark incised on base, Qianlong period, casting flaws, neck reduced **11,550.00**
  7¾" h, baluster, yellow body, two carved birds and flowering peony and prunus branches extending around sides, issuing from rockwork base, 19th C, price for pair . . **1,650.00**

PELOTON

History: Wilhelm Kralik of Bohemia patented Peloton art glass in 1880. Later it was also patented in America and England.

Peloton glass is found with both transparent and opaque grounds, with opaque being more common. Opaque colored glass filaments (strings) are applied by dipping or rolling the hot glass. Generally, the filaments (threads) are pink, blue, yellow, and white (rainbow colors) or a single color. Items also may have a satin finish and enamel decorations.

Reference: Ellen T. Schroy, *Warman's Glass,* Wallace–Homestead, 1992.

Tumbler, yellow, pink, red, light blue, and white, 3¾" h, $125.00.

Biscuit Jar, 6¾" h, ribbed body, pale blue ground, multicolored filaments, white lining, SP rim, cover, and bail handle **500.00**
Bowl, 3½" d, 2½" h, pinched top, ribbed sides, clear ground, white, pink, blue, and olive green filaments, fiery opal pastel orchid lining. **175.00**
Finger Bowl, clear, multicolored filaments. **65.00**
Pitcher, 6½" h, sq blown clear body, applied colorless, pink, yellow, blue, and white striped yellow filaments, applied clear handle **175.00**

Punch Cup, turquoise ground, multicolored filaments, enameled florals, set of six **300.00**

Rose Bowl, 2½" d, 2¼" h, crimped top, opaque white ground, pink, yellow, blue, and white filaments **250.00**

Toothpick
2½" h, clear ground, green filaments **100.00**
3" h, clear, white filaments **125.00**

Tumbler, 3¾" h, clear ground, yellow, pink, red, light blue, and white filaments. **125.00**

Vase
3¼" h, 3" d, ball shape, flared ruffled top, orchid pink ground, blue, pink, yellow and white filaments **175.00**
4¼" h, 4¾" d, squatty, ribbed, tricorn folded down rim, clear ground, rose, yellow, blue and white filaments, white lining **300.00**
6¾" h, 3" d, stick, yellow ground, white, rose, blue, and yellow filaments, white lining **225.00**

Water Set, blown water pitcher, polished pontil, five tumblers, light yellow amber ground, multicolored filaments. . . **650.00**

PERFUME, COLOGNE, AND SCENT BOTTLES

History: Decorative bottles to hold scents have been made in various shapes and sizes. They reached a "golden age" during the second half of the 19th century.

An atomizer is a perfume bottle with a spray mechanism. Cologne bottles usually are larger and have stoppers which also may be used as applicators. A perfume bottle has a stopper that often is elongated and designed as an applicator.

Scent bottles are small bottles used to hold a scent or smelling salts. A vinaigrette is an ornamental box or bottle with a perforated top used to hold aromatic vinegars or smelling salts. Fashionable women of the late 18th and 19th centuries carried them in purses or slipped them into gloves in case of a sudden fainting spell.

References: Joanne Dubbs Ball and Dorothy Hehl Torem, *Commercial Fragrance Bottles,* Schiffer Publishing, 1993; Jacquelyne Jones–North, *Commercial Perfume Bottles,* Schiffer Publishing, 1987; Jacquelyne Jones–North, *Czechoslovakian Perfume Bottles & Boudoir Accessories,* Antique Publications, 1990; Tirza True Latimer, *The Perfume Atomizer: An Object With Atmosphere,* Schiffer Publishing, 1991; Hazel Martin, *A Collection Of Figural Perfume & Scent Bottles,* published by author, 1982; Jacquelyne North, *Perfume, Cologne, and Scent Bottles,* Schiffer Publishing, 1987; Jean Sloan, *Perfume and Scent Bottle Collecting With Prices, Second Edition,* Wallace–Homestead, 1989.

Collectors' Clubs: International Perfume & Scent Bottle Collectors, 310 Maple Ave., Vienna, VA 22180; Mini–Scents, 1123 N. Flores St., Apt. 21, West Hollywood, CA 90069; Perfume and Scent Bottle Collectors, 2022 East Charleston Blvd., Las Vegas, NV 89104.

ATOMIZERS

DeVilbiss
Amber, etched floral design **150.00**
Black Amethyst, art glass, goldstone spider web dec, no bulb **80.00**
Galle, 8" h, cameo glass, lavender flowers and foliage, shaded yellow and frosted grounded. **1,250.00**
Moser, 4½" h, sapphire blue, gold florals, leaves, and swirls, melon ribbed body, orig gold top and bulb . . **250.00**

COLOGNES

Baccarat, 5⅞" h, clear, panel cut, matching stopper **75.00**
Cobalt Blue Overlay, 4½" h, thousand eye, faceted base, matching stopper **110.00**
Cut Glass, 7" h, cranberry cut to clear, cane cut, matching stopper **250.00**
Nash Glass, Chintz pattern, paperweight stopper **225.00**
Pairpoint, 8" h, applied vertical cranberry ribbing, elaborate flower form cranberry and clear stopper **110.00**
Peachblow, 4¾" h, floral dec, acid finish, cut stopper **375.00**
Sterling Silver Overlay, clear ground . **150.00**

PERFUMES

Clichy
3¹¹⁄₁₆" h, ext. dec with alternating blue and white swirled bands, hallmarked sterling silver lid, no stopper **165.00**
3¹⁵⁄₁₆" h, ext. dec with alternating blue and white swirled bands, stopper and base dec with 16K gold chased with delicate patterns, base marked "D.J.," fitted leather carrying case **990.00**
Mary Gregory, 4⅝" h, cranberry, white enameled girl dec, clear ball stopper **165.00**
Rene Lalique, 5½" h, Sirenes, frosted mermaids with traces of gray patine, molded signature on base, no cover **250.00**
Saint Louis, 3¹⁹⁄₁₆" h, cherub sulphide surrounded by ornate faceting on all sides, gilded copper cap, glass stopper. **358.00**
Steuben, Rosa, black jade stopper . . **660.00**
Venetian
2⅜" h, globular bottle, Lion of Venice portrait cane on surface of opaque

yellow and silver glass, crowned with an ornate cap dec with flowers, no stopper. **330.00**
3¹⁵⁄₁₆″ h, vertical bands of pistachio, white, and blue glass and green aventurine, bottle ext. enhance with ornate cutting. **303.00**
Verre–de–Soie, 4¾″ h, jade green . . **300.00**

Scent Bottle, glass, light yellow, painted abstract floral in red, orange, and blue, shaped triangular motif, silver cap, 2½″ h, $150.00.

SCENTS

Agate, 3″ h, flattened globe form, silver hinged rim and screw cap marked "Black, Starr & Frost" **250.00**
Chelsea, child's
  3″ h, romantic Georgian couple, dove finial **250.00**
  3¼″ h, harlequin, figural **1,300.00**
Czechoslovakian, multicolored jewels, enameled top **100.00**
Early American Glass
  2½″ h
    Amethyst, teardrop shape with emb sunburst design **220.00**
    Opaque white and amethyst looping, blown, snail shell shape, cased with clear and clear applied rigaree. **165.00**
  2⅞″ h, fiery opalescent, teardrop shape with emb sunburst design . . **625.00**
  3″ h, cobalt blue, teardrop shape, ribbed. **95.00**
  4⅜″ l, clear, blown, dec with cranberry and white stripes with white and gold metallic twist. **80.00**
Ivory, carved
  1½″ h, miniature, gourd shape, Oriental. **65.00**

3¾″ h, figural, woman, holding basket of flowers in one hand, fan in other, polychrome dec, Japanese **85.00**
Opalescent, blown, cast pewter lid . . **165.00**
Ruby Glass, cylindrical, SS cap dated 1884 . . . . **90.00**
Victorian, repousse brass dec, chain with finger ring, Nacre **145.00**

VINAIGRETTES

Cut Glass, 3⅞″ l, cobalt blue, yellow flashing, SS overlay, emb SS cap. . . **125.00**
Gold, 2½″ l, flattened cartouche shape, putto playing lute, another playing with hound, carnelian intaglio base with two lovebirds and chaplet, inscribed "Vivons Fidelle," English, Mid 18th C **650.00**
Sterling Silver
  ⅞″ l, tooled purse shape, gilded int., John Turner, Birmingham hallmarks, 1792 . . . . **240.00**
  1″ l, tooled purse shape, gilded int., Joseph Taylor, Birmingham hallmarks, 1821 . . . . **205.00**
  1¼″ l, tooled purse shape, gilded int., S Pemberton, Birmingham hallmarks, 1790 . . . . **215.00**
Victorian, tiger claw, surmounted by figure of tiger holding garnet in chased high karat gold mount **3,850.00**

PETERS AND REED POTTERY

History: J. D. Peters and Adam Reed founded their pottery company in South Zanesville, Ohio, in 1900. Common flowerpots, jardinieres, and cooking wares comprised their early major output. Occasionally art pottery was attempted, but it was not until 1912 that their Moss Aztec line was introduced and widely accepted. Other art wares included Chromal, Landsun, Montene, Pereco, and Persian.

Peters retired in 1921 and Reed changed the name of the firm to Zane Pottery Company. Marked pieces of Peters and Reed Pottery are unknown.

Bowl, 5″ d, 2″ h, brown, green highlights **25.00**
Candlesticks, pr, 10″ h, mirror black glaze **24.00**
Doorstop, cat, yellow **375.00**
Ewer, 11″ h, brown, raised grapes, orange and yellow dec **45.00**
Jardiniere
  Chromal Landsun dec, price for pair **650.00**
  Lions, #249 . . . . **45.00**
Jug, bulbous, grape clusters and vine dec, standard glossy brown glaze, handled **50.00**
Mug, blended glaze **25.00**

Vase, Art Nouveau, leaf and lily pattern, green ground, pink overtones, matte glaze, 5¾" h, $95.00.

Pitcher, 4" h, man with banjo, standard glossy brown glaze	35.00
Rose Bowl, wreath and vine dec, standard glossy brown glaze, ftd.	40.00
Vase	
3" h, 4" w, yellow, blue speckles ..	20.00
5" h, Zane Ware, underglaze rose dec.	40.00
6" h, 6½" w, mirror black glaze . . .	40.00
7½" h, Landsun blue	30.00
8½" h, rust, black, blue, and yellow swirl.	45.00
10" h, gray blended	35.00
Wall Pocket, Moss Aztec	75.00

PEWTER

History: Pewter is a metal alloy consisting mostly of tin with small amounts of lead, copper, antimony, and bismuth added to improve formability and hardness. The metal can be cast, formed around a mold, spun, easily cut, and soldered to form a wide variety of utilitarian articles.

Pewter ware was known to the ancient Chinese, Egyptians, and Romans. English pewter supplied the major portion of the needs of the American colonies for nearly 150 years before the American Revolution. The Revolution ended the embargo on raw tin and allowed the small American pewter industry to flourish. This period lasted until the Civil War.

The listing concentrates on the American and English pewter forms most often encountered by the collector.

Reference: Donald L. Fennimore, *The Knopf Collectors' Guides to American Antiques: Silver & Pewter,* Alfred A. Knopf, 1984.

Collectors' Club: Pewter Collectors Club of America, 29 Chesterfield Road, Scarsdale, NY 10583.

Museum: The Currier Gallery of Art, Manchester, NH.

Advisor: Robert Limons.

Baptismal Bowl, L L Williams, Philadelphia, PA, ftd, 6½" d	**750.00**
Basin	
Barns, Blakslee, Philadelphia, PA	
6⅝" d, 1½" h, partial eagle touch, wear and battering	175.00
9" d, eagle stamp on int.	500.00
Jones, Gershom, Providence, RI, eagle touch, dents, wear, and scratches, 7¾" d, 1⅞" h	375.00
Unmarked, American	
5" d, 3¼" h, ftd	250.00
6" d, 2" h	105.00
8" d, attributed to Abraham Hasselberg or John Brunstrom, Philadelphia, PA, Lovebird mark	550.00
13" d, attributed to Abraham Hasselberg or John Brunstrom, Philadelphia, Lovebird mark	825.00

Candlesticks, pr, unmarked, English, weighted bases, 9¼" h, $100.00.

Candlestick	
Dunham, Rufus, Westbrook, ME, 6" h	175.00
Gleason, Roswell, Dorcester, MA, "R. Gleason" touch, 7" h	375.00
Unmarked, American	
8" h, beaded trim	275.00
8" h, pushups, price for pair	330.00
9¾" h, price for pair	440.00
Charger	
Austin, Nathaniel, MA, c1800, 13½" d	750.00
Hamlin, Samuel, Providence, RI, c1800, 13½" d	800.00
Melville, David, 1804–10, Newport, RI, dents, 14" d	450.00

Townsend, John, London, smooth rim, 15″ d 250.00

Unknown Maker, Continental, angel touch mark, scalloped rim, minor wear, 12½″ d. 110.00

Ciborium (Pyx), Joseph Liddell, Jr, New York City, c1750, worn mark, some pitting, 7¾″ d, ... 1,980.00

Coffeepot

Dixon, James, England, octagonal, wooden handle and finial, marked "James Dixon & Sons," 10½″ h. . . 172.00

Dunham, R, 11″ h 275.00

Gleason, Roswell, Dorchester, MA, wooden finial wafer with glued repair, repair to bottom edge, 11″ h. . 200.00

Porter, F, #1, 7½″ h 250.00

Smith & Co, Boston, pedestal foot, wood handle, 10″ h. 265.00

Trask, Israel, Beverly, MA, lighthouse, bright cut engraving, 7″ h 350.00

Trask, O, cut engraving, 11½″ h . . 275.00

Unmarked, American, C–shaped wooden handle, dents and soldered repair on bottom, 11½″ h 130.00

Communion Chalice, unmarked, American, handles removed, 6¼″ h, price for pair. 200.00

Communion Set, unknown maker, 11″ flagon, two 6″ h chalices, price for three piece set 225.00

Creamer, unmarked, American, teapot shape, 5⅞″ h 250.00

Flagon, unknown maker, Continental 9½″ h, thumb piece, engraved floral and amorous couple on bench design, German inscription and "F C S 1809," soldered repair. 165.00

Flagon, castle touchmarks, 11″ h, $75.00.

10″ h, German eagle touch mark, thumb piece, lid engraved "GOP 1842". 200.00

11¾″ h, twist ring top lid, spout flap and shield with "B W". 145.00

12½″ h, thumb piece, lid engraved "A R G 1811," fleur de lis touch mark 200.00

Food Mold, unmarked, English, cylindrical, int. flutes and fruit design top

6″ h 72.00

6½″ h 85.00

Hot Water Plate, Henry and Richard Joseph, English, touch marks, slightly battered, 8″ d 165.00

Inkstand, unknown maker, ftd, 3½″ h, 5½″ w, 9½″ l. 165.00

Inkwell, unknown maker, hinged lid, missing insert, 2¼″ h 90.00

Lamp, fluid

Dunham, Rufus, Portland, ME, whale oil burner, "R. Dunham" touch, 5⅝″ h 330.00

Gleason, Roswell, missing burner, 7″ h, price for pair 350.00

Graves, H H, CT, brass single spout burner, snuffer with chain, partially obliterated "Graves" touch, 7½″ h 315.00

Hyde, Martin, New York City, sparking, single spout burner, ring handle, burner with chain, marked "M. Hyde," 4¼″ h. 280.00

Porter, Allen, Westbrook, ME, brass and tin whale oil burner, "A. Porter" touch, 8⅜″ h 715.00

Unknown Maker, pear shape font, molded stem, saucer base, twin tube burner, 12″ h 225.00

Unmarked, American, sparking

Brass and pewter burning fluid burner, snuffer caps missing, 4″ h. 200.00

Single spout burner, ring handle, snuffer missing, minor battering, 4¼″ h 60.00

Single spout burner, snuffer on chain, cast ear handle, burner resoldered, 4″ h. 50.00

Whale oil burner, 5¼″ h 165.00

Measure

Unknown Maker, English, side spout, battered, resoldered handle, 7″ h. . 30.00

Warne, John, English, brass rim, battered, old repair, quart, 5¾″ h 95.00

Mug, quart

Boardman, Thomas Danforth, Hartford, CT, tankard, partial "T.D.B." touch, some battering, soldered repairs, 4″ h. 500.00

Danforth, Samuel, Hartford, CT, 1795–1913, marked with eagle and Hartford. 1,430.00

Hamlin, Samuel, 1767–1801, Hartford, Middletown, CT, and Providence, RI, Laughlin 330 and 331 to left of handle, dent at base, 5⅞″ h . . . 605.00

Pitcher
- Porter, Freeman, Westbrook, ME, 2 qt, 6″ h . . . 225.00
- Unknown Maker
  - American, hinged lid, battered and damaged, 7½″ h . . . 60.00
  - Continental, swirl design, hinged lid, angel touch mark, 6½″ h . . . 75.00

Plate, French or English, castle touchmark, scalloped rim with beaded edge, 19th C, 9¾″ d, price for set of six, $300.00.

Plate
- Austin, Nathaniel, Charlestown, MA, 1763–1800, smooth rim, rampant lion mark, 8″ d, price for pair . . . 2,310.00
- Austin, Richard, Boston, MA, 8″ d . . . 375.00
- Barns, B, Philadelphia, PA, 7¾″ d . . . 325.00
- Boardman, Thomas Danforth, Hartford, CT
  - Eagle in oval touch, 9⅜″ d . . . 440.00
  - Lion touch with "Boardman," scratches, 8⅞″ d . . . 300.00
- Danforth, Edward, Middletown, CT, wear and scratches, 8″ d . . . 250.00
- Danforth, Samuel, Hartford, CT, 7¾″ d . . . 275.00
- Danforth, Thomas, Philadelphia, PA, touch with eagle, very minor wear, 7¾″ d . . . 415.00
- Danforth, William, Middletown, CT, partial eagle touch, wear and scratches, 8¾″ d . . . 275.00
- Gleason, Roswell
  - 9¼″ d, price for pair . . . 450.00
  - 10⅞″ d . . . 250.00
- Griswold, Ashbill, Meriden, CT, 8″ d, price for pair . . . 550.00
- Jones, Gershom, Providence, RI, anchor touch marks, wear, damage, and repair, 8⅜″ d . . . 120.00
- Kilbourne, Samuel, Baltimore, MD, 7½″ d . . . 350.00
- Pierce, Samuel, Greenfield, MA, 1792–1830, 11¼″ d . . . 500.00
- Sheldon and Feltman, Albany, 10 1¼″ d . . . 250.00
- Skinner, John, Boston, 1760–90, smooth brim, 9¼″ d . . . 360.00
- Spackman, Jack, London, 8½″ d . . . 100.00
- Unknown Maker
  - American, attributed to Philadelphia, PA area, Love touch, 8½″ d . . . 330.00
  - Continental, engraved design, initials and date "B S 1790," 12½″ d . . . 145.00

Porringer
- Boardman, Thomas and Sherman, 1810–50, cast old English handle, 4″ d . . . 475.00
- Boardman, Thomas Danforth, cast old English handle, "TD & SB" touch, 4″ d . . . 600.00
- Hamlin, Samuel E, Jr, Providence, RI, cast handle, eagle touch and "Hamlin, Providence," dent in bowl, handle possibly resoldered, 4¼″ d . . . 500.00
- Unknown Maker, American
  - 3¼″ d . . . 220.00
  - 4½″ d
    - Cast crown handle, attributed to NY or New England . . . 330.00
    - Cast heart handle, attributed to Lee or Gleason . . . 330.00
  - 5½″ d, cast flowered handle, attributed to RI or CT . . . 250.00

Porringer Taster, Thomas & Sherman Boardman, 1810–50, old English handle, 2¼″ d . . . 375.00

Pot, Sheffield, English, wood handle, 8″ h . . . 120.00

Salt Shaker, unknown maker, 4¼″ h . . . 100.00

Spittoon, Hall & Cotton, Middlefield, CT, handled, hole underneath handle, 3″ h, 8¼″ d . . . 110.00

Syrup Pitcher, unmarked, attributed to Hall & Cotton, Middlefield, CT, ear handle, shell thumb piece, 8⅛″ h . . . 200.00

Tall Pot
- Calder, William, Providence, RI, "Calder" touch, wood handle, 11″ h . . . 360.00
- Sellew and Co, Cincinnati, well shaped ear handle, 10″ h . . . 420.00

Tankard, unknown maker
- American, 6¼″ h . . . 155.00
- European, cov, spherical thumb piece, engraved initials and 1778, soldered repair, 8⅝″ h . . . 75.00

Tea Caddy, B G S & Co, American,
1825–30, almond shape, bright cut
designs, touch mark, wear, pitted,
3¾″ h **200.00**

Teapot
Boardman and Hart, NY, wood ear–
shaped handle, tiny split in edge of
foot, 7½″ h **250.00**
Calder, Providence, wood C–shaped
handle, wood finial, "Calder, Providence" touch, old repairs, 9¼″ h . . **275.00**
Danforth, No. 3, 10″ h **330.00**
Dixon, James and Sons, English
5½″ h, reeded, fruit finial **75.00**
9″ h, repousse pedestal **200.00**
Dixon, James, English, octagonal,
wooden handle and finial, marked
"James Dixon & Sons," 8″ h **160.00**
Dunham, Rufus, Westbrook, ME, pear
shaped, wood C–shaped handle,
wood finial, "R. Dunham" touch,
8¼″ h **470.00**
Gerhardt & Co, paneled lighthouse,
one cup, 6½″ h **200.00**
Gleason, Roswell, 1822–71, Dorches-
ter, MA, marked at base, imperfec-
tions, 8¼″ h **285.00**
Porter, A, squatty form, 7″ h **250.00**
Porter, Freeman, Westbrook, ME, No.
1, 8″ h **330.00**
Richardson, George, Boston
Globular, ear–shaped wood handle,
touch "G. Richardson," minor
dents, 7⅝″ h **500.00**
Straight sided, C–shaped wood
handle, touch "G. Richardson,
Warranted," 9¼″ h **615.00**
Richardson, George, Cranston, RI,
No. A Warranted, 7¾″ h **300.00**
Sellew and Co, Cincinnati, wood C–
shaped handle, touch, split in bot-
tom edge, 7½″ h **220.00**
Simpson, Samuel, Yalesville, CT,
wood handle, bulbous shape, "S.
Simpson" touch, 7¾″ h **320.00**
Smith and Feltman, Albany, NY, 9½″
h **275.00**
Smith, Eben, Beverly, MA, oval, cut
engraved, 7″ h **300.00**
Unknown Maker, pear shape,
stamped 5 above crown and X
mark, 6″ h **155.00**
Unmarked, American, wood handle,
minor damage to hinge, some re-
soldering, 6⅝″ h **140.00**
Wilcox, R C, cylindrical, C–shaped
wooden handle, marked "R. C. Wilcox & Co," dents, split in bottom
seam, tip of spout battered, 8¾″ h **100.00**
Woodbury and Colton, Philadelphia,
PA, pedestal, 9¾″ h **250.00**
Tobacco Box, Thomas Stanford, cast

eagle feet, engraved label with scroll
work "Thomas Stanford, Gospel Hill,
1838," wear, finial and one foot sol-
dered, 4⅜″ h **115.00**
Tray, Thomas Compton, London, oval,
10½ x 14″ **225.00**
Tumbler, Thomas Danforth Boardman,
Hartford, CT, partial eagle touch 2¾″
h **175.00**
Water Pitcher
Flagg and Homan, well shaped, ear
handle, 9″ h **400.00**
Sellew and Co, Cincinnati, hinged lid,
well shaped, ear handle, 9¼″ h . . . **750.00**

PHOENIX BIRD CHINA

History: Phoenix Bird pattern is a blue-and-
white china exported from Japan during the early
1900s to 1940s. A limited amount was made during
the "Occupied Japan" period.

Initially, it was available at Woolworth's Five-and-
Ten, through four wholesale catalog companies, or
by selling subscriptions to Needlecraft magazine.
Myott Son & Co., England, also produced this pat-
tern under the name "Satsuma" around 1936.
These earthenware items were for export only.

Once known as "Blue Howo Bird China," the
Phoenix Bird pattern is the most sought after of
seven similar patterns in the Hō–ō bird series.
Other patterns are: Flying Turkey (head faces forward with heartlike border); Howo (only pattern with
name on base); and Twin Phoenix (border pattern
only, center white). The Howo and Twin Phoenix
patterns are by Noritake and are occasionally
marked "Noritake." Flying Dragon (birdlike), an
earlier pattern, comes in green and white as well
as the traditional blue and white and is marked with
six Oriental characters. A variation of the Phoenix
Bird pattern has a heartlike border and is called
Hō–ō.

Phoenix Bird pattern has over 500 different
shapes and sizes. Also varying is the quality found
in the execution of design, shades of blue, and
quality of the ware itself, from restaurant-thick to
egg shell-thin. However, because of the wide range
of categories, value is most often determined by a
piece's uniqueness of form, condition, then quality
of execution of print. All these factors must be considered in pricing. The maker's mark tends to add
value; over 110 marks have been cataloged.

Post–1970 pieces were produced in limited
shapes with precise detail but are on a milk-white
ground and usually don't have a maker's mark.
When a mark does appear on a modern piece, it
appears stamped in place.

Reference: Joan Collett Oates, *Phoenix Bird
Chinaware*, published by author, *Book One*, 1984,
Book Two (A Through M), 1985, *Book Three (N
through Z and Post–1970)*, 1986; *Book Four (With
A Section On Flying Turkey)*, 1989.

Collectors' Club: Phoenix Bird Collectors of America, 685 S. Washington, Constantine, MI 49042.

Additional Listings: See *Warman's Americana & Collectibles* for more examples.

Advisor: Joan C. Oates.

Tea Set, child's, #2, $85.00.

Bath Salts Jar, cov	40.00
Berry Bowl, 8¾" d, scalloped	65.00
Berry Server, drain holes	48.00
Cake Tray, cut-out handles	55.00
Casserole, cov, round	145.00
Children's Dishes	
Creamer and Sugar, cov, #2	38.00
Teapot, cov, #5	40.00
Chop Plate, "B", 11¼" d	65.00
Condensed Milk, cov	75.00
Demitasse Cup and Saucer	18.00
Dinner Plate	
9¾" d	45.00
10" d, hp, Flying Turkey pattern, scalloped	55.00
Fruit Bowl, 8¾" d, plain edge	45.00
Gravy Boat, underplate, #4	65.00
Gravy Tureen, cov, underplate, #1	135.00
Hot Water Pot, cov	48.00
Margarine Platter, small, oval	35.00
Meat Platter, 15" l, oval	75.00
Milk Pitcher, #3	45.00
Muffin #3 Cover, ten steam holes	20.00
Mustard Pot, cov, #6	45.00
Nut Cup, ftd, scalloped	20.00
Pancake, cov, two steam holes	125.00
Relish Dish, oval, HOWO pattern	35.00
Salt and Pepper Shakers, pr, scalloped	28.00
Sauce Boat, #2	55.00
Soup Dish, 7⅜" d	40.00
Teapot, Post 1970, rattan handle	35.00
Teastrainer, #4	50.00
Teastrainer and base, #3	65.00
Toothpick, #2	45.00
Vegetable Bowl, oval	48.00
Vegetable Tureen, cov, handled	135.00

PHOENIX GLASS

History: Phoenix Glass Company, Beaver, Pennsylvania, was established in 1880. Known primarily for commercial glassware, the firm also produced a molded, sculptured, cameo-type line from the 1930s until the 1950s.

References: Ellen T. Schroy, *Warman's Glass,* Wallace-Homestead, 1992; Jack D. Wilson, *Phoenix & Consolidated Art Glass, 1926–1980,* Antique Publications, 1989.

Collectors' Club: Phoenix & Consolidated Glass Collectors, PO Box 81974, Chicago, IL 60681.

Cookie Jar, 9" h, Con-Cora, white milk glass, gilt dec	50.00
Floor Vase, 18" h, Bushberry pattern, light green	450.00
Lamp	
Ceiling, 15" sq, flying birds, heavy custard glass, metal mounts	1,450.00
Table	
17½" h, Pine Cone pattern, brown, fixtures in both top and base	165.00
28" h, Lovebirds, green opalescent glass, brass fixtures	200.00
Umbrella Stand, 18" h, Thistle pattern	
All white, orig paper label	425.00
Pearlized blue ground	425.00

Vase, ivory ground, yellow flowers, green leaves, 12½" h, $225.00.

Vase	
6" h, dragonflies and cattails, custard ground	95.00
7" h	
Bluebell pattern, brown	115.00
Fern pattern, white ferns, gray-green ground	80.00
Pine Cone pattern, spherical, red dec, clear ground	195.00
9" h, Gold Fish, four color	550.00
10" h, Wild Geese, pearlized white birds, light green ground	175.00
10½" h, Zodiac, raised white figures, peach colored ground	700.00

11" h
Vine pattern, custard ground, gilt
highlights **225.00**
Wild Rose, blown out, pearlized
dec, dark rose ground, orig label **225.00**
12" h, Dancing Girls, satin custard
ground, blown out color enhanced
figures, minor flake on inside rim . . **275.00**
14" h, Philadendron, blue, ormolu
mounts **400.00**
Water Set, 8" h water pitcher, eight 5¼"
h cone shaped tumblers, Catalonian,
irid ruby red, price for nine piece set **600.00**

PHONOGRAPHS

History: Early phonographs were commonly
called "talking machines." Thomas A. Edison invented the first successful phonograph in 1877.
Other manufacturers followed with their variations.

References: Robert W. Baumbach, *Look For
the Dog: An Illustrated Guide to Victor Talking Machines,* Stationery X–Press, 1990; Arnold
Schwartzman, *Phono–Graphics: The Visual Para-
phernalia of the Talking Machine,* Chronicle Books,
1993.

Periodicals: *The Horn Speaker,* PO Box 1193,
Mabank, TX 75147; *The New Amberola Graphic,*
37 Caledonia St., St. Johnsbury, VT 05819.

Collectors' Clubs: Antique Phonograph Collectors Club, 502 E. 17th St., Brooklyn, NY 11226;
California Antique Phonograph Society, PO Box
67, Durate, CA 91010; Michigan Antique Phonograph Society, Inc., 2609 Devonshire, Lansing, MI
48910; Vintage Radio & Phonograph Society, Inc.,
PO Box 165345, Irving, TX 75016.

Museums: Edison National Historic Site, West
Orange, NJ; Seven Acres Antique Village & Museum, Union, IL.

Apollo, oak case, blue fluted metal horn,
crank wind **400.00**
Boston Talking Machine, Little Wonder
Disc Phonograph, castiron case and
horn, single spring, 1909–12 . . . . . . **375.00**
Brunswick, Model 105, mahogany case,
two headed reproducer, oval fretwork
grill, crank wind **275.00**
Columbia
Baby Regent, square mahogany table, four carved cabriole legs,
drawer in turntable int., louvered
speaker horn **1,150.00**
Graphophone
12½" l, oak case, metal horn, celluloid retailer's mark "Deninger
Cycle Co, Rochester, NY," cylin-
der disc **450.00**
15" l, oak case, columned corners,
nickel plated platform, metal

**Victor V, windup, oak case, nickel
plated horn, 16¼" sq case, 23½" d horn,
$1,500.00.**

horn, stenciled cast iron
mechanism **725.00**
Home Grand, oak case, nickel plated
works, six spring motor **1,400.00**
Decca Junior, portable, leather cov
case, carrying handle **190.00**
Edison
Excelsior, coin operated, spring
wound **2,500.00**
Gem Model D, maroon, two and four
minute K reproducer, early 1900s . **1,700.00**
Opera, stationary reproducer and
moving mandrel, wood horn **2,500.00**
Standard, oak case, hanging metal
horn, cylinder disc, 13" l **385.00**
Standard Model A, oak case, red
metal horn, 11" sq **450.00**
Triumph, triple spring, mahogany
case, wood cygnet horn **2,500.00**
Harvard, trumpet style horn **300.00**
Kalamazoo Duplex, reproducer, orig
horns and decals, patent date 1904 . **3,300.00**
Odeon Talking Machine Co, table
model, crank wind, brass bell horn,
straight tone arm **500.00**
Silvertone, Sears & Roebuck, two repro-
ducers, 1914 . . . . **200.00**
Sonora Disc Console Phonographs
Gothic Deluxe, Normandy, walnut
case, triple spring, goldplated metal
parts, automatic stop, storage for
eighty records **350.00**
Luzerne, Renaissance style case,
storage for eighty records **200.00**
Talk–O–Phone Company, The Brooke,
table model, oak case, beaded dec,
triple spring, steel horn with brass bell,

detachable metal horn bracket, combination brake and speed regulator . . **550.00**

Victor

Monarch, table model, corner columns, brass bell horn, reproducer **1,400.00**

Talking Machine, style VIC III, oak case and horn, 14″ sq. **1,100.00**

VI, mahogany case, fluted Corinthian corner columns, carved capitals, gold dec, reproducer, triple spring, bell brass morning glory horn **1,500.00**

Wizard, cylinder, table model, oak case, morning glory horn **850.00**

PHOTOGRAPHS

History: A vintage print is a positive image developed from the original negative by the photographer or under the photographer's supervision at the time the negative is made. A nonvintage print is a print made from an original negative at a later date. It is quite common for a photographer to make prints from the same negative over several decades. Changes between the original printing and subsequent prints usually can be identified. Limited-edition prints must be clearly labeled.

References: Stuart Bennett, *How To Buy Photographs*, Salem House, 1987; O. Henry Mace, *Collector's Guide To Early Photographs*, Wallace–Homestead, 1990; Lou W. McCulloch, *Card Photographs, A Guide to Their History And Value*, Schiffer Publishing, 1981; Norman E. Martinus and Harry L. Rinker, *Warman's Paper*, Wallace–Homestead, 1994; Floyd and Marion Rinhart, *American Miniature Case Art*, A. S. Barnes and Co., 1969; Susan Theran, *Prints, Posters & Photographs: Identification and Price Guide*, Avon Books, 1993; Susan Theran and Katheryn Acerbo (eds.), *Leonard's Annual Price Index of Prints, Posters & Photographs, Volume 1, July 1, 1991–June 30, 1992*, Auction Index, 1992; John Waldsmith, *Stereoviews: An Illustrated History and Price Guide,* Wallace–Homestead, 1991.

Periodicals: *CameraShopper,* 313 N. Quaker Lane, PO Box 37029, W. Hartford, CT 06137; *The Photograph Collector,* Photographic Arts Center, 163 Amsterdam Ave., #201, New York, NY 10023-0099.

Collectors' Clubs: American Photographic Historical Society, Inc., 1150 Avenue of the Americas, New York, NY 10036; Association of International Photography Art Dealers, 1609 Connecticut Ave. NW, #200, Washington, DC 20009-1034; National Stereoscopic Association, PO Box 14801, Columbus, OH 43214; Photographic Historical Society of Canada, PO Box 54620, Toronto, Ontario M5M 4N5 Canada; Photographic Historical Society of New England, PO Box 189, Boston, MA 02165; The Daguerreian Society, PO Box 2129, Green Bay, WI 54306-2129; The Photographic Historical Society, Inc., PO Box 39563, Rochester, NY

14604; Western Photographic Collectors Assoc., Inc., PO Box 4294, Whittier, CA 90607.

Museums: Center for Creative Photography, Tucson, AZ; International Center of Photography, New York, NY; International Museum of Photography at George Eastman House, Rochester, NY; International Photographic Historical Association, San Francisco, CA; National Portrait Gallery, Washington, DC.

Additional Listings: See *Warman's Americana & Collectibles* for more examples.

Tin Type, Confederate soldier holding sword, 3 x 3½″, $250.00. Photograph courtesy of Morton M. Goldberg Auction Galleries.

Album

Railroad, thirty–nine 2¾ x 7½″ silver prints of New England railroads, including New York, New Haven, and Hartford, Central New England, Boston and Maine, Boston and Albany, Central Vermont, Rutland, and Bangor and Aroostook, photographer's title on endpaper, description and notations on verso, oblong 8vo album with gilt lettering and leatherette ties, 1930s **220.00**

Albumen Print, W L Germon, portrait of Abraham Lincoln and Son, oval, 8½ x 6½″, photographer's gilt lettered identification and studio address on mount recto, period frame, 1860s **880.00**

Ambrotype, postmortem, quarter plate, little girl with peaceful expression, holding wreath with hand tinted leaves and flowers, leather half case, 1860s **190.00**

Cabinet Card, Mathew Brady, Portrait of General James "Pete" Longstreet, photographer's Washington, DC studio imprint on mounts recto and verso, 1860s. 250.00

Carbon Print, F M Sutcliffe, Whitby Harbor, 13½ x 17″, notations on verso, 1880s. 2,200.00

Chlorobromide Print, Floyd B Evans Nature's Labyrinth, 13½ x 16″, penciled photographer's signature on mount recto, photographer's address label and several camera club and exhibition labels affixed to mount verso, c1944. . . . . 467.00

Chromogenic Print, Gisele Freund, Portrait of Matisse, 15¾ x 11¾″, photographer's inked signature and chopmark on recto, copyright handstamp on verso, 1940s, printed later. 412.00

Daguerreotype, Samuel Root, quarter plate, portrait of Elizabeth Risley Naylor, wearing plaid dress with fringe and lace gloves, sealed, leather case, separated at hinge, c1859 . . . . 220.00

Dye Transfer Print, Erwin Blumenfeld, Cubistic Purple Nude, from orig transparency, 12½ x 10″, estate stamp, initials "FY" and notations "19/50" on verso, 1930s, printed 1984. . . . . 880.00

Gold Toned Silver Print, Harold Haliday Costain, Desert night scene, approx 7 x 9″, 1930s 412.00

Gum Print, Wilbur Porterfield, Night's Curtain, 10¼ x 13½″, title and date penciled by photographer on mount recto, penciled notations and gallery handstamp on mount verso, 1906. . . 715.00

Orotone, Edward S Curtis, The Fisherman, Wisham, approx 14 x 11″, sgd and copyrighted by photographer in the negative, orig studio frame, c1900. . . . . 5,060.00

Photomontage, Harold Leroy Harvey, man on stairs, toned silver print, 14 x 11″, penciled notations on verso, c1932. . . . . 495.00

Platinum Print
Anderson, P Douglas, Chinatown, San Francisco Street Towers, 11¼ x 7¼″, photographer's penciled signature on mount recto and penciled notations on mount verso, c1926. . 330.00

Bravo, Manuel Alvarez, two women, 11½ x 10″, photographer's penciled signature on recto, 1930s, printed later 1,210.00

Salt Print, Felix Teynard, Medinet–Abou, Thebes, 9½ x 12″, orig mount with title, photographer's credit, and publisher printed on recto, 1850s 1,760.00

Silver Print
Becker, Murray, The Hindenberg Disaster, 14 x 11″, sgd and inscribed by photographer on image, photog-

rapher's notations in ink on verso, John Faber's handstamp on verso, 1937, printed 2958. . . . . 2,860.00

Van Vechten, Carl, portrait of Mary Martin, 9½ x 6¾″, photographer's blindstamp on recto and inked handstamp and notations on verso, 1949. 880.00

Weston, Edward, Death Valley, 7½ x 9½″, photographer's penciled notations on verso, 1938 . . . . 1,760.00

Tintype, hand painted, man's portrait, whole plate, elaborate period frame, 1860s. 100.00

Toned Platinum Print, Clarence White, woman's portrait, 9 x 7″, photographer's red monogram on recto, pencil signature and date on Japanese tissue affixed to mount recto, 1906. . . . 605.00

Toned Silver Print, Karl Moon, Portrait of Native American Elder, 9½ x 7½″, photographer's signature and Fred Harvey Studio blindstamp with copyright and date on recto, 1912 . . . . . . 715.00

PICKARD CHINA

History: The Pickard China Company was founded by Wilder Pickard in Chicago, Illinois, in 1897. Originally the company imported European china blanks, principally from the Havilands at Limoges, which they then hand painted. The firm presently is located in Antioch, Illinois.

Collectors' Club: Pickard Collectors Club, 300 E. Grove St., Bloomington, IL 61701.

Bowl, 10½″ d, ruffled, poppies and leaves, gold trim, artist sgd, 1905 . . . 175.00

Cake Plate, violets, trees with pink blossoms, lake and mountains background, two handles, artist sgd "Felix". 350.00

Candy Dish, 5″ d, fluted, gold dec . . . 65.00

Chocolate Pot, cov, 9″ h, conical, pink carnations, green leaves, gold arches, pink and white flowers, scrolling, gold handle, rim band, and knob 235.00

Coffee Set, cov coffeepot, creamer, and sugar, artist sgd, price for set 300.00

Creamer and Sugar, 4¼″ h, Violets, c1898, artist sgd "H Reury," Silesia blank, price for pair 325.00

Gravy Boat, 8″ w, Acorn, c1905–10, artist sgd "Vokel" **295.00**

Hatpin Holder, allover gold design of etched flowers, c1925 . . . . **45.00**

Lemonade Set, tankard pitcher, five tumblers, bluebells and foliage, lemon–yellow ground, price for six piece set **100.00**

Marmalade Jar, cov and underplate, 6″ h, hp, dogwoods and leaves, gold trim, artist sgd. **85.00**

Perfume Bottle, yellow primroses, shaded ground, artist sgd and dated 1905, gold stopper, Limoges blank . . **200.00**

Pitcher, Water Lily pattern, green and gold **395.00**

Cake Plate, scenic, purple, green, blue and gold tones, gold trim, sgd "hand-painted china, W Pickard" and "B & C Limoges, France" gold mark, $300.00.

Plate

   7½″ d, hp, currants, 1898 . . . . **75.00**

   8¼″, poppies, gold tracery and rim, artist sgd "Challinor". **150.00**

Platter, 12″ d, hp, landscape, artist sgd "Marker". **225.00**

Powder Box, 4″ d, roses, artist sgd . . **100.00**

Punch Bowl, 12″ d, orange grapes and plums design, artist sgd "F Walton". . **1,295.00**

Relish Dish, 9½″ l, 4″ w, pink and green leaves, open handles, maple leaf mark **70.00**

Stein, 7″ h, large bunches of grapes and leaves, black ground, gold handle, rim, and base, artist sgd, c1898 . . . . **275.00**

Teaset, peonies dec, artist sgd "Vibon-nik," c1895, Limoges blank, price for three piece set **550.00**

Tile, 6¾″ d, Holland, Dutch Merchant Ship, GDA France mark, c1905 . . . . **395.00**

Tray, 11″ d, circular, bisque, teal blue,

gold grapes and leaves, engraved, artist sgd "Coufall," 1905 mark **200.00**

Urn, 11½″ h, allover gold, 3″ band of grapes and strawberries, artist sgd, Belleek blank **500.00**

Vase

   7¾″ h, cylindrical, moonlight lake and pine forest scene, artist sgd "Challinor," Nippon blank **250.00**

   9″ h, large golden yellow, pink, and deep rose chrysanthemums and green leaves, soft turquoise blue shaded to green ground, gold trim, artist sgd, 1898 . . . . **300.00**

PICKLE CASTORS

History: A pickle castor is a table accessory used to serve pickles. It generally consists of a silver-plated frame fitted with a glass insert, matching silver-plated lid, and matching tongs. Pickle castors were very popular during the Victorian era. Inserts are found in pattern glass and colored art glass.

Reference: Ellen T. Schroy, *Warman's Glass,* Wallace-Homestead, 1992.

Clear, castle scene in medallions, silverplated frame, $135.00.

Amber, Bag Ware pattern, silver frame with relief masks, tongs, and cov . . . **230.00**

Blue, finecut design, tongs and frame . **210.00**

Cranberry, thumbprint, enameled daisies, twig feet, elaborate floral cutout sides, cov, and tongs, 13″ h **325.00**

Crown Milano, forget–me–ot dec, silver-plate finish frame, orig tongs. **985.00**

Northwood, Netted Apple Blossom insert, ornate SP ftd frame **275.00**

Pattern

   Daisy & Button, clear, quadruple plate holder, cov, and tongs **130.00**

Paneled and Diamond Point, clear, triple plate holder, cov, and tongs . . . **80.00**

Pigeon Blood, Beaded Drape insert, Consolidated Glass Co, orig cov and frame. **425.00**

Rubena Crystal, Mount Washington, enameled floral dec, wild roses, bleeding hearts, and daisies, green floral, silverplate frame, orig tongs, 10½" h. **875.00**

Rubena Verde, Hobbs Hobnail, SP frame, cov, tongs **495.00**

PIGEON BLOOD GLASS

History: Pigeon blood refers to the deep orangish-red colored glassware produced around the turn of the century. Do not confuse it with the many other red glasswares of that period. Pigeon blood has a very definite orange glow.

Reference: Ellen T. Schroy, *Warman's Glass,* Wallace-Homestead, 1992.

Salt and Pepper Shakers, pr, metal tops, 2¾" h, $110.00.

Berry Bowl, 9" d, master, Torquay, SP rim. **110.00**

Butter Dish, cov, Venecia, enameled dec **350.00**

Celery, 6" h, Torquay, SP rim **225.00**

Creamer, Venecia, enameled dec . . . **125.00**

Decanter, 9½" h, orig stopper **75.00**

Hand Cooler, 5" l, cut panels, two compartments with silver fittings **135.00**

Pickle Castor, Beaded Drape insert, SP cov and frame, Consolidated Glass Co. **425.00**

Pitcher, 9½" h, Bulging Loops, applied clear handle, ground pontil. **220.00**

Salt and Pepper Shaker, pr, Bulging Loops, orig top **145.00**

Sugar Shaker, Bulging Loops, orig top **150.00**

Syrup, Beaded Drape, Consolidated Glass Co, orig hinged lid **245.00**

Toothpick, Bulging Loops **125.00**

Tumbler, 3¼" h, alternating panel and rib **75.00**

PINK SLAG

History: True pink slag is found only in the molded Inverted Fan and Feather pattern. Quality pieces shade from pink at the top to white at the bottom.

Reference: Ellen T. Schroy, *Warman's Glass,* Wallace-Homestead, 1992.

Reproduction Alert: Recently, pieces of pink slag made from molds of the now defunct Cambridge Glass Company have been found in the Inverted Strawberry and Inverted Thistle pattern. This is not considered "true" pink slag and brings only a fraction of the Inverted Fan and Feather pattern prices.

Punch Cup, Inverted Fan and Feather pattern, ftd, $285.00.

Berry Bowl

Individual, ftd, price for six piece set **825.00**

Master, 10" d, ftd **740.00**

Butter Dish, cov, 7⅝" d, 7" h cov, 2¼" h base with four molded feet, fiery opalescence coloring **1,485.00**

Creamer **450.00**

Cruet, 6¾" h **950.00**

Jelly Compote, 5" h, 4½" d, scalloped top. **350.00**

Marmalade Jar, cov **875.00**

Pitcher, water **750.00**

Punch Cup, 2½" h, ftd **275.00**

Salt Shaker **300.00**

Sauce Dish, 4¼" d, 2½" h, ball feet . . **210.00**

Sugar, cov **550.00**

Toothpick **400.00**

Tumbler, 4½" h **400.00**

PIPES

History: The history of pipe making dates as early as 1575. Almost all types of natural and man-made materials, some that retained smoke and some that did not, were used to make pipes. Among the materials were amber, base metals, clay, cloisonné, glass, horn, ivory, jade, meerschaum, parian, porcelain, pottery, precious metals, precious stones, semiprecious stones, assorted woods, *inter alia*. Chronologically, the four most popular materials and their generally accepted introduction dates are: clay, c1575; woods, c1700; porcelain, c1710; and meerschaum, c1725.

National pipe styles exist around the globe, wherever tobacco smoking is a custom or habit. Pipes reflect a broad range of themes and messages, e.g., figurals, important personages, commemoration of historical events, mythological characters, erotica and pornographica, the bucolic, the bizarre, the grotesque, and the graceful.

Pipe collecting began in the mid–1880s; William Bragge, F.S.A., Birmingham, England, was an early collector. Although firmly established through the efforts of freelance writers, auction houses, and museums (but not the tobacco industry), the collecting of antique pipes is an amorphous, maligned, and misunderstood hobby. It is amorphous because there are no defined collecting bounds; maligned because it is conceived as an extension of pipe smoking, now socially unacceptable [many pipe collectors are avid nonsmokers]; and misunderstood because of its association with the "collectibles" field.

References: R. Fresco–Corbu, *European Pipes*, Lutterworth Press, 1982; E. Ramazzotti and B. Mamy, *Pipes et Fumeurs des Pipes. Un Art, des Collections, Sous le Vent*, 1981; Benjamin Rapaport, *A Complete Guide To Collecting Antique Pipes*, Schiffer Publishing, 1979.

Periodicals: *Pipe Collectors Of The World*, Box 11652, Houston, TX 77293; *The Complete Smoker Magazine*, PO Box 7036, Evanston, IL 60204; *The Pipe Smoker's Ephemeris*, 20–37 120th Street, College Point, NY 11356.

Collectors' Clubs: International Association of Pipe Smokers' Clubs, 47758 Hickory, Apt. 22305, Wixom, MI 48393; New York Pipe Club, PO Box 265, Gracie Station, New York, NY 10028; North Texas Pipe Club, 1624 East Cherry St., Sherman, TX 75090; Pipe Collectors Club of America, PO 5179, Woodbridge, VA 22194; Sherlock Holmes Pipe Club Ltd. USA, PO Box 221, Westborough, MA 01581-0221; Society for Clay Pipe Research, PO Box 817, Bel Air, MD 21014; Southern California Pipe & Cigar Smokers' Association, 1532 South Bundy Dr., Apt. D, Los Angeles, CA 90025.

Museums: Museum of Tobacco Art and History, Nashville, TN; National Tobacco–Textile Museum, Danville, VA; Pipe Smoker's Hall of Fame, Galveston, IN; U.S. Tobacco Museum, Greenwich, CT.

CHEROOT HOLDER

Meerschaum
5⅝″ l, small girl and dog, damaged stem 100.00
6⅛″ l, Venus and Cupid, amber stem, fitted case, minor damage. 150.00

7⅛″ l, two galloping horses, amber stem, fitted case. 360.00

PIPE

Briar, Queen Victoria, 6¼″ l, head, carved, silver trim, case, hallmarked 75.00
Clay, 18″ l, figural, young man with curly hair, wooden slim stem, French, Gambler. 65.00
Glass, large ovoid bowl, long shaped stem, red and ivory dec 75.00

Meerschaum, hand holding goblet, amber stem and goblet, carved Meerschaum hand, Wm. Burnbaum, NY, 3¼″ l, $285.00.

Meerschaum, amber stem, fitted case
4¾″ l, Meerschaum and amber bowl, gold and silver Art Nouveau ferule 175.00
5¼″ l ferule, head of Mephistopheles, damaged stem. 250.00
6⅛″ l, head of gentleman, plumed beret, stained 330.00
8⅝″ l, Bacchanalian scene 660.00
11⅝″ l, buck, doe, and fawn beside bellflower bowl, amber and meerschaum stem, amber mouth piece, fitted case, minor damage. 470.00
16⅜″ l, presentation model, pierced relief monogram. 190.00
Opium, 7¾″ l, cranes, red stem, brass fittings, Oriental, c1800 . . . . 85.00
Porcelain
9″ l, Graf Zeppelin, marked "P.O.B." 125.00
12″ l, floral, relief dec 125.00
29″ l, Hunter, sleeping 125.00
Pottery, monk, postwar 45.00
Regimental, 149th Infantry Regiment 1881, 10″ l, blacksmith tools in rear. . 85.00

TAMPS

Brass, 2¼″ l, Robin Hood, England . . 35.00

Ivory, 2¾″ l, column **15.00**
Silverplated, 1⅝″ l, man bending at waist, marked "E.P.N.S." **25.00**

POCKET KNIVES

History: Alcas, Case, Colonial, Ka-Bar, Queen, and Schrade are the best of the modern pocketknife manufacturers, with top positions enjoyed by Case and Ka-Bar. Knives by Remington and Winchester, firms no longer in production, are eagerly sought.

Form is a critical collecting element. The most desirable forms are folding hunters (one and two blades), trappers, peanuts, Barlows, elephant toes, canoes, Texas toothpicks, Coke bottles, gun stocks, and Daddy Barlows. The decorative aspect also heavily influences prices. Values are for pocketknives in mint condition.

References: Jacob N. Jarrett, *Price Guide To Pocket Knives, 1890–1970,* L-W Books, 1993; Bernard Levine, *Levine's Guide To Knives and Their Values, Third Edition,* DBI Books, 1993; Bernard Levine, *Pocket Knives: The Collector's Guide To Identifying, Buying, and Enjoying Vintage Pocketknives,* Apple Press, 1993; C. Houston Price, *The Official Price Guide To Collector Knives, Tenth Edition,* House of Collectibles, 1991; Jim Sargent, *Sargent's American Premium Guide To Pocket Knives & Razors, Identification and Values, 3rd Edition,* Books Americana, 1992; Ron Stewart and Roy Ritchie, *The Standard Knife Collector's Guide, 2nd Edition,* Collector Books, 1993.

Periodicals: *Knife World,* PO Box 3395, Knoxville, TN 37927; *The Blade,* PO Box 22007, Chattanooga, TN 37422.

Collectors' Clubs: American Blade Collectors, PO Box 22007, Chattanooga, TN 37422; Canadian Knife Collectors Club, 3141 Jessuca Court, Mississauga, ON L5C 1X7 Canada; Dare Blade Collectors' Society, 3938 Pineway Dr., Kitty Hawk, NC 27949; The National Knife Collectors Association, PO Box 21070, Chattanooga, TN 37421.

Museum: National Knife Collectors Museum, Chattanooga, TN.

Additional Listings: See *Warman's Americana & Collectibles* for more examples.

CASE

Case uses a numbering code for its knives. The first number (1–9) is the handle material; the second number (1–5) designates the number of blades; the third and fourth numbers (0–99) the knife pattern. Stag (5), pearl (8 or 9), and bone (6) are the most sought in handle materials. The most desirable patterns are 5165—folding hunters, 6185—doctors, 6445—scout, muskrat—marked muskrat with no number, and 6254—trappers.

In the Case XX series a symbol and dot code are used to designate a year.

Union Cutlery Co., marked "OLCUT, U.C.C., Olean, NY," 1911–23, $100.00.

02221 ½, slick black, stamped "Tested XX," 1920–40, 3¼″ l **200.00**
06244, red bone, stamped "XX," 1940–64, 3¼″ l **50.00**
06263SSP, bone, polished blade, stamped "USA," 1965–69, 3⅛″ l **30.00**
11011, walnut, 10 dot, 1970 . . . . **30.00**
22087, slick black, stamped "USA," 1965–69, 3¼″ l **30.00**
31093, yellow composition, stamped "XX," 5″ l, 1940–64 . . . . **300.00**
3299 ½, flat yellow, "A" blade, stamped "XX," 1940–64, 4⅛″ l **100.00**
42056, Office Knife, composition, stamped "W. R. Case & Son," 3⅜″ l **150.00**
5172, geniune stag, stamped "Tested XX," 5½″ l, 1920–40 . . . . **1,500.00**
53131PU, stag, stamped "W. R. Case & Son," 3⅝″ l **1,400.00**
61005 ½, green bone, clip blade, stamped "Tested XX," 3⅜″ l, 1920–40 . . . . **400.00**
6232, Rogers Bone, late, stamped "XX," 1940–64, 3⅝″ l **75.00**
6347SHSP, green bone, long pull, stamped "XX," 1940–55, 3⅞″ l **200.00**
6394 ½LP, bone, stamped "XX," 1940–64, 4¼″ l **750.00**
7278, tortoise, stamped "Case Bros. Little Valley NY," 3¼″ l **300.00**
8220, genuine pearl, stamped "Tested XX," 1920–40, 2¾″ l **400.00**
B1095, imitation onyx, stamped "Case's Stainless," 1945 . . . . **350.00**
B1098, waterfall, stamped "Tested XX," 5½″ l, 1920–40 . . . . **500.00**
R1049L, candy stripe, stamped "Tested XX," 4$\frac{1}{16}$″ l, 1920–40. . . . . **500.00**
W1216, metal wire, stamped "Case Tested Pat. 9-21-26," 3¼″ l. **150.00**
Muskrat, bone, stamped "USA," 3⅞″ l, 1965–69. **50.00**

KA–BAR (Union Cutlery Co, NY)

The company was founded by Wallace Brown at Tidioute, PA, in 1892. It was relocated to Olean, NY, in 1912. The products have many stampings, including Union [inside shield]; U–R Co. Tidioute [variations]; Union Cutlery Co., Olean, NY; Olcut, Olean, NY; Keenwell, Olean, NY; and Ka–Bar. The larger knives with a profile of a dog's head on the handle are the most desirable. Pattern numbers rarely appear on a knife prior to the 1940s.

24107	**1,000.00**
31187, two blades	**150.00**
61126L, dog's head	**850.00**
61161, light celluloid handle	**100.00**
61187, Daddy Barlow	**150.00**
6191L	**600.00**
6260KF	**100.00**

KEEN KUTTER (Simons Hardware, St. Louis, MO)

833, equal end jack, black jigged imitation bone, Keen Kutter, 3⅛″ l	**25.00**
1773 ¾, Daddy Barlow, bone, easy opener, pick, E C Simmons, 5″ l	**225.00**
K231, moose, peach seed bone, Keen Kutter, 4″ l	**125.00**
K1998 ¾, Texas toothpick, cracked ice celluloid, Keen Kutter, 5″ l	**125.00**

QUEEN

10, Winterbottom bone, two blades, 3½″ l	**28.00**
19, fisherman's Big Q, Rogers bone, 5″ l	**80.00**
38, swell center jumbo, Big Q, jigged bone, 5¼″ l	**200.00**

REMINGTON, last made in 1940

R953, toothpick, brown bone, grooved bolster, saber blade, 5″ l	**500.00**
R1285, swell center, tortoiseshell, 3″ l	**160.00**
R1915, candy stripe, long pull, 3⅜″ l	**150.00**
R3050, jack, buffalo horn, 4″ l	**300.00**
R3715, whittler, pyremite, 3⅞″ l	**260.00**
R7854, pearl handle with engraved Purina checkerboard, bail, 3″ l	**300.00**

WESTERN STATES

1235, genuine horn, two blades, 3½″ l	**45.00**
17233, pyralin, candy stripe, teardrop shield, two blades, 3⅜″ l	**50.00**
6100L, lockback, bone, dog head shield, regular jig, bail, 5⅜″ l	**350.00**
6130, bone oval shield, 4½″ l	**250.00**
7400, heavy utility, butter and molasses with bull head shield, four blades, 4¾″ l	**500.00**
A100, folding hunter, Christmas tree, single blade, clip, oval shield, 5⅜″ l	**250.00**

WINCHESTER

1703, Daddy Barlow, brown bone, single blade, 5⅛″ l	**250.00**
2039, jack, celluloid, 3″ l	**100.00**
2089, office, white celluloid, 3¾″ l	**150.00**
2302, senator, pearl bail, 2¼″ l	**90.00**
2990, dog leg, stag, 2¾″ l	**130.00**
3002, whittler, green celluloid, 3¾″ l	**275.00**
4951, utility, stag, 3⅝″ l	**400.00**

POISON BOTTLES

History: Poison bottles were designed to warn and prevent accidental intake or misuse of their poisonous substances, especially in the dark. Poison bottles generally were made of colored glass, embossed with "Poison" or a skull and crossbones, and sometimes were coffin-shaped.

John H. B. Howell of Newton, New Jersey, designed the first safety closure in 1866. The idea did not become popular until the 1930s, when bottle designs became simpler and the user had to read the label to identify the contents.

References: Ralph and Terry Kovel, *The Kovels' Bottle Price List, 9th Edition,* Crown Publishers, 1992; Carlo and Dorothy Sellari, *The Standard Old Bottle Price Guide,* Collector Books, 1989.

Periodicals: *Antique Bottle and Glass Collector,* PO Box 187, East Greenville, PA 18041; *Bottles & Extras,* PO Box 154, Happy Camp, CA 90369.

Bowker's Pyrox Poison, clear	**30.00**
Carbolic Acid, 3 oz, cobalt blue, hexagonal, flat back	**45.00**

Blown, aqua, embossed "Poison," 3 × 14 panel side, 12¾″ h, $25.00.

Chemical Cat, Chases Rats & Mice, 8 oz	5.00
Chloroform, 5¾" h, green, ribbed, label, 1900	70.00
Coffin, 3½" h, cobalt blue, emb, 1890	100.00
Diamond Antiseptics, 10¾" h, triangular shape, golden amber, emb.	385.00
Durfee Embalming Fluid Co, 10⅞" h, clear	50.00
Goffe Potash Water, torpedo shape, cobalt blue.	440.00
Imperial Fluid Company Poison, 1 gallon, clear	95.00
Jacob Hulle, Strychnine, 3½" h, octagonal, blue, marked "Not To Be Taken".	15.00
Lysol, 3¼" h, cylindrical, amber, emb "Not To Be Taken"	10.00
Mercury Bichloride, 2¹¹⁄₁₆" h, rect, amber	15.00
Norwich Coffin, 3⅜" h, amber, emb, tooled lip.	90.00
Not To Be Taken, 4⅜" h, hexagonal, amber	15.00
Owbridge's Embrocation Hull, 5" h, hexagonal, cobalt blue	30.00
Owl Drug Co, 3⅜" h, cobalt blue, owl sitting on mortar	65.00
P D & Co, 2½" h, rect, amber, skull and crossbones.	55.00
Plumber Drug Co, 7½" h, cobalt blue, lattice and diamond pattern	90.00
Poison, 3½" h, hexagonal, ribbed, cobalt blue.	18.00
Sharp's Ammonia, 9¼" h, apple green	120.00
Tinct Iodine, 3" h, amber, skull and crossbones.	40.00
USA Hospital Dept, Acetate Potassa, 6½" h, cylindrical, aqua	55.00
Wilberts Javex, 9" h, amber, concave and ribbed	45.00

POLITICAL ITEMS

History: Since 1800 the American presidency has always been a contest between two or more candidates. Initially, souvenirs were issued to celebrate victories. Items issued during a campaign to show support for a candidate were actively being distributed in the William Henry Harrison election of 1840.

Campaign items cover a wide variety of materials—buttons, bandannas, tokens, pins, etc. The only limiting factor has been the promoter's imagination. The advent of television campaigning has reduced the emphasis on individual items. Modern campaigns do not seem to have the variety of materials which were issued earlier.

References: Herbert Collins, *Threads of History,* Smithsonian Institution Press, 1979; Stan Gores, *Presidential and Campaign Memorabilia With Prices, Second Edition,* Wallace-Homestead, 1988; Theodore L. Hake, *Encyclopedia of Political Buttons, United States, 1896–1972,* Americana & Collectibles Press, 1985; Theodore L. Hake, *Political Buttons, Book II, 1920–1976,* Americana & Collectibles Press, 1977; Theodore L. Hake, *Political Buttons, Book III, 1789–1916,* Americana & Collectibles Press, 1978; Note: Theodore L. Hake issued a revised set of prices for his three books in 1991; Ted Hake, *Hake's Guide to Presidential Campaign Collectibles,* Wallace-Homestead, 1992; Keith Melder, *Hail To The Candidate: Presidential Campaigns From Banners to Broadcasts,* Smithsonian Institution Press, 1992; Edmund B. Sullivan, *American Political Badges and Medalets, 1789–1892,* Quarterman Publications, 1981.

Collectors' Clubs: American Political Items Collectors, PO Box 134, Monmouth Junction, NJ 08852; Indiana Political Collectors Club, PO Box 11141, Indianapolis, IN 46201.

Periodicals: *Political Collector,* PO Box 5171, York, PA 17405; *The Political Bandwagon,* PO Box 348, Leola, PA 17540-0348.

Museums: National Museum of American History, Washington, DC; Smithsonian Museum, Washington, DC; Western Reserve Historical Society, Cleveland, OH.

Note: The abbreviation "h/s" is used to identify a head and shoulder photo or etching of a person.

Additional Listings: See *Warman's Americana & Collectibles* for more examples.

Advisor: Theodore L. Hake.

Advertising Trade Card	
Melcher & Miller Boots and Shoes, Lewiston, ME, metamorphic, forms Cleveland or Blaine portraits, 1884 copyright, W S Parker.	35.00
Muzzy Starch, black and white Grover Cleveland and Thomas Hendricks jugate photos.	15.00
Ashtray, 5" d, "Vote Republican In '52," white, gold band, cartoon illus of man hitchhiking next to exhausted Democratic donkey with GOP elephant lumbering down road, caption "My Ass Is Tired".	15.00
Badge, 2½ x 2½", Republican National Convention, celluloid and brass hanger with black and white McKinley photo, red, white, and blue fabric, reverse with "Philadelphia, Pa/June 19, 1900".	100.00
Bandanna	
Bryan–Sewall, jugate photos, eagle, shield, rooster, White House illus, and slogans, cotton, black and white, 1896.	80.00
Herbert Hoover, 14 x 18", sepia photo, red, white, and blue border	45.00
Bank, Roosevelt, 1½ x 3½ x 2½", cast	

Broadside, silk, President Taylor's Inaugural Address, March 5, 1849, printed by J. Murphy & Co., Baltimore, MD, light green border, frayed on edges, soiled, $350.00.

iron, Teddy on one side, orig gold
paint, c1908 . . . . 100.00
Blotter, Willkie, 4 x 9″, black and white,
campaign slogans and inscription
"Contributed By A Citizen Of Amster-
dam NY 1940" 15.00
Book, *Life of John Quincy Adams,* W H
Seward, Derby, Miller & Co, 1849, 404
pgs, hardcover, 5 x 8″ 45.00
Booklet, 4 x 9″, *A Sketch of the Presi-
dent,* black and white, 8 pgs. 25.00
Bookmark, Taft–Sherman, 2½ x 2¾″,
diecut, aluminum, teddy bear shape,
cutout heart with Taft portrait, Sher-
man portrait on reverse 75.00
Bow Tie, 6″ l, "Vote For Ike," fabric, red,
white lettering 18.00
Bumper Sticker, 4 x 7″, "Elect JFK–60
President," orange and black, license
plate design 8.00
Cabinet Photo
   Bryan, 4 x 6½″, sepia, c1896 . . . . . 30.00
   McKinley and wife, 4¼ x 6½″, sepia,
   Canton, Ohio home, 1896–1900 . . 20.00
Car Attachment, "Keep Coolidge," 2½″
d, tin plate with black and white por-
trait and slogan, silvered metal,
threaded shaft. 175.00
Card Game, The Watergate Scandal,
black and white cards, 4 page instruc-
tion sheet, copyright 1973 . . . . 15.00
Carte de Visite, 2½ x 3½″, Lincoln, Mary,
and two sons, sepia, 1860s 30.00
Clicker, 2½″ l, Click with Dick, litho tin,
blue and white. 15.00

Flue Cover, 8″ d, "For President Al
Smith," tin, blue and cream, small
flakes of face 75.00
Gearshift Knob, 2″ d, Woodrow Wilson,
celluloid, amber, metal ring surrounds
rubber disk with Wilson portrait,
c1916. . . . . 75.00
Invitation, 7 x 9¾″, Cleveland–Hen-
dricks, inaugural ball, 1885. . . . . . . 45.00
Lapel Stud
   Harrison, silvered tin rim, black and
   white celluloid insert 25.00
   McKinley–Hobart, sepia photos,
   cream ground, red, white, and blue
   border. 18.00
Letter Opener, 8″ l, Vote Demo! Hubert
Humphrey For President, plastic,
white, blue image, red lettering. . . . 8.00
License Plate, 6 x 12″, "I Like Ike,"
metal, black and white 25.00
Medal
   Buchanan, 1⅞″ d, copper, buck leaping over cannon and "Ans/Breckin-
   ridge" on one side, other with
   Washington portrait and slogan . . . 150.00
   Jimmy Carter, 2¾″ d, bronze, raised
   bust, Presidential seal on back with
   inscription "39th President Of The
   United States Of America/Inaugu-
   rated January 20, 1977" 20.00
Megaphone, 7½″ l, Richard Nixon, plas-
tic, white, blue lettering, 1972 . . . . . 15.00
Menu, 6 x 8″, Theodore Roosevelt, Cin-
cinnati Fall Festival Assn, dinner, stiff
paper, black engraving, pink Presi-
dential seal, 1902 . . . . 25.00
Mirror, 2¼″ d, Taft, bust photo, black and
white, "It's Up To The Man On the
Other Side To Put This Tried & Safe
Man At The Head Of The
Government" 200.00
Mug, 3¾″ h, Bryan, milk glass, oval
transfer, floral border dec, 1896 . . . 60.00
Necktie
   Landon, "For President Alfred M Lan-
   don," brown, round photo, white
   lettering. 25.00
   Reagan/Bush, 24″ l, "The 50th Inau-
   gural/January 21, 1985/Washing-
   ton, DC," jugate, red synthetic,
   white design 15.00
Newspaper, *Daily Patriot,* Monday, June
17, 1844, Concord, 4 pgs, announcing
Democratic–Republican nominations 50.00
Note Pad, 2 x 2¾″, Cleveland, cover with
Cleveland and wife portrait, Baldwin &
Gleason 1886 copyright. 10.00
Pen, 5½″ l, Herbert Humphrey, dark
blue, silver inscription "Businessmen
For Humphrey/Thank You/Hubert H
Humphrey". 8.00

Pennant

Truman, 12″ l, red, white oval of Truman and lettering, "For President" in center, 1948 . . . . 25.00

Wilson, 21″ l, blue, white and flesh tone, "Our President," 1912–16 . . . 25.00

Pinback Button, McKinley, memorial, black and white, black ribbon, paper insert, 1³⁄₁₆″ d, $20.00.

Pinback Button

Bryan, 1¾″ d, sepia portrait, St Louis Button Company, 1896 . . . . 30.00

Coolidge–Dawes, ⅞″ d, jugate, black and white, oval portrait, text, 1920 45.00

Dewey–Warren, 1¾″ d, jugate, black and light gray 25.00

Eisenhower–Nixon, 3½″ d, jugate photos, red, white, and blue 25.00

Harding and Coolidge, red, white, and blue litho 10.00

McKinley and Roosevelt, 1¼″ d, jugate, blue and gold, 1900 . . . . . . 25.00

Roosevelt–Garner, "Return our country to the People," jugate, black and white, 1932 . . . . 300.00

Smith and Robinson, red, white, and blue litho 12.00

Stevenson For President, blue tone photo, red, white, and blue design 20.00

Taft–Sherman, jugate, black and white oval photos with wreath design 75.00

Theodore Roosevelt, ⅝″ d, shaded brown portrait 15.00

Truman–Barkley, sepia portraits and red, white, and blue design 150.00

Warren G Harding, sepia portrait, red rim 15.00

Wilson–Marshall, 1¼″ d, jugate black and white photos, red, white, and blue shield on top 400.00

Plaque, 4½ x 6″, wood, lead bust of Lincoln, painted gold 55.00

Plate

9″ d

Blaine, black on white, floral motif, 1884 . . . . 35.00

McKinley, glass, frosted portrait, c1896 . . . . 55.00

10½″ d, Eisenhower Inauguration, glazed china, black and white, inscribed "34th President Of The US/ Inaugurated Jan 20, 1953," "Decorated By Delano Studios/Setauket/ NY" on reverse 30.00

Platter, 9 x 11½″, Taft–Sherman, oval, china, jugate portraits, red, white, and blue flags, purple roses, eagle with shield, gold floral border 35.00

Post Card

Bryan, 3½ x 5½″, black and white, unused, c1908 . . . . 15.00

Nixon, 3½ x 5½″, black and white glossy photo, dated "Sept 29, 1952" 10.00

Taft, mechanical, black, white, and yellow elephant, pull tail and black and white portrait slides out, brief message, October 24, 1908 postmark 35.00

Poster

Kennedy–Johnson, 27 x 41″, red, white, and blue, black and white jugate photo, inscribed "Democratic National Committee, Washington 6, DC" 75.00

McGovern, 21 x 27″, black and white photo, red caption "I Believe Him," hand written "McGovern/1972 Dem" 12.00

Mondale, 14 x 20″, paper, black and white photo, blue lettering 15.00

Reagan–Bush, 16 x 22″, stiff paper, full color, 1984 . . . . 18.00

Richard Nixon, 14 x 20″, stiff paper, black and white photo 25.00

Program

Franklin D Roosevelt, inauguration ceremonies, 1937, 8 pgs, 6 x 9″ . . 40.00

Garfield–Arthur Inauguration, 16 pgs, 1881 . . . . 35.00

Puzzle

Roosevelt–Garner, jugate, cardboard, red, white, and blue, slogan "Together To Revive Prosperity," dated March 4, 1933, orig glassine envelope 40.00

The Puzzle of Watergate, black and white cov, shrink–wrapped, copyright 1973 . . . . 20.00

Ribbon, Taft and Sherman, 2 x 6″, fabric, gold on blue, flag on top 50.00

Salt and Pepper Shakers, pr, Eisenhower, figural, ceramic, beige and tan,

head lifts off for one shaker, body
serves as other, c1952 . . . . **30.00**
Sheet Music
  Fremont's Great Republican March,
    black on white, 6 pgs, 1856. . . . . . **40.00**
  Kennedy Victory Song, 9 x 12", 4 pgs,
    blue tone photo on cov **25.00**
Stickpin
  Benjamin Harrison, 2" l, brass **15.00**
  Blaine, cardboard photo, 1884 . . . . **50.00**
  Coolidge, green and silver logo, "Cal/
    24/Coolidge". **50.00**
  McKinley, 2" l, gold and silver, en-
    graved, c1896 . . . . **20.00**
  William H Taft, brass diecut letters . **25.00**
Tab
  Hoover–Curtis, metal, blue, white let-
    ters, 1928 . . . . **8.00**
  Landon–Knox, diecut, elephant,
    1936. . . . . **10.00**
Tape Measure, 1¾" l, "President Nixon
  Now More Than Ever," gold glass
  case, metal tape, red, white, and blue
  inscription, orig plain gold box. **5.00**
Ticket
  Democratic, 3½ x 5½", black printing
    on white, 1916. . . . . **10.00**
  Grant and Colfax, 3¼ x 5¼", black
    printing on white. **25.00**
  Horace Greely, Liberal Republican
    Ticket, 6 x 12", paper, Greely image
    between Justice and Liberty fig-
    ures, 1872. . . . . **55.00**
  Republican Convention, National Pro-
    gressive Convention/Colosseum/
    1912, Good For Third Day Only,
    black and white Lincoln, Washing-
    ton, and Jefferson illus, blue
    background **50.00**
Toy, windup, 5" h, Jimmy Carter, "Jimmy
  The Walking Peanut," plastic, painted
  features, orig box, late 1970s **35.00**
Wristwatch, Jimmy Carter, metal case,
  expandable band, caricature illus,
  Goober Time Co, 1976 . . . . **60.00**

POMONA GLASS

History: Pomona glass, produced only by the
New England Glass Works and named for the Roman goddess of fruit and trees, was patented in
1885 by Joseph Locke. It is a delicate lead, blown
art glass which has a pale, soft beige ground and
a top one–inch band of honey amber.

There are two distinct types of backgrounds.
First ground, made only from late 1884 to June
1886, was produced by fine cuttings through a wax
coating followed by an acid bath. Second ground
was made by rolling the piece in acid-resisting particles and acid etching. Second ground was made
in Cambridge until 1888 and until the early 1900s

in Toledo, where Libbey moved the firm after purchasing New England Glass Works. Both methods
produced a soft frosted appearance, with fine curlicue lines more visible on first ground pieces. Designs are used on some pieces, which were etched
and then stained in color. The most familiar design
is blue cornflowers.

Do not confuse Pomona with "Midwestern Pomona," a pressed glass with a frosted body and
amber band.

References: Joseph and Jane Locke, *Locke Art
Glass: A Guide For Collectors,* Dover Publications,
1987; Ellen T. Schroy, *Warman's Glass,* Wallace–
Homestead, 1992.

**Punch Cup, Cornflower, second grind,
2⅛" d, $85.00.**

Bowl, ruffled, first ground, amber edge **65.00**
Celery Vase, 6½" h, 4½" d, first ground,
  Cornflower, blue stained flower dec. . **485.00**
Creamer, second ground, Daisy and
  Butterfly, applied clear handle, three
  applied clear feet. **275.00**
Cruet, 5½" h, first ground, Blueberry,
  gold leaves, applied clear handle,
  clear ball stopper. **285.00**
Dish, 4 x 3", Blueberry, handle, ruffled,
  gold leaves. **125.00**
Finger Bowl, 2½" h, 5" w, Blueberry,
  ruffled **90.00**
Goblet, 6" h, first ground, little amber
  stain remains **115.00**
Lemonade Glass, 4½" h, first ground,
  Cornflower, blue stained flower dec. . **175.00**
Pitcher
  7" h, second ground, Cornflower, blue
    stained flower dec **75.00**
  7½" h, bulbous, DQ, twisted rope han-
    dle and collar, polychrome floral
    motif **110.00**
  7½" h, 6½" w, second ground, Pansy
    and Butterfly, excellent staining . . . **275.00**
Punch Cup and Underplate, 2½" h x 2½"
  w cup, 4½" d underplate, second
  ground, excellent staining. **225.00**
Toothpick, first ground, Cornflower, blue
  stained flower dec **245.00**
Tumbler
  Blueberries, second ground **165.00**

Midwestern, dec 80.00
Vase, 3″ h, 6″ w, fan, first ground, Cornflower, blue stained flower dec and violet spray 240.00

PORTRAIT WARE

History: Plates, vases, and other articles with portraits on them were popular in the second half of the 19th century. Although male subjects, such as Napoleon or Louis XVI, were used, the ware usually depicted a beautiful woman, often unidentified.

A large number of English and Continental china manufacturers made portrait ware. Because most ware was hand painted, an artist's signature often is found.

Box, cov, 6″ d, center cartouche of female holding music, gilt ground, raised gold dot border, green and gold inner border, cobalt blue and gilt trim, Royal Vienna, beehive mark 240.00
Cup and Saucer
  3½″ h, cup with medallion of Louis XVI, Madame de Lamballe, and Marie Antoinette, blue celeste and jeweled ground, saucer with central crest, Sevres, 19th C, price for pair **2,200.00**
  6½″ h, cov cup, portrait reserve, floral spray, apple green ground, gilt highlights, Sevres style 225.00
Plaque, 17¼″ h, 14½″ w, bust of young girl, white ground, leaves and berry dec, gold rim, sgd "G Landgraf," Crown Derby, c1881 . . . . 5,000.00

Plate, woman in yellow–gold gown, maroon border with poppies, emb gold dec, sgd Wagner, Vienna, crown mark, 9½″ d, $675.00.

Plate
  8¼″ d, Victorian lady, red flowers in hair, gold border, Limoges 95.00
  8½″ d, monarch, floral border, tin glaze, Delft, sgd "H V Cumberland 1748" 1,150.00
  9″ d, Marie Antoinette and Louis XVI, cobalt borders, three oval floral reserves, stamped "Chatteau de Tuilleries," Sevres, mid 19th C, price for pair 550.00
  9½″ d
    Bust of Josephine, green border, gold traces, marked "Z S & Co Bavaria". 70.00
    Madame de Lamballe wearing puce dress, floral border, turquoise and gold rim, Sevres 295.00
  9¾″ d, Queen Louise, blue–green border, gold trim, shaped rim, marked "Z S & Co Bavaria" 100.00
  10″ d, souvenir, Louisiana Purchase, earthenware, blue and white, high glaze, fair buildings on rim, Victoria Art Company, NY
    Jefferson 225.00
    Napoleon 275.00
  12¾″ d, woman wearing brocade robe, playing dulcimer, pastel ground, gold rim, pierced for hanging. 110.00
Tea Set, cup and saucer, creamer, and sugar, child portrait, lavendar, Old Paris, c1880, price for four piece set 110.00
Vase
  3½″ h, miniature, young girl with bonnet, Bavaria. 110.00
  8″ h, lady with peacock, maroon and gold ground, turquoise accents, marked "Royal Windsor". 350.00
  11½″ h, glass, painted oval reserve of bejeweled woman, urn shape, green, gilt painted dec, applied gilt handles, Continental, mid 19th C. . 250.00

POSTERS

History: The poster was an extremely effective and critical means of mass communication, especially in the period before 1920. Enormous quantities were produced, helped in part by the propaganda role posters played in World War I.

Print runs of two million were not unknown. Posters were not meant to be saved. Once they served their purpose, they tended to be destroyed. The paradox of high production and low survival is one of the fascinating aspects of poster history.

The posters of the late 19th and early 20th centuries represent the pinnacle of American lithography printing. The advertising posters of firms such as Strobridge or Courier are true classics. Philadelphia was one center for the poster industry.

Europe pioneered in posters with high artistic and aesthetic content. Many major artists of the 20th century designed posters. Poster art still plays a key role throughout Europe today.

References: John Barnicoat, *A Concise History of Posters*, Harry N. Abrams, 1976; Tony Fusco, *The Official Identification and Price Guide To Posters*, House of Collectibles, 1990; George Theofiles, *American Posters of World War I: A Price and Collector's Guide*, Dafram House Publishers; Walton Rawls, *Wake Up, America!: World War I and The American Poster*, Abbeville Press, 1988; Stephen Rebello and Richard Allen, *Reel Art: Great Posters From The Golden Age of The Silver Screen*, Abbeville Press, 1988; Susan Theran, *Prints, Posters & Photographs: Identification and Price Guide*, Avon Books, 1993; Susan Theran and Katheryn Acerbo (eds.), *Leonard's Annual Price Index of Prints, Posters & Photographs, Volume 1, July 1, 1991–June 30, 1992*, Auction Index, 1992; Jon R. Warren, *Warren's Movie Poster Price Guide, 1993 Edition*, American Collector's Exchange, 1992; Bruce Lanier Wright, *Yesterday's Tomorrows: The Golden Age of Science Fiction Movie Posters, 1950–1964*, Taylor Publishing, 1993.

Museum: Motion Picture Arts Gallery, New York, NY.

Additional Listings: See *Warman's Americana & Collectibles* for more examples.

Advisor: George Theofiles.

ADVERTISING

Avalon Cigarettes, 10 x 16″, smiling girl, Anon, c1940.	45.00
EVM Bicycle, 19 x 27″, full color, Art Nouveau border, c1910.	175.00
Fireman's Fund Insurance Co, 14 x 18″, color litho decal transfer, fireman rescuing girl, flaming background, c1920.	150.00
Lux, 21 x 11″, full color, man putting on shirt, black background, c1930.	125.00
Raleigh Cigarettes, 12 x 18″, full color, couple dancing, Anon, c1935.	65.00
Sonny Sugar Cones, 18 x 8″, boy and sugar cone illus, Anon, c1923.	75.00

CIRCUS, SHOWS, AND ACTS

Christy Bros Big 5 Ring Wild Animal Shows, The Wonder Show, 27 x 41″, c1925.	150.00
Hollywood Peep Show, 27 x 41″, burlesque strip revue, c1950.	125.00
Hot From Harlem, 22 x 28″, black burlesque show, color, Anon, c1947	250.00
Larry Brenner's Fantasies of 1929, 14 x	
22″, Vaudeville and dance revue, Donaldson litho.	80.00
Ringling Bros Barnum & Bailey Liberty Bandwagon, 30 x 19″, color litho, ornate wagon with Merue Evans portrait, 1943.	225.00
Wallace Bros Circus, 28 x 41″, full color, snarling tiger and lion, c1950	75.00

Movie, insert, *Metropolis,* Paramount, 1926, 14 × 36″, $33,000.00.

MOVIE

Action In Arabia, 27 x 41″, George Sanders and Virginia Bruce, 1944	75.00
Bad Boy, 27 x 41″, James Dunn and Louise Fazenda, Fox, 1934	150.00
Cheaters At Play, 27 x 41″, Thomas Meighan and Charlotte Greenwood, Fox, 1931.	275.00
Double Danger, 27 x 41″, Preston Foster and Whitney Bourne, RKO, 1938	110.00
False Paradise, 27 x 41″, Hopalong Cassidy, United Artists, 1947	125.00
Goodbye Mr. Chips, 27 x 41″, Robert Donat and Greer Garson, MGM, 1939	450.00
I'll Be Seeing You, 27 x 41″, Ginger Rogers, Joseph Cotton, and Shirley Temple, United Artists, 1945.	150.00
Love Takes Flight, 22 x 28″, Bruce Cabot and Beatrice Roberts, Grand National, 1937.	135.00
Pursuit Of The Graf Spee, 22 x 28″, John Gregson and Anthony Quayle, Rank, c1955.	150.00

Smouldering Fires, 14 x 22″, Pauline
Frederick and Laura La Plante, Universal, 1925 . . . .   **125.00**
Up The River, 27 x 41″, Preston Foster,
Tony Martin, and Arthur Treacher,
Fox, 1938. . . . .   **125.00**

PUBLISHING

Clack Book—April 1896, 19 x 12″, full
moon smiling down on rows of cats. .   **150.00**
Free—NY Sunday Journal—It's A Hot
Combination, 20 x 15″, gentlemen
holding musical notes, red and green
Christmas type background, 1899. . .   **125.00**
Harper's July, 14 x 22″, German sentry,
1895 . . . .   **150.00**
Philadelphia Enquirer's Boys and Girls
Christmas Book, 19 x 24″, Victorian
lady holding hands with child, multi-
colored, 1901 . . . .   **125.00**
Success Magazine—Christmas Number
1900, 10 x 15″, Three Wise Men illus,
J C Lyendecker. **225.00**

THEATRICAL

Dangers Of A Great City, 21 x 28″, color
litho, several men fighting in office,
Anon, c1900. . . . .   **150.00**
Key Largo, 14 x 22″, Paul Muni portrait,
black and red motif, Anon, c1930 . . .   **65.00**
No No Nanette, 15 x 22″, surprised gen-
tleman being embraced by young
lady, Theatre Mogador, Paris, c1925   **375.00**
The Gambler Of The West, 20 x 30″,
Strobridge, 1906 . . . .   **190.00**

WORLD WAR I

Be Patriotic, Sign Your Country's Pledge
To Save To Food, 20 x 30″, Columbia
figure wrapped in stars and stripes,
1918 . . . .   **90.00**
Hold Up Your End, 20 x 30″, nurse hold-
ing stretcher, yellow background,
1918 . . . .   **125.00**
I Shall Expect Every Man Who Is Not A
Slacker, 29 x 43″, Navy Dept, 1918. .   **200.00**
If You Want To Fight—Join The Marines,
30 x 41″, woman with charging ma-
rines background, Howard Chandler
Christy, 1915 . . . .   **575.00**
Joan Of Arc Saved France Women Of
America, Save Your Country, 30 x
40″, Joan of Arc image, 1918 . . . . . .   **150.00**
Remember The Flag Of Liberty Support
It!, 20 x 30″, full color, immigrant family
on dock **100.00**
US Marines—Soldiers Of The Sea, 29 x
40″, Marines signaling from beach,
Marine life vignettes, 1915 . . . .   **175.00**

Your Country Needs You—Join The
Navy, 17 x 20″, saluting sailor, Statue
of Liberty background, Rolf Arm-
strong, 1916. . . . .   **100.00**

WORLD WAR II

All Soldiers Can't Be In The Infantry—
But..., 17 x 25″, charging soldier,
1944 . . . .   **125.00**
Battle Stations! Keep 'Em Fighting, 31 x
41″, Naval bugler, 1942 . . . .   **125.00**
Buy War Bonds, 14 x 22″, Uncle Sam
leading battle, N C Wyeth, 1942 . . . .   **125.00**
I'm Counting On You! Don't Discuss
Troop Movements, Ships Sailings,
War Equipment, 20 x 28″, Uncle Sam
with finger to lip, blue background,
1943 . . . .   **95.00**
Save Your Cans—Help Pass The Am-
munition, 25 x 33″, soldiers feed
empty tomato cans through belts,
1942 . . . .   **200.00**
To Have And To Hold—War Bonds, 20 x
28″, soldier with streaming flag,
c1943. . . . .   **175.00**
United For Victory, 22 x 28″, locomotive
and red, white, and blue stars and
stripes illus, Anon, c1944 . . . .   **100.00**
We're In The Army Now, 10 x 15″, three
women and terrier illus, Anon, c1943   **75.00**

POT LIDS

History: Pot lids are the lids from pots or small
containers which originally held ointments, po-
mades, or soap. Although a complete set of pot
and lid is desirable to some collectors, lids are the
most collectible. The lids frequently were decorated
with multicolored underglaze transfers of rural and
domestic scenes, portraits, florals, and landmarks.

The majority of the containers with lids were
made between 1845–1920 by F. & R. Pratt, Fenton, Staffordshire, England. In 1920, F. & R. Pratt
merged with Cauldon, Ltd. Several lids were reissued by the firm using the original copper engraving plates. They were used for decoration and
never served as actual lids. Reissues by Kirkhams
Pottery, England, generally have two holes for
hanging and often are marked as reissues. Cauldon, Coalport, and Wedgwood were other firms
making reissues.

References: Susan and Al Bagdade, *Warman's
English & Continental Pottery & Porcelain, 2nd Edi-
tion,* Wallace–Homestead, 1991; A. Ball, *The Price
Guide to Pot–Lids And Other Underglaze Multicolor
Prints On Ware, Second Edition,* Antique Collec-
tors' Club, 1991 value update; Ronald Dale, *The
Price Guide To Black and White Pot–Lids,* Antique
Collectors' Club; Barbara and Sonny Jackson,
American Pot Lids, published by authors, 1987.

Note: Sizes are given for actual pot lids; size of any framing not included.

Arctic Expedition, multicolored, T J & J
    Mayer, 3″ d, rim chip 320.00
Bloater Paste, black label, white iron-
    stone, 4½″ d, marked "England". . . .   25.00
Dr Hassall's Hair Restorer, 1¾″ d   . . .   250.00
Dublin Industrial Exhibition, multico-
    lored, 3¾″ d 50.00
Embarking For The East, multicolored,
    Pratt, 4⅛″ d, orig jar 100.00
Linaleton's Eye Ointment, 1⅝″ d 210.00
Morris's Imperial Eye Ointment 200.00
Mrs Ellen Hale's Celebrated Heal All
    Ointment, black on white, 4″ d 350.00
Napirima, Trinidad, T J & J Mayer,
    c1853, medium 165.00
Persuasion, multicolored, 4⅛″ d 150.00
Picnic On The Banks Of The River,
    Gothic Ruins, Pratt, 4¾″ d 90.00
Prepared Only By Hooks, Windsor Oint-
    ment, bird on branch 120.00

The Late Prince Consort, 4⅛″ d, $160.00.

Queen Victoria on Balcony, T J & J
    Mayer, large 265.00
Residence of the Late Sir Robert Peel,
    Pratt 150.00
Roman Eye Balsam, purple, glass base   210.00
Tam O'Shanter and Souter Johnny, 4″
    d, framed 275.00
Trouchet's Corn Cure Safe Reliable,
    lighthouse 125.00
Trysting Place, The, small 165.00
View of Windsor Castle, Pratt, 6½″ d   .   150.00
Village Wedding, The, multicolored,
    Pratt, 4¼″ d 80.00
Ville De Strasbourg, Pratt type 75.00
Walmer Castle, Kent, Tatnell & Son, 4½″
    d 200.00

Wellington, T J & J Mayer, c1850,
    medium 100.00

PRATT

PRATT WARE

PRATT
FENTON

History: The earliest Pratt earthenware was made in the late 18th century by William Pratt, Lane Delph, Staffordshire, England. In 1810–18, Felix and Robert Pratt, William's sons, established their own firm, F. & R. Pratt, in Fenton in the Staffordshire district. Potters in Yorkshire, Liverpool, Sunderland, Tyneside, and Scotland copied the ware.

The wares consisted of relief molded jugs, commercial pots and tablewares with transfer decoration, commemorative pieces, and figure and animal groups.

Much of the early ware is unmarked. The mid–19th-century wares bear several different marks in conjunction with the name Pratt, including "& Co."

References: Susan and Al Bagdade, *Warman's English & Continental Pottery & Porcelain, Second Edition,* Wallace–Homestead, 1991; John and Griselda Lewis, *Pratt Ware 1780–1840,* Antique Collectors' Club, 1984.

Additional Listing: Pot Lids.

Creamer, 5¼″ h, cow and milkmaid, yel-
    low and black sponged cow, under-
    glaze enamels, translucent green
    stepped rect base, horns chipped . . .   440.00
Cup Plate, 3⅛″ d, dalmatian, white,
    black spots 65.00
Figure
    Autumn, 9″ h, young woman, classical
        robes, holding armful of fruit, rock-
        work base, flaring rect plinth molded
        with leaf band, polychrome enamel
        trim, early 19th C 360.00
    Owl, 5½″ h, alert expression, incised
        plumage, molded head and leg de-
        tails, creamware, ochre, green, and
        brown spots, chips around base,
        cracked, c1785 . . . .   5,280.00
Jar, 7¾″ h, molded oval panels of pea-
    cocks in landscapes, blue, brown,
    green, and ochre, lower section with
    vertical leaves, band of foliage on rim,
    c1790. . . . .   600.00
Jug, 7¾″ h, large oval molded reserve,
    exotic barnyard fowl, stiff leaf–tip band
    at edge of reserve, molded rim band
    with flowering branches, base with
    long stiff leaves alternating with slen-
    der flowering branches, polychrome
    enamel highlights, c1800 . . . .   1,430.00

Plate, Philadelphia Public Building, blue, 8½″ d, $150.00.

Miniature, 4¾″ l, dish, center molded with sprig of two ochre plums, green leaf, brown stem, feather molded rim, underglaze blue edging, small rim chip, c1800.	330.00
Mug, 4″ h, colorful tavern scene transfer, hairline crack	55.00
Mustard Jar, dark blue hunt scene, tan ground	55.00
Pitcher, 7¼″ h raised couple, mother, children, and trees dec, yellow, blue, brown, and green, 18th C.	340.00
Plaque, 6¼ x 7¼″, Louis XVI portrait, oval form, beaded border, polychrome enamels, c1793, rim nicks, glaze wear	880.00
Plate, 9″ d, Haddon Hall, classical figure border	100.00
Sauce Boat, 6⅜″ l, figural, dolphin, translucent green glaze over scales, brown eyes and fins, oval foot, yellow band border, chips, small hairlines in foot, c1790.	770.00
Tea Caddy, 6¼″ h, rect, raised figural panels front and back, fluted and yellow trimmed lid, blue, yellow, orange, and green dec.	330.00

PRINTS

History: Prints serve many purposes. They can be a reproduction of an artist's paintings, drawings, or designs. Prints themselves often are an original art form. Finally, prints can be developed for mass appeal as opposed to aesthetic statement. Much of the production of Currier & Ives fits this latter category. Currier & Ives concentrated on genre, urban, patriotic, and nostalgia scenes.

Prints are beginning to attract a wide following. This is partially because prices have not matched the rapid rise in oil and other paintings.

References: William P. Carl, *Currier's Price Guide to American and European Prints at Auction, Second Edition,* Currier Publications, 1991; Karen Choppa and Paul Humphrey, *Maud Humphrey: Her Permanent Imprint On American Illustration,* Schiffer Publishing, 1993; Victor J. W. Christie, *Bessie Pease Gutmann: Her Life and Works,* Wallace-Homestead, 1990; Frederic A. Conningham and Colin Simkin, *Currier & Ives Prints, Revised Edition,* Crown Publishers, 1970; William R. Holland and Douglas L. Congdon–Martin, *The Collectible Maxfield Parrish,* Schiffer Publishing, 1993; Denis C. Jackson, *The Price & Identification Guide to J. C. Leyendecker & F. X. Leyendecker,* published by author, 1983; Denis C. Jackson, *The Price & Identification Guide To: Maxfield Parrish, Eighth Edition,* published by author, 1992; M. June Keagy and Joan M. Rhoden, *More Wonderful Yard-Long Prints,* published by authors, 1992; William D. Keagy et al., *Those Wonderful Yard-Long Prints & More,* published by authors, 1989; Robert Kipp, *Currier's Price Guide to Currier & Ives Prints, Second Edition,* Currier Publications, 1991; Stephanie Lane, *Maxfield Parrish: A Price Guide,* L-W Book Sales, 1993; J. L. Locher (ed.), *M. C. Escher, His Life And Complete Graphic Work,* Harry N. Abrams, 1992; Coy Ludwig, *Maxfield Parrish,* Schiffer Publishing, 1973, 1993 reprint with value guide; Rita C. Mortenson, *R. Atkinson Fox, His Life and Work,* Volume 1 (1991), Volume 2 (1992), L-W Book Sales; Richard J. Perry, *The Maxfield Parrish Identification & Price Guide,* Starbound Publishing, 1993; Ruth M. Pollard, *The Official Price Guide To Collector Prints, 7th Edition,* House Of Collectibles, 1986; *Print Price Index '94: 1992–1993 Auction Season,* Gordon and Lawrence Art Reference, 1993; Susan Theran, *Prints, Posters & Photographs: Identification and Price Guide,* Avon Books, 1993; Susan Theran and Katheryn Acerbo (eds.), *Leonard's Annual Price Index of Prints, Posters & Photographs, Volume 1, July 1, 1991–June 30, 1992,* Auction Index, 1992.

Collectors' Clubs: American Antique Graphics Society, 5185 Windfall Rd., Medina, OH 44256; American Historical Print Collectors Society, PO Box 201, Fairfield, CT 06430; Prang-Mark Society, PO Box 306, Watkins Glen, NY 14891.

Periodicals: *Audubon Newsletter,* 4700 N. Habana Ave., Tampa, FL 33614; *Journal of the Print World,* 1008 Winona Rd., Meredith, NH 03253-9599; *The Illustrator Collector's News,* PO Box 1958, Sequim, WA 98382; *The Print Collector's Newsletter,* 119 East 79th St., New York, NY 10021.

Museums: Audubon Wildlife Sanctuary, Audubon, PA; John James Audubon State Park and Museum, Henderson, KY; National Portrait Gallery, Washington, DC.

Reproduction Alert: Reproductions are a problem, especially Currier & Ives prints. Check the dimensions before buying any print.

Additional Listing: See Wallace Nutting.

Allen, James E, Teeming Ingots, sgd "James E. Allen" in pencil lower right, dated in ink on folder, titled on Society insert, etching on laid paper, published by Society of American Etchers, orig folder, 12 x 9⅞" plate size, matted, unframed, 1935 . . . . **1,100.00**

Barnet, John, Niagara Falls, American Side, identified in inscriptions in matrix, litho, hand colored on paper, sheet size 27 x 38⅝", framed, 1855 . **1,210.00**

Baumann, Gustave, Big Timber Upper Pecos, sgd "Gustave Baumann" in pencil with hand in heart chop lower right, titled in pencil lower left, numbered "15 of 100" in pencil lower center, identified on labels on back, color woodblock on laid paper, 9¾ x 11¼", framed **1,100.00**

Benson, Frank Weston
  Flying Pintail II, sgd "Frank W. Benson" in pencil lower left, etching and drypoint on paper, 4⅞ x 5⅞" plate size, framed, 1927 . . . . **300.00**
  Six Bluebills, sgd "Frank W. Benson" in pencil lower left, identified "Friends of Contemporary Prints" label on reverse, drypoint on paper, 3¾ x 4⅞" plate size, framed **500.00**

Coleman, Glenn O, Street Dance, edition of 50, sgd, numbered, and dated "9/50 1928 Glenn O. Coleman" in pencil lower left, sgd in the stone lower center, litho on cream wove paper, 12⅛ x 15⅞" image, matted, unframed **1,760.00**

Cornell, James & Sons, London, publisher, The New York and London Packet Ship Victoria 1000 Tons Entering New York Harbor, sgd "Clifford R James" in pencil lower right, identified in inscription in the plate, intaglio process printed in colors on chine appliqué, 16¼ x 22", burl frame **330.00**

Currier and Ives, Publishers
  American Homestead Summer, minor stains in margins, repaired tear in top margin, matted and framed, 15¾" h, 19½" w, c1868 . . . . **220.00**
  The Celebrated Boston Team Mill Boy and Blondine..., fully identified in inscription lower margin, chromolithograph on paper, sheet size 24½ x 36⅝", framed, staining, losses, stray pencil marks, 1882. . . . . . . **330.00**
  The Great Ocean Yacht Race between the Henrietta, Fleetwing and Vesta...," Charles Parsons, lithog-

rapher, fully identified in inscriptions in lower margin, label from the Old Print Shop, NY, on back, lithograph printed in colors, additional hand coloring, heavy paperboard, 23⅛ x 32¾" sheet size, framed **2,200.00**

The Ivy Bridge, pen and ink presentation inscription in border, stains, framed, 12¾" h, 17" w **75.00**

The King of the Turf, St Julian, litho, hand colored, 29¾ x 37¾", stains, framed **610.00**

The Miniature Ship "Red, White and Blue," fully identified in inscriptions in lower margin, lithograph, hand coloring on paper, sheet size 12 x 16", framed, toning, minor wrinkles, not examined out of frame **140.00**

The US Sloop of War, *Kearage* Seven Guns, sinking the Pirate *Alabama* Eight Guns, fully identified in inscriptions in lower margin, lithograph, hand colored heightened by gum arabic on paper, 13½ x 17¼" sheet size, matted, unframed, 1864 . . . . **220.00**

Currier, Nathaniel
  Amos, litho, hand colored, enhanced colors, 17¼ x 13½", pine frame. . . **140.00**
  Clipper Ship *Nightingale,* Charles Parsons, lithographer, fully identified in inscription in lower margin, label from Old Print Shop, NY, on reverse, lithograph, hand coloring on paper, 18¾ x 25" sheet size, framed, 1854 . . . . **3,025.00**
  The Sinking of the *Cumberland* [*sic*] by the Iron Clad *Merrimac* off Newport News, VA, March 8, 1862, fully identified in inscription in lower margin, lithograph, hand coloring, 12 x 15½" sheet size, framed. **440.00**

Dehn, Adolph Arthur, Moonrise in Concarneau, sgd and dated "Adolph Dehn, 1927" in pencil lower right, edition of 10, litho, tint stone on paper, 10½ x 15¼" image size, framed **165.00**

Endicott & Co
  New York Clipper Ship Challenge fully identified in inscription beneath image, label from Old Print Ship, NY, on reverse, lithograph printed in colors, additional hand coloring, 23½ x 32½" sheet size, framed, 1852 . . . . **3,300.00**
  View of Newburyport, Massachusetts, after John Badger Bachelder, identified in inscription on reverse, lithograph, hand colored, gum arabic, heavy paper, 22¾ x 29½" sheet size, framed. **412.00**

Fenn, Harry, Trees by a River, sgd

Emil Ganso, Spring, color litho, sgd, edition of 15, fine impression, ink stains in margins, minor discoloration in margins, c1937, 11½ x 16″, $935.00. Photograph courtesy of William Doyle Galleries.

"Harry Fenn" in pencil lower right, monotype, black ink, heavy wove paper, 10⅜ x 7½″ plate size, matted, framed 715.00

Gearhart, Frances Hammel, Incoming Fog, sgd "Frances H. Gearhart" in pencil lower right, titled in pencil lower left, color woodblock on Japan paper, 10 x 11″ matted, minor creasing, tape to edges. 1,430.00

Grosz, George, Dunes and Grass, sgd "George Grosz" in pencil lower right, titled on mat, drypoint, added ink, wove paper, 10 x 12⅞″ plate size, framed 360.00

Hassam, Frederick Childe, Old Lace, monogrammed and annotated "imp." lower right, monogrammed, inscribed, and dated "Cos Cob 1915" in plate lower right, etching and drypoint on paper, 6⅞ x 6⅞″ plate size, unmatted, unframed, 1915. . . . . 990.00

Heath, Howard, Vase of Flowers, sgd "Howard Heath" in pencil lower right, block print in colors on Tableau wove paper, 20⅛ x 15¼″, matted, unframed 385.00

Helleu, Paul Cesar, Head of a Woman, sgd "Helleu" in pencil lower right, drypoint, brown and gray ink, wove paper, 16¼ x 10⅜″ plate size, framed, good, abrasions, soiling to margins and on reverse 1,210.00

Hennings, E. Martin, Beneath the Cottonwoods, sgd "E. Martin Hennings" in pencil lower right, numbered "4/100" and titled in lower left, litho on wove paper with watermark, 10 x 10″ image size, framed 1,430.00

Icart, Louis, Smoke, sgd "Louis Icart" in pencil, inscribed with date and "les Graveurs Modernes..." upper right, publisher's drystamp lower left, drypoint in colors, added color, 14⅛ x 19⅜″ plate size, framed, surface abrasions, repaired and unrepaired tears to margin, staining, 1926 . . . . 615.00

Kellogg, Lucy, handcolored litho, good old curly maple veneer frame, old glass, 11¾″ h, 10″ w, ... 105.00

Landeck, Armin, Manhattan Nocturne, sgd "Landeck" in pencil lower right, sgd and dated in the plate lower left, initialed lower center, etching and drypoint on laid paper, published by Society of American Etchers, 7⅛ x 12″, matted, unframed, 1938. . . . . 880.00

Lazzell, Blanche, The Blue Vase, sgd and dated "Blanche Lazzell 1927" in pencil lower right, monogrammed in matrix lower left, titled in pencil lower left, annotated "Nov. 7, 1927" lower center, and "19½" (twice) on the reverse, block print in colors on paper, 14 x 12¼″ image size, framed 9,350.00

Lewis, Martin
Lost Railroad, sgd "Martin Lewis" in pencil lower right, in the plate lower left, collector's annotations in margins and reverse, etching, drypoint, aquatint, and sandpaper ground on wove paper, 9⅞ x 16⅞″ plate size, framed, 1933. . . . . 3,575.00

Rain on Murray Hill, sgd "Martin Lewis–imp–" in pencil lower right and in the plate lower right, drypoint on wove paper, 7¾ x 11¾″ plate size, matted, unframed, 1928 . . . . 6,100.00

Lum, Bertha, Wedding Banners, sgd "Bertha Lum" in pencil within image lower center, inscribed and dated "...1924..." in pencil lower center, numbered "no. 46" in pencil lower right, color woodcut on paper, 8⅝ x 11¼″, matted, unframed. 330.00

Marsh, Reginald, Jersey City Landscape, final state, sgd "Reginald Marsh" in pencil lower right, sgd and dated "Reginald March 1939" in the plate, titled in pencil lower left, annotated "Etch'd & Engraved–Ed. 40" in pencil lower center, etching and engraving on paper, 7¹³⁄₁₆ x 11¹⁵⁄₁₆″ plate size, unmatted, unframed. 715.00

Matisse, Henri, Danseuse au Tabouret, from Dix Danseuses portfolio, published by Galerie d'Art Contemporain, Paris, total edition of 150, sgd and numbered "45/130 Henri Matisse" in pencil lower left, litho on Arches wove paper, 19¾ x 12⅞″ sheet size, pale light staining at mat opening, collector's annotations to margins, 1927. . . 9,350.00

Mottram, C, engraver, after John William Hill, Boston, 1857, identified in inscriptions in the plate, collotype, hand coloring on paper, 28¾ x 41¾", framed 1,045.00

Parrish, Maxfield, Waterfall, 7 x 10" . . 125.00

Prang, Louis & Co, Old Warehouse–Dock Square, Boston, Built 1680, Taken Down 1860, identified in inscription, lithograph printed in colors on paper, 10½ x 14¾", framed, fading. 550.00

Rice, William S, sgd "W. S. Rice" in pencil lower right, titled in pencil lower left, color woodblock on paper

Dawn, 5¾ x 3¼", framed 500.00

Eucalyptus–Northbrae, 7¾ x 3½", framed 615.00

Ripley, Aiden Lassell

Goose Shooting, sgd "A. Lassell Ripley" in pencil lower right, titled with copyright in pencil lower left, drypoint on paper, 8¾ x 13¾" sight size, framed. 880.00

Grouse and Vines, sgd "A Lassell Ripley" in pencil lower right, titled and dedicated in pencil lower left, etching with drypoint on paper, 6½ x 8½" plate size, framed 360.00

Rungius, Carl

Alaskan Wilderness, sgd "E. Rungius" in pencil lower right, titled in pencil lower left, drypoint on cream wove paper, 7⅞ x 10⅝" plate size, framed 1,320.00

A Woodland Stag, sgd "C. Rungius" in pencil lower right, identified on label on reverse, edition of 50, drypoint on wove paper, 6⅛ x 8⅜" plate size, matted, unframed, 1926 1,045.00

Spruance, Benton M, Flight from the Beach, sgd and dated "Spruance 39" in pencil and initialed "BS" in the stone lower right, titled in pencil lower center, numbered in pencil lower left, litho on wove paper, 13⅝ x 9⅝" sight, framed 1,045.00

Steffen, Bernard Joseph, Haying, sgd "Bernard J. Steffen" in pencil lower right, titled on AAA label on reverse of frame, published by Associated American Artists, NY, litho on paper, 8½ x 12¾" image size, framed 275.00

Sutherland, Thomas, engraver after William John Higgins, South Sea Whale Fishing, identified in inscriptions beneath image, etching, aquatint, hand coloring on paper, 17¼ x 22¼", framed, scattered foxing, toning, 1825 . . . . 440.00

Thaulow, Fritz, Sunday Evening in the Village, sgd "Fritz Thaulow" in pencil lower right, numbered in pencil and publisher's drystamp lower left, colored aquatint on paper, 18¾ x 23½" plate size, framed 385.00

Tissot, James Jacques Joseph, Reverie, sgd "J. Tissot" in pencil lower left, sgd and dated in plate upper right, artist's stamp in red upper right, etching on laid paper, 9⅛ x 4½" plate size, framed 1,540.00

Toby, Mark

The Grand Parade, sgd "Tobey" in pencil lower right, numbered "32/150" in lower left, publisher's drystamp "Transworld Art" lower left, litho in color on paper, 9¼ x 10⅝" image, framed 880.00

Winter Leaves, sgd "Tobey" in pencil lower right, numbered "32/150" in pencil lower left, titled on reverse, publisher's drystamp "Transworld Art" lower left, etching with colors intaglio and relief–printed color on paper, 14 x 10⅞" plate size, framed 475.00

Ury, Lesser, Nighttime in the Cafe, sgd "L. Ury" in pencil lower left, litho on paper, 14½ x 10" image size, framed 1,430.00

Wengenroth, Stow

Greenport, 8 p.m., sgd "Stow Wengenroth" in pencil lower right, annotated "Ed/24" in pencil lower left, litho on wove paper, 9⅞ x 15⅞" image sight, framed, 1953 . . . . 1,320.00

House at Port Clyde, sgd "Stow Wengenroth" in pencil lower right, annotated "Ed/50" in pencil lower left, litho on wove paper, 9¹⁵⁄₁₆ x 13⅜" image size, shrink wrapped, unmatted, unframed, 1938. . . . . 360.00

Inlet Light, sgd "Stow Wengenroth" in pencil lower right, edition of 181, litho on wove paper, 8¼ x 12¾" image size, framed, 1938. . . . . 470.00

The Chickadees, Corea, Maine, sgd "Stow Wengenroth" in pencil lower right, annotated "Ed/50" in pencil lower left, litho on wove paper, 11⅛ x 15¾" image size, matted, unframed, 1953. . . . . 440.00

Whistler, James Abbott McNeill, Drouet Sculpteur, sgd and dated "Whistler 1859" in the plate lower right, titled in plate lower center, etching and drypoint, thin wove paper, 8⅞ x 5⅞" plate size, framed, 1859. . . . . 880.00

Yoshida, Toshi, Festival in Spring, woodblock on paper, pencil sgd, 30/200, 15 x 10", framed, 1962 . . . . 90.00

PRINTS—JAPANESE

History: Buying Japanese wood-block prints requires attention to detail and skilled knowledge of the subject. The quality of the impression (good, moderate, or weak), the color, and condition are critical. Various states and strikes of the same print cause the price to fluctuate. Knowing the proper publisher and censor's seals is helpful in identifying an original print.

Most prints were recopied and issued in popular versions. These represent the vast majority of the prints found in the marketplace. These popular versions should be viewed solely as decorative since they have little value.

A novice buyer should seek expert advice before buying. Talk with a specialized dealer, museum curator, or auction division head.

The listings below concentrate on details to show the depth of data needed for adequate pricing. Condition and impression are good, unless indicated otherwise.

O = Oban, 10 x 15″	C = Chuban, 7 x 10″
t = tat-e, large in width	H = Hosoban, 5½″ x 13″
y = yoke-e, large in length	T = Triptyck

Reference: Gloria and Robert Mascarelli, *Warman's Oriental Antiques,* Wallace-Homestead, 1992.

Collectors' Club: Ukiyo-E Society of America, Inc., FDR Station, PO Box 665, New York, NY 10150.

Museum: Honolulu Academy of Fine Arts, Honolulu, HI.

Eisen, *Ukiyo nijuyonko* series, Yang Hsiang shown teasing cat, sgd *Keisai Eisen–ga,* with *kiwame* and publisher's seal, good impression, slight wrinkling, Ot 725.00
Gakutei, seated geisha playing the *biwa,* from *Hanazo bantsuki* series, sgd *Gakutei,* color slightly faded, C 950.00
Harunobo, courtesan showing the neck of her kamoro before a screen dec with farmers harvesting rice, titled *Jin, Virtue,* from *The Five Cardinal Virtues* series, sgd *Suzuki Harunobo ga,* Ct .   7,750.00
Hiroshi Yoshida, titled *Skakuji,* title in plate, toned, soiled margins, framed, sgd in pencil 65.00
Hiroshige
  Kanagawa–Dai no tei, hilltop view, from *Tokaido Gojusan–tsugi* series, sgd *Hiroshige–ga,* red gourd shaped seal with *kiwame* and *Takenouchi* seals, fair impression, good color, backed, left margin trimmed, Oy. 125.00
  Mishima asagiri, "Morning Mist, Mishima," from *Toto meisho* series, "Fa-

mous Places of the Eastern Capital," sgd *Hiroshege ga,* with *Hoseido/Senkakudo,* publisher's seals, margins trimmed, slightly rubbed, and soiled, Oy 675.00
Hokusai, *Sinsho Suwa–ko,* "Lake Suma in Shinano Province," from *Fugaku sanjurokkei* series, "Thirty–six views of Mt Fuji," sgd *Zen Hokusai Iitsui hitsu,* publisher's seal *Eijudo,* Oy. . . .   4,250.00
Kawase Hasui, *Ebisu Harbor, Sado Island in Winter, Tabi miyage dinishi* series, sgd *Hasui,* seated *kawase,* dated Taishi 10 (1921), *Watanabe* publisher's seal, Oy 1,200.00
Kikumaro, courtesan seated by hibachi, surrounded by female attendants, blossoming prunus and sparrow, sgd *Kikumaro hitsu,* fair impression, poor color, stained, Ot. 275.00
Kunichika, *Music Lessons,* c1860, oban, spotting, fair condition, framed 50.00
Kunisada, Kakemono–e, high ranking courtesan walking in elaborate kimono, sgd *Kochoro Kunisada hitsu,* with *aratame/negetsu* seal, c1865, good impression, fair color, faded, toned, trimmed, backed 225.00
Kuniyoshi
  Oda Kazuma, titled *Matsue Ohashi/ The Great Bridge of Matsue,* group of figures crossing bridge in snowstorm, sgd *Kazuma hitsu,* red artist's seal, right margin with title and dated Taisho 13 (1924), very good impression and color, Oy 850.00
Maekawa, Sempan, Bird in Hand, color woodcut, 1955, sgd in pencil lower

Kunisada, Utgawa, 1786–1868, 13½ x 9½″, $900.00.

right, artist's red chop, unframed, 11¼
x 16⅝" **750.00**
Nakayama, Tadashi, Three Zebras,
color woodcut, sgd in pencil lower left,
1959, numbered 30/50, 28 x 22" **1,200.00**
Saito, Kiyoski, Buddha, color woodcut,
sgd in ink within the image, 1962, titled
and numbered 96/200, artist's red
chop, 20¾ x 15" **900.00**
Sekino, Junichiro
My Daughter, color woodcut, 1952,
sgd in pencil lower right, numbered
and annotated 98/100 Ile etat, art-
ist's red chop, 18 x 14½" **900.00**
Portrait, woodcut, sgd in pencil lower
right, numbered 28/30, unframed,
29 x 18¼" **1,900.00**
Terukata, titled *On The Veranda*, c1910,
elaborate black design on kimono,
slight toning, good color and
condition **55.00**
Toyokuni I, three courtesans and their
attendants strolling on busy street,
sgd *Toyokuni-ga, kiwame* and *Iwato-
ya Kisaburo* publisher's seal, fair
impression, pool color, faded, fair
state, Ot. **400.00**
Utamaro, one courtesan standing one
another in front, sgd *Utamaro hitsu*,
with *kiwame, negetsu, (1806)* and
publisher's seals, fair impression,
poor color, faded, wrinkled, Ot **300.00**
Yakamura Koko (Toyonari), three-quar-
ter view of actor *Matsumoto Koshiro*
as *Sekibei*, sgd *Koka-ga,* publisher's
seal and blind printed date Taisho 8
(1919), good impression and color,
Ot **900.00**
Yoshida, Toshi
Irozaki Morning, color woodcut, sgd in
pencil unframed, 9½ x 13½" **50.00**
Silver Pavilion, color woodcut, sgd in
pencil, 14½ x 9¾" **150.00**
Yoshitoshi, Triptych Set, titled *Taiheiki
Sengatake honjun no zu*, showing samurai *Takuma Morimasa* bound in
ropes held by warriors, sgd *Ikahaisai
Yoshitoshi hutsu* with *aratame/ne-
getsu (c1867)* and publisher *Tsuna-
jima Kamekuchi* seals, fair impression
and color, fair state, Ot **300.00**

PURPLE SLAG (MARBLE GLASS)

History: Challinor, Taylor & Co., Tarantum,
Pennsylvania, c1870s–1880s, was the largest pro-
ducer of purple slag in the United States. Since the
quality of pieces varies considerably, there is no
doubt other American firms made it as well.

Purple slag also was made in England. English
pieces are marked with British Registry marks.

Other color combinations, such as blue, green,
or orange, were made but are rarely found.

Additional Listings: Greentown Glass (chocolate slag) and Pink Slag.

Reproduction Alert: Purple slag has been
heavily reproduced over the years and still is reproduced at present.

**Tumbler, ten sided paneled body, 3¼"
h, $50.00.**

Cake Stand, Flute **75.00**
Compote, 4½" d, crimped top **65.00**
Creamer, Flower and Panel **85.00**
Goblet, Flute **40.00**
Match Holder, Daisy and Button **40.00**
Mug, rabbit **65.00**
Plate, 10½" d, closed lattice edge . . . **80.00**
Spooner, Scroll with Acanthus **65.00**
Sugar, cov, Flute **185.00**
Toothpick, Inverted Fan and Feather . **65.00**

PUZZLES

History: The jigsaw puzzle originated in the
mid–18th century in Europe. John Silsbury, a London mapmaker, was selling dissected map jigsaw
puzzles by the early 1760s. The first jigsaw puzzles
in America were English and European imports and
were aimed primarily at children.

Prior to the Civil War, several manufacturers,
e.g., Samuel L. Hill, W. and S. B. Ives, and Mc-
Loughlin Brothers, included puzzle offerings as part
of their line. However, it was the post–Civil War
period that saw the jigsaw puzzle gain a strong
foothold among the children of America.

In the late 1890s and the first decade of the 20th
century, puzzles designed specifically for adults
first appeared. Both forms have existed side by
side ever since. Adult puzzlers were responsible
for two 20th-century puzzle crazes: 1908–9 and
1932–33.

Prior to the mid–1920s, the vast majority of jigsaw puzzles were cut using wood for the adult mar-

ket and composition material for the children's market. In the 1920s the die–cut, cardboard jigsaw puzzle evolved. By the time of the puzzle craze of 1932–33, it was the dominant puzzle medium.

Jigsaw puzzle interest has cycled between peaks and valleys several times since 1933. Mini-revivals occurred during World War II and in the mid–1960s, when Springbok entered the American market.

References: Linda Hannas, *The Jigsaw Book*, Dial Press, 1981, out of print; Harry L. Rinker, *Collector's Guide To Toys, Games and Puzzles,* Wallace–Homestead, 1991; Anne D. Williams, *Jigsaw Puzzles: An Illustrated History and Price Guide*, Wallace–Homestead, 1990.

Collectors' Clubs: American Game Collectors Association, 49 Brooks Ave., Lewiston, ME 04240; National Puzzler's League, PO Box 82289, Portland, OR 97282.

Additional Listings: See *Warman's Americana & Collectibles* for an expanded listing.

ADULT

Wood

F. B., Shenandoah Valley, VA, "Tap–Tap," 8¾ x 5¾", 132 pcs, colored magazine photograph of dance chorus line rehearsing on stage, mid–1930s, cloth bag **22.50**

Milton Bradley, Premier Jigsaw Puzzles, "Tyrolean Waters," 15 x 11", 300 pcs, interlocking cut, some figural pcs, minor cutting along color lines, 1937. . . **25.00**

Cooke, Frances A., Weston, MA, No. 23, "Speak for it!," 13⅛ x 8½", 213 pcs, grassy meadow scene, seated young girl holds out hand containing a biscuit, young dog stands in front of her, second dog curled up in her other arm, print marked "Heywood Hardy 1887," c1910, orig box, portion of label lost to silverfish **35.00**

Gencraft/Glendex, "Tree Island," 14 x 10", 304 pcs, New England landscape scene, interlocking, 1960s, cardboard box **20.00**

Great Lakes Exposition, Cleveland Centennial, June 27 to Oct. 4, 1936, 2⅛ x 3⅛ x¾", information stenciled on top of block in blue and red, three dimensional layered cutting. **45.00**

Jost, Jr., J. W., Jost Jig–Saw Puzzle, No. 107, "Their First Lesson," 16 x 12", 220 pcs, figural pcs (2 stars, bird on branch, spaniel, horse, rooster, elephant, "D", and "G"), some line cutting, orig box. **20.00**

Parker Brothers, Pastime Picture Puzzle, "First American Flag Raising On The Schoolhouse," 22 x 15½", over 500 pcs, crowd in colonial dress stands before log cabin schoolhouse, approx 40 figural pcs, Sawed by 16, dated 10/29/25, orig box **60.00**

Parker Brothers, Pastime Contest, untitled, 4⅞ x 3¼", 27 pcs, Indian painting hide before campfire, includes four page booklet folded in half providing suggested contest rules, orig box . . . **10.00**

Selchow & Righter Co., New York, Pandora Jig Saw Puzzle, "The Tavern," 5⅞ x 7⅞", 72 pcs, several abstract figural pcs, orig box **15.00**

Straus, Joseph K., Series No. 222, "Rural Beauty," 11¾ x 8⅞", over 200 pcs, interlocking, dark green wrapped cardboard box, orange end label, no Straus identification, early **10.00**

Unknown cutter, "QUOITS," 7¾ x 11¼", 123 pcs, cartoon image of four gentlemen (gentry) playing quoits, print marked in lower left corner "Copyright 1904/ J. I. Austin Co., Chicago," R. Mattloch illustrator, fleur–de–lis figural signature piece, orig packaging missing. **25.00**

Unknown cutter, untitled, 9⅜ x 12⅛", approx 135 pcs, scene of World War I soldier in uniform holding girl in white dress with red, white, and blue ribbon and playing with a campaign hat upon returning home, Gayle Hoskins illustrator, orig packaging missing. **30.00**

Unknown cutter, untitled, 12⅛ x 5⁵⁄₁₆", 126 pcs, woman reclining on couch rests head on shoulder of seated lover, sixteen century costumes, tiger skin on floor, Gilbert 4686 Alarm box on bottom reads "Old Ladies Home/ Two Lovers. pretty/Mrs. W. P. Lunt/ over 100 pieces," first quarter 20th C **20.00**

J. Ottmann Lithograph Co., NY, Dissected Circus, sliced cardboard, 24 pcs, c1900, 18½ x 12¾", cardboard box, $85.00.

Whatami Puzzle Co., Arlington, MA, untitled, 24 x 14¾", label reads "374 pcs. $3.50," semi–cartoon of English fox hunt party approaching and passing through wooden gate in stone fence line, woman, daughter, and dog watch in lower right corner, Cecil L. Alden illustrator, print marked "1900," c1900, orig box **50.00**

Die–cut, Cardboard

Note: Cardboard puzzles from the post–1945 period sell for between $1.00 and $4.00 per box depending on company and subject matter.

Automatic Products Co., Transportation Bldg., Indianapolis, IN, Tip–Top Jig–Saw Puzzle, "Paradise Valley," 11⅝ x 15¾", 391 pcs, fox type illus of garden terrace with mountains in background, orig box **10.00**

E. J. Brach & Sons Art Study Jigs Saw Puzzles (For Study and Recreation/Featuring/Six Famous Painting/By World Famous Artists/Price/15¢ Each/Produced Exclusively For/E.J. Brach & Sons, Chicago), untitled, 10¾ x 8", 98 pcs, young Dutch girl selling flowers standing before doorway, paper envelope. **7.50**

Milton Bradley, Mayfair Jig Picture Puzzle, No. 4934, "A Scene in Venice," over 200 pcs, cardboard box **5.00**

Consolidated Paper Box, Picture Perfect Puzzle, "War at Sea," 19½ x 15¹⁄₁₂", 378 pcs, British Spitfire and bomber battle Nazi planes while sinking German freighter, K. Graf illustrator, red, white and blue color theme box, central guide picture on lid flanked by four stars on left and three stars and Savings Bond logo on right, 1942–45 . . .   **20.00**

Einson–Freeman, Every Week Jig–Saw Puzzle, No. 24, "Sails and Sea Gulls," 10½ x 14½", racing yacht at full sail surrounded by sea gulls, 1933, cardboard box.   **15.00**

Fort Wayne Paper Box Co., Ft. Wayne, IN, Wayne Jig–A–Jig Puzzle, No. 23, "Bringing Home The Flock," over 300 pcs, Van Truesdael illustrator, orig box **6.00**

Regent Specialties, Inc., DeLuxe Picture Puzzle, "Silver Moon," approx 16 x 20", approx 400 pcs, 1930s, cardboard box.   **12.50**

Santway Photo–Craft Company, Watertown, NY, The Muddle: The Jig Puzzle with the Interlocking Border, "Fine Art Series L–Lake Louise Campfire," over 300 pcs, orig box **8.00**

George P. Schlicher & Sons, Allentown, PA, Black and White Picture Puzzle, No. 10, "The Bridge," 14¼ x 8⅝", over 200 pcs, E. Berninger illustrator, cardboard box. **10.00**

Smoller–Mazur Co., Madison, WI, Gamo–Jig (The Gamest Game of Them All/New Subject Weekly/Over 325 Pieces/Interlocking), No. 34, "A Gift From Heaven," orig box. **15.00**

TUCO Deluxe Picture Puzzle: A Quality Puzzle For Particular People, "Peonies," 14¾ x 19", 357 pcs, picture copyrighted 1937, guide picture on box with white border, orig box **5.00**

Viking Manufacturing Co., Picture Puzzle Weekly, C–3, "The Breath of Spring," 10 x 13½", elderly man gets fishing gear out of chest in attic while cat looks on, orig box. **10.00**

University Distributing Company, Jig of the Week, No. 25, "So Near Yet So Far," young boy stands outside pet shop window short of money to buy the puppy he sees, 1933, cardboard box **12.50**

CHILDREN

Pre–1940

McLoughlin Brothers, Picture Puzzle, "Little Bo–Peep," 5½ x 7¼", 20 pcs, wood, guide picture on front of cardboard box. **45.00**

Peter G. Thomson, Cincinnati, Sliced Objects, 72 strips each measuring approx 7 x 1¼", letter to left and portion of drawing to write, spells BRIDGE (requires twelve strips), BOAT, CAR, CHURCH (Cincinnati Cathedral), ENGINE, FORT (Fort Sumter), FOUNTAIN (Taylor Davidson Fountain, Cincinnati), HOUSE, JAIL, PARK, PLANE, STATUE, AND YACHT, box lid shows children playing with sliced puzzle **65.00**

Wilder Mfg. Co., St. Louis, MO, Movie–Land Cut Ups, set of four, each puzzle 10 x 8", piece count ranges from 12 to 20, die–cut, cardboard, featuring scenes from movie: "Our Gang," "Harry Langdon," "Mickey (Himself) McGuire," and "Only the Brave," copyright 1930, orig box. **80.00**

Post–1940

Consolidated Paper Box, Children of All Nations, cardboard, Set No. 2, three puzzles, approx 50 pcs each, cardboard box with children's parade theme 4.00

H–G Toys, Long Beach, NY, No. 496–02, Star Trek Jigsaw Puzzle, "Attempted Hijacking of USS Enterprise and Its Officers," approx 14 x 18", over 300 pcs, cartoon drawing, guide picture on box. 8.00

Leo Hart Company, Rochester, NY, "Wings of Victory... Three Hart Picture Puzzles of War Planes" (Curtiss Commando, Curtiss Dive Bomber, Grumman Skyrocket), Series 200, each puzzle measures 9⅝ x 7", 40 pcs, five figural pcs in each puzzle, copyright 1943, orig box. 45.00

Transogram, Funny Page Jig–Saw Puzzle, Series No. 6, "Fritzi Ritz in Mistaken Identity," approx 10 x 14", late 1930s, box cover features cartoon characters 40.00

J. L. Wright, Inc., Chicago, IL, Lincoln Log Historical Jig Saw Puzzle, No. 503, "The Rail Splitter," Lincoln, approx 50 pcs, orig box. 15.00

Frame Tray

Saalfield Publishing Co., No. 7319, "Bonny Braids: Dick Tracy's New Daughter," 10¼ x 11½", 28 pcs, cartoon drawing, minor fraying on corners. 30.00

Whitman, No. 2606, "Rip Foster Picture Puzzle," 11⅜ x 14⅞", 36 pcs, three figural pcs (airplane, battleship, and handgun), image shows mother, father, and son in space suits flying among planets, rocket ship in background. 25.00

Whitman, No. 4228, "Pip the Piper Frame Tray Puzzle," 11⅜ x 14½", 17 pcs, photograph of characters from television show, orig cellophane wrap (torn) with 29¢ price sticker 12.50

ADVERTISING

Chevrolet, '60 CHEVYS: FOR 1960 CHEVY'S GOT 'EM ALL!, 5½ x 3¼", 12 pcs, plastic bag with cardboard top flap, bag—5 x 5", flap—4⅞ x 2", back of flap with Shilling Chevrolet Company adv, puzzle—cardboard, pictures 1960 Corvair in front of U.S. Capitol 30.00

Chicago Mail Order Co., "Glorious Girl" Jig–Saw Puzzle, given free with any Glorious Girl dress or coat purchased from Spring and Summer catalog, offer expired July 31, 1993, 6⅝ x 6⅛", 40 pcs, cardboard, cartoon drawing of

Advertising, Turkish Trophies cigarettes, American Tobacco Co., NY, tobacco insert, over 200 puzzles in series, each puzzle approx 20 pcs, c1909, 2½ x 3¼", $10.00.

children playing, paper envelope with guide picture. 20.00

Cunningham Radio Tubes, 12 x 10", cardboard, frame tray format, central, bust portraits of Kate Smith and Rudy Vallee, printed biographical comments about each, advertising in border around central picture, orig packaging missing 55.00

DIF Washing Powder, 8½ x 12", cardboard, First in War, Washington leading the troops, Einson–Freeman, S–131, copyright 1933, paper envelope with guide picture on back 10.00

Esso, English, 5 x 7", 35 pcs, cardboard, S.A.V.E. The Tiger campaign, vertical format, bust portrait of the Tiger pointing a finger, portion of S.A.V.E. THE TIGER button in lower right, 1970s, no packaging. 20.00

Lucas Paints and Varnishes, Giant Painter Puzzle, 5½ x 7", cardboard, painter kneeling in miniature village, can of paint by right knee, holding house in left hand, 1920s, orig box (2¼ x 4 x ⅞") duplicated puzzle picture on lid. 80.00

MS NEUW AMSTERDAM, 13¹⁄₁₆ x 9⅞", 100 pcs, cardboard, map of western Caribbean with insert of ship in upper right quadrant, promotion for DDA "You're Part Of It" Travel Award Winner, 1980s, cardboard can 20.00

Olympic Airways, "Catch Olympics flying Greek party to Paris. Any night.," 5¾ x 9", 18 pcs, cardboard, orig box 7.50

Orange Disc Anthracite Coal, 8⅝ x 12⅛", cardboard, puzzle distributed free with each ton of coal, Summer, Einson–Freeman, S115, Welsh illustrator, paper envelope with guide picture 30.00

Quaker Oats Company, cardboard, The Quaker Oats Company/Makers of/ Puffed Wheat and Puffed Rice/Presenting/Dick Daring, 12 x 8¾", 100 pcs, cardboard, schematic drawings of Dick Daring's city headquarters, insert of puzzle surface, paper envelope 30.00

Sundial Bonnie Laddie Shoes, Sundial "Lucky Pup" Jig Saw Puzzle, 10¾ x 8¾", frame tray type with Bonnie Laddie on the right, features characters from Lucky Pup television show, 1948, envelope with guide picture . . . 40.00

Taco Bell, 5 x 8", 15 pcs, cardboard, fast food premium, frame tray format, Parasaurolophus, one of series, 1993 . . 4.00

White Rose Tea, Puzzle No. 1 (two puzzles known in series), untitled, 7¹⁄₁₆ x 9¹⁄₁₆", 49 pcs, cardboard, scene of boy taking his sick dog to a veterinarian, figural pcs, 1932–33, envelope with guide picture. 15.00

MULTIPURPOSE PUZZLES

Christmas Card, 7 x 10½", 20 pcs, cardboard, unknown manufacturer, "Wishing you a full–of–fun Christmas!/From Aunt Lizzy, Uncle Joe, Joey & Richy 1980," squirrel, rabbit, and chipmunk building a snowman, orig packaging missing 2.00

Mystery, Janus Games, Inc., New York, NY, The Janus Mystery Jigsaw Puzzle, No. 3, Ellery Queen "The Case of His Headless Highness," 21½ x 14¾", 510 pcs, cardboard, figural gun and daggar pcs, mystery story on back of box 15.00

Post Card Souvenir, "Greeting/To/ From/At Niagara Falls," 8 x 5", 13 pcs counting vertical border strip, cardboard, two World War II fighter planes fly over falls, canvas mailing envelope, orig unopened cellophane packaging. 20.00

JIGSAW PUZZLE EPHEMERA

Booklet, Perry S. Graffam (editor), *50 Jigsaw Projects*, published as part of The Home Workshop Library by General Publishing Co., 1949, pgs 5–14 devoted to how to cut jigsaw puzzles 7.50

Catalog List, Supplementary List for the Spring 1926 Famous Pastime Puzzles Manufactured exclusively by Parker Brothers, Inc., Salem, Massachusetts, 8½ x 11½", four pgs, 22 illus . . 15.00

Magazine Article, *Life*, July 10, 1944, cover pictures Admiral Nimitz, "Speaking of Pictures...These Have Been Cut Into Unusual Jigsaw Puzzles," pgs 12–14, article about PAR puzzles cut for movie stars and politicians 10.00

Magazine Cover, *Woman's Home Companion*, August 1993, illus of seated cat knocking apart puzzle of dog, Diana Thorne illustrator 25.00

Saalfield Publishing Co., Akron, OH, Tillie the Toiler, Set #915, 4 puzzle set, diecut cardboard, 50 pcs each puzzle, c1935, 9¾ x 8", cardboard box, guide picture, $65.00.

Quezal

QUEZAL

History: The Quezal Art Glass Decorating Company, named for the "quezal," a bird with brilliantly colored feathers, was organized in 1901 in Brooklyn, New York, by two disgruntled Tiffany workers, Martin Bach and Thomas Johnson. They soon hired two more Tiffany workers, Percy Britton and William Wiedebine.

The first products, unmarked, were exact Tiffany imitations. In 1902 the "Quezal" trademark was first used. Quezal pieces differ from Tiffany pieces in that they are more defined and the decorations are more visible and brightly colored. No new techniques came from Quezal.

Johnson left in 1905. T. Conrad Vahlsing, Bach's son–in–law, joined the firm in 1918 but left with Paul Frank in 1920 to form Lustre Art Glass Company, which copied Quezal pieces. Martin Bach died in 1924, and by 1925 Quezal ceased operations.

Wares are signed "Quezal" on the base of vases and bowls and on the rims of shades. The acid–etched or engraved letters vary in size and may be found in amber, black, or gold. A printed label of a quetzal bird was used briefly in 1907.

Reference: Ellen T. Schroy, *Warman's Glass,* Wallace–Homestead, 1992.

Lamp Shade, gold, green, and white pulled feather design, gold irid int., dated 1901–1920, 5¾″ h, $175.00.

Candlesticks, pr, 7¾″ h, irid blue, sgd 575.00
Chandelier, gilt metal
14″ drop
  Four elaborate scroll arms, closed teardrop gold, green, and opal shades inscribed "Quezal" at collet rim, very minor roughness at rim edge 2,000.00
  Two sgd matching opal and gold irid feather dec shades 360.00
16″ h, three shouldered flared opal shades, rib mold design, gold irid int., collet rim inscribed "Quezal," classic shaped socket, wheel with chain drop. 440.00
Lamp
Mantel, 17″ h, diamond quilted mold design, brilliant gold irid surface and int., collet rim inscribed "Quezal," bronzed metal French candelabra imp "Fabrication Francaise/Made in Paris France," price for pair. 715.00
Table, 22″ h, two opal glass shades, gold and green leaf and vine motif, random gold threading, irid gold linings, collet rim inscribed "Quezal," two arm lyre mounting, gilt metal and onyx lamp standard with eagle finial 375.00

Lamp Shade, 5¼″ h, pulled feather dec, price for set of three 440.00
Taster, 2¾″ h, oval, gold irid, four pinched dimples, sgd "Quezal" on base 150.00
Toothpick, 2¼″ h, melon ribbed, pinched sides, irid blue, green, purple, and gold, sgd 200.00
Vase
7¾″ h, Favrile, gold, ftd, sgd on base 425.00
8″ h, blue irid, double bulbed, flared rim, inscribed "Quezal" on base . . 550.00
Wall Sconce, three light, bell form opal glass shades, green, gold pulled feathers and random allover threading, each sgd, scrolling arms and foliate wall mount 500.00

QUILTS

History: Quilts have been passed down as family heirlooms for many generations. Each is an individual expression. The same pattern may have hundreds of variations in both color and design.

The advent of the sewing machine increased, not decreased, the number of quilts which were made. Quilts are still being sewn today.

The key considerations for price are age, condition, aesthetic beauty, and design. Prices are now at a level position. Exceptions are the very finest examples, which continue to bring record prices.

References: American Quilter's Society, *Gallery of American Quilts, 1849–1988,* Collector Books, 1988; Suzy McLennan Anderson, *Collector's Guide to Quilts,* Wallace-Homestead, 1991; Cuesta Benberry, *Always There: The African–American Presence in American Quilts,* Kentucky Quilt Project, 1992; Barbara Brackman, *Clues in the Calico: A Guide To Identifying and Dating Antique Quilts,* EPM Publications, 1989; Liz Greenbacker and Kathleen Barach, *Quilts: Identification and Price Guide,* Avon Books, 1992; Alda Leake Horner, *The Official Price Guide to Linens, Lace and Other Fabrics,* House of Collectibles, 1991; Carter Houck, *The Quilt Encyclopedia Illustrated,* Harry N. Abrams and Museum of American Folk Art, 1991; William C. Ketchum, Jr., *The Knopf Collectors' Guides to American Antiques: Quilts,* Alfred A. Knopf, 1982; Jean Ray Laury and California Heritage Quilt Project, *Ho For California: Pioneer Women and Their Quilts,* E. P. Dutton, 1990; Dana G. Morykan and Harry L. Rinker, *Warman's Country Antiques & Collectibles, Second Edition,* Wallace-Homestead, 1994; Patsy and Myron Orlofsky, *Quilts in America,* Abbeville Press, 1992; Lisa Turner Oshins, *Quilt Collections: A Directory For The United States And Canada,* Acropolis Books, 1987; Rachel and Kenneth Pellman, *The World of Amish Quilts,* Good Books, 1984; Schnuppe von

Gwinner, *The History of the Patchwork Quilt,* Schiffer Publishing, 1988.

Periodicals: *Quilters Newsletter,* Box 394, Wheat Ridge, CO 80033; *Vintage Quilt Newsletter,* PO Box 744, Great Bend, TX 67530-0744.

Collectors' Clubs: American Quilt Study Group, Suite 400, 660 Mission St., San Francisco, CA 94105-4007; The American Quilter's Society, PO Box 3290, Paducah, KY 42001; The National Quilting Association, Inc., Po Box 393, Ellicott City, MD 21043.

Museums: Doll & Quilts Barn, Rocky Ridge, MD; Museum of the American Quilter's Society, Paducah, KY; National Museum of American History, Washington, DC; New England Quilt Museum, Lowell, MA.

Feather Pinwheel, appliqued, cotton, red and olive green on white field, feather quilting, American, 19th C, 82 x 84", $440.00. Photograph courtesy of Skinner, Inc.

American Flag, pieced, red, white, blue, brown, and green, c1910, 83 x 72½"	850.00
American Shield, pieced, stars and stripe border, c1885, 84 x 75"	1,000.00
Amish, geometric design, black and burgundy, c1925, 75½ x 64½"	750.00
Basket, pieced, red, white, and blue, youth size, American, c1895, 81 x 68"	300.00
Birds on a Nest, pieced, indigo on white field, two bar border, seven stitches per running inch, OH, late 19th C, 78 x 80"	425.00
Carolina Lily, pieced, red and blue, white ground, hand sewn design, machine sewn appliqued stems, wear and stains, 71 x 71"	200.00

Crazy Quilt, Victorian, pieced and embroidered, American

67 x 77", patterned squares, embroidered motifs, novelty stitch border, inscribed "To JHS from SJM, September 14, 1889"	1,500.00
68 x 70", maroon, purple, black, cream, yellow, brown, and blue patches, abstract patterns within large squares, embroidered birds, butterflies, flowers, short proverbs, and date "1885," multicolored quilting, fringed border three sides, late 19th C	575.00

Floral Design

Appliqued, bold design, red, teal blue, goldenrod, and pink calico, machine sewn applique, hand quilting, made by Margaret Holloway, central MO, c1870, small stains and repair, 72 x 84"	1,100.00
Appliqued and Pieced, green and two shades of red, white rebound silk, c1900, 78 x 77"	225.00

Friendship, pieced, wool and other fabrics, circular designs, embroidery and names of makers, dated 1916, made at Crown Hill Mennonite Church, Orrville, OH, minor wear and small stains, 69 x 81" 330.00

Irish Chain

Pieced, three stripe border, beige, tan, red, goldenrod, and white, made by Myra Ellis, Crystal Springs, MS, 1894, small repairs, 75 x 76"	300.00
Pieced and Appliqued, printed cotton mustard, red, and green patches, leaf medallion pattern enclosed by swag and tassel border, conforming diamond and parallel line quilting, 82 x 85"	470.00

Log Cabin, pieced, strip border, conforming quilting, 82 x 82", $375.00.

Log Cabin, pieced, sunshine and shadow, multicolored prints and solid red, purchased in Osage City, KS, machine sewn binding, overall wear, 76 x 89″ 385.00

Lone Star, pieced, red, navy, and teal blue, goldenrod ground, pencil quilt pattern intact, machine stitched binding, made by Mary Green Knietzing, Louisville, KY, 1922, 78 x 88″ 615.00

Oak Leaf Pinwheels, appliqued, four large medallions and five eight–pointed stars in tan and olive green, olive green border stripe, machine and hand sewn, hand quilted, minor stains, 80 x 107″ 360.00

Optical, twenty miniature triangle filled patches, red and blue matching border, American, c1890, 80 x 60″ 375.00

Philadelphia Pavement, pieced, multicolored prints, calico, and white, Chesapeake Bay, MD, area, machine sewn binding, some stains and minor wear, 74 x 77″ 370.00

Pinwheels, star centers, applique, plume pinwheels, red and khaki stars and grid, white gound, Eureka, MO origin, stains, 80 x 83″ 615.00

Spools, pieced, multicolored prints, made by Maud Severson, Lincoln, NE, c1890, small stains, 73 x 83″ . . .   165.00

Squares, colorful multiple sized squares, orange, yellow, and brown printed fabric border, c1930, 85½ x 70¼″ 165.00

Squares, Stars, and Hearts, crib size, red, white, and blue, pieced, c1910, 60 x 41″ 150.00

Star of Bethlehem, solid red, blue, green, mustard, and lavender patches, conforming feather, leaf, and diamond quilting, American, c1940, 76 x 65″ 525.00

Stylized Flower, appliqued and reverse appliqued, nine patches, green swag border, c1865, 82 x 83″ 3,250.00

Theorum, embroidered, turkey red embroidery, white field, allover diamond pattern stitch, cable border, sgd and dated "February 6, 1914 by Florence Mohr," 73 x 74″ 300.00

Thousand Pyramid Medallion, pieced, multicolored prints, solid pink and white, pencil pattern intact, made by Martha Ann Ford Ashby, (1829–1912), Parkville, MO, 75 x 75″ 440.00

Virginia Reel, pieced, cotton, two bar border, allover diamond quilting, PA, 1890–1910, 68 x 73″ 250.00

Whitework, cotton, eight stitches per running inch, 20th C, 72 x 87″ 300.00

HB
Quimper
1883-1910

PORQUIER-BEAU
1898

c 1898

HB
c 1898

HR
Quimper
1895-1922

HENRiot
Quimper
AFTER 1922

QUIMPER

History: Quimper faience, dating back to the 17th century, is named for Quimper, a French town where numerous potteries were located. Several mergers resulted in the evolution of two major houses—the Jules Henriot and the Hubaudiébre–Bousquet factories.

The peasant design first appeared in the 1860s, and many variations exist. Florals and geometrics, equally popular, also were produced in large quantities. During the 1920s the Hubaudiébre–Bousquet factory introduced the Odetta line which utilized a stone body and Art Deco decorations.

The two major houses merged in 1968, each retaining its individual characteristics and marks. The concern suffered from labor problems in the 1980s and recently was purchased by an American group.

Marks: The HR and HR Quimper marks are found on Henriot pieces prior to 1922. The Henriot Quimper mark was used after 1922. The HB mark covers a long span of time. The addition of numbers or dots and dashes refers to inventory numbers and are found on later pieces. Most marks are in blue or black. Pieces ordered by department stores, such as Macy's and Carson Pirie Scott, carry the store mark along with the factory mark, making them less desirable to collectors. A comprehensive list of marks is found in Bondhus's book.

References: Susan and Al Bagdade, *Warman's English & Continental Pottery & Porcelain, Second Edition,* Wallace–Homestead, 1991; Sandra V. Bondhus, *Quimper Pottery: A French Folk Art Faience,* published by author, 1981; Millicent Mali, *Quimper Faience,* Airon, 1979; Marjatta Taburet, *La Faience de Quimper,* Editions Sous le Vent, 1979, French text.

Museums: Musee des Faiences de Quimper, Quimper, France; Victoria and Albert Museum, French Ceramic Department, London, England.

Advisors: Susan and Al Bagdade.

Ashtray, 5½" d, female peasant in center, floral band, blue, yellow, green, and dark red, blue sponged border, "HB Quimper" mark. **40.00**

Barber Bowl, 12" l, 9" w, female peasant in center, floral garland border, red and blue 4 dot design, pierced for hanging, "HR Quimper" mark. **550.00**

Bookends, pr, 8½" h, Modern Movement, old man and woman, two children, man wearing cobalt blue coat and trousers, woman with cobalt bodice and striped skirt, "HenRiot Quimper France, Bachelet" marks **750.00**

Butter Tub, cov, 6½" d, 3½" h, attached underplate, cov with male peasant, blue floral sprays, and seashell finial, floral band on tub, "HR Quimper" mark **175.00**

Cake Stand, 10½" d, 3½" h, female peasant with basket, red crisscross panels with blue outline, red, yellow, and blue floral border, shaped blue rim, "HB Quimper" mark **775.00**

Candlestick
  7" h, male or female peasant, floral band on base, green glaze, "HenRiot Quimper France, 114" mark, price for pair **350.00**
  8⅛" h, figural male peasant, green shirt, blue and gold vest, orange–gold pantaloons, basket on head, "HenRiot Quimper France" mark. . **295.00**
  8⅝" h, stylized figural female peasant with green dot shirt, yellow–gold striped skirt, brown potted baskets on arms form holders, "HB Quimper" mark, price for pair **575.00**

Chamberstick
  5¼" d, 2¼" h, female peasant on dish, iron–red, green, blue, and yellow flowers, blue sponged handle and cone, "HenRiot Quimper France" mark. **175.00**
  7" l, 5" w, leaf shape, seated male

playing bagpipe, yellow and blue florals and bands, "HB Quimper" mark. **240.00**

Cruets, 6½" h, joined at base, male peasant on one spout, female on other, blue ground, wood stoppers, "HB Quimper France" mark **75.00**

Cup and Saucer
  Female peasant and scattered florals, blue and yellow banded border, "HenRiot Quimper France" mark. . **50.00**
  Hex, red, blue, and green florals in blue outlined panels, blue handle, "HenRiot Quimper France" mark. . **40.00**
  Scattered florals and 4 blue dot design, doll size, "HenRiot Quimper France 118" mark **95.00**

Dish, 9¾" l, figural fish face and tail, male peasant with pipe and staff in center, scattered florals, blue half circle and dot border, "HenRiot Quimper" mark. **175.00**

Eggcup, 2" h, figural swan, blue, green, yellow, and rust florals and swan outline, c1895, "HB Quimper" mark. . . . **95.00**

Figure
  6" h, dancing couple in black, pink, blue, yellow, and white Modern Movement colors, "HenRiot Quimper France 309 P.C." mark **90.00**
  10¾" h, standing boy, black wide brimmed hat, blue jacket, black vest with yellow and gold trim, gray pants with black stripes, "HenRiot Quimper France," and "JB" and arrow marks **295.00**
  12" h, Modern Movement, standing child, cobalt bodice, black sleeves, maroon striped skirt, brown wooden shoes, "HenRiot Quimper Blandin" mark. **475.00**
  13" h, 16" w, Modern Movement bust of Breton woman, white and black dress with yellow Broderie bib, "HB Q.F. Porson 110/220" mark **375.00**

Fish Platter, 23" l, 8½" w, painted dancing peasants in center, bagpipers at side, 2 figures leaning on fence, scattered flowers, blue acanthus border, orange rim, "HB Quimper" mark. . . . **1,500.00**

Gravy Boat, 3" h, 7" w, spout at each end, peasant woman on side, rose band on top, yellow ground, blue sponged handles, "HB Quimper France" mark **50.00**

Inkwell, double, 7" l, 4" h, female peasant on top, scattered floral bands, shell terminal on backplate, "HenRiot Quimper France 73" mark **450.00**

Jardiniere, 14" l, 5¼" h, center medallion christening scene with mother, father, and child on front, reverse medallion with fishermen scene, scattered florals and black ermine tails, molded handles with Brittany crests, four small feet, "HB Quimper" mark 1,200.00

Match Safe, 4½" h, bellows shape, female peasant knitting and ermine tails on front, floral sprays on sides, "HB" mark 215.00

Menu
5½" h, multicolored frontal view of female peasant with basket, black Brittany crest, "Porquier Beau Quimper" mark 300.00

7⅜" h, male peasant leaning against wall, molded yellow and gold fleur de lis, blue outlined rim and "Menu" 500.00

Pitcher
3½" h, female peasant under spout, scattered florals and 4 blue dot design, "HB" mark 130.00

8½" h, trumpet shape, male peasant on front, yellow and blue striped border, blue sponged handle, "France 196"mark 80.00

Plate
6½" sq, rolled edge, female peasant with bucket on head, floral panels at corners, ermine tails between, blue sawtooth rim, "HB" mark 300.00

9" d, female peasant holding bunch of flowers, flanked by multicolored florals, blue and yellow banded border, unmarked 60.00

9½" d
Blue and brown frontal view of male peasant with stick in center, farm scene background, yellow zigzag border, "HenRiot Quimper France" mark 160.00

Female peasant with infant on shoulder, waving, child at side, border with alternating panels of Brittany crests and floral sprays, orange and yellow scalloped rim, "HR Quimper" mark on front and back 495.00

Mayflower ship in center, red and blue dash border, "HenRiot Quimper France 77" mark 275.00

10" d, pr, sailor on one, female dancing peasant on other, blue ribbon border, "HenRiot Quimper AG" mark, price for pair. 145.00

10⅞" d, "Mieux vaut L'honneur que les honneurs" in center, ivory ground, blue and yellow band border with flowers, "HB Quimper France" mark 40.00

Platter
12½" d, Art Deco style, yellow and brown busts of male musicians,

cream ground, black and yellow banded border, "HB Quimper" mark. 225.00

13½" l, 10" w, oval, navy, gold, teal blue, and purple raised Breton Broderie design, cream ground, c1925, "HB Quimper" mark. 450.00

Porringer, 8" w handle to handle, male or female peasant in bowl, blue and yellow banded int. border, pierced for hanging, "HR" mark, price for pair. . 300.00

Quintel, 5" h, center medallion of seated peasant woman with basket of eggs, blue floral sprigs, yellow ground, "HenRiot Quimper France 119" mark 165.00

Relish Tray, 10" l, oval, male peasant with pipe or female with basket on arm, red crisscross panels and red or blue flowerheads, blue outlined rim, "HB Quimper France" mark, c1930, price for pair. 230.00

Salt, 3½" h, 4" w, figural double swan shape, crests on sides, tan ground, "HenRiot Quimper" mark 45.00

Snuff Bottle
3" h, flower shape with watch face on front, male peasant on reverse, blue neck and edge, unmarked . . . 495.00

3" l, Maltese Cross shape, dark blue outlines with red and green crisscross design, reverse with red and green herringbone and blue radiating lines, yellow neck and edge, unmarked 875.00

3¼" l, shield shape, female peasant on front, blue rose and red floral

Tray, three section, peasant woman and multicolored florals, blue and orange rim, blue dash handle with orange trim, hairline, "HenRiot Quimper France 96" mark, 11" l, 11½" w, $225.00.

spray on reverse, blue sponged neck and edge, crack on face, "HenRiot Quimper France" mark. . **200.00**

Teapot, 10½″ h, flat sided, full view of male with hand in pocket and female with knitting, reverse with female with hay bail and male with arms folded, blue dash spout, rim, and handle, repaired lid, lip, and handle, "HB" mark **600.00**

Tea Tile, 8¾″ w, octagonal, female peasant in center, vertical florals, orange and blue striped border, green sponged rim, "HenRiot Quimper" mark **275.00**

Tray, 11″ l, 11½″ w, three section, peasant woman and multicolored florals, blue and orange rim, blue dash handle with orange trim, hairline, "HenRiot Quimper France 96" mark **225.00**

Tureen, 9¼″ h, 12¼″ w handle to handle, seated peasant woman, seated male peasant with horn, and florals, red crisscross design, blue striped handles, "HB Quimper" mark **595.00**

Vase

7½″ h, male peasant with flute, scattered flowers, "HenRiot Quimper, France" **295.00**

8¼″ h, blue and orange crosshatching at top, female peasant on front, white ground, blue sponged handles, "HenRiot Quimper France" mark. **165.00**

12″ h, horn shape, frontal view of female peasant with hands in apron, vertical florals and 4 blue dots, red linked "S" design at waist and rim, three curved blue sponged legs, "HR Quimper" mark **600.00**

Vegetable Bowl, cov, 13″ l, oval, scattered blue flowers, red 4 dots pattern, yellow banded rims, AP design, unmarked. **385.00**

Wall Pocket, 10¼″ l, female peasant on front, iron–red, blue, green, and yellow flowers, blue and yellow outline rim, open blue flowerhead at hole, "HR Quimper" mark **300.00**

RADIOS

History: The radio was invented over 100 years ago. Marconi was the first to assemble and employ the transmission and reception instruments that permitted sending electric messages without the use of direct connections. Between 1905 and the end of World War I many technical advances were made to the "wireless," including the invention of the vacuum tube by DeForest. By 1920 technology progressed. Radios filled the entertainment needs of the average family.

Changes in design, style, and technology brought the radio from the black boxes of the 1920s to the styled furniture pieces and console models of the 1930s and 1940s, to the midget models of the 1950s, and finally to the high–tech radios of the 1980s.

References: Robert F. Breed, *Collecting Transistor Novelty Radios*, L–W Book Sales, 1990; Marty and Sue Bunis, *Collector's Guide To Antique Radios, Second Edition*, Collector Books, 1992; Marty and Sue Bunis, *Collector's Guide To Transistor Radios*, Collector Books, 1994; Philip Collins, *Radio Redux: Listening In Style*, Chronicle Books, 1992; Philip Collins, *Radios: The Golden Age*, Chronicle Books, 1987; Alan Douglas, *Radio Manufacturers of the 1920s*, Vol. 1, (1988), Vol. 2 (1989), Vol. 3 (1991), Vestal Press; Roger Handy, Maureen Erbe, and Aileen Farnan Antonier, *Made In Japan: Transistor Radios of the 1950s and 1960s*, Chronicle Books, 1993; David Johnson, *Antique Radio Restoration Guide, 2nd Edition*, Wallace–Homestead, 1992; David and Betty Johnson, *Guide To Old Radios, Pointers, Pictures, And Prices*, Wallace–Homestead, 1989; David and Robert Lane, *Transistor Radios: A Wallace–Homestead Price Guide*, Wallace–Homestead, 1994; Harry Poster, *Poster's Radio & Television Price Guide: 1920–1990, Second Edition*, Wallace–Homestead, 1993; Ron Ramirez with Michael Prosise, *Philco Radio: 1928–1942*, Schiffer Publishing, 1993; John Sideli, *Classic Plastic Radios of the 1930s and 1940s: A Collector's Guide to Catalin Radios*, E. P. Dutton, 1990; Scott Wood (ed.), *Evolution of the Radio*, Vol. 1 (1991), Vol. 2, (1993), L–W Book Sales, 1991.

Periodicals: *Antique Radio Classified*, PO Box 2, Carlisle, MA 01741; *Radio Age*, 636 Cambridge Road, Augusta, GA 30909; *The Horn Speaker*, PO Box 1193, Mabank, TX 75147; *Transistor Network*, RR. 1, Box 36, Bradford, NH 03221.

Collectors' Clubs: Antique Radio Club of America, 300 Washington Trails, Washington, PA 15301; Antique Wireless Association, 59 Main St., Bloomfield, NY 14469; New England Antique Radio Club, RR. 1, Box 36, Bradford, NH 03221; Vintage Radio & Phonograph Society, Inc., PO Box 165345, Irving, TX 75016.

Museums: Antique Wireless Museum, Bloomfield, NY; Caperton's Radio Museum, Louisville, KY; Muchow's Historical Radio Museum, Elgin, IL; Museum of Broadcast Communication, Chicago, IL; Museum of Wonderful Miracles, Minneapolis, MN; New England Wireless and Steam Museum, Inc., East Greenwich, RI; Voice of the Twenties, Orient, NY.

Advisor: Lewis S. Walters.

Additional Listings: See *Warman's Americana & Collectibles* for more examples.

Atwater Kent, Model 318, table model, dome **175.00**

Columbia, table model, oak **135.00**

Atwater Kent, #318, table model, dome, $175.00.

Crosley
 Model 4–29, battery operated, 1926   **155.00**
 Model 10–135 . . . . **95.00**
Fada, two color Bakelite case
 115, bullet shape, deep ochre, red
  trim, 10½ x 5¼ x 6″ **600.00**
 652, round end, rect caramelized
  body, red knobs, slide rule dial . . . **650.00**
General Electric, Model 81, 8 tube,
 1934 . . . . **250.00**
Metrodyne Super 7, 1925 . . . . **210.00**
Philco
 Model 37–84, Cathedral, schematic
  design, 1937 . . . . **145.00**
 Model 551, 1928 . . . . **125.00**
RCA Radiola 20, 1925 . . . . **160.00**
Spartan, Model 5218 . . . . **85.00**
Stromberg Carlson, Model 636A, con-
 sole, 1928 . . . . **170.00**
Westinghouse, Model WR–602 . . . . . **90.00**
Zenith, Zephyr, 6–S–147, multiband . **175.00**

RAILROAD ITEMS

History: Railroad collectors have existed for decades. The merger of the rail systems and the end of passenger service made many objects available to private collectors. The Pennsylvania Railroad sold its archives at public sale.

Railroad enthusiasts have organized into regional and local clubs. Join one if you are interested. Your local hobby store can probably point you to the right person. The best pieces pass between collectors and rarely enter the general market.

References: Stanley L. Baker, *Railroad Collec-*
tibles: An Illustrated Value Guide, 4th Edition, Collector Books, 1990, 1993 value update; Phil Bollhagen (comp.), *The Great Book of Railroad Playing Cards, 1991 Version,* published by author, 1991; Arthur Dominy and Rudolph A. Morgenfruh, *Silver At Your Service,* published by authors, 1987; Richard Luckin, *Mimbres to Mimbreno: A Study of Santa Fe's Famous China Pattern,* RK Publishing, 1992; Everett L. Maffet, *Silver Banquet II: A Compendium on Railroad Dining Car Silver Serving Pieces,* Silver Press, 1990; Douglas W. McIntrye, *The Official Guide To Railroad Dining Car China,* Walsworth Press, 1990, out of print; Larry R. Paul, *Sparkling Crystal: A Collector's Guide To Railroad Glassware,* Railroadiana Collectors Assoc., 1990.

Periodicals: *Key, Lock and Lantern,* PO Box 15, Spencerport, NY 14559; *Main Line Journal,* PO Box 121, Streamwood, IL 60107; *Rail Fan and Railroad Magazine,* PO Box 700, Newton, NJ 07860.

Collectors' Clubs: Chesapeake & Ohio Historical Society, Inc., PO Box 79, Clifton Forge, VA 24422; Illinois Central Railroad Historical Society, 14818 Clifton Park, Midlothian, IL 60445; Railroad Enthusiasts, 456 Main Street, West Townsend, MA 01474; Railroadiana Collectors Association, 795 Aspen Drive, Buffalo Grove, IL 60089; Railway and Locomotive Historical Society, PO Box 1418, Westford, MA 01886; Twentieth Century Railroad Club, 329 West 18th St., Suite 902, Chicago, IL 60616.

Museums: Baltimore and Ohio Railroad, Baltimore, MD; Museum of Transportation, Brookline, MA; California State Railroad Museum, Sacramento, CA; Frisco Railroad Museum, Van Buren, AR; National Railroad Museum, Green Bay, WI; New York Museum of Transportation, West Henrietta, NY; Old Depot Railroad Museum, Dassel, MN.

Additional Listings: See *Warman's Americana & Collectibles* for more examples.

Advertising Mirror, The Travelers Insurance Co., The Railroad Men's Reliance, Hartford, CT, multicolored, 2¾ x 1⅝″, $70.00.

Baggage Tag, SOO Line, celluloid, leather strap, "Tag Your Grip, Take a Trip, The New Train," 1½ x 2½" **18.00**

Book, John Bourne, *History and Description of the Great Western Railway*, 1846. . . . . **2,850.00**

Builder's Plate, brass

American Locomotive Works, from New York, New Haven & Hartford engine #573, oval, 1909, 15½" l . . **1,430.00**

Schenectady Locomotive Works, from Rutland #240, 1899 . . . . **715.00**

Calendar, Burlington Route, 1938, litho illus, steam and diesel trains in mountain landscape, vignette of covered wagons above, full pad, 18 x 27". . . . **45.00**

Cap Badge, C&O RY, brakeman, emb black enameled lettering, pebbled silver ground, arched top, milled border, 4¼ x 1½" **30.00**

China

Butter Pat, Pennsylvania RR, backstamp. **75.00**

Cereal Bowl, Union Pacific, Challenger pattern, no backstamp, Syracuse China, 6¼" d **25.00**

Cup and Saucer, Chicago Burlington & Quincy, Chuck Wagon pattern, backstamp, Syracuse China **250.00**

Eggcup, Pullman Co, Calumet pattern, ftd, Burley & Co, no backstamp, 2¾" h. **75.00**

Gravy Boat, Northern Pacific, Monad pattern, no backstamp, Shenango, 6" l **125.00**

Ice Cream Dish, Baltimore & Ohio, Capitol pattern, ftd, no backstamp . **50.00**

Plate, dinner, Wabash RR, Banner pattern, no backstamp, Syracuse China, 9½" d **235.00**

Platter, Delaware & Hudson, Adirondak pattern, no backstamp, Syracuse China, 9¾ x 7¾" **50.00**

Sauce Dish, Atchison Topeka & Santa Fe, Mimbreno pattern, backstamp, "Made expressly for Santa Fe dining car service," Syracuse China, 5½" d **75.00**

Coach Seat, New Haven 8600 series, double **28.00**

Doors, pr, wood, passenger car vestibule. **28.00**

Engine Status Board, NY&NERR, used in Norwich, CT engine shop, tracked locomotive fleet's mechanical conditions, 60" sq **330.00**

Fire Bucket, leather, marked "CRR" . **132.00**

Grade Crossing Sign, wood, circular, black "RR" and "X", white ground. . **12.00**

Headlight, from New Haven diesel engine #0900. . . . . **182.00**

Kerosene Can, NPR, emb label, painted

Hat, L.I.R.R. Conductor, $25.00.

black, spout top front, screw filler cap top center, bail handle, 8¾" d, 11" h . **35.00**

Lantern

Atlantic & St Lawrence Railroad, clear fixed globe, cast lettering, 1859. . . **880.00**

B&MRR, etched fixed globe **465.00**

MCRR, clear etched fixed globe . . **300.00**

NY&NERR, brass topped, bell bottom **635.00**

Unmarked, brass topped, bell bottom, blue globe. **275.00**

Napkin, Milwaukee Road, cotton, printed magenta "Hiawatha" and Indian emblem, tan ground, 10½ x 16¼" **15.00**

Oiler, GN RY, long spout, name incised on handle, stop flow lever, Eagle, 10½" h. **48.00**

Photograph

Lehigh Valley #6 Black Diamond Express, hand colored, 34 x 25" **470.00**

NY&NE Solid Pullman Vestibuled Train, mahogany and gold frame, 36 x 21" **125.00**

Portland & Ogdensburg Railroad, seven trainmen with locomotive "#1, The Presumpscot," framed . . **60.00**

White Train Between Boston and New York, 30 x 20" **275.00**

Playing Cards, WP&YR, orig box, 1900 **62.00**

Pocket Watch

American Waltham Watch Co, size 16, open face, gold filled case, damascened Vanguard movement, 23 jewels, wind indicator, adjusted for six positions **450.00**

Elgin Watch Co, size 16, B W Raymond movement, open face, gold filled case, 19 jewels, damascened plate, wind indicator, 1913. . . . . . . **450.00**

Hamilton Watch Co, model 999, made for the Ball Watch Co, size 18, open face, gold filled case, 21 jewels, damascened plates, inscribed gold lettering, c1895 . . . . **300.00**

Presentation Lantern, silverplated, globe etched "Fireman Steamer No. 1," marked "made by SB Underhill NY," 19th C, 17" h, 7" d. **385.00**

Rebuilder's Plate, cast iron, Southern Iron & Equipment Co. **685.00**

Rule Book, MStP&SSM Rules and Regulations of the Operating Department, May 1, 1912 . . . . **20.00**

Scale Model, NYC&HR gondola freight car, 69" l, with track. **250.00**

Shaving Mug, B of RRT, brakewheel, lantern, crossed signal flags, script gold leaf member's name, floral designs, gold handle and trim, 3½" h . . **175.00**

Silver Holloware

Bud Vase, Great Northern RY, candlestick style, marked on side and bottom, International, #05082, 1951, 7¼" h. **150.00**

Coffeepot, Chicago & Northwestern RY, pine cone finial, bottom marked, International, #05073, 1949, 14 oz. **75.00**

Syrup Pitcher, attached tray, Illinois Central RR, Mississippi Valley Route, diamond and circle logo, hinged lid, Wallace, #0301, 10 oz **175.00**

Steam Whistle, brass, 19" h **230.00**

Streetcar Sign, "Springfield Limited" one side, "Holyoke Limited" other side. . . **55.00**

Timetable

1928, Louisville and Nashville Railroad, booklet, color. **30.00**

1946, Charleston and Western Carolina System **12.00**

Ventilator Window, arched, stained and leaded glass, from NY&NERR dining car "Boston". **165.00**

Water Bucket, metal, bail handle **22.00**

Whistle Post, black "W", white ground **25.00**

Wrench, marked "E.E.P." **11.00**

RAZORS

History: Razors date back several thousand years. Early man used sharpened stones. The Egyptians, Greeks, and Romans had metal razors.

Razors made prior to 1800 generally were crudely stamped WARRANTED or CAST STEEL, with the maker's mark on the tang. Until 1870 almost all razors for the American market were manufactured in Sheffield, England. Most blades were wedge shaped; many were etched with slogans or scenes. Handles were made of natural materials: various horns, tortoiseshell, bone, ivory, stag, silver, and pearl. All razors were handmade.

After 1870 razors were machine made with hollow ground blades and synthetic handle materials. Razors of this period usually were manufactured in Germany (Solingen) or in American cutlery factories. Hundreds of molded celluloid handle patterns were produced.

Cutlery firms produced boxed sets of two, four, and seven razors. Complete and undamaged sets are very desirable. Most popular are the 7–Day sets, with each razor etched with a day of the week.

The fancier the handle or more intricately etched the blade, the higher the price. Rarest handle materials are pearl, stag, sterling silver, pressed horn, and carved ivory. Rarest blades are those with scenes etched across the entire front. Value is increased by certain manufacturer's names, e.g., H. Boker, Case, M. Price, Joseph Rogers, Simmons Hardware, Will & Finck, Winchester, and George Wostenholm.

Abbreviations:

hgb = hollow ground blade

wb = wedge blade

References: Ronald S. Barlow, *The Vanishing American Barber Shop,* Windmill Publishing, 1993; Robert A. Doyle, *Straight Razor Collecting, An Illustrated Price Guide,* Collector Books, 1980, out of print; Phillip L. Krumholz, *Value Guide For Barberiana & Shaving Collectibles,* Ad Libs Publishing, 1988; Jim Sargent, *Sargent's* American *Premium Guide To Pocket Knives & Razors, Identification and Values, 3rd Edition,* Books Americana, 1992.

Periodical: *Blade Magazine,* PO Box 22007, Chattanooga, TN 37422.

Additional Listings: See *Warman's Americana & Collectibles* for more examples.

American, Geneva Cutlery Co., Geneva, NY, carved bone handle, 6¼" l, $45.00.

AMERICAN BLADES

Case & Sons, Manganese, clear smoked handles 65.00
Case Bros, Tested XX, Little Valley, NY, hollow point, slick black handles, mother–of–pearl inlaid tang 400.00
Cattaraugus Cutlery Co, Little Valley, NY, square point, blue handles with white liners. 25.00
J B F Champlin & Son, square point, brown streaked celluloid handles . . . 85.00
Crandall Cutlery Co, Bradford, PA, square point, blade etched "I Must Kut," cream colored handles with beaded borders. 65.00
Kane Cutlery Co, Kane, PA, hollow point, cream and rust twisted rope handles, c1884 . . . . 40.00
Kinfolks Inc, square point, imitation ivory handles with silver endcaps and marked "Real Red Point Razor". . . . 75.00
Standard Knife Co, Little Valley, NY, arc mark, round point, yellow mottled handles with beaded borders, 1901–3 . . 145.00
Union Cutlery Co, Olean, NY, A J Case Shoo–Fly, tiger eye handle, c1912 . . 125.00

ENGLISH BLADES, SHEFFIELD

Chris Johnson, wide hgb, plated brass handle 55.00
George Wostenholme, etched adv on blade, emb ivory handle. 30.00
Joseph Rodgers & Sons, wb, stag handle with inlaid rect escutcheon plate . 125.00
Turniss Cutler & Stacey Sheffield, pressed horn handle, two intertwined snakes, maker's mark on blade 615.00
Wade & Butcher, hg, etched in ribbon "Wade & Butcher," sterling silver Art Nouveau handle with raised scroll across front and back and monogram 325.00

GERMAN BLADES

Cosmos Mfg Co, hgb, ivory handle, raised nude picking purple grapes, green leaves. 100.00
J A Henckels Twin Works, bone handle, rounded and shaped, corn, plain blade, orig box with silver emb "J A Henckels Twin Works, Germany" . . . 50.00
Imperial Razor, blade etched with US Battleship Oregon scene, dark blue celluloid handle. 40.00
F A Koch & Co, ivory handle, colored scene with deer, branches, and oak leaves 45.00
Wadsworth Razor Co, semi wb, carved bone handle, c1870. . . . . 55.00

SETS OF RAZORS

Crown & Sword, seven day set, blades etched "The Crown & Sword Razor Extra Hollow Ground," black handles with raised "Crown and Sword," homemade wood case with felt lining, emb "RAZORS" plaque on top 45.00
G W Ruff's Peerless, pr, hg, ivory handles, leather over wood case with "Gentlemen's Companion Containing 2 Razors Special Hollow Ground," red lining 55.00

SWISS BLADES

John Engstrom, frameback, seven interchangeable wafer blades, black horn handle, c1880. . . . . 65.00
Tornablom, hgb, ivory handle 30.00

RECORDS

History: With the advent of the more sophisticated recording materials, such as 33⅓ RPM long-playing records, 8–track tapes, cassettes, and compact discs, earlier phonograph records became collectors' items. Most have little value. The higher priced examples are rare (limited production) recordings. Condition is critical.

References: Steven C. Barr, *The Almost Complete 78 RPM Record Dating Guide (II),* Yesterday Once Again, 1992; L. R. Docks, *1900–1965 American Premium Record Guide, 4th Edition,* Books Americana, 1992; *Goldmine's 1994 Annual, Third Edition,* Krause Publications, 1993; Anthony J. Gribin and Matthew M. Schiff, *Doo–Wop: The Forgotten Third of Rock 'n' Roll,* Krause Publications, 1992; Fred Heggeness, *Country Western Price Guide,* FH Publishing, 1990; Vito R. Marino and Anthony C. Furfero, *The Official Price Guide To Frank Sinatra Records and CDs,* House of Collectibles, 1993; Jerry Osborne, *The Official Price Guide To Movie/TV Soundtracks and Original Cast Albums,* House of Collectibles, 1991; Jerry Osborne, *The Official Price Guide To Records, Tenth Edition,* House of Collectibles, 1993; Neal Umphred, *Goldmine's Price Guide To Collectible Jazz Albums, 1949–1969,* Krause Publications, 1992; Neal Umphred, *Goldmine's Price Guide To Collectible Record Albums, 1949–1989, Third Edition,* Krause Publications, 1993; Neal Umphred, *Goldmine's Rock 'n' Roll 45 RPM Record Price Guide, Second Edition,* Krause Publications, 1992.

Periodicals: *Cadence,* Cadence Building, Redwood, NY 13679; *DISCoveries Magazine,* PO Box 309, Fraser, MI 48026; *Goldmine,* 700 E. State Street, Iola, WI 54990; *Jazz Beat Magazine,* 1206 Decatur St., New Orleans, LA 70116; *Joslin's Jazz Journal,* PO Box 213, Parsons, KS 67357; *Record Collectors Monthly,* PO Box 75, Mendham, NJ

07945; *Record Finder,* PO Box 1047, Glen Allen, VA 23060; *The New Amberola Graphic,* 37 Caledonia St., St. Johnsbury, VT 05819.

Collectors' Clubs: Association For Recorded Sound Collections, PO Box 10162, Silver Spring, MD 20914; International Association of Jazz Record Collectors, PO Box 75155, Tampa, FL 33605.

Additional Listings: See *Warman's Americana & Collectibles* for more examples.

Note: Most records, especially popular recordings, have a value of less than $3.00 per disc. The records listed here are classic recordings of their type and are in demand by collectors.

Allen, Rex, Under Western Skies, Decca, 8402	**16.00**
Ames Brothers, In The Evening By The Moonlight, Coral, 56017	**12.00**
Annette, Songs From Annette, Mickey Mouse, 24	**40.00**
Bailey, Pearl, I'm With You, Coral, 56078	**16.00**
Beach Boys, Surfin' Safari, Capitol, DT–1808	**30.00**
Berry, Chuck, After School Session, Chess, 1426	**50.00**
Calloway, Cab, Hi De Hi, Hi De Ho, RCA Victor	**16.00**
Cash, Johnny, Johnny Cash With His Hot & Blue Guitar, Sun, 1220	**20.00**
Cole, Nat King, The King Cole Trio, Volume 2, Capitol, H–29	**20.00**
Crosby, Bing, Jerome Kern Songs, Decca, 5001	**20.00**
Day, Doris, You're My Thrill, Columbia, 6071	**20.00**
Domino, Fats, Rock and Rollin', Imperial, 9009	**65.00**
Ellington, Duke, Masterpieces By Ellington, Columbia, 4418	**30.00**
Everly Brothers, Songs Our Daddy Taught Us, Cadence, 3106	**30.00**
Fabian, Hold That Tiger, Chancellor, 5003	**20.00**
Fisher, Eddie, I'm In The Mood For Love, RCA Victor, 3058	**16.00**
Fitzgerald, Ella, Songs In A Mellow Mood, Decca, 8068	**20.00**
Gillespie, Dizzy, Dizzy Gillespie, Volume 1, Atlantic, 138	**150.00**
Goodman, Benny, Carnegie Hall Jazz Concert, Columbia, 160	**45.00**
Haley, Bill, & His Comets, Rock With Bill Haley and The Comets, Essex, 202	**75.00**
Ink Spots, The Ink Spots, Volume 1, Decca, 5056	**20.00**
Lee, Peggy, Black Coffee, Decca, 5482	**35.00**
Little Richard, Here's Little Richard, Specialty, 2100	**75.00**
Mathis, Johnny, Warm, Columbia, 1078	**14.00**
McGuire Sisters, By Request, Coral, 56123	**20.00**

Page, Patti, Tennessee Waltz, Mercury, 25154	**16.00**
Platters, The Platters, Mercury, 20146	**50.00**
Reese, Della, Melancholy Baby, Jubilee, 1026	**10.00**
Righteous Brothers, Some Blue–Eyed Soul, Moonglow, 1002	**8.00**
Shirelles, Tonight's The Night, Scepter, 501	**35.00**
Sinatra, Frank, Songs By Sinatra, Columbia, 124	**50.00**
Torme, Mel, California Suite, Capitol, P–200	**30.00**
Twitty, Conway, Conway Twitty Songs, MGM, E–3744	**40.00**
Vaughn, Sarah, Hot Jazz, Remington, 1024	**35.00**
Williams, Hank, Hank Williams Sings, MGM, E–107	**75.00**

REDWARE

History: The availability of clay, the same used to make bricks and roof tiles, accounted for the great production of red earthenware pottery in the American colonies. Redware pieces are mainly utilitarian—bowls, crocks, jugs, and so on.

Lead-glazed redware retained its reddish color, but a variety of colored glazes were obtained by the addition of metals to the basic glaze. Streaks and mottled splotches in redware items resulted from impurities in the clay and/or uneven firing temperatures.

"Slipware" is a term used to describe redwares decorated by the application of slip, a semiliquid paste made of clay. Slipwares were made in England, Germany, and elsewhere in Europe for decades before becoming popular in the Pennsylvania German region and elsewhere in colonial America.

References: Kevin McConnell, *Redware: America's Folk Art Pottery,* Schiffer Publishing, 1988; Dana G. Morykan and Harry L. Rinker, *Warman's Country Antiques & Collectibles, Second Edition,* Wallace–Homestead, 1994.

Apple Butter Jar, 5¾″ h, glazed int.	**30.00**
Bank	
3¼″ h, apple shape, red and yellow paint	**140.00**
7½″ h, chest of drawers shape, yellow slip knobs and name "Albert Stewart," molded label "Savings Bank"	**145.00**
Bottle, 5¾″ h, pinched sides and tooling, green glaze, brown flecks, green striping, incised label "Made by I S Stahl, 11–1–1939"	**55.00**
Bowl	
4″ d, brown streak dec, red glaze, double handle	**225.00**
6½″ d, white stripe dec, brown glaze	**50.00**

Bowl, glazed int., 8″ d, 3½″ h, $85.00.

10″ d, slip dec, brown, white, and green	1,430.00
10″ d, 4″ h, brown sponged glaze	95.00
12½″ d, 2½″ h, sgraffito, eagle, flowers, and "1827," late 19th–early 20th C.	425.00
Charger	
13″ d, molded bust of Washington, star ringed medallion, coggeled rim, brown fleck glaze	475.00
14½″ d, coggeled edge, yellow slip dec.	285.00
Coffeepot, 11¼″ h, molded and tooled dec, dome top, English	385.00
Cooler, 18″ h, ovoid, glaze flaking, mounted as lamp	70.00
Creamer	
3¾″ h, three coggle rings, light brown glaze	110.00
4″ h, brown dec, yellow glaze, stamped "John Bell"	2,700.00
Cup, 3¾″ h, flared lip, applied handle, clear glaze with mottled amber, minor wear and glaze flakes	85.00
Cuspidor, 8 x 4¼″, tooled bands, brown and green running glaze, brown dashes, some wear and edge chips	250.00
Dish, 11½″ l, 9″ w, rect, slip dec, inscribed "Beef"	385.00
Flask, 6½″ h, tooled lines and brown splotched glaze, old hairline in side, chip on lip	220.00
Flowerpot, 8¾″ h, brown sponged glaze, tooled and finger crimped rim, mismatched saucer	225.00
Food Mold	
5″ d, miniature, red glaze	125.00
6″ d, Turk's head, amber glaze	55.00
7½″ d, Turk's head, green glaze, amber spots	85.00
8½″ d, Turk's head, molded leaf design, amber glaze	30.00
Jar	
4⅜″ h, glazed int., handle	45.00
5½″ h, ovoid, black, brown, and amber mottled glaze	60.00

5¾″ h, shiny glaze, dark amber and brown splotches, ribbed strap handle	50.00
6″ h, brown streak dec, red glaze, handled, two coggle rings near neck	165.00
7½″ h, glazed int., handle	35.00
8″ h, cov, incised band dec, applied twist handles, c1810	75.00
8¾″ h, ovoid, dark brown mottled glaze	30.00
9″ h	
Dark brown alkaline dec, light brown glaze	150.00
Manganese dec, ovoid	400.00
Tooled lines, ovoid, shoulder handles, clear glaze, dark brown splotches	165.00
9¾″ h, ovoid, speckled mustard glaze	650.00
11″ h, ovoid, mounted as lamp	50.00
Jug	
6″ h, ovoid, dark brown glaze, minor allover glaze flakes	165.00
6¼″ h, ovoid, rich dark glaze, strap handle	65.00
6¾″ h, squatty ovoid, mustard shading to brown glaze	275.00
7″ h, ovoid, dark brown speckled glaze	75.00
8″ h, ovoid, dark green metallic glaze, glaze flakes	75.00
9½″ h, ovoid, greenish–amber glaze, orange spots	200.00
10¾″ h, ovoid, glazed, c1845	25.00
12″ h, ovoid, dark green speckled glaze	55.00
Milk Bowl	
8″ d, rim spout	145.00
9″ d, white slip dec, greenish–amber glaze, surface chips	250.00
Milk Pan, 17″ d	60.00
Miniature, chest of drawers, 11¼″ w,	

Flowerpot, crimped edges, green and brown glaze, attached base, I. S. Stahl, 1938, 4½″ d, 2¼″ h, $85.00.

5¾" d, 10¼" h, yellow slip dec, brown speckles, scalloped apron, six small drawers, incised on back "Annie Maria Marsden 1884" 825.00
Mug, 5¼" h, butter print style applied star design, strap handle, tooled lip, clear glaze with greenish highlights, good patina, minor glaze flakes and wear 125.00
Pie Plate
7⅞" d
Amber glaze, brown flecks 100.00
Dark brown fleck glaze 75.00
8" d, white slip, green, and brown plaid design. 575.00
8¼" d, clear orange glaze 30.00
9½" d, four line yellow slip dec, coggeled rim. 220.00
10¼" d, yellow slip design, coggeled rim 385.00
Pipkin, 8¼" h, manganese and colored slip dec, c1800 . . . . 95.00
Pitcher
6⅛" h, mottled dark brown metallic glaze 55.00
7¼" h, ovoid, green glazed int. . . . 25.00
8" h, molded stylized floral detail, cherub heads, dark brown glaze, imp "Nathaniel Sellers, Upper Hanover, PA," 200.00
8¼" h, greenish amber glaze, ribbed strap handle 225.00
8½" h, mottled brown glaze, sgd "John Bell, Waynesboro" 950.00
Plate
6¼" d, coggeled edge 140.00
8¾" d, coggeled rim, yellow slip date "1908" 165.00
10½" d, incised distelfink, flowers, and German inscription and name, dark amber glaze 200.00
Preserving Jar, cov, 10" h, green, orange spots, Galena. 110.00
Scoop, 14" l 175.00

RED WING POTTERY

History: The Red Wing pottery category covers several potteries from Red Wing, Minnesota. In

1868 David Hallem started Red Wing Stoneware Co., the first pottery with stoneware as its primary product and with a red wing stamped under the glaze as its mark. The Minnesota Stoneware Co. started in 1883. The North Star Stoneware Co., 1892–96, used a raised star and the words Red Wing as its mark.

The Red Wing Stoneware Co. and the Minnesota Stoneware Co. merged in 1892. The new company, the Red Wing Union Stoneware Co., made stoneware until 1920, when it introduced a pottery line which it continued until the 1940s. In 1936 the name was changed to Red Wing Potteries, Inc. During the 1930s it introduced several popular lines of hand-painted pattern dinnerware which were distributed through department stores, Sears, and gift stamp centers. Dinnerware declined in the 1950s, being replaced with hotel and restaurant china in the early 1960s. The plant closed in 1967.

References: Stanley Bougie and David Newkirk, *Price Guide & Supplement for Red Wing Dinnerware (1990–1991 Edition)*, published by authors, 1990; Dan and Gail DePasquale and Larry Peterson, *Red Wing Collectibles*, Collector Books, 1985, 1994 value update; Dan and Gail DePasquale and Larry Peterson, *Red Wing Stoneware*, Collector Books, 1983, 1992 value update; Dana G. Morykan and Harry L. Rinker, *Warman's Country Antiques & Collectibles, Second Edition*, Wallace–Homestead, 1994; David A. Newkirk, *A Guide To Red Wing Markings*, Monticello Printing, 1979; Dolores Simon, *Red Wing Pottery With Rumrill*, Collector Books, 1980, out of print; Gary and Bonnie Tefft, *Red Wing Potters and their Wares, Second Edition*, Locust Enterprises, 1987.

Collectors' Club: Red Wing Collectors Society, Inc., PO Box 124, Neosho, WI 53059.

Additional Listings: See *Warman's Americana & Collectibles* for more examples.

Bean Pot, cov, 1 gallon, Saffron ware, allover blue and red sponged dec . . . 250.00
Butter Crock, gray line 175.00
Casserole, cov, Saffron ware, brown sponged band on lid and bowl, handled, marked "Made In Red Wing" in circle on bottom 185.00
Chamber Pot, cov, white glaze, cobalt blue bands, unsgd. 100.00
Churn, 8 gallon, cobalt blue "8" and double leaf design, unsgd 325.00
Crock
10 Gallon, white glaze, stamped cobalt blue pair of double leaves and "Union Stoneware Co, Red Wing, Minn" in oval, cobalt blue handwritten "10" 250.00
20 Gallon, salt glaze, cobalt blue quill work leaf design and "20," 22½" h 165.00
Jug
½ Gallon, common, brown Albany slip, seamed at bottom, raised "Min-

nesota Stoneware Co, Red Wing"
on bottom **40.00**
1 Gallon
  Blue sponged dec, molded, wire
  bail with turned wood handle, incised "Minnesota Stoneware Co,
  Red Wing Minn" in bottom. **875.00**
  Two tone, shoulder style, brown
  glazed conical top, white bottom,
  imp "Red Wing Stoneware Co" in
  bottom. **135.00**
Milk Pan, brown Albany glaze, incised
  "RWSCo" on bottom, 7″ d **45.00**
Pitcher
  Blue and white, emb cherry band
  design. **400.00**
  Saffron ware, brown and white stripes,
  marked "Red Wing Saffron Ware"
  on bottom **115.00**

RELIGIOUS ITEMS

History: Objects for the worshiping or expression of man's belief in a superhuman power are collected by many people for many reasons.

Icons are included since they are religious mementos, usually paintings with a brass encasement. Collecting icons dates from the earliest period of Christianity. Most antique icons in today's market were made in the late 19th century.

Collectors' Club: Foundation International for Restorers of Religious Medals, PO Box 2652, Worcester, MA 01608.

Museum: American Bible Society, New York, NY.

Reproduction Alert: Icons are heavily reproduced.

Vase, tapered cylinder, straight neck, relief floral design, red matte glaze, stamped "Red Wing, Union Stoneware Co, Red Wing, Minn," 8¼″ h, $50.00.

Figure, Madonna and Child, carved ivory, French Gothic, $17,600.00.

Refrigerator Jar, cov, stacking, stoneware, cobalt blue bands and "Red
Wing Refrigerator Jar". **135.00**
Spittoon, blue and white, sponged dec,
unsgd. **450.00**
Syrup Jug, 1 gallon, shoulder style,
white glaze, pour spout, incised "Minnesota Stoneware Co, Red Wing
Minn" in bottom. **50.00**
Water Cooler, cov, 3 gallon, salt glazed,
cobalt blue freehand "3" and stenciled
"Ice Water," petal lid with cobalt blue
bands, Red Wing Union red wing
trademark. **400.00**

Bible, *The Illuminated Bible,* 1846, New
York, morocco gilt, two engraved ti-
tles, 1,600 plates, 8 x 10″. **275.00**
Bible Box
  Oak, 23½ x 15½ x 8″, slant lid, carved
  front panel dec, butterfly hinges,
  orig lock and hasp, dated 1703 . . .   **350.00**
  Pine, 17¼″ l, chip carved dec, rose
  head wrought iron nail construction,
  old dark patina. **125.00**
  Softwood, 22 x 17 x 10″, dovetailed,
  relief carved designs, iron strap
  hinge and lock, old green, red, and
  orange repaint **145.00**
Chalice, communion, pewter, Leonard,
Reed & Barton, 1835–40, price for
pair **350.00**

Cross, 3¼" h, Russian Orthodox, brass,
early 19th C **175.00**
Crucifix, 19" h, wood and gesso, poly-
chrome repaint **200.00**
Figure
Angel, 18" h, carved alabaster, Ren-
aissance style, standing, staring
downward, hands clasped, good
patina, 19th C, price for pair **1,760.00**
Virgin Mary, plaster, painted, giltwood
case, late 19th C **110.00**
Flagon, communion, 14½" h, pewter, sil-
ver plating, marked "Reed & Barton"   **45.00**
Holy Water Font, 10" h, 11" w, wall type,
carved marble, clam shell shaped
bowl above pair of winged cherubs,
Italian, late 19th C **550.00**
Icon
Greek
Saint George and dragon, 5⅝ x
7½", wood, polychrome paint . . .   **225.00**
Virgin Mother and Child, 10 x 7½",
gilded ground **350.00**
Visitation scene, 15 x 12" **450.00**
Russian
Saints Peter and Paul, 8½ x 7", re-
pousse silver oaklad, applied
raised enameled halos **775.00**
Winged figure with sword, 14 x 10"   **500.00**
Painting, 39½ x 32", Saint Jerome, oil
on canvas, unsigned, Continental
School, 19th C, framed, scattered
punctures, losses, scattered retouch,
surface grime **330.00**
Plaque, 3⅝ x 5¾", Christ crucified,
Frank Gardner Hale, Boston, enamel,
polychrome rendering, olive velvet
border, framed, sgd **110.00**

REVERSE PAINTING ON GLASS

History: The earliest examples of reverse painting on glass were produced in 13th-century Italy.
By the 17th century the technique had spread to
Central and Eastern Europe. It spread westward
as the glass industry center moved to Germany in
the late 17th century.

The Alsace and Black Forest region developed
a unique portraiture style. The half and three-quar-
ter portraits often were titled below the portrait.
Women tend to have general names. Most males
are of famous men.

The English used a mezzotint method, rather
than freestyle, to create their reverse paintings.
Landscapes and allegorical figures were popular.
The Chinese began working in the medium in the
17th century, eventually favoring marine and patriotic scenes.

Reverse painting was done in America. Most
were by folk artists, unsigned, who favored portraits, patriotic and mourning scenes, floral com-

positions, landscapes, and buildings. Known American artists include Benjamin Greenleaf, A.
Cranfield, and Rowley Jacobs.

In the late 19th century commercially produced
reverse paintings, often decorated with mother-of-
pearl, became popular. Themes included the
Statue of Liberty, the capitol in Washington, D.C.,
and various world's fairs and expositions.

Reference: Shirley Mace, *Encyclopedia of Silhouette Collectibles On Glass,* Shadow Enterprises, 1992.

**Jerome Napoleon, Baltimore, MD, 12¾
x 15¾", $300.00.**

PORTRAITS

Adelle, orig frame, 13½ x 10½" **425.00**
Beta, polychrome, two tone brown
ground, orig frame, 12" h, 9½" w. . . .   **330.00**
Frederike, orig frame, 13½ x 10⅝" . .   **385.00**
Geisha, facing pair, geisha seated next
to table, vase with flower, bamboo
dec, mirrored ground, Chinese Export, 19th C, framed, losses, 16" h,
11½" w, price for pair. **615.00**
Lincoln, Abraham, portrait, framed,
21½" h, 18" w **425.00**
Rosinia, polychrome, dark green
ground, orig frame, 9⅛" h, 6½" w . . .   **425.00**
Speiniolin, polychrome, two tone brown
ground, orig frame, wear and flaking,
10⅛ x 7⅝" **140.00**
Washington, George, silhouette, intri-
cately painted border, maple veneer

frame, gilded liner with minor damage, 12¾" h, 11" w **250.00**

SCENES

Geisha, facing pair, Geisha walking, acolyte on one side, antelope on other, heron standing on rockwork, scenic background, Chinese Export, 19th C, framed, 23" h, 16" w, price for pair **1,320.00**

George Washington on horseback, 20th C, minor wear, old frame, 14½" w, 10½" h. **60.00**

Perry's Lake Erie Victory, September 10th, 1813, naval battle scene, multicolored, 7 x 9" **250.00**

Ship, side-wheeler steamship *Ohio*, poplar frame, 10½" h, 12½" w **275.00**

RIDGWAY

History: Throughout the 19th century the Ridgway family, through a series of partnerships, held a position of importance in Shelton and Hanley, Staffordshire, England. The connection began with Job and George, two brothers, and Job's two sons, John and William. In 1830 John and William separated, with John retaining the Cauldon Place factory and William the Bell Works. By 1862 the porcelain division of Cauldon was carried on by Coalport China Ltd. William and his heirs continued at the Bell Works and the Church [Hanley] and Bedford [Shelton] works until the end of the 19th century.

Many early pieces are unmarked. Later marks include the initials of the many partnerships.

References: Susan and Al Bagdade, *Warman's English & Continental Pottery & Porcelain, Second Edition*, Wallace–Homestead, 1991; G. A. Godden, *Ridgway Porcelains*, Antique Collectors' Club, 1985.

Additional Listings: Staffordshire, Historical, and Staffordshire, Romantic.

Bowl, 8⅞" d, floral and foliage band, Imari colors, No. 21138 . . . . **300.00**

Cake Stand, 9½" d, 2¼" h, Oriental floral design, butterflies, gilt trim, marked "Ridgway, Old Derby," stains, gilt

Pitcher, Oriental scene, blue transfer, John & William Ridgway, 1814–30, 7½" h, $125.00.

wear, one has chip and hairline, price for pair **125.00**

Dinner Service, underglaze blue, multicolored enameled floral sprays and border, scrolled ground, gadrooned rim, cov soup tureen with stand, soup ladle, 3 cov sauce tureens with stands, 2 sauce ladles, 3 cov vegetable dishes, 18 soup plates, 27 dinner plates, 12 salad plates, 15 dessert plates, 2 pudding bowls, fruit bowl, cheese dish, dish strainer, 2 serving dishes, printed mark "Fancy Stone China" with title and initials, No. 1289, price for 101 pieces. **4,600.00**

Meat Platter, 18½ x 15½", Tyrolean, light blue transfer, molded well and tree, marked "William Ridgway" **195.00**

Plate, 8½" d, rust, rose, and purple Oriental type flowers with yellow centers, gray green branches, scalloped edge, No. 2004, c1830 . . . . **60.00**

Platter, 13 x 11", Asiatic Palaces, dark blue transfer, marked "William Ridgway, Son & Co." **160.00**

Teapot, cov, Royal Vistas, black transfer, green yellow overglaze, copper luster trim **185.00**

Vase, 7¼" h, squatty, molded, swans' head handles terminating in scrolls, flared quatrefoil foot, painted landscape panel, turquoise ground, gilt trim, No. 4290, c1830–40, price for pair **700.00**

RING TREES

History: A ring tree is a small, generally saucer-shaped object made of glass, porcelain, metal, or wood with a center post in the shape of a hand, branches, or cylinder for hanging or storing finger rings.

GLASS

Bristol, 3″ h, 3¼″ d, turquoise blue, lacy yellow leaves and large gold leaves dec 80.00
Cameo, 3¼″ h, 4″ d, acid cut, red flowers, leaves, and stems, leaf ground, St Louis 145.00
Clear, 3″ h, 3¾″ d, cut floral dec, black enameled cut bands 60.00
Cranberry, 3¼″ h, 3½″ d, hp, multicolored flowers, gold leaves. 115.00
Moser, black amethyst, 4″ h, 3¾″ d, heavily enameled blue, white, orange, and yellow flowers and green leaves, allover lacy gold dec, unsgd 115.00
Pink Cased, 3½″ h, 3½″ d, enameled blue and white flowers and branches dec, clear post 75.00
Vaseline Opalescent, 2½″ h, 3¼″ d, striped 60.00

METAL

Tiffany & Co, angel, SS 450.00
Wilcox, open hand, saucer base, engraved edge, sgd 55.00

Porcelain, Geisha Girl, Temple pattern variant, marked "Kutani," $35.00.

PORCELAIN

German, hand on saucer, dec 25.00
Limoges, multicolored blossoms, white ground, marked "T & V Limoges" . . . 40.00
Minton, 3″ h, pastel flowers, gold trim, marked "Minton, England" 40.00
Nippon, gold hand, rim dec 35.00
Parian Ware, 4″ h, child's hand, fingers extended 45.00

Royal Worcester, 2¾″ h, 4½″ l, oval dish, three pronged holder, hp pink and yellow flowers, beige ground, c1898 . . . 145.00
Schlegelmilch, RS Poland, violets, pearlized finish 90.00

POTTERY

Austria, hp pink and green floral dec, gold trim, marked "M Z Austria" 65.00
Wedgwood, 2¾″ h, jasperware, center post, white cameos of classical ladies, floral border, blue ground, marked . . 145.00
Zsolnay, 3½″ h, irid gold 75.00

ROCKINGHAM AND ROCKINGHAM BROWN GLAZED WARES

History: Rockingham ware can be divided into two categories. The first consists of the fine china and porcelain pieces made between 1826 and 1842 by the Rockingham Company of Swinton, Yorkshire, England, and its predecessor firms: Swinton, Bingley, Don, Leeds, and Brameld. The Bramelds developed the cadogan, a lidless teapot. Between 1826 and 1842 a quality soft paste body with a warm, silken feel was developed by the Bramelds. Elaborate specialty pieces were made. By 1830 the company employed 600 workers and listed 400 designs for dessert sets and 1,000 designs for tea and coffee services in their catalog. Unable to meet its payroll, the company closed in 1842.

The second category of Rockingham ware includes pieces produced in the famous Rockingham brown glaze that became an intense and vivid purple-brown when fired. It had a dark, tortoiseshell mottled appearance. The glaze was copied by many English and American potteries. American manufacturers who used Rockingham glaze include D. & J. Henderson of Jersey City, New Jersey; United States Pottery in Bennington, Vermont; potteries in East Liverpool, Ohio; and several potteries in Indiana and Illinois.

Reference: Susan and Al Bagdade, *Warman's English & Continental Pottery & Porcelain, Second Edition,* Wallace–Homestead, 1991.

Museum: The Bennington Museum, Bennington, VT.

Additional Listings: Bennington and Bennington-Type Pottery.

Bank, 6½" h, figural, Rockingham glaze, imp "Anna L Curtis Pittsfield, Mass," minor imperfections	275.00
Bedpan, 15" l, Rockingham glaze, chips	35.00
Bottle	
Book shape, 6" h, Rockingham glaze, chipped	110.00
Shoe shape, 6" h, emb "Ann Reid 1859"	250.00
Toby, 8½" h, two tone Rockingham glaze	35.00
Bowl	
10¼" d, 2¾" h, Rockingham glaze, small chips	50.00
10½" d, 2¾" h, Rockingham glaze, shallow	85.00
Creamer, 2½" h, acid etched, Wedgwood, c1875, rim nick	85.00
Cuspidor, 7½" d, Rockingham glaze, molded shells, surface flake	35.00
Dish	
8¾" l, 7" w, oval, Rockingham glaze, wear and small edge flakes	40.00
9" sq, Rockingham glaze, rim with molded scroll design	45.00
Figure, 9¾" h, dog, green and brown running glaze	330.00
Mixing Bowl	
10" d, 4¼" h, Rockingham glaze, slightly flared rim, ftd, minor chip on base	50.00
10½" d, 4¾" h, Rockingham glaze, worn	40.00
12" d, 5¾" h, Rockingham glaze, worn, hairlines	120.00

Muffin Tray, 14¾" h, Rockingham glaze, 19th C	110.00
Mug, 3½" h, cuspidor shape	185.00
Mustache Cup, 4¼" h, Rockingham glaze, toby	115.00
Pie Plate	
8⅜" d, Rockingham glaze	60.00
9½" d, Rockingham glaze, America, 19th C, price for set of four	110.00
10" d, Rockingham glaze	75.00
Pitcher	
3⅛" h, miniature, Rockingham glaze, hound handle, pinpoint edge flakes	280.00
4⅜" l, Rockingham glaze, squatty, C scroll handle	72.00
6⅜" h, Rockingham glaze, molded Gothic Arch design	60.00
6¾" h, Rockingham glaze, molded panels, ftd, wear and chips	60.00
7½" h, Rockingham glaze, tooled band at rim, beaded trim, poorly repaired chips in spout	55.00
7¾" h, Rockingham glaze, paneled, mask spout, Bennington, hairlines, rim chip	110.00
7⅞" h, Rockingham glaze, minor edge chips	55.00
8" h, Rockingham glaze, molded peacocks, rim chips	85.00
9½" h, Rockingham glaze, hound handle, hanging game, eagle spout, attributed to OH, hairline in base	140.00
Platter, 15" l, oval, Rockingham glaze	170.00
Pot, cov, 4⅝" h, bulbous, Rockingham glaze, side spout, handle	280.00
Soap Dish, 5¼" d, round, Rockingham glaze, molded lip	40.00
Teapot, cov, 3¼" h, widow finial, Wedgwood, c1875, chips	90.00
Vegetable Dish, 11" d, Rockingham glaze, America, 19th C, price for pair	110.00

Plate, 8¼" d, blue transfer, romantic scene, imp "Brameld," $85.00.

ROCK 'N' ROLL

History: Rock music can be traced back to early rhythm and blues music. It progressed and reached its golden age in the 1950s and 1960s. Attention and most of the memorabilia issued during that period focused on individual singers and groups. The two largest sources of collectibles are items associated with Elvis Presley and the Beatles.

In the 1980s two areas—clothing and guitars—associated with key Rock 'n' Roll personalities received special collector attention. Sotheby's and Christie's East regularly feature Rock 'n' Roll memorabilia as part of their collectibles sales. At the moment, the market is highly speculative and nostalgia driven.

It is important to identify memorabilia issued during the lifetime of an artist or performing group as opposed to material issued after they died or disbanded. This latter material is identified as "fantasy" items and will never achieve the same degree of collectibility as its period counterparts.

References: Jeff Augsburger, Marty Eck, and Rich Rann, *The Beatles Memorabilia Price Guide, Second Edition,* Wallace–Homestead, 1993; Rosalind Cranor, *Elvis Collectibles,* Collector Books, 1983, out of print; L. R. Docks, *1900–1965 American Premium Record Guide, Fourth Edition,* Books Americana, 1992; Barbara Fenick, *Collecting The Beatles: An Introduction and Price Guide To Fab Four Collectibles, Records and Memorabilia,* Vol. 1 (1984) and Vol. 2, Perian Press; Alison Fox, *Rock & Pop,* Boxtree (London), 1988; Anthony Gribin and Matthew Schiff, *Doo-Wop: The Forgotten Third of Rock 'n' Roll,* Krause Publications, 1992; Paul Grushkin, *The Art of Rock—Posters From Presley To Punk, Revised Edition,* Abbeville Press, 1991; David K. Henkel, *The Official Price Guide to Rock and Roll,* House of Collectibles, 1992; Jerry Osborne, *The Official Price Guide To Records, Tenth Edition,* House of Collectibles, 1993; Jerry Osborne, Perry Cox, and Joe Lindsay, *The Official Price Guide to Memorabilia of Elvis Presley And The Beatles,* House of Collectibles, 1988; Michael Stern, Barbara Crawford, and Hollis Lamon, *The Beatles: A Reference & Value Guide,* Collector Books, 1994; Neal Umphred, *Goldmine's Price Guide To Collectible Record Albums, 1949–1989, Third Edition,* Krause Publications, 1993; Neal Umphred, *Goldmine's Rock 'n Roll 45 RPM Record Price Guide, 2nd Edition,* Krause Publications, 1992.

Periodicals: *Beatlefan,* PO Box 33515, Decatur, GA 30033; *Good Day Sunshine,* 397 Edgewood Avenue, New Haven, CT 06511.

Collectors' Clubs: Beatles Connection, PO Box 1066, Pinellas Park, FL 34665; Beatles Fan Club of Great Britain, Superstore Productions, 123 Marina St, Leonards on Sea, East Sussex, England TN38 OBN; Elvis Forever TCB Fan Club, PO Box 1066, Pinellas Park, FL 34665; Graceland News Fan Club, PO Box 452, Rutherford, NJ 07070; Working Class Hero Club, 3311 Niagara St., Pittsburgh, PA 15213.

Reproduction Alert: Records, picture sleeves, and album jackets, especially for the Beatles, have been counterfeited. Sound may be inferior. Printing on labels and picture jackets usually is inferior to the original. Many pieces of memorabilia also have been reproduced, often with some change in size, color, and design.

Additional Listings: See the Beatles, Elvis Presley, and Rock 'n' Roll in *Warman's Americana & Collectibles.*

Psychedelic Drawing, Jimi Hendrix, 1969, $6,875.00.

Album, The Ink Spots, 5 x 7", blue stiff paper cov, black and white glossy photos, text on members, and list of record releases, Gale Inc, 1950s . . .   30.00

Autograph
Buddy Holly, photo, color, pencil signature, 1959 . . . .   1,350.00
Doors, photo, sgd by members   . . .   1,250.00
Elvis Presley, document, contract with MGM Studios, 1961 . . . .   850.00
Janis Joplin
  Album Cover, blue signature, "Love Janis Joplin," matted and framed. 2,990.00
  Stationery, WFIL–TV, red signature 1,015.00
Jim Morrison, stationery, WFIL–TV, black signature 1,135.00
Jimi Hendrix, poster, inscribed "To Archie Be Groovy Jimi Hendrix, Noel Redding, and Mitch Mitchell," 1967, framed 1,135.00
John Lennon, signature matted with two 5 x 7" color photos, engraved name plate 550.00
Queen, album cov, *A Night At The Opera,* bold signature by members, matted and framed. 975.00
Rolling Stones, magazine centerfold photo, pen and ink signatures 495.00
Smokey Robinson, 8 x 10", black and white glossy, sgd "To William/God Bless/You/Smokey Robinson". . . .   15.00
Bandanna, 22" l, Rod Stewart, "Camouflage Tour 1984," cotton, red 15.00
Banner, concert, Stevie Nicks, Sun Country Cooler & Westwood One Ra-

dio Networks Present Stevie Nicks, nylon, green **345.00**

Bracelet, 6½" l, gold colored metal links and four charms, orig display card, Rayburt Productions Inc, 1967 . . . . . **45.00**

Cigarette Lighter, Rod Stewart decal, chrome, c1975. . . . . **30.00**

Coloring Book, Beatles, 8¼ x 10¼", Saalfield Publishing Co, 1964 . . . . . . **50.00**

Costume, Gene Simmons, vinyl, molded thin plastic mask, Collegeville Costumes, 1978 Aucoin Management Inc copyright **50.00**

Exhibit Card
Bill Haley and His Comets, 3¼ x 5¼", 1950s **30.00**
Diana Ross, 1960s **15.00**

Figure, Dave Clark 5, 3" h, hard plastic, Remco, c1964, price for set of 4 . . . . **75.00**

Flag, Beatles, 8 x 10", rayon, blue and white, group's heads, marked "LTE," c1960. . . . . **75.00**

Game
Beatles, Flip Your Wig, orig box . . . **75.00**
The Monkees Game, Transogram, 1967 Rayburt Productions Inc **110.00**

Magazine
Changes, #1, 1969, Bob Dylan . . . **25.00**
Fifteen Fever, January, 1966 . . . . . **30.00**
Strobe, July, #1, 1969, Janis Joplin Up Front **35.00**
Teen World, June, 1962 . . . . **25.00**

Makeup Kit, Kiss, Kiss Your Face, unused. **50.00**

Nodder, Beatles, hp, holding instruments, gold base, orig box, Car Mascots Inc, 1964, price for set of 4 . . . . **1,725.00**

Photo
Buddy Holly, black and white glossy **100.00**
James Dean, 8 x 10", color, 1955 . . **55.00**
The Four Aces, 5 x 7", black and white glossy, blue signature "Sincerely The Four Aces," 1950s **20.00**

Pinback Button, I Love Freddy and the Dreamers, 3½" d, black and white photos, red and white letters, Premier Talent Associates Inc copyright, c1960. . . . . **25.00**

Post Card
Blood, Sweat & Tears, John Handy, Son House, 14 x 20", red, yellow, and black **4.00**
Monkees, 5½ x 8½", glossy photo, black signatures, Monkees Fan Club text on reverse, orig mailing label, late 1960s. **35.00**

Poster
Beatles, 24 x 17¼", Here Come The Beatles, Monday, August 29, Candlestick Park, 1966. . . . . **1,495.00**
Bill Haley & His Comets, The Drifters, Flamin' Groovies, 14 x 22", mon-

ochrome photo of radio personality Tom Donahue **20.00**

Black Sabbath, 23 x 23", Born Again, red and blue **8.00**

Chubby Checker, 21 x 27", July 15–21, Atlantic Steel Pier, red, white, and purple, c1970 . . . . **40.00**

Chuck Berry, 14 x 20", yellow, red, blue, and black **25.00**

Donovan, 14 x 21½", sepia photo . **30.00**

Family Dog, 14 x 20", Denver, Sept 22–23, 1967 . . . . **75.00**

Janis Joplin, 14 x 19", Mt Tamalpias Outdoor Theater, San Francisco, marked "Copyright Also–Gut–67" . **150.00**

Jefferson Airplane, 16¾ x 23", red and blue, abstract design of plane wing **15.00**

Led Zepplin, 36 x 24", Ampex adv for first album, two tone photo image, 1969. . . . . **115.00**

Martha & The Vandellas, 14 x 23", blue, chartreuse, and red **25.00**

Rod Stewart, 36 x 48", Tonight I'm Yours, 1981. . . . . **18.00**

Rolling Stones, 14 x 22", monochrome photo, metallic silver lettering **50.00**

Youngbloods, 14 x 20", silhouette of couple dancing, magenta, blue, green, and orange **25.00**

Program
Alan Freed Presents The Big Beat, 9 x 12", 24 pgs, 1950s **110.00**
Fleetwood Mac, Tango in the Night, 32 pgs **12.00**
Herman's Hermits, 10 x 13", 16 pgs, 1960s. **50.00**
Paul Revere and The Raiders, 11 x 11", 24 pgs, glossy black and white and color photos, 1960s **55.00**
Rod Stewart, Blondes Have More Fun, 1978–79, 96 pgs. **20.00**
Woodstock, 8½ x 11", Concert Hall Publications, c1970 . . . . **25.00**

Puppet, finger, Mike Nesmith, 5" h, hard plastic body, vinyl head, Remco, 1970 Columbia Pictures Industries Inc copyright **55.00**

Puzzle, Yellow Submarine, Jaymar, 1968 King features Syndicate copyright, orig box **75.00**

Record, 33⅓ rpm
Little Richard, Good Golly Miss Molly, Lucille, 1957 . . . . **55.00**
The Shirelles, Baby It's You, Cameo label **25.00**

Record Sleeve, Jerry Lee Lewis, 7 x 7", glossy paper, 1958 . . . . **25.00**

Sheet Music
Bob Dylan, Like A Rolling Stone, 9 x 12", 4 pgs, 1965. . . . . **50.00**
Herman's Hermits, Mrs Brown You've

Got A Lovely Daughter, 9 x 12″, 28
pgs, 1965 . . . .   20.00
Ticket Stub
Buddy Holly, Clear Lake, Iowa, 1959   110.00
Pink Floyd, Marquee Club, London,
1968 . . . .   35.00
The Doors, Whisky–a–Go–Go, Los
Angeles, 1967 . . . .   50.00
Yearbook
Dick Clark, 8½ x 11″ 42 pgs, 1957 .   35.00
Hit Parader, 1967 . . . .   15.00

Catalog Cover, Sears, Roebuck & Co,
1932 . . . .   65.00
Magazine, cover illus
Country Gentleman, October 6, 1917   60.00
Literary Digest, August 17, 1918   . .   40.00
Magazine Tear Sheet, Jell–O adv,
Country Gentleman, 1922 . . . .   10.00
Poster
Freedom of Speech, WWII, 1943   . .   35.00
Maxwell House Coffee adv, 1932–33   325.00
Sheet Music, *Over There*, 1918   . . . .   45.00

ROCKWELL, NORMAN

History: Norman Rockwell (February 3, 1894–
November 1978) was a famous American artist and
illustrator. During the time he painted, from age 18
until his death, he created over 2,000 works.

His first professional efforts were illustrations for
a children's book. He next worked for *Boy's Life,*
the Boy Scout magazine. His most famous works
were used by *Saturday Evening Post* for its cover
illustrations.

Norman Rockwell painted everyday people in
everyday situations, mixing a little humor with sentiment. His paintings and illustrations are treasured
because of this sensitive approach. Rockwell
painted people he knew and places with which he
was familiar. New England landscapes are found
in many of his illustrations.

References: Denis C. Jackson, *The Norman
Rockwell Identification And Value Guide To: Mag-
azines, Posters, Calendars, Books, 2nd Edition,*
published by author, 1985; Mary Moline, *Norman
Rockwell Collectibles, Sixth Edition,* Green Valley
World, 1988.

Collectors' Club: Rockwell Society of America,
597 Saw Mill River Rd., Ardsley, NY 10502.

Museums: Museum of Norman Rockwell Art,
Reedsburg, WI; Norman Rockwell Museum, Stock-
bridge, MA; Norman Rockwell Museum, North-
brook, IL; Norman Rockwell Museum, Philadelphia, PA.

Reproduction Alert: Because of the popularity
of his works, they have been reproduced on many
objects. These new collectibles should not be confused with original artwork and illustrations. However, they do allow a collector more range in collecting interests and prices.

Additional Listings: See *Warman's Americana
& Collectibles* for more examples.

HISTORIC

Book
My Adventures as an Illustrator, Rockwell, 1960 . . . .   20.00
Tom Sawyer, Heritage Press, 1936   20.00
Calendar, 1941, boy and dog illus, Hercules Powder Company adv, 13 x
30¼″ 175.00

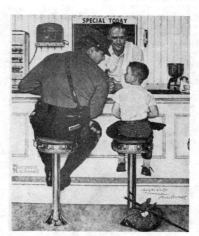

**Print, The Runaway, *Saturday Evening
Post* cover, Sept. 20, 1958, sgd by
Rockwell, 11 x 14″, $350.00.**

MODERN

Coin, Ford Motor Co, 50th Anniversary   35.00
Figure
Gorham Fine China, Four Seasons,
Childhood, 1973, set of four 500.00
Grossman Designs, Inc, Tom Sawyer,
Series No. 1, 1976 . . . .   100.00
Plate, Scotty Gets His Tree, Christmas
Series, Rockwell Society of America,
1974 . . . .   175.00
Print
Gilding The Eagle, Eleanor Ettinger,
Inc, litho, 21 x 25½″ 3,225.00
Music Hath Charms, Circle Fine Arts,
limited edition, sgd and numbered   3,000.00

ROGERS & SIMILAR STATUARY

History: John Rogers, born in America in 1829, studied sculpturing in Europe and produced the first plaster-of-paris statue, *The Checker Players,* in 1859. It was followed by *The Slave Auction* in 1860.

His works were popular parlor pieces of the Victorian era. He produced at least 80 different subjects, and the total number of groups made from the originals is estimated to be over 100,000.

Casper Hennecke, one of Rogers's contemporaries, operated C. Hennecke & Company from 1881 until 1896 in Milwaukee, Wisconsin. His statuary often is confused with Rogers's work since both are very similar.

It is difficult to find a statue in undamaged condition and with original paint. Use the following conversions: 10% minor flaking; 10% chips; 10% to 20% piece or pieces broken and reglued; 20% flaking; 50% repainting.

References: Paul and Meta Bieier, *John Rogers' Groups of Statuary,* published by authors, 1971; Betty C. Haverly, *Hennecke's Florentine Statuary,* published by author, 1972; David H. Wallace, *John Rogers: The People's Sculptor,* Wesleyan Univ., 1976.

Periodical: *The Rogers Group,* 4932 Prince George Avenue, Beltsville, MD 20705.

Conquering Jealousy, $200.00.

ROGERS

Charity Patient	650.00
Mail Day, 1864	650.00
Picket Guard, The, 1861	750.00
Referee, The, 1880, repainted	350.00
School Days, 1877	700.00
Taking the Oath and Drawing Rations	425.00
Weighing the Baby	450.00

ROGERS TYPE

By Jingo, minor chipping	125.00
Can't You Talk	135.00
First Love, repainted	165.00
Holy Family	225.00
Romeo and Juliet	150.00

ROOKWOOD POTTERY

History: Mrs. Marie Longworth Nicholas Storer, Cincinnati, Ohio, founded Rookwood Pottery in 1880. The name of this outstanding American art pottery came from her family estate "Rookwood," named for the rooks (crows) which inhabited the wooded grounds.

There are five elements to the Rookwood marking system—the clay or body mark, the size mark, the decorator mark, the date mark, and the factory mark. Rookwood art pottery can best be dated from factory marks.

In 1880–82 the factory mark was the name "Rookwood" incised or painted on the base. Between 1881 and 1886 the firm name, address, and year appeared in an oval frame. Beginning in 1886, the impressed "RP" monogram appeared and a flame mark was added for each year until 1900. After 1900 a Roman numeral, indicating the last two digits of the year of production, was added at the bottom of the "RP" flame mark monogram. This last mark is the one most often found on Rookwood pottery today.

Though the Rookwood pottery filed for bankruptcy in 1941, it was soon reorganized under new management. However, efforts at maintaining the pottery proved futile, and it again was sold in 1956 and in 1959. The pottery was moved to Starkville, Mississippi, in conjunction with the Herschede Clock Co. It finally ceased operation in 1967.

Rookwood wares changed with the times. The variety is endless, in part because of the great variations in glazes and designs due to the creativity of the many talented artists.

References: Anita J. Ellis, *Rookwood Pottery: The Glorious Gamble,* Rizzoli International and Cincinnati Art Museum, 1992; L–W Book Sales (ed.), *A Price Guide To Rookwood,* L–W Book Sales, 1993; Herbert Peck, *The Book of Rookwood Pottery,* Crown Publishers, 1968; Herbert Peck, *The Second Book of Rookwood Pottery,* published by author, 1985.

Collectors' Club: American Art Pottery Association, 125 E. Rose Ave., St. Louis, MO 63119.

Bookends, pr
5½" h, shape #2275, William P
McDonald, 1943. . . . . 250.00
5¾" h, white glaze, elephants, shape
#2444C, 1931. . . . . 285.00
7½" h, brown and white glossy glaze,
St Francis, shape #6883 . . . . . . 275.00
8" h, Art Deco Oriental figure, glossy
pale blue, blue headpiece, black
comb, red accents, shape #2362,
William P McDonald. 825.00

**Bowl, brown matte glaze, emb water lily
design, four feet, 6" d, 4" h, $150.00.**

Bowl
7" d, matte turquoise with green speckled glaze, relief geometric and linear band at rim, shape #957D,
1910. 220.00
7¾" d, 3½" h, hammered glaze Lim-
oges style underglaze pink blossoms dec, gold highlights, shape
#166, Laura A Fry 770.00
Candlestick, 6" h, Limoges style underglaze trumpet vine dec, shape
#S1022W, Harriet R Strafer, 1892,
crazing. 220.00
Chocolate Pot
8½" h, cameo glaze, crab apples on
branch dec, shape #251W, Harriet
R Strafer, 1890, crazing, hairline . . 440.00
10" h, standard glaze, oak leaves and
acorns dec, shape #722, Lenore
Asbury, 1904. . . . . 495.00
Ewer
6½" h, standard glaze, white wild rose
blossom sprig, yellow green glaze,
Grace Young, 1889, small base
nick 330.00
7" h, standard glaze, yellow daffodils
dec, shape #433C, Josephine E
Zettel, 1897, crazing. 330.00
12" h, standard glaze, yellow fruit

blossoms, contrasting green glazing, shape #471B, William P Mc-
Donald, 1893, crazing, glaze
scratches 550.00
Flower Boat, 16" l, standard glaze, pansies dec, shape #3745, Matt A Daly,
1890 . . . . 880.00
Humidor, 6" h, standard glaze, carved
and dec salmon pansies, 1889,
crazing. 470.00
Jar, cov, 7" h, globular form, slate blue,
berries and leaves dec on cov,
c1910. . . . . 425.00
Jardiniere, 7¼" h, 8¼" d, standard
glaze, blooming wild roses dec, double handled, shape #484D, Amelia
Sprague, 1898 . . . . 770.00
Mug
5" h, "Chief Goes to War, Sioux" portrait, shape #656, Edith R Felten,
1900. 1,265.00
6" h, light standard glaze, blooming
chrysanthemums dec, shape #501,
William P McDonald, 1889 . . . . . . 385.00
Paperweight, monkey 85.00
Perfume Jug, Limoges style underglaze
green leaves and butterfly dec, inscribed "Miss Hanna," shape #12E,
Albert R Valentien, 1883 . . . . 110.00
Pitcher
5½" h, Limoges style underglaze
bamboo and butterfly dec, gold
flecked glaze, shape #220, Martin
Rettig, 1885. . . . . 385.00
9¼" h, blue glaze, Limoges style underglaze apple blossoms dec, Al-
bert R Valentien, 1881 . . . . 550.00
Presentation Stein, cov, 6¾" h, standard
glaze, stylized ferns dec, presented to
Lucian Wulsin by the Commercial
Club of Cincinnati, pewter lid, shape
#783, Constance A Baker, 1895. . . . 1,540.00
Tea Set, 5½" h teapot, navy blue bands,
shape #2469, 1919, random crazing 330.00
Vase
4" h, Iris glaze, pink flowers, leaves
strung along shoulder, Geneova O
Reed, 1901, crazing. 500.00
6" h, standard green glaze, stylized
cream floral garland, shape #346B,
Matt A Daly, 1888 . . . . 440.00
6⅜" h, Iris glaze, violets dec, shape
#483, Fred Rothenbusch, 1903,
base chip, crazing 660.00
6½" h, Limoges style underglaze blue
and white floral sprig dec, cream
ground, imp anchor mark, Albert R
Valentien, 1882, crazing 770.00
6¾" h
Iris glaze, poppy blossom and buds,
shape #926D, Clara D Linde-
man, 1904, crazing. 880.00

Standard glaze, green tone, fruit
blossom on branch, shape
#535E Y, Kataro Shirayamadani,
1890, glaze scratch **825.00**
Tiger Eye, asters dec, shape
#535E, Amelia B Sprague, 1894,
rim irregularity, crazing **825.00**
7" h, flared cylindrical form, painted
lilies of the valley dec, gray shading
to peach ground, c1905 . . . . **660.00**
7¾" h
Iris glaze, grape leaves on vine
dec, Fred Rothenbusch, 1903,
crazing **825.00**
Pink to gray glaze, incised floral and
line dec, shape #2143, sgd with
15 rays **440.00**
8" h
Standard glaze, autumn leaf de-
sign, 1902, Sallie E Coyne **700.00**
Wax matte glaze, red–yellow tulips,
green leaves, blue outlines, dusty
rose ground, shape #932E, artist
sgd, 1925 . . . . **525.00**
8¼" h, scenic vellum, gray silhouetted
trees and birds, orange winter sunset, shape #951D, E T Hurley,
1906, crazing, hairline **1,210.00**
8½" h, vellum, shades of green with
blue, shape #900C, Sallie E Coyne,
1915, base chip, peppering,
crazing **1,210.00**
8¾" h, vellum, Dogwood, beige to
gray ground, beige branches, ivory
flowers, yellow and pale blue highlights, shape #9040, E T Hurley,
1910, crazing **770.00**
9½" h, vellum, apple blossoms, light
blue green ground, cream petals,
tan pollen details, pink buds, green
leaves, blue gray outlines, shape
#2746, Lenore Asbury, 1928 . . . . **1,430.00**
10¼" h, five fish swimming in current,
green blue glaze, shape #907D, E
T Hurley, 1903, crazing, nick at
base **2,200.00**
10½" h, standard glaze, maple leaf
sprigs, shape #922B, Matt A Daly,
1901, glaze scratches, crazing . . . **385.00**
11¼" h, wax matte glaze, red and yellow peony, green leaves, pink–blue
ground, shape #1369C, Elizabeth
N Lincoln, 1928 . . . . **990.00**
12¼" h, Iris glaze, pink orchids, olive
stems, green leaves, shape #940B,
Albert R Valentien, 1903, crazing . . **2,200.00**
14½" h, high glaze, underglazed wide
band of stylized white flowers, red
accents, stylized green leaves,
shape #614B, Elizabeth Barrett,
1935 . . . . **825.00**

Whiskey Jug, stopper
7¼" h, standard glaze, gooseberries,
leaves, and vines dec, shape
#747C, Howard Altman, 1900 . . . . **495.00**
8¼" h, standard glaze, ear and corn
and wheat dec, shape #889B, Mary
Nourse, 1899 . . . . **440.00**

ROSE BOWLS

History: A rose bowl, a decorative open bowl
with a crimped, pinched, or petal top, held fragrant
rose petals or potpourri which served as an air
freshener in the late Victorian period. Practically
every glass manufacturer made rose bowls in a
variety of patterns and glass types, including fine
art glass.

Reference: Ellen T. Schroy, *Warman's Glass*,
Wallace-Homestead, 1992.

Additional Listings: See specific glass categories.

Spatter Glass, tortoise shell spatter, applied gold dec, 3¾" d, 3" h, $125.00.

Glass
Acid Etched, 4¼" d, 3¾" h, pinched
sides, enameled purple violets, gold
stems and dec, Mont Joye **145.00**
Amberina, 6" h, tricorn rim, DQ int. and
ext., three applied amber reeded
feet. **550.00**
Art Deco, 6½" h, frosted, enameled
intertwining yellow and green
design. **55.00**
Baccarat, 3" h, cranberry, lacy enamel
dec. **150.00**
Bohemian, 8½" d, Deer and Castle
pattern, ruby flashed, clear and
frosted **225.00**

Crystal, 7″ d, spherical, diagonal optics, Continental **60.00**
Opalescent, 4¼″ h, pink and rose pansies, green leaves, cream ground, sgd, Smith Bros **300.00**
Rose Overlay, 3⅛″ d, 3″ h, white int., four crimp top, clear wafer foot, heavy gold flowers and branches, enameled "E" and spider web dec on base, Thomas Webb & Sons . . **275.00**
Satin, 4½″ d, 2¾″ h, Rivulet pattern, eight crimp top, MOP, shaded pink **250.00**
Spangled, 3⅜″ d, 3½″ h, eight crimp top, cased deep rose, heavy mica coral like dec, white int.. . . . . **110.00**
Stretch, 3½″ d, 5″ h, pink, melon ribbed **50.00**
Porcelain, 2½″ h, shell molded, Royal Worcester, shape #G908. . . . . **65.00**
Pottery, glossy brown glaze, wreath and vine dec, ftd, Peters and Reed **40.00**

ROSE CANTON, ROSE MANDARIN, ROSE MEDALLION

History: The pink rose color has given its name to three related groups of Chinese export porcelain. Rose Mandarin was produced from the late 18th century to approximately 1840. Rose Canton began somewhat later, extending through the first half of the 19th century. Rose Medallion originated in the early 19th century and was made through the early 20th century.

Rose Mandarin derives its name from the Mandarin figure(s) found in garden scenes with women and children. The women often feature gold decorations in their hair. Polychrome enamels and birds separate the scenes.

Rose Medallion has alternating panels of figures and birds and flowers. The elements are four in number, separated evenly around the center medallion. Peonies and foliage fill voids.

Rose Canton is similar to Rose Medallion except the figure panels are replaced by flowers. People are present only if the medallion partitions are absent. Some patterns have been named—Butterfly and Cabbage, Rooster, etc. The category actually is a catchall for all pink enamel ware not fitting into the first two groups.

Reference: Gloria and Robert Mascarelli, *Warman's Oriental Antiques,* Wallace—Homestead, 1992.

Reproduction Alert: Rose Medallion is still made, although the quality does not match the earlier examples.

ROSE CANTON

Brush Pot, 4½″ h, scenic, ladies, reticulated, gilt trim **265.00**

Plate, 10⅛″ d, marked "Made In China," $40.00.

Charger, 13″ d, floral panels, 19th C . **200.00**
Garden Set, 18″ h, barrel form **1,320.00**
Plate
  8½″ d, floral dec **75.00**
  9¾″ d, 19th C, price for pair **550.00**
Soup Tureen, cov, lozenge shape, gilt floral ground, figural scenes **300.00**
Sugar, cov, handle **100.00**

ROSE MANDARIN

Chamberstick, 3½″ h, floral dec, snuffer, Canton, 19th C **330.00**
Cup and Saucer, scenic panels, butterfly and floral border **150.00**
Fruit Bowl and Undertray, 10¼″ l x 3½″ h bowl, 10″ l undertray, late 19th C . . **1,870.00**
Plate, 9½″ d, central medallion of ladies and seated robed mandarin, garden scene, dragon dec border **385.00**
Punch Bowl
  13″ d, 19th C, imperfections **1,320.00**
  15½″ d, 19th C **1,870.00**
Rice Bowl, cov, ring type undertray, Canton, price for pair. **110.00**
Serving Dish, 10½″ l, shaped, 19th C **360.00**
Shrimp Dish, 10½″ d, 19th C **550.00**
Vase, 9½″ h, figures and precious ornaments below Rose Canton floral designs, crazed ground, one rim repaired, c1860, price for pair **495.00**
Vegetable Dish, 11″ l, central figural panel, Rose Canton borders, c1840, price for pair. **1,540.00**

ROSE MEDALLION

Bowl
  13″ d, 5½″ h **990.00**
  14½″ d, 6½″ h **1,100.00**

Chamber Bowl, 15½" d, flat rim, dec int.......................... 275.00
Dresser Box, 3⅞" d, cov, circular, Canton...................... 110.00
Garden Seat, 17½" h, landscape dec panels, 19th C, minor losses 2,420.00
Planter, 10 x 12" 385.00
Platter, oval
  11½ x 15" 440.00
  12 x 15" 330.00
  12½ x 16", oval, stamped "Made in China"..................... 385.00
Teapot, cov, 5¼" h, Canton 110.00
Tray, 10" l, oval, reticulated border, alternating floral and figural reserves dec 225.00
Tureen, cov, 14" l, 9" h, woven handles 990.00
Umbrella Stand, 24" h, China, 19th C 1,540.00
Vase
  6½" h, bottle shape, price for pair . 250.00
  12" h, 19th C, price for pair 615.00
  13½" h, Ku–form, landscape dec panels, China, 19th C, imperfections................ 470.00
Wash Basin, 18½" d, China, 19th C, restored.................... 880.00

ground, gold trim, artist sgd, 1922, price for 10 pc set 135.00
Cup and Saucer, San Souci pattern, white 12.00
Figure
  Clown, 6" h 225.00
  Deer, 3½" h, sitting 135.00
  Fairy Queen, 10½" h, sgd "L. Friedrich–Granau".............. 325.00
  Heron
    12¼" h 350.00
    13¾" h 400.00
  Nude, 14" h, kneeling, sgd "Klimsch" 775.00
  Ram, 9" h, mottled gray 195.00
Planter, 7½" l, 4" w, raised tree bark design, unglazed white ext., glazed int. 95.00
Plate
  8" d, Moss Rose pattern, price for set of six 85.00
  9⅞" d, lady's head and shoulder portrait, pale yellow and white ground, faux green, turquoise, blue, and red hardstone jewels 350.00
  10" d, girl and lamb dec, multicolored 35.00
  10¾" d, green and gold berry and leaf border, price for set of twelve 175.00
Platter, 15" l, Greenblum pattern 25.00

ROSENTHAL

History: Rosenthal Porcelain Manufactory began operating at Selb, Bavaria, in 1880. Specialities were tablewares and figurines. The firm is still in operation.

Reference: Susan and Al Bagdade, *Warman's English & Continental Pottery & Porcelain, Second Edition*, Wallace-Homestead, 1991.

Cake Plate, 12" w, grape dec, scalloped ruffled edge, open ruffled handles... 65.00
Chocolate Set, cov chocolate pot, 10" d handled plate, four cups and saucers, transitional Art Deco–Art Nouveau dec, brown shaded to beige, cream

Vase, Copenhagen series, sterling silver overlay, marked, c1890, 10¼" h, $395.00.

Vase
  6" h, black cats, white ground 40.00
  6½" h, dancing nude dec, multicolored, artist sgd 80.00
  9⅞" h, vertical ribs, banded top and base, polychrome floral bouquet in center, marked "Rosenthal" 50.00
  11" h, hp, multicolored roses 120.00

Roseville
u.s.a.

ROSEVILLE POTTERY

History: In the late 1880s a group of investors purchased the J. B. Owens Pottery in Roseville, Ohio, and made utilitarian stoneware items. In 1892 the firm was incorporated and joined by George F. Young, who became general manager. Four generations of Youngs controlled Roseville until the early 1950s.

A series of acquisitions began: Midland Pottery of Roseville in 1898, Clark Stoneware Plant in Zanesville (formerly used by Peters and Reed), and Muskingum Stoneware (Mosaic Tile Company) in Zanesville. In 1898 the offices also moved from Roseville to Zanesville.

In 1900 Roseville introduced its art pottery—Rozane. Rozane became a trade name to cover a large series of lines. The art lines were made in limited amounts after 1919.

The success of Roseville depended on its commercial lines, first developed by John J. Herald and Frederick Rhead in the first decades of the 1900s. In 1918 Frank Ferrell became art director and developed over 80 lines of pottery. The economic depression of the 1930s brought more lines, including Pine Cone.

In the 1940s a series of high-gloss glazes were tried to revive certain lines. In 1952 Raymor dinnerware was produced. None of these changes brought economic success. In November 1954 Roseville was bought by the Mosaic Tile Company.

References: John W. Humphries, *A Price Guide To Roseville Pottery By The Numbers,* published by author, 1993; Sharon and Bob Huxford, *The Collectors Encyclopedia Of Roseville Pottery,* First Series, (1976, 1993 value update), Second Series (1980, 1993 value update), Collector Books; Dana G. Morykan and Harry L. Rinker, *Warman's Country Antiques & Collectibles, Second Edition,* Wallace–Homestead, 1994.

Collectors' Clubs: American Art Pottery Association, 125 E. Rose Ave., St. Louis, MO 63119; Roseville's of the Past, PO Box 681117, Orlando, FL 32868.

Additional Listings: See *Warman's Americana & Collectibles* for more examples.

Ashtray
Corinthian, 2″ h		65.00
Zephyr Lily, blue		70.00

Basket
Apple Blossom, green, 310–10		140.00
Bittersweet, 10″ d, 810		110.00
Bleeding Heart, 10″ d, 360		135.00
Columbine, 365–7		135.00

Gardenia, 8″ d, 608		75.00
Imperial I, 6″ d		75.00
Iris, blue, 10″ d		95.00
Ixia, blue, 10″ h, 346		150.00
Jonquil, hanging		320.00
Magnolia, blue, 8″ h, 384		110.00
Rozane, pink, 6″ d		110.00

Bookends, pr, Pine Cone, blue 150.00

Bowl
Blackberry, 8″ d		175.00
Bushberry, green, 411–4		55.00
Cherry Blossom, 6″ d		225.00
Clematis, blue–green, 445–4		35.00
Dahlrose, oval, handle, 10″ l		100.00
Florane, orange and black, 8″ d		45.00
Fuchsia, 4″ d, 346		55.00
Gardenia, 4″ d, 600		35.00
La Rose, 6″ d		50.00
Luffa, 4″ d		75.00
Pinecone, 3″ d, 632		55.00
Water Lily, 3″ d, 663		35.00
Zephyr Lily, blue, 8″ l, 474		80.00

Candleholder, pr
Blackberry, 4½″ h		300.00
Cremona, 4½″ h		50.00
Earlam, blue, 6″ h		65.00
Foxglove, 4½″ h, 1150		125.00
Tuscany, 4″ h		45.00

Candlestick, pr
Carnelian II		125.00
Rozane, blue, 6″ h		65.00
Velmoss Scroll, 8″ h		150.00

Compote
Corinthian, 10″ d		80.00
Florentine, ftd, 10″ d		85.00

Console Bowl
Blackberry, 13″ d		225.00
Pine Cone, 15″ d, 323		200.00
Wisteria, 12″ d		250.00

Cornucopia
Bushberry, green, 153–6		40.00
Snowberry, blue, 6″ h, 1CC		40.00

Ewer
Bittersweet, 816–8		75.00
Clematis, blue, 17–10		100.00
Freesia, blue, 15″ h		350.00
Magnolia, blue, 13–6		55.00
Peony, golden yellow, 8–10		130.00
Rozane, 10″ h, hp, sgd, c1900		175.00
White Rose, 10″ h, 990		175.00
Zephyr Lily, green, 15″ h, 24		200.00

Flower Frog
Donatello		10.00
White rose, 41		30.00

Flowerpot and Saucer
Bushberry, 5″ h		175.00
Donatello, imp mark, 5″ h		125.00

Jardiniere
Baneda, 9½″ h		450.00
Cherry Blossom, 10″ h		550.00
Dogwood, 8″ h		275.00
Rozane		310.00

Pitcher
Bleeding Heart, 1323	....	150.00
Fuchsia, 8" h, 1322	....	250.00
Pine Cone, 9" h, 415	....	300.00
White Rose, 1324	....	75.00

Planter
Bittersweet, 6" d, 808	....	65.00
Futura, 7" l	....	175.00
Magnolia, blue, 8" l, 389	....	75.00
Pine Cone, 8" l, 468	....	100.00
Thornapple, 5" l, 262	....	55.00
Spittoon, ivory, 5" h, ink stamp mark	.	150.00
Urn, Sunflower, black paper label, 5½" h	....	300.00

Vase, Silhouette, fan shaped, green, No. 783, 7" h, $165.00.

Vase
Apple Blossom, green, 381–6	....	65.00
Baneda, 8" h	....	250.00
Blackberry, 12½" h	....	800.00
Carnelian II, red, 5" h	....	95.00
Cherry Blossom, 10" h	....	300.00
Corinthian, 6" h	....	60.00
Dahlrose, sq, 10" h	....	150.00
Donatello, gray and beige, 10" h	..	275.00
Foxglove, green, 16" h	....	350.00
Futura, 8" h, 427–8	....	300.00
Luffa, 7" h	....	125.00
Morning Glory, 7" h	....	200.00
Mostique, 10" h	....	125.00
Pine Cone, blue, paper label, 8" h	.	250.00
Primrose, 8" h, 765	....	150.00
Rozane, 15" h, hp, sgd, c1900	....	175.00
Snowberry, bud, blue, 7" h, 1BV	..	40.00
Sunflower, bulbous, curved handles, 5" h	....	175.00
Thornapple, blue, 6" h, 812	......	45.00
Topeo, 9½" h	....	175.00
Tuscany, pink, 8" h	....	75.00
Water Lily, 10" h, 81	....	110.00
Wisteria, 7" h	....	275.00
Zephyr Lily, green, 131–7	......	40.00

Wall Pocket
Dogwood II, double	....	155.00
Florentine, 7" h	....	85.00
Freesia, blue	....	125.00
Peony, blue, 8" h, 1293	....	135.00

BAVARIA

ROYAL BAYREUTH

History: In 1794 the Royal Bayreuth factory was founded in Tettau, Bavaria. Royal Bayreuth introduced its figural patterns in 1885. Designs of animals, people, fruits, and vegetables decorated a wide array of tablewares and inexpensive souvenir items.

Tapestry ware, rose and other patterns, were made in the late 19th century. The surface of the ware feels and looks like woven cloth. Tapestry ware was made by covering the porcelain with a piece of fabric tightly stretched over the surface, decorating the fabric, glazing the piece, and firing.

The Royal Bayreuth crest mark varied in design and color. Many wares were unmarked. It is difficult to verify the chronological years of production due to the lack of records.

Royal Bayreuth still manufactures dinnerware. It has not maintained production of earlier wares, particularly the figural items.

References: Susan and Al Bagdade, *Warman's English & Continental Pottery & Porcelain, Second Edition,* Wallace-Homestead, 1991; Mary J. Mc-Caslin, *Royal Bayreuth: A Collector's Guide,* Antique Publications, 1993.

Collectors' Club: Royal Bayreuth International Collectors' Society, PO Box 325, Orrville, OH 44667.

Corinthian
Chamberstick, 4½" h, enameled Grecian figures, black ground.	55.00
Creamer and Sugar, classical figures, black ground.	75.00
Pitcher, 12" h, red ground, pinched spout	225.00
Salt and Pepper Shakers, pr, 3½" h, mythological scene, black satin ground, blue mark	110.00
Toothpick Holder, three handles	95.00
Vase, 9" h, green ground	295.00

Devil and Cards
Creamer, 3¾" h 185.00
Mug, large 295.00
Salt, master 325.00
Lobster
Celery Tray, 12½" l, figural, blue mark. 245.00
Creamer, figural 140.00
Pitcher, 7¾" h, figural, orange–red, green handle. 175.00
Salt and Pepper Shakers, pr 125.00

Plate, 7¾" d, Rose Tapestry pattern, multicolored, gold trim, marked, $150.00.

Miscellaneous Patterns
Bowl, 6" d, multicolored tavern scene 95.00
Creamer, figural
Bird of Paradise 230.00
Fish Head 165.00
Owl 350.00
Cup and Saucer, multicolored tavern scene 90.00
Hatpin Holder, courting couple, cutout base with gold dec, blue mark. . . . 395.00
Mug, 5¾" h, tavern scene 125.00
Pitcher
4" h, multicolored hunting scene . 70.00
5½" h, elk head 210.00
Plate, 6¼" d, musicians 60.00
Pot, cov, miniature, handle, pheasant scene. 150.00
Ring Box, cov, pheasant scene, glossy finish 75.00
Toothpick, Brittany Girl, 3 ftd, blue mark. 150.00
Vase
3½" h, peasant ladies and sheep

scene, silver rim, three handles, blue mark. 50.00
4¼" h, multicolored donkey and boy scene 95.00
6" h, orange and black sunset and cottage scene. 210.00
Nursery Rhyme
Bell, Ring Around The Rosey, children dancing. 295.00
Planter, Jack and the Beanstalk, round, orig liner 225.00
Plate
6½" d, Jack and the Beanstalk, blue mark 145.00
7½" d, Little Bo Peep, blue mark 85.00
Poppy
Chocolate Set, chocolate pot and three cups, figural, red, price for four piece set. 700.00
Sand Babies, inkwell, babies skipping rope, blue mark. 325.00
Snow Babies
Bowl, 6" d 325.00
Creamer, gold trim 90.00
Milk Pitcher, corset shape 175.00
Tea Tile, 6" sq, blue mark 90.00
Vase, 5½" h 145.00
Sunbonnet Babies
Cake Plate, 10¼" d, babies washing 400.00
Cup and Saucer, babies fishing . . . 225.00
Demitasse Cup and Saucer, babies cleaning 275.00
Dish
7" d, babies washing 135.00
8" d, babies ironing, ruffled edge, blue mark. 165.00
Fruit Bowl, 9¾" d, babies washing and hanging wash 90.00
Mustard Pot, babies sweeping, blue mark. 395.00
Tea Tile, babies fishing, blue mark . 195.00
Tomato
Creamer and Sugar, figural, blue mark. 65.00

ROSE TAPESTRY

Bowl, 10½" d, pink and yellow roses . 675.00
Cache Pot, 2¾" h, 3¼" d, ruffled top, gold handles. 200.00
Creamer, 4" h, three color roses, pinched spout, blue mark. 150.00
Hairpin Box, pink and white 235.00
Nut Dish, 3¼" d, 1¾" h, three color roses, gold feet, green mark. 160.00
Pitcher, 5¾" h, pink roses 420.00
Plate, 6" d, three color roses, blue mark 145.00
Ring Box, cov, 3" l, triangular, puffy top, blue mark. 295.00
Tray, 7¾" l, three color roses, handled, blue mark. 225.00

TAPESTRY, MISCELLANEOUS

Box, 3¾" l, 2" w, courting couple, multicolored, blue mark. 235.00
Chocolate Pot, pastoral scene, moun-
tain goats 425.00
Ewer, 3½" h, scene of two ladies at
pond, multicolored, blue and green
ground, gold trim. 135.00
Hatpin Holder, scene of swimming
swans and sunset, saucer base, blue
mark 245.00
Pitcher, formal garden scene, lady and
cavalier 425.00
Tumbler, 4" h, barrel shape, blue mark
Castle in mountains scene 195.00
Gazebo, deer standing in stream,
foliage. 195.00

Bonn
1920

ROYAL BONN

History: In 1836 Franz Anton Mehlem founded
a Rhineland factory that produced earthenware
and porcelain, including household, decorative,
technical, and sanitary items. In 1890 the name
Royal was added to the mark. All items made after
1890 include the name "Royal Bonn." The firm reproduced Hochst figures between 1887 and 1903.
These figures, produced in both porcelain and earthenware, were made from the original molds from
the defunct Prince-Electoral Mayence Manufactory
in Hochst. The factory was purchased by Villeroy
and Boch in 1921 and closed in 1931.

Reference: Susan and Al Bagdade, *Warman's
English & Continental Pottery & Porcelain, Second
Edition*, Wallace-Homestead, 1991.

Cake Plate, 10¼" d, dark blue floral
transfer 20.00
Cheese Dish, cov, multicolored floral
dec, cream ground, gold trim 75.00
Cup and Saucer, relief luster flowers,
marked. 30.00
Ewer, 12½" h, hp bird, orchids, and dragonfly, gold lizard handle 175.00
Marmalade Jar, 5" h, floral dec, beige
ground, SP cov and bail handle 65.00
Plate
8½" d, red and white roses, green
leave, earthtone ground, crazing,
c1900 . . . . 15.00
9" d, floral dec, gilt traces 60.00
10¼" d, fisherman in river, trees and
cliffs landscape, relief scrollwork
border, c1860 . . . . 12.00

**Teapot, red, black, and light blue floral
dec, gold finial and trim, marked "1755"
in crowned cartouche and "Bonn," 4½"
h, $65.00.**

Tea Tile, 7" d, hp pink, yellow, and purple pansies, white ground, green border, marked "Bonn–Rhein". 25.00
Urn, cov, 13" h, hp multicolored flowers,
green and yellow ground, two gold
handles, artist sgd. 100.00
Vase
7¼" h, four magenta roses, shaded
yellow to rust ground, single rose on
reverse, marked "Royal Bonn" . . . 225.00
8¼" h, portrait of lad with wreath of
roses in hair, gold emb dec, brown
and gold shaded ground, artist sgd
"G Muller". 550.00
9½" h, multicolored flowers reserve,
red ground, gold trim, two small
handles on neck 175.00
12" h, multicolored bird and iris
design. 85.00
14" h, pear shape, hp rose and leaf
design, cream ground, two animal
head handles, round base with supports, marked "FM" 350.00

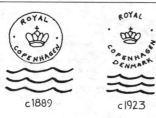

c1889   c1923

Figure, Oriental couple, #1847, 8½" h, $675.00.

ROYAL COPENHAGEN

History: Franz Mueller established a porcelain factory at Copenhagen in 1775. When bankruptcy threatened in 1779, the Danish king acquired ownership, appointing Mueller manager and adopting the name "Royal Copenhagen." The crown sold its interest in 1867; the company remains privately owned today.

Blue Fluted, Royal Copenhagen's most famous pattern, was created in 1780. It is of Chinese origin and comes in three styles: smooth edge, closed lace edge, and perforated lace edge (full lace). Many other factories copied it. Flora Danica, named for a famous botanical work, was introduced in 1789 and remained exclusive to Royal Copenhagen. Botanical illustrations were done freehand; all edges and perforations were cut by hand.

Royal Copenhagen porcelain is marked with three wavy lines (which signify ancient waterways) and a crown (added in 1889). Stoneware does not have the crown mark.

Reference: Susan and Al Bagdade, *Warman's English & Continental Pottery & Porcelain, Second Edition,* Wallace-Homestead, 1991.

Additional Listing: See Limited Edition Collector Plates.

Bowl, 10" w, cupid on chariot pulled by three maidens. 375.00
Butter Pat, Symphony pattern, price for set of six 18.00
Candlestick, pr, 9" h, blue floral design, white ground, bisque lion heads, floral garlands. 150.00
Cup and Saucer, Floral Danica pattern, price for set of twelve. 7,150.00
Dinner Service, partial, Floral Danica

pattern, compote, six cups and saucers, eight dinner plates, three salad plates, pierced serving bowl, round platter, rect platter, price for set 14,850.00
Figure
  4" l, Scottie dog, green slipper in mouth, No. 3476 . . . . 85.00
  6¾" h, girl knitting, No. 1314 . . . . . 350.00
  8½" h, fawns on fluted columns, rabbit and lizard below, price for pair. . . . 355.00
  9" h, mermaid on rock, cream, gray base, No. 4431 . . . . 850.00
Fish Plate, 10" d, different fish swimming among marine plants, molded and gilt border, light green highlighting, gilt dentil edge, crown circular mark, price for set of ten. 8,250.00
Inkwell, Blue Fluted pattern, matching tray 125.00
Pickle Tray, 9" l, Half Lace pattern, blue triple wave mark 65.00
Pitcher, 4" h, floral dec, cobalt blue ground. 50.00
Plate
  6½" d, blue and white lace pattern, blue triple wave mark, 1786 . . . . . 45.00
  7½" d, salad, Flora Danica pattern, botanical specimen, molded gilt border, dentil edge, blue triple wave and green crown mark, price for set of six 3,575.00
  7⅝" d, salad, Flora Danica pattern, pink and green, gilt dentil rim, underglaze blue triple wave mark, price for set of twelve. 3,575.00
  10" d, dinner, Flora Danica pattern, botanical specimen, molded gilt border, dentil edge, pink highlights, blue triple wave and green crown circular mark, black enamel titles,

model number, and artists' marks, price for set of six 440.00

Platter, Flora Danica pattern
13″ d, flower specimen, shaped pierced border with gilt accents, blue wave mark 550.00
18″ l, oval, botanical specimen, sloping border, blue triple wave and green crown circular mark. 2,200.00

Salad Bowl, 9⅞″ d, Flora Danica pattern, botanical specimen, molded gilt border, dentil edge, pink highlights, blue triple wave and green crown mark. . . 825.00

Sauceboat and Stand, 9¼″ l, oval, fish design, two applied handles, gray ground, attached stand, blue wave mark 395.00

Soup Plate, 9½″ d, scalloped rim, pierced lattice border, three molded cartouche panels with flowers, bouquet of garden flowers, scattered blossoms, and insects, enamel and gilt dec, underglaze blue wave mark, price for set of four 440.00

Teapot, 8½″ h, open lace trim lid, faces on spout and handle 350.00

Tray, 10″ l, Blue Fluted pattern 55.00

Vase
6″ h, coral and gray crackle glaze . 40.00
7″ h, blackberries and blossom design................... 50.00
10″ h, ovoid, blue painted windmill, hilly landscape, c1900 .... 800.00
18″ h, fish, shaded blue ground ... 750.00

ROYAL CROWN DERBY

History: Derby Crown Porcelain Co., established in 1875 in Derby, England, had no connection with earlier Derby factories which operated in the late 18th and early 19th centuries. In 1890 the company was appointed "Manufacturers of Porcelain to Her Majesty" (Queen Victoria) and from that date has been known as "Royal Crown Derby."

Derby porcelains from 1878 to 1890 carry only the standard crown printed mark. After 1891 the mark carries the "Royal Crown Derby" wording. In the 20th century "Made in England" and "English Bone China" were added to the mark.

A majority of these porcelains, both tableware and figures, were hand decorated. A variety of printing processes were used for additional adornment. Today, Royal Crown Derby is a part of Royal Doulton Tableware, Ltd.

References: Susan and Al Bagdade, *Warman's English & Continental Pottery & Porcelain, Second Edition,* Wallace-Homestead, 1991; John Twitchett and Betty Bailey, *Royal Crown Derby,* Antique Collectors' Club, 1988.

Cup, saucer, and plate, Mikado pattern, blue dec, white ground, marked "XXVII," $35.00.

Creamer, 1½″ h, miniature, cobalt blue, orange, and white floral dec, mark . . 110.00

Dinner Set, 12 dinner plates, 11 soup plates, 12 salad plates, 12 bread and butter plates, 14 tea cups, and 18 saucers, exotic bird pattern, blue, price for 79 piece set 1,450.00

Dish, 9″ d, scattered rose sprays, floral border, late 18th C. 150.00

Ewer, 7½″ h, cobalt blue, profuse gold gilt and floral dec, sgd 200.00

Mug, grapes and vines dec, blue and gold 130.00

Plate, luncheon
8½″ d, Imari pattern, shaped rim, printed and imp marks, c1923, price for set of twelve 330.00
9″ d, Imari palette, price for set of eight. 500.00

Potpourri, 6″ h, urn form, mounted masks, allover floral and gilt dec, pierced top with finial. 75.00

Sauce Dish, Imari pattern, iron red, co-

balt blue, and burnished gilt, matching
stand, price for pair **1,200.00**
Tea Set, teapot, sugar, two cake trays,
13 cake plates, 11 tea cups and saucers, and 10 demitasse cups with 12
saucers, red, blue, and gold Imari
floral dec, price for 50 piece set **2,200.00**
Toothpick Holder, 3½″ h, green, hp floral
reserve. **135.00**
Urn, 11½″ h, cobalt blue, red, and gold
floral pattern, painted red crown
mark **400.00**
Vase
7″ h, dark red and gold, handled,
c1884 . . . . **185.00**
13″ h, raised gold floral and scroll dec,
blue and red ground, gold handles,
ftd, marked "Royal Crown Derby,"
price for pair **410.00**

ROYAL
DOULTON
FLAMBE

ROYAL DOULTON

History: Doulton pottery began in 1815 under
the direction of John Doulton at the Doulton &
Watts pottery in Lambeth, England. Early output
was limited to salt-glazed industrial stoneware.
John Watts retired in 1854. The firm became Doulton and Company and production was expanded
to include hand-decorated stoneware, such as figurines, vases, dinnerware, and flasks. In 1872 the
firm began marking its ware "Royal Doulton."

In 1878, John's son, Sir Henry Doulton, purchased Pinder Bourne & Co. in Burslem and the
companies became Doulton & Co., Ltd., in 1882.
Decorated porcelain was added to Doulton's earthenware production in 1884. The Royal Doulton
mark was used on both wares.

Most Doulton figurines were produced at the Burslem plants from 1890 until 1978, when they were
discontinued. A new line of Doulton figurines was
introduced in 1979.

Beginning in 1913, an "HN" number was assigned to each new Doulton figurine design. The
"HN" numbers refer to Harry Nixon, a Doulton artist. "HN" numbers were chronological until 1940,
after which blocks of numbers were assigned to
each modeler. From 1928 until 1954, a small number appeared to the right of the crown mark; this
number added to 1927 gives the year of manufacture of the figurines.

Dickens ware, in earthenware and porcelain,
was introduced in 1908. The ware was decorated
with characters from Charles Dickens's novels. The
line was withdrawn in the 1940s, except for plates,
which continued until 1974.

Character jugs, a 20th-century revival of early
Toby models, were designed by Charles J. Noke
for Doulton in the 1930s. They come in four major
sizes and feature fictional characters from Dickens,
Shakespeare, and other English and American
novelists, as well as historical heroes.

Doulton's Rouge Flambee (also Veined Sung) is
a highly glazed, strong-colored ware noted most
for the fine modeling and exquisite colorings, especially in the animal items. The process used to
produce the vibrant colors in this ware is a Doulton
secret.

Production of stoneware at Lambeth ceased in
1956; production of porcelain continues today at
Burslem.

References: Susan and Al Bagdade, *Warman's
English & Continental Pottery & Porcelain, Second
Edition,* Wallace–Homestead, 1991; Jean Dale,
*The Charlton Standard Catalogue of Royal Doulton
Figurines, Third Edition,* Charlton Press, 1993;
Jean Dale, *The Charlton Standard Catalogue of
Royal Doulton Jugs,* Charlton Press, 1991; Louise
Irvine, *Royal Doulton Bunnykins Figures,* UK Inter-
national Ceramics, 1991; Jocelyn Lukins, *Collect-
ing Royal Doulton Character & Toby Jugs,* Venta
Books, 1985; Kevin Pearson, *The Character Jug
Collectors Handbook, Fifth Edition,* Kevin Francis
Publishing, 1991; Kevin Pearson, *The Doulton Fig-
ure Collectors Handbook, Third Edition,* Kevin
Francis Publishing, 1993; Ruth M. Pollard, *The Of-
ficial Price Guide To Royal Doulton, Sixth Edition,*
House of Collectibles, 1988; Princess and Barry
Weiss, *The Original Price Guide to Royal Doulton
Discontinued Character Jugs, Sixth Edition,* Har-
mony Books, 1987.

Periodicals: *Collecting Doulton,* BBR Publishing, 2 Strafford Avenue, Elsecar, Barnsley, S. Yorkshire, England S74 8AA; *Doulton Divvy,* PO Box
2434, Joliet, IL 60434.

Collectors' Clubs: Heartland Doulton Collectors, PO Box 2434, Joliet, IL 60434; Mid–America
Doulton Collectors, PO Box 483, McHenry, IL
60050; Royal Doulton International Collectors
Club, PO Box 6705, Somerset, NJ 08873; Royal
Doulton International Collectors Club, 850 Progress Ave., Scarborough, Ontario, Canada M1H
3C4.

Animal Mold, 12½″ l, fish, Flambe ware **800.00**
Beaker, coronation, majolica style dec,
silver rims, 1902 London hallmarks,
price for pair **165.00**
Bowl, 7¾″ d, 3⅜″ h, Dickens ware, three
characters, marked **145.00**
Character Jug, large
Cardinal **140.00**
Guy Fawkes, Canadian **165.00**

Figure, The Judge, HN2443, 6″ h, $225.00.

Poacher, D6781	350.00
Veteran Motorist	120.00

Character Jug, miniature

Blacksmith	50.00
Pickwick	60.00

Character Jug, small

Mephistopheles	750.00
Pearly King	30.00
Toby Philpots	75.00

Child's Feeding Dish, Bunnykins in country store. ... 135.00

Cuspidor, 7″ h, Isaac Walton ware, polychrome dec, transfer printed, fisherman on ext., verses on int. lip, printed mark ... 315.00

Dinnerware

Arcadia pattern, white, scalloped border, polychrome floral design, 12 dinner plates, 10 luncheon plates, 12 bread and butter plates, 10 cups and saucers, price for 54 pieces .. 440.00

Coventry pattern, service for eight, price for 40 piece set ... 250.00

Covington pattern, cov teapot, 8 bread and butter plates, 8 dessert plates, 6 cups and saucers, price for 29 pieces ... 195.00

English Renaissance pattern, service for twelve, price for set ... 425.00

Floradora, 4 dinner plates, 4 luncheon plates, 4 coffee cups and saucers, price for 16 pieces ... 55.00

Figure

Blyth Morning, HN2021	165.00
Curly Locks, HN2049	380.00
Fair Lady, HN2193	180.00
Fleur, HN2368	210.00
Flora, HN2349	210.00
Grand Manor, HN2723	225.00
Jennifer, HN2392	210.00
Kate Hardcastle, 8″ h, HN2028	195.00
Lobsterman, The, 7″ h, HN2317	110.00
Mask Seller, The	140.00
Memories, HN2030	460.00
Minuet, HN2019	310.00
Teatime	135.00
Tiger, crouching, Rouge Flambe #111	600.00

Fish Plates

9″ d

Set of 10, swimming fish centers, gild bands and rims, pale yellow ground, sgd "J. Hallmark," price for set ... 700.00

Set of 12, different fish centers, gilt rim, one repaired, price for set .. 490.00

9½″ d, set of 12, different fish scene centers, sgd "J. Birbeau Sen.," price for set. ... 1,100.00

Humidor, cov, 6″ h, Chang ware, squatty, molded ribs, brilliant shades of red, blue, yellow, and white, thick crackle finish, sgd in overglaze "Chang/Royal/Doulton" and "Noke" with monogram, c1925. ... 1,955.00

Jar, cov, 7″ h, raised hunt scene and dogs reserves. ... 150.00

Pitcher

6⅛″ h, continuous Venice scene dec 200.00

12½″ h, Coaching Days series, continuous scene with coach attendants stopping at woods, dark green rims. ... 250.00

Plate, 10½″ d, set of 24, Gibson Girl, black transfer, each with different titled scene from orig Charles D Gibson drawings, reserve center, transfer printed cobalt blue stylized foliage border, printed lion and crown mark, c1901, price for set ... 1,320.00

Tankard, 9½″ h, hinged pewter lid, incised frieze of herons among reeds, blue slip enamel, imp mark, sgd, int. rim chip, c1875. ... 1,430.00

Teacup and Saucer, cobalt, heavy gold dec ... 95.00

Teapot, cov, 5½″ h, formed spout, incised frieze of goats, blue dec stiff leaf and floret border, imp mark, sgd, dated 1880. ... 1,540.00

Tobacco Jar, cov, 8″ h, plated rim, handle, and cov, incised frieze of cattle, goats, and donkeys, imp mark, sgd, worn plating, dated 1880 ... 990.00

Toby Jug, 9″ h, Winston Churchill, #8360 ... 90.00

Umbrella Stand

23½″ h, stoneware, enamel dec, applied floral medallions within diamond formed panels, framed by button motifs, imp mark, glaze crazing, c1910. ... 500.00

24" h, blue and white pottery, fan form, chinoiserie dec, hairlines, 19th C . . **715.00**

Vase

7¼" h, Shakespearean series, Hamlet, cream colored ground, green rims **35.00**

8" h, baluster shape, floral relief dec, price for pair **165.00**

10½" h, Edward VII commemorative **85.00**

11¾" h, cov, Athenic pattern, baluster form, red glaze, acorn and leaf dec, silver mounted neck, sweeping scroll handle, foliate thumb piece, hinged lid, ftd, Gorham Mfg Co, Providence, c1905 . . . . **1,430.00**

18½" h, baluster form, panels dec with orange tiger lilies and yellow daisies, divided by green scrolling vines, design repeated on neck, dark blue green ground, artist sgd "EJG" and "184," price for pair **1,100.00**

ROYAL DUX

History: Royal Dux porcelain was made in Dux, Bohemia (Czechoslovakia), by E. Eichler at the Duxer Porzellan–Manufaktur, established in 1860. Many items were exported to the United States. By the turn of the century Royal Dux figurines, vases, and accessories were captivating consumers, especially Art Nouveau designs.

A raised triangle with an acorn and the letter "E" plus Dux, Bohemia was used as a mark between 1900 and 1914.

Reference: Susan and Al Bagdade, *Warman's English & Continental Pottery & Porcelain, Second Edition*, Wallace–Homestead, 1991.

Centerpiece, figural

13½" l, oval, swans, sailboat, and boy and girl at each end **275.00**

14¾" h, standing maiden with arms folded across her breast, wearing voluminous green gown continuing to dish, glazed pink and cream, gilt highlights, imp factory mark, No. 1313, c1900 . . . . **920.00**

17¼" h, conch shell on floral plinth with three maidens wearing gold colored gowns, oval base with leaf dec, gilt highlights, c1900 . . . . **450.00**

Bust, floral headdress, dress highlighted in brown and gold, pink trim, pink triangle, No. 448, 9" h, $385.00.

19" h, two maidens wearing flowing gowns, large stem with one maiden standing on either side, arms raised to support blossom form vessel, pale green, pink, and tan, gilt highlights, imp factory marks and numbers, c1900 . . . . **1,925.00**

Figure

9" h, Victorian couple, lady in brown dress with pink sash, holding flower, man in brown toga with sash, holding palette and ewer, brown sandals, pink triangle mark, minor chips **350.00**

14" h, young Greek athlete standing on backs of two horses **500.00**

Flower Bowl, 9½" d, 9" h, kneeling girl pouring water from jug, wearing pink dress, water lily bowl, pink triangle and acorn mark **650.00**

Jardiniere, 10¼" h, figural, boy and girl, hanging drapery form bowl, polychrome matte finish, repairs **250.00**

Tray, figural, irid blue, center maiden holding basket on her back **300.00**

Vase

11" h, art pottery, green and gold floral dec, lemon ground, #8947IV **60.00**

36" h, Mideastern couple, standing beside palm trees, late 19th C, restoration, one with hairline crack in base, price for pair **715.00**

ROYAL FLEMISH

History: Royal Flemish was produced by the Mount Washington Glass Co., New Bedford, Massachusetts. The process was patented by Albert Steffin in 1894.

Royal Flemish has heavy raised gold enamel lines on frosted transparent glass that separates areas into sections, often colored in russet tones. It gives the appearance of stained-glass windows, with elaborate floral or coin medallions in the design.

Collectors' Club: Mount Washington Art Glass Society, 60 President Ave., Providence, RI 02906.

Advisors: Clarence and Betty Maier.

Biscuit Jar, orange tones, silverplated top, bail handle, 8″ h, $1,750.00.

Ewer, 10½″ h, 8″ w, 5″ d, circular semi–transparent panel on front with youth thrusting spear into chest of winged creature, reverse panel shows mythical fish creature with tail changed into stylized florals, raised gold dec, outlines, and scrolls, rust, purple, and gold curlicues, twisted rope handle with brushed gold encircles neck, hp minute gold florals on neck, burnished gold stripes on rim spout and panels ... **4,950.00**

Jar, 8″ h, classical Roman coin metallic dec, simulated stained glass panels, SP rim, bail, and cov, paper label "Mt. W.G.Co. Royal Flemish" **1,750.00**

Vase

4″ h, orange–amber stained glass window background, gold enameled Griffin and scrolling **1,210.00**

6″ h, double bulbed, frosted, colorful pansies, allover gold enameling. . . **1,210.00**

7½″ h, 7½″ d, squatty, smaller squatty form as collar, fourteen pastel pansies, clear frosted ground, four rayed suns, painted foliage–like gold tracery **1,385.00**

12½″ h, 7½″ d, wild roses, flowers, scrolls, raspberries and floral dec, round medallions with heavily dec raised gold flowers, bright rust colored enameled dec, allover floral and scroll dec on long neck, sgd "Royal Flemish," paper label reads

"pat. applied for Mt. Washington Glass Company" with double headed eagle. **3,700.00**

ROYAL RUDOLSTADT

History: Johann Fredrich von Schwarzburg–Rudolstadt was the patron of a faience factory located in Rudolstadt, Thuringen, Germany, from 1720 to c1790. The pottery's mark was a hayfork and later crossed two–prong hayforks in imitation of the Meissen mark.

In 1854 Ernst Bohne established a factory in Rudolstadt. His pieces are marked "EB."

The "Royal Rudolstadt" designation originated with wares imported by Lewis Straus and Sons (later Nathan Straus and Sons) of New York from the New York and Rudolstadt Pottery between 1887 and 1918. The factory's mark was a diamond enclosing the initials "RW" and which was surmounted by a crown. The factory manufactured several of the Rose O'Neill (Kewpie) items.

Reference: Susan and Al Bagdade, *Warman's English & Continental Pottery & Porcelain, Second Edition,* Wallace–Homestead, 1991.

Bottle, cov, 9¼″ h, gourd form, encrusted flowers, Ernest Bohne Sohne, late 19th or early 20th C, chips, price for pair. **315.00**

Bowl, floral dec, ftd, marked "R. W. Germany". **65.00**

Bust, 15″ h, classical figure, glazed to simulate marble. **150.00**

Cake Plate, 12″ d, pink, white roses, gold handles and trim **75.00**

Candlesticks, pr, 7″ h, ivory, emb acanthus leaves, petal shape cups, crown mark on base **50.00**

Ewer, 10″ h, ivory, floral dec, gold handle and trim **100.00**

Figure

6″ h, muse Polyhymnia, playing lyre, gilt highlights, rockwork base, underglaze blue crossed hayfork mark. **275.00**

8¼″ h, muse Euterpe, wearing classical garb, flowers in hair, lute at her feet, holding scroll of poetry and flute **200.00**

Hatpin Holder, lavender and roses . . **25.00**

Plate, 8⅞" d, ivy leaf dec, gold trim, marked "Germany, R W Rudolstadt," $35.00.

Nut Set, master bowl, six small bowls, white and green roses, fluted, ftd, B under crown mark, price for 7 piece set 250.00
Pitcher, 10" h, floral dec 45.00
Plate, 8½" d, pink, yellow, and white roses, gold molded pie crust rim 30.00
Teapot, cov, 5½" h, ivory, pink, lavender, and green hp floral dec 95.00
Tea Set, child's, cov teapot, creamer, cov sugar, four cups and saucers, and four plates, price for 15 piece set . . . 275.00
Urn
  10" h, mythological scene, Hector and Andro crowning maiden, cobalt blue ground, gold handles, artist sgd, with stand 125.00
  22½" h, baluster form, sculpted classical maidens, lion mask handles, mounted as lamp 725.00
Vase
  4" h, floral dec, elephant handles . . 90.00
  17" h, urn shaped, floral dec, double handles, detachable base, marked "RW Germany" 110.00

1749 -1864

ROYAL VIENNA

History: Production of hard-paste procelain in Vienna began in 1720 with Claude Innocentius du

Paquier, a runaway employee of the Meissen factory. In 1744 Empress Maria Theresa brought the factory under royal patronage; subsequently the ware became known as Royal Vienna. The firm went through many administrative changes until it closed in 1864. The quality of its workmanship always was maintained.

Many other Austrian and German firms copied the Royal Vienna products, including the use of the "Beehive" mark. Many of the pieces on today's market are from these firms.

Reference: Susan and Al Bagdade, *Warman's English & Continental Pottery & Porcelain, Second Edition.* Wallace–Homestead. 1991.

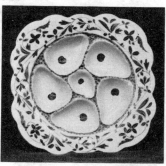

Oyster Plate, six cavities, scalloped edge, shaded light pink, vine and floral motif, gold trim, 9¾" sq, $175.00.

Cabinet Vase
  6" h, oval portrait of maiden, gilt floral dec, irid blue ground, gilt handles 425.00
  7" h, oval reserve of Lemiramis, irid red and black ground, gold encrusted, Eolzner, late 19th C 775.00
Chocolate Pot, cov, 10" h, large reserve with artist decorating a vase, woman looking on, cream ground, gilt handles and trim, Knoeller 325.00
Cup and Saucer, frieze figures and horses dec, cobalt blue border 135.00
Floor Vase, cov, 51" h, classical dec, women bathing, cobalt blue ground, gilt dec 10,000.00
Urn
  4¼" h, double handled, gilt foliate dec, marked "Una Gitana" and beehive mark. 350.00
  13½" h, cov, cupid bound to tree on one, other with cupid in attendance to maiden, maroon ground, gold trim, sq plinth, sgd "Forster," price for pair 1,550.00

18¼" h, two reserves of romantic couple and three muses, cobalt blue ground, gold trim, sq plinth, two handles **880.00**

19¾" h, two winged female cat handles, reserve of king and subjects examining sphere, emerald green ground with gild dec, sgd "C. Forster," crack in base **1,250.00**

30" h, cov, gilt intertwined serpent handles, gilt scroll dec and band and classical figures on cobalt blue ground, square plinth painted with figural reserves on two sides, repaired, c1900 . . . . **4,000.00**

Vase

3" h, children of four seasons dec, blue beehive mark **250.00**

3½" h, Meditation, artist sgd "Wagner," beehive mark **395.00**

8" h, portrait, Art Nouveau young woman surrounded by rococo swirls and emb flowers, pale yellow, brown, and purple ground, two handles **150.00**

10¼" h, cov, maiden portrait, green ground, gilt handles and trim, c1900 . . . . **375.00**

and R. W. Binns formed a new company and revived the ornamental wares.

In 1862 the firm became the Royal Worcester Porcelain Co. Among the key modelers of the late 19th century were James Hadley, his three sons, and George Owen, an expert at pierced clay pieces. Royal Worcester absorbed the Grainger factory in 1889 and the James Hadley factory in 1905. Modern designers include Dorothy Boughty and Doris Lindner.

References: Susan and Al Bagdade, *Warman's English & Continental Pottery & Porcelain, Second Edition,* Wallace–Homestead, 1991; David, John, and Henry Sandon, *The Sandon Guide To Royal Worcester Figures, 1900–1970,* Alderman Press, 1987; Henry Sandon, *The Dictionary of Worcester Porcelain, Volume II: 1852 To The Present Day,* Antique Collectors' Club; John Sandon, *The Dictionary of Worcester Porcelain, Volume I: 1751–1851,* Antique Collectors' Club.

Museum: Charles William Dyson Perrins Museum, Worcester, England.

Figure, November, 7½" h, $175.00.

c1876-1891

1891

ROYAL WORCESTER

History: In 1751 the Worcester Porcelain Company, led by Dr. John Wall and William Davis, acquired the Bristol pottery of Benjamin Lund and moved it to Worcester. The first wares were painted blue under the glaze, followed closely by painting on the glaze in enamel colors. Among the most famous 18th-century decorators were James Giles and Jefferys Hamet O'Neale. Transfer–print decoration was developed by the 1760s.

A series of partnerships took over upon Davis's death in 1783: Flight (1783–93), Flight & Barr (1793–1807), Barr, Flight & Barr (1807–13), and Flight, Barr & Barr (1813–40). In 1840 the factory was moved to Chamberlain & Co. in Diglis. Decorative wares were discontinued. In 1852 W. H. Kerr

Cake Compote, three gold floral panels, cream ground, gilt and floral base . . . **210.00**

Candelabra, 11½" h, Queen Anne, three branch, tree form holders surrounded by boy, girl, and pug dog, shape #787, printed and imp mark, restorations, c1887 . . . . **220.00**

Candlesticks, pr, 10½" h, spiral columnar form, shape #1050, printed and imp marks, gilt and glaze ware, c1884 . . . . **550.00**

Dinnerware, painted gilt spirals on cobalt blue bands, gilt rims, 12 dinner plates, 12 soup plates, 12 dessert plates, 12 salad plates, 12 bread and butter plates, 12 cups and saucers, creamer, sugar bowl, 7 demitasse cups and saucers, gravy boat with underplate, 3 cov vegetable tureens, and 5 graduated platters, price for 91 piece set 850.00

Dish, 6" h, nautilus shell on coral support, 1867, slight chips, price for pair 660.00

Ewer, 7¼" h, floral dec, ivory matte glaze, bronzed and gilt winged serpent form handle............. 190.00

Figure
3⅜" h, Watteau, seated female figure playing lute, shape #547, printed and imp marks, c1900 .... 350.00

6¼" h, musicians, resting on tree trunks, one playing horn, other with tambourine, printed marks, c1953, price for pair 220.00

8" h, lady, standing, wearing hand muff, shape #1016, imp marks, c1884.................... 350.00

8½" h, gentleman, standing, holding monocle, George II style costume, shape #1016, printed and imp marks, c1886.................. 330.00

9¾" h, boy and girl with waterpot and pitcher, shape #1046, printed and imp mark, sgd "Hadley," boy restored, c1884................ 275.00

10" h, Sorrow, holding dead bird, shape #58, printed mark, base restored, c1893................ 150.00

26½" h, redware, The Bather Surprised, standing by tree, rect base with cut corners, imp on back "T. Brock, London 1868," factory mark under base, one hand restored at finger, base rim chip, minor nicks, c1868.................... 1,100.00

Jar, cov, 15" h, soft beige, purple, lavender, and yellow irises, green leaves, gold highlights, handles, green and gold reticulated cov 100.00

Jug, 10" h, mask spout, molded foliate handle, polychrome bird perched within foliage dec, gilt highlights, shape #1366, printed mark, c1889.. 525.00

Pitcher, 7¾" h, ivory satin glaze, floral dec, gilt loop handle............. 70.00

Planter, 7½ x 10", figural, swan 265.00

Platter, 19¼" l, white ironstone, brown leaf dec 50.00

Service Plate, 10½" d, gold overlay on green and gold border, beige ground, price for set of twelve............ 1,155.00

Soup Plate, Miranda pattern, price for set of twelve................. 275.00

Spill Vase, 4¾" h, molded Oriental landscape scenes, branch handles and feet, pierced top gallery, shape #956, printed mark, gilt rim wear, c1894... 550.00

Tea Set, Oriental water garden scene with birds and butterflies, bronze, silver, and gold dec, teapot, cov sugar with plated rim, creamer, 4 cups and saucers, and 15" d tray, printed and imp marks, minor chips to teapot spout and cov, one saucer with gilt rim retouched, c1883, price for twelve piece set 880.00

Tureen, cov, 15" l, 9" h, rect, blue and gilt dec, elephant shaped handles, raised ft, ladle, price for three pieces 225.00

Vase
5½" h, double, pilgrim, red enamel ground, gold foliage, printed and imp mark, c1877 .... 415.00

9¼" h, everted trumpet shape, scalloped gilt fluted foliate rim, applied gilt foliate scrolls, cream ground, circular stepped base with gilt blossoms on pale blue ground, c1890 . 125.00

11¾" h, cov, floral design with insects, shape #1481, printed and imp marks, one cover restored, gilt wear with retouched rims, c1890, price for pair 330.00

12½" h, baluster, pinched neck, flaring rim, swag and tassel dec on neck, large gilt floral dec on body. . 225.00

13¾" h, bulbous shape, floral dec, phoenix handles, shape #1570, printed marks, gilt wear, wing restored, c1893................ 385.00

18" h, double gourd shape, yellow ground, applied gilt writhing dragon with green glass eyes.......... 1,870.00

ROYCROFT

History: Elbert Hubbard founded the Roycrofters in East Aurora, New York, at the turn of the century. Considered a genius in his day, he was an author, lecturer, manufacturer, salesman, and philosopher.

Hubbard established a campus which included a printing plant where he published *The Philistine*, *The Fra*, and *The Roycrofter*. His most famous book was *A Message to Garcia*, published in 1899. His "community" also included a furniture manufacturing plant, a metal shop, and a leather shop.

References: Nancy Hubbard Brady, *The Book of The Roycrofters*, House of Hubbard, 1977; Nancy Hubbard Brady, *Roycroft Handmade Fur-*

niture, House of Hubbard, 1973; Charles F. Hamilton, *Roycroft Collectibles*, A. S. Barnes & Company, 1980; Kevin McConnell, *Roycroft Art Metal*, Schiffer Publishing, 1990; Paul McKenna, *A New Pricing Guide For Materials Produced by The Roycroft Printing Shop, Second Edition*, Tona Graphics, 1982.

Collectors' Clubs: Foundation for the Study of Arts & Crafts Movement, Roycroft Campus, 31 S. Grove St., East Aurora, NY 14052; Roycrofters–At–Large Association, PO Box 417, East Aurora, NY 14052.

Museum: Elbert Hubbard Library–Museum, East Aurora, NY.

Additional Listings: Arts and Crafts Movement and Copper.

Match Holder, hammered copper, nested ashtray, c1915, 3¼″ h, 3¼″ d, $85.00.

Armchair, 41½″ h, mahogany, five splats, leather upholstered seat, carved orb mark	465.00
Bookends, pr, 3½″ w, 5¼″ h, copper, flat panels with curled crest over repousse flower, logo signature, slight corrosion	95.00
Bookstand, rect overhanging top, two lower shelves, keyed tenons, vertical side slats, ftd base, metal tag, top separation, finish wear, 26¼″ w, 14″ d, 26¼″ h	475.00
Bowl, 10¼″ d, 4⅛″ h, hammered copper, rolled rim, shouldered bowl, three pointed ft, red patina, imp mark, traces of brass wash	440.00
Candle Lamp, blue art glass, baluster form, flaring foot, stamped "Roycroft," electrified	140.00
Desk Set, hammered copper, paper knife, pen tray, stationery holder, perpetual desk calendar, pair of book-	

ends, flower holder, match holder with nested ashtray, c1915, price for set . | **550.00** |
Goodie Box, 23″ w, 12¼″ d, 9¼″ h, mahogany, hinged rect lid, iron hardware, imp logo, cracked back panel, c1910	**385.00**
Magazine Pedestal, No. 080, overhanging sq top, canted sides, keyed tenons, five shelves, carved oak leaf design, maker's mark on sides, top split, edge roughness, wear and worming, c1906.	**3,520.00**
Sideboard, 56″ w, 24″ d, 43″ h, oak, carved crest rail, panel constructed back with plate rack, slab top, central bank with two deep drawers and one shallow drawer, flanked on either side by single shallow drawer over tall open shelf, wrought copper handles and escutcheons.	**4,950.00**
Table Lamp, 15″ h, No. 902, hammered copper and mica, 10″ d dome shade, riveted strapwork over mica band, imp mark, cleaned.	**1,430.00**
Vase	
9½″ h, hammered copper, cylindrical form, fluted rim, band and repeating bellflowers dec, green highlights, imp logo, c1915.	**175.00**
19″ h, 8″ d, No. 201, American Beauty, hammered copper, elongated cylindrical neck with rolled rim, flaring to form top of two part riveted bulbous base, stamped on base, c1920 . . .	**880.00**

RUBENA GLASS

History: Rubena crystal is a transparent blown glass which shades from clear to red. It also is found as the background for frosted and overshot glass. It was made in the late 1800s by several glass companies, including Northwood and Hobbs, Brockunier & Co. of Wheeling, West Virginia.

Rubena was used for several patterns of pattern glass, including Royal Ivy and Royal Oak.

Reference: Ellen T. Schroy, *Warman's Glass*, Wallace-Homestead, 1992.

Butter Dish, cov, Royal Oak, sq, acorn finial, Northwood	**150.00**
Compote, 14″ h, 9″ d, rubena overshot bowl, white metal bronze finished figural standard.	**150.00**
Creamer, Royal Ivy	**125.00**
Cruet, frosted	**375.00**
Decanter, 9″ h, bulbous body, narrow neck, applied clear handle	**150.00**
Pickle Castor, enameled daisy dec, ornate sgd frame with two handles, pickle fork holder in front	**235.00**
Sugar, Royal Oak, frosted	**175.00**
Syrup, frosted	**525.00**

Tumbler, Royal Ivy, 3¾″ h, 2½″ w, $75.00.

Tumbler
Hobnail, frosted, 4″ h 65.00
Medallion Sprig 100.00
Vase, 9½″ h, six crimp gold trim top,
chrysanthemum dec, gold leaves,
price for pair. 275.00

RUBENA VERDE GLASS

History: Rubena Verde, a transparent glass that shades from red in the upper section to yellow-green in the lower, was made by Hobbs, Brockunier & Co., Wheeling, West Virginia, in the late 1880s. It often is found in the inverted thumbprint (IVT) pattern, termed "Polka Dot" by Hobbs.

Reference: Ellen T. Schroy, *Warman's Glass,* Wallace-Homestead, 1992.

Butter Dish, cov, Daisy and Button base,
Thumbprint lid. 225.00
Celery Vase, 6¼″ h, Inverted
Thumbprint. 225.00
Compote, 6″ h, Honeycomb 125.00
Cruet, 6″ h, Hobnail, clear faceted
stopper. 250.00

Pickle Castor, Hobb's Hobnail, SP
frame, cov, and tongs 495.00
Pitcher, 7¼″ h, glossy, bulbous, quatrefoil top, applied amber handle, white
casing, ground polished pontil, Hobbs
Brockunier, c1870. . . . . 850.00
Syrup, 6¾″ h, Inverted Thumbprint, orig
hinged pewter cov. 300.00
Tumbler, Inverted Thumbprint pattern 120.00
Vase, 7″ h, bulbous body, scalloped rim,
enameled floral dec. 225.00

RUBY STAINED GLASS, SOUVENIR TYPE

History: Ruby stained glass was produced in the late 1880s and 1890s by several glass manufacturers, primarily in the area of Pittsburgh, Pennsylvania.

Ruby stained items were made from pressed clear glass which was stained with a ruby red material. Pieces often were etched with the name of a person, place, date, or event and sold as souvenirs at fairs and expositions.

In many cases one company produced the pressed glass blanks and a second company stained and etched them. Many patterns were used, but the three most popular were Button Arches, Heart Band, and Thumbprint.

References: William Heacock, *Encyclopedia of Victorian Colored Pattern Glass, Book 7: Ruby-Stained Glass From A to Z,* Antique Publications, 1986; Ellen T. Schroy, *Warman's Glass,* Wallace-Homestead, 1992.

Reproduction Alert: Ruby staining is being added to many pieces through the use of modern stain-glass coloring kits. A rash of fake souvenir ruby stained pieces was made in the 1960s; the best-known example is the "bad" button arches toothpick.

Tumbler, Button Arches, Carnival, July 29, 1904, J. M. Craig on reverse, 3⅞″ h, 2⅞″ d, $25.00.

Vase, webbed, 4″ h, $225.00.

Bread Tray, Triple Triangle, "Cape Cod" 65.00
Candy Dish, cov, "Columbia Exposition, 1893". 65.00
Creamer, miniature
    Arched Ovals, "Lakemont Park, 1908". 24.00
    Heart Band, "Union City" 22.00
Goblet
    Ruby Thumbprint, "Mother" 30.00
    Shriner Convention, Syria insignia and "Pittsburgh, PA" on front, "St Paul, MN, 1908" on back, words on sides, 5¼" h, 3" d. 100.00
Napkin Ring, Diamond with Peg, "1907". 85.00
Pitcher, tankard, Button Arches, "Pittsburgh" 125.00
Sauce Dish, Cathedral, "Niagara Falls" 20.00
Spooner, York Herringbone, "World's Fair, 1893". 45.00
Toothpick Holder, "1908 Indiana State Fair". 40.00
Tumbler, Dakota, "From Atlantic City" 45.00

ВРАТЬЕВЪ

Baterin's factory
1812-1820

КорНИЛОВЫХЪ

Korniloff's factory
c 1835

RUSSIAN ITEMS

History: During the late 19th and early 20th centuries Russia contained skilled craftsmen in lacquer, silver, and enamel wares. Located mainly in Moscow during the Czarist era (1880–1917) was a group of master craftsmen led by Fabergé, who created exquisite enamel pieces. Fabergé also had an establishment in St. Petersburg and enjoyed the patronage of the Russian Imperial family and royalty and nobility throughout Europe.

Almost all enameling was done on silver. Pieces are signed by the artist and the government assayer.

The Russian Revolution in 1917 brought an abrupt end to the century of Russian craftsmanship. The modern Soviet government has exported some inferior enamel and lacquer work, usually lacking in artistic merit. Modern pieces are not collectible.

References: Vladimir Guliayev, *The Fine Art of Russian Lacquered Miniatures*, Chronicle Books, 1993; A. Kenneth Snowman, *Fabergé: Lost and Found*, Harry N. Abrams, 1993.

Museums: Cleveland Museum of Art, Cleveland, OH; Forbes Magazine Collection, New York, NY; Hillwood, The Marjorie Merriweather Post Collection, Washington, D.C.; Virginia Museum of Fine Arts, Lillian Thomas Pratt Collection, Richmond, VA; Walters Art Gallery, Baltimore, MD.

Advisors: Barbara and Melvin Alpren.

Russian Icon, Our Lady of Kazanskaya, repousse silvered metal riza, 8½ x 10⅜", $325.00.

ENAMELS

Cigarette Case, 3½" l, 2¼" w, 84 standard, silver gilt, robin's egg blue enamel, feathered guilloche ground, opaque white enamel borders, diamond chips on clasp, gilt int., Ivan Britzin, St Petersburg, 1908–17, small losses and chips to enamel 1,200.00
Coffee Spoon, blue dot border in bowl, stylized polychrome enamel foliage, gilt stippled ground, twisted gilt stem, crown finial, G Tokmakov, c1890 ... 290.00
Kovsh, 3" l, silver gilt, Art Nouveau style enameling, pointed prow, hooked handle, Marie Semenova, Moscow, c1900. .... 1,900.00
Letter Opener, 10½" l, cylindrical handle, enameled translucent green guil-

loche ground, overlaid gilt trellis dec,
horse head finial, red cabochon eyes,
seed pearl border, agate blade 895.00
Sugar Spoon, 84 standard, enameled
lavender, sky blue, white, translucent
red, green, and cobalt blue stylized
scrolling foliage, gilt stippled ground,
sky blue enamel dot border, enameled crown finial on stem, I Gubkin,
1893 . . . .   500.00
Tea Spoon, turquoise ground, filigree
cloisons, white enamel dot border, red
and white enamel flower in center of
bowl, red flower on handle, gilt stem,
V Akhimov, 1896. . . . .   290.00
Trinket Box, oval, silver gilt, en plein
enameling, slip—on lid, Moscow,
c1900. . . . .   1,950.00

MISCELLANEOUS

Bronze
Figure, 8½" h, Pirate—Woman, after
Alexei Gratcheff, CF Woeffel
foundry mark, 1889 . . . .   990.00
Group, 11½" h, fox hunter and dogs,
Nicholai Lieberich, late 19th C, sgd
"Sculp Lieberich" and "Fabr CF
Woeffel/St Petersburg". 2,475.00
Glass
Candle Lamp, opaque glass, enameled dec, three handle baluster
form, matching clear shades with
wheel cut dec, ormolu mounts,
price for pair 470.00
Christening Cup, 5½" h, etched,
equestrian figure of Peter the Great,
1905. . . . .   330.00
Jar, cov, 5" h, cut, cobalt blue, ten
sides, gilt dec, price for pair. 990.00
Icon, silver, gilt, and enamel
12¼ x 10¾", Holy Mother and Child,
20th C. 625.00
12½ x 10¼", Mother of God 330.00
Iron, group, 15" h, Cossack rider and
woman, farewell embrace, foundry
marks on base, patinated. 525.00
Papier Mâché
Box, painted winter scene of trokia
pulling sleigh, pre—Revolution, 7" w,
4¼" h, 2" h 200.00
Etagere, 20¼" l, 14" w, 38½" h, ebon-
ized and parcel gilt, top shelf
painted after "Boyar Wedding" over
two open shelves, octagonal
straight legs, shaped feet 1,100.00

PORCELAIN

Bouillon Cup and Saucer, 5" d, AG Popov, Moscow, 19th C, floral designs,
gilt trim, price for set of eight 550.00

Butter Dish, 6" l, modeled as rams, 19th
C, price for pair. 360.00
Coffee Pot, 8" h, attributed to Safronov,
early 19th C, male portraits on gilt
ground, rim damage 440.00
Cup and Saucer
Gardner, F, Moscow, early 20th C, 3"
h, gilt on white designs, price for set
of six 385.00
Imperial Porcelain Factory
Alexander II, c1855–81, Serves
style 220.00
Nicholas I, c1825–55, floral relief   220.00
Kuznetsov, MS
3½" h, floral dec, magenta ground,
reticulated base, price for set of
six. 500.00
4½" h, blue glazed, honoring coro-
nation of Nicholas II, 1878,
hairline. 200.00
5" h, modeled as samovar, cover
with finial damage. 300.00
Dessert Plate, I E Kuznetsov, 19th C,
floral rim, magenta ground, printed
mark, Islamic script, price for set of
six 250.00
Dessert Set, Kornilov Bros, St Peters-
burg, 20th C, twelve 8" d plates, 11" d
round platter, stylized geometric bor-
der, price for thirteen piece set 770.00
Dish, cov, 8" l, M S Kuznetsov, 19th C,
molded as bunch of grapes, grape leaf
underplate, chipped. 385.00
Ewer, 9" h, Markov, 19th C, orange
ground, cov chip 250.00
Figure
7" h, King and Queen, attributed to
Safronov, 19th C, prices for pair . .   440.00
9" h, bisque, F Gardner, Moscow, 19th
C, peasant woman, printed mark. .   550.00
11½" h, bisque, F Gardner, Moscow,
19th C, hunter and child, imp and
stamped marks 770.00
Plate
8½" h, F Gardner, Moscow, c1800,
figural landscape scene, price for
pair. 935.00
9" d, A G Popov, Moscow, 19th C,
bucolic scene, sepia, two chips, one
crack, minor wear, price for set of
ten 660.00
10" d
Catherine II, Imperial Porcelain
Factory, 18th C, floral spray,
white ground 825.00
Paul I, Imperial Porcelain Factory,
c1800, floral spray, white ground   715.00
11" d, F Gardner, Moscow, 19th C,
blue and white, transfer dec, garden
scene, price for pair 315.00
Portrait Plate, 8" d, Safronov, early 19th

C, depicting Empress Elizabeth, hairline. **315.00**
Tankard, 8" h, figural, Turk's head, marked "F. Gardner, Moscow," 19th C, restored. **1,210.00**
Tea Set
Gardner, F, Moscow, 19th C, teapot, five cups and saucers, three bowls, flowers, dark magenta ground, printed mark and Islamic script . . . **525.00**
Popov, A G, Moscow, late 19th C, 4" h teapot, creamer, sugar with stand, five cups and saucers, floral dec, gilt trimmed borders, int. border dec. **935.00**
Vase
9" h, cov, bottle shape, Nicholas II, Imperial Porcelain Factory, St Petersburg, c1900, rococo reserves, blue floral encrusted ground **1,100.00**
10" h, F Gardner, Moscow, 19th C, campagna form, painted scenes, price for pair **1,980.00**
Water Pipe, 19th C, five sections, flowers and portraits, magenta ground . . **175.00**

SILVER

Belt, turquoise links spaced with silver gilt links, large turquoise clasp, hallmarks, 29" l **165.00**
Icon
9½ x 8", Virgin and Child, silver riza Astrakhan, 1799 maker LCB in trefoil, western style. **360.00**
12½ x 10½", Virgin Iverskaya, 18th/ 19th C. **550.00**

SABINO GLASS

History: Sabino glass, named for its creator Ernest Marius Sabino, originated in France in the 1920s and is an art glass which was produced in a wide range of decorative glassware: frosted, clear, opalescent, and colored glass. Both blown and pressed moldings were used. Hand-sculpted wooden molds that were cast in iron were used and are still in use at the present time.

In 1960 the company introduced a line of figurines, 1 to 8 inches high, plus other items in a fiery opalescent glass in the Art Deco style. Gold was added to the batch to attain the fiery glow. These pieces are the Sabino that is most commonly found today. Sabino is marked with the name in the mold, an etched signature, or both.

Blotter, 6" l, rocker type, crossed American and French flags **275.00**
Clock, 6⅛" h, opalescent, arched case, overlapping geometric devices, molded festoons centered by circular

Dragonfly, 6" h, $85.00.

chapter ring, molded "SABINO," c1925. . . . . **1,725.00**
Figure
Butterfly, opalescent, relief molded "Sabino". **20.00**
Fish, large **110.00**
Maiden, 7¾" h, opalescent, draped in contraposto with raised right arm, etched "Sabino Paris" **880.00**
Pekingese, 1¼" h, begging, opalescent, relief molded "Sabino" **25.00**
Rabbit, 1 x 2" **55.00**
Venus de Milo, large **65.00**
Knife Rest, duck **20.00**
Napkin Ring, birds, opalescent **45.00**
Powder Box, small **40.00**
Scent Bottle, Petalia **50.00**
Vase
7½" h, blue, spherical, six indented panels, molded with stylized sunflower blossoms, etched "Sabino France". **1,320.00**
9⅞" h, opalescent, rounded rect form, Art Deco female nude each side, joining hands around vessel, etched "Sabino Paris" **1,870.00**
14⅛" h, opalescent, La Danse, ovoid, molded in high relief, band of cavorting female nudes, inscribed "Sabino Paris," 20th C **3,575.00**

ℂ 𝒮 SALOPIAN

SALOPIAN WARE

History: Salopian ware was made at Caughley Pot Works, Salop, Shropshire, England, in the 18th century by Thomas Turner. The ware is polychrome on transfer. One time classified as Polychrome Transfer, it retains the more popular name of Salopian. Wares are marked with an "S" or "Salopian" impressed or painted under the glaze. Much of it was sold through Turner's Salopian warehouse in London.

Creamer, 6″ h, black transfer, maiden with urn, yellow and burnt orange highlights, black and white frieze, black, white, orange, and yellow floral border around rim, c1790 . . . . **225.00**

Cup and Saucer, handleless, pearlware, polychrome enamels, shepherd transfer, chips and hairlines **100.00**

Cup and Saucer, handleless, bird on branch, 1¾ x 2⅞″ cup, 4¾″ d saucer, $150.00.

Milk Pitcher, 5″ h, black transfer, castle and cows, yellow–gold and blue accents, black and white geometric design int., blue rim, c1790 . . . . **335.00**

Plate, 7¼″ d, white stag center, floral border, black transfer, polychrome enamel accents **110.00**

Serving Dish, 11″ l, blue floral dec, late 18th C **375.00**

Teabowl and Saucer, green transfer, woodchopper on cup, barnyard scene on saucer **110.00**

Teapot, 5⅜″ h, dark brown transfer, milkmaid milking cow in meadow scene, floral dec lid, polychrome accents **150.00**

Waste Bowl, 5″ d, 2½″ h, Britannia, black transfer, polychrome enamel accents, emb ribs **125.00**

SALT AND PEPPER SHAKERS

History: Collecting salt and pepper shakers, whether late-19th-century glass forms or the contemporary figural and souvenir types, is becoming more and more popular. The supply and variety are practically unlimited; the price for most sets is within the budget of cost-conscious young collectors. Finally, their size offers an opportunity to assemble a large collection in a small amount of space.

One can specialize in types, forms, or makers. Great art glass artisans such as Joseph Locke and Nicholas Kopp designed salt and pepper shakers in the normal course of their work. Arthur Goodwin Peterson's *Glass Salt Shakers: 1,000 Patterns* provides the reference numbers given below. Peterson made a beginning; there are hundreds, perhaps thousands, of patterns still to be cataloged.

The clear-colored and colored-opaque sets command the highest prices, clear and white sets the lowest. Although some shakers, e.g., the tomato or fig, have a special patented top and need it to hold value, it is not detrimental to the price to replace the top of a shaker.

The figural and souvenir type is often looked down upon by collectors. Sentiment and whimsy are prime collecting motivations. The large variety and current low prices indicate a potential for long-term price growth.

Generally older shakers are priced by the piece, figural and souvenir types by the set. The pricing method is indicated at each division. All shakers are assumed to have original tops unless noted. Identification numbers are from Peterson's book.

References: Gideon Bosker, *Great Shakes: Salt and Pepper For All Tastes*, Abbeville Press, 1986; Gideon Bosker, *Salt and Pepper Shakers: Identification and Price Guide*, Avon Books, 1994; Melva Davern, *The Collector's Encyclopedia of Salt & Pepper Shakers: Figural And Novelty*, First Series (1985, 1991 value update), Second Series (1990, 1993 value update), Collector Books; Helene Guarnaccia, *Salt & Pepper Shakers*, Vol. I (1985, 1993 value update), Vol. II, (1989, 1993 value update), Vol. III (1991), Vol. IV (1993), Collector Books; Mildred and Ralph Lechner, *The World of Salt Shakers, 2nd Edition*, Collector Books, 1992; Arthur G. Peterson, *Glass Salt Shakers: 1,000 Patterns*, Wallace–Homestead, 1970, out of print; Mike Schneider, *The Complete Salt and Pepper Shaker Book*, Schiffer Publishing, 1993.

Collectors' Clubs: Antique and Art Glass Salt Shaker Collectors Society, 2832 Rapidan Trail, Maitland, FL 32751; Novelty Salt & Pepper Shakers Club, 581 Joy Road, Battle Creek, MI 49017.

Museum: Judith Basin Museum, Stanford, MT.

Additional Listings: See *Warman's Americana & Collectibles* for more examples.

ART GLASS (PRICED INDIVIDUALLY UNLESS OTHERWISE NOTED)

Burmese, 4″ h, branches and leaves dec, metal top, Mt Washington **65.00**

Cockleshell, 2¾″ h, figural, lusterless, ribbed, hp blue, white, and amber enameled floral dec, orig metal shell form top, Mt Washington **140.00**

Squatty, 2″ h, ribbed, leaves and flowers dec, metal top with seven prongs, very

Art Glass, satin, vaseline, enameled daisies, Mount Washington, dated 1889, price for pair, $200.00.

minor roughage around top edge, Mt Washington 105.00

IVORY (PRICED INDIVIDUALLY)

Eskimo, 2⅝" h, walrus, carved, bear's head one side, walrus head other side, seal on top, one bear fang missing, age crack in side, screw–in bottom piece missing 55.00
Italian, 5⅛" l, carved, gilt metal mounted, pipe form, lion head with open mouth, wearing hinged crown, four paw feet, sgd "C Gazza," late 19th C 285.00

OPALESCENT GLASS (PRICED INDIVIDUALLY UNLESS OTHERWISE NOTED)

Bubble Lattice, mold blown, cranberry, orig tops, price for pair 325.00
Coin Spot, cylindrical, cranberry, orig top 100.00
Hobnail, cranberry, orig top, price for pair 58.00
Leaf Umbrella, cased blue, orig top, Northwood 75.00
Seaweed, Hobbs, cranberry 45.00
Twelve Panel, 2⅞" h, robin's egg blue, pink carnations, mold blown, orig lid, Pairpoint, c1895–1900 . . . . 95.00

OPAQUE GLASS (PRICED INDIVIDUALLY UNLESS OTHERWISE NOTED)

Argonaut Shell, custard, orig tops, Northwood, price for pair 350.00
Inverted Fan & Feather, custard, orig tops, Northwood, price for pair 495.00
Panelled Sprig pattern, milk white, color trim, orig tops, Northwood, price for pair 150.00
Ribbed Drape, custard, orig tops, Jefferson, price for pair 175.00

Ring Band, custard, orig top, undecorated, Heisey 55.00
Ring Neck Mold, tall cylinder shape, white, cat sitting in foliage gazing at spider web dec, Wave Crest 195.00
Sunset, 3" h, white, Dithridge 30.00

PATTERN GLASS (PRICED INDIVIDUALLY UNLESS OTHERWISE NOTED)

Bulging Loops, pigeon blood, orig tops, price for pair 175.00
Cosmos, milk white, molded blossoms, blue band dec, orig tops, Consolidated Lamp and Glass Co, price for pair 125.00
Klondike, frosted, amber cross, orig tops, price for pair 100.00
Maine, stippled flower panels, orig tops, price for pair 65.00
Michigan, enameled dec, orig top . . . 32.00
Minnesota, ruby stained, orig top . . . 50.00
Peacock Feather, orig tops, price for pair 50.00

POTTERY (PRICED BY SET)

Dedham Pottery, 2¾" h, rabbit pattern, crackled finish, unmarked. 110.00
Roycroft, 2¾" h, deep green border around top, rust and deep green geometric designs, black outlining, black linear orb mark on ivory ground, both marked in black "Buffalo Pottery 1926" and "Roycroft," salt shaker with hairline in base 275.00
Staffordshire, 4¼" h, Mideast scene, medium blue transfer. 195.00
Torquay, cottage, egg shaped, "Snowdon" on front, "Cymru–amwyth" on back. 70.00

SALTGLAZED WARES

History: Saltglazed wares have a distinctive "pitted" surface texture made by throwing salt into the hot kiln during the final firing process. The salt vapors produce sodium oxide and hydrochloric acid, which react on the glaze.

Many Staffordshire potters produced large quantities of this type of ware during the 18th and 19th centuries. A relatively small quantity was produced in the United States. Saltglazed wares still are made today.

Reference: Susan and Al Bagdade, *Warman's English & Continental Pottery & Porcelain, Second Edition,* Wallace–Homestead, 1991.

Bottle, 10½" h, molded eagle and shield, imp "M & W, Gr" 360.00

Shaker, figural, Toby holding mug, cream color, unmarked, 5½″ h, $165.00.

Centerpiece, 15″ h, figural, gentlemen standing on two tiers, some playing instruments, others holding dec objects, two reticulated wells on bottom, circular base with flowerheads dec, six ball feet, German, 19th C 460.00
Creamer, 3¼″ h, pear shape, raised leaf and putti dec, lyre handle, claw feet, 18th C 740.00
Cuspidor, 8½″ d, brown highlights . . . 55.00
Dish, 9″ d, circular, scroll and latticinio dec 300.00
Food Mold, 12¾″ d, turk's head, gray saltglazed ext., int. with brown Albany slip and molded fluted design 330.00
Jar, ovoid
  7½″ h, tan glaze, brushed blue tulip 220.00
  8″ h, flared mouth 30.00
  11″ h, traces of blue paint 110.00
Jug, 11″ h, two tone, brown top, molded raised label "The Ohio Stoneware Co Akron, Ohio". 90.00
Miniature, churn, cov, 5½″ h 55.00
Pitcher, 10¾″ h, brownish–gray, strap handle, pinched spout 165.00
Plate, 9¾″ d, emb diaper and reticulated border 300.00
Salt, helmet shape, latticinio star and lion, bird and shell dec, claw feet, 18th C. 880.00
Soup Tureen, cov, 9⅜″ l, oval, three mask and claw feet with latticinio and scroll dec, loop handles, glazed 1,375.00
Teapot, 7″ h, ball shape, raised branch dec, bird finial, 18th C 2,860.00
Water Pitcher, pear shape, rain, calla lily, and leaf dec 75.00

SALTS, OPEN

History: When salt was first mined, the supply was limited and expensive. The necessity for a receptacle in which to serve the salt resulted in the first open salt, a crude, hand–carved, wooden trencher.

As time passed salt receptacles were refined in style and materials. In the 1500s both master and individual salts existed. By the 1700s firms such as Meissen, Waterford, and Wedgwood were making glass, china, and porcelain salts. Leading manufacturers in the 1800s included Libbey Glass Co., Mount Washington, New England Glass Company, Smith Bros., Vallerystahl, Wave Crest, Webb, and many outstanding silversmiths in England, France, and Germany.

Open salts were used as the only means of serving salt until the appearance of the shaker in the late 1800s. The ease of procuring salt from a shaker greatly reduced the use and need for the open salts.

References: William Heacock and Patricia Johnson, *5,000 Open Salts: A Collectors Guide,* Richardson Printing Corporation, 1982, 1989 value update; L. W. and D. B. Neal, *Pressed Glass Dishes Of The Lacy Period 1825–1850,* published by the authors, 1962; Allan B. and Helen B. Smith have authored and published ten books on open salts, beginning with *One Thousand Individual Open Salts Illustrated* (1972) and ending with *1,334 Open Salts Illustrated: The Tenth Book* (1984). Daniel Snyder did the master salt sections in Volumes 8 and 9. In 1987 Mimi Rudnick compiled a revised price list for the ten Smith books.

Periodical: *Salty Comments,* 401 Nottingham Rd., Newark, DE 19711.

Collectors' Clubs: New England Society of Open Salt Collectors, PO Box 177, Sudbury, MA 01776; Open Salt Collectors of the Atlantic Region, PO Box 5112, Lancaster, PA 17604-0112.

CONDIMENT SETS WITH OPEN SALTS

Bristol Glass, cov mustard pot, pepper shaker with orig lid, open salt, milk white, pink and blue flowers and green leaves dec, 4¼ x 5¾″ SP holder. . . . 135.00
German Silver, two castors, two salts, and two salt spoons, Renaissance style with swan supports, c1900, .800 fine 770.00
Silver, six circular salts, six pear shaped castors, and six matching spoons, each with pierced leaf capped domed covers, repousse foliate dec, three shell capped scroll feet, and monogram, Jacobi & Jenkins, c1900. . . . . 1,035.00

FIGURALS

Boat, glass, opaline blue, enameled white garland and scrolling dec. 80.00

Peacock, glass, amethyst wings, green
base **70.00**
Seahorse, porcelain, brilliant turquoise,
white base, supports shell shaped
salt, Belleek, first black mark **350.00**
Sleigh, lacy glass, medium fiery opales-
cent, raised standing American eagle
at each corner, American shield on
sides, scrolled feet, c1840 . . . . **350.00**
Triton, with beard and tail, rising above
rocky oval base, silverplated, holding
cut crystal dolphin shaped bowl, Con-
tinental, price for pair. **550.00**
Viking ship, 3¼" l, silver, glass liner,
Continental, price for pair. **80.00**

**Individual, Limoges, scalloped edge,
white ground, gold trim, marked "D & C
France," 1⅝" d, 1¾" h,
$12.00.**

INDIVIDUAL

Battersea Enamel, 2½" d, 19th C,
damaged **130.00**
Bohemian Glass, 4⅛" d, cut floral and
foliate dec, gilt highlights, price for set
of four **160.00**
Bristol Glass, 1¾" d, 1⅜" h, semi-
opaque, round, enameled blue, red,
and gold dec, white ground **40.00**
Cut Glass, 2⅛" d, 2" h, green cut to
clear, silver rim, clear sq ft **80.00**
Gold Iridescent, 1½" d, 1" h, Tiffany Fav-
rille, sgd "LCT #625," price for set of
six **660.00**
Opalescent Glass, ½" d, 1¼" h, pink to
white opalescent ext., gold lustre int.,
fluted top, Monot Stumpf, Pantin,
French **70.00**
Pattern Glass
Fourteen Diamond, 3" l, double ogee,
colorless lead glass, pontil scar, attributed to New England, 18th C,
price for pair **85.00**
King's Crown **35.00**

Moon & Star, flint **90.00**
Satin, pink shaded to raspberry, MOP,
DQ **125.00**
Threaded Glass, 1¾" d, 1¼" h, char-
treuse green, clear applied snail
feet. **70.00**
Porcelain, Lenox Belleek, price for set of
ten. **55.00**
Silver
Austrian, Art Deco style, circular, partially fluted border, conical foot, vermeil int., liner, Klingshot, .800 fine,
price for set of six **225.00**
English
3⅜" l, George III, gadrooned rim,
pierced gallery sides, four claw
feet, cobalt blue glass liners,
marks worn, Richard Smith and
Robert Sharp, London, 1788,
price for set of four **460.00**
3¾" l, George III, bombe rect form,
crested, everted gadrooned rims,
gilt int., stepped pedestal base,
Richard Sibley, London, 1818,
price for set of six **1,265.00**
4⅛" l, George IV, rect form, gad-
rooned rim, shells flanked by
leaves at angles, gilt int., crested
sides, lobed pedestal base, Paul
Storr, London, 1821, price for
pair. **660.00**
Italian, 3" h, Neoclassical, base
marked with crowned cross in oval,
late 18th C, price for pair. **660.00**

MASTERS

Colored Glass
Cranberry
3½" w, 2¾" h, four petal top, clear
applied shell rigaree, SP stand. . **160.00**
3¾" d, 5½" h, vaseline ruffled top,
second vaseline ruffle around
middle, SP basket stand and
spoon **170.00**
4" d, 2¼" h, fluted edge, clear ap-
plied shell feet, clear rigaree
around center. **92.00**
Crystal, 1¼" d, ¾" h, set in 2½" d ornate gold colored holder with blue,
red, yellow, and white enameled circle with lion dec in corners, salt
spoon **125.00**
Orange, 3½" d, 2½" h, applied crystal
rigaree, SP stand. **150.00**
Opalescent Glass
Blue, Beatty Rib **68.00**
Vaseline, 3½" d, 2" h, applied shell
rigaree around center, SP stand
with ball feet **140.00**
Pattern Glass
Argus, flint **35.00**

Leaf and Dart, cov	95.00
Lily of the Valley, open, three footed	60.00
Lincoln and Drape, with tassel	125.00
Log Cabin, flint	28.00
Loop & Dart, round ornaments	45.00
Loop, flint	30.00
Paneled Thistle	12.00
Sawtooth, flint	25.00
Valencia, blue, waffle	45.00
Sterling Silver, pierced borders, drapery and lion paw feet, matching spoons, Black, Starr & Frost, price for pair	195.00

SAMPLERS

History: Samplers served many purposes. For a young child they were a practice exercise and permanent reminder of stitches and patterns. For a young woman they demonstrated her skills in a "gentle" art and preserved key elements of family genealogy. For the mature woman they were a useful occupation and functioned as gifts or re-membrances, e.g., mourning pieces.

Schools for young ladies of the early 19th century prided themselves on the needlework skills they taught. The Westtown School in Chester County, Pennsylvania, and the Young Ladies Seminary in Bethlehem, Pennsylvania, are two examples. These schools changed their teaching as styles changed. Berlin work was introduced by the mid 19th century.

Examples of samplers date back to the 1700s. The earliest ones were long and narrow, usually done only with the alphabet and numerals. Later examples were square. At the end of the 19th century, the shape tended to be rectangular.

The same motifs were used throughout the country. The name is a key element in determining the region. Samplers are assumed to be on linen unless otherwise indicated.

References: Ethel Stanwood Bolton and Eva Johnston Coe, *American Samplers*, Dover, 1987; Glee Krueger, *A Gallery of American Samplers: The Theodore H. Kapnek Collection*, Bonanza Books, 1984 edition; Dana G. Morykan and Harry L. Rinker, *Warman's Country Antiques & Collectibles, Second Edition*, Wallace–Homestead, 1994; Betty Ring, *American Needlework Treasures: Samplers and Silk Embroideries From The Collection of Betty Ring*, E. P. Dutton, 1987; Anne Sebba, *Samplers: Five Centuries of a Gentle Craft*, Thames and Hudson, 1979.

Museums: Cooper–Hewitt Museum, National Museum of Design, New York, NY; Smithsonian Institution, Washington, D.C.

1788, Elisa Chapman, cotton homespun, silk stitches, inner floral wreath encircling verse, stylized trees, buildings, birds, and vining border, "Elisa Chapman 9 years old work'd May

1788," soft colors, gold painted frame, 18½ x 14½"	475.00

1796
Stone, Elizabeth, linen ground, pink, green, and cream silk threads, rows of alphabets, zig–zag border, trees, figures, "Elizabeth Stone was born in Danvers Janury (sic) 30th worked this in the 10th year of her age 1796," 7½" w, 11½" h	3,100.00
Wilde, Polly, MA, green, pink, cream, umber, blue, and black silk threads, "Polly Wilde Sampler Wrought in Salem, June 1796," and further inscribed "Maffachufetts State Salem...," rows of alphabets, middle section of two floral urns, center lion, lower section of two seated facing ladies, trees, birds, florals, and animals, two inner borders of pyramid shaped devices, framed, 13¾ x 12½".	8,800.00
1798, Lydia Ashleys, MA, pink, green, yellow, and burnt umber silk threads, "Lydia Ashleys sampler, aged eleven years, worked September 1798," framed, some color loss, 10 x 7".	1,045.00
1799, Elizabeth Somerby, linen–woolsey ground, pink, blue, and cream, green ground, rows of alphabets, flowering border, floral urns, "Wrought by Elizabeth Somerby aged 8 years, 1799," repairs, attributed to MA, 17½ x 14½".	3,300.00
1808, Lois Newhall, linen, silk cream shaded threads, central panel enclosed by floral and cornucopia border, "Lois Newhall aged 12 years Lynn 2nd day September 1808," fading, framed, incomplete, 15½ x 16".	615.00
1810, Mary Perry, green, gold, red, and blue silk threads, linen ground, "MP", unframed, 6½ x 10¼"	330.00
1812, Ann Wild, green, blue, gold, black, and white silk threads, linen homespun, vining border, verse, pots of flowers, conical tree, "Ann Wild, Aged nine years, Decr. 1812," dark stains, bleeding of black floss, framed, 12¾ x 18"	310.00

1817
Jewell, MaryAnn, linen homespun, intricate brown, gold, green, white, black, and light blue silk stitches, vining border, verse, cottage, barn, farm, people, and wild animals, "MaryAnn Jewell finished this work, April 24th, 1817 at Mrs. Venthams Boarding School, Winton, Aged Years," framed, 12¾ x 17"	1,595.00
Perkins, Louisa, Boston, green silk thread, linen ground, bands of al-	

phabet and verse over inscription, "Louisa Perkins at Miss Williams School, Boston, June 18th, 1817," unframed, some discoloration, bleeding, 14 x 12½″ **440.00**

1820

Handley, Olive, linen, blue, green, and yellow threads, alphabet and verse, floral and vine border, "Worked by Olive Handley, aged 11 years, 1820," discoloration, fading, framed, 16¼ x 17¼″. **1,100.00**

Meck, Anna, linen homespun, red, blue, sage, and black silk stitching, alphabets, stylized flowers, animals, and people, poplar frame, 18 x 21½″ **330.00**

Read, Abigail, New England, blue, green, pink, yellow, coral, cream, and black silk threads, linen ground, "Abigail E. Read," framed, paper label on reverse inscribed "Daughter of George and Abigail, sister of Elisa T. Read. Abigail E. Read born August 2, 1814, died January 28, 1881," 17¾ x 17¼″ **5,500.00**

1823, Catharine Foster, linen homespun, pink, olive, ivory, gray, green, and gold silk threads, flowering border, verse, birds, angels, flowers, and "Catharine Foster, Aged 12, 1823," some moth damage, orig molded black frame, 15½ x 15″ **700.00**

1825

Kellar, Catherine, America, linen homespun, alphabets, stylized pots of strawberry–like flowers, "Catherine Kellar worked this in the twelve year of her age 1825," matted, gilt frame, 21¼ x 28″ **245.00**

Unidentified Maker, Chester County, PA, blue, green, yellow, cream, and peach silk threads, natural linen and green gauze ground, quilted silk ribbon trim, corner rosettes, framed, minor fiber loss, 23½ x 27½″. **8,800.00**

1827, Sarah Hunts, dark linen homespun, green, pink, white, and blue silk stitches, verse, alphabets, baskets of flowers, and strawberry border, "Sarah Hunts sampler Age 15 years, Waterford, May the 31, 1827," unframed, 23½ x 17″. **1,100.00**

1828

Lyndall, Elizabeth, homespun, flowering vine border, butterflies, birds, flowers, and verse "Gratitude," stains, faded colors, possibly Quaker, framed, 23¼ x 22¾″ **900.00**

Pierce, Hannah S, Jamaica, linen, alphabets, house, trees, and flowers, inscribed above "Hannah S Pierce,

Jamaica Age 13, 1828," 16½ x 16¾″. **935.00**

Smith, Mary Ann, homespun, green, tan, yellow, white, black, and beige silk and linen threads, vining floral border, rows of alphabets, stylized flowers and birds with verse, "Mary Ann Smith aged 7 Y 7M, Sept. 2nd 1828," stains and some facing, matted and framed, 11½ x 13½″ . . **500.00**

1830, Margaret Jane Morice, Sackville, NJ, linen, alphabet, numerals, verse, flowers, insects, birds, and beasts, 24 x 15″ **495.00**

1833, Marie Clark, New England, linen, alphabets, family register, poetic verse, trees, pots of flowers, and grass, floral and foliate border, 21½ x 20″. **525.00**

1837, Sarah Jane Rest, multicolored threads, potted flowers, birds, buildings, trees, verse, and inscription, vining border, $525.00.

1837, Wealthy A. Gregory, silk on linen homespun, side by side design with rows of alphabets and numerals on left half, right side with memorial to Sidney J Gregory, verse, stylized people, trees, and church scene of Sidney ascending to heaven, "Wealthy A. Gregory, Aged 12 years, 1837," attributed to Pembrook, MA, minor stains, framed, 19¼ x 17¾″ **1,250.00**

1838, Martha E Maynard, linen, polychromed silk threads, alphabets, poetic verse and inscribed "Wrought by

Martha E Maynard Age 11 years 1838," floral vine border, 20½ x 16" **880.00**

1842

Chapin, Charlotte, MA, pink, green, blue, yellow, brown, and black silk threads, "Wrought by Charlotte Chapin in the 12th year of her age 1842," foxing to ground, some discoloration, 18¼ x 15¼". **1,540.00**

Gould, Emma Ann, natural linen homespun, blue, green, red, black, and pink silk stitches, alphabets, birds, heart, and vining border, "Emma Ann Gould, age 8 years 1842," stapled to cardboard, unframed, 15¼ x 10½". **610.00**

1845, Ellen Sullivan, dark linen homespun, green, brown, gold, and blue silk threads, vining strawberry border, stylized Adam and Eve, church, windmill, angels, flowers, animals, trees, and "Ellen Sullivan, her work age 11 years, 1845," small holes, brown marker used to highlight some designs, modern frame, 12⅝ x 17¼" . . **700.00**

1846, homespun, silk stitches, stylized border with flowers and pastel colors, center rectangle with basket of flowers, inscription "Yjadejvan Ydejvana Fernandez Anode 1846, Viva Jesus, y Marya Meyzo, Trinindad, Belasco," framed, 22½ x 21½". **495.00**

1860, Harriet Adams, homespun, green, brown, gold, and red silk stitches, baskets of flowers, floral bouquets, and vining floral border, "Harriet Adams, March 13, 1860," beveled bird's eye veneer frame, 17½ x 15". **475.00**

1876, Mary Margret Callishaw, linen, wool stitches, vining border, alphabets, flowers, verse, and "Mary Margret Callishaw '76," matted, framed, 15¾ x 16¾" **275.00**

Undated

Attributed to Hollowell, ME, natural linen homespun, variety of embroidery silk threads in shades of brown, green, blue, red, yellow, and white, vining strawberry border, rows of alphabets and numerals, vase of flowers, butterfly and bird, framed, 9⅝ x 13¼". **1,350.00**

Frith, Ann, linen homespun, wool stitches, alphabets, numerals, house, animals, flowers, "Ann Frith, aged 9 years," linen slightly puckered, minor wear, small holes, some stitches missing, beveled walnut frame, 12¼" w, 15⅞" h. . . . **825.00**

Sewall, Lucy P, linen homespun, rows of alphabets in several different stitches, name "Lucy P. Sewall, Ag

9 years" all in beige silk nearly the color of the linen ground, satin stitch floral border in bluish green, beige, and white, minor stains, attributed to ME, modern frame, 18⅝ x 20". . **700.00**

Smith, Elizabeth, wool homespun, small precise brown, green, gold, and white silk stitches, vining floral border, stylized birds, trees, flowers, spotted dog, windmill, verse and name, small hole in upper right, modern frame, 14¾ x 14¼". **1,000.00**

SANDWICH GLASS

History: In 1818 Deming Jarves was listed in the Boston Directory as a glass factor. The same year he was appointed general manager of the newly formed New England Glass Company. In 1824 Jarves toured the glassmaking factories in Pittsburgh, left the New England Glass Company, and founded a glass factory in Sandwich.

Originally called the Sandwich Manufacturing Company, it was incorporated in April 1826 as the Boston & Sandwich Glass Company. From 1826 to 1858 Jarves served as general manager. The Boston & Sandwich Glass Company produced a wide variety and quality of wares. The factory used the free–blown, blown three–mold, and pressed glass manufacturing techniques. Clear and colored glass both were used.

Competition in the American glass industry in the mid–1850s forced a lowering of quality of the glass wares. Jarves left in 1858, founded the Cape Cod Glass Company, and tried to maintain the high quality of the earlier glass. At the Boston & Sandwich Glass Company emphasis was placed on mass production. The development of a lime glass (nonflint) led to lower costs for pressed glass. Some free–blown and blown–and–molded pieces, mostly in color, were made. Most of this Victorian-era glass was enameled, painted, or acid etched.

By the 1880s the Boston & Sandwich Glass Company was operating at a loss. Labor difficulties finally resulted in the factory closing on January 1, 1888.

References: Raymond E. Barlow and Joan E. Kaiser, *The Glass Industry In Sandwich*, Vol. 2, Vol. 3, and Vol. 4 distributed by Schiffer Publishing; Ruth Webb Lee, *Sandwich Glass: The History Of The Sandwich Glass Company*, Charles E. Tuttle, 1966; Ruth Webb Lee, *Sandwich Glass Handbook*, Charles E. Tuttle, 1966; George S. and Helen McKearin, *American Glass*, Crown Publishers, 1941 and 1948; L. W. and D. B. Neal, *Pressed Glass Dishes Of The Lacy Period 1825–1850*, published by authors, 1962; Ellen T. Schroy, *Warman's Glass*, Wallace–Homestead, 1992; Catherine M. V. Thuro, *Oil Lamps II: Glass Kerosene Lamps*, Wallace–Homestead, 1983.

Museum: Sandwich Glass Museum, Sandwich, MA.

Additional Listings: Blown Three Mold and Cup Plates.

Basin, 3⅛″ d, 1″ h, blue, paneled, c1840–55	275.00
Butter Dish, cov, clear, flint, Gothic pattern	175.00
Candlestick, pr	
Columnar, clambroth	500.00
Dolphin	
Canary, two step	950.00
Opaque blue and white, 9¾″ h, stepped base	650.00
Hexagonal base, 7½″ h, purple–blue petal socket, translucent white. . . .	550.00
Loop base, hexagonal socket, canary.	450.00
Waterfall base, lacy, clear	650.00
Condiment Set, mustard, cruet, and shaker, clear, flint, Gothic pattern, orig wire holder	165.00
Creamer and Sugar, clear, flint, Gothic pattern, sugar with cov.	80.00
Cup Plate	
Blue, Lacy Ship	125.00
Violet Blue, Lacy Heart	325.00
Goblet, set of 14, clear, flint, Gothic pattern	660.00
Lamp, fluid	
6″ h, free blown, bulb, pressed lacy circular base, c1803	260.00
6¾″ h, Loop and Petal pattern, clear sapphire blue font, translucent white base.	850.00
8½″ h, Waffle pattern, opaque blue and white, camphene burner, whale oil.	950.00
9″ h, clear, Loop pattern, whale oil, price for pair	250.00
9½″ h, clear flint, bull's eye and fleur–	

de–lis font, brass stem, marble base	125.00
9¾″ h, opaque white font, brass stem, marble base, gold dec	110.00
10⅞″ h, clear, flint, Sweetheart pattern, monumental base, price for pair.	990.00
12½″ h, double overlay, pressed Baroque base with tortoise shell spatter, c1870, imperfections.	7,140.00
13″ h, double cut overlay, emerald green to clear, brass reeded standard, double stepped marble base	330.00
19½″ h, tulip, sand finish opaque cobalt blue font, clambroth columnar standard, square base, frosted globe, imperfections, price for pair	1,650.00
Paperweight	
Commemorative, 3½″ w, 1¼″ h, clear and frosted, portraits of Queen Victoria and consort, 1851.	195.00
Poinsettia, blue flower, purple ground	850.00
Pitcher, 10″ h	
Amberina Verde, fluted top	280.00
Electric Blue, enameled floral dec, fluted top, threaded handle	390.00
Reverse Amberina, fluted top	390.00
Plate	
6″ d	
Daisy	160.00
Shell pattern, lacy	160.00
7″ d, Rayed Peacock Eye	95.00
Salt, boat, clear	350.00
Spoon Holder, clear, flint, Gothic pattern	40.00
Sugar, cov, translucent blue, Lacy Gothic pattern	1,200.00
Tumbler, 3½″ h, clear, flint, Gothic pattern	225.00
Vase, 9⅝″ h, clear, flint, Loop pattern, scalloped top	110.00

Salt Shaker, Christmas Pearl, opaque, agitator top, $115.00.

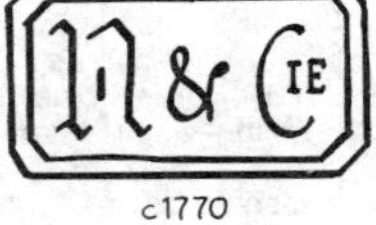

c1770

SARREGUEMINES

SARREGUEMINES CHINA

History: Sarreguemines ware is a faience porcelain, i.e., tin-glazed earthenware. The factory was established in Lorraine, France, in 1770, under the supervision of Utzcheider and Fabry. The factory was regarded as one of the three most prominent manufacturers of French faience. Most of the wares found today were made in the 19th century. Later wares are impressed Sarreguemines and Germany due to a change of boundaries and location of the factory.

Reference: Susan and Al Bagdade, *Warman's English & Continental Pottery & Porcelain, Second Edition,* Wallace-Homestead, 1991.

Vases, fisheye pattern, green ground, marked and numbered 14032DT C531 under foot, 11½″ h, price for pair, $550.00. Photograph courtesy of Leslie Hindman Auctioneers.

Basket, 9″ h, quilted, green, heavy leopard skin crystallization 250.00
Bowl, 9¼″ sq, raised fruits 100.00
Centerpiece, 14¾″ h, 14¾″ d, bowl with pierced ringlets to sides, supported by a center stem flanked by sea nymphs either side, mounted atop circular base on four scrolled feet, polychrome dec, imp marks, chips, restorations, c1875. . . . . 880.00
Pitcher, 8½″ h, grinning male face, imp marks, minor crazing, c1890. . . . . . . 385.00
Plate
  7½″ d, dec with music and characters from French children's songs, price for set of twelve 350.00
  8″ d, Exposition Universelle transfer scenes, price for set of four. 65.00
Sugar Bowl, cov, 6″ d, mocha, marbleized red and black on white, age lines, 19th C 175.00
Tankard, cov, 11″ h, stoneware, continuous country scene of dancing and celebrating villagers, branch handle, pewter lid with porcelain medallion and painted polychrome coat of arms, dated 1869. . . . . 300.00
Urn, 31¼″ h, gilt metal mounted majol-

ica, baluster form, cobalt blue glazed, mounted with the figure of a crowned lion holding sword, lion and mask handled sides, pierced foliate rim, raised on four scrolling foliate cast ft, imp "Majolica Sarreguemines," second half 19th C 1,760.00
Vase, 8½″ h, Mideastern motif 400.00

SARSAPARILLA BOTTLES

History: Sarsaparilla refers to a number of tropical American, spiny, woody vines of the lily family whose roots are fragrant. An extract was obtained from these dried roots and used for medicinal purposes. The first appearance in bottle form dates from the 1840s. The earliest bottles were stoneware, later followed by glass.

Carbonated water often was added to sarsaparilla to make a soft drink or to make consuming it more pleasurable. For this reason, sarsaparilla and soda became synonymous even though they were two different entities.

References: Ralph and Terry Kovel, *The Kovels' Bottle Price List, 9th Edition,* Crown Publishers, 1992; Carlo and Dot Sellari, *The Standard Old Bottle Price Guide,* Collector Books, 1989.

Periodical: *Antique Bottle and Glass Collector,* PO Box 187, East Greenville, PA 18041.

Additional Listings: See *Warman's Americana & Collectibles* for a list of soda bottles.

A H Bull Extract of Sarsaparilla, 6⅞″ h, aqua 75.00
Ayers Concentrated Sarsaparilla, 7¾″ h 65.00
Bristols Extract of Sarsaparilla, 5½″ h, aqua, open pontil 65.00

Mission Beverage, Pioneer Beverages, San Francisco–Oakland, CA, clear, 7 oz, 8¼″ h, $215.00.

Buffum Sarsaparilla Mineral Water,
aqua, ten sided, pontil **200.00**
Carl's Sarsaparilla & Celery Compound,
7⅜" h, aqua **60.00**
Corwitz Sarsaparilla, 9½" h, aqua . . . **55.00**
Dr AS Hopkins Compound Ext, 9" h,
aqua **75.00**
Dr Cronk's Sarsaparilla Beer, 10" h, pot-
tery, gray, twelve sided **80.00**
Dr Guysott's Compound Extract, 9½" h,
olive amber. **60.00**
Dr Ira Baker's, clear **100.00**
Dr Townsend's Sarsaparilla, olive . . . **155.00**
Edward Wilder's, Sarsaparilla & Potash,
8½" h. **175.00**
Foley's Sarsaparilla, light amber **35.00**
Gold Medal Sarsaparilla, 9" h, amber **65.00**
Hambolt's, aqua, label, open pontil . . **75.00**
John Bull Extract of Sarsaparilla, 9½" h,
aqua **30.00**
Kennedy's Sarsaparilla, 9½" h, amber,
label. **140.00**
Masury's Sarsaparilla Compound, qt,
aqua, emb **275.00**
McLean's Sarsaparilla, 9¼" h, light
green. **75.00**
Radway's Sarsaparilla Resolvent . . . **20.00**
Rush's Sarsaparilla, 8¾" h, aqua . . . **40.00**
Sand's Sarsaparilla, 6" h, rectangular,
aqua **125.00**
Walker's, aqua **135.00**
Whipple's Sarsaparilla, 9⅛" h, aqua . **75.00**
Yager's Sarsaparilla, 8¾" h, amber . . **55.00**

SATIN GLASS

History: Satin glass, produced in the late 19th
century, is an opaque art glass with a velvety matte
(satin) finish which was achieved through treat-
ment with hydrofluoric acid. A large majority of the
pieces were cased or had a white lining.

While working at the Phoenix Glass Company,
Beaver, Pennsylvania, Joseph Webb perfected
Mother-of-Pearl (MOP) satin glass in 1885. Similar
to plain satin glass in respect to casing, MOP satin
glass has a distinctive surface finish and an integral
or indented design, the most common being diamond quilted (DQ).

The most common colors are yellow, rose, or
blue. Rainbow coloring is considered choice. Satin
glass, both plain and MOP, has been widely reproduced.

Reference: Ellen T. Schroy, *Warman's Glass*,
Wallace-Homestead, 1992.

Additional Listings: Cruets, Fairy Lamps, Miniature Lamps, and Rose Bowls.

Basket, 7" h, blue, MOP, Raindrop, ruffled top, pedestal base, applied cam-
phor handle **300.00**

Bowl, 4" d, 3" h, deep rose shading to
bluish white, MOP, Mt Washington . . **90.00**
Bride's Basket, 15½" h, deep rose,
enamel swan and floral dec, heavy
bronze holder with birds perched at
top. **420.00**
Cologne Bottle, 5½" h, peach, globular,
SS top **250.00**
Ewer, 8" h, 3½" d, shaded blue, MOP,
Herringbone, frosted applied handle,
rose petal satin finish. **200.00**
Finger Bowl, 4¼" d, 2¾" h, pink, MOP,
Thumbprint, ruffled top. **150.00**
Rose Bowl
Hand painted lavender floral dec,
blue, white int. **75.00**
Plain, 4½" h, blue, MOP, DQ **70.00**
Spooner, 6¼" h, rainbow, MOP, DQ . **275.00**
Sugar Shaker, 6¼" h, blue, MOP, Rain-
drop, SP top. **415.00**

**Tumbler, Rainbow pattern, DQ, MOP,
paneled, 3¾" h, $825.00.**

Vase
3" h, green, vertical stripes of gilt floral
dec, frosted clear foot, attributed to
Stevens & Williams or Webb **250.00**
3½" h, 3" d, fan shape, ruffled top,
chartreuse green, MOP, swirl, white
int., frosted wafer foot. **250.00**
4½" h, swelled bulbous base extend-
ing to flat flared rim, yellow shading
to white, swirl dec, attributed to Stevens & Williams **100.00**
5" h, pink, MOP, Thumbprint, ruffled
top **100.00**
6½" h, brown shaded to white, dia-
mond quilted pattern, blue, white,
and orange enameled forget–me–
not dec, MOP int. **825.00**
7" h, blue, Diamond Quilted Herring-
bone, ruffled top. **75.00**
7¼" h, white, MOP, Raindrop, melon
ribbed, ruffled top. **100.00**
7½" h, 3½" d, 4" l slender neck, bul-

bous, yellow, white int., large polished pontil, Hobbs. **145.00**
8″ h, blue, MOP, Raindrop, bulbous **225.00**
8¾″ h, yellow shading to white, MOP, DQ. **125.00**
9½″ h, 5″ w, blue shading to white, Coinspot, lightly crimped rim pulled down to shoulder at three places, Mt Washington. **675.00**
12½″ h, pink, MOP, Thumbprint, gourd shape **240.00**

SATSUMA

History: Satsuma, named for a war lord who brought skilled Korean potters to Japan in the early 1600s, was a hand-crafted Japanese faience glazed pottery. It is finely crackled, has a cream, yellow-cream, or gray-cream color, and is decorated with raised enamels in floral, geometric and figural motifs.

Figural satsuma was made specifically for export in the 19th century. Later satsuma, referred to as satsuma-style ware, is Japanese porcelain also hand decorated in raised enamels. From 1912 to the present, satsuma-style ware has been mass-produced. Much of the ware on today's market is of this later period.

Reference: Gloria and Robert Mascarelli, *Warman's Oriental Antiques,* Wallace-Homestead, 1992.

Bouillon Cup and Saucer, hp landscape scene, double handle. **25.00**
Bowl
4¾″ d, pinched floriform rim, floral int., cobalt ext. with flowering prunus . . **275.00**
5″ d, figures and pavilion, mountainous landscape scene, Showa period. **165.00**
5½″ d, cobalt blue ground, gilt dec, 19th C, gilt worn. **220.00**
6″ d, wisteria dec **275.00**
8″ d, two elderly people and two boys, Japanese, 19th C. **330.00**
Box, 5″ l, figure dec, Meiji period **200.00**
Bucket, 12″ h, fan and floral dec **165.00**
Cabinet Vase, 3″ h, bulbous, two figural reserves, deep green and gold ground, four short feet, late 19th C . . **325.00**
Cache Pot, 6½″ h, figural and landscape scene. **110.00**
Container, cov, 8½″ h, lantern shaped, trailing purple wisteria, green leaves, beige ground, gilt highlights, Showa period **125.00**
Cup and Saucer, bird and floral motif, cobalt blue border, Kinkozan, Japanese. **110.00**
Dinnerware, Kutani porcelain, arhats in multicolored brocaded robes, gold

halos, chocolate brown ground, jeweled enameled details, twelve 5⅜″ d bowls, 9″ pedestal bowl, creamer, eleven cups and saucers, gravy with attached underplate, eleven 6¼″ plates, eleven 7¾″ plates, twelve 10″ plates, 12½″ l platter, eleven 7¾″ soup plates, cov sugar, 11 x 7½″ oval vegetable, price for set **875.00**
Dish
4½″ l, fan shape, floral dec, gilt ground, Meiji period, price for pair . **175.00**
6″ sq, figural dec, Meiji period, Japanese **850.00**
10¾″ d, shallow, wide everted rim, figural and cherry blossom tree dec int., enamels and gilt, early 20th C **165.00**
Ginger Jar, 6½″ h, floral dec, Meiji period **50.00**

Jar, cov, maroon ground, white flowers, gold leaf trim, c1830, 8½″ h, $135.00.

Jar
4″ h, globular, silver ground, figures, 19th C. **220.00**
24″ h, cov, figural reserves, foo dog finial, Meiji period, price for pair. . . **8,250.00**
Jug, 4″ h, polychrome bird and floral dec, Meiji period. **35.00**
Teapot, Meiji period
5″ h, polychrome floral dec, beige ground, green glazed bamboo handle. **35.00**
6¼″ h, floral dec, bamboo form handle and finial. **350.00**
Tea Service, 7″ h teapot, creamer, cov sugar, six cups and saucers, figures in landscape, gilt floral dec, blue ground, price for fifteen piece set . . . **575.00**
Tray
10″ l, raised immortals and white dragon design, gilt ground, Meiji period. **500.00**
15½″ l, oval, raised sides, figural and landscape dec. **500.00**

Vase

5" h, painted floral dec, Japanese .	230.00
6¼" h, floral dec, Japanese	40.00
7" h, landscape reserves, Japanese, 19th C.	70.00
8½" h, ovoid, floral and landscape frieze dec, sgd, Japanese, late 19th C, price for pair	425.00
9" h, bottle form, Showa period . . .	225.00
9¾" h, floral and bird dec, elephant head handles, sgd on bottom, price for pair	650.00
10" h, urn shape, figural design, late 19th C, price for pair.	138.00
11¾" h, warriors dec, two dragon handles.	325.00
13" h, double gourd form, two panels, seated man and warrior with crashing waves, band of overlapping patterns, gilt highlights, mounted as lamp, late 19th C	920.00
14½" h, baluster, two painted panels of woman in landscape, cobalt blue ground, gilt dec	176.00
15" h, baluster form, dragon dec, gray ground, Japanese, 19th C.	193.00
22" h, ovoid, rolled rim, painted panel of enamels and gilt dec, low relief dragon and dancing women, Meiji period.	1,093.00
42" h, figural dec, Japanese	4,400.00
Watch Holder, 11" h, figural, parrot . .	250.00

SCALES

History: Prior to 1900 the simple balance scale commonly was used for measuring weights. Since then scales have become more sophisticated in design and more accurate. A variety of styles and types include beam, platform, postal, and pharmaceutical.

Collectors' Club: International Society of Antique Scale Collectors, Suite 1706, 176 W. Adams St., Chicago, IL 60603.

Apothecary, 19½" l, 15¾" h, walnut, fitted ivory dec.	200.00
Balance	
14" l, brass and iron	140.00
26" h, brass, B & H Bracey Cardiff .	330.00
39½" h, brass, column standard . .	325.00
Candy, National Store Co, tin pan, c1910.	85.00
Counter Top, The Standard Computing Scale Company, Detroit, MI, 34" h, brass trim, orig	150.00
Egg, Oaks Mfg Co	8.00
Hanging, 26" d, 150 lb tray, marked "R F Forschner Company, Makers, New York, New York".	130.00

Fairbanks, marked "IZ8," retains 50% of the orig paint, 15½" l, 8¾" h, $50.00.

Jeweler, brass, ten weights, green velvet lined box.	150.00
Platform	
J L Mott Iron Works, for Merchant, John Chatillon & Sons, NY, 66" h, cast iron, painted, stenciled dial, replaced needle	210.00
National Automatic Weighing Machine Co, 68" h, cast iron, painted, relief patterns, porcelain sign and dial.	990.00
Peerless Weighing Machine Co, Peerless Junior, 63" h, porcelainized steel, tiled platform, gold lettering on reverse	330.00
Watling Scale Co, porcelain case, red and yellow, attached coin–operated horoscope.	110.00
Postal, 4¼" h, desk type, sterling silver, cased, marked "Shreve & Co," 1900–22	250.00
Store, National Store Speciality Co, Lancaster, PA, 2 lbs	150.00

SCHLEGELMILCH PORCELAINS

History: Erdmann Schlegelmilch founded his porcelain factory in Suhl in the Thuringia region in 1861. Reinhold, his brother, established a porcelain factory at Tillowitz in Upper Silesia in 1869. In the 1860s Prussia controlled Thuringia and Upper Silesia, both rich in the natural ingredients needed for porcelain.

By the late 19th century an active export business was conducted with the United States and Canada due to a large supply of porcelain at reasonable costs achieved through industrialization and cheap labor. Both brothers marked their pieces with the RSP mark, a designation honoring Rudolph Schlegelmilch, their father. Over 30 mark variations have been discovered.

The Suhl factory ceased production in 1920, unable to recover from the effects of World War I. The Tillowitz plant, located in an area of changing international boundaries, finally came under Polish socialist government control in 1956.

References: Susan and Al Bagdade, *Warman's English & Continental Pottery & Porcelain, Second Edition,* Wallace–Homestead, 1991; Mary Frank Gaston, *The Collector's Encyclopedia Of R.S. Prussia and Other R.S. and E.S. Porcelain,* First Series (1982, 1993 value update), Second Series (1986, 1992 value update), Third Series (1994), Collector Books; Clifford S. Schlegelmilch, *Handbook Of Erdmann And Reinhold Schlegelmilch, Prussia–Germany And Oscar Schlegelmilch, Germany, 3rd Edition,* published by author, 1973.

Collectors' Club: International Association of R.S. Prussia Collectors Inc., 22 Canterbury Dr., Danville, IN 46122.

Reproduction Alert: Many "fake" Schlegelmilch pieces are appearing on the market. These reproductions have new decal marks, transfers, or recently hand-painted animals on old, authentic R.S. Prussia pieces.

plates, pheasant, hp, marked "E. S. Germany," price for six piece set . . .	**195.00**
Portrait Plate, 8½″ d, Queen Josephine, marked "E. S. Germany"	**125.00**
Scuttle Mug, 3½″ h, pink poppies . . .	**100.00**
Shaving Mug, swallows over mountain and lake scene, marked "E. S. Germany"	**85.00**
Tankard, 11½″ h, pink and yellow roses, marked "Handpainted R. S. Germany"	**495.00**
Vase	
4″ h	
Church scene, sampler	**95.00**
Windmill, house, boy walking, shadow leaves, early green wreath mark	**200.00**
10½″ h, swallows, cream ground, gold highlights, marked "E. S. Germany"	**165.00**

R. S. Germany, cake plate, pink roses, green and cream ground, green mark, 10″ w handle to handle, $40.00.

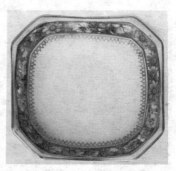

R. S. Poland, sauce dish, chamfered corners, multicolored floral band, gold line highlights, red and green mark, 4½ x 4⅛″, $35.00.

c 1910-1956

R. S. GERMANY

Celery, 10½″ l, Bird of Paradise	**195.00**
Cup and Tray, 9½″ d, pheasants	**135.00**
Ice Cream Set, tray and five serving	

c 1945-1956

R. S. POLAND

Bowl, 5⅜″ d, ⅞″ h, round, shallow sides, multicolored Rembrandt's *Night Watch* scene, gray–blue ground	**145.00**

Dresser Set, glossy, pink roses, 13 x 9"
tray, pair 6¼" h candlesticks, 5" h hatpin holder, price for four piece set. . . **400.00**
Ewer, 6¼" h, golden pheasants dec, left
handed. **460.00**
Flower Holder, pheasants, brass frog
insert **675.00**
Vase
3½" h, 1½" d, miniature salesman's
sample, crowned cranes dec. . . . **815.00**
4" h, miniature salesman's sample,
cavaliers dec **315.00**
8½" h, 4¾" d, large white and tan
roses, shaded brown and green
ground **165.00**
10" h, cottage, woman, and sheep
dec, ornate handles, gold rim **640.00**

**R. S. Prussia, bowl, Basket of Roses,
cream ground, gold beading and trim,
green wreath with red star and R. S.
Prussia mark, 10¾" d, $135.00.**

c 1870s - 1880   c 1870s - 1914

R. S. PRUSSIA

Berry Set, painted white flowers, green
luster, red mark, price for seven piece
set. **285.00**

Bowl
10½" d
Art Nouveau scrolls, lobed floral
medallion, gold outlines, ornate,
medallion mold. **380.00**
Roses and daisies dec, deep rose
trim **250.00**
Victorian woman with fan **1,200.00**
11" d
Castle scene **495.00**
Lilies, fish scale mold, scalloped,
purple and orange luster **395.00**
Swans, relief evergreens, lavender
shading, mold 405 . . . . **395.00**
Cake Plate
9½" d, open handles, cobalt blue trim,
gold enameled flowers and trim, as-
ters dec. **275.00**
11" d, cutout handles, pastel colors,
six pearlized large sunflowers, large
multicolored roses bouquet in cen-
ter, gold floral border, red mark . . . **350.00**
Cake Set, frosty colors, silver, gold, and
frosty white lilies, red mark, price for
five piece set **225.00**
Celery, 12¼" l, floral spray, beading,
gold trim, open handles, daffodil
mold **110.00**
Centerpiece Bowl, carnations dec int.
and ext. **275.00**
Charger, 12" d, Leaf Variation, roses
and daisies dec, deep green, lavender
highlights, mold 10C **225.00**
Cracker Jar, cov
Red Roses, mold 509A **200.00**
Roses and Snowballs, mold 456 . . **400.00**
Sunflower, white pearl luster, green
flower centers and highlights, red
mark. **150.00**
Creamer and Sugar, round, ftd, cupids
playing round horns, pink roses,
heavy gold, orange wreath and star
mark, price for pair **500.00**
Dessert Set, pink poppies with aqua,
yellow, and amethyst tints, plain mold,
pedestal cup and saucer, pedestal
creamer and sugar, two 9¾" w handled plates, eleven 7¼" d plates, 9
cups and saucers, and oversized
creamer and sugar, price for set. . . . **1,950.00**
Dresser Tray, icicle mold, hanging bas-
ket dec. **360.00**
Hatpin Holder, floral and scroll dec, gold
trim, three ftd **170.00**
Jam Jar, underplate, Tiffany color dog-
wood with pink carnations, Morning
Glory mold **265.00**
Milk Pitcher, 5" h, pink carnations dec,
Morning Glory mold. **165.00**
Plate
8¼" d, white dogwood dec with raised
gold branches **95.00**

8½" d, swan, lavender and blue, satin finish. **195.00**

9" d, Viersa, heavy cobalt blue trim, roses dec, mixed florals in four medallions, gold floral trim, mark 52, mold 343 . . . . **340.00**

11" w handle to handle, Leaf Variation, roses and daisies dec, deep green lavender highlights, open handles. **200.00**

Syrup Pitcher, underplate, roses and dogwood dec, pearlized luster, R M mark **295.00**

Tea Set

Colonial scenes, Egg on Pedestal, light blue luster and gold trim, Colonial scenes, two scenes on teapot, one scene matches scene on creamer, other matches scene on sugar, unmarked, mold 601, price for three piece set **750.00**

Floral dec, hp, emb gold trim, lavender and pale green ground, cov teapot, creamer and sugar, price for three piece set. **265.00**

Urn, cov, cottage and mill scenes, price for pair. **3,475.00**

Vase, 9½" h, cottage scene, young woman coming out of door, green and blue ground, gold jewels, double handles, red mark. **250.00**

Plate

6¾" d, cherubs dec **80.00**

7½" d, The Cage, cobalt blue, heavy gold **695.00**

Powder Dish, Night Watch, green shading **410.00**

Tea Set, cov teapot, creamer, and cov sugar, dogwood dec, blue and gold trim, price for three piece set **300.00**

Vase

6¾" h, handled, sunflowers dec . . . **110.00**

12" h, ovoid body tapering to short wide neck with flat rim, open angled gold handles at shoulder, dancing classical ladies in woodland setting dec, price for pair. **2,400.00**

R. S. TILLOWITZ

Box, cov, 4" d, Melon Eaters scene . . **150.00**

Relish Tray, 8" l, oval, hp, shaded green, white roses, green leaves, center handle, blue mark. **35.00**

Vase

6" h

Black and white pheasants dec, plain mold **260.00**

Golden pheasants dec, plain mold **260.00**

10¾" h, ovoid body, flared rim, allegorical scene of Peace Bringing Plenty, dark shaded green and brown ground, deep red gilt trimmed top border. **1,800.00**

R. S. Suhl, dish, classical ladies in white, pink, and yellow, green ground, light green ext., 8" l, 4⅝" w, $475.00.

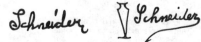

R. S. SUHL

Coffee Set, figural scenes, gold trim, cov coffeepot, creamer and sugar, six cups and saucers, some pcs marked "Angelica Kauffmann," price for 15 piece set **1,700.00**

SCHNEIDER GLASS

History: Brothers Ernest and Charles Schneider founded a glassworks at Epiney-sur-Seine, France, in 1913. Charles, the artistic designer, previously had worked for Daum and Galle.

Although Schneider art glass is best known, the firm also made table glass, stained glass, and lighting fixtures. The art glass exhibits simplicity of design; bubbles and streaking often are found in larger pieces. Other wares include cameo cut and hydrofluoric acid–etched designs.

Schneider signed its pieces with a variety of script and block signatures, "Le Verre Francais," or "Charder." Robert, son of Charles, assumed the art direction in 1948. Schneider moved to Loris in 1962.

Bowl
    5½" d, 3" h, Cluthra, amethyst, turquoise, and clear, irregular bubbles, side acid stamped "Schneider" with underline, base marked "France" **470.00**
    11" d, 5½" h, Cluthra, wide squatty bulbous body, closed rim, bubbled and striated pink, white, and clear, applied clear medial swagged band, acid stamped "Schneider" . . **1,100.00**
    14¾" d, 14" h, flaring, mottled yellow ground, streaked and mottled blue border, cylindrical opaque glass stem with internal ribs in light gray to black, wrought iron ring base mounting with three radiating ribs, down scrolled feet with three leaves, three pieces of opaque rust, amber, and yellow glass fruit, sgd on stem base, base rusted **990.00**
Compote, 9" d, 4¾" h, wide flaring conical body, flattened rim and knop, round foot, faux marble design, pink, maroon, and yellow striations, amethyst knop and foot, engraved "Schneider" **420.00**
Ewer, 12¾" h, elongated oval, handle, mottled chartreuse dec, shaded brown and orange overlay, cameo etched stylized foliate designs of four snails, embedded candy cane signature at base edge **1,210.00**
Finger Bowl and Underplate, 4½" d bowl, 7¼" d underplate, mottled red, burnt umber and clear, stamped mark **330.00**
Vase
    6½" h, sphere, flaring rim, thick clear glass, ribbed walls internally dec with random pattern of bubbles, orange overlaid shoulder, wheel carved band of stylized flowers, mottled deep violet pedestal base, inscribed "Schneider," acid stamped "France" **3,300.00**
    7" h
        Bulbous, cylindrical neck, yellow and pink mottled ground, brown casing, two applied crimped orange handles, engraved "Schnei-

der" and logo, slightly ground rim **440.00**
Sphere, flaring trumpet form neck, cameo, mottled orange and yellow, blue–brown overlay, cut repeating design of stylized leaves and blossoms, cameo sgd "Charder". **420.00**
13½" h overall, 5 x 6" sphere, blue, white, and colorless body, purple shaded to lavender overlay, etched Art Deco stylized blossoms, wrought metal scrolling foliate trifid base side sgd "Le Verre Francais" and "Charder". **660.00**

Vase, fluted, light amber, sgd, 7½" h, 7" d, $135.00.

14" h, tapering cylindrical, baluster neck, orange overlay, five clusters of pendant grapes, geometric pattern cut foot over yellow mottled ground, inset cane at base **600.00**
14⅜" h, sphere, cylindrical neck, circular foot, clear glass streaked with lemon yellow shading to deep purple, applied orange glass ring turnings on neck and waist, four applied angular handles of clear glass streaked with pumpkin orange, intaglio sgd **3,850.00**
15¼" h, attenuated ovoid, clear internally dec, overall pattern of air bubbles, two applied black handles at shoulder with terminals finely wheel carved as bouquet of flowers, tendril extending to mottled purple circular foot, intaglio sgd "Schneider," c1925 . . . . **3,575.00**
24" h, mottled and bubbled pastel yellow and colorless body, amber–orange overlay, acid etched five repeating elements of grapes or berry clusters above and below honey-

comb patterned borders, swirled cane mark embedded in base **900.00**

SCHOENHUT TOYS

History: Albert Schoenhut, son of a toymaker, was born in Germany in 1849. In 1866 he ventured to America to work as a repairman of toy pianos for Wanamaker's in Philadelphia, Pennsylvania. Finding the glass sounding bars inadequate, he perfected a toy piano with metal sounding bars. His piano was an instant success, and the A. Schoenhut Company had its beginning.

From that point, toys seemed to flow out of the factory. Each of his six sons entered the business. The business prospered until 1934, when misfortune forced the company into bankruptcy. In 1935 Otto and George Schoenhut contracted to produce the Pinn Family Dolls.

At the same time, the Schoenhut Manufacturing Company was formed by two other Schoenhuts. Both companies operated under a partnership agreement that eventually led to O. Schoenhut, Inc., which continues today.

Some dates of interest: 1872—toy piano invented; 1903—Humpty and Dumpty and Circus patented; 1911–1924—wooden doll production; 1928–1934—composition dolls.

References: Carol Corson, *Schoenhut Dolls*, Hobby House Press, 1993; Richard O'Brien, *Collecting Toys, 6th Edition*, Books Americana, 1993.

Collectors' Club: Schoenhut Collectors Club, 45 Louis Ave., West Seneca, NY 14224.

Animal

Buffalo, Style III, leather horns, missing tail. **575.00**
Cow, 8½" l, Style I **475.00**
Elephant, 8" l, wood, gray, glass eyes, circus dec on head, missing tail and left tusk. **35.00**
Hippopotamus, 9½" l, Style I **260.00**

Elephant, glass eyes, repainted trunk, $100.00.

Leopard, 7" l, Style I, ball jointed neck, glass eyes. **350.00**
Lion, 7½" l, Style III **550.00**
Poodle, 4¼" h, 9¼" l, glass eyes . . **150.00**
Rhinoceros, 8¾" l, Style II **325.00**
Tiger, 7¼" l, Style I, ball jointed neck, glass eyes. **275.00**
Catalog, 1913, black and white and color illus **80.00**
Circus
Accessories
Chariot, 14" l, pressed paperboard, red stained platform, clown and burro. **3,400.00**
Humpty Dumpty Cage Wagon, 12" l, orange–red, stenciled lettering. . . . **1,300.00**
Humpty Dumpty Set, reduced size, animals, ring masters, lady acrobat, clowns, hobo, and tent, 1924, price for set. **2,200.00**
Set, clown, two elephants, tiger, camel, giraffe, horse, donkey, and two pedestals, price for ten piece set **660.00**
Performer
Acrobat, man, 7¾" h, holding barbell. **425.00**
Bare Back Rider, lady, 6¾" h, wood. **85.00**
Clown, 7¼" h, worn face **40.00**
Ring Master, 8½" h **170.00**
Doll
14" h, wood socket head, painted blue eyes and facial features, blonde hair, spring jointed wood body, stamped "Foreign Countries" **420.00**
14½" h, baby, painted features, mohair wig, bent limb body, imp 11913 mark. **440.00**
15" h, open–closed mouth, painted teeth, blonde mohair wig. **195.00**
16" h, boy, wood, wire strung, brown intaglio eyes, closed mouth, wistful expression, molded brown hair, coat and pants, orig shoes and socks, imp mark "Schoenhut/Jan 17 '11 USA/& Foreign Countries". . **770.00**
19" h, intaglio eyes, closed mouth, mohair wig, damaged hands, paint chips, repainted **250.00**
21½" h, blue sleep eyes, open closed mouth, painted teeth, nurse outfit, blue stamp mark **600.00**
22" h, pouty mouth, brown painted intaglio eyes. **850.00**
Personalities
Barney Google, 7¼" h, orig paper label, missing one ear. **325.00**
Boob McNutt, 8½" h **1,550.00**
Maggie, 9" h, with rolling pin **200.00**
Max and Moritz, 7½" and 8" h, price for pair **600.00**

Piano and Bench, 23¾" h, 23½" l, fine
condition, 1920s **130.00**

SCIENTIFIC INSTRUMENTS

History: Chemists, doctors, geologists, naviga-
tors, and surveyors used precision instruments as
tools of their trade. Such objects are well designed
and beautifully crafted. The principal medium is
brass. Fancy hardwood cases also are common.

References: Crystal Payton, *Scientific Collectibles Identification & Price Guide*, published by author, 1978; Anthony Turner, *Early Scientific Instruments, Europe 1400–1780*, Sotheby's Publications, 1987.

Periodicals: *Rittenhouse,* American Scientific
Instrument Enterprise, PO Box 151, Hastings–on–
Hudson, NY 10706; *Scientific, Medical & Mechan-
ical Antiques,* 11824 Taneytown Pike, Taneytown,
MD 21787.

Collectors' Clubs: Maryland Microscopical Society, 8261 Polk St., McLean VA, 22102; The
Oughtred Society, 8338 Colombard Court, San
Jose, CA 95135; Zeiss Historica Society, PO Box
631, Clifton, NJ 07012.

Museum: National Museum of American History
Branch, Smithsonian Institution, Washington, D.C.

Barometer
   French, 41¼" h, hardwood, floral dec,
     orig white and red paint, "Richard"
     label **715.00**

**Surveyor's Compass, brass, J. Gilbert,
England, compass and sight only,
needle off pivot, 12" l, 5⅜" d, $325.00.
Photograph courtesy of Richard A.
Bourne Co., Inc.**

TS & JD Negus, NY, stick, brass, orig
   case **450.00**
Binoculars, Carl Hellstam & Co, 1920   **55.00**
Chronometer, ship's, Hamilton, 5" d, orig
   case **400.00**
Compass, Telltale, 5½" d, brass, mid
   19th C **850.00**
Globe, table, celestial
   Gilman Joslin, Boston, second quarter
     19th C, 14½" h, imperfections **2,420.00**
   Merriam Moore & Co, Troy, NY, sec-
     ond quarter 19th C, 12" h,
     imperfections. **1,210.00**
Inclinometer, French, cased, marked
   "Made by H Bellieni of Nancy," dated
   1900 . . . . **125.00**
Octant
   13" l, H Duren, NY, ebony, brass arm,
     ivory scales and label, mahogany
     case with "A Stowell" label, early
     19th C. **500.00**
   17¾" l, rosewood, ivory scales, brass
     radial arm, ivory nameplate with in-
     cised "Joseph Clark 79" **600.00**
Protractor, Crane & Vinton, Brattleboro,
   VT, 23¼" l, brass and steel, dated
   1858 . . . . **165.00**
Quadrant
   Frye & Shaw, NY, 12" l, cased, brass
     radial arm, ivory scales and name-
     plate, orig label **800.00**
   J Bassnett, Liverpool, 13¼" l, ebony,
     brass radial arm, ivory scales and
     label "John Martin". **410.00**
Sextant, Lewis, South Shields, brass,
   cased with green felt lining. **375.00**
Slide Rule, Keuffel & Esser **22.50**
Surveyor's Compass, 13" l, wood,
   marked "Made by Thomas Green-
   ough, Boston N. England," mid 18th
   C, minor imperfections. **1,210.00**
Surveyor's Transit
   Brunson, Kansas City, MO, ball bear-
     ing dustproof spindle, 18"
     telescope **325.00**
   Keuffel & Esser, NY, Corp of Engi-
     neers issue, table model for map
     reading **400.00**
Telegraph, ship's, 17" h, brass, lamps   **630.00**
Telescope
   Bardou & Son, Paris, 35¾" l, two in-
     terchangeable lenses, 63" h tripod,
     mahogany case **1,430.00**
   Heath & Co, London, single draw, ta-
     pered wood barrel, wrapped cord. . **250.00**
   L H Marriott, single draw, orig leather
     wrapped barrel, marked "Welling-
     ton N Z," dated 1844 . . . . **225.00**
   S & B Solomons, high power, re-
     placed leather barrel, orig tripod . . **880.00**
Theolodite, surveyor's, Troughton &
   Simms, London, sighting telescope,

compass, spirit levels, beveled azimuth scale, mahogany tripod, fitted box, 19th C. **4,400.00**

SCRIMSHAW

History: Norman Flayderman defined scrimshaw as "the art of carving or otherwise fashioning useful or decorative articles as practiced primarily by whalemen, sailors, or others associated with nautical pursuits." Many collectors expand this to include the work of Eskimos and the War of 1812 French POWs.

Collecting scrimshaw was popularized during the presidency of John F. Kennedy.

References: E. Norman Flayderman, *Scrimshaw, Scrimshanders, Whales And Whalemen,* N. Flayderman & Co., 1972, out of print; Stuard M. Frank, *Dictionary of Scrimshaw Artists,* Mystic Seaport Museum, 1991; Nina Hellman and Norman Brouwer, *A Mariner's Fancy: The Whaleman's Art of Scrimshaw,* South Street Seaport Museum, Balsam Press, and the University of Washington Press, 1992; Martha Lawrence, *Scrimshaw: The Whaler's Legacy,* Schiffer Publishing, 1993; Richard C. Malley, *Graven By The Fishermen Themselves,* Mystic Seaport Museum, 1983.

Museums: Cold Spring Whaling Harbor Museum, Cold Spring Harbor, NY; Kendall Whaling Museum, Sharon, MA; Mystic Seaport Museum, Mystic, CT; National Maritime Museum, San Francisco, CA; Old Dartmouth Historical Society, New Bedford, MA; New Bedford Whaling Museum, New Bedford, MA; Pacific Whaling Museum, Waimanalo, HI; Sag Harbor Whaling & Historical Museum, Sag Harbor, NY; San Francisco Maritime National Historical Park, San Francisco, CA; South Street Seaport Museum, New York, NY; Whaling Museum, Nantucket, MA.

Reproduction Alert: The biggest problem in the field is fakes. A very hot needle will penetrate the common plastics used in reproductions. Ivory will not generate static electricity when rubbed; plastic will. Patina is not a good indicator; it has been faked with tea, tobacco juice, burying in a raw rabbit hide, and other ingenious ways. Usually an old design will not be of consistent depth of cut as the ship rocked and tools dulled; however, skilled forgers have even copied this.

Bodkin, 5⅜" l, whale ivory, inlaid tortoise shell bands, mid 19th C **175.00**
Box, 7" l, ivory triangles and hearts, incised "Mae Hyde 1851". **135.00**
Busk, 12¹⁵/₁₆" l, bone engraved full-length portrait of woman, American man of war ship passing by lighthouse and fort, sgd "Zerviah," early 19th C   **880.00**
Cane
  32" l, wood shaft, whale's tooth handle, last half 19th C **55.00**

32½" l, rope carved wood shaft, turned whale ivory knob, mid 19th C **80.00**
33⅛" l, whalebone shaft, inlaid walrus ivory handle, second quarter 19th C **165.00**
36" l, whalebone shaft, silver collar, sculpted beast head handle, mid 19th C. **880.00**
Carpenter's Level, 26½" l, walnut, geometric wood inlays and border, brass bound, nameplate with "WT," 19th C   **400.00**
Chest, 19" w, 12" d, 11" h, walrus and elephant ivory, lift top, two drawers, applied whale figures, hearts, stars, tulips, compass roses, ship, and triangles dec, whaling scene engraved on lead panel int., last half 19th C. . . **3,500.00**
Coat Rack, 29½" l, wood, three whale tooth hooks mounted on panbone, mid 19th C **800.00**

Stamp, whale ivory, full whale stamp, inscribed "Maria, 1837," 1¼" d, 1¾" h, $450.00.

Corset Busk
  11⅛" l, second quarter 19th C **150.00**
  12⅞" l, engraved Scotsman with bagpipes, whaling scene, sailor, hearts, and geometric designs, 19th C . . . **550.00**
Dipper, 16" l, made by Captain William W Eldredge, third quarter 19th C. . . . **770.00**
Ditty Box, cov, 6⅜" l, panbone, wood top and bottom, engraved scene **550.00**
Figure, 5¼" h, bird, mounted on whale tooth section with carved swans, 19th C. **225.00**
Jagging Wheel
  4½" l, three–tined fork, heart motif, mid 19th C **350.00**
  7⅛" l, whale ivory, reticulated, first half 19th C. **880.00**

Jewelry Box, 6½″ l, whale's tooth, three—tined fork and wheel, mid 19th C. 425.00

Knife Box, 14⅜″ l, wood and whale ivory inlays, includes thirteen pieces of bone handled flatware, 19th C 500.00

Knitting Needles, 16½″ l, inlaid coconut wood rings, clenched hands holding snake ends, 19th C 850.00

Mirror, 13¼″ l, hand, wood frame, whalebone, animal bone, baleen, and mother of pearl inlay, mid 19th C . . . 250.00

Needle Holder, 3″ h, whale ivory, pierced, mounted on green velvet, c1840. . . . . 600.00

Pastry Tool, 6¾″ l, whale ivory, three-tined fork, crimper, and pinned hanger, early 19th C 450.00

Powder Horn, 10″ l, engraved panoramic whaling and hunting scenes, ship, whaleboat, and Indian tepee around bottom, 19th C 880.00

Ring, sculpted clasped hands, last half 19th C 220.00

Rolling Pin
15¼″ l, ebony and whale ivory handles, mid 19th C. 250.00
15½″ l, ivory handles, mid 19th C . 275.00

Sealing Wax Stamp, 2½″ l, whale ivory, mid 19th C 125.00

Seam Rubber, 4¾″ l, reglued handle, mid 19th C 130.00

Sewing Basket, 8¾ x 9¼″, hexagonal, whale ivory and whalebone, reticulated, acorn finial, mid 19th C 4,400.00

Straightedge, 9″ l, incised garland dec, mid 19th C 135.00

Swift, 15¼″ h, stepped wood base, mid 19th C 710.00

Vase, 6¾″ h, whale's tooth, mounted on whale ivory base, engraved sailing ship, 19th C, price for pair 500.00

Walrus Tusk
13½″ l, patriotic symbols, map of New Bedford harbor. 275.00
26″ l, engraved whales, ships, etc. . 440.00

Whale's Tooth
5″ l, engraved figure of young man, waving hat, third quarter 19th C. . 275.00
6″ l, engraved rooster, eagle, and ship on one side, other with humorous dog's head, mid 19th C. 330.00

SEBASTIAN MINIATURES

History: Sebastians are hand-painted, lightly glazed figurines of characters from literature and history. They range in size from 3 to 4 inches. Each figurine is made in limited numbers. Other series include children and scenes from family life.

Prescott W. Baston, the originator and designer of Sebastian figures, began production in 1938 in Marblehead, Massachusetts. Sebastian Studios are located in Hudson, Massachusetts. Prescott Baston died on May 25, 1984.

Each year a Sebastian Auction is held in Boxborough, Massachusetts, at the Sebastian Collector's Society meeting. Prices are determined from this source plus the work of the Sebastian Exchange Board, which develops a price list that is the standard reference for the field.

References: Dr. Glenn S. Johnson, *The Sebastian Miniature Collection & A Guide To Identifying, Understanding, and Enjoying Sebastian Miniatures*, Lance Corp., 1982; Paul J. Sebastian (comp.), *1991–92 Value Register Handbook For Sebastian Miniatures*, The Sebastian Exchange, 1990.

Collectors' Club: Sebastian Collector's Society, 321 Central Street, Hudson, MA 01749.

Lobsterman, Marblehead paper label, $45.00.

Abraham Lincoln, seated	125.00
Baby Buggy of 1850	90.00
Betsy Ross, #129	85.00
Davy Crockett, #249	225.00
Evangeline, #12	125.00
George and Martha Washington, price for pair.	110.00
Gibson Girl, #316–A	90.00
Henry Hudson, #311	175.00
Kennel Fresh, ashtray, #239	300.00
Little Gorge, American National Bank, Nashville, TN, 1966, #350–A	225.00
Manager	20.00
Mark Twain, #315	100.00
Parade Rest, #216	100.00
Raphael's Madonna	20.00
Santa Claus	25.00
Thomas Jefferson, #124	85.00
Town Crier	25.00
Uncle Sam	25.00

1778

c 1793-1804

Jevres
25
1825

DECORE A SEVRES

DECORATOR MARK
1873

1000

SÈVRES

History: The principal patron of the French porcelain industry in early-18th-century France was Jeanne Antoinette Poisson, Marquise de Pompadour. She supported the Vincennes factory of Gilles and Robert Dubois and their successors in their attempt to make soft-paste porcelain in the 1740s. In 1753 she moved the porcelain operations to Sèvres near her home, Chateau de Bellevue.

The Sèvres soft-paste formula used sand from Fontainbleu, salt, saltpeter, soda of alicante, powdered alabaster, clay, and soap. Louis XV allowed the firm to use the "double L's." Many famous colors were developed, including a cobalt blue. The great scenic designs on the ware were painted by such famous decorators as Watteau, La Tour, and Boucher. In the 18th century Sèvres porcelain was the world's foremost diplomatic gift.

In 1769 kaolin was discovered in France and a hard-paste formula developed. The baroque gave way to rococo, a style favored by Jeanne du Barry, Louis XV's next mistress. Louis XVI took little interest in Sèvres. Many factories began to turn out counterfeit copies. In 1876 the factory was moved to St. Cloud and was eventually nationalized.

Reference: Susan and Al Bagdade, *Warman's*

English & Continental Pottery & Porcelain, Second Edition, Wallace–Homestead, 1991.
Reproduction Alert.

Bowl, 10⅜″ d, scattered floral sprigs center, int. and ext. rim with floral garland suspended from rose, purple and blue bowknots pendant, berried floral wreaths, gilt dotted band, scalloped rim, blue enamel interlaced L's, incised "25".	660.00
Box, cov, 2 x 3½″, floral dec	220.00
Chocolate Cup and Saucer, cov, painted scattered sprays of flowers, blue line and gilt dash borders, gilt dentil rim.	275.00
Cup and Saucer, pink rose spray, foliate garland rim, late 18th C	225.00
Dish, 9¾″ d, central floral design with fruit, border reserve of oval panels painted with floral groups surrounded by gilt floral sprigs and scrolls, green ground, gilt edged rim, c1750	175.00
Figure, 6½″ h, allegorical Winter figure, putti at fire, C–scroll base, mid 18th C	470.00

Figurines, unglazed white pair, marble and gilt metal bases, 8″ h, $3,000.00.

Pin Box, 6½″ l, oval, cartouche of romantic couple on cov, blue ground	275.00
Plate	
9″ d, center reserve of pansies, trailing roses border, cobalt dec rim, late 18th C.	350.00
9½″ d, center reserve of Passage Su Rhin, turquoise and red floral motif, jeweled cobalt blue border, gilt highlights, sgd "Moreau," 19th C	375.00
Platter, 13¼″ l, oval, painted military camp scene reserve, scrolling gilt border, cobalt scalloped rim	605.00

Potpourri Bottle, 11″ h, baluster, enlongated neck, reserves of frolicking putti and rose garland monogram, blue celeste ground, gilt highlights, 19th C, price for pair **550.00**

Saucer, 5¼″ d, floral garland tied with bow and floral spray dec, 18th C. . . . **220.00**

Soup Plate, 9½″ d, scattered flower sprigs, three kidney shape flower panels surrounded by apple green border with gilt tooled floral garlands, c1775, price for set of six **1,400.00**

Tray, 16″ l, oval, putti with bales of wheat center, rim with floral reserves, blue celeste ground, scrolled and rocaille handles, late 18th C. **1,500.00**

Tureen, cov, 10½″ h, fruit and flower bouquets surrounded by blue feathered borders, cluster of artichoke and onion finial, four scroll feet, gilt foliate handles tied with blue ribbon, crack in base, reglued knob, c1765. . . . . **1,125.00**

Urn

8″ h, cov, medallion of woman, dark green ground, ormolu mounts, artist sgd. **295.00**

10½″ h, figures in landscape scene cartouche, flowers in reserve, azure blue ground, ormolu salamander handles, base, collar, and finial, sgd "G Poitewin" **1,540.00**

14″ h, baluster, courting couple and landscape reserves, yellow ground with gilt dec, scrolled handles, 19th C, price for pair **1,760.00**

Vase

11″ h, lobed ovoid, earthenware, streaked cobalt blue and turquoise glaze, gilt bronze collar cast with berried leafage, gilt bronze ring turned foot rim, c1900. . . . . **1,375.00**

21½″ h, landscape and figures in garden reserves, two wreath handles, gilt metal dec. **550.00**

29″ h, scene of wedding of Napoleon and Josephine, gilt designs, apple green ground, ormolu mounts, sgd "David," cov missing **4,675.00**

SEWING ITEMS

History: As late as 50 years ago, a wide variety of sewing items was found in almost every home in America. Women of every economic and social status were skilled in sewing and dressmaking. Even the most elegant ladies practiced the art of embroidery with the aid of jeweled gold and silver thimbles. Sewing birds, an interesting convenience item, were used to hold cloth (in the bird's beak) while sewing. Made of iron or brass, they could be attached to a table or shelf with a screw-type fixture. Later models featured a pincushion.

References: Carter Bays, *The Encyclopedia of Early American Sewing Machines,* published by author, 1993; Victor Houart, *Sewing Accessories: An Illustrated History,* Souvenir Press (London), 1984; Dana G. Morykan and Harry L. Rinker, *Warman's Country Antiques & Collectibles, Second Edition,* Wallace-Homestead, 1994; Gay Ann Rogers, *American Silver Thimbles,* Haggerston Press, 1989; Gay Ann Rogers, *An Illustrated History of Needlework Tools,* Needlework Unlimited, 1983, 1989 price guide; Gay Ann Rogers, *Price Guide Keyed To American Silver Thimbles,* Needlework Unlimited, 1989; James W. Slaten, *Antique American Sewing Machines: A Value Guide,* Singer Dealer Museum, 1992; Estelle Zalkin, *Zalkin's Handbook Of Thimbles & Sewing Implements,* Warman Publishing Co., 1988.

Collectors' Club: International Sewing Machine Collectors Society, 1000E Charleston Blvd., Las Vegas, NV 89104; Thimble Collectors International, 6411 Montego Bay Dr., Louisville, KY 40228.

Museums: Fabric Hall, Historic Deerfield, Deerfield, MA; Museum of American History, Smithsonian Institution, Washington, D.C.; Sewing Machine Museum, Oakland, CA; Shelburne Museum, Shelburne, VT.

Additional Listings: See Thimbles and *Warman's Americana & Collectibles* for more examples.

Booklet, *Directions For Using The Light Running New Home Sewing Machine,* Orange, MA, 1890, 16 pgs, engravings **10.00**

Button Cabinet, 24″ h, 18″ w, 13″ d, Banasch's Sewing Supplies, Cincinnati, OH, door with mounted button display int., forty drawers with buttons **250.00**

Needlecase and Seam Ripper, silver, 4¼″ l, $150.00.

Buttonhook, sterling, repousse, floral
and scroll dec. **30.00**
Display Case, Boye Crochet Hook,
wood, dovetailed, glass front **275.00**
Hem Marker, mini–skirt, hemline
marker, plastic container with powder,
and instruction sheet, orig white, blue,
and purple box, Orco Products Inc,
c1960. . . . . **45.00**
Needle Case
Boye, includes needles **295.00**
Figural, 2" h, porcelain, robed mother
holding nursing child, enamel dec . **275.00**
Quilting Frame, 41 x 95", pine, old blue
paint, red and yellow striping **385.00**
Sewing Box
9" d, 7" h, poplar, cylindrical, orig yellow varnish and red and black stenciled dec, arrows and foliage de-
sign, turned handle. **665.00**
10" h, Victorian, late 19th C, lacquered
papier mâché, painted roundels of
dogs among gilt and mother of pearl
designs, lift top, fitted compartment,
cabinet enclosing three drawers,
minor losses **1,210.00**
14" l, Anglo Indian, 19th C, bone inlaid
sandalwood, coffered top, int. fitted
with compartments. **1,100.00**
Sewing Rocker, 28½" h, Empire, ma-
hogany, worn rush seat, old finish. . . **55.00**
Spinning Wheel, 39" h, 20" d wheel,
hardwood, bobbin tension adjust-
ment, old finish **110.00**
Spool Chest, walnut, maple inlay, four
drawers, replaced brass ring pulls, old
dark finish, 23½" w, 14¼" d, 17½" h **500.00**
Thread Caddy
Hardwood, 6" h, ftd, turned, wire pins,
pin cushion top, old finish **30.00**
Treen, two compartments, worn var-
nish, sgd and numbered "C G
Pease Mfg, Concord, Lake Co.
Ohio 593". **275.00**
Watch Fob, Broom Sewing Machine,
1½" d, silvered metal, raised sewing
machine, marked on back, "The Baltimore Automatic Broom Sewing Ma-
chine," early 1900s **50.00**

SHAKER

History: The Shakers, so named because of a
dance used in worship, are one of the oldest com-
munal organizations in the United States. This religious group was founded by Mother Ann Lee, who
emigrated from England and established the first
Shaker community near Albany, New York, in
1784. The Shakers reached their peak in 1850 with
6,000 members.

Shakers lived celibate and self-sufficient lives.

Their philosophy stressed cleanliness, order, simplicity, and economy. Highly inventive and moti-
vated, the Shakers created many utilitarian household forms and objects. Their furniture reflected a
striving for quality and purity in design.

In the early 19th century, the Shakers produced
many items for commercial purposes. Chairmaking
and the packaged herb and seed business thrived.
In every endeavor and enterprise, the members
followed Mother Ann's advice: "Put your hands to
work and give your heart to God."

References: Michael Horsham, *The Art of the
Shakers,* Apple Press, 1989; Dana G. Morykan and
Harry L. Rinker, *Warman's Country Antiques & Col-
lectibles, Second Edition,* Wallace-Homestead,
1994; Charles R. Muller and Timothy D. Rieman,
The Shaker Chair, Canal Press, 1984; Timothy D.
Rieman and Jean M. Burks, *The Complete Book
of Shaker Furniture,* Harry N. Abrams, 1993; June
Sprigg and Jim Johnson, *Shaker Woodenware: A
Field Guide,* Berkshire House, 1991; June Sprigg
and David Larkin, *Shaker Life, Work, and Art,*
Stewart, Tabori & Chang, 1987.

Periodical: *The Shaker Messenger,* PO Box
1645, Holland, MI 49422.

Museums: Hancock Shaker Village, Pittsfield,
MA; Shaker Historical Museum, Shaker Heights,
OH; Shaker Village of Pleasant Hill, Harrodsburg,
KY 40330; The Shaker Museum and Library, Old
Chatham, NY.

Basket
10 x 29 x 18", laundry, slat handle . **125.00**
17" d, 24" h, woven splint, faded black
and red, Union Village **65.00**
Beeswax Molds, 2" d, wood, Mt Leba-
non, price for pair **125.00**

**Blanket Box, child's, pine, single
drawer, bracket feet, orig red stain,
Canterbury, NH, early 19th C, 33¼" w,
16¼" d, 24¾" h, $8,250.00. Photograph
courtesy of Skinner, Inc.**

Blanket Chest, 37½" w, 16½" d, 18" h, pine, dovetailed case, bracket feet, large till with dovetailed drawer, refinished, back feet repair, Mt Lebanon . 1,320.00

Box, 5½" l, oval, painted black, Harvard 90.00

Candlestand, 19¾" d, walnut, turned column, tripod base with cutout legs, replaced top, refinished 665.00

Chair, 39¼" h, side, ladderback, hardwood, three slat back with turned finials, old dark brown finish, back feet with wooden levelers 880.00

Churn, 14½" h, stave constructed, wood bands, worn old red finish, handle, Mt Lebanon. 255.00

Cupboard, 27¾" w, 35¾" h, hanging, poplar and cherry, paneled doors, replaced cornice molding, Union Village 610.00

Desk, elder's, 31½" w, 22" d, 34¼" h, country Hepplewhite style, slant top, mortised and pinned apron, sq tapered legs 1,200.00

Footwarmer, 7 x 8", walnut, dovetailed case, black velvet top, tin lined int. with whale oil lamps, wire bail handle, ball feet, Mt Lebanon. 275.00

Grain Shovel, 36" l, wood, refinished, Sabbathday Lake 265.00

Grater, 29" l, tin, punched, wood back board, Mt Lebanon 55.00

Herb Box, 6 x 8", cherry, dovetailed, four part int., sliding lid, old finish, Union Village 75.00

Rocker
33" h, ladderback, replaced paper rush seat, refinished red stain, Mt Lebanon, No. 3 . . . . 250.00

34" h, woven back and seat, old refinish, Mt Lebanon, NY label. 425.00

43" h, arm, ladderback, four slat back with traces of black graining, simple turning, replaced ivory taped seat, Union Village. 550.00

Sewing Box
6⅝" h, hard and soft woods, drawer, spool compartment with ivory eyelets, pincushion finial, red stain and varnish 550.00

8¾" h, walnut and maple, one drawer, tambour door, ebonized trim, int. with pullout shelf with pincushion, four post spool holders, two thimble caddies. 440.00

Sewing Stand, 8" h, hardwood, tiered, twelve wire pin spool holders, cherry colored finish 195.00

Storage Box
6¾" d, beech and pine, yellow varnish, copper tack trim 65.00

7¾" d, bentwood, ash and pine, old patina 75.00

10½" d, bentwood, finger construction, minor wear and age crack . . . 525.00

String Holder, 4⅜" d, 3⅜" h, cylindrical, walnut and maple, laminated, Enfield, CT. 250.00

Swift, 20" h, table clamp, orig yellow varnish. 210.00

Table, 20½ x 37", 28" h, poplar and pine, dovetailed drawer, sq tapered legs, refinished 880.00

Work Table, 27¼ x 44", country Hepplewhite style, poplar base, pine top, breadboard section on one end, mortised and pinned apron, sq tapered legs, drop leaf, Sabbathday Lake . . . 175.00

c 1908

SHAVING MUGS

History: Shaving mugs hold the soap, brush, and hot water used to prepare a beard for shaving. They come in a variety of materials, including tin, silver, glass, and pottery. One style is the scuttle, so called because of its "coal scuttle" shape, with separate compartments for water and soap.

Shaving mugs were popular between 1880 and 1925, the period of the great immigration to the United States. At first barbershops used a common mug for all customers. This led to an epidemic of a type of eczema known as barber itch.

Laws were passed requiring each individual to have his own mug. Initially names and numbers were used. This did not work well for those who could not read. The occupational mug developed because illiterate workers could identify a picture of their trade or an emblem of its tools. Fraternal emblems also were used and were the most popular of the decorative forms. Immigrants especially liked the heraldry of the fraternal emblems since it reminded them of what they had left behind in Europe.

European porcelain blanks were decorated by American barber supply houses. Prices ranged from 50 cents for a gold name mug to $2.50 for an elaborate occupational design. Most of the artwork was done by German artists who had immigrated to America.

The invention of the safety razor by King C. Gil-

lette, issued to 3.5 million servicemen during World
War I, brought an end to the shaving mug era.

References: Susan and Al Bagdade, *Warman's
English & Continental Pottery & Porcelain, 2nd Edi-
tion,* Wallace-Homestead, 1991; Ronald S. Barlow,
The Vanishing American Barber Shop, Windmill
Publishing, 1993; Phillip L. Krumholz, *Value Guide
For Barberiana & Shaving Collectibles,* published
by author, 1988; Robert Blake Powell, *Occupa-
tional & Fraternal Shaving Mugs of The United
States,* published by author, 1978.

Collectors' Club: National Shaving Mug Collectors Association, 320 S. Glenwood St., Allentown,
PA 18104.

**Eagle, "James De Gemoro, 1926,"
Felda China, Germany, $150.00.**

BARBERSHOP: FRATERNAL

B of R R T, orange, gray, and red engine, engineer in cab, gilt dec, marked
"J & C Bavaria" 250.00
F of A, gilt deer's head, two crossed
American flags, and floral designs, gilt
dec, fuchsia rim, marked "Germany" 25.00
Loyal Order of Moose, gold circle with
gray moose head, purple and green
floral dec, gilt rim and base, marked
"Germany" 200.00
Masonic, emblem with floral circle, pink
rose garland dec, marked "C T Al-
twasser, Germany" 90.00
P O S of A, emblem with gold star, gilt
dec 30.00
United Mine Workers, clasped hands
emblem flanked by crossed picks and
shovels and floral dec, rose garland
around top, marked "Germany" 155.00

BARBERSHOP: OCCUPATIONAL

Baker, three men wearing white hats
and aprons preparing bread, gilt sprig
dec, marked "P Eiseware" 145.00

Bartender, three men and bar scene, gilt
sprig dec, marked "Austria" 375.00
Blacksmith, anvil and hammer on wood
stump, gilt sprigs, marked "T & V Lim-
oges France" 200.00
Brewery Delivery Wagon, man driving
horse–drawn delivery wagon, sign on
wagon reads "G Ehrets Extra," green,
blue, and brown background, marked
"T & V Limoges France" 525.00
Butcher, butcher with cleaver cutting
meat, meat hanging in background,
marked "Eugene Berninghaus, Cin-
cinnati, Ohio" 350.00
Carpenter, hammer, saw, and plane, gilt
dec, marked "S D Show Barber Sup-
ply Co, Wichita, Kansas" 130.00
Coachman, man sitting on blue cushion
outside carriage, holding whip and
reins, brown horses, gilt dec. 190.00
Cobbler, black man's and woman's boot,
gilt sprig dec, marked "CFH GDM
France" 110.00
Dentist, man wearing gray suit standing
over man sitting in chair, dental office
background, gilt sprig dec, marked
"OCKCI" 22.00
Doctor, man sitting in horse–drawn car-
riage, gilt sprig dec 140.00
Dry Goods Clerk, man with mustache
wearing black suit, female customer,
three bolts of fabric, wall background
with shelves of fabric, marked "CFH
GDM". 575.00
Engineer, red, gray, and yellow engine
pulling gray and black tender, gilt sprig
dec, marked "Limoges France, The
World Our Field, Koken St Louis,
Trademark" 160.00
Farmer, man standing by horses plow-
ing field, farm buildings, and trees, gilt
dec, marked "Decorated by Koken
Barber Supply Co St Louis, MO Con-
gress Chair, best in the world" 325.00
Farrier, man wearing blue vest and
pants, white horse, anvil, and tools,
gilt dec, marked "T & V Limoges
France" 425.00
Fireman, fire truck with driver, marked
"Germany". 1,000.00
Governor, eagle, draped American
flags, and globe, "Governor Eugene
N Foss" flanked by purple roses,
marked "T & V Limoges France" . . . 550.00
Grocery Clerk, man and woman, store
counter background, gilt sprigs. 325.00
Jeweler, cherub holding gold horn up-
side down, clocks and watches falling
from horn, gilt dec, marked "D & C" . 950.00
Livery, man driving horse and buggy,

marked "Livery" and "Eugene
Berninghaus" 200.00
Musician, lyre, mandolin, and tambour-
ine, colorful leaf background, rolled
banner with name, worn gilt 250.00
Seaman, gray and white battleship   . .   450.00
Stove Retailer, fancy wood cook stove
dec, marked "D & C" 715.00
Tailor, man with tape measure around
neck cutting piece of fabric, gilt dec,
marked "T & V Limoges France" . . .   475.00

Tinsmith, crossed tin shears and poker
with tin oven, gilt sprigs 200.00
Trainman, red plank caboose, gilt dec,
marked "H & B T RR" 140.00
Undertaker, man wearing gray suit and
hat, horses pulling hearse, marked "K
F" 650.00
Writer, black desk inkwell with sander,
pen, and brass handle 350.00

BARBERSHOP: OTHER

Automobile, red and yellow convertible
touring car, blue, green, and brown
background, marked "Welmar
Germany" 550.00
Bicycle Racer, pink and yellow flowers,
gilt banner with "Bicycle Racers Madison Square Garden," trophy with
inscription 500.00
Buggy, man sitting in open carriage,
buildings in background, gilt sprig
dec 275.00
Floral and Name, "Jas Cassaday,"
marked "CFH GDM France" 30.00
Good Luck, horse shoe, blue ribbon, red
roses, and four leaf clover, marked "T
& V Limoges France" 60.00
Hunter, holding gun, two dogs, fenced
pasture background 210.00

Scroll, "H B Nester" in black letters outlined in gold, pink and green floral dec,
marked "D/France" 25.00
Victorian Lady, wearing blue and yellow
dress, black background, violet pin-
striping, gilt dec 145.00
Winter Scene, five deer standing in
snow covered pasture, trees, sheds,
and wooded background 30.00

SCUTTLES

American Indian, holding flag 25.00
Coronation of H M King Edward VIII,
18th May 1937, British seal with monarch, flags on reverse 25.00
Lucky Spots, green oval with hand holding four ace cards and dice 22.00

SHAWNEE POTTERY

History: The Shawnee Pottery Co. was founded in 1937 in Zanesville, Ohio. The company acquired a 650,000-square-foot plant that formerly housed the American Encaustic Tiling Company. Shawnee produced as many as 100,000 pieces of pottery per day until 1961, when the plant closed.

Shawnee limited its chief production to kitchen-ware, decorative art pottery, and dinnerware. Distribution was primarily through jobbers and chain stores.

Shawnee can be marked "Shawnee," "Shawnee U.S.A.," "USA #—," "Kenwood," or with character names, e.g., "Pat. Smiley," "Pat. Winnie," etc.

References: Jim and Bev Mangus, *Shawnee Pottery: An Identification and Value Guide*, Collector Books, 1994; Mark Supnick, *Collecting Shawnee Pottery: A Pictorial Reference And Price Guide*, L-W Book Sales, 1989, 1992 value update; Duane and Janice Vanderbilt, *The Collector's Guide To Shawnee Pottery*, Collector Books, 1992.

Collectors' Club: Shawnee Pottery Collectors Club, PO Box 713, New Smyrna Beach, FL 32170.

Teapot, cov, Granny Anne, blue bow,
gold apron, white ground, 8½" h, 7½"
w, $30.00.

Bottle Pitcher, Snowflake, green 45.00
Bowl, 7" d, Kenwood, emb silverware,
#941 . . . .   25.00
Canister, Fernware, blue 55.00
Casserole, cov, King Corn 60.00
Cookie Jar, cov
Dutch Girl, yellow dress, cold paint   150.00
Lucky, cold paint 125.00
Mugsey 525.00
Queen Corn 195.00
Winnie, shamrock 200.00
Creamer
King Corn 25.00
Puss N' Boots, red and green trim   .   85.00
Figurine, bear 35.00
Grease Jar, cov
Adv, Great Northern 60.00
Water Bucket 60.00

Jug
King Corn		75.00
PA Dutch Tulip		175.00

Mixing Bowl, King Corn
#5		45.00
#6		50.00

Pitcher
Bo Peep, marked "17–6–6"		125.00
Smiley, gold trim, peach flower		500.00

Planter, windmill	35.00
Plate, King Corn, #68	45.00
Range Set, Winnie and Smiley	135.00
Relish Dish, Queen Corn	10.00

Salt and Pepper Shakers, pr
Chanticleer	55.00
Flowerpot	25.00
King Corn	24.00
Owl	20.00
Puss N' Boots	15.00

Sugar, cov, King Corn	45.00

Teapot
Granny Anne, peach apron	75.00
King Corn	90.00
Tom–Tom, blue and red	75.00

SILHOUETTES

History: Silhouettes (shades) are shadow profiles produced by hollow cutting, mechanical tracing, or painting. They were popular in the 18th and 19th centuries.

The name came from Etienne de Silhouette, a French Minister of Finance, who tended to be tight with money and cut "shades" as a pastime. In America the Peale family was one of the leading silhouette makers. An impressed stamp marked "PEALE" or "Peale Museum" identifies their work.

Silhouette portraiture lost popularity with the introduction of daguerreotype prior to the Civil War. In the 1920s and 1930s a brief revival occurred when tourists to Atlantic City and Paris had their profiles cut as souvenirs.

References: Shirley Mace, *Encyclopedia of Silhouette Collectibles on Glass*, Shadow Enterprises, 1992; Dana G. Morykan and Harry L. Rinker, *Warman's Country Antiques & Collectibles, Second Edition*, Wallace–Homestead, 1994; Blume J. Rifken, *Silhouettes in America, 1790–1840, A Collectors' Guide*, Pardigm Press, 1987.

Museums: Essex Institute, Salem, MA; National Portrait Gallery, Washington, D.C.

Boy
4½″ h, 3⅝″ w, reverse cut, white paper, black cloth backing, old gilt frame	65.00
5⅝″ h, 4⅝″ w, hollow cut paper, black cloth backing, marked "Charles —," emb letter "M," fold line, edge tears, framed	85.00

Couple, man and woman
4¾″ h, 3¾″ w, hollow cut paper, good detail, ink details on man, stains and insect damage, orig frames, price for pair	330.00
5⅛″ h, 4½″ w, hollow cut paper, ink and watercolor details, emb brass frames, price for pair	715.00
5¼″ h, 4″ w, hollow cut, black paper backing, Alexander and Isabel Loomis McNeil, ink highlights, eglomise mats, orig gilt frames, identified on reverse in pencil, accompanied by further genealogical information, price for pair	660.00
6½″ h, 10″ w, hollow cut paper, ink and watercolor details, pair framed together, sgd "Doyle," eglomise glass with two ovals and gilded frame	412.00

Family, 8″ h, 7″ w, husband, wife with baby on knee, grandparents, two children, hollow cut, watercolor and pencil details, black cloth backing, paper professionally cleaned, orig bird's eye maple frames with turned dark wood buttons on corner blocks, price for set of five	9,900.00

Gentleman
5¼″ d, ink, pencil, and ink wash on paper, stains and faded pencil inscription, orig round turned frame, convex glass	72.00
5¼″ h, 4½″ w, ink and gold wash on paper, black lacquered frame with gilded trim	470.00
5½″ h, 4¾″ w, black painted silhouette on chalk, fine detail, orig black lacquered frame with gilded trim, convex glass	440.00
6¾″ h, 5½″ w, Alexander Hamilton, hollow cut, identified on reverse, imp stamp "Peale's Museum," oval, minor imperfections	220.00
12¾″ h, 7¼″ h, full length, cut black paper, top hat, edges ragged, blue stains, framed	200.00
13½″ h, 7½″ w, William Kerr, Esq., label inscribed "by Forrest St. Muray Howe 19th March," discoloration	275.00
14″ h, 10″ w, full length cut figure, lithographed scenic ground, framed	415.00
16½″ h, 12½″ w, young gentleman, full length cut, top hat, riding crop, black and white litho background, identified as Alexander McNair, 1776–1826, brief biography on back of mahogany veneered beveled frame, minor stains	775.00

Military Officer
5″ h, 4″ w, Brigadier General Henry Knox, watercolor and ink on paper, unsigned, framed	440.00

5⅝" h, 6" w, ink and watercolor on
paper, orange and gold uniforms,
marked "F. Perring 1840" and
"C.C.–1804," repainted black and
gold frames, price for pair **330.00**
10½" h, 8" h, General Henry Dear-
born, full length, gilt highlights,
imperfections. **165.00**

Woman
5¾" h, 5" w, young features, hollow
cut paper, faded pen and ink detail,
flaking eglomise glass, black frame **55.00**
6¾" h, 5" w, young features, hollow
cut paper, braided hair in bun,
framed **140.00**
7¾" h, 6" w, young features, hollow
cut paper, black cloth backing, high
collar, stains and fold line, mahogany veneer frame. **90.00**
11½" h, 8½" w, full length, cut, holding
a book, gilt highlights, giltwood
frame, some foxing, imperfections **220.00**

SILVER

History: The natural beauty of silver lends itself
to the designs of artists and craftsmen. It has been
mined and worked into an endless variety of useful
and decorative items. Pure silver is too soft to be
fashioned into strong, durable, and serviceable
utensils. Therefore, a way was found to give silver
the required degree of hardness by adding alloys
of copper and nickel.

Silversmithing in America goes back to the early
17th century in Boston and New York. It began in
the early 18th century in Philadelphia. Boston was
influenced by the English styles, New York by the
Dutch.

References: Louise Bilden, *Marks Of American
Silversmiths In the Ineson-Bissell Collection*, Uni-
versity of VA Press, 1980; Frederick Bradbury,
Bradbury's Book of Hallmarks, J. W. Northend,
1987; Maryanne Dolan, *1830's–1900's American
Sterling Silver Flatware: A Collector's Identification
& Value Guide*, Books Americana, 1993; Rachael
Feild, *Macdonald Guide To Buying Antique Silver
and Sheffield Plate*, Macdonald & Co., 1988; Don-
ald L. Fennimore, *The Knopf Collectors' Guides To
American Antiques: Silver & Pewter*, Alfred A.
Knopf, 1984; Tere Hagan, *Silverplated Flatware:
An Identification & Value Guide, Revised 4th Edi-
tion*, Collector Books, 1990; Kenneth Crisp Jones
(ed.), *The Silversmiths of Birmingham and Their
Marks, 1750–1980*, N.A.G. Press, 1981, distributed
by Antique Collectors Club; Joel Langford, *Silver:
A Practical Guide To Collecting Silverware and
Identifying Hallmarks*, Chartwell Books, 1991; Ev-
erett L. Maffett, *Silver Banquet II*, Silver Press,
1990; Benton Rabinovitch, *Antique Silver Servers
For The Dining Table*, Joslin Hall Publishing, 1991;
Dorothy T. Rainwater, *Encyclopedia of American*
Silver Manufacturers, 3rd Edition, Schiffer Publish-
ing, 1986; Dorothy T. and H. Ivan Rainwater, *Amer-
ican Silverplate*, Schiffer Publishing, 1988; Jeri
Schwartz, *The Official Identification And Price
Guide To Silver and Silver-Plate, Sixth Edition*,
House of Collectibles, 1989; *Sterling Silver, Silver-
plate, and Souvenir Spoons, Revised*, L–W Book
Sales; Peter Waldon, *The Price Guide To Antique
Silver, 2nd Edition*, Antique Collectors' Club, 1982
(price revision list 1988); Seymour B. Wyler, *The
Book Of Old Silver, English, American, Foreign*,
Crown Publishers, 1937 (available in reprint).

Periodicals: *Silver*, PO Box 1243, Whittier, CA
90609; *The Silver Update*, 3366 Oak West Dr., Ellicott City, MD 21043.

Museums: Bayou Bend Collection, Houston,
TX; Boston Museum of Fine Arts, Boston, MA; Currier Gallery of Art, Manchester, NH; Yale University
Art Gallery, New Haven, CT; Wadsworth Antheneum, Hartford, CT.

Additional Listing: See Silver Flatware in *Warman's Americana & Collectibles* for more examples
in this area.

**American, Marquand & Company, NY,
c1835, Restauration, fruit bowl, wirework body, trailing band of cast grapes
and leaves on rim, pierced scrolling foliage feet, 11¼" w, approx 36 oz,
$2,860.00. Photograph courtesy of Wil-
liam Doyle Galleries.**

AMERICAN, 1790–1840
Mostly Coin

Coin silver is slightly less pure than sterling silver. Coin silver has 900 parts silver to 100 parts
alloy. Sterling silver has 925 parts silver. American
silversmiths followed the coin standards. Coin silver is also cured Pure Coin, Dollar, Standard, or
Premium.

Bailey and Kitchen, Philadelphia, PA,
1833–46, creamer, spheroid body,
scrolled handle, flaring open concave
spout, conforming circular stepped
base, monogrammed. **350.00**

Brasher, Ephraim, New York, NY, 1744–1810, creamer and sugar, bright cut dec, 5½" creamer, 4¾" ftd sugar, repair, imperfections 1,540.00

Caldwell, J. E., Philadelphia, PA, late 19th C, bowl, 11" d, pierced everted rim, chased int., scrolling flowers, monogram, 25 troy oz 900.00

Cann and Dunn, c1838, coffee service, 9½" h coffeepot, cov cream pitcher, cov sugar, pear shaped, fluted sides, floral chased and repousse arabesque panels, applied chased twig form handle, four pierced C–scroll feet, melon finial, coffeepot engraved "Presented to Mrs. H. N. Prewett by the Mayor and citizens of New Orleans," 67 troy oz 2,640.00

Dummer, Jeremiah, Boston, 1645–1718, caudle cup, engraved "NsM" at base, marked "I.D." in heart cartouche, 6 troy oz 2,100.00

Farnman, R. and H., Boston, MA, c1807, teapot, 12" l, Federal style, oval body, banded design engraved on shoulder, hinged lid, urn finial, wood handle . . . 650.00

Farr, John C., Philadelphia, PA, c1843, presentation pitcher, pear shaped body, large pouring lip, applied S–scroll handle, spreading foot with egg and dart border, front engraved "Presented to J. C. & L. Redmond as a mark of respect by their attached domestics, Frankford, May 1, 1843" . . . 605.00

Farrington and Hunnewell, Boston, MA, 1835–55, cake slice, medallion, 6 troy oz 100.00

Hanners, George, Boston, MA, c1720, porringer, 4¾" d, marked twice, small dent 2,640.00

Harding and Co., Newel, Boston, MA, 1822–32, tray, 21" l, engraved Bates family coat of arms, wide wreath of oak leaves and acorns, conforming cast border, cast and pierced feet, marked at base, 103 troy oz 4,400.00

Hurd, Jacob, Boston, MA, 1740–50, sugar nippers, 4¼" l, scissor form, spurred ring grips, shaped arms, shell tips, circular hinge, engraved initials, marked on inside tip, 10 dwts 3,250.00

Jacobi and Jenkins
  Chamberstick, 5½" d, repousse, marked "A. Jacobi," 5 troy oz 385.00
  Platter, 14" l, oval rim, monogram, 20 troy oz 330.00

Jones, J. B., Boston, c1840, teapot, creamer, and sugar, repousse floral sprays, 64 troy oz, price for set. 1,430.00

Kirk, S. and Son, 19th C
  Bowl, 9" d round, repousse, monogram, 11 troy oz 200.00

Tea Service, 15" h hot water kettle on stand, teapot, hot milk pitcher, creamer, sugar, and waste bowl, repousse, engraved crest, later burner, 136 troy oz, price for set . . 6,100.00

Lownes, Joseph, Philadelphia, PA, c1820, tea and coffee service, two teapots, 10½" h coffeepot, creamer, cov sugar, waste bowl, each marked at base, 128 troy oz, price for set . . . 3,520.00

Myers, Myer, New York, NY, 1723–95, teaspoon, engraved initials on handle 225.00

Richardson, Nathaniel and Joseph Jr, Philadelphia, PA, c1790, creamer and sugar urn, engraved monogram, marked twice on base "1 NR" in rect, creamer 8" h, 6 troy oz, cov sugar urn 9" h, 14 troy oz, price for pair 2,310.00

Sargent, J., Hartford, CT, c1795, spoons, coffin end, price for set of six teaspoons, six tablespoons, minor wear and dents, 12 troy oz 660.00

Stanwood, H. B., Boston, MA, mid 19th C, water pitcher, 13" h, chased grapevine and foliage, 44 troy oz 1,430.00

Stoutenburgh, Tobias, NY, 1749, wine taster, tapered circular form, opposed scroll handles, three engraved initials and date. 1,430.00

Warner, A. E., 19th C, sugar basket, 4½" h, repousse, 10 troy oz 330.00

William, Robert and William, Philadelphia, early 19th C, serving spoon, shell pattern, some wear, 14 troy oz, price for set of six 275.00

Wilson, Robert and William, Philadelphia, PA
  Porringer, 1¾" h, c1825–46, marked "R & W Wilson" on reverse of handle, lion rampant mark on side, 6 troy oz 385.00
  Salt, 3" h, c1835, chased floral swag, oak leaf handle, 7½" troy oz 220.00
  Tablespoon, c1825, price for set of five. 135.00

Woodard & Grosjean for Jones Ball & Poor, Boston, tea tray, rect, segmented molded floral rim, center engraved cipher surrounded by floral frame, opposed floral bifurcated handles, 30" l 4,290.00

SILVER, AMERICAN, 1840–1920
Mostly Sterling

There are two possible sources for the origin of the word sterling. The first is that it is a corruption of the name Easterling. Easterlings were German silversmiths who came to England in the Middle Ages. The second is that it is named for the starling (little star) used to mark much of the early English silver.

Sterling has 925/1,000 parts per silver. Copper comprises most of the remaining alloy. American manufacturers began to switch to the sterling standard about the time of the Civil War.

Adams, W., New York, NY, c1842, water pitcher, 17″ h, urn shape, allover floral and scroll repousse dec, C–shape handle with ram's head and leaf dec, circular plinth with loop and dart dec, 48 oz **1,850.00**

Armcraft, Battleboro, MA, tea ball, sterling **55.00**

Ball, Black & Co., New York, NY, c1870, tea set, 6″ h teapot, creamer, and sugar, oval cylindrical, beaded border, engraved foliage, marked "E & S" and "Old Silver," 57 troy oz **700.00**

Baltimore Sterling Silver Co., c1892–1910, tea and coffee service, repousse floral motif, blossom form finial, cast paw feet, 10½″ h coffeepot, teapot, cream pitcher, cov sugar, waste bowl, 99 troy oz **3,520.00**

Dominick & Haff, New York, NY, 1891, entree dish, 12″ l rect, scrolled rim and feet, foliate handles, 64 troy oz **2,970.00**

Durgin Co., William B., Concord, NH, tea and coffee service, retailed by J. E. Caldwell Co., tea and coffee pots, creamer, cov sugar, waste bowl, engraved Colonial Revival style, ivory finials, monogram, some dents, 87 troy oz **1,430.00**

Fletcher and Gardnier, Philadelphia, PA, c1820, hot water kettle on stand, 15½″ h, domed cov, chased vine band, ovoid body with leafy band, scrolled legs, sq base, paw feet, later Tiffany burner, monogram, dents, 103 troy oz **3,200.00**

Gale, William, and Son, NY, 1852, kettle on stand, 16¾″ h, baluster form, twisted wire trim, monogram, burner may be replaced, 59 troy oz **935.00**

Gorham, Providence, RI
Bowl, 1898, 12″ d, lobed hexagonal form, reticulated C–scroll border, 17 troy oz **360.00**
Centerpiece, 1869, 10¾″ h, 9¾″ d, central figural handle, ribbed petal form bowl, 31 troy oz **1,650.00**
Coffee Service, coffeepot, hot water kettle on stand, creamer, and sugar, half reeded Regency style, 73 troy oz **990.00**
Ewer, c1860–70, 11″ h, tapering baluster form, shoulders encircled by beading, C–scroll handle with foliate dec, floral framed repousse re-

serve, retailed by E. A. Tyler, New Orleans, 18 troy oz **770.00**

Flatware Service
Chantilly pattern, c1902, six luncheon forks, salad forks, luncheon knives, teaspoons, and soup spoons; cake lifter, cased, price for 31 pieces, 31 troy oz **470.00**
Versailles pattern, dinner, luncheon, dessert, salad, and seafood forks, teaspoons, demitasse spoons, tablespoons, luncheon knives, butter knives, large serving spoons, carving set, fifteen assorted serving pieces, some monograms, price for 118 pieces, 163 troy oz **4,400.00**

Loving Cup, c1895, 9¾″ h, urn form, chased and repousse floral and foliate motifs, three scrolling handles, domical foot, engraved to winner of New Orleans golf tournament, 54 troy oz **605.00**

Picture Frame, c1890, 9″ h, Rococo taste, scrollwork frame **265.00**

Salad Fork and Spoon, 10″ l, Imperial Chrysanthemum pattern, monogram, 8 troy oz **360.00**

Sauceboat, c1873, 4½″ h, baluster form, acanthus leaf borders, 13 troy oz **275.00**

Tea and Coffee Service, c1926, tea and coffee pots, creamer, cov sugar, waste bowl, flattened baluster form, engraved inscription and initial, 80 troy oz **1,100.00**

Tea Set, fluted Federal style, monogram, 31 troy oz **415.00**

Tray, 25″ l, oval, molded rim, 83 troy oz **1,210.00**

Vase, early 20th C, 15″ h, trumpet shape, applied and engraved prunus dec, hammer textured ground, 14 troy oz **360.00**

Water Pitcher, c1870, 10″ h, Greek Revival design, inscriptions, 26 troy oz **825.00**

International, tea and coffee service, tea and coffee pots, creamer, cov sugar, waste bowl, Colonial style, chased floral and scroll dec, 90 troy oz **1,100.00**

Leinonen, Karl F., Boston, MA, Arts and Crafts era, tray, 12¼″ d round, hammered finish, banded rim, imp marks, 26 troy oz **500.00**

Meriden, Britannia Sterling, Meriden, CT Basket, shaped edge, ftd oval, swing handle, engraved detail, 44 troy oz **880.00**

Punchbowl, 6½″ h, George II style monteith after D. Henchman, 56 troy oz **715.00**

Oakes, Edward E., Boston, MA, c1920,

porringer, 4½" d, 2" h, hammered bowl, raised rim, curvilinear handle, applied oak leaves, imp marks, 9 troy oz **935.00**
Redlich, bowl, shaped circular rim, chased roses, monogram, 14 troy oz **500.00**
Reed & Barton
Bowl, 11" d, Francis I pattern, 42 troy oz, price for pair. **990.00**
Clock, 8½" h, table type, shaped frame, oval dial, etched foliage, numbers missing, small dent. **385.00**
Tea and Coffee Service, tapering baluster form, urn shaped finial, circular base, 9½" h coffeepot, teapot, cov sugar, cream pitcher, and waste bowl, 86 troy oz, price for set **1,320.00**
Shiebler
Serving Spoon, chrysanthemum and cornucopia design, monogram, 5 troy oz **360.00**
Toast Server, chrysanthemum and cornucopia design, monogram, 5 troy oz **385.00**
Shreve, Crump and Low, San Francisco, CA
Candlesticks, pr, 7" h, Queen Anne style, 22 troy oz **550.00**
Cocktail Shaker, 10½" h, cylindrical body, peened surface, removable fishtail pourer, gilt and enameled medallions on sides, bell mark, 20 ozs, 4 dwts **500.00**
Ice Bucket, Arts and Crafts, c1910, 6" h, flaring cylindrical body, applied horizontal staves, swing handle, finger strap below at back, hammered surface, applied monogram on spout, 17 ozs, 6 dwts **400.00**
Teapot, Art Nouveau, 9¼" h, undulating vines, 19 ozs, 10 dwts. **420.00**
Smith, Frank, compote, 10¼" d, pierced and shaped rim, chased leaf and scroll dec, monogram, 22 troy oz . . . **825.00**
Starr, Theodore B., New York, NY, 1900–24
Bowl, 11" d, shaped circular rim with chased and pierced carnations dec, 20 troy oz **660.00**
Tea and Coffee Service, kettle on stand, tea and coffee pots, creamer, sugar, and waste bowl, globular, scalloped gadroon rim and paw feet, monogram, minor dents, 126 troy oz **1,980.00**
Stone, Arthur J., Gardner, MA
Bowl, 7¼" d, 3¾" h, by Herbert A Taylor, c1920, faint hammered pattern, circular foot, imp marks, 14 troy oz **605.00**
Tray, serving, 12½" sq, rounded corners, 35 troy oz **825.00**

Tiffany & Co, New York, NY
Bowl
Oval, c1875, 12" l, egg and dart molded rim, 24 troy oz. **525.00**
Round, 1938–47, low, applied Arts and Crafts floral stripes, 26 troy oz **880.00**
Cake Plate, 10¾" d, etched neoclassical design, monogram, 21 troy oz **770.00**
Center Bowl, 12" d, 3" h, everted rim, chased C–scrolls, brass insert, 41 troy oz **1,155.00**
Compote, low, applied reticulated chrysanthemum rim, surface scratches, 35 troy oz, price for pair **1,980.00**
Demitasse Service, 1907–38, coffeepot, creamer, sugar, tray, twelve cups and saucers with Lenox porcelain liners, 101 troy oz. **4,400.00**
Flatware Service, King William pattern, luncheon forks, salad forks, butter knives, luncheon knives, teaspoons, tablespoons, and sugar tongs, price for 32 pieces, approx 38 troy oz weighable **525.00**
Fork, 7" l, shaped handle, daisies in relief, monogram verso, price for set of eight, 13½" troy oz **550.00**
Punch Ladle, 13" l, Wave Edge pattern, monogram, 9 troy oz. **440.00**
Vase
3" h, 1891–1902, melon form, etched violet design, monogram, 6 troy oz **615.00**
12" h, tapering cylindrical form, etched linear rim dec, base dents, price for pair, 48 troy oz. . **1,760.00**
Vegetable Dish, cov, 9½" d round, molded domed cov, 35 troy oz. . . . **880.00**
Water Pitcher, c1865, 9" h, band of neoclassical designs, 22 troy oz . . **935.00**
Towle, hot water kettle on stand, 13" h, 40 troy oz. **415.00**
Wallace, c1917
Dresser Set, Carthage pattern, c1917, three brushes, comb, hand mirror, jar, and tray, hammered and linear design, monogram, imp marks, dents, price for seven piece set. . . . **275.00**
Hot Water Kettle On Stand, 14" h, pear form, scrolled legs, 43 troy oz **525.00**
Teaspoon, Carthage pattern, c1917, hammered and linear design, set of twelve in orig case, imp marks, approx 7 troy oz **275.00**
Wood & Hughes, NY, c1880
Center Bowl, 13" l, leaf form, fruiting grapevines applied at rim, inscription, 34 troy oz. **4,500.00**
Meat Fork, retailed by A. B. Griswold, New Orleans **150.00**

Continental, teapot on stand, c1879, blossom finial, swing handle stamped "Houret 79," scrolled and chased stand, paw feet, 10" h, $1,210.00. Photograph courtesy of Leslie Hindman Auctioneers.

SILVER, CONTINENTAL

Continental silver does not have a strong following in the United States. The strong feeling of German silver cannot compare with the lightness of the English examples. In Canada, Russian silver finds a strong market.

Austrian, Pressburg, 19th C, maker F.V., inkstand, shaped rect, inkpot, pounce pot, and central raised dish, engraved foliate and lapis finials, silver gilt, 7" l, 10 troy oz **660.00**
Danish, Georg Jensen
 Bowl, leaf and seed openwork base, Model 19A, 7" h, 23 troy oz. **2,200.00**
 Salad Fork and Spoon
  Acorn pattern, approx 5 troy oz . **525.00**
  Cactus pattern, imp "Georg Jensen, Denmark," 9½" l, 6 troy oz **420.00**
 Tea and Coffee Service, tea and coffee pots, creamer, and sugar, hammered lower body, chased overlapping barbed leaves, Model #45C, circular tray, Model #251, 106 troy oz. **9,350.00**
Dutch
 Bowl, 13" l, shaped oval, foliate and geometric reticulated piercing, 14 troy oz **440.00**
 Marrow Scoop, Amsterdam, 19th C, 9¼" l, plain design, double ends, 1 troy oz **375.00**

Tea and Coffee Service, 1896, hot water kettle on stand, tea and coffee pots, creamer, milk jug, sugar, waste bowl, two vases, repousse tavern scenes, dents, stand loose, marker AV/34, 110 troy oz **2,750.00**
 Tea Caddy, 5½" h, repousse, figural stopper. **145.00**
French
 Asparagus Tongs, late 19th C, 10" l, engine turned dec, 950 standard, marked "JG". **220.00**
 Vegetable Dish, cov, 19th C, round, foliate scrolled legs and handles, 8" h, 38 troy oz **880.00**
German
 Bread Basket, 19th C, 15" l, oval, pierced openwork and repousse ornaments, floral garland borders entwining flower filled baskets at ends holding agricultural implements draped over ribbons tied in French knots, alternating with cartouche at either side with scene of kneeling suitor and intended in Alpine landscape, each scene spaced with facing pair of birds and flowers, base with medallion of two infants playing with baby ducks, 800 standard, 15 ozs. **525.00**
 Compote, 11" d, 9¾" h, pierced scalloped rim, reeded vasiform standard, circular base, price for pair . . **385.00**
 Figure, 21" l, pheasants, maker JLS in monogram, glass eyes, female with tail down, male with strutting tail, 800 fine, 52 troy oz, price for pair. **2,530.00**
 Flatware, Menner, early 20th C, dinner forks, luncheon forks, salad forks, dessert forks, teaspoons, tablespoons, soup spoons, egg spoons, demitasse spoons, dinner knives, luncheon knives, dessert knives, butter knives, ladles, carving set, serving forks, serving spoons, stirrers, other serving pieces, monogram, price for 244 pieces, approx 284 troy oz weighable silver **2,200.00**
 Goblet, 3¾" h, 19th C, chased foliage, 3½ troy oz. **360.00**
 Tea and Coffee Service, H. Mau & G. Rutger, tea and coffee pots, creamer, waste bowl, cov jar, and tray, fluted pear form, 152 troy oz **1,870.00**
 Wine Cooler, 11½" h, Baroque, late 19th C, waisted, chased nautical dec, inscribed, 60 troy oz **2,860.00**
Italian
 Candlestick, 9½" h, Neoclassical, attributed to Naples, early 19th C,

knopped shaft, spreading base, engraved diaper bands, marked "GP," city mark, head of woman with "N" over 8, 20 troy oz. **2,100.00**

Plaque, 9½ x 7", Renaissance, Madonna and Child Enthroned, Geneoa, 16th C, repousse, velvet mount with inscription, worn **1,540.00**

Russia, ladle, 12¼" l, 18th C taste, oblong bowl, fiddle form handled, marked "A. K. 1890," 8 troy oz **200.00**

SILVER, ENGLISH

From the 17th century to the mid 19th century, English silversmiths set the styles which American silversmiths copied. The work from the period exhibits the highest degree of craftsmanship. Active collection of English silver takes place in the American antiques marketplace.

Charles I, Apostle spoon, London, 1633, 7½" l, fig shaped bowl, hexagonal stem, surmounted by saint figure, 3 troy oz **1,600.00**

Charles II, tumbler, 2¾" d, hammered sides, slightly convex bottom, marks rubbed, 2 ozs **250.00**

Edward VII
Belt, H. & A., Birmingham, 1901, Art Nouveau style **200.00**
Tea Set, W. Comyns, London, c1903, teapot, creamer, sugar, and two demitasse cups and saucers, silver mounted on Staffordshire Pottery. . **500.00**

Edwardian
Center Bowl, Mapin and Webb, London, c1903, 10" d, 10" h, Baroque style, truncated baluster form, repousse with acanthus leaf tips, scrolling acanthus form lug handles, stepped socle base, 72 troy oz. **2,200.00**
Dish Ring, Carrington & Co, London, 1910–11, 7½" d, waisted cylinder, pierced and engraved, 14 troy oz. . **450.00**

Elizabeth II, tray, A. & Bro. Ltd., Birmingham, 1952, 27½" l, octagonal, molded border, 133 troy oz **2,420.00**

George I
Caudle Cup, London, c1925, 5" h, plain lip, cast S–scroll handles, reeded and gadrooned body, scole base, rubbed maker's mark, 9 troy oz. **200.00**
Pepper Pot, John Albright, London, 1721–22, 3" h, cylindrical, molded borders, domed engraved cov, 3 troy oz **525.00**

George II
Candlesticks, J. Cafe, London, 1751–2, 8¼" h, knopped stem, square

shell and scroll base, engraved crest, price for set of four, 66 troy oz. **4,290.00**

Coffee Pot, attributed to C. Wright, London, 1769–70, 13" h, baluster form, later chased gadroons, engraved armorial, 40 troy oz **2,100.00**

Hot Water Kettle on Stand, T. Stoddart, Newcastle, 1746–47, globular form, later chased swags, 63 troy oz. **1,210.00**

Sauce Boat, helmet form, floral and scroll repousse dec, lyre handle, shell feet, 16½ oz. **2,200.00**

Salver, G Hindmarsh, London, 1732–33, 16" d, scrolled border, scrolled feet, engraved armorial, 56 troy oz **2,530.00**

George III
Basin, William Simmons, London, c1809, 16½" w, 3½" h, oval, gadrooned lip quartered by shell form clasps, plain body, engraved coronet, 50 ozs **3,250.00**
Calling Card Tray, attributed to Edward Capper, London, c1768, 6¾" d, shell and S–scroll molded border enclosing plain surface, raised on double C–scroll legs, pad feet, 7 ozs **200.00**
Chocolate Pot, Robert Gray & Son, Glasgow, Edinburgh mark, 1804, 11½" h, pyriform, leaf capped scroll handle, hinged lid, foliate finial, circular foot, body engraved with cartouches centered by scrolling foliate medallions, one inscribed 1847, 23 ozs, 4 dwts, foot repaired **850.00**
Coffeepot
Bateman, W., London, 1808, 10" h, spout damage, 28 troy oz **1,210.00**
Woods, Christopher, London, 1770–71, 10¼" h, pear shaped body, acanthus clad scrolling spout, domical lid, spiral finial, spreading circular foot, engraved griffin crest, fully marked on bottom, 26 troy oz **1,540.00**
Wright, C., London, 1768, 11" h, baluster form, later chased flowers, engraved armorial, repaired, 39 troy oz **1,430.00**
Cup, cov, J. Robins, London, 1799–1800, 14" h, half reeded urn form body, two handles, acorn finial, engraved arms, 54 troy oz **1,430.00**
Cup, Irish, Dublin, 18th C, 6" h, harp and hibernia in rect, date Roman "M" in shaped reserve, maker crowned "W" in shamrock, vasiform, two scrolled handles, later chased farm scenes, 25 troy oz. . . **1,100.00**
Kettle on Stand, attributed to B. Bre-

wood, London, 1755–56, inverted pear form, engraved crest, filigree base, burner inset missing, 39 troy oz. **1,650.00**

Ladle, Michael Keating, Dublin, 1786, 13½" l, circular fluted bowl, turned down tip at handle, bright cut star, bellflower and wrigglework engraving, 8 troy oz. **385.00**

Shoe Buckle, W Fearn & W Chawner, London, 1811, price for pair **370.00**

Skewer, Hester Bateman, London, 1782–93, 11½" l, ring and cartouche handle, engraved birdhead crest, 3 troy oz. **425.00**

Spoon, London, Smith & Fearn hallmarks, 1795, 11⅜" l, sauce strainer in bowl, engraved animal and monogram on handle **375.00**

Sugar Bowl, Crispin Fuller, London, 1804, 4½" h, oval neoclassical style, engraved dec, dents, 8 troy oz. **330.00**

Sugar Tongs, unknown maker, London, 1803 . . . . **75.00**

Tablespoon, John Shields and John Pittar, Dublin, 1760 and 1767, 9¼" l, downturned tip, bright cut engraved handle, linear border design, 16 troy oz, price for set of six **500.00**

Teapot, Jas Young, London, 1784–85, 5" h, oval cylindrical form, engraved design and arms, 14 troy oz. **660.00**

Tea Set, R & S Hennell, London, 1802–3, teapot and stand, creamer and sugar, globular, engraved design and crest, 37 troy oz **825.00**

Waiter, R Hennell I, London, 1784–85, 6" l, oval, pierced rim, engraved crest, 5 troy oz. **275.00**

George IV
Fruit Basket, Robert Hennell, London, 1820, 14¾" l, pierced basket with applied border chased with scrolls and fluted garlands, sides of fluted swirls terminating in acanthus leaves, swing openwork handle, pierced band of flowers and scrolls base, central face engraved with rampant cat, inscribed below "Touch Not The Cat Bot A Glove," 45 ozs, 16 dwts **5,000.00**

Salt, Charles Price, London, 1822, 3¾" d, double border of scrolls and flowers, tripod hoof feet, gilt int., price for set of four, 15 ozs **375.00**

Stuffing Spoon
Eley & Fearn, London, 1822, 12" l **165.00**
W. Welch, Exeter, 1825–26, 12" l, monogram handle. **140.00**

Toast Rack, John Cope Folkard, London, 1820, 6½" h, oval gadrooned and shell dec handle, seven slice rack, gadrooned stand with floral and shell corners, lion paw feet, 13 troy oz **125.00**

George V
Compote, F N & S, London, 1913, 5" h, 10" d, round, openwork design, minor dent, 16 troy oz. **420.00**

Muffineer, Birmingham, 1934, 8" h, oct Queen Anne style, acorn finial, maker's mark "TS" in two ovals, 7 troy oz **275.00**

Queen Anne
Caudle Cup, Timothy Ley, London, 1705, 4¾" h, two handles, stamped and chased designs, engraved initials, minor dents, 8 troy oz **1,320.00**

Chocolate Pot, London, c1709, 10" h, hinged knop finial, domed hinged cov, reeded rolled thumbpiece, flaring cylindrical body, treen S–scrolled handle, side spout, 24 troy oz. **4,500.00**

Taperstick, M. Cooper I, London, 1813–14, 5" h, knobbed stem, octagonal base, later chased, 4 troy oz. **275.00**

Regency, mug, W. Rudkins, London, 1809–10, 5" h, baluster form, later rococo chasing, 11 troy oz **475.00**

Victorian
Basket, Robinson, Edkins & Aston, Birmingham, 1845, 10" d, chased and engraved, 18 troy oz **615.00**

Bowl
C. S./H., London, 1901–02, shaped oval, repousse flowers, gilt int., 12 troy oz. **440.00**
N. & H., Birmingham, 1893, 3½" h, reticulated, Adams style, swags and ram's heads, later glass liner, 9 troy oz **110.00**

Dish, S M & Co, London, 1894–95, 8" l, rococo style relief dec, 13½ troy oz. **500.00**

Plate, Mortimer & Hunt, London, 1843, 10" d, serpentine gadrooned border with engraved crest, 19 troy oz. **275.00**

Sugar Caster, JA/JS, London, 1884–5, Georgian style, 9" h, maker's mark in quatrefoil, 9 troy oz **200.00**

Tea Service, Charles T. Fox and George Fox, London, 1839, 10½" h hot water pot, teapot, creamer, and sugar, repousse, floral spray and leaf scrolls, leaf scrolled handles, 86 troy oz **2,800.00**

Wine Cooler, Barnard, London, c1840, 9½ x 11½", Greek vase shape, bulging lobed body with acanthus leaves, emb and chased border of English rose, Scotch thistle, and Irish shamrock at top, overhanging lip with alternating leaves, squat stem with border of tongues and leaves, circular foot chased with acanthus on matted ground, S–curved handles ending in acanthus leaf terminals, rubbed date letter, 74 ozs **3,850.00**

SILVER, ENGLISH, SHEFFIELD

Sheffield Silver, or Old Sheffield Plate, was made by a fusion method of silver plating used from the mid 18th century until the mid 1880s, when the silver electroplating process was introduced.

Sheffield plate was discovered in 1743 when Thomas Boulsover of Sheffield, England, accidentally fused silver and copper. The process consisted of sandwiching a heavy sheet of copper between two thin sheets of silver. The result was a plated sheet of silver which could be pressed or rolled to a desired thickness. All Sheffield plate articles were worked from these plated sheets.

Most of the silver-plated items found today marked "Sheffield" are not early Sheffield plate. They are later wares made in Sheffield, England.

Basket, unidentified maker, 1828, 7″ h, reticulated, handle, 11 troy oz. **275.00**
Caster, Edward VII, maker J. R., 1909, sterling overlay bottle (damaged), 6 troy oz **360.00**
Epergne, Victorian, John Harrison & Co, Ltd., 1870, 21″ h, three branch, triangular base with leaf capped scrolling feet, scrolling leafy apron between each foot with center shell, beaded leafy ridges rise to plinth capped with applied, pierced, and chased grape leaves and clusters, three entwined grape canes issuing above and terminating in a central cup to support Waterford leaded glass cut bowl with irregular fan borders above diaperwork, sides with three adventitous removable numbered canes applied with cut and chased grapes supporting smaller side bowls, confirming vintage ornament below, 123 ozs, 12 dwts. **7,150.00**
Fruit Knives and Forks, 1817, Regency, MOP handles, fitted case, price for twelve knives and twelve forks **330.00**
Hot Water Urn
George III, 18th C, 18″ h, vasiform, two handles, minor dents and rosing **360.00**
Regency, early 19th C, 19″ h, reeded, female mask handles, repairs **880.00**
Meat Dish and Cov, Regency, first quar-

ter 19th C, 22″ w, 11½″ h, oval, domed cov, engraved Prince of Wales plumes and motto "Royal Welch (sic) Fusiliers," shaped oval tray, well and tree surface, allover gadrooned moldings, minor dents, base repair. **1,540.00**
Plateau, attributed to TJ Creswick, mid 19th C, 17½″ l, Rococo style, mirror plate in shell and scroll border, conforming spreading border, spreading shell form sides, mask, and scroll feet, feet cut down **625.00**
Urn, cov, George III, c1800, 17½″ h, Adam style, minor rosing, price for pair **1,870.00**

Silver Plated, dressing mirror, American Aesthetic Movement, Meriden Company, c1880, stylized floral motif, 18½″ w, 20″ h, $1,870.00. Photograph courtesy of William Doyle Galleries.

SILVER, PLATED

Plated silver production by an electrolytic method is credited to G. R. and H. Elkington, England, in 1838.

In electroplating silver, the article is completely shaped and formed from a base metal and then coated with a thin layer of silver. In the late 19th century, the base metal was Britannia, an alloy of tin, copper, and antimony. Other bases are copper and brass. Today the base is nickel silver.

In 1847 the electroplating process was introduced in America by Rogers Bros., Hartford, Connecticut. By 1855 a number of firms were using the method to produce silver-plated items in large quantities.

The quality of the plating is important. Extensive use or polishing can cause the base metal to show through. The prices for plated silver items are low, making it a popular item with younger collectors.

Bowl, 9" h, Derby Silver Company, foliate repousse, surmounted by figure of squirrel on oak branch **330.00**

Butter Dish, tiny delicate double rows of beading around base, on edges, and dome lid, cut glass drip tray, Meriden Silver Plate Co **75.00**

Centerpiece, 17½" h, Victorian, Reed and Barton, center cased glass vase, pink ext., white int., white Mary Gregory type enamel figure of woman with wings carrying garland, two handles with figural butterflies and pond lilies, pr of figural storks on rect base, sgd, refinished silver **900.00**

Champagne Bucket, Simpson, Hall, Miller & Co., 9" d, cylindrical, bracket handles, applied scroll border band, monogram **265.00**

Claret Jug, 11½" h, Victorian, 19th C, minor nicks **300.00**

Cruet Set, 10¾" h, Victorian, 19th C, cut glass bottles, minor nicks **350.00**

Egg Caddy, Simpson, Hall, Miller & Co., emb floral platform holding six egg cups, dec prongs, feet with raised lion's masks, heart shaped ball handle, six egg spoons with shell shaped bowls **225.00**

Epergne, 21" h, Victorian, 19th C, central stem, four scrolled arms with foliage design, supporting Anglo–Irish cut glass bowl, engraved crest, minor chips **1,100.00**

Jardiniere, 25½" h, Baroque style, oblong, pair of leaf capped scroll handles, body emb with broad leaf of acanthus leaves and foliate scrollwork, supported by pr griffins, stepped oval platform base, metal liner **1,200.00**

Meat Cover, 18 x 10½", Victorian, domed body, bright cut with panel of foliage swags and roses, beaded base edge, twisted branch handle, monogram, maker's marks **225.00**

Pitcher, 8¾" h, English, Victorian, late 19th C, large pouring lip, compressed circular body, repousse scrollwork and shell motifs, four scroll feet **305.00**

Sardine Box, small Greek key border on box, lid with figural fish finial, fancy feet, monogram, glass liner **90.00**

Sweetmeat, 7" h, Victorian, peasant carrying basket, price for matched pair . . **1,350.00**

Teapot, circular, floral repousse dec, glass handle **125.00**

Tray, serving
   21½ x 15¼", American, oval, raised everted edge, loop handles **200.00**

   24" l, American, rococo, scrollwork and shell raised border, emb foliate surface **285.00**

Vase, James W. Tufts, c1885, 8" h, Neoclassical style, amphora form body, applied handles in form of fists clenching batons, price for pair **70.00**

Water Set, American, late 19th C, 21½" w x 25" h, cylindrical cov pitcher, finely ribbed upper and lower bands, wide center band engraved with cranes, arched frame, ornately scroll molded feet, flaring ribbed circular dish base with space for two matching goblets, inset drip tray, paw feet, full figure flying horse as front projection **2,320.00**

SILVER DEPOSIT GLASS

History: Silver deposit glass, consisting of a thin coating of silver actually deposited on the glass by an electrical process, was popular at the turn of the century. The process was simple. The glass and a piece of silver were placed in a solution. An electric current was introduced which caused the silver to decompose, pass through the solution, and remain on those parts of the glass on which a pattern had been outlined.

Reference: Ellen T. Schroy, *Warman's Glass,* Wallace-Homestead, 1992.

Salt Shaker, hexagonal base, partial paper label reads "Sterling Deposit," 3¼" h, 2" w, $18.00.

Bowl, 10½" d, cobalt blue ground, flowers and foliage, silver scalloped edge **85.00**

Cologne Bottle, 3⅜" h, clear ground, bulbous, floral and flowing leaf motif . . . **165.00**

Decanter, 13¼" h, clear ground, Continental silver mounts, grape clusters, and leaves dec, orig stopper **90.00**

Ice Tub, clear ground, floral and foliage dec, closed tab handles, matching sterling silver ice tongs **125.00**

Perfume Bottle, 4½″ h, clear ground,
vine and grape leaf dec **60.00**
Sugar Shaker, clear ground, vine and
grape leaf dec, SP top **65.00**

SILVER OVERLAY

History: Silver overlay is silver applied directly
to a finished glass or porcelain object. The overlay
is cut and decorated, usually by engraving, prior to
being molded around the object.

Glass usually is of high quality, either crystal or
colored. Lenox used silver overlay on some porcelain pieces. The majority of design motifs are
from the Art Nouveau and Art Deco periods.

Reference: Ellen T. Schroy, *Warman's Glass*,
Wallace-Homestead, 1992.

Basket, 5½″ l, 6″ h, deep cranberry
body, allover floral and lattice design,
sterling handle **600.00**
Decanter, 16″ h, spiral oval vessel, acid
etched surface, leaf form dec, sterling
rim and pour lip, conforming spiral
stopper.   **220.00**
Flask, 5″ h, clear bottle shaped body,
scrolling hallmarked silver, hinged
cov **275.00**
Inkwell, 3¾ x 3″, bright green ground,
rose, scroll, and lattice overlay,
matching cov, monogrammed "E". . .   **650.00**
Jardiniere, 2¾″ h, orange–amber
ground, Art Nouveau style overlay cut
blossoms, buds, and scrolled devices,
Austrian **470.00**
Perfume Bottle, 6 x 4″, deep emerald
green ground, abstract scroll sterling
overlay, sgd "Sterling Silver Deposit,"
numbered. **600.00**
Rose Bowl, 5″ w, 4½″ h, emerald green
ground, heavy floral design of roses,

**Tumbler, sterling grape, vine, and leaf
motif, marked "455," 5″ h, $85.00.**

buds, leaves, stems, and scrolls, sgd
"999/1000 fine," Alvin mark, patent
mark, numbered **725.00**
Teapot, 5½″ w, 2¼″ h, white Limoges
body, elaborate floral and scroll
design **100.00**
Tea Set, 8¾″ h, Lenox porcelain body,
Reed & Barton silver overlay, price for
three piece set **315.00**
Vase
4½″ h, 3″ w, pinched body, deep cranberry body, wild rose overlay,
crests, monogram, dated 1899,
sgd, patented, Alvin mark **150.00**
5½″ h, black satin ground, sterling sil-
ver overlay of cattails, flowers, and
bud. **300.00**
8″ h, glossy rose red cased to white
ground, silver overlay imp "Sterling
680," small bruise on side. **360.00**
8¼″ h, 3″ w, flaring, emerald green
ground, carnation and arch design
overlay **600.00**
12¼″ h, 7″ w, clear ground, Art Deco
roses, buds, and leaves, band at
top and base **575.00**
Violet Bowl, 3″ d, 3″ h, cranberry ground,
allover heavy scroll design **325.00**

SILVER RESIST

History: Silver resist ware was first produced
about 1805. It is similar to silver luster in respect to
the silvering process and differs in that the pattern
appears on the surface.

The outline of the pattern was drawn or stenciled
on the ware's body. A glue or sugar-glycern adhesive was brushed over the part not to be lustered, causing it to "resist" the lustering solution
which was applied and allowed to dry. The glue or
adhesive was washed off. When fired in the kiln,
the luster glaze covered the entire surface except
for the pattern.

Coffee Set, silver resist dec of grapes
and leaves, rust enamel highlights,
yellow ground, 7⅜″ h cov coffeepot,
cream pitcher, ftd sugar, six coffee
canns and saucers, Wedgwood,
printed and imp mark, c1927, price for
set. **360.00**
Cordial Set, 9¼″ h decanter, silver resist
Venetian canal scene, price for de-
canter and four cordials **175.00**
Decanter, 11″ h, cobalt blue ground,
floral and foliage dec, spike stopper,
c1900. . . . .   **160.00**
Jug, satyr, 4½″ h, enameled dec face,
floral design, English, c1830. . . . . . .   **440.00**
Plate, 8¼″ d, luncheon, Wedgwood,
price for set of twelve. **165.00**

Pitcher, pine branch and pine cone dec, marked "Wedgwood & Barlston Eturia," 5" h, $70.00.

Spill Vase, 3½" h, pottery, gourd form, paneled, Continental, price for pair . .	50.00
Wine Set, green glass ground, silver resist scroll dec surrounding water birds, c1900, price for decanter and ten matching cups.	120.00

SMITH BROS. GLASS

History: After establishing a decorating department at the Mount Washington Glass Works in 1871, Alfred and Harry Smith struck out on their own in 1875. Their New Bedford, Massachusetts, firm soon became known worldwide for its fine opalescent-decorated wares, similar in style to those of Mount Washington.

Their glass often is marked on the base with a red shield enclosing a rampant lion and the word "Trademark."

Reference: Ellen T. Schroy, *Warman's Glass,* Wallace-Homestead, 1992.

Reproduction Alert: Beware of examples marked "Smith Bros."

Biscuit Jar, cov, 7" h, creamy satin ground, daisies, yellow shaded centers, green foliage, SP cov, rampant lion base, sgd "SB" in cov	375.00
Bowl, 8½" d, leaves and acorn dec, SP rim, rampant lion mark	375.00
Creamer and Sugar, 2¾" h creamer, 3¼" h cov sugar, slightly ribbed satin glass, tiny yellow and orange flowers, SP trim, sugar marked, price for pair	420.00
Mustard Jar, 2" h, ribbed, gold prunus dec, white ground	300.00
Rose Bowl, 4½" h	
Burmese painted ground, pansies, heavy raised gold dec	425.00

Rose Bowl, Shasta Daisy pattern, gold rim with white beads, 3⅞" d, 4" h, $150.00.

Creamy satin ground, daisies, yellow shaded centers, green foliage, white beaded rim	195.00
Vase	
6" h, cone shape, enameled dec, two interlocking circles, one with silver background and two red birds perched on limb laden with apple blossoms which continues around body, other circle with landscape scene	385.00
8" h, Greenaway style figure and dog dec, sgd	395.00
8½" h, bulbous melon shape, blue wisteria blossoms, gold enameling, unsgd	
Lustered Crown Milano	350.00
Lusterless Crown Milano	385.00

SNOW BABIES

History: Snow babies, small bisque figurines spattered with glitter sand, were made originally in Germany and marketed in the early 1900s. There are several theories about their origin. One is that German doll makers copied the designs from the traditional Christmas candies. Another theory, the most accepted, is that they were made to honor Admiral Robert Peary's daughter, who was born in Greenland in 1893 and was called the "Snow Baby" by the Eskimos.

References: Ray and Eilene Early, *Snow Babies,* Collector Books, out of print; Mary Morrison, *Snow Babies, Santas, and Elves: Collecting Christmas Bisque Figures,* Schiffer Publishing, 1993.

Baby	
In Sleigh, sitting, both arms raised, reindeer in front	150.00
Riding bear, red, white, and maroon, 2⅞" h	150.00
Sitting, 2" h	195.00

Sledding
Single baby pulled by huskies, 2¾″
h. 90.00
Three seated babies, bisque sled 165.00
Standing
Holding tennis racket, stamped
"Germany". 115.00
Playing banjo, stamped
"Germany". 135.00
Waving 160.00
Bear
On four paws 95.00
Standing, 2½″ h 115.00
Elf, 1½″ h 65.00

Bear on skis, 2″ h, $50.00.

Girl, seated on snowball, red skirt, arms
raised. 120.00
Ice Skaters, boy and girl, 2″ h, price for
pair 250.00
Sheep, 2″ h 70.00
Snowman 60.00

SNUFF BOTTLES

History: Tobacco usage spread from America to
Europe to China during the 17th century. The Europeans and Chinese preferred to grind the dried
leaves into a powder and sniff it into their nostrils.
The elegant Europeans carried their snuff in boxes
and took a pinch with their fingertips. The Chinese
upper class, because of their lengthy fingernails,
found this inconvenient and devised a bottle with a
fitted stopper and attached spoon.

In the Chinese manner, these utilitarian objects
soon became objets d'art. Snuff bottles were fashioned from precious and semiprecious stones,
glass, porcelain and pottery, wood, metals, and
ivory. Glass and transparent stone bottles often
were enhanced further with delicate hand paintings, some done on the interior of the bottle.

Reference: Gloria and Robert Mascarelli, *War-*

man's Oriental Antiques, Wallace-Homestead,
1992.

Collectors' Club: International Chinese Snuff
Bottle Society, 2601 North Charles Street, Baltimore, MD 21218.

Agate
Flattened purse form 275.00
Fruit form, golden relief carved gourds
and vines with tendrils, jadeite top,
c1850 . . . . 75.00
Honey colored, carved circular panels
with characters on each side, ma-
lachite top 330.00
Oriental, 2⅞″ h, carved, green jade
top 290.00
Oval, 2½″ h, coral stopper, Chinese 125.00
Parallel colored bands, crystalline
inclusion 950.00
Bone, 3⅜″ h, conical shape, carved,
brown top, Chinese 180.00
Bronze, flask shape, chain 135.00
Glass
Blue overlay, eight horses of Mu
Wang, snowflake ground, c1880 . . 110.00
Green overlay, snowflake ground, chi-
long on each side. 55.00
Handpainted, continuous lake scene,
sgd "Zhon Leyna" 1,150.00
Red overlay, bifed tail chilong on milk
glass, carnelian stopper, c1850. . . 250.00
Star design, 2½″ h, dark smoky int.,
green stone inset in enameled silver
lid, cracked 85.00
Hornbill, Chinese
2⅛″ h, flattened pear shape, carved
fruit and floral dec, painted charac-
ter int. 750.00
2⅜″ h, oval, carved birds and bush,
Chinese 1,100.00

**Malachite, carved roses, 2½″ h,
$275.00.**

2½" h, flattened oval shape, carved
figures and hawks 1,320.00
2¾" h
Cicada form, carved 1,600.00
Flattened oval shape, carved relief
figures 950.00
Inkstone, black, allover relief carved fig-
ure, pine tree rising from rocky base,
foot rim, 1880–1920 . . . . 165.00
Ivory
Carved, vase of flowers, repaired . . 55.00
Figural, removable head, finely in-
cised detail 110.00
Jade
Plain panels, circular grain border,
18th C. 475.00
Relief carved vintage design, 2½" h,
pale green, hairline 95.00
Simple form, mask handles, foot rim,
18th C. 220.00
Peking Glass
2¾" h, red and white, pale green jade
top 220.00
3" h, green and white, pale green jade
top 165.00
3⅛" h, blue, white, and red, pale
green jade top 165.00
Pewter, circular, gilt handles, Chinese 450.00
Porcelain
Allover flower dec, geometric ground,
sgd "Ch'ien Lung Nien Chih,"
1820–1900 . . . . 465.00
Figural, Lui Hai, famille rose dec . . 330.00
Flask shape, oval, raised black design, lavender ground, orig case . . 120.00
Miniature, enameled, carved stopper,
c1850 . . . . 175.00
Vase shape, tan glaze, teak and cat's
eye top 275.00
Silver, figural, emb design on robe, head
stopper, c1900 . . . . 385.00
Stone, 2⅛" h, carved, gray–white,
dragon design, colorful top, small
wood stand 160.00
Wood, hardwood, two compartments,
allover carved vertical fluting, matching malachite tops, c1900 . . . . 165.00

SOAPSTONE

History: The mineral steatite, known as soapstone because of its greasy feel, has been utilized
for carving figural groups and designs by the
Chinese and others. Utilitarian pieces also were
made. Soapstone pieces were very popular during
the Victorian era.

Bookends, pr, rect, carved flowerpot on
stand, flower, and foliage 80.00
Bowl, 11½" d, irregular oval, carved fig-

**Vase, Chinese, four openings, red
tones, c1900, 6¾" h, 9½" w, $135.00.**

ure dec, carved teak stand, Chinese,
19th C 225.00
Box, cov, 2⅜ x 3⅛", oval, brass inlaid
crossed lines design 35.00
Figure
6¾" h, bird in flowering tree, carved 45.00
8¾" h, polar bear carrying seal,
mounted on turntable, dated 1,300.00
10" h, man with walking staff, carved 55.00
Plaque, 9½" h, birds, trees, flowers, and
rocks 115.00
Seal, 12" h, foo dog, price for pair . . . 220.00
Teapot, 5" h, carved figures, vines, and
flowers 350.00
Vase
4¾" h, double, carved animals . . . 110.00
6¼" h, carved, reticulated floral designs, Chinese, early 20th C 60.00
10¼" h, carved, high relief floral design, Chinese, early 20th C 75.00

SOUVENIR AND
COMMEMORATIVE CHINA AND
GLASS

History: Souvenir, commemorative, and historical china and glass include those items produced
to celebrate special events, places, and people.
Among the china plates, those by Rowland and
Marcellus and Wedgwood are the most eagerly
sought. Rowland and Marcellus, Staffordshire, England, made a series of blue-and-white historic
plates with a wide rolled edge depicting scenes
beginning with the Philadelphia Centennial in 1876
and continuing to the 1939 New York World's Fair.
Wedgwood collaborated in 1910 with Jones,
McDuffee and Stratton to produce a series of historic dessert–sized plates depicting scenes
throughout the United States.
Many localities issued plates, mugs, glasses,
etc., for anniversary celebrations or to honor a local
historical event. These items seem to have greater

value when sold in the region from which they originated.

Commemorative glass includes several patterns of pressed glass which celebrate persons or events. Historical glass includes campaign and memorial items.

References: Bessie M. Lindsey, *American Historical Glass*, Charles E. Tuttle Company, 1967; Ellen T. Schroy, *Warman's Glass*, Wallace-Homestead, 1992; Frank Stefano, Jr., *Wedgwood Old Blue Historical Plates And Other Views Of The United States Produced For Jones, McDuffee & Stratton Co., Boston, Importer: A Check–List with Illustrations*, published by author, 1975.

Collectors' Clubs: Souvenir China Collectors Society, Box 562, Great Barrington, MA 01230; Statue of Liberty Collectors' Club, PO Box 535, Chautauqua, NY 14722.

Additional Listings: Cup Plates, Pressed Glass, Political Items, and Staffordshire, Historical. Also see *Warman's Americana & Collectibles* for more examples.

Candy Container, "Remember the Maine," pressed glass, 7" l, 2¾" w, 3½" h, $110.00.

Butter Dish, Liberty Bell, glass	**140.00**
Creamer, 6" h, Williamsburg, VA, blue illus, white ground, English	**25.00**
Creamer and Sugar, Illinois State Penitentiary–Joliet, custard glass.	**85.00**
Cup, "Hotel Richmond, Richmond, Virginia," ceramic, Germany.	**18.00**
Dish	
Rawlins County Court House, Atwood, KS, ceramic.	**15.00**
Remember the *Maine*, glass, green, cov.	**125.00**
Ewer, Rapids, MI, silver overlay, blended glaze, cut bottom, elk dec . .	**25.00**
Jug, Garden of the Gods, Mt Evans .	**15.00**
Mug, Independence Hall, William Jennings Bryan, milk glass	**30.00**
Paperweight, glass	
Plymouth Rock, clear	**65.00**
Washington Monument, 5½" h, blue,	

sq base, oval medallion with bust of Washington, inscribed "Cornerstone, July 4th–48, Dedicated Feb 21, '85".	**165.00**
Plate	
7" d, Kankakee State Hospital, ceramic, multicolored scene, cobalt blue ground, gold border, Germany, c1915.	**75.00**
7½" d, Marietta College 125th Anniversary, 1960, blue, Wedgwood. . .	**20.00**
9" d, Columbus, glass, emb "1892"	**50.00**
9½" sq, Grant, glass, amber, emb "Patriot & Soldier"	**50.00**
10" d, Lewis & Clark Centennial Expo 1905, flow blue, Staffordshire	**50.00**
10½" d, Atlantic City, NJ, Rowland and Marcellus	**45.00**
Teapot, "Niagara Falls," two views of falls, yellow iridescent, copper luster neck, white spout and handle, gold tracings, Germany.	**55.00**
Tile, 4" d, Detroit Women's League, glass, multicolored irid dec.	**130.00**
Tumbler, Dewey, glass, Banded Icicle pattern, portrait base	**50.00**
Vase	
Boys Town, NE, decal, incised "BT"	**20.00**
Dryden, KS, clay, oil well dec, marked, numbered, orig paper label	**25.00**
Niagara Falls, scrolled enameled panel, scenic background, allover enameled pink apple blossoms, purple highlights, brass base.	**425.00**

SOUVENIR AND COMMEMORATIVE SPOONS

History: Souvenir and commemorative spoons have been issued for hundreds of years. Early American silversmiths engraved presentation spoons to honor historical personages or mark key events.

In 1881 Myron Kinsley patented a Niagara Falls spoon, and in 1884 Michael Gibney patented a new flatware design. M. W. Galt, Washington, D.C., issued commemorative spoons for George and Martha Washington in 1889. From these beginnings a collecting craze for souvenir and commemorative spoons developed in the late 19th and first quarter of the 20th century.

References: Dorothy T. Rainwater and Donna H. Felger, *American Spoons, Souvenir and Historical*, Schiffer Publishing, 1990; Dorothy T. Rainwater and Donna H. Fegler, *A Collector's Guide To Spoons Around The World*, Everybodys Press, 1976; Dorothy T. Rainwater and Donna H. Fegler, *Spoons From Around the World*, Schiffer Publishing, 1992; *Sterling Silver, Silverplate, and Souvenir*

Spoons With Prices, Revised, L-W Book Sales, 1991–92 prices.

Periodical: Spoony Scoop Newsletter, 84 Oak Avenue, Shelton, CT 06484.

Collectors' Clubs: American Spoon Collectors, 4922 State Line, Westwood Hills, KS 66205; Northeastern Spoon Collectors Guild, 52 Hillcrest Ave, Morristown, NJ 07960.

Additional Listings: See Warman's Americana & Collectibles for more examples.

Salem, 1692, Daniel Low, SS, $125.00.

Bar Harbor, emb bowl, fish handle, Shepard mark.	32.00
California, SP	7.50
Chicago, SS	12.50
Claremont Commemorative of the Hudson Fulton Celebration, SS, Tiffany & Co, 1909	20.00
Colorado, SS	20.00
Decatur, IL, SS	40.00
Fort Dearborn, SS	12.00
Fort Worth, TX, SS	15.00
Grand Army of Republic, engraved bowl.	65.00
Helena, MT, SS	22.00
Honolulu, SS	25.00
Hutchinson, KS, SS	24.00
Jamestown Expo	35.00
Lake Okaboji, cutout Indian head handle	45.00
Maryland, SP	7.50
Mexico, SS	15.00
New Orleans, SS	20.00
Palm Springs Aerial Tramway, SP, John Brown, marked "Antico".	100.00
Portland, OR, SS	25.00
Queen Elizabeth, 1953 Coronation	15.00
Rip Van Winkle	30.00

San Antonio, TX, SS	35.00
Seattle, WA, SS	20.00
Seeing St Louis, SS	45.00
Statue of Liberty, NY	40.00
Thousand Islands, SS, fish handle, engraved bowl, Watson.	40.00
Winona Hotel, IN, SS	35.00

SPANGLED GLASS

History: Spangled glass is a blown or blown-molded variegated art glass, similar to spatter glass, with the addition of flakes of mica or metallic aventurine. Many pieces are cased with a white or clear layer of glass. Spangled glass was developed in the late 19th century and still is being manufactured.

Originally spangled glass was attributed only to the Vasa Murrhina Art Glass Company of Hartford, Connecticut, which distributed the glass for Dr. Flower of the Cape Cod Glassworks, Sandwich, Massachusetts. However, research has shown that many companies in Europe, England, and the United States made spangled glass, and attributing a piece to a specific source is very difficult.

Reference: Ellen T. Schroy, Warman's Glass, Wallace-Homestead, 1992.

Tumbler, tortoise shell mottling, large brown spots, traces of mica flakes, white ground, cased white int., 3¾" h, $75.00.

Basket, 9" w, lobed body, pink shading to white, mica flecks, applied clear handle	140.00
Candlestick, 18" h, spangled black amethyst, hollow baluster, gently down sloping lip, Vasa Murrhina	220.00
Condiment Set, 2 x 5½ x 6" h, cruet with orig stopper, cov mustard pot, and cov pepper pot, SP holder and covers, cranberry and green spatter, silver mica flecks, price for set	225.00
Creamer, 3¼" d, 4¾" h, bulbous,	

molded swirled ribs, cylindrical neck, pinched spout, blue ground, swirled mica flecks, clear applied reeded handle 225.00

Pitcher, 8" h, bulbous, six wide blown out ribs, heart shaped pouring spout, silver mica suspended between double gather of clear and rose colored glass, applied clear handle, hp flower and leaves dec, gold trim, white lining, Hobbs Brockunier, patented 1883. . . 650.00

Rose Bowl, 4" d, 3¼" h, spherical, eight crimp top, oxblood, pink, and cream spatter, silver mica flecks, swirling striped design, white lining 110.00

Toothpick Holder, butterscotch, gold mica flecks, white lining 175.00

Tumbler, 3¾" h, pink, gold, and brown spatter, mica flecks, white lining 75.00

Vase, 8⅝" h, tapering baluster, green and deep green Aventurine swirl design, white lining, clear applied petal feet, clear applied upright leaves around base 60.00

SPATTER GLASS

History: Spatter glass is a variegated blown or blown-molded art glass. It originally was called "End-of-Day" glass, based on the assumption that it was made from leftover batches of glass at the end of the day. However, spatter glass was found to be a standard production item for many glass factories.

Spatter glass was developed at the end of the 19th century and is still being produced in the United States and Europe.

References: William Heacock, James Measell, and Berry Wiggins, *Harry Northwood: The Early Years 1881–1900*, Antique Publications, 1990; Ellen T. Schroy, *Warman's Glass*, Wallace-Homestead, 1992.

Reproduction Alert: Many modern examples come from Czechoslovakia.

Basket
5" d, 7" h, cased, pink ground, green aventurine spatter, emb pinwheel pattern around sides, clear applied twisted handle 140.00

5" d, 7¾" h, ftd flaring cylindrical form, pointed and fluted rim, gold and pink spatter, white lining, clear frosted applied angular thorn handle. 155.00

5¼" d, 6¼" h, bulbous, star shaped rim, maroon, white, green, and yellow spatter, emb rosette and swirl pattern, clear applied twist handle . 100.00

Bowl, 8¼" d, 5¼" h, crimped rim, white

Vase, hexagonal, purple and yellow spatter, cased white int., marked "Czechoslovakia," 4⅝" h, $25.00.

and peach spatter, ornate ftd ormolu base 225.00

Creamer and Sugar, red, orange, and yellow, white lining, clear applied handle, price for pair. 120.00

Epergne, 10" d, 17" h, cranberry opalescent to green, ruffled bowl, ornate nickel plated metal base, single ruffled lily vase fits in center mount 400.00

Jack In The Pulpit Vase, 4¼" d, DQ, green ground, white, green, and pink spatter 100.00

Miniature Lamp, Beaded Swirl, red and gold spatter, tiny glass burst in outer casing 85.00

Pitcher
5" h, bulbous, tri–lobed rim, maroon, yellow, and white spatter, white lining, clear applied reeded handle . . 90.00

8" h, melon ribbed body, ruffled rim, cased, blue, pink, yellow, and black splashes, deep cranberry shades to pink ground, applied handle 300.00

Plate, 11¾" d, tortoise shell, amber ground, darker mottling, free blown . . 95.00

Sugar, cov, Ribbed Pillar, pink spatter, Northwood 45.00

Tumbler, white spatter, cranberry ground 58.00

Vase
8" h, baluster, ringed neck, flared mouth, red, yellow, and green spatter, brown lining. 85.00

11" h, 6½" d, sapphire blue ground, blue spatter, ruffled top with clear edging, price for pair. 400.00

Watch Holder, 3¾" x 4¼" dish, ruffled rim, blue spatter, 7" h ormolu metal watch holder. 165.00

SPATTERWARE

History: Spatterware is made of common earthenware, although occasionally creamware was used. The earliest English examples were made about 1780. The peak period of production was 1810 to 1840. Marked pieces are rare. Firms known to have made spatterware are Adams, Barlow, and Harvey and Cotton.

The amount of spatter decoration varies from piece to piece. Some objects simply have decorated borders. These often are decorated with a brush, requiring several hundred touches per square inch to achieve the spatter effect. Other pieces have the entire surface covered with spatter. Aesthetics of the final product are a key to value.

Collectors today focus on the patterns—Cannon, Castle, Fort, Peafowl, Rainbow, Rose, Thistle, Schoolhouse, etc. On flatware the decoration is in the center. On hollow pieces it occurs on both sides.

Color of spatter is another price key. Blue and red are the most common. Green, purple, and brown are in a middle group. Black and yellow are scarce.

Like any soft paste, spatterware was easily broken or chipped. Prices are for pieces in very good to mint condition.

References: Susan and Al Bagdade, *Warman's English & Continental Pottery & Porcelain, Second Edition,* Wallace-Homestead, 1991; Kevin McConnell, *Spongeware and Spatterware,* Schiffer Publishing, 1990; Dana G. Morykan and Harry L. Rinker, *Warman's Country Antique & Collectibles, Second Edition,* Wallace-Homestead, 1994; Carl and Ada Robacker, *Spatterware and Sponge,* A. S. Barnes & Co., 1978.

Reproduction Alert: "Cybris" spatter is an increasing collectible ware made by Boleslow Cybris of Poland. The design utilizes the Adams-type peafowl and was made in the 1940s. Many contemporary craftsmen also are reproducing spatterware.

Teapot, Peafowl, red, blue, yellow, and black peafowl, blue spatter, 1830–50, 6″ h, $250.00.

Bowl, 7¾″ d, 4½″ h, stick spatter, marked "Villeroy & Boch," wear	105.00
Creamer, 4½″ h, blue spatter, hairline in bottom	55.00
Cup, handleless, Peafowl, green, red, blue, and black peafowl, brown and green spatter	70.00
Cup and Saucer, handleless	
Deer, red spatter cup, black deer on red spatter saucer, stains, pinpoint flakes	360.00
Peafowl, blue, yellow, red, and black	165.00
Rooster, blue, red, black, and yellow ochre rooster, blue spatter, saucer marked "T," stains, minor wear, small flakes on table ring	440.00
Rose, purple spatter, red, green, and black rose, pinpoint flake on saucer table ring	260.00
Schoolhouse, red, green, and brown	175.00
Pitcher, 8¾″ h, blue and white, minor roughness on rim and chips on base	135.00
Plate	
7½″ d, Rose, blue, red, green, and black dec, Adams	330.00
8¼″ d, blue spatter, eagle and shield transfer	150.00
Platter, 14″ l, stick spatter, polychrome floral enameling, marked "Auld Heather Ware, Scotland"	425.00
Saucer	
Columbine, rosebud, and thistle center, 5⅞″ d, red, blue, green, purple, and black design, purple spatter border	95.00
Peafowl	
4⅛″ d, red, blue, yellow ochre and black peafowl, red spatter, wear, minor stains, small rim repairs	60.00
5⅜″ d, red, green, blue, and black peafowl, red spatter, rim chips, minor stains	160.00
5¾″ d, red, blue, yellow, and black peafowl, green spatter, imp "Stoneware B. & T.," stains	110.00
Sugar, cov	
4¼″ h, Peafowl, blue, purple, red, green, and black dec	145.00
4⅜″ h, Rainbow, red and blue spatter, stains, wear, some damage, glued break in lid	150.00
4¾″ h, Peafowl, red, orange, green, and black design, blue spatter, applied ring handles, chips and hairlines, mismatched glued lid	125.00
5″ h, purple spatter	275.00
Teapot, 5¾″ h, Rooster, red, blue, yellow, and black dec	275.00
Waste Bowl, 6½″ d, blue spatter, blue transfer eagle and shield, hairline on base	125.00

SPONGEWARE

History: Spongeware is a specific type of decoration, not a type of pottery or glaze.

Spongeware decoration is found on many types of pottery bodies—ironstone, redware, stoneware, yellow ware, etc. It was made in both England and the United States. Marked pieces indicate a starting date of 1815, with manufacturing extending to the 1880s.

Decoration is varied. In some pieces the sponging is minimal, with the white underglaze dominant. Other pieces appear to be sponged solidly on both sides. Pieces from 1840 to 1860 have sponging which appears in either a circular movement or a streaked horizontal technique.

Examples are found in blue and white, the most common colors. Other prevalent colors are browns, greens, ochers, and a greenish-blue. The greenish-blue results from blue sponging which has been overglazed in a pale yellow. A red overglaze produces a black or navy color.

Other colors are blue and red (found on English creamware and American earthenware of the 1880s), gray, grayish-green, red, dark green on stark white, dark green on mellow yellow, and purple.

References: Susan and Al Bagdade, *Warman's English & Continental Pottery & Porcelain, Second Edition,* Wallace-Homestead, 1991; Kevin McConnell, *Spongeware and Spatterware,* Schiffer Publishing, 1990; Earl F. and Ada Robacker, *Spatterware and Sponge,* A. S. Barnes & Co., 1978.

Coffeepot, blue sponged dec, c1830, $275.00.

Bowl, 8½″ d, green and brown sponging, tan ground 45.00
Creamer, 3″ h, green, blue, and cream 100.00
Cup and Saucer, blue flower dec on cup 55.00
Food Mold, brown and cream 55.00
Marble, 2″ d, gray, blue sponging, late 19th C 220.00

Milk Pitcher, 7½″ h, black sponging, white ground 185.00
Mixing Bowl, 10″ d, brown sponging, Rockingham 100.00
Mug, 5″ h, baluster, pale gray, cobalt stained dip ext., looped handle with pinched terminal, c1775 . . . . 1,585.00
Pitcher
8″ h, green, blue, and cream 175.00
8¼″ h, blue and white dec, blue stripes 225.00
9½″ h, blue and white sponging . . . 145.00
10″ h, barrel shape, green, gold, and brown sponging 95.00
11″ h, blue and brown sponging, hairline 60.00
Planter, 7″ h, 13″ d, hanging, molded, Continental, late 19th/early 20th C, price for pair 300.00
Plate, 9½″ d, red, green, and black central flower dec, red and green sponged border 190.00
Platter, 13¼″ l, octagonal, central red and blue foliate chain, blue band border, off white ground, imp factory mark, Elsmore & Foster, Tunstall, 19th C 110.00
Sugar Bowl, cov, 4″ h, floral reserve, brown sponging, English, 19th C. . . . 85.00
Teapot, 7¼″ h, olive green and white dec 300.00
Umbrella Stand, 21″ h, American, 19th C 600.00
Vegetable Bowl, 8½″ l, dark blue sponging, white ground, c1820 . . . . 225.00

SPORT CARDS

History: Baseball cards date from the late 19th century. By 1900 the most common cards, known as "T" cards, were those produced by tobacco companies such as the American Tobacco Co., with the majority of the tobacco–related cards being produced between 1909 and 1915. During the 1920s American Caramel, National Caramel, and York Caramel candy companies issued cards identified in lists as "E" cards.

From 1933 to 1941 Goudey Gum Co. of Boston and in 1939 Gum Inc. were the big producers of baseball cards. Following World War II, Bowman Gum of Philadelphia (B.G.H.L.I.), the successor to Gum, Inc., lead the way. Topps, Inc., (T.C.G.) of Brooklyn, New York, followed. Topps bought Bowman in 1956 and enjoyed almost a monopoly in card production until 1981.

In 1981 Topps was challenged by Fleer of Philadelphia and Donruss of Memphis. All three companies annually produce sets of cards numbering 600 cards or more.

Football cards have been produced since the 1890s. However, it was not until 1933 that the first bubble gum football card appeared in the Goudey Sport Kings set. In 1935 National Chickle of Cambridge, Massachusetts, produced the first full set of gum cards devoted exclusively to football.

Both Leaf Gum of Chicago and Bowman Gum of Philadelphia produced sets of football cards in 1948. Leaf discontinued production after its 1949 issue. Bowman Gum continued until 1955.

Topps Chewing Gum entered the market in 1950 with its college stars set. Topps became a fixture in the football card market with its 1955 All–American set. From 1956 through 1963 Topps printed a card set of National Football League players, combining them with the American Football League players in 1961.

Topps produced sets with only American Football League players from 1964 to 1967. The Philadelphia Gum Company made National Football League card sets during this period. Beginning in 1968 and continuing to the present, Topps has produced sets of National Football League cards, the name adopted by the merger of the two leagues.

References: James Beckett, *The Official 1994 Price Guide To Baseball Cards, Fourteenth Edition*, House of Collectibles, 1994; James Beckett, *The Official 1994 Price Guide To Basketball Cards, Third Edition*, House of Collectibles, 1993; James Beckett, *The Official 1994 Price Guide To Football Cards, Thirteenth Edition*, House of Collectibles, 1993; James Beckett, *The Official 1994 Price Guide To Hockey Cards, Third Edition*, House of Collectibles, 1993; James Beckett, *The Sport Americana Baseball Card Price Guide, No. 15*, Edgewater Book Co., 1993; James Beckett, *The Sport Americana Basketball Card Price Guide and Alphabetical Checklist, #3*, Edgewater Book Co., 1993; James Beckett, *The Sport Americana Football Card Price Guide, No. 10*, Edgewater Book Co., 1993; James Beckett, *The Sport Americana Hockey Card Price Guide #3*, Edgewater Book Co., 1993; James Beckett, *The Sport Americana Team Football and Basketball Card Checklist, No. 1*, Edgewater Book Co., 1990; Gene Florence, *Florence's Standard Baseball Card Price Guide, Sixth Edition*, Collector Books, 1994; Jeff Fritsch and Jane Fritsch–Gavin, *The Sport Americana Team Football and Basketball Card Checklist, Number 2*, Edgewater Book Co., 1993; Allan Kaye and Michael McKeever, *Baseball Card Price Guide 1995, Second Edition*, Avon Books, 1994; Allan Kaye and Michael McKeever, *Basketball Card Price Guide 1994*, Avon Books, 1993; Allan Kaye and Michael McKeever, *Football Card Price Guide, 1994*, Avon Books, 1993; Allan Kaye and Michael McKeever, *Hockey Card Price Guide 1994*, Avon Books, 1993; Troy Kirk, *Collector's Guide To Baseball Cards*, Wallace–Homestead, 1990; Jeff Kurowski (ed.), *Sports Collectors Digest Baseball Card Price Guide, 7th Edition*, Krause Publications, 1993; Jeff Kurowski (ed.), *Standard Catalog Of Baseball Cards, Third Edition*, Krause Publications, 1992; Jeff Kurowski and Tony Prudom, *Sports Collectors Digest Pre–War Baseball Card Price Guide, 1887–1947*, Krause Publications, 1993; Mark Larson, *Sports Collectors Digest Minor League Baseball Card Price Guide*, Krause Publications, 1993; Mark Larson (ed.), *Sports Collectors Digest: The Sports Card Explosion*, Krause Publications, 1993; Bob Lemke and Sally Grace, *Sportscard Counterfeit Detector, Second Edition*, Krause Publications, 1993; Norman E. Martinus and Harry L. Rinker, *Warman's Paper*, Wallace–Homestead, 1994; Sports Collectors Digest, *Football, Basketball, & Hockey Price Guide*, Krause Publications, 1991; Sports Colllectors Digest, *Getting Started In Card Collecting*, Krause Publications, 1993; Sports Collectors Digest, *101 Sports Card Investments*, Krause Publications, 1993.

Periodicals: *Allan Kaye's Sports Cards News & Price Guides*, 10300 Watson Rd., St. Louis, MO 63127; *Baseball Update*, Suite 284, 220 Sunrise Highway, Rockville Centre, NY 11570; *Beckett Baseball Card Monthly*, Suite 200, 4887 Alpha Rd., Dallas, TX 75244; *Beckett Basketball Card Magazine*, Suite 200, 4887 Alpha Rd., Dallas, TX 75244; *Beckett Football Card Magazine*, Suite 200, 4887 Alpha Rd., Dallas, TX 75244; *Beckett Hockey Card Monthly*, Suite 200, 4887 Alpha Rd., Dallas, TX 75244; *Canadian Card News & Price Guide*, 700 E. State St., Iola, WI 54990; *Malloy's Sports Collectibles*, 17 Danbury Rd., Ridgefield, CT 06877; *Sport Card Economizer*, RFD 1, Box 350, Winthrop, ME 04364; *Sports Card Price Guide Monthly*, 700 E. State St., Iola, WI 54990; *Sports Cards*, 700 East State Street, Iola, WI 54990; *Sports Collectors Digest*, 700 East State Street, Iola, WI 54990; *The Old Judge*, PO Box 137, Centerbeach, NY 11720; *Tuff Stuff*, PO Box 1637, Glen Allen, VA 23060; *Your Season Ticket*, 106 Liberty Rd., Woodsboro, MD 21798.

American Carmel Co., Tom Griffith, outfield, Brooklyn Nationals, $6.00.

BASEBALL

BOWMAN ERA
1948 Bowman (black and white)
Complete set (48)	1,600.00
Common player (1–36)	9.00
Common player (37–48)	13.50
14 Allie Reynolds	23.00
29 Joe Page	23.00
36 Stan Musial	400.00
48 Dave Koslo	27.00

1949 Bowman
Complete set (240)	7,400.00
Common player (1–144)	8.00
Common player (145–240)	30.00
33 Warren Spahn	80.00
36 Pee Wee Reese	95.00
50 Jackie Robinson	375.00
224 Satchel Paige	575.00

1950 Bowman
Complete set (252)	4,500.00
Common player (1–72)	25.00
Common player (73–252)	8.00
35 Enos Slaughter	57.50
98 Ted Williams	350.00
232 Al Rosen	32.00

1952 Bowman (color)
Complete set (252)	4,200.00
Common player (1–216)	6.75
Common player (217–252)	15.00
1 Yogi Berra	180.00
101 Mickey Mantle	1,100.00
116 Duke Snider	90.00
218 Willie Mays	575.00

1954 Bowman
Complete set (224)	2,000.00
Common player (1–128)	4.50
Common player (129–224)	6.75
66B Jim Piersall	45.00
132 Bob Feller	42.50
161 Yogi Berra	80.00
177 Whitey Ford	50.00

TOPPS ERA
1951 Topps, blue backs
Complete set (52)	950.00
Common player (1–52)	16.00
3 Richie Ashburn	75.00
30 Enos Slaughter	57.50
37 Bobby Doerr	50.00

1954 Topps
Complete set (250)	3,700.00
Common player (1–50)	6.75
Common player (51–75)	13.50
Common player (76–250)	6.75
1 Ted Williams	200.00
17 Phil Rizzuto	34.00
94 Ernie Banks	375.00
132 Tom Lasorda	75.00

1956 Topps
Complete set (340)	3,500.00
Common player (1–100)	3.80
Common player (101–180)	5.25

Common player (181–260)	7.25
Common player (261–340)	5.75
20 Al Kaline	57.50
31 Hank Aaron	125.00
63 Roger Craig	13.50
79 Sandy Koufax	190.00
260 Pee Wee Reese	70.00

1958 Topps
Complete set (495)	2,500.00
Common player (1–110)	3.70
Common player (111–198)	2.70
Common player (199–352)	2.30
Common player (353–440)	2.00
Common player (441–474)	1.90
Common player (475–495)	2.00
1 Ted Williams	115.00
52A Roberto Clemente	90.00
70B Al Kaline YL	80.00

1960 Topps
Complete set (572)	1,800.00
Common player (1–110)	1.70
Common player (111–198)	1.35
Common player (199–286)	1.55
Common player (287–440)	1.70
Common player (441–506)	2.30
Common player (507–552)	5.50
Common player (553–572)	6.75
1 Early Wynn	10.00
148 Carl Yastrzemski	135.00
300 Hank Aaron	57.50

FOOTBALL

BELL BRAND, 1960
Complete Set (39)	900.00
Common player (1–18)	10.00
Common player (19–39)	15.00
2 Gene Selawski	450.00

BOWMAN GUM COMPANY
1948
Complete Set (108)	2,500.00
3 John Lujack	100.00
36 Bulldog Turner	90.00

1953
Complete Set (96)	1,000.00
Common player (1–96)	6.25
Common player SP	8.50
26 Otto Graham	55.00
43 Frank Gifford	150.00

1955
Complete Set (160)	550.00
Common player (1–64)	1.50
Common player (65–160)	2.00
52 Pat Summerall	22.50
152 Tom Landry	75.00

FLEER GUM COMPANY
1960
Complete Set (132)	275.00
Common Player (1–132)	.75
58 George Blanda	15.00
124 Jack Kemp	150.00

1962
Complete Set (88)	275.00
Common player (1–88)	1.75
46 George Blanda	17.00
79 Jack Kemp	55.00

LEAF GUM
1948
Complete Set (98)	2,500.00
Common player (1–49)	6.25
Common player (50–98)	35.00
34 Sammy Baugh	125.00

1949
Complete Set (49)	600.00
Common player (1–150)	7.50
15 Sid Luckman	45.00

PHILADELPHIA GUM COMPANY
1964
Complete Set (198)	375.00
Common player (1–198)	.50
91 Merlin Olsen	32.50

1966
Complete Set (198)	350.00
Common player (1–198)	.40
31 Dick Butkus	60.00
38 Gale Sayers	100.00

TOPPS CHEWING GUM INC
1951
Complete Set (75)	400.00
Common player (1–75)	5.00
2 Bill Wade	10.00
48 George Young	7.00

1955
Complete Set (100)	1,250.00
Common player (1–92)	5.00
Common player (93–100)	9.00
Common player SP	6.50
16 Knute Rockne	100.00
27 Red Grange	110.00
37 Jim Thorpe	125.00

1958
Complete Set (132)	500.00
Common player (1–132)	1.00
22 John Unitas	70.00
73 Frank Gifford	37.50

1960
Complete Set (132)	250.00
Common player (1–132)	.75
51 Bart Starr	14.00
113 Y. A. Tittle	9.00

1963
Complete Set (170)	450.00
Common player (1–170)	.55
Common player SP	1.85
14 Jim Brown	55.00
44 Deacon Jones	22.50
98 Fran Tarkenton	42.50

SPORTS COLLECTIBLES

History: Individuals have been saving sports-related equipment since the inception of sports.

Some was passed down from generation to generation for reuse. The balance occupied dark spaces in closets, attics, and basements.

In the 1980s two key trends brought collectors' attention to sports collectibles. First, decorators began using old sports items, especially in restaurant decor. Second, card collectors began to discover the thrill of owning the "real" thing. Although the principal thrust was on baseball material, by the beginning of the 1990s all sport categories were collectible, with golf and football especially strong.

References: Gwen Aldridge, *Baseball Archaeology: Artifacts From The Great American Pastime,* Chronicle Books, 1993; Mark Baker, *Sport Collectors Digest Baseball Autograph Handbook, 2nd Edition,* Krause Publications, 1991; Mark Baker, *Team Baseballs: The Complete Guide to Autographed Team Baseballs,* Krause Publications, 1992; Peter Capano, *Baseball Collectibles,* Schiffer Publishing, 1989; Bruce Chadwick and David M. Spindel, *The Dodgers: Memories and Memorabilia from Brooklyn to L.A.,* Abbeville Press, 1993; Bruce Chadwick and David M. Spindel, *The Giants: Memories and Memorabilia from a Century of Baseball,* Abbeville Press, 1993; Douglas Congdon–Martin and John Kashmanian, *Baseball Treasures: Memorabilia From The National Pastime,* Schiffer Publishing, 1993; Ralf Coykendall, Jr., *Coykendall's Sporting Collectibles Price Guide,* Lyons & Burford, 1991; Ralf Coykendall, Jr., *Coykendall's Second Sporting Collectibles Price Guide,* Lyons & Burford, 1992; Ted Hake and Roger Steckler, *An Illustrated Price Guide To Non–Paper Sports Collectibles,* Hake's Americana & Collectibles Press, 1986; Buck Kronnick, *The Baseball Fan's Complete Guide To Collecting Autographs,* Betterway Publications, 1990; Mark Larson, *The Complete Guide To Baseball Memorabilia,* Krause Publications, 1992; Roderick A. Malloy, *Malloy's Sports Collectibles Value Guide: Up–To–Date Prices For Noncard Sports Memorabilia,* Attic Books, Ltd., 1993; Norman E. Martinus and Harry L. Rinker, *Warman's Paper,* Wallace–Homestead, 1994; Ron Menchine, *A Picture Postcard History of Baseball,* Almar Press, 1992; John M. and Morton W. Olman, *Golf Antiques & Other Treasures of the Game, Expanded Edition,* Market Street Press, 1993; Donald M. and R. Craig Raycraft, *Value Guide To Baseball Collectibles,* Collector Books, 1992; Beverly Robb, *Collectible Golfing Novelties,* Schiffer Publishing, 1992; George Sanders, Helen Sanders, and Ralph Roberts, *The Sanders Price Guide To Sports Autographs, 1994 Edition,* Scott Publishing, 1993; Shirley and Jerry Sprung, *Decorative Golf Collectibles: Collector's Information, Current Prices,* Glentiques, 1991; Mark Wilson (ed.), *The Golf Club Identification and Price Guide III,* Ralph Maltby Enterprises, 1993.

Periodicals: *Baseball Hobby News,* 4540 Kearney Villa Rd., San Diego, CA 92123; *Beckett Focus on Future Stars,* Suite 200, 4887 Alpha Rd., Dallas, TX 75244; *Boxing Collectors Newsletter,* 59 Boston

St, Revere, MA 02151; *Fantasy Baseball,* 700 E. State St., Iola, WI 54990-0001; *Golfiana Magazine,* PO Box 688, Edwardsville, IL 62025; *Malloy's Sports Collectible,* 15 Danbury Rd., Ridgefield, CT 06877; *Old Tyme Baseball News,* PO Box 833, Petoskey, MI 49770; *Sporting Collector's Monthly,* PO Box 305, Camden, DE 19934; *Sports Collectors Digest,* 700 East State Street, Iola, WI 54990; *The Diamond Angle,* PO Box 409, Kaunakakai, HI 97648; *Tuff Stuff,* PO Box 1637, Glen Allen, VA 23060; *U.S. Golf Classics & Heritage Hickories,* 5407 Pennock Point Rd., Jupiter, FL 33458.

Collectors' Clubs: Baseball Glove Collector, 14507 Rolling Hills Lane, Dallas, TX 75240; Boxiana & Pugilistica Collectors International, PO Box 83135, Portland, OR 97203; Society for American Baseball Research, PO Box 93183, Cleveland, OH 44101-5183; Golf Collectors' Society, PO Box 491, Shawnee Mission, KS 66202; Golf Club Collectors Association, 640 E. Liberty St., Girard, OH 44420-2308.

Museums: Aiken Thoroughbred Racing Hall of Fame & Museum, Aiken, SC; International Boxing Hall of Fame, Canastota, NY; Metropolitan Museum of Art, The Jefferson Burdich Collection, New York, NY; Naismith Memorial Basketball Hall of Fame, Springfield, MA; National Baseball Hall of Fame & Museum, Inc., Cooperstown, NY; National Bowling Hall of Fame & Museum, St. Louis, MO; New England Sports Museum, Boston, MA; PGA/World Golf Hall of Fame, Pinehurst, NC; The Kentucky Derby Museum, Louisville, KY.

BASEBALL

Autograph, Giants Infielder Pee Wee Reese and Manager Herman Hanks	35.00
Badge, 6″ w, Baltimore Orioles, full color team photo, 1966	50.00
Book, *Satchel Paige Biography,* Hal Lebovitz, 1948, 96 pgs	50.00
Certificate, Giants, Fred Fitzsimmons, United Half Million Miles Club	8.00
Game	
All–Star Baseball, orig box, Cadaco–Ellis, 1959 copyright	25.00
Play Ball, bagatelle, plastic and metal, Steven Mfg Co, 1964	30.00
Necktie Rack, 11″ l, wood, brown burnt wood art and inscription, brass hanging rings, baseball theme, 1920s	100.00
Nodder, Senators, Mo Lain, 1962	75.00
Pennant	
Boston Red Sox, 29″ l, felt, red, white ink inscription, 1950s	30.00
Chicago White Sox, 28½″ l, red felt, white inscriptions and image, 1960s	25.00
Philadelphia Phillies, 30″ l, felt, white, red inscription, full color team photo, 1968	20.00

Planter, 5½″ h, china, baseball and baseball player swinging bat, white, maroon and blue accents, yellow bat, glossy finish, 1950s	30.00
Post Card, 3½ x 5½″, full color view of South Side Ball Park, Chicago, 1913 postmark	25.00
Record	
Joe E Brown, How To Play Baseball, 78 rpm record, 12½ x 14″ cardboard album with four illus instruction pgs, 1940–50	50.00
Take Me Out To The Ball Game, 78 rpm, Golden Records, paper cover, 1952 copyright	25.00
Schedule, Giants, 1926 season, spring training trip, games, railroad itinerary, autographed by Fred Fitzsimmons	38.00
Score Card, A High Fly, artist sgd drawing "W D," c1895	25.00
Wallet, 3½ x 4½″, leather, brown, emb baseball scenes, white accents, early 1950s	55.00

BASKETBALL

Coloring Set, Pro Basketball Coloring Set, nine sketches and supplies, National Basketball Players Assn, 1970–80	25.00
Figure, 6½″ h, Chicago Bulls, composition, painted, gold base, NBA symbol, orig box, 1969 copyright	50.00
Game, Star Basketball, bagatelle, multicolored board, Star Paper Box Co, c1926	40.00
Nodder, 6″ h, Harlem Globetrotters, composition, green sq base, early 1960s	250.00

BOXING

Autograph, Raging Bull/Jake LaMotta, 8 x 10″, full color glossy, bold blue ink signature	30.00
Bottle Opener, 4½″ l, ceramic, boxing glove, dark purple, white decal, silvered metal opener	15.00
Photo	
Jersey Joe Walcott, 5¼ x 7¼″, black and white glossy, 1951–52 heavyweight champion	50.00
Rocky Graziano, 8 x 10″, black and white glossy, 1947–48 middleweight champion	25.00
Post Card, Jack Dempsey, 3½ x 5½″, sepia portrait, reverse with Dempsey's New York City Restaurant adv, 1940s	100.00
Program, 8 x 10½″, Turner vs Gavilan,	

July 7, 1952, Municipal Stadium, Philadelphia, 8 pgs **55.00**
Ticket Envelope, 4¼ x 9½", Louis vs Walcott, June 23, 1948 world championship bout **50.00**

FOOTBALL

Glass, 4¾" h, clear, Baltimore Colts World Champions, 1959, reverse with game score listing **25.00**
Magazine, *Harvard Alumni*, November, 1937, Harvard's loss to Army article . **5.00**

Football, Christmas tree ornament, celluloid, orange and gray, marked "T, Japan," 4½" h, $12.00.

Nodder, 6½" h, football player, composition
  Baltimore Colts, emb "Colts" and horseshoe, sq blue wood base, 1961–62 . . . . **100.00**
  Michigan State, green and white uniform, round white base, 1960s . . . **25.00**
  Princeton Tigers, orange and black uniform, round green base, "Tigers" decal, mid 1960s **75.00**
Program, 9 x 12", Army–Navy, December 2, 1939, Municipal Stadium, Philadelphia, 104 pgs **15.00**
Yearbook, 8½ x 11", 1965 New York Jets, 40 pgs **25.00**

GOLF

Advertising Sign, 13½ x 12", The Original Canadian Dry, cardboard, golfing scene, 1920s **75.00**
Badge, Woman's Golf Association, 67th Western Open, red and black, 1970, price for pair **8.00**

Book, *Putting Made Easy, The Mark G Harris Method,* P A Vaile, Reilly & Lee, 1935, first edition **25.00**
Door Stop
  8" h, cast iron, golfer figure, Hubley Manufacturing Company, 1920s . . **350.00**
  8½" h, cast iron, black caddy figure, 1920s **400.00**
Magazine, *American Golfer*, June, 1932 . . . . **8.00**
Noisemaker, 2¾" d, 6½" l, litho tin, full color image, male golfer, marked "Germany" on handle, 1930s **25.00**
Program, Fort Worth Open Golf Championship, Glen Garden Country Club, Fort Worth, TX, 1945 . . . . **100.00**
Weathervane, 14" h, 19" l, brass, golfer in swing position and caddy, 1920s . . **850.00**

HORSE RACING

Glass, 5¼" h, colorful frosted design for 1975 and 1980 runnings, reverse with list of Annual winners from 1875, price for pair **25.00**
Mug, 5½" h, plastic, 1983 Kentucky Derby, blue logo and inscription, General Electric Plastics **15.00**
Program, 1942 Kentucky Derby, Saturday, May 2 annual 68th Derby, Churchill Downs, Louisville, 6 pgs . . . **25.00**
Tray, 13½ x 21½", litho tin, 1974 Kentucky Derby, Churchill Downs, full color race scene **25.00**

OLYMPICS

Book, *Olympische Spiele 1964,* summary of Innsbruck, Austria Winter Olympics and Tokyo Summer Olympics, 384 pgs, German text, 7½ x 10½" **30.00**
Handkerchief, 8½ x 9", XI Olympaide/ Berlin 1936, white, color ring symbol **50.00**
Pennant, 26" l, gray felt, white inscriptions, color rings symbol, 1932 . . . . . **45.00**
Plate, 6¼" d, XVIth Olympiad, white china, full color symbols, scalloped edge, gold trim, marked "Royal Albert Bone China/England" **55.00**
Poster Stamp, 2 x 2½", Olympic Games/ Stockholm 1912, June 29–July 22, full color image **20.00**
Press Badge, 1½ x 2", metal, 1952 Summer Olympics, Helsinki, Finland, metal, tower and ring symbol, enamel accents, attached yellow and black striped ribbon **75.00**
Program, 1936 Summer Olympics, Berlin, 96 pgs **75.00**

STAFFORDSHIRE, HISTORICAL

History: The Staffordshire district of England is the center of the English pottery industry. There were 80 different potteries operating there in 1786, with the number increasing to 179 by 1802. The district includes Burslem, Cobridge, Eturia, Fenton, Foley, Hanley, Lane Delph, Lane End, Longport, Shelton, Stoke, and Tunstall. Among the many famous potters were Adams, Davenport, Spode, Stevenson, Wedgwood, and Wood.

In historical Staffordshire the view is the most critical element. American collectors pay much less for non-American views. Dark-blue pieces are favored. Light views continue to remain undervalued. Among the forms, soup tureens have shown the highest price increases.

References: David and Linda Arman, *Historical Staffordshire: An Illustrated Check List,* published by authors, 1974, out of print; David and Linda Arman, *First Supplement, Historical Staffordshire: An Illustrated Check List,* published by authors, 1977, out of print; Susan and Al Bagdade, *Warman's English & Continental Pottery & Porcelain, Second Edition,* Wallace-Homestead, 1991; Ada Walker Camehl, *The Blue China Book,* Tudor Publishing Co., 1946 (Dover, reprint); A. W. Coysh and R. K. Henrywood, *The Dictionary Of Blue And White Printed Pottery, 1780–1880* (1982) and *The Dictionary of Blue and White Printed Pottery, Vol. II* (1989), Antique Collectors' Club, 1982; Ellouise Larsen, *American Historical Views On Staffordshire China, 3rd Edition,* Dover Publications, 1975.

Museum: Hershey Museum, Hershey, PA.

Notes: Prices are for proof examples. Adjust prices by 20% for an unseen chip, a faint hairline, or an unseen professional repair; by 35% for knife marks through the glaze and a visible professional repair; and by 50% for worn glaze and major repairs.

The numbers in parentheses refer to items in the books by Linda and David Arman, which constitute the most detailed list of American historical views and their forms.

The company operated four potteries at Stoke and one at Tunstall. American views were produced at Tunstall in black, light blue, sepia, pink, and green in the 1830–40 period. William Adams died in 1865. All operations were moved to Tunstall. The firm continues today under the name of Wm. Adams & Sons, Ltd.

Log Cabin, medallions of Gen. Harrison on border, teapot, pink (458)	450.00
Seal of United States, dark blue, 7½" pitcher (443)	1,200.00
U.S. Views	
Shannondale Springs, Virginia, U.S., pink, 7⅞" plate (451)	85.00
The Falls of Niagara, black, 19½" platter (453)	1,200.00

Clews, plate, Christmas Eve, dark blue transfer, imp mark, 6¾" d, $175.00.

ADAMS

W.ADAMS&SONS **ADAMS**

The Adams family has been associated with ceramics from the mid 17th century. In 1802 William Adams of Stoke–upon–Trent produced American views.

In 1819 a fourth William Adams, son of William of Stoke, became a partner with his father and was later joined by his three brothers. The firm became William Adams & Sons. The father died in 1829 and William, the eldest son, became manager.

CLEWS

From sketchy historical accounts that are available, James Clews took over the closed plant of A. Stevenson in 1819. His brother Ralph entered the business later. The firm continued until about 1836, when James Clews came to America to enter the pottery business at Troy, Indiana. The venture was a failure because of the lack of skilled workmen and the proper type of clay. He returned to England but did not reenter the pottery business.

Cities Series, dark and medium blue
Columbus, dark blue, 14½″ platter
(21) **3,500.00**
Philadelphia, dark blue, 9⅞″ plate
(26) **525.00**
Washington, dark blue, 7¾″ plate
(30) **425.00**
Doctor Syntax, dark blue
Doctor Syntax and the gypsies, soup
tureen (51) **2,200.00**
Doctor Syntax mistakes a gentle-
man's house for an inn, 9¾″ soup
plate (42). **250.00**
Doctor Syntax star gazing, 8¾″ plate
(61) **225.00**
Don Quixote Series, dark blue
Don Quixote's Library, vegetable dish
(68) **750.00**
Sancho Panza's debate with Teresa,
9″ plate (78). **150.00**
Landing of Lafayette at Castle Garden,
dark blue (1)
Cup Plate, 3½″, oval medallion . . . **400.00**
Pitcher, 5½″ **1,850.00**
Plate, 7⅞″ **295.00**
Platter, 21¾″, well and tree **1,200.00**
Teapot **700.00**
Peace and Plenty, dark blue (34)
Cup Plate, 4½″ **900.00**
Plate, 7⅞″ **350.00**
Picturesque Views Series
Bakers Falls, Hudson River, pink, 9″
plate (101). **75.00**
Fort Edward, Hudson River, light blue,
4⅛″ cup plate (102) **75.00**
Hudson, Hudson River, slate blue, cov
vegetable dish (107). **750.00**
Penitentiary in Allegheny, near Pitts-
burgh, brown, 17½″ platter (117) . . **475.00**
Troy From Mount Ida, mulberry, 10″
plate (120). **195.00**
Pittsfield Elm, dark blue, soup, 10½″
(33) **250.00**
States or America and Independence
Series, dark blue
Building, Deer on Lawn, 10½″ plate
(2) **225.00**
Dock, large building and ships, 19½″
platter (4) **1,700.00**
Mansion, small boat with flag in fore-
ground, 14¾″ platter (12) **1,200.00**

works formerly were owned by the Wedgwood family. The firm produced transfer scenes in a variety
of colors, such as black, light blue, pink, sepia,
green, maroon and mulberry. Over 40 different
American views of Connecticut, Massachusetts,
Pennsylvania, New York, and Ohio were issued.
The firm is believed to have closed about 1844.

**J. & J. Jackson, plate, American Sce-
nery Series, The Race Bridge, Philadelphia, (486), $65.00.**

American Scenery Series, all colors
Girard's Bank, black, 6½″ plate (474) **110.00**
Hartford, CT, black, 10″ soup (476) **145.00**
Harvard Hall, MA, pink, 7″ plate
(477). **165.00**
Iron Works at Saugerties, 12″ platter
(478). **275.00**
View of Newburgh, black, 17½″ platter
(463). **575.00**
Water Works, Philadelphia, dark
brown, 9″ plate (487) **175.00**
Yale College, deep dish (493) **125.00**

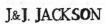

J.&J. JACKSON

J. & J. JACKSON

Job and John Jackson began operations at the
Churchyard Works, Burslem, about 1830. The

THOMAS MAYER

In 1829, Thomas Mayer and his brothers, John
and Joshua, purchased Stubbs' Dale Hall Works

of Burslem. They continued to produce a superior grade of ceramics.

Arms of the American States, dark blue
Connecticut, gravy tureen (498) . . . **3,800.00**
New Jersey, 19″ platter (503) **7,500.00**
Rhode Island, 8½″ plate (507) **795.00**
Lafayette at Franklin's Tomb, dark blue,
sugar bowl (510). **850.00**

CHARLES MEIGH

Job Meigh began the Meigh pottery in the Old Hall Pottery in 1780. Later his sons and grandsons entered the business. The firm's name is recorded as Job Meigh & Sons, 1823; J. Meigh & Sons, 1829; Charles Meigh, 1843.

The American Cities and Scenery series was produced by Charles Meigh between 1840 and 1850. The colors are light blue, brown, gray, and purple. Sometimes the colors appear in combination.

Albany, NY, 13½″ platter (544) **275.00**
Baltimore, brown, 12″ wash bowl (546) **225.00**
Capitol at Washington, tureen, round,
cover (550). **650.00**
City Hall, New York, 10¼″ plate (551) **75.00**
Hudson City, 10¼″ soup (552) **75.00**
Utica, NY, light blue, 7¼″ plate (556) . **75.00**
Village of Little Falls, 8¼″ plate (558) . **75.00**
Yale College, New Haven, 9½″ plate
(560) **75.00**

MELLOR, VENEABLES & CO.

Little information is recorded on Mellor, Veneables & Co. except that they were listed as potters in Burslem in 1843. Their Scenic Views series with the Arms of the States Border does include the arms for New Hampshire. This state is missing from the Mayer series. However, the view was known in England and collectors search for a Mayer example.

Arms of States, white body, light color
transfers (529)
Maryland, teapot **650.00**
Pennsylvania, sugar bowl **350.00**
Scenic Views, Arms of States Border,
light blue, pink, brown, purple
Albany, 15″ platter (516) **250.00**
The President's House from the River,
14″ pitcher (520) **300.00**
Tomb of Washington, Mt. Vernon,
7½″ plate. **90.00**
View of Capitol at Washington, 11″
vegetable dish (526). **300.00**

JOHN & WILLIAM RIDGWAY - c.1814-1830

J.W. R.
Stone China
W. RIDGWAY

J. & W. RIDGWAY AND WILLIAM RIDGWAY & CO.

John and William Ridgway, sons of Job Ridgway and nephews of George Ridgway, who owned Bell Bank Works and Couldon Place Works, produced the popular Beauties of America series at the Couldon plant. The partnership between the two brothers was dissolved in 1830. John remained at Couldon.

William managed the Bell Bank Works until 1854. Two additional series were produced based upon the etchings of Bartlett's American Scenery. The first series had various borders, including narrow lace. The second series is known as Catskill Moss.

Beauties of America is in dark blue. The other series are found in the light transfer colors of light blue, pink, brown, black, and green.

J. & W. Ridgway, Beauties of America, City Hall of New York, dark blue transfer, 9½″ d, $250.00.

American Scenery
Albany, wash bowl (279) 325.00
Columbia Bridge on the Susquehanna, soup tureen (281) 650.00
Peekskill Landing, Hudson River, purple, 10″ open vegetable dish (287) 175.00
Valley of the Shenandoah from Jefferson's Rock, brown, 7″ plate (289)................... 95.00
Wilkes–Barre, Vale of Wyoming, light blue, 11″ coffeepot (294)........ 450.00
Beauties of America, dark blue
Almshouse, Boston, soup tureen (254)................... 3,000.00
Bank, Savannah, gravy tureen (257) 1,500.00
City–Hall, NY, 10″ plate (260) ... 225.00
Exchange, Charleston, vegetable dish (265)................... 1,200.00
Octagon Church, Boston, 9¾″ soup (271)................... 395.00
Catskill Moss
Anthony's Nose, 6″ plate (295) ... 75.00
Caldwell, Lake George, 5″ sauce dish (298)................... 50.00
Kosciusko's Tomb, 10″ plate (305) . 75.00
Valley of Wyoming, cup (317) 40.00
Columbian Star, Harrison's Log Cabin
End View, brown, 11″ platter (276) . 450.00
Side View, green, 10¼″ plate (277) 245.00

death in 1815, John's son Spencer became a partner and the firm operated under the name of John Rogers & Sons. John died in 1816. His son continued the use of the name until he dissolved the pottery in 1842.

Boston Harbor, dark blue (441)
Cup Plate 1,400.00
Cup and Saucer 650.00
Waste Bowl 900.00
Boston State House, medium dark blue (442)
Plate, 10″ 265.00
Platter, 16⅝″ 1,100.00
Wash Bowl and Pitcher 2,400.00

c 1816-1830

ROGERS

ROGERS

John Rogers and his brother George established a pottery near Longport in 1782. After George's

R.S.W.

STEVENSON

As early as the 17th century the name Stevenson has been associated with the pottery industry. Andrew Stevenson of Cobridge introduced American scenes with the flower and scroll border. Ralph Stevenson, also of Cobridge, used a vine and leaf border on his dark-blue historical views and a lace border on his series in light transfers.

The initials R. S. & W. indicate Ralph Stevenson and Williams are associated with the acorn and leaf border. It has been reported that Williams was Ralph's New York agent and the wares were produced by Ralph alone.

Acorn and Oak Leaves Border, dark blue
Columbia College, New York, 7½″ plate (350)................. 475.00
State House, Boston, 5″ toddy plate (360)................... 725.00
Water Works, Philadelphia, 10″ soup (363)................... 650.00

Stevenson, platter, Alms House, Boston, vine border, dark blue, (365), 16¼″ l, $1,250.00.

Floral and Scroll Border, dark blue
  Almshouse, NY, 10″ plate (394) . . . **750.00**
  Catholic Cathedral, NY, 6½″ plate
    (395) **1,650.00**
  New York from Heights near Brooklyn,
    17″ platter (399) **2,250.00**
  View of New York From Weehawk,
    soup tureen (404) **10,000.00**
Lace Border
  Erie Canal at Buffalo, 10″ soup (386) **100.00**
  New Orleans, sugar bowl (387) . . . **150.00**
  Riceborough, GA, wash bowl (388) **375.00**
Vine Border
  Almshouse, NY, 14¼″ platter (366) **1,650.00**
  Battery, NY, 6⅞″ plate (367) **850.00**
  Columbia College, NY, 8″ plate (372) **475.00**
  Hospital, Boston, 9″ plate (378) **325.00**
  Pennsylvania Hospital, Philadelphia,
    soup tureen (383) **8,500.00**

c1828-1830

Stubbs, plate, Spread Eagle border, Fair Mount Near Philadelphia, 10¼″ d, $200.00.

State House, Boston, 14½″ platter
  (331) **750.00**
Upper Ferry Bridge over the River
  Schuylkill (332)
  Dish, round **750.00**
  Platter, 19″ **800.00**
  Vegetable Dish **750.00**
  Wash Bowl **1,100.00**

S. TAMS & CO.

The firm operated at Longton, England. The exact date of its beginning is not known but is believed to be about 1810–15. The company produced several dark blue American views. About 1830 the name became Tams, Anderson, and Tams.

Capitol, Washington
  Bowl, deep (514) **1,500.00**
  Wash Pitcher (514) **1,500.00**
United States Hotel, Philadelphia, 10″
  soup (515) **1,000.00**

UNKNOWN MAKERS

Antislavery, light blue, 9¼″ plate (608) **150.00**
Erie Canal inscription (597)
  Cup Plate, 3¾″ **1,500.00**
  Pitcher, 5¼″ **1,000.00**
Famous Naval Heroes
  Pitcher, dark blue, 7″ (604) **750.00**
  Washbowl (604) **1,200.00**
Franklin Flying a Kite, light blue, toy
  plate (603) **95.00**
Great Fire, City of New York, plate, series of three, each (605–607) **125.00**
Mount Vernon, Washington's Seat, dark
  blue, sugar bowl (600) **850.00**

STUBBS

In 1790 Stubbs established a pottery works at Burslem, England. He operated it until 1829, when he retired and sold the pottery to the Mayer brothers. He probably produced his American views about 1825. Many of his scenes were from Boston, New York, New Jersey, and Philadelphia.

Rose Border, dark blue
  Boston State House and New York
    City Hall, 6½″ pitcher (335) **1,200.00**
  City Hall, NY, 6″ plate (336) **400.00**
Spread Eagle Border, dark and medium
  blue
  City Hall, NY, 6½″ plate (323) **400.00**
  Fair Mount Near Philadelphia, 22″
    platter (324) **900.00**
  Highlands, North River, 10″ plate
    (325) **2,500.00**
  Hoboken in New Jersey, salt shaker
    (326) **700.00**

WOOD

Enoch Wood, sometimes referred to as the Father of English Pottery, began operating a pottery at Fountain Place, Burslem, in 1783. A cousin, Ralph Wood, was associated with him. In 1790 James Caldwell became a partner and the firm was known as Wood and Caldwell. In 1819 Wood and his sons took full control.

Enoch died in 1840. His sons continued under the name of Enoch Wood & Sons. The American views were first made in the mid 1820s and continued through the 1840s.

It is reported that the pottery produced more signed historical views than any other Staffordshire firm. Many of the views attributed to unknown makers probably came from the Woods.

Marks vary, although always with the name Wood. The establishment was sold to Messrs. Pinder, Bourne & Hope in 1846.

Celtic China, light transfer colors
Columbus, GA, 3⅞″ cup plate (238) ... 450.00
Shipping Port on the Ohio, KY, 12″
  platter (249)................ 500.00
Transylvania University, Lexington,
  KY, 10″ soup (250) 125.00

Enoch Wood & Sons, plate, shell border, Catskill Mountains, dark blue transfer, (162), 7½″ d, $350.00.

West Point, Military Academy, open-
  work dish (252) 350.00
Floral Border, irregular, dark blue
  Commodore MacDonnough's Victory
    (154)
    Coffeepot 1,500.00
    Cup and Saucer 450.00
  Entrance of the Erie Canal into the
    Hudson at Albany (156)
    Plate, 6½″ 750.00
    Soup, 10″ 825.00
  Erie Canal, Aqueduct Bridge at Roch-
    ester, 5½″ pitcher, with first canal
    view (157)............... 1,500.00
  Wadsworth Tower, sugar bowl (155) 550.00
Four Medallion, Floral Border Series,
  light transfers
  Castle Garden, 8″ plate (225) 75.00
  Monte Video, 7½″ plate (229) 75.00
  Race Bridge, Philadelphia, gravy tur-
    een (233) 300.00
General Jackson (224)
  Cup Plate 750.00
  Pitcher, 4″, luster 1,500.00
  Plate, 7″ 900.00
Shell Border, circular center, dark blue
  Belleville on the Passaic River, soup
    tureen (159)............... 6,000.00
  Castle Garden Battery, NY, 18½″ plat-
    ter (160) 2,500.00
  Catskill Mountains, Hudson River,
    custard cup with handle (162) 600.00
  City of Albany, State of New York, 10″
    plate (163)............... 450.00
  Highland, Hudson River, vegetable
    dish (167) 1,200.00
  Mount Vernon, 5¾″ plate (173) ... 700.00
  Railroad, Baltimore and Ohio, incline,
    9″ plate (182)............. 750.00
  West Point Military Academy, 12″ plat-
    ter (188) 1,500.00
  White House, Washington, D.C., cup
    plate (189)............... 2,500.00
Shell Border, irregular center, dark blue
  Cadmus, 10″ soup (125) 450.00
  Commodore MacDonnough's Victory,
    coffeepot (130) 1,500.00
  Constitution and Guerriere, 10″ plate
    (131)................. 800.00
  Erith on the Thames, vegetable dish
    (136)................. 800.00
  Union Line, 10″ soup (144) 450.00
  Wadsworth Tower (147)
    Coffeepot 1,200.00
    Cup and Saucer 400.00
    Waste Bowl 500.00
Washington's Tomb, dark blue (190B)
  Creamer 700.00
  Soup, 10″ 900.00
  Sugar Bowl 750.00
  Teapot 900.00

STAFFORDSHIRE ITEMS

History: A wide variety of ornamental pottery items originated in England's Staffordshire district, beginning in the 17th century and extending to the present. The height of production was from 1820 to 1890.

These naive pieces are considered folk art by many collectors. Most items were not made carefully; some were even made and decorated by children.

The types of objects are varied, e.g., animals, cottages, and figurines (chimney ornaments). The key to price is age and condition. The older the piece, the higher the price is a general rule.

References: Susan and Al Bagdade, *Warman's English & Continental Pottery & Porcelain, Second Edition,* Wallace-Homestead, 1991; Pat Halfpenny, *English Earthenware Figures, 1740–1840,* Antique Collectors' Club; Charles Kenyon Kies, *Collecting Victorian Staffordshire Pottery Figures,* Antique Publications, 1989; P. D. Gordon Pugh, *Staffordshire Portrait Figures Of The Victorian Era,* Antique Collectors' Club; Dennis G. Rice, *English Porcelain Animals Of The 19th Century,* Antique Collectors' Club, 1989.

Spill Vase, "The Rivals," cobalt, orange, green, and pink, orange int., c1855, 12″ h, $500.00.

Animal Covered Dish, hen
3¼″ h, orange, green, black, and white **110.00**
10½″ l, orange, green, black, red, and white **305.00**
Cup Plate
3⅝″ d, medium blue transfer, man at fence **85.00**
3¾″ d, dark blue transfer, three children **85.00**

3⅞″ d, dark blue transfer, English country scene, pink luster wash over floral border, pinpoint on table ring **80.00**
Figure
5¼″ h
Cat, black and tan sponging, glass eyes **275.00**
Man with whip, polychrome dec . **105.00**
8⅛″ h, zebra, black, white, green, and brown, late **255.00**
8¾″ h, Returning Home, couple on horseback, polychrome, damage, repaired **200.00**
9″ h, cat, seated, 19th C, price for pair **440.00**
9½″ h, judge dozing over pontificating vicar, 19th C **450.00**
9¾″ h, Saint George on horseback **125.00**
12½″ h, man on horseback, white, traces of color **200.00**
14″ h, spaniel, black glazed, gilt dec, 19th C, price for pair **440.00**
Mug
1½″ h, yellow glazed, inscribed "ABC," early 19th C **400.00**
2″ h, yellow glazed, inscribed, early 19th C
A New Carriage for Anne **425.00**
A Nightingale for Eliza **400.00**
A Rocking Horse for John **550.00**
A Trifle for Richard **425.00**
2⅛″ h, transfer dec, inscribed "Lovejoy the first Martyr to American Liberty," imperfections **375.00**
2⅞″ h, brown transfer, "STU" with children, early cycles, polychrome enamel **115.00**
Plate
7⅛″ d, molded floral border, black transfer, The Sluggard, blue, orange, yellow, and green enamel, purple luster rim **105.00**
8¾″ d, black transfer, General Jackson, The Hero of New Orleans, molded feather edge, pink luster trim, minor wear **1,155.00**
9½″ d, green transfer, General WH Harrison, Hero of the Thames 1813, back labeled "James Tams & Co. Importers, Philadelphia," stains . . . **1,980.00**
Soup Plate, 10½″ d, red transfer, Hartford CT, Jacksons, price for set of four **440.00**
Spill Holder, 11″ h, cow with calf, 19th C, imperfections, price for pair **420.00**
Tankard, 5¾″ h, pearlware, blue transfers, portrait of Shakespeare, central actors depicting Act IV, scene I from *The Tempest,* early 19th C, minor rim discoloration **550.00**

Toby Jug, 10″ h, seated sailor, holding
    clay pipe and beer stein, 19th C **110.00**
Toddy Plate, 5⅜″ d, ironstone, molded
    flowers and wheat rim, Franklin's
    Proverbs, Make Hay While The Sun
    Shines in black, polychrome enamel,
    green rim stripe, imp "Meakins" **90.00**

STAFFORDSHIRE, ROMANTIC

History: In the 1830s two factors transformed
the blue-and-white printed wares of the Staffordshire
potters into what is now called "Romantic
Staffordshire." Technical innovations expanded
the range of transfer–printed colors to light blue,
pink, purple, black, green, and brown. There was
also a shift from historical to imaginary scenes.
These patterns had less printed detail and more
white space, adding to the pastel effect.

Shapes in the 1830s are predominately rococo
with rounded forms, scroll handles, and floral finials.
With time, patterns and shapes became simpler
and the earthenware bodies coarser. The late
1840s and 1850s saw angular gothic shapes and
the weight and texture of ironstone.

The most dramatic post-1870 change was the
impact of the Japanese design craze with zigzag
border elements and such motifs as bamboo, fans,
and cranes. Brown printing dominated this style,
sometimes with polychrome enamel highlights.

Wares are often marked with pattern or potter's
names, but marking was inconsistent and many
authentic unmarked examples exist. The addition
of "England" as a country of origin mark in 1891
helps to distinguish 20th-century wares made in the
romantic style.

References: Susan and Al Bagdade, *Warman's
English & Continental Pottery & Porcelain, Second
Edition,* Wallace-Homestead, 1991; Petra Williams,
Staffordshire: Romantic Transfer Patterns,
Fountain House East, 1978; Petra Williams, *Staffordshire
II,* Fountain House East, 1986.

Advisors: Mark R. Brown and Tim M. Sublette.

Caledonia, William Adams, 1830s
  Plate
    7½″ d **90.00**
    10½″ d **135.00**
  Platter, 17″ l **500.00**
  Soup Plate, two color **165.00**
Canova, Thomas Mayer, c1835; G Phillips,
  c1840
  Plate, 10½″ d **95.00**
  Pudding Bowl, two color **225.00**
  Vegetable, cov **350.00**
Columbia, W Adams & Sons, 1850
  Creamer **110.00**
  Cup and Saucer **55.00**
  Cup Plate **55.00**
  Plate, 10″ d **55.00**
  Relish **65.00**

Coral Border, Thomas Dimmock, 1830s,
    chestnut basket, without tray **275.00**
Dado, Ridgways, 1880s
  Creamer, brown **75.00**
  Cup and Saucer, polychrome **75.00**
  Plate
    7½″ d, brown **35.00**
    8½″ d, polychrome **55.00**
    10½″ d, polychrome **70.00**
  Platter, 11½″ l, polychrome **150.00**
  Sugar, brown **85.00**

**Italian Villas, J. Heath, soup dish, 7¾″
d, $50.00.**

Japonica, maker unknown, 1830s
  Creamer **125.00**
  Sugar **135.00**
Marmora, William Ridgway & Co, 1830s
  Platter, 16½″ l **325.00**
  Sauce Tureen, matching tray **350.00**
  Soup Plate **90.00**
Melbourne, Gildea & Walker, 1881
  Sauce Tureen, matching tray **165.00**
  Soup Plate **50.00**
  Vegetable, cov **150.00**
Millennium, Ralph Stevenson & Son,
  1830s, plate, 10½″ d **135.00**
Palestine, William Adams, 1836
  Creamer **135.00**
  Cup and Saucer
    Single color **55.00**
    Two color **135.00**
  Cup Plate **55.00**
  Plate
    5″ d **45.00**
    6″ d **45.00**
    7″ d **45.00**
    8½″ d **50.00**
    9½″ d
      Single color **55.00**
      Two color **110.00**
    10″ d **100.00**

Platter
　13″ l 325.00
　15″ l 350.00
　17″ l 375.00
Sugar 165.00
Tall Pot 600.00
Teapot 350.00
Vegetable, open
　10″ l 135.00
　12″ l 200.00
Union, William Ridgway Son & Co, 1840s
　Plate, 10 1/ 2″ d 65.00
　Platter, 15″ l 175.00
Venus, Podmore, Walker & Co, 1850s
Plate
　7½″ d 45.00
　10″ d 55.00
Sugar 110.00

STAINED AND/OR LEADED GLASS PANELS

History: American architects in the second half of the 19th century and the early 20th century used stained and leaded glass panels as a chief decorative element. Skilled glass craftsmen assembled the designs, the best known being Louis C. Tiffany.

The panels are held together with soft lead cames or copper wraps. When purchasing a panel, check the lead and have any repairs made to protect your investment.

Periodicals: *Glass Art Magazine,* PO Box 260377, Highlands Ranch, CO 80126; *Glass Patterns Quarterly,* PO Box 131, Westport, NY 40077.

Collectors' Club: Stained Glass Association of America, 4050 Broadway, Suite 219, Kansas City, MO 64111.

Museum: Corning Museum of Glass, Corning, NY.

Leaded
　Firescreen, 48½″ w, 32″ h, three panels, clear glass top half, hammered white glass lower half, central applied Art Nouveau floral design, green bull's eye highlights... 2,750.00
　Panel, 96″ h, 20″ w, rect, rippled and opaque glass, turquoise, white, and avocado, clear glass ground, stylized flowering plant motif, c1910, price for set of six panels 6,000.00
　Window, 90″ w, 95″ h, three panels, woodland and stream scene, blue, green, and mauve slag glass, iron frame 4,675.00
Stained
Panel
　24 x 14″, red, white, green, pink, and blue floral design, two layers

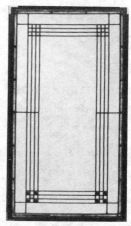

Stained and Leaded, Frank Lloyd Wright, c1915, rectilinear and grid design, gold and white accents, 49½ x 21½″, price for pair estimated at $2,500.00 to $3,500.00. Photograph courtesy of Leslie Hindman Auctioneers.

of striated and fractured glass, green patinated bronze frame, stamped "Tiffany Studios New York," price for pair.......... 2,200.00
26 x 21″, Richard the Lion Hearted on horseback, 1883 .... 660.00
54⁵⁄₁₆ x 19 9/16″, two panels depicting death of St Norbert: one panel of Saint lying in state, surrounded by flaming torches, monks, and members of abbey, coat of arms and inscription above; second panel shows translation of Saint's relics from Magdeburg to Premonstransian Abbey of Strahow, procession of men and soldiers in Baroque costume, city of Prague, banner, and inscriptions above, both panels with scrolling strapwork cartouche flanked by pendant swags of fruit, inscriptions, minor breaks and losses, each mounted in electrified box frame, part of forty one windows orig created for Abbey of Parc at Heverlee–Louvain, Southern Lowlands, by Flemish workshop of Jean De Caumont, 1640, price for pair................... 10,350.00

Window
    32 x 42″, Art Nouveau, yellow, blue,
      and orange geometric, oak
      frame, c1900 . . . .   **275.00**
    61½″ h, 61″ l, over entry type, blue
      and orange shield and geometric
      design, c1920. . . . .   **470.00**

STANGL POTTERY BIRDS

History: Stangl ceramic birds were produced from 1940 until the Stangl factory closed in 1972. The birds were produced at Stangl's Trenton plant and shipped to its Flemington, New Jersey, plant for hand painting.

During World War II the demand for these birds and Stangl pottery was so great that 40 to 60 decorators could not keep up with the demand. Orders were contracted out to private homes. These orders then were returned for firing and finishing. Colors used to decorate these birds varied according to the artist.

As many as ten different trademarks were used. Almost every bird is numbered; many are artist signed. However, the signatures are used only for dating purposes and add very little to the value of the birds.

Several birds were reissued between 1972 and 1977. These reissues are dated on the bottom and valued at approximately half of the older birds.

References: Harvey Duke, *The Official Identification And Price Guide To Pottery And Porcelain, Seventh Edition,* House of Collectibles, 1989; Harvey Duke, *Stangl Pottery,* Wallace-Homestead, 1992; Joan Dworkin and Martha Horman, *A Guide To Stangl Pottery Birds,* Willow Pond Books, 1973; Norma Rehl, *The Collectors Handbook of Stangl Pottery,* Democrat Press, 1982.

Collectors' Club: Stangl Bird Collectors Association, PO Box 419, Ringoes, NJ 08551.

Additional Listings: See *Warman's Americana & Collectibles* for more examples.

3580, Cockatoo, 8⅞″ h, $65.00.

3250E, Drinking Duck **75.00**
3276S, Bluebird, 5″ h **80.00**
3286, Hen, 3¼″ h **45.00**
3400, Love Bird, 4″ h **55.00**
3401S, Wren, gold **30.00**
3402S, Oriole on limb with leaves, price
  for pair **115.00**
3407, Owl, 4″ h **275.00**
3444, Cardinal, female, pine cones dec,
  6½″ h. **80.00**
3447, Warbler, yellow, 5″ h **75.00**
3453, Mountain Bluebird, 6⅛″ h **450.00**
3454, Key West Quail Dove, 9″ h   . . .   **275.00**
3491, hen pheasant **165.00**
3580, Cockatoo, 8⅞″ h **90.00**
3582, Parakeet, blue/green, price for
  pair **175.00**
3589, Indigo Bunting, 3¼″ h **60.00**
3591, Brewer's Blackbird, 3½″ h **80.00**
3593, Nuthatch, 2½″ h **55.00**
3629, Broadbill Hummingbird, 4½″ h   .   **100.00**
3715, Blue Jay, 10¼″ h **500.00**
3749S, Scarlet Tanager, pink body, 4¾″
  h. **175.00**
3755S, Audubon Warbler, 4¼″ h **125.00**
3811, Chestnut–backed Chickadee, 5″
  h. **75.00**
3849, Goldfinch, 4″ h **100.00**
3852, Cliff Swallow, 3¾″ h **125.00**

STATUES

History: Beginning with primitive cultures, man produced statues in the shape of people and animals. During the Middle Ages most works were religious and symbolic in character and form. The Renaissance rediscovered the human and secular forms.

During the 18th and 19th centuries it was fashionable to have statues in the home. Many famous works were copied for popular consumption.

Statuette or figurine denotes smaller statues, one-fourth life size or smaller.

Reference: Lynne and Fritz Weber (eds.), *Jacobsen's Thirteenth Painting and Bronze Price Guide, January 1992 to January 1994,* Weber Publications, 1994.

Alabaster, 19″ h, angel, carved, Renaissance style, clasped hands, patina,
  19th C, price for pair **1,760.00**
Bronze
  9″ h, Napoleon, standing at attention,
    rouge marble base, sgd
    "Guillamin" **695.00**
  12½″ h, athlete, partially clad muscular figure, clasped right hand, rockwork base, sgd base, French School, after Luca Madrassi, late
    19th C.   **715.00**
  12⅞″ h, True Blue, marked "National

41" h, Semeur, patina, cast signature, Luis Domenech, c1900 . . . . **1,320.00**
Parian, 15½" h, Mary, standing, extended arms, detachable forearms . . **55.00**
Pottery, 37" h, Court Official, wearing arched hat and amber tunic, glazed, rock work base, T'ang Dynasty **15,000.00**
Terra Cotta, 10" h, Moses, seated, sgd "Alva Studios," c1955 . . . . **165.00**

STEIFF

History: Margarete Steiff, GmbH, established in Germany in 1880, is known for very fine quality stuffed animals and dolls, as well as other beautifully made collectible toys. It is still in business, and its products are highly respected.

The company's first products were wool-felt elephants made by Margarete Steiff. In a few years the elephant line was expanded to include a donkey, horse, pig, and camel.

By 1903 the company also was producing a jointed mohair Teddy Bear, whose production dramatically increased to over 970,000 units in 1907. Margarete's nephews took over the company at this point. The bear's head became the symbol for its label, and the famous "Button in the Ear" round, metal trademark was added.

Newly designed animals were added: Molly and Bully, the dogs, and Fluffy, the cat. Pull toys and kites also were produced, as well as larger animals on which children could ride or play.

Become familiar with genuine Steiff products before purchasing an antique stuffed animal. Plush in old Steiff animals was mohair; trimmings usually were felt or velvet. Unscrupulous individuals have attached the familiar Steiff metal button to animals that are not Steiff.

Bronze, Le Devoir, shield with "Honor Patria," sgd E. Picault, 11½" h, $575.00.

Security League, New York, C. 1915," marble base **215.00**
22¾" h, standing nude, sq plinth, sgd "Talconnet" **665.00**
52" h, standing nude youth, dark brown patina, attributed to George Kolbe **5,750.00**
55½" h, Le Drapeau de Prophate, Arabian figure, inscribed "Henri Ple" on base **6,500.00**
Cast Iron, 28½" h, angel, crossed arms, applied wings, shaped base, Victorian, mid 19th C **665.00**
Gesso, 31" h, standing figure with draped gilt cloth, arm extended, 19th C. **2,200.00**
Marble
  18½" h, Andro Richter as a boy, carved. **385.00**
  25" h, winged infant holding dove, wearing draped cloth, circular base, third quarter 19th C **880.00**
  33" h, maiden, preparing to bathe, circular base, Italian, late 19th C. . . . **2,640.00**
  37½" h, maiden looking upwards, anchor at side, sq integral base, third quarter 19th C **1,100.00**
  56" h, white marble, Woman: The Water Carrier, classical dress, fluted columnar base, purchased from Florentine Craftsman, New York City. **3,300.00**
  58½" h, carved, semi–nude maiden, chained to rocky outcrop, Italian, 19th C. **11,000.00**
Metal
  24" h, Joan of Arc on horseback, patina, French, late 19th C **275.00**

References: Peggy and Alan Bialosky, *The Teddy Bear Catalog*, Workman Publishing, 1984, Revised Edition; Jurgen & Marianne Cieslik, *Button In Ear: The History of Teddy Bear and His Friends,* distributed by Theriault's, 1989; Peter Consalvi, Sr., *Collector Steiff Values*, Hobby House Press, 1994; Margaret Fox Mandel, *Teddy Bears And Steiff Animals*, First Series (1984, 1993 value update), Second Series (1987), Collector Books; Margaret Fox Mandel, *Teddy Bears, Annalee Animals & Steiff Animals, Third Series,* Collector Books, 1990; Dana G. Morykan and Harry L. Rinker, *Warman's Country Antiques & Collectibles, Second Edition,* Wallace–Homestead, 1994; Linda Mullins, *Teddy Bear & Friends Price Guide, Fourth Edition,* Hobby House Press, 1993; Christel & Rolf Pistorius, *Steiff: Sensational Teddy Bears, Animals & Dolls,* Hobby House Press, 1991; Jean Wilson, *Steiff Toys Revisited,* Wallace–Homestead, 1989.

Collectors' Club: Steiff Collectors Club, PO Box 798, Holland, OH 43528.

Additional Listings: Teddy Bears. See Stuffed

Toys in *Warman's Americana & Collectibles* for more examples.

Bull Dog, 6″ h, mohair, 1960s	30.00
Camel, 14″ l, brown–gold mohair, black glass eyes, gold painted cast iron frame with wheels, repair to rear hump.	450.00
Donkey, 8″ h, plush, glass eyes, button on ear, 1960s	50.00
Fox Terrier, 4¼″ h, sitting, mohair wire hair, glass eyes, buttons on ear and collar	245.00

Cat, glass eyes, pink nose, paw marks, blue ribbon collar with bell, 7″ l, 5¾″ h, $65.00.

Frog, 4″ h, mohair, 1950s	50.00
Goat, 8″ l, mohair, 1950s	45.00
Groundhog, 5″ h, mohair, 1950s	40.00
Koala Bear, 8″ h, mohair, glass eyes, button in ear, 1960s.	75.00
Lamb, 12½″ l, felt face, ears, and legs, four wheels, orig white tag and button in ear, orig bell, 1908.	1,700.00
Opossum, 5″ l, Joggi	35.00
Pekingese, 6″ l, Pinky, mohair, 1960s	50.00
Pig, 14″ l, oinker, mohair, shoe button eyes, worn mesh nose, 1910	400.00
Polar Bear, jointed legs	550.00
Poodle, 13″ l, plush, glass eyes, four cast iron wheels, c1910	600.00
Reindeer, 10″ l, mohair, leather collar with bell, shoe button eyes, four cast iron wheels, button in ear, c1908 . . .	800.00
Sheep, 37″ l, mohair and velour, glass eyes, 1910	650.00
Squirrel, 9″ h, rust tipped mohair, fully jointed, button in ear, 1930s	300.00
Teddy Bear	
16″ h, hump, light golden mohair, black shoe button eyes, c1906 . . .	1,000.00

24″ h, Mr. Bear, light yellow mohair, shoe button eyes, fully jointed, black nose, mouth, and claws, replaced pads, c1910	715.00

1892-1921

STEINS

History: A stein is a mug especially made to hold beer or ale, ranging in size from the smaller ³/₁₀ liters and ¼ liters to the larger 1, 1½, 2, 3, 4, and 5 liters, and in rare cases to 8 liters. (A liter is 1.05 liquid quarts.)

Master steins or pouring steins hold 3 to 5 liters and are called krugs. Most steins are fitted with a metal hinged lid with thumblift. The earthenware character-type steins usually are German in origin.

References: Susan and Al Bagdade, *Warman's English & Continental Pottery & Porcelain, Second Edition,* Wallace-Homestead, 1991; John L. Hairell, *Regimental Steins,* published by author, 1984; Gary Kirsner and Jim Gruhl, *The Stein Book,* Glentiques, 1984; Eugene Manusov, *Encyclopedia of Character Steins,* Wallace-Homestead, 1976, out of print; Eugene V. Manusov and Mike Wald, *Character Steins: A Collector's Guide,* Cornwall Books, 1987; James R. Stevenson, *Antique Steins: A Collectors' Guide, Second Edition,* Cornwall Books, 1989; Mike Wald, *HR Steins,* SCI Publications, 1980.

Periodical: *Stein Line,* PO Box 48716, Chicago, IL 60648-0716.

Collectors' Club: Stein Collectors International, 3530 Mimosa Court, New Orleans, LA 70131.

Faience, earthenware, tin glaze	
1 L, line design, pewter lid inscribed "1849," ball thumblift, Hannoverisch Munden factory, mid 19th C . .	500.00
1¼ L, floral cart, pewter lid with inscribed wreath and "1731," ball thumblift, Berlin factory, early 18th C	1,500.00
Glass	
Cut	
¼ L, flat panels, prism lid, cavalier thumblift, ground and polished . .	125.00
½ L, line pattern, clear, silver lid, small flakes	350.00

¾ L, wheel cut, hunter with dog, clear, bird thumblift, bubble pattern base, c1820 . . . . 800.00
1 L, cut dec, floral and "Zur Erinnerung," c1840 . . . . 250.00
Enameled
  ½ L, cavalier, pewter lid 100.00
  1 L, floral dec 175.00
Mettlach, etched
2057, Bacchanalian revelers, pewter lid and thumblift 400.00
2090, cat, dog, verse, and card motif, gnome thumblift 350.00
2100, two medieval figures, mask thumblift, H Schlitt 500.00
2281, Renaissance beer drinkers, pewter and china lid, bust thumblift 440.00

Pottery, ½ L, Schw. Reiter Regiment Pring Carl V Bavern, 1896–99, pewter lid and thumblift, $250.00.

Porcelain
½ L, Regimental, 45 Fld Artl, Bahrenfeld, lithophane, eagle thumblift, sgd "Res Brodt" 350.00
1 L, creamware, hp floral and verse, pewter lid 75.00
2 L, leaf pattern, pewter lid, glaze chips and rim chips 350.00
3 L, blue and white ball and star pattern, face spout, pewter lid 450.00
Pottery, relief
½ L
  Musical scene and instruments, pewter lid 45.00
  People at table, 1101 . . . . 75.00
1 L
  Hunting scene, 420 . . . . 65.00
  Lovers, pewter lid, 64 . . . . 100.00

Stoneware, relief
½ L
  Drinking scene, B & C 3884 . . . . 55.00
  Hand painted, cavalier, pewter lid 150.00
  People around table, 385 . . . . . . 65.00
1 L, etched and threaded, verse, pewter lid 85.00

1903–32

STEUBEN GLASS

History: Frederick Carder, an Englishman, and Thomas G. Hawkes of Corning, New York, established the Steuben Glass Works in 1904. In 1918 the Corning Glass Company purchased the Steuben company. Carder remained with the firm and designed many of the pieces bearing the Steuben mark. Probably the most widely recognized wares are "Aurene," "Verre De Soie," and "Rosaline," but many other types were produced.

The firm continues operating, producing glass of exceptional quality.

References: Paul Gardner, *The Glass of Frederick Carder,* Crown Publishers, 1971; Paul Perrot, Paul Gardner, and James S. Plaut, *Steuben: Seventy Years Of American Glassmaking,* Praeger Publishers, 1974; Ellen T. Schroy, *Warman's Glass,* Wallace-Homestead, 1992.

Museums: Corning Museum of Glass, Corning, NY; Rockwell Museum, Corning, NY.

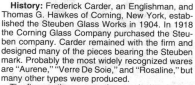

AURENE

Bowl, 6" d, blue, irid surface 275.00
Candlesticks, pr, 10" h, gold, rope twist form, engraved "Aurene 686" 880.00
Console Set, 10" d w bowl, pr 6" h 3581 wide rim candleholders, blue Aurene on calcite, decumbent rim, triangular Steuben labels, price for three piece set 1,870.00
Cordial Set, 7¼" h cylindrical decanter, four glasses, 6" d conforming tray, gold, sgd and numbered 2025, price for six piece set 990.00
Lamp Shade, 5" h, 2½" d rim, gold, ten ribbed flared trumpet form, silver fleur de lis mark at rims, price for set of three 360.00

Narcissus Bowl, 10″ d, blue, shallow bowl, bright blue irid, applied nipple feet, base engraved "Aurene 2586" **660.00**

Planter, 12″ d, blue, inverted rim, three applied prunt feet, engraved "Aurene 2586". **770.00**

Punchbowl, 12″ d, 5⅛″ h, gold, applied dished foot, irid stretched at rim, inscribed "Aurene 2852," chips on foot edge **615.00**

Tumbler, 6″ h, gold, engraved "Steuben Aurene 1044" **250.00**

Aurene, vase, bulbous, flared rim, sgd, 8¼″ h, $600.00.

Vase

4½″ h, gold, pinched ball top, four applied prints below, pale turn of century irid coloring, base engraved "Aurene 150," price for pair. **770.00**

5″ h, blue, bulbous, flared, subtle ribbing, fine int. luster, silver–blue irid, base engraved "Steuben". **715.00**

6¼″ h, blue, ten ribbed flared oval body, irid luster, inscribed "Steuben". **770.00**

8″ h, gold, decumbent collar, trumpet form 1124, strong iridescence, engraved "Aurene," numbered **525.00**

8½″ h, blue, flattened cone, raised pedestal foot, white vines and gold Aurene hearts, base engraved "Steuben Aurene 2697," tooling blemish. **1,430.00**

12½″ h, blue, ruffled trumpet, flawless white calcite, bright blue irid int., triangular Steuben label. **1,150.00**

JADE

Beverage Set, pitcher, four matching mugs, green, alabaster handles, sgd, price for five piece set **800.00**

Bowl, 11½″ l, 6¼″ h, Grotesque, blue jade, Frederick Carder design, minor int. surface wear, fleur de lis mark. . . **3,850.00**

Candlesticks, pr, 10″ h, No. 2956, jade candlecup and base, alabaster shaft, gold foil labels. **500.00**

Center Bowl, 15½″ d, broad decumbent rim, shallow bowl, green. **330.00**

Compote, 10″ h, yellow, ftd **1,400.00**

Lamp Base, 25″ h, broad ruffled top, tapered jade shaft, applied jet black rigaree handles, two gilt metal socket lamp fittings, stepped platform base, Carder Steuben Catalog No. 8002 . . **315.00**

Parfait, 6″ h, applied alabaster foot . . **250.00**

Planter, 5½″ h, 9″ l, rect block, green, alabaster lion head medallions on ends **360.00**

Rose Bowl, 7″ d, 7″ h, spherical, smooth jade crystal. **330.00**

Vase, 7″ h, green, swirled flared body, fleur de lis mark on base **165.00**

MISCELLANEOUS

Basket, No. 644, crystal, latticework, berry prunts **435.00**

Bowl

4½″ h, Grotesque, shaded clear to green **325.00**

8″ d, 4″ h, Mat Su Noke, crystal 2687 form, amethyst Cintra Oriental applied handles and rim, small annealing line **525.00**

Candelabra, 10″ h, No. 8050, two arm, crystal, c1952, price for pair. **990.00**

Center Bowl

12″ d, 4″ h, Florentina, mat finish, flattened rim, internal dec, broad pink peach blossoms, minute reflective particles **2,200.00**

14″ l, 6¾″ h, Ivorene, Grotesque, slumped twelve ribbed bowl, inscribed "Steuben" on base **550.00**

15″ d, 5″ h, crystal, six ball feet, large John Dreves design, engraved "Steuben" mark. **220.00**

Champagne, Cerise, ruby swirled, crystal stem and wafer, price for set of four **100.00**

Compote, 13¾″ h, No. 2968, amethyst, ribbed, crystal knop, matching cov, pear finial, early "Steuben Glass Works" label. **225.00**

Exhibition Sculpture, 18″ l, Salmon Run, designed by James Houston, engraved by George Thompson, number fourteen in series of twenty, orig red leather and velvet box **13,200.00**

Lamp Base, 11″ h shaft, 25″ h overall, silver speckled Moss Agate shaft with crackled dark amethyst and blue, red, amber, green, and black swirls, beaded and foliage gilt metal platform base, conforming cap, two socket fittings **1,760.00**

Vase

6″ h, Pomona, green, tree trunk, thorny three prong bud base **200.00**

8¼″ h, flared trumpet, Bristol Yellow, airtrap bubbles, applied brilliant yellow random reeding, acid "Steuben" mark on base. **220.00**

8½″ h, fan, Spanish Green, flattened cone, raised pedestal foot, etched fleur de lis mark on base. **220.00**

ROSALINE

Bowl, 8″ l, 7″ w, 3¼″ h, one end folded in, other pinched spout, inscribed "F. Carder Steuben 723" on edge of polished pontil. **335.00**

Cocktail, 7″ h, flared, twisted alabaster stem, fleur de lis mark, price for pair **360.00**

Compote, 4″ h, ruffled, alabaster stem and foot **275.00**

Goblet, crystal foot, price for set of three **180.00**

VERRE DE SOIE

Basket, raspberry prunts, unsgd **345.00**

Bonbon, 6″ h, compote form, overall irid surface, swirled celeste blue finial, twisted stem **825.00**

Compote, cov

6¾″ h, No. 3343, frosted celeste blue twisted stem, full bodied pear finial **1,250.00**

8″ h, 6″ w, pale green body, celeste blue edge, applied green leaves, full bodied peach finial **1,250.00**

Perfume Bottle, 4½″ h, melon ribbed, deep amber stopper **325.00**

Vase, 10″ h, classic form, notched rim, all over floral motif **360.00**

STEVENGRAPHS

History: Thomas Stevens of Coventry, England, first manufactured woven silk designs in 1854. His first bookmark was produced in 1862, followed by the first Stevensgraphs, perhaps in 1874 but definitely in 1879 at the York Exhibition. The first "portrait" Stevensgraphs (of Disraeli and Gladstone) were produced in 1886, and the first postcards incorporating the silk-woven panels in 1904. Stevens offered many other items with silk panels, including valentines, fans, pin cushions, needle cases, etc.

Stevensgraphs are miniature silk pictures, matted in cardboard, and usually having a trade announcement, or "label," affixed to the reverse. Thomas Stevens's name appears on the mat of the early Stevensgraphs directly under the silk panel. Many of the later "portraits" and the larger silks (produced initially for calendars) have no identification on the front of the mat other than the phrase "woven in pure silk" and have no label on the back. Other companies, notably W. H. Grant of Coventry, copied this technique. Their efforts should not be confused with Stevensgraphs.

American collectors favor the Stevengraphs of American interest, such as "Signing of the Declaration of Independence," "Columbus Leaving Spain," and "Landing of Columbus." Sports-related Stevengraphs, such as "The First Innings" (baseball) and "The First Set" (tennis), are also popular, as well as portraits of Buffalo Bill, President and Mrs. Cleveland, George Washington, and President Harrison.

The bookmarks are longer than they are wide, have mitered corners at the bottom, and are finished with a tassel. Originally, Stevens's name was woven into the fold-over at the top of the silk, but soon the identification was woven into the fold-under mitered corners. Almost every Stevens bookmark has such identification, except the ones woven at the World's Columbian Exposition in Chicago, 1892–93.

Postcards with very fancy embossing around the aperture in the mount almost always have Stevens's name printed on them. Embossed cards from the "Ships" and "Hands Across the Sea" series generally are not printed with Stevens's name. The most popular postcard series in the United States are "Ships" and "Hands Across the Sea," the latter incorporating two crossed flags and two hands shaking. Seventeen flag combinations have been found, but only seven are common. Stevens produced silks that were used in the "Alpha" Publishing Co. cards. Many times the silks were the top or bottom half of regular bookmarks.

References: Geoffrey A. Godden, *Stevengraphs and Other Victorian Silk Pictures,* Associated University Presses, 1971; Chris Radley, *The Woven Silk Postcard,* privately printed, 1978; Austin Sprake, *The Price Guide to Stevengraphs,* Antique Collectors' Club, Baron Publishing, 1972.

Collectors' Club: Stevengraph Collectors' Association, 2103–2829 Arbutus Road, #2103, Victoria, British Columbia, Canada, V8N 5X5.

Museums: Herbert Art Gallery and Museum, Coventry, England; Paterson Museum, Paterson, NJ.

Note: Prices are based on pieces in mint or close to mint condition.

Advisor: John High.

BOOKMARK

For A Good Boy, I had a little doggy . **60.00**

For A Good Girl, Sweet Maggie had a little bird **60.00**

Little Bo–Peep 50.00
Little Jack Horner 50.00
Little Red Riding Hood 50.00
The Late Ear of Beaconsfield, Peace
with Honour 25.00

19th C

STEVENS AND WILLIAMS

History: In 1824 Joseph Silvers and Joseph Stevens leased the Moor Lane Glass House at "Briar Lea Hill" (Brierley Hill), England, from the Honey-Borne family. In 1847 William Stevens and Samuel Cox Williams took over, giving the firm its present name. In 1870 the firm moved to its Stourbridge plant. In the 1880s the firm employed such renowned glass artisans as Frederick C. Carder, John Northwood, other Northwood family members, James Hill, and Joshua Hodgetts.

Stevens and Williams made cameo glass. Hodgetts developed a more commercial version using thinner-walled blanks, acid etching, and the engraving wheel. Hodgetts, an amateur botanist, was noted for his brilliant floral designs.

Other glass products and designs manufactured by Stevens and Williams include intaglio ware, Peach Bloom (a form of peachblow), moss agate, threaded ware, "jewell" ware, tapestry ware, and Silveria. Stevens and Williams made glass pieces covering the full range of late Victorian fashion.

After World War I the firm concentrated on refining the production of lead crystal and achieving new glass colors. In 1932 Keith Murray came to Stevens and Williams as a designer. His work stressed the pure nature of the glass form. Murray stayed with Stevens and Williams until World War II and later followed a career in architecture.

References: Ellen T. Schroy, *Warman's Glass,* Wallace-Homestead, 1992; R. S. Williams-Thomas, *The Crystal Years,* Stevens and Williams Limited, England, Boerum Hill Books, 1983.

Additional Listing: Cameo Glass.

Bookmark, Wesley, black and white, $50.00.

POST CARD

Anne Hathaway's Cottage 40.00
Hands Across The Sea, man and woman's hands
  R.M.S. *Carmania*, Great Britain and
  USA flags. 40.00
  U.S.M.S. *Philadelphia*, USA and Norway flags. 100.00
Houses of Parliment 60.00
Princes Street, Edinburgh 60.00
R.M.S. *Lusitania* 70.00
R.M.S. *Saxona* 40.00

STEVENGRAPH

Are You Ready? 150.00
John L. Sullivan, story label 100.00
Rt. Hon. J. Chamberlain, M.P., flower
  spray. 125.00
The Final Spurt 175.00
The First Innings 300.00
The First Over 250.00

Biscuit Jar, cov, 7¾" h, 5½" d, cream opaque, large amber and green applied ruffled leaves, rich pink int., SP rim, lid, and handle 275.00
Bowl, 7⅞" d, jade green shading to alabaster disk base, stamped "Brierley Royal Crystal/S & W" mark 250.00
Calling Card Receiver, 10" l, applied amber handle, rolled edge, translucent opalescent ground, three applied berries, blossoms, and green leaves, three applied amber feet 725.00
Finger Bowl and Underplate, Rainbow Swirl, three swirls of yellow, blue–purple, and rose, crimped edge. 575.00
Jardiniere, 6½" d, 10" h, pink opalescent, cut back, two spatter flowers and

sunflower, three applied opalescent
thorn feet, leaves, and stems, minor
damage 350.00
Pitcher, 7″ h, amber, applied fruit,
leaves, and thorny stem 480.00
Plate, 4¾″ d, ruffled shell shape, Swirl
pattern, shaded pink to green, MOP
satin finish 195.00
Rose Bowl, 5″ h, 3½″ d, egg shape,
shaded brown ground, rich cream lining, gold prunus blossoms and
branches dec, box pleated top 475.00

**Vase, ruffled, ruby red throat, deep gold
shading to peach to buff, multicolored
dec, 8″ h, $400.00.**

Vase
4¾″ h, 3½″ d, blue overlay top,
opaque ivory ext., three clear applied leaves and two red cherries. . 170.00
9¼″ h, amber acorn and oak leaf overlay, background shades from amber to pink to pale white, applied
amber rigaree rim and shell feet . . 750.00
9½″ h, Pompelian Swirl, blue shaded
to pink to deep red, white lining . . . 850.00
10″ h, shaded pink cased to white, applied thorn handles and feet, blue
below white enameled flowers, yellow, lavender, and gold accents,
one foot chipped, price for pair . . . 440.00
10½″ h, baluster, lime green satin
cased to white, swirl dec 300.00
11¼″ h, Verre de Soie, cased pink
satin glass, trapped swirl design . . 715.00
13″ h, 5″ w at shoulder, slender green
and white swirled neck, Watermelon Pompelian Swirl, green shading
to pink to deep rose base, attributed
to Frederick Carder 975.00

13¼″ h, 6″ w, bulbous, Peachblow,
deep red shading to pale amber–
yellow, pale cream lining 725.00

STICKLEYS

History: There were several Stickley brothers:
Albert, Gustav, Leopold, George, and John
George. Gustav often is credited with creating the
Mission style, a variant of the Arts and Crafts style.
Gustav headed Craftsman Furniture, a New York
firm, much of whose actual production took place
near Syracuse. A characteristic of Gustav's furni-
ture is exposed tenon ends. Gustav published *The
Craftsman*, a magazine supporting his antimachine
points of view.

Originally Leopold and Gustav worked together.
In 1902 Leopold and John George formed the L.
and J. G. Stickley Furniture Company. This firm
made Mission-style furniture and cherry and maple
Early American–style pieces.

George and Albert organized the Stickley Brothers Company, located in Grand Rapids, Michigan.

References: David M. Cathers, *Furniture Of The
American Arts and Crafts Movement*, New American Library, 1981; Donald A. Davidoff and Robert
L. Zarrow, *Early L. & J. G. Stickley Furniture: From
Onondaga Shops to Handcraft*, Dover Publications,
1992; Bruce Johnson, *The Official Identification
And Price Guide To Arts And Crafts*, Second Edition, House of Collectibles, 1992; L-W Book Sales
(ed.), *Furniture Of The Arts & Crafts Period*, L-W
Book Sales, 1992; Mary Ann Smith, *Gustav Stickley: The Craftsman*, Dover Publications, 1983,
1992 reprint.

Periodical: *Arts and Crafts Quarterly,* 9 Main St.,
Lambertville, NJ 08530.

Collectors' Club: Foundation for the Study of
Arts & Crafts Movement, Roycroft Campus, 31 S.
Grove St., East Aurora, NY 14052.

Museum: Craftsman Farms Foundation, Inc.,
Morris Plains, NJ.

Chair
Arm, matching footstool, L & JG Stickley, No. 420 and 394, c1915,
shaped flat arm over seat rail,
arched apron, branded "The Work
of....," footstool with sq post legs,
arched apron, Handcraft decal, refinished, 31½″ w x 42″ h chair, 19¼
x 15 x 16″ h stool, price for pair . . . 1,210.00
Dining, oak
Gustav Stickley, No. 1291, c1901,
medium–dark finish, rabbit ear,
horizontal crest rail, keyed tenons, red decal, 18¾″ w, 37¾″ h 525.00
L & JG, No. 950, c1915, medium
finish, shaped wood seat, decal,
metal tag, seat split, 16¾″ w, 35″
h 330.00

Stickley Bros, No. 479½, c1905, some refinishing, edge roughness, Quaint Furniture brass tags, 18¼″ w, 37″ h, price for set of six **935.00**

Morris, oak

Gustav Stickley, No. 336, c1903, dark finish, adjustable back, pyramidal pegs, arms with cut corners, sq legs, arched seat apron, red decal, old refinish, 31½″ w, 39″ h **4,950.00**

L & JG Stickley

No. 448, c1910, orig medium finish, fixed back, seven slats under each arm, Handcraft decal, worn finish, 31½″ w, 41¾″ h .. **1,540.00**

No. 830, c1910, adjustable back, flat arms, sq legs, orig medium finish and box spring, Handcraft decal, reupholstered, 29¼″ w, 41″ h **3,520.00**

Morris Chair, No. 369, Gustav Stickley, adjustable back, slant arm, brand mark, refinished, c1912, 32½″ w, 41½″ h, $4,750.00. Photograph courtesy of Skinner, Inc.

Cigar Box, Stickley Bros, No. 64, c1908, copper, cedar lined, hinged lid, brass trim, imp number, cleaned, inner liner oiled, 11½″ w, 7¼″ d, 6½″ h **935.00**

Clock, mantel, Gustav Stickley, c1902, overhanging top, single door, Seth Thomas works mounted on block, copper numerals, green stained frame, copper hardware, orig finish,

red decal, restoration, 13½″ w, 8″ d, 21″ h **6,600.00**

Magazine Cabinet, Gustav Stickley, No. 72, c1812, oak, orig medium–light finish, overhanging top, arched side aprons, branded mark, 22″ w, 13″ d, 41½″ h **1,870.00**

Magazine Stand, L & JG Stickley, No. 47, oak, light–medium finish, unsgd, refinished, stains, 18″ w, 15″ d, 42″ h **715.00**

Plant Stand, Stickley Bros, No. 131, c1910, sq top, splayed sq legs, crossed trestle feet, stenciled model no., refinished, 12″ w, 34″ h **825.00**

Rocker, Gustav Stickley, oak

No. 303, c1907, dark brown finish, cane seat rail, unsgd, refinished, rocker repaired, 17″ w, 33″ h **220.00**

No. 311, c1903, V–back, orig dark finish, red decal, finish wear, 26¼″ w, 35¼″ h **605.00**

No. 337, c1904, Harvey Ellis design, orig medium–dark finish, red decal, minor roughness, 16¾″ w, 34½″ h **220.00**

No. 373, c1904, spindle back, red decal, edge roughness, refinished, 19″ w, 41″ h **880.00**

No. 2597, c1902, V–back, orig medium–light finish, orig leather upholstery, black finish tacks, red decal, repair to one rocker, 26″ w, 34⅝″ h **715.00**

Settle, oak

Gustav Stickley, No. 172, c1901, medium brown finish, orig leather upholstery, brass dome top tacks, minor splitting, water stains, 55⅓″ l, 20¾″ d, 32¼″ h **2,090.00**

L & JG Stickley Onondaga Shop, No. 738, c1902, molded crest rail over thirteen canted vertical slats, molded even–arm over four vertical slats, two part drop seat, cushion, orig medium finish, 76¼″ w, 30⅛″ d, 38¾″ h **4,510.00**

Stickley Bros, No. 119, c1915, orig medium finish, green leather upholstery, fifteen canted back slats, three slats under each arm, unsgd, 77⅝″ l, 34¼″ h **1,540.00**

Sideboard, Stickley Bros, No. 8868½, oak, orig medium finish, hammered brass hardware with copper finish, unsgd, surface staining, 54″ w, 22″ d, 44½″ h **1,210.00**

Stool, foot, oak

Gustav Stickley, No. 302, rush, sq, flaring feet, unsgd, refinished, 12¼″ w, 4½″ h **275.00**

L & JG Stickley

No. 394, c1915, orig medium finish, remnants of "The work of..." de-

cal, edge roughness, 19″ w, 15″ d, 16″ h	305.00
No. 397, c1918, orig spring cushion and upholstery, medium finish, conjoined decal, 20″ w, 14″ d, 16½″ h.	470.00

Table, oak
Center, L & JG Stickley, No. 580, c1910, sq top, cut corners, sq legs, medial shelf, arched and crossed stretchers, refinished, 36″ w, 29¼″ h	715.00
Child's, Gustav Stickley, No. 658, c1910, sq legs, crossed stretchers, evidence of paper label, round top refinished, roughness, 24″ d, 19¾″ h	330.00
Drop Leaf, Gustav Stickley, No. 671, c1912, demilune drop leaves, medium finish, paper label, refinished, 32″ l, 30″ h.	1,430.00

Library
L & JG Stickley, No. 598, c1910, medial shelf, keyed tenons, orig medium brown finish, Handcraft decal, watermark, worn finish, 48″ w, 30″ d, 29¼″ h	825.00
Stickley Bros., No. 2696½, c1910, single drawer, brass pulls, varnished top, Quaint Furniture brass tag, 50″ l, 36″ w, 29½″ h. .	1,650.00
Occasional, L & JG Stickley, c1918, arched crossed stretchers, conjoined decal, orig finish, minor surface abrasions, stains, 30″ d, 29″ h	660.00

STIEGEL-TYPE GLASS

History: Baron Henry Stiegel founded America's first flint glass factory at Manheim, Pennsylvania, in the 1760s. Although clear glass was the most common color made, amethyst, blue (cobalt), and fiery opalescent are found. Products included bottles, creamers, flasks, flips, perfumes, salts, tumblers, and whiskeys. Prosperity was short lived. Stiegel's extravagant living forced the factory to close.

It is very difficult to identify a Stiegel-made item. As a result the term "Stiegel type" is used to identify glass made at that time period in the same shapes and colors.

Enamel decorated ware also is attributed to Stiegel. True Stiegel pieces are rare. An overwhelming majority is of European origin.

References: Frederick W. Hunter, *Stiegel Glass*, 1950, available in Dover reprint; Ellen T. Schroy, *Warman's Glass,* Wallace-Homestead, 1992.

Reproduction Alert: Beware of modern reproductions, especially in enamel wares.

Mug, enameled, center shield with carpenter's and blacksmith's tools, floral dec on sides, "Das ihre bare Huff and Wassen, Schmidt Handwerck 1790," 6⅛″ h, $375.00.

ENAMELED

Bride's Bottle
4¾″ h, enameled dec	55.00
6¼″ h, enameled floral dec, pewter top	65.00
Decanter, 8½″ h, center floral dec, stopper.	30.00

Flask
3⅝″ l, oval, clear, enameled floral design, slight chemical deposit	120.00
4¼″ l, oval, clear, enameled floral dec, one flat side.	165.00
Flip, clear, enameled vining flowering plant	
3½″ h	165.00
4¾″ h	190.00
Mug, 4⅜″ h, enameled floral dec, applied strap handle, half pint.	165.00

ENGRAVED

Flip, 4½″ h, clear, blown, engraved potted tulip	135.00
Mug, cov, floral motif, strap handle . .	400.00
Tumbler, clear, blown	
3⅛″ h, engraved bird on branch . . .	165.00
3⅝″ h, copper wheel engraved rim, ribbed base.	155.00

OTHER

Christmas Light, Expanded DQ	
3½″ h, light green	75.00
4¼″ h, smoky amethyst	30.00
Flask, 4¾″ h, amethyst, pattern molded, flattened globular, diamond daisy pattern and fluting	4,620.00
Perfume Bottle, daisy in hexagon pattern, flake on neck.	4,000.00

Salt, clear, blown mold

| 2⅝" h, ribbed, open bubble on int. | . | **45.00** |
| 2⅞" h, Expanded DQ | . . . . | **55.00** |

Scent Bottle, 3" l, cobalt blue, swirled . . . **95.00**

STONEWARE

History: Made from dense kaolin clay and commonly salt glazed, stonewares were hand-thrown and high-fired to produce a simple, bold vitreous pottery. Stoneware crocks, jugs, and jars were produced for storage and utility purposes. This use dictated shape and design—solid, thick-walled forms with heavy rims, necks, and handles with little or no embellishment. When decorated, the designs were simple: brushed cobalt oxide, incised, slip trailed, stamped, or tooled.

Stoneware has been made for centuries. Early American settlers imported stoneware items at first. As English and European potters refined their earthenware, colonists began to produce their own wares. Two major North American traditions emerged based only on the location or type of clay. North Jersey and parts of New York comprise the first area; the second was eastern Pennsylvania spreading westward and into Maryland, Virginia, and West Virginia. These two distinct locations, style of decoration, and shape are discernible factors in classifying and dating early stoneware.

By the late 18th century, stoneware was manufactured in all sections of the country. During the 19th century, this vigorous industry flourished until glass "fruit jars" appeared along with the widespread use of refrigeration. By 1910, commercial production of salt-glazed stoneware came to an end.

References: Georgeanna H. Greer, *American Stoneware: The Art and Craft of Utilitarian Potters,* Schiffer Publishing, 1981; Jim Martin and Bette Cooper, *Monmouth-Western Stoneware,* published by authors, 1983, 1993 value update; Dana G. Morykan and Harry L. Rinker, *Warman's Country Antiques & Collectibles, Second Edition,* Wallace-Homestead Book Co., 1994; Don and Carol Raycraft, *Country Stoneware And Pottery,* Collector Books, 1985, 1992 value update; Don and Carol Raycraft, *Collector's Guide To Country Stoneware & Pottery,* First Series (1985, 1992 value update), Second Series (1990, 1992 value update), Collector Books; George Sullivan, *The Official Price Guide To American Stoneware,* House of Collectibles, 1993.

Periodical: *Bottles & Extras,* PO Box 154, Happy Camp, CA 96039.

Collectors' Club: American Stoneware Association, 930 Country Lane, Indiana, PA 15701.

Museum: Museum of Ceramics at East Liverpool, East Liverpool, OH.

Batter Pitcher

9" h, cobalt blue brushed floral and foliage dec, wire bail and wood handle, imp "Cowden & Wilcox, Harrisburg" **1,710.00**

9¼" h, dark brown Albany slip dec, wire handle, imp "4".	**90.00**
9½" h, brushed floral dec, sgd "John Burger, Rochester".	**310.00**
10⅜" h, blue feather foliage designs, incised rope spiral handle, dark drips of brown glaze, incised "James Holloway"	**1,320.00**

Bird Fountain

5½" h, cobalt blue trim, hairline and small chips	**325.00**
6" h, cobalt blue trim	**330.00**
9¼" h, jug shape, dark brown Albany slip, imp "Dalton Pottery"	**85.00**

Butter Crock, 6¼" h, cobalt blue slip floral design, misfired to grayish–blue, imp "New York Stoneware Co Fort Edward, NY". **30.00**

Churn

15¼" h, ovoid, imp "3," brushed cobalt blue dec, applied shoulder handles.	**330.00**
16½" h, ovoid, red clay body, gray salt glaze, brushed cobalt blue floral dec and "4".	**85.00**
18¾" h, tan clay, tooling, two tone amber and brown slip with stenciled design, wear and chips, New Geneva.	**150.00**

Cooler

| 23½" h, ovoid, stenciled cobalt blue label "Alderman and Scott, Belpre, Ohio" and "16" in wreath, double ear handles, applied tooled ornaments around bung hole, hairlines and repair . . . . | **825.00** |

26½" h, cobalt blue slip simple flower

Crock, T. Harrington, Lyons, 3 gallon, semi–ovoid, imp label, cobalt blue bull's eye starburst dec, $2,970.00. Photograph courtesy of Arthur Auctioneering.

and flourish, imp screw head design at double ear handles and bung hole, chips, hairline on one handle **200.00**

Crock

8″ d, 8″ h, cobalt blue brushed foliage band, imp "R C R Phila" in border cartouche **495.00**

9⅞″ h, 3 gal, cobalt blue calligraphic design, sgd "Cooperative Pottery Company, Lyons, NY," 1902–5 . . . **110.00**

10⅛″ h, 3 gal, cobalt blue leafy spray, marked "Haxstun & Co, Fort Edward, NY," 1875–82 . . . . **125.00**

10¼″ h, blue chicken pecking corn, orange peel texture, Hudson River type, NY, c1855 . . . . **475.00**

10½″ h, cobalt blue quill work dragonfly and "3" **75.00**

12″ d, 7½″ h, cov, cobalt blue brushed dec **485.00**

13″ h

Baby bird dec, 5 gal, sgd "J Burger Jr, Rochester, NY," 1880–90 . . **1,950.00**

Cobalt blue brushed vintage dec and "6" **75.00**

13¾″ h, cobalt blue quill work label "6 Butter 1870" and flourish dec, applied handles **385.00**

Inkwell, 1½″ h, incised "Union," cobalt blue stars dec, sgd "N Boors Vanport PA," early 20th C **880.00**

Jar

8″ h, ovoid, imp label "Sipe Nichols & Co, Williamsport, Pa," cobalt blue brushed design, surface flakes . . . **275.00**

8¾″ h, ovoid, gray salt glaze, brushed cobalt blue design **160.00**

9″ h, ovoid, brushed cobalt blue wavy and straight lines and "1½" **220.00**

9¼″ h, ovoid, stenciled blue label, "Hamilton & Jones, Greensboro, Pa 1½" **110.00**

10¾″ h, cobalt blue bird, sgd "West Troy Pottery, NY," 1879–80 . . . **175.00**

11″ h

Cobalt blue floral dec, handles, marked "Charlestown," c1865 . . **175.00**

Three leaf clover motif, 2 gal, marked "W Roberts, Binghamton, NY," 1848–88 . . . . **160.00**

11¼″ h, bird dec, 4 gal, sgd "Whites, Utica," 1856–82 . . . . **450.00**

12¾″ h, ovoid, imp circular label "Norton & Fenton, Bennington, Vt," cobalt blue brushed floral dec **385.00**

13¼″ h, cobalt blue quill work, buildings, fence, and rooster, imp "J & E Norton, Bennington, Vt 3" **800.00**

14¾″ h, brushed cobalt blue floral dec around shoulder, imp "3" **225.00**

15″ h, ovoid, cobalt blue wreath and floral dec **125.00**

17″ h, ovoid, mottled grayish–tan glaze, tan spots, tooled lines, applied handles, imp "D Albright 6" . . **165.00**

18½″ h, imp label "Hamilton, Greensboro, Pa. 8," applied shoulder handles, good brushed cobalt blue floral dec, badly cracked **855.00**

Jug

6¼″ h, squat form, incised bird and branch, cobalt blue slip and "1869," blue stripes on strap handle, imp "J Matheis" **3,325.00**

9½″ h, cobalt blue calligraphic cartouche, ½ gal, c1865 . . . . **250.00**

11½″ h, cobalt blue quill work flourish and date "1867" **200.00**

12″ h, cobalt blue stenciled "H J Miller & Co, Alexandria, VA," 1 gal **250.00**

13″ h, ovoid, imp label with cobalt blue highlight, "I M Mead & Co 2" **160.00**

13½″ h, ovoid, brushed cobalt blue floral design **130.00**

14½″ h

Cobalt blue brushwork rose design, imp label "Fort Edward NY 2," fitted as lamp **190.00**

Ovoid, two–tone brown and gray salt glaze, tooled lines, ribbed strap handle, imp "Boston" **700.00**

15″ h, ovoid, cobalt blue quill work tulip and "2," imp "Burger & Lang, Rochester, NY" **55.00**

16″ h, ovoid, cobalt blue slip design **220.00**

16¼″ h, ovoid, imp label "W E Welding, Brantford 3," cobalt blue brushed floral design **385.00**

17¼″ h, imp "Nichols and Boynton, Burlington, Vt. 4," cobalt blue quill work stylized floral design, large chip on lip, hairline in handle, flake on base **126.00**

18″ h, blue leaf spray, 5 gal, sgd "Lyons Cooperative Pottery," 1902–5 . . . . **130.00**

19½″ h, ovoid, brushed cobalt blue labels "10" and "1882" on one side, "W. Lunn" on reverse, double ear handles, lip and one handle glued **190.00**

Pitcher

7″ h, ovoid, brushed cobalt blue slip floral dec, strap handle **635.00**

7½″ h, bulbous, cobalt blue and gray splotched glaze **100.00**

10″ h, ovoid, cobalt blue brushed leaf design, imp label "Lyons," hairline in rim at handle **385.00**

10½″ h, cobalt blue brushed floral dec, spout chip **660.00**

14″ h, incised archaic Great Seal of the United States, crimped rim, 1826 . . . . **3,500.00**

Preserving Jar
   6¾″ h, cobalt blue stenciled label "Hartford City Salt Co, Dealers in Salt & General Merchandise, Hartford City, W. Va," chips and hairlines **275.00**
   8″ h, ovoid, cobalt blue brushed and stenciled design, small flake on base **170.00**
   10″ h, cobalt blue brushed shoulder design **115.00**

STONEWARE, BLUE AND WHITE

History: Blue and white stoneware refers to molded, salt-glazed, domestic, utilitarian earthenware with a blue glaze produced in the late 19th and early 20th centuries. Earlier stoneware was usually hand thrown and either undecorated, hand decorated in Spencerian script floral and other motifs, or stenciled. The stoneware of the blue and white period is molded with a design impressed, embossed, stenciled, or printed.

Although known as blue and white, the base color is generally grayish in tone. The blue cobalt glaze may coat the entire piece, appear as a series of bands, or accent the decorative elements.

All types of household products were available in blue and white stoneware. Bowls, crocks, jars, pitchers, mugs, and salts are just a few examples. The ware reached its height between 1870 and 1890. The advent of glass jars, tin containers, and chilled transportation brought its end. The last blue and white stoneware was manufactured in the 1920s.

Reference: Kathyrn McNerney, *Blue & White Stoneware,* Collector Books, 1981, 1993 value update.

Collectors' Club: Blue & White Pottery Club, 224 12th St. NW, Cedar Rapids, IA 52405.

Reproduction Alert: The vast majority of blue and white stoneware found in antiques shops and flea markets are unmarked reproductions from Rushville Pottery, Rushville, OH.

Bean Pot, 6⅜″ h, molded dec and figures, emb "Boston Baked Beans," int. crazing **185.00**
Berry Bowl, 4½″ d, diffused blues . . . **55.00**
Bowl, 1½ gal, white, blue flourish, Sipe and Son, Williamsport, PA, c1860 . . . **450.00**
Butter Crock, 4½″ d, diffused blues . . **85.00**
Chamber Pot, 11″ d, petal scallop design with stenciled wildflowers, applied handle **175.00**
Coffeepot, 11½″ h, blue and white swirl design, blue tipped knob, spur handle, iron base **450.00**
Crock, 8″ h, 7½″ d, diffused blues, bail handle, Brereton Coal Co adv **110.00**

Pitcher, Swan, 8¼″ h, $165.00.

Custard Cup, 2½″ d, 5″ h, fishscale design **75.00**
Hot Water Bottle, 10¾″ h, cylindrical, flat side, white glaze, blue stenciled label "Chas E Brauer, Catawba Sanatorium, Va." **125.00**
Jar, molded, blue and white sponged dec, c1900 . . . . **175.00**
Jug, 2 gal, white, blue running bird, "2," and "Whites Utica" **550.00**
Milk Crock, 9″ d, lovebird design, restored bail and handle grip **155.00**
Mixing Bowl, 9½″ d, gadrooned arches **150.00**
Mug, 5″ h, flying bird design **200.00**
Pie Plate, 10½″ d, brick wall design, imp star and "Patented" on bottom **125.00**
Pitcher
   6½″ h, poinsettia, sq woven cane background, daubed handle **225.00**
   8″ h, blue and white molded tree bark with rose and bust **110.00**
   9″ h, raised rope medallion with butterfly dec, orange peel finish, diffused blues **250.00**
Roaster, 19″ l, diffused blues, applied handles, flat finial **225.00**
Rolling Pin, 13″ l, swirl, orig wood handles **450.00**
Soap Dish, cat's head **145.00**
Teapot, 9″ h, swirl design with high relief ball dec, double wire bail, highset lid **425.00**
Water Jug, 7″ h, ball shape, diffused blues, stopper **200.00**

STRETCH GLASS

History: Stretch glass was produced by many glass manufacturers in the United States between the early 1900s and the 1920s. The most prominent makers were Cambridge, Fenton (who probably manufactured more stretch glass than any of the others), Imperial, Northwood, and Steuben. Stretch glass can be identified by its iridescent, onionskinlike effect. Look for mold marks. Imported pieces are blown and show a pontil mark.

References: Ellen T. Schroy, *Warman's Glass,* Wallace-Homestead, 1992; Berry Wiggins, *Stretch Glass,* Antique Publications, 1972, 1987 value update.

Collectors' Club: Stretch Glass Society, PO Box 770643, Lakewood, OH 44107.

STRING HOLDERS

History: The string holder developed as a utilitarian tool to assist the merchant or manufacturer who needed tangle-free string or twine to tie packages. The early holders were made of cast iron, with some patents dating to the 1860s.

When the string holder moved to the household, lighter and more attractive forms developed, many made of chalkware. The string holder remained a key kitchen element until the early 1950s.

Chalkware, Dutch Girl, green hat, blue eyes, 6⅜" w, 7" h, $35.00.

Bowl, fluted body, vaseline, flat rim with applied gold band of pheasants in medallions and flowers, 9¾" d, 3¼" h, $45.00.

Bowl
  8½" d
    Blue, paneled 50.00
    White 25.00
  9½" d, blue, ribbed int., ftd 35.00
  10" d, green, rolled rim 25.00
Candy Dish, cov, topaz, Fenton 60.00
Compote, 6½" d, 5½" h, bright green, zipper notched pedestal base. 50.00
Console Bowl, 11½" d, orange, rolled rim. 35.00
Creamer and Sugar, tangerine, Rings pattern, price for pair 75.00
Hat, 4" h, purple, Imperial 55.00
Nappy, 7" w, vaseline, Fenton 35.00
Plate
  8¼" d, gold Aurene, attributed to Steuben 80.00
  8½" d, blue 35.00
Sandwich Server, sq. green, center handle 25.00
Vase
  5½" h, pink, baluster, Imperial 75.00
  6" h, green, fan shape, ribbed 40.00

Advertising
  Higgins German Laundry Soap, 6" h, cast iron, four wall or counter mounts 60.00
  Post Toasties, round, tin front 50.00
Bennington, figural, dog 165.00
Bentwood, 3¼" h, 3⅜" d, cylindrical, painted blue and red, Norwegian inscription, stylized flowerheads, late 19th C 135.00
Bronze, Victorian
  Beehive, japanned 75.00
  Seymour's Patent, No. 3, hanging, c1870. 125.00
  Smith's Patent, No. 10½, paw feet, cutter on side. 175.00
  Webb's Patent, No. 65, hemispherical, heart motif, pedestal base. . . . 350.00
Cast Iron
  6" d, hanging, ball type 55.00
  7" h, girl ice skating, polychrome paint. 375.00
Chalkware
  Cat, 6½" h, black and cream, red ball of string. 30.00
  Cut Glass, notched prisms, SS Gorham top. 185.00
  Scotty Dog 45.00
  Porcelain, 7" h, mammy, stamped "Japan," 1930s 75.00

Wood, treen, English
    Barrel form, cutter **110.00**
    Cylindrical, hexagon base **90.00**

SUGAR SHAKERS

History: Sugar shakers, sugar castors, or muffineers all served the same purpose: to "sugar" muffins, scones, or toast. They are larger than salt and pepper shakers, were produced in a variety of materials, and were in vogue in the late Victorian era.

Reference: William Heacock, *Encyclopedia of Victorian Colored Pattern Glass, Book III, Syrups, Sugar Shakers & Cruets, From A to Z*, Antique Publications, 1976, 1991–92 Value & Rarity Guide, revised by William Gamble.

CHINA

Nippon, white, gold beading **60.00**
Schlegelmilch, RS Prussia, 5″ h, scalloped base, pearl finish, roses, red mark **235.00**
Wedgwood, white classical design, blue ground **50.00**

Opalescent Glass, Swirl, cranberry, white metal top, 4¾″ h, $95.00.

GLASS

Bristol, 6¼″ h, tall tapering cylinder, pink, blue flowers and green leaves dec . . **65.00**
Cut, Russian pattern alternating with clear panels, orig silver top. **375.00**
Cut Velvet, DQ, blue satin, white lining, orig top. **395.00**
Depression, Early American Sandwich pattern, clear, orig top, Duncan & Miller **95.00**
Opalescent
    Bubble Lattice, blue, bulbous ring neck, orig top. **225.00**
    Coin Spot, blue, orig top **175.00**
    Daisy & Fern, clear, Parian Swirl mold, orig top **100.00**

Leaf Umbrella, cased crystal, orig top, Northwood. **295.00**
Royal Ivy, frosted rubena, orig top . **160.00**
Spanish Lace, cranberry, orig top . **150.00**
Opaque
    Forget Me Not, pink, orig top, Challinor **165.00**
    Quilted Phlox, blue, orig top, Northwood. **270.00**
    White, 4½″ h, 3″ d, tapering cylinder shape, enameled pastel fern dec, orig top, Wave Crest **195.00**
Satin, Leaf Mold, cased blue, orig top, Northwood. **285.00**
Spatter, Leaf Mold, vaseline, cranberry spatter, Northwood **450.00**

CAMBRIAN POTTERY
c 1783 - 1810

DILLWYN & CO. SWANSEA
c 1811 - 1817

BEVINGTON & CO.
c 1817 - 1824

SWANSEA

History: This superb pottery and porcelain was made at Swansea (Glamorganshire, Wales) as early as the 1760s, with production continuing until 1870.

Marks on Swansea vary. The earliest marks were SWANSEA impressed under glaze and DILLWAN under glaze after 1805. CAMBRIAN POTTERY was stamped in red under glaze from 1803 to 1805. Many fine examples, including the Botanical series in pearlware, are not marked but may have the botanical name stamped under glaze.

Fine examples of Swansea often may show imperfections, such as firing cracks. These pieces are considered mint because they left the factory in this condition.

Reference: Susan and Al Bagdade, *Warman's English & Continental Pottery & Porcelain, Second Edition*, Wallace-Homestead, 1991.

Reproduction Alert: Swansea porcelain has been copied for many decades in Europe and England. Marks should be studied carefully.

Plate, blue and white Oriental design, gold rim, imp mark, c1785, 7¼" d, $125.00.

Bowl, 6⅜" d, gilt cartouches with idyllic landscape scenes, gilt line borders, William Billingsley, c1815, red Swansea mark **750.00**

Cup and Saucer, ribbed, gold fluted border and handle, white int., c1820 ... **150.00**

Plate, wild rose and trailing blue flowers, elaborate gilt diaper and foliage well, molded flower wreath and C–scroll border reserved with gilt green berried foliage, gilt line rim, William Pollard, red stencil mark, c1820 .... **990.00**

Tureen, 6⅝" h, multicolored floral sprays, gilt scrolling and borders, double handles, gilt triple ram's head finial, c1820 .... **1,525.00**

Vase, 6¾" h, floral band, gilt borders, flared base with painted flowers, applied bee handles, imp "Swansea" and trident mark, c1815–20, restored, price for pair **4,725.00**

SWORDS

History: The first swords in America came from Europe. The chief cities for sword manufacturing were Solingen in Germany, Klingenthal in France, and Hounslow and Shotley Bridge in England. Among the American importers of these foreign blades was "Horstmann," whose mark is found on many military weapons.

New England and Philadelphia were the early centers for American sword manufacturing. By the Franco-Prussian War, the Ames Manufacturing Company of Chicopee, Massachusetts, was exporting American swords to Europe.

Sword collectors concentrate on a variety of styles: commissioned versus noncommissioned officers' swords, presentation swords, naval weapons, and swords from a specific military branch, such as the cavalry or infantry. The type of sword helped identify a person's military rank and, depending on how he had it customized, his personality as well.

Following the invention of repeating firearms in the mid 19th century, the sword lost its functional importance as a combat weapon and became a military dress accessory. Condition is a key criterion determining value.

References: Harold L. Peterson, *The American Sword 1775–1945*, Ray Riling Arms Books Co., 1965; Gerald Welond, *A Collector's Guide to Swords, Daggers & Cutlasses*, Chartwell Books, 1991.

Collectors' Club: The Association of American Sword Collectors, PO Box 288, Parsonburg, MD 21849.

Museum: Fort Ticonderoga Museum. Ticonderoga, NY.

Artillery, N. P. Ames, bronze handle, blade marked with eagle and "United States 1838 W. S.," brass mounted leather scabbard, 26" l, $425.00.

American

Cane, 27" l, cherry wood, Toledo Rapier blade, retains bark **200.00**

Cavalry officer's saber, c1870, 32" l blade, slender curved highly polished black struck maker's mark, sgd by retailer "The M. C. Lilley & Co, Columbus, O," finely etched on matted panels both sides, owner's name "Capt. L. P. Hunt, 10th Cavalry U.S.A.," gilt brass hilt cast in relief, three bar guard, orig wire bound fishskin guard, orig nickel plated scabbard with presentation quality gilt brass mounts, orig sword knot and belt **2,100.00**

Medical Officer's, carried by Assistant Surgeon Holmes Offley Paulding, 1874 Expedition against the Sioux, 28¼″ l, slender straight etched blade by Ames Mfg, regulation brass hilt applied with silver letters "MS" on one langet and inscribed by the owner "H.O.P, U.S.A 1874" on other, orig nickel plated scabbard, regulation mount, blade rubbed **5,500.00**

US Cavalry, 35½″ gray steel blade, steel handguard, steel and wood scabbard covered in tan canvas, marked "U.S., 1913, SA", flaming bomb and 7XX serial number **250.00**

Brescian, hunting, second half 17th C, steel hilt pierced and chiseled with scrolling foliage centering on flowers, guard detached, later blade **1,000.00**

French

Officer's, Regulation, dated 1816, 37″ l, curved fullered dated Klingenthal blade etched on one side of the forte with fleur de lis above and below the inscription "Gardes du Corps Monsieur," martial tropies below, other side with radiant human mask, further trophies, Royal Arms of France between, brass hilt including semi–basket guard, orig grip and steel scabbard **1,200.00**

Steel hilted small sword, mid 18th C, 29½″ l, slender tapering blade of hollow triangular section, each side etched below the hilt with patterns of strapwork and scrolls including a putto with heart on a plumline and the inscription "De la Manufacture de la Marque au Raisin a Sohlingen" (partly rubbed), steel hilt chiseled in relief with pierced scrollwork, trophies of arms on both halves of guard, orig wire bound grip with "Turk's heads". **1,500.00**

German

NCO's, army, Nazi era, nickeled silver "P" guard, 34″ l curved blade, engraved panel depicting war trophies, black painted steel scabbard. **200.00**

Officer's, dress

Early Nazi Luftwaffen, 28″ l, silver plated handle, gold swastikas on crossguard and pommel, scabbard with blue leather wrapping, attached belt hanger **350.00**

1940 production period, 33″ l, gold plated lion head handle, gold fittings, Nazi eagle crossguard, "P" handguard with engraved oak leaves and acorns, black bakelite twisted wire wrapped grip, black enameled scabbard. **400.00**

Processional, early 17th C style, 42½″ l, two handles, blade formed by two lugs ahead of leather cov ricasso, writhen straight quillons with fishtail terminals, small inner and outer rings, wooden grip, spirally fluted pommel. **2,750.00**

Japanese

Sin–Gunto, WW II period, 26½″ l, zig-zag temper line, brass chrysanthemum Tsuba, sharkskin grips, brass Menuki in a floral design, wooden scabbard with mounted brass, SN32XXXX **450.00**

Wakizashi, 13½″ l, iron Tsuba with mountain stream scene, wooden scabbard lacquered, minor nicks . . **120.00**

Turkish silver hilted sword and scabbard, Yataghan, c19th C, 34½″ l, long single edged steel blade, hilt and scabbard ornately chased and incised arrangements of flowers and weapons within scrolling cusped panels, mosque, and inscription at base of scabbard **2,415.00**

TEA CADDIES

History: Tea once was a precious commodity. Special boxes or caddies were used as containers to accommodate different teas, including a special cup for blending.

Around 1700 silver caddies appeared in England. Other materials, such as Sheffield plate, tin, wood, china, and pottery, also were used. Some tea caddies became very ornate.

Porcelain

Chinese Export, 3 x 3″, sq, allover roosters and flower dec **325.00**

Imari, 4¾ x 4″, silver cov **355.00**

Meissen, 5½″ h, rect, relief molded, rocaille and C–scroll cartouche, figure on horseback and port scene, damaged top, c1755. . . . . **675.00**

Royal Vienna style, 6″ h, rect, neo–classical figural reserves, green ground, late 19th C. **275.00**

Quillwork, 4½″ h, octagonal, inlaid frame, quillwork panels on lid and sides, front panel with reverse painted convex glass lens, three dimensional scene of woman and flowers, damage, glued repairs, some small pieces missing. **650.00**

Stoneware, 5¼″ h, hexagonal ovoid

Burl Walnut, line inlaid, chamfered corners, two compartments, inlaid ivory escutcheon, brass hinges, 7½ x 4¾ x 4⅜", $575.00.

form, cylindrical cov, relief and gilt birds and flowering branches, brown lacquered, c1715 . . . . **36,000.00**
Tin, 8" h, gold stenciled floral dec, molded lid, brass bail handle **75.00**
Wood
George III
  5½ x 8½ x 5", mahogany, rect, conforming case, brass bail handle, compartment int., bracket feet, late 18th C. **250.00**
  6½ x 10 x 6", mahogany, bombé style, bail handle, foliate escutcheon, compartment int., late 18th C. **750.00**
Georgian
  5 x 7 x 4", satinwood, rect, inlaid shell patera, early 19th C. **660.00**
  5 x 10 x 5", mahogany, rect, satinwood banded top, two compartments, 19th C. **350.00**
Regency
  5 x 7½ x 4½", mahogany, rect, satinwood stringing, compartment int., early 19th C **325.00**
  7 x 13 x 6", mahogany, sarcophagus form, center well with cov boxes **190.00**
William IV, 6" h, exotic wood, apple form, carved, diamond fruitwood escutcheon **425.00**

TEA LEAF IRONSTONE CHINA

History: Tea Leaf Ironstone china flowed into America from England in great quantities in the 1860 to 1910 period and graced the tables of working-class America. It traveled to California and Texas in wagons and by boat down the Mississippi River to Kentucky and Missouri. It was too plain for the rich homes; its simplicity and strength appealed to wives forced to watch pennies. Tea Leaf found its way into the kitchen of Lincoln's Springfield home; sailors ate from it aboard the *Star of India*, now moored in San Diego and still displaying Tea Leaf.

Tea Leaf was not manufactured exclusively by English potters in Staffordshire, contrary to popular opinion. Although there were more than 35 English potters producing Tea Leaf, at least 26 American potters helped satisfy the demand. However, American potters perpetuated the myth by using back stamps bearing the English coat of arms and the marking "Warrented." The American housewife favored imported ware to that made by Americans.

Anthony Shaw (1850–1900) first registered the pattern in 1856 as Luster Band and Sprig. Edward Walley (1845–56) already was decorating ironstone with luster trefoil leaf, a detached bud, and trailing green vine. Walley's products are designated Pre–Tea Leaf and are sought by eclectic collectors. Other early variants include "Morning Glory" and "Pepper Leaf" or "Tobacco Leaf" by Elsmore & Forster (Foster) (1853–57) and "Teaberry" by Clementson Bros. (1832–1916). Clover leaf, cinquefoil, and pinwheel all may be found in a collection specializing in early ware.

The most prolific Tea Leaf makers were Anthony Shaw and Alfred Meakin (1875–). Johnson Bros. (1883–), Henry Burgess (1864–92), and Arthur J. Wilkinson (1897–) all shipped much of their ware to America and followed close behind Shaw and Meakin.

Although most of the English Tea Leaf used copper luster, Powell and Bishop (1868–78) and their successors, Bishop and Stonier (1891–1936), worked exclusively in gold luster. Beautiful examples of gold luster by H. Burgess still are being found. Mellor, Taylor & Co. (1880–1904) used gold luster on their children's tea sets. Other English potters also used gold luster. Recently discovered are gold luster pieces by W. & E. Corn, Thomas Elsmore, and Thomas Hughes.

J. & E. Mayer, Beaver Falls, Pennsylvania, were English potters who immigrated to America and produced a large amount of copper luster Tea Leaf. The majority of the American potters decorated with gold luster, with no brown underglaze like that found under the copper luster.

East Liverpool, Ohio, potters, such as Cartwright Bros. (1864–1924), East End Pottery (1894–1909), Knowles, Taylor & Knowles (1870–1934), and others, decorated only in gold luster. This is also true of Trenton, New Jersey, potters, such as Glasgow Pottery, American Crockery Co., and Fell & Thropp Co. Since no underglazing was used with the gold, much of it has been washed away.

By the 1900s Tea Leaf's popularity had waned. However, the sturdy ironstone did not disappear. It was stored in barns and relegated to attics and basements. Much of it was disposed of in dumps, where one enterprising collector has dug up some beautiful pieces.

A frequent myth about Tea Leaf is that pieces marked "Wedgwood" are THE Wedgwood—Josiah. This is not true! Dealers and collectors who perpetuate this myth should be confronted. Enoch Wedgwood was the only potter of that name to produce Tea Leaf. Enoch Wedgwood's product is beautiful, with large showy leaves. He deserves full credit for his work.

References: Susan and Al Bagdade, *Warman's English & Continental Pottery & Porcelain, Second Edition,* Wallace-Homestead, 1991; Annise Doring Heaivilin, *Grandma's Tea Leaf Ironstone,* Wallace-Homestead, 1981; Jean Wetherbee, *A Look At White Ironstone,* Wallace-Homestead, 1980, out of print; Jean Wetherbee, *A Second Look At White Ironstone,* Wallace-Homestead, 1985, out of print.

Collectors' Club: Tea Leaf Club International, PO Box 14133, Columbus, OH 43214.

Museums: Lincoln Home, Springfield, IL; Sherman Davidson House, Newark, OH; Ox Barn Museum, Aurora, OR.

Reproduction Alert: There are reproductions that are collectible and then there are *reproductions*! Avoid the latter. Collectible reproductions were made by Cumbow China Decorating Co. of Abington, Virginia, from 1932 to 1980. Wm. Adams & Sons, an old English firm that made Tea Leaf in 1960s, made reproduction Tea Leaf from 1960 to 1972. Red Cliff, which decorated Hall China blanks with Tea Leaf and clearly marked them, worked in the late 1960s and early 1970s.

Ruth Sayer started making Tea Leaf reproductions in 1981. Although her early pieces were not marked, all of it now is marked with a leaf and the initials "RS" on the bottom. In 1968 Blakeney Pottery, a Staffordshire firm, manufactured a poor-quality reproduction of Meakin's Bamboo pattern and marked it "Victoria." It was distributed through a Pennsylvania antiques reproduction outlet.

Baker, open vegetable	
Johnson Bros, piecrust edge, round, 8¾" d	80.00
Meakin, Chelsea pattern, 9" sq	52.00
Butter Dish, cov, Shaw, Hexagon Sunburst pattern, orig liner	225.00
Butter Pat	
Edwards, sq	15.00
Meakin, Chelsea pattern, price for pair	35.00
Chamber Pot	
W & E Corn	150.00
Wedgwood, plain, round	180.00
Children's Dishes	
Cup and Saucer, handleless, Shaw, Lily of the Valley	240.00
Milk Mug, Tobacco Leaf variant, unmarked, 2½" d, 2½" h	275.00

Tea Set, Knowles, Taylor & Knowles, American, teapot, sugar, four cups, saucers, and plates, price for 14 piece set	750.00
Compote	
Mellor Taylor, 7⅞" d, 4½" h	235.00
Shaw, Sunburst pattern, 9½" d, 4" h	450.00
Creamer	
Elsmore & Forster, Pepper Leaf variant	105.00
Unmarked, Pinwheel variant, 5" h, repaired	140.00
Cup and Saucer, handled cup	
Furnival, price for set of six	260.00
Red Cliff, price for set of four	90.00
Shaw, Basketweave, price for pair	160.00
Egg Cup	
Meakin, Boston, low, ftd, repaired	190.00
Unmarked	270.00

Gravy Boat, unmarked, 6" l, $45.00.

Gravy Boat, Mayer, American	55.00
Hot Water Pitcher, chamber set type	
Johnson Bros, Chelsea pattern	140.00
Wilkinson, Bow Knot pattern	250.00
Nappy	
Meakin, sq, price for set of eight	95.00
Powell & Bishop, gold luster, price for pair	25.00
Pitcher	
Cumbow, American, 6½" h	50.00
East End Pottery, American, copper luster, 7¾" h	125.00
Shaw, Chinese pattern	190.00
Wedgwood, 9" h, sq ridged	130.00
Relish Dish	
Shaw, Cable pattern	90.00
Wedgwood, Chelsea pattern	55.00
Sauce Ladle, Shaw	200.00
Sauce Tureen, base, cov, ladle, and underplate	
Mellor Taylor, Lions Head, small chip on ladle	250.00
Wilkinson, simple square shape	425.00
Shaving Mug	
Shaw, Lily of the Valley pattern	265.00
Wilkinson	110.00

Soap Dish	
Mellor Taylor, open	**150.00**
Shaw, Cable pattern, base, cov, and	
liner	**200.00**
Soup Bowl, Shaw, 11" d	**27.00**
Soup Ladle, Meakin	**290.00**
Soup Tureen, base, cov, ladle, and un-	
derplate	
Meakin, Fishhook pattern	**725.00**
Shaw, Cable pattern	**575.00**
Spittoon, Shaw, hairline and chip ...	**450.00**
Sugar, cov	
Edwards, Victory pattern	**140.00**
Mayer, American, copper luster, emb	**60.00**
Shaw, Pear shape, early, rare	**230.00**
Teapot, Meakin, Bamboo pattern ...	**195.00**
Toothbrush Holder	
Meakin	**135.00**
Unmarked, American, hairline	**80.00**
Wilkinson	**105.00**
Vegetable, cov	
East End Pottery, American	**70.00**
Shaw, Daisy pattern	**100.00**
Wash Bowl and Pitcher	
Mayer, copper luster	**190.00**
Mellor Taylor, Lions Head pattern .	**360.00**

TEDDY BEARS

History: Originally thought of as "Teddy's Bears," the name comes from President Theodore Roosevelt. These stuffed toys are believed to have originated in Germany and in the United States during the 1902–3 period.

Most of the earliest Teddy Bears had humps on their backs, elongated muzzles, and jointed limbs. The fabric used was usually mohair; the eyes were either glass with pin backs or black shoe buttons. The stuffing was generally excelsior. Kapok (for softer bears) and wood–wool (for firmer bears) also were used as stuffing materials.

Quality older bears often had elongated limbs, sometimes with curved arms, oversize feet, and felt paws. Noses and mouths were black and embroidered onto fabric.

The earliest Teddy Bears are believed to have been made by the original Ideal Toy Corporation in America and a German company, Margarete Steiff, GmbH. Bears made in the early 1900s by other companies can be difficult to identify because they had a strong similarity in appearance and because most tags or labels were lost through childhood play.

Teddy Bears are rapidly increasing as collectibles and their prices are increasing proportionally. As in other fields, desirability should depend upon appeal, quality, uniqueness, and condition. One modern bear already has been firmly accepted as a valuable collectible among its antique counterparts: the Steiff Teddy put out in 1980 for the company's 100th anniversary. This is a reproduction of that company's first Teddy and has a special box, signed certificate, and numbered ear tag; 11,000 of these were sold worldwide.

References: Peggy and Alan Bialosky, *The Teddy Bear Catalog, Revised Edition,* Workman Publishing, 1984; Kim Brewer and Carol–Lynn Rössel Waugh, *The Official Price Guide To Antique & Modern Teddy Bears,* House of Collectibles, 1990; Jurgen and Marianne Cieslik, *Button In Ear: The Story of Teddy Bear and His Friends,* distributed by Theriault's, 1989; Peter Consalvi, Sr., *Collector Steiff Values,* Hobby House Press, 1994; Pam Hebbs, *Collecting Teddy Bears,* Pincushion Press, 1992; Dee Hockenberry, *Bear Memorabilia: Reference & Price Guide,* Hobby House Press, 1992; Margaret Fox Mandel, *Teddy Bears And Steiff Animals,* First Series, (1984, 1993 value update), Second Series (1987), Collector Books; Margaret Fox Mandel, *Teddy Bears, Annalee Animals & Steiff Animals, Third Series,* Collector Books, 1990; Linda Mullins, *The Raikes Bear & Doll Story,* Hobby House, 1991; Linda Mullins, *Teddy Bear & Friends Price Guide, 4th Edition,* Hobby House Press, 1993; Linda Mullins, *Teddy Bears Past & Present, Vol. II,* Hobby House Press, 1992; Cynthia Powell, *Collector's Guide To Miniature Teddy Bears: Identification & Values,* Collector Books, 1994.

Periodicals: *Antiques & Collectables,* PO Drawer 1565, El Cajon, CA 92022; *National Doll & Teddy Bear Collector,* PO Box 4032, Portland, OR 97208-4032; *Teddy Bear And Friends,* 6405 Flank Dr., Harrisburg, PA 17112.

Museum: Teddy Bear Museum of Naples, Naples, FL.

Additional Listing: See Steiff.

BEARS

9½" h, plush, straw filled, black boot button eyes, brown stitched nose and mouth, felt pads, swivel limbs, button in left ear, Steiff, c1910	**885.00**
11" h, blonde mohair, glass eyes, embroidered nose and mouth, fully jointed, excelsior and cotton stuffing, 1920–30.	**145.00**
12" h, Teddy Bar, open mouth, glass eyes, Steiff.	**100.00**
14" h, blonde mohair, shoe button eyes, fully jointed, black embroidered nose, mouth, and claws, blank ear button, excelsior stuffing, c1906.	**1,650.00**
19" h, yellow mohair, black embroidered nose and claws, fully jointed, excelsior and kapok stuffing, replaced eyes and pads, 1920s	**165.00**
23" h	
Blonde curly mohair, shoe button eyes, beige nose, claws, and mouth, ear button, fully jointed, excelsior stuffing, Steiff, c1905	**2,200.00**

Tan, humpback, dressed with child's
size lederhosen 165.00
23½" h, gold plush fur, black boot button
eyes, black stitched nose and mouth,
felt pads, swivel limbs, growler, button
in left ear, Steiff, c1915 . . . . 4,425.00
24" h, blonde plush mohair, shoe button
eyes, rust broadcloth, embroidered
nose and claws, accentuated hump,
fully jointed, excelsior stuffing, Ideal,
early 20th C 1,210.00

Ideal, brown mohair, felt pads, c1920,
24" h, $325.00.

TEPLITZ CHINA

History: Around 1900 twenty-six ceramic manufacturers were located in Teplitz, a town in the
Bohemian province of Czechoslovakia. Other potteries were located in the nearby town of Turn.
Wares from these factories were molded, cast, and
hand decorated. Most are in the Art Nouveau and
Art Deco styles. Most pieces do not carry a specific
manufacturer's mark. They are simply marked "Teplitz," "Turn-Teplitz," and "Turn."

Reference: Susan and Al Bagdade, *Warman's
English & Continental Pottery & Porcelain, Second
Edition.* Wallace-Homestead. 1991.

Water Pitcher, black and cream enamel
swirls, green textured ground, marked
"Stellmacher Turn–Teplitz Austria,"
$1,200.00.

BEAR-RELATED ITEMS

Bank, 5" h, mechanical, bear and tree
stump, cast iron, Judd Manufacturing
Co, 1870s. 750.00
Book, *Ver Beck's Book of Bears,* Frank
Ver Beck, J B Lippincott, 1906, 96
pgs, hard cov, 8½ x 10½" 50.00
Bottle Warmer, teddy bear dec, 1940–
50 . . . . 60.00
Bowl, Jolly Bear, opalescent,
Northwood 75.00
Coffee Set, Victorian, teddy bears play-
ing, price for set 325.00
Dish, 6" d, china, white, full color illus of
young bear finishing school black-
board picture, teacher's paw reaching
for him, pine tree branch and pine
cone border, early 1900s 55.00
Plate, milk glass, two big bears and one
small bear. 38.00

Bust, 22½" h, young woman, elaborate
dress, fan, flowers and hat with reticulated border, putto on shoulder,
Ernst Wahliss, c1900, repaired 1,650.00
Ewer, 9¾" h, curvilinear, red painted
berries, gold highlights, faint irid, free
form squares, flowing lines, gently
curving handle, c1900 . . . . 350.00
Figure
8" h, 8½" l, two children, young boy in

hat with pink ribbon pushing young girl carrying umbrella and basket, soft beige ground, pink and blue highlights, sgd "Teplitz Bohemia," imp "4007" **400.00**
21" h, gentlemen, 18th century style dress **660.00**
Vase
5½" h, ovoid, painted Art Nouveau portrait, imp mark, stamped in red, blue Turn mark **550.00**
5¾" h, spider web and jeweled upper section, butterfly dec, irid blue— green **1,050.00**
9¼" h, stylized blue and white iris dec, green ground, blue linear floral pattern, gold accents, stamped "Turn— Teplitz—Bohemia/RS + K/Made in Austria". **385.00**
11½" h, stylized blue and green scene of sun through trees, lower band with ivory and blue insect and floral dec, gold accents, stamped "Turn— Teplitz—Bohemia/RS + K/Made in Austria". **470.00**
17⅛" h, Secessionist style, ovoid, cylindrical, red, cast stylized roses, trailing tendrils, sea green glaze, gray blue and navy blue, gilt, imp factory marks and numbers for Riessnier, Stellmacher, and Kissel, c1905 . . . . **990.00**
17¾" h, swollen cylinder, molded free form loop handles, stylized tree and flower dec, green, brown, pink, and gold, imp mark. **825.00**

TERRA-COTTA WARE

History: Terra-cotta is ware made of a hard, semifired ceramic clay. The color of the pottery ranges from a light orange-brown to a deep brownish red. It is usually unglazed, but some pieces can be found partially glazed or decorated with slip designs, incised, or carved. Examples include utilitarian objects as well as statuettes and large architectural pieces. Fine early Chinese terra-cotta pieces recently have brought substantial prices.

Architectural Fragment, 38" l, lintel supports, from Solomon Blumenfeld Flats, 1884 . . . . **550.00**
Bust, 22" h, young woman, Chas Eugene Breton, 1916. . . . . **650.00**
Figure, 10" h, bulldog, polychromed, glass eyes **150.00**
Jug, 7½" h, marked "Cambridge Ale" . . . **150.00**
Medallion, 142mm d, Benjamin Franklin portrait, sgd "J.B Nini 1770," period frame, unobtrusive crack **825.00**

Figurine, boy leaning on fence, Italian, 4½" h, $50.00.

Plaque, 12 x 22", relief neoclassical figures **35.00**
Sculpture, 12" h, hunting dog, head, brown glaze, J Uffrecht & Co, late 19th C, compressed U & C/'879, slight chips **715.00**
Tray, 9 x 7", hp, pilgrims resting, gilt dec, 1920 . . . . **75.00**
Urn, 29½" h, molded putti and foliage dec, green glaze, waisted neck, two handles, circular foot **375.00**
Vase, 6" h, raised daisy dec, green glazed int.. . . . . **35.00**

TEXTILES

History: Textiles are cloth or fabric items, especially anything woven or knitted. Those that survive usually represent the best since these were the objects that were used carefully and stored by the housewife.

Textiles are collected for many reasons—to study fabrics, understand the elegance of a historical period, and for decorative and modern use. The renewed interest in clothing has sparked a revived interest in textiles of all forms.

References: Gideon Bosker, Michele Mancini, and John Gramstad, *Fabulous Fabrics of the 50s, and Other Terrific Textiles of the 20s, 30s, and 40s*, Chronicle Books, 1992; Alda Leake Horner, *The Official Price Guide to Linens, Lace and Other Fabrics*, House of Collectibles, 1991; William C. Ketchum, Jr., *The Knopf Collectors' Guides to American Antiques: Quilts*, Alfred A. Knopf, 1982; Dana G. Morykan and Harry L. Rinker, *Warman's Country Antiques & Collectibles, Second Edition*, Wallace-Homestead Book Co., 1994; Betty Ring, *Needlework: An Historical Survey, Revised Edition*,

Main Street Press, 1984; Carleton L. Safford and Robert Bishop, *America's Quilts And Coverlets*, Bonanza Books, 1985; Jessie A. Turbayne, *Hooked Rugs: History and the Continuing Tradition*, Schiffer Publishing, 1991; Jessie A. Turbayne, *The Hookers' Art: Evolving Designs In Hooked Rugs*, Schiffer Publishing, 1993; Helene Von Rosenstiel, *American Rugs And Carpets: From The Seventeenth Century To Modern Times*, William Morrow And Company, 1978; Sigrid Wortmann Weltge, *Women's Work: Textile Art From The Bauhaus*, Chronicle Press, 1993.

Periodicals: *International Old Lacers Bulletin*, PO Box 481223, Denver, CO 80248; *The Lace Collector*, PO Box 222, Plainwell, MI 49080; *The Textile Museum Newsletter*, The Textile Museum, 2320 S. St. NW, Washington, DC 20008.

Collectors' Clubs: Costume Society of America, 55 Edgewater Dr., PO Box 73, Earleville, MD 21919; Stumpwork Society, PO Box 122, Bogota, NJ 07603.

Museums: Cooper-Hewitt Museum, New York, NY; Currier Gallery of Art, Manchester, NH; Museum of American Textile History, North Andover, MA; Ipswich Historical Society, Ipswich, MA; Museum of Art, Rhode Island School of Design, Providence, RI; Philadelphia College of Textiles & Science, Philadelphia, PA; The Lace Museum, Mountain View, CA; The Textile Museum, Washington, DC; Valentine Museum, Richmond, VA.

Additional Listings: See Clothing, Linens, Quilts, and Samplers.

Jacquard Coverlet, floral medallions, eagle and tree border, corner block reads "Made by J. Lutz, E Hempfield Township for Rebecca Hershey, 1839," 99 x 77", $675.00.

Bag, drawstring, cotton homespun
  Pen and ink drawn floral dec, poem, "Mary Littlefield 1816" on one side, landscape on rev, fragile, wear, stains, small tears, 9" h, 10½" w . . **225.00**
  Wool and silk green, brown, and beige floral embroidery, white silk facing, fragile, stains and damage, 8½" sq **125.00**
Blanket, wool, American, 19th C
  Blue and white, woven in one piece, hand sewn hems, small holes, 62 x 80" **115.00**
  Indigo, madder, and natural white broken point twill weave, goose eye pattern, initials "SMB," 82 x 68". . . **225.00**
  Madder and natural white twill weave, 75 x 68" **190.00**
Coverlet
  Jacquard
    Two Piece, double weave
      Floral medallions, navy blue and tomato red, wear, edge damage, and small holes, 81 x 92" **440.00**
      Floral with compotes of fruit borders and eagles in corners with "E. Pluribus Unum" and "Mary A. Martin, Jefferson Co. N.Y. 1847," navy blue, black, and white, no fringe, 86 x 92" **1,705.00**
      Star and flower with bird and rose borders, corners labeled "G. Stich, Newark, Ohio 1839," navy blue, tomato red, and natural white, worn, very worn fringe, small holes and stains, 70 x 84" **320.00**
    Two Piece, single weave
      Floral medallions, rose borders, corners labeled "Woven by H. Wolf, Ohio AD 1854 for Margaret Haman," medium blue, teal blue, tomato red, gold, and natural white, overall and edge wear, some fringe loss **360.00**
      Floral with turkey in tree corners, "Manufactured by Henry Oberly, Womelsdorf, Penn," tomato red and natural white, some overall wear, fringe removed, ends rebound, 78 x 90" **560.00**
      Floral with vining borders and corners, "Coverlet, Wm. H. VanGordon, Weaver, Covington, Miami Co, Ohio 1849," medium blue and white, overall and top edge wear, some moth damage, 73 x 90" **440.00**
      Flowers and stars with bird and house borders, corners labeled "Somerset, Ohio 1845, L. Hesse, Weaver," tomato red, navy blue, natural white, and

teal green, overall and edge wear, fringe loss, light stains, 64 x 80″ **250.00**

Foliage medallions, rose borders, corners labeled "Made by Jacob Saylor, Saltcrick Townsp. Pickaway Co. Ohio 1854," blue, red, olive, and natural white, minor end wear, 74 x 82″. **440.00**

Four large medallions, steamship borders, labeled "B. Lichty, Bristol, Wayne Co, Ohio 1845," medium blue and natural white, wear, rebound, seam resewn, minor fringe damage and repair, 71″ sq. **580.00**

Four rose medallions, bird and star border, corners labeled "Andre Kump, Hanover 1839, J. Bachman," red, navy blue, and natural white, light stains, minor moth damage, 87″ sq . . **360.00**

Star and flower medallions, vintage border and corner labeled "W. in Mt. Vernon Knox County, Ohio by Jacob and Michael Ardner 1852," rust red and natural white, edge wear, small holes, incomplete fringe, 76 x 82″ **470.00**

Stars and flowers with bird and urn, corners labeled "G. Foore, 1843," navy blue and natural white, worn, fringe loss, 76 x 96″ **220.00**

Overshot, two piece

Optical pattern, navy blue and natural white, wear, moth damage, and stains, 74 x 88″ **90.00**

Snowflake and pine tree pattern, deep navy blue and natural white, some edge wear, holes and stains, 74 x 88″. **250.00**

Star, diamond, and stripe design, red, navy blue, gold, olive, and natural white, some edge wear, small holes and stains, 74 x 88″ **250.00**

Stars, trees, flowers, and stick soldiers, navy, salmon red, gold, and natural white, wear, edge damage, missing fringe, 70 x 89″ **315.00**

Memorial, silk figure, classical figure mourns before monument dedicated to George Washington, backboard labeled "John Gibbs, Portsmouth," c1800, 9⅜ x 8″, framed **1,100.00**

Needlework Picture, embroidered silk panel

Man and woman in garden, deer, lion, rabbit, squirrel, snail, butterfly, insects, and sun, gilt and walnut frame, early 18th C, 11 x 14½″ . . . **625.00**

Portrait of young Queen Victoria, holding scepter, c1840, period frame, 33 x 24″ **145.00**

Prayer, flowers, and bees, dated "November The 27, 1736," shadow box frame, 12¾ x 8½″ **165.00**

Pocketbook, needlework, America, late 19th C

Irish stitched, crewel flame pattern, pink, gold, yellow, and brown, gold linen tape binding, moth damage, 4 x 6⅝″ **200.00**

Queen stitched, silk threads, green, peach, gold, and bittersweet flower and strawberry pattern, brocaded silk fabric sides, 3½ x 5½″ **250.00**

Rug, hooked, American, 19th C

Brick pattern, braided circles border, 78 x 44½″ **935.00**

Cat, white cat, pink, blue, and green leafy floral border, variegated gray ground, 39 x 46″ **3,850.00**

Pictorial, three masted ship *Blue Nose,* polychrome yarn, burlap ground, some wear and soiling, 34 x 45″. **250.00**

Show Towel, birds, flowers, pitchers, and chairs, Fyanna Wenger, 1842, 17 x 51″ **300.00**

Tapestry

Aubusson Panel

Floral medallion and swags, salmon border, 19th C, 112 x 47″. **3,575.00**

Pair of hanging bouquets, deep burgundy ground, lattice and scroll borders, vibrant colors, Louis Philippe, mid 19th C, 115 x 78″. . . . **15,400.00**

Flemish, late 16th or early 17th C

Biblical, king wearing turban, soldier standing by burning altar, mountains in distance, floral urn and game park borders, 116″ x 67″. . **4,950.00**

Hunt scene, riders and dogs hunt deer and various animals and fowl in woodland, floral urn and trophies border, repairs **15,400.00**

THIMBLES

History: Thimbles often are thought of as common household sewing tools. Many are. However, others are miniature works of art, souvenirs of places, people, and events, or gadgets (thimbles with expanded uses, such as attached threaders, cutters, or magnets).

There were many thimble manufacturers in the United States prior to 1930. Before we became a "throwaway" society, hand sewing was a never-ending chore for the housewife. Garments were mended and altered. When they were beyond repair, pieces were salvaged to make a patchwork quilt. Thimble manufacturers tried to create a new thimble to convince the home sewer that "one was not enough."

By the early 1930s only one manufacturer of gold and silver thimbles remained in business in the United States: the Simons Brothers Company of Philadelphia, which was founded by George Washington Simons in 1839. Simons Brothers thimbles from the 1904 St. Louis World's Fair and the 1893 Columbian Exposition are prized acquisitions for any collector. The Liberty Bell thimble, in the shape of the bell, is one of the most novel.

Today, the company is owned by Nelson Keyser and continues to produce silver and gold thimbles. The Simons Brothers Company designed a special thimble for First Lady Nancy Reagan as a gift for diplomats' wives who visited the White House. The thimble has a picture of the White House and the initials "N. D. R."

Thimbles have been produced in a variety of materials: gold, silver, steel, aluminum, brass, china, glass, vegetable ivory, ivory, bone, celluloid, plastics, leather, hard rubber, and silk. Common metal thimbles usually are bought by the intended user, who makes sure the size is a comfortable fit. Precious metal thimbles often were received as gifts. Many of these do not show signs of wear from constant use. This may result from an ill fit of the thimble or from it simply being too elegant for mundane work.

During the 20th century thimbles were used as advertising promotions. It is not unusual to find a thimble that says "You'll Never Get Stuck Using Our Product" or a political promotion stating "Sew It Up—Vote for John Doe for Senator."

References: Helmut Greif, *Talks About Thimbles,* Fingerhutmuseum, Cregligen, Germany, 1983 (English edition available from Dine-American, Wilmington, DE); Edwin F. Holmes, *A History Of Thimbles,* Cornwall Books, 1985; Myrtle Lundquist, *The Book Of A Thousand Thimbles,* Wallace-Homestead, 1970, out of print; Myrtle Lundquist, *Thimble Americana,* Wallace-Homestead, 1981, out of print; Myrtle Lundquist, *Thimble Treasury,* Wallace-Homestead, 1975, out of print; Averil Mathis, *Antique and Collectible Thimbles and Accessories,* Collector Books, 1986, 1991 value update; Gay Ann Rogers, *American Silver Thimbles,* Haggerston Press, 1989; Gay Ann Rogers, *Price Guide Keyed To American Silver Thimbles,* Needlework Unlimited, 1989; John Von Hoelle, *Thimble Collectors Encyclopedia,* Wallace-Homestead, 1986, out of print; Estelle Zalkin, *Zalkin's Handbook Of Thimbles & Sewing Implements,* Warman Publishing, 1988.

Periodical: *Thimbletter,* 93 Walnut Hill Road, Newton Highlands, MA 02161.

Collectors' Clubs: Empire State Thimble Collectors, 8289 Northgate Dr., Rome, NY 13440-1941; The Thimble Guild, PO Box 381807, Duncanville, TX 75138-1807; Thimble Collectors International, 6411 Montego Bay Dr., Louisville, KY 40228.

Advisor: Estelle Zalkin.

Reproduction Alert: Reproductions can be made by restrikes from an original die or cast from a mold made from an antique thimble. Many reproductions are sold as such and priced accordingly. Among the reproduced thimbles are a prerevolution Russian enamel thimble and the Salem Witch thimble (the repro has no cap and the seam is visible).

Sterling Silver, honeycomb design, size 10, Pat. May 28, 1889, $115.00.

Advertising		
Brass, advertisement or inscription		**5.00**
Plastic, 1930–1950		
One color	....	**1.00**
Two colors, red top	....	**2.00**
Sterling Silver	....	**35.00**
Gold, 1900–40		
Plain band	....	**75.00**
Scenic band	....	**100.00**
Semiprecious stones on band	....	**200.00**
Ivory		
Modern scrimshaw	....	**20.00**
Vegetable ivory	....	**60.00**
Metal, common		
Brass		
Cloisonne design, China	......	**10.00**
Fancy band	....	**15.00**
Cast pot metal, "For A Good Girl"	.	**5.00**
Silver, 1900–40		
Continental, synthetic stone cap	.	**25.00**
Cupid in high relief	....	**150.00**
Enameled band	....	**75.00**
Engraved, two birds on branch	..	**25.00**
Flowers in high relief	....	**35.00**
Italian, stones on band, modern	.	**35.00**
Raised design		
Bleeding heart	....	**25.00**
Wild rose	....	**35.00**
Scenic band	....	**35.00**

Simons, Cupid and garlands . . .	150.00
Souvenir	
Liberty Bell, 1976 issue	100.00
Palm Beach	150.00
Statue of Liberty, France	35.00
World's Fairs	
1892, Columbian, buildings . . .	500.00
1904, St. Louis World's Fair . .	500.00
1933, Chicago World's Fair . . .	150.00
Porcelain	
Meissen, hp, modern, Germany . . .	150.00
Royal Worcester, hp, modern, artist sgd, England	50.00
Scrimshaw, antique, whalebone or whale tooth	200.00

THREADED GLASS

History: Threaded glass is glass decorated with applied threads of glass. Before the English invention of a glass threading machine in 1876, threads were applied by hand. After this invention, threaded glass was produced in quantity by practically every major glass factory.

Threaded glass was revived by the art glass manufacturers, such as Durand and Steuben, and continues to be made today.

Finger Bowl, fluted rim, chartreuse, 5″ d, $65.00.

Creamer
4⅛″ h, aqua, threaded neck and lip, applied handle **1,485.00**
4¾″ h, clear, threaded neck and lip, applied ribbed handle, slight blue tint, Pittsburgh **150.00**
Lamp Shade, 11⅜″ d rim, 13⅜″ d, 7″ h, broad mushroom shape, amber mottled glass, internal random red–maroon threading, allover irid, Austrian . **530.00**
Mug, 4¾″ h, clear, second gather of glass with swirled ribs, applied handle, copper wheel engraved initials and wreath, threaded neck, attributed to New England Glass Co **1,540.00**

Pitcher
3⅞″ h, clear, applied threading at neck, applied handle **135.00**
6¾″ h, aqua, threaded neck and lip, applied handle **425.00**
7″ h
Lily Pad, aqua, threaded neck, applied tooled foot and handle **5,500.00**
Pittsburgh, aqua, threaded neck and lip, applied hollow handle . . **550.00**
7¼″ h, aqua, lily pad, threaded neck, second gather of glass with trailed lily pad dec, applied handle **5,725.00**
Vase, 6¾″ h, attributed to Loetz, irid opal amber body, red threading, oil spot lower half, applied handles, polished pontil **330.00**

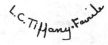

TIFFANY

History: Louis Comfort Tiffany (1849–1934) established a glasshouse in 1878 primarily to make stained glass windows. There he developed a unique type of colored iridescent glass called Favrile. His Favrile glass differed from other art glass in manufacture as it was a composition of colored glass worked together while hot. The essential characteristic is that ornamentation is found within the glass. Favrile was never further decorated. Different effects were achieved by varying the amount and position of colors which project movement in form and shape.

In 1890, in order to utilize surplus materials at the plant, Tiffany began to design and produce "small glass," such as iridescent glass lamp shades, vases, stemware, and tableware, in the Art Nouveau manner.

Commercial production began in 1896. Most Tiffany wares are signed with the name L. C. Tiffany or the initials L.C.T. Some pieces also carry the word "Favrile" as well as a number. A number of other marks can be found, e.g., Tiffany Studios and Louis C. Tiffany Furnaces.

Louis Tiffany and the artists in his studio also are well known for the fine work in other areas—bronzes, pottery, jewelry, silver, and enamels.

References: Victor Arwas, *Glass, Art Nouveau and Art Deco,* Rizzoli International Publications, 1977; Vivienne Couldrey, *Tiffany: The Art of Louis Comfort,* Wellfleet Press, 1989; *The Art Work of Louis C. Tiffany,* Apollo Books, 1987; Alastair Duncan, *Louis Comfort Tiffany,* Harry N. Abrams, Inc., 1992; Robert Koch, *Louis C. Tiffany, Rebel In Glass,* Crown Publishers, 1966; Ellen T. Schroy, *Warman's Glass,* Wallace-Homestead, 1992; John

A. Shuman III, *The Collector's Encyclopedia of American Art Glass*, Collector Books, 1988, 1991 value update.

Museums: Chrysler Museum, Norfolk, VA; Corning Glass Museum, Corning, NY; University of Connecticut, The William Benton Museum of Art, Storrs, CT.

BRONZE

Bookends, pr, gilt bronze
  Bookmark style, imp "Tiffany Studios
  New York 1056". 550.00
  Buddha, ovals, coppery patina, monogram, inscribed 11–23–31, base stamped "Tiffany Studios New York 1025" 360.00
Buckle, cloak, 3¼" l, enamel polychrome dec, molded foliate motif, ovals imp "L. C. T./265". 1,870.00
Chandelier Mount, ceiling drop, wheel ring, seven sockets, shade supports, and chain connectors, adjustable 29" h, 22" d wheel. 1,100.00
Clock, desk, 4¼ x 3¾ x 3", Venetian, dark gilt bronze sq, Tiffany & Co clock, base imp "1679" 715.00
Desk Set, gilt bronze
  Bookprinter pattern, No. 1002 long blotter ends, No. 1056 bookends, No. 864 inkwell, No. 1097 letter opener, No. 1055 pen tray, No. 1031 scissors, each imp "Tiffany Studios New York" and numbered, price for six piece set 1,540.00
  Grapevine pattern, amber slag glass accents, No. 801 Box, No. 807 Box, No. 940 calendar, No. 844 inkwell, No. 1006 letter holder, No. 1004 pen tray, No. 872 postal scale, minor damage, price for seven piece set 1,320.00
Inkwell
  4" h, squatty, three legged pot, six gold jewels, turtleback medallion cov, gold favrile ink reservoir inscribed "LCT," gilt bronze base marked "Tiffany Studios New York" 1,870.00
  5" h, Chinese, dark brown patina, imp "Tiffany Studios New York 1753". .   470.00
Lamp Base, 8" h, fluid, urn style, quatraform, oil canister and base marked "Tiffany Studios New York 29937" . .   275.00
Picture Frame
  6¾ x 9", Chinese, broad dark alligatored finish, imp "Tiffany Studios New York 1761". 385.00
  12½ x 14½", etched, spring flower pattern, beaded and wire twist borders, imp "Tiffany Studios New York," slightly bent. 2,310.00

Pot, 4¾" d, 3¾" h, cast metal, deeply molded frieze of robed men standing before classical architectural elements, imp "S113/Tiffany Studios/ From the Antique/1607". 470.00
Sconce, 16" w, 16" h, Oriental influence, three brilliant blue irid glass tiles mounted in gilt bronze frame, triple bulb sockets, imp "Louis C Tiffany Furnaces Inc.," price for pair 4,125.00
Vase, 15" h, alternating ribs, vertical panels, curvilinear devices, imp "Tiffany & Co 28215B" 990.00

GLASS

Bonbon
  4¾" h, 2" h, pastel blue, bright blue flared border, leaf dec bowl, foot inscribed "L. C. Tiffany Favrile" 660.00
  5" d, 3" h, stretched pastel blue–green opal, ribbed bowl, internal herringbone leaf dec, inscribed "L. C. T. Favrile 1700". 550.00
Bowl
  5¾" d, 2¾" h, scalloped, eight ribs, cobalt blue, strong blue irid, inscribed "L. C. T.". 440.00
  7" h, 2" h, scalloped, ten ribs, shallow, heavy walled cobalt blue, inscribed "L. C. T. Favrile" 715.00
  10" d, 3½" h, gold, twelve ribbed scalloped dish, stretched irid surface, inscribed "L. C. Tiffany Favrile 1925" 415.00
Box, cov, 3¼ x 6¾ x 4", green slag glass, metal Grapevine pattern, beaded hinged cov, imp "Tiffany Studios New York". 440.00
Candleholder, 4¼" h, stretched irid pastel pink rim, striped opal and colorless holder, hollow knop, cupped pedestal foot engraved "L.C.T. Favrile 1817" .   440.00
Center Bowl
  12¼" d, 3" h, pastel aqua, geometric flower devices within diamond quilted pattern, flared opal bowl, inscribed "L. C. Tiffany Favrile 1561," foot edge ground 990.00
  12½" d, 3¾" h, herringbone leaf pattern, aqua–green opalescent pastel, stretched irid rim, inscribed "L.C. Tiffany Favrile 1925" 660.00
Center Bowl and Flower Arranger, 12¼" d x 3" h bowl, expanded diamond, brilliant purple–blue stretched irid, inscribed "L. C. Tiffany Favrile 1561," 3" h two tier blue frog marked "L. C. T. Favrile 6" 1,540.00
Champagne, 8" h, flared, irid gold, double knopped stem, sgd "L.C.T. F1774". 275.00

Compote
3¼″ h, 8″ l, oval, stretched pastel
green irid on crystal bowl, stem, and
foot, inscribed "L. C. T. Favrile
1919C". 385.00
9½″ h, blue, goblet form, conforming
cov, inscribed "L. C. Tiffany Inc Fa-
vrile/9202M," finial ground. 470.00
Exhibition Piece, 6½″ h, red fused to
black, irid shoulder dec, imp "L. C. Tiffany Favrile Panama Pacific Ex.
2343J," cracked 1,540.00
Finger Bowl and Underplate, 4⅜″ d gold
irid bowl, swirled prunt pattern, conforming 5½″ d underplate, marked
"LCT R4654/R4544," price for two
piece set 415.00
Plate, 8″ d, blown eighteen ribs, central
five petaled irid gold blossom, triple
border bands, inscribed on back "L.
C. T. K2357". 715.00
Salt, 2¾″ d, ruffled, irid gold, inscribed
"LCT," price for set of five 550.00
Stemware, six champagnes and six cordials, irid gold Favrile, wheel cut
grapevine border, each sgd
"L.C.T." or "LCT Favrile," price for
twelve piece set 1,870.00
Taster, 2¼″ h, swirled prunt pattern, lustrous gold, each sgd "L.C.T. Favrile,"
price for set of six 1,430.00
Vase
4″ h, subtle eight rim body, pulled
thorny nubs at shoulder, silver blue
irid shading to purple base, inscribed "LCT Q9186". 880.00
6½″ h, optic ribbed opal shaded to
pale lavender, conforming foot, inscribed "L. C. T. Favrile". 615.00
8″ h, double bulbed, cobalt blue body,
swirled irid surface, inscribed "L. C.
T. Favrile A581E". 615.00
8½″ h
Lobed oval opal glass, green and
gold pulled irid feather, inscribed
"L. C. Tiffany Favrile 7804E" . . . 1,430.00
Tel el Amarna, Egyptian Revival Favrile, emerald green cased to
white, black border, irid silver,
gold, and green linear shoulder
frieze, base inscribed "1347H L.
C. Tiffany–Favrile" 4,100.00
9″ h, baluster
Amber–gold, wheel–cut grape leaf
border inside rim, irid surface, inscribed "Louis C. Tiffany Inc. Favrile 1824". 550.00
Gold Favrile, six pulled and hooded
feathers around base, ruby red
jewels and tiara dec at top, base
labeled and inscribed "L.C.T.
1456A" 1,100.00

10″ h, ruffled trumpet, eighteen ribs,
cobalt blue, overall irid, inscribed
"L.C.T. Favrile o 9715". 990.00
10½″ h, floriform, apricot pulled green
leaf dec rising from bulbed stem, repeated on cupped pedestal foot, irid
int., inscribed "LCT M 8975". 2,200.00
10¾″ h, ten ribs, favrile trumpet blossom, white opal, gold irid under
folded foot, inscribed "L. C. Tiffany
Favrile 1669". 1,320.00
12″ h, bud, elongated flared irid body,
five pulled green pointed leaf forms,
applied pedestal foot, inscribed
"L. C. Tiffany Inc. Favrile 1503–
5975N". 935.00
18″ h, angular, irid gold Favrile, engraved Art Deco design, repeating
stylized foliate devices, selectively
polished lower edge, base inscribed
"1822 P Louis C. Tiffany Favrile". . 3,960.00

Table Lamp, 12 sided shade with frosted amber glass panels centering molded linenfold plaques, bronze base, 23″ h, 16″ d shade, $6,875.00. Photograph courtesy of James D. Julia, Inc.

LAMPS

Boudoir, 15″ h, 8″ d dome amber cased
to opal shade, subtle irid surface, gold
Favrile baluster form lamp, leaf form
lamp inclusions, lightly engraved outlines, glass foot inscribed "L.C. Tiffany
Favrile" 1,210.00
Desk, 14″ h, 7″ d bronze shade cut with
stars, six opal glass bent panel liners,
bronze cantilever base stamped "Tiffany Studios New York 417". 2,530.00

Floor, 54″ h, counterbalance, gold dore finish, bulbed five ftd base, adjustable ball lever socket, sgd "Tiffany Studios" on foot 825.00

Fluid, 22″ h, 16″ d opal tam–o–shanter shade, irid green and gold Wave pattern Damascene, rim sgd "L.C.T.," three arm spider and urn form base, four ribbed legs, quatraform base, oil font marked "Tiffany Studios New York 6816," electrified 3,250.00

Luminor, 8″ h, Moorish, oct opal glass shade, double pulled feather gold and green irid design, gold heat cap, inscribed "LCT Favrile," wooden lamp base, conforming oct gilt bronze border, minor wear. 1,980.00

Student, 29″ h, 10″ d translucent green favrile glass shade, blown into two bronze shade frames, numbered 22503, adjustable fluid burner arms, central fuel canister, orig bronze framework, twist and beaded dec, frame imp 25574. . . . . 12,100.00

Table

Acorn, 17″ h, 12″ d favrile glass leaded shade, mottled yellow, band of green–blue heart shaped elements, two socket bronze base, imp "Tiffany Studios New York" 6,050.00

Damascene, 21½″ h, 16″ d cased opal favrile glass shade, green pulled rippled gold irid dec, early three arm and socket bronze base, wire twist and cast turtleback dec, imp "Tiffany Studios New York 25882" and "TG&D Co" logo 4,400.00

Grapevine, 16″ h, 14″ d bronze dome shade, eight green favrile bent panels, rim tag reads "Tiffany Studios New York," three arm spider over Tiffany spun bronze tobacco leaf fluid lamp 5,225.00

Lily, 9″ h, three green pulled feather on opal lily blossom shades, sgd "L.C.T.," squat form 320 base, dark patina, candleholder lappet base, rewired, new sockets, one shade cracked. 1,100.00

Lotus, 21″ h, 15½″ d bell form shade, green and white favrile glass leaded segments, rib reinforcements, bronze bell frame, ribbed five ftd base, numbered and imp "Tiffany Studios New York," some segments cracked. 19,800.00

Pomegranate, 18″ h, 16″ d leaded glass dome shade, deep green favrile segments, yellow border belt, spun bronze converted fluid lamp base, conforming three arm shade supports, imp "Tiffany Studios New York". 4,400.00

Swirling Leaf, 24″ h, 18″ d green slag leaded Favrile brickwork domed shade, straight apron, wide belt of amber and white opal curving leaf forms, small rim tag "Tiffany Studios New York," three socket 533 paneled dark bronze base, imp marks. 5,100.00

Turtleback, 23½″ h, 18″ d mottled dichroic gold brickwork dome shade, shoulder bent of twenty–one opal gold irid tiles, horizontal rim tab imp "Tiffany Studios New York 1482," three socket six panel 533 base, imp mark 8,250.00

c1960

TIFFIN GLASS

History: A. J. Beatty & Sons built a glass manufacturing plant in Tiffin, Ohio, in 1888. On January 1, 1892, the firm joined the U.S. Glass Co. and was known as factory "R". Quality and production at this factory were very high and resulted in fine Depression-era glass.

Beginning in 1916 wares were marked with a paper label. From 1923 to 1936, Tiffin produced a line of black glassware called Black Satin. The company discontinued operation in 1980.

References: Fred Bickenheuser, *Tiffin Glassmasters, Book I,* Glassmasters Publications, 1979; Fred Bickenheuser *Tiffin Glassmasters, Book II,* Glassmasters Publications, 1981; Fred W. Bickenheuser, *Tiffin Glassmasters, Book III,* Glassmasters Publications, 1985; Ellen T. Schroy, *Warman's Glass,* Wallace-Homestead, 1992.

Collectors' Club: Tiffin Glass Collectors Club, PO Box 554, Tiffin, OH 44883.

Bud Vase

Cherokee Rose, crystal, 8″ h 45.00
June Night, crystal, ftd 45.00

Champagne

Adam, pink 30.00
Cherokee Rose, crystal, 5½ oz . . . 20.00
Flanders, pink 42.00
Persian Pheasant, #17358, crystal 27.00

Cigarette Holder, Copen Blue 65.00

Cocktail

Fuchsia, crystal 18.00

June Night, crystal 18.00
Console Set, 8″ d bowl, pr 8″ h candlesticks, cobalt blue, silver overlay, cutout and applied sterling silver band of dancing Dutch children and windmills, made for Rockwell, sgd, price for three piece set 150.00
Cordial, Persian Pheasant, #17358, crystal 40.00
Cornucopia, Copen Blue, 8¼″ 75.00
Creamer, June Night, crystal 20.00
Cup and Saucer
    Flanders, crystal, ftd cup 35.00
    Fontaine Twilight 125.00
    La Fleure, yellow 45.00
Goblet
    Cerice, crystal 24.00
    Flanders, pink 48.00
    Persian Pheasant, #17358, crystal 45.00
    Shawl Dancer, crystal 38.00
Juice, Cerice, crystal, #071, ftd 18.00
Lemonade Pitcher, Arcadian, green handle and foot. 375.00
Plate, Cherokee Rose, crystal, 8″ d . . 18.50
Sherbet, Cherokee Rose, crystal 20.00
Sherry
    Persian Pheasant, #17358, crystal, wide mouth 21.00
    Shawl Dancer, crystal 52.00
Sugar
    Cerice, crystal 25.00
    La Fleure, yellow 37.50

c1875

c1880

c1872-1951

TILES

History: The use of decorated tiles peaked during the latter part of the 19th century. Over one hundred companies in England alone were producing tiles by 1880. By 1890 companies had opened in Belgium, France, Australia, Germany, and the United States.

Tiles were not limited to adorning fireplaces. Many were installed into furniture, such as washstands, hall stands, and folding screens. Since tiles were easily cleaned and, hence, hygienic, they readily were used on the floors and walls of entry halls, hospitals, butcher shops, or any place where sanitation was a concern. Many public buildings and subways also employed tiles to add interest and beauty.

Condition is an important fact in determining price. A cracked, badly scuffed and scratched, or heavily chipped tile has very little value. Slight chipping around the outer edges of a tile is, at times, considered acceptable by collectors, especially if these chips can be covered by a frame.

It is not uncommon for the highly glazed surface of some tiles to have become crazed. Crazing is not considered a deterrent as long as it does not detract from the overall appearance of the tile.

References: J. & B. Austwick, *The Decorated Tile,* Pitman House, 1980; Susan and Al Bagdade, *Warman's English & Continental Pottery & Porcelain, Second Edition,* Wallace-Homestead, 1991; Julian Barnard, *Victorian Ceramic Tiles,* N.Y. Graphic Society, 1972; Terence A. Lockett, *Collecting Victorian Tiles,* Antique Collectors Club, 1979; Hans Van Lemmen, *Tiles: A Collectors' Guide,* Seven Hills Books, 1985; Noel Riley, *Tile Art: A History of Decorative Ceramic Tiles,* Chartwell Books, 1987.

Periodical: *Flash Point,* PO Box 1850, Healdsburg, CA 95448.

Collectors' Club: Tiles & Architectural Ceramics Society, Ironbridge Gorge Museum, Ironbridge, Telford, Shropshire, England TF8 7AW.

Advertising
    Baker's Chocolate, 6¼″ sq, lady carrying serving tray, blue, white yellow, green, and lavender, tan ground, Grueby 355.00
    Northwestern Terra Cotta Works, 4 x 5¼″, detailed, rough corners 250.00
Alcock, S, 7 x 14½″, enamel dec after oil painting entitled Sea Shells by Albert Joseph Moore, sgd in lower corner "S Alcock," wood and cloth frame 1,210.00
American Encaustic Tiling Co, Zanesville, OH
    4¼″ sq, white, black design of horseman riding through brush 30.00
    6″ sq, Ulysses Grant bust, peacock green glaze, framed. 300.00
Batchelder, Ernest A, Los Angeles, CA, 8″ sq, incised landscape scene, matte blue glaze. 220.00
California Faience Co, 5½″ sq, clo-

Claycraft, CA, brown, blue, and green, imp "Claycraft from CA, Aztec design," 1920, 8 x 6", $65.00.

isonne style dec, glossy and matte blue and brown glaze 275.00
Fine Art Ceramic Co, Indianapolis, IN, 5½ x 8¾", Abraham Lincoln bust, black and white, framed 385.00
Grueby, 6" sq, brown and ochre turtle, mottled brown ground, sgd, framed . . 600.00
J & J G Low, Chelsea, MA
4¼" sq, swirled foliate, teal blue . . . 50.00
6" sq, Galileo bust, wearing hat, framed 220.00
6⅛ x 4½", rect, woman, blue–green, titled "Autumn" 75.00
Kensington, 6" sq, classic female head, brown 40.00
Marblehead, 6" sq, green, brown border of dashes, dark brown edge band, matte glaze 660.00
Minton China Works
6" sq, cows crossing stream, brown and cream 75.00
8" sq, brown and pale blue transfer scene, framed 65.00
Owens, 6" sq, Egyptian Revival style, relief molded tulip blossom, imp mark 45.00
Pardee, C
4¼" sq, imp stylized cat and leaf sprig, blue ground 220.00
6" sq, Grover Cleveland portrait, gray lavender 120.00
Paul Revere Pottery, Boston, MA
3¾" sq, incised Boston street scene, pink, blue, brown, white, and gray, inscribed and sgd 385.00
4⅜" d, round, swan, yellow, brown, green, and white, slight age crack 125.00
Rookwood
5¾" d, round, seagulls in flight, 1943 60.00
12" sq, sailing ship, bluish–green sea, oak frame 1,210.00
Sherwin & Cotton
6 x 9", Abraham Lincoln, brown . . . 135.00

6 x 12", Quiltmaker and Ledger, orange, price for pair 250.00
Trent Tile Co, Trenton, NJ
4¼" sq, young woman, head portrait, clear caramel glaze, framed 110.00
U.S. Encaustic Tile Works, Indianapolis, IN, 6 x 8", panel, Dawn, green, framed 150.00
Wedgwood, England
6" sq, Red Riding Hood, black and white 100.00
8" sq, Tally Ho, man riding horse, blue and white 75.00
Weller, 8½" sq, four tile landscape scene, polychrome slip glaze, framed, c1925 . . . . 3,080.00
William DeMorgan, London, England, 6" sq, peacock, blue and green, glossy glaze, framed 355.00

TINWARE

History: Beginning in the 1700s many utilitarian household objects were made of tin. Tin is nontoxic, rust resistant, and fairly durable, so it can be used for storing food. It often was plated to iron to provide strength. Because it was cheap, tinware and tin-plated wares were in the price range of most people.

An early center of tinware manufacture in the United States was Berlin, Connecticut. Almost every small town and hamlet had its own tinsmith, tinner, or whitesmith. Tinsmiths used patterns from which to make items. They cut out the pieces, hammered and shaped them, and soldered the seams. If a piece was to be used with heat, a copper bottom was added because of the low melting point of tin. The Industrial Revolution brought about machine-made, mass-produced tinware pieces. The handmade era ended by the late 19th century.

This category is a catchall for tin objects which do not fit into other categories in our book.

Reference: Dana G. Morykan and Harry L. Rinker, *Warman's Country Antiques & Collectibles, Second Edition,* Wallace-Homestead Book Co., 1994.

Museum: Cooper-Hewitt Museum National Museum of Design, Smithsonian Institution.

Additional Listings: See Advertising, Kitchen Collectibles, Lanterns, Lamps and Lighting, and Tinware: Decorated.

Bed Warmer, 42½" l, brass trim, turned wooden handle, old black paint 85.00
Bird Cage, 13½" d, 20½" h, old blue paint 195.00
Candle Box, 15" l, match compartment on one end, c1830 . . . . 150.00
Candle Mold, 10½" h, twelve tube, handle 75.00

**Candle Mold, six tube, strap handle,
$60.00.**

Candle Sconce
9¼" h, simple crimped crest, price for
pair. 210.00
13" h, oval fluted sunburst reflectors,
"S" curve arms, crimped drip pans,
price for pair 1,000.00
Coffeemaker
9¾" h, removable drip top, black
wooden handle, pewter finial. 72.00
13¾" h, two pc, drip top, brass spigot,
cast leaf and ring handles, pitted . . 85.00
Coffeepot
10½" h, parrot beak spout, cut–out
heart shaped air hold, stamped "J
Brinkhouse". 440.00
11½" h
Double spout, emb brass label
"Maxim's patent coffee pot...,"
rust damage, holes in one spout 62.00
Pewter handle, spout, and lid, some
rust, battered finial 72.00
Colander, 4¼" h, heart shape, circle
feet 130.00
Cookie Cutter
6" l, bird 75.00
7¾" l, horse 110.00
Food Cover, 12 x 15", oval, oval,
platter, reticulated base, light rust . . . 30.00
Food Mold, 7¼" l, oval, fruit 50.00
Foot Warmer, 7½ x 9 x 5¾" h, punched
dec, turned posts, butternut frame. . . 220.00
Grater, 13½" l, punched dec, pine back,
cutout handle, old finish 140.00
Hair Comb, anniversary type, 9" h,
American, 19th C 358.00
Lamp, 11" h, betty, matching stand, han-
ger, and wick pick, both stamped
"J.D.," (J. Deer), stand with crimped
rusted top edge, damage, soldered
repair. 250.00
Memorial Sign, 18½" h, shield shape,
emb detail, worn black paint, "Daniel
Taylor Jr. O.B. Dec. 9th 1825 AE 55
years" 110.00

Miniature Kitchen, 19" l, various accessories, pots, pans, pump, etc., worn
polychrome paint, corn husk doll. . . . 315.00
Parade Torch, 38" l, barrel shaped font,
three burners, tin handle, some
damage 30.00
Pitcher, 11" h, punched and tooled sun-
burst dec, scrolled ear handle. 145.00
Serving Tray, 30¾ x 21¾" h, painted,
gilt rim, bronze leaves, hunting scene
vignettes, floral sprigs, minor losses,
English, 19th C 1,870.00
Spoon Holder, 10" h, 15" w, punched
dec 250.00
Teapot
5¾" h, oval, punched tulip and inter-
section wavy line border design,
ribbed handle, hinged lid, three ring
finial 225.00
8" h, pewter finial 115.00

TINWARE: DECORATED

History: The art of decorating sheet iron, tin, and
tin-coated sheet iron dates back to the mid 18th
century. The Welsh called the practice pontipool,
the French To'le Peinte. In America the center for
tin-decorated ware in the late 1700s was Berlin,
Connecticut.

Several styles of decorating techniques were
used: painting, japanning, and stenciling. Designs
were done by both professionals and itinerants.
English and Oriental motifs strongly influenced
both form and design.

A special type of decoration was the punch work
on unpainted tin practiced by the Pennsylvania
tinsmiths. Forms included coffeepots, spice boxes,
and grease lamps.

Reference: Dana G. Morykan and Harry L.
Rinker, *Warman's Country Antiques & Collectibles,
Second Edition*, Wallace-Homestead, 1994.

Bowl, 7¾" w, 12¾" l, 3⅝" h, oval, orig
dark brown japanning, red, yellow,
and white floral dec, minor wear 350.00
Box, brass bail, cast pewter feet, very
worn black paint, gold striping and
flowers, interior lift out tray, engraved
brass label in lid: "H. W. Butterworth,
Phila, 1850," minor damage, hinges
loose 115.00
Bread Tray, 14" l, orig green paint, yel-
low striping, polychrome stenciled
bronze powder fruit, flowers, and foli-
age dec 55.00
Bucket, helmet shape, worn old black
paint, gilt Chinoiserie dec, European,
battered and damage, 20" h 300.00
Candle Box, 9" l, worn orig red, black
striping, traces of orig floral dec,
hinged lid 75.00

Milk Can, stenciled red and gold stylized floral design, black japanning, 8½" h, $175.00.

Canister, 8¼" h, worn orig black paint, red, green, and yellow floral dec, cap resoldered 115.00
Clock, 17" h, hanging, orig red and black graining, floral stenciled dec, brass works, silvered brass face marked "Seth Thomas," wear to case, seam separation 250.00
Coffeepot, 10½" h, orig dark brown japanning, floral dec, yellow, two shades of red, white, and green, minor wear 3,100.00
Creamer, 4⅛" h, worn dark brown japanning, red, green, and yellow floral dec 450.00
Cuspidor, 8¼" d, smoked white, red stripes, gold stenciled dec, worn gold rim bands 70.00
Desk Set, 8" l, old worn black paint, brass bail handle, paw feet, three part int. with ink bottle, sander, one repaired wire hinge. 95.00
Document Box, dome top
  6¾" l, orig dark brown japanning, yellow striping, white band with red, green, and yellow floral dec, some wear. 70.00
  7" l, orig dark brown and black japanning, red, green, yellow, black, and white floral dec, minor wear, lid seam loose 200.00
  9" l, orig worn brown japanning, polychrome and gold stenciled floral dec, some battering 125.00
  10" l, orig brown japanning, white band, red and yellow swags, red, black, and green floral dec, some wear, good colors. 415.00
Food Warmer
  7½ x 6½", worn brown japanning, gold

stenciled lyre, wooden base and top 95.00
8¼" h, cylindrical, orig brown japanning, stenciled floral dec, font and whale oil burner, two pans, minor wear. 275.00
Match Holder, 7⅜" h, traces of orig black paint, red and yellow dec 62.00
Miniature, 3" l, deed box, flat top, orig brown japanning, white band, yellow striping, yellow, red, and green dec. . 330.00
Spice Box, 7¼" d, round, six (of seven) original interior canisters, worn original brown japanning, gold stenciled labels. 115.00
Sugar Bowl, 3½" h, worn orig red paint, brown and yellow comma type foliage, foot slightly battered 165.00
Tea Caddy
  4¼" h, orig red paint, stylized black, white, and yellow florals, minor wear 1,800.00
  4½" h, oval, worn orig black paint, yellow and red floral dec, red ground lid with black comma dec 165.00
  8¼" l, dark ground, worn stenciled bronze powder dec, int. lift out tray fits over two lidded compartments, orig emb brass handle, minor damage. 200.00
Tea Canister, 7" h, orig dark brown japanning, yellow and orange–red dec, worn 115.00
Tray
  9⅜" w, 12¼" l, orig dark green–blue paint, gilt floral rim, center with detailed painting of village with stream, boat, and people, minor edge battering 450.00
  10⅞" w, 14⅜" l, orig black paint, gilt floral rim, well detailed painting of farmers meeting on country road. . 375.00

TOBACCO CUTTERS

History: Before prepackaging, tobacco was delivered to merchants in bulk form. Tobacco cutters were used to cut the tobacco into desired sizes.

Cast Iron, Brighton 3, $35.00.

Cupples Arrow & Superb	50.00
E C Simmons Keen Kutter	225.00
Griswold Tobacco Cutter, Erie, PA	55.00
John Finzer & Bros, Louisville, KY	25.00
Sprague Warner & Co	75.00
Unknown Maker	
5½" h, brass, ship's telegraph form	185.00
11½" l, silhouette, horse, iron blade, pine handle and base, 19th C	385.00
13" l, walnut, human head form terminal, flared rect base, wrought iron blade, tapered sq handles, 19th C	385.00
15" l, 6¾" w, wrought iron and sheet metal, forged cylindrical shaft, crescent shape blade, U shape handle, turned pine grip, mid 19th C	45.00

TOBACCO JARS

History: A tobacco jar is a container for storing tobacco. Tobacco humidors were made of various materials and in many shapes, including figurals. The earliest jars date to the early 17th century. However, most examples in today's market were made in the late 19th or early 20th centuries.

Reference: Deborah Gage and Madeleine Marsh, *Tobacco Containers & Accessories*, Gage Bluett & Company, 1988.

Collectors' Club: Society of Tobacco Jar Collectors, 3021 Courtland Blvd., Shaker Heights, OH 44122.

Bisque, 8 x 8", figural, bust of baby, Germany	125.00
Brass, 5½" h, tin cased int., early 19th C	40.00
Jasperware, 6" h, blue and white	65.00
Majolica, figural	
5" h, bust of American Indian	135.00
6" h, bear smoking pipe	125.00

Porcelain, figural, skater, high glaze, marked "8876," 6¼" h, $230.00.

Milk Glass, cylindrical, enameled floral dec, brass hinged Art Nouveau style cov	90.00
Old Paris, 6¼" h, figural, turk's head, painted, tasseled turban form cov, c1835.	715.00
Porcelain, figural	
Emperor Franz Joseph, full regalia	1,000.00
Humpty Dumpty	115.00
Pottery, cov, 6" h, 4" d, Winking Scotchman, blue beret with plaid band and orange tuft, green collar.	140.00
Rookwood, 8¾" h, pipes, cigarettes, and matches dec, standard glaze, sgd "Jeannette Swing," dated 1903.	500.00
Silver and Glass, 8⅛" h, octagonal, ivory finial, stamped "Made in France for J E Caldwell," 57 oz, Tetard Freres, c1930.	1,500.00
Terra-Cotta, 11" h, figural, Bismark, sitting in easy chair.	250.00

TOBY JUGS

History: A toby jug is a drinking vessel usually depicting a full-figured, robust, genial drinking man. They originated in England in the late 18th century. The term "Toby" probably related to the character Uncle Toby from *Tristam Shandy* by Laurence Sterne.

References: Susan and Al Bagdade, *Warman's English & Continental Pottery & Porcelain, Second Edition*, Wallace-Homestead, 1991; Vic Schuler, *British Toby Jugs*, Kevin Francis Publishing (London), 1986.

Additional Listing: Royal Doulton.

Reproduction Alert: Within the last 100 years or more, tobies have been reproduced copiously by many potteries in the United States and England.

Bennington Type, 9½" h, standing	110.00
China, 9¼" h, green coat, blue vest, British.	110.00
Lustre Ware	
6½" h, blue coat, spotted vest, 19th C	155.00
9¾" h, standing, blue coat, gold vest	265.00
Majolica, 8¾" h, monk	145.00
Staffordshire	
3¾" h, pearlware, polychrome enamel, chips on hat rim.	165.00
7⅛" h, yellow coat, yellow spotted vest, 19th C.	125.00
8½" h	
Blue coat, spotted vest	285.00
Holding mug on knee, underglaze blue and polychrome enamel.	440.00
9" h, Falstaf, 19th C	210.00
9¼" h, orange coat, 19th C	145.00

Hearty Good Fellow, red coat, yellow breeches, 11½″ h, $285.00.

9½″ h	
Green coat, caryatid handle	255.00
Watch man, early 19th C	175.00
9¾″ h, King wearing striped suit, 19th C	235.00
10″ h	
Brown coat, spatterware hat and base, 19th C	355.00
Creamware, underglaze brown, black, yellow, and tan sponging, holding mug on knee, barrel between feet, small edge chips . . .	440.00
10¼″ h, yellow ware, white slip, black, tan, brown, and blue glaze, holding bottle in right hand, mug in left, old professional repair	385.00
11″ h, Hearty Good Fellow, standing, blue coat.	230.00
11¼″ h	
Blue coat, yellow vest, angular plinth, 19th C	295.00
Home Brewed Ale, sitting on barrel	385.00
11½″ h, Hearty Good Fellow, standing, red coat, aqua vest	265.00

TOOLS

History: Before the advent of the assembly line and mass production, practically everything required for living was handmade at home or by a local tradesman or craftsmen. The cooper, the blacksmith, the cabinetmaker, and the carpenter all had their special tools.

Early examples of these hand tools are collected for their workmanship, ingenuity, place of manufacture, or design. Modern-day craftsmen often search out old hand tools for use to authentically re-create the manufacture of an object.

References: *A Price Guide To Keen Kutter Tools,* L-W Books, 1993; Ronald S. Barlow, *The Antique Tool Collector's Guide to Value,* Windmill Publishing, Third Edition, 1991; Herbert P. Kean and Emil S. Pollak, *A Price Guide To Antique Tools,* Astragal Press, 1992; Herbert P. Kean and Emil S. Pollak, *Collecting Antique Tools,* Astragal Press, 1990; Kathryn McNerney, *Antique Tools, Our American Heritage,* Collector Books, 1979, 1993 value update; Dana G. Morykan and Harry L. Rinker, *Warman's Country Antiques & Collectibles, Second Edition,* Wallace-Homestead, 1994; Emil and Martyl Pollak, *A Guide To American Wooden Planes and Their Makers, Second Edition,* Astragal Press, 1991; Emil and Martyl Pollak, *Prices Realized on Rare Imprinted American Wood Planes, 1979–1992,* Astragal Press, 1993; R. A. Salaman, *Dictionary of Tools,* Charles Scribner's Sons, 1974; John Walter, *Antique & Collectible Stanley Tools: A Guide To Identity and Value,* Tool Merchants, 1990; John M. Whelan, *The Wooden Plane: Its History, Form, and Function,* Astragal Press, 1993; Jack P. Wood, *Early 20th Century Stanley Tools: A Price Guide,* L-W Book Sales, n.d.; Jack P. Wood, *Town-Country Old Tools and Locks Keys and Closures,* L-W Books, 1990.

Periodicals: *Fine Tool Journal,* RD #2, Box 245B, Pittsford, VT 05763; *Stanley Tool Collector News,* 208 Front St., PO Box 227, Marietta, OH 45750; *Tool Ads,* PO Box 33, Hamilton, MT 59840.

Collectors' Clubs: Collectors of Rare & Familiar Tools Society, 38 Colony Ct., Murray Hill, NJ 07974; Early American Industries Assoc., PO Box 2128, Empire State Plaza Station, Albany, NY 12220; Early American Industries-West, 8476 West Way Dr., La Jolla, CA 92038; Mid-West Tool Collectors Assoc., 808 Fairway Dr., Columbia, MO 65201; Missouri Valley Wrench Club, 613 N. Long St., Shelbyville, IL 62565; New England Tool Collectors Assoc., 303 Fisher Rd., Fitchburg, MA 01420; Ohio Tool Collectors Assoc, PO Box 261, London, OH 43140; Pacific Northwest Tool Collectors, 2132 NE 81st St., Seattle, WA 98115; Potomac Antique Tools & Industries Association, 6802 Newbitt Pl., McLean, VA 22101; Rocky Mountain Tool Collectors, 2024 Owens Ct., Denver, CO 80227; Society of Workers in Early Arts & Trades, 606 Lake Lena Blvd, Auburndale, FL 33823; Southwest Tool Collectors Assoc., 7032 Oak Bluff Dr., Dallas, TX 75240; Three Rivers Tool Collectors, 39 S. Rolling Hills, Irwin, PA 15642; Tool Group of Canada, 7 Tottenham Rd., Ontario, Canada MC3 2J3.

Museums: American Precision Museum Association, Windsor, VT; Mercer Museum, Doylestown, PA; Shelburne Museum, Shelburne, VT; World of Tools Museum, Waverly, TN.

Adze, shipwright's, lipped	30.00
Archimedean Drill, wood center grip and head, two ball flywheel.	75.00
Bench, cobbler's, NH, early 19th C . .	600.00
Board Rule, octagonal	60.00
Bow Saw, 24″ I blade, maple	40.00

Archimedean Drills, top: German, pre WWII, 9¾" l, $35.00; bottom: gentleman's style, ebonized, 7¾" l, $25.00.

Broad Axe, 8½" w, wood handle, marked "Hopkins & Co, Hartford, Warranted Cast Steel"	75.00
Caliper	
Hand Forged, double, locking circle and wing nuts	125.00
Spring Style, 8" l, inside	10.00
Carpenter's Rule	
H Chapins Son, folding, #39	25.00
Stanley, #78½, boxwood, 2 ft, 4 fold, brass bound	85.00
Chisel, shipwright's, 2¾" w blade	60.00
Divider, wing style	
18" l, wood	65.00
22" l, metal, hand forged, chamfered	45.00
Felling Axe, Rockaway pattern	15.00
Furniture Clamp, bar type, 60" l	20.00
Hammer	
Blacksmith's, top swage	10.00
Cobbler's	5.00
Slater's, hand forged	25.00
Tinsmith's	12.00
Mallet	
Carpenter's	8.00
Wheelwright's	15.00
Mortise Chisel, gooseneck	35.00
Plane	
Auburn Tool Co, plow, rosewood, handle	250.00
Colton & B Sheneman, sash	100.00
F Dallicker, large rabbet	175.00
H H Read, Wilmington, VT, smoothing	65.00
Marley, NY, planemaker's, dovetail	400.00
Stanley, 7" l, #2, smooth, cast iron, rosewood handle and knob	175.00
Pocket Level, Davis Level & Tool Co, 3½" l, acorn finials both ends	95.00
Rake, wood, twelve prongs, three graduating semicircular braces, c1850, 77" l	130.00
Saw, coachmaker's, 72" l, plank, framed	175.00
Slide Rule, Pickett	1,850.00
Sliding Bevel, 6" l, I J Robinson, brass framed, rosewood infill	225.00

Spirit Level, carpenter's	
Davis Level & Tool Co, 18" l, cast iron	100.00
Stanley, 24" l, mahogany, brass bound	50.00
Square, hand forged, hand struck numbers, 18th C	15.00
Tool Chest, paneled lid, brass trim, two trays	1,200.00
T–Square, 48" l, mahogany, fixed head	8.00
Wheelbarrow, wood, iron wheel and braces, removable sides, sgd	75.00

TOOTHPICK HOLDERS

History: Toothpick holders, indispensable table accessories of the Victorian era, are small containers used to hold toothpicks.

They were made in a wide range of materials: china (bisque and porcelain), glass (art, blown, cut, opalescent, pattern, etc.), and metals, especially silver plate. Makers include both American and European firms.

Toothpick holders were used as souvenir items by applying decals or transfers. The same blank may contain several different location labels.

References: William Heacock, *Encyclopedia Of Victorian Colored Pattern Glass, Book I, Toothpick Holders From A To Z, Second Edition*, Antique Publications, 1976, 1992 value update; William Heacock, *1,000 Toothpick Holders: A Collector's Guide*, Antique Publications, 1977; William Heacock, *Rare & Unlisted Toothpick Holders*, Antique Publications, 1984; National Toothpick Holders Collectors Society, *Toothpick Holders: China, Glass, and Metal*, Antique Publications, 1993.

Collectors' Club: National Toothpick Holders Collectors Society, 1224 Spring Valley Lane, West Chester, PA 19380.

Additional Listings: See *Warman's Americana & Collectibles* for more examples.

Advisor: Judy Knauer.

Glass	
Amber, frosted, Gonterman Swirl	195.00
Amberina, Daisy and Button	145.00
Blue Opalescent, Iris and Meander, 2½" h, 2½" d	90.00
Cranberry Opalescent, Reverse Swirl	235.00
Crystal, petticoat hat, gold dec	50.00
Custard, Inverted Fan and Feather	495.00
Daum Nancy, winter scene, sgd	750.00
Libbey, floppy hat, frosted, sgd "Libbey Glass Co, Toledo, Ohio" and "Columbian Exposition 1893"	225.00
Pink Cased, Sunset pattern, 2¼" h, 2" d	85.00
Vaseline, Thousand Eye	45.00
Vaseline Opalescent, Ribbed Spiral	115.00
White Opalescent, Criss Cross	165.00

China, hp, Nippon blank, three gold handles, sgd "G. Hills," blue sunrise Nippon mark, $60.00.

White Overlay, blue lining, egg shaped, amber rigaree leaf feet. . .	65.00
Porcelain	
Royal Bayreuth, triangular, penguin on each side, blue mark	235.00
RS Prussia, swimming swans scene	110.00
Wedgwood, Jasperware, dark blue, raised white crest with castle, lady with dog, man with dog, 1¾" h, 1¾" d	65.00

TORTOISESHELL ITEMS

History: For many years amber and mottled-colored tortoiseshell has been used in the manufacture of small items such as boxes, combs, dresser sets, and trinkets.

Note: Anyone dealing in the sale of tortoiseshell objects should be familiar with the Endangered Species Act and Amendment in its entirety. As of November 1978, antique tortoiseshell objects can be legally imported and sold with some restrictions.

Box	
4" w, oval	125.00
5 x 3½", rect, mid 19th C	175.00
Calling Card Case, 4 x 3", MOP and ivory inlaid dec, c1825	220.00
Cigar Box, rounded rect, gold inlaid dec	250.00
Coin Purse, 3 x 2", silver inlay	150.00
Compact	12.50
Eyeglass Case, 5" l, rounded ends, eyeglasses	165.00
Letter Opener, 12" l, silver fox head handle	225.00
Mirror, hand, oval	110.00
Pill Box	
2½" l, small ivory feet	80.00
3" w, rect, c1825	100.00
Pin Box, 3½" w, silver corner dec and inscription "Pin" on top	225.00

Ring Box	110.00
Snuff Box	
½ x 2 x 1¼", pique dec	110.00
1½ x 2", oval, silver dec	325.00
1½ x 3¼ x 1¼", oval, applied gold basket of flowers	650.00
2½ x 4"	175.00
4" w	110.00
Tea Caddy	
Casket form, compartment int., squat ivory bun feet, mid 19th C	2,200.00
Octagonal, 4¼" w, Georgian	1,400.00
Shaped front, flattened ball feet, 7½" l	1,250.00
Work Box, 8¾ x 5½", Colonial, rect, fitted needlework int.	550.00

TOYS

History: In America the first cast-iron toys began to appear shortly after the Civil War. Leading 19th-century manufacturers included Hubley, Dent, Kenton, and Schoenhut. In the first decades of the 20th century, Arcade, Buddy L, Marx, and Tootsie Toy joined these earlier firms. Wooden toys were made by George Brown and other manufacturers who did not sign or label their work.

In Europe, Nuremberg, Germany, was the center for the toy industry from the late 18th through the mid 20th century. Companies such as Lehman and Marklin produced high-quality toys.

Every toy is collectible. The key is the condition and working order if mechanical. Examples listed are considered to be in good to very good condition to mint condition unless otherwise specified.

References: Linda Baker, *Modern Toys, American Toys, 1930–1980*, Collector Books, 1985, 1993 value update; Bill Bruegman, *Toys of the Sixties*, Cap'n Penny Productions, 1991; Steve Butler and Clarence Young, *Autoquotes, The Complete Reference For: Promotions, Pot Metal & Plastic with Prices*, Autohobby Public, 1993; Robert Carter and Eddy Rubinstein, *Yesterday's Yesteryears: Lesney "Matchbox" Models*, Haynes Publishing Group (London), 1986; Roger Case and Tom Hammel (eds.), *1994 Toys & Prices*, Krause Publications, 1993; Jurgen and Marianne Cieslik, *Lehmann Toys*, New Cavendish Books, 1982; Don Cranmer, *Collectors Encyclopedia, Toys-Banks*, L-W Books, 1986, 1993 value update; Edward Force, *Corgi Toys*, Schiffer Publishing, 1984, 1991 value update; Edward Force, *Dinky Toys*, Schiffer Publishing, 1988, 1992 value update; Edward Force, *Matchbox and Lledo Toys*, Schiffer Publishing, 1988; Edward Force, *Solido Toys*, Schiffer Publishing, 1993; Richard Friz, *The Official Identification And Price Guide To Collectible Toys, Fifth Edition*, House of Collectibles, 1990; Gordon Gardiner and Alistair Morris, *The Illustrated Encyclopedia of Metal Toys*, Harmony Books, 1984; Lillian Gottschalk, *American Toy Cars & Trucks*, Abbeville

Press, 1985; David C. Gould and Donna Crevar-Donaldson, *Occupied Japan Toys With Prices,* L-W Book Sales, 1993; Bill Hanlon, *Plastic Toys: Dimestore Dreams of the '40s & '50s,* Schiffer Publishing, 1993; Jay Horowitz, *Marx Western Playsets: The Authorized Guide,* Greenberg Publishing, 1992; Dana Johnson, *Matchbox Toys 1948 to 1993: Identification and Value Guide,* Collector Books, 1994; Joe Johnson and Dana McGuinn, *Toys That Talk: Over 300 Pullstring Dolls & Toys— 1960s To Today,* Firefly Publishing, 1992; Dale Kelley, *Collecting The Tin Toy Car, 1950–1970,* Schiffer Publishing, 1984; Constance King, *Metal Toys & Automata,* Chartwell Books, 1989; Samuel H. Logan and Charles W. Best, *Cast Iron Toy Guns and Capshooters,* published by authors, 1990; Ernest and Ida Long, *Dictionary of Toys Sold in America,* 2 vols., published by authors; David Longest, *Character Toys and Collectibles,* Collector Books, 1984, 1992 value update; David Longest, *Character Toys and Collectibles, Second Series,* Collector Books, 1987, 1990 value update; David Longest, *Toys: Antique & Collectible,* Collector Books, 1990, 1992 value update; Charlie Mack, *Lesney's Matchbox Toys: Regular Wheel Years, 1947–1969,* Schiffer Publishing, 1992; Charlie Mack, *Lesney's Matchbox Toys: The Superfast Years, 1969–1982,* Schiffer Publishing, 1993; Charlie Mack, *Matchbox Toys: The Universal Years, 1982–1992,* Schiffer Publishing, 1993; Albert W. McCollough, *The New Book of Buddy L Toys,* Vol. I (1991), Vol. II (1991), Greenberg Publishing; Kevin McGimpsey and Stewart Orr, *Collecting Matchbox Diecast Toys: The First Forty Years,* Major Productions Limited (England), 1989; Brian Moran, *Battery Toys,* Schiffer Publishing, 1984; Richard O'Brien, *Collecting Toys: A Collectors Identification and Value Guide, 6th Edition,* Books Americana, 1993; Richard O'Brien, *The Story of American Toys,* Abbeville Press, 1990; Bob Parker, *Hot Wheels: A Collector's Guide,* Schiffer Publishing, 1993; Maxine A. Pinsky, *Greenberg's Guide to Marx Toys,* Vol. I (1988), Vol. II (1990), Greenberg Publishing Co.; David Pressland, *The Art of the Tin Toy,* New Cavendish Books, 1976; David Pressland, *The Book of Penny Toys,* New Cavendish Books, 1991; David Richter, *Collector's Guide To Tootsietoys,* Collector Books, 1991; Harry L. Rinker, *Collector's Guide To Toys, Games, And Puzzles,* Wallace-Homestead, 1991; Nancy Schiffer, *Matchbox Toys,* Schiffer Publishing, 1983; Martyn L. Schorr, *The Guide To Mechanical Toy Collecting,* Performance Media, 1979; Robin Langley Sommer, *I Had One Of Those: Toys Of Our Generation,* Crescent Books, 1992; Bruce and Diane Stoneback, *Matchbox Toys: A Guide To Selecting, Collecting, and Enjoying New and Vintage Models,* Chartwell Books, 1993; Jack Tempest, *Post-War Tin Toys: A Collector's Guide,* Wallace-Homestead, 1991; Toyshop Magazine, *Toyshop 1994 Annual, Second Edition,* Krause Publications, 1993; Tom Tumbusch, *Tomart's Price Guide To Hot Wheels,* To-mart Publications, 1993; Carol Turpen, *Baby Boomer Toys and Collectibles,* Schiffer Publishing, 1993; Peter Viemeister, *Micro Cars,* Hamilton's, 1982; Gerhard G. Walter, *Metal Toys from Nuremberg: The Unique Mechanical Toys of the Firm of Georg Kellermann & Co. of Nuremberg 1910–1979,* Schiffer Publishing, 1992; Blair Whitton, *Paper Toys of The World,* Hobby House Press, 1986; Blair Whitton, *The Knopf Collector's Guide to American Antiques: Toys,* Alfred A. Knopf, 1984.

Periodicals: *Antique Toy World,* PO Box 34509, Chicago, IL 60634; *Canadian Toy Mania,* PO Box 489, Rocanville, Saskatchewan, Canada SOA 3LO; *Collectible Toys & Values,* Attic Books, 15 Danbury Rd., Ridgefield, CT 06877; *Collecting Toys,* 21027 Crossroads Circle, Waukesha, WI 53187; *Die Cast & Tin Toy Report,* PO Box 301, Easton, CT 06612; *Model & Toy Collector Magazine,* 137 Casterton Ave., Akron, OH 44303-1552; *Plastic Figure & Playset Collector,* PO Box 1335, La Crosse, WI 54602-1355; *Plastic Warrior,* 905 Harrison St., Allentown, PA 18103; *Robot World & Price Guide,* PO Box 184, Lenox Hill Station, New York, NY 10021; *The Plane News,* PO Box 845, Greenwich, CT 06836; *Toybox Magazine,* 8393 E. Holly Rd., Holly, MI 48442; *Toy Collector & Price Guide,* 700 E. State St., Iola, WI 54990; *Toy Collector Marketplace,* 1550 Territorial Rd., Benton Harbor, MI 49022; *Toy Gun Collectors of America Newsletter,* 312 Starling Way, Anaheim, CA 92807; *Toy Shop,* 700 East State Street, Iola, WI 54990; *Toy Trucker & Contractor,* HC 2, Box 5, LaMoure, ND 58458; *US Toy Collector Magazine,* PO Box 4244, Missoula, MT 59806; *Yo-Yo Times,* PO Box 1519, Herndon, VA 22070.

Collectors' Clubs: AC Gilbert Heritage Society, 594 Front St., Marion, MA 02738; American Game Collectors Assoc., 49 Brooks Ave., Lewiston, ME 04240; American International Matchbox Collectors & Exchange Club, 532 Chestnut St., Lynn, MA 01904; Antique Engine, Tractor & Toy Club, Inc., 5731 Paradise Rd, Slatington, PA 18080; Antique Toy Collectors of America, 13th Floor, Two Wall Street, New York, NY 10005; Capitol Miniature Auto Collectors Club, 10207 Greenacres Dr., Silver Spring, MD 20903-1402; Diecast Exchange Club, PO Box 1066, Pineallas Park, FL 34665; Ertl Collectors Club, Highways 136 & 120, Dyersville, IA 52040; Farm Toy Collectors Club, PO Box 38, Boxholm, IA 50040; Majorette Diecast Toy Collectors Assoc., 13447 NW Albany Ave., Bend, OR 97701-3160; Matchbox Collectors Club, PO Box 287, Durham, CT 06422; Matchbox International Collectors Assoc, 574 Canewood Crescent, Waterloo, Ontario, Canada N2L 5P6; Matchbox USA, 62 Saw Mill Rd., Durham, CT 06422; New Moon Matchbox and Label Club, 425 East 51st St., New York, NY 10022; San Francisco Bay Brooklin Club, PO Box 61018, Palo Alto, CA 94306; Schoenhut Collectors Club, 45 Louis Ave., West Seneca, NY 14224; Southern California Toy Collectors Club, Suite 300, 1760 Termino, Long Beach, CA 90804.

Museums: American Museum of Automobile Miniatures, Andover, MA; Eugene Field House & Toy Museum, St. Louis, MO; Evanston Historical Society, Evanston, IL 60201; Forbes Magazine Collection, New York, NY; Hobby City Doll & Toy Museum, Anaheim, CA; Matchbox & Lesney Toy Museum, Durham, CT; Matchbox Road Museum, Newfield, NJ; Museum of the City of New York, New York, NY; Smithsonian Institution, Washington, DC; Spinning Top Exploratory Museum, Burlington, WI; Margaret Woodbury Strong Museum, Rochester, NY; Toy & Miniature Museum of Kansas City, Kansas City, MO; Toy Museum of Atlanta, Atlanta, GA; Washington Dolls' House & Toy Museum; Western Reserved Historical Society, Cleveland, OH.

Additional Listings: Characters, Disneyana, Dolls, and Schoenhut. Also see *Warman's Americana & Collectibles* for more examples.

American National Pumper, pedal car fire truck, equipped with simulated dial dashboard, hand brake, bell, and ladders, c1928, 60″ l, 32″ h, $16,500.00. Photograph courtesy of James D. Julia, Inc.

Alps, Japan
Happy Car, friction, tin, plaid bucket seats, orig box, 8½″ l **125.00**
Strutting Peacock, windup, litho tin, spreads and lifts tail feathers and walks, 7″ l **235.00**
Arcade
Ambulance, cast iron, blue, "City Ambulance" on side, orig sticker, 5¾″ l, 2½″ h **375.00**
Chevrolet Utility Stake Truck, black, gray stake body, driver, 8¾″ l, 4″ h   **400.00**
Convertible, cast iron, painted, black, white trim, mesh grill, 6¾″ l **700.00**
Fire Truck, cast iron, molded driver and standing fireman, nickel plated grill and bumper, rubber tires, 9½″ l **275.00**
Greyhound Bus, 8¾″ l, 2¾″ h **200.00**
Ice Truck, cast iron, blue, nickel plated grill, rubber tires, 6⅝″ l, 3¼″ h **350.00**

Model T Coupe, cast iron, high roof, 6½″ l **950.00**
Railroad Wrecker, cast iron, painted, red wheels, brown platform **300.00**
Sedan, cast iron, painted, rubber tires, nickel plated grill, 6½″ l **220.00**
Showboat, cast iron and metal, red decks, green hull, white sides, orig label, 10½″ l **475.00**
Yellow Cab, cast iron, black highlights, 8″ l, 3⅝″ h **775.00**
Bandai, Japan
Mercedes Benz 300SL, friction, pressed tin, 8″ l **140.00**
Mercury with Siren, friction, tin, orig box, 6½″ l **85.00**
Monkey Cycle, windup, litho tin, lifts and rings bell, eyes pop in and out, attached vinyl flag, orig box, 5″ l . .   **225.00**
Bergmann, Althof
Camel, bell toy, painted tin, off set wheel action, 1875–85, 9¼″ l **1,650.00**
Patriotic Boy, hoop toy, windup, cloth dressed painted doll with tinplate arms and legs, holding 13 star American flag, encased within two 7″ d wheels, 9″ h **7,150.00**
Bing
Convertible Coupe, windup, pressed tin, painted, black, litho tin driver, 6¼″ l **375.00**
Monoplane, compressed air engine, free flight, silver body, wire framework wings, tail, and wheel supports, fabric cov wings and tail, c1912, 51½″ l **5,500.00**
Bonnet, Victor, France, bell toy, seated clown rings bell, c1925, 10″ h **1,045.00**
Buddy L, Fast Delivery Truck, No. 3313, pressed steel, yellow, chrome grill, black rubber tires, red "Shell" decals, marked "Buddy L–East Moline," orig box, 13″ l **145.00**
Chein
Drum Major, windup, litho tin, multicolored, 9″ h **150.00**
Ferris Wheel, windup, litho tin, minor rust on base int., 16½″ h **145.00**
Mechanical Drummer, No. 109, windup, litho tin, multicolored, orig box **230.00**
Musical Roundabout, lever action, litho tin, 10¼″ h **225.00**
Roller Coaster, windup, litho tin, colorful, two cars, 19½″ l **185.00**
Three Little Pigs Washer, litho tin and wood, multicolored, slight pitting and scratches, 8″ h **125.00**
Cragston, battery operated
Lady Pup Tending Her Garden, litho tin and cloth, bends forward and waters flower, orig box, 7 x 8″ **385.00**

Mr. Fox the Magician Blowing Magical Bubbles, fox wearing glasses, green cape, red coat, rect base, 7¼" l, 9½" h **200.00**

Dayton Toy, Son–ny Parcel Post Truck, painted steel, c1926, 26¼" l, 11½" h **275.00**

Distler, J, Germany

Fire Ladder Truck, windup, litho tin, red, yellow and black trim, 9½" l . . **150.00**

Limousine, windup, litho tin, dark blue, pastel blue trim, light green spoked wheels, uniformed chauffeur, front lamps, glazed front windscreen, opening rear doors, c1920, 12" l . . **1,100.00**

Fallows, elephant, bell toy, painted tin, flexible mohair trunk, some chipping, slight rust, Nov 14, 1882 patent date, 6½" l **465.00**

Fischer, Germany, Saloon Car, penny toy, litho tin, chauffeur driver, 4" l . . . **100.00**

Freidag, dump truck, cast iron, molded driver, red cab, orange dump, 8" l, 3⅝" h **700.00**

Girard Toys, Whiz Sky Fighter, windup, tin, stenciled, red, yellow, gold, and blue, minor scratches, 9" l **350.00**

lamps, hp driver, pressed tin wheels, c1910, 7½" l **5,150.00**

Hubley

Borden's Milk Truck, cast iron, 5¾" l, 3⅜" h **450.00**

Dumb Truck, #471, cast iron, MIB . **75.00**

Fire Pumper, cast iron, c1919, 11¾" l, 7" h **275.00**

Huber Tractor, cast iron, painted, dark green, red wheels, gold lettering . . **600.00**

Indian Motorcycle, cast iron, painted, nickel plated engine, green, dark blue rider, partial orig label, 9" l . . . **625.00**

P–38 Fighter, No. 881, diecast metal, red, manual spinning propeller, landing gear wheels, orig box **275.00**

Racer, painted, green, nickel plated driver, 6⅜" l **130.00**

Ideal

Globemaster, litho tin and plastic, transport plane, plastic vehicles and figures, orig box, 20" l box. **70.00**

Robert The Robot, battery operated, remote control, plastic, hands grasp objects, walks, talks, arms swing, and head lights up, orig box, c1955, 14" h. **250.00**

Germany, Mickey Mouse Hurdy Gurdy, litho tin, windup, 6" l, 3" w, 8" h, $18,700.00. Photograph courtesy of James D. Julia, Inc.

Irwin, Mechanical Walking Bear, #622, windup, plastic, 5¼" l, 4½" h, orig box, $175.00.

Gunthermann

Horseless Carriage, windup, litho tin, green and black, red and wood grained seats, driver, spoked wheels with white rubber tires, c1900, 5½" l **1,575.00**

Limousine, Georgian Window, windup, litho tin, cream and brown, red trim, adjustable front wheels, hinged rear doors, roof rack, front

Kellerman, Germany, Policeman Motor- cycle, penny toy, litho tin, 3" l **750.00**

Kenton, fire chief car, cast iron, molded driver, orig red paint, 5½" l, 2½" h. . . **775.00**

Lehmann, tin

Alabama Coon Jigger, windup, litho, blue, red, and yellow, orig box, 10" h **700.00**

Climbing Miller, weight driven, hp, green, red, and yellow, orig box, 16½" h **375.00**

Daredevil, windup, man driving red cart pulled by zebra, 7″ l, 4½″ h. . . . **325.00**

New Century Cycle, windup, litho, painted, missing steering rod, 5″ l . **230.00**

Nu–Nu, windup, litho and painted, blue, white, and gold, orig box, 4½″ l. **1,600.00**

Paddy and His Pig, windup, hp, red, brown, and gray, 6″ l **575.00**

Wild West Bucking Bronco, windup, hp and stenciled, orig box, 7½″ h. . **850.00**

Zeppelin, windup, litho tin, marked "EPL–1," c1907, 8″ l. **425.00**

Zikra, windup, driver moves up and down on cart, bucking zebra, orig box. **1,100.00**

Linemar

Donald Duck Tricycle, windup, litho tin, celluloid Donald, bell ringing action, orig box **575.00**

Jungle Trio, battery operated, litho tin, vinyl, and rubber, two monkeys, one beats drum, other with cymbals, elephant blows whistle with trunk, orig box, 8″ h **1,000.00**

Minnie Mouse Rocker, windup, litho tin, Minnie sitting on rocker knitting, rubber ears, 7″ h **410.00**

Pluto Drum Major, windup, litho tin, yellow–orange, green, and red, 6½″ h **110.00**

Popeye on Skates, windup, litho tin **725.00**

Running Pluto, friction, litho tin, yellow, red, and black, missing ears and tail, orig box, 4¼″ l **185.00**

Siren 1902 Ford Jalopy, friction, litho tin, convertible with swing down windshield, two celluloid riders, orig box, 8¼″ l **180.00**

Sky–View Taxi, friction, litho tin, siren, orig box, 5″ l **125.00**

Super Susie, battery operated, plush bear with litho tin grocery checkout, orig box, 5 x 9″. **700.00**

Tramp, friction, litho tin, tan and green, orig box, 3¾″ h **210.00**

Walking Gorilla, battery operated, plush and litho tin, eyes light, mouth opens, orig box, 7½″ h **475.00**

Lionel, Peter Rabbit Handcar, windup, steel, composition figure and basket, painted, 10″ l. **300.00**

Lutz, Germany

Horse, tin, brown, painted mane, tail, eyes, and bridle, separate tin collar, rect wheeled base with small cast iron wheels, c1880, 7½″ h. **3,350.00**

Open Carriage, ornate chassis and wheels, yellow, c1875, 17″ l **700.00**

Marklin

Hansom Cab, litho tin, dark blue, orange trim, black roof with hinged hatch, mustard coachman's seat, hinged folding doors, red lined yellow spoked wheels, etched glass windows, c1900, 17″ l. **4,350.00**

Ocean Liner, orig paint, 37″ l, 14″ h **12,000.00**

Mamod, toy steam engine, alcohol burner, red base, England, $40.00.

Marx

Allstate Service Truck, friction, litho tin, crank operated winch, plain box, 4¾″ l. **65.00**

Amos 'N Andy Fresh Air Taxi, windup, litho tin, orange and black car, dressed figures, orig box, 8″ l **1,300.00**

Auto Transport, pressed steel, red, blue, and yellow, two plastic cars, orig box, 13¾″ l **140.00**

Balking Mule, windup, tin, clown in cart pulled by donkey, moves back and forth and up and down, 7¾″ l, 5½″ h **200.00**

B. O. Plenty, windup, litho tin, multicolored, 8¾″ h. **145.00**

Charlie McCarthy, windup, litho tin, black and white, head turns as car moves, 7″ l **350.00**

Climbing Fireman, windup, litho tin, multicolored, orig box, 22″ h **225.00**

Donald Duck Duet, litho tin, multicolored, replaced drumsticks, 11″ h. . **240.00**

Dumbo, windup, litho tin, multicolored, orig box, 4½″ h **375.00**

Ferdinand The Bull, windup, vibrating motion, tail spins, rubber horns, 6″ l. **445.00**

Figaro, windup, litho tin, black, white, orange, and yellow, replaced ears, 5″ l. **110.00**

George The Drummer Boy, windup, litho tin, multicolored, orig box, 9¼″ h **290.00**

Harold Lloyd Walker, windup, litho tin, multicolored, 11" h 150.00

Home Dairy Truck, red, white, blue, and yellow, orig box, 11" l 160.00

Hopalong Cassidy Rocker, windup, litho tin, multicolored, minor scratches, 10" h. 325.00

Joe Penner, windup, litho tin, multicolored, 8" h 320.00

Jumping Jeep, windup, litho tin, green and yellow, 6" l 110.00

Leaping Lizzie, windup, litho tin, black and white lettering, minor wear, 7" l 240.00

Magic Barn and Tractor, windup, litho tin, multicolored, orig box, 10½" l. . 250.00

Main Street, windup, litho tin, multicolored, minor scratches, orig box, 24" l 450.00

Marine Corps Truck, gray–green, black chassis, plastic marine figures, orig box, 13¼" l 150.00

Mickey Jack–in–the–Box, black and white Mickey with pie cut eyes and ruffled collar, box with paper litho waving Minnie illus, missing lid, 12" h 330.00

Mickey Mouse Express, windup, multicolored, minor scratches, 9¼" lw 250.00

Mickey's Delivery, friction, cart and figure, painted celluloid head, 6" l. . 450.00

Midget Racer, windup, litho tin, blue, 5" l 160.00

Monkey Cyclist, windup, crank lever, cycle moves forward, cardboard arms, orig box, 6 x 6" 225.00

Moon Mullins and Kayo Handcar, windup, steel and litho tin, painted, orig box, 6½" l 600.00

Mortimer Snerd, windup, litho tin, multicolored, 8¾" h 250.00

Mr. Mercury Robot, battery operated, litho tin, plastic arms and ears, grasps objects, orig box, 12" h. . . . 1,200.00

Northwest Airplane, battery operated, litho tin and plastic, multicolored, orig box, 15" l 110.00

Old Jalopy, windup, litho tin, multicolored, 7" l. 170.00

Pinocchio The Acrobat, windup, litho tin, multicolored, minor scratches and wear, 16½" h. 210.00

Rookie Cop Motorcycle, windup, cycle moves in circles, siren noise, orig box, 8½" l 385.00

Rookie Pilot, windup, litho tin, multicolored, minor scratches, 7½" l . . . 450.00

Sheriff Sam Whoopee Car, windup, litho tin and plastic, red and white, orig box, 6" l 110.00

Siren Police Patrol, windup, pressed steel, painted and stenciled, green and yellow, electric headlights, 15" l 110.00

Tom Corbett Space Cadet Rocketship, windup, engine sound and sparks, c1940, 12" l 235.00

Toy Town Express, multicolored, 12" l 185.00

Tractor Trailer, windup, litho tin, multicolored, orig box, 16" l 185.00

Tricky Taxi on Busy Street, windup, taxi scoots around busy city life illus base, orig box, 1930s, 6 x 10" base, 4½" l taxi. 550.00

Whee–Whiz Auto Racer, windup, dish shape track, four cars, up and down rocking motion, c1925, 13" d 475.00

Whoopee Car, windup, litho tin, multicolored, 8½" l 280.00

WWI Doughboy Tank, windup, soldier pops up firing gun, swivel machine gun, 1930s, 9½" l 245.00

Meier, J P, penny toy, litho tin

Cab, blue, red wheels, 4⅝" l 230.00

Carousel, windup, red canopy, green base, 2¾" h. 700.00

Horsedrawn ambulance, penny toy, mounted soldier, 4" l 435.00

Landau Carriage, windup, two horses, 5" l 400.00

Locomotive, green, red, and gray, 2¾" l 140.00

Sailboat, life preserver printed with "Hamburg," missing wheeled platform, 3" l 325.00

Truck, yellow ladder, 3¼" l 275.00

Metalcraft

Coke Truck, pressed steel, painted and stenciled, red and yellow, ten miniature glass Coke bottles, 11" l 350.00

Delivery Truck, green, black cab, metal wheels, marked "Hardy's Salts, St. Louis" on side, 8¼" l, 5¼" h 900.00

Shell Motor Oil Stake Truck, pressed steel, painted, red and yellow, 12¼" l 450.00

Spirit of St. Louis Hanger, #890, orig box and stencils. 240.00

Peter Puppet Playthings, marionette

Clarabelle, composition, painted, cloth costume, red, white, and blue, 14" h. 160.00

Flub–A–Dub, composition and cloth, multicolored, slight crazing, 12" l . . 100.00

Indian, composition and cloth, painted, orig box, 13" h. 35.00

Schoenhut, upright piano and bench, 1920s, 23¾" h, 23½" l 130.00

Schuco, windup, painted tin

Boy, drinks beer, holds blue ceramic mug, brown suit, green hat, 5" h . . 125.00

Mercedes 190SL, No. 2095, plastic
int., orig key and box, 8½" l **695.00**
Monkey, plays violin, green shirt, red
pants, brown hair, 4¼" h. **100.00**
Synchromatic 5700 Packard Hawk
Convertible, battery operated,
green, red int., orig box, 10½" l . . . **880.00**
Steelcraft
Army Scout Plane, 22" l **250.00**
Lockheed Sirius Airplane, pressed
steel, white baked enamel body,
red wings, rubber tires, 21½" l,
21¾" w **1,100.00**
U S Mail Airplane, pressed steel, three
motors, orig canvas mailbag, 23½"
l, 26½" w. **550.00**
Strauss, Ferdinand
Flying Zeppelin, windup, aluminum,
orig box, 16" l **375.00**
Ham and Sam Band, windup, litho tin,
diecut piano legs, 1921–22 . . . . . . **660.00**
Inter–State Bus, windup, litho tin,
green and yellow, 10" l **500.00**
Jitney Bus, windup, litho tin, green
and yellow, missing radiator cap,
9½" l **300.00**
Santee Claus, windup, litho tin, Santa,
sleigh, and reindeer, 11" l **1,800.00**
Tombo Coon Jigger, windup, litho tin,
multicolored, minor scratches, 10"
h **350.00**
Tootsietoy
Aces of the Air, cast metal, painted,
two seaplanes and one biplane, orig
box, 4" l. **475.00**
Buck Rogers Flash Blast Attack Ship,
No. 1033, diecast, white and red,
emb name, orig box, 4½" l **400.00**
Unique Art
Dog Patch Band, windup, brightly colored, missing Mammy's baton, 9"
h **400.00**
G I Joe Jouncing Jeep, windup, or-
ange, green, and yellow, 7" l **140.00**
Jazzbo Jim, windup, black man play-
ing banjo, dancing on rooftop, 9½"
h **450.00**
Kiddie Cyclist, windup, litho tin, multicolored, pitting and scratches, 9" h **325.00**
Li'l Abner Band, windup, Mammy sitting on piano, Pappy plays drums,
Daisy plays piano, Abner dances,
orig box. **695.00**
Unknown Maker
Germany
Black Dancer, penny toy, litho tin,
animated, figure moves when
platform handle is turned, early
20th C, 3⅝" h **660.00**
Boy pulling girl in two wheeled cart,
windup, litho and painted tin,
some paint loss, c1900, 7½" l . . **715.00**

Chinaman seated on stump,
windup, tin, musical, plays mandolin, eyes and tongue move,
8¼" h **440.00**
Dux Astroman, battery operated,
plastic, bends over, arms move,
and chest flashes, orig box, 12"
h. **1,200.00**
Girl in stroller, penny toy, litho tin,
early 20th C, 2¾" h. **350.00**
Porter, penny toy, pushes trunk, 3
x 3". **440.00**
Wheelbarrow, penny toy, litho tin,
early 20th C, 3⅝" l **10.00**
Japan
Clown Unicyclist, windup, clown on
unicyle, moves legs and arms, 6"
h. **230.00**
Happy Life, windup, celluloid girl on
rocking chair, duck, and umbrella, carnival illus base, 9½" h,
4 x 6" base. **300.00**
Pioneer Spirit, friction, litho tin, figure driving covered wagon with
team of horses, two battery op-
erated lanterns, 11" l. **145.00**
Texas Sporting Convertible, friction,
green, siren, orig box, 1950s, 6" l. **110.00**
Watrous, bell toy, Army and Navy, cast
iron, nickel finish, gold painted soldier,
silver painted sailor, Spanish American War period, slight rust, c1901,
8¾" l **495.00**
Wolverine, windup, litho tin
Drum Major, No. 27, multicolored,
13¾" h **130.00**
Zilotone, painted, six orig discs, minor
paint chips, 7" h. **575.00**
Wyandotte, Fire Dept Car, spring–wind
mechanism, pressed steel, painted,
13" l. **475.00**

TRAINS, TOY

History: Railroading has always been an important part of childhood, largely because of the romance associated with the railroad and the emphasis on toy trains.

The first toy trains were cast iron and tin; windup
motors added movement. The Golden Age of toy
trains was 1920 to 1955, when electric-powered
units were available and names such as Ives,
American Flyer, and Lionel were household words.
The construction of the rolling stock was of high
quality. The advent of plastic in the late 1950s lessened this quality considerably.

Toy trains were designated by a model scale or
gauge. The most popular are HO, N, O, and standard. Narrow gauge was a response to the modern
capacity to miniaturize. Its popularity has lessened
in the last few years.

Condition of trains is critical. Items in fair condition (scratched, chipped, dented, rusted, or warped) and below generally have little value to a collector. Restoration is accepted, provided it is done accurately. It may enhance the price one or two grades. Prices listed below are for very good to mint condition unless noted.

References: Paul V. Ambrose, *Greenberg's Guide To Lionel Trains, 1945–1969, Volume III*, Greenberg Publishing, 1990; Susan and Al Bagdade, *Collector's Guide To American Toy Trains*, Wallace-Homestead, 1990; John O. Bradshaw, *Greenberg's Guide To Kusan Trains*, Greenberg Publishing, 1987; Pierce Carlson, *Collecting Toy Trains*, Pincushion Press, 1993; W. G. Claytor, P. Doyle, and C. McKenney, *Greenberg's Guide To Early American Toy Trains*, Greenberg Publishing, 1993; Joe Deger, *Greenberg's Guide To American Flyer S Gauge*, Vol. I, Fourth Ed. (1991), Vol. II (1991), Vol. III (1992), Greenberg Publishing; Richard Friz, *The Official Identification And Price Guide To Toy Trains*, House of Collectibles, 1990; Bruce Greenberg, *Greenberg's Guide to Ives Trains, 1901–1932*, Vol. I: I and Wide Gauge (1991) and Vol. II: O Gauge (1992), Greenberg Publishing; Bruce Greenberg, (edited by Christian F. Rohlfing), *Greenberg's Guide To Lionel Trains: 1901–1942*, Vol. 1 (1988), Vol. 2 (1988), Greenberg Publishing; Bruce Greenberg *Greenberg's Guide To Lionel Trains: 1945–1969*, Vol. 1: Eighth Edition (1992), Vol. 2: Second Edition (1993), Greenberg Publishing; Greenberg Publishing Co., *Greenberg's Lionel Catalogues, Volume V: 1955–1960*, Greenberg Publishing, 1992; Greenberg Publishing, *Greenberg's Marx Train Catalogues: 1938–1975*, Greenberg Publishing, 1992; George Horan and Vincent Rosa, *Greenberg's Guide To Lionel HO 1957–1966, Vol. I, Second Edition*, Greenberg Publishing, 1993; John Hubbard, *The Story of Williams Electric Trains*, Greenberg Publishing Co., 1987; Steven H. Kimball, *Greenberg's Guide To American Flyer Prewar O Gauge*, Greenberg Publishing, 1987; Roland La Voie, *Greenberg's Guide To Lionel Trains, 1970–1991, Volume I* (1991), *Volume II* (1992), Greenberg Publishing Co.; Lionel Book Committee, *Lionel Trains: Standard Of The World, 1900–1943*, Train Collectors Association, 1989; Dallas J. Mallerich III, *Greenberg's American Toy Trains: From 1900 With Current Values*, Greenberg Publishing, 1990; Dallas J. Mallerich, III, *Greenberg's Guide to Athearn Trains*, Greenberg Publishing, 1987; Eric J. Matzke, *Greenberg's Guide To Marx Trains, Volume 1* (1989), *Volume II* (1990), Greenberg Publishing Co.; Robert P. Monaghan, *Greenberg's Guide to Markin OO/HO*, Greenberg Publishing, 1989; Richard O'Brien, *Collecting Toy Trains: An Identification and Value Guide, No. 3*, Books Americana, 1991; John R. Ottley, *Greenberg's Guide To LGB Trains*, Greenberg Publishing, 1989; Alan R. Schuweiler, *Greenberg's Guide to American Flyer, Wide Gauge*, Greenberg Publishing, 1989; John D. Spanagel,

Greenberg's Guide to Varney Trains, Greenberg Publishing, 1991; Robert C. Whitacre, *Greenberg's Guide To Marx Trains Sets, Volume III*, Greenberg Publishing, 1992.

Note: Greenberg Publishing Company (7566 Main Street, Sykesville, MD 21784) is the leading publisher of toy train literature. Anyone interested in the subject should write for a catalog and ask to be put on its mailing list.

Periodicals: *Classic Toy Trains*, 21027 Crossroads Cir., PO Box 1612, Waukesha, WI 53187; *Lionel Collector Series Marketmaker*, Trainmaster, PO Box 1499, Gainsville, FL 32602.

Collectors' Clubs: American Flyer Collectors Club, PO Box 13269, Pittsburgh, PH 15234; Lionel Collectors Club of America, PO Box 479, LaSalle, IL 61301; Lionel Operating Train Society, 18 Eland Ct., Fairfield, OH 45014; Marklin Club–North America, PO Box 51559, New Berline, WI 53151-0559; Marklin Digital Special Interest Group, PO Box 51319, New Berlin, WI 53151-0319; The National Model Railroad Assoc., 4121 Cromwell Road, Chattanooga, TN 37421; The Toy Train Operating Society, Inc., Suite 308, 25 West Walnut Street, Pasadena, CA 91103; Train Collector's Assoc., PO Box 248, Strasburg, PA 17579.

Museum: Toy Train Museum of the Train Collectors Assoc., Strasburg, PA 17579.

Additional Listings: See *Warman's Americana & Collectibles* for more examples.

Ives, set #691, The Ives Railway Lines, motor #3250, orig box, $360.00. Photograph courtesy of Bider's Antiques, Inc.

AMERICAN FLYER

Car
910 Gilbert Chemicals Tank Car,
small paint chip on end and dome — **180.00**
3007 gondola, litho, O gauge . . . . — **30.00**
23743 track maintenance car, S
gauge, orig box . . . . — **160.00**
24026 Central of Georgia, box, S
gauge, minor rubs on catwalk
ends. — **100.00**
Locomotive
3110, AFL rubber stamped tender,
nickel trim, O gauge . . . . — **90.00**
21910, 21910–1, and 21910–2, SF
PA ABA, S gauge, minor chips,
price for set of three . . . . — **950.00**
Set
466 Comet PA A unit, 960 combine,
two 962 vista domes, 963 observation, knuckle coupler, blue
stripes, S gauge, AFL decal missing, two replaced steps, paint
retouches . . . . — **230.00**
470 Santa Fe A unit, 471B unit, 473
dummy A, 961 coach, two 962 vista
domes, 963 observation, minor
chips, rubs, and wear to decals,
knuckle coupler, red stripes, S
gauge. — **1,150.00**
499 New Haven Mainline Electric, 921
CB & Q hopper, 911 C & O gondola,
920 Southern gondola, 958 Mobil
Gas tanker, 985 B & M box car, 935
BM caboose, S gauge, decals
faded, horn missing, minor wear . . — **250.00**
49602 Northern Pacific PA ABA, com-
bine, coach, pair vista domes, observation, orig boxes and set box,
S gauge . . . . — **1,000.00**

IVES

Car
130 combine, litho, red and black
striped roof, flaking. . . . . — **1,200.00**
184 club car, olive, S gauge, c1927 — **100.00**
Locomotive
25 locomotive and tender, 4 bands,
missing bell and harp, black and
white. . . . . — **550.00**
3200, green, gold, and red trim, paint
flaking on roof . . . . — **400.00**
Set
3238 locomotive, 60 baggage, 61
Yale, 62 Harvard, emb lettering,
black, red, and gold trim, red and
yellow litho, gray and yellow roofs . — **750.00**
3250 locomotive, 64 Union Line box
car, 66 tank car, 65 stock car, 67
caboose, brown, yellow litho, gray

roof, weak rubber stamping, wheels
oxidized . . . . — **350.00**

LIONEL

Car
211 lumber car, orig box missing one
end, S gauge. . . . . — **130.00**
217 caboose, red, orig box, S gauge — **1,100.00**
219 derrick, yellow cab, pea green
boom, red roof, S gauge. . . . . — **400.00**
220 floodlight car, green, nickel trim,
orig box, S gauge. . . . . — **775.00**
6820 flat, Little John helicopter, repro
tips, orig bracket . . . . — **150.00**
Locomotive
238E PA Torpedo, gunmetal, 265W
tender, postwar trucks, O gauge . . — **260.00**
400E locomotive, gunmetal, frame
warped and repaired, rewheeled,
400T tender, S gauge. . . . . — **900.00**
2035 locomotive, 6466W tender . . — **160.00**
2356 Southern ABA, power A with orig
box, small nick in B unit, O gauge . — **725.00**
Set
385E locomotive, 385W tender, gunmetal, 1767 baggage, 1766 pullman, 1768 observation, red and
maroon, some plastic window in-
serts missing, S gauge . . . . — **1,300.00**
1835E locomotive, 1835W tender,
310 baggage, 309 pullman, 312 observation, blue and silver, bend in
smokestack, missing whistle, slight
bowing, S gauge . . . . — **600.00**

TRAMP ART

History: Tramp art was prevalent in the United
States from 1875 to the 1930s. Items were made
by itinerant artists who left no record of their identity. They used old cigar boxes and fruit and vegetable crates. The edges of items were chip-carved
and layered, creating the "Tramp Art" effect. Finished items usually were given an overall stain.
Today they are collected primarily as folk art.
  Reference: Helaine Fendelman, *Tramp Art: An
Itinerant's Folk Art Guide*, E. P. Dutton & Co., 1975.

Box
6″ h, two drawers, alligatored varnish
finish. . . . . — **250.00**
8″ h, drawer, sliding lid . . . . — **140.00**
9½″ l, hinged lid . . . . — **95.00**
10″ l, worn finish, white porcelain
buttons . . . . — **110.00**
13½″ l, worn maroon velvet panels,
gilded tin trim, lid mirror and int. lining missing, some edge damage . . — **115.00**
Clock, tall case, 67½″ h, 16½″ w, sea
shell and painted dec, c1915 . . . . . . — **3,500.00**

Picture Frame, chip carved, 26 x 20″, $165.00.

Frame, 17½″ h, 14″ w, laminated jigsaw
work, chip carved, double eagle crest,
old brown finish, porcelain button
trim **250.00**
Jardiniere, 13¼″ h, painted, America,
early 20th C **110.00**
Miniature, chest of drawers, 13″ h, three
drawers, porcelain pulls, old alligatored finish, back labeled "I bought
this July 2, 1955," old repairs to crest **140.00**
Table, 25″ h, 40¼″ d, pine, sunburst
pieced top, molded skirt, stepped
base, 25 x 40¼″ **550.00**

TRANSPORTATION MEMORABILIA

History: The first airlines in the United States
depended on subsidies from the government for
carrying mail for most of their income. The first
non–Post Office Department flight for mail carrying
was in 1926 between Detroit and Chicago. By 1930
there were thirty-eight domestic and five international airlines operating in the United States. A typical passenger load was ten. After World War II,
four-engine planes with a capacity of 100 or more
passengers were introduced.

The jet age was launched in the 1950s. In 1955
Capitol Airlines used British-made turboprop airliners in domestic service. In 1958 National Airlines
began domestic jet passenger service. The giant
Boeing 747 went into operation in 1970 as part of
the Pan American fleet. The Civil Aeronautics
Board, which regulates the airline industry, ended
control of routes in 1982 and fares in 1983.

Transoceanic travel falls into two distinct
periods—the era of the great clipper ships and the
era of the diesel-powered ocean liners. The later
craft reached their "Golden Age" in the period between 1900 and 1940.

An ocean liner was a city unto itself. Many had
their own printing rooms to produce a wealth of
daily memorabilia. Companies such as Cunard,
Holland-America, and others encouraged passengers to acquire souvenirs with the company logo
and ship name.

Certain ships acquired a unique mystic. The
Queen Elizabeth, *Queen Mary,* and *United States*
became symbols of elegance and style. Today the
cruise ship dominates the world of the ocean liner.

References: Aeronautica & Air Label Collectors
Club of Aerophilatelic Federation of America, *Air
Transport Label Catalog,* published by club; Stan
Baumwald, *Junior Crew Member Wings,* published
by author; Trev Davis and Fred Chan, *Airline Playing Cards: Illustrated Reference Guide, 2nd Edition,* published by authors, 1987; Lynn Johnson
and Michael O'Leary, *En Route: Label Art From
The Golden Age of Air Travel,* Chronicle Books,
1993; Karl D. Spence, *How To Identify and Price
Ocean Liner Collectibles,* published by author,
1991; Karl D. Spence, *Oceanliner Collectibles,*
published by author, 1992; Richard R. Wallin, *Commercial Aviation Collectibles: An Illustrated Price
Guide,* Wallace-Homestead, 1990.

Periodical: Airliners, PO Box 52-1238, Miami,
FL 33152-1238.

Collectors' Clubs: Aeronautica & Air Label Collectors Club, PO Box 1239, Elgin, IL 60121-1239;
National Assoc. of Timetable Collectors, 125 American Inn Rd., Villa Ridge, MO 63089; Oceanic Nav-
igation Research Society, PO Box 8005, Studio
City, CA 91608-0005; Steamship Historical Society
of America, Inc., Suite #4, 300 Ray Drive, Providence, RI 02906; The Gay Airline Club, PO Box
69A04, West Hollywood, CA 90069; Titanic Historical Society, PO Box 51053, Indian Orchard, MA
01151; Titanic International, PO Box 7007, Free-
hold, NJ 07728; Transport Ticket Society, 4 Glad-
ridge Close, Earley, Reading Berks, England RG6
2DL; World Airline Historical Society, 3381 Apple
Tree Lane, Erlanger, KY 41018.

Museums: Owls Head Transportation Museum,
Rte. 73, Box 277, Owls Head, ME; South Street
Seaport Museum, New York, NY; University of Bal-
timore, Steamship Historical Society Collection,
Baltimore, MD.

Additional Listings: See Automobilia and Railroad Items in *Warman's Antiques And Their Prices*
and Aviation Collectibles, Ocean Liner Collectibles,
and Railroad Items in *Warman's Americana & Collectibles.*

AVIATION

Booklet, *Young Wings,* Junior Literary
Guild, July 1932, 5 x 7½″, Amelia Ear-
hart photo on front cov. **15.00**

Pinback Button

Douglas Corrigan, 1¾" d, black and white portrait, red, white, and blue patriotic design border, 1930s **25.00**

Lakehurst Naval Air Station, red, white, and blue, attached ribbon and aluminum airship, 1930s. **75.00**

Lindbergh, Sept 3–4, 1927, celebration, Salt Lake City, 1½" d, blue and white. **200.00**

Wright Brothers, Home Celebration, June 17–18, 1909, Dayton, OH, ⅞" d, multicolored. **100.00**

Plate, 8½" d, Lindbergh Commemorative, full color portrait, inscribed "First to navigate the air in continuous flight from New York to Paris–1927," Limoges. **50.00**

Pocket Watch

Graf Zeppelin, 2" d, silvered metal, black and white illus on dial, rim inscription **200.00**

Lindbergh, 2" d, silvered metal, black and white dial illus, inscribed "New York To Paris Airplane Model". **200.00**

Sheet Music

Amelia Earhart, 9 x 12", Amelia Earhart's Last Flight, bluetone cov, 1939 copyright. **40.00**

Lindbergh, 9 x 12¼", Triumph Lindbergh and WE, portrait on front cov, 1927. .... **50.00**

Timetable, Graf Zeppelin, lists round trip times from Germany to Buenos Aires, South America, reverse with Graf Zeppelin air mail service adv, 1934. . **50.00**

OCEAN LINER

Ashtray, RMS Queen Elizabeth I, Cunard Line, wood ship's wheel, center color photo with glass insert. **30.00**

Belt Buckle, Queen Elizabeth II, Cunard Line, chrome plated brass, black outline of ship, red lettering. **15.00**

Booklet, St Lawrence Route to Europe, Canadian Pacific, 1930, 16 pgs, 8 x 11". **25.00**

Candy Container, 5 x 8 x 1¾", Queen Mary, Cunard Line, tin, McDowell illus, Benson's Candy **25.00**

Chair, arm, 40" h, Normandie, curvilinear form, orig needlepoint upholstery, pyramidal feet, designed by Jean Rothschild, price for pair **8,800.00**

Deck Plan, SS Hamburg, fold out, 1930 **35.00**

Dish, 5" l, Queen Mary, Cunard Line, oval, ceramic, color portrait, gold edge, Staffordshire **35.00**

Menu

Andrea Doria **15.00**

Queen Elizabeth **20.00**

Ashtray, ocean liner Normandie, French Line, porcelain, black lettering, backstamp, 4⅝" d, $125.00.

Menu Holder, 5⅝" h, Normandie, glass, frosted, molded high relief satyr mask with ram's horns entwined with grapes, enameled highlights, Lalique **425.00**

Model, 72 x 9 x 27", Titanic, mahogany, brass railing, boom cranes, funnel ladders, mahogany case with hinged doors and table. **5,940.00**

Pennant, 25½" l, SS Princess Anne, maroon, white VFC logo, cruise ship illus, c1930. .... **8.00**

Print, 13 x 10", The Sinking of the Normandie in New York Harbor, silver .. **825.00**

Stock Certificate, Cunard Steam Ship Co, Ltd. **7.50**

Toy, 25½" l, tinplate, windup, hp, beige, yellow, and red, deck cabin, four life boats, and ladder with scrollwork, Bing, Germany **135.00**

Vase, 10½" h, Normandie, silvered metal, trumpet form, sq base with beaded foot, Compagnie Generale Transatlantique monogram, imp "E Brandt" and "G Bastard" **1,100.00**

TRUNKS

History: Trunks are portable containers that clasp shut for the storage or transportation of personal possessions. Normally "trunk" means the ribbed flat or dome-top models of the second half of the 19th century. Unrestored they sell for between $50 and $150. Refinished and relined the price rises to $200 to $400, with decorators being a principal market.

Early trunks frequently were painted, stenciled, grained, or covered with wallpaper. These are collected for their folk art qualities and as such experience high prices.

Reference: Martin and Maryann Labuda, *Price & Identification Guide to Antique Trunks*, published by authors, 1980.

Flat top, tin over wood, brass banded ends, wood rim, int. shelf missing, 29¼ x 15½ x 16¼", $95.00.

Dome Top

16" l, leather covered wood, brass stud dec, bail handle	**30.00**
26½" l, 13" d, 11½" h, New England, c1830, grain painted, initials "DH" in top, lined with MA newspapers. .	**250.00**
29" w, 15½" d, 12½" h, pine, spatter design dec, mustard paint, missing latch piece.	**200.00**
32" w, 16½" d, 13¾" h, New England, early 19th C, putty dec, green and salmon, imperfections.	**525.00**

Flat Top

14 x 8", Chinese, 19th C, pigskin, red, painted Oriental maidens and landscapes within quatrefoils, brass loop handles and lock.	**125.00**
39⅓ x 19¼", rect, camphor wood, dovetailed, brass bound corners, escutcheon and shaped hasp, handles, fitted int.	**550.00**
46" l, campaign, brass bound leather, c1850	**400.00**

VALENTINES

History: Early cards were handmade, often containing both handwritten verses and hand-drawn pictures. Many cards also were hand colored and contained cutwork.

Mass production of machine-made cards featuring chromolithography began after 1840. In 1847 Esther Howland of Worcester, Massachusetts, established a company to make valentines which were hand decorated with paper lace and other materials imported from England. They had a small "H" stamped in red in the top left corner. Howland's company eventually became the New England Valentine Company (N.E.V. Co.).

George C. Whitney and his brother founded a company after the Civil War which dominated the market from the 1870s through the first decades of the twentieth century. They bought out several competitors, one of which was the New England Valentine Company.

Lace paper was invented in 1834. The 1835 to 1860 period is known as the "golden age" of lacy cards.

Embossed paper was used in England after 1800. Embossed lithographs and woodcuts developed between 1825 and 1840, with early examples being hand colored.

References: Roberta B. Etter, *Tokens Of Love*, Abbeville Press, 1990; Ruth Webb Lee, *A History of Valentines*; Frank Staff, *The Valentine And Its Origins*, out of print.

Collectors' Club: National Valentine Collectors Association, Box 1404, Santa Ana, CA 92702.

Additional Listings: See *Warman's Americana & Collectibles* for more examples.

Advisor: Evalene Pulati.

Diecut, c1865, 8 x 4¾", $25.00.

Cameo, Berlin and Jones, 5 x 7", 1860	**35.00**
Cobweb, Dobbs, 8 x 10", hand colored, 1860	**250.00**
Cutwork, Pennsylvania German, 16" sq, hand colored, 1820	**450.00**
Easel Back	
6 x 9", fancy cutwork border, 1900 .	**15.00**
8½", girl carrying red honeycomb paper parasol	**45.00**
Lacy Folder, 3 x 5"	
Hand assembled, emb, 1850	**25.00**
Howland, sgd, 1855	**35.00**
Layered	
3 x 5", lacy, N.E.V. Co, 1875	**25.00**
5", hearts and flowers, c1860	**28.00**
Mechanical, R Tuck, large paper doll, 1900	**25.00**

Pulldown, German
5 x 10", five layers, c1920	**45.00**
8 x 12", large ship, 1910	**85.00**

Sailor's, shell work
8½" w, heart and forget me not designs, octagonal double hinged case, late 19th C, minor imperfections. **1,430.00**
13¾" d, compass rose and heart patterns, octagonal double hinged case, 19th C, losses. **2,860.00**

Sheet, emb, Union soldier embracing girl, c1860. . . . . **65.00**

Stand–Up Diecut, mechanical
9" h, boy and girl	**18.50**
10" h, boy fishing	**25.00**

VALLERYSTAHL GLASS

History: Vallerystahl (Lorraine), France, has been a glass-producing center for centuries. In 1872 two major factories, Vallerystahl glassworks and Portieux glassworks, merged and produced art glass until 1898. Later, pressed glass–covered animal dishes were introduced. The factory continues operation today.

Reference: Ellen T. Schroy, *Warman's Glass,* Wallace-Homestead, 1992.

Animal Dish, Cov
Hen on nest, aqua opaque, sgd . . . **60.00**

Animal Dish, cov, blue milk glass, squirrel finial, $65.00.

Rabbit, white, frosted	**60.00**
Swan, blue milk glass	**100.00**
Box, cov, Irish Setter, frosted, inside rim with two chips	**95.00**
Butter Dish, cov, turtle, milk white, snail finial.	**100.00**
Candlesticks, pr, Baroque pattern, amber	**75.00**
Compote, 6¼" sq, blue milk glass . . .	**75.00**
Dish, cov, figural, lemon, milk white, sgd	**65.00**
Mustard, cov, swirled ribs, scalloped, blue milk glass, matching cov with slot for spoon	**25.00**
Plate, 6" d, Thistle pattern, green . . .	**65.00**
Salt, cov, hen on nest, white opal . . .	**35.00**
Sugar, cov, 5" h, Strawberry pattern, milk white, gold trim, salamander finial.	**75.00**
Tumbler, 4" h, blue	**40.00**
Vase, 10" h, ribbed body, hp wine blossoms connected by gold branches of thorns, gold accents, ruffled top	**120.00**

VAL SAINT-LAMBERT

History: Val Saint-Lambert, a 12th-century Cistercian abbey, was located during different historical periods in France, the Netherlands, and Belgium (there from 1930 to the present). In 1822 Francois Kemlin and Auguste Lelievre, along with a group of financiers, bought the abbey and opened a glassworks. In 1846 Val Saint-Lambert merged with the Société Anonyme des Manufactures de Glaces, Verres à Vitre, Cristaux et Gobeletaries. The company bought many other glassworks.

Val Saint-Lambert developed a reputation for technological progress in the glass industry. In 1879 Val Saint-Lambert became an independent company employing 4,000 workers. Val Saint-Lambert concentrated on the export market, making table glass, cut, engraved, etched, and molded pieces, and chandeliers. Some pieces were finished in other countries, such as the silver mounts added in the United States.

Val Saint-Lambert executed many special commissions for the artists of the Art Nouveau and Art Deco periods. The tradition continues. The company also made cameo-etched vases, covered boxes, and bowls. The firm celebrated its 150th anniversary in 1975.

Reference: Ellen T. Schroy, *Warman's Glass,* Wallace-Homestead, 1992.

Atomizer, Art Deco style, cut glass, transparent green, marked "Val St. Lambert for Saks," missing bulb, 6″ h, $145.00.

Atomizer, 6¾″ h, acid etched, raised floral garland, light cranberry flashing, gold washed fittings, bulb missing . . .	260.00
Bowl	
6½″ d, cov, cameo, deep cut purple florals, frosted ground, sgd "Val St Lambert".	750.00
10″ d, 4″ h, red flashed overlay, sgd	350.00
Compote, 3½″ d, amberina, ruby rim, mottled glass bowl, applied amber foot and handles	165.00
Dresser Box, colored	95.00
Finger Bowl	
4″ d, price for set of twelve	135.00
4½″ d, crystal, half pentagon cut edge, sgd.	40.00
Lamp, hanging, 10″ h, amber, cut grapevine design, late 19th C	440.00
Pitcher, clear, paneled, cut diamond design, sgd	85.00
Tumble–Up, decanter and matching tumbler, amber–crystal, marked	95.00
Vase, 8¼″ h, double gourd, opaque, taupe flowers	140.00

VAN BRIGGLE POTTERY

History: Artus Van Briggle, born in 1869, was a talented Ohio artist. He joined Rookwood in 1887 and studied in Paris under Rookwood's sponsorship from 1893 until 1896. In 1899 he moved to Colorado for his health and established his own pottery in Colorado Springs in 1901.

Van Briggle's work was influenced heavily by the Art Nouveau "school" he saw in France. He produced a great variety of matte glazed wares in this style. Colors varied.

The "AA" mark, a date, and "Van Briggle" were incised on all pieces prior to 1907 and sometimes into the 1910s and 1920s. After 1920, "Colorado Springs, Colorado" or an abbreviation was added. Dated pieces are the most desirable.

Artus died in 1904. Anne Van Briggle continued the pottery until 1912.

References: Barbara Arnest (ed.), *Van Briggle Pottery: The Early Years*, The Colorado Springs Fine Art Center, 1975; Scott N. Nelson, Lois Crouch, Euphemia Demmin, and Robert Newton, *Collector's Guide To Van Briggle Pottery*, Halldin Publishing, 1986; Richard Sasicki and Josie Fania, *Collector's Encyclopedia of Van Briggle Art Pottery*, Collector Books, 1993.

Collectors' Club: American Art Pottery Association, 125 E. Rose Ave., St. Louis, MO 63119.

Museum: Pioneer Museum, Colorado Springs, CO.

Reproduction Alert: Van Briggle pottery still is made today. These modern pieces often are confused for older examples. Among the glazes used are Moonglo (off-white), Turquoise Ming, Russet, and Midnight (black).

Vase, Lorelei, matte glaze, slight greenish cast to ext., darker green face and bust, marked "A. Van Briggle, 1898" in rust underglaze, 7⅜″ h, $1,000.00.

1901–1920

Bowl
4″ d, No. 733, turquoise blue, dated 1916. . . . . 325.00

6¼" d, 3¼" h, No. 735, flaring shoulder, interlocking and repeating ring and X—raised in relief on body, tapering to cylindrical foot, dark blue mottled matte glaze, incised mark . . 360.00
Chamberstick, 5½" h, molded leaf shape, hood over candle socket, green glaze. 115.00
Figure
   7" h, female nude holding shell, matte Persian rose glaze, incised "Van Briggle". 250.00
   10½" h, 16" l, Lady of the Lakes, matte Persian rose glaze, incised marks, crazing, int. discoloration. 300.00
Night Light, 8½" h, figural, stylized owl, bulb cavity, light refracting glass eyes, turquoise blue matte glaze, unsgd. . . 415.00
Vase
   5⅛" h, Shape 361, matte blue and green glaze, Anna Van Briggle, 1905, incised marks, minute base nicks. 360.00
   6" h
     No. 836, five stylized relief flowers at shoulder, tapering to base, caramel glaze, moss green mottling, inscribed mark and dated 1913 . 470.00
     No. 838, Persian Rose, dated 1917 . . . . 325.00
   7½" h
     No. 890, matte Persian rose glaze, incised and inscribed marks. . . . 330.00
     Shape 29, matte green glaze, Artus Van Briggle, 1902, incised marks 990.00
   9½" h, No. 754, designed by Anna Gregory Van Briggle
     Matte Persian rose glaze 330.00
     Matte turquoise glaze, incised marks 385.00
   11" h, Lorelei, matte turquoise glaze, incised marks, initialed, 1902. . . . 550.00
   13¾" h, No. 719, turquoise blue glaze, relief tulip design, inscribed marks, chip at rim, c1907 . . . . 880.00

1928–1968

Ashtray, 6½" w, Hopi Indian maiden kneeling, grinding corn, turquoise Ming glaze 75.00
Bust, 6½" h, child reading book 50.00
Lamp, Damsel of Damascus 175.00
Paperweight, 3" d, rabbit, maroon . . . 65.00
Rose Bowl, 5" d, blue–green, spade shaped leaves around top 40.00
Vase, 10¾" h, Lorelei, turquoise, baluster form, hand molded face inside rim, incised "Van Briggle/K/Colo Spgs" . . 360.00

VENETIAN GLASS

History: Venetian glass has been made on the island of Murano, near Venice, since the 13th century. Most of the wares are thin walled. Many types of decoration have been used: embedded gold dust, lacework, and applied fruits or flowers.

Reference: Ellen T. Schroy, *Warman's Glass*, Wallace-Homestead, 1992.

Reproduction Alert: Venetian glass continues to be made today.

Wine, Colonial couple in scrolled medallions, swirled stems, c1880–90, price for set of six, $200.00.

Bowl, 7½" w, 6⅛" h, deep quatreform bowl, applied quatreform rim, blue and clear internal dec, trapped air bubble squares, circles, and gold inclusions, c1950. . . . . 360.00
Centerpiece Set, two 8½" h baluster ftd ewers, 7½" d ftd compote, red and white latticino stripes with gold flecks, applied clear handles and feet, price for three pieces. 125.00
Decanter, 13" h, figural clown, bright red, yellow, black, and white, aventurine swirls, orig stopper 250.00
Figure
   8" l, rabbit, clear, cobalt blue and gold ribbon design alternating to white latticino bands 65.00
   8½" l, elephant, clear, red, amber, white, and black accents. 110.00
   15" h, bird, exotic, tomato red back, aqua and gray breast, silver dust accents, amber tail and crest. 125.00
Goblet, water, amber swirled bowls, blue beaded stems, price for set of eight . 160.00
Sherbet, 4" d, 4½" h, ruby bowl, clear stem, gold knob 195.00
Sherry, amber swirled bowls, blue beaded stems, price for set of eight . 90.00

Vase

10″ h, green ground, controlled bubbles, sgd "Barovier & Tosa" **495.00**

10½″ h, spherical, circular foot, angular handles from rim to shoulder, pink ground, white lattice pattern . . **715.00**

14½″ h, irregular gourd form, elongated neck, enclosed powders of red, royal blue, yellow, white, and turquoise, latticino patches, large star shaped murrina, gold foil inclusions, designed by Dino Martins for Oriente Series produced by Auerelian Toso, Murano, c1948 . . . . **7,763.00**

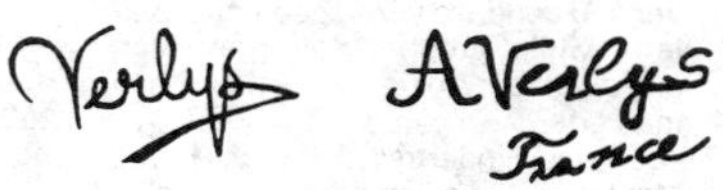

VERLYS GLASS

History: Originally made by Verlys France, established from 1931 to 1960, this Lalique-influenced art glass was produced in America by the Holophane Co., 1935–51, with select pieces by the A. H. Heisey Co., 1955–57. Holophane acquired molds and glass formulas from Verlys France and began making the art glass in 1935 at its Newark, Ohio, facility. It later leased molds to the Heisey Co. and in 1966 finally sold all molds and rights to the Fenton Art Glass Co.

The art glass was made in crystal, topaz, amber, rose, opalescent, and Directoire Blue. Heisey added turquoise. Most pieces have the relief designs etched (frosted).

Verlys France signed the glass with mold-impressed "Verlys France" and "A Verlys France." Holophane (also known as Verlys of America) signed with the mold-impressed "Verlys" and a scratched script signature of "Verlys." The A. H. Heisey Co. used only a paper label which reads "Verlys by Heisey."

Reference: Carole and Wayne McPeek, *Verlys of America Decorative Glass, 1935–1951,* published by authors, 1972, Revised Edition, 1992.

Advisor: Wayne McPeek.

Ashtray, Rose, amber frosted, 4⅛″ d, ⅝″ h, center rose, script sgd **160.00**

Bookend, Girl and Deer, clear frosted, 6½ x 3⅛ x 5¼″, girl kneeling with arm around deer, script sgd **650.00**

Bowl

Americana, clear frosted, 12¾″ l, 4⅝″ h, oval, spread wing eagle, four stars, script sgd, artist sgd "Carl Schmitz" **1,100.00**

Birds, dusty rose frosted, 11⅝″ d, 2¼″ h, birds and bees, mold sgd "Verlys" **400.00**

Cupidon, clear frosted, 6″ d, 2″ h, cupid with bow and arrow, script sgd. **125.00**

Flowers, opalescent frosted, 8¼″ w, 4¼″ h, six sided, flowers and border panels, script sgd. **450.00**

Girl–Lamb–Ewe, clear frosted, 13⅛″ d, high relief, script sgd, artist sgd and dated "Carl Schmitz, 1940". . . **650.00**

Moderne, clear frosted, 12½″ l, 9″ w, 2¾″ h, rect, Chinese floral design in bottom, script sgd. **400.00**

Orchid, opalescent frosted, 14″ d, 1⅝″ h, three orchids, mold sgd "Verlys" **455.00**

Poissons, Directoire blue frosted, 19¼″ l, 7⅞″ w, 3¾″ h, oval, high relief fish, tails forming handles, mold sgd "Verlys" **850.00**

Thistle, turquoise by Heisey, frosted, 8⅝″ d, 2⅞″ h, allover thistle flower pattern, not sgd **400.00**

Candlesticks, pr, 3½″ h, 2⅜″ h, Americana, three eagles form stick, script sgd **550.00**

Plaque

Christ, clear frosted, 7½ x 3½ x ⅞″, crucifix, wood base, script sgd. . . . **600.00**

St Theresa, clear frosted, 5¼ x 3¼ x ⅞″, profile of St Theresa holding roses and crucifix, script sgd. **500.00**

Vase

Alpine Thistle, topaz frosted, 8⅜″ h, 9″ d, flared top, high relief alpine thistle flower, mold sgd "Verlys" **800.00**

Fleur de Chine, clear frosted, 11¼″ h, 6″ d, intaglio Chinese man, woman, tree, and bush, script sgd "Verlys," artist sgd "Carl Schmitz". **650.00**

Gems, Directoire blue frosted, 6½″ h, 6¾″ d, allover berry pattern, matching flower holder, mold sgd "Verlys" **500.00**

Love Bird, opalescent frosted bowl, 4¼″ h, 6½″ l, 2¾″ w, clear design around base, mold sgd "Verlys" . . **275.00**

Mandarine, clear frosted, 9½″ h, 5¹⁄₁₆″ d, Chinaman with umbrella, script sgd. **500.00**

Mermaid, opalescent, 11″ h, 6½″ d, clear neck and flipped top, six mermaids around bottom, mold sgd "Verlys" **1,400.00**

Thistle, amber, 9⅞″ h, 6¼″ d, high relief thistle flower, six clear arched panels in lower section, mold sgd "Verlys" **650.00**

1874 - PRESENT

1885 - PRESENT

VILLEROY & BOCH

History: Pierre Joseph Boch established a pottery near Luxemburg, Germany, in 1767. Jean Francis, his son, introduced the first coal-fired kiln in Europe and perfected a water power–driven potter's wheel. Pierre's grandson, Eugene Boch, managed a pottery at Mettlach; Nicholas Villeroy also had a pottery nearby.

In 1841 the three potteries were merged into the firm of Villeroy & Boch. Early production included a hard-paste earthenware comparable to English ironstone. The factory continues to use this hard-paste formula for its modern tablewares.

Reference: Susan and Al Bagdade, *Warman's English & Continental Pottery & Porcelain, Second Edition,* Wallace-Homestead, 1991.

Additional Listings: Mettlach.

Canister, cov, 7″ h, barrel shape, German kitchen necessity names on each, price for set of ten **300.00**

Vases, pr, Art Deco, green, brown, and white, gold outlining, 6¼″ h, $200.00.

Dinner Service, partial, transfer printed, Cloverleaf pattern, blue dec, scattered cloverleaves, mottled blue and white ground, sponged blue border, two dinner plates, six soup plates, small oval platter, sq serving bowl, handled circular serving bowl, and cov circular tureen, chips, repairs, cracks, black printed factory marks and numerals, price for set **250.00**
Figure, 53″ h, Venus, scantily clad seated figure, ribbon tied headdress, left arm raised across chest, resting on rock, inscribed "Villeroy & Boch," damage to foot and base **1,870.00**
Tray, 11¼″ d, metal gallery with geometric cutouts, ceramic base with border and central stylized geometric pattern, white ground, soft gray high gloss glaze, blue accents, base marked. **200.00**
Tureen and Undertray, 16½″ d, 14″ h, Mettlach, polychrome, couples flanked by stylized floral and geometric motifs, gray ground **275.00**
Vase, 15″ h, bulbous, cylindrical, deep cobalt blue glaze, splashes of drizzled white, three handled silver plated mount cast with leaves, berries, and blossoms, molded, pierced foot, vase imp "V & B," "S" monogram, numbered. c1900. price for pair. **2,750.00**

WARWICK

History: Warwick China Manufacturing Co., Wheeling, West Virginia, was incorporated in 1887 and continued until 1951. The company was one of the first manufacturers of vitreous glazed wares in the United States. Production was extensive and included tableware, garden ornaments, and decorative and utilitarian items.

Pieces were hand painted or decorated by decals. Collectors seek portrait items and fraternal pieces for groups such as the Elks, Eagles, and Knights of Pythias.

Some experimental, eggshell–type porcelain was made before 1887. A few examples are in the market.

Cuspidor, 6½″ h, floral dec, marked "IOGA". **70.00**
Egg Cup, large, Tudor Rose **15.00**
Gravy Boat, red currants, green leaves, gold trim. **50.00**

Pitcher, monk playing fiddle, brown tones, standard glaze, marked "IOGA," 4¼" h, $85.00.

Marmalade Jar, cov, pale yellow florals, brown ground, handles 100.00
Mug, 4½" h, singing monk, brown ground 45.00
Pitcher, 12" h, white, hp gold trim . . . 50.00
Plate
  9½" d, monk drinking wine, brown ground 75.00
  10" d, gypsy lady portrait, multicolored, white ground 65.00
Spooner, platinum banded dinnerware 60.00
Tea Set, teapot, creamer, and cov sugar, gold bands, price for three piece set 115.00
Vase
  10½" h, urn shape, gypsy girl portrait, blue blouse and hair ribbon, brown shaded ground, twig handles. 150.00
  11" h, red hibiscus, brown ground . 75.00

WATCHES, POCKET

History: Pocket watches can be found from flea markets to the specialized jewelry sales at Butterfield & Butterfield, William Doyle Galleries, and Skinners. Condition of the movement is first priority; design and detailing of the case are second.

In pocket watches, listing aids are size (18/0 to 20), number of jewels in the movement, open or closed (hunter) face, and whether the case is gold, gold filled, or some other metal. The movement is the critical element since cases often were switched. However, an elaborate case, especially of gold, adds significantly to value.

Pocket watches designed to railroad specifications are desirable. They are 16 to 18 in size, have a minimum of 17 jewels, adjust to at least five positions, and conform to many other specifications. All are open faced.

Study the field thoroughly before buying. There is a vast amount of literature, including books and newsletters from clubs and collectors. Abbreviations: S = size; gf = gold filled; yg = yellow gold; j = jewels.

References: August C. Bolino, *The Watchmakers of Massachusetts,* Kensington Historical Press, 1987; Howard Brenner, *Collecting Comic Character Clocks and Watches,* Books Americana, 1987; Roy Ehrhardt and Joe Demsey, *Cartier Wrist & Pocket Watches, Clocks: Identification & Price Guide 1992,* Heart of America Press, 1992; Roy Ehrhardt and Joe Demsey, *Patek Phillipe,* Heart of America Press, 1992; Roy Ehrhardt and William Meggers, *American Pocket Watches Identification And Price Guide: Beginning To End... 1830–1980,* Heart of America Press, 1987; Roy Ehrhardt and William Meggers, *American Pocket Watch Serial Number Grade Book, 1993 Prices,* Heart of America Press, 1993; The Ehrhardts, *European Pocket Watches, Book 2: Identification and Price Guide,* Heart of America Press, 1993; Cedric Jagger, *The Artistry Of The English Watch,* Charles E. Tuttle Co., 1988; Reinhard Meis, *Pocket Watches: From the Pendant Watch To The Tourbillon,* Schiffer Publishing, 1987, originally published in German; Cooksey Shugart and Richard E. Gilbert, *Complete Price Guide To Watches, Thirteenth Edition,* Cooksey Shugart Publications, 1993.

Periodical: *Watch & Clock Review,* 2403 Champa St, Denver, CO 80205.

Collectors' Clubs: American Watchmakers Institute Chapter 102, 3 Washington Sq., Apt. 3C, Larchmont, NY 10538; Early American Watch Club Chapter 149, PO Box 5499, Beverly Hills, CA 90210; National Association of Watch & Clock Collectors, 514 Poplar Street, Columbia, PA 17512. *Bulletin* (bimonthly) and *Mart* (bimonthly).

Museums: American Clock & Watch Museum, Bristol, CT; Hoffman Clock Museum, Newark, NY; National Association of Watch and Clock Collectors Museum, Columbia, PA; The Time Museum, Rockford, IL.

Cartier
  Platinum, Art Deco, 19 jewel 8 adjustment movement sgd "European Watch & Clock Co," circular rock crystal case, center engine turned oyster enamel dial sgd "Cartier France," blue steel arrow hands, outer chapter ring with rose diamond Roman numerals, triangular bail sgd "05220" and "3943". 8,050.00
  Yellow Gold, 14K, 17 jewel Movado movement, No. 253988, white dial, Arabic numbers and subsidiary dial for seconds 475.00
E Bourquin & Fil, Geneva, 18K yg, No. 24264, circular case, travel rest, elaborate monogram, black face, white Arabic numerals, five minute chapter rim, subsidiary seconds, gold arrow hands, movement sgd 920.00

Election, Art Deco, 18K yg, 17 jewels, nickel movement, engine turned silvered dial, Arabic numbers and subsidiary dial for seconds accented by red, black, and white enamel border, enamel loss 275.00

Hunting Case, key wind

Auguste Lavalette, 14K yg, circular case, forest green and black enamel dec, rose diamond cartouche, Greek key banding and scrolling field, white enamel dial, black Roman numerals, subsidiary seconds, and arrow hands, sgd on dust cov 500.00

Louis Humbert, 18K yg, circular case, gold and black enamel foliage dec, white enamel dial, black Roman numerals, subsidiary seconds, fancy blue arrow hands, 14K yg chain with slide 805.00

Elgin, lady's, 6 S, 7j movement, gold filled, demi–hunting, engraved "Miss Sally to Mary, 1896," case marked "Fahays 10K," $185.00.

Lady Elgin, Art Nouveau, 14K yg, floral overlay on green guilloche enamel, two small accent diamonds, dragon watch pin with enameled green highlights, some enamel loss 1,210.00

Lapel, niello silver pin suspending open face watch, faceted crystal, openwork frame accented with gold beads, c1900. . . . .   715.00

LeRoy & Fils, Art Nouveau, 18K yg, No. 51484, black-and-white enameled mythological scene, brown enamel dial, Roman numerals, white enamel accent figures, minor scratches to enamel. 660.00

Meylan, CH, 18K yg, minute repeater, 31 jewels movement marked "No.

5208," white porcelain dial, subsidiary dial for seconds, movement and case sgd "Meylan," retailed by H Kohn & Sons, Hartford, CT 2,970.00

Movado, 14K white gold, silver dial, Arabic numbers and subsidiary dial for seconds, octagonal shaped case, platinum watch fob with diamond centered locket. 770.00

Patek Philippe, 18K yg

No. 91113, open face, white porcelain dial, Arabic numbers, Louis XIV hands, second hand sweep, jeweled nickel movement, signed on dial, movement, and dust cover, made for Henry Bohm Co, Denver, CO, chips to crystal, minor case scratches 1,540.00

No. 149813, white porcelain dial, subsidiary dial for seconds, scrolled hands, cobalt blue and white enamel border, back monogram, signed on dial, case, and movement. 2,970.00

Vacheron and Constantin, 18K yg, 21 jewels, 18 size, triple sgd 1,980.00

WATCHES, WRIST

History: The definition of a wristwatch is simple: "a small watch that is attached to a bracelet or strap and is worn around the wrist." However, a watch on a bracelet is not necessarily a wristwatch. The key is the ability to read the time. A true wristwatch allows you to read the time at a glance, without making any other motions. Early watches on a bracelet worn on the arm had the axis of their dials, from 6 to 12, perpendicular to the band. Reading them required some extensive arm movement.

The first true wristwatch appeared about 1850. The key date is 1880, though, when the stylish decorative wristwatch appeared and almost universal acceptance occurred. The technology to create the wristwatch existed in the early nineteenth century with Brequet's shock-absorbing "Parachute System" for automatic watches and Ardien Philipe's winding stem.

The wristwatch was a response to the needs of the entreprenuerial age with its emphasis on punctuality and planned free time. By approximately 1930 the sales of wristwatches surpassed that of pocket watches. Swiss and German manufacturers were quickly joined by American makers.

The wristwatch has undergone many technical advances during the twentieth century, including such features as self-winding (automatic), shock-resistance, electric operation, etc. It truly is the most significant and dominant clock of the century.

References: Howard S. Brenner, *Identification and Value Guide Collecting Comic Character Clocks and Watches,* Books Americana, 1987; Hy

Brown with Nancy Thomas, *Comic Character Timepieces: Seven Decades of Memories,* Schiffer Publishing, 1992; Gisbert L. Brunner and Christian Pfeiffer–Belli, *Wristwatches,* Schiffer Publishing, 1993; *The Classic Watch: The Great Watches and Their Makers From The First Wrist Watch To Present Day,* The Wellfleet Press, 1989; Roy Ehrhardt and Joe Demsey, *Cartier Wrist & Pocket Watches, Clocks: Identification & Price Guide 1992,* Heart of America Press, 1992; Roy Ehrhardt and Joe Demsey, *Patek Phillipe,* Heart of America Press, 1992; Roy Ehrhardt and Joe Demsey, *Rolex Identification and Price Guide, 1993,* Heart of America Press, 1993; Sherry and Roy Ehrhardt and Joe Demsey, *Vintage American & European Wrist Watch Price Guide, Book 6,* Heart of America Press, 1993; Helmut Kahlert, Richard Mühee, and Gisbert L. Brunner, *Wristwatches: History of a Century's Development,* Schiffer Publishing, 1986; Gerd J. Lang and Reinhard Meis, *Chronograph Wristwatches: To Stop Time,* Schiffer Publishing, 1993; Cooksey Shugart and Richard E. Gilbert, *Complete Price Guide To Watches, Thirteenth Edition,* Cooksey Shugart Publications, 1993.

Periodical: *International Wrist Watch,* 242 West Ave., Darien, CT 06820.

Collectors' Clubs: International Wrist Watch Collectors Chapter 146, 5901C Westheimer, Houston, TX 77057; National Association of Watch & Clock Collectors, 514 Poplar Street, Columbia, PA 17512; The Swatch Collectors Club, PO Box 7400, Melville, NY 11747-7400. *Bulletin* (bimonthly) and *Mart* (bimonthly).

Museums: American Clock & Watch Museum, Bristol, CT; Hoffman Clock Museum, Newark, NY; National Association of Watch and Clock Collectors Museum, Columbia, PA; The Time Museum, Rockford, IL.

Audemars Piguet, 18K yg, Swiss jewel movement, gold ribbed dial and frame, leather band, c1960. . . . . **1,210.00**
Borel, Ernest, gentleman's, No. 42013, 18K pink gold, Imca Star model, Roman and abstract chapters. **310.00**
Bulova, 14K yg, 21 jewels, flared lugs, gold filled Speidel band **165.00**
Cartier
  No. 781004328, 18K yg, square cut corner case, white dial, Roman numerals. **1,760.00**
  Santos, stainless steel and 18K yg, white enamel dial, Roman numerals, blued steel hands, flexible rect plaque–like band, deployant buckle. **1,320.00**
Concord, 14K yg, Retro, 17 jewels, brickwork gold bracelet, diamond and channel set ruby buckle highlighted with white gold, marked "Tiffany and Co" on dial, 15.1 dwt. **935.00**
Cyma, Swiss, lady's, white gold, 15 jew-

els, diamond and platinum frame accented by blue stones **450.00**
Ditisheim, Paul, platinum, 17 jewels, silvered dial with markers, faceted crystal **1,045.00**
Duoplan, No. 69/78, 9K yg, rect black dial, abstract chapters, leather strap . **660.00**
Elgin, No. 304995, 14K yg, jeweled nickel movement, white dial, Roman numerals, subsidiary dial for seconds, crystal missing **250.00**
Gruen
  14K rose gold, curved white dial, abstract chapters, subsidiary dial for seconds **330.00**
  14K white gold, Quadron, silvered dial, Arabic chapters, subsidiary dial for seconds, leather strap, slightly yellowed dial. **275.00**
Hamilton
  14K white gold, 19 jewels, silvered dial, diamond markers, subsidiary dial for seconds, leather strap **660.00**
  Gold filled, Piping Rock, silver dial, subsidiary dial for seconds within black bezel, Roman numerals, Speidel band **770.00**
  Platinum, tank, silvered dial, Arabic numbers, subsidiary dial for seconds, leather strap **525.00**
LeCoultre, lady's, 18K yg, wrist alarm, two tone dial, Arabic and abstract chapters. **990.00**
Marshall Field, lady's, 14K yg, dial marked, brickwork pattern bracelet, diamond border, 21.9 dwt. **360.00**
Movado, 18K rose gold, 15 jewels, black and white dial, abstract and Arabic numbers, day and date window **800.00**
Patek Philippe & Co, 18K yg
  Gentleman's
    Cream dial, abstract chapters, subsidiary dial for seconds, leather strap, numbered 6034 on lugs, retailed by Cartier. **3,960.00**
    Silvered dial, No. 974263, abstract chapters, subsidiary dial for seconds, leather strap, redone dial, crystal slightly cracked. **2,860.00**
    White metal dial, subsidiary dial for seconds, leather strap, retailed by Tiffany & Co, 1950s **1,980.00**
  Lady's
    No. 944875, 18K yg, white dial, dome shoulders, cord band, 18K gold fittings and clasp, retailed by Tiffany & Co. **935.00**
    No. 9200177, platinum, 18 jewel, cream color dial, Arabic numbers, dial sgd "Tilden Thurber & Co," double black cord bracelet, gold filled deployant buckle. **770.00**

Rolex, gentleman's, 14K yg, Oyster Perpetual, raised gold markers, center seconds sweep, leather band, c1950 .... 880.00

Sellita, lady's, 14K yg, 17 jewels, textured and polished gold band, 18.0 dwt 200.00

Universal Geneve, stainless steel, tricompass, moonphase calendar chronograph 770.00

Vacheron & Constantin, silvered two tone dial, Arabic and abstract chapters, subsidiary dial for seconds, stainless steel strap 990.00

WATERFORD

History: Waterford crystal is quality flint glass commonly decorated with cuttings. The original factory was established at Waterford, Ireland, in 1729. Glass made before 1830 is darker than the brilliantly clear glass of later production. The factory closed in 1852. After 100 years it reopened and continues in production.

Biscuit Barrel, cov, 7½" h 130.00

Bowl
  6" d, allover diamond cutting 70.00

Fruit Bowl, everted rim, standard base, 5¾" h, 6¾" d, $300.00.

7½" w, 10½" l, 3¼" h, oval, scalloped 200.00
8" d, DQ, thumbprint stem 125.00
13½" l, 4½" h, Kennedy, sgd 550.00
Cake Plate, 10" d, 5¼" h, sunburst center, geometric design 80.00
Cake Server, cut glass handle, orig box 80.00
Celery Bowl, oval 80.00
Champagne Flute, 6" h, Coleen pattern, price for twelve piece set 450.00
Compote, 5½" h, allover diamond cutting above double wafer stem, price for pair 400.00
Cordial, 2½" h, Coleen pattern, price for twelve piece set 300.00
Creamer and Sugar, 4" h creamer, 3¾" d sugar, price for pair
  Sawtooth variant 90.00
  Tralee pattern 70.00
Decanter
  11" h, Lismore, roly poly, circular stopper 110.00
  12¾" h, allover diamond cutting, monogrammed, price for pair.. 300.00
Goblet, 5½" h, Coleen pattern, price for twelve piece set 850.00
Honey Jar, cov 70.00
Lamp, table, 23" h, 13" d umbrella shade, blunt diamond cutting, Pattern L-1122.................... 440.00
Mantle Luster, 10¼" h, row of prisms 140.00
Napkin Ring, 2" h, price for twelve piece set 225.00
Old Fashioned, 3½"h, Comeragh pattern, price for pair 65.00
Pitcher, 6¼" h, Coleen pattern 110.00
Salt and Pepper Shakers, pr, 4" h, diamond and rosette dec 65.00
Vase, 8" h, alternating diamond cut panels and horizontal notches 100.00
Wine
  5½" h, white, Patrick, price for eight piece set.................. 220.00
  7⅜" h, clear, Coleen pattern, price for twelve piece set............. 725.00
  7½" h, red, Coleen pattern, price for twelve piece set............. 900.00

WAVE CREST WARE

c1892

WAVE CREST

History: The C. F. Monroe Company of Meriden, Connecticut, produced the opal glassware known as Wave Crest from 1898 until World War I. The company bought the opaque, blown-molded glass blanks for decoration from the Pairpoint Manufacturing Co. of New Bedford, Massachusetts, and other glassmakers, including European factories. Florals were the most common decorative motif. Trade names used were "Wave Crest Ware," "Kelva," and "Nakara."

References: Wilfred R. Cohen, *Wave Crest: The Glass of C. F. Monroe*, Collector Books, 1987, out of print; Elsa H. Grimmer, *Wave Crest Ware*, Wallace-Homestead, 1979, out of print.

Biscuit Jar, barrel shape, rococo cartouche, pastel floral design, SP top, $275.00.

Biscuit Jar, cov
  7″ h, 6″ d, soft yellow and white satin ground, pink, blue, and yellow pansies dec, emb pattern, resilvered top, rim, and handle **225.00**
  7½″ h, 5″ w, Helmshmid swirl, alternating bands of pale blue Rococo design, bands of pale yellow Wild Roses, thorns, and buds, all glass top **1,250.00**
Box, hinged
  6″ d, octagonal, shaded peach to pale yellow ground, enameled purple iris, sgd "Nakara". **950.00**
  7″ d, round
    Crystal ground, Christmas Holly dec, irid int. **1,450.00**
    Pale yellow ground, Baroque Shell dec, sq central medallion on top of purple violets, pale green leaves and traceries, enameled violet bands, orig pink lining. . . .   **895.00**
    White ground, Helmshmid Swirls, raised pink gold dec, gold accents, pink blossoms, green leaves, black stripe **885.00**
  7 x 6½″, swirl, pearly white, shaggy peach, pink, and white astors, moss green leaves, ornate ftd brass base **945.00**
  8″ w, cut, sterling fittings, swivel mirror inside lid, sgd "CFM C" **1,500.00**

Cigar Humidor, cov
  Lime green ground, pink floral dec, purple enamel accents, orig key, sgd "Wavecrest," banner mark . . .   **1,750.00**
  Opal ground, molded florals, hp blue enameled forget–me–nots, hp pink "Cigars," Indian on horseback on cov, gilt metal hinged mounts, red Wavecrest flag on base **660.00**
Creamer and Sugar, bulbous, blue floral design, metal rims and bail. **115.00**
Dresser Set, 5″ d cov powder jar, 5″ d hair receiver, Kate Greenaway type cherubs, stamped "Nakara CFM Co"   **825.00**
Dresser Tray, 5″ d, circular, pink wild roses, white to light green ground, raised floral and scroll design, oval mirror, marked "Wavecrest". **425.00**
Fernery, 5 x 9″, rect, white shading to blue ground, pink wild roses, raised scrolls, gold metal rim, shield mark . .   **350.00**
Jewel Box, 5 x 5½″ d, hinged, dark green, heavy floral enamel, marked "Kelva". **350.00**
Ring Box, floral design, sgd **495.00**
Salt and Pepper Shakers, pr, one olive green ground with pink daisies, other pink ground with blue daisies, marked "Nakara".   **410.00**
Sugar Shaker, 5″ h, pale yellow and white ground, rust and red flowers, leaves, and branches, orig top **225.00**
Trinket Dish, 1½ x 5″, blue and red flowers. **175.00**
Vase
  3¼″ h, dark green shiny lines, white shading to green ground, sea green florals, beaded rim **525.00**
  10″ h, pale pink accents on white, pink, and orange chrysanthemums, enameled foliage, beaded white top rim **600.00**
Whisk Broom Holder, hp daisies in pink luster scrolled medallion, red banner mark **250.00**

WEATHER VANES

History: A weather vane indicates wind direction. The earliest known examples were found on late-17th-century structures in the Boston area. The vanes were handcrafted of wood, copper, or tin. By the last half of the 19th century, weather vanes adorned farms and houses throughout the nation. Mass-produced vanes of cast iron, copper, and sheet metal were sold through mail-order catalogs or at country stores.

The champion vane is the rooster. In fact, the name weathercock is synonymous with weather vane. The styles and patterns are endless. Weathering can affect the same vane differently. For this reason, patina is a critical element in collecting vanes.

Whirligigs are a variation of the weather vane. Constructed of wood and metal, often by unskilled craftsmen, whirligigs not only indicate the direction of the wind and its velocity but their unique movements served as entertainment for children, neighbors, and passersby.

References: Robert Bishop and Patricia Coblentz, *A Gallery of American Weathervanes and Whirligigs*, E. P. Dutton, 1981; Ken Fitzgerald, *Weathervanes and Whirligigs*, Clarkson N. Potter, 1967; Dana G. Morykan and Harry L. Rinker, *Warman's Country Antiques & Collectibles, Second Edition*, Wallace–Homestead, 1994.

Reproduction Alert: Reproductions of early models exist; they are being aged and sold as originals.

Cow, molded copper, full bodied, 27″ l, $1,000.00. Photograph courtesy of James D. Julia, Inc.

WEATHER VANES

Banner, copper and iron, floriform standard, American, late 19th C, 94″ h. . .	440.00
Black Hawk, molded copper, attributed to Cushing & White, Waltham, MA, late 19th C, 24½″ l, 15″ h	935.00
Butterfly, sheet metal, American, late 19th C, imperfections, 23″ l, 16½″ h	1,540.00
Cock, copper, American, late 18th/early 19th C, traces of bolle, fine verdigris surface, old repair, some losses, 23″ h, 42″ l	3,300.00
Cow, copper, molded, 27″ l	1,100.00
Duck, sheet metal, hollow, 36″ l	275.00
Eagle	
Copper, sitting on ball, old patina, 12¾″ w	310.00
Molded copper, American, early 20th C, 55″ w, 40″ h.	2,310.00

Molded gilt copper, American, early 20th C, 25″ w, 23″ d, 19″ h	500.00
Fish, wood, metal fins, orig white paint, Duxbury, MA, 22″ l	250.00
Grasshopper	
Copper, American, 20th C, verdigris surface, 35″ l	770.00
Gilded zinc, American, 20th C, 20¼″ l	360.00
Henry Hudson's Ship *Half Moon*, molded copper, American, early 20th C, bears inscription "Half Moon," good surface, 44″ h, 45″ l	1,870.00
Hermaphrodite Brig, painted wood and metal, New England, c1930, 16″ h, 25″ l	715.00
Horse, running	
Cast Iron, American, c1900, 23½″ w, 30″ h.	2,640.00
Copper	
33″ l, hollow body, old dark patina, modern base	2,310.00
42″ l, repousse, cast zinc head, directional arrows	1,320.00
Copper and zinc	
Attributed to A L Jewell & Co, Waltham, MA, 19th C, fine verdigris surface, 27¼″ w, 18″ h	1,430.00
Unknown Maker, American, 19th C, later gilding, 31″ l	880.00
Molded copper and zinc, American Late 19th C, verdigris surface, 28″ l	880.00
Mid 19th C, full bodied figure of Ethan Allen, 41″ l	1,540.00
Lighthouse, wood, New England origin, late 19th C, 19 14″ h, 16¾″ l	65.00
Mariner, standing, pointing, holding spy glass, sheet metal, painted black, American, 19th C, found in upstate New York.	615.00
Merino Sheep, molded copper, American, early 20th, verdigris surface, repaired bullet holes, 28½″ l	4,125.00
Moose, zinc and copper, silhouette, Maine, 20th C, wooden base, 39″ l, 28½″ h.	330.00
Ox, zinc and copper, American, mid 19th C, regilded, some losses to forefront, 19½″ h, 34½″ l	3,850.00
Peacock, painted dec on wood and wire, American, early 20th C, flat silhouette form, 49″ l, 14″ h	935.00
Rooster	
Cast and sheet iron, detailed body, flat tail, regilt, 37″ h	1,540.00
Copper	
16½″ w, 24″ l, hollow, molded . . .	250.00
20″ w, 18″ h, attributed to France, late 19th C, gilded.	2,420.00
21″ h, molded	800.00

Sheet Metal, folky design, 10" h, 13"
l 175.00
Steel, silhouette, old dark finish,
weathered polychrome paint, 32¼"
h 400.00
Schooner, 31" l, carved and painted
wood, American, 20th C, painted tin
sails and wire rigging, wear, 31" l . . . 1,100.00
Scroll, gilded copper, zinc, and iron,
American, 19th C, 55" w, 7" d, 47" h 990.00
Shore Bird, gilt metal, Long Island, NY,
20th C, imperfections, 24" w, 18½" h 1,210.00
Weaver's Shuttle, molded gilt copper,
America, 19th C, fine verdigris sur-
face, 64" l. 2,750.00
Wolf, wood, carved, orig paint, c1930,
18¼" h, 16" w. 200.00

WHIRLIGIGS

Canoe and two Indians, New England,
c1900, carved wood, polychrome dec,
imperfections, 21" w, 3" d, 11" h 660.00
Dewey Boy, American, c1900, carved
and painted, 12" h 935.00
Figures, double, carved and painted
wood, zinc flywheel, American, late
19th C, imperfections, 32" h 1,320.00
Kicking Mule, 48" l, painted wood, imperfections, 20th C 275.00
Man, carved, metal cap, vestiges of orig
paint, American, 19th C, imperfec-
tions, 14¾" h 500.00
Roman Soldier, carved, American,
c1900, 12" h. 220.00

WEBB, THOMAS & SONS

History: Thomas Webb & Sons was established
in 1837 in Stourbridge, England. The company
probably is best known for its very beautiful English
cameo glass. However, many other types of colored glass were produced, including enameled
glass, iridescent glass, pieces with heavy glass ornamentation, cased glass, and other art glass besides cameo.

References: Charles R. Hajdamach, *British
Glass, 1800–1914,* Antique Collectors' Club, 1991;
Ellen T. Schroy, *Warman's Glass,* Wallace-Home-
stead, 1992.

Additional Listings: Burmese, Cameo, and
Peachblow.

Bowl
6" d, 2½" h, cameo, ruffled edge, emerald green layered in white, cameo
cut and carved with daisies and
blackberry dec, intricate floral ribbon border below, marked with

**Ewer, enamel dec, turquoise and brown
body, gilt and orange–amber scrolling,
13" h, $605.00. Photograph courtesy of
Skinner, Inc.**

"Webb" four sided medallion on
base. 1,650.00
6¼" d, 3¾" h, Burmese, floral dec, ap-
plied crystal rim, sgd "Thos.
Webb" 1,120.00
Perfume Bottle
4" l, cameo, teardrop form, yellow layered in white, floral spray dec,
cameo carved monogram
"R.E.W.," dated 1886, hinged silver
rim and lift cap. 1,760.00
4¼" h, undulating body, yellow over-
laid in white, cut and carved as
swimming dolphin, inscribed registry mark "Rd. 18100," rim and cap
missing. 4,950.00
5¾" h, cameo, globular, frosted clear
layered in red and white, cameo cut
and carved with allover fuchsia
blossoms, buds, leafy stems, and
butterfly, double linear borders
above and below, hallmarked silver
threaded rim and ball cap 1,815.00
6½" l, fish shape, rock crystal, diamond cut body, carved fin and head
details, registry mark "Rd. 16711,"
threaded silver rim and fishtail cap
with hallmarks 2,860.00
11" l, elongated lay down type, yellow
amber layered in white, cameo cut
and carved with allover sweet pea
blossoms, buds, and leafy stems,
wide border of vertical slats above
and below, hallmarked "SM," silver
threaded rim and ball cap 2,310.00
Punch Cup, 2¾" h, 2¼" d, Alexandrite,
barrel shape, blue shaded to rose to
citron, citron applied handle, ground
pontil, belltone. 560.00

Rose Bowl, 2¾" d, 2¼" h, miniature, acid finish, salmon pink evenly shaded to yellow, reheated yellow top edge, six crimp top, brown leaves and foliage, white and blue enameled flowers, unsgd. 310.00

Vase

2" h, miniature, cameo, bulbous body, cranberry red cased to opal, overlaid in white, cameo cut with morning glory vines, blossoms, and butterfly, unsgd, attributed to Thomas Webb 1,100.00

3¼" h, 4" d, Burmese, acid finish, salmon pink evenly shaded to yellow, bowl shape, hexagonal top, red berries, green leaves, unsgd. 330.00

4" h, 2¾" d, Burmese, acid finish, salmon pink evenly shaded to yellow, ruffled, brown leaves and foliage, white and blue enameled flowers, unsgd. 300.00

4¼" h, 2½" d, Burmese, acid finish, salmon pink evenly shaded to yellow, four petal top, coral flower buds, green leaves, unsgd 375.00

6¾" h

Cameo, bell shaped, yellow layered with bright red, white overlay, cameo etched and carved cyclamen blossoms, leafy stems, insect in flight at back, arrow border 1,320.00

Peachblow, 3½" d, glossy, deep rose pink shading to lighter pink, cream int., gold branches and prunus flowers with butterfly dec, gold trim. 385.00

7" h, cameo, oval body, bright blue layered in white, cut and carved grasses and blossoming leafy plants interspersed by beetles and eight–legged insects, salamander, and bullfrog. 9,350.00

7½" h, 4½" d, satin, MOP, DQ pattern, green shading to white, glossy white opalescent int., sgd "Patent" 475.00

7¾" h, 3¾" d, peachblow, glossy, deep rose to lighter pink, gold branches and flowers dec, ivory lining. 340.00

8¼" h, cameo, sepia stained simulated ivory with three overlapping medallions carved with Oriental floral, bird, and butterfly designs, elaborate borders, attributed to George Woodall, large circular mark "Thomas Webb & Sons Limited" 3,850.00

8½" h, 4" d, Burmese, acid finish, salmon pink evenly shaded to yel-

low, orange berries, green and brown leaves, unsgd 765.00

8¾" h, cameo, cylindrical, clear cased to bright citron yellow, layered in white, cameo cut and carved with two crested exotic birds among bamboo shoots and broad leafed foliage, chevron borders above, wide elaborate borders below, unsgd. 4,400.00

9⅝" h, cameo, trumpet form, crystal overlaid in cranberry red, acid cut with four symmetrically repeating lily blossoms on scrolling leafy stems, "Webb" mark cameo cut above pedestal foot 550.00

10" h, 5½" d, Burmese, acid finish, salmon pink evenly shaded to creamy yellow, green ivy leaves dec, sgd 1,000.00

WEDGWOOD

WEDGWOOD
c1759-1769

WEDGWOOD
c1900

WEDGWOOD

History: In 1754 Josiah Wedgwood entered into a partnership with Thomas Whieldon of Fenton Vivian, Staffordshire, England. Products included marbled, agate, tortoiseshell, green glaze, and Egyptian black wares. In 1759 Wedgwood opened his own pottery at the Ivy House works, Burslem. In 1764 he moved to the Brick House (Bell Works) at Burslem. The pottery concentrated on utilitarian pieces.

Between 1766 and 1769 Wedgwood built the famous works at Etruria. Among the most renowned products of this plant were the Empress Catherina of Russia dinner service (1774) and the Portland Vase (1790s). Product lines were caneware, unglazed earthenwares (drabwares), piecrust wares, variegated and marbled wares, black basalt (developed in 1768), Queen's or creamware, Jasperware (perfected in 1774), and others.

Bone china was produced under the direction of Josiah Wedgwood II between 1812 and 1822 and revived in 1878. Moonlight luster was made from

1805 to 1815. Fairyland luster began in 1920. All luster production ended in 1932.

A museum was established at the Etruria pottery in 1906. When Wedgwood moved to its modern plant at Barlaston, North Staffordshire, the museum was continued and expanded.

References: Susan and Al Bagdade, *Warman's English & Continental Pottery & Porcelain, Second Edition,* Wallace-Homestead, 1991; David Buten and Jane Clancy, *Eighteenth-Century Wedgwood: A Guide For Collectors And Connoisseurs,* Main Street Press, 1980; Robin Reilly, *The Collector's Wedgwood,* Portfolio Press/A Robert Campbell Rowe Book, 1980; Robin Reilly and George Savage, *Dictionary Of Wedgwood,* Antique Collectors Club, 1980; Peter Williams, *Wedgwood: A Collector's Guide,* Wallace-Homestead, 1992; Geoffrey Wills, *Wedgwood,* Chartwell Books, 1989.

Periodical: *ARS Ceramica,* 5 Dogwood Court, Glen Head, NY 11545.

Collectors' Clubs: Wedgwood Collectors Society, PO Box 14013, Newark, NJ 07198; The Wedgwood Society, The Roman Villa, Rockbourne, Fordingbridge, Hants, England, SP6 3PG.

Museums: Art Institute of Chicago, Chicago, IL; Birmingham Museum of Art, Birmingham, AL; Cincinnati Museum of Art, Cincinnati, OH; Cleveland Museum of Art, Cleveland, OH; Henry E. Huntington Library and Art Gallery, San Marino, CA; Nassau County Museum System, Long Island, NY; Nelson-Atkins Museum of Art, Kansas City, MO; Potsdam Public Museum, Potsdam, NY; Rose Museum, Brandeis University, Waltham, MA; Wadsworth Atheneum, Hartford, CT.

BASALT

Bough Pot, 4¼" h, D–shaped, pierced cov, white slip ovals below banding of applied black florets, imp mark, early 19th C, relief loss 935.00

Bust
8¾" h, Newton, imp title and "MADE IN ENGLAND" mark, c1900 . . . . . 330.00
12½" h, Shakespeare, imp mark and title, late 19th C, base rim nick . . . 825.00
14½" h, Byron, modeled by Wyon, imp marks, title, and sculptor, mid 19th C 440.00
17" h, Germanicus, circular base, imp marks and title, late 18th C, chips . 3,080.00
18¼" h, Minerva, modeled clad in armor, titled, imp "ENGLAND" mark, c1900, restored helmet chip 825.00
Candlesticks, pr, 11" h, Triton, modeled as part human, part fish, holding sconce formed as whorled shell, imp mark, 1974 . . . . 825.00
Cream Pitcher, 3⅝" h, Lady Templetown's Poor Maria, imp turning, imp upper–lower case mark, c1785 . . 370.00
Cup and Saucer, 2½" h, engine turned

border, cup with relief of children, imp marks, c1800 . . . . 360.00

Figure
9½" h, titled "Skills of the Nation—The Potter," Colin Melbourne, No. 146 from limited edition of 1,000, imp and printed marks, c1980 . . . . 440.00
17" h, Hiawatha, modeled holding metal spear, imp title and mark, late 19th C, chips to headdress 990.00
18½" h, Faun and Bacchus, imp title and mark, late 19th C 2,970.00
18¾" h, Venus and Doves, titled and imp marks, 19th C, minor chips to toes 1,650.00

Inkwell
2⅛" h, drum shape, engine turned body, imp mark, c1775, base rim nick 415.00
5¼" h, bowl supported on three dolphin feet, imp "Etruria England" marks, c1895, restored finial 525.00

Lamp, oil, cov, 8⅝" h, oval, carved fluting over applied acanthus and bellflower relief, female figure seated to one end with book in hand as handle, imp mark, mid 19th C, minor chips to book 550.00

Plaque
Oval, black relief
5½ x 7¼", Hercules and the Erymanthean Boar, imp marks, brass frame 550.00
8½ x 11½", Judgment of Hercules, imp mark, late 18th C, mounted in wood frame. 825.00
Rect, 7⅛ x 11¼", black relief, dancing nymph, imp mark, rim chips, mounted to wood frame 220.00
Portrait Medallion, 1⅝ x 1⅞" oval, Caesar, imp mark and title, c1800, price for set of twelve. 615.00
Tea Kettle, cov, 7" h, bail handle, draped border, engine turning, widow finial, imp mark, late 18th C, chip to finial . . 660.00
Teapot, cov, 5¼" h, central medallions, classical relief over stiff leaf border, imp marks and date letters, c1865 . . 360.00
Tea Set, Cambridge Ware, white banded dec, 4" h cov teapot, 6" h cov coffeepot, 2⅛" h creamer, 3" h cov sugar, imp mark, c1885 . . . . 880.00
Vase
4¾" h, Bamboo Ware, enamel dec, modeled as four spill vases mounted on simulated earth base, imp marks, 19th C 660.00
8½" h, iron red and black dec, central classical female figure border of gadroons, dot drops, loop handles, imp mark, early 19th C, base rim ground 1,045.00

9¾" h, grape vine molded loop handles, Bacchus head terminals, trophy relief on neck, "Triumph of Cybele" to one side, Cybele in car drawn by lions on other, imp mark, c1800 . . . . **1,100.00**

BONE CHINA

Jar, cov, 5½" h, encrusted black ground, gilt leaves, central enamel dec, fruit and floral banding, printed mark, mid 19th C, gilt wear, cov restored **250.00**
Vase
4½" h, enamel and gilt Japan pattern, printed marks, mid 19th C, gilt rim wear, price for pair **330.00**
5½" h, trumpet, blue glazed ground, gilt bordered enamel medallions, sgd "J Thorley," printed mark, late 19th C. **400.00**

CANEWARE

Basket, cov, 3½" h, basketweave body, strap handle, imp mark, early 19th C **385.00**
Butter Dish, cov, 8½" h, applied drabware ferns, imp mark, c1800, restored **330.00**
Candlesticks, pr, 6" h, smear glazed, basketwork body, imp mark, early 19th C **200.00**
Chamberstick, 2⅛" h, applied rosso antico scrolled floral and foliage dec, imp mark, early 19th C **315.00**
Coffee Cann and Saucer, banded black basalt relief of hieroglyphs of winged discs, sphinx, and Apis, imp marks, c1810, cann restored. **250.00**
Creamer, 3⅝" h, white applied fern dec, glazed, imp "WEDGWOOD" mark, c1830. **250.00**
Cup and Saucer, 5" d saucer, Bacchanalian boys in relief, engine turned borders, red enamel foliate and line banding, imp upper–lower case marks, c1790. **715.00**
Game Pie Dish, cov, 8¼" h, oval, latticework cov, foliate and twig finial, imp mark, c1800, chips **440.00**
Potpourri, cov, 3½" h, smear glazed, imp marks, early 19th C **200.00**
Spill Vase, 3½" h, white applied fern dec, glazed, imp "WEDGWOOD" marks, c1830. **235.00**
Sugar Bowl, cov, 4" h, engine turned body, bamboo form finial, imp mark, c1775, cov repaired. **330.00**
Teabowl and Saucer, 3¼" d saucer, fluted engine turning, blue enamel banding, imp marks, c1800 . . . . . . **415.00**
Teapot, cov, 4¾" h, Bacchanalian boys

in relief, simulated bamboo spout, handle, cov, and banding, blue enamel trimwork, imp upper–lower case mark, c1790, restoration. **225.00**
Vase, 4½" h, modeled four spills mounted on simulated earth base, imp mark, early 19th C, restored, foot rim ground **750.00**
Wine Cooler, engine turned body, mask handles, imp mark, early 19th C, stain, price for pair **935.00**

CREAMWARE

Bidet, 18" l, imp mark, early 19th C . . **110.00**
Bough Pot, cov, 6⅛" h, yellow ground, brown slip dec, applied florets to border, imp mark, early 19th C **360.00**
Cup Plate, black transfer, imp mark, 19th C **75.00**
Egg Standish, 10¼" h, Viking head and swan ends, two cov cups, gilt trim, imp marks, mid 19th C, chips **385.00**
Jelly Mold, 6½" h, wedge form, floral enamel dec, imp mark, c1800, hairline, glaze nicks **2,310.00**
Pap Feeder, 2¼" h, imp mark, late 18th C **90.00**
Tea Caddy, cov, 5" h, black transfer tea party and shepherd dec, imp mark, late 18th C **550.00**
Vase
7¼" h, agate, creamware bodies, black basalt plinth base, gilt dec widow finials, imp wafer mark, c1770, restorations, price for pair. . **2,860.00**
8½" h, Porphyry, three handles, speckled blue glaze, pear shape, gilt accented handles, applied florets, basalt plinth base, imp wafer mark, chips to relief, gilt wear, price for pair. **5,170.00**
Whiskey Keg, 10¾" h, puce ground, yel-

Drabware, teapot, smear glaze, architectural design in relief, 4½" h, $250.00.

low enamel panel, gilt title "I. Whisky," disc cov, metal spigot, imp mark, c1865. . . . . **330.00**

DRABWARE

Bowl, 4¾" h, glazed, gilt banding, ball finials, two handles **220.00**

Chess Figures, 4" h, king and queen, imp mark, c1794, chip to crown, price for pair. **1,045.00**

Creamer, 4½" h, applied white and lilac dec, imp marks, early 19th C **125.00**

Inkstand, 8¼" h, inkpot, sander, and central cov, glazed, imp mark, early 19th C, restored inkpot, glaze loss, gilt trim wear, hairlines **220.00**

Sugar Bowl, cov, 5" h, widow finial, 19th C. **195.00**

Tea Canister, cov, 4" h, glazed, imp mark **200.00**

Teapot, cov
3½" h, white classical and foliate relief, imp marks, 19th C, chips **200.00**
6" w, white applied floral dec, imp mark, mid 19th C, nicks to spout, chip restored **135.00**

Jasperware, pitcher, white classical figures, blue ground, marked "#36, Wedgwood, Made in England, 1951," on bottom, 4¾" h, $75.00.

JASPER

Bowl, 10¼" h, black dip, Dancing Hours applied dec, imp mark and date 1968 **550.00**

Cache Pot, 3¼" h, matching underplate, scallop form rims, blue ground, white jasper leaf border, basketweave engine–turning, imp upper–lower case marks, c1790, rim ground, nicks, and hairlines **385.00**

Candlesticks, pr, 10¼" h, pale blue, molded white classical females, holding cornucopia form bases supporting leafy scones, imp marks, c1800, restorations, chips **1,980.00**

Chess Set, white figures, lilac and dark blue dip bases, 4" h king, c1785, price for thirty–four piece set **36,300.00**

Cup, 2½" l, Comma, solid yellow jasper, white applied latticework, imp mark, late 18th C **1,320.00**

Custard Cup, cov, 2½" h, solid blue, white rope handle and applied latticework, pierced cov, imp mark, late 18th C, nick to int. cov collar **880.00**

Figure, 6½" l, Sphinx, white figure, dark blue base with applied floral trim, imp mark, late 18th C, restorations, base rim chips **3,575.00**

Flower Pot, 3½" h, pale blue, engine turned dice body, white applied quatrefoils and leafy border, imp mark, c1790, foot rim chip and lines. **525.00**

Incense Urn, cov, 7¼" h, lilac dip, white classical relief leafy borders, fruiting garlands terminating in ram's heads to pedestal base, pierced insert and lattice cov, imp mark, date letters, c1870, rim chip. **1,540.00**

Monocular, 2¾" h, blue and white, ivory body, classical relief, cut steel beading, late 18th C, jasper and ivory cracked **1,430.00**

Plaque
7 x 9½", solid blue oval, white relief of Feast of the Gods, imp mark, c1790, crazed, wood frame. **12,100.00**
7 x 10¼", solid blue oval, white applied relief of The Triumph of Bacchus, imp mark, c1779, mounted in wood frame. **14,300.00**
16" d, pale blue circular, white Centaur and Bacchante, self framed with white relief, late 18th C, rim repair, staining, firing lines **13,200.00**

Sugar Bowl, cov, 4" h, solid pale blue, white jasper relief of domestic employment, engine turning to cov, upper–lower case mark, c1790. . . . . **880.00**

Teabowl and Saucer, green, white applied classical figures, foliate borders on cup, palmette enclosed flowers on 3" d saucer, imp mark, late 18th C . . **715.00**

Teapot, cov, 5½" h, lilac, white applied leaves, band of scrolled flowers, imp mark, late 18th C, damage to handle and spout **615.00**

Tea Set, crimson dip, white applied classical relief, 3½" h cov teapot, 2" h creamer, 3¼" h cov sugar, imp mark, c1920, losses **770.00**

Trembleuse, 4½" h cup, green, undercut

white fluting floral swags and relief inverted grasses, sunflower finial, imp
marks, late 18th C, restored rim, finial
chips 1,100.00
Vase
6″ h, column form, pale blue, white
applied Corinthian columns below
floral swags terminating at skulls,
imp mark, late 18th C, rim chips,
ground top rim, missing cov 250.00
7″ h, tricolor, solid pale blue body, lilac
dipped, white applied relief flaming
torches, imp mark, late 18th C, rim
nick, cov missing 1,100.00
9½″ h, Canopic, green dip, white
banded hieroglyphs and zodiac
symbols, imp mark, c1800,
restorations 3,300.00
10″ h, Portland, dark blue, white classical figures, base with half–length
figure in Phrygian cap, imp mark,
19th C. 2,310.00

LUSTERS

Butterfly, Melba bowl, 8″ d, butterflies on
MOP ext., orange luster int., Pattern
Z4832, printed mark, c1920 . . . . . . 550.00
Dragon, cup, 2″ h, three handles, blue
ext., gilt reptiles, eggshell int. with
central dragon, printed mark, c1920 . 275.00
Fairyland
Plaque
5 x 10½″, Picnic By A River, printed
marks, c1922, wood frame. 4,400.00
11½ x 16″, The Stuff That Dreams
Are Made Of, wood frame,
c1920 . . . . 13,200.00
Punch Bowl, 11″ d, Firbolgs, ruby ext.
ground, MOP Thumbelina int.,
printed mark and no., c1920 . . . . 3,575.00
Vase
7¾″ h, Butterfly Woman, black luster ground, trumpet shape,
printed marks, c1920, foot rim
restored. 2,420.00
11¾″ h, Imps On A Bridge, flame
luster ground, green Roc birds,
crimson imps, violet shading,
Shape No. 3451, printed marks,
c1925 . . . . 6,600.00
19″ h, cov, Temple On A Rock, gold
printing, painted purple, red, yellow, green, blue, black, and
brown, Dragon Bead borders,
purple luster cov with gold stars,
Shape No. 2046, printed mark,
c1920 . . . . 17,600.00
Moonlight
Basket, 5¾″ h, strap handle, pierced
disc cov, repair to cov, imp mark,
c1810 . . . . 300.00

Butter Dish, cov, 4″ h, attached un-
derdish, imp mark, c1810, repaired
chips. 275.00
Cup and Saucer, 2⅜″ d cup, imp
mark, c1810 . . . . 200.00
Goblet, 3¼″ h, imp mark, c1810 . . 195.00

MAJOLICA

Dish, 3⅞″ w, triangular, wood simulated
pattern, imp mark and date letters. . . 90.00
Flowerpot, 7¾″ h, glazed, four caryatid
figures, side panel with circular cartouche enamel dec of Music, Science,
and Art, armored battles and marine,
imp mark and date letters, ball finial,
rim restoration, glaze wear. 935.00
Snuffer Tray, 1⅝″ h, imp mark and date
letters. 75.00
Spittoon, 7¼″ h, blue, yellow, and brown
glaze, imp mark and date letters,
c1885, restored rim chip. 150.00
Tumbler, 4¼″ h, molded hunt scene, imp
mark and date letters. 100.00
Wall Pocket, 5¼″ l, modeled as female
and satyr–head masks, match holders, imp mark and registry code,
c1872, price for pair. 715.00

**Pearlware, bough pot, mottled brown
glaze, fern and acanthus leaf dec, imp
Wedwood mark, 18th C, 8½″ h, $800.00.**

PEARLWARE

Figure
7⅜″ h, Apollo, enamel dec, imp mark,
early 19th C, chips restored 550.00
7½″ h, eagle, enamel dec, imp mark,
early 19th C, chips, beak restored 990.00
8″ h, cupid, seated on rock circular
base, turquoise ground, imp mark,
c1870 . . . . 250.00
Garniture, 5⅜″ to 6″ h, porphyry style,
buff and black bodies, gilt dec applied

acanthus leaves, rosette border, pierced disc cov, imp marks, late 18th C, two vases restored, gilt retouched, price for three piece set **1,320.00**
Root Pot, cov, 5½" h, checker molded handing, surface agate dec, imp mark, c1800, rim hairlines **3,750.00**

QUEEN'S WARE

Coffeepot, cov, 9¼" h, red transfer printed landscape, imp mark, early 19th C **525.00**
Tea Infuser, 12¼" h, red transfer printed foliate design, metal spigot, imp mark and titled "Beane's Patent," 1889, crazing, finial reglued. **470.00**

ROSSO ANTICO

Coffeepot, cov, 7¼" h, enamel dec, imp mark, c1850, spout restored. **415.00**
Inkstand, 4" h, applied black basalt leaf and berry border on stand, supported by three dolphin feet, central pot insert, imp mark, early 19th C, foot rim restored **525.00**
Sugar Bowl, cov, 4½" h, classical black basalt relief between foliate panels, widow finial, imp mark, c1820. . . . . .   **440.00**
Teapot, cov, 8½" w, relief banded hieroglyphs of winged discs, sphinx, Apis, and canopic urn above strapwork border, black basalt trim, cov with fluted body and crocodile finial, imp mark, c1810, top of spout restored, inside cov and foot rim nicks, hairline crack   **625.00**
Vase, 6½" h, modeled as open mouth fish, enamel and gilt dec squid designs, imp marks and date letters, c1870, rim chips, restoration, price for pair **1,870.00**

STONEWARE

Cream Pitcher, 6½" l, brown ground, white prunus pattern relief, imp mark, early 19th C **330.00**
Ginger Jar, cov, 9¼" h, brown ground, turquoise enamel dec Oriental designs, gilt and white enameled sea dragon finial, imp date letter mark, c1871. . . . .   **625.00**
Jardiniere and Stand, 6" h, brown ground, gilded kylin's mask handles, herringbone banding and trim, enamel dec Oriental floral designs, imp marks, mid 19th C, minor gilt wear. **620.00**
Orange Basket, cov, 7¼" h, blue dip squares, pierced body, weave molded strap handle, imp mark, date letters, c1860. . . . .   **935.00**

Teapot, cov, 7¾" h, brown ground, leaf molded oval body, white applied stems and florets, imp marks, early 19th C, relief loss, spout restored . . .   **500.00**
Urn, 7½" h, smear glazed white ground, crater, green classical and foliate relief, pierced disc cov, imp mark, 19th C, plinth nick. **770.00**

WELLER POTTERY

History: In 1872 Samuel A. Weller opened a small factory in Fultonham, near Zanesville, Ohio, to produce utilitarian stoneware, such as milk pans and sewer tile. In 1882 he moved his facilities to Zanesville. In 1890 Weller built a new plant in the Putnam section of Zanesville along the tracks of the Cincinnati and Miskingum Railway. Additions followed in 1892 and 1894.

In 1894 Weller entered into an agreement with William A. Long to purchase the Lonhuda Faience Company, which had developed an art pottery line under the guidance of Laura A. Fry, formerly of Rookwood. Long left in 1895, but Weller continued to produce Lonhuda under a new name, Louwelsa. Replacing Long as art director was Charles Babcock Upjohn. He, along with Jacques Sicard, Frederick Hurten Rhead, and Gazo Fudji, developed Weller's art pottery lines.

At the end of World War I, many prestige lines were discontinued and Weller concentrated on commercial wares. Rudolph Lorber joined the staff and designed lines such as Roma, Forest, and Knifewood. In 1920 Weller purchased the plant of the Zanesville Art Pottery and claimed to be the largest pottery in the country.

Art pottery enjoyed a revival when the Hudson Line was introduced in the early 1920s. The 1930s saw Coppertone and Graystone Garden ware added. However, the Depression forced the closing of the Putnam plant and one on Marietta Street in Zanesville. After World War II, cheap Japanese imports took over Weller's market. In 1947 Essex Wire Company of Detroit bought the controlling stock. Early in 1948 operations ceased.

References: Sharon and Bob Huxford, *The Collectors Encyclopedia Of Weller Pottery*, Collector Books, 1979, 1994 value update; Ann Gilbert McDonald, *All About Weller: A History And Collectors Guide To Weller Pottery, Zanesville, OH*, Antique Publications, 1989.

Collectors' Club: American Art Pottery Association, 125 E. Rose Ave., St. Louis, MO 63119.

Additional Listings: See *Warman's Americana & Collectibles* for more examples.

Wall Pocket, Roma, 10¼″ h, $85.00.

Basket
Copra, 12½″ h	325.00
Tivoli, 8½″ h	125.00

Bowl
Coppertone, frog shaped, with flower frog, 11″ d	385.00
Eocean, 5″ d	100.00
Fleron	40.00
Monochrome	25.00
Candleholder, double, Marvo	50.00
Centerpiece Bowl, matching flower frog, Lavonia	65.00
Clock, Louwelsa, floral dec, 12″ h	700.00
Comport, Lustre, pale green, 6½″ h	55.00

Console Set
Elberta, price for four pieces	150.00
Lily of the Valley, price for three pieces	95.00
Ewer, Sicard, experimental, hand thrown, 4½″ h	1,200.00

Flower Frog
Muskota	135.00
Woodcraft, 3½″ h, 6″ w	85.00
Jar, cov, Chase, blue	300.00

Jardiniere
Flemish, four lion heads with garlands, 11″ d	375.00
Greora, bulbous, "S" handles, green mottling on orange ground, 8″ d	160.00
Louwelsa, blooming flowers dec, Virginia Adams, artist sgd, #228, 11¼″ h, 13″ d	140.00
Woodcraft, woodpecker and squirrel, ear damaged, 9½″ d	350.00

Mug
Etna Grape, 5½″ h	95.00

Louwelsa, blister, sgd "Minnie Mitchel"	175.00

Pitcher
Louwelsa, tankard, large pears hanging from vine, #580, 12¼″ h	165.00
Marvo	120.00
Planter, Woodsware, molded dec, three baby foxes, small glaze chip on one fox's paw, hairline crack, 4½″ h, 7″ d	35.00
Punch Bowl, Louwelsa	350.00

Vase
Ardsley, double	85.00
Barcelona, 7″ h	450.00
Blue ware, 8½″ h	210.00
Bonito, 9″ h	120.00
Cameo, bulbous apple shape, green, 7″ h	60.00
Coral, 6½″ h	25.00
Eocean Rose, squatty, sgd	285.00
Etna	95.00
Experimental, fish handles, 7″ h	475.00

Forest
8″ h, pillow	165.00
10½″ h	245.00

Hudson
8″ h, floral dec	275.00
11″ h, six sided, cream to gray, white flowers and leaves	225.00
Lorbeek	75.00

Louwelsa
7″ h, pillow, floral dec	200.00
8¾″ h, owl perched on pine branch dec, #555	440.00
10½″ h, Native American portrait, Levi J Burgess, artist sgd, #602	1,045.00
11″ h, chrysanthemums, artist Pillsbury	500.00
12¾″ h, blooming lilies dec, #801	220.00
13″ h, blooming poppies dec	330.00
14″ h, colorful oriole perched among apple blossoms	330.00
Lustre, bud, pale yellow, 6″ h	45.00
Malverne, bud, 8½″ h	150.00
Marbleized, 11″ h	150.00
Roma, paneled, four sided, 12″ h	200.00
Rosemont II, Dorothy England, sgd, 4″ h	245.00
Woodcraft, 8½″ h	45.00

Wall Pocket
Fairfield	175.00
Lavonia, lady	325.00
Warwick	175.00

WHALING

History: Whaling items are a specialized part of nautical collecting. Provenance is of prime importance since whaling collectors want assurances that their pieces are from a whaling voyage. Since a ship's equipment seldom carries the ship's identification, some individuals have falsely attributed a whaling provenance to general nautical items. Know the dealer, auction house, or collector from whom you buy.

Special tools, e.g., knives, harpoons, lances, spades, etc., do not overlap the general nautical line. Makers' marks and condition determine value for these items.

References: Nina Hellman and Norman Brouwer, *A Mariner's Fancy: The Whaleman's Art of Scrimshaw,* South Street Seaport Museum, Balsam Press, and University of Washington Press, 1992; Martha Lawrence, *Scrimshaw: The Whaler's Legacy,* Schiffer Publishing, 1993; Thomas G. Lytle, *Harpoons And Other Whalecraft,* Old Dartmouth Historical Society, 1984.

Museums: Cold Spring Harbor Whaling Museum, Cold Spring Harbor, NY; Kendall Whaling Museum, Sharon, MA; Mystic Seaport Museum, Mystic, CT; National Maritime Museum Library, San Francisco, CA; New Bedford Whaling Museum, New Bedford, MA; Pacific Whaling Museum, Waimanalo, HI; Sag Harbor Whaling & Historical Museum, Sag Harbor, NY; South Street Seaport Museum, New York, NY.

Additional Listings: Nautical Items and Scrimshaw.

Bill of Sale
Whaleship *William Rotch,* October 29, 1819, New Bedford, hull purchase	125.00
Whaling Schooner *Rainbow,* August 31, 1865	160.00
Binnacle Lamp, bark *Ben Avon,* brass, oil burner, 1885	220.00
Blubber Pike, 52" l, curved iron, orig wood handle, 19th C	140.00
Branding Iron, 20" l, whaleship *Ship R M,* handwrought iron, mounted letters	275.00
Compass, bark *Ben Avon,* Telltale, 1885	275.00
Dirk, sheath, H Richardson, c1870	355.00

Document, whaleship *Cadmus,* gives permission to voyage Pacific Ocean, sgd by President Andrew Jackson, framed, 1831 . . . . 880.00

Harpoon, toggle	
17½" l, wood and bone, late 19th C, price for pair	440.00
29¾" l, marked on side "JDD"	600.00
38¼" l, orig wood and canvas sheath	440.00
99" l, mounted on yellow painted pole	550.00

Lantern, ship's masthead, copper	
15" h	85.00
19" h	55.00

Log Book
Bark *Otranto,* commences at New Bedford January 17, 1847 thru April 30, 1849, contains whale stamps and ship stamps	3,080.00
Whaleship *Phoenix,* October 4, 1847 thru October 18, 1847	660.00

Photograph, 10 x 12½", whaleship under sail, orig wood frame and tan matting 75.00

Whalebone Products
Cane, 36" l, L shape handle with carved sleeping boy issuing from whale's tooth, last half 19th C	880.00
Carpenter's Square, 5½" l, third quarter 19th C	75.00
Double Block, 3⅞" l, orig ropework, 19th C	550.00
Figure, 6⅜" l, whale, late 19th C	75.00
Plane, 2" w, 8½" l, mustard pigment highlights, 19th C	660.00
Seam Rubber, 5⅛" l, carved, mid 19th C	255.00

Whale's Tooth
4⅛" l, engraved Arctic whaling scene, "Wrath of Right," last half 19th C	385.00
4¾" l, pinpoint scrimshaw work, engraved people, Washington, and "The Gentle/Man of the/Country," third quarter 19th C, pr	330.00
6½" l, engraved figure of lady reading book, mid 19th C	330.00
7⅛" l, engraved whaling scene, names, dates	990.00

Whale Stamp, wood, turned whale ivory handle, mid 19th C 575.00

Branding Iron, cast and wrought iron, "E. S. Mitchell" brand, Dartmouth, c1850, 32¾" l, $80.00.

WHIELDON

WHIELDON

History: The Staffordshire potter, Thomas Whieldon, established his shop in 1740. He is best known for his mottled ware, molded in forms of vegetables, fruits, and leaves. Josiah Spode and

Josiah Wedgwood, in different capacities, had connections with Whieldon.

Whieldon ware is a generic term. His wares were never marked and other potters made similar items. Whieldon ware is agate–tortoiseshell earthenware, in limited shades of green, brown, blue, and yellow. Most pieces are utilitarian items, e.g., dinner ware and plates, but figurines and other decorative pieces can be found.

Reference: Susan and Al Bagdade, *Warman's English & Continental Pottery & Porcelain, Second Edition,* Wallace-Homestead, 1991.

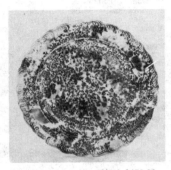

Plate, feather edge, 9½″ d, $450.00.

Dish, 5½″ l, leaf shape, gray and brown
  mottling, splashes of green and yellow
  on white, three small feet, c1770. .... **400.00**
Miniature, plate, 3″ d, creamware, brown
  sponging, pinpoints **300.00**
Pitcher, 8¾″ h, green, brown, and gray–
  blue glaze, applied flower and scroll
  design, three mask and paw feet,
  matching cov with repaired bird finial,
  1755–60. .... **8,000.00**
Plate
  9¼″ d, molded rim, brown, blue, gray,
    green, and amber tortoise shell,
    small chips, some edge repair. ... **225.00**
  9⅝″ d, green, blue, and brown, black
    tortoise shell glaze, emb rim **215.00**
Platter, 10⅜″ l, blue and green, brown
  tortoise shell glaze, emb rim. **300.00**
Saucer, 5″ d, molded floral sprigs, brown
  tortoise shell glaze with blue and
  green, small chips, edge repair. **155.00**
Tea Caddy, 4¼″ h, creamware, straight
  sided panels, molded scrolled leaf designs, translucent green and brown
  stripes, rim chip, edge roughness,
  18th C **385.00**
Teapot, 4⅞″ h, Pineapple, molded body,

crab stock handle finial, green and
  yellow glazes, c1765, minor glaze
  wear **5,500.00**

WHIMSIES, GLASS

History: Glassworkers occasionally spent time during lunch or after completing their regular work schedule creating unusual glass objects, known as whimsies, e.g. candy striped canes, darners, hats, paperweights, pipes, witch balls, etc. Whimsies were taken home and given as gifts to family and friends.

Because of their uniqueness and infinite variety, whimsies can rarely be attributed to a specific glass house or glassworker. Whimsies occurred wherever glass was made, from New Jersey to Ohio and westward. Some have suggested that style and color can be used to pinpoint a region or factory, but no one has yet developed an identification key that is adequate.

One of the most collectible types of whimsies is glass canes. Glass canes range from very short, under 1 foot, to lengths of 10 feet and beyond. They come in both hollow and solid form. Hollow canes can have a bulb-type handle or the rarer "C"- or "L"-shaped handle. Canes are found in many fascinating colors, with the candy striped being a regular favorite with collectors. Many canes are also filled with various colored powders, gold and white being the most common and silver being harder to find. Sometimes they were even used as candy containers.

References: Joyce E. Blake, *Glasshouse Whimsies,* published by author, 1984; Joyce E. Blake and Dale Murschell, *Glasshouse Whimsies: An Enhanced Reference,* published by authors, 1989.

Collectors' Club: The Whimsey Club, 4544 Cairo Drive, Whitehall, PA 18052.

Advisors: Joyce E. Blake and Lon Knickerbocker.

Baton, 41″ l, candy stripe dec, 1890 . **225.00**
Bird Fountain, clear, blown
  5¼″ h, cobalt blue finial **75.00**
  6⅜″ h, figural bird finial on conical font,
    damaged spiral below finial. **105.00**
Buttonhook, 6⅜″ l, clear, blown, applied
  flowers and other color dec **45.00**
Cane
  36″ l, aqua, threaded aqua stem, mid
    19th C. **70.00**
  41″ l, fluted and twisted stem, c1895 **35.00**
  46½″ l, aqua, spiraled, mid 19th C . **70.00**
  48″ l, candy stripe dec, plaster lined,
    c1895. .... **95.00**
Doorstop, 6¼″ w, 5″ h, internally dec
  pulled colors and bubbles, late 19th
  C. **75.00**
Funnel, blown, opalescent, twenty vertical ribs, folded lip, 19th C **55.00**

Handcooler, perfume type

1⅞" l, cobalt blue, enameling, gilded brass fittings with chain	95.00
2½" l, cranberry cased in clear, floral enameling, gilded brass fittings and chain	40.00
3⅛" l, green, shaped like pea pod, polychrome enameling and gilt, gilded fittings and chain	110.00

Hat, blown three-mold

2" h, cobalt blue, folded rim, stone in brim, McKearin GII–18	470.00
2¼" h, clear, folded rim, McKearin GIII.	140.00
2½" h, 5" w, broken swirl, twenty ribs, pontil scar, attributed to Midwest, 1820–50	525.00
2¾" h, clear, fifteen ribs, applied cobalt blue rim.	115.00

Inkwell, 7⅞" h, clear, blown, applied foot, baluster stem, divided bowl, rigaree dec, two protruding ink pots with folded lips, gallery rim on top compartment, domed lid with finial, minor stain in ink pots, few pinpoint flakes, attributed to Pittsburgh area. .	2,035.00
Pestle, 4" h, cobalt blue, blown, ribbed handle, wear and flakes at snapped pontil	85.00
Rolling Pin, 14½" l, traces of orig painted sailing ship, amethyst, mid 19th C. . .	140.00

Witch Ball, decanter vase with wafer type foot, white Nailsea loopings, $665.00.

Witch Ball

4" d, deep olive	55.00
4¾" d, amber	85.00
5" d, amber, blown	55.00
5½" d, clear, blown, white loopings .	110.00
6" d, clear, gray tint, white loopings, 1820–50	165.00

WHISKEY BOTTLES, EARLY

History: The earliest American whiskey bottles were generic form bottles blown by pioneer glassmakers in the 18th century. The Biningers (1820s to 1880s) were the first bottles specifically designed for whiskey. After the 1860s distillers favored the cylindrical "fifth" form.

The first embossed brand name bottle was the amber E. G. Booz Old Cabin Whiskey bottle which was issued in 1860. Many stories have been told about this classic bottle. Unfortunately, most are not true. Research has proved that "booze" was a corruption of the words "bouse" and "boosy" from the 16th and 17th centuries. It was only a coincidence that the Philadelphia distributor also was named Booz. This bottle has been reproduced extensively.

Prohibition (1920–33) brought the legal whiskey industry to a standstill. Whiskey was marked "medicinal purposes only" and distributed by private distillers in unmarked or paper-label bottles.

The size and shape of whiskey bottles are standard. Colors are limited to amber, amethyst, clear, green, and cobalt blue (rare). Corks were the common closure in the early period, with the inside screw top being used in the 1880 to 1910 period.

Bottles made prior to 1880 are the most desirable. In purchasing a bottle with a label, condition is a critical factor. In the 1950s distillers began to issue collectors' special edition bottles to help increase sales.

References: Ralph and Terry Kovel, *The Kovels' Bottle Price List, 9th Edition*, Crown Publishers, 1992; Carlo and Dorothy Sellari, *The Standard Old Bottle Price Guide*, Collector Books, 1989.

Periodicals: *Antique Bottle and Glass Collector*, PO Box 187, East Greenville, PA 18041; *Bottles & Extras*, PO Box 154, Happy Camp, CA 96039.

Museum: The Seagram Museum, Waterloo, Ontario, Canada.

Additional Listings: See *Warman's Americana & Collectibles* for a listing of Collectors' Special Editions Whiskey Bottles.

A M Bininger & Co, 19 Broad St, NY, 12½" h, golden amber, sheared mouth, smooth base	375.00
Argonaut, E Martin & Co, 11" h, amber	25.00
Bellmore Whiskey, qt, clear, label . . .	25.00
Black Cat, 11½" h, cylindrical, clear, cut and polished fluted panels, orange enameled lettering, black and white enameled cat, tooled mouth with ring, ground pontil scar	275.00
Burbank Bond Whiskey, pt, rect, amber	5.00
Casper's Whiskey, 11⅞" h, cobalt blue	225.00
Chestnut Grove Whiskey, qt, red amber, applied handle	80.00
Dr Abernathy's Green Ginger Brandy, 11" h, amber.	35.00

Gordon's Dry Gin, London, England, green, slightly tapered sides, 8¾" h, $35.00.

Duffy Malt Whiskey Company, 4" h, amber	25.00
E G Booz's Old Cabin Whiskey, qt, golden amber	250.00
Extra Bourbon of the Excelsior, 10" h, aqua	55.00
Four Roses, 3" h, bulb shape, clear, white enameling	45.00
Glen Garry Blended Scotch Whiskey, stoneware	25.00
G Rottanzi Liquor Dealer, 6½" h, clear	75.00
H Pharazyn, 12½" h, figural, Indian, golden amber, inward rolled mouth, smooth base	375.00
J H Cutter Old Bourbon, 11¾" h, amber	25.00
J T Gayen Altona, 13¾" h, deep reddish amber, round collared mouth, smooth base	800.00
Manhattan Club Pure Rye Whiskey, qt, amber	35.00
OK Old Bourbon Castle Whiskey, 12" h, amber, blob top	275.00
Old Continental Whiskey, 9¼" h, yellow amber	650.00
Potter & Bodine, 11¼" h, olive amber	75.00
Ridgeway Straight Corn Whiskey, miniature, stoneware	50.00
Schiele Old 91 Whiskey, 4¼" h, clear	20.00
Spring Hill Bourbon, 11" h, purple	85.00
Star Whiskey, 8⅛" h, medium amber, open pontil	350.00
Turner Brothers, 9⅞" h, barrel shape, yellow amber	110.00
Wharton's Whiskey, 5½" h, cobalt blue	145.00

WHITE PATTERNED IRONSTONE

History: White patterned ironstone is a heavy earthenware first patented in 1813 by Charles Mason, Staffordshire, England, using the name "Pat-

ent Ironstone China." Other English potters soon began copying this opaque, feldspathic, white china.

All white ironstone dishes first became available in the American market in the early 1840s. The first patterns had simple Gothic lines similar to the shapes used in transfer wares. Pattern shapes, such as New York, Union, and Atlantic, were designed to appeal to the American housewife. Motifs, such as wheat, corn, oats, and poppies, were embossed on the forms as the American western prairie influenced design. Eventually over 200 shapes and patterns, with variations of finials and handles, were made.

White patterned ironstone is identified by shape names and pattern names. Many potters only named the shape in their catalogs. Pattern names usually refer to the decoration motif.

References: Dana G. Morykan and Harry L. Rinker, *Warman's Country Antiques & Collectibles, Second Edition,* Wallace–Homestead, 1994; Jean Wetherbee, *A Look At White Ironstone,* Wallace-Homestead, 1980, out of print; Jean Wetherbee, *A Second Look At White Ironstone,* Wallace-Homestead. 1985, out of print.

Coffeepot, Grape Medallion, $200.00.

Cake Plate, 9" d, Brocade, handled, Mason	125.00
Chamber Pot, Wheat & Blackberry, Meakin	35.00
Coffeepot, Washington shape, John Meir	125.00
Covered Vegetable	
Blackberry	45.00
Cable and Ring, Savoy shape, T & R Boote	50.00
Prairie Flowers, Livesley & Powell	85.00
Creamer	
Fig, Davenport	60.00
Wheat in the Meadow, Powell & Bishop, 1870	40.00

Cup and Saucer, handleless

Ceres, Elsmore & Forster	48.00
Oak Leaf, Pankhurst, 1863	50.00
Ewer, Scalloped Decagon, Wedgwood	140.00

Gravy Boat

Bordered Fuchsia, Anthony Shaw .	40.00
Wheat & Blackberry, Meakin	25.00

Pitcher

Berlin Swirl, Mayer & Elliot	115.00
Japan pattern, Mason, c1815	275.00
Syndenham, 7⅞" h, T & R Boote . .	185.00
Wheat, W E Corn	65.00

Plate

8½" d, Ceres, Elsmore & Forster . .	12.00
9½" d, Gothic, Adams	18.00

Platter

20 x 15", Columbia, octagonal	125.00
20¾ x 15⅝", Wheat, Meakin	50.00

Punch Bowl

Adriatic, scalloped edge	335.00
Berry Cluster, J Furnival	125.00

Relish

Ceres, Elsmore & Forster, 1860 . . .	40.00
Wheat, W E Corn	30.00
Sauce, Vintage, Challinor	15.00

Soup Tureen, cov, Lily of the Valley,

Shaw	225.00
Sugar, cov, Hyacinth, Wedgwood . . .	40.00

Teapot

Hyacinth, Wedgwood	85.00
Ivy, 10" h, imp "William Adams" . . .	75.00
Niagara, Walley	110.00
Trent, T & R Boote	90.00

Toothbrush Holder

Bell Flower, Burgess	45.00
Cable and Ring, Cockson & Seddon	40.00

WILLOW PATTERN CHINA

History: Josiah Spode developed the first "traditional" willow pattern in 1810. The components, all motifs taken from Chinese export china, are: a willow tree, an "apple" tree, two pagodas, a fence, two birds, and three figures crossing a bridge. The legend, in its many versions, is an English invention based on the design components.

By 1830, there were over 200 plus makers of willow pattern china in England. The pattern has remained in continuous production. Some of the English firms that still produce willow pattern china are: Burleigh, Johnson Bros. (Wedgwood Group), Royal Doulton's continuation of the Booths pattern, and Wedgwood.

By the end of the 19th century, pattern production spread to France, Germany, Holland, Ireland, Sweden, and the United States. In the United States, Buffalo Pottery made the first willow pattern beginning in 1902. Many other companies followed, developing willow variants using rubberstamp simplified patterns as well as overglaze de-

cals. The largest American manufacturers of the traditional willow pattern were Royal China and Homer Laughlin, usually preferred because it is dated. Shenango pieces are most desired among restaurant-quality ware.

Japan began producing large quantities of willow pattern china in the early 20th century. Noritake began about 1902. Its early pieces used a Nippon "Royal Sometuke" mark. Most Japanese pieces are porous earthenware with a dark blue pattern using the traditional willow design, usually with no inner border. Noritake did put the pattern on china bodies. Unusual forms include salt and pepper shakers, one-quarter-pound butter dishes, and canisters. "Occupied Japan" may add a small percentage to the value of common table wares. Maruta and Moriyama marked pieces are especially valued. The most sought after Japanese willow is the fine quality NKT Co. ironstone with a copy of the old Booths pattern. Recent Japanese willow is a paler shade of blue on a porcelain body.

The most common dinnerware color is blue. However, pieces can also be found in black (with clear glaze or mustard-color glaze by Royal Doulton), brown, green, mulberry, pink (red), and polychrome. Although colors other than blue are hard to find, there is less demand; thus, prices may not necessarily be higher.

The popularity of the willow design has resulted in a large variety of willow-decorated products: candles, fabric, glass, graniteware, linens, needlepoint, plastic, tinware, stationery, watches, and wall coverings. All this material has collectible value.

References: Robert Copeland, *Spode's Willow Pattern and Other Designs After The Chinese*, Studio Vista, 1980, 1990 reprint; Mary Frank Gaston, *Blue Willow: An Identification & Value Guide*, Revised Second Edition, Collector Books, 1990, 1992 value update; Veryl Marie Worth and Louise M. Loehr, *Willow Pattern China: Collector's Guide, 3rd Edition*, H. S. Worth Co., 1986.

Periodicals: *American Willow Report*, PO Box 900, Oakridge, OR 97463; *The Willow Word*, PO Box 13382, Arlington, TX 76094.

Collectors' Clubs: International Willow Collectors, 2903 Blackbird Rd., Petoskey, MI 49770; Willow Society, 39 Medhurst Rd., Toronto, Ontario, Canada M4B 1B2.

Reproduction Alert: The Scio Pottery, Scio, Ohio, currently manufactures a willow pattern set sold in variety stores. The pieces have no marks or back stamps, and the transfer is of poor quality. The plates are flatter in shape than those of other manufacturers.

Additional Listings: Buffalo Pottery. See *Warman's Americana & Collectibles* for more examples.

Berry Bowl, small

Blue, Homer Laughlin Co	6.00
Pink, marked "Japan"	5.00
Bowl, 9" d, Mason	48.00

Teapot, child's, marked "Made in Japan," $40.00.

Cake Plate, tab handles, Royal China Co	12.00
Charger, 13" d	35.00
Chop Plate, Royal China Co	20.00
Creamer and Sugar, Royal China Co	15.00
Cup and Saucer	
Booths	30.00
Buffalo Pottery	25.00
Homer Laughlin	10.00
Japanese, decal inside cup, pink	25.00
Shenango	15.00
Gravy Boat, orig ladle, Royal China Co	25.00
Mug	15.00
Pie Plate, 10" d	50.00
Plate	
Bread and Butter	
Homer Laughlin Co	5.00
Royal China Co	5.00
Dinner	
Allerton, 10" d	25.00
Johnson Bros, 10" d	15.00
Royal China Co, 9" d	7.00
Salad, Royal China Co	4.00
Platter, 12" l, Homer Laughlin Co	25.00
Soup Bowl, Royal China Co	6.00
Teapot, Johnson Bros	60.00
Vegetable	
9" d, Royal China Co	12.00
10½" l, pink, Royal China Co	20.00

WOODENWARE

History: Many utilitarian household objects and farm implements were made of wood. Although they were used heavily, these implements were made of the strongest woods and were well taken care of by their owners.

This category serves as a catchall for wood objects which do not fit into other categories.

References: Dana G. Morykan and Harry L. Rinker, *Warman's Country Antiques & Collectibles, Second Edition,* Wallace–Homestead, 1994; George C. Neumann, *Early American Antique Country Furnishings: Northeastern America, 1650–*1880's, L–W Book Sales, 1984, 1993 reprint; June Sprigg and Jim Johnson, *Shaker Woodenware: A Field Guide,* Berkshire House, 1991.

Additional Listings: See *Warman's Americana & Collectibles* for more examples.

Whimsey with egg shaped darner, turned, two loose rings on pedestal base, 4½" h, $45.00.

Bank, 2¼" h, 3⅞" w, 2⅛" d, stylized village scene, wood peg construction	150.00
Bowl	
11¾ x 16¼", 4¼" h, burl, ash, oblong, cutout open handles	880.00
13¾ x 23½", 4¾" h, boat shape, dark patina int., dark blue paint ext.	575.00
25" d, 6" h, yellow pine, octagonal, dovetailed joints with metal pins, old dark brown patina	220.00
Box	
3½ x 8¾", 7¾" h, mahogany, inlaid marquetry stars on sides and lid	180.00
8" l, pine and poplar, sliding lid, old finish, scratch carved "P B Gaff" on lid	50.00
8⅝" l, beech, rect, floral dec, wood pin hinges, orig polychrome paint	560.00
9½" d, bentwood, round, old dark green paint	200.00
12¾" l, pine, orig black paint, orange striping, stenciled "Deborah W Holway"	110.00
13 x 9½ x 19½", pine, dovetailed, wall type, two drawers, open heart hanger, 18th C	660.00
Bride's Box	
15" l, pine, orig light blue paint with polychrome floral dec, insect damage	300.00
15¾" l, pine, orig paint, polychrome	

buildings, house, and tree, white
ground, damaged lid. 225.00
18¾″ l, pine, orig paint with polychrome floral designs, black
ground, lid with couple holding
hands and German inscription
"Thou Goest with me and I with
thee..." 2,310.00
Butter Paddle
10″ l, shaped handle with bird's head
hook end, scrubbed patina 500.00
11″ l, maple, curl and hook handle,
worn finish. 75.00
Candle Box
14″ l, pine, black and white striping
and alligatored finish, orig red paint,
sliding lid. 200.00
16½″ h, hardwood, rounded crest,
sliding front lid, old finish. 275.00
19¼″ l, country, pine and poplar, three
finger hole sliding lid, old red paint 180.00
Candle Stand, 29″ h, adjustable ratchet,
iron socket with pushup, early 19th C 40.00
Cane, 38¼″ l, carved, high relief figures
and animals, c1870 . . . . 1,100.00
Cookie Board, 12¼ x 7″, George Washington, rooster, equestrian figure, and
woman, metal cutting edge. 85.00
Dough Box, cov, 36″ l, 27″ h, poplar,
whittled leg stand, old refinish. 250.00
Drying Rack, 24″ w, 30½″ h, poplar,
three bars, chamfered posts, shoe
feet, old black paint 165.00
Frame, 13 x 16⅞″, beveled, worn orig
reddish brown flame graining 100.00
Loom Light, 44″ l extended, hanging,
ratchet type, double, American, 19th
C 175.00
Mannequin, 48″ h, female, carved, mid
19th C 2,750.00
Milk Pan Rack, 44½″ h, 45½″ w, 7″ d,
pine, green paint, c1850. . . . . 55.00
Mortar and Pestle, maple, turned . . . 55.00
Nodder, 5″ h, peafowl, carved, polychrome paint. 75.00
Paddle, 4¾″ l, burl, soft finish 335.00
Pipe Box, 20½″ h, mahogany, truncated
case, cutout crest, hinged lid, old
finish 330.00
Salt Box, 9½″ w, 7″ d, 8¾″ h, hanging,
pine, dovetailed, cutout crest, lift lid,
homemade hinges, old dark paint
over green 140.00
Spice Box
9″ l, cherry, dovetailed, four compartment int., sliding lid, refinished. . . . 110.00
12½″ w, poplar, dovetailed, scalloped
crest with hanging hole, divided int.,
hinged lid 770.00
Spoon
5″ l, burl, soft finish 165.00
6¼″ l, carved, engraved design on

bowl, shaped handle with letter
"K". 60.00
17″ l, curly maple, long handle 95.00
Sugar Bucket
9½″ h, stave constructed, old dark
repaint 110.00
9¾″ h, stave constructed, worn blue
paint. 165.00
11½″ h, stave constructed, old red
paint, missing handle 95.00
12″ h, stave constructed, light green
repaint 275.00
Toy, pull
10″ l, grasshopper, animated, old dark
patina. 150.00
11″ l, pair of oxen, alligatored brown
and blue paint 660.00
Tub Stand, 28 x 36″, three arms, mortised construction, pencil post legs,
old blue paint traces 30.00
Walking Stick
31″ l, carved, diamond design shaft,
round knob 35.00
32¾″ l, pine, ebonized finish, bone
knob. 40.00
Weathervane, 24″ h, horse, prancing,
old weathered white paint, modern
base, 1900s 80.00
Whirligig, 15″ l, horse, worn polychrome
paint, 20th C. 225.00

WORLD'S FAIRS AND EXPOSITIONS

History: The Great Exhibition of 1851 in London
marked the beginning of the World's Fair and Exposition movement. The fairs generally feature exhibitions from nations around the world displaying
the best of their industrial and scientific achieve-
ments.

Many important technological advances have
been introduced at world's fairs. Examples include
the airplane, telephone, and electric lights. The ice
cream cone, hot dog, and iced tea were products
of vendors at fairs. Art movements often were
closely connected to fairs, with the Paris Exhibition
of 1900 generally considered to have assembled
the best of the works of the Art Nouveau artists.

References: *American Art, New York World's
Fair 1939*, Apollo Books, 1987; Carl Abbott, *The
Great Extravaganza: Portland and the Lewis and
Clark Exposition*, Oregon Historical Society, 1981;
Stanley Appelbaum, *The New York World's Fair,
1939/1940*, Dover Publications, 1971; Patricia F.
Carpenter and Paul Totah, *The San Francisco Fair,
Treasure Island, 1939–1940*, Scottwall Associates,
1989; Richard Friz, *World's Fair Memorabilia*,
House of Collectibles, 1989, out of print; Kurt Krue-
ger, *Meet Me In St. Louis—The Exonumia Of The
1904 World's Fair*, Krause Publications, 1979;

Frederick and Mary Megson, *American Exposition Postcards, 1870–1920: A Catalog and Price Guide,* The Postcard Lovers, 1992; Howard Rossen and John Kaduck, *Columbia World's Fair Collectibles,* Wallace-Homestead, 1976, revised price list 1982, out of print; Larry Zim, Mel Lerner, and Herbert Rolfes, *The World of Tomorrow: The 1939 New York World's Fair,* Harper & Row Publishers, 1988.

Periodical: *World's Fair,* PO Box 339, Corte Madera, CA 94925.

Collectors' Clubs: 1904 World's Fair Society, 529 Barcia Dr., St. Louis, MO 63119-1518; World's Fair Collectors' Society, Inc., PO Box 20806, Sarasota, FL 34276.

Museums: Atwater Kent Museum, Philadelphia, PA; Buffalo & Erie County Historical Society, Buffalo, NY; California State University, Madden Library, Fresno, CA; 1898 Chicago World's Fair Columbian Exposition Museum, Columbus, WI; Museum of Science & Industry, Chicago, IL; Presidio Army Museum, San Francisco, CA 94129; The Queens Museum, Flushing, NY.

1876, Philadelphia, Centennial

Bookmark, woven silk, green on white, "Women's Pavilion" 30.00

Handkerchief, 21 x 22½", silk, white, blue border and allover repeating design of diamond with "76" inside, leaf spray, and spreadwing bird. . .   45.00

Mug, glass, Liberty Bell, snake handle, "Manufactured At The Centennial Exhibition by Gillender & Sons" on bottom 250.00

Pin, 1¾" h, spreadwing eagle, "1876" in star on breast, openwork shield with Liberty Bell below, "Liberty & Freedom to All" around shield. . . .   30.00

1893, Chicago, Columbian Exposition

Match Box, 4¼" l, Satsuma, red and gold hp Machinery Hall image on lid, red, gold, and white stylized dec, striker on underside, sgd inside . . .   200.00

Plate, milk glass, serrated edge with openwork trefoils, center with painted bust of Columbus and "1492–1892". 35.00

1901, Buffalo, Pan–American Exposition

Advertising Mirror, pocket, celluloid, Castle Copal illus, Berry Bros Ltd Varnish Mfrs 65.00

Demitasse Spoon, SS, gold wash, buffalo and Indian on handle, meeting of the continents in bowl 22.00

Dish, 5¾ x 5¼", heavy copper, Indian with bow and arrow, right side of dish formed by edge of bow, left side by Indian and feathers, "Pan–American 1901," copper and verdigris finish. 40.00

Pencil, 12½" l, oversized, red, white,

and blue, "Souvenir of Pan–American Exposition 1901 American Pencil Co. N.Y.". 25.00

Punch Cup, ruby flashed, "Pan–Am 1901 Buffalo, B. F. Hardenvergh" .   30.00

Tape Measure, celluloid, Expo flag and "Souvenir Pan–American Exposition, Buffalo, N.Y., 1901" on front, back with Meeting of the Continents design, missing metal end tab 40.00

1904, St. Louis, Louisiana Purchase Exposition

Mug, 3¾" h, glass, green, engraved "Anna E. Conklin, World's Fair, St. Louis, 1904," ornate gilt dec, tiny rim flake 55.00

Tapestry, multicolored, Festival Hall and the Cascades above "1904" in circle flanked by American and French flags, leaf borders 100.00

1905, Portland, Lewis & Clark Exposition, pinback button, Sighting the Pacific 1805, J I Case Threshing Machine Co, Racine, WI, Case logo and Lewis and Clark with Miss Liberty fair logo, multicolored 125.00

1909, New York, Hudson–Fulton Celebration, stickpin, "Clermont" image at top, "Hudson–Fulton Celebration, 1609–1807, New York, Sep. 25–Oct 12 1909" on pendant. 10.00

1915, San Francisco, Panama–Pacific International Exposition

Badge, guest, "Pennsylvania, Panama–Pacific Exposition Commission," gilt, enameled blue, blue ribbon. 150.00

1933, Chicago, Century of Progress, paperweight, adv, glass globe with flattened base, 3" d, $40.00.

Pocket Watch, nickel plated, "Official Souvenir" printed on face, fair logo of Liberty atop world with torch and laurel branch emb on case 200.00

1933, Chicago, Century of Progress
Ashtray, miniature rubber Firestone tire frame, glass insert, 5½" d 38.00

Pipe, 5¼" l, bottle shaped, varnished wood, aluminum trim 50.00

Pocket Knife, "Coca–Cola in Bottles," brown celluloid handles, two blades..................... 55.00

Thermometer, 3⅜" d, round, enameled steel, "Chicago World's Fair, Fort Dearborn".............. 25.00

1939, New York, New York World's Fair
Bank, stainless steel, oval, Federal Building image on front........ 75.00

Bud Vase, clear glass, ruby band at center, gold trim and lettering "New York World's Fair 1940" 20.00

Pie Server, George Washington image on handle, fair logo on server 32.00

Viewer, 5 x 6½", three dimensional, The World of Tomorrow, orig envelope, expands to 25"........ 150.00

1939, San Francisco, Golden Gate International Exposition
Comb, amber plastic, pocket size, emb goldtone metal case with brass medallion in center........... 32.00

Lamp, 9" h, made from two halves of abalone shell and half mussel shell, polished 28.00

1964, New York, New York World's Fair
Coaster Set, 4" d, wood, multicolored fair views, descriptions on backs, orig package, price for set of six .. 15.00

Record, 45 rpm, Official Souvenir Record from Walt Disney's "It's A Small World," four languages, orig case, 1964 Walt Disney Productions copyright.............. 8.00

YELLOW WARE

History: Yellow ware is a heavy earthenware of differing weight and strength which varies in color from a rich pumpkin to lighter shades which are more tan than yellow. Although plates, nappies, and custard cups are found, kitchen bowls and other cooking utensils are most prevalent.

The first American yellow ware was produced at Bennington, Vermont. English yellow ware has additional ingredients which make its body much harder. Derbyshire and Sharp's were foremost among the English manufacturers.

References: John Gallo, *Nineteenth and Twentieth Century Yellow Ware,* Heritage Press, 1985; Joan Leibowitz, *Yellow Ware: The Transitional Ce-*ramic, Schiffer Publishing, 1985, 1993 value update; Lisa S. McAllister and John L. Michael, *Collecting Yellow Ware,* Collector Books, 1993; Dana G. Morykan and Harry L. Rinker, *Warman's Country Antiques & Collectibles, Second Edition,* Wallace–Homestead, 1994.

Mug, chocolate brown stripe above white band, 3" d, $125.00.

Creamer, 4½" h, green and brown sponging 75.00

Cuspidor, 7½" h, 5" d, green, blue, and tan sponging................. 60.00

Figure
10" l, lion, rect base, brown details, chips on nose and base 110.00

10¼" h, seated dog, brown sponging, good detail, open front legs, incised name "Percy Wilton" on edge of base, small chips, small glued base repair 165.00

11" h, seated dog, unglazed, worn old paint and varnish, black coat, green base, chips, reglued to base, crack in tail..................... 165.00

14½" l, lion, olive amber glaze, brown accents, oval base with firing warp, good detail, OH, small chip on int. of base, chipped ears......... 275.00

Food Mold, 6" l, ear of corn 65.00

Jar, cov, 12¼" h, brown running glaze, chipped lid 85.00

Jug, 9" h, mocha, blue dec 525.00

Match Holder, 6" l, beetle shape, removable lid, chips 75.00

Medallion, 6¼" h, oval, white molded bust of Washington 250.00

Miniature, chamber pot, 1¾" h, mocha, white band, brown stripes, blue seaweed dec 195.00

Mixing Bowl, 14¼" d, white band with brown stripes 110.00

Mug, 3⅞" h, white band, ribbed strap handle 145.00

Pitcher, 4¾″ h, molded Gothic Arch design, brown sponging, flaked spout . . **40.00**

Salt, 3″ d, ftd, mocha, white band, brown seaweed dec **225.00**

ZANE WARE
MADE IN U.S.A.

ZANE POTTERY

History: In 1921 Adam Reed and Harry McClelland bought the Peters and Reed Pottery in Zanesville, Ohio. The firm continued production of garden wares and introduced several new art lines: "Sheen," "Powder Blue," "Crystalline," and "Drip." The factory was sold in 1941 to Lawton Gonder.

Reference: Jeffery, Sherrie, and Barry Hersone, *The Peters and Reed and Zane Pottery Experience,* published by authors, 1990.

Additional Listings: Gonder and Peters and Reed.

Vase, daisy motif, unglazed terra cotta, green glazed int., 6″ h, 4½″ d, $35.00.

Bowl
   5″ d, brown and blue **45.00**
   5¼″ d, Wilse Blue, dragonfly dec . . **50.00**
   6½″ d, blue, marked "Zanesware" . **25.00**
Figure, 10⅛″ h, cat, black, green eyes **500.00**
Jardiniere
   7⅛″ h, 8½″ d, waisted cylindrical form, blue and green landscape scene, maroon matte glaze, c1907. . . . . . **165.00**
   34″ h, green matte glaze, artist sgd "Frank Ferreu". **300.00**
Vase
   5″ h, green, cobalt blue drip glaze . **25.00**
   7″ h, flowing medium green over dark forest green ground **85.00**

LA MORO

ZANESVILLE POTTERY

History: Zanesville Art Pottery, one of several potteries located in Zanesville, Ohio, began production in 1900. A line of utilitarian products was first produced. Art pottery was introduced shortly thereafter. The major line was La Moro, which was hand painted and decorated under glaze. The impressed block print mark La Moro appears on the high-glazed and matte-glazed decorated ware. The firm was bought by S. A. Weller in 1920 and became known as Weller Plant No. 3.

References: Evan and Louise Purviance, *Zanesville Art Tile In Color,* Wallace-Homestead, 1972, out of print; Louise and Evan Purviance and Norris F. Schneider, *Zanesville Art Pottery In Color,* Mid-America Book Company, 1968.

Bowl, 6½″ d, fluted edge, mottled blue glaze **45.00**
Jardiniere
   7⅛″ h, 8½″ d, waisted cylindrical form, landscape scene, blue, green, and maroon matte glaze, c1908. . . . . . **175.00**
   8¼″ h, ruffled rim, cream to light amber peony blossoms, shaded brown ground **75.00**
Plate, 4½″ d, applied floral dec **25.00**
Portrait Vase, 10¼″ h, light gray horse portrait, light olive green to blue green ground, peachblow in back, matte ext., glossy brown int., sgd "R. G. Turner". **825.00**
Vase, 11½″ h, gilt dec, cobalt ground **20.00**

ZSOLNAY POTTERY

History: Vilmos Zsolnay (1828–1900) assumed control of his brother's factory in Pécs, Hungary, in the mid 19th century. In 1899 Miklos, Vilmos's son, became manager. The firm still produces ceramic ware.

The early wares are highly ornamental, glazed, and have a cream color ground. "Eosin" glaze, a deep rich play of colors reminiscent of Tiffany's iridescent wares, received a gold medal at the 1900

Paris exhibition. Zsolnay Art Nouveau pieces show great creativity.

Originally no trademark was used. Beginning in 1878 a blue mark depicting the five towers of the cathedral at Pécs was used. The initials "TJM" represent the names of Miklos's three children.

Zsolnay's recent series of iridescent glazed figurines, which initially were inexpensive, now are being sought by collectors and show a steady increase in value.

Reference: Susan and Al Bagdade, *Warman's English & Continental Pottery & Porcelain, Second Edition,* Wallace-Homestead, 1991.

Bowl, boat shaped, reticulated rim, floral and leaf design int., gold wash highlights, castle mark, $325.00.

Bowl, 10″ d, cherubs dec, curved leaf handles 500.00
Compote, 11″ d, ribbed, four caryatids modeled as angel supports, blue–green irid glaze 1,000.00
Dish, 8½″ w, fan shape, reticulated, beige, gold, and pink dec, rolled in edge, steeple mark 185.00
Ewer, 7½″ h, cream, yellow, and beige dec, gold base, gold reticulated neck band, ornate handle 115.00
Mug, 4½″ h, irid blue luster 80.00
Pitcher, 15″ h, Art Nouveau style, floriform, winding stem handle, peacock–green irid glaze, imp "Zsolnay Pecs–5517/1003" 4,180.00
Plate
8½″ d, shell shape, reticulated, red and gold flowers, beige ground, steeple mark 180.00
12″ d, pink and blue flowers on light yellow center, reticulated gold trimmed border extending to rim, marked "Zsolnay Pecs" 245.00
Puzzle Jug, 6½″ h, pierced roundels, irid dec, cream ground, castle mark, imp "Zsolnay" 165.00
Sculpture, 8½″ h, mother and child, green irid glaze 310.00
Vase
5⅞″ h, irid gold and blue swirl glaze, raised medallion mark, c1903 . . . . 305.00
6⅞″ h, double gourd shape, four mice dec, red and mustard irid glaze, four handles, imp mark and "6020" . . . 990.00
8″ h, blue and green irid, six handles 800.00
8⅛″ h, double gourd form, forest landscape dec with leafy trees, purple, green, red, blue, and amber glaze, incised factory marks, c1900 . . . . . 2,475.00
11¾″ h, cylindrical, three dark olive frogs sitting under water, mottled purplish spotted irid ground 5,500.00
15″ h, Art Nouveau design, reticulated, four red blossoms, green leaves, raised circular medallion, marked "Zsolnay Pecs 6531 M" . . 10,340.00
17″ h, irid gold, green, and brown glaze, high relief dec, raised medallion mark, c1903, minor glaze chip near base 2,640.00

INDEX

See Warman's Americana & Collectibles, 6th Edition (1993)
for expanded listings of categories preceded by †.

- C -

Harry and the Rinkettes. Left to right: Nancy M. Butt, Jocelyn C. Mousely, Harry L. Rinker, Jr., Terese J. Yeakel, Harry L. Rinker, Ellen T. Schroy, and Dana Gehman Morykan.

HARRY L. RINKER is consulting editor for Wallace-Homestead Book Company; editor of *Warman's Antiques and Collectibles Price Guide* and *Warman's Furniture*; author of *Collector's Guide to Toys, Games, and Puzzels, How to Make the Most of Your Investments in Antiques and Collectibles,* and *Rinker on Collectibles*; co-author with Frank Hill of *The Joy of Collecting with Craven Moor,* with Norman E. Martinus of *Warman's Paper,* and with Dana Gehman Morykan of *Warman's Country Antiques & Collectibles, Second Edition*; syndicated columnist of "Rinker on Collectibles," and executive director of The Institute for the Study of Antiques and Collectibles.